Robotics Research

Robotics Research

The Fourth International Symposium

edited by
Robert C. Bolles
and
Bernard Roth

The MIT Press
Cambridge, Massachusetts
London, England

Publisher's note: This format is intended to reduce the cost of publishing
certain works and to shorten the gap between editorial preparation and publication.
The text has been photographed from copy prepared by the authors.

Printed and bound by Halliday Lithograph in the United States
of America.

Library of Congress Cataloging-in-Publication Data

Robotics research.

   (The MIT Press series in artificial intelligence)
   Papers of the Fourth International Symposium on
Robotics Research, held at the University of
California at Santa Cruz on Aug. 14, 1987; sponsored
by the National Science Foundation and the System
Development Foundation.
   1. Robotics—Research—Congresses. I. Bolles,
Robert C. II. Roth, Bernard. III. International
Symposium on Robotics Research (4th: 1987: University
of California at Santa Cruz) IV. National Science
Foundation (U.S.) V. System Development Corporation
(Palo Alto, Calif.) VI. Series.
TJ210.3.R636 1988   629.8 '92   88–629
ISBN 0–262–02272–9

Contents

Series Foreword

Artificial intelligence is the study of intelligence using the ideas and methods of computation. Unfortunately, a definition of intelligence seems impossible at the moment because ietligence appears to be an amalgam of so many information-processing and information-representation abilities.

Of course psychology, philosophy, linguistics, and related disciplines offer various perspectives and methodologies for studying intelligence. For the most part, however, the theories proposed in these fields are too incomplete and too vaguely stated to be realized in computational terms. Something more is needed, even though valuable ideas, relationships, and constraints can be gleaned from traditional studies of what are, after all, impressive existence proofs that intelligence is in fact possible.

Artificial intelligence offers a new perspective and a new methodology. Its central goal is to make computers intelligent, both to make them more useful and to understand the principles that make intelligence possible. That intelligent computers will be extremely useful is obvious. The more profound point is that artificial intelligence aims to understand intelligence using the ideas and methods of computation, thus offering a radically new and different basis for theory formation. Most of the people doing work in artificial intelligence believe that these theories will apply to any intelligent information processor, whether biological or solid state.

There are side effects that deserve attention, too. Any program that will successfully model even a small part of intelligence will be inherently massive and complex. Consequently, artificial intelligence continually confronts the limits of computer-science technology. The problems encountered have been hard enough and interesting enough to seduce artificial-intelligence people into working on them with enthusiasm. It is natural, then, that there has been a steady flow of ideas from artificial intelligence to computer science, and the flow shows no sign of abating.

The purpose of this MIT Press Series in Artificial Intelligence is to provide people in many areas, both professionals and students, with timely, detailed information about what is happening on the frontiers in research centers all over the world.

Patrick Henry Winston
J. Michael Brady

Preface

The papers in this volume are a record of the Fourth International Symposium on Robotics Research, held at the University of California at Santa Cruz on August 9 through August 14, 1987. The participants, who came from Australia, Europe, Japan, and the United States, discussed their research and shared their views on the current state of robotics. The symposium was scheduled so that all participants could attend the presentation of each paper; there were no parallel sessions. In addition, blocks of time were set aside for individuals or small groups to discuss research informally, to make new friendships, and to take part in athletic activities. The relaxed atmosphere generated by these informal activities carried over into the formal sessions, encouraging the free interchange of ideas and opinions. The symposium was sponsored jointly by the National Science Foundation and the System Development Foundation.

This series of symposia has been a great success; in fact, we believe it has been the major catalyst in the establishment of the close ties that now link the members of the international robotics-research community. (Some tangible indications of these ties are the increase in the number of robotics researchers who have worked in foreign countries, the increase in the number of papers published under joint international authorship, and the increase in the number of references to foreign research.) The proceedings of these symposia have provided the entire robotics community with descriptions of the latest research results and directions.

The organization of this volume differs from that of the symposium. As the table of contents shows, we have arranged the papers in eight parts. Part I contains descriptions of four state-of-the-art robotic systems, including one that plays ping-pong and another that can turn a somersault. Part II includes papers describing new actuators, sensors, and other devices (among them a magnetically levitated wrist). Part III covers control strategies, some of which combine teleoperation and autonomous techniques. Part IV contains papers describing the kinematics of arms and hands and procedures for calibrating these devices. The papers in part V describe techniques for visually recognizing objects and techniques for automatically programming vision systems to recognize an object when given a three-dimensional model of it. Part VI concentrates on error models and on techniques for estimating task parameters from image sequences. Part VII includes a number of papers describing high-level programming techniques for manipulators. The final papers, in part VIII, describe algorithms for planning collision-free paths through complex environments.

As at previous symposia, the number of participants was limited to encourage scientifically rewarding interactions. The difficult decisions about whom to invite were made by an international committee consisting of S. Arimoto, R. Bolles, M. Brady, O. Faugeras, G. Giralt, H. Miura, L. Paul, and B. Roth. This committee proposed a list of invitees based on technical, institutional, and geographic criteria. The committee selected 68 symposium participants and four observers from the sponsoring organizations.

The symposium banquet was held at the Monterey Bay Aquarium in Monterey, California. During this event a best-paper award was presented to Victor Scheinman for his description of an automatic assembly system called Robotworld. The judging panel for this award was composed of the members of the editorial board of the *International Journal of Robotics Research*.

Many people helped make the symposium a success. We particularly want to thank Cherry Powers-Moser, who did a tremendous amount of planning and then helped to ensure that the meeting ran smoothly by handling numerous details. We also want to thank Prasad Akella, who helped in the day-to-day running of the meeting.

The goal of the International Symposia on Robotics Research is to provide an informal forum for the open exchange of ideas and for the continuing development of close links among researchers from various countries. Over the years, the paper-selection committees have attempted to incorporate new, young researchers into the community and to restrict the publication of papers by authors who have contributed to previous volumes. We continue to search for ways to broaden the participation base while maintaining both the high quality and the personal interactions that have been hallmarks of the first four symposia. We will issue an open call for papers to be presented at the fifth symposium. All papers will be subjected to peer review. To maintain the workshop-like atmosphere of the first four symposia, attendance will be by invitation only and will be limited to approximately 100 researchers, including the authors selected through the peer-review process. The fifth symposium will be held in Tokyo on August 28 through August 31, 1989; the deadline for the submission of papers is January 15, 1989.

Robert C. Bolles
Menlo Park, California

Bernard Roth
Stanford, California

Robotics Research

I SYSTEMS

The integration of hardware and software into a working system is the essence of robotics. All four of the papers in part I describe state-of-the-art systems. Although they were designed for different tasks and with different motivations, they share the distinction of being at the forefront of robotics research and its application.

Hodgins and Raibert describe recent results from Raibert's ongoing efforts to understand locomotion by constructing legged systems and analyzing the scientific principles that govern their performance. The videotape that accompanied the presentation of their paper featured a biped running in a circle and then, while still in full stride, responding to an operator command by bounding into the air and performing a complete somersault. Although the paper describes this action nicely, it cannot convey the delight generated by the videotape.

In a similar vein, the papers by Andersson and Scheinman describe systems that have to be seen to be appreciated. Andersson combines vision and manipulation in his tour-de-force application of robot technology to the playing of ping-pong against a human opponent. Scheinman describes Robotworld, a novel, self-contained world for assembly and inspection robots. Using as many as twenty magnetically levitated, lightweight, fast-moving, simple robot manipulators and vision systems, he has created a miniature factory of the future.

Lozano-Pérez et al. describe a robot system that recognizes and manipulates (mostly) planar-faced objects that can be jumbled together in a pile. In addition, they discuss the difficult choices involved in designing and implementing such complex systems.

Biped Gymnastics

Jessica Hodgins
Computer Science Department
Carnegie-Mellon University
Pittsburgh, PA

Marc H. Raibert
Artificial Intelligence Laboratory
Massachusetts Institute of Technology
Cambridge, MA

In this paper we examine the nature of the forward flip and a variant called the front aerial, and we describe how a hydraulically powered biped running machine executes them. We found that the control system can produce a flip by using a fixed pattern of open-loop actuator commands together with algorithms described previously for the control of normal running.

1 Introduction

The forward somersault or *flip* is a gymnastic maneuver in which the performer runs forward, springs off the ground with both feet, rotates the body forward through 360 degrees, and lands in a balanced posture on one or both feet. See figure 1. Human gymnasts can do a forward flip as an isolated maneuver or as part of a floor routine in which the flip is preceded and followed by other maneuvers. The best gymnasts can do double flips. The average teenager can learn to do a forward flip in a few weeks with proper coaching and practice.

To perform a flip, the biped machine runs forward, thrusts with both legs to jump while pitching the body forward, shortens its legs to tuck once airborne, untucks in time to land on its feet, and continues running. The process is initiated by a human operator who uses a joystick to specify the desired running speed on the approach. Once the system reaches an acceptable speed, the operator presses a button that enables the flip sequence—the control program initiates the maneuver when the machine passes a specified location on the circular track in the laboratory. On a good day the machine completes nine out of ten flips successfully.

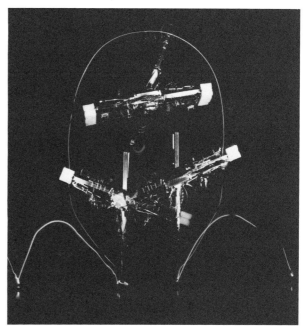

Figure 2: Photograph of planar biped doing a flip. Lines indicate the path of a foot and the flashes are synchronized with liftoff, the highest point of flight, and touchdown. The machine was running from right to left.

Figure 1: Forward somersault or *flip* as performed by a human gymnast. Drawings reprinted from Tonry (1983).

The experiments reported in this paper show that a relatively simple control program can accomplish a forward flip. The operations used to perform a flip are each similar to actions that are routinely used to produce normal running. The entire flip maneuver is accomplished by modifying three strides in an otherwise normal sequence of strides. The method used to provide pitch acceleration and maximum thrust to produce a flip depends on predetermined open-loop control data. Symmetries used to simplify the dynamics of normal running also apply to flips and aerials, and were used to develop the control.

In this paper we examine the nature of the forward flip

and a variant called the front aerial, and describe how a planar biped running machine executes them. The flip is interesting to study because it is an extremely dynamic form of locomotion that incorporates an extended ballistic phase. It provides an opportunity to examine control techniques for such dynamic activity and to assess their strengths and weaknesses. We developed the control programs that produce flips and aerials by extending previous methods for controlling locomotion. So a second reason we find flips interesting is that they serve to further validate the generality and utility of the previous locomotion control algorithms. Finally, the challenging nature of the project and the visual impact of the result make it lots of fun.

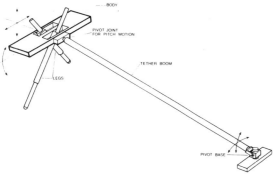

PLANAR BIPED WITH TETHER

Figure 3: Diagram of planar biped used for experiments. The machine travels by running on a 2.5 m radius circle on the laboratory floor. The body is an aluminum frame on which are mounted hip actuators, hydraulic accumulators, and computer interface electronics. The hip has two low friction hydraulic actuators that position the legs fore and aft. Actuators within the legs change the leg lengths and air springs make the legs springy in the axial direction. Onboard accumulators on the hydraulic supply and return lines increase the instantaneous actuator rate. Sensors on the machine measure the lengths of the legs and air springs, the positions and velocities of the hydraulic hip actuators, and contact between each foot and the floor. A tether mechanism constrains the body to move with three degrees of freedom—fore and aft, up and down, and pitch rotation. Sensors on the tether mechanism measure vertical displacement of the body, forward displacement, and pitch rotation. The tether also supports an umbilical cable that carries hydraulic connections, electrical power, and a connection to the control computer.

2 Mechanics of the Flip

The planar biped running machine, shown in figure 3, has two telescoping legs connected to the body by pivot joints that form hips. Each hip has a hydraulic actuator that positions the leg fore and aft. An actuator within each leg changes the leg length, while an air spring makes the leg springy in the axial direction. The biped's motion is constrained to be planar by a tether mechanism that allows it to move fore and aft, up and down, and to rotate about the pitch axis. The biped is described more fully in Hodgins, Koechling, and Raibert (1985).

A flip is a maneuver in which the flight phase includes one full rotation of the body and legs. The control of such maneuvers must ensure that the system neither over-rotates nor under-rotates. A basic equation governing the behavior

Figure 4: Cartoon of planar biped doing a forward flip. The machine was running from right to left. 1) Approach with normal alternating gait, 2) hurdle step to gain altitude and prepare for double support, 3) the body has accelerated forward to initiate the flip and the legs have shortened to increase pitch rate, 4) landing step reduces pitch and vertical rates, and 5) resume normal alternating gait. The body configurations are from actual data recorded during a flip. The dots indicate the path of the center of mass at 12 ms intervals.

of the body during the flight phase of a flip is

$$n\pi = \frac{\dot{\phi}\dot{z}}{g},\qquad(1)$$

where

n is the number of full pitch rotations of the body,
$\dot{\phi}$ is the pitch rate of the body,
$\dot{z}$ is the vertical velocity of the body, and
g is the acceleration of gravity.

Equation (1) relates the vertical velocity of the body to its angular velocity. For n full rotations of the body during the flight phase, the rate of body pitch rotation $\dot{\phi}$, times the duration of the flight phase $2\dot{z}/g$, equals the angular displacement of the body $2n\pi$.

Equation (1) relies on several simplifying assumptions. We assume that the legs do not swing with respect to the body during the flight phase, so $\dot{\phi}$ represents the angular rates of both the body and the legs. We further assume that the pitch angle of the body is zero at both liftoff and touchdown, the altitude of the body is the same at liftoff as it is at touchdown, and that there is negligible wind resistance and, therefore, constant angular momentum during flight.

We also assume the pitch rate of the system is constant during the flip. Actually, angular rate may change even though angular momentum is constant. For instance, humans reduce their moment of inertia to increase their rotation rate by tucking the arms and legs. The ice skater's spin is a most dramatic demonstration of this phenomena. Tucking reduces the moment of inertia by concentrating the masses nearer to the center of mass of the system than when untucked.

If the angular rate and moment of inertia of the system in the untucked configuration are $\dot{\phi}_1$ and J_1 and the moment of inertia in the tucked configuration is J_2, then conservation of angular momentum requires the angular rate in the tucked configuration to be $\dot{\phi}_2 = (J_1/J_2)\dot{\phi}_1$. The planar biped tucks † by shortening its legs to minimum length during the

---

† In describing the actions of the biped running machine we use the terminology of gymnastics. When the biped *tucks* it reduces its moment of inertia by shortening its legs. When it *throws* the body a hip torque is applied that increases the body's rotation rate. We use the gymnastic terminology with some trepidation, lest we oversimplify and mislead the reader by suggesting too strong an analogy between the planar biped and a human. The human versions of each of these actions and the human's physical system itself are substantially richer and more elaborate than the planar biped versions we describe here. Moreover, we may find that the suggested functional analogies are

flight phase. To justify the assumption of constant angular rate during the flip, we further assume that the system tucks instantaneously just after liftoff and that it untucks instantaneously just before touchdown. This simplification results in constant pitch rate during the flight phase of a flip. Later we consider the case of slower tucking and untucking.

Frohlich (1979; 1980) points out in his elegant papers on the physics of diving, that a system with several masses can change orientation and angular rate without any angular momentum. This is done by windmilling the arms, peddling the legs, or folding the joints of the body in one sequence and unfolding the body in another sequence. Such configuration effects are not considered here.

Flip Strategies

Equation (1) shows a direct trade-off between the pitch rate and vertical rate of the body at liftoff. The values at liftoff are important because the ballistic nature of the task makes liftoff the last moment the control system can affect either the linear or angular momentum until the next landing. The vertical velocity of the body determines the altitude and the duration of the flight phase, whereas the angular rate determines how far around the body will rotate during that time. Keep in mind that the control system must ensure that the system doesn't over-rotate or under-rotate if it is to continue balanced running. The angular rate can be influenced after liftoff, but for now we assume that the control system does not do so. If the control system increases the vertical rate at liftoff, then a lower pitch rate is needed to rotate the body around in time for landing, and vice versa. This trade-off between vertical velocity and angular velocity suggests three strategies for producing a flip.

One strategy is to maximize the vertical velocity while adjusting the body pitch rate to provide the correct amount of rotation in the available time. Gymnastics coaches seem to teach this strategy to humans for the forward flip. The second strategy is to maximize the body pitch rate while adjusting the vertical velocity to produce a flight phase that takes the correct amount of time. The third strategy is to compromise on both angular and vertical rates, perhaps by introducing an additional constraint on the maneuver or an optimization criterion. The control system we implemented uses the first of these three strategies—maximize flight duration and adjust pitch rate accordingly.

Angular Rate During Flip

Because a system doing a flip will typically have nonzero body pitch angle at both the beginning and end of the flight phase, the total required rotation of the body may deviate substantially from the nominal one revolution that was used in (1). When the liftoff and touchdown pitch angles have the right sign—nose down at liftoff and nose up at touchdown—the distance the body must rotate is reduced. Equation (1) can be modified to incorporate this reduction in the required rotation angle, $\Delta\phi$. Another correction to (1) is required because the legs do not maintain a fixed orientation with respect to the body during flight. At liftoff the body has rotated into a nose down orientation, so the legs are near their extreme forward position with respect to the body. See figure 4. During the flip the legs are rotated forward over the top to place them near the back end of their travel. This rotation of the legs causes backward rotation of the body. We use the notation that when a leg is of length r its moment of inertia is given by $J_l(r)$. If we assume the

legs reorient through an angle $\Delta\theta$ with respect to the body, that reorientation takes place when each leg has minimum length r_{min}, and that the body has moment of inertia J_b, then reorientation adds $2\Delta\theta J_l(r_{min})/J_b$ to the required rotation of the body. Modifying (1) to account for these factors, the basic flip equation becomes

$$\frac{\Delta\phi_{total}}{2} = n\pi + \frac{\phi_{td} - \phi_{lo}}{2} + \frac{\Delta\theta J_l(r_{min})}{J_b} = \frac{\dot{\phi}\dot{z}}{g}. \quad (2)$$

where ϕ_{lo} and ϕ_{td} are the body pitch angles at liftoff and touchdown, assuming positive values for nose down.

To compute the angular rate during the flip we need to know the angular momentum of the system. The angular momentum of the system is the sum of the angular momenta of the body and legs. To simplify the analysis we make the approximation that the center of mass of the system remains located at the hip throughout all maneuvers.

The angular momentum of the legs at liftoff is a function of the configuration at liftoff and the forward and vertical speeds. During normal running the net angular momentum of the legs is small because the legs sweep out of phase—one moves forward while the other moves backward. In a flip, however, the legs move together as they sweep backward during stance, giving them substantial angular momentum. The planar biped has telescoping legs as shown in figure 3. Calculation of angular momentum for such legs is simple because the orientation and angular rate for all parts of the leg are determined by the hip-foot axis. The angular velocity of the stance leg is

$$\dot{\theta} = \frac{\dot{z}_f x_f - \dot{x}_f z_f}{x_f^2 + z_f^2}, \quad (3)$$

where x_f is the forward position of the foot with respect to the center of mass and z is the altitude of the body. During stance when the foot is stationary on the ground $\dot{x}_f = \dot{x}$ and $\dot{z}_f = \dot{z}$. The angular momentum of each leg at liftoff is

$$H_l = \dot{\theta} J_l(r), \quad (4)$$

where the moment of inertia of each leg about the hip is

$$J_l(r) = J_{l1} + m_{l1} r_1^2 + J_{l2} + m_{l2}(r - r_2)^2. \quad (5)$$

J_{l1}, J_{l2}, m_{l1}, m_{l2}, r_1, and r_2 are physical parameters of the leg and are given in table 1. The angular momentum of the body is just $\dot{\phi} J_b$.

The pitch rate of the system once airborne can be found by equating the angular momentum just before liftoff and just after the tuck. If the legs have length r_{lo} just before liftoff, then the angular momentum of the system is

$$\dot{\phi}(J_b + 2J_l(r_{min})) = \dot{\phi}_{lo} J_b + 2\dot{\theta}_{lo} J_l(r_{lo}). \quad (6)$$

If the legs shorten immediately after liftoff to length r_{min} and do not swing with respect to the body, then the pitch rate after the tuck is

$$\dot{\phi} = \frac{\dot{\phi}_{lo} J_b + 2\dot{\theta}_{lo} J_l(r_{lo})}{J_b + 2J_l(r_{min})}. \quad (7)$$

3 Control

To control flips we start with normal biped running and the control algorithms described in Hodgins, Koechling, and Raibert (1985). Briefly, the normal control system positions the legs during flight to regulate the forward running speed, thrusts axially with the stance leg to drive the up-and-down

---

faulty in significant details.

Parameter	Symbol	Value
Body mass	m_b	11.45 kg
Body moment of inertia	J_b	0.40 kg-m^2
Upper leg mass	m_{l1}	1.055 kg
Upper leg moment of inertia at COM	J_{l1}	0.0204 kg-m^2
Distance from hip to upper leg COM	r_1	0.0838 m
Lower leg mass	m_{l2}	0.608 kg
Lower leg moment of inertia at COM	J_{l2}	0.0237 kg-m^2
Distance from foot to lower leg COM	r_2	0.317 m
Min leg length	r_{min}	0.44 m
Max leg length	r_{max}	0.67 m
Min leg moment of inertia about hip	$J_l(r_{min})$	0.062 kg-m^2
Max leg moment of inertia about hip	$J_l(r_{max})$	0.126 kg-m^2

Table 1: Physical parameters of planar biped.

Step	Action
Approach	Run forward at 2.5 m/s with alternating gait
Hurdle	Hop with maximum thrust Prepare to land on two legs Extend legs further forward than normal
Flip	Jump with maximum thrust Pitch body forward with large hip torque Shorten legs once airborne Lengthen and position both legs for landing
Landing	Hop with small or negative thrust Return pitch rate to zero and restore posture
Following	Resume running with alternating gait

Table 2: Summary of actions taken by planar biped to do a flip.

bouncing motion, and exerts hip torque between the stance leg and the body to keep the body in an upright posture. Using these algorithms the machine runs with an alternating gait that uses each leg for support, one at a time, with a flight phase separating each stance phase. The control actions needed for the flip are superimposed upon the normal running behavior produced by this set of control algorithms.

Three steps of the normal running sequence are modified to perform a flip. The three modified steps are the *hurdle step*, *flip step*, and *landing step*. The hurdle step is used to prepare for the maneuver by developing extra hopping height and by making a transition from the normal running gait that uses the legs in alternation, to the double support needed for the flip. The flip step uses both legs together to power the jump, and accelerates the body about the pitch axis for the actual rotating maneuver. The landing step dissipates the high angular and vertical rates and returns the system to the standard alternating gait. The activities that take place in these three steps are summarized in table 2 with additional detail given in the appendix. We now describe these three steps and how the control system uses them to generate a flip.

Maximum Jump Altitude

Earlier we suggested three possible strategies for establishing the trade-off between pitch velocity and vertical velocity. We decided to control the flip using the first strategy, which attempts to achieve a maximum vertical velocity and an intermediate pitch rate. The rationale for this decision was

that it would be easier to remove excess vertical energy with a hard landing than it would be to remove excess angular energy. The large hip torque needed to remove angular energy might demand more traction than would be available, and we were unsure of the ability of the pitch control servo to correct large rate errors.

To get maximum altitude during the flip the control program does three things. It jumps high on the hurdle step to increase the vertical energy in the system, it converts forward speed into vertical speed by placing the foot further forward than normal on the landing just before the flip, and it delivers maximum thrust during the flip step.

The control system delivers maximum thrust to the leg on the hurdle step to increase the altitude that will be reached during the next flight phase. Since the legs are springy they absorb a portion of the system's vertical energy on landing and then return the absorbed energy to help power the next flight. A hurdle step with increased altitude will result in a flip step with increased altitude as well. Gymnastics coaches generally do not recommend a high hurdle step (George 1980).

Maximum thrust is developed during the hurdle step by setting the hydraulic servovalve that extends the leg to its maximum value as soon as the stance phase begins. On a normal step thrust is delayed to the middle of stance, but thrusting throughout all of stance provides more time for the leg actuator to compress the leg spring and accelerate the body upward.

In principle, this strategy of using the springy legs to recover the vertical thrust energy from one step and propagate it ahead to the next step can be used to overcome the limited power of the leg actuator. Rather than use a single hurdle step there could be several, with the liftoff altitude and flight time increasing on each one. In practice, leg spring losses increase monotonically with hopping height. Therefore, the highest hop possible occurs when the maximum thrust the actuator can deliver during one stance phase just equals the leg losses that occur during one hop. In any case, the planar biped uses just one hurdle step.

The second thing the control program does to maximize altitude is to convert some of the forward kinetic energy into vertical kinetic energy. This is done by extending the legs further forward than normal just before the stance phase of the flip step. In normal running, the control system positions the foot to leave the forward and vertical speeds of the body unchanged from one step to the next. The foot position that achieves this result is called the *neutral point* (Raibert 1986a). When the control system places the foot forward of the neutral point, the forward speed declines and the vertical speed increases as shown in figure 5.

If the foot were positioned to change the forward speed from $\dot{x}_a$ to $\dot{x}_b$ and if there were no mechanical losses in the leg, then the vertical velocity would increase from $\dot{z}_a$ to $\dot{z}_b = \sqrt{\dot{x}_a^2 - \dot{x}_b^2 + \dot{z}_a^2}$ and the duration of flight would increase by $2(\sqrt{\dot{x}_a^2 - \dot{x}_b^2 + \dot{z}_a^2} - \dot{z}_a)/g$. On a typical flip $\dot{x}_a = 2.5$ m/s and $\dot{x}_b = 1.5$ m/s, so the flight phase could increase by 0.2 seconds if the leg were lossless. We have not measured how much this actually increases flight duration.

The third method of increasing altitude for the flip is to deliver maximum thrust on the flip step itself. During this step there are two legs in support, both of which thrust with maximum hydraulic servovalve settings from the beginning of the stance phase to the end.

Figure 6 shows data recorded from the sensors and actuators of the planar biped as it performed a forward flip. Examining these data, we find that a good approach at 2.5 m/s,

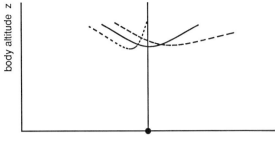

Figure 5: Trajectory of body for various foot positions. During normal running the foot is positioned so that the forward velocity of the body is the same at the end of the stance phase as it was at the beginning of the stance phase (solid line). During a flip the foot is extended forward to transfer some of the forward kinetic energy into vertical kinetic energy, thereby increasing the altitude of the flip and the time available to rotate the body (dotted line). It is also possible to convert vertical velocity into forward velocity, a procedure that can be used upon landing after the flip. For each trajectory shown in the plot, the foot is located at the solid circle (•). Adapted from Stentz (1983).

a good hurdle step, and a good two-legged jump resulted in a vertical velocity at liftoff of 3.4 m/s, an altitude of 1.04 m, and a flight time of about 0.67 s.

The description so far has centered on maximizing the duration of flight. Assuming this method produces a consistent duration of flight from one flip to the next, it remains to provide one full rotation of the body in the time available. The next section addresses this task.

Desired Body Rotation

We implemented a simple control program for providing the correct amount of pitch rotation. The human driver adjusts the running speed which gives the legs a certain angular momentum, the hip actuator throws the body to give it angular momentum, and once airborne the legs shorten into a tuck to increase the angular pitch rate.

The angular momentum of the body is $\dot{\phi}J_b$. The body is given angular momentum by exerting a large nose-down pitch torque about the hip during the final part of the stance phase, just before the flip. This is called throwing the body. When a gymnast throws, he or she typically uses the arms, head, and trunk. The planar biped has no head or arms so it is restricted to throwing the body. The control system uses two parameters to regulate how much throw the body is given. One parameter is the magnitude of pitch torque. The other parameter is a threshold for the pitch rate—when the pitch rate exceeds this value, the control system turns off the pitch torque. The actual pitch rate exceeds the threshold value by some amount which we have found to be repeatable.

It is undesirable for the body to over-travel the limited motion of the hip joint during the period of throw. If the body runs out of travel and hits the mechanical stop before liftoff, the collision and resulting ground forces dissipate the angular momentum of the body. To avoid this the control system initiates the throw early enough so that the pitch rate reaches the threshold value at approximately the same time the feet leave the ground at the end of stance. A third parameter specifies this delay.

Acceptable values for these three parameters—the delay for initiation of pitch torque, the magnitude of pitch torque, and the threshold pitch rate to terminate pitch torque—were

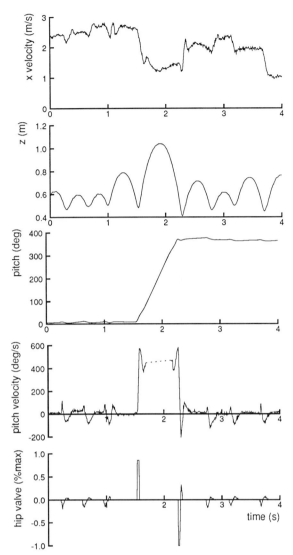

Figure 6: Data recorded during a biped flip. The top two curves show that forward speed is converted into vertical motion. The second graph shows that the flip step is the highest in the sequence. The bottom curves of pitch velocity and hip torque illustrate the inherent symmetry in the flip. Data recorded at 6 ms, the cycle time of the control system.

determined empirically through a series of attempted flips. We started with zero delay, maximum pitch torque, and a very large pitch rate threshold. After about 20 attempts with manual adjustment after each, we arrived at values that provided acceptable rotational behavior for a flip.

When the body reaches its peak altitude during the flight phase of the flip, the control system swings the legs part way forward to center the hip joints. As the body approaches the floor, the control system lengthens the legs to untuck for landing and orients the legs to position the feet. The vertical altitude of the body at which the control system begins to lengthen and orient the legs is specified by another parameter, which was adjusted manually throughout the course of attempting several flips. The leg orientation on this landing is calculated as in normal running, where the goal is to provide balance and to control forward running speed.

For the flip shown in figure 6, the biped approaches with a forward running speed of about 2.5 m/s. After 36 ms of the stance phase of the flip step the control system sets the hip servovalve output signals to 85% of maximum. The hip servovalve is turned off when $\dot{\phi} = 7.85\,\text{rad/s}$. At liftoff the body has developed angular momentum $H_b = 3.9\,\text{kg-m}^2/\text{s}$ and each of the two legs has angular momentum $H_l = 0.42\,\text{kg-m}^2/\text{s}$. The total angular momentum at liftoff is $H = 4.7\,\text{kg-m}^2/\text{s}$. Once the system tucks, the total moment of inertia is $J = 0.52\,\text{kg-m}^2$ and the rotation rate is $\dot{\phi} = 9.97\,\text{rad/s}$. Equation (2) suggests a pitch rate of 9.92 rad/s for the measured values $\phi_{lo} = -.40\,\text{rad}$, $\phi_{td} = .10\,\text{rad}$, and $\Delta\theta = .33\,\text{rad}$.

Once the system lands after the flip, the control system must eliminate the large vertical and angular energies that were needed for the flip. The control system reduces the vertical energy in two ways. It returns the desired forward running speed to the value used before the flip, converting some of the vertical kinetic energy back into forward kinetic energy. This accelerates the system forward while reducing the height of the next hop. The control program also specifies a smaller than usual leg thrust to absorb some of the vertical energy.

To return the body pitch angle and pitch rate to their normal values the control program exerts hip torques between both legs and the body using a linear PD servo:

$$\tau = -k_p(\phi - \phi_d) - k_v(\dot{\phi}), \qquad (8)$$

where

τ is the hip torque and
ϕ is the pitch angle of the body,
ϕ_d is the desired pitch angle of the body (level),
$\dot{\phi}$ is the pitch rate of the body, and
k_p, k_v are gains.

This is the same mechanism that is used to maintain the body posture in normal running. After the landing step, the control program switches back to an alternating gait with the control algorithms for normal running.

Figure 7: Aerial as performed by a human gymnast. Drawings reprinted from Tonry (1983).

Aerials

The front aerial is a variant of the flip. It differs from the flip in that the performer takes off from one leg rather than two, the legs are spread during the pitch rotation rather than kept together, and the landing takes place on one leg. See figure 7. For humans, an aerial is a variant of the cartwheel, in which the hands do not touch the ground. The aerial is considerably easier than a flip for humans, because humans can spread the legs a large amount to reduce the amount of body rotation needed during the flight phase.

For the biped, the aerial is harder than the flip. Just one leg is used to power the flight phase, so the time of flight for an aerial is about 80% of that for a flip. The flight time for a typical flip is 0.67 s compared to 0.55 s for an aerial. This makes it difficult to get adequate rotation during the

time available in the flight phase. On the other hand, there is no need to swing the legs forward during the flight phase, because the angles between the legs and the body at liftoff are already correct for landing. This reduces the amount the system has to rotate during flight by about 0.10 rad as compared to a flip.

The planar biped control program for aerials differs from that for the flip in only one important characteristic; both the body and the swing leg are thrown to develop angular momentum about the pitch axis. Because the legs move in opposite directions during the approach for an aerial, the net angular momentum of the legs is small. The stance leg sweeps backward while the swing leg sweeps forward. The control program throws the swing leg along with the body to increase the contribution of the legs to the angular momentum of the system. See figure 8. The procedure for throwing the body is the same as for the flip, but with just one hip actuator exerting torque. Examining the data shown in figure 9 we find that the leg thrown has angular momentum just before liftoff of $H_l = 0.60\,\text{kg-m}^2$. At that time the angular momentum for the stance leg is $H_l = 0.19\,\text{kg-m}^2$, for the body is $H_b = 3.74\,\text{kg-m}^2$, and for the total system is $H_{aerial} = 4.52\,\text{kg-m}^2$. The total is slightly less than for the flip $H_{flip} = 4.7\,\text{kg-m}^2$.

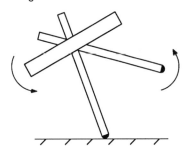

Figure 8: To develop angular momentum in the aerial the control system accelerates both the body and the swing leg in the same direction during the final part of the stance phase.

Step	Action
Approach	Run forward at 2.5 m/s with alternating gait
Hurdle	Hop with maximum thrust Extend leg further forward than normal
Aerial	Hop with maximum thrust Swing free leg backward Pitch body forward with large hip torque Shorten legs once airborne Lengthen and position forward leg for landing
Landing	Hop with small or negative thrust Return pitch rate to zero and restore posture
Following	Resume running with normal alternating gait

Table 3: Summary of actions taken by planar biped to do an aerial.

The planar biped executes aerials using the control sequence outlined in table 3. Data for one aerial are shown in figure 9. The machine has performed aerials successfully many times. In every case, however, the time available for rotation was so short that the control system could not orient the landing leg to properly position the foot for best stability on landing. The system kept its balance on landing, but

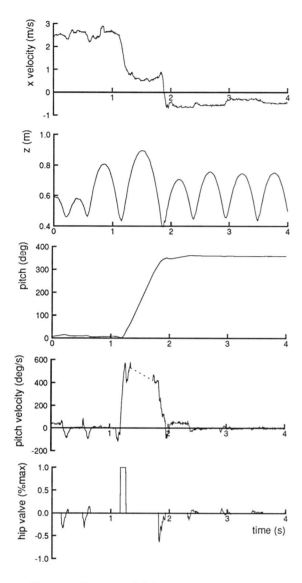

Figure 9: Data recorded during a biped aerial. The top curve of x velocity shows how the forward speed is converted to vertical motion, and how after the aerial the foot is not positioned well enough for the machine to continue traveling forward although it does continue running. The second graph shows that the aerial step is the highest in the sequence, although the difference between the hurdle step and the aerial step is not as dramatic as it was for the flip.

with a noticeable reduction in forward running speed after the maneuver, as can be seen in the top curve of figure 9.

4 Discussion

Adjusting Pitch Rate During Flight

The control system we implemented for the biped flip makes no attempt to adjust pitch rate once the system is airborne. It keeps the legs tucked during most of the flight phase, resulting in constant moment of inertia and constant angular rate. The amount of rotation during the flight phase is a function of the system's state at liftoff.

It should be possible to control a flip more precisely by

manipulating the rate of rotation during the flight phase. Because angular momentum must be conserved during the flight phase, the control system can manipulate the rate of rotation by changing the length and moment of inertia of the legs. To synchronize foot contact with full body rotation, the control system could measure the altitude of the body and rotational progress of the flip to determine the moment to untuck the legs.

The simplest model assumes that the legs lengthen instantaneously. If $2J_l(r_{min}) + J_b$ is the moment of inertia of the system with the legs short and $2J_l(r_{max}) + J_b$ is the moment of inertia with the legs long, then to synchronize full rotation with the moment of landing the legs should lengthen when

$$\Delta\phi = \dot\phi\left(\frac{2J_l(r_{min}) + J_b}{2J_l(r_{max}) + J_b}\right)\left(\frac{\dot z + \sqrt{\dot z^2 + 2g(z - z_{td})}}{g}\right) \quad (9)$$

where

$\Delta\phi$ is the remaining rotation required before landing,
$\dot\phi$ is the angular rate of the body,
z is the vertical position of the body,
z_{td} is the expected vertical position of the body at touch-down, and
$\dot z$ is the vertical velocity.

The control system could evaluate (9) throughout the flight phase of the flip to determine when the legs should lengthen.

The utility of (9) depends on the ability to lengthen the legs in zero time. For the planar biped the maximum rate at which the planar biped can lengthen its legs is primarily determined by the maximum rate at which oil can flow through the hydraulic servovalves. Equation 9 can be extended to accommodate a fixed rate of leg lengthening.

How far does the body rotate during leg lengthening at a fixed rate? Suppose the legs change length from r_a to r_b at a fixed rate $\dot r_k$. Define t_a and t_b so that $r(t_a) = r_a$ and $r(t_b) = r_b$. If the pitch rate is initially $\dot\phi_a = \dot\phi(t_a)$, then the angular rate during leg lengthening is a function of leg length

$$\dot\phi(t) = \dot\phi_a\left(\frac{2J_l(r_a) + J_b}{2J_l(r) + J_b}\right). \quad (10)$$

Substituting for $r = r_a + (t - t_a)\dot r_k$ and integrating we determine how much ϕ changes during lengthening

$$\Delta\phi' = \int_{t_a}^{t_b}\frac{\dot\phi_{lo}(2J_l(r_b) + J_b)}{2J_l(r_a + (t - t_a)\dot r_k) + J_b}dt$$
$$= \frac{a}{\dot r_k b}\left\{\arctan\left(\frac{r_b - r_2}{b}\right) - \arctan\left(\frac{r_a - r_2}{b}\right)\right\}, \quad (11)$$

where $J_l(r)$ is defined in (5), r_2 and m_{l2} are constants defined in table 1, and

$$a = -\frac{\dot\phi_{lo}(J_b + 2J_l(r_b))}{2m_{l2}}$$

$$b = \sqrt{(r_b - r_2)^2 - \frac{J_b + 2J_l(r_b)}{2m_{l2}}}.$$

If the legs are length r_a during a flip, then they should lengthen to r_b at rate $\dot r_k$ when

$$\Delta\phi = \dot\phi\left(\frac{2J_l(r_a) + J_b}{2J_l(r_b) + J_b}\right)\left(\frac{\dot z + \sqrt{\dot z^2 + 2g(z - z_{td})}}{g} - t_b + t_a\right)$$
$$+ \frac{a}{\dot r_k b}\left\{\arctan\left(\frac{r_b - r_2}{b}\right) - \arctan\left(\frac{r_a - r_2}{b}\right)\right\}. \quad (12)$$

Symmetry of the Flip

The locomotion algorithms that are normally used to generate running in the planar biped are based on a principle of control that we call *running symmetry* (Raibert 1986b). The basic idea is that a legged system will travel in steady state when the accelerations it experiences have odd symmetry during each stride. Odd functions integrate to zero, resulting in no net change in running speed or in posture. For systems with a symmetric mechanical shape, the control system can produce the desired pattern of odd accelerations by causing the body and limbs to move along trajectories that are even and odd functions of time. These symmetries apply to steady state running, to pairs of steps, and to multilegged running (Raibert 1986b; 1986c).

For a legged system to run with symmetry throughout a series of steps, the vertical and angular velocities of the body must be coordinated during the flight phases. In normal running the constraint is

$$\frac{\phi}{\dot{\phi}} = \frac{\dot{z}}{g} \qquad (13)$$

assuming constant angular rate during flight. An implication of (13) is that the pitch angle of the body at the end of the flight phase is equal and opposite to the pitch angle at the beginning of the flight phase $\phi_{td} = -\phi_{lo}$. Despite temporary but radical departures from the steady state, the flip and aerial conform to these symmetries.

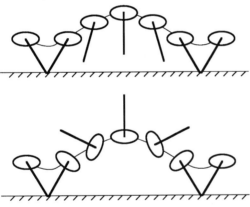

Figure 10: Diagram of symmetric behavior during the flight phase for a normal step and for a flip. In both cases the forward displacement and pitch angle of the body are described by odd functions of time, and the altitude of the body is described by an even function of time.

For flips and aerials (13) becomes

$$\frac{\phi + n\pi}{\dot{\phi}} = \frac{\dot{z}}{g}, \qquad (14)$$

which is related to (1) and (2). Equation (14) implies the same constraint as does (13), but with n additional full rotations of the body during flight. See figure 10. Reorientation of the legs with respect to the body during flight is ignored here, but the nonzero pitch angles at liftoff and touchdown are included. The torque exerted at the hip to accelerate the body about the pitch axis to start the flip forms a symmetric pair with the torque exerted at the hip to decelerate the body upon landing. The bottom curves in figures 6 and 9 illustrate this symmetry.

Recognition that flips, too, should conform to symmetry helped us to reason through the design of the flip control programs and to generalize our understanding of symmetry. For instance, at first we worried about getting adequate traction after the flip to dissipate the large angular momentum. Symmetry considerations permitted us to see that if there were adequate traction at liftoff to generate the angular momentum, then there should be adequate traction at touchdown to dissipate the angular momentum. A similar consideration was useful in reasoning about the vertical motion.

Open-loop Control

The flip and aerial belong to a class of movements that are dynamic and ballistic. Other members of the class are those that occur in tumbling, diving, and high jumping. These movements are dynamic in that substantial speed and kinetic energy are a major factor in their production. The movements are ballistic in that there are intervals during which the actuators cease to have any direct influence on the key variables of the task. For instance, during the flight phase of a flip no actuator can change the altitude, vertical rate, or angular momentum of the system. In contrast, for the task of making a manipulator move along a trajectory there is a separate motor to drive the motion of each joint directly and continuously.

Another attribute of these tasks is that outside disturbance plays a relatively minor role. The environment for the movement is essentially unchanging during and between movements, changing only slightly from one repetition to the next. If the initial conditions are precisely established and if the same forces are exerted by each actuator on each repetition, then the behavior repeats in nearly identical form time after time. Sensing and feedback are important in executing such tasks, but in a more relaxed role than the inner loop of a high bandwidth servomechanism. At the same time, open-loop feedforward control signals can play a more important role in such behavior.

The approach we have taken to control flips and aerials relies on the repeatability of the system, on constancy of the environment, and on correctly establishing the initial conditions for the movement. This allows the use of a rather inflexible open-loop actuation pattern to produce the behavior. For instance, to accelerate the pitch rotation of the body the control system waits 36 ms after the start of the flip step, sets the output signal for the hip servovalves to 85% of maximum, waits until the pitch rate reaches 7.85 rad/s, and then turns the hip servovalves off. This control is not devoid of feedback, however, feedback is used sparingly. It uses the pitch rate to determine when to stop throwing the body, and it uses the underlying running pattern to synchronize each flip action to the behavior of the machine.

The control system we implemented for flips is somewhat like a multichannel tape recorder, with the output signal from each channel wired directly to one actuator. To begin a movement the control system establishes the initial conditions for the movement and "it presses the play button" on the tape recorder. In biological contexts this model of motor control has been called the *motor tape* (Evarts et al. 1970). It is thought that under certain circumstances the nervous system may produce behavior not through sensors and high-gain feedback loops, but by issuing sequences of open-loop commands that go directly to the muscles. In the pure form of the model the commands are issued independent of progress in executing the movement. It is not known whether the motor tape accurately models actual biological motor behavior.

The flip control system is like the motor tape model in that it uses a sequence of motor commands that are issued directly to the actuators, without a local servo. The magnitude of actuator signals for thrust in the hurdle and flip steps and the throw delay and magnitude are specified in this manner. The flip control system is unlike the motor tape in that the timing of control actions are synchronized to events in the locomotion cycle, and thereby, to the progress of the movement. For example, the maximum vertical thrust does not begin until the normal locomotion control algorithm has entered stance. The starting time and magnitude of hip torque for pitch acceleration are determined with a fixed sequence like the motor tape, but hip torque is terminated when pitch rate reaches a desired value.

The use of feedforward without high bandwidth feedback is not new. It is used to send spacecraft to the moon, Mars, and beyond. At a predetermined moment the engines ignite for a predetermined period to take the craft out of Earth orbit and send it toward the remote rendezvous. In space travel there is no attempt to adjust thrust continuously throughout the trip to stay exactly on course with precisely the desired speed, because such an approach would require far too much energy. Occasional adjustments are made instead.

There are two characteristics of space travel that make this approach feasible. First, unexpected external disturbances have a minor influence on the behavior of the spacecraft. Second, variability in the actuators and internal mechanism is relatively small. These conditions imply that for the same initial conditions and the same actuator output signals the actual behavior of the system is very nearly the expected behavior, and that behavior of the system will reliably repeat on successive executions. These conditions apply to the symmetric maneuvers described in this paper.

Formulating Strategies

We have described the specific control used to make the biped running machine do forward flips and aerials. The essential features of the approach are a strategy for executing the flip and a set of low-level actions and parameters that implement the strategy. The strategy we chose is based on several decisions:

- Maximize time of flight, with pitch rate adjusted accordingly.
- Extend the legs forward on the flip step to convert forward speed into vertical speed.
- Adjust the start of pitching torque to synchronize the end of hip travel with liftoff.
- Shorten the legs during flight to increase pitch rate.
- Reduce thrust to absorb vertical energy on landing.
- Use normal pitch control algorithm to absorb angular energy on landing.

Each of these decisions was made by humans based on knowledge of the mechanics of the problem and intuition. It is not hard to imagine that future control systems may be able to formulate strategies such as these automatically. Such systems will embody a model of the mechanical system to be controlled, a working knowledge of the physics that govern behavior of the model, and an ability to reason. Heuristics and optimizations may be important. The need for techniques that bridge the gap between the task level of a motor act and the actuator control level is a deep and important problem in robotics and artificial intelligence.

If strategies for performance of a task were found automatically, optimal behavior might be easier to find. A given strategy for performing a particular task may not be the only or the best strategy, and it may be difficult to know if a better strategy exists. Richard Fosbury demonstrated this point

in 1968. He introduced a previously unknown form for doing the high jump, the *Fosbury Flop*, winning an Olympic gold medal in the process. Six years later Dwight Stones used the Fosbury Flop to set a new high jump world record of $7'7\frac{1}{4}''$ (Doherty 1976). In 1973 a flip was used in long jump competition. It was soon declared illegal because it was "not what has traditionally been known as long jumping" but perhaps it would have become a second example of a radically different and significantly better strategy (Ecker 1976). Formal techniques may some day permit us to find all possible strategies for a task and to identify the best possible solution.

Acknowledgements

This work was supported by the Defense Advanced Research Projects Agency, Engineering Applications Office, ARPA Order No. 4148, and by a grant from the System Development Foundation.

References

Doherty, J. K. 1976. *Track and Field Omnibook* (Tafnews Press: Los Altos Cal.)

Ecker, T. 1976. *Track and Field: Technique through Dynamics* (Tafnews Press: Los Altos Cal.)

Evarts, E. V., Bizzi, E., Burk, R. E., Delong, M., Thach, W. T., Jr. 1971. Central control of movement. *Neurosciences Research Progress Bulletin* 9.

Frohlich, C. 1979. Do springboard divers violate angular momentum conservation? *American Journal of Physics* 47:583–592.

Frohlich, C. 1980. The physics of somersaulting and twisting. *Scientific American* 242:154–164.

George, G. S. 1980. *Biomechanics of Women's Gymnastics* (Prentice-Hall Inc.: Englewood Cliffs, N. J.).

Hodgins, J., Koechling, J., Raibert, M. H. 1985. Running experiments with a planar biped. *Third International Symposium on Robotics Research*, Cambridge: MIT Press.

Raibert, M. H. 1986a. *Legged Robots That Balance* (MIT Press: Cambridge Mass.)

Raibert, M. H., 1986b. Running with symmetry. *Int. J. of Robotics Research* 5:4.

Raibert, M. H. 1986c. Symmetry in running. *Science*, 231:1292–1294.

Raibert, M. H., Hodgins, J., Brown, H. B., Chepponis, M., Goldberg, K., Koechling, J., Miller, J. 1986. *Dynamically Stable Legged Locomotion–Progress Report: January 1985–August 1986*. Robotics Institute, Carnegie-Mellon University.

Stentz, A. 1983, Behavior during stance. In *Dynamically Stable Legged Locomotion—Third Annual Report*, M. H. Raibert et al. Robotics Institute, Carnegie-Mellon University, CMU-RI-TR-83-20, pp. 106–110.

Tonry, D. 1983. *Tumbling* (Harper & Row: New York).

Appendix: Details of Control Sequence for Flip

State	Trigger Event	Action	Flip Action
Approach			
FLIGHT 150	Leg 1 not touching ground	Shorten leg 1 Don't move hip 1 Lengthen leg 2 for landing Position leg 2 for landing	
Hurdle Step			
LOADING 1210	Leg 2 touches ground	Keep leg 1 short Don't move hip 1 Hold leg 2 at landing length Zero hip torque leg 2	
COMPRESSION 1220	Leg 2 air spring shortened	Keep leg 1 short Position leg 1 for landing † Erect body with hip 2	Reduce desired speed Max thrust: leg 2
THRUST 1230	Leg 2 air spring lengthening	Keep leg 1 short Position leg 1 for landing Erect body with hip 2	Max thrust: leg 2
UNLOADING 1240	Leg 2 air spring near full length	Keep leg 1 short Position leg 1 for landing Shorten leg 2 Zero hip torque leg 2	
FLIGHT 1250	Leg 2 not touching ground	Lengthen both legs for landing Position both legs for landing	
Flip Step			
LOADING 2110	Both legs touch ground	Hold both legs at landing length	Zero both hip torques
COMPRESSION 2120	Both air springs shortened		Max thrust: both legs Zero both hip torques
THRUST 2130	Compression + delay (36 ms)		Max thrust: both legs Exert large pitch torque: both legs (85% of max)
THRUST 2131	Pitch velocity > desired pitch velocity (7.85 rad/s)		Max thrust: both legs Zero both hip torques
UNLOADING 2140	Both air springs near full length	Shorten both legs Zero both hip torques	
FLIGHT A 2150	Both legs not touching ground		Shorten both legs Don't move either hip
FLIGHT B 2151	Vertical velocity zero		Keep both legs short Center both hips
FLIGHT C 2152	Body altitude < threshold (.7 m)	Lengthen both legs for landing Position both legs for landing †	
Landing Step			
LOADING 3210	Both legs touch ground	Hold both legs at landing length Zero both hip torques	
COMPRESSION 3220	Both air springs shortened	Keep both legs at landing length Erect body: both hips	
THRUST 3230	Both air springs lengthening	Erect body: both hips	Reduced thrust: both legs
UNLOADING 3240	Both air springs near full length	Shorten both legs Zero both hip torques	
Resume normal running			

† Expected T_s is adjusted by a factor of $1/\sqrt{2}$ to account for two legs in support during the flip step.

Investigating Fast, Intelligent Systems with a Ping-Pong Playing Robot

Russell L. Andersson

AT&T Bell Laboratories
Crawford's Corner Road (Rm. 4B607)
Holmdel, NJ 07733

A robotic system that plays ping-pong has been constructed as an experiment in intelligent real time planning and control. The primary advance is a specialized form of "expert system" designed for numeric and symbolic processing of real time applications. A vision system tracks the ball in 3-D at 60 Hz, requiring special consideration of the dynamic nature of the images, as well as techniques for static accuracy. The low-level robot controller uses partial dynamics for planning and control. We will overview the system, concentrating mainly on the expert component.

1. Introduction

The robot ping-pong experiment described in this paper was created to investigate how to build robot systems that can display reasonably intelligent behavior in dynamically changing environments. Artificial intelligence (AI) programs can exhibit symbolic reasoning, but only at slow rates. Speed is not the only issue, however, because the AI systems concentrate on symbols to the exclusion of numbers, and we require numbers to run robots. Robot controllers use directly coded numeric algorithms to attain the speed required to drive the robot, and consequently fail to display very interesting or complex behavior patterns. Our intent here is to provide an intermediate level between the AI system and the robot controller, which is able to do numeric and simple symbolic processing at the rates required for operation in the dynamic environment, thus reproducing the skilled behavior patterns of an athlete or assembly-line worker.

We use robot ping-pong as an example because it is a stable, well-defined problem with many degrees of freedom and stringent performance requirements. Robot ping-pong has no best solution: best can only be defined in terms of some arbitrary evaluator. The only true evaluator is: who won the point? The robot controller must pick a suitable return from those feasible for a given incoming trajectory, and update it as additional data arrives. The planned return must satisfy the constraints of the robot and the rules of ping-pong. The robot system must act long before accurate data is available.

The robot plays ping-pong according to international standard robot ping-pong rules proposed by [Billingsley, 1984] (Figure 1). Reaction time ranges from 0.4 to 0.8 sec. Only five degrees of freedom are required for ping-pong because the paddle can be rotated about its normal vector, but the direction of this degree of freedom varies. One of the system's challenges is to take advantage of this degree of freedom.

We use an upside-down Unimation PUMA 260 robot; with a reach of 0.4 m, it is a smaller and faster relative of the

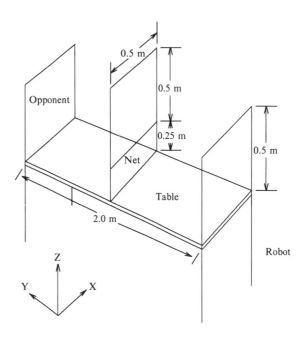

Figure 1. Robot Ping-Pong Table. The players, background, and table are black. The ball must travel sequentially through the square frame at one end, through the center frame, then bounce once and travel through the frame at the table's other end.

PUMA 560. To create a workable robot configuration, we put the paddle at the end of a 0.45 m stick, mounted perpendicular to the axis of joint six. The configuration enhances reach and reduces the velocity required of joint six.

We have implemented the system on a network of Motorola 68020s connected by the S/Net [Ahuja, 1983], a high bandwidth, low latency inter-processor connect. A multiprocessing and multitasking operating system called MEGLOS supports real time programming [Gaglianello & Katseff, 1985]. Each processor contains a "CLOX" board, which emulates a global wall clock, enabling high timing accuracy to be maintained across the entire system [Andersson, 1986]. A block diagram is shown in Figure 2.

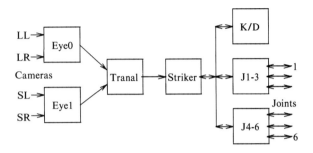

Figure 2. Simplified Block Diagram. The cameras (long-range left, short-range right, *etc.*) feed the vision processors, Eye0 and Eye1. XYZT data is sent to the trajectory analyzer, Tranal, which produces predictions of the ball's path for the expert system processor, striker. A kinematics and dynamics slave processor (K/D) and two joint servo processors drive the robot.

The paper is divided into three major sections. First, we will describe the real time expert system's design. Next, we will describe the vision system, including some experimental data. Finally, we will describe the robot controller and its trajectory planning and following methods. Due to length limitations, we can only overview the system; see [Andersson, 1988] for a full description.

2. Real Time Expert System

This section describes the generic design of the real time expert system at the heart of the robot ping-pong player. Most of the discussion will be ping-pong-independent, but we will occasionally use ping-pong as an example.

2.1 Functionality Required

To understand why something should be organized the way it is, we must first understand what it must do. We will review the specific capabilities required of the real time expert system.

2.1.1 Initial planning. The expert system must select initial values for program variables whose values are not directly determined from the sensor data. For example, the return velocity of a ping-pong ball can be arbitrary within certain bounds. The values of these "free" variables will greatly influence the values of other program variables.

We have to avoid problems whose existence can not be detected until we have committed them. The expert system must intelligently pick values for the free variables to minimize the likelihood of subsequent problems, before much information is available to guide the selection.

2.1.2 Temporal updating. Once an initial plan has been formulated, the expert system must update it as new data becomes available at 60 Hz. We will refer to the modification of the plan as temporal updating. Changes in the input data must be mapped into appropriate degrees of freedom in the plan so that the resulting plan continues to be feasible.

In addition, the expert system must evaluate the current plan, and modify it preemptively to avoid problems. For example, if a particular joint is getting close to its maximum torque output, the expert system should begin to change program variables in advance to compensate for the problem.

2.1.3 Exception handling. When the ball bounces, hits the net, or the spin suddenly becomes understood, dramatic changes in plan are required. The expert system must rapidly identify a strategy to solve the problem. It must have a means for causing changes in the program's existing flow of execution. The implementation of the strategy must be monitored, and alternative strategies chosen if the initial approach proves infeasible.

2.2 Rule-Based Systems

Conventional AI research often makes use of rule-based systems. Rule-based systems have a number of advantages when applied to certain problems. The rules separate the knowledge base from the inference engine required to use it, allowing inference engines to be reused. The inference engine provides data matching and search algorithms which are task independent.

Global blackboards and flat name spaces enable each rule to access any variable without regard to the program's structure (since there is none), so the rule base may take advantage of all available information.

Because each rule is complete in its own right, it is presumably easy to understand and modify. The rules may be machine-readable, and thus amenable to programmed modification.

A rule-based system can provide flexible control. By merely manipulating a few variables, a non-local goto may be obtained without cries of protest from structured programmers, or the explicit designation of the target of the goto. Sudden changes in control flow are useful in exception handling, when a different activity must suddenly be scheduled.

2.3 Real Time Expert System Architecture

The real time expert system problem domain has specialized characteristics that affect the system design. Transparently, a real time rule-based system must be optimized for speed.

Real time robotic systems require the synthesis of a plan. Because the system creates new data rather than examining old data, it is appropriate to work from the problem towards the solution. The data is known and fixed in quantity, eliminating the need for pattern matching between rules and variables.

A robot system requires more sequencing than a situation analysis system. Data dependencies among subtasks force one subtask after another to be solved, suggesting a data-flow architecture rather than independent parallel tasks. A rule-based system must implement sequencing with goal and state variables that obscure its original advantages of clarity and easy modification.

We may now outline the real time expert system's basic features. The expert system is implemented in the programming language "C," which efficiently executes numeric programs. Readability and ease of modification (by man or machine) are obtained by appropriately structuring the program and data.

2.3.1 Notes. To provide the visibility of rule-based systems, data storage revolves about a central blackboard consisting of tuples:

(symbol, value)

The value may represent either some figure of merit for the strength of the symbol, or some numeric value as in *(joint_1, 40.2 deg)*.

All symbols on the blackboard are unique, so each tuple may be represented by a variable, and a **note** (binary flag) that indicates whether or not it contains a value. Notes and the variables are implemented as global data in the C program.

2.3.2 Program flow implementation. The notes represent the state of the task: what data is available and what subtasks have been completed or need to be done. The program counter implicitly stores part of the state of the blackboard, since program execution may reach a location only after testing some subset of the state.

The important characteristics of the program flow architecture are:

A. During normal operation, the program runs very fast, with the state encoded in the program counter.

B. Whenever necessary, the system can easily and efficiently be redirected to another task.

The basic approach is shown in Figure 3 and Table 1. Did_task_1 and so on are notes indicating just that. After task_1 returns, the program counter implicitly records that task_1 has been performed, so did_task_1 does not have to be retested. Instead, did_task_2 will be tested and task_2 run immediately. The structure is hierarchical as shown with did_task_1a.

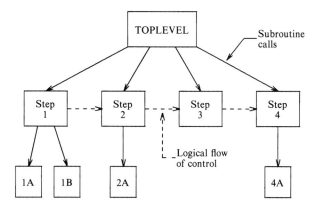

Figure 3. Program Flow Architecture. The **TOPLEVEL** routine examines the blackboard to decide what routines to call, creating the apparent flow of control shown. By changing the notes, we can easily redirect control.

If the flow of control must be drastically changed, the program reconfigures the notes, then executes a *longjmp*.

```
setjmp (main_jmp_buf);        /* in TOPLEVEL */
if (invisible (did_task_1))
    task_1 ();
if (invisible (did_task_2))
    task_2 ();
...

task_1 ()
{
    if (invisible (did_task_1a))
        task_1a ();
    ...
    scribble (did_task_1);
}
```

Table 1. Program Flow Fragment. The main program (TOPLEVEL) calls the subtasks selected by the notes. A longjmp causes control to return to the setjmp.

Longjmp and setjmp (at the head of Table 1) are C library calls. Longjmp causes all subroutine calls since the setjmp was executed to be removed from the stack, and the program continues as if the setjmp had just completed. The expert system quickly drives back down through the program hierarchy until the right section of code to execute is found.

2.4 Model Data Structure

A specialized data structure, the "model," stores both symbolic and numeric information. Different outputs may be written to the blackboard by each model invocation. A simple example is a symbolic/numeric version of square root which maps an input value to one of the tuples:

(sqrt_is, *value*)
(input_negative, *by_how_much*)

The model data structure is a generalized quadtree or octree. Each node in the model data structure can have a different set of inputs, and a different degree of quantitization. A model's accuracy may be different in different portions of the input space, allowing resolution to be allocated to critical areas. Models can be built by a human-input program or by specialized programs.

2.5 Initial Planning

In this section, we will discuss the initial planning problem, that is, how to go from the first data point to the first plan. The reason that we have an initial planning problem is that the problem is underconstrained, that is, we have more degrees of freedom than equations to determine values for them. However, we do have many constraints on the entire set of variables, though not necessarily directly upon the free variables. The angle of the stick supporting the paddle is one example of a free variable. Its value dramatically affects the kinematic and dynamic reachability of the resulting configuration.

The constraints on the initial plan tend to be highly non-linear, for example, those derived by mapping joint angle constraints to Cartesian constraints. Some may not be computable in closed form and require extensive search techniques to discover.

The solution to this conundrum comes with the realization that the initial plan need not be perfect. The subsequent temporal updating process will improve the global optimality of the plan, when all the constraints are visible.

Notice that the initial sensor data is similarly flawed, and is essentially guaranteed incorrect. We should not devote excessive time and effort to finding the optimal plan based on suboptimal data.

2.5.1 Selecting among alternatives. We will now consider how to select among a few alternatives. We begin by subjectively evaluating all applicable input data over the possible alternatives. Models are used to map input data to one or more figures of merit. We select the alternative with the highest weighted average figure of merit. Our approach is to simply make the evaluators display the right characteristics, and include as many factors as possible. Our domain is synthesis, not analysis. There is no **right** answer.

2.5.2 Selecting a continuous value. We select values of continuous variables with the same attitude with which we select among alternatives. Our approach is to explicitly compute optimal values from restricted views of the problem (and correspondingly small numbers of inputs). We then find the weighted average to form a consensus.

The continuous variable's evaluators produce not figures of merit, but values in the output space. They are the semantic equivalent of: if x, then do y. Rules are still with us, but increasingly camouflaged.

2.6 Temporal Updating

Once we have formulated an initial plan and begun its execution, we must continue to update it as additional sensor data becomes available. The temporal updating process has two objectives: to change the plan in response to new sensor data, and to propagate information about the later stages of processing up to the earlier ones, and so achieve a more globally optimal solution to the problem.

The free variables must be carried over from one iteration of the program to the next. The temporal updating process must have knowledge of the plan in progress as it formulates a new one. Knowledge of the prior plan is essential to ensure that decisions are made on the same basis as they were made in the past, and to generate continuous transitions.

We will refer to the planning routines that comprise the heart of the temporal updating process as tuners. Each tuner adjusts a few free variables in response to global program conditions.

2.6.1 Evaluators. During the first stage of initial planning, the input data was evaluated using models. Similarly, during temporal updating, as many program variables as possible and reasonable ought to be evaluated.

The evaluators used in updating are again implemented as models, but with yet a third output semantics. The output represents a preferred relative change in the input. For example, consider the model shown in Figure 4, which evaluates the value of joint 3 of the robot (the elbow). As may be seen, the same evaluator can produce several evaluations, conveying symbolic as well as numeric information. We can encode a time-varying strategy in the shape of the curve, without requiring any additional state, making the implementation simpler and more robust.

2.6.2 Tuners. Rather than have a single massive tuner, we partition the task into tuner modules operating on individual or related free variables. Partitioning makes the system more manageable, and the granularity it imposes is necessary during exception handling.

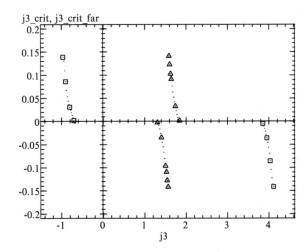

Figure 4. Updating Evaluator for Joint 3. The model's horizontal axis represents joint 3's position in radians. The vertical axis specifies a proposed correction. The central curve, marked with triangles, proposes a change when the wrist is becoming too far away from the shoulder. The curve marked with squares keeps the joint from hitting the limit stops.

A tuner alters its output variables to attempt to correct problems. The tuner does not have to examine all possible problems, only those it believes it can solve. Each correction is described by what amounts to a rule.

Data from the previous iteration is available to aid in computing corrections. Rather than computing a particular value from scratch, we can often just use its value from the previous iteration, even though we will introduce some slight error and inconsistency by doing so.

A tuner must try to ensure that by solving one problem, it is not making another much worse. Jacobians and other related partial derivatives are an excellent way of comparing the scale of the problem and solution. If the Jacobian is much greater than 1, we must be careful to avoid overcorrecting the symptom. If the Jacobian is much less than 1, the cure will be significantly larger than the symptom. The best tactic under these circumstances is to not make the change at all, and let a different tuner solve the problem.

Recall that we are not under any obligation to make a change at all, let alone some "optimal" correction. The tuner's behavior is loosely specified; our objective is to create tuners which exhibit the desired effects.

2.7 Exception Recovery

In a complex, dynamic environment, problems occur regularly, as new sensor data forces responses of which the robot is incapable (despite the temporal updating), or as a result of unimplementable initial plans. The exception recovery mechanism (Figure 5) must solve the problem and return to the normal task as rapidly as possible. We use the tuners to determine and execute the actual correction.

Normal numeric programs produce *symbolic* error descriptions: "divide by zero" or "sqrt argument < 0," a reversal from what one would expect of a supposedly numeric program. Exceptions can arise when particular constraints are

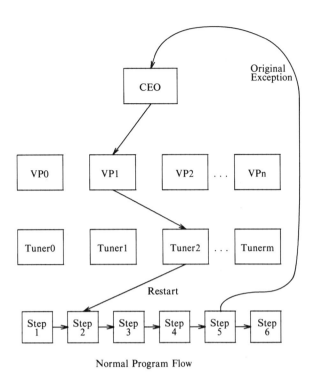

Figure 5. Exception Handling Architecture. An exception occurs in Step 5, causing CEO, VP1, and Tuner2 to be invoked in that order. After Tuner2 is run, VP1 adjusts the blackboard and does a longjmp; TOPLEVEL causes control to pass to Step 2.

violated, for example, that the joint angles of the robot stay within certain bounds. The system architect must establish a correspondence between the failure condition and a task level problem. For example, a particular square root of a negative number may correspond to the robot target position being out of reach.

Numeric data about the degree of error is required to allow us to solve the problem. If the arm is too far away, we need to know that it is 11.4 mm too far. A single model can conditionally generate a temporal updating tuple, an exception tuple, or nil, simplifying implementation.

After an implementation routine has determined that an exception has occurred and characterized the type and degree of the problem, it initiates the exception recovery process by calling the master exception handler, **CEO**.

The CEO executes global checks on the recovery process, for example, it can break off processing to meet an upcoming deadline. Otherwise, the CEO will choose a **VP** capable of handling that particular class of problems, using the symbolic information about the problem's classification. The selection is recorded using notes.

The VP is responsible for picking the actual tuner to attempt a correction, based on model-generated factors. The two most important factors are: that the problem be sensitive to the attempted correction, and the length of time required to effect a correction. Even though a given problem may be solved in several ways, the exception handler should use a correction which is unlikely to cause further harm. The length of time

required becomes a more important factor as the available time becomes smaller; time spent in exception recovery reduces the arm motion time.

The selected tuner is called directly by the VP to find new values for the selected variables. After the tuner has been run, notes are modified to cause program flow to resume (via longjmp and top-level) at the point of use of the just-tuned variables.

Once a single exception has taken place, additional exceptions may occur, especially if major changes in sensor data occur late in a motion. Additional exceptions may also result from an earlier exception's cure.

Notes recorded during the original exception allow the subroutine calling sequence to be rapidly re-established. The VP can then consider several cases.

If the same problem has recurred, the severity of the problem may be examined and compared to the original value. If the problem has been mitigated, it is worthwhile to call the same tuner again; otherwise, a new strategy should be selected with that tuner excluded. A global algorithm makes this decision, ensuring that the error recovery process will not result in an infinite loop, even across a collection of VPs.

When a new problem occurs, the VP may utilize additional specialized strategies, call upon an additional VP, or allow the CEO to designate a new primary VP. There are many options for both CEO and VPs. The point of this architecture is that we can express complex strategies effectively, and can continue to improve them.

3. Vision System

The vision system is charged with the task of predicting the exact future trajectory of the ball through four dimensional space-time at 60 Hz. We use four cameras to achieve a large field of view; they are organized as a short-range and a long-range stereo pair.

To separate the ball from the background image, we use gray-scale thresholding:

$$pixel_{out} = \max(pixel_{in} - threshold, 0) \qquad (1)$$

Gray scale processing maximizes accuracy. Equation 1 is implemented in real time by a look-up table.

We locate the ball's gray-scale centroid in each of the four cameras 60 times a second, using the moment generator system described in [Andersson, 1985a][Andersson, 1985b]. To compensate for the lenses' distortion, we use a simple lens calibration technique that analyzes the residual errors after the basic camera calibration (for a complete discussion of lens calibration, see [Tsai, 1986]). The short-range cameras' root-mean-square error is reduced from 6.3 mm to 0.9 mm; the long-range cameras' from 1.6 mm to 1.1 mm.

3.1 Lighting Compensation

The vision system computes the centroid of the ball's intensity distribution. We need to know the ball's center of mass. The mass and intensity centroids do not coincide because the lighting is strongly oriented towards the two overhead flood lights. The distance between centroids varies between zero and the radius of the ball, 18.9 mm; they are normally about 10 mm apart. This error is substantial compared to the system's other errors; we must compensate for it.

Our approach is to compute an uncompensated estimate of the ball's position, compute the location of the intensity centroid relative the mass centroid, then subtract the relative position from the ball's initial position estimate. The lighting calculations are done in 3-space, but the actual compensations take place on the camera image plane. After we have computed the corrections, we must perform the stereo triangulation a second time to find the final XYZ position. We are able to compensate for the lighting because of the simplicity of the sphere and because of the regularity of the moment computation.

Once all of the corrections have been applied, the system's nominal static accuracy is approximately 1 mm, with repeatability considerably better than that.

3.2 Imaging Dynamic Scenes

The images viewed by the TV cameras vary rapidly with time. Unlike our past experience in computer vision, a model of the camera's dynamic characteristics must be used to obtain accurate data. We need to understand what the TV camera will output as a function of the actual scene, so that we can define a self-consistent object position and time.

3.2.1 Camera types. TV cameras are designed for relatively slowly changing scenes. The electrical output of a camera is a complex function of the time-varying light input over the time interval $(-\infty, now)$ that depends on the camera's design.

For example, vidicons have a decay function such that the output at any time might be affected by a bright image many frames ago; the effect is similar to the persistence of CRT displays. Each point of the image is sampled at a different time as the beam sweeps over it, so a vertical bar moving horizontally results in a picture of a diagonal bar.

CCD cameras operate as pipelined device, integrating one image while reading out the previous one. Every pixel is integrated over the same time interval, so the bar stays vertical.

Unfortunately, we use a third type of camera, MOS (Hitachi KP-231A), which has less well behaved timing characteristics. Each pixel is reset as it is being read out, therefore the start of the sampling interval is different for each pixel. The cameras change a horizontally moving vertical bar into a diagonal one just as a vidicon does.

3.2.2 Motion blur and integration time. If we take the moments of the smear left on the camera by a single moving surface patch, we get the average position of the patch during the interval of observation. If the velocity of the patch is constant during the sampling interval, the computed centroid corresponds to the temporal center of the frame's sampling interval.

Since moments are a linear operator, the moments of the sum of two images equals the sum of the moments of the images. The moments of two patches tell us the position of the centroid of the two patches at the center of the sampling interval. The entire image is nothing but the sum of the effects of many such patches. Consequently, the moments of an object moving at constant velocity tell us the position of the object at the center of the sampling interval.

3.2.3 MOS cameras. Since MOS cameras reset each pixel as it is being read, each pixel's sampling interval is different. At 3.0 m/sec, the 16 msec difference in the sampling interval between the top and bottom of the image causes a 5 cm shift in the ball's apparent position. The effect is especially noticeable when the ball jumps from the bottom of the long-range stereo pair to the top of the short-range pair. (We

ignore the minor effect due to X position.) The sampling time can be computed from the ball's Y coordinate.

3.2.4 Application to stereo. When we are doing stereo, we have two different sampling times. The concept of stereo is predicated upon the assumption that we have two observations of the same body at the same position. Because the two cameras' effective sampling times are different, we have violated this assumption. In practice, both Y values are similar since we have the cameras oriented predominantly in the same plane. We use the average of the two Y values.

3.3 Three Dimensional Trajectory Analysis

Unlike research with general scenes, we do not have to worry about correspondence, since we track only one object. The ball's 3-D location is computed from two 4×3 perspective transform matrices using closed-form least squares. The ball's trajectory must be computed each $\frac{1}{60}$ sec as a new position is available, and the trajectory used to predict the future path.

The need for prediction imposes a great demand upon the trajectory fitting process. It is not enough to fit some high order polynomial to the data: it will track the noise, and generate grossly unstable predictions. We must perform a noise reducing fit, and use actual knowledge of the trajectories to perform the extrapolation.

The requirement for accurate treatment of the motion model is a distinct difference from prior work in motion interpretation, which typically makes a constant velocity assumption. Although we will not discuss it here, the trajectory analysis uses quadratic fits, but feeds forward corrections to compensate for higher-order terms.

3.4 Operation in Play

The final test of the vision system is its performance on live balls in play. The real time expert system is given the time, position, velocity, and spin at which the ball will cross the robot's end of the table (where Y=0). A trajectory out of the middle of a volley is shown in Figure 6. The human opponent has hit a reasonably hard 6.1 m/sec shot at the robot, which the latter has returned. The prediction error data in Figure 7 shows the error on a moving ball. After 5 sec, the ball is 2 m away, and the depth error is predictably higher.

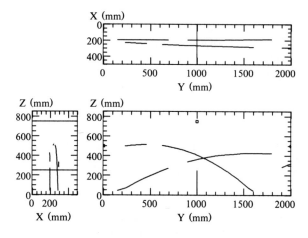

Figure 6. Trajectory of Incoming Volley. The human hits the first shot from right to left.

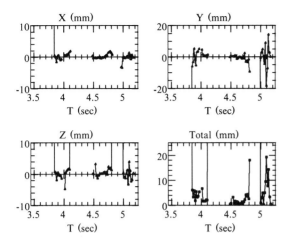

Figure 7. Prediction Errors

4. Robot Controller

The controller (Figure 8) must operate the actuator as close as possible to its capabilities. We will do our planning in joint space (rather than Cartesian, for example), because the limits on the robot's performance are expressed primarily in this space.

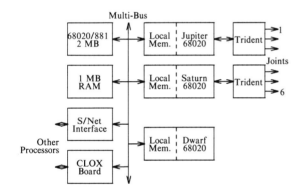

Figure 8. Robot Controller Architecture. The expert system runs in the processor at top left. The dwarf performs background kinematics and dynamics. The slave processors can not access the Multi-Bus, but can be accessed from it. The trident contains the optical encoder circuits and digital to analog converters.

Polynomials are a natural choice for a motion representation because their properties are well known, and closed-form solutions may often be derived. Only a single polynomial is needed to represent the entire trajectory, so the trajectory is inherently very smooth and easy to evaluate. The derivatives are easy to compute, and may be represented in the same form. We use fifth order, or quintic, polynomials to match the six degrees of freedom (positions, velocities, and accelerations at the beginning and end of the motion) required for trajectory planning [Craig, 1986][Paul, 1981].

A representation's utility is measured by what may be done with it; given an instance of the representation, what properties of it may be described? For example, suppose that a joint is near its maximal acceleration, and we wish to find the final position which minimizes the acceleration. Knowing this position, the expert system can attempt to alter the problem so that this final position is attained, thus minimizing the stress on the joint.

We can find the acceleration-minimizing final position of a quintic trajectory:

$$p_{a,\min} = \frac{10t_f(v_i+v_f)+(a_i-a_f)t_f^2}{20} + p_i \qquad (2)$$

We can similarly find the final velocity which minimizes the acceleration required to get to a final position at a specified time:

$$v_{a,\min} = \frac{44(p_f-p_i)-20t_f v_i+(3a_f-a_i)t_f^2}{24t_f} \qquad (3)$$

4.1 Dynamics and Control

Once a trajectory has been proposed, it must be evaluated to determine if it can be successfully executed by the robot, and then it must be executed as accurately as possible. We use partial manipulator dynamics for both tasks.

We compute the joint inertias, gravity loads, and some coupling inertias. At present, only the coupling inertias to and from the wrist joints are computed. The equations are based on those of [Izaguirre & Paul, 1986]. At present, we do not feed-forward centripetal and Coriolis effects. Timing analysis indicates that the dwarf processor will be able to handle the full dynamics; we have simply not implemented it yet. Our equations are formulated for an arbitrary load, because the ping-pong paddle is very asymmetrical.

During the planning process, we must establish if a given proposed trajectory is feasible. By feasible, we mean: can the actuators cause the robot to accurately follow this trajectory? The manipulator dynamics can be used to make this determination, but it requires simulating the entire motion.

Instead, we do a quasi-worst-case analysis with the maximum value of each parameter at the beginning and end of the trajectory. (We neglect the coupling torques.) We are clearly throwing away system performance by this simplification, and furthermore, we run the risk of not catching actual limits.

Our servo control is based on a PD (position and derivative) controller; we feed-forward terms due to the acceleration of the same joint and the other joints, gravity load, and friction. We compute the feed-forward torques and inertias at the 26 msec major cycle rate (on the dwarf), using the acceleration at the midpoint of the 26 msec cycle.

The joint servos execute the PD routine every 830 μsec, computing the feed-forward due to friction and acceleration (of that joint alone), then adding the feed-forward for that 26 msec cycle. This approach greatly reduces the computation required of the joint servo and the amount of data that needs to be transferred among the processors. The side effect is a small increase in the apparent disturbing torque.

4.2 Analysis of an Actual Hit

Figure 9 shows the Cartesian velocity of the paddle's center. The desired trajectory and the actual trajectory are overlaid. Most of the velocity is in the Y direction towards the opponent. The peak paddle acceleration is 2.5 G. At the contact time (3.5 sec), the total position error from all sources was 3 mm (J6 was 0.3° off), while the arm was moving at 1500 mm/sec. The effective timing accuracy was 2 msec. The velocity error was 40 mm/sec (5°/sec on J6). We believe that joint flexibility contributes significantly to these errors.

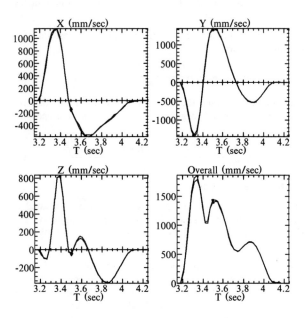

Figure 9. Cartesian Velocities During Motion

5. Summary

The experimental result is a ping-pong system able to beat human beings. Volleys of 21 hits by man and machine have been observed — a credit to the performance of both.

Tracking moving objects has been shown to introduce significantly more complexity than encountered in conventional static image processing. Interpreting a dynamic image sequence is certainly not just a matter of examining enough snap-shots. The camera's temporal model is increasingly important as our tasks become truly dynamic. The real-world trajectories of objects moving on the short time scale of robot applications, i.e., cycle times on the order of a second, do not conform to simplified motion models.

We have described an architecture for constructing complex and robust real time systems that process continuous streams of sensor data to solve poorly specified problems. The stream of sensor data greatly affected the design of the system. It allowed us to simplify the initial planning process, and concentrate on obtaining initial plans which are "good guesses." The temporal updating process propagates information from later stages of processing up to the earlier stages, so that the plan can be globally optimized. An exception handling scheme rapidly assesses and corrects exceptions as they occur; the temporal updating process reduces the frequency of exceptions.

The regular program organization and the program development tools facilitate continuing performance enhancement by humans or programs. Much use was made of a common data structure, the "model," to represent both numeric and symbolic information. The expert system lets us

exploit the system designer's knowledge in real time.

The system fills the gap between the slow, symbolic AI systems, and the fast, numeric robot controllers, much as humans have a range of processing levels from rational to trained reflexes. It leads the way towards future fast and intelligent systems.

References

Ahuja, S.R., "S/Net: A High Speed Interconnect for Multiple Computers," IEEE Journal of Selected Areas in Communication, Vol. SAC−1, No. 5, p. 751−756, November 1983.

Andersson, R.L., "Real-Time Gray-Scale Video Processing Using a Moment-Generating Chip," IEEE Journal of Robotics and Automation, Vol. RA−1, No. 2, p. 79−85, June 1985.

Andersson, R.L., "Real time video moment generator chip," in N.H.E. Weste, K. Eshraghian, "Principles of CMOS VLSI Design: A Systems Perspective," Addison-Wesley, p. 407−424, 1985.

Andersson, R.L., "Living in a Dynamic World," Proceedings of the ACM−IEEE Fall Joint Computer Conference, p. 97−104, November 1986.

Andersson, R.L., "A Robot Ping-Pong Player: Experiment in Real-Time Intelligent Control," The MIT Press, 1988.

Billingsley, J., "Machineroe joins new title fight," Practical Robotics, p. 14−16, May/June 1984.

Craig, J.J., "Introduction to Robotics: Mechanics and Control," Addison-Wesley, 1986.

Gaglianello, R.D., Katseff, H.P., "Meglos: An Operating System for a Multiprocessor Environment," Proceedings of the Fifth International Conference on Distributed Computing Systems, May 1985.

Izaguirre, A., Paul, R.P., "Automatic Generation of the Dynamic Equations of the Robot Manipulators Using a LISP Program," IEEE International Conference on Robotics and Automation, Vol. 1, p. 220−226, April 1986.

Paul, R.P., "Robot Manipulators: Mathematics, Programming, and Control," The MIT Press, 1981.

Tsai, R.Y., "An Efficient and Accurate Camera Calibration Technique for 3D Machine Vision," Proceedings of the IEEE Computer Society Conference on Computer Vision and Pattern Recognition, p. 364−374, May 1986.

ROBOTWORLD
A MULTIPLE ROBOT VISION GUIDED ASSEMBLY SYSTEM

Victor Scheinman

Automatix Incorporated
499 Seaport Court
Redwood City, CA 94063

ROBOTWORLD is a multiple robot, vision guided assembly system suitable for electronic assembly, small or large part mechanical assembly, machine vision inspection and many other robotic applications. The robots are lightweight (generally less than 3kg.), fast (up to 1.5 meters per second, 4 g's), strong (can be configured with up to 30kg. force capability), accurate (absolute accuracy .03mm, can use existing data bases without point touch-up), repeatable (typical repeatability about .01mm), reliable (fewer moving parts than any ther current robot), safe (low moving mass) and low cost. ROBOTWORLD systems support many robots (up to 20) working in the same work envelope which can be of different sizes and shapes.

Introduction

Imagine a world tailored to meet the needs of robots. An environment dedicated to maximizing the performance and productivity of robotic elements and accessories and at the same time being reasonable in cost and support requirements. The current ROBOTWORLD system is the product of an ongoing advanced development program to investigate and implement a robotic system tailored to the needs of robots and the specific automation task, rather than the needs of people and their automation environment, the traditional factory or the assembly line.

System Philosophy

One way to understand the goals of the ROBOTWORLD system is by analogy to the relationship between the current state of robotics and fixed automation. Most robots in industry today are being used in a dedicated mode. They are purchased, tooled and programmed to perform a single task. Some may be programmed for a family of variations, but the majority of robot installations are scarcely distinguishable from fixed automation or CNC machinery at best. Once reduced to practice, the apparant flexibility of an industrial robot is usually lost. In fact, robots are frequently slower, more expensive, and more complex than a dedicated machine performing the same task.

The advantage of robotics is that when presented with a new problem, the robot significantly facilitates automating the process. Whatever the process is, it is certain to involve the movement of objects and material along trajectories in particular sequences which may be dependent on a number of conditions and variables. Using a robot not only saves an extraordinary amount of development time by eliminating the need to reinvent positioning devices and controllers, but because of the generality of the solution, major modifications of motion and sequence can be accomodated during development with only software changes.

Through the robot application program the functional equivalent of a custom automated machine is created. This may result in a 200kg robot being use to move 1gm parts, but because the cost of application development dominates most automation efforts, the robotic approach is often the logical choice.

In the instance which the capabilities of the robot do not fully encompass the requirements of the task, the situation is far from ideal and the advantages of the robotic approach to automation are much less apparant. This situation can result in a system with the compromised performance of a robot at the cost of fixed automation, with the advantages of neither!

ROBOTWORLD is to current robotics as robotics is to fixed automation. The ROBOTWORLD system seeks to create an idealized environment for robotic automation, a "world" for modular robotic elements. This environment is established complete with reference frames, power and control facilities, mounting and motion surfaces, sensor and communication interfaces, and computation and programming resources. The engineer has great freedom in introducing into it and implementing as many or as few axes, sensors, or other robotic devices and accessories of the appropriate scale and performance as required to perform his automation task with the efficiency and performance he might expect of the best custom automation equipment. (Figure 1).

Whereas traditional automation systems operate in buildings and facilities primarily scaled to human workers and tailored to human needs, ROBOTWORLDS being exclusively for robots can be scaled and tailored to robot needs. This results is many significant scale and configuration differences.

Design and Development Issues

The following are some of the more important design and development issues we addressed.

> Scale
> Modularity
> Resources
> Precision Reference and Workspace
> Integrated Use of Vision
> Multiple Robotic Devices
> Flexible and Versatile Software
> Complete Facility

Scale: We studied the scale of assembly tasks. The majority of automatic assembly tasks today are on small parts. By making the robots more closely scaled to the specific task requirements we found that the productivity could be increased and the system floor space greatly reduced. For example, smaller structures generally have higher natural frequencies and shorter settling times than larger structures. End point positioning accuracy is generally greater with shorter kinematic chains. Smaller, more compact, robots can work in less space with closer spacing of workstations and feeders. What once might have been a room full of traditional robots, automation equipment and people might now be substituted by a compact desk size multilevel ROBOTWORLD system.

Modularity: We found that there are good, better and best robots for each task, although the selection process is by no means simple. By designing robots so that they can be tailored to the specific task without excessive inventory cost the more optimum robot can be configured for each task. We focused on multiple robot applications with the philosophy that if robot cost is low enough, then productivity and application simplicity can be achieved by paralleling and serializing operations among multiple moderate performance robots rather than integrating many operations into a high performance single robot workstation.

Resources: We decided that just as a good employer provides a supportive work environment for his employees, so should the ROBOTWORLD provide for its robots. We provided a rigid, precise reference space, controlled power and signal interfaces for multiple robots, sensor inputs, easy setup and calibration capabilities, and a flexible, high level programming environment.

Precision References and Workspace: Rather than put extreme demands on the worktable, tooling, grippers, feeders, and workpieces, we took the approach that you build a precise, controlled environment, and have a good reference and measuring system within that environment. Then you don't have to be very concerned about what you did in that environment as you could get the system to find out about and monitor it's own state better than you could with outside means.

Integrated use of Vision: We adopted vision as our primary built-in system sense resource and we rely on it heavily. The ROBOTWORLD system cannot run without vision, for it is the means by which we gather precise knowledge of the true state of the system and is the basis of most calibrations. Vision is also intimately used in many assembly operations.

Multiple Devices: A typical robotic installation is generally a small part robot and a large part tooling, accessories, and software. Just as a commitment to traditional automatic assembly requires addressing the issues of many operations at once, so does a commitment to robotic assembly. We feel that the current collections of single robot workcells will eventually be replaced with the integrated robotic factory. If ROBOTWORLD is to be that factory, then it has to be multiple device in every way. Thus it supports multiple devices, has multi-tasking motion control, and is configured as such even in the basic system.

Flexible and Versatile Software: We insisted on software with capability and features for control of multiple robots and other devices, as well as integrated vision and communications. The user should have only one language to learn and worry about. The language should be high level, expandable, and have good real time performance even with frequent use of image processing and other computation intensive facilities.

Complete Facility: We took the approach that the one facility should provide all the resources one might normally need. All of these resources should be efficiently integrated into the system, so that access to and use of them is easy and simple to learn. Support and maintenance is also facilitated by use of software and hardware interface standards and common components throughout the system.

Component Descriptions

The ROBOTWORLD system in its present state of development consists of three major component groups (Figure 2):

> "World"
> System Controller
> Set of Modular Robotic Elements

The "world" of the ROBOTWORLD system consists of a frame, a drive surface and a work surface.

The frame consists of rigid, welded tubular steel structure having a four legged rectangular box configuration with four posts supporting the upper precision drive surface. A work surface is also mounted some adjustable distance below the drive surface. Within this volume, the robot world, most of the precision, sensor guided, high speed robotic operations take place. Doors and panels completely surround the lower part of the structure and enclose all of the system electronics, controllers, and other "world" resources.

The precision drive surface provides the motion surface for the air bearing supported mobile modules. This rigid, flat, steel structure acts as the stator for the electromagnetic based direct drive X-Y motion modules (Sawyer linear motors) and also provides a precision reference grid etched into the entire steel surface. This grid is accurate to about .1mm over the entire surface, and sets the basic standard of placement accuracy for the X-Y motion axes of the mobile modules. Local calibrations can further increase this accuracy. The stable drive surface, made of steel, naturally has about one third the thermal expansion coefficient of aluminum, the primary structural material in most other robots.

The system controller is the "brains" of the ROBOTWORLD system. Motion control, vision and other sensor processing, and communications capability issues were addressed in the selection and development of this important system resource. A multiprocessor (MC68000 and MC68020 based) machine vision unit (Automatix, Inc. AV-5) with parallel processing architecture and a flexible high level programming environment with a "C" based interpretive language (Automatix' RAIL^{tm}) is used as the core of the controller.

To this unit we add one or more motion controller boards. This large circuit board features an MC68000 series CPU and a high speed bipolar ALU with multi-tasking, path planning, control and I/O capability. Up to 16 axes of micro-stepping control and 10 axes of closed loop d.c. servo control are available from this controller. Multiple axes (any number) may be software configured and linked together in any number of groups from 1 to 16. All linked axes are smoothly moved in linearly interpolated fashion, including controlled acceleration, constant velocity and deceleration segments. Real time path modification features with update rates to 60 per second permit smooth transitions near via points and end point corrections from sensor inputs. Additional boards may be added for additional axes. Effective controller performance when controlling X-Y motion module axes is a command resolution of .002mm and a control command accuracy of .01mm.

A separate internal rack mounted power control unit houses up to 32 switching power amplifiers to drive up to 32 d.c. servos or actuators or 16 stepper axes. Because of the very modest power requirements of most of the modules (typically less than 50 watts), the entire ROBOTWORLD system can run on a single standard 120VAC, 15A circuit.

The modular elements are the robotic devices and accessories which work in the precise controlled environment of the "world". They can be fixed or mobile, powered or passive, but they are all precisely defined and interface in a common manner with the "world" and with the system controller.

Examples of these modules include:

Mobile Modules- All of these items have X-Y motion axes in common. The static and dynamic performance of these modules is a function of their mass, the load mass, the travel of the additional axes, their overall length, and the umbilical cable mass and drag. Presently, the basic X-Y module size is about 12cmx12cm with a static thrust of about 4.5kgf. Total module mass is typically about 1.1kg for a simple 2 axis mobile platform to 1.5kg for a 2 axis mobile camera module or a 4 axis placement module with 5cm Z travel. Basic 2 axis module motion accuracy is about .01mm. Larger modules with longer Z travel have lower basic accuracy than smaller, shorter kinematic chain length, modules. Since dynamic performance is based on thrust and mass, larger modules will generally have lower acceleration and damping resulting in lower performance. Larger X-Y motors can be built to regain performance in these larger modules (Figure 3).

Other modules which we have built are a direct drive servoed rotary indexer using an NSK/Motornetics motor, a controlled motion conveyor featuring a flat belt conveyor with speed, acceleration and travel directly controllable from the ROBOTWORLD controller, and an assortment of fixed and mobile CCD camera modules.

Application Examples

Although this development effort has focused on technology and capability development, we have already delivered ROBOTWORLDS to perform a very nice mechanical assembly application and an electronic assembly application. A brief description of the application and implementation will give the reader some indication of the performance of the ROBOTWORLD system.

In the case of the mechanical assembly application, the user, a large corporation, wanted to assemble a new type of fluid flow control valve. This valve is made in many slightly different configurations depending on flow requirements. A total of over 50 configurations are made up from a parts supply of about 20 different parts. The average valve has 12 parts. Using 3 placement modules with 5cm Z travel, a direct drive rotary indexing table, and simple part feeders all controlled directly from the ROBOTWORLD controller, the user configured and programmed the system himself to produce assemblies at the rate of about one every 5 seconds. The three placement modules work at four placement areas and share feeders. An additional placement module will increase production to one assembly in less than 4 seconds.

For electronic assembly, another user wants to assemble high reliability, surface mount component circuit boards for space applications. Typical lot sizes are less than 10 boards with one board lot sizes common. The assembly process is complicated by part traceability requirements, detailed part and board preparation and test specifications, and a multistep placement, bond and solder procedure. Technician error rate is great on these boards because of all the requirements. We configured a ROBOTWORLD to visually acquire and inspect all parts and boards, do some board and part preparation, place parts, and then finally inspect the finished assemblies. The system is driven from user supplied data bases. To permit it to be quickly configured to work on a wide variety of boards of different sizes and shapes no conveyor guides, board stops, or other precision mechanical locations or orientations are required. The drawing in Figure 4 is a conceptual application example of an enhanced and future version of such a ROBOTWORLD system application.

Issues for the Future

Clearly the major issue for the future is task planning and efficient use of resources. At the present time, most planning is done in a rather straightforward way; the programmer decides the sequence and order of operations, and the layout of the "world". The resultant plan usually has many surprises in store even for tasks with only two robots. Collisions usually don't produce any damage and safety is not a human concern because of the small size, low mass and controlled workspace. SILMA Inc., Los Altos, CA has done some ROBOTWORLD simulation work and it is clear that good graphics, simulation and planning tools are a necessity.

The flexible cable to each mobile module provides power, signals and air. Although not an important issue with a few modules in the workspace, they are a major limitation to greatly increasing the robotic density of the system. It appears that eliminating the cable is not an insurmountable problem and represents a nice development challenge.

Alternative drive systems are attractive. Although Sawyer motor technology is appealing because of it's simplicity and proven performance, there are other multi-axis drive technologies which have the potential for higher performance (greater accelerations and peak velocity) and may be less costly to produce. These should be investigated.

Intimate use of high resolution vision in assembly operations must be carefully thought out as even image processing times of less than 100ms can significantly affect cycle time if extra motion is also required, particularly in single camera shared resource applications requiring vision based correction. In a vision calibrated system and with vision guided and corrected operations, system accuracy is directly related to image resolution.

References

Reynolds, G. "ROBOTWORLD- An Overview", Automatix Inc. Internal Memorandum, Sept. 1984.

Robotics Today, "Robotworld: A Self-contained Work Environment for Assembly, October 1986.

Sawyer, Bruce A. "Magnetic Positioning Device", U.S. Patent 3,376,578, April 1968.

Scheinman, Victor D. " ROBOTWORLD-The Latest Advance in Assembly System Technology" Automatix Inc. Literature, March 1987.

Tsai, Lung-Wen and Ciardella, R.L., "Linear Step Motor Design Provides High Plotter Performance at Low Cost", Hewlett-Packard Journal, 1979

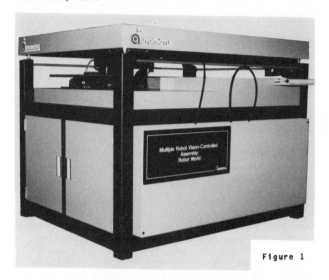

Figure 1

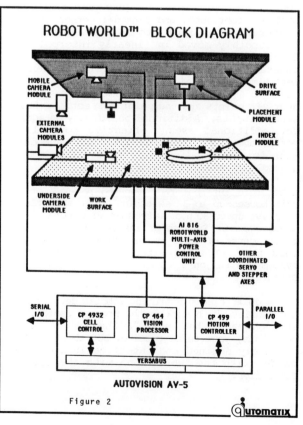

Figure 2

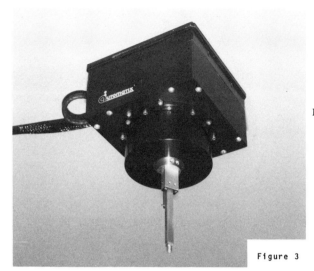

ROBOTWORLD
4 axis Placement Module

Dimensions:
L,W,H-   12cm x 12cm x 12cm
Z travel- 5cm
Mass-   1.5kg

Figure 3

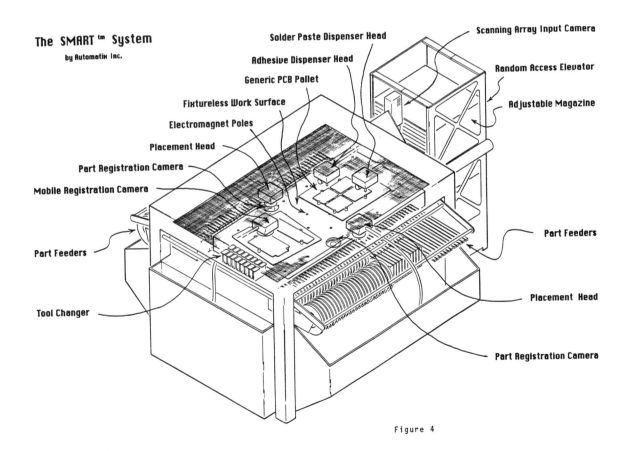

The SMART ™ System
by Automatix Inc.

Solder Paste Dispenser Head

Adhesive Dispenser Head

Generic PCB Pallet

Fixtureless Work Surface

Electromagnet Poles

Placement Head

Part Registration Camera

Mobile Registration Camera

Part Feeders

Tool Changer

Scanning Array Input Camera

Random Access Elevator

Adjustable Magazine

Part Feeders

Placement Head

Part Registration Camera

Figure 4

ROBOTWORLD
Surface Mount Assembly System Concept

Handey: A Task-Level Robot System

Tomás Lozano-Pérez, Joseph L. Jones, Emmanuel Mazer*, Patrick A. O'Donnell, W. Eric L. Grimson
MIT Artificial Intelligence Laboratory, USA

Pierre Tournassoud
INRIA, France

Alain Lanusse
E.T.C.A., Arcueil, France

*On leave from LIFIA, Grenoble, France.

Abstract. We describe Handey, a robot system capable of locating a part in an unstructured pile of objects, choose a grasp on the part, plan a motion to reach the part safely, plan a sequence of regrasp motions, and plan a motion to place the part at a commanded position. The system requires as input a polyhedral world model including models of the part to be manipulated, the robot arm, and any other fixed objects in the environment. In addition, the system builds a depth map, using structured light, of the area where the part is to be found initially. Any other objects present in that area do not have to be modeled.

1. Introduction

The word robot should conjure up the image of a system with (at least) three generic capabilities:

- The ability to perceive its environment and to locate objects of interest.
- The ability to act on its environment.
- The ability to plan actions to achieve its goals.

Surprisingly, very few systems in the, admittedly short, history of robotics have possessed all of these capabilities in non-trivial form. Most of the ones that have had this combination of capabilities have been mobile robots, for example, Shakey [Nilsson 69], and Hilare [Giralt et al 79]. In the area of manipulation, some early systems possessed these capabilities, for example, the Stanford Hand-Eye System [Feldman 69; Paul 72], MIT Copy Demo [Winston 72], Edinburgh's Freddy [Ambler et al 1975], and a very few recent systems, for example, [Ikeuchi, et al 86]. In all cases, these systems operated in a very restricted domain of objects and their component modules were tailored to specific tasks.

In this paper, we describe a new integrated robot system, called Handey, under development at MIT. Handey's domain is that of simple assembly of (mostly) planar-faced objects. The user starts by building accurate object models for all the parts to be manipulated. The user then specifies a sequence of MOVE commands, each of which specifies an object and its destination. Handey locates each part on its worktable, chooses how to grasp it, and takes it to the destination. The unique features of Handey are its ability to operate on a wide class of objects and to operate in a cluttered environment. Also, Handey's modules are designed to be reasonably general purpose; they are not tailored to a specific task. Figure 1 illustrates a sample plan found by Handey; the task consists of picking up one of the L-shaped objects and placing it on top of the other so that they form a block.

Handey consists of the following major modules:

- *Object modeling*: Handey can model a fairly general class of polyhedral objects, including an interactive facility for defining object models from depth data.

- *Range finder*: Handey uses a triangulation range-finder based on projected laser planes.
- *Model-based object localization*: Handey can locate known polyhedral objects in complex scenes that may involve obscuration of the target object.
- *Collision-free path planning*: Handey can plan motions for a six degree of freedom revolute manipulator in cluttered environments.
- *Grasping*: Handey can choose grasping positions on objects in cluttered environments and plan regrasping motions if necessary.
- *Robot Control*: Handey uses a traditional trajectory controller capable of joint-interpolated or cartesian motions.

Handey's current limitations are: the lack of any capability for planning or executing compliant motions, the inability to postpone decisions, and its limited ability to deal with errors. Eliminating these limitations is the the subject of ongoing work.

Before proceeding to a description of Handey, we must answer an important question: "What is to be learnt by building an integrated robot system such as Handey?" There are several good reasons. The first is to uncover problems in the interaction between the modules. The second is to stress-test the modules; the use of module within a system tends to uncover hidden assumptions in the design. The third is that the resulting system can be a tool in investigating high-level planning in Artificial Intelligence.

2. An overview of Handey

The basic command for Handey is of the form: MOVE *object* TO *destination*. In this section we describe briefly the steps Handey must go through to execute a single MOVE command. Subsequent sections will focus on the individual steps in more detail.

Handey requires that a metrically-accurate polyhedral model of the object be available. The object is assumed to be located in arbitrary pose within the field of view of the range sensor. The destination will typically be outside of the field of view.

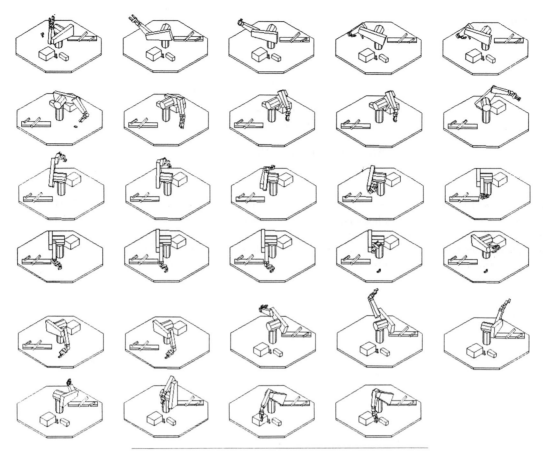

Figure 1. A plan found by Handey. The first image is on the top left; it shows the initial position of the part identified by the edge matcher. The final position of the part, specified by the user, is on the bottom right.

Handey executes the following steps in fixed order:

- *Locate the object*: A depth map is built of the area under the range sensor's view. The recognition module locates the object within the scene and returns a transformation that describes the object's position relative to robot's coordinate system.

- *Choose a grasp on the object*: The grasping module searches for a grasp on the object that is both stable and can be reached by the robot at both the origin and destination. Choosing a grasp will require taking into account the obstacles present in the depth map and in the world model. If a single grasp cannot be used both at the origin and at the destination, then choose a grasp compatible with the origin only; regrasping will be necessary.

- *Approach the grasp location and grasp the part*: Plan a collision-free path from the robot's current position to the chosen grasp position. Grasp the part.

- *Regrasp the object*: If regrasping is necessary, plan a sequence of regrasping motions that will enable the robot to reach a grasp that is legal at the destination. An empty area of the worktable is used to perform these motions.

- *Plan an approach path to the destination*: Plan a collision-free path from the robot's current position to a point near the destination.

- *Place the object at the destination*: Generate a force-guarded motion to place the object at the destination. In a future version of the system, a compliant motion strategy should be used.

Subsequent sections explain the operation of the different modules and how they are used to carry out these steps.

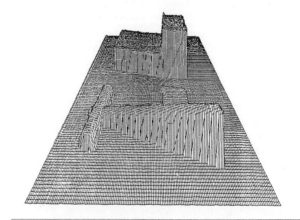

Figure 2. A very simple depth map

3. Locating the object

The first step in executing a MOVE command is localizing the object using depth information obtained from a range sensor. The range sensor is a light-striping triangulation sensor. It is used to produce a depth map of a small region on the worktable. The object to be MOVE'd is assumed to be present in this area.

After the depth map is constructed (Figure 2), the map is processed as if it were an image, except that "brightness" corresponds directly to elevation above the worktable. A standard "edge" operator [Canny 86] is run over the image and extended linear segments are identified in the resulting array. Note that this process identifies 3D edge segments, not just their projection in an image.

The method used for object localization is a simple hypothesize-verify algorithm based on matching linear segments in the depth map to edges in the polyhedral model of the part. This method is a variation of the method described in [Lozano-Pérez and Grimson 86], using edge data instead of face data. The basic step in the matcher is to take two edges in the model and consider all possible assignments of these edges to pairs of data edges. If the pairs of model edges are non-collinear, such an assignment of data edges to model edges is sufficient to solve for at most four transformations that map the model coordinate system into the data coordinate system. The ambiguity in the transformation arises due to the possible assignment of direction vectors to the edges. Given such a transformation, we can predict the location of other model edges in the data and verify their presence. The assignment that predicts the location of the most data edges is chosen.

The matcher attempts to consider only a few assignments of data edge pairs to model edge pairs. To reduce the set of such assignments it exploits two basic geometric constraints. First, a data edge should match a model edge only if their lengths are compatible, that is, if the length of the data edge is less than or equal to that of the model edge. Second, a pair of data edges can be matched to a pair of model edges if the parameters describing the relative pose of the edges in the pairs are consistent, taking into account the measurement error. Exploiting these constraints significantly reduces the number of matches that need to be considered.

We can describe the relative pose of two 3D edges using

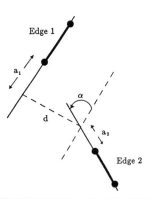

Figure 3. Definition of the four parameters that define the relationship between two edge segments.

the following parameters (Figure 3): α — the angle between the lines supporting the edge segments; d — the length between the lines measured along the common perpendicular to the lines; a_1 and a_2 — the distance from the base of the common perpendicular to the nearest end of the edge. Note that we only know the *line* on which a data edge lies; to obtain a *vector* we would need to know an additional sign. Therefore, there is a potential ambiguity in the parameters arising from the missing sign. This has to be treated carefully when testing whether two pairs are consistent.

Figure 4 shows examples of the matcher in operation, using edges extracted from depth maps similar to that in Figure 2.

Figure 4. (a) The x, y projection of edge fragments obtained by running the Canny edge detector on a depth map. (b) The projected object model located by the edge matcher superimposed on the edge fragments. This example corresponds to Figure 1.

4. Planning collision-free motions

At a number of points in the operation of the system, a collision-free path is required from one specified location to another. Handey uses a simplified version of the path planner described in [Lozano-Pérez 86]. This path planner uses the robot's joint space as the configuration space.

The obstacles are mapped into a quantized version of this configuration space by a simple numerical method illustrated in Figure 5 for a two-link manipulator. Given a value for θ_1, we can compute the range of forbidden values of θ_2 due to each of the obstacles. The set of forbidden ranges of θ_2 for each value of θ_1 comprise an approximation to the exact configuration space. This space can then be searched for a path. For a manipulator with three joints, the process described above (applied to joints two and three) is repeated for all possible (quantized) values of the first joint angle.

The version of the path planner used by Handey never computes configuration spaces of dimension greater than three, but it allows motions requiring six degrees of freedom. Essentially, we assume that a path from the start to the goal exists such that the last three joints of the arm retain their starting values until some intermediate point where they are changed to their values at the goal and never changed after that. It is easy to construct cases where this assumption will fail, but it works in a large percentage of actual cases.

The actual planning proceeds as follows: An approximate arm model is built in which the last three links are replaced by a box. This box must be large enough to enclose the last three links, the hand, and any object in the hand, not only at their start and goal positions but also at intermediate positions between the two. The three-dimensional configuration space for this model can then be built. We then find the closest free points in this configuration space to both the start and goal positions. A path is found between these two free points. Note that the complete robot is guaranteed to be safe along this path, for the whole range of values of the last three joints between the start and the goal. Therefore, we can simply interpolate the values of the last three joints between the start and goal values. Then, we plan a path using the original model of the robot between the free point closest to the start and the start itself. We also plan a path from the free point closest to the goal to the goal itself. In these two paths, the values of the last three joints are fixed. The concatenation of these three paths form the desired path.

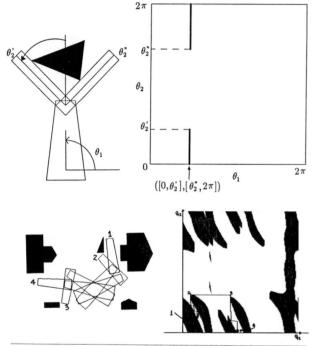

Figure 5. (a) The configuration space obstacles for a two-link manipulator are built by quantizing θ_1 and finding forbidden ranges of θ_2. (b) A sample configuration space with a path obtained by the path-planning algorithm.

5. Grasping

The most intensive interaction between perception, planning and action in Handey happens in grasping. After the target object's location has been determined, Handey must choose a pair of features, such as a pair of parallel faces, for grasping. Then, it must choose a path to reach those features that avoids any nearby objects. In addition to any known objects in the model, the hand must avoid colliding with any obstacles detected in the depth map, even if their identity is unknown.

A grasp that is suitable for picking up the object may not be suitable for placing it at the destination. Handey attempts to find a grasp consistent with both states. If there is not a single grasp suitable for both, then a sequence of grasps and intermediate motions may be necessary.

We model the hand by two opposing rectangular fingers which can close on an object by sliding along a crosspiece. A legal grasp has each finger in contact with a grasp feature on the object. The feasible grasp feature pairs are: two parallel faces of the object, or a face and a parallel edge, or a face and a vertex. The current version of Handey limits its attention to pairs of parallel faces.

The criteria for a legal grasp are as follows:

- The grasp must be stable. That is, the location and magnitude of the forces and torques exerted by the fingers must produce a balanced system of forces and be sufficient to overcome the effect of gravitational forces on the grasped object.

- The grasp must be reachable, both at the pickup point and the putdown point. That is, there must be a clear path to achieve contact with the chosen grasp features at the original location of the grasped object. Also, the grasp must not produce a collision when the object is placed at its destination.

In the current implementation of Handey we use very simple heuristics to guarantee stability. Our rationale is that for small objects and strong fingers, almost all grasps are stable. Since we limit ourselves to pairs of parallel faces, the forces are automatically balanced. Furthermore, we require that there be a user-specified minimum area of contact between the fingers and one of the grasped faces.

In general, to guarantee the stability of a grasp one must compute the forces and torques generated by the fingers, including the frictional forces and torques, and compare them to the gravity forces and torques acting on the object. Only if the applied forces and torques can balance the gravitational forces and torques will the grasp be stable. A procedure for computing the forces and torques for a particular two-fingered grasp is given in [Barber et al 86.]. Future versions of Handey will incorporate a more careful stability test.

We have placed more emphasis on guaranteeing reachability. There are three phases in computing a reachable grasp. The first phase is choosing the grasp features and a gross orientation for the hand. The second is planning the detailed grasping motion. The third is regrasping, when necessary. The following sections examine these phases in turn.

5.1 Choosing a grasp

Before attempting a detailed plan of the grasp, Handey examines different classes of candidate grasps and evaluates their feasibility both at the pickup point and the putdown point. A grasp class is characterized by a choice of object surfaces. A grasp is feasible if there exists a path for the hand to reach some point on the face while avoiding the obstacles reflected in the depth map. The two sets of constraints (at pickup and putdown) can be treated simultaneously by transforming the obstacles at the putdown position into the pickup position using the inverse of the transformation relating the putdown to the pickup pose (see Figure 6). These transformed obstacles are added to the depth map (by simulating the action of the range finder on the models). A safe path for the hand in this environment will be safe both on pickup and putdown.

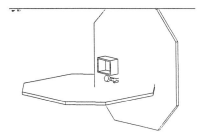

Figure 6. The obstacles at the putdown pose are transformed into the pickup pose. A legal grasp in this environment is legal for both poses.

We assume that the robot hand moves in a plane parallel to the faces being grasped and midway between them. This is called the *grasp plane*. When approaching a grasp the fingers remain parallel to the grasp plane and centered about it but are otherwise free to rotate and translate in the plane. The restriction to motion in the grasp plane is intended to minimize the risk of collision with the object to be grasped.

The grasp plane is bounded by a rectangle whose size determines the range of motion allowed the hand during grasping. The rectangular volume the hand can sweep out while constrained to move in the grasp plane is the grasp volume. In fact we must consider separately three grasp volumes – one for each finger and one for the crosspiece. Only these volumes need to be investigated for potential collisions.

Consider a point specified by the depth map which lies within or above a grasp volume. The point can be thought of as the origin of a ray which extends downward through the table. That portion of the ray which lies within the grasp volume is projected onto the grasp plane. Following this procedure for all such points marks the portion of the grasp plane where objects intrude into a grasp volume, that is, places where the hand cannot go. For ease of computation the projected line segments are discretized – becoming filled cells in a grid imposed on the grasp plane.

A necessary condition for the existence of a grasp is that there exist empty cells in this grid inside the intersection of the grasp faces (projected onto the grasp plane). These empty cells must also be connected to empty cells in the designated start region for the hand. The grasp class with the most free space is selected. The centroid of the empty cells on the face becomes the target grasp point.

If a grasp compatible with both pickup and putdown is not found, the obstacles from the putdown phase are removed from the depth map and the process described above is repeated. Regrasping will then be necessary.

5.2 Planning the grasping motion

We limit the grasping motion to be within the grasp plane and the representation of the obstacles is as filled cells in a grid overlaid on this plane. To plan the actual grasp approach motion, we use a planner specialized for planning the motion of the hand in the grasp plane. The planner uses a method loosely modeled on the potential field method for obstacle avoidance [Khatib 85].

The straightforward potential field method, although applicable, is not convenient in this situation because the obstacles are a large number of points, rather than a few extended obstacles. Also, the method described here is less likely to get stuck in local minima of the potential field.

The goal of the grasp motion planner is to bring a designated point on the fingertip as close as possible to the chosen grasp point on the grasp faces, without causing a collision between the hand and other objects. In the absence of intervening filled grid cells in the grasp plane the motion of the hand would be a simple translation along the vector connecting the finger and object grasp points. We call the unit vector in this direction the free motion vector.

Surrounding the hand at some distance and moving with it are bump lines. A bump line is a line segment on the grasp plane which is checked each iteration to see if it crosses a filled grid cell. A bump vector is a unit vector perpendicular to a bump line pointing away from the hand (see Figure 7). Also associated with each bump line is a multiplier used for limiting motion along its bump vector. This multiplier is related to the distance between the hand and the bump line.

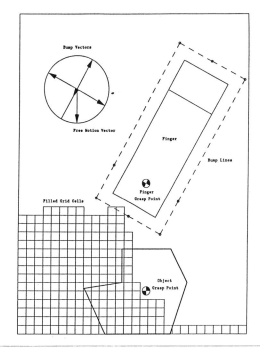

Figure 7. The grasp approach planner algorithm.

After investigating all the bump lines for collisions with filled cells we construct a unit circle and map onto it the bump vectors and free motion vector. In Figure 7, we show the product of the bump vectors and their multipliers. For non-colliding bump lines the multiplier is 1, for colliding bump lines it is 0. Not shown are bump lines which surround the hand at a greater distance; they may have collision multipliers greater than 1.

There are several possible ways to combine these vectors to pick a direction to move the hand. One way is simply to move along the non-zero bump vector closest in direction to the free motion vector. (This however leads to stairstep motion of the hand.) Another way is to move along the free motion vector as far as is allowed by the scaled bump vectors, choosing the former procedure only if latter computed no motion.

The bump lines also provide a convenient way of computing a "torque" to rotate the hand. Any colliding bump line produces a torque whose magnitude is proportional to the cross product of the bump vector and a vector connecting the finger grasp point and the center of the bump line. The total torque on the hand is just the sum of torques generated by each colliding bump line.

The combination of incremental translation and rotation defines the position of the hand at the next iteration. But, before actually moving the hand, the planner makes sure that a kinematic solution exists for that position of the hand.

In each iteration the distance between the finger and the object grasp points is checked. If this distance drops below a preselected threshold the grasp motion planner stops and returns the path it has discovered. However, as this method may fail to find a suitable grasp, the planner must be terminated after a certain number of iterations in any case. Even after such a termination a grasp is legal only if the finger and the grasp object face overlap sufficiently.

An example of planner output is shown in Figure 8.

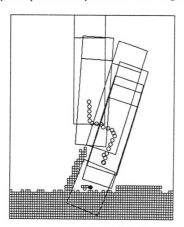

Figure 8. The grasp approach planner in operation.

5.3 Regrasping

In regrasping, one wants to find a sequence of pickup and put-down motions that will reorient the object so that it can be placed at the destination without collision. An example of a regrasping plan is shown in Figure 9. The regrasping algorithm used in Handey is described in detail in [Tournassoud, Lozano-Pérez, and Mazer 87]. Here, we give a brief summary of its operation.

A great deal of work has been done on the problem of choosing a single stable grasp on an object [Paul 72, Lozano-Pérez 76, 81, Taylor 76, Brou 80, Wingham 77, Laugier 81, Hanafusa and Asada 82, Laugier and Pertin-Troccaz 83, Cutkosky 84, Fearing 84, Abel, Holzmann and McCarthy 85, Baker, Fortune and Grosse 85, Holzmann and McCarthy 85, Barber et al. 86, Nguyen 86a, 86b, Jameson and Leifer 86] As far as we are

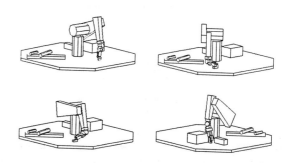

Figure 9. A one-step regrasping operation: (a) the initial grasp, which is constrained by the presence of other objects in the environment, (b) the intermediadte placement on the table surface, (c) the new grasp, and (d) the final assembly operation.

aware, however, the only previous systematic exploration of regrasping, as defined above, was by Paul [72] in the context of the Stanford Hand-Eye system.

Our approach to regrasping is as follows: We characterize the possible grasps of an object and its stable placements on the table. Both grasps and placements are described by the discrete choice of a surface of contact, combined with the choice of a continuous parameter. The regrasping problem is then solved by computing transitions in a space where we represent all compatible conjunctions of grasps and placements.

A *grasp*, G_i, is characterized by a choice of a pair of parallel grasp surfaces and some grasp point on the surfaces. The designated fingertip point is placed on the grasp point. This leaves one degree of freedom to be chosen, namely, the angle ϑ specifying the rotation of the fingers about the surface normal. Similarly, an object *placement*, P_j, is characterized by the choice of a surface to place on the table. The position of the projection of the object's center of mass is constrained to be a given point on the table. This leaves one degree of freedom to be chosen, namely, the angle φ specifying the rotation of the object about the table's normal.

We define the grasp-placement table to contain the combinations of all grasps and placements. Each entry in the table corresponds to a (G_i, P_j) pair. The table entry is the range of legal values of (ϑ, φ), call this $\overline{q_{ij}}$. A regrap sequence can be viewed as in Figure 10. The legal motions in the table are characterized by the Propositions below:

• Proposition 1:

A transition between the grasps $(G_{i_1}:\vartheta_1)$ and $(G_{i_2}:\vartheta_2)$ is legal if and only if there exists a placement $(P_j:\varphi)$ such that:

$$(\vartheta_1, \varphi) \in \overline{q_{i_1 j}}$$
$$(\vartheta_2, \varphi) \in \overline{q_{i_2 j}}$$

This simply states that we can, with a grasp of class G_{i_2}, pick up an object that has been ungrasped with a grasp of class G_{i_1}.

• Proposition 2:

Equivalently, a transition between the placements $(P_{j_1}:\varphi_1)$ and $(P_{j_2}:\varphi_2)$ is legal if and only if there exists a grasp $(G_i:\vartheta)$ such that:

$$(\vartheta, \varphi_1) \in \overline{q_{i j_1}}$$
$$(\vartheta, \varphi_2) \in \overline{q_{i j_2}}$$

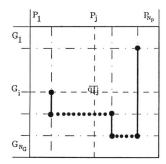

Figure 10. The grasp-placement table with an indicated regrasp sequence.

This transition is indeed a move with an invariant grasp $(G_i : \vartheta)$ between two placements of the object.

One version of the Regrasping Problem can now be stated as follows: given some initial grasp $(G^{ini} : \vartheta^{ini})$ and some goal one $(G^{goal} : \vartheta^{goal})$, find a sequence of grasps $(G_{i_0} : \vartheta_0), ..., (G_{i_n} : \vartheta_n)$, such that $(G_{i_0} : \vartheta_0) = (G^{ini} : \vartheta^{ini})$, $(G_{i_n} : \vartheta_n) = (G^{goal} : \vartheta^{goal})$, and there exists a legal transition between two consecutive grasps. If there are solutions to the problem, we want the given sequence to be of minimum length.

6. Calibration

The operation of Handey requires having accurate calibrations between several coordinate frames. The key systems that maintain their own coordinate frame are the range sensor and the modeling system. We are interested in the mapping between these coordinate frames and the cartesian frame supported by the robot controller. This section describes the calibration of the range sensor frame relative to the robot frame.

The calibration procedure assumes that the z axis of the range sensor's frame is parallel to the z axis of the robot's frame and that the height of the table is known in both reference systems. These assumptions are enforced by the mechanical construction of the range sensor. So the calibration problem is a two dimensional problem consisting of computing a rotation about the z axis and a linear offset in the x-y plane.

Phase one: Computing the rotation. A cube is placed in the robot's gripper so that the cube is aligned with the gripper, but its position relative to the gripper is arbitrary. The robot is commanded to move the cube in the field of view of the range sensor. Let (xw_1, yw_1) be the coordinates of the robot wrist in the x-y plane of the robot frame and (xv_1, yv_1) be the coordinates of the centroid of the single face of the cube visible to the range sensor (the z value is not used).

Then, the robots moves to $(xr_1 + dx, yr_1)$ without changing orientation. dx is chosen so that the cube remains in the field of view of the range sensor, (xv_2, yv_2) are the new coordinates of the face centroid given by the range sensor. The vector $(xv_2 - xv_1, yv_2 - yv_1)$ is parallel to the x axis of the robot frame, this allows us to compute the rotation between the sensor frame and the robot frame as: $R = Rot(\hat{z}, atan2(xv_2 - xv_1, yv_2 - yv_1))$, where $Rot(\mathbf{v}, \theta)$ is the homogeneous transformation representing a rotation by θ radians about the vector $\mathbf{v}$.

Phase two: Computing the offset. Since nothing is assumed concerning the relative location of the wrist and of the centroid of the cube face, let (fx, fy) be the projection of this vector in the x-y plane of the robot frame. The goal of the next motion is to compute fx and fy. The robot is commanded to rotate the hand about the robot frame's z axis by an angle of π, while keeping the wrist position fixed. Therefore, the cube face's centroid moves to the opposite end of a circle centered on the projection of the wrist. Call the new centroid location (xv_3, yv_3). We can now write: $(fx, fy) = 0.5 R^{-1}(xv_2 - xv_3, yv_2 - yv_3)$. The offset between the origin of the robot frame and the origin of the sensor frame is given by: $(o_x, o_y) = (xr_2, yr_2) + (fx, fy) + R^{-1}(xv_2, yv_2)$. If h_r is the height of the table in the robot frame and h_v and the height in the sensor frame then $o_z = h_r - h_v$ is the z offset between the two frames.

Finally the transform that maps points in the sensor frame to points in the robot frame can be written as:

$$Trans(o_x, o_y, o_z)R^{-1},$$

where $Trans(x, y, z)$ is the homogeneous transformation corresponding to a translation of the origin to (x, y, z).

7. Discussion

Building Handey has been quite difficult. This reflects the usual difficulty of building large systems. We feel that it was feasible at all due to the use of very simple and robust algorithms for the constituent modules, such as the path planner and recognition module.

The most significant lesson we have drawn from our experience so far with Handey is the need for a systematic and efficient way of dealing with the number of options available while constructing a plan. It is instructive to consider the number of geometrically different ways one could go about stacking two blocks. Consider the block symmetries, the hand symmetries, multiple kinematic solutions, multiple grasp points, and multiple paths. In most cases we don't care which solution is chosen but, unfortunately, many of the possible solutions can be impossible due to the presence of nearby objects or limitations in the robot's joint angles, etc. Handey simply lists all possible solutions, ranks them heuristically, and tries them sequentially until one works. While adequate in the short term, this strategy leaves much to be desired. In earlier work [Lozano-Pérez and Brooks 85], we have considered the use of constraints as a mechanism for making these decisions. Constraint propagation and satisfaction, however, can be extremely difficult and computationally expensive. This area requires a great deal of further work.

Future work on Handey will also attempt to expand its capability to do sensor-guided assembly and to do meaningful error detection and recovery.

Acknowledgments

This work was funded primarily by the Office of Naval Research under contracts N00014-85-K-0214 and N00014-86-K-0685. Additional support was provided by an NSF Presidential Young Investigator Award (Lozano-Pérez) and the French CNRS (Mazer). The visits of Lanusse and Tournassoud to MIT were funded by their home organizations in France: E. T. C. A. and INRIA respectively.

Bibliography

Abel, J. M., Holzmann, W. and McCarthy, J. M., "On grasping planar objects with two articulated fingers," *Proc. IEEE Intl. Conf. on Robotics and Automation*, St. Louis, 1985, pp. 576–581.

A. P. Ambler, H. G. Barrow, C. M. Brown, R. M. Burstall, and R. J. Popplestone, "A versatile system for computer-controlled assembly." *Artificial Intelligence*, Vol 6, 1975, pp 129–156.

Baker, B. S., Fortune, S., and Grosse, E., "Stable prehension with a multi-fingered hand," *Proc. IEEE Intl. Conf. on Robotics and Automation*, St. Louis, 1985, pp. 570–575.

J. Barber, R. A. Volz, R. Desai, R. Rubinfeld, B. Schipper, and J. Wolter, "Automatic two-fingered grip selection," in *Proc. IEEE Conf. Robotics and Automation*, San Francisco, 1986, pp. 890–896.

Brou, P, "Implementation of High-Level Commands for Robots," M. S. Thesis, Electrical Engineering and Computer Science, MIT, 1980.

J. Canny, "A Computational Approach to Edge Detection," *IEEE Trans. on PAMI*, Vol 8, No 6, 1986, pp. 679-698.

Cutkosky, M. R., "Mechanical properties for the grasp of a robotics hand," CMU-RI-TR-84-24, Carnegie Mellon Robotics Institute, 1984.

Fearing, R, "Simplified grasping and manipulation with dextrous robot hands," *Proc. Amer. Control Conf.*, 1984, pp. 32–38.

G. Giralt, R. P. Sobek, R. Chatila, "A multilevel planning and navigation system for a mobile robot: A first approach to Hilare," in *Proc. 6th IJCAI*, Tokyo, 1979.

Hanafusa, H., and H. Asada, "Stable prehension of objects by the robot hand with elastic fingers," *Proc. 7th Int. Symp. Industrial Robots*, Tokyo, 1977, pp. 361-368.

Holzmann, W. and McCarthy, J. M., "Computing the friction forces associated with a three-fingered grasp," *IEEE Intl. Conf. on Robotics and Automation*, St. Louis, 1985, pp.594-600.

K. Ikeuchi, H. K. Nishihara, B. K. P. Horn, P. G. Sobalvarro, S. Nagata, "Determining grasp configurations using photometric stereo and the PRISM binocular stereo system." *Robotics Research*, Vol 5, No 1, 1986, pp 46–65.

Jameson, J. W., and Leifer, L. J., "Quasi-Static Analysis: A method for predicting grasp stability," *IEEE Intl. Conf. on Robotics and Automation,* San Francisco, 1986, pp. 876–883.

O. Khatib, "Real-time obstacle avoidance for manipulators and mobile robots," in *Proc. IEEE Conf. Robotics and Automation*, St. Louis, 1985, pp. 500–506.

Laugier, C, "A program for automatic grasping of objects with a robot arm," *Proc. 11th Int. Symp. Industrial Robots,* Tokyo, 1981.

Laugier, C. and Pertin-Troccaz, J., "Automatic Robot Programming: The Grasp Planner," *Proc. Intl. Conf. on Advanced Software in Robotics,* Liege, 1983.

Lozano-Pérez, T, "The design of a mechanical assembly system," MIT AI TR 397, Artificial Intelligence Laboratory, MIT, 1976.

Lozano-Pérez, T, "Automatic planning of manipulator transfer movements," *IEEE Trans. Systems, Man, Cybernetics*, SMC-11, 10, 1981, pp. 681-689.

T. Lozano-Pérez, "A Simple Motion Planning Algorithm for General Robot Manipulators," in *Proc. 5th AAAI*, Philadelphia, 1986, pp. 626–631.

T. Lozano-Pérez and R. A. Brooks, "An Approach to Automatic Robot Programming," MIT AI Lab., AIM 842, 1985.

T. Lozano-Pérez and W. E. L. Grimson, "Off-line planning for on-line object localization," in *Proc. of FJCC.*, Dallas, 1986.

Nguyen, V. D., "The synthesis of stable grasps in the plane," *Proc. IEEE Intl. Conf. on Robotics and Automation*, San Francisco, 1986, pp. 884–889.

Nguyen, V. D., "Constructing force-closure grasps," *Proc. IEEE Intl. Conf. on Robotics and Automation*, San Francisco, 1986, pp. 1368–1373.

N. Nilsson, "A mobile automaton: an application of artificial intelligence," in *Proc. 1st IJCAI*, 1969, pp. 509–520.

R. P. Paul, "Modeling, trajectory calculation, and servoing of a computer controlled arm," Stanford AI Lab., AIM 177, 1972.

P. Tournassoud, T. Lozano-Pérez, and E. Mazer, "Regrasping," in *Proc. IEEE Conf. Robotics and Automation*, 1987.

Wingham, M, "Planning how to grasp objects in a cluttered environment," M.Ph. Thesis, Edinburgh, 1977.

P. H. Winston, "The MIT Robot," in *Machine Intelligence* 7, Edinburgh University Press, 1972, pp 431–463.

II DEVICES

At the heart of every robotic system is a set of basic devices. Early robotics researchers sometimes suggested that the design of these devices was not important because the computer controllers could compensate for design limitations. We now know that, in fact, the basic devices are of primary importance. Good devices can sometimes be controlled by rudimentary controllers, but poor devices generally cannot be adequately controlled by even the most sophisticated controllers. The papers in part II focus on the design of good robotic devices.

Jacobsen treats the all-important problem of actuators. He discusses the design trade-offs and selection criteria for actuators, which ultimately determine system performance. In the past, various pneumatic, artificial-muscle-type actuators were proposed, and prototypes were developed. Few of these ever resulted in a successful commercial product. The major problem was short lifetimes, especially at elevated pressures. Inoue describes one such actuator—the Rubbertuator—which he believes has overcome many of the earlier difficulties.

Although most actuators drive single, decoupled degrees of freedom, there are actuators that can produce several motions simultaneously. Hollis et al. describe a magnetic actuator that drives six degrees of freedom under fine-motion control and with specified variable compliance. They present the necessary analysis for the kinematics, dynamics, and control of their actuator, and discuss its use as a magnetically levitated six-degree-of-freedom wrist.

The next two papers deal with sensing. Nakamura et al. revisit the well-known six-axis force sensor. They give a fresh analysis that is aimed at answering questions related to the optimal placement of strain guages and the stiffness of elastic elements. Bicchi and Dario make the case that artificial hands should perform tactile sensing by means of remote force and torque measurements (intrinsic tactile sensing) rather than relying exclusively on surface-mounted pressure-sensing tactile arrays (extrinsic sensing). They describe an experimental finger that incorporates both types of sensors.

Idesawa discusses high-precision optical range finders. He uses a one-dimensional mark detection system and triangulation to achieve high-precision miniature devices.

BEHAVIOR BASED DESIGN OF ROBOT EFFECTORS

Stephen C. Jacobsen*, Craig C. Smith**, Klaus B. Biggers*, Edwin K. Iversen*

*Center for Engineering Design,
Department of Mechanical Engineering,
University of Utah, Salt Lake City, Utah

**Department of Mechanical Engineering,
Brigham Young University, Provo, Utah

This paper explores important issues in the design of effector systems, which are those parts of a robot that interact with the environment through mechanical movements. Effector subsystems include actuators, structures, loads, sensors, and servo-level controllers.

The effector design problem is reviewed, as simply and intuitively as possible, using second-, third-, and fifth-order linear models of a system with only one external degree of freedom. The design approach discussed includes the following five steps: (1) IDENTIFY SYSTEM BEHAVIORAL OBJECTIVES. These objectives are expressed for a specific system being designed. Certain behavioral characteristics, such as speed and strength, are easily defined while others are difficult to express quantitatively, such as quickness, grace, trajectory execution accuracy, ability to maintain stability when touching objects, response to external loading insults, saturation avoidance, and functioning without structural oscillations. (2) DEFINE QUANTITATIVE PERFORMANCE CRITERIA. These criteria are generated based on behavioral objectives. (3) ESTABLISH A MINIMUM COMPLEXITY SYSTEM MODEL. The model should have sufficient complexity to exhibit behaviors of interest and is expressed in terms of basic model and controller parameters. (4) DETERMINE PARAMETER CONSTRAINT EQUATIONS. The quantitative performance criteria and the system model are combined to form eleven simultaneous parameter constraint equations in terms of system variables. (5) APPLY PARAMETER CONSTRAINT EQUATIONS. Two design scenarios are reviewed which use the constraint equations to define various relationships between known and unknown system variables. Two example design scenarios are: (A) With the structure, load, sensor, and controller parameters defined, determine the actuator characteristics required to produce the desired effector system behavior; or (B) With the actuator, structure, and load parameters defined, determine maximum performance possibilities.

Well–known techniques are used with only a slight change in approach aimed at emphasizing that in designing these systems the generation of a clear understanding of desired system behavior must be a dominant priority. Results are presented via a set of fairly complicated, nonlinear equations composed of system parameters and performance objectives. To avoid masking realities, little attempt has been made to refine the format of constraint equations. Generalizations, clean mathematical representations, and closed form solutions, which are of course desirable, are deferred to later work.

INTRODUCTION

Background

Over the past decade, a major focus of the Center for Engineering Design (CED) at the University of Utah has been the design of actuation systems for robots, teleoperators, prosthetic limbs, and medical devices. Each project has required the development of systems with different combinations of behavioral characteristics such as strength, speed, precision, grace, efficiency, size, and weight. Necessarily, the projects have included consideration of the six subsystems of a robot shown in Figure 1.

Block 3 represents the effector, the distinguishing feature which separates a robot from other smart machines. The effector includes actuators, structures, a servo-level controller, and internal sensors. The actuators, which are energy transforming devices, can be electric, hydraulic, or pneumatic systems controlled by amplifiers and/or valves. Actuators may also include other mechanisms such as reducers and drives.

Block 4 represents the environment, which can impose external loads on the effector by touching or pushing. Block 2 represents the mid- and high-level controller, which plans

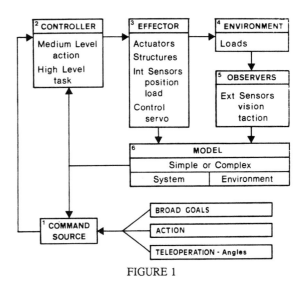

FIGURE 1

The Six Subsystems of a Robot

actions and tasks. Block 5 includes external sensors which observe the environment, such as vision systems, tactile sensors, and acoustic systems. Block 1 represents the command source, and Block 6 is the model, which provides information to the higher level controller and the command source. The model can be as simple as a group of potentiometer settings in an analog electronic system, or as complex as a complete representation of the dynamics of the system.

Problems with Effector Development

Successful effector systems have been developed by the CED for the Utah Arm, the Utah/M.I.T. Dextrous Hand, entertainment robots, and high performance servo-pumps for use in medical devices. The CED is a design-oriented group which has believed itself quite good at developing effectors. This belief was somewhat shaken when, during a workshop, a sponsor asked the question,"What is a good actuator and how is one designed?" (Kelly, 1985). No one responded very well and attempted answers were fuzzy and circular. The discussion demonstrated clearly that it is not yet easy to talk about effectors in a comprehensive way. As a result of the discussions, it became clear that the reasons for lack of progress in the development of effectors stem from: (1) lack of need, (2) problems with complexity, and (3) a general underestimation of the importance of effecting systems.

(1) Need: The performance demands on effectors have only recently begun to stretch the limits of available physical systems. Thus, it has been possible to consider effectors as merely simplified elements in block diagrams. In short, effectors have been neglected because neglecting them has been possible. **(2) Complexity:** Effectors have also been neglected because their characteristics are difficult to understand and represent. Effectors are complex thermodynamic machines, which are typically only one interactive element of an even larger, more complex system. **(3) Underestimation:** Finally, and most significantly, the importance of effectors, and the limitations they will impose on future robots, has not been clearly articulated by researchers interested in this area.

The Real Question

It was interesting that during the Kelly actuator discussions the question "What is a good actuator?" raised a set of concerns and antagonisms which have been growing over the past decade. Typical comments on this issue have been "Why all this talk from engineers about problems with machinery that moves? Surely, problems with actuators can't represent a major obstacle to progress in robotics." "Clearly, actuators don't rank in difficulty with Artificial Intelligence, vision, and other topics in robotics." "Motors just can't be a problem, they're just motors." "Where's the fundamental content, anyway?" "When we want them, we'll simply build them." "There has been too much talk and no clear answers. This problem should be solved or go away."

Out of these discussions, three important points emerged:

(1) With sufficient effort, the actuator problem can be completely understood, certainly for linear systems. The relationships between effector configuration and behavior can be rigorously defined. This is the focus of this paper.

(2) The development of new effector systems, appropriate for future robots, does rank in importance and difficulty with other major engineering problems. Barriers to progress range from the development of better approaches to the dynamic control of energy conversion to basic issues in machine design (i.e., packaging, heat transfer, friction, wear, efficiency, etc.).

(3) Systems of the future must exhibit extraordinary behavioral capabilities while simultaneously being reliable, efficient, and economic. If these problems are not addressed now, in a fundamental way, the effector problem will become a major obstacle to future progress in the area of robotics.

Objectives

The goal of this paper is to explore issues important to the systematic design of effectors. Of specific importance is how to assemble effector system elements into machinery which will produce desired behaviors.

The paper addresses the effector design problem using no new approaches, only an examination of some fundamental concepts via an application of performance criteria to an effector model. The objective is to improve our understanding of concepts and to expand the vocabulary necessary to discuss effectors systematically.

Results are not expressed in a particularly pretty or comprehensive form. Generalized representations such as nondimensional groups and universal graphs are deferred for later work. The system model is not dismembered into elements in an attempt to understand overall behaviors in terms of component characteristics such as internal impedances. It is the behavior of the entire system, when assembled, which is of primary importance.

APPROACH

A Simple Effector System

Our goal is to understand the behavioral characteristics of an effector system in the simplest possible way. Of importance is understanding how to trade off component and controller parameters in order to achieve desired performance characteristics. The following review serves to acquaint the reader with a typical servo experiment.

The usual approach is to assemble a servo–system such as that shown in Figure 2. The system includes a one-degree-of-freedom arm with motor, amplifier, reducer, sensors (colocated with the reducer output), a compliant arm, and a controller. Alternatively, the example could utilize a hydraulic or pneumatic actuator in place of the electric motor.

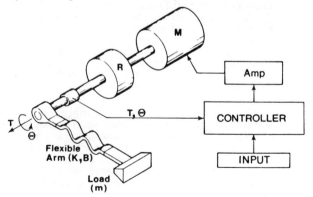

FIGURE 2

Simple One-dimensional Model of a One-link Effector Arm

A process of optimization (compromise) is then undertaken to determine acceptable system parameter settings, i.e., via knob twisting. As variables are changed, a number of behaviors can result as depicted in Figure 3. Figure 3 is a simplified schematic which shows the load, the flexible arm structure, and the armature mass as elements which under various conditions combine to exhibit sluggish, rapid, oscillatory, or unstable behaviors. Note that the armature mass M_A is actuated by the feedback system, which includes position and force sensors (shown as the eye) and a motor (shown as the coil).

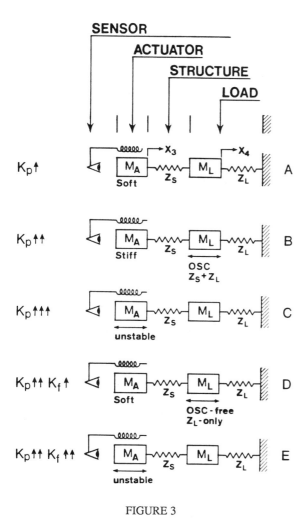

FIGURE 3

Simple Servo-system Behaviors

First, the position feedback loop gain, K_p, is increased from zero. If the position loop gain is too low the system will be soft, slow, and positional accuracy will be low (Case A in Figure 3). As K_p is increased the system exhibits sufficient stiffness to improve positional accuracy while remaining stable. Typically, the resulting stiff system does not interact well with touched objects and can encounter combinations of servo and structural oscillations when speed demands are high enough for actuator loadings to deform structures (Case B, Figure 3). If K_p is further increased, the system becomes unstable and the actuator mass M_A oscillates against the load mass M_L through the structural impedance Z_s (Case C, Figure 3).

In an attempt to correct the problem, a force feedback loop is usually added in order to modify passive qualities of the system's response. As the force feedback gain, K_f, is increased, the system becomes increasingly softer, more graceful, and the fundamental oscillation frequency of the load decreases and approaches that of the free load without an

actuator. Now the system interacts more successfully with external objects but steady state position error is increased (Case D, Figure 3). If K_f is further increased, problems with high frequency structural oscillations and instability emerge (Case E, Figure 3).

Root locus plots, shown later in the paper, further discuss these behaviors. Note that these behavioral trade-offs strongly suggest the development of nonlinear adaptive controllers in which the gains of selected feedback loops are dynamically adjusted according to system behavioral demands (Jacobsen, 1973; Jacobsen, 1986; Meek, 1986; Fullmer, 1986; Seamons, 1986; Hooker, 1987).

A Linear Effector Model

A general linear model of the system in Figure 2 is shown in Figure 4. The model contains ten elements: a motor, amplifier, reducer, drive, sensors, structure, load, touch load, and a linear feedback control system.

This model has sufficient complexity to exhibit behaviors of interest while also being relatively simple. In the following sections, the system is separated into second- and third-order approximate models in order to examine sequentially the influence of actuators, structures, loads, and controllers on behavior.

Design Sequence

Of importance here is that this problem is not merely one of addressing an existing plant to be controlled. The entire problem must be impartially re-explored not only in the area of control strategy but also in the design of actuators, structures, and load.

The design approach includes five steps:

First — Identify, in general terms, the desired system behavior versus anticipated types of inputs (including externally produced disturbances). Important behaviors can be characterized by terms such as quickness, gracefulness, trajectory quality, ability to maintain stability while touching objects, absence of structural oscillations during operation, as well as others.

Second — Define quantitative performance criteria (QPC's) which, if satisfied, will constrain the system to exhibit desired behaviors. Typical performance criteria include rise-time, overshoot, steady state error, relative stability and others.

Third — Formulate a model which is complex enough to generate behaviors of interest and exhibit the relationships between the system and these behaviors, yet which is simple enough to allow solutions to be obtained systematically.

Fourth — Combine results of steps 1–3 to define a set of parameter constraint equations which can then be used in different design scenarios.

Fifth — Explore design scenarios, such as:

(A) Given structure, load, and desired system behavioral characteristics, what is a good actuator?

(B) What behavior is possible given the characteristics of the actuator, load, controller, and structure?

Or, in more simple terms: Use the desired system behavior (1) to generate quantitative performance criteria (2) which when used with the system model (3) can generate a set of constraint equations (4) which are useful in the solution of various design scenarios (5).

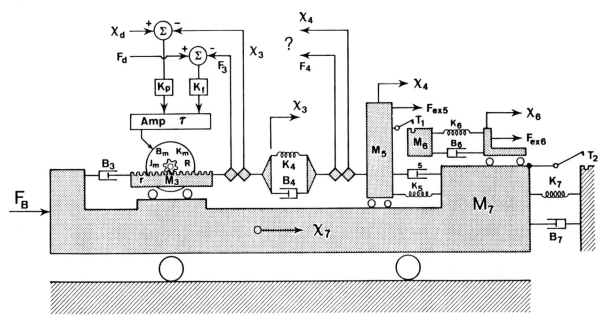

FIGURE 4

One-dimensional Linear Effector Model

A LINEAR EFFECTOR MODEL

Introduction

Figure 4 shows a simple linear model of the system in Figure 2, which includes one external degree-of-freedom. The model includes no stiction, backlash, saturation, drive compliance (in the shaft between the motor armature and the pinion gear), or other complications.

The actuator, which consists of the motor, reducer, sensors, and drive, is represented in the model as a second-order system with a torque delay caused by the motor inductance. Additional delays could be caused via the amplifier, drive compliance, and backlash, but they are not considered here.

The motor is a permanent magnet, DC electric motor (see Table 1) connected to a reducer and drive (rack and pinion gears), which includes inertial and damping characteristics (M_3, B_3). The diamond-shaped elements interposed between the rack and structure, and between the structure and load mass, are transducers which measure force and position. The inverse of the radius of the pinion gear, r, is defined as the reduction parameter G.

The structure is represented by parallel spring and damping elements (B_4, K_4), which permit the representation of structural oscillations between the actuator and load. The load is a second-order parallel combination of the mass, spring, and damper (M_5, B_5, K_5), and it can be contacted by a second-order touch impedance defined by a mass, spring, and damper (M_6, B_6, K_6). Note that touch is engaged by the binary parameter T_1 ($T_1 = 1$, connected) and pushing (with impedance) via movement of the variable X_6. An external force (with zero impedance) can also be applied via F_{ex5}.

Although the position of the base X_7 is assumed fixed in this case (parameter $T_2 = 1$), for later studies it can be freed to include base dynamics (M_7, B_7, K_7) and the application of external force F_B. Observe that, in future work, the model can be cascaded to represent higher complexity systems by connecting the load mass (M_5) in one system to the base mass

(M_7) of the next system. Of course, successive systems would typically be free with their ground impedances (K_7, B_7) set at zero.

The simple linear control structure includes position and force loops adjusted by gains K_p and K_f. The system input is X_d and the output for this paper is considered as X_3. If the output is considered as X_4 and information from noncolocated sensors X_4 and F_4 is used, then more complicated stability issues arise (Cannon, 1984).

Of course, initial conditions can be specified in order to simulate specific effector experiments. For example, with an appropriate initial velocity on X_4 and suitable load impedance, the model can be used to simulate system response to external insults.

Case I – The Total System

Case I is the total fifth-order system obtained by using parameter values listed in Table 1. Equations representing system elements are described by Equations 1.

Third-order (Case II) and second-order (Case III and IV) approximations of Case I will be used to generate eleven constraint equations.

Motor:

$$P_1 \frac{d\theta}{dt} = \frac{K_m}{R} V_{in} - P_2 T_{dr} \qquad (1a)$$

where V_{in} is the voltage applied to the motor.

Reducer:

$$T_{dr} = \frac{1}{G} F_{dr} \qquad (1b)$$

where F_{dr} is the force applied to the rack by the pinion gear, and

$$\theta = G\,X_3 \qquad (1c)$$

Drive:

$$F_{dr} = P_3\,X_3 + F_{st} \qquad (1d)$$

where F_{st} is the force applied to the structure.

Structure:

$$F_{st} = P_4\,(X_3 - X_4) \qquad (1e)$$

Load:

$$F_L = P_5\,X_4 - F_{ex5} \qquad (1f)$$

Controller:

$$V_{in} = K_p\,(X_d - X_3) + K_f\,(F_d - F_{st}) \qquad (1g)$$

Where

$$P_1 = \left[\frac{L}{R}J_m\right]s^2 + \left[J_m + \frac{L}{R}B_m\right]s + \left[B_m + \frac{K_m^2}{R}\right] \qquad (1h)$$

$$P_2 = \left[\frac{L}{R}\right]s + 1 \qquad (1i)$$

$$P_3 = [M_3]s^2 + [B_3]s \qquad (1j)$$

$$P_4 = [B_4]s + K_4 \qquad (1k)$$

$$P_5 = [M_5]s^2 + [B_5]s + K_5 \qquad (1l)$$

Equations 1

The Case I equations are combined below as Equations 2.

$$\left(D_5 s^5 + \cdots + D_1 s + D_0\right)X_3 = \varphi_p(gs^2 + bs + a)X_d \qquad (2a)$$

where

$$\begin{bmatrix} D_0 \\ \vdots \\ \vdots \\ \vdots \\ D_5 \end{bmatrix} = \tilde{\beta}\begin{bmatrix} M_A \\ B_A \\ B_L \\ \varphi_P \\ \varphi_F \\ 1 \end{bmatrix} \qquad (2b)$$

and

$$M_A = G^2 J_m + M_3 \qquad (2c)$$

$$B_A = G^2 B_m + B_3 \qquad (2d)$$

$$B_L = G^2\left(\frac{(K_m)^2}{R}\right) \qquad (2e)$$

$$\varphi_F = \left(1 + G\frac{K_m}{R}K_f\right) \qquad (2f)$$

$$\varphi_P = \left(G\frac{K_m}{R}K_p\right) \qquad (2g)$$

$$G = 1/r \qquad (2h)$$

and

$$\tilde{\beta} = \begin{bmatrix} 0 & 0 & 0 & a & e & 0 \\ 0 & a & a & b & c & \left(\frac{L}{R}\right)e \\ a & b+\left(\frac{L}{R}\right)a & b & g & d & \left(\frac{L}{R}\right)c \\ b+\left(\frac{L}{R}\right)a & g+\left(\frac{L}{R}\right)b & g & 0 & f & \left(\frac{L}{R}\right)d \\ g+\left(\frac{L}{R}\right)b & \left(\frac{L}{R}\right)g & 0 & 0 & 0 & \left(\frac{L}{R}\right)f \\ \left(\frac{L}{R}\right)g & 0 & 0 & 0 & 0 & 0 \end{bmatrix} \qquad (2i)$$

$$\begin{bmatrix} a \\ b \\ c \\ d \\ e \\ f \\ g \end{bmatrix} = \begin{bmatrix} K_4 + K_5 \\ B_4 + B_5 \\ B_4 K_5 + B_5 K_4 \\ B_4 B_5 + K_4 M_5 \\ K_4 K_5 \\ M_5 B_4 \\ M_5 \end{bmatrix} \qquad (2j)$$

Equations 2

Ten System Elements Are Defined by Twenty-six Parameters

TABLE 1

Model Parameters

K_m	53.2×10^{-3} N·m/W$^{1/2}$	Motor*
R	.631 Ω	Motor*
J_m	38.1×10^{-6} kg·m^2	Motor*
B_m	17×10^{-6} N·m·s/rad	Motor*
L	.0975 mH	Motor*
τ	0	Amplifier
G	108.7 m^{-1} ($\frac{1}{r}$)	Reducer
B_3	3.46 N·s/m	Drive
M_3	0	Drive
B_4	3.464 N·s/m	Structure
K_4	2.83×10^5 N/m	Structure
M_5	2.65 kg	Load
B_5	17.32 N·s/m	Load
K_5	113.2 N/m	Load
M_6	0	Touch Load
B_6	0	Touch Load
K_6	0	Touch Load
T_1	0	Touch Load
K_p	Variable	Controller
K_f	Variable	Controller
Sf,Sp	Unity	Sensors
M_7,B_7,K_7,T_2	Fixed	Base

*Pitman Corp Motor, Model 5113.

The D's are coefficients of the system's characteristic equation and s is the Laplace transform operator. φ's are nondimensional controller gains and a through g are constants composed of the lumped parameter coefficients of the structure and load. M_A, B_A, and B_L are motor, reducer, and drive system characteristics.

Root Loci Illustrating Case I Behavior

In order to examine the behavior of the fifth-order system in a qualitative way, a number of root loci are plotted for a typical system whose parameters are quantitatively defined in Table 1. (Note that for illustration purposes all root locus plots are distorted by an expansion of the real axis and some poles and/or zeros are off the figure.)

Figure 5 contains a root locus plot for the Case I system with only the position feedback loop in operation ($K_f = 0$). Observe that as the gain of the position loop, K_p, is increased from 0 to ∞, five poles migrate to two finite zeros and three infinite zeros.

The two finite zeros marked "A" represent an oscillation of the load together with the actuator which occurs at relatively low frequencies. The complex poles marked "B" are the result of oscillatory interactions between the actuator and structure, which ultimately result in unstable operation as those poles cross the imaginary axis. The fifth pole migrates out the negative real axis (recall Figure 3, Cases A, B, and C).

Note that the behavior of poles and zeros on the negative real axis can be important, since they shift the intersection of asymptotes with the real axis.

Case I, Kf=0 V/N, Varying Kp

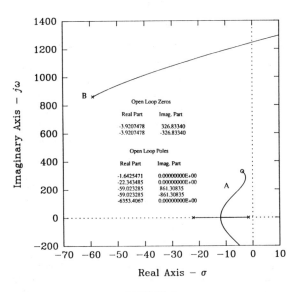

FIGURE 5

Root Locus of Case I System

(Fifth-order System with Position Feedback Only)

Figure 6 shows a root locus for Case I with $K_p = 30,000$ V/m and the force feedback gain K_f varying from 0 to ∞ V/N. Observe again two types of oscillation. The low magnitude poles labelled A represent a load oscillation which

becomes progressively more free (slower and less damped than the case in Figure 5 where only K_p is a variable) as the force feedback gain is increased. These poles approach the eigenvalues of the load with the actuator unattached (which show up as zeros on the plot). The higher frequency poles labelled B represent oscillations which occur as a result of interactions between the actuator and the load through the compliant structure. As K_f increases, the B poles continue out toward the imaginary axis and can, if the system is not properly designed, produce undesirable instabilities before the desired level of softness is achieved (recall Figure 3, Cases D and E).

Note again that the motivation for adding force feedback is to soften the system's behavior. This in fact occurs as K_f is turned up and the A poles, which represent the load (swinging against gravity in Figure 2), decrease in magnitude (frequency) and remain less damped than without force feedback.

Case I, Kp=30000 V/m, Varying Kf

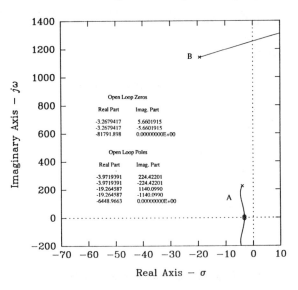

FIGURE 6

Root Locus of Case I System
for $K_p = 30,000$ V/m
and K_f Varying from 0 to ∞ V/N

Use of Reduced Models

Generating quantitative relationships between system parameters and behavior is difficult using the fifth-order model. Therefore, the fifth-order case is separated into three simpler cases.

Case II is a third-order system which focuses on oscillations between the actuator and structure. Case III is a second-order system which addresses behavior of the load assuming a rigid structure. Case IV is a second-order system used to examine system response to insults to the structure and actuator assuming the motor is fast and the load is slow. These reduced equations are then used, together with quantitative performance criteria (QPC's), to develop system parameter constraint equations.

Case II — Compliant structure with a slow load. This case is generated by assuming that the load mass (M_5) is large such that its motions are slow (assumed fixed) compared to the dynamics of the actuator and structure. Case II is described by Equations 3 and 4.

Actuator:

$$\left\{ [P_6] s^3 + [P_7]s^2 + [P_8] s + [P_9] \right\} X_3 = G\frac{K_m}{R} V_{in} \qquad (3a)$$

Controller with $F_d = 0$:

$$V_{in} = K_p X_d - \left\{ [K_f B_4] s + [K_p + K_f K_4] \right\} X_3 \qquad (3b)$$

where

$$P_6 = \frac{L}{R} \left[M_A \right] \qquad (3c)$$

$$P_7 = M_A + \frac{L}{R} \left[B_A + B_4 \right] \qquad (3d)$$

$$P_8 = B_A + B_L + B_4 + \frac{L}{R} \left[K_4 \right] \qquad (3e)$$

$$P_9 = K_4 \qquad (3f)$$

Equations 3

For later use, combining Equations 3a and 3b yields Equation 4a.

$$\left[A_3s^3 + A_2s^2 + A_1s + A_0 \right] X_3 = \varphi_P X_d + G\frac{K_m}{R} K_f F_d \qquad (4a)$$

$$A_3 = \frac{L}{R} \left[M_A \right] \qquad (4b)$$

$$A_2 = M_A + \frac{L}{R} \left[B_A + B_4 \right] \qquad (4c)$$

$$A_1 = B_A + B_L + \varphi_F B_4 + \frac{L}{R} \left[K_4 \right] \qquad (4d)$$

$$A_0 = \varphi_F K_4 + \varphi_P \qquad (4e)$$

$$T(s) = \frac{X_3}{X_d} \qquad (4f)$$

Equations 4

Where A_n represents the coefficients of the characteristic equation, and $T(s)$ is the third-order system's closed loop transfer function.

Case III — Rigid structure with moving load. This case, described by Equations 5 and 6, is generated by assuming that L is very small and K_4 is very large, i.e., a rigid structure.

Actuator:

$$\left\{ [P_{10}]s^2 + [P_{11}]s + [P_{12}] \right\} X_3 = G\frac{K_m}{R} V_{in} + F_{ex5} \qquad (5a)$$

Controller:

$$V_{in} = K_p X_d + K_f F_d + K_f F_{ex5} - P_{13} X_3 \qquad (5b)$$

where

$$P_{10} = M_A + M_5 \qquad (5c)$$

$$P_{11} = B_A + B_L + B_5 \qquad (5d)$$

$$P_{12} = K_5 \qquad (5e)$$

$$P_{13} = \left[K_f M_5 \right] s^2 + \left[K_f B_5 \right] s + \left[K_f K_5 + K_p \right] \qquad (5f)$$

Equations 5

For later use, combining Equations 5a and 5b yields Equation 6a.

$$\left\{ [M_1]s^2 + [B_1]s + [K_1] \right\} X_3 = \varphi_P X_d + G\frac{K_m}{R} K_f \left[F_d + F_{ex5} \right] \qquad (6a)$$

where

$$M_1 = M_A + \varphi_F M_5 \qquad (6b)$$

$$B_1 = B_A + B_L + \varphi_F B_5 \qquad (6c)$$

$$K_1 = \varphi_F K_5 + \varphi_P \qquad (6d)$$

Equations 6

Figure 7 shows a typical root locus of Case III, the second-order system, with K_p fixed. As in the previous plot, note that the load oscillations become more free as K_f is increased. At very large values of K_f the A poles approach the load zeros and the actuator is functionally absent, i.e., the system behaves as the free load.

Case III, Kp=30000 V/m, Varying Kf

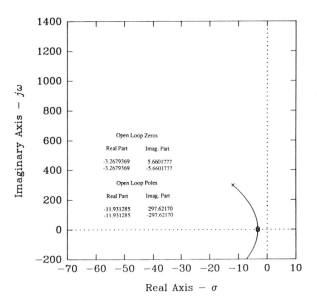

FIGURE 7

Root Locus for Case III with $K_p = 30,000$ V/m and K_f Varying

Figure 8 shows a typical root locus of Case II, the third-order system used to represent structural oscillations. Note that as K_f is increased, the complex poles (B poles) approach the imaginary axis.

Case II, Kp=30000 V/m, Varying Kf

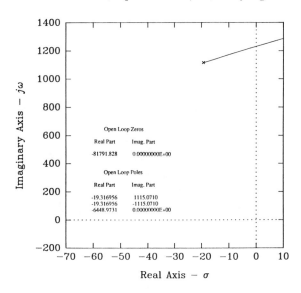

FIGURE 8

Root Locus for Case II with K_p = 30,000 V/m
and K_f Varying

Cases I, II, and III Superimposed

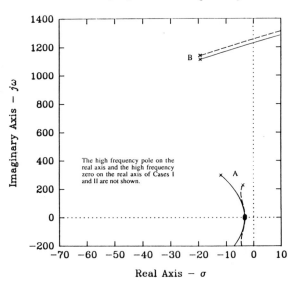

FIGURE 9

Cases II and III (Solid Lines) Superimposed on
Case I (Dotted Lines)

Figure 9 is a root locus plot in which the second- and third-order models have been overlayed onto the fifth-order model with K_p fixed and K_f varying. The objective of this figure is to illustrate the validity of the assumptions which allow the separation of the fifth-order system into the second- and third-order models. Note that the large magnitude B poles overlay closely, indicating that using the third-order structural model is acceptable for the system under consideration. In this case, the second-order model does not agree quite as well for low values of K_f. For higher K_f the agreement is quite good. Increasing K_4 and B_4 would move the A poles of Figure 7 closer to the A poles of Figure 6. Then, however, the agreement for intermediate values of K_f would not be as accurate.

Case IV — Compliant structure with slow load and fast motor. This case is generated by assuming that the motor inductance (L) is zero and is described by Equations 7.

$$\left\{ [M_2]s^2 + [B_2]s + [K_2] \right\} X_3 = P_4\,\varphi_F X_4 +$$

$$\varphi_P X_d + \left[G\frac{K_m}{R} K_f \right] F_d \qquad (7a)$$

$$M_2 = M_A \qquad (7b)$$

$$B_2 = B_A + B_L + \varphi_F B_4 \qquad (7c)$$

$$K_2 = \varphi_P + \varphi_F K_4 \qquad (7d)$$

Equations 7

CHARACTERIZING SYSTEM BEHAVIOR

Behaviors

Clearly, system behavioral requirements, rather than the convenience of the designer, should drive design decisions. Most often, however, quantitative performance criteria

(QPC's) are favored as a starting point for design. QPC's, which are intentionally structured for convenient use in optimization procedures, can be simple, such as rise time and bandwidth, or more comprehensive, such as quadratic forms on integral functions of error and time. Using well-defined QPC's without reflection can divert focus from the main objective of any design procedure, which is the production of a system which achieves desired behavioral characteristics.

Approaching effector design from a behavior-based viewpoint can be extremely valuable, since it alters the designer's mentality by forcing acceptance of nonlinear issues and by encouraging the inclusion of experimental validation procedures into development methodologies. Finally, a behavior-based viewpoint makes clear the advantages of designing systems which behave appropriately as a result of intrinsic physics rather than as a result of compensation via ad hoc feedback loops.

Definition of Behaviors

Certain behavioral characteristics, such as speed and strength, are easily defined. However, many are hard to think about, being multidimensional, nonlinear, and difficult to quantify for convenient use in analytical optimization procedures. Examples of behavioral characteristics that are hard to define include quickness, grace, trajectory execution precision, ability to maintain stability when touching objects, response to external loading insults, saturation avoidance, and functioning without structural oscillations.

Some behaviors can be characterized as active in that they are a result of control inputs, and others can be considered as passive since they are responses to environmental insults or influences. It is important to understand the difference, since passive responses, many times ignored, may actually have much higher demands in terms of bandwidth and power and thus emerge as fundamental determinants of system success.

Consider desired behaviors for the one-degree-of-freedom effector in Figure 2. A typical goal statement for the one-link arm would be that the system should have appropriate active responses to inputs being strong, fast, accurate, and graceful. The system should also exhibit minimal high-frequency oscillation (hum) between the actuator and structure and should not oscillate (shake) while in contact with objects.

The system should be compliant (appropriately passive) and experience minimal internal loads when pushed out of the way. Finally, system elements should not saturate or overheat in operation.

These are in fact complex goals which involve the simultaneous satisfaction of multiple conflicting constraints (SSMCC). The really difficult problem is to translate these behaviors into quantitative performance criteria so that they can be applied to the system model.

FORMULATION OF DESIGN EQUATIONS

Comments

Previous sections introduced a comprehensive model and a number of individual cases useful as a basis for <u>design</u>. This section introduces a number of quantitative performance criteria which can be used to generate <u>design equations</u>. The final section, <u>Design Scenarios</u>, briefly introduces the application of design equations to specific situations. This final section, which is rough and conceptual, is by no means a complete treatment of all issues. It serves to introduce an enormous amount of work which remains to be completed before the design of effector systems can be a truly rigorous procedure.

Basis for Design Equations

The model includes ten system elements with twenty-six parameters as shown in Table 1. In this paper, position variables include the angular position of the motor (θ), the deflection of the drive (X_3), and the deflection of the load (X_4). Inputs are the desired position (X_d), the desired force (F_d), the externally applied push forces (F_{ex5} and F_{ex6}), the externally applied base force (F_B), the binary touch parameter (T_1 -- which engages the contact between the load and the touch impedances), the shove variable (X_6), and the base shaking variable (X_7 together with T_2).

Desired Effector Behaviors

For the model shown in Figure 4, eleven desired behaviors are considered along with the quantitative performance criteria they generate. Note that for each of the behaviors, many different quantitative performance criteria can be defined. Each QPC will succeed, to various degrees, in imposing desirable behaviors on the system. In this paper we select the simplest possible QPC's. In later papers, more comprehensive but less mathematically convenient QPC's will be applied.

QPC 1 — Structural smoothness, ζ_2, is defined here as the absence of high-frequency structural oscillation or instability. These oscillations are caused by interactions between the actuator and load through the structural impedance. A smoothness constraint equation can be generated based on a number of approaches. However, to maintain simplicity in this case, smoothness will be characterized by the damping ratio, ζ_2, of the complex poles in the third order model of Case II.

From Equations 4 the system is represented by Equation 8.

$$\left\{ s^3 + \left[\frac{A_2}{A_3} \right] s^2 + \left[\frac{A_1}{A_3} \right] s + \left[\frac{A_0}{A_3} \right] \right\} X_3 = \left[\frac{\varphi_P}{A_3} \right] X_d$$

Equation 8

Equation 9 shows a form which allows a convenient (traditional) definition of pole locations.

$$\left[(\tau_2) s + 1 \right] \left\{ s^2 + \left[2\zeta_2 \, \omega_{n2} \right] s + \left[\omega_{n2} \right]^2 \right\} = \tau_2 Z_9 X_d$$

Equation 9

Expanding the terms of Equation 9 yields Equation 10.

$$\left\{ s^3 + \left[Z_6 \right] s^2 + \left[Z_7 \right] s + \left[Z_8 \right] \right\} X_3 = \left[Z_9 \right] X_d$$

Equation 10

Where

$$Z_6 = \frac{2\zeta_2 \, (\omega_{n2}) \, \tau_2 + 1}{\tau_2} \qquad (11a)$$

$$Z_7 = \frac{\tau_2 \, (\omega_{n2})^2 + 2\zeta_2 \, (\omega_{n2})}{\tau_2} \qquad (11b)$$

$$Z_8 = \frac{(\omega_{n2})^2}{\tau_2} \qquad (11c)$$

Equations 11

Equating like terms yields Equations 12.

$$Z_6 = \frac{A_2}{A_3} = \frac{M_A + \frac{L}{R} [B_A + B_4]}{\frac{L}{R} [M_A]} \qquad (12a)$$

$$Z_7 = \frac{A_1}{A_3} = \frac{B_A + B_L + \varphi_F B_4 + \frac{L}{R} [K_4]}{\frac{L}{R} [M_A]} \qquad (12b)$$

$$Z_8 = \frac{A_0}{A_3} = \frac{\varphi_F K_4 + \varphi_P}{\frac{L}{R} [M_A]} \qquad (12c)$$

Equations 12

If one chooses marginal stability for the structural oscillations, then $\zeta_2 = 0$ and

$$\frac{A_2}{A_3} = \frac{1}{\tau_2} \qquad (13a)$$

$$\frac{A_1}{A_3} = (\omega_{n2})^2 \qquad (13b)$$

$$\frac{A_0}{A_3} = \frac{(\omega_{n2})^2}{\tau_2} \qquad (13c)$$

Equations 13

The results in Equation 13 are the same as would be obtained using a Routh array, as shown in Equation 14.

$$A_2 A_1 = A_0 A_3$$

Equation 14

One can set ω_{n2} and τ_2 in Equations 13 as desired to further constrain system variables.

QPC 2 — Structure/actuator stability assurance, AI, is an alternative to QPC 1 and applies to Case II as shown in Figure 10. By placement of the zero (via adjustment of K_4 and B_4), the asymptote intersection (AI) with the real axis can be moved into the left half plane thereby indemnifying the system against instability regardless of the value of K_f.

Case II, Kp=30000 V/m, Varying Kf

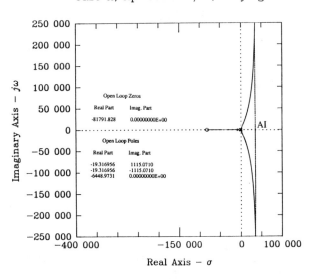

FIGURE 10

Schematic of Root Locus Plot for Case II
Showing the Location of Intersection of Asymptotes
with the Real Axis

Recall that the closed loop transfer function, T(s) in Equations 4, can be written in the form:

$$T(s) = \frac{K_{10}\,G_1(s)}{1 + K_{10}\,G_1(s)}$$

Equation 15

Then the open loop transfer function can be shown for K_p fixed and K_f varying as Equations 16.

$$K_{10}\,G_1(s) = \frac{\left[G\frac{K_m}{R} K_f B_4 \frac{1}{A_3}\right]\left[s + \frac{K_4}{B_4}\right]}{\left[s^3 + \left(\frac{A_2}{A_3}\right)s^2 + \left(\frac{A_4}{A_3}\right)s + \left(\frac{A_5}{A_3}\right)\right]} \quad (16a)$$

Where

$$A_4 = B_A + B_L + B_4 + \frac{L}{R}\left[K_4\right] \quad (16b)$$

$$A_5 = \varphi_P + K_4 \quad (16c)$$

Equations 16

The intersection can then be determined by selecting the second terms in the numerator and denominator polynomials defining sums of poles and zeros as shown by Equations 17.

$$AI = \frac{-\dfrac{A_2}{A_3} + \dfrac{K_4}{B_4}}{2} \quad (17a)$$

or in expanded terms

$$B_4\left[M_A + \frac{L}{R}(B_A + B_4)\right] = K_4\frac{L}{R}\left[M_A\right] \quad (17b)$$

Equations 17

QPC 3 — Static force accuracy, A_{SF}, is derived from Equations 4 with $X_d = 0$. This yields Equations 18 and 19 as:

$$A_0 X_3 = G\frac{K_m}{R} K_f F_d$$

Equation 18

$$F_{st} = K_4 X_3 = F_a$$

Equation 19

Combining these, Equation 20 is derived:

$$\frac{F_a}{F_d} = \frac{K_f K_4}{K_f K_4 + K_p + \dfrac{RK_4}{GK_m}}$$

Equation 20

Equation 20 shows that a system with a high reduction and no position feedback ($K_p = 0$) will be statically accurate in terms of force generation.

QPC 4 — Quickness, Q_L, is probably best represented by the inverse of the time required for the system to transfer the load between two end states. A more simple indicator of quickness used in this paper is the inverse of rise time, as shown by Equation 21.

$$\frac{1}{RT} = Q_L = \frac{\omega_{nL}}{\alpha}$$

Equation 21

The term alpha is defined by Equation 22.

$$\alpha = \left[0.8 + 2.5\zeta_L\right]$$

Equation 22

The natural undamped frequency is defined by Equation 23.

$$\omega_{nL} = \sqrt{K_1/M_1}$$

Equation 23

The quickness equation can then be written as Equation 24.

$$\boxed{(Q_L)^2 \, \alpha^2 \, M_1 = K_1}$$

Equation 24

QPC 5 — Positional accuracy, A_p, is an indicator of a system's ability to position itself in its working space within a specified tolerance. Here, accuracy will be defined by

Equation 25 as one minus the steady state error.

$$A_p = \left[\frac{X_3}{X_d}\right]_{\text{Steady State}} = \frac{\varphi_P}{K_1}$$

Equation 25

Rearranging and combining with Equations 6 produces the constraint Equation 26.

$$K_5 \, \varphi_F \, A_p = \varphi_P \, (1 - A_p)$$

Equation 26

QPC 6 — Load movement grace, ζ_L, depends on the specific application of the system. For example, it might be desirable to achieve a good step response while positioning a load, or, as in the case of an entertainment robot, it might be desirable to have the system swing freely or "dangle" well. For this case, a reasonable indicator of grace will be the damping ratio (ζ_L) of the load in Case III.

The constraint is shown below as Equation 27.

$$\boxed{4\zeta_L^2 \, M_1 \, K_1 = B_1^2}$$

Equation 27

where $\zeta_L = 0.707$ produces a good step response and ζ_L less than 0.1 yields a system with good dangle.

QPC 7 — Strength, S_{LM}, indicates the capability of the system to move its load through an excursion of Δ without exceeding power requirement P.

From Equations 5 the static deflection versus input voltage is shown in Equation 28.

$$P_{12} X_3 = G \frac{K_m}{R} V_{in}$$

Equation 28

If the input voltage is V_m and the maximum deflection is Δ (also called strength), then Equation 29 results as the constraint.

$$\boxed{S_{LM} = \Delta = \frac{G K_m}{\sqrt{R} \, K_5} \sqrt{P}}$$

$$P = V_{in} \, i_m$$

Equation 29

where i_m is the armature current and power is the product of motor current and voltage.

QPC 8 — Saturation avoidance, S_A, constrains the system to stay within the voltage of V_m when the system undergoes a maximal step input of Δ.

From Equations 5, the controller relationship together with $V_{in} = V_m$, and $X_d = \Delta$, Equation 30 results.

$$\boxed{V_m = K_p \Delta - X_3 \left[K_f M_5\right]}$$

Equation 30

The acceleration $\ddot{X}_3$ is shown by Equation 31.

$$\ddot{X}_3 = \frac{G \frac{K_m}{R} V_m}{M_A + M_5}$$

Equation 31

Then the constraint is as shown in Equation 32.

$$S_A = V_m = K_p \Delta \left[\frac{M_A + M_5}{M_A + \varphi_F M_5}\right]$$

Equation 32

QPC 9 — Response of the load to insults, ζ_3, ω_{n3}, and Δ_3, is used to describe the response of the load to external disturbances. Thus QPC 9 is an indicator of the expected passive behavior. It can be used, for example, to determine the behavior of a leg contacting the ground during running or walking motions.

QPC 9 assumes that F_d, X_d, B_5, and K_5 are all zero, that M_5 is a vehicle mass, and that F_{ex5} is the vehicle weight ($g_c M_5$). This produces Equations 33

$$\left\{ [M_3]s^2 + [B_3]s + [K_3] \right\} X_3 = G \frac{K_m}{R} K_f \, g_c M_5 \quad (33a)$$

where

$$M_3 = M_A + \varphi_F M_5 \quad (33b)$$

$$B_3 = B_A + B_L \quad (33c)$$

$$K_3 = \varphi_p \quad (33d)$$

Equations 33

The load response can then be constrained by setting the damping ratio ζ_3, the natural frequency ω_{n3}, and the static deflection Δ_3 in Equations 34.

$$4(\zeta_3)^2 M_3 K_3 = (B_3)^2 \qquad (34a)$$

$$(\omega_{n3})^2 M_3 = K_3 \qquad (34b)$$

$$K_p \Delta = g K_f M_5 \qquad (34c)$$

Equations 34

QPC 10 — Response of the _structure_ to insults, ζ_5, is similar to QPC 9, but it describes the behavior of the structure to externally imposed disturbances. During encounters with external loadings, structural force can grow dramatically until the actuator catches up with the insult. The system can experience an insult from a load as represented by a ramp of variable X_4 as in Equations 7. Equation 35 shows the response X_3 to input X_4 with φ_P, X_d, and F_d all set to zero.

$$X_3 = \frac{P_4 \, \varphi_F}{\left\{ [M_2]s^2 + [B_2]s + [K_2] \right\}} X_4$$

Equation 35

The structural force F_{st} can then be determined via Equation 36.

$$F_{st} = P_4 (X_3 - X_4)$$

Equation 36

Although not completed here, Equation 36 can be used to control force overshoot in response to ramp inputs X_4 by setting its damping ratio ζ_5 at an appropriate value such as 0.707.

In this case, given the speed limitations of actuators (which simultaneously must also be strong), the structural parameters B_4 and K_4 can be chosen to soften (minimize) actuator loading during rapid transients. This improves passive performance at the expense of active speed, as shown in the next paragraph defining force generation quickness.

QPC 11 — Force generation quickness, Q_4. In Case IV, the actuator applies force to the load through the structure. If the structure has been softened by application of QPC 10, its force generation speed can be degraded [the actuator must store energy in the structure (B_4 and K_4) in order to transfer force to the load]. QPC 11 uses a quickness criterion Q_4 similar to QPC 4 to impose a speed constraint on the force generation capability of the system.

The actuator generates force on a static load through the structure by moving X_3. This situation is represented by Equations 7 with X_4 and X_d equal to 0 and with F_d as the input. The quickness of force control is then shown by Equations 37 (RT = rise time).

$$\frac{1}{RT} = Q_4 = \frac{\omega_{n4}}{\alpha_4} \qquad (37a)$$

where

$$\alpha_4 = (0.8 + 2.5 \, \zeta_4) \qquad (37b)$$

Equations 37

Using the definition of natural undamped frequency produces the constraint Equation 38.

Where Q_4 and α_4 must be specified,

$$Q_4^2 \, \alpha_4^2 \, M_2 = K_2$$

Equation 38

Comments

In addition to the eleven behaviors mentioned above, many others can be used to generate QPC's and constraint equations. Their selection depends on the specific intended application of the effector. Just a few examples are:

(1) Pushing capability, which can quantify the system's capability to generate external forces.

(2) Stability margin when touching objects, i.e., tolerance to changes in load impedance.

(3) Response to shaking of the base (variable X_7 on Figure 4).

(4) The system's tolerance to degrading functional nonlinearities such as backlash and stiction.

(5) Various active and passive bandwidth measures.

Of course, other _static_ system descriptors are also important. Examples of these are: size, weight, geometry, kinematics, structural strength, acoustic noise generation, etc. It should also be remembered that performance measures are functions of more fundamental characteristics of the materials and components which comprise the system. For example, the following all have an effect on the final achievable performance of the overall system: (1) field strengths which can be generated by magnetic materials, (2) magnetic characteristics of iron, (3) electrical properties of field generating coils, (4) power capacities and speed of commutation systems, (5) losses in bearings, and (6) inertial characteristics of armatures.

Ideally, as the relationships between fundamental characteristics and system model parameters are better defined, the design synthesis can proceed directly from a statement of desired behaviors into static characteristics such as size and weight. Actuators can then be more precisely designed to optimize the complete system in which they function.

Interesting Cases

Various combinations of Equations 8 through 38, when combined with system equations, can be used to generate constraint equations. For example, using QPC's 1, 4, 5, 6, 7, and 8 (via Equations 39 through 44), structural stability, quickness, accuracy, grace, strength, and linearity can be constrained.

Assuming $\zeta_s = 0$ yields Equation 39.

$$\left(\frac{L}{R}\right) M_A \left(\varphi_F K_4 + \varphi_P\right)$$
$$= \left[M_A + \left(\frac{L}{R}\right)(B_A + B_4)\right]\left[(B_A + B_L)\right.$$
$$\left. + \varphi_F B_4 + \left(\frac{L}{R}\right) K_4\right]$$

Equation 39

Rearranging and combining Equations 24, 26, and 27 with system equations produces the very interesting set of Equations 40, 41, and 42. Equation 40 is a mass equation. Equation 41 is a damping equation and Equation 42 is a stiffness equation.

$$Z_1 \varphi_P - M_5 \varphi_F = M_A$$

Equation 40

$$Z_2 \varphi_P - B_5 \varphi_F = B_A + B_L$$

Equation 41

$$Z_3 \varphi_P - K_5 \varphi_F = 0$$

Equation 42

Where the performance goals are embedded in the equalities,

$$Z_1 = \frac{1}{A_p (Q_L)^2 (\alpha)^2} \qquad (43a)$$

$$Z_2 = \frac{2\zeta_l}{A_p Q_L \alpha} \qquad (43b)$$

$$Z_3 = \left(\frac{1}{A_p}\right) - 1 \qquad (43c)$$

The strength equation from QPC 7 yields Equations 43.

$$S_{LM} = (G K_m \sqrt{P}) / (\sqrt{R} K_5) \qquad (43d)$$

Equations 43

And finally, the saturation avoidance equation from QPC 8 yields Equation 44.

$$V_{max} \ (M_A + \varphi_F M_5) = K_p \Delta (M_A + M_5)$$

Equation 44

DESIGN SCENARIOS

Use of Constraints

Obviously, the generation of constraint equations is only a beginning which can, as shown above, become quite complicated. In undertaking a real design procedure, the constraint equations must be carefully selected in an attempt to produce desired behaviors. Then constraints can be used in an appropriate computational format to determine design limits. Later papers will address the selection of constraints and their quantitative implementation.

Objectives

Our objective is to develop the capability to execute systematic design scenarios in terms of system variables, which include:

(1) 26 model parameters,
(2) 2 controller gains, and
(3) 12 performance goals.

In each scenario, some of the variables are specified and others are unknown. The object in each scenario is to determine the range of values permissible for unknowns given the knowns. Then the selection of physical hardware can begin.

Prior to discussing the scenarios it is advantageous to reorganize constraint equations by eliminating φ_P and φ_F from Equations 40, 41, and 42. The simple design number shown in Equation 45 results, where desired performance is carried by parameters Z_1, Z_2, Z_3, the load is defined by M_5, K_5, B_5, and actuator characteristics are defined in terms of M_A, B_A, and B_L.

$$\frac{Z_3 M_5 - Z_1 K_5}{Z_3 B_5 - Z_2 K_5} = \frac{M_A}{B_A + B_L}$$

Equation 45

With some effort, similar equations can be generated for combination with other sets of constraint equations (design rules). Equation 45 is particularly well structured since it so cleanly states the requirements for a system which obeys constraints on quickness, accuracy, and grace.

Two example scenarios are included below to introduce concepts briefly. In these discussions only six QPC's (1 and 4 through 8) are used. Later papers will expand the number of QPC's used.

Scenario A — "What's a good actuator?"

In this scenario the goal is to determine those actuator characteristics required to produce the desired effector system behavior given the characteristics of structure, load, and controller. In this case, the sixteen known parameters are K_4, B_4, M_5, B_5, K_5, M_6, B_6, K_6, T_1, T_2, τ, M_7, B_7, K_7, S_p, S_f, and the six QPC's ζ_s, S_{LM}, Q_L, A_p, ζ_L, and S_A. The ten unknown parameters are L, J_m, B_m, K_m, R, B_3, M_3, G, K_p, and K_f.

The constraint equations are used to limit possible values of the unknown parameters, thus defining limits on what the motor, reducer, drive, and controller can be. Note that if performance requirements are too aggressively selected the analysis might ask for a motor which cannot exist due to physical realities.

By pursuing scenario A in greater depth, general design rules can be generated which permit not only a better selection of commercially available system components, but a better understanding of the design of motors, drives, and controllers which are more appropriate for use in robotic applications.

Scenario B — "What are the limits of a given system's performance?"

In this scenario the goal is to determine what performance is possible for various feedback gains given the system characteristics. In this case all parameters are defined except for the performance criteria ζ_s, S_{LM}, Q_L, A_p, ζ_L, and S_A, and the controller gains K_p and K_f. The objective is generating an understanding of the relationships between controller settings and the limits of system performance.

CONCLUSIONS

The Paper

Being able to answer questions like "What's a good actuator?" and "How well can a specific effector system perform?" will be one of the fundamental determinants of success in the design of future robots. Attempting to answer these complex questions motivated this paper, which is the first of a number of related publications from the CED.

The paper applies a relatively conventional design methodology to a carefully structured, fifth-order, one-degree-of-freedom study model so that important issues can be identified and understood. Using this approach, simple effector systems can be designed in a comprehensive way, beginning with a systematic understanding of system behavioral objectives which guide selection of system elements and their controller (i.e., servo science).

Clearly, the design procedures will be complex for more comprehensive systems which include multiple degrees-of-freedom, nonideal elements, nonlinear kinematics, and other realities. However, in these more complicated cases, numerical methods will be applied, together with an expanded data base on actual subcomponents in order to facilitate the design of effectors.

Future Work

Work in the CED is now pursuing answers to questions in three areas:

(1) **Thoroughly understanding the linear, one-degree-of-freedom model in Figure 4. Specifically:**

  (a) Response to shove – How well can the output X_3 be maintained in the presence of external disturbances represented, for example, as a step in F_{ex5} or F_{ex6} or as an initial velocity of M_5? Should the response be characterized by the behavior of displacement or force?

  (b) Stability margin when touching external loads – What is the effect on performance of changing the load impedance by touching?

  (c) Response to base shaking – Using X_d as an input, how well can the effector maintain its output, X_3, with a disturbed base X_7?

  (d) Performance in operation with a compliant base – With a soft footing ($T_2 = 0$ and M_7, B_7, K_7 "soft") how well can the output X_3 be controlled by the input X_d?

  (e) Operation with noncolocated sensors – As sensors are separated from actuators across dynamic structures, how are resulting delays tolerated?

  (f) Intrinsic qualities – Can they be used to design in desirable system characteristics? For example, can structural damping, B_4, as presented in QPC 2, be used to eliminate the instability caused by interactions between the actuator and structure?

  (g) Understanding the behavior of systems in specific simplified operating regimes – For example, how will the system behave while (1) operating at high speed with small loads (i.e., as an indicator with small M_5, B_5, K_5); (2) operating massy loads (i.e., as a free arm with B_5 and K_5 small); and (3) running against viscous loads (i.e., as a speaker cone with B_5 large)?

(2) **The study of more complicated systems with:**

  (a) Higher order models – How will the system behave with more complicated motors, reducers, drives, structures, loads, sensors, and controllers?

  (b) Additional degrees-of-freedom – How should a cascade of the model be controlled? (Cascade is when successive models are connected at base and load masses.) Can a cascade be balanced so that an intrinsic passivity is created which causes masses to respond to disturbances in a coordinated fashion?

  (c) Surviving nonlinearities – How can saturation, backlash, stiction, and delays be tolerated? Can additional elements such as K_3 be used to counteract problems such as backlash?

  (d) Adaptive control capabilities used for both calibration maintenance and behavior modification in response to inputs. For example: can a variation of actuator and load damping be used to avoid instabilities?

  (e) Alternate components – Can a simple, fluid-based actuator model be inserted in order to allow the design of hydraulic or pneumatic systems?

(3) **Efforts to make results more useful for general design procedures:**

  (a) Nondimensional groups, like those used in mechanics, will be defined to better represent system elements, such as motors, structures, and loads. Such normalized representations will simplify the understanding of system behavior, as well as form the basis for a more useful method of characterizing system elements supplied by manufacturers.

  (b) Quantitative performance criteria that can impose constraints which produce desired effector system behavior will be defined.

  (c) Actuator parameters, such as K_m, R, L, and G, will be related to static actuator characteristics, such as size and weight, for use in comprehensive design procedures.

ACKNOWLEDGEMENTS

The authors wish to acknowledge the support of the Systems Development Foundation, the Defense Advanced Research Projects Agency (DARPA/USAF, Wright-Patterson), and the Naval Ocean Systems Center of the Office of Naval Research.

The authors also thank the Artificial Intelligence Laboratory at the Massachusetts Institute of Technology for their collaborative efforts.

REFERENCES

An, C.H., Hollerbach, J.M.: "Dynamic Stability Issues in Force Control of Manipulation," Proc. I.E.E.E. Int. Conf. Robotics and Automation, Raleigh, NC, March 30 – April 3, 1987.

Biggers, K.B., Jacobsen, S.C., Gerpheide, G.E.: "Low-Level Control of the Utah/M.I.T. Dextrous Hand," Proc. I.E.E.E. Int. Conf. Robotics and Automation, San Francisco, CA, April 7–10, 1986.

Book, W.J., Maizza-Neto, O., Whitney, D.E.: "Feedback Control of Two Beam, Two Joint Systems with Distributed Flexibility," Trans. A.S.M.E. J. Dyn. Sys. Meas. and Control, pp. 424–421, December 1975.

Book, W.J.: "Recursive Lagrangian Dynamics of Flexible Manipulator Arms Via Transformation Matrices" I.F.A.C. Symp. CAD Multivariable Technological Sys., W. Lafayette, IN, Vol. 5, No. 17 (1983).

Book, W.J.: "Recursive Lagrangian Dynamics of Flexible Manipulator Arms," 2nd Sym. of Robotics Research, Kyoto, 1984.

Cannon, D.H., Schmitz, E.: "Initial Experiments on the End-Point Control of a Flexible One-Link Robot," International Journal of Robotics Research, Vol. 3, No. 3, pp. 62–75, Fall 1984.

Coy, J.R.: "Dynamic Performance and Control of an Electromechanical Actuator," M.S. Thesis, Department of Mechanical Engineering, Brigham Young University, Provo, UT, 1987.

Fullmer, R.R., Meek, S.G., Jacobsen, S.C.: "Generation of the 7 Degree-of-Freedom Controller Equations for a Prosthetic Arm," Presented at the Conference on Applied Motion Control, University of Minnesota, Minneapolis, MN, 11–13 June 1985.

Hollerbach, J.M.: "A Recursive Formulation of Lagrangian Manipulator Dynamics," I.E.E.E., Trans. Systems, Man, Cybernetics, Vol. 10, No. 11 (1980).

Hollerbach, J.M.: "Dynamic Scaling of Manipulator Trajectories," A.S.M.E. J. Dyn. Syst. Meas. and Control, Vol. 106, No. 1 (1984-a).

Hooker, D.J.: "Robot and Payload Weight Compensation for a Compliant Robot in Free Space," M.S. Thesis, Department of Mechanical Engineering, Brigham Young University, Provo, UT, July 1987.

Hooker, D.J., Seamons, M.B., Smith, C.C.: "Position and Orientation Control of a Compliant Robot with Weight Compensation," Society of Engineering Science, 24th Annual Meeting, Salt Lake City, UT, September 1987.

Jacobsen, S.C.: "Control Systems for Artificial Limbs," Ph.D. Thesis, Massachusetts Institute of Technology, Cambridge, MA, 1973.

Jacobsen, S.C., Meek, S.G., Fullmer, R.R.: "An Adaptive Myoelectric Filter," 6th Conference I.E.E.E./Eng. in Med. and Biol. Soc., 1984.

Jacobsen, S.C., Iversen, E.K., Knutti, D.F., Johnson, R.T., Biggers, K.B.: "Design of the Utah/MIT Dextrous Hand," I.E.E.E. International Conference on Robotics and Automation, San Francisco, CA, March 1986.

Johnson, D.A.: "A Simulation of Force Feedback Control of Robotic Assembly," M.S. Thesis, Department of Mechanical Engineering, Brigham Young University, Provo, UT, December 1984.

Kelly, C., III: Personal communication, 1985.

Meek, S.G.: "An Adaptive Myoelectric Filter," M.S. Thesis, University of Utah, Salt Lake City, UT, 1980.

Reese, B.S.: "Excitation of Rotary Mechanical Systems for System Identification," M.S. Thesis, Department of Mechanical Engineering, Brigham Young University, Provo, UT, December 1984.

Seamons, M.B.: "Compliant Position Control for a Robot Manipulator in Free Space," M.S. Thesis, Department of Mechanical Engineering, Brigham Young University, Provo, UT, March 1986.

Seering, W.P., Eppinger, S.D.: "Understanding Bandwidth Limitations in Robot Force Control," Proc. I.E.E.E. Int. Conf. on Robotics and Automation, Raleigh, N.C., March 30–April 3, 1987.

Smith, C. C.: "Robot Control for Assembly," Alliance with Industry Conference, Brigham Young University, Provo, UT, November 1985.

Whitney, D.E.: "Resolved Motion Rate Control of Manipulators and Human Prostheses," I.E.E.E. Trans. Man-Machine Systems, 10, 1969-a.

Whitney, D.E.: "Force Feedback Control of Manipulator Fine Motions," 1976 Fine Automatic Control Conf., San Francisco, 1976.

Whitney, D.E.: "Force Feedback Control of Manipulator Fine Motions," A.S.M.E. J. Dyn. Sys. Meas. and Control, 1977.

Rubbertuators and Applications for Robots

Kanji Inoue
Bridgestone Corporation
3-1-1, Ogawahigashi-Cho, Kodaira-Shi
Tokyo 187, Japan

A rubber pneumatic-controlled actuator called the Rubbertuator which functions in a manner highly resembling the movements of human muscle has been developed by BRIDGESTONE. The Rubbetuator is very light with a high-power-to weight ratio. It has spring characteristics and force and compliance can be controlled by air pressure. With these characteristics, the Rubbertuator performs as very unique actuator when it is used for robots. The structure and characteristics of the Rubbertuator, control with the Rubbertuator and its application to robots are outlined.

1. Introduction

The actuator is an indispensable part in a robot which corresponds to the muscles of a human being.
Presently, three types of actuators are in use: (1) the electrical actuator, (2) the hydraulic actuator and (3) the pneumatic actuator. Each has the following characteristics:

The electrical actuator is the most widely used of the three today, as its energy source is most often accessable and, owing to the advance in electronics, it is the most easily controlled.
For such reasons, it is becoming widely used in the development of motors, such as high power-to-weight ratio DC motors, direct-drive motors and AC servo motors which are easily maintained.

Next, is the hydraulic actuator. This type is frequently used as a compact component in high powered systems capable of attaining high levels of oil pressurization and thereby providing a high power-to-weight ratio. In addition, accompanying improvements in servo valve design, including such innovations as the development of actuators with built-in servo valves, the hydraulic actuator is becoming easier to use. However, it does have the drawback of being difficult to maintain.

In contrast to other types of actuators, with the pneumatic-control actuators, up until now, it has been difficult to obtain high power output; there have also been problems in obtaining accurate position control.

For these reasons, and because of its simplicity and relatively low cost, use of the pneumatic actuator has been limited to simple, fixed-sequence robots.

A rubber pneumatic-controlled actuator called the Rubbertuator is a new actuator developed by BRIDGESTONE, taking advantage of inherent simplicity and compliance control characteristics of pneumatic-contolled actuators, enabling position control or force control,which is difficult to perform with such a current pneumatic actuator as the air cylinder.

2. Structure

Fig. 1 shows the structure of the Rubbertuator. It consists of a rubber tube which is covered with a sleeve of inter-twined fiber cord. Metal fittings are affixed to both ends of the tube.

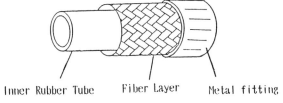

Inner Rubber Tube   Fiber Layer   Metal fitting

Fig.1 Structure

As precedents for this type of actuator, there are the conventional Mackevin artificial muscle and the rubber artificial muscle developed by Waseda University. Although both have commendable designs, they have failed to reach the stage for practical use due to lack of durability.

The newly developed Rubbertuator, however, has the same basic structure as the Mackevin artifical muscle, but the durability and performance of its rubber and cord layers has been improved to the level for practical use. Fig. 2 shows how the unit increases in width and contracts in length when the pressure inside the Rubbertuator is increased. This is due to force conversion of the cord fabric, which simulates the action of a pantogragh.

Reducing Pressure

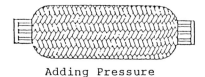

Adding Pressure

Fig. 2 Operating Principle

3. Characteristics

The following Formula (1), is used to indicate the basic characteristics of the Rubbertuator.

$$F = (\pi D_0{}^2/4) P \{a(1-\varepsilon)^2 - b\} \qquad (1)$$

F : Contraction force
D_0 : Effective diameter before displacement
P : Internal pressure (gauge pressure)
ε : Contraction rate
a,b: Original constant of actuator

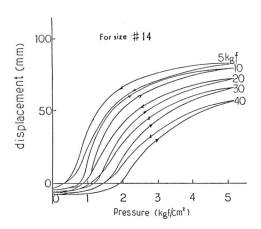

Fig. 3 Pressure - Contraction

In Formula (1), we can see that the static characteristics of the Rubbertuator can be indicated by the three parameters: F, P and ε.

The actually measured values for the static characteristics of the Rubbertuator are shown in Figs. 3, 4 and 5.

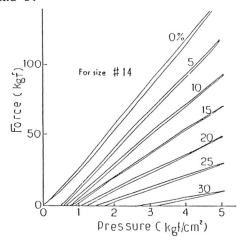

Fig. 4 Pressure - Contraction Force

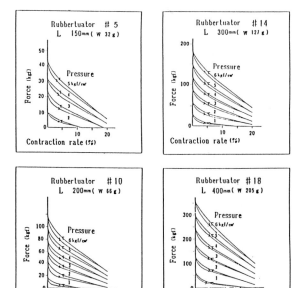

Fig. 5 Contraction Rate - Contraction Force

Fig. 3 shows the relation between the pressure and contraction rate of the Rubbertuator under fixed contraction force (load). A negative displacement value is indicated in low pressure areas because the initial angle of the cord varies in accordance with the load, thus causing the Rubbertuator to extend in length.

Fig. 4 shows the relation between the pressure and the contraction force of the Rubbertuator at a fixed contraction rate. A blind sector occurs in the area where the contraction rate is high, as pressure is required to extend the rubber.

Fig. 5 shows the relation of the contraction rate and contraction force of the Rubbertuator under a fixed pressure and indicates that the Rubbetuator has spring characteristics which vary with pressure. It also shows that, in comparison to the conventional pneumatic cylinder with same diameter, the contraction force of the Rubberuator is approx. ten times stronger when the contraction rate is zero and approximately four times stronger when the contraction rate is 20%.

Each of these figures indicates that the Rubbertuator features high hysteresis. The high rate of hysteresis is due to the original cord hysteresis inherent in the rubber, friction between the rubber and cords, and friction between the cords themselves.

As the Figs. 3 - 5 show, Formula (1), in indicating the qualitative characteristics of the Rubbertuator, reveals a large quantitative error. However, as the non-linear characteristics and hysteresis of rubber are difficult to imitate, it is nearly impossible to create a precise mathematical model. Nonetheless, Formula (1) is presently being improved through experiment in order to fit individual design purposes. In view of the data shown above, the major features of the Rubbertuator can be summarized as follows:

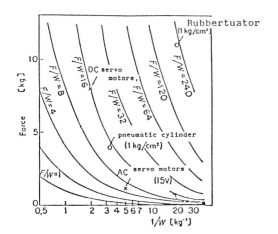

Fig. 6 Comparison of Tensile Strength v.s.

Power-to-weight Ratio for Various Actuators

(1) It is a lightweight product with a high power-to-weight ratio; Fig. 6 summarizes the power-to-weight ratio of actuators. (The artificial muscle used in this figure is based on research by Waseda University.)

(2) It features elasticity and has spring characteristics;

(3) It easily performs position control; With the pneumatic cylinder, position control is difficult due to high piston friction. However, with the Rubbertuator, which does not have sections that rub together, comparatively high precision control is accomplished with ease, as we will explain later. Also, as the Rubbertuator does not require lubrication, it is relatively pollution free.

(4) Force and compliance can be controlled by pressure;

(5) The Rubbertuator is intrinsically explosion proof.

(6) Maintenance is accomplished with relative ease.

With these features, the Rubbertuator is capable of applications in robots which are difficult for other types of actuators to perform. However, it also has the following limitations:

(1) It has a small stroke (contraction rate is 20%)

(2) It does not meet the requirements of a high speed, high precision actuator.

4. Control

Since the Rubbertuator generates force only in the direction in which it contracts, when used in robot, two Rubbertuator units with one degree of freedom should be combined as shown in Fig. 7 in order to perform pulling and pushing motions. If this is not sufficient, use a spring on one of the two Rubbertuators. If $P_0 + \triangle P$ pressure is applied to one of the Rubbertuator units, and $P_0 - \triangle P$ pressure is applied to the other, rotation can be obtained in proportion to $\triangle P$.

The equation of motion for this system is obtained as follows:
Contraction forces of a pair of the Rubbertuators are:

$$F_1 = (\pi D_0^2/4)(P_0 + \triangle P)\{a(1-\varepsilon_1)^2 - b\} \quad (2)$$
$$F_2 = (\pi D_0^2/4)(P_0 - \triangle P)\{a(1-\varepsilon_2)^2 - b\} \quad (3)$$
$$\varepsilon_1 = \varepsilon_0 + r\theta/L \quad , \quad \varepsilon_2 = \varepsilon_0 - r\theta/L \quad (4)$$

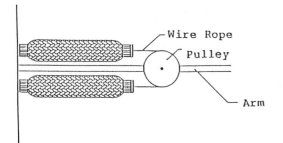

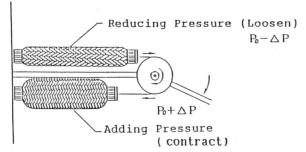

Fig. 7   Example of One-axis Drive Rotation

F_1, F_2: Contraction forces of the Rubbertuators
ε_1, ε_2: Contraction rates of the Rubbertuators
ε_0 : Contraction rate at $P = 0$
L : Orinigal length of the Rubbertuator
r : Radius of pulley
θ : Rotation around pulley

Torque exerted on pulley (T) is:
$$T = r(F_1 - F_2) \qquad (5)$$
Substituting F_1 and F_2 in (5) with (2) (3) and (4) We can obtain:

$$T = K_2 \triangle P - K_1 \theta$$

Therefore, the equation of motion for the system is indicated as follows:

$$J\ddot{\theta} + C\dot{\theta} + K_1\theta = K_2\triangle P \qquad (6)$$
J : Moment of inertia
C : Equivalent coefficient of viscosity
K_1: Proportional constant to P_0
K_2: Proportional constant to $\triangle P$

The existence of the third term, $K_1\theta$, in the equation (6) is unique, compared to the motor servo system or cylinder servo system. This means that it can perform position control with open loop by means of $\triangle P$. Although high accuracy is difficult to obtain due to the frictional force in the driving system or hysterisis in the Rubbertuator, the open loop control is enough when precise position control is not expected.

The other feature in the equation (6) is that compliance ($1/K_1$) can be controlled with intial pressure P_0, since K_1 is proportional to P_0.

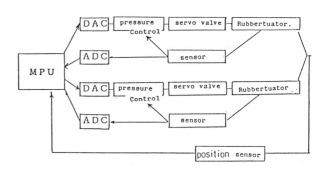

Fig. 8   Structure of Servo Control Section

Fig. 8 gives the structure of the servo control section of the Rubbertuator. This is made up of a digital control section which performs software servo operations and of an analog control section which performs pressure control.

The transfer function of $\triangle P$ and θ is

$$\frac{\Theta(s)}{\triangle P(s)} = \frac{K_2}{Js^2 + Cs + K_1}$$

Also, the transfer function of the servo valve, which can be approximated as time lag of the first order, is expressed as

$$\frac{\triangle P(s)}{U(s)} = \frac{K_V}{T_V s + 1}$$

U(s): Input value (Electric current)

Open loop transfer function is as follows:

$$G(s) = \frac{K_V \cdot K_2}{(T_V s + 1)(Js^2 + Cs + K_1)} \qquad (9)$$

Position control is performed as follows:

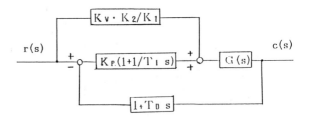

K_P : Proportional Gain
T_I : Integral Time
T_D : Differential Time
r(s): Target Valve
c(s): Controlled Valve

BRIDGESTONE performs this control with its own software.

Fig. 9 shows an example of position control using a servo controller.

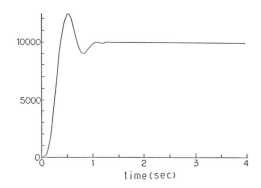

Fig. 9   Position control Diagram
(in step response)

The vertical axis indicates the pulse
count of the rotary encoder.
(1 pulse = 360°-2^{16})   In this example,
positioning precision is controlled to
within ± 2 pulses which, in terms of the
Rubbertuator displacement, equals a few
μm.   Such a high level of control
precision cannot be obtained with other
types of pneumatic actuators.

5. Application to Robots

BRIDGESTONE has developed two types of
robots with the Rubbertuators for
industrial use and has put them into the
market.   One is the horizontal multi-
joint robot called RASC and the other is
the suspended multi-joint robot called
SOFT ARM.   The specifications, structure
and major features of SOFT ARM are
outlined as follows:

Specifications of SOFT ARM

Standard specifications are shown in
Table 1.   The scope of operations for
Type 2 of SOFT ARM is shown in Fig. 9.
System configuration is shown in
Fig. 10.

Item Type		Type 1	Type 2
Model		FAS-402	FAS-501
Structure		Suspension type multijoint robot	
Degree of freedom		4	5
Drive system		Rotation drive by rubbertuator	
Rotation angle and arm length	First (shoulder) Angle	± 180°	± 180°
	Length	250mm	250mm
	Second (upper arm) Angle	± 50°	± 50°
	Length	410mm	410mm
	Third (lower arm) Angle	± 50°	± 50°
	Length	385mm	370mm
	Forth (Up&down wrist movement) Angle	± 45°	± 45°
	Length	90mm	55mm
	Fifth (Turning wrist movement) Angle		± 90°
	Length		–
Lifting capability		1 kg	3 kg
Position repeating precision		± 1.5mm	± 1.5mm
Installation method		Suspension from a horizontal base	
Ambient temperature and humidity		0–50°C,85% RH (without dew formation)	
Air pressure source		6 kgf/cm² (clean air free of himidity and oil mist)	
Weight		31.0 kg	32.0 kg

Table 1 Standard specifications
of SOFT ARM

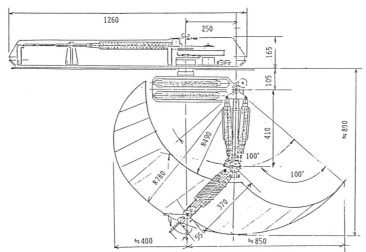

Fig. 9 The scope of operations and structure of Type 2 of SOFT ARM

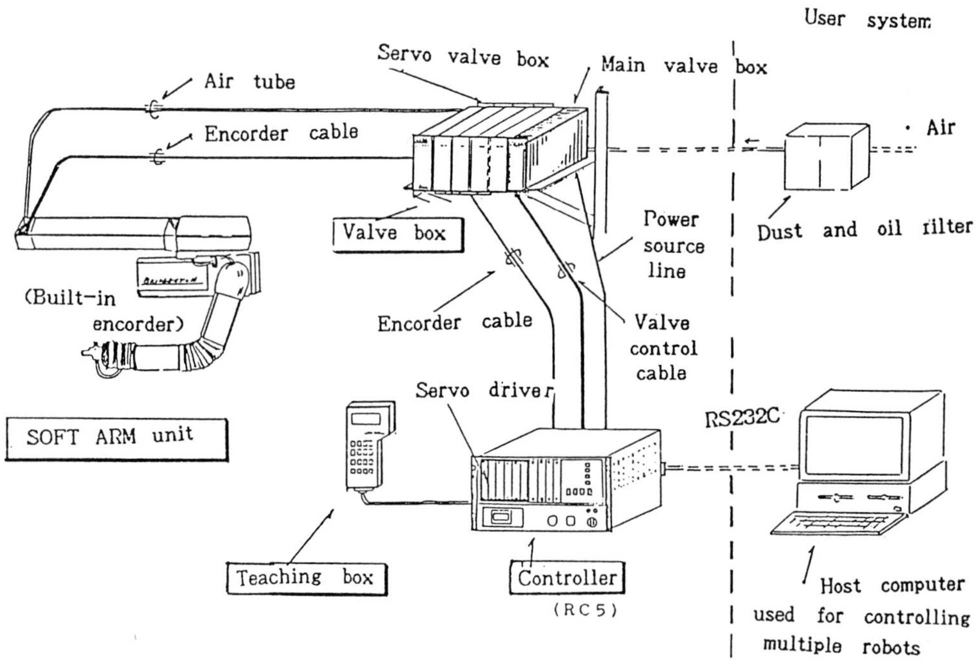

Fig. 10 System configuration

Structure of SOFT ARM

The structure of Type 2 of SOFT ARM is shown in Fig. 9. This robot consists of a shoulder, an upper arm, a lower arm and wrists, all of which are equiped with the Rubbertuators as artificial muscles. By means of pulling and pushing motions generated by a pair of the Rubbertuators, the joint located downstream of the muscles is driven, and this configuration resembles a human arm very much.

Major features of SOFT ARM

(1) Simple, Lightweight Structure with High Capacity performance.

- All axial functions of the SOFT ARM are driven by Rubbertuators which weigh between 122 and 250 grams per unit. These enable the structure to be simple and the construction to be lightweight. The SOFT ARM also features an easy-to-install suspension-type design that can be set up without requiring major modifications to existing assembly lines and equipment.

  The weight of the standard 5-axial type SOFT ARM robot is approximately 32.0 Kg.

- The overall lifting capability can be greatly increased in relation to the actual robot weight.

- The arm weight is approximately 5 Kg which is extremely light. It can be manipulated easily by an operator, or it can be taught certain sequences directly.

- The robot is easily transported, installed and relocated. It can also be modified for a wide range of various applications. Installation and maintenance are easily performed.

(2) High Elasticity

- The entire SOFT ARM robot unit is elastic and has a gentle "soft touch" when making contact with surrounding objects. As a result, even when it hits other equipment accidentally, it will rarely damage it.

- During operation, the SOFT ARM can be stopped manually and freely set at positions other than its programmed positions. The robot unit itself recognizes and responds directly to external stimuli.

- Because of its flexibility and elasticity, precision positioning can be easily guided by eternal stoppers.

(3) Explosion-Proof

  - As the SOFT ARM is operated
    pneumatically, electrical circuitry
    need not be installed on the robot
    unit itself. Thus, it can be used
    freely in activities in which there
    is danger of explosion, such as in
    painting or coating.

(4) Specifications Easily Modified

  - The SOFT ARM features a modular
    construction and can be easily
    reassembled in various ways to
    match desired applications.

  - The standard specifications for the
    axial operating area can be modified
    and set in accordance with the job
    requirement.

  - The arm can be modified to adapt to
    work requirements. (Effective use of
    the highly versatile and flexible
    features of the SOFT ARM can keep
    costs of the robot system to a
    minium.)

6. Conclusion

The Rubbertuator is a product of high
quality featuring excellent
characteristics such as high durability,
high reliability, high power-to-weight
ratio and level of compliance control
which other actuators in its class do
not feature. It will have applications
in a variety of fields and will attain a
high level of practical use. SOFT ARM
with the Rubbertuators as artificial
muscles, has a different range of
application than conventional high
speed, high precision robots. Any
comments on the Rubbertuators or SOFT
ARM will be appreciated.

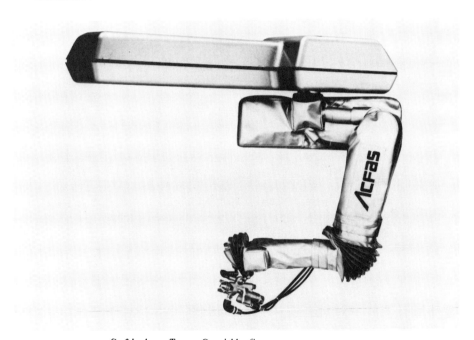

Soft Arm Type 2 with Cover

A Six Degree-of-Freedom Magnetically Levitated
Variable Compliance Fine Motion Wrist

R. L. Hollis, A. P. Allan,† and S. Salcudean

IBM Thomas J. Watson Research Center
Yorktown Heights, NY 10598 USA

It has been shown that dramatic improvements in positioning precision and system response can be achieved by dividing a robot manipulator system into coarse and fine domains. Success of this strategy depends critically on the design of the fine manipulator. In this paper we describe work in progress to create a high performance six degree-of-freedom magnetically levitated fine motion wrist with programmable compliance. Design considerations, discussion of the major elements of the device, and control methods are presented. A prototype wrist has been built and controlled in both position and compliance modes. The results obtained, including synthesis of several mechanisms, establish the feasibility of this approach.

Introduction

We begin by providing some of the motivation for undertaking work on the six degree-of-freedom magnetically levitated "magic" wrist. Our basic observation is founded on some of the inadequacies of available industrial robot manipulators. We first examine manipulation for assembly from the standpoint of both position and force control.

Difficulties with Position Control

It has long been recognized that robot control by computed position goal tracking has many limitations in the "real world". A major limitation is static accuracy, that is, a general inability of the robot to go very close to where it is programmed to go. Typically the robot's positional feedback occurs only from joint angle sensing. The position of the robot end effector is subject to a series of measurement errors which can occur in the joints, and from bending in the links and joints. Problems are made worse by temperature excursions and variable payload masses. These considerations typically limit accuracies to the order of 100 μm. Sometimes, calibration [1] or direct sensing of the manipulator endpoint by laser tracking [2] can decrease this limit.

Besides the static accuracy problem, dynamic effects, particularly during settling after a swift move, tend to limit overall job throughput severely. Another, often ignored, dynamic effect is the manipulator's susceptibility to external disturbances such as room vibrations. All these considerations limit the useability of robots for many industrial applications such as microelectronic or micromechanical assembly. Metrology methods for characterizing robot performance under position control are surveyed in [3].

Difficulties with Compliance or Force Control

For automatic assembly and other domains, the robot manipulator must often come into physical contact with its environment to generate significant forces and torques. Position control alone is insufficient for the robot to achieve its useful purpose. To alleviate this difficulty, robots can potentially be endowed with some form of compliant behavior, and/or control by force servoing. Several notable efforts to achieve these

functions are reported in the literature. Among them are open-loop or "intrinsic" stiffness control provided by adjustment of actuator position loop proportional gains [4], stiffness control in laboratory or "world" coordinates [5], closed-loop servoing to a force goal using information from distally mounted force sensors [6], hybrid position/force control along separate axes [7], and generalization of stiffness control to include dynamic effects [8, 9]. For a historical perspective and review of current research in this area, see [10].

Most work on compliance or force control has failed to provide satisfactory performance. Whereas much has been very interesting and valuable, applications to manufacturing have been few. This has to do with the mechanical nature of the manipulator itself. When compliance or force control of a standard industrial robot is attempted, the results are usually dominated by high masses and inertias [8] which are difficult to overcome by the weak and poorly performing actuators, as well as by stiction and Coulomb friction [11, 12], which lead to deleterious limit cycle effects. Most force controlled robots balk when confronted with stiff environments, resulting in hammering or chattering. These dynamic effects were studied in [13]. Additional problems arise with the low effective computational bandwidth of the typical digital control system.

Coarse-Fine Manipulation

For high performance, the conventional position- or force-controlled robot must be augmented by the addition of a dextrous hand or fine motion device. The robot manipulation task is divided into coarse and fine domains, and the manipulator itself has redundant coarse and fine degrees of freedom. Here, some form of endpoint sensing must be used to measure relevant task parameters directly in order to guide the manipulator system to achieve the desired goal. This paradigm is depicted in Figure 1 and is described in [14].

For a wide range of robotic assembly tasks, especially in the electronics industry, it is only necessary to provide fine compliant motion over limited distances, *e.g.* over distances of the order of the features on the parts to be manipulated. Compliant motion capability over the entire manipulator motion range is not required. Thus, in such a coarse-fine system, the coarse manipulator (CM) can operate in a strictly position-

---

†Now at E. I. DuPont deNemours and Co., Engineering Development Laboratory, 101 Beach St., Wilmington, Delaware, 19898.

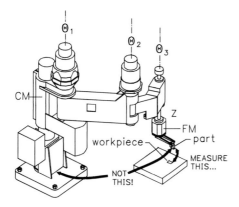

Figure 1.   Coarse-Fine Manipulation: coarse and fine robotic devices are used in tandem along with endpoint sensing to achieve very high precision and programmable compliance over a limited range.

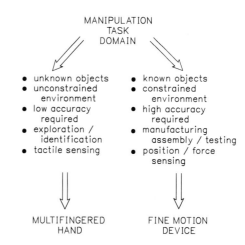

Figure 2.   Two Approaches to Manipulation: multifingered hands vs. fine motion devices.

controlled mode, while the fine manipulator (FM) attached to it can be position, compliance or force-controlled. In effect, the CM acts merely as a transportation system for the FM which actually carries out the work. Since the mass and moments of inertia of the FM can be several orders of magnitude smaller than the CM, and the motion of the FM can be made *completely free of static friction*, it is possible to achieve programmable robot motion which is both very fast and very precise.

The Fine Manipulator

In a coarse-fine system, there is considerable choice in the design of the fine manipulator. Much fascinating work is focussed today on the design and control of multifingered hands for manipulation [15, 16]. For industrial applications, however, approaches based on fine motion devices may have more promise. Figure 2 shows a loose factoring of the manipulation domain into two scenarios. If the objects to be manipulated are unknown, and the environment is relatively unconstrained, a multifingered hand with tactile sensing offers the best approach. Here, high accuracy is seldom required, and the hand is used mostly in an exploratory way, or for identification of unknown objects. A different set of conditions arises in the manufacturing environment, where accuracy requirements may be high, but objects such as manufactured parts are well characterized and may be constrained by fixtures, or the partially assembled workpiece. We believe these considerations lead more naturally to a fine motion device.

Design and control of the FM device is crucial to success at the system level. Several approaches have been taken to building fine manipulation devices which can be attached to robots, including hydraulic [17, 18] and electric DC servomotor [4] five degree of freedom (5-DOF) wrists, an electric moving-coil wrist with two active and three passive DOFs [19], and brushless DC motor four-bar linkage and ball-screw linear bearing 3-DOF designs described in [20]. Control of a flexible manipulator with a small fast-motion device was described in [21]. A 2-DOF fine motion device based on DC motors has recently been reported [22].

Previous work in our laboratory has concentrated on two- and three-DOF electromagnetic devices [23, 24]. Application experiments with the two-DOF devices were reported in [14, 25], where it was shown that parts alignment accuracy improvements nearly two orders of magnitude better than with the CM alone could be obtained. While we are continuing to refine

and develop the 3-DOF electromagnetic fine positioners for planar alignment tasks in manufacturing, a new approach to FM devices was considered with features which include:

- 6 degrees of freedom redundant with those of the CM
- a positional resolution very much smaller than the CM for high precision
- minimal mass so as to not adversely load the CM
- extremely high acceleration to make it possible to synthesize compliance, correct for vibrational disturbances in the environment, and maximize job throughput
- a motion range as large as possible, to avoid extra motion of the CM
- zero static friction to avoid loss of accuracy and difficulties with control

In this paper we discuss a new fine motion robot wrist with these characteristics.

Design

Active Magnetic Suspension

In our previous work on fine positioning devices we were very careful to eliminate stiction effects by supporting the moving element with flexures [24] or air bearings. These methods are difficult to extend to six degrees of freedom and still retain the inherent elegance of a single moving part. Therefore, it was decided to eliminate the mechanical suspension and to float the wrist using active magnetic levitation. Except for a thin flexible ribbon cable for power, there is no mechanical connection between the wrist, with its gripper or tooling and endpoint sensing means, and the robot arm. Figure 3 is a photograph of the prototype wrist.

Magnetic bearings have existed for some time, but these are generally narrow-gap *electromagnetic* devices designed to provide maximum stiffness in a single position and orientation. For the magic wrist, a quite different *electrodynamic* moving coil approach was chosen with magnetic gaps wide enough to allow 6-DOF motion through a limited range of positions and angles.

Actuation

Many configurations were considered for the wrist actuator layout. The only essential requirement is that the

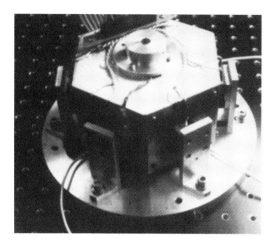

Figure 3. Photograph of Prototype Magic Wrist: forcer elements, stator with sensor cables, and flotor with ribbon power cable are evident. Scale can be inferred from the one-inch hole pattern of the table top.

electrodynamic forcing elements be arranged in such a manner that in combination they can exert an arbitrary force direction and arbitrary torque direction on the moving element. The hexagonal ring form shown in Figure 3, and schematically in Figure 4 was selected. A stator element comprised of an inner and outer ring of permanent magnet structures is fixed to the robot. Nested between these rings is a flotor element ring containing flat-wound coils. (We propose the term "flotor" in analogy to "rotor" of conventional motor terminology.) A hexagonal platform on top of the moving flotor (not shown in Figure 4) carries the gripper or tooling end effector necessary to perform the task. We will refer to the combination of an individual magnet structure and its associated coil as a "forcer".

Referring to Figure 4, there are six forcers alternately arranged horizontally and vertically around the ring. Each of these forcers generates a force along a single horizontal or vertical direction.

Internal Position Sensing

In Figure 4(a), the flotor is at its zero configuration, with co-incident robot and wrist coordinate frames located at the wrist center (shown displaced to the right for clarity) specified by the triads of unit vectors $^R\mathbf{b}$ and $^W\mathbf{b}$. In Figure 4(b), the flotor and its associated coordinate frame W is shown displaced and rotated from the frame R fixed in the stator. The prototype wrist has a radius $\rho_f = 67$ mm, allowing maximum translations and rotations of approximately ± 5 mm and $\pm 4°$.

For positioning and control, it is necessary to know the relationship between the W and R frames. This is accomplished by a set of three position sensors located at $120°$ intervals around the periphery. A triplet of radial light beams $120°$ apart generated by three LED projectors attached to the flotor impinge on three two-dimensional lateral effect photodiodes as shown in Figure 5. The position sensing resolution of the light spots is roughly 0.5 μm, giving, after appropriate transformation, translational and rotational resolutions for the wrist of approximately 1 μm and $0.001°$.

Docking Mechanism

The wrist need not operate during the coarse motion phases of the robot activity. That is, fine compliant motion need only be

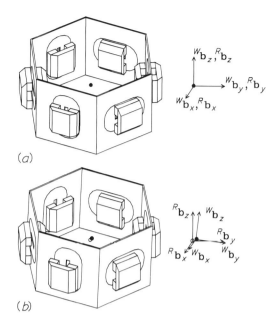

Figure 4. Magic Wrist Configuration: (a) at zero position and orientation, showing coincident robot and wrist frames, (b) displaced and rotated.

executed when the coarse robot is stationary or quasi-stationary after it has completed its motion. Therefore, a simple mechanical "docking mechanism" for fixing the position of the fine motion wrist with respect to the coarse robot will be included in later versions. When it is desired to dock the wrist, it is moved into a fixed detenting position and locked into place. The wrist coils are then turned off, saving power, and allowing the coils to cool. When required, the wrist is "flown" away from its docking position under active control whereupon it is again ready to perform some compliant fine motion task.

Workspace Considerations

Up to this point, we have discussed a hexagonal ring structure for the wrist, but if the workspace of such a wrist is examined, difficulties are found. Consider the wrist as a moving point in the non-convex six-dimensional configuration space illustrated in Figure 6(a). Thus if we want to move in a straight line in "joint space" between configuration A and configuration B, we may run into the limits of the workspace. For example, if we rotate the wrist by small angles in roll, pitch, and yaw, a seemingly feasible translational move may be blocked by the limit stops.

If, however, we make the wrist spherical, as shown in Figure 6(b), the six-dimensional configuration space can be written as the product of two three-dimensional spaces, one for rotation and one for translation. Full translational freedom is retained even if the wrist is rolled, pitched, and yawed, and *vice versa* for rotational freedom. A slightly different spherical wrist than that shown in Figure 6(b) is a spherical sector taken "above the equator" in order to make the center more accessible.

Because a spherical wrist is more difficult to construct, we are deferring it until after we have demonstrated stable control of the hexagonal magic wrist. We have, however, successfully fabricated spherically-shaped coils.

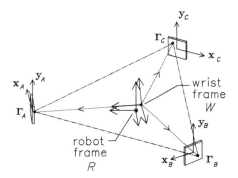

Figure 5.   Internal Position Sensors: three radial light beams fall on a set of three two-dimensional lateral effect photodiodes to give complete position and orientation sensing for the wrist.

Forcing Element Performance

The basic electromechanical unit which provides force or torque to the wrist is a flat coil electrodynamic drive unit, or *forcer*, shown in Figure 7. Four rectangular neodymium iron boron (NdFeB) magnets with energy product $B_{max}H_{max} = 35$ megagauss-oersteds provide a high average gap field of 6 kG. A pair of permeable 1008 steel back plates returns the flux. The coils are wound from specially made flat copper wire with high temperature Epotek™ 377 epoxy insulations. Coil current I interacts with the field to produce a force $f = BIL$, where L is the effective length of wire in the magnetic gap. If necessary, thin copper sheets can be bonded to the coil faces to form passive dampers which work like homopolar generators. Flat coil forcer units similar to this are used as actuators in disk files, where the gap length is minimized to increase the effective field and reduce stray fields. In the magic wrist, there is a tradeoff between high magnetic efficiency with a narrow gap *vs.* the necessity of allowing free motion in all six degrees of freedom, *i.e.*, achievable force *vs.* workspace size.

Flux Distribution

We have studied the gap flux distribution as a function of gap length and magnet dimensions both experimentally and by solving Poisson's equation over a two-dimensional grid, as shown in Figure 8. One of the flat-wound forcer coils at its nominal position and orientation is shown in the figure. As the wrist moves within its workspace, the coil position and orientation with respect to the field distribution changes. The total force on the coil is always given by the line integral

$$\mathbf{f} = -I \int \mathbf{B} \times d\mathbf{l}, \tag{1}$$

where $d\mathbf{l}$ is an element of wire in the coil. The force vector $\mathbf{f}$ is approximately in the plane of the coil and approximately normal to the long axis of the coil. The curved ends of the coils contribute some to $\mathbf{f}$, but also generate internal forces. Small torques about the coil center may safely be neglected. There are design trade-offs between field uniformity, field strength, and workspace constraints which can be explored. Proper design and characterization of the forcer is crucial for high performance. The measured force constant for a single forcer in nominal position is $f \cong 6.2$ N/A.

As we have surmised, the force $\mathbf{f}_k(I_k)$ for each forcer k varies with the position and orientation of the flotor with respect to the stator. We have determined from an experimental test setup, which allowed us to measure force over the entire expected range of coil motion, that the variation in $\mathbf{f}_k(I_k)$ is no

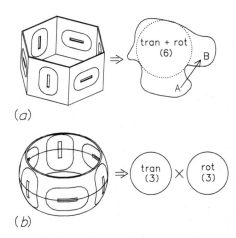

Figure 6.   Workspace Considerations: (a) hexagonal wrist with non-convex workspace, (b) spherical wrist with independent translational and rotational workspaces.

more than 15% . For control purposes, this variation can be accommodated by a simple parameterized model, or simply ignored.

Thermal Considerations

Numerous thermal tests were run on vertical and horizontal coils without cooling (other than natural convection). It was found that temperatures of 120 °C could be sustained indefinitely, and operation up to 140 °C for periods of several minutes was feasible. Much higher coil temperatures are possible with ceramic loaded epoxies and polyimide insulation, and we are pursuing these possibilities. Operating at 120 °C corresponds to $I \cong 2$ A, with power dissipation $P = I^2R \cong 20$ W. This current level in each of the three coils producing force in the $^W\mathbf{b}_z$ direction allows the wrist to support a static payload of 32.5 N (7.3 lb.) indefinitely with a power expenditure of 60 W.

Control Tests in One Dimension

Realizing we must crawl before we can fly, a digital PID control loop was implemented with a lateral effect sensor on the one-dimensional test setup used for forcer characterization. At a loop rate of approximately 1 KHz, very fast, stable control was achieved, with accelerations up to 30 *g*'s. By means of software control, the feedback gain coefficients were changed to vary the compliance from very soft to very stiff. In effect, this amounted to changing the spring constant K in the Hooke's Law relation $f = -Kx$, where f is the force and x is the displacement. If the one-dimensional tests are extrapolated to indicate performance for the completed wrist, it seems likely that accelerations up to 100 *g*'s are attainable using recently completed power amplifiers.

Kinematic and Dynamic Relations

Controlling the magic wrist requires a kinematic transformation, as well as a dynamic one. The direct kinematic transformation determines the position and orientation of the wrist given the projections of the LED light beams on the lateral cells; the inverse kinematic transformation determines the lateral cell projections given the wrist's position and orientation. For a given position and orientation of the wrist, the direct dynamic transformation determines the forces and torques that act upon the wrist as a function of the currents through the

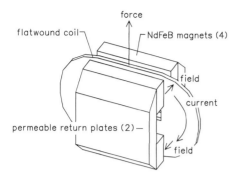

Figure 7.   *Forcer Design: a current sheet generated by the flat-wound coil interacts with the field of the permanent magnets to create a driving force.*

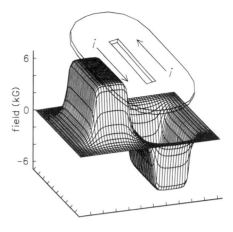

Figure 8.   *Forcer Magnetic Field Distribution: the normal component of the magnet B-field is plotted in physical relation to a flat-wound coil.*

wrist's six coils; the inverse dynamic transformation determines the coil currents that produce desired force and torque vectors acting on the wrist. For the purpose of our analysis here, each forcer unit k is modelled by a single sheet of uni-directional current moving in direction $\mathbf{I}_k$ attached to the flotor, interacting with a uniform inwardly-directed magnetic field $\mathbf{B}_k$ fixed in the stator.

Coordinate Systems

As illustrated in Figure 9 and Figure 10 , we shall deal with two coordinate systems: the *robot coordinate system*, attached to the wrist stator, and the *wrist coordinate system*, attached to the wrist flotor (see also Figure 4). The origin of the robot coordinate system is located at the intersection of the normals to the centers of the lateral effect cell planes, while its orthonormal frame $(^R\mathbf{b}_x, {}^R\mathbf{b}_y, {}^R\mathbf{b}_z)$ is defined as follows: $^R\mathbf{b}_x$ coincides with the normal to the center of lateral effect cell A, $^R\mathbf{b}_z$ is perpendicular to the plane determined by the centers of the lateral effect cell planes, and $^R\mathbf{b}_y = {}^R\mathbf{b}_z \times {}^R\mathbf{b}_x$. The origin of the wrist coordinate system coincides with the intersection of the lines coincident with the LED light beams, while the vectors $^W\mathbf{b}_x$, and $^W\mathbf{b}_y$ of its orthonormal frame $(^W\mathbf{b}_x, {}^W\mathbf{b}_y, {}^W\mathbf{b}_z)$ lie in the plane of the beams with $^W\mathbf{b}_x$ coinciding with light beam A. Throughout the rest of this paper, any vector expressed in robot frame will carry the prefix R, while any vector in wrist frame will carry the prefix W.

When the LED light beams of the wrist are projected onto the centers of the lateral effect cell planes, the wrist coordinate system and the robot coordinate system coincide. Otherwise, any vector $^W\mathbf{r}$ in the wrist coordinate system can be expressed as a vector $^R\mathbf{r} - {}^R\mathbf{r}_0$ in the robot coordinate system through the following simple coordinate transformation:

$$^R\mathbf{r} - {}^R\mathbf{r}_0 = {}^RQ_W\,{}^W\mathbf{r} \ , \tag{2}$$

where the matrix ^RQ_W represents a proper rotation (i.e. ^RQ_W is orthogonal and $\det{}^WQ_R = 1$). The columns of ^RQ_W are the co-ordinates of the wrist frame vectors $(^W\mathbf{b}_x, {}^W\mathbf{b}_y, {}^W\mathbf{b}_z)$ in robot frame, and $^R\mathbf{r}_0$ is the displacement of the wrist coordinate system origin.

First, note that with respect to the robot frame, the magnetic field vectors and the planes of the lateral cells are fixed (see Figure 9). The matrix of magnetic field vectors can be written as follows:

$$\left[\,{}^R\mathbf{B}_1 \ \ldots \ {}^R\mathbf{B}_6\,\right] = \tag{3}$$

$$= \begin{bmatrix} -1 & -1/2 & 1/2 & 1 & 1/2 & -1/2 \\ 0 & -\sqrt{3}/2 & -\sqrt{3}/2 & 0 & \sqrt{3}/2 & \sqrt{3}/2 \\ 0 & 0 & 0 & 0 & 0 & 0 \end{bmatrix} \cdot$$

$$\mathrm{diag}(B_1, \ldots, B_6),$$

where $B_1, \ldots, B_6$ are the magnetic field magnitudes and $\mathrm{diag}(B_1, \ldots, B_6)$ denotes the matrix that has $B_1, \ldots, B_6$ on the diagonal and zeros elsewhere.

Let (x_A, y_A) , (x_B, y_B), and (x_C, y_C) be the coordinates of the light spots projected by the LED's on the planes of the lateral effect cells A, B, and C, respectively, and let ρ_l be the distance from the origin of the robot frame to the centers of the lateral effect cells (see Figure 5 and Figure 9). Then, it is clear that the matrix of light spot positions on the A, B, and C lateral effect cell planes is given by:

$$\left[\,{}^R\mathbf{r}_A \ {}^R\mathbf{r}_B \ {}^R\mathbf{r}_C\,\right] = \rho_l \begin{bmatrix} 1 & -1/2 & -1/2 \\ 0 & \sqrt{3}/2 & -\sqrt{3}/2 \\ 0 & 0 & 0 \end{bmatrix} + \tag{4}$$

$$\begin{bmatrix} \begin{bmatrix} 0 & 0 \\ 1 & 0 \\ 0 & 1 \end{bmatrix}\begin{bmatrix} x_A \\ y_A \end{bmatrix} & \begin{bmatrix} -\sqrt{3}/2 & 0 \\ -1/2 & 0 \\ 0 & 1 \end{bmatrix}\begin{bmatrix} x_B \\ y_B \end{bmatrix} & \begin{bmatrix} \sqrt{3}/2 & 0 \\ -1/2 & 0 \\ 0 & 1 \end{bmatrix}\begin{bmatrix} x_C \\ y_C \end{bmatrix} \end{bmatrix} .$$

Second, with respect to the wrist coordinate system, the current directions, the coil center points and the directions of the LED light beams are fixed (see Figure 10). The matrix of current vectors in the wrist frame is given by

$$^WD = \left[\,{}^W\mathbf{I}_1 \ \ldots \ {}^W\mathbf{I}_6\,\right] \cdot \mathrm{diag}(I_1 \ldots I_6) = \tag{5}$$

$$\begin{bmatrix} 0 & -\sqrt{3}/2 & 0 & 0 & 0 & \sqrt{3}/2 \\ 0 & 1/2 & 0 & -1 & 0 & 1/2 \\ 1 & 0 & 1 & 0 & 1 & 0 \end{bmatrix} \cdot \mathrm{diag}(I_1 \ldots I_6) \ ,$$

where $I_1 \ldots I_6$ are the coil current magnitudes. The matrix of coil center points in the wrist coordinate system is found to be:

$$^WC \triangleq \left[\,{}^W\mathbf{c}_1 \ \ldots \ {}^W\mathbf{c}_6\,\right] = \tag{6}$$

$$= \rho_f \begin{bmatrix} 1 & 1/2 & -1/2 & -1 & -1/2 & 1/2 \\ 0 & \sqrt{3}/2 & \sqrt{3}/2 & 0 & -\sqrt{3}/2 & -\sqrt{3}/2 \\ 0 & 0 & 0 & 0 & 0 & 0 \end{bmatrix} ,$$

where ρ_f is the distance from the intersection point of the LED beams to the coil centers (see Figure 10). Finally, the matrix

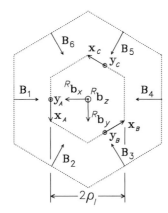

Figure 9.   Robot Frame Vectors: the magnetic field vectors and the lateral effect cell coordinate systems are fixed in the wrist stator.

of light spot positions on the A, B, and C lateral effect cell planes can also be expressed in the wrist coordinate system by using the directions of the LED light beams.
Indeed,

$$\left[{}^W\mathbf{r}_A \; {}^W\mathbf{r}_B \; {}^W\mathbf{r}_C\right] = \tag{7}$$

$$\begin{bmatrix} 1 & -1/2 & -1/2 \\ 0 & \sqrt{3}/2 & -\sqrt{3}/2 \\ 0 & 0 & 0 \end{bmatrix} \operatorname{diag}\left[\lambda_A, \lambda_B, \lambda_C\right] \; ,$$

where λ_A, λ_B and λ_C are the distances, measured along the beams, from the point of intersection of the LED light beams to the lat cells.

We can now fully develop the kinematic and dynamic transformations needed for control.

Kinematic Transformations

The inverse kinematic transformation can be easily obtained from (4) , (7) and the coordinate transformation (2) . For each lateral effect cell, we obtain a linear system of equations with 3 unknowns. For example, in the case of cell A, we have

$$\begin{bmatrix} 0 & 0 \\ 1 & 0 \\ 0 & 1 \end{bmatrix} - {}^R Q_W \begin{bmatrix} 1 \\ 0 \\ 0 \end{bmatrix} \begin{bmatrix} x_A \\ y_A \\ \lambda_A \end{bmatrix} = {}^R\mathbf{r}_0 - \rho_l \begin{bmatrix} 1 \\ 0 \\ 0 \end{bmatrix} . \tag{8}$$

In developing the direct kinematic transformation, we shall use the notation ${}^R\mathbf{r}_{MN} \triangleq {}^R\mathbf{r}_N - {}^R\mathbf{r}_M$, for any two points M and N. Note that, given the positions ${}^R\mathbf{r}_A$, ${}^R\mathbf{r}_B$, and ${}^R\mathbf{r}_C$ of the LED light spots on the lateral effect cell planes, the origin ${}^R\mathbf{r}_0$ of the wrist coordinate system must be the intersection of the loci of points that lie in the plane spanned by ${}^R\mathbf{r}_{AB}$ and ${}^R\mathbf{r}_{AC}$ and that subtend the line segments $\mathbf{r}_{AB}$, $\mathbf{r}_{AC}$ at angles of $120°$. These loci are arcs of circle centered at ${}^R\mathbf{r}_M$ and ${}^R\mathbf{r}_N$, where

$${}^R\mathbf{r}_M = \frac{1}{2}\left({}^R\mathbf{r}_A + {}^R\mathbf{r}_B\right) + \frac{1}{2\sqrt{3}} \frac{{}^R\mathbf{r}_{AB} \times \left[{}^R\mathbf{r}_{AB} \times {}^R\mathbf{r}_{AC}\right]}{\|{}^R\mathbf{r}_{AB} \times {}^R\mathbf{r}_{AC}\|} , \tag{9}$$

$${}^R\mathbf{r}_N = \frac{1}{2}\left({}^R\mathbf{r}_A + {}^R\mathbf{r}_C\right) + \frac{1}{2\sqrt{3}} \frac{\left[{}^R\mathbf{r}_{AB} \times {}^R\mathbf{r}_{AC}\right] \times {}^R\mathbf{r}_{AC}}{\|{}^R\mathbf{r}_{AB} \times {}^R\mathbf{r}_{AC}\|} . \tag{10}$$

Since $\|{}^R\mathbf{r}_{MA}\| = \|{}^R\mathbf{r}_{M0}\|$ and $\|{}^R\mathbf{r}_{NA}\| = \|{}^R\mathbf{r}_{N0}\|$, we have that

$${}^R\mathbf{r}_0 = {}^R\mathbf{r}_A + 2\left[{}^R\mathbf{r}_{AN} - \frac{<{}^R\mathbf{r}_{AN} , \; {}^R\mathbf{r}_{MN}>}{\|{}^R\mathbf{r}_{MN}\|^2} \; {}^R\mathbf{r}_{MN}\right] . \tag{11}$$

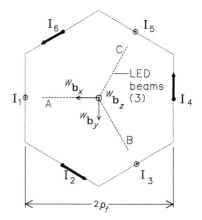

Figure 10.   Wrist Frame Vectors: the coil currents and LED beams are fixed in the wrist flotor.

It now follows that the columns of ${}^R Q_W$ are given by:

$${}^R Q_W = \tag{12}$$

$$\left[\frac{{}^R\mathbf{r}_{0A}}{\|{}^R\mathbf{r}_{0A}\|} \quad \frac{{}^R\mathbf{r}_{AB} \times {}^R\mathbf{r}_{AC}}{\|{}^R\mathbf{r}_{AB} \times {}^R\mathbf{r}_{AC}\|} \times \frac{{}^R\mathbf{r}_{0A}}{\|{}^R\mathbf{r}_{0A}\|} \quad \frac{{}^R\mathbf{r}_{AB} \times {}^R\mathbf{r}_{AC}}{\|{}^R\mathbf{r}_{AB} \times {}^R\mathbf{r}_{AC}\|} \right] ,$$

and this completes the direct kinematic transformation.

Dynamic Transformations

In order to compute the required dynamic transformations, we have to obtain the coil current vectors and the coil centers in the robot coordinate system. From the transformation of coordinates equation (2) , the matrix of current vectors in the robot frame is given by

$${}^R D = \left[{}^R\mathbf{I}_1 \; ... \; {}^R\mathbf{I}_6\right] \cdot \operatorname{diag}(I_1 \; ... \; I_6) = {}^R Q_W \; {}^W D \; , \tag{13}$$

while the coordinates of the coil center points are given by:

$${}^R\mathbf{c}_i = {}^R\mathbf{r}_0 + {}^R Q_W \; {}^W\mathbf{c}_i \; , i = 1, ... , 6 . \tag{14}$$

From (13) and (14) , it follows that the unit Lorentz forces acting on the wrist coils are given by

$${}^R\mathbf{f}_i = {}^R\mathbf{I}_i \times {}^R\mathbf{B}_i = \left({}^R Q_W \; {}^W\mathbf{I}_i\right) \times {}^R\mathbf{B}_i , \quad i = 1, ... , 6 , \tag{15}$$

while the torques on the wrist due to these forces are given by

$${}^R\boldsymbol{\tau}_i = \left({}^R\mathbf{c}_i - {}^R\mathbf{r}_0\right) \times {}^R\mathbf{f}_i = \tag{16}$$

$$= \left({}^R Q_W \; {}^W\mathbf{c}_i\right) \times {}^R\mathbf{f}_i \; , \quad i = 1, ... , 6 .$$

Combining the above equations, we obtain the following linear system that relates the coil currents to the forces and torques acting on the wrist:

$$\begin{bmatrix} {}^R\mathbf{f}_1 & {}^R\mathbf{f}_2 & ... & {}^R\mathbf{f}_6 \\ {}^R\boldsymbol{\tau}_1 & {}^R\boldsymbol{\tau}_2 & ... & {}^R\boldsymbol{\tau}_6 \end{bmatrix} \begin{bmatrix} I_1 \\ I_2 \\ . \\ . \\ . \\ I_6 \end{bmatrix} = \begin{bmatrix} {}^R\mathbf{f}_d \\ {}^R\boldsymbol{\tau}_d \end{bmatrix} . \tag{17}$$

In order to obtain a desired force ${}^R\mathbf{f}_d$ and desired torque ${}^R\boldsymbol{\tau}_d$ acting on the wrist, we need to solve (17) for I_i , $i = 1, ... , 6$. In some cases, it may be of interest to specify a desired torque in wrist frame. It is easy to show that the transformation (2) can be used in (17) to arrive at

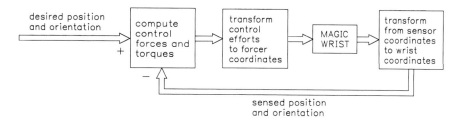

Figure 11.   Basic Control Scheme.

$$\begin{bmatrix} {}^{R}\mathbf{f}_1 & {}^{R}\mathbf{f}_2 & \cdots & {}^{R}\mathbf{f}_6 \\ {}^{W}\boldsymbol{\tau}_1 & {}^{W}\boldsymbol{\tau}_2 & \cdots & {}^{W}\boldsymbol{\tau}_6 \end{bmatrix} \begin{bmatrix} I_1 \\ I_2 \\ \cdot \\ \cdot \\ \cdot \\ I_6 \end{bmatrix} = \begin{bmatrix} {}^{R}\mathbf{f}_d \\ {}^{W}\boldsymbol{\tau}_d \end{bmatrix} \,. \tag{18}$$

Control Strategy

A very general feedback control diagram for the wrist is shown in Figure 11. A simple controller designed to achieve programmable compliance is based on a proportional-derivative scheme. If we let the roll, pitch and yaw angles be denoted by ϕ, θ and ψ, respectively, $\boldsymbol{\xi} \triangleq \left[{}^{R}\mathbf{r}_0^{T} \; \phi \; \theta \; \psi \right]^{T}$ and $\boldsymbol{\xi}_d$ is a desired set point, then the PD controller can be implemented by setting

$$\begin{bmatrix} {}^{R}\mathbf{f}_d \\ {}^{R}\boldsymbol{\tau}_d \end{bmatrix} = K_P (\boldsymbol{\xi} - \boldsymbol{\xi}_d) + K_D \frac{d}{dt} (\boldsymbol{\xi} - \boldsymbol{\xi}_d) \,, \tag{19}$$

in equation (17) and solving for the six current magnitudes. Stiffness and damping can be programmed by appropriate selection of the gain matrices K_P and K_D. The controller can be simplified by assuming that the rotation matrix ${}^{R}Q_W$, which is implicit in (17), is the identity (this assumption is reasonable for small angle rotations), thus reducing significantly the task of finding the coil currents.

The PD control scheme described above neglects the wrist's dynamics, but is attractive due to its simplicity. More sophisticated controllers can be obtained when the dynamic equations of the wrist are taken into consideration. With the usual parametrizations of rotation– such as Euler angles and direction cosines– the equations of rotation of a levitated body are extremely complicated and have geometric singularities for small angles, thus making the design of a controller quite difficult. A technique used in the design of large angle satellite attitude controllers has been to resort to the Euler *parameters* or Euler *quaternion* [26, 27]. The Euler parameter vector $\boldsymbol{\beta}$ is defined by

$$\boldsymbol{\beta} \triangleq \left[\beta_0 \; \beta_1 \; \beta_2 \; \beta_3 \right]^{T} = \left[\beta_0 \; {}^{R}\hat{\boldsymbol{\beta}}^{T} \right]^{T} \tag{20}$$

$$= \left[\cos(\phi/2) \; \sin(\phi/2) \, {}^{R}\mathbf{s}^{T} \right]^{T} \,,$$

where ${}^{R}\mathbf{s}$ is the axis of rotation ($\|{}^{R}\mathbf{s}\| = 1$) and ϕ is the angle of rotation. Note that $\|\boldsymbol{\beta}\| = 1$ and that (20) is closely related to the symmetric 3-parameter representation of rotation known as the Rodrigues formula [28]. When the Euler quaternion is used, the dynamics of the wrist have the following simple form [27, 29]:

$$^{R}\ddot{\mathbf{r}}_0 = \frac{1}{m} \, {}^{R}\mathbf{f} + {}^{R}\mathbf{g} \,, \tag{21}$$

$$^{W}\dot{\boldsymbol{\omega}} = -J^{-1} ({}^{W}\boldsymbol{\omega} \times J \; {}^{W}\boldsymbol{\omega}) + J^{-1} \, {}^{W}\boldsymbol{\tau} \,,$$

$$\dot{\beta}_0 = -\frac{1}{2} \, {}^{R}\hat{\boldsymbol{\beta}}^{T} \; {}^{W}\boldsymbol{\omega} \,,$$

$$^{R}\dot{\hat{\boldsymbol{\beta}}} = \frac{1}{2} \, (\beta_0 \; {}^{W}\boldsymbol{\omega} + {}^{R}\hat{\boldsymbol{\beta}} \times {}^{W}\boldsymbol{\omega}) \,,$$

where m and $J = \mathrm{diag}[\, J_1, J_2, J_3 \,]$ are the mass and the matrix of principal moments of inertia of the wrist, ${}^{W}\boldsymbol{\omega}$ is the angular velocity of the wrist, ${}^{R}\mathbf{f}$ is the force with which the coils act on the wrist, ${}^{R}\mathbf{g}$ is the gravitational vector, and ${}^{W}\boldsymbol{\tau}$ is the applied torque. In deriving (21), we have made three assumptions: first, that the center of mass of the wrist and the origin of the wrist coordinate system coincide; second, that the wrist frame vectors are defined along principal axes of inertia; and third, that the robot moves slowly enough, so as to be able to consider its coordinate system to be inertial. The above assumptions are not strictly speaking satisfied, but they simplify our discussion.

Following the technique presented in [30], (21) can be transformed *exactly* into a linear system, via a nonlinear memoryless transformation of the input and state [29]. The drawback of this approach is twofold: first, it is computationally quite demanding, and, second, the nonlinear transformation of the input depends explicitly on the angular velocity vector ${}^{W}\boldsymbol{\omega}$. This vector cannot be measured directly with the sensors the wrist is currently equipped with, and obtaining it by differentiation of the sensed angles may lead to very noisy estimates. One could consider designing a nonlinear observer for ${}^{W}\boldsymbol{\omega}$, but such an approach seems quite difficult.

What may turn out to be the best alternative for the control system design, at least for small angular velocities, is to use the linearized version of (21) about ${}^{R}\hat{\boldsymbol{\beta}} = 0$, ${}^{W}\boldsymbol{\omega} = 0$. First, observe that integration of (21) keeps $\|\boldsymbol{\beta}\|$ constant, so $\beta_0^2 + {}^{R}\hat{\boldsymbol{\beta}}^{T} \, {}^{R}\hat{\boldsymbol{\beta}} \equiv 1$. Now, since the quaternion $\boldsymbol{\beta}$ and its negative $- \boldsymbol{\beta}$ represent the same rotation, we can always select ${}^{R}\hat{\boldsymbol{\beta}}$ (obtained from the rotation matrix ${}^{R}Q_W$) such that $\beta_0 \geq 0$, so we can substitute $\beta_0 = (1 - {}^{R}\hat{\boldsymbol{\beta}}^{T} \; {}^{R}\hat{\boldsymbol{\beta}})^{1/2}$ into the fourth equation of (21). Linearization of (21) then leads to the following system:

$$\frac{d}{dt} \begin{bmatrix} {}^{R}\mathbf{r}_0 \\ {}^{R}\dot{\mathbf{r}}_0 \\ {}^{R}\hat{\boldsymbol{\beta}} \\ {}^{W}\boldsymbol{\omega} \end{bmatrix} = \begin{bmatrix} 0 & I & 0 & 0 \\ 0 & 0 & 0 & 0 \\ 0 & 0 & 0 & 1/2I \\ 0 & 0 & 0 & 0 \end{bmatrix} \begin{bmatrix} {}^{R}\mathbf{r}_0 \\ {}^{R}\dot{\mathbf{r}}_0 \\ {}^{R}\hat{\boldsymbol{\beta}} \\ {}^{W}\boldsymbol{\omega} \end{bmatrix} + \begin{bmatrix} 0 & 0 \\ 1/mI & 0 \\ 0 & 0 \\ 0 & J^{-1} \end{bmatrix} \begin{bmatrix} {}^{R}\mathbf{f} \\ {}^{W}\boldsymbol{\tau} \end{bmatrix} \,, \tag{22}$$

where all the submatrices are 3 by 3. The currents producing a desired input vector in (22) can be obtained by means of (18).

Designing an observer-based controller for the system (22) can be done via several design techniques for linear multivariable systems (see, for example, [31]). Variable compliance control can be achieved by software changes in the controller parameters, by keeping in mind that the rotation parameter ${}^{R}\hat{\boldsymbol{\beta}}$ is the

72   Hollis et al.

axis of rotation multiplied by the sine of the half-angle of rotation.

Emulation of Mechanisms

The notion of synthesizing other mechanisms using a robot with a programmable control system has been discussed by several authors, *e.g.* [32, 8, 9]. Many simple and useful mechanisms can be emulated with the magic wrist, a small set of which is illustrated in Figure 12. If the stiffness K is set to be high along all motion directions but one, then a unidirectional plunger is synthesized. If all stiffnesses are large except two in translation, a slider mechanism results. By setting all the rotational stiffnesses high, only translational motion is allowed. Conversely, by setting the translational stiffnesses high, a ball and socket rotator is created. By allowing some rotational, and some translational motion, a remote center compliance (RCC) device is synthesized. All of these synthesized mechanisms result from restricting degrees of freedom, and have many useful applications in robotic assembly. Unlike conventional mechanical mechanisms, these are all selectable by program control in real time, and can be altered several times even within a single job cycle.

Control Implementation and Experiments

Position and orientation finding routines based on (9), (10), (11), and (12), and a feedback PD controller based on (21) were written in C, using 16 bit fixed-point arithmetic. These routines were compiled on a Masscomp workstation and downloaded to a 10 MHz SBE card with a 68020 CSA processor and iSBX I/O cards. The experimental GPAC [33] system was used to download and debug the real-time code.

The magic wrist was *"flown"* *successfully*, in spite of the low sampling rate (250 Hz) and the relatively coarse positioning resolution (2.5 μm translational resolution) imposed by the 16 bit fixed-point implementation. Both *position* and *compliant* control were demonstrated. Of the mechanisms described in Figure 12, all but the RCC device were synthesized, with chatter-free control even when the wrist was in contact with stiff (massive steel bar) environments. Mechanism synthesis was achieved by executing small AML/X [34] programs that reside in GPAC's programming system– the Masscomp workstation. These programs change the position gains of the PD controller *while the wrist is in operation*. Simply typing in commands like "rotator," "xytable," etc. serve to select the mechanism to be emulated.

Our control experiments have just begun; present efforts are directed towards achieving a higher sampling rate, which will lead to more accurate velocity signals and will allow us to obtain stiffer controllers.

Summary and Conclusions

We have discussed some of the difficulties inherent in single-stage manipulation using position control and compliance control. In the case of position control, static accuracy and dynamic problems associated with high masses and inertias, bending, temperature effects, and joint friction were cited. In the case of compliance control or force servoing, dynamic and control problems associated with high masses and inertias, joint friction, and contact with a stiff environment were cited. We have argued that many of these difficulties can be circumvented by adopting a two-stage manipulation scheme with both *coarse* and *fine* domains. This approach will be effective if precise positioning or compliant behavior is needed only over limited

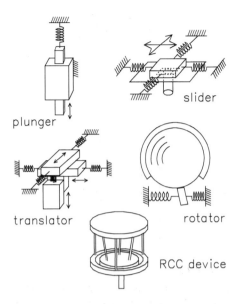

Figure 12.   Synthetic Mechanisms: by varying the control gains the magic wrist can pretend to be these mechanisms.

ranges of motion. Distinctions were raised between the applicability of dextrous hands for this purpose, *vs.* fine motion devices.

Within the scope of these considerations, particular emphasis was placed on the design of a six degree-of-freedom magnetically levitated fine motion wrist (FM) with the potential for extraordinary capabilities. In a robot system, this wrist would be inserted between a coarse manipulator (CM) wrist and the gripper or other end-effector. The CM wrist rotational axes would be programmed to coincide with those of the FM. The geometry and magnetics of the wrist were discussed at some length, and performance results in one dimension were given. A scheme for sensing the wrist position and orientation was described. A complete description of the kinematic and dynamic equations necessary for control was presented. Several possible approaches to control were briefly discussed. Simulation software has been written to test various control strategies. A prototype wrist, including power drive amplifiers and sensing electronics has been built, and controlled in both position and compliance modes, with extremely encouraging results.

We expect that the wrist described here, with its frictionless magnetic suspension, extremely high acceleration, precise positioning capability, and programmable compliance will find many applications in automatic assembly and testing for microelectronics. Beyond immediate application, it would seem in many respects the magic wrist provides the basis for a truly useful fine motion *universal mechanism*.

References

[1]   R. Podoloff, W. Seering, and B. Hunter, "An Accuracy Test Procedure for Robotic Manipulators Utilizing a Vision Based, 3-D Position Sensing System," *Proc. American Control Conf.*, San Diego, June (1984).

[2]   K. Lau, R. Hocken, and L. Haynes, "Robot Performance Measurements Using Automatic Laser Tracking Techniques," 1986.

[3]   K. Lau and R. J. Hocken, "A Survey of Current Robot Metrology Methods," *Annals of the CIRP*, **33** [2], 1984, pp. 485-488.

[4]   H. Van Brussel and J. Simons, "The Adaptable Compliance Concept and its use for Automatic Assembly by Active Force Feedback Accomodations," *9th International Symposium on Industrial Robots*, Washington, D.C., 1979, pp.167-181.

[5]   J. K. Salisbury, "Active Stiffness Control of a Manipulator in Cartesian Coordinates," *Proc. 19th IEEE Conf. on Decision and Control*, 1980, pp. 95-100.

[6]   D. E. Whitney, "Force Feedback Control of Manipulator Fine Motions," *ASME J. of Dynamic Systems, Measurement, and Control*, June, 1977, pp. 91-97.

[7]   M. H. Raibert and J. J. Craig, "Hybrid Position/Force Control of Manipulators," *ASME J. of Dynamic Systems, Measurements and Controls*, **102**, June 1981, pp. 126-133.

[8]   Neville Hogan, "Impedance Control: An Approach to Manipulation," Parts I-III, *ASME J. of Dynamic Systems, Measurement, and Control*, **107**, Mar. 1985, pp. 1-23.

[9]   O. Khatib, "A Unified Approach for Motion and Force Control of Robot Manipulators: the Operational Space Formulation," *IEEE J. of Robotics and Automation*, **3** [1], 1987, pp. 43-53.

[10]   D. E. Whitney, "Historical Perspective and State of the Art in Robot Force Control," *Int. J. of Robotics Research*, **6** [1], Spring, 1987, pp. 3-14.

[11]   A. Gogoussis and M. Donath, "Coulomb Friction Joint and Drive Effects in Robot Mechanisms," *Proc. IEEE Conf. on Robotics and Automation*, Raleigh, N.C. Mar 31-Apr 3, 1987, pp. 828-835.

[12]   W. T. Townsend and J. K. Salisbury, "The Effect of Coulomb Friction and Stiction on Force Control," *Proc. IEEE Conf. on Robotics and Automation*, Raleigh, N.C. Mar 31-Apr 3, 1987, pp. 883-889.

[13]   C. H. An and J. M. Hollerbach, "Dynamic Stability Issues in Force Control of Manipulators," *Proc. IEEE Conf. on Robotics and Automation*, Raleigh, N.C. Mar 31-Apr 3, 1987, pp. 890-896.

[14]   R. H. Taylor, R. L. Hollis, and M. A. Lavin, "Precise Manipulation with Endpoint Sensing," International Symposium on Robotics Research, Kyoto, Japan, August 20-23, 1984, and *IBM J. Res. Develop.* **29**[4], pp. 363-376, July, 1985.

[15]   J. Kenneth Salisbury and John J. Craig, "Articulated Hands: Force Control and Kinematic Issues," *Int. J. of Robotics Research*, **1**[1], 1982, pp. 4-17.

[16]   S. C. Jacobsen, J. E. Wood, D. F. Knutti, and K. B. Biggers, "The Utah/M.I.T. Dextrous Hand: Work in Progress," *Int. J. of Robotics Research*, **3**[4], 1984, pp. 21-50.

[17]   M. R. Cutkosky and P. K. Wright, "Position Sensing Wrists for Industrial Manipulators," *12th International Symposium on Industrial Robots*, 1982, pp. 427-438.

[18]   Andre Sharon and David Hardt, "Enhancement of Robot Accuracy Using Endpoint Feedback and a Macro-Micro Manipulator System," *American Control Conference proceedings*, San Diego, California, June 6-8, 1984, pp. 1836-1842.

[19]   Kazuo Asakawa, Fumiaki Akiya, and Fumio Tabata, "A Variable Compliance Device and its Application for Automatic Assembly," *Autofact 5 conference proceedings*, Detroit, Michigan, Nov. 14-17, 1983, pp. 10-1 to 10-17.

[20]   Ronald Benton, "Enabling Technology for Flexible Assembly Systems," *Sixteenth Nat'l Conf. on Material and Process Engineering*, Albuquerque, NM, October 1984.

[21]   S. W. Tilley and R. A. Cannon, "End-Point Force Control of a Very Flexible Manipulator with Fast End Effector," *Proc. ASME Winter Annual Mtg.*, Anaheim, CA, 1986.

[22]   H. Kazerooni and J. Guo, "Direct-Drive, Active Compliant End-Effector (RCC)," *Proc. IEEE Conf. on Robotics and Automation*, Raleigh, N.C. Mar 31-Apr 3, 1987, pp. 758-766.

[23]   R. L. Hollis, "A Fine Positioning Device for Enhancing Robot Precision," *Robots 9 Conference Proceedings*, Detroit, Michigan, June 2-6, 1985, pp. 6-28 to 6-36.

[24]   R. L. Hollis, "Design for a Planar XY Robotic Fine Positioning Device," **PED-Vol. 15: Robotics and Manufacturing Automation**, *Proc. ASME 1985 Winter Annual Mtg*, Miami, Nov. 19-22, 1985, pp. 291-298.

[25]   R. L. Hollis, R. H. Taylor, M. Johnson, A. Levas and A. Brennemann, "Robotic Circuit Board Testing Using Fine Positioners with Fiber-Optic Sensing," *Proc. Int'l Symposium on Industrial Robots*, Tokyo, Japan, Sept. 11-13, 1985, pp. 315-322.

[26]   J. L. Junkins and J.D. Turner, **Optimal Spacecraft Rotational Maneuvers,** Elsevier, 1986.

[27]   J.L. Junkins, and J.D. Turner, "Optimal Continuous Torque Attitude Maneuvers", *AIAA Journal of Guidance Contr.*, **3** [3], May-June 1980, pp210-217.

[28]   R.M. Rosenberg, **Analytical Dynamics of Discrete Systems**, Plenum Press, 1977.

[29]   T.A.W. Dwyer, "Exact Nonlinear Control of Large Angle Rotational Maneuvers", *Trans. Auto. Control*, **AC-29** [9], pp769-774, September 1984.

[30]   L.R. Hunt, R.Su, and G. Meyer, "Global Transformations of Nonlinear Systems", *Trans. Auto. Control.*, **AC-28**, pp. 24-31, Jan., 1983.

[31]   M. Vidyasagar, **Control Systems Synthesis: A Factorization Approach**, MIT Press, Cambridge, MA, 1985.

[32]   Jehuda Ish-Shalom "The CS Language Concept: A New Approach to Robot Motion Design," *Proc. of 23rd Conf. on Decision and Control*, Las Vegas, NV, Dec. 1984, pp. 760-767, and *Int'l J. of Robotics Research*, **4**[1], Spring, 1985, pp. 42-58.

[33]   J. U. Korein, G. E. Maier, R. H. Taylor, and L. F. Durfee, "A Configurable System for Automation Programming and Control," *Proc. IEEE Intl. Conf. on Robotics and Automation*, pp. 1871-77, April, 1986.

[34]   L. R. Nackman, M. A. Lavin, R. H. Taylor, W. C. Dietrich, and D. D. Grossman, "AML/X: A Programming Language for Design and Manufacturing," *Proc. Fall Joint Computer Conference,*, pp. 145-159, November, 1986.

DESIGN AND SIGNAL PROCESSING OF SIX-AXIS FORCE SENSORS

Yoshihiko Nakamura[†‡]   *Tsuneo Yoshikawa*[†]   *Ichiro Futamata*[†]

† *Automation Research Laboratory, Kyoto University*
Uji, Kyoto, 611 Japan

‡ *Center for Robotic Systems in Microelectronics*
University of California Santa Barbara
California, 93106 USA

Three criteria are proposed to evaluate the elastic components of force sensors, that is, the strain gage sensitivity, the force sensitivity, and the minimum stiffness. The strain gage sensitivity is defined as the Euclidean norm of a row vector of the sensor compliance matrix. The force sensitivity is the minimum singular value of the sensor compliance matrix. The minimum rigidity means the reciprocal of the maximum singular value of the compliance matrix at the origin of the sensor coordinates. When the number of strain gages is more than six, there is variety in inverting strain gage signals into the force information. By using this fact, it is also proposed to design the elastic component so that Wheatstone bridges should work as a part of the analog inverting circuit. A six-axis force sensor is designed as an example to show the design procedure based on the proposed criteria and signal processing method.

1. INTRODUCTION

Force Control has been discussed from the beginning of the robotics research [Scheinman, 1969; Inoue, 1971] and recognized as an important control scheme for using robots in the advanced applications [Goto, 1986; Hatamura, 1986].

Concerning the force sensing of manipulators, to measure the strain of driving joint axis [Nakano, 1974] and to measure the driving current of direct drive manipulators [Arai, 1986] were proposed. However, when they are used to measure the force applied to the end effector, they have such a drawback that the friction force and inertial force should be eliminated to get the effective signal [Uchiyama, 1985]. A direct and simple method to measure the end effector force is to equip a force sensor close to the end effector of a robot.

Force sensing has a long research history as well as force control, and many force sensors have been developed so far [Loewen, 1951; Kinoshita, 1984; Flatau, 1976; Watson, 1975; Kasai, 1981; Asakawa, 1985; De Fazio, 1986; Uchiyama 1986; Ono, 1985 (a)]. Several six-axis force sensors are commercially available at present [Ono, 1985 (b), LORD Corporation ,1985]. Since a major problem in developing force sensors is the design of elastic component which has been heuristic and dependent on the experience of designers, the theoretical evaluation of the designed force sensor and the comparative evaluation between developed force sensors have not been made sufficiently. Uchiyama and Hakomori [1985 (b)] proposed to evaluate the structure of elastic component of force sensor by the condition number of sensor compliance matrix. This evaluation method made the first contribution not just to the evaluation of the developed force sensors but to the theoretical principle of force sensor design.

In this paper, we propose to evaluate the structure of the elastic component of force sensor by three criteria, that is, the strain gage sensitivity, the force sensitivity and the minimum stiffness. The strain gage sensitivity means the sensitivity of each strain gage for forces and moments within the measurement range given as the design specification. The force sensitivity evaluates the force information of the whole sensor and is used to check if the output signal can include effective signals in all of six axes. The mechanical stiffness of force sensor is liable to be low because of the elastic component. The evaluation of the stiffness is required to consider the mechanical stiffness at the design stage. The minimum stiffness implies the stiffness in the most compliant direction.

Next, we propose an inverse transformation utilizing Wheatstone bridges. To know the force and moment exerted on the end effector

from the obtained strain gage signals, a common method is to compute the inverse matrix or the pseudoinverse of the sensor compliance matrix and multiply it to the strain gage signal [Uchiyama, 1985 (b)]. The drawback of this method is to require a large amount of computation. On the other hand, it is also proposed to design the elastic component so that a strain gage should be sensitive only to a corresponding force axis [Ono, 1985 (b)]. This method does not require the computation for inverse transformation, but it seems to be a drawback that the structure of elastic component becomes complex. In this paper, we propose to determine the structure of elastic component and the location of strain gages so that Wheatstone bridges, which are usually used for thermal compensation, work as a part of the inverse transformation circuit to compute the force and moment exerted on the end effector.

Finally, a six-axis force sensor is designed as an example to show the design procedure based on the above principles.

2. FORCE SENSING

2.1 Basic Equations

Let O_h-xyz represent the hand coordinates which is a coordinate frame fixed at the end effector of a robot manipulator and O_s-xyz indicate the sensor coordinates which means a coordinate frame fixed at the force sensor, as shown in Fig.1. We represents a vector from O_s to O_h described in the sensor coordinates by r_o. A_o shows an orthogonal matrix which includes unit vectors in x, y and z directions of the hand coordinates described in the sensor coordinates as the first, second and third column vectors in order. The force and moment applied to the end effector are represented by F_h and N_h which mean the force and moment applied at the origin of the hand coordinates. F_h and N_h can equivalently be transformed in the following way to F_s and N_s which mean the force and moment applied to the origin of the sensor coordinates:

$$F_s = A_o F_h \tag{1}$$

$$N_s = A_o N_h + r_o \times (A_o F_h) \tag{2}$$

Assuming elastic strain for the elastic component of force sensor, strain ϵ_i $(i = 1, \ldots, m)$ of strain gages can be represented by the following linear equation of F_s and N_s [Uchiyama, 1985 (b)]:

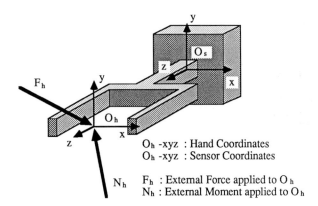

O_h -xyz : Hand Coordinates
O_h -xyz : Sensor Coordinates

N_h F_h : External Force applied to O_h
       N_h : External Moment applied to O_h

Fig.1   Principle of Force and Moment Measurement

$$\epsilon = C f, \tag{3}$$

$$\epsilon = col.(\epsilon_i) \in R^m$$
$$f = (F_s^T \ N_s^T)^T \in R^6$$

where m is the number of strain gages and $C \in R^{m \times 6}$ is called the sensor compliance matrix. Force sensing is the problem to obtain F_h and N_h from measured ϵ and eqs. (1) through (3). Therefore, it would be desirable to design force sensors based on the relationship of eqs. (1) through (3). However, since A_o and r_o in eqs. (1) and (2) depend on tasks, force sensors cannot be designed without specifying tasks. In this paper, we discuss the design of force sensors by simplifying the problem into the problem to obtain F_s and N_s from measured ϵ and eq.(3). To generalize the discussion, the following equation is used as the basic equation:

$$\bar{\epsilon} = \bar{C} \bar{f} \tag{4}$$

$$\bar{\epsilon} = \epsilon / \epsilon_{max}$$
$$\bar{f} = (F_s^T / F_{max} \ N_s^T / N_{max})^T$$
$$\bar{C} = 1/\epsilon_{max} \ CH$$
$$H = diag.(F_{max}, F_{max}, F_{max}, N_{max}, N_{max}, N_{max})$$

which is obtained by normalizing eq. (3) by means of maximum force F_{max}, maximum moment N_{max} given as the design specification, and maximum strain ϵ_{max} which is determined by the proportional limit of the elastic material. Note that although the proportional limit of steel is 0.12 % for example, ϵ_{max} should be determined so that the strain at the places where strain gages are not fixed should not exceed the proportional limit.

2.2 Structure Evaluation by Condition Number

In order that $\bar{f}$ can be computed from $\bar{\epsilon}$ for an arbitrary force, $m \geq 6$ and $rank \, \bar{C} = 6$ are required [Uchiyama, 1985 (b)]. In this event, the singular value decomposition [Iri, 1982] of $\bar{C}$ is represented by

$$\bar{C} = U\Sigma V^T \tag{5}$$

$$\Sigma = \begin{pmatrix} \sigma_1 & 0 & \dots & 0 \\ 0 & \sigma_2 & \dots & 0 \\ \vdots & \vdots & \ddots & \vdots \\ 0 & 0 & \dots & \sigma_6 \\ 0 & 0 & \dots & 0 \\ \vdots & \vdots & \ddots & \vdots \\ 0 & 0 & \dots & 0 \end{pmatrix} \in R^{m \times 6}$$

where $U \in R^{m \times m}$ and $V \in R^{6 \times 6}$ are orthogonal matrices and σ_i satisfies $\sigma_1 \geq \sigma_2 \geq \dots \geq \sigma_6 > 0$. For $m = 6$, $\bar{f}$ is computed from measured $\bar{\epsilon}$ by

$$\bar{f} = \bar{C}^{-1} \bar{\epsilon} \tag{6}$$

Uchiyama and Hakomori [1985 (b)] showed that if computation error $\Delta \bar{f}$ included in $\bar{f}$ is caused only by measurement error $\Delta \bar{\epsilon}$ contained in $\bar{\epsilon}$, $\Delta \bar{\epsilon}$ and $\Delta \bar{f}$ satisfy the following equation:

$$(cond \, \bar{C})^{-1} \leq \frac{\|\Delta \bar{f}\|/\|\bar{f}\|}{\|\Delta \bar{\epsilon}\|/\|\bar{\epsilon}\|} \leq cond \, \bar{C} \tag{7}$$

where $\|\cdot\|$ represents the Euclidean norm and $cond \, \bar{C} = \sigma_1 / \sigma_6$ is called the condition number. The above equation implies that $cond \, \bar{C}$ and $(cond \, \bar{C})^{-1}$ are respectively the maximum and minimum magnification ratios from the relative error of $\bar{\epsilon}$ to the relative error of $\bar{f}$. Based on this result, Uchiyama and Hakomori proposed to use the condition number of the sensor compliance matrix as the index for the structural evaluation of force sensors and made it a goal to design a force sensor with $cond \, \bar{C} = 1$. This evaluation method provided, for the first time, the designers of force sensor who had depended on their intuition and experience with a theoretical principle for force sensor design. However, we have to point out that the structure evaluation by condition number has the following problems:

1) Suppose that two force sensors have sensor compliance matrices $\bar{C}^1$ and $\bar{C}^2$ respectively. If $\bar{C}^1 = \frac{1}{2}\bar{C}^2$ is satisfied, the condition numbers of both force sensors are equal to each other. Although $\bar{C}^2$ seems better than $\bar{C}^1$ from the viewpoint of so called *sensor sensitivity*, condition number cannot evaluate the difference.

2) Assume $\bar{C}^1 = \begin{pmatrix} 1 & 0 \\ 0 & 1 \end{pmatrix}$. Now, we put another strain gage on the same location as ϵ_1. Then, the sensor compliance matrix becomes $\bar{C}^2 = \begin{pmatrix} 1 & 0 \\ 1 & 0 \\ 0 & 1 \end{pmatrix}$. Since the condition numbers become $cond \, \bar{C}^1 = 1$ and $cond \, \bar{C}^2 = \sqrt{2}$, $\bar{C}^1$ will be evaluated better than $\bar{C}^2$. Although $\bar{C}^2$ may have a redundant strain gage, $\bar{C}^2$ seems not to have less sensing performance than $\bar{C}^1$.

3) In case of $m > 6$, eq.(6) can be replaced by

$$\bar{f} = \bar{C}^{\#} \bar{\epsilon} \tag{8}$$

where $\bar{C}^{\#} \in R^{6 \times m}$ is the pseudoinverse of $\bar{C}$. $\bar{f}$ and $\bar{\epsilon}$ satisfy the following relationship:

$$\|\bar{f}\|^2 = \bar{\epsilon}^T (\bar{C}^{\#})^T \bar{C}^{\#} \bar{\epsilon} = \bar{\epsilon}^T U (\Sigma^{\#})^T \Sigma^{\#} U^T \bar{\epsilon} \tag{9}$$

$$\Sigma^{\#} = \begin{pmatrix} 1/\sigma_1 & 0 & \dots & 0 & 0 & \dots & 0 \\ 0 & 1/\sigma_2 & \dots & 0 & 0 & \dots & 0 \\ \vdots & \vdots & \ddots & \vdots & \vdots & \ddots & \vdots \\ 0 & 0 & \dots & 1/\sigma_6 & 0 & \dots & 0 \end{pmatrix} \in R^{6 \times m}$$

which yields the following equation for nonzero $\bar{\epsilon}$:

$$0 \leq \frac{\|\bar{f}\|}{\|\bar{\epsilon}\|} \leq \frac{1}{\sigma_6} \qquad (10)$$

The same relationship can be obtained for $\Delta\bar{f}$ and nonzero $\Delta\bar{\epsilon}$.

$$0 \leq \frac{\|\Delta\bar{f}\|}{\|\Delta\bar{\epsilon}\|} \leq \frac{1}{\sigma_6} \qquad (11)$$

From eqs.(10) and (11) the relationship between the relative errors is represented as follows:

$$0 \leq \frac{\|\Delta\bar{f}\|/\|\bar{f}\|}{\|\Delta\bar{\epsilon}\|/\|\bar{\epsilon}\|} < \infty \qquad (12)$$

Therefore, the condition number offers nothing about the relative errors.

4) If $m > 6$ and $rank\,\bar{C} = rank\,[\bar{C},\ \bar{\epsilon}]$ are fulfilled, the inverse transformation of eq.(4) is given not only by eq.(8), but more generally by the following equation:

$$\bar{f} = \bar{C}^-\bar{\epsilon} \qquad (13)$$

where $\bar{C}^- \in R^{6\times m}$ is the generalized inverse matrix of $\bar{C}$. In case of $rank\,\bar{C} = 6$, $\bar{C}^-$ becomes the reflective generalized inverse matrix and $rank\,\bar{C}^- = 6$ [Kodama, 1981]. $\bar{C}^-$ is not unique like $\bar{C}^\#$, but its general form is represented as follows [Kodama, 1981]:

$$\bar{C}^- = \bar{C}^\# + (Z - \bar{C}^\#\bar{C}Z\bar{C}\bar{C}^\#) \qquad (14)$$

where $Z \in R^{6\times m}$ is an arbitrary matrix. The condition number does not give any suggestion about the variety of the inverse transformation.

In the following section, taking the above problems into consideration, we propose a new structure evaluation method based on three principles, that is, the strain gage sensitivity, the force sensitivity and the minimum stiffness.

3. STRUCTURE EVALUATION OF ELASTIC COMPONENT

3.1 Strain Gage Sensitivity

First, we assume that the specification of measurement range is given as follows:

$$\|\bar{f}\| \leq 1 \qquad (15)$$

Then, $\bar{\epsilon}_i$ satisfies the following inequality:

$$|\bar{\epsilon}_i| \leq \|\bar{C}_i\| \qquad (16)$$

where $\bar{C}_i$ means the i-th row vector of $\bar{C}$. Therefore, in order that $|\epsilon_i|$ does not exceed ϵ_{max}, the following equation should be fulfilled:

$$\|\bar{C}_i\| \leq 1 \qquad (17)$$

Since $\|\bar{C}_i\|$ can be considered as the maximum sensitivity of the i-th strain gage for all of $\bar{f}$ that satisfy eq.(15), we call $\|\bar{C}_i\|$ the *strain gage sensitivity*. To increase S/N ratio of sensor signals, it is desirable to design the elastic component so that it will give large

output signals. Consequently, it is the first design principle to bring the strain gage sensitivity to one as long as it satisfies eq.(17).

3.2 Force Sensitivity

When all the forces that satisfy $\|\bar{f}\| = 1$ are applied, minimum singular value σ_6 represents from eqs.(4) and (5) the minimum magnitude of $\bar{\epsilon}$. Accordingly, in the conservative sense, we call minimum singular value σ_6 *the force sensitivity*. Since it is desirable that a force sensor can generate enough output signals in all directions, it is the second design principle to make the force sensitivity as large as possible.

Now, we investigate the relationship of the force sensitivity with the strain gage sensitivity. From eq.(5), the following equation is derived:

$$\begin{aligned} trace\,\bar{C}\bar{C}^T &= trace\,U\Sigma\Sigma^T U^T \\ &= trace\,\Sigma\Sigma^T U^T U \\ &= \sum_{i=1}^{6}\sigma_i^2 \end{aligned} \qquad (18)$$

On the other hand, the following equation also holds:

$$trace\,\bar{C}\bar{C}^T = \sum_{i=1}^{m}\|\bar{C}_i\|^2 \qquad (19)$$

From eqs.(18) and (19), the strain gage sensitivity and the singular values satisfy the following relationship:

$$\sum_{i=1}^{6}\sigma_i^2 = \sum_{i=1}^{m}\|\bar{C}_i\|^2 \qquad (20)$$

Therefore, when the strain gage sensitivities are fixed, the force sensitivity takes the following maximum value at $\sigma_1 = \sigma_2 = \ldots = \sigma_6$:

$$\sigma_{6\,max} = \sqrt{\frac{1}{6}\sum_{i=1}^{m}\|\bar{C}_i\|^2} \qquad (21)$$

In this case, if the strain gage sensitivities are optimized, that is, $\|\bar{C}_i\| = 1\ (i = 1,\ldots,m)$, the potential maximum value of force sensitivity becomes

$$\sigma_{6\,max} = \sqrt{\frac{m}{6}} \qquad (22)$$

This is the theoretical maximum value of force sensitivity.

Next, we consider the relationship of the force sensitivity with the magnification of measurement error. We assume the inverse transformation by the generalized inverse matrix of sensor compliance matrix as shown in eq.(13). Suppose that the strain gage signal is represented as the sum of true value $\bar{\epsilon}$ and measurement error $\Delta\bar{\epsilon}$. Then, the force information is computed as the sum of true value $\bar{f}$ and error $\Delta\bar{f}$.

$$\bar{f} + \Delta\bar{f} = \bar{C}^-(\bar{\epsilon} + \Delta\bar{\epsilon}) \qquad (23)$$

Subtracting eq.(13) from eq.(23), the following equation is obtained:

$$\Delta\bar{f} = \bar{C}^-\Delta\bar{\epsilon} \qquad (24)$$

Representing an arbitrary matrix by $Z = V(Z_1\ Z_2)U^T$, $Z_1 \in R^{6\times 6}$, $Z_2 \in R^{6\times(m-6)}$ and substituting eqs.(5) and the arbitrary matrix into eq.(14), the following equation is obtained:

$$\bar{C}^- = V\Sigma^- U^T \qquad (25)$$

$$\Sigma^- = \begin{pmatrix} 1/\sigma_1 & \cdots & 0 \\ \vdots & \ddots & \vdots & Z_2 \\ 0 & \cdots & 1/\sigma_6 \end{pmatrix} \in R^{6 \times m}$$

If the magnification ratio of measurement error is defined for nonzero $\Delta\bar{\epsilon}$ by

$$\alpha = max \frac{\|\Delta\bar{f}\|}{\|\Delta\bar{\epsilon}\|}, \qquad (26)$$

then it is observed from eqs.(13), (14) and (25) that α depends on Z_2 and becomes equal to $1/\sigma_6$ in case of $Z_2 = 0$, that is, $\bar{C}^- = \bar{C}^\#$, but α never becomes smaller than $1/\sigma_6$. In other words, the measurement error magnification ratio of inverse transformation by the pseudoinverse means the lower limit of the measurement error magnification ratio by the generalized inverse matrix, and it becomes equal to the reciprocal of the force sensitivity.

3.3 Minimum Stiffness

The measurement principle of force sensor is to measure the strain produced in the elastic component and compute the applied force and moment from it. Since the low stiffness of elastic component generally means the high force sensitivity, the elastic component is apt to be with low stiffness. However, low stiffness of force sensor makes the total stiffness of robotic mechanisms low. Therefore, it is one of the important points in elastic component design to answer such a contradictory requirement that both of the force sensitivity and the mechanical stiffness should be maximized simultaneously. In this subsection, a computational method of mechanical stiffness of force sensor is proposed to enable the stiffness evaluation at design stage. As shown in Fig.2, we assume that the elastic component is approximated by a curve which passes through the center of elastic component *(the axis of elastic component)* and all the stress is caused only by bending moment along the axes perpendicular to the axis of elastic component *(the axes of elastic strain)*. The axis of elastic component is chosen as x-axis and a vector from the point where forces are exerted to x is represented by r_x. If we represent by $e_x \in R^3$ a unit vector in the direction of the axis of elastic strain, the bending moment at x is calculated by

$$M_x = e_x^T(N_s - r_x \times F_s) \qquad (27)$$

The elastic strain energy of the whole elastic component is computed by the following equation [Timoshenko, 1965]:

$$U = \int_x \frac{M_x^2}{2EI_x} dx \qquad (28)$$

where E means the modulus of elasticity of the material and I_x is the second moment of area at x. Substituting eq.(27) into (28), the following equation is obtained:

$$U = \frac{1}{2}f^T G f \qquad (29)$$

$$G = \int_x \frac{1}{EI_x} h_x h_x^T dt$$

$$h_x = \begin{pmatrix} -R_x^T e_x \\ e_x \end{pmatrix}$$

$$R_x = \begin{pmatrix} 0 & -r_{x3} & r_{x2} \\ r_{x3} & 0 & -r_{x1} \\ -r_{x2} & r_{x1} & 0 \end{pmatrix}$$

$$r_x = \begin{pmatrix} r_{x1} & r_{x2} & r_{x3} \end{pmatrix}^T$$

Displacement u at the point where $f = (F_s^T \ N_s^T)^T$ is applied is calculated based on *Castigliano's theorem* [Timoshenko, 1965] as follows:

$$u = \left(\frac{\partial U}{\partial f}\right)^T = Gf \qquad (30)$$

Equation (30) is normalized as follows:

$$\bar{u} = \bar{G}\bar{f} \qquad (31)$$

$$\bar{u} = \frac{1}{N_{max}}Hu$$

$$\bar{G} = \frac{1}{N_{max}}H^T GH$$

$\bar{G}$ implies the normalized compliance matrix at the point where the force is applied. If we represent the singular values of $\bar{G}$ by $\sigma_{G1} \geq \sigma_{G2} \geq \ldots \geq \sigma_{G6} > 0$, $1/\sigma_{G6}$ means the stiffness in the stiffest direction and $1/\sigma_{G1}$ implies the stiffness in the most compliant direction. Therefore, we call $1/\sigma_{G6}$ *the maximum stiffness* and $1/\sigma_{G1}$ *the minimum stiffness*. Consequently, to keep the minimum stiffness large is the third design principle.

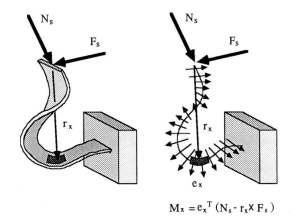

$$M_x = e_x^T (N_s - r_x \times F_s)$$

Fig. 2   Computation of Elastic Strain Energy

4. INVERSE TRANSFORMATION BY WHEATSTONE BRIDGE

The theoretical minimum number of strain gages to measure six elements of force and moment is six. However, it is practically usual to put more than six strain gages as Sheinman put sixteen strain gages on all the surfaces of four prisms which make a cross-shaped force sensor [Ono, 1985 (a)]. This is because of (1) thermal compensation effect, (2) reducing the effect of strain gage location error, and (3) simplifying the inverse transformation. On the other hand, Ono et al.[Ono, 1985 (a), (b)] designed the structure of elastic component so that the sensor compliance matrix becomes a diagonal matrix. In this section, using the fact that the generalized inverse matrix allows a variety of inverse transformation in the case of $m > 6$ as shown in eqs.(13) and (14), we propose to design an elastic component and determine the strain gage location so that Wheatstone bridges work as a part of the analog inverse transformation circuit. Figure 3 shows the schematic drawing of Wheatstone bridge. The equilibrium condition of Wheatstone bridge to give $V = 0$ is described by [Smith, 1976]

$$\frac{r_2}{r_1} = \frac{r_3}{r_4} \tag{32}$$

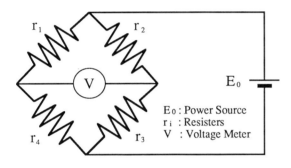

Fig. 3   Wheatstone Bridge

Now, we put strain gages for all of $r_1, \ldots, r_4$ and assume that resistance change is proportional to strain. Then we have the following equation:

$$V = k \left(\epsilon_{r1} - \epsilon_{r2} + \epsilon_{r3} - \epsilon_{r4} \right) \tag{34}$$

If the initial resistance values are $r_1 = r_2 = r_3 = r_4$ and each resistance value changes from r_i to $r_i + \Delta r_i$, the bridge output becomes [Shiota, 1983]

$$V \propto \Delta r_1 - \Delta r_2 + \Delta r_3 - \Delta r_4 \tag{33}$$

where k is a constant and ϵ_{ri} means the strain which corresponds to Δr_i. When twenty four strain gages and six Wheatstone bridges are used, transfer function $B \in R^{6 \times 24}$ of the circuit becomes

$$B = k \begin{pmatrix} 1 & -1 & 1 & -1 & 0 & 0 & 0 & 0 & \ldots & 0 & 0 & 0 & 0 \\ 0 & 0 & 0 & 0 & 1 & -1 & 1 & -1 & \ldots & 0 & 0 & 0 & 0 \\ 0 & 0 & 0 & 0 & 0 & 0 & 0 & 0 & \ldots & 0 & 0 & 0 & 0 \\ 0 & 0 & 0 & 0 & 0 & 0 & 0 & 0 & \ldots & 0 & 0 & 0 & 0 \\ 0 & 0 & 0 & 0 & 0 & 0 & 0 & 0 & \ldots & 0 & 0 & 0 & 0 \\ 0 & 0 & 0 & 0 & 0 & 0 & 0 & 0 & \ldots & 1 & -1 & 1 & -1 \end{pmatrix} \tag{35}$$

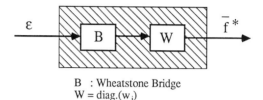

B : Wheatstone Bridge
W = diag.(w_i)

Fig. 4   Analog Inverse Circuit

Figure 4 shows the block diagram of the circuit including six Wheatstone bridges and corresponding gain adjustment amplifiers w_i ($i = 1, \ldots, 6$). If $\bar{C}$ is designed so that the transfer function of the circuit could satisfy the following equation by adjustment of gain matrix $W = diag.(w_i) \in R^{6 \times 6}$:

$$WB = \frac{1}{\epsilon_{max}} \bar{C}^-, \tag{36}$$

then output $\bar{f}^*$ of the circuit becomes equal to $\bar{f}$. It is difficult to give the general structure of elastic component that meets eq.(36). However, it is comparatively easy to make $\bar{C}$ satisfy eq.(36) by designing a symmetric structure and adjusting strain gage location. In the next section, an example of such structure is to be shown. Note that symmetric structure of elastic component simplifies analysis and is useful to evaluate the strain gage sensitivity, the force sensitivity and the minimum stiffness analytically. A drawback of this method is the fact that however faithfully $\bar{C}$ may fulfill eq.(36) in theoretical analysis, it is practically difficult for $\bar{C}$ to satisfy eq.(36) because of the machining error, the strain gage location error and the effect of neglected strain which cannot be considered in theoretical analysis. Therefore, this method may inherently contain some measurement error. In spite of this drawback, since the inverse transformation can be done by analog circuit, this method will be effective specially in the case where force feed back control must be done by high sampling frequency.

5. A DESIGN EXAMPLE OF FORCE SENSOR

Figure 5 shows an example of designed elastic component. Design specification was $F_{max} = 10\,N$ and $N_{max} = 100\,Nmm$. Steel was chosen as elastic material. Considering safety coefficient 3, the proportional limit was determined as $\epsilon_{max} = 0.02\%$, since the proportional limit of steel is 0.12% and the maximum strain at the part where strain gages are not fixed is approximately twice as large as the maximum strain at the part where strain gages are fixed. The sensor compliance matrix was analytically calculated and became as follows:

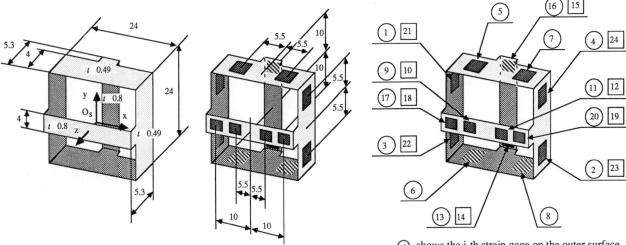

(a) Designed Elastic Component   (b) Strain Gage Location   (c) Strain Gage Numbers

Fig. 5   Designed Six-Axis Force Sensor

$$\bar{C} = \begin{pmatrix}
-a_1 & -a_2 & 0 & 0 & 0 & -a_3 \\
a_1 & a_2 & 0 & 0 & 0 & -a_3 \\
-a_1 & a_2 & 0 & 0 & 0 & a_3 \\
a_1 & -a_2 & 0 & 0 & 0 & a_3 \\
a_4 & a_5 & 0 & 0 & 0 & a_6 \\
a_4 & -a_5 & 0 & 0 & 0 & -a_6 \\
-a_4 & a_5 & 0 & 0 & 0 & -a_6 \\
-a_4 & -a_5 & 0 & 0 & 0 & a_6 \\
0 & 0 & a_7 & 0 & -a_8 & 0 \\
0 & 0 & -a_7 & 0 & a_8 & 0 \\
0 & 0 & a_7 & 0 & a_8 & 0 \\
0 & 0 & -a_7 & 0 & -a_8 & 0 \\
0 & 0 & a_9 & -a_{10} & 0 & 0 \\
0 & 0 & -a_9 & a_{10} & 0 & 0 \\
0 & 0 & -a_9 & -a_{10} & 0 & 0 \\
0 & 0 & a_9 & a_{10} & 0 & 0 \\
0 & 0 & a_{11} & 0 & -a_{12} & 0 \\
0 & 0 & -a_{11} & 0 & a_{12} & 0 \\
0 & 0 & -a_{11} & 0 & -a_{12} & 0 \\
0 & 0 & a_{11} & 0 & a_{12} & 0 \\
-a_{13} & -a_{14} & 0 & 0 & 0 & -a_{15} \\
-a_{13} & a_{14} & 0 & 0 & 0 & a_{15} \\
a_{13} & a_{14} & 0 & 0 & 0 & -a_{15} \\
a_{13} & -a_{14} & 0 & 0 & 0 & a_{15}
\end{pmatrix} \qquad (37)$$

$$a_1 = 0.930 \qquad a_2 = -0.0372 \qquad a_3 = 0.391$$
$$a_4 = 0.0372 \qquad a_5 = 0.930 \qquad a_6 = -0.391$$
$$a_7 = 0.419 \qquad a_8 = -0.917 \qquad a_9 = -0.837$$
$$a_{10} = -0.614 \qquad a_{11} = -0.837 \qquad a_{12} = 0.614$$
$$a_{13} = -0.930 \qquad a_{14} = 0.0372 \qquad a_{15} = -0.391$$

where $E = 2.1 \times 10^5 \, N/mm^2$ was used as the modulus of elasticity of steel. Accordingly, the strain gage sensitivities were calculated as follows:

$$\|\bar{C}_i\| = \begin{cases} 1.01 & (i = 1, \dots, 12, 21, 22, 23, 24) \\ 1.04 & (i = 13, \dots, 20) \end{cases} \qquad (38)$$

The singular values of $\bar{C}$ were obtained as follows:

$$col.(\sigma_i) = (2.63 \ 2.51 \ 2.21 \ 1.86 \ 1.35 \ 1.23)^T \qquad (39)$$

Therefore, the force sensitivity was 1.23. Incidentally, the condition number was 2.14. Compliance matrix $\bar{G}$ was also analytically computed and obtained as follows:

$$\bar{G} = 10^{-4} diag.(2.02, 2.02, 1.16, 1.01, 1.01, 0.686) \qquad (40)$$

The maximum stiffness and the minimum stiffness became 1.46×10^4 and 4.95×10^3 respectively. The value of the minimum stiffness means that if $F_{max} = 10N$ is applied in the weakest direction, it will produce $2.02 \times 10^{-3} mm$ of displacement, which seems a fairly high stiffness. On the other hand, gain matrix W of the inverse transformation circuit using Wheatstone bridges was obtained as follows:

$$W = \frac{1}{k \, \epsilon_{max}} diag.(-0.269, 0.269, 0.597, 0.406, -0.406, 0.640) \qquad (41)$$

and the singular values of generalized inverse matrix $\bar{C}^-$ became

$$col.(\sigma_i^-) = (1.28 \ 1.20 \ 0.811 \ 0.811 \ 0.538 \ 0.538)^T \qquad (42)$$

where the maximum singular value was 1.28 and the condition number was 2.38. Although these values are a little greater than maximum singular value $1/\sigma_6 = 0.813$ and condition number 2.14 of pseudoinverse $\bar{C}^\#$, the measurement error magnification by these values is not serious and, therefore, Wheatstone bridges and the gain matrix W could be acceptable for the analog inverse transformation circuit for the force sensor.

6. CONCLUDING REMARKS

The design of elastic component of force sensor can be done based on the following three evaluation principles:

1) *the strain gage sensitivity*: $\|\bar{C}_i\|$ is called the strain gage sensitivity. $\|\bar{C}_i\| \leq 1$ gives a condition so that the material does not make any plastic deformation. It is a design principle to bring the strain gage sensitivity to one as close as possible.

2) *the force sensitivity*: The minimum singular value of $\bar{C}$ is called the force sensitivity. It is a design principle to make the force sensitivity as large as possible because it guarantees that a force sensor can generate enough output signals in all force directions. When the strain gage sensitivities are optimized, that is, $\|\bar{C}_i\| = 1$ $(i = 1, \ldots, m)$, the potential maximum value of force sensitivity becomes equal to $\sqrt{m/6}$, which means the theoretical maximum value of the force sensitivity. Since the measurement error magnification ratio of inverse transformation by the pseudoinverse becomes equal to the reciprocal of the force sensitivity and it means the lower limit of the measurement error magnification ratio by the generalized inverse matrix, high force sensitivity is effective for reducing the measurement error magnification.

3) *the minimum stiffness*: The compliance matrix at the point where forces are applied is obtained based on *Castigliano's theorem*. The reciprocal of the maximum singular value of the compliance matrix is called the minimum stiffness, which implies the stiffness in the most compliant direction. It is a design principle to keep the minimum stiffness large.

There is a large number of degrees of freedom in the design of elastic component of force sensor. The above principles are not enough to identify a unique structure of the elastic component. We have to also consider practical requirements such as the light weight of elastic component, the compact shape which is fit for packaging, the simple structure which makes easy to machine elastic components and put strain gages, and so on. However, we are convinced that the above three design principles will show a clear design direction to the designers of the elastic components of force sensors. We showed a fact that there is variety in inverse transformation of force signals in the case where the number of strain gages is larger than six and proposed to design an elastic component and determine the strain gage location so that Wheatstone bridges work as a part of the analog inverse transformation circuit. Since the inverse transformation can be done by analog circuit, this method will be effective specially in the case where force feed back control must be done by high sampling frequency. An example of six-axis force sensor design was shown to illustrate the design procedure based on the proposed design principles and inverse transformation method. In the example, the strain gage sensitivity, the force sensitivity and the minimum stiffness were analytically computed by making several assumptions. Finite element method will enable more accurate evaluation of these three values and make it possible to realize an interactive CAD system for designing force sensors.

ACKNOWLEDGEMENT

We express our sincere gratitude to Dr. Susan Hackwood and Dr. Gerardo Beni for their encouragement and support of this work at the Center for Robotic Systems in Microelectronics, University of California Santa Barbara. This work was partially supported by the National Science Foundation under contract number 8421415. However, any opinions, findings, conclusions, or recommendations expressed in this paper are those of the authors and do not reflect the views of the foundation.

BIBLIOGRAPHY

Arai, H. and Tachi, S., "Operational Force Measurement and Active Force Assistance in Human Operation of Direct Drive Manipulators," Journal of Japan Robotics Society, Vol.4-3, pp.209-219, 1986 *(in Japanese)*

Asakawa, K., "Realization of Highly Accurate Tasks by Sensor Feedback," Journal of Precision Engineering, Vol.51-11, pp.2034-2039, 1985 *(in Japanese)*

De Fazio, T.L., Seltzer, D.S. and Whitney, D.E., "The IRCC Instrumented Remote Center Compliance," *Robot Sensors*, Vol.2, ed. Alan Pugh, IFS Ltd., Bedford, UK, pp.33-44, 1986

Flatau, C.R., "Force Sensing in Robots and Manipulators," Proc. 2nd International CISM-IFToMM Symposium on the Theory and Practice of Robots and Manipulators, pp.294-306, Warsaw, 1976

Goto, T., Inoyama, T. and Takeyasu, K., " Precise Insert Operation by Tactile-Controlled Robot," *Robot Sensors* , Vol.2, ed. Alan Pugh, IFS Ltd., Bedford, UK, pp.45-52, 1986

Hatamura, Y., " Force Torque Sensor, " Journal of Japan Society of Mechanical Engineers, Vol.89-814, pp.1055-1058, 1986 *(in Japanese)*

Inoue,H., "Computer Controlled Bilateral Manipulator," Bulletin of Japan Society of Mechanical Engineers, Vol.14-69, pp.199-207, 1971

Iri, M., Kodama, S. and Suda, N., "Singular Value Decomposition and its Application to System Control," Journal of Society of Instrument and Control Engineers, Vol.16, pp.391-397, 1982 *(in Japanese)*

Kasai, M. et al., "Trainable Assembly System with an Active Sensory Table Possessing 6 Axes," Proc. 11th International Symposium of Industrial Robots, pp.393-404, 1981

Kinoshita, G., "A Survey of Tactile Sensor Development," Journal of Japan Robotics Society, Vol.2-5, pp.430-437, 1984 *(in Japanese)*

Kodama, S. and Suda, N., *Matrix Theory for System Control*, Society of Instrument and Control Engineers, Tokyo, 1981 *(in Japanese)*

Loewen, E.G., Marshall, E.R. and Shaw, M.C., "Electric Strain Gage Tool Dynamometers," Proc. SESA, Vol.8, No.2, pp.1-16, 1951

LORD Corporation, Force/Torque Wrist Sensing Systems, Technical Note F/T Series 6/85, 1985

Nakano, E., Ozaki, S., Ishida, T. and Kato, I., " Coorperative Control of a pair of Anthropomorphous Manipulators: MELARM," Proc. 4th International Symposium on Industrial Robots, pp.251-260, Tokyo, 1974

Ono, K., Hatamura, Y., Ogata, K., Takada, R. and Kusaki, T., "Development of 6 Axis Force Sensor LSA6000," Proc. 3rd Annual Conference of Japan Robotics Society, pp.19-20, 1985 (a)*(in Japanese)*

Ono, K., "6 Axis Force Sensor for High Performance Robot Manipulators," *Automation*, Vol.30-2, Nikkan Kogyo Shinbunsha Ltd., Tokyo, pp. 48-52, 1985 (b)*(in Japanese)*

Scheinman, V.D., "Design of a Computer Controlled Manipulator," Stanford Artificial Intelligence Project Memo AIM-92, Stanford University, 1969

Shiota, Y. and Taniguchi, Y., *Sensors*, Sangyo Tosyo Ltd., Tokyo, 1983 *(in Japanese)*

Smith, R.J.,*Circuits, Devices, and Systems (the third edition)*, John Wiley & Sons Inc., 1976

Timoshenko, S. and Young, D.H., *Theory of Structures*, McGraw-Hill Book Company, New York, 1965

Uchiyama, M., Yokota, M. and Hakomori, K., "Kalman Filtering the 6-axis Robot Wrist Force Sensor Signal," Proc. '85 International Conference on Advanced Robotics, pp.153-160, Tokyo, 1985 (a)

Uchiyama, M. and Hakomori, K., "A Few Considerations on Structure Design of Force Sensors," Proc. 3rd Annual Conference on Japan Robotics Society, pp.17-18, 1985 (b) *(in Japanese)*

Uchiyama, M., "Robot Sensors," in the Text of Seminar on Fundamental Robotics, Society of Instrument and Control Engineers, pp.89-113, 1986 *(in Japanese)*

Watson, P.C. and Drake, S.H., "Pedestal and Wrist Sensors for Automatic Assembly," Proc. 5th International Symposium of Industrial Robots, pp.501-511, 1975

INTRINSIC TACTILE SENSING FOR ARTIFICIAL HANDS

A. Bicchi[o][^] and P. Dario[o]

[o] Centro "E. Piaggio", Faculty of Engineering, University of Pisa, Italy
[^] Dipartimento di Ingegneria delle Costruzioni, University of Bologna, Italy

In this paper "intrinsic" tactile sensing, i.e. contact sensing based on pure force and torque measurements and geometric calculations, is discussed with reference to the design of sensorized fingertips for artificial hands. Pros and cons of the intrinsic approach are examined, as opposed to "extrinsic" tactile sensing systems, usually consisting of sensitive arrays distributed over the sensor surface. While either sensing method could prove best for specific applications, the integration of the two for a general-purpose artificial fingertip sensor is recommendable. Some general considerations are made about The design of intrinsic tactile sensing systems, and the derived guidelines used for the development of an intrinsic sensor conceived to be a part of a multifunctional sensorized finger. A description of this sensor is provided in the paper along with the experimental evaluation of its performances.

INTRODUCTION

Dexterous manipulation and haptic perception are the fundamental aims of the evolution of present robotic end effectors toward a future artificial hand system, even if the development of end effectors intended for carrying out those two functions has proceeded thus far along almost distinct pathways |Dario 1987|.

The design of an artificial hand system requires substantial progresses in three main areas: actuators for hand motion, sensors of the actual state of the hand-environment system, and AI techniques for managing the perceptual and decisional processes, involved in manipulatory tasks.

In the sensing domain, we can distinguish between proprioceptive sensing (i.e. getting information on the hand itself, such as joint angles or torques) and exteroceptive sensing, which is related to the interactions between the hand and its environment. In the hand (both human and robotic), exteroceptive sensing is essentially distributed force sensing, although other sensing capabilities (such as proximity, temperature, chemical, etc.) could be also implemented.

In this paper we discuss some different aspects of tactile sensing for artificial hands and pursue solutions to the dual requirements of controlling robotic manipulation and perception.

So far, artificial tactile sensing has been investigated mostly through an **"extrinsic"** approach (i.e. by means of pressure sensing arrays distributed over the sensor surface). Harmon |1982| showed as most research efforts have been directed to replicate the sensory properties of the human skin, by spreading sensing sites over the hand surfaces where contacts with the environment are expected to occur ("active surfaces").

On the other hand, "intrinsic" tactile sensing is contact sensing based on pure force and torque measurements and geometric calculations, as proposed first by J.K. Salisbury |1984|. The tactile system developed by Salisbury had no distributed sensing capabilities in the active surface, but rather a force sensing device remote from the contact, and the software means necessary to infer the desired tactile information from force data.

A summary of the possible advantages and drawbacks of tactile sensors of the two classes is proposed in Table 1.

TYPE FEATURES	EXTRINSIC	INTRINSIC
SPATIAL RESOLUTION	INHERENTLY FINITE	THEORETICALLY INFINITE
BANDWIDTH	LIMITED	HIGH
CONTACT FORCE MEASUREMENT	GENERALLY INACCURATE	FAST, LINEAR, NONHYSTERETIC
FRICTIONAL EFFECTS	AT PRESENT, NOT SENSED	MEASURED
SLIPPAGE DETECTION	NONE	POSSIBLE
SENSOR SURFACE SHAPE	FREE	ONLY SIMPLE SHAPES
SENSOR COVER COMPLIANCE	ALLOWED	IT PRODUCES ERRORS
PARATACTILE SENSITIVITY	POSSIBLE	IMPOSSIBLE
ENCUMBRANCE	MANY WIRES	RATHER BULKY, FEW WIRES

TABLE 1

An intrinsic tactile sensor (ITS) is very useful for manipulation control, because it is able to monitor the resultant of contact forces in real time. For this reason, an ITS is suitable for such tasks as object contouring, assembly operations, etc.

ITS handles very well also frictional forces, whose effects it can distinguish and measure. Based on this information, if a proper model of friction between the sensor's active surface and the body is available, an "a priori" strategy can be selected to prevent slippage.

If the contact can be hypothesized as punctual, i.e. if the contacting surfaces are rigid enough and have different spatial curvatures, and if the contact takes place in no more than one point at a time, the ITS can resolve with high (theoretically infinite) spatial resolution the contact point.

Conversely, an extrinsic tactile sensor (ETS) has inherently finite spatial resolution and it is not able, in general, to sense frictional forces, by which it is often even deceived.

An advantage of ETSs is that they are capable of managing contacts, over large areas, which are likely to occur if a very compliant fingertip cover is used to enhance grasp stability. Furthermore, an ETS permits the extraction of "tactile images", which are very useful in order to recognize local features of objects.

A few ETS also incorporate sensing elements capable of detecting some very useful "paratactile" characteristics, such as the thermal properties of the object being touched |Dario et al. 1984||Siegel 1986|.

In this paper some general issues related to the design of an ITS are discussed, and the fabrication and testing of a prototype of such sensor are described some preliminary work aimed at integrating this ITS sensor with the ETSs being developed in our laboratory is also outlined.

GENERAL CONSIDERATIONS ON "INTRINSIC" TACTILE SENSING

Basically, an ITS system consists of three elements: a force sensor, an active surface, and an electronic computing unit.

A force sensor is a device which measures, in a particular coordinate frame, the six components of the generalized (force and torque) force vector which is exerted through the sensor itself. Similar devices have been already studied and applied in robotics, mostly as sensorized pedestals or wrists |Bejczy 1983|.

The active surface of a sensor is the set of points where the contacts with the environment are expected to occur. In an ITS, the active surface is integral with the force sensor, to which the mechanical effects of the contact forces are transmitted.

An accurate geometrical description of the active surface in the force sensor coordinate frame is mandatory.

Although there are infinite load configurations statically equivalent to a given generalized resultant force vector, there is only one such pure force (no torque).

With reference to Figure 1, let $F_1 - F_6$ be the resultant force components which are sensed by the force sensor along its coordinate frame axes X_1, X_2, X_3.

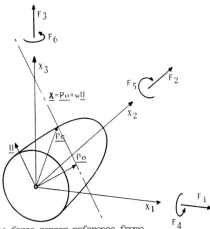

FIG.1. The force sensor reference frame

If a pure force load is assumed (i.e., if punctual contacts transmitting no local torques are hypothesized), then such force must lay on the line |Salisbury 1984|:

$$\underline{X} = \underline{Po} + w \, \underline{U} \qquad \qquad 1)$$

where:

$$\underline{Po} = \left(\frac{F_2 F_6 - F_3 F_5}{|\underline{F}|^2} \; ; \; \frac{F_3 F_4 - F_1 F_6}{|\underline{F}|^2} \; ; \; \frac{F_1 F_5 - F_2 F_4}{|\underline{F}|^2} \right)$$

$$\underline{U} = \frac{1}{|\underline{F}|} (F_1 ; F_2 ; F_3)$$

$$|\underline{F}|^2 = (F_1^2 + F_2^2 + F_3^2)$$

Intersecting this line with the active surface $f(X_1, X_2, X_3) = 0$, so as to obtain the value of w corresponding to the contact point, is the task of the computing unit of an ITS system.

In the particular case of a spherical active surface, having its center in the origin of the force sensor coordinate frame, and radius R, the expression for w is:

$$w = \pm \left(R^2 - \frac{(F_2 F_6 - F_3 F_5)^2 - (F_3 F_4 - F_1 F_6)^2 - (F_1 F_5 - F_2 F_4)^2}{|\underline{F}|^4} \right)^{\frac{1}{2}} \qquad 2)$$

and the contact point $\underline{Pc} = (X_1, X_2, X_3)$ can be calculated from (1). The sign ambiguity in (2) is easily solved, if only compressive forces are assumed on the active surface.

It is apparent that the spatial resolution of an ITS is only theoretically infinite, even in the point-contact hypothesis. In fact, the ultimate resolution is limited by the errors with which the above expressions are calculated. Assuming that the errors made in the determination of the geometric constants of the active surface are small with respect to the inaccuracies in force measurement, the criteria for the error propagation in algebraic calculations give the following upper limit for the error:

$$\frac{|d\underline{F}|}{|\underline{F}|} \le 2 \max \frac{|dFi|}{|Fi|} \; ; \; i=1,3 \; = 2 \, Ef \qquad 3)$$

$$|dX_1| \le \frac{2}{|\underline{F}|^2} \, Ef \; 2(|F_2 F_6| + |F_3 F_5|) + K \, |F_1| \qquad 4)$$

$$|dX_2| \le \frac{2}{|\underline{F}|^2} \, Ef \; 2(|F_3 F_4| + |F_1 F_6|) + K \, |F_2| \qquad 5)$$

$$|dX_3| \leq \frac{2}{|\underline{F}|^2} \; Ef \; 2(|F_1 F_5|+|F_2 F_4|) + K \; |F_3| \qquad \qquad 6)$$

where:

"$|Q|$" is the absolute value of the scalar quantity "Q"

"dQ" indicates the absolute error on the quantity "Q";

$Ef = \max \; \dfrac{|dFi|}{|Fi|}$; $i = 1,6$ is the maximum relative error made by the sensor in the measurement of $F_1 - F_6$;

$$K = \frac{|\underline{F}|^4 R^2 + 2 \; (|F_2 F_6|+|F_3 F_5|)^2 + (|F_3 F_4|+|F_1 F_6|)^2 + (|F_1 F_5|+|F_2 F_4|)^2}{w \; |\underline{F}|}$$

It should be pointed out that the foregoing expressions have been actually evaluated neglecting the errors due to the use of finite precision computing units.

The application of (3)–(6) to the cases of contact with and without friction will help in understanding the entity of such errors:

Case a): Contact without friction ($F_4 = F_5 = F_6 = 0$);

$$|dXi| \leq 2 R \frac{|Fi|}{|\underline{F}|} Ef \; , \quad i = 1,3 \qquad \qquad 7)$$

The maximum error in the localization of the contact point is:

$$|\underline{dP}| \leq (dX_1^2 + dX_2^2 + dX_3^2)^{\frac{1}{2}} = 2 R \; Ef \qquad \qquad 8)$$

For example, with R=10 mm, Ef = 1%, the accuracy is 0.2 mm; the maximum angular error in the determination of the contact force vector ($|\underline{dP}|/R$) is 1 degree.

Case b): Contact with friction.

Let, for example, $F_1 = Fo \cos(q)$, $F_2 = Fo \; sen(q)$, $F_3 = F_4 = F_5 = 0$, $F_6 = R \; Fo \; sen(q)$, where "$tang(q)$" is the Coulomb friction coefficient. Then:

$$|\underline{dP}| \leq 2 R \; Ef \; f(q) \quad \text{where} \quad \begin{array}{l} f(q) = 1.08 \text{ for } tang(q) = 0.1 \\ f(q) = 1.62 \text{ for } tang(q) = 0.3 \\ f(q) = 2.30 \text{ for } tang(q) = 0.5 \end{array} \qquad 9)$$

It appears from these expressions that the precision of an ITS is essentially related to the accuracy of the force sensor (1/Ef). Owing to this fact and to the problems associated with the miniaturization of the sensing device, the development of an ITS system requires extreme attention to the design of the force sensor.

FORCE SENSORS FOR "INTRINSIC" TACTILE SENSING

A force sensor consists of a mechanical structure fixed to a rigid frame at one end, while an external force system is applied to the other end. When the classical linear elasticity hypotheses hold, it is possible to deduce the state of stress, and ultimately the load originating it, from strain measurements.

The state of strain in a point of a mechanical structure is described by 6 components of the strain tensor; in general they are correlated to the stress tensor through relations accounting also for the effects of temperature. However, most available strain transducers measure only one component of the strain tensor along some peculiar direction; moreover, the temperature effects on strain are most often kept under control by means of "dummy" transducers, or even inherently compensated for. Thus, the electrical output Vi of the i-th strain transducer can be written:

$$Vi = Gi \sum_{j=1}^{6} Aij \; Fj = \sum_{j=1}^{6} \left[Gi \; Aij \; |Fj,n| \right] \left[\frac{Fj}{|Fj,n|} \right] = \sum_{j=1}^{6} Cij \; Pj \qquad 10)$$

where Gi is the transducer conversion factor and Aij depend on the geometry and elastic properties of the sensor structure. In order to normalize these equations, in (10) are introduced the "nominal values" Fj,n of the components $F_1 - F_6$, i.e. the maximum values that those quantities are supposed to attain during the task operations |Von Brussel et al. 1985|.

If several such transducers are placed in the mechanical structure of the force sensor, we obtain a linear algebraic system, expressed in matrix notation as:

$$\underline{V} = C \; \underline{P} \qquad \qquad 11)$$

Some methods of linear algebra can be applied to this system in order to study the optimal configurations of a force sensor. In general, at least 6 strain transducers are needed to solve Eq.(13) for the six components of $\underline{P}$, provided that those transducers are placed so that the rows of the C matrix are linearly independent. We say that a force sensor using just 6 transducers has a "minimal" configuration, as opposed to "extended" configurations using more transducers.

The attention of the investigators who dealt with the development of force sensing devices has been focused thus far mostly on "extended" configurations |Bejczy 1983| |Von Brussel et al. 1985| |Brock and Chiu 1985| |Hirzinger 1987|. The requirements in terms of simplicity, low cost and small number of wires, for a force sensor to be incorporated in a robot end effector suggest, instead, to investigate "minimal" force sensor configurations.

According to (13), we might place arbitrarily 6 strain transducers on whatever mechanical structure to build a force sensor (excluding the unlikely case in which the associated matrix "C" is singular). The Cij components of the matrix C may be calculated by means of the elasticity theory relations in any but the simplest cases. However, it is possible to evaluate those components with an accurate calibration of the sensor, consisting in the application of well known loads and in the measurement of the responses of each basic transducer to each component of $\underline{P}$.

Once the matrix C associated with the sensor is known, an algorithm can be written to solve for $\underline{P}$ any $\underline{V}$ measurement: Gaussian elimination is generally the preferable method |Wilkinson 1965|.

Any configuration of 6 basic transducers will be then equally suitable for a force sensor? The answer is no, of course. Optimization criteria for the disposition of the 6 basic transducers are provided by the analysis of the force sensor accuracy. Both $\underline{V}$ and C are not known with absolute precision. Measuring transducer signals generally implies electrical noise and analog-to-digital conversion inaccuracies: a relative error is defined as the ratio of the norm of the error vector $\underline{dV}$ to the norm of the measurements vector $\underline{V}$:

$\|d\underline{V}\|/\|\underline{V}\|$ (the Euclidean norm, indifferent to reference changes, is the preferable choice in this case). Also the calibration operations, notwithstanding the care one can pay, introduce some errors in estimated C_{ij}. A relative error on C is defined as $\|dC\|/\|C\|$, where the definition of spectral norm is assumed. From the theory of linear systems solution |Wilkinson 1965|, we observe that these errors "propagate" through the algorithms to the solution $\underline{P}$, being amplified by the "condition number" N_c of the C matrix:

$$\frac{\|d\underline{P}\|}{\|\underline{P}\|} \le \left(\frac{\|d\underline{V}\|}{\|\underline{V}\|} + \frac{\|dC\|}{\|C\|}\right) \frac{N_c}{1-N_c \|dC\|/\|C\|} \qquad 14)$$

where: $N_c = \|C\|\,\|C^{-1}\|$

The condition number of a matrix is always greater than, or equal to, 1; the latter case occurs only when the matrix has orthogonal columns. A well conditioned sensor, having small N_c, will not magnify the errors intrinsic to its fabrication. It should be noted that, while decreasing $\|d\underline{V}\|/\|\underline{V}\|$ and $\|dC\|/\|C\|$ is a matter of instrumentation quality (thus, ultimately, of mere cost), N_c depends only on the quality of the sensor design. Small N_c guarantee also other good qualities to the sensor, such as uniform accuracy over the whole allowed range of contact points and contact force intensities. Hence, the number $1/N_c$ can be assumed as a figure of merit for different configurations of basic transducers in a force sensor.

It should be noted that increasing the basic sensitivity of transducers to strain by a constant factor (for instance, by using solid state, instead of foil, strain gauges) would not affect sensor accuracy (as N_c remains unchanged), but only the measurement range, allowing smaller forces to be sensed.

Unfortunately, the condition number of a matrix is, in general, a very involved function of matrix entries. Thus, the optimization of the sensor design is not achievable in close form. Only in particular cases we get some intelligible hints; for instance, if C is diagonal:

$$N_c(C) = \|C\|\,\|C^{-1}\| = \frac{max(C_{ii},\ i=1,6)}{min(C_{ii},\ i=1,6)} \qquad 15)$$

Given a minimum C_{ii} (the sensitivity to the force vector component P_i), there is no advantage in having better sensitivities to other components, as this would make accuracy even worse. The equalization of sensitivities is then strongly recommendable, confirming the intuitive guess.

Even in the general case, however, a numerical evaluation of N_c for a certain number of configurations varying about a reference design can help in understanding the roles played by some design parameters. An example of the application of this approach is given in the next paragraph.

DESIGN OF AN ITS FOR ARTIFICIAL FINGERTIPS.

The concept of a fingertip ITS has been recently implemented by Brock and Chiu (1985), who designed a sensor incorporating 16 very sensitive (but costly and fragile) semiconductor strain gauges.

As anticipated in the introduction, our goal in studying IT sensing was the design and realization of a precise, reliable, cost effective device to be integrated in a thoroughly sensorized, real size fingertip for artificial hands. We tried to fulfill the specifications for this application (miniaturization, robustness, low number of connecting cables, in addition to precision and time response) emphasizing sensor simplicity.

We elected to employ strain gauges as "basic" strain transducers in our prototype sensor, since this technique has proved reliable, accurate and economical in innumerable applications. A thin walled cylindrical cantilever beam was chosen as the mechanical structure of the force sensor. The sensor structure is depicted in Figure 2, along with the associated coordinate frame X_1, X_2, X_3.

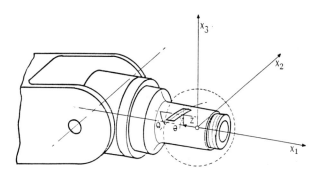

FIG. 2. The mechanical structure of the force sensor. The dashed line sketches the active surface.

In order to realize a "minimal" force sensor, six gages are to be bonded to the beam surface: their position will be uniquely determined by the cylindrical coordinates Z, θ of the strain gauge center, and by the angle Q the gage axis forms with the X axis.

By measuring the unbalancement of a Wheatstone bridge having the i-th gauge as a leg, a signal V_i given by (12) will be obtained:

$$V_i = \sum_{J=1}^{6} C_{ij} P_j = G \sum_{J=1}^{6} A_{ij}\, |F_j, n| \frac{F_j}{|F_j, n|} \qquad 12')$$

where G is a constant depending upon the gage factor, the excitation voltage and the bridge amplifier gain (which can be reasonably assumed the same for each gage).

Assuming the hypotheses currently adopted in the theory of elasticity in order to describe the strains in a cylindric cantilever beam loaded with normal and shear forces, and with torsional and bending torques, the i-th row of the C matrix can be written as:

$$
\begin{aligned}
C_{i1} &= G\,|F_1, n|\ [\cos^2(Q_i) - \mu \sin^2(Q_i)]\ W_n \\
C_{i2} &= G\,|F_2, n|\ \{Z_i\,[\cos^2(Q_i) - \mu \sin^2(Q_i)]\cos(\theta_i)\,W_f + \\
        &\qquad + \sin(2\,Q_i)\sin(\theta_i)\,W_s\} \\
C_{i3} &= G\,|F_3, n|\ \{Z_i\,[\cos^2(Q_i) - \mu \sin^2(Q_i)]\sin(\theta_i)\,W_f + \\
        &\qquad + \sin(2\,Q_i)\cos(\theta_i)\,W_s\} \\
C_{i4} &= G\,|F_4, n|\ \sin(2\,Q_i)\,W_t \qquad\qquad\qquad\qquad 16) \\
C_{i5} &= G\,|F_5, n|\ [\cos^2(Q_i) - \mu \sin^2(Q_i)]\cos(\theta_i)\,W_f \\
C_{i6} &= G\,|F_6, n|\ [\cos^2(Q_i) - \mu \sin^2(Q_i)]\sin(\theta_i)\,W_f
\end{aligned}
$$

where "μ" is the Poisson coefficient of the beam material, and Wn, Wf, Ws, Wt are constants depending on the elastic properties of the material and on the geometry of the beam section:

$$Wn = \frac{1}{2\,E\,\pi\,R\,s} \quad ; \quad Wf = 2\,Wn/R; \qquad (17)$$

$$Ws = 2\,(1+\mu)\,Wn \quad ; \quad Wt = (1+u)\,Wn/R$$

where E is the material Young's modulus, R is the cylinder radius and s the cylinder wall thickness.

The condition number associated with this sensor is a complicated function of the nineteen parameters at designer's disposal ($Qi, \theta i, Zi$ (i=1,6) and R). This function is by far too complex to be minimized symbolically, although this procedure would have led to the absolute "optimal" sensor in this class.

Thus, we followed a semiheuristic procedure: a basic configuration was chosen "intuitively", and only three parameters Q, d and R, described in Figure 3, were left for optimization.

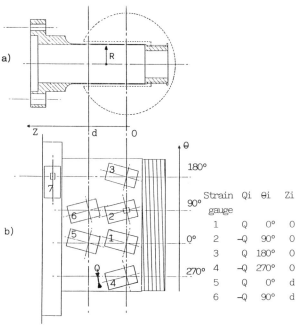

FIG. 3 Cross section a) and plane development b) of the force sensor

Substituting these values in (14), we obtain the C matrix for our sensor:

$$C = \begin{bmatrix} C_1 & 0 & C_3 & -C_4 & 0 & C_6 \\ C_1 & -C_2 & 0 & C_4 & C_5 & 0 \\ C_1 & 0 & -C_3 & -C_4 & 0 & -C_6 \\ C_1 & C_2 & 0 & C_4 & -C_5 & 0 \\ C_1 & C_7 & C_3 & -C_4 & 0 & C_6 \\ C_1 & -C_2 & -C_8 & C_4 & C_5 & 0 \end{bmatrix} \qquad (18)$$

where:

$C_1 = G\,|F_1,n|\,[\cos^2(Q) - \mu \sin^2(Q)]\,Wn$

$C_2 = G\,|F_2,n|\,\sin(2\,Q)\,Ws$

$C_3 = G\,|F_3,n|\,\sin(2\,Q)\,Ws$

$C_4 = G\,|F_4,n|\,\sin(2\,Q)\,Wt$

$C_5 = G\,|F_5,n|\,[\cos^2(Q) - \mu \sin^2(Q)]\,Wf$

$C_6 = G\,|F_6,n|\,[\cos^2(Q) - \mu \sin^2(Q)]\,Wf$

$C_7 = G\,|F_2,n|\,[\cos^2(Q) - \mu \sin^2(Q)]\,Wf\,d$

$C_8 = G\,|F_3,n|\,[\cos^2(Q) - \mu \sin^2(Q)]\,Wf\,d$

Moving through the space of the parameters Q, d and R, the figure of merit Nc(C) varies unpredictably. However, Nc (C) is likely to have several local minima, while it certainly tends to infinite as C approaches singularities. Notwithstanding that ideal configurations (Nc=1) might well not exist, placing Nc(C) in one of the lowest "hollows" of its locus can be assumed as a design target.

A computer program which, given a set of initial parameters, moves in the parameter space and "tumbles down" into the hollows it encounters, has been purposely written. The flow chart of this optimization program is sketched in Figure 4.

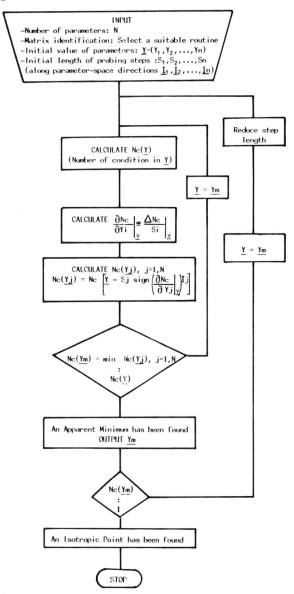

FIG. 4. A simplified flow-chart of the design optimization program

The program, suitable for general matrices with any number of parameters, adapts automatically the probing step length, and it stops in the points where the Nc value of the point itself and the NC's of neighbouring points differ less than an adjustable threshold value.

By applying this program to the matrix (18), some different local minima (obtained by varying the starting points) have been found. The parameters corresponding to these local minima are reported below.

	LOCAL MINIMA			ACTUAL DIMENSIONS
R	4.1	6.6	7.2	5.0
Q	11.5°	19.5°	20.0°	14.0°
d	9.7	13.5	14.6	10.0
Nc	4.9	3.7	3.6	4.2

While the best choice for Q, d and R would have been the third column (Nc = 3.6), we traded off a little accuracy in order to comply with practical fabrication constraints. Thus, we chose the design parameters R=5mm, d=11mm, Q=14° corresponding to Nc=4.2

Actually, the basic configuration illustrated in Figure 4 has not been chosen only for reducing the dimensionality of the design problem. In fact, by premultiplying both terms of the equation describing the sensor, $\underline{V} = C\underline{P}$ by the matrix M:

$$M = \begin{bmatrix} 1 & 1 & 1 & 1 & 0 & 0 \\ -1 & 0 & 0 & 0 & 1 & 0 \\ 0 & 1 & 0 & 0 & 0 & -1 \\ -1 & 1 & -1 & 1 & 0 & 0 \\ 1 & 0 & -1 & 0 & 0 & 0 \\ 0 & 1 & 0 & -1 & 0 & 0 \end{bmatrix} \quad 19)$$

we obtain

$$M\,\underline{V} = \begin{bmatrix} V_1+V_2+V_3+V_4 \\ V_5-V_1 \\ V_2-V_6 \\ V_2-V_1+V_4-V_3 \\ V_1-V_3 \\ V_2-V_4 \end{bmatrix} = M\,C\,\underline{P} = \begin{bmatrix} 4C_1 & 0 & 0 & 0 & 0 & 0 \\ 0 & C_7 & 0 & 0 & 0 & 0 \\ 0 & 0 & C_8 & 0 & 0 & 0 \\ 0 & 0 & 0 & 4C_4 & 0 & 0 \\ 0 & -2C_2 & 0 & 0 & 2C_5 & 0 \\ 0 & 0 & 2C_3 & 0 & 0 & 2C_6 \end{bmatrix} \underline{P} \quad 20)$$

Thus, an almost uncoupled sensor is obtained with the same hardware, allowing shorter time response by reducing the computational burden associated with the solution of the linear system.

The different algorithms which solve the linear system associated with the sensor can be implemented in subroutines invoked alternatively, according to the prevalence of either accuracy or response swiftness requirements in the current task phase.

Of course, the accuracy of force measurement is strongly dependent, in this case, on how well the real sensor matrix approximates (16). In fact, the actual MC matrix (estimated by means of appropriate calibration procedures) will have small elements instead of the expected zeroes, since machining the sensor body, bonding the transducers, etc. will not allow the exact elimination of the Cij. In order to use the fast force sensing method, these small quantities must be ignored, and the corresponding error will add to calibration inaccuracies; the overall error $\|dMC\|/\|MC\|$, propagating to the solution in accordance to (14), will be normally much larger than the original $\|dC\|/\|C\|$, emphasizing constructive inaccuracies.

EXPERIMENTAL

As a first implementation of the above considerations on the design of the force sensor element of an ITS, a prototype fingertip incorporating the ITS has been realized in our laboratory. The fingertip was designed in view of a future integration with an ETS.

The present prototype consists of a hollow cylinder made out of aluminum alloy, which supports a sphere at one end. As depicted in Figure 2, a flange located at the other end connects the fingertip to the distal phalanx of an articulated finger |Bicchi 1984||Dario et al. 1985|.

Six foil-type strain gauges are bonded to a thin walled portion of the cylinder, according to the disposition shown in Figure 3 and to the dimensional data reported above. A seventh strain gauge is fixed to a part of the cylinder having much thicker wall, so that its output can be used to compensate for possible thermal drift.

The thickness of the thin walled cylinder has been dimensioned to withstand a maximum load of 30 N (it should be noted that the wall thickness does not affect the sensor Condition Number, i.e. its accuracy); if larger bending loads are applied orthogonal to the cylinder axis, the cylinder is prevented from collapsing by a stiff coaxial cylinder.

The force sensor fits into a cylindrical cavity in the sphere. The center of the sphere (that is the active surface of the ITS) lies in the same plane as the centers of the strain gauges in the first row.

The sphere radius is 13 mm; the active surface (where contacts can be detected) is 92% of the sphere surface, corresponding to a solid angle of 11,58 spherical radians.

Each strain gauge is individually wired in a Wheatstone quarter-bridge arrangement; the bridge output is amplified, A/D converted and sent to a DEC PDP 11/73 computer.

Some experimental tests have been carried out in order to assess sensor performances. Although neither very accurate construction or precise instrumentation were used in the present prototype, experimental results were fairly good, probably owing to the "robust" design resulting from the condition number approach.

The accuracy of force measurement in the prototype was about 2% of the measured value; the minimum detectable force was 0.1 N.

The location of the contact point can be calculated with a precision variable with the intensity of the contact force: Figure 5 (a)(b) shows the graphic displays corresponding to a point contact load of 1 N and 10 N, respectively, on the top of the fingertip sphere.

The measured forces were, respectively, 1.0 N and 10.1 N; the position errors were, respectively, 0.2 mm and 0.05 mm. For the general case of a contact force in the range 0.1 N–30 N, the precision is better than 1 mm.

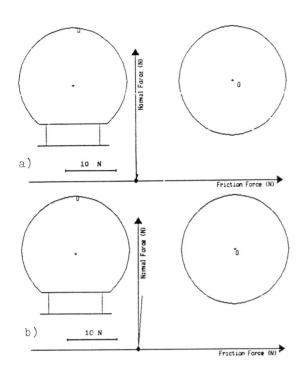

FIG. 5 (a,b). The graphic display of two experimental tests, showing the calculated position of the contact point and the contact force components for two different loads.

Finally, some preliminary experiments have been carried out in order to evaluate the feasibility of slippage control through IT sensing. A plane surface was pressed against the sensor with constant normal force, while an increasing force tended to slide the surface over the sensor. Resultant normal and tangential forces on the fingertip surface were monitored; the ratio, R_{nt}, between normal and tangential force is plotted vs. time in Figure 6, referring to the case of a rubber surface.

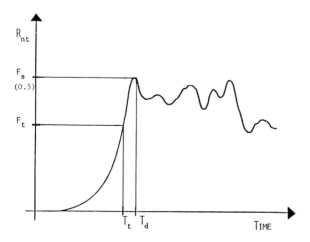

FIG. 6. Monitoring of friction and slippage by the ITS.

As the sliding force increases, the contact opposes an increasing counteracting friction force, until, at time Td, the static friction coefficient (Fs) is overcome and stick-slip occurs.

Two slippage control modes are possible. A first strategy is appropriate when the material and the superficial characteristics of the manipulated objects have been experimentally evaluated in advance. By comparing current Rnt ratios measured during the manipulation tasks, with a threshold value set on the basis of a safe estimate of Fs, adequate actions can be undertaken by the controller. In the general case in which object properties are not known a priori, slippage detection is still possible by detecting the abrupt variations of the Rnt ratio due to the first occurrence of dynamic friction.

CONCLUSIONS

The approach to tactile sensing presented in this paper has, in principle, general validity: an ITS is capable of detecting data on the contact between the end effector and the manipulated object informative and accurate enough to allow the controller not only to manage manipulation tasks, but also to infer information useful for perceptual purposes. As anticipated in the introduction, however, since the peculiar characteristics of the ITS are reliability, robustness and fast operation, while the main (although, at present, mostly potential) advantages of ETS are their capability of measuring locally minute stress or strain, and their sensitivity to physical and chemical parameters other than force, an ideal configuration of an advanced robot hand would include both types of sensors. In such configuration, the primary role of the ITS would be providing data useful for the low level control of manipulation, while the function of the ETS should be detecting exteroceptive data on the manipulated object. According to this schematization, that has some analogies with the organization of the nervous central system in humans, the accurate control of contact conditions is a prerequisite to true tactile exploration |Bicchi et al. 1985||Dario and Buttazzo 1987|. While the ITS measures accurately the overall contact conditions, as is actually necessary in order to carry out any manipulative task, an ETS located at the fingertip surface can sense a number of significant parameters relative to the local features of the explored object. If we accept the anthropomorphic analogy, we could tolerate that the accuracy of some of the measurements obtained by the ETS is relatively low: in fact, provided that a substantial level of intelligence is incorporated in the top levels of the hierarchical control, even semiqualitative, redundant information could be organized in order to obtain a coherent model of the explored object.

In order to verify the practical value of this approach, we have designed a testbed for the analysis of the fundamentals of haptic perception which is intended to implement most of the concepts outlined above. The main component of the experimental testbed is an articulated robot finger incorporating many different sensors, each having a primary function distinct from that of the other sensors. However, some of the data provided by the different sensors, just like in biological systems, may overlap. Devising appropriate methods and techniques for dealing with sensor redundancy in the proposed robot system are the ultimate goal of this research.

Figure 7 illustrates a scheme of the version of the fingertip being currently developed |Dario et al. 1987|. The fingertip incorporates the ITS presented in this paper, and a new ETS comprising, at present, an optical tactile sensor capable of measuring locally the normal and tangential components of contact forces |Femi et al. 1987|, as well as an array of undulated, piezoelectric polymer film transducers for ultrasonic imaging. A further interesting feature of the new finger is the shape memory alloy–based actuator located within the phalanxes, that, allowing to eliminate most of the tendon routings, is specifically intended for generating the smooth motions required for fine manipulation.

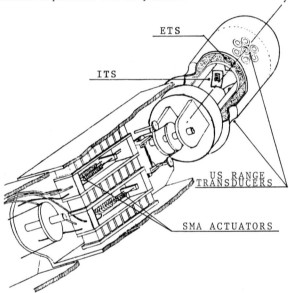

Fig. 7. Schematic view of a sensorized fingertip incorporating both the ITS described in this paper and a new ETS.

ACKNOWLEDGMENTS

The authors wish to thank G. Vassura for helpful discussions on the design of the ITS, and F. Vivaldi for the technical assistance in sensor fabrication.

The work described in this paper was supported in part by the Italian Government (MPI 40%), and by NATO Scientific Affairs Division (C.R.G. 224/85).

REFERENCES

Bejczy, A.K., "Smart hand–Manipulator control through sensory feedback," JPL D–107 Report, January 15, 1983.

Bicchi, A., Thesis for the Doctor's Degree in Mechanical Engineering on "Design of a pluriarticulated finger for tactile exploration", University of Pisa, Italy, 1984.

Bicchi, A., Dario, P., Pinotti, P.C., "On the Control of a Sensorized Artificial Finger for Tactile Exploration of Objects," Robot Control (SYROCO '85)", Edited by L. Basanez, G. Ferraté, G.N. Saridis. IFAC Publication–Pergamon books Ltd, pp. 251–256.

Brock, D., Chiu, S., "Environment perception of an articulated robot hand using contact sensors," Proc. ASME Winter Annual Meeting, Miam, Nov. 1985.

Dario, P., De Rossi, D., Domenici, C., Francesconi, R., "Ferroelectric polymer tactile sensors with anthropomorphic features," Proc. 1st IEEE int. Conf. on Robotics, Atlanta, GA, pp. 332–340, March 1984.

Dario, P., Bicchi, A., Vivaldi, F., Pinotti, P.C., "Tendon actuated exploratory finger with polymeric, skin–like tactile sensor. Proc. 2nd IEEE Int. Conf. on Robotics and Automation, St. Louis, pp. 701–706, March 1985.

Dario, P., "Contact sensing for robot active touch, "Proc. SDF Benchmark Symp. on Robotics Research, Santa Cruz, CA, MIT Press, Aug. 1987.

Dario, P., Bicchi, A., Femi, D., Fiorillo, A.: "Multiple sensing fingertip for robot active touch," Proc. of 3rd Int. Conf. on Advanced Robots, Versailles, Oct. 1987.

Dario, P. and Buttazzo, G.: "An anthropomorphic robot finger for investigating artificial tactile perception". Int. J. Robotics Res., 1987.

Femi, D., Dario, P., Lombardi, P., Francesconi, R.: "An optical fiber–based multicomponent tactile sensor", Proc. 10th IASTED Int. Symp. on Robotics and Automation, Lugano, June 1987.

Harmon, L.D., "Automated tactile sensing," Int. J. Robotics Res., Vol. 1, No. 2, pp. 3–32, 1982.

Hirzinger, G., "The space and telerobotic concepts of DFVLR rotex," Proc. IEEE Int. Conf. on Robotics and Automation, Raleigh, NC, pp. 443–449, March 1987.

Salisbury, J.K., "Interpretation of contact geometries from force measurements," Proc. 1st Int. Symp. on Robotics Research, Bretton Woods, NH, MIT Press, Sept. 1984.

Siegel, D.M., Garabieta, I., Hollerbach, J.M., "An integrated tactile and thermal sensor", Proc. IEEE Int. Conf. on Robotics and Automation, San Francisco, CA, pp. 1286, 1291, April 1986.

Von Brussel, H., Belien, H., Thielemans, H., "Force sensing for advanced robot control," Proc. 5th Conf. on Robot Vision and Sensory Control, Amsterdam, pp. 59–68, Oct. 1985.

Wilkinson, J.H., "The algebraic eigenvalue problem," Clarendon Press, Oxford 1965.

Optical Range Finding Methods for Robotics

Masanori Idesawa

Riken:The Institute of Physical and Chemical Research

2-1, Hirosawa, Wako-shi, Saitama, 351-01 JAPAN

Various type of spacial information acquisition means are required for robotics. Optical range finding method seems to be a suitable mean for this purpose. Triangulation is the most important and stable method in optical range finding. Active method, in which light beam or light sheet is projected onto an object to be tested, is adopted to remove the problem of correspondence in the triangulation. Semiconductor position sensitive detector (PSD) is used widely in the optical range finding system. Measuring accuracy of the distance is largely depend on the precision of the image position detection. Requirements for range finding apparatus are summarized as high precision, miniaturized, easy to use, high stability and so forth. In order to increase the image position sensing accuracy by PSD, a high precision mark position sensing method with kaleido-scopic mirror tunnel system and a new hybrid type position sensitive detector (RH-PSD) are introduced. In order to realize high precision and miniaturized 3-D position measuring system, 1-D mark direction sensing method which consist of a 1-D image position sensing element, a cylindrical lens and a parallel mirror tunnel is proposed. Furtheremore, to realize a miniaturized proximity range sensor based on the triangulation, a new type of optical range sensing method (RORS) is proposed. In addition, a range sensing method for surface tracing with ring pattern projection is proposed.

1. Introduction

In order to provide more flexible capabilities for machines such as automation systems, robot systems, etc., an ability to obtain the spacial information is strongly required. Range data acquisition means seem to be one of the indispensable functions to obtain the spacial information. Various kinds of range sensing means are required for robot control(Fig.1). For instance, in the searching or aproaching mode, spacial information in relatively wide area from distant position is needed to find out an object to be handled and to grasp the circumstances around the object, but required precision is not so high. On the other hand, in the attacking or handling mode, precise spacial information from the close position is required in order to keep the appropriate relation between effector and an object to be handled in limited space.

It is considered that the optical method can provide an effective mean to detect the spacial infomation because of its noncontact and nondetractive detecting capabilities. Many types of optical range sensing methods have been proposed and examined for the above purposes [Jarvis, 1983]. Triangulation is the most important principle in the optical distance measurement. It is applied widely in optical range sensing to obtain quite stable measurement. In order to

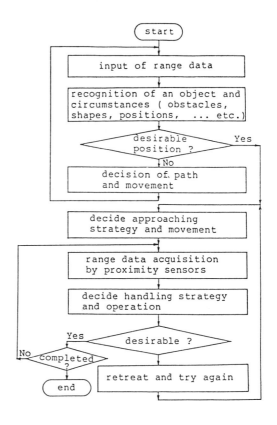

Fig.1 Robot control and range data acquisition

avoid the problem of correspondence in triangulation, light beam projecting method is adopted. In the light beam projecting method, measuring accuracy is limited by the mark position detecting precision. To increase the resolution of the mark position detecting apparatus with PSD, some methods are introduced.

A miniaturized optical range sensing method (**RORS**), which is based on the triangulation, has been developed recently by the author and is introduced in this paper. Furthermore, it is often required to follow the surface of an object in a machine operation such as in 3-D shape measurement, painting robots , etc.. In such cases, it is preferable that the range finding system can detect not only the distance but also the partial inclinations of the surface.

2. Optical Range Finding Methods

An optical method seems to be powerfull for noncontact measurement and many types of measuring method for 3-D shape have been examined (Fig. 2). Distance detection is the most essential operation in 3-D shape measurement and the principle of triangulation has been used widely (Fig.3). In the triangulation, an object to be measured is observed from two independent position; detecting image positions of the interesting point on the observation plane; 3-D position of the

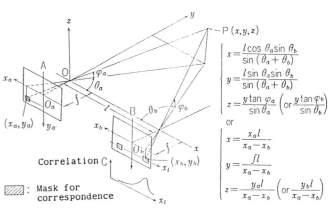

$$\begin{cases} x = \dfrac{l\cos\theta_a\sin\theta_b}{\sin(\theta_a+\theta_b)} \\[2mm] y = \dfrac{l\sin\theta_a\sin\theta_b}{\sin(\theta_a+\theta_b)} \\[2mm] z = \dfrac{y\tan\varphi_a}{\sin\theta_a}\left(\text{or }\dfrac{y\tan\varphi_b}{\sin\theta_b}\right) \end{cases}$$

or

$$\begin{cases} x = \dfrac{x_a l}{x_a-x_b} \\[2mm] y = \dfrac{fl}{x_a-x_b} \\[2mm] z = \dfrac{y_a l}{x_a-x_b}\left(\text{or }\dfrac{y_b l}{x_a-x_b}\right) \end{cases}$$

⬛⬛: Mask for correspondence

Fig.3 Principle of triangulation

interesting point is determined as a vertex of the triangle. According to this principle, it is possible to detect 3-D position from stereoscopic images, however, it is very difficult to detect the corresponding point between two views. Concerning to this corresponding problem, many attempts such as binocular stereo vision based on eye and neuron model[Ohmori, 1986] have been tried.. In order to avoid this correspondence problem, active method in which measuring light is projected on to an object is introduced.

In the light beam projection method, a light beam is projected onto an object to be measured; and bright spot is produced on the object surface; the bright spot is observed by the image detector and the image position of the bright spot on the observation plane is detected. 3-D position of the bright spot is determined by the triangulation. By sweeping the object surface by the bright spot, 3-D shapes are measured point by point. In this method, measuring accuracy is influenced by precision of image position detection. In order to increase mark position detecting accuracy, a high precision mark position detection method had developed .

In the light sheet projection method [Shirai, 1971], a light sheet is projected on to an object to be tested and a line image which corresponding to the sectional shape of the object can be obtained.

In the moiré topography [Takasaki,1970], a line grating is projected onto an object to be measured and shadow grating is produced on the surface of an object; the deformed shadow grating is observed through the another line grating and superimposed image is produced; the superimposed image consisting contour line image of the object to be measured. Thus the contour line image is taken easily by the moiré topography , however, it is difficult to automate a measuring

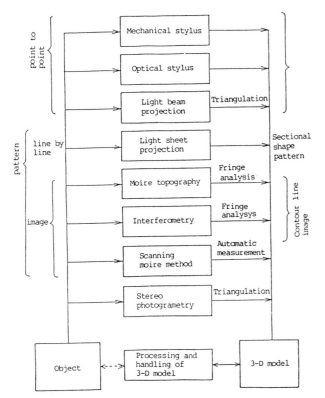

Fig.2 Various methods for 3-D shape measurement

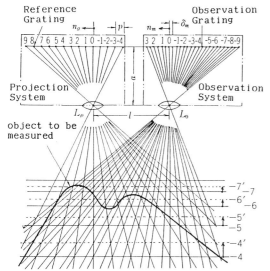

(a) movement of contour line level by changing the phase of the observation (virtual) grating

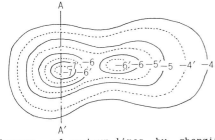

(b) changes of contour lines by changing the phase of the observation (virtual) grating

Fig.4 Principle of scanning moiré method

process because identification of fringe order which corresponding to height of contourline is impossible only from a contour line image. In order to solve this ambiguity problem, scanning moiré method had developped (Fig.4)[Idesawa, 1977], in which electrical sampling technique is used instead of the second grating in the conventional type moiré topography system. By changing the phase of sampling, sign of contour line (depression or elevation) is identified and it becomes possible to automate the measuring process.

In the space coding method [Inokuchi, 1984], several coded grating are projected time sequentially onto an object to be tested and their binary images are taken and accumulated as a corresponding bit for each pixel. Then the accumulated code which representing distance information can be obtained for each pixel.

In the interferometric method, it is possible to produce interferometric fringe pattern representing deformation or shape of an object surface in high precision of wave length of light. In this method, sign identification of

fringe pattern also becomes a difficult problem. In order to remove this ambiguity, phase changing method of reference light, inclining method of an object and so on are proposed. Interferometric method is an indespensable techniques in high precision measurement of surface and it is applied widely, for instance surface testing of silicon wafer and so forth. It is possible to generate a hologram or deformed grating corresponding to an ideal shapes by computer[Yatagai, 1977]. The generated hologram or deformed grating can be used as a reference of shape and actually used in process testing of super high precision mirror manufacturing.

Optical position measuring methods can provide an effective tool for non-contact measurement of shape, deformation, movement and so forth. Many of them are based on the trianguration in the wide sense.

3. High Precision Mark Position Detecting Methods for PSD

In the light beam projecting method, surface of an object to be measured is swept by a bright spot and image positions of the bright spot are detected by the several image position detecting apparatuses. Then the 3-D position of a bright spot is determined based on the principle of triangulation. In this method, the measuring accuracy of 3-D position is influenced considerably by the detecting accuracy of image position on the observation plane.

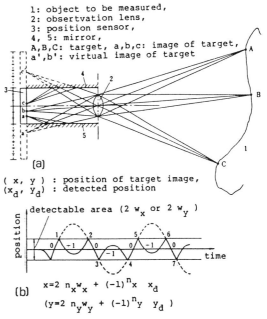

1: object to be measured,
2: observation lens,
3: position sensor,
4, 5: mirror,
A,B,C: target, a,b,c: image of target,
a',b': virtual image of target

(a)

(x, y) : position of target image,
(x_d, y_d) : detected position

$$x = 2 n_x w_x + (-1)^{n_x} x_d$$
$$(y = 2 n_y w_y + (-1)^{n_y} y_d)$$

Fig.5 Principle of high precision mark position sensing method with kaleidoscopic mirror tunnel

A semiconducter position sensitive detector (PSD) [Peterson, 1978] has been used widely for a mark position determimation apparatus. In these apparatus, position sensing accuracy is mainly limited by the stability and the accuracy of the signal processing circuit and A/D converter.

3-1. A High Precision Position Sensing Method with Kaleidoscopic Mirror Tunnel System

Noticing to the high stability and reproducibility of an optical system, the following method had been invented [Idesawa, 1984].

Figure 5 (a) represents principle of the invented method in which light reflecting mirrors are put around a photo sensitive element like a kaleidoscopic mirror tunnel. With this arrangement the effective photosensitive area of the position sensing apparatus could be extended as shown by broken lines. For instance, marks on different position **A**, **B**, and **C** on an object are detected on corresponding points **a**, **b**, and **c** on the photo sensitive plane respectively. If there were no mirrors around the photosensitive area, the image of marks **A** and **C** would fall on the places exterior to the phot-sensitive area as indicated by broken lines, and therefore, could not be detected by the photo-sensitive element. If pieces of information are given as to which side of the sourounding mirror reflects the beam of light from the marks **A** and **C**, and as to how often the beams of light are reflected, the position of image points **a** and **c** can be converted to the positions of points **a'** and **b'** with recourse to the mathematical method. Figure 5 (b) represents a conceptual diagram showing a trajectory of detected position when target is moving on a sinusoidal wave. the actual range of the photo-sensitive element extend from $-w_x$ to $+w_x$. In this figure, the numerical characters appearing between the opposite sides of the mirror represent the times of reflection, and are reffered as reflection time index n_x or n_y. The sign of the reflection time index shows on which side the first reflection occures; upper or lower side in this figure.

An outer range position x on which the beam of light falls can be determined in the terms of the coordinate x_d in the actual photo-sensitive area and of the reflection time index n_x and n_y from the formula shown in Fig. 5 (b). In order to determine the outer-range position of the light spot from the corresponding inner-range position, it is necessarry to obtain the reflection time index n_x and n_y in X and Y directions. Necessary information can be obtained in consideration of the continuity of

movement of the mark, in consideration of the regurarity in the movement of the mark or with the aid of another position detecting apparatus.

By adopting the proposed method, it is expected that the effective sensing area can be extended to several times wider than that of original one. Thus relative precision of mark detection can be increased extremly without any special improvement of accuracy and stability of signal processing system. A trial apparatus for 2-D mark position detection has been manufactured and it was proven that the effective sensing area could be enlarged and the relative precision of position detection could be increased extremly. It is expected that the proposed method can provide a usefull toll for high precision 3-D range data acqusition in the field of advanced robot vision.

3-2. Hybrid Type Position Sensitive Detector (RH-PSD)

Recently, a hybrid (analogue and digital) type semiconductor position sensitive detector **RH-PSD** (Riken Hybrid type Position Sensitive Detector) has been invented by the author. Auxiliary output terminals are added between the output terminals in the conventional type **PSD** as shown Fig.6 (a). By selecting appropriate pair of output terminals (Fig.6 (b)), each devided interval or several continuous intervals can works entirely the same as an ordinary type PSD. By selecting output terminals which

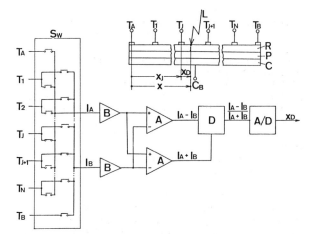

Fig.6 Principle of RH-PSD(Riken Hybrid Type Position Sensitive Detector
(a) conceptual figure showing sectional configuration of RH-PSD element, (b) schematic drawing of the signal processing circuit for RH-PSD (R: resistance layer, P: photo-sensitive layer, C: bias layer, L: incident light, Ta, Tb, T1,..., Tj: output terminals, Cb: bias terminal, Sw: output terminal selecting circuit, X: image position, Xj: position of the j-th output terminal, Xd: detected position in the j-th interval, B: buffer amplifier, A: operational amplifier, D: divider, A/D: analogue to digital converter, Ia,Ib: output current)

including wider range, the devided interval on which target image is falling can be decided. Then, the output terminals including the target image are selected and the image position in the interval(Xd) is detected. Finally, image position is determined from the position of the selected interval(Xj) and the detected position in the selected interval (Xd). Since, the physical positions of the output terminals can be fabricated extremly precise and can be selected digital mode, therefore, it can be considered that the position detecting accuracy is influenced only by that in the selected interval. For instance, suppose that n(15) output terminals are added in equi-spacing between the output terminals of the ordinary PSD and the precision of the A/D converter is m(10) bits, the precision in total sensing area may be $(n+1) \times 2^m$ (16x1024). It means that the position detecting precision can be increased to n+1(16) times than that of in the ordinary type PSD without any improvement of the precision of the A/D converter and signal operation circuit.

4. 1-D Mark Direction Sensing Method

Generally, 2-D type image position sensitive element has lower position detecting resolusion than that of 1-D (linear) type image position sensitive element. Because of this reason, 3-D position measuring system composed of several 1-D mark direction sensing apparatus which are consist of 1-D type image position sensing element has been tried.

4-1. 3-D Position Measuring System with 1-D Mark Direction Detecting Apparatuses

Figure 7 shows a conceputual construction of 1-D mark direction sensing apparatus consist of a cylindrical lens and a 1-D image position sensitive element. A

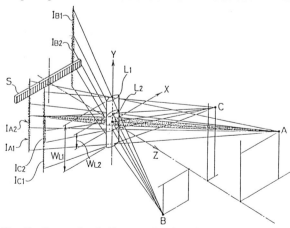

Fig.7 Conceptual figure showing imaging condition by a cylindrical lens {L1,L2: cylindrical lens, WL1,WL2: width of the cylindrical lens, S: 1-D image position sensing element, A,B,C: different mark positions, IA1,IA2,IB1,IB2,IC1,IC2: line images of marks on the observation plane}

cylindrical lens projecting a bright spot as a line image on the observation plane and the position of the line image is detected by the 1-D image position sensitive element which is placed on the observation plane. Thus the direction of the plane on which bright spot lying can be defined.

Figure 8 shows the typical arrangement of 3-D position measuring system with three 1-D mark direction sensing apparatus. The directions of the planes on which bright spot lying are defined from the detected line image positions for each 1-D mark direction sensing apparatus. 3-D

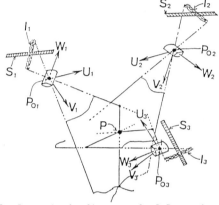

Fig.8 Conceptual figure of 3-D mark position detecting system with three 1-D mark direction sensing device { Si: 1-D image position sensing element, P: mark to be detected, Ii: image of the mark on the observation plane, Poi: position of the nodal point of the cylindrical lens, Ui,Vi,Wi: direction vector of 1-D mark direction sensing device (i=1,2,3)}

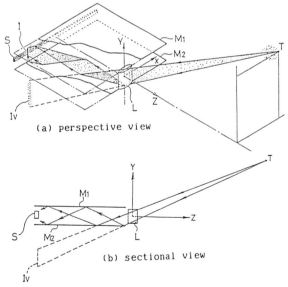

(a) perspective view

(b) sectional view

Fig.9 Conceptual configuration of the miniaturized 1-D mark direction sensing device with parallel mirror tunnel
(a) perspective figure, (b) sectional figure { L: cylindrical lens, S: 1-D image position sensing element, M1,M2: parallel mirror tunnel, T: target mark, I: image of the target on the observation plane, Iv: virtual image of the target}

position of the bright spot can be
determined as an intersection of these
three planes.

4-2. 1-D Mark Direction Sensing Device with Parallel Mirror Tunnel

As shown in Fig. 7, detectable angle on
the plane on which bright spot lying is
limited by the width of the cylindrical
lens. In order to enlarge the
detectable angle, it is required to use a
cylindrical lens which has wider width
and it is inconvenient to make such mark
detecting apparatus smaller. A new method
to miniaturize a 1-D mark direction
detecting apparatus has been developed
and its conceptual arrangement is shown
in Fig. 10. A parallel mirror tunnel
system is placed between clyndrical lens
and 1-D image position detective element
so that it reflect the light rays which
would fall on exterior place of the image
sensitive element without the mirror
tunnel, and direct them to the image
sensitive element. By this method, the
width of 1-D mark direction sensing
apparatus can be kept narrower without
sacrifice to the detectable angle.

According to the developed method, some
prototypes of 1-D mark direction
detecting apparatus were manufactured and
it has been proven experimentally that
the practical limitation of the
detectable angle can be removed and width
of the apparatus can be reduced extremely
by the developed method.

5. Miniaturized Optical Range Sensing Method:RORS

In the triangulation, in order to keep
measuring accuracy, appropriate base line
length is required. It seems to be
difficult to realize a miniaturized range

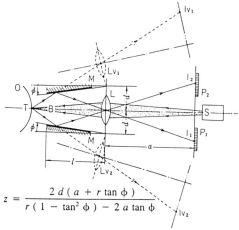

$$z = \frac{2 d (a + r \tan \phi)}{r (1 - \tan^2 \phi) - 2 a \tan \phi}$$

Fig.10 Principle of the miniaturized optical range
sensing method RORS
{ S: light source, B: light beam, L: observation
lens, M1,M2: mirrors, P1,P2: position sensor,
Lv1,Lv2: virtual lenses, O: object to be tested,
I1,I2: images of target, Iv1,Iv2: virtual images
of target}

sensor based on this principle. By
applying newly growing technologies, such
as micro-electronics, opto-electronics,
fiber-optics, etc, many attempts have
been made to realize small size and
accurate range sensors [Kanade, 1983]
[Nakamura, 1983], however, their sizes
cannot be miniaturized sufficiently and
the accuracy and stability are not enough
for use in advanced noncontact
measurements. In order to realize a
compact optical range sensing probe, the
author developed a new type of optical
range sensing scheme called RORS (Riken
Optical Range Sensing Scheme) [Idesawa,
1983, 1985] whose principle is shown in
Fig. 10 and is based on triangulation. A
mirror tunnel such as cylindrical or
circular conical mirror is placed between
an objective lens and an object to be
tested; a light beam is projected through
the objective lens and bright spot is
produced on an object to be tested; the
bright spot is observed throgh the
objective lens after reflection with the
mirror tunnel; distance along to the
optical axis can be determined according
to the principle of triangulation. The
width of an optical system can be reduced
to remarkably smaller than that of by the
ordinary type triangulation, and it may
be suitable to miniaturize an optical
range sensor such as an optical stylus,
proximity sensor and so on.

6. Optical Range Finding Method for Surface Tracing :RORST

In the case of 3-D shape measurement, it
is necessary to follow the surface of an
object to be measured. An optical stylus
which can detect not only distance but
also partial inclination of a surface may
be desirable for surface tracing. And
also isotropical detecting
characteristics may be desirable for
these purposes. The author proposed two
methods: in the first method, qualitative
information of the surface inclination is
detected by using reflection properties
of light on a rough surface. In the
second method, an axially symmetrical
light sheet is projected onto an object
and quantitative information of
inclination can be determined based on
the triangulation.

6-1. Considerations on the Detection of Surface Inclination in the RORS Scheme

The author has tried to provide a
capability of the inclination detection
for a range sensor based on the RORS.
Figure 11(a) represents a conceptual
aspect of intensity distribution at the
bright spot on the rough surface produced
by projecting a light beam. Figure 11(b)
shows a mathematical model of intensity
distribution on the plane which includs
normal of surface at the bright spot and
an axis of an incident light beam.

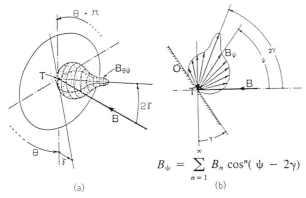

$$B_\psi = \sum_{n=1}^{\infty} B_n \cos^n(\psi - 2\gamma)$$

(a)   (b)

Fig.11 Conceptual aspect of intensity distribution at the bright spot on the rough surface produced by projecting a light beam
(a)conceptual intensity distribution, (b)mathematical model of the intensity distribution (B: incident light beam, T: bright spot, O: object to be tested, B_ψ, $B_{\theta\psi}$: intensity distribution, θ: maxmum gradient azimuth, γ: angle of inclination)

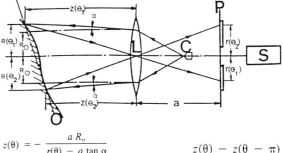

$$z(\theta) = -\frac{a R_o}{r(\theta) - a \tan\alpha}$$

$$R(\theta) = \frac{R_o \, r(\theta)}{r(\theta) - a \tan\alpha}$$

$$g(\theta) = \frac{z(\theta) - z(\theta - \pi)}{R(\theta) + R(\theta - \pi)}$$

Fig.12 Principle of inclination detecting method by ring pattern projection: RORST (Riken Optical Range Sensing Scheme for Surface Tracing) (S: light source, C: conical lens, L: objective lens, O: object tobe tested, P: observation plane, a :projection angle of the axially symmetrical sheet beam, a : distance between objective lens and the observation plane, Ro: radius of the sheet beam at the objective lens, $r(\theta_i)$ (i-1,2): radial position of the ring pattern for azimuth θ_i (i=1,2), [$R(\theta_i)$,$z(\theta_i)$](i=1,2): positions of points on the ring pattern for azimuth θ_i(i=1,2) in a cylindrical coordinates }

Quantity of light (integration of intensity for certain areas) which is received by a fixed area at a certain position is influenced by the inclination of the surface to be tested. Therefore, it is expected and confirmed by the basic experiment that the qualitative information of surface inclination can be taken by detecting the intensity of target images at several parts on the observation plane.

6-2. Surface Tracing Range Sensor by ring Pattern Projection

In order to detect quantitative information of the surface inclination, a new type of range sensing scheme called **RORST** (Riken ' Optical Range Sensing Scheme for Surface Tracing) has been proposed [Idesawa, 1985] [Kinosita, 1985]. Figure 12 represents a principle of **RORST**: an axially symmetrical (cylindrical or circular conical) light sheet is projected and ring shaped pattern is produced on the surface of an object to be investigated. The projected ring shaped pattern is observed through an objective lens and radial position of the ring pattern image on the observation plane is detected for each azimuth(θ). Range information in the cylindrical coordinates ($z(\theta)$,$R(\theta)$) is determined based on the triangulation (Fig. 12).

By detecting the radial position of the target pattern image for several azimuths, 3-D coordinates of points along the projected ring pattern can be obtained by the above formulas. Furthermore, mean gradient of the surface for each azimuth ($g(\theta)$) can be estimated as shown in Fig.12. In addition, the isotropical characteristics of the gradient detection can be realized by

this method. An axially symmetrical light beam can be produced by the combination of a conical lens and an objective lens.

From the basic experiments, it is confirmed that the range sensor which can detect not only the distance but also the gradient of a surface can be realized by the proposed method.

7. Conclusion

In this paper, the author introduced some optical range finding methods which have been proposed and examined by the **Riken** groupe. Topics were focused on the techniques to realize high precision and miniaturized optical range sensor.

High precision mark position sensing methods for the image position detecting apparatus using **PSD** are proposed. Basically, **PSD** is considered as an analogue device and special technology is required and is difficult to increase position detecting accuracy in the conventional technologies. The proposed methods can give one of the solution for this problem.

Generally, 1-D type image position detecting element has higher position detecting precision than that of 2-D type. A miniaturized 1-D mark direction detecting method with parallel mirror tunnel has been proposed. The author believes that the miniaturized 1-D mark direction detecting apparatus based on the proposed method can provide a usefull tool for 3-D position measuring system.

A new type of optical range sensing scheme (**RORS**) which is based on the principle of triangulation has been proposed. From the experimental results, it has been confirmed that a miniaturized and accurate range sensor can be realized based on the RORS. It is expected that the RORS can provide a miniaturized and accurate range sensor which is suitable for use as an optical stylus, a position detector, a proximity sensor and in other advanced noncontact measurements.

Furthermore, the author has thought to provide an inclination detecting capability in an optical range sensor as well as an optical range finding method using an axially symmetrical light sheet projection which can detect partial inclination of surface. Some basic experiments have been performed and has proven that not only range information, but also the gradient of the surface can be detected effectively by the proposed methods.

The author believes that the presented methods can provide useful range finding means in the field of robotics and automation.

Acknowledgements

The author would like to thank Dr. E. Goto and Dr. T. Soma of Riken for their encouragement. He also would like to appreciate to Prof. T. Yatagai, some concerning works have been done with him. Concerning to the development of miniaturized range sensor based on the RORS has been performed partially under the support from the Shimadzu foundation.

References

[Idesawa,1984] M. Idesawa : High precision mark position sensing method suitable for 3-D range data acquisition, Proc. 7th Intl. Conf. on Pattern Recognition, 451(1984)

[Idesawa,1977] M. Idesawa et al. : Scanning moire method and automatic measurement of 3-D Shapes, Appl. Opt., Vol.9, No.4, 2152/2162(1977)

[Idesawa,1985] M. Idesawa : A new type of optical range sensing method for surface tracing, 2nd Intl. Symp. on Optical and Electrical applied Science and Engineering, Dec. 1985(Cannes, France)

[Idesawa,1983] M. Idesawa; Range sensor, Japanese Patt. Appl. No. 58-161088, Optical distance measuring apparatus, US Patent No.4,637,715

[Idesawa,1985] M. Idesawa; A new type of miniaturized optical range sensing scheme: RORS, J. of Robot Society of Japan, Vol. 3,No.2, 87(1985) (in Japanese)

[Inokuchi,1985] S. Inokuchi, K. Sato and F. Masuda; Range-Imaging System for 3-D Object Recognition, 7th Intl. Conf. on Pattern Recognition,

[Ishii,1976] M. Ishii, et al. : Feature extraction of three dimensional object and visual processing in a hand-eye system using laser tracker, Pattern Recognition, Vol.8, 229/237(1976)

[Itoh,1986] Y. Itoh and M. Idesawa : A study on robot path planning from a solid model, Jour. Robotic Systems, 3(2), 191/203(1986)

[Jarvis,1983]R. A. Jarvis: Perspective on Range Finding Techniques for Computer Vision, IEEE Trans. Pattern Analysis and Machine Intelligence, PAMI-5-5, 505/512(1983)

[Kanade,1983] T. Kanade and T. M. Sommer; An optical proximity sensor for measuring surface position and orientation for robot manupulation, C.M.U. Tech. Rept. CMU-RI-TR-83-15

[Kinoshita,1985] G. Kinoshita and M. Idesawa; Optical Range Finding System by Projecting Ring Beam Pattern, Proc. '85 ICAR, 177 (1985)

[Nakamura,1983] Y. Nakamura and H. Hanafusa; A New Optical Proximity Sensor for Three Dimensional Autonoumous Trajectory Control of Robot Manipulators, '83 ICAR 179(1983)

[Ohmori,1986] T. Ohmori: Binocular stereo vision System Using an Eye and Neuron Model, Journal of Robotic Systems, 3-2,149/163(1986)

[Peterson,1978] G. P.Petersson and L. E. Lindholm; Position sensitive detector with high linearity, IEEE J. of Solid State Circuit, Vol. SC13, No.3,392(1978

[Shirai,1971] Y. Shirai; Recognition of Polyhedrons with a Range Finder, Bulletin of the Electrotechnical Laboratory, Vol.35, No. 3(1971)

[Takasaki,1970] H. Takasaki : Moire topography, Appl. Opt., Vol.3, No.4, 1467/1472(1970)

[Yatagai,1977] T. Yatagai and M. Idesawa : Use of synthetic deformed grating in moire topography, Optics Communications, Vol.20,No.2,243(1977)

III CONTROL

The papers in part III consider eight different types of control problems associated with manipulation. The variety of the problems serves to underscore the difficulty and richness inherent in the quest to develop appropriate controllers and dynamic models for robotic manipulators.

Atkeson et al. describe a type of adaptive control in which a manipulator's performance is used to modify the model of the controlled system. They apply their ideas to the problem of improving a robot's ability to throw a ball at a target. Dubowsky and Tanner consider the control of a manipulator being carried on a moving base. They show how to compensate for those aspects of the base's motion that act as a disturbance, which could degrade manipulator performance. Daniel et al. discuss the use of self-tuning for the real-time control of compliant manipulators. De Schutter and Leysen develop the mathematics for determining task frame trajectories for use in contour tracking. Khatib develops the mathematics of a decoupled force-control system consisting of several

manipulators in simultaneous contact with a single movable object. His results can be applied to object manipulation carried out by a group of cooperating manipulators or fingers of a multi-fingered hand.

The remaining papers treat the control of master-slave manipulators. Oomichi et al. present the details of a master-slave, bilateral, force-controlled manipulator system that features finger mechanisms that provide for delicate and dexterous movements with both tactile and force feedback. Sato and Hirai describe a master-slave system that relies on object-oriented models and rule-based motion software to enhance the system performance and man-machine communications. Arai et al. propose a universal configuration for a master so that it can be used with a variety of different types of slave manipulators. All three of these papers on master-slave systems contain interesting results and ideas that are equally useful for researchers interested in computer-controlled robotic manipulators.

Model-Based Robot Learning

Christopher G. Atkeson, Eric W. Aboaf, Joseph McIntyre,
and David J. Reinkensmeyer

Artificial Intelligence Laboratory, Massachusetts Institute of Technology
NE43-759, 545 Technology Square, Cambridge, MA 02139

Abstract: Models play an important role in learning from practice. Models of a controlled system can be used as learning operators to refine commands on the basis of performance errors. The examples used to demonstrate this include positioning a limb at a visual target, throwing a ball at a target, and following a defined trajectory. Better models lead to faster correction of command errors, requiring less practice to attain a given level of performance. The benefits of accurate modeling are improved performance in all aspects of control, while the risks of inadequate modeling are poor learning performance, or even degradation of performance with practice.

1 Introduction

An important component of human motor skill is the ability to improve performance by practicing a task. Commands are refined on the basis of performance errors. It is often suggested that such learning reduces the need for an accurate internal model, a model of the mechanical plant in the control system (see Arimoto, 1984b; Wang and Horowitz, 1985; and Harokopos, 1986 for examples). This is not the case. Internal models play an important role in generating command corrections from performance errors. As an internal model is made more accurate, learning efficiency is improved, as is initial performance.

This paper will show, in a series of examples, how internal models can be used as learning operators. The examples are 1) positioning a limb at a visual target, 2) throwing a ball at a target, and 3) following a defined trajectory. The essence of the model-based learning algorithms used to improve performance on these tasks is that internal models are used to transform performance errors into command corrections.

The type of learning described in this paper – refining commands on the basis of practice – complements many other types of adaptive processes. Feedback controller designs can be improved by adaptive control algorithms. Internal models can be incrementally improved using system identification techniques. Trajectories can be optimized for particular tasks. Robot plans and programs can be debugged as errors are discovered during execution. This paper focuses on improving execution of a given task plan by refining the commands given to the robot.

Model-Based Learning Algorithm Structure

The model-based learning algorithms described here all have the same form. Commands are refined on the basis of performance errors. A command is applied to the controlled system (Figure 1A). Performance errors may result from errors in the command. A model of the inverse of the controlled system is used to estimate the errors in the command based on the measured performance or output errors (Figure 1B). If the inverse model of the controlled system is perfect, the command errors would be correctly estimated and completely eliminated after one attempt at performing the task. (Of course, if a perfect model of the controlled system is available then the initial command would also have been perfect). Perfect knowledge of the controlled system is not usually available, and the model of the inverse of the controlled system will be incorrect. Due to the modeling errors, the command correction will be incomplete, and learning will be an iterative process of refining the command.

There are three steps to the learning algorithms: command initialization, execution, and modification. The initial command is generated by applying the inverse model of the controlled system to the desired performance. During execution, a command is applied to the system and the actual performance is monitored. The command correction is calculated by applying the inverse model to the performance errors. The refined command is now executed. The cycle of command execution and modification is repeated until desired performance is achieved.

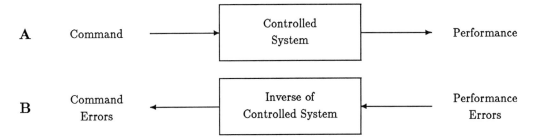

Figure 1: The inverse of the controlled system is used to estimate command errors from performance errors.

2   A Kinematic Example

The task of positioning the limb at a visual target will be used to provide a specific example of how model-based learning works. A robot arm and a target are viewed by a vision system (Figure 2). The robot arm servos to a commanded set of joint angles, $\boldsymbol{\theta}$, and the vision system measures the tip position, $\mathbf{x}$, in vision system coordinates. The controlled system in this case transforms commanded joint angles into a measured tip position (Figure 1A):

$$\mathbf{x} = L(\boldsymbol{\theta}) \qquad (1)$$

The forward kinematics, $L()$, is in general a nonlinear transformation. For the purposes of this example we will assume there are no singularities or redundancies to resolve in the field of view of the vision system. For each desired tip position there is one and only one appropriate set of joint angles.

A *model* of the inverse kinematics is used to transform the desired tip position, $\mathbf{x}_d$, into an initial joint angle command, $\boldsymbol{\theta}^0$, in the command initialization stage:

$$\boldsymbol{\theta}^0 = \hat{L}^{-1}(\mathbf{x}_d) \qquad (2)$$

A caret (ˆ) is used to indicate a model or an estimate of a quantity. The initial joint angle command is applied in the first execution stage, and the corresponding tip position is measured:

$$\mathbf{x}^0 = L(\boldsymbol{\theta}^0) \qquad (3)$$

The true system, $L()$, and its inverse are unknown, and only imperfect models are available. Due to modeling errors, the actual tip position, $\mathbf{x}^0$, will not match the desired tip position, $\mathbf{x}_d$.

At this point we must decide how to transform the measured tip position error into a correction to the set of commanded joint angles. Performance errors must be mapped into command corrections. The same model of the inverse kinematics that was used to generate the initial command, $\hat{L}^{-1}()$, will be used to estimate the command error (Figure 1B).

The command error, $\delta\boldsymbol{\theta}$, is the difference between the currently commanded joint angles, $\boldsymbol{\theta}^0$, and the (unknown) correct set of joint angles, which will be indicated as $\boldsymbol{\theta}^*$. The command error can be computed in terms of the actual and desired performances using the true system inverse:

$$\delta\boldsymbol{\theta}^0 = \boldsymbol{\theta}^0 - \boldsymbol{\theta}^* = L^{-1}(\mathbf{x}^0) - L^{-1}(\mathbf{x}_d) \qquad (4)$$

As we do not have perfect knowledge of the true system inverse, we must use a model of the system inverse to estimate the command error:

$$\widehat{\delta\boldsymbol{\theta}}^0 = \hat{L}^{-1}(\mathbf{x}^0) - \hat{L}^{-1}(\mathbf{x}_d) \qquad (5)$$

The command is updated by simply subtracting the estimate of the command error from the previous command:

$$\boldsymbol{\theta}^1 = \boldsymbol{\theta}^0 - \widehat{\delta\boldsymbol{\theta}}^0 \qquad (6)$$

If the model of the system inverse was perfect the command error would be estimated correctly and completely eliminated on the next attempt. However, a model is rarely perfect, so command correction must be an iterative process of estimating a command error using an imperfect model, removing the estimated command error, applying the refined command, and using the resulting performance error and the model to estimate remaining errors in the command. Equations (3), (5), and (6) can be indexed with i to indicate that they are applied on each practice attempt, reflecting the iterative nature of the algorithm:

1. Command initialization:

$$\boldsymbol{\theta}^0 = \hat{L}^{-1}(\mathbf{x}_d) \qquad (7)$$

2. Command execution:

$$\mathbf{x}^i = L(\boldsymbol{\theta}^i) \qquad (8)$$

3. Command error estimation:

$$\widehat{\delta\boldsymbol{\theta}}^i = \hat{L}^{-1}(\mathbf{x}^i) - \hat{L}^{-1}(\mathbf{x}_d) \qquad (9)$$

4. Command modification:

$$\boldsymbol{\theta}^{i+1} = \boldsymbol{\theta}^i - \widehat{\delta\boldsymbol{\theta}}^i \qquad (10)$$

Steps 2, 3, and 4 are repeated until satisfactory performance is achieved.

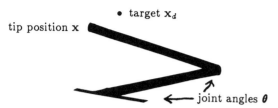

tip position $\mathbf{x}$

• target $\mathbf{x}_d$

joint angles $\boldsymbol{\theta}$

Figure 2: A robot arm and a target are viewed by a vision system.

Convergence

The quality of the inverse model used as the learning operator determines how fast model-based learning converges. Fixed point theory can be used to analyze the general nonlinear case (Wang 1984, Wang and Horowitz 1985). A learning algorithm can be viewed as a mapping of commands on the ith attempt to commands on the next attempt:

$$\boldsymbol{\theta}^{i+1} = F(\boldsymbol{\theta}^i) \qquad (11)$$

The previously described algorithm can be put into this form by substituting equation (8) into (9) and (9) into (10). The model-based learning algorithm modifies the ith command by adding a correction based on the performance error transformed by the inverse model:

$$\boldsymbol{\theta}^{i+1} = \boldsymbol{\theta}^i - \left(\hat{L}^{-1}(L(\boldsymbol{\theta}^i)) - \hat{L}^{-1}(\mathbf{x}_d) \right) \qquad (12)$$

Note that when the desired performance, $\mathbf{x}_d$, is achieved using the correct command, $\boldsymbol{\theta}^*$, then $L(\boldsymbol{\theta}^*) = \mathbf{x}_d$ and equation (12) reduces to the fixed point $\boldsymbol{\theta}^{i+1} = \boldsymbol{\theta}^i = \boldsymbol{\theta}^*$.

We can ask whether this fixed point is stable by analyzing a linearization of equation (12) at the point $(\boldsymbol{\theta}, \mathbf{x}) = (\boldsymbol{\theta}^*, \mathbf{x}_d)$. For a small perturbation $\delta\boldsymbol{\theta}$ from the fixed point,

$$L(\boldsymbol{\theta}^* + \delta\boldsymbol{\theta}) = \mathbf{x}_d + J(\boldsymbol{\theta}^*)\delta\boldsymbol{\theta} \qquad (13)$$

where J is the Jacobean matrix of derivatives of $L()$. Similarly, for a small perturbation $\delta\mathbf{x}$ from the fixed point,

$$\hat{L}^{-1}(\mathbf{x}_d + \delta\mathbf{x}) = \hat{L}^{-1}(\mathbf{x}_d) + \hat{J}^{-1}(\mathbf{x}_d)\delta\mathbf{x} \qquad (14)$$

where $\hat{J}^{-1}$ is the Jacobean matrix for the inverse model $\hat{L}^{-1}()$. If on the ith trial the command is perturbed from $\boldsymbol{\theta}^*$ by $\delta\boldsymbol{\theta}^i$ so that $\boldsymbol{\theta}^i = \boldsymbol{\theta}^* + \delta\boldsymbol{\theta}^i$, the error in the next command, $\delta\boldsymbol{\theta}^{i+1} = \boldsymbol{\theta}^{i+1} - \boldsymbol{\theta}^*$, can be computed by substituting equations (13) and (14) into equation (12):

$$\delta\boldsymbol{\theta}^{i+1} = (1 - \hat{J}^{-1}(\mathbf{x}_d)J(\boldsymbol{\theta}^*))\delta\boldsymbol{\theta}^i \qquad (15)$$

If $\hat{J}^{-1}$ is a correct inverse of J the command error will be completely corrected after one attempt, in the linear case. The command error $\delta\boldsymbol{\theta}$ will decrease when all of the eigenvalues of the matrix $(1-\hat{J}^{-1}J)$ are less than one in absolute value, with the rate of decrease determined by the magnitude of the eigenvalues. If the magnitude of any eigenvalue is greater than one, the learning process will be unstable and performance degraded rather than improved by learning. The magnitude of the eigenvalues of $(1 - \hat{J}^{-1}J)$ depend on how accurately $\hat{J}^{-1}$ inverts J, and thus the convergence rate of the learning algorithm depends on how closely the learning operator inverts the controlled system.

Input vs. output disturbance estimation

Although our performance errors are due to errors in modeling the controlled system, the model-based learning algorithm was derived by assuming that an unknown error was added to the command. In the kinematic tip positioning example a constant command disturbance would correspond to constant joint angle offsets added to the commanded joint angles. The learning algorithm just described can be viewed as an iterative procedure to estimate a command disturbance.

An alternative version of the model-based learning algorithm is suggested by assuming that the major source of errors are output (performance) disturbances rather than input (command) disturbances. In the kinematic example just presented, the camera measuring tip position could have an unknown offset, Δ. This offset could initially be assumed to be zero, and after each positioning attempt an estimate of the offset could be refined by subtracting the tip position error:

$$\Delta^i = \Delta^{i-1} - (\mathbf{x}^{i-1} - \mathbf{x}_d) \qquad (16)$$

The estimated output offset would be added to the desired tip position when the next joint angle command was computed:

$$\boldsymbol{\theta}^i = \hat{L}^{-1}(\mathbf{x}_d + \Delta^i) \qquad (17)$$

Equations (16) and (17) replace equations (9) and (10) in the input disturbance version of the model-based learning algorithm to form the output disturbance version.

Representing possible modeling errors as either input or output errors is a modeling decision that depends on the assumed source of the modeling errors. In the output disturbance version of the model-based learning algorithm, as in the input disturbance version, the performance error is mapped through an inverse model of the controlled system to calculate a command correction. The output disturbance model-based learning algorithm has similar convergence properties as the input disturbance algorithm.

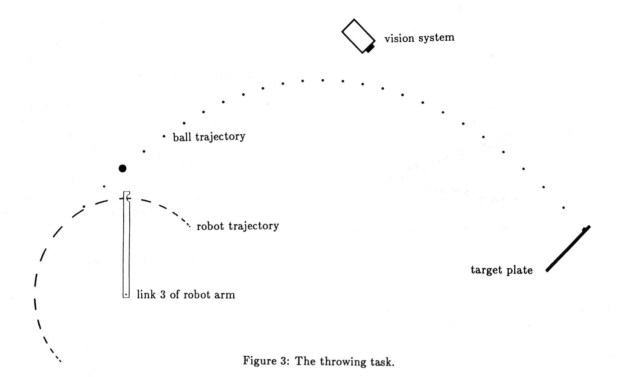

Figure 3: The throwing task.

3   Learning to Throw

Model-based learning can be used to improve performance on a complete task, in addition to improving positioning. As an example of task level learning, a robot arm was programmed to throw balls at a target. The robot throwing accuracy improved with practice.

Figure 3 illustrates the apparatus used in the throwing experiments. The target was at the center of a large metal plate, which was placed approximately 5 meters from the base of the robot. For this throwing task only the height of the ball when it hit the target plate was monitored and improved by a learning algorithm.

The last link of a three joint direct drive arm was used as a catapult to throw a ball. The robot was positioned so that the last link of the arm rotated in a vertical plane. The last joint was servoed to a fifth order polynomial trajectory that began at rest at 225° and ended at rest at 45°. A 4cm diameter rubber ball was placed onto a 3.5cm diameter hole at the end of the last link. The ball left the hole as the robot arm decelerated during the throw. No release mechanism was used. The release position of the ball was assumed to be when the last link was at 135°. The distance the ball was thrown was controlled by changing the duration of the throwing movement, which changed the release velocity. A shorter duration and therefore faster movement threw the ball higher and further, and a longer duration movement threw the ball lower and closer.

A video camera was used to record where the ball hit the target plate. The impact of the ball was sensed by a force sensor on which the target plate was mounted. This signal was used to choose video frames to be stored for later analysis. After the throw, the location of the ball on the target plate was manually measured from the appropriate video frame.

The initial release velocity command was calculated by measuring the distance to the target and using a simple ballistics model, incorporating only gravity, to predict the required flight trajectory given the assumed release position and initial direction of ball flight. The corresponding trajectory duration was computed and the calculated trajectory executed. On the first throw the ball hit the target plate 28cm above the target. The model-based learning algorithm based on estimating an output offset (equations (16) and (17)) was used to improve performance on the throwing task. This output offset learning algorithm corresponds to our intuition that we should aim lower if we are hitting too high, and vice versa. The role of the internal model is to calculate how much the aim should be changed. The ballistics model used to generate initial performance was also used to calculate the appropriate release velocity as the aim was offset by the estimated disturbance amount. The open squares in Figure 4 show the throwing performance during model-based learning. In this particular experiment the ball hit the target on the eighth throw.

The open triangles in Figure 4 indicate the performance of a model-based learning algorithm that improves the model as well as refining the command. This algorithm will be discussed in a later paper.

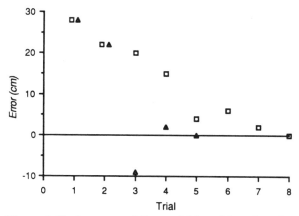

Figure 4: Performance of the model-based learning algorithm on a throwing task.

4   Trajectory Learning

Trajectory execution of a robot can be improved using a model-based learning algorithm (Atkeson and McIntyre 1986a, 1986b). A model of the robot inverse dynamics is used as the learning operator that transforms trajectory following errors into feedforward command corrections. This form of learning is useful for refining repetitive motions, and can also be used to refine groups of similar motions. Model-based trajectory learning was implemented on the MIT Serial Link Direct Drive Arm and greatly reduced trajectory following errors in a small number of practice movements.

The robot model used as the learning operator in the trajectory learning experiments was identified from movements of the MIT Serial Link Direct Drive Robot Arm (Atkeson, An, and Hollerbach 1986). The dynamics of this direct drive robot arm are dominated by rigid body dynamics, so a Newton-Euler model structure was used. The Newton-Euler rigid body dynamics equations for a robot can be written as

$$\boldsymbol{\tau} = \hat{R}^{-1}(\boldsymbol{\theta}, \dot{\boldsymbol{\theta}}, \ddot{\boldsymbol{\theta}}) = \mathbf{I}(\boldsymbol{\theta}) \cdot \ddot{\boldsymbol{\theta}} + \dot{\boldsymbol{\theta}} \cdot \mathbf{C}(\boldsymbol{\theta}) \cdot \dot{\boldsymbol{\theta}} + \mathbf{g}(\boldsymbol{\theta}) \quad (18)$$

where $\boldsymbol{\theta}(t)$ is the desired trajectory of the joint angles, $\boldsymbol{\tau}(t)$ is the vector of required torques to achieve the desired trajectory, $\mathbf{I}(\boldsymbol{\theta})$ is the inertia matrix of the arm, $\mathbf{C}(\boldsymbol{\theta})$ is the Coriolis and centripetal force tensor, and $\mathbf{g}(\boldsymbol{\theta})$ is the gravitational force vector (Hollerbach, 1984). For other types of robots it is argued that additional sources of dynamics are important (Goor, 1985; Good, Sweet, and Strobel, 1985). In these cases we can still model the robot dynamics and invert the model.

As before, there are several stages of the algorithm. The initial feedforward command is generated by applying the model of the robot inverse dynamics to the desired trajectory (as in equation (7)):

$$\boldsymbol{\tau}_{ff}^{0}(t) = \hat{R}^{-1}(\boldsymbol{\theta}_d(t), \dot{\boldsymbol{\theta}}_d(t), \ddot{\boldsymbol{\theta}}_d(t)) \quad (19)$$

During command execution the applied command is the sum of the feedforward command, $\boldsymbol{\tau}_{ff}$, and the output of the feedback controller, $\boldsymbol{\tau}_{fb}$:

$$\boldsymbol{\tau}^i(t) = \boldsymbol{\tau}_{ff}^i(t) + \boldsymbol{\tau}_{fb}^i(t) \quad (20)$$

The total applied command, $\boldsymbol{\tau}$, is used as the basis for the next feedforward command. As described in the previous sections, the command error is estimated using the model of the robot inverse dynamics (as in equation (9)):

$$\widehat{\delta\boldsymbol{\tau}}^i(t) = \hat{R}^{-1}(\boldsymbol{\theta}^i(t), \dot{\boldsymbol{\theta}}^i(t), \ddot{\boldsymbol{\theta}}^i(t)) - \hat{R}^{-1}(\boldsymbol{\theta}_d(t), \dot{\boldsymbol{\theta}}_d(t), \ddot{\boldsymbol{\theta}}_d(t))$$
$$(21)$$

and the next feedforward command is the modified total command (as in equation (10)):

$$\boldsymbol{\tau}_{ff}^{i+1}(t) = \boldsymbol{\tau}^i(t) - \widehat{\delta\boldsymbol{\tau}}^i(t) \quad (22)$$

Other Approaches to Trajectory Learning

Recent work in a number of laboratories has focused on how to refine feedforward commands for repetitive movements on the basis of previous movement errors. Work on repeated trajectory learning includes (Arimoto et al 1984, 1985; Casalino & Gambardella 1986; Craig 1984; Furuta & Yamakita 1986; Hara et al 1985; Harokopos 1986; Mita & Kato 1985; Morita 1986; Togai & Yamano 1986; Uchiyama 1978; Wang 1984; Wang & Horowitz 1985). These papers discuss only linear learning operators and emphasize the stability of the proposed algorithms. There has been little work emphasizing performance, i.e. the convergence rate of the algorithm. Simulations of several of these algorithms have revealed very slow convergence and large sensitivity to disturbances and sensor and actuator noise (C. G. Atkeson, unpublished results).

An Implementation of the Trajectory Learning Algorithm

The model-based trajectory learning algorithm has been implemented on the MIT Serial Link Direct Drive Arm (Atkeson and McIntyre 1986a, 1986b). This three joint arm is described in (Atkeson, An, and Hollerbach 1986). To explore the effectiveness of the model-based trajectory learning algorithm we will present results on learning a particular trajectory.

The Test Trajectory: All three joints of the Direct Drive Arm were commanded to follow a fifth order polynomial trajectory with zero initial and final velocities and accelerations and a 1.5 second duration. Figure 5 shows the shape of the trajectory for each joint, and Table 1 gives the initial and final joint positions, the peak joint velocities, and the peak joint accelerations.

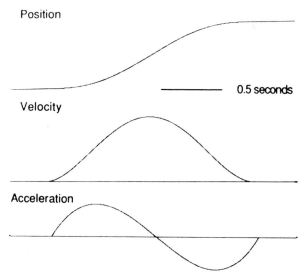

Figure 5: The test trajectory.

Joint	Initial Position *radians*	Final Position *radians*	Peak Velocity *radians/s*	Peak Acceleration *radians/s²*
1	0.5	4.5	5.0	±10.3
2	5.0	1.0	-5.0	±10.3
3	4.0	-0.5	-5.6	±11.5

Table 1: Test trajectory parameters.

The Feedback Controller: An independent digital feedback controller was implemented for each joint and was not modified during learning.

Initialization Of The Feedforward Command: The initial feedforward torques were generated from a rigid body dynamics model. The model and the estimation of its parameters are described in (Atkeson, An, and Hollerbach, 1986). The calculated feedforward torques are shown in Figure 6A.

Initial Trajectory Performance: As an index of trajectory following performance the velocity errors (the difference between the actual joint velocity and the desired joint velocity) for the first movement are shown in Figure 7A. We have plotted the raw velocity error data to give an idea of the relative size of the trajectory errors and sensor noise.

Calculating Acceleration and Filtering: In order to use the rigid body inverse dynamics model to compute joint torques it was necessary to compute the joint accelerations. Joint positions and velocities were measured directly. A digital differentiating filter combined with an 8Hz low pass filter was applied to the velocity data to estimate accelerations.

To reject noise and non-repeatable disturbances and to compensate for high frequency unmodelled dynamics it was necessary to filter the trajectory errors and controller output. In this implementation we applied low pass digital filters with an 8Hz cutoff to the data

used in the learning process. We filtered the references used by the learning operator with the same filter used on the data. It was also necessary to correct for inconsistencies between the velocity sensors and the position measurements, which was done by adjusting the position reference to the feedback controller until the integrated velocity error matched the position error.

Final Trajectory Performance: The robot executed two additional training movements which are not shown, and its performance on the fourth attempt of the test trajectory was assessed. Figure 6B shows the modified feedforward commands used on the fourth movement, and should be compared with the predicted torques shown in Figure 6A. Figure 7B shows the velocity errors for the fourth movement, and should be compared with the initial movement velocity errors in Figure 7A. There has been a substantial reduction in trajectory following error after only three practice movements.

5   Issues For Further Research

Some of the questions that warrant further research include the effect of modeling errors and non-repeatable disturbances on convergence, and learning of non-repetitive tasks.

As discussed previously, the convergence of model-based learning algorithms depends on the quality of the model. Accurate models support efficient learning. Inaccurate models may cause learning algorithms to degrade performance rather than improve it.

Reducing or filtering the estimated command correction will make model-based learning more robust to modeling errors. Convergence will be slowed, however. Further research is required into the appropriate tradeoff between handling modeling errors and fast convergence. Filtering of the model-based command update also plays an important role in reducing the effect of non-repeatable disturbances.

If intermediate sensory signals are available, then breaking the control system into modules and having each module learn independently may improve learning performance. We plan to explore this issue in the throwing task. If measurements are available of when and where the ball is released, then independent models of the throwing motion and the ball flight characteristics can be made. These independent models can be used to choose an appropriate release velocity separately from refining the trajectory that attains that release velocity.

It is possible to modify models as well as commands during learning. In the examples presented in this paper the same models were used repeatedly even after it became clear during learning that the models had large errors. We have explored some methods of model refinement during practice. The open triangles of Figure 4 show the faster convergence of a model-based learning algorithm that improves the model as well as the command.

Joint 1 Feedforward Torque

Joint 2

Joint 3

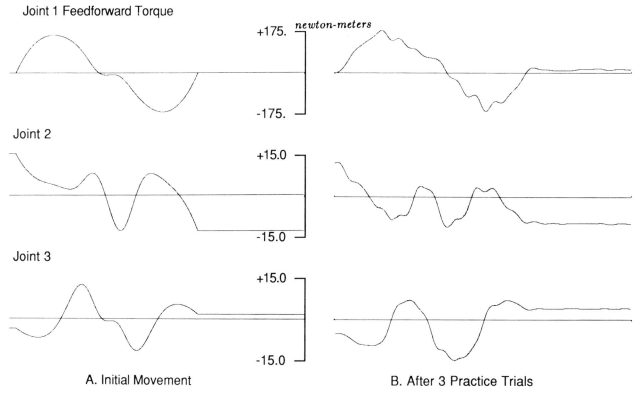

A. Initial Movement

B. After 3 Practice Trials

Figure 6: Feedforward Torques

Joint 1 Velocity Error

Joint 2

Joint 3

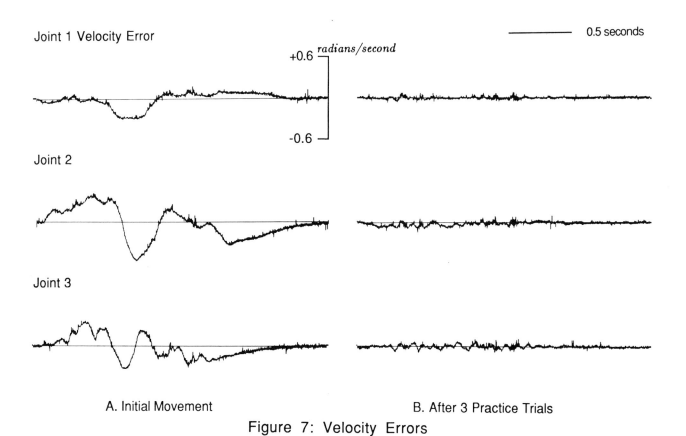

A. Initial Movement

B. After 3 Practice Trials

Figure 7: Velocity Errors

The model-based learning algorithms are ideally suited to refining repetitive commands for the same tasks. The learning algorithms can also be applied to refining commands for different tasks by assuming that similar command errors will be made on similar tasks. An estimate of the command error on one task will be useful for improving the command for other tasks that share features with the original task.

6 Conclusion

The main message of this paper is that models play an important role in learning from practice. Better models lead to faster correction of command errors. The incorporation of learning in a control system is not a license to do a poor modeling job of the controlled system. The benefits of accurate modeling are better performance in all aspects of control, while the risks of inadequate modeling are poor learning performance or even degradation of performance with practice.

The approach to robot learning presented here is based on explicit modeling of the robot and the task being performed. An inverse model of the task is used as the learning operator that processes the errors. Such model-based command refinement algorithms usefully complement other approaches to adaptive control.

Studying model-based learning algorithms serves two purposes: 1) to improve robot performance, and 2) to increase our understanding of the role of practice and internal models in human motor learning.

Acknowledgments

This article describes research done at the Whitaker College, Department of Brain and Cognitive Sciences, and the Artificial Intelligence Laboratory of the Massachusetts Institute of Technology. Support was provided in the Whitaker College by grants AM26710 and NS09343 from the NIH. Support for the A. I. Laboratory's research is provided in part by the Advanced Research Projects Agency of the Department of Defense under Office of Naval Research contract N00014-85-K-0124, and the Office of Naval Research University Research Initiative Program under Office of Naval Research contract N00014-86-K-0685. Support for CGA was provided by a Whitaker Health Sciences Fund MIT Faculty Research Grant. Support for EWA was provided by an Office of Naval Research Graduate Student Fellowship. Support for JM was provided by an NIH training grant NIH-GM07484 and a Whitaker Health Sciences Fund Doctoral Fellowship.

References

Arimoto, S., S. Kawamura, and F. Miyazaki, "Bettering Operation of Robots by Learning", *Journal of Robotic Systems* **1** (1984a) 123-140.

Arimoto, S., S. Kawamura, and F. Miyazaki, "Can Mechanical Robots Learn by Themselves?", Proc. of 2nd Inter. Symp. Robotics Research (Kyoto, Japan, August, 1984b).

Arimoto, S., S. Kawamura, F. Miyazaki, and S. Tamaki, "Learning Control Theory for Dynamical Systems", Proc. 24th Conf. on Decision and Control (Fort Lauderdale, Florida, Dec. 11-13, 1985).

Atkeson, C. G., C. An, and J. M. Hollerbach, "Estimation of Inertial Parameters of Manipulator Loads and Links", *International Journal of Robotics Research* **5** (1986) 101-119.

Atkeson, C. G. and J. McIntyre, "Robot Trajectory Learning Through Practice", IEEE Conf. on Robotics and Automation (San Francisco, CA, April 7 - 10, 1986a).

Atkeson, C. G. and J. McIntyre, "Applications of Adaptive Feedforward Control in Robotics", Proc. 2nd IFAC Workshop on Adaptive Systems in Control and Signal Processing (Lund, Sweden, July 1-3, 1986b).

Casalino, G. and L. Gambardella, "Learning of Movements in Robotic Manipulators", Proc. 1986 IEEE International Conference on Robotics and Automation (San Francisco, CA, April 7-10, 1986a) pp. 572-578.

Craig, J. J., "Adaptive Control of Manipulators Through Repeated Trials", Proc. American Control Conference (San Diego, June 6-8, 1984) pp. 1566-1574.

Furuta, K. and M. Yamakita, "Iterative Generation of Optimal Input of a Manipulator", Proc. 1986 IEEE International Conference on Robotics and Automation (San Francisco, CA, April 7-10, 1986) pp. 579-584.

Good, M.C., Sweet, L.M., and Strobel, K.L., "Dynamic models for control system design of integrated robot and drive systems", *ASME J. Dynamic Systems, Meas., Control,* **107** (1985) 53-59.

Goor, R.M., "A new approach to robot control", Proc. American Control Conf (Boston, June 19-21, 1985) pp. 385-389.

Hara, S., T. Omata, and M. Nakano, "Synthesis of Repetitive Control Systems and its Application", Proc. 24th Conf. on Decision and Control (Fort Lauderdale, Florida, Dec. 11-13, 1985).

Harokopos, E. G., "Optimal Learning Control of Mechanical Manipulators in Repetitive Motions", Proc. 1986 IEEE International Conference on Robotics and Automation (San Francisco, CA, April 7-10, 1986) pp. 396-401.

Hollerbach, J. M., "Dynamic Scaling of Manipulator Trajectories", *Journal of Dynamics Systems, Measurement, and Control* **106** (1984) 102-106.

Mita, T., and E. Kato, "Iterative Control and its Application to Motion Control of Robot Arm – A Direct Approach to Servo-Problems", Proc. 24th Conf. on Decision and Control (Fort Lauderdale, Florida, Dec. 11-13, 1985).

Morita, A., "A Study of Learning Controllers For Robot Manipulators With Sparse Data", M.S. thesis, Mechanical Engineering, Massachusetts Institute of Technology (February 27, 1986).

Togai, M. and O. Yamano, "Learning Control and Its Optimality: Analysis and Is Application to Controlling Industrial Robots", Proc. 1986 IEEE International Conference on Robotics and Automation (San Francisco, CA, April 7-10, 1986) pp. 248-253.

Uchiyama, M., "Formation of High-Speed Motion Pattern of a Mechanical Arm by Trial", *Transactions of the Society of Instrument and Control Engineers (Japan)* **19** (1978) 706–712.

Wang, S. H., "Computed Reference Error Adjustment Technique (CREATE) For The Control of Robot Manipulators", 22nd Annual Allerton Conf. on Communication, Control, and Computing (October, 1984).

Wang, S. H., and I. Horowitz, "CREATE - A New Adaptive Technique", Proc. of the Nineteenth Annual Conference on Information Sciences and Systems (March, 1985).

A STUDY OF THE DYNAMICS AND CONTROL OF MOBILE MANIPULATORS SUBJECTED TO VEHICLE DISTURBANCES

Steven Dubowsky
Professor of Mechanical Engineering
Massachusetts Institute of Technology
Cambridge, MA 02139

Albert B. Tanner
Captain, Department of Mechanical Engineering
United States Military Academy
West Point, NY 10996

Manipulators mounted on vehicles have many potential applications. However, such manipulators are subject to base motion disturbances which can degrade their performance. Conventional controllers may not be able to compensate for the base motion. This paper presents a control technique to compensate for base motion disturbances. It is shown that the technique which uses relatively limited sensory information, can substantially improve mobile manipulator performance. The technique is demonstrated in simulations and experimentally using a manipulator mounted on a moving platform.

INTRODUCTION

Current manipulators generally operate while mounted on fixed bases and are therefore not subject to base motion disturbances. However, many potential future applications of robotic manipulators will require that they operate while being carried by moving vehicles. Some of these potential applications may require manipulators to operate while their vehicles move over rough terrain [Committee, 1983]. Under such conditions, the manipulators would be subject to large dynamic disturbances due to the vehicle's motion. These disturbances can seriously degrade the manipulator's performance. They can cause the manipulator to leave its prescribed path, saturate its actuators, and induce high stresses in its elements [Lynch, 1985 and Tanner, 1987]. This work shows that conventional control strategies would have difficulty controlling mobile manipulators subject to large base motions.

There has been very little prior research into studying the control problems in mobile manipulators caused by dynamic disturbances [Lynch, 1985, Joshi and Desrochers, 1986, Li and Frank, 1986]. In order for future mobile robotic systems to successfully accomplish tasks while their vehicles are in motion, new control techniques must be developed. In this paper, a control strategy based on using relatively limited sensory information from the vehicle is studied. The results show that for the cases studied, this strategy can effectively compensate for vehicle motion dynamic disturbances and greatly improve system performance.

Experiments were performed which confirmed the results of the simulations. Furthermore, they show that the technique can be practically implemented in real-time using relatively little computation effort.

ANALYTICAL DEVELOPMENT

The System

For this research, a prototype mobile manipulator system was designed to perform a proposed material handling task [Committee, 1983 and Holly, 1983], see Figure 1. The manipulator's mechanical properties were selected to achieve a given set of specifications and constraints [Tanner, 1987]. It is designed to be constructed with steel tube links and powered by direct drive hydraulic actuators. The actuator capacities were chosen to meet task acceleration requirements, overcome gravity, and reject disturbances without saturating. The manipulator's links were designed to also have structural natural frequencies well above the system's operating speed. The lowest structural natural frequency with the maximum payload is approximately 95 rad/sec. A complete description of this system is contained in reference [Tanner, 1987] and some of its characteristics are given in Table 1.

The task of the manipulator is to remove objects weighing between 40 and 60 pounds, from various locations in a rack which is fixed to the vehicle, place them into a chamber, and return to the rack, see Figure 2. It is assumed that the vehicle is far more massive than the manipulator system. As a result, it is assumed that the motion of the manipulator does not effect the vehicle. If the masses of the manipulator and vehicle are of the same order of magnitude the problem is substantially more difficult [Vafa and Dubowsky, 1987].

A typical trajectory is shown in Figure 2. The manipulator's cycle time, approximately 6 seconds, is somewhat shorter than the time required to manually perform this task [Holly, 1983]. The crucial point in the system's performance is the accuracy of the manipulator when the payload is inserted into the chamber. Based on the geometry of the chamber and payload, the position tolerances in Table 2 were calculated as a function of insertion distance. Once the payload enters the chamber by more than 6.0 inches, it is assumed that it will slide into the chamber along its walls under simple force control without jamming. At this point position control is no longer required.

	Mass	Inertia
Pay Load	M_p	J_p
Link 1	M_1	J_1
Link 2	M_2	J_2

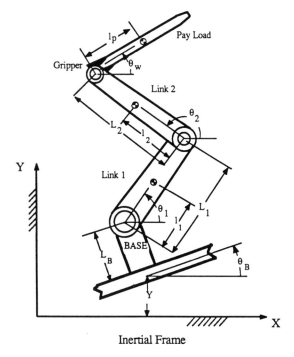

Figure 1. Mobile Manipualtor System Model.

Table 1: Basic Manipulator Mechanical Properties

Links	1	2	Wrist	Payload
Outer Radii (in.)	4.4	3.9	5.0	5.0
Inner Radii (in.)	3.4	3.0	0.0	0.0
Length (in.)	36.0	36.0	3.0	30.0
Mass $(lbf - sec^2/ft)$	9.3	6.8	0.8	2.6
Moments of Inertia $(lbf - sec^2 - ft)$	7.3	5.2	0.03	1.5

Actuators	1	2	Wrist	Payload
Weight (lbf)	100.	40.	43.	-
Capacity (lbf-ft)	5913.	1808.	570.	-

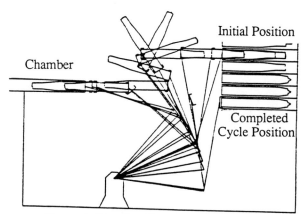

Figure 2. Baseline Task Trajectory.

Table 2: Insertion Tolerances

Insertion Distance (in.)	0.0	2.4	6.0
Vertical Tolerance (in.)	1.4	1.0	0.6
Angular Tolerance (deg.)	15.0	15.0	0.0

When the vehicle is operating at high speed over rough terrain it will experience high amplitude random rotations and translations. The manipulator system being studied would be required to perform its task during this time. For this study the manipulator was treated as a planar three degree-of-freedom system and it was assumed that the vehicle would translate and rotate in the plane of the manipulator. Typical measured values of the vehicle's vertical acceleration experienced by the manipulator is shown in Figure 3 as a function of time [Musell, 1986]. The measured vehicle pitch angular acceleration has a form similar to vertical acceleration and a maximum amplitude of approximately $\pm 4.0 rad/sec^2$. These profiles were used in this study to model the vehicle motions.

System Equations of Motion

To study the system's response, a dynamic model of the system including the effects of base motion was developed using Lagrange's equation:

$$\frac{d}{dt}\left[\frac{\partial T}{\partial \dot{q}_i}\right] - \frac{\partial T}{\partial q_i} + \frac{\partial U}{\partial q_i} = Q_i \qquad i = 1, 2, 3 \qquad (1)$$

where:

T is the the system kinetic engery,

U is the system potential energy,

Q_i is the ith generalized force,

q_i is the ith generalized coordinate.

The angles θ_1, θ_2, and θ_w were selected as generalized coordinates, see Figure 1. The vehicle's motion was described by a vertical motion and a pitch rotation with respect to inertial space (Y and θ_b respectively). Using these variables and the parameters defined in Figure 1 yields the following nonlinear equation of motion for the θ_1 generalized coordinate.

$$(M_1 L_b l_1 + M_2 L_b L_1 + M_p L_b L_1) cos(\theta_b - \theta_1)\ddot\theta_b +$$
$$(M_1 L_1^2 + M_2 L_1^2 + M_p L_1^2 + J_1)\ddot\theta_1 + (M_2 L_1 l_2 + M_p L_1 L_2)$$
$$cos(\theta_1 - \theta_2)\ddot\theta_2 + M_p L_1 l_p cos(\theta_1 - \theta_w)\ddot\theta_w +$$
$$(M_1 l_1 + M_2 L_1 + M_p L_1)cos\theta_1(\ddot Y + g) -$$
$$(M_1 L_b l_1 + M_2 L_b L_1 + M_p L_b L_1)sin(\theta_b - \theta_1)\dot\theta_b^2$$
$$+(M_2 L_1 l_2 + M_p L_1 L_2)sin(\theta_1 - \theta_2)\dot\theta_2^2 + M_p L_1 l_p sin(\theta_1 - \theta_w)\dot\theta_w^2$$
$$= T_1 - T_2$$
$$(2)$$

The equations for the θ_2 and θ_w generalized coordinates have forms similar to Equation (2), see reference [Tanner, 1987]. The variables T_1, T_2 and T_w are the torques applied by the first, second, and wrist actuators, respectively. In the system equations of motion, the terms which contain Y and θ_b and/or their derivatives are due to the vehicle's motions. It is through these distrubance terms that the vehicle motions dynamically couple into the manipulators motion.

The system's equations of motion were used in a computer simulation to model the full nonlinear behavior of the system. They were also linearized about a nominal manipulator position and velocity for designing the manipulator's control systems. If θ_i^n, $\dot\theta_i^n$ and $\ddot\theta_i^n$ are the selected nominal operating points, and $\delta\theta_i$, $\delta\dot\theta_i$ and $\delta\ddot\theta_i$ are small perturbations about these points, then:

$$\theta_i = \theta_i^n + \delta\theta_i \qquad i = 1,2,w \qquad (3)$$

The resulting linearized equation of motion for the θ_1 generalized coordinate is:

$$(M_1 l_1^2 + M_2 L_1^2 + M_p L_1^2 + J_1)\delta\ddot\theta_1 + (M_2 L_1 l_2 + M_p L_1 L_2)$$
$$cos(\theta_1^n - \theta_2^n)\delta\ddot\theta_2 + M_p L_1 l_p cos(\theta_1^n - \theta_w^n)\delta\ddot\theta_w =$$
$$\{-(M_1 L_b l_1 + M_2 L_b L_1 + M_p L_b L_1)[sin(\theta_b - \theta_1^n)\ddot\theta_b +$$
$$cos(\theta_b - \theta_1^n)\dot\theta_b^2] + (M_2 L_1 l_2 + M_p L_1 L_2)[sin(\theta_1^n - \theta_2^n)\ddot\theta_2^n -$$
$$cos(\theta_1^n - \theta_2^n)(\dot\theta_2^n)^2] + M_p L_1 l_p [sin(\theta_1^n - \theta_w^n)\ddot\theta_w^n -$$
$$cos(\theta_1^n - \theta_w^n)(\dot\theta_w^n)^2] + (M_1 l_1 + M_2 L_1 + M_p L_1)sin\theta_1^n(\ddot Y + g)\}\delta\theta_1$$
$$+(M_2 L_1 l_2 + M_p L_1 L_2)[cos(\theta_1^n - \theta_2^n)(\dot\theta_2^n)^2 - sin(\theta_1^n - \theta_2^n)\ddot\theta_2^n]\delta\theta_2$$
$$-2(M_2 L_1 l_2 + M_p L_1 L_2)sin(\theta_1^n - \theta_2^n)\dot\theta_2^n\delta\dot\theta_2 +$$
$$M_p L_1 l_p [cos(\theta_1^n - \theta_w^n)(\dot\theta_w^n)^2 - sin(\theta_1^n - \theta_w^n)\ddot\theta_w^n]\delta\theta_w -$$
$$2M_p L_1 l_p sin(\theta_1^n - \theta_w^n)\dot\theta_w^n\delta\dot\theta_w + T_1 - T_2$$
$$(4)$$

The linearized equations for the θ_2 and θ_w generalized coordinates have forms similar to Equation (4). These linearized equations of motion can be written in state space form as:

$$\dot X = AX + BU + LW \qquad (5)$$

where:

X is the system state vector,

U is a vector of actuator torques

W is a vector of vehicle motions.

The matrices A, B and L depend upon the vehicle's motion and the nonimal state space trajectory used for the linearization.

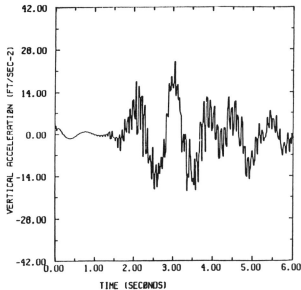

Figure 3. A Sample of Measured Vehicle Vertical Accelerations, $\ddot Y$, as Function of Time.

Control System Design

A linear full state feedback controller was selected as the basic manipulator controller. This controller is shown in block diagram form in Figure 4. Also shown in the figure are the base motion disturbance terms, W, and a feedfoward compensation term T_{comp} which is discussed later. For this case, the actuator torques will be given by the 6 element vector U:

$$U = R - KX \qquad (6)$$

where R is the command vector, and K is a matrix of controller gains. The controller gains were selected to obtain closed-loop system eigenvalues (poles) corresponding to frequencies which are as high as possible, but less than one third of the lowest structural resonances, which are approximatly 95 rad/sec. Futhermore, the damping ratios for the closed-loop poles were chosen to be 0.707. Based on these objectives, the gain matrix, K, was selected using an eigenstructure assignment method [Tanner, 1987]. Several other controllers were designed and tested. A discussion of these controllers are beyond the scope of this paper.

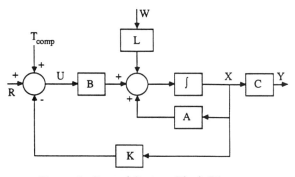

Figure 4. Control System Block Diagram.

SIMULATION RESULTS

Performance without Base Motion Disturbances

Simulations of the full nonlinear system were conducted to verify the performance of the system without vehicle motion disturbances. These simulations showed that the system, without any base motion disturbances, meets all performance specifications. Figure 5 shows the motion of the manipulator's joints during the six second loading cycle shown in Figure 2. The actuator torques for this motion are well below the actuator saturation levels given in Table 1. Figures 6 and 7 show that the payload's vertical tip and angle errors are within their allowable tolerances during insertion.

Our studies also showed that while the closed-loop system poles change as the manipulator moves, these poles remain within the limits imposed by the structural resonences during the entire cycle. It was also shown that the manipulator was able to handle payloads of different weights without problems.

Based on the simulation results, it was concluded that the system would successfully perform its tasks in the absence of base motion disturbances.

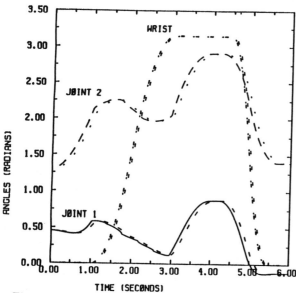

Figure 5. Joint Angles Commands and Response for Typical Task, as a Function of Time.

Performance with Base Motion Disturbances

Without Compensation

Next, simulations for the basic system were conducted with base motions. In these cases, the system's performance was found to be unsatisfactory. A typical result is shown in Figure 8. It shows an unacceptable vertical tip position error during the critical insertion phase of the motion. This error would prevent the payload from successfully entering the chamber. These results demonstrate the degrading effect that base motion disturbances

can have on a mobile manipulator with a conventional feedback controller.

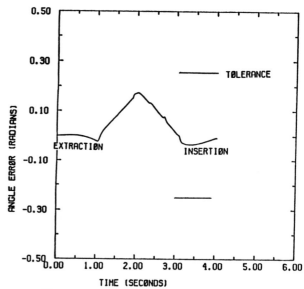

Figure 6. Payload Angle Error for Baseline Task Without Base Motions.

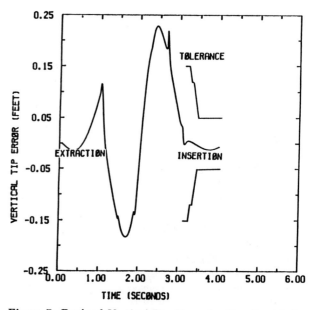

Figure 7. Payload Vertical Tip Error for Baseline Task Without Base Motions.

With Sensory Compensation

To overcome the problems found in the system with only feed back control, a feed foward compensator, which uses sensory information of base motion, was developed. As shown below, this compensator can counter the effects of the dynamic forces generated by the disturbances to yield good performance in the presence of base motions, and still have low enough gains to prevent the excitation of system's structural resonances.

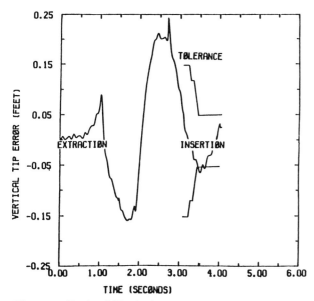

Figure 8. Payload Vertical Tip Error for Baseline Task
With Base Motions and Without
Compensation.

First, it was assumed that all the motions of the base
(θ_b, $\dot\theta_b$, $\ddot\theta_b$, and $\ddot Y$) could be measured. The base motion
dynamic disturbances acting on the manipulator are func-
tions of these variables. These values were then used to
calculate feed forward torques, T_{comp} in Figure 4, which
would cancel the dynamic forces and moments due to the
base motions. Obviously this procedure will be effective
as long as all the base motions are accurately measured,
the compensation torques are within the actuator torque
limits, and an accurate dynamic model of the manipulator
is available.

Simulations were conducted for the nonlinear system with
compensation which used all the vehicle motion variables
and an accurate dynamic model of the system. As expected, the results were virtually identical to cases when
there were no base motions, see Figures 5 and 7. For these
cases the actuators did not saturate.

In practice, measuring all the base motion variables would
be difficult. The vehicle, which was assumed for this
study, has the ability to measure $\dot\theta_b$ using rate gyros and
obtains θ_b by integration. However, the angular accelerations, $\ddot\theta_b$, are very difficult to measure and are subject to
noise. Furthermore, it should be noted that the dynamic
disturbances are not functions of Y or $\dot Y$. Therefore, the
system's performance of only using $\ddot Y$, θ_b, and $\dot\theta_b$ in the
compensation was examined. First, the relative magni-
tudes of the disturbance forces due to the various terms
were calculated for typical conditions. These calculations
showed that the $\ddot Y$ disturbance terms are substantially
larger than any of the other terms. Based on this, a compensation technique called partial compensation was developed. This method does not rely on the measurement
of $\ddot\theta_b$. Figure 9 is typical of the performance of the system
with base motion disturbances and partial compensation.

It can be seen that the vertical tip error, which was unacceptable without compensation (see Figure 8), is now
within the required limits.

The sensitivity of the compensation method to the accuracy of the model used in the compensation was studied.
It is often difficult to obtain an accurate dynamic model
of robotic systems, especially when the payload characteristics are not known. Simulations were conducted for the
partial and full compensation methods utilizing models
with ten percent errors in their parameters and various
payloads. The results show that the manipulator using
either compensation method could successfully perform
its tasks. These results suggest that the method is not
very sensitive to modeling errors.

Our simulation results show that this proposed technique,
which uses measurements of the base motions, is effective
in reducing the errors caused by the base motion disturbances even when the vehicle is moving over very rough
terrain.

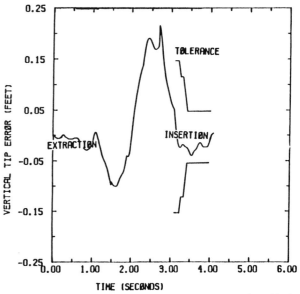

Figure 9. Payload Vertical Tip Error for Baseline Task
With Base Motions and With Compensation.

EXPERIMENTAL STUDIES

Experimental Description

The practicality of the compensation method was experimentally demonstrated in our laboratory. A schematic
of the experimental system is shown in Figure 10. The
system consists of a PUMA 260 manipulator mounted
on a vertical motion platform [Fresko, 1986]. Two micro
PDP11/73 computers are used, one to control the platform's motion and one to control the manipulator.

The platform, see Figure 11, consists of a plate driven
by a hydraulic piston whose motion is controlled by its
computer. The platform is capable of producing motion
profiles with amplitudes up to 10 inches and frequencies

116   Dubowsky and Tanner

up to 10 Hertz. During these tests the platform's accelerations were limited in software to two g's to prevent damage to the manipulator. The platform computer receives the platform acceleration signals, filters them, and sends them to the manipulator control computer for use in the compensator. The manipulator control computer is connected to the manipulator through special interface boards which receive position information from the manipulator's encoders and sends commands to the motors' amplifiers. The manipulator control algorithm are implemented using high level languages. This permits complex control algorithms to be tested easily [Dubowsky and Kornbluh, 1983 and Whaley, 1985]. In this case the control algorithms, with and without dynamic compensation, were writen in PASCAL.

The command trajectory used in these studies is very similar to the one used in the simulations. The calculation of the compensation torques require the mass properties of the manipulator and these were determined experimentally.

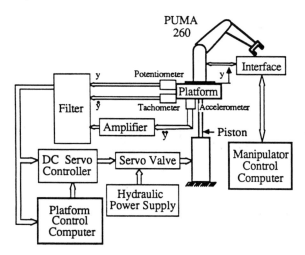

Figure 10. Experimental System Schematic Diagram.

Experimental Results

Figures 12 and 13 show typical experimental results. The manipulator was commanded to move through its task while the platform oscillated sinusoidaly with an amplitude of 4.5 inches and at a frequency of 0.8 Hertz. In Figure 12 the tip error without compensation is shown. Figure 13 shows the same case with compensation. Comparing these figures clearly shows that the effectiveness of the compensation approach in reducing the errors due to base motion disturbances. The computation effort required by this approach, even when it is implemented in a high level language, is not excessive.

CONCLUSIONS

This study has shown that important control problems arise when a manipulator is carried on a mobile platform.

The base motion creates dynamic disturbances which can seriously degrade the manipulator's performance. Clearly these base motion disturbances need to be considered in the design of future mobile manipulator systems. For the cases considered in this study, conventional control algorithms have difficulty rejecting these disturbances. However, both simulation and experimental studies showed that the effects of these disturbances could be significantly reduced by using a dynamic feed forward compensation method based on measured base motions. The experimental studies showed that such a control approach is practical.

ACKNOWLEDGEMENTS

Captain Tanner's studies were supported by a U.S. Army Fellowship and the research was funded by the U.S. Army Research Institute under contract MDA903-83-C-0196 and by DARPA (US Army Human Engineering Laboratory Agents) under Oak Ridge National Laboratory subcontract 19X-55970C. The authors would like to acknowledge the contributions of M. Fresko, N. Hootsmans and I. Paul to the development of the experimental equipment.

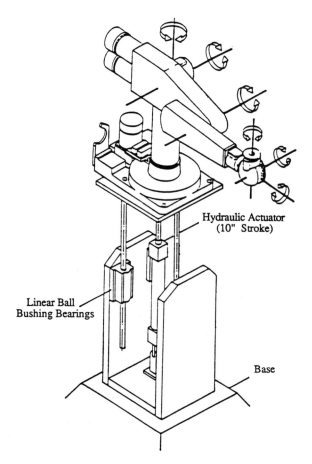

Figure 11. Experimental System Mechanical Elements Diagram.

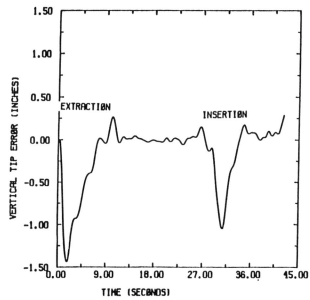

Figure 12. Payload Vertical Tip Error for Experimental System With Base Motions and Without Compensation.

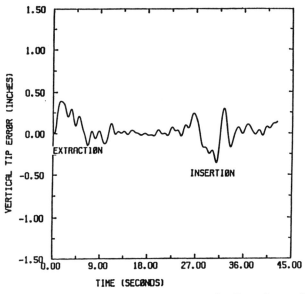

Figure 13. Payload Vertical Tip Error for Experimental System With Base Motions and With Compensation.

REFERENCES

[1] Committee on Army Robots and Artificial Intelligence, "Applications of Robotics and Artificial Intelligence to Reduce Risk and Improve Effectiveness: A Study for the United States Army," Published by the National Academy Press, Washington, D.C. 1983.

[2] Dubowsky, S. and Kornbluh, R., "On the Development of High Performance Adaptive Control Algorithms for Robotic Manipulators," Proceedings of the Second International Symposium of Robotics Research, Kyoto, Japan, August, 1984.

[3] Fresko, M., "The Design and Implementation of a Computer ControlledPlatform With Variable Admittance," MS Thesis, MIT, Cambridge, MA, January, 1986.

[4] Holly, J. W., Automatic Ammunition Loading Systems for Large Caliber Weapons Mounted in Close Combat Armored Vehicles, Tank Automotive Command, Warren, Michigan, 1983.

[5] Joshi, J., and Desrochers, A. "Modeling and Control of a Mobile Robot Subject to Disturbances," Proceedings of the 1986 IEEE Inter. Conf. on Robotics and Automation, San Francisco, CA, March, 1986.

[6] Li, Y. and Frank, A.A., "A Moving Base Robot," Proceedings of the American Control Conference, Seattle, WA, June, 1986.

[7] Lynch, R., "Analysis of the Dynamics and Control of a Two Degree of Freedom Robotic Manipulator Mounted on a Moving Base," M.S. Thesis, Department of Mechanical Engineering, MIT Cambridge MA, October, 1985.

[8] Musell, R., "Actual Disturbances Measured on the Abrams Tank," United States Army Tank Automotive Command, A Private Communciation, Warren, Michigan, 1986.

[9] Tanner, A.B., "Study of Robotic Manipulators Subject to Base Disturbances," M.S. Thesis, Department of Mechanical Engineering, MIT Cambridge MA, January, 1985.

[10] Vafa, Z., and Dubowsky, S., "On the Dynamics of Manipulators in Space Using the Virtual Manipulator Approach," Proceedings of the 1987 IEEE Inter. Conf. on Robotics and Automation, Raleigh, NC, March, 1987.

[11] Whaley, J.L., "An Experimental System for Testing Robotic Manipulator Control Alogrithms: A Demonstration of Adaptive Control," MS Thesis, MIT, Cambridge, MA, November, 1985.

The Control Of Compliant Manipulator Arms

R. W. Daniel, M. A. Irving, A. R. Fraser, M. Lambert

Oxford University
Department Of Engineering Science
Parks Road
Oxford OX1 3PJ
England

Three compliant robot arms designed and built at Oxford University are described. The control of a two link compliant arm using inverse dynamics and on-line model identification are given. A new control algorithm aimed at using SIMD parallel computer architectures is also described together with some results of using this algorithm on a one link model compliant arm.

The paper is concluded with a description of a large direct drive compliant arm built at Oxford and of the control issues which this research vehicle will enable us to address in the near future.

This paper is an overview of some recent work at Oxford University[1] on the design and control of compliant robot arms. Several related projects are described briefly as fuller accounts are in preparation. The descriptions are necessarily brief, but accurately reflect the interests of the robotics research group in force and motion control issues. The chosen theme is compliance, why it should be of interest to roboticists, and our experiences in dealing with it in the real world.

1 Compliance: A Bug or Feature?

1.1 Compliance As A Bug

A number of researchers have looked into the problem of controlling compliant robot arms [Book 1975, Cannon 1984, Kanoh 1985, Truckenbrodt 1981] . The most often quoted reason for the interest in this subject is the improvement in performance which would ensue from using lightweight structures instead of the heavy rigid members used in current robot arms. Reducing the mass of an arm will enable actuators to accelerate the arm more quickly but will incur the penalty of compliance in what was orig-

inally a rigid structure. However, extremely fast industrial direct drive arms are now being developed which do not exhibit large degrees of compliance. This feature is usually achieved by using semi-direct drive technology, with the advantage that the arm does not need to carry the mass of its motors.

It seems then that for lightweight assembly it is possible to design arms that are both rigid and fast. There are, however, many industrial processes in which compliance cannot be swept aside as a design bug. In some applications, large deformations *inevitably* arise and need to be controlled eg large space structures, continuous contact processes such as deburring.

Now consider the problem depicted in figure 1. This depicts the situation that exists in UK Magnox gas cooled nuclear reactors, into which it is required to place manipulator arms to carry out routine inspection and maintenance. Access is restricted because of the reactor shielding, the arm must pass through 11 inch diameter standpipes. Large loads may need to be carried (up to 35 kg), sometimes with great precision (0.1 mm). The restriction on the access routes means that there is a limit to the stiffness that can be achieved for such a structure, and the effects of compliance must be taken into account if precise end-point control is required. A small two link arm has been constructed at Oxford University to model

[1] The authors would like to thank the UK Central Electricity Generating Board and the Science and Engineering Research Council for financial support. We would also like to thank Nippon Seiko K.K. for their help and enthusiasm.

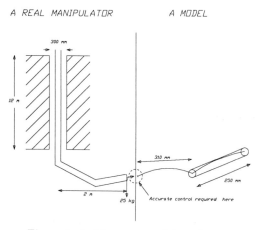

Figure 1: Inside a gas cooled nuclear reactor

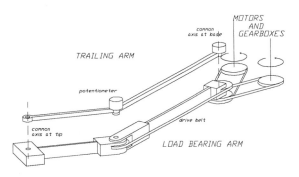

Figure 2: A model two link arm

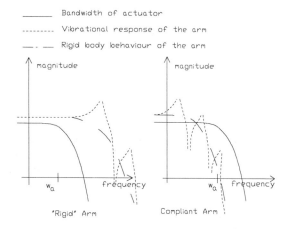

Figure 3: Relative bandwidths of rigid and compliant arm controllers

the control of such an arm when precise end point control is required. Figure 2 represents the model arm, which uses a stiff lightweight trailing arm to measure true tip position. The double arm configuration is a mechanical analogue of the situation that arises when a non-contact form of tip position sensing is used. In a real application, such as arc welding inside a nuclear reactor, an optical technique for position sensing could be used. However, it does not matter whether contact or non-contact position sensing is used, some form of kinematic model must be employed within the control loop in order to move the flexible arm. A major problem then exists due to mismatch between the kinematic model of the trailing arm and the true kinematics of the deformed arm. The aim of the model arm was to investigate the use of true tip measurement to achieve accurate control of position. Thus when large loads are to be moved accurately tip position must be used, resulting in a non-collocated control problem, together with problems of kinematic mismatches. This paper will not detail the problems of kinematic mismatch between physical and model arms, but will concentrate on the ability of the controller to remove vibrations. Figure 10 is a photograph of the arm showing the effect of such vibrations when not under control.

1.2 Compliance As A Feature

However, is compliance ever desirable? In the previous section we noted that in many applications compliance inevitably arises and has to be dealt with appropriately. In this section we argue that it can be a virtue, easing the problem of dealing with contacts between the arm and the external world. Consider the problem of controlling collisions. One possible method of controlling both desired and undesired collisions (as may occur during an assembly process) is to use a passive technique of force control such as that provided by Remote Center Compliance. Another method is to employ force control. However, to achieve force control at the tip of a non-compliant robot arm, torques applied to the robot joints must be able to decelerate the arm before external contact constraints are able to generate large impulsive forces, which could break the wrist or any wrist force/torque sensors. To achieve this, the bandwidth of the actuators plus control system must be greater than the lowest natural frequencies present in the arm structure. However, a rule of thumb used for designing robot control schemes is that the natural frequencies present in the robot structure must be at least ten times higher than the bandwidth of the arm. Conflicting demands are then placed on the controller of a rigid arm if it is to be used in a force control loop. If collisions between the arm and its environment are envisaged then pure force control would be limited to low bandwidth applications like following contours along surfaces covered with soft material or contact with highly compliant objects.

Extra compliance can be added to the end effector, such as that provided by Remote Center Compliance. It is possible to control tip force by using a spring plus position transducer arrangement. However, we have found in practice that it is then possible to obtain unstable interactions between the kinematics of the arm and the kinematics of the sensor. The instability arises from the finite resolution used to measure arm position. This can lead to significant hunting as the arm tracks a force using in effect its position controller.

A different approach is to reduce the bandwidth of the arm by deliberately introducing compliance into the structure and increasing the bandwidth of the control system. The first few vibrational modes of the arm then enter into the control calculation. This situation is depicted in figure 3 where the left hand diagram represents a rigid arm controller unable to control high frequency transients caused by collisions, and the right hand diagram represents a flexible arm. If the arm is *highly* compliant, impacts with the arm will cause safe deformation. Contrast this with a rigid arm, whose inertia will cause large transient forces on impact, perhaps destroying its delicate force sensors attached to the arm.

If control over the force exerted at the tip of an arm is required, even during collisions, a possible design approach would be to deliberately introduce compliance into the structure. The force exerted by the actuators would then be controlled up to some desired frequency. Next, the degree of compliance would be chosen so that the stiffness of the end point of the arm rolls off significantly within the actuator bandwidth. The bandwidths of the arm and controller could then be matched for a smooth transition from a controlled stiffness for low and medium frequencies to a high degree of compliance at high frequency. However, the penalty of introducing compliance is that control inevitably becomes much more difficult, and unless special measures are taken, the positioning accuracy of the arm tip will deteriorate.

2 A One-Link Compliant Arm

The behaviour of compliant structures are radically altered by changing boundary conditions. A robot arm may be expected to pick up a payload and to change configuration, resulting in different end masses and inertias for the arm. As the arm performs motion throughout its work volume, its configuration will change, altering the mode shapes of the individual links. To investigate the effects of changing operating conditions, a one link direct drive model arm has been built with the facility

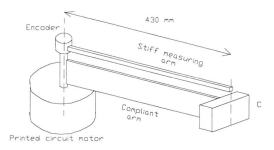

Figure 4: A one link model

for clamping different end masses and link inertias to its end point [Fraser, 1987]. Figure 4 is a diagram of the model arm constructed from 1mm x 40mm spring steel, the position of the end point is measured by means of a light, stiff trailing arm connected to the tip via a sliding joint. The motor used is of the printed circuit armature type to minimise its hub inertia.

Research at Oxford into the control of such a compliant structure while subject to perturbations to its dynamic equations is concentrating on:

- An investigaton into the use of time dependent perturbation analysis for predicting the changes in the dynamics of a flexible link when subject to changes in its boundary conditions. Possible changes that may occur are the picking up of objects, changes in configuration in a multi-link device, and contact with objects in the work volume [Fraser, 1987].

- Predictive self-tuning control of compliant arms [Lambert, 1987].

The prediction of changes in the dynamics of a compliant structure is the subject of a Ph. D. thesis approaching completion at Oxford, and has implications for the design of self-tuning controllers, especially for continuous adaptation is required. Since this paper is concerned with the control aspects of compliant structures, we will describe the new predictive algorithm developed at Oxford, which has been successfully used to control the single link compliant arm.

2.1 Generalized Predictive Control

Robot arms typically follow pre-programmed paths. The desired trajectory is usually presented to the dynamic control system in the form of a sequence of sampled set points $(\theta_{t_k}|k = 1\ldots, t_{k+1} - t_k = \delta t)$ projected into the future. Information about the future set point can be used to generate considerable phase advance and allow anticipative controls. Generalised Predictive Control provides such a facility. Another feature of compliant systems is the fact that without end-point sensing the position of the arm is not known to any accuracy. If end-point sensing is used, the classic non-collocated sensor problem arises. GPC was developed to deal with the problem of self tuning for non-minimum phase process plants. Similarly the major problem of structures with non-collocated sensing is non-minimum phase zeros. Another criterion which is important in the design of a robot control algorithm is that it be efficient and readily broken down into parallel tasks for implementation in real time. The current implementation of GPC at Oxford runs on a multiple-68020 system communicating via a VME bus, and despite being a fairly complex algorithm has achieved sample rates beyond 100 Hz whilst self tuning in real time. Figure 5 is a sketch of the components used [Lambert, 1987].

GPC is similar to Generalised Minimum Variance Control [Clarke and Gawthrop, 1975] and most other quadratic cost control schemes (such as LQG [Clarke, Kanjilal, and Mohtadi, 1985]) in that it minimises a quadratic cost functional. However, it differs from other schemes in that the control is chosen to minimise a quadratic cost under the constraint that the predicted control u is only allowed to change a small number of times in the future 'the con-

trol horizon'. Hence at every control calculation only a small number of switches are allowed to the minimisation routine during the prediction horizon. This *prediction horizon* is the distance into the future over which the controller attempts to predict the output behaviour of the arm given past data, and possibly future set points. The *control horizon* is the distance into the future during which the algorithm is allowed to change the predicted control input at each sample point. The version of GPC found to be most effective in the control of compliant systems has a control horizon of one sample ie the control u is assumed to be constant throughout the prediction horizon after an initial incremental change. This results in the cost function

$$J(N_p) = \sum_{j=1}^{N_p} [\hat{y}(t+j) - \hat{w}(t+j)]^2 + \lambda[\Delta u]^2 \quad (1)$$

where N_p is the prediction horizon, $\hat{y}(t+j)$ the predicted value of the output j samples into the future given that the input is constant, $\hat{w}(t+j)$ the predicted set point j samples in the future and Δu the increment in the control at the present sample interval (λ is a weighting allowing control over performance). Control over the plant is achieved by repeating this calculation at each sample interval, resulting in a receding horizon control scheme, performing a simple minimisation at each sample. A Linear Quadratic Gausian controller minimises a cost function involving a *sequence* of controls, the control horizon equalling the prediction horizon, but this requires the solution of a Ricatti equation.

The function given above is in incremental form [Tuffs and Clarke, 1985] which is able to reject constant disturbances, allowing integral action to be incorporated directly into a self tuning algorithm rather than identifying offsets (as required if conventional self-tuning is used).

The solution to the GPC minimisation problem is

$$u = [G^T G + \lambda]^{-1} G^T (\mathbf{w} - \mathbf{f}) \quad (2)$$

where G is the step response sequence of the arm, $\mathbf{w}$ the vector of future set point estimates, and $\mathbf{f}$ the predicted free response of the arm based on past measurements of inputs and outputs. Equation 2 gives the control u as the result of an inner product between a step response and a vector of measurements. The free response $\mathbf{f}$ may be obtained by convolving past inputs with the impulse response. Convolution is highly suited to parallel implementation on an SIMD machine and so GPC could be written in a form where at each control interval a processor may be assigned to a fixed sample position relative to the current sample instant, either in the past (to obtain the state for the free response) or the future (to obtain the predicted outputs). If this algorithm is then coupled to a least squares incremental estimator, a highly efficient self tuning controller results.

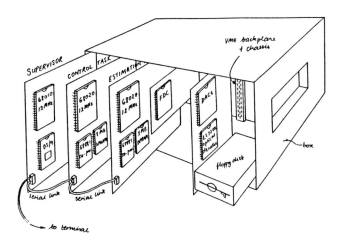

Figure 5: Physical layout of the self-tuning controller

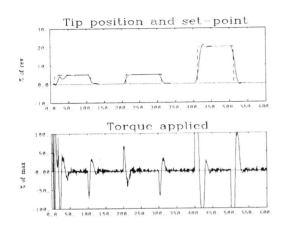

Figure 6: Response of the single link arm while self tuning

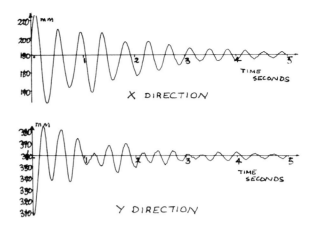

Figure 7: The vibrational behaviour of the two link model

Figure 6 is from a 6 second run of GPC with three step changes in position as the set points. The vertical axis of the position graph is in percentage points of one revolution ie 1% represents 3.6 degrees. The structure of the model was fixed as the ratio between two fourth order polynomials in the backward shift operator z^{-1} and was initialized to zero. A recursive least squares estimation algorithm was used to generate the prediction model with a prediction horizon of 10 samples. The figure shows that the estimator converged within 0.5 seconds (note the wild swings in control torque during the estimation process). The predictive nature of GPC can be seen from the anticipative controls produced (the arm starts to respond to a step before the step change being required). The effect of control saturation can also be seen in the third step.

3 The Control Of A Two Link Arm

Figure 2 shows a two link planar arm designed to model (and exaggerate) the problems of compliance in a large nuclear reactor manipulator. The links are made of 1mm x 40mm spring steel and driven by toothed rubber belts, the drive being provided by printed circuit motors via harmonic gearboxes with ratios 78:1. The dominant natural modes of the arm are at 2.2 and 2.9 Hz when joint

two is at 90 degrees. The arm is able to support its own weight, which differs from the majority of compliant arms reported in the literature. A plot of vibrational behaviour in true x and y co-ordinates of the arm tip is given in figure 7. Tip position is obtained by using a light mechanical trailing arm. The driven arm has no position sensing but is instrumented for strain at the link roots.

True tip position may only be obtained by using non-collocated sensors and thus results in non-minimum phase behaviour. However, root strain is collocated and does not exhibit the opposite going transient behaviour characteristic of non-minimum phase systems. There is another reason for requiring root strain, and that is the problem of the motor-drive characteristics. Real actuators have inertia, friction and backlash. If a system has dynamic non-linearities, then it is good engineering practice to use tight inner loop control to reduce the effects of non-linearities inside the loop to a minimum (motor tacho feedback is often used to provide this desirable feature in rigid robots). This, together with the benign zeros of the root strain transfer function, means that some form of strain feedback becomes very desirable for the control of real compliant systems.

To demonstrate the efficacy of using root strain as a tight inner loop control, figure 8 shows the performance of the arm while following a closed trajectory consisting of straight lines *but using a controller designed on the assumption that the arm is rigid*. This uses simple inverse dynamic control — the torques required of the motors are calculated on the basis of desired acceleration, the desired acceleration being generated by a P+D positional controller. A tight inner loop strain controller compensates for the non-linearities present in the actuation system and moves the vibrational poles due to the

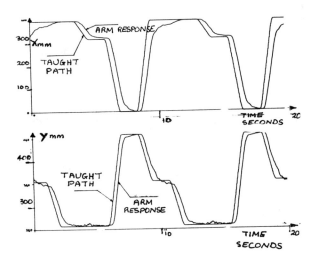

Figure 8: Tip position of two link arm under control

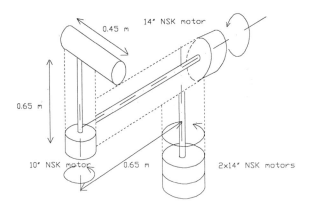

Figure 9: A three degrees of freedom compliant arm: The Rotabot

compliant arm well into the left half plane.

4   A Three Degrees of Freedom Industrial Compliant Arm: The Rotabot

A three degrees of freedom direct drive compliant arm has also been designed and built at Oxford. Its kinematics are illustrated in figure 9 and a photograph of the arm is shown in figure 11. The arm is fairly large for a direct drive robot and is able to carry up to 35kg when no wrist is present.

The kinematics have been chosen to allow the structure to carry the weight of the motors (it is statically balanced) and the compliance is exhibited by long thin shafts connecting the motor to the joints. The links are designed to be stiff in bending with a predicted tip deflection at full load of only 40 microns. However, the Rotabot is highly compliant in torsion, achieved by using a skeletal structure to carry the bending moment, shown in dotted outline. There were two reasons for choosing torsional compliance to dominate:

1. If both bending and torsion are present, whirling adds major complications to the dynamics.

2. Absolute position sensing cannot be used near sin-

gularities because of mismatches between the kinematics of the compliant arm and the position sensing mechanism. This can lead to catastrophic kinematic instabilities in the control system as the two systems enter different poses.

The control problem is now one of a full space-filling robot with compliance in three degrees of freedom. Control of the arm is under development and results will be reported in a future paper.

5 Conclusion

We have argued that compliance is an important feature for arms which need to interact with their environment and that it is possible to implement self-tuning control *in real time* using existing computer harware. A new control algorithm developed for self-tuning non-minimum phase plants, and hence particularly suited to the control of arms with tip position sensing, has been described. It has been shown that this algorithm is able to take advantage of the pre-programmed nature of most robot trajectories and may be expressed in a form suited to parallel computation.

A real two link highly compliant arm has been described,

which is capable of supporting its own weight. The problems of non-linearities in the drive system of real arms have been discussed and tight inner-loop control over root strain suggested as a method of alleviating this problem.

The final arm described is a three degrees of freedom direct drive compliant arm capable of lifting 35kg in a working volume of diameter 3m. This arm uses an exoskeleton to obtain accurate tip position data, while torsional compliance in the links allows the structure to absorb impacts with its environment.

References

Book, W.J., Maizza-Neto, O., Whitney, D.E., Feedback control of two beam, two joint systems with distributed flexibility, *Trans ASME J. Dyn Meas and Control*, pp 424-431, December 1975.

Cannon, D.H., Schmitz, E., Initial experiments on the end-point control of a flexible one-link robot, *International Journal Of Robotics Research*, Vol 3, No 3, pp 62-75, Fall 1984.

Clarke, D.W., Gawthrop, P.J., Self-tunign control, *Proc IEE* Vol 122 No 9 pp 929-934, 1975.

Clarke, D.W., Kanjilal, P.P., Mohtadi, C., A generalized LQG approach to self-tunign control, *Int. J. Control* Vol 41 No 6 pp 1509-1523, 1985.

Clarke, D.W., Mohtadi, C., Tuffs, P.S., Generalized predictive control. Part 1: The basic algorithm. Part 2: Extensions and Interpretations, *Automatica*, To appear.

Fraser, A.R., Perturbation analysis of compliant robot arm dynamics, *D. Phil Thesis Oxford University Department Of Engineering Science*, In preparation.

Kanoh, H., Gil Lee, H., Vibration control of one-link flexible arm, *Proceedings of 24th Conference on Decision and Control*, Ft. Lauderdale, FL. pp 1172-1177, December 1985.

Lambert, M.R., Adative control of flexible systems, *D. Phil Thesis Oxford University Department Of Engineering Science*, In preparation.

Truckenbrodt, A., Truncation problems in the dynamics and control of flexible mechanical systems, *Proc. IFAC 8th Triennial World Congress on Dontrol Science and Technology*, Kyoto Japan, pp 1909-1915, 1981.

Tuffs, P.S., Clarke, D. W., Self-tuning control of offset: a unified approach. *IEE Proceedings*, Vol 132, Pt D, No 3, pp 100-110, May 1985.

Figure 10: Photograph of the model two link arm vibrating

Figure 11: Photograph of the Rotabot

Tracking in Compliant Robot Motion: Automatic Generation of the Task Frame Trajectory Based on Observation of the Natural Constraints

J. De Schutter, J. Leysen

Katholieke Universiteit Leuven

Departement of Mechanical Engineering

Celestijnenlaan 300B

B-3030 Leuven

Belgium

Abstract
A compliant motion is specified in terms of artificial constraints (desired velocities and forces) defined with respect to a task frame or compliance frame. The location of this task frame, however, may vary during the task execution. Therefore, the user has to specify the trajectory of the task frame in addition to the artificial constraints. This is usually error prone and difficult for the user to specify.

This paper presents a general procedure to automatically generate the task frame trajectory, even without any user specified information. The idea consists of observing on-line the evolution of the natural constraints (motion and force constraints), and then aligning the task frame with these constraints. This automatic 'tracking' reduces the effort required from the user during the programming phase. It is particularly useful in situations where there is partial information on the task frame trajectory.

1. Introduction
If the motion of a robot manipulator is modified or even generated based on the interaction with the environment, it is termed compliant. Although different types of sensing information can be used such as vision, proximity sensing or contact force measurement, the term compliant motion is mostly reserved for force or tactile feedback.

There are three important aspects in active force feedback : sensor design, task specification or programming, and task execution or control. In the past, research work has focused on the design of force sensors [Van Brussel, 1985] and, more recently on the control aspects of compliant motion tasks. See e.g. [Whitney, 1987], [De Schutter, 1987a], or [Khatib, 1987] for an overview of force control. On the contrary, the problem of programming compliant motions has received much less attention. In this respect, Mason [Mason, 1981] has formalized the hybrid control concept which is now widely accepted as a basis for characterizing compliant motion tasks. Hirzinger proposes to extend the on-line

programming of robots by teaching also compliant tasks [Hirzinger 1985]. Asada [Asada, 1987] also generates compliant motion programs using 'teaching-by-showing'. On the other hand, De Schutter [De Schutter, 1986a,b] develops a completely off-line formalism for specifying compliant motions. Based on the same view this article describes an additional tool to support the off-line specification of compliant tasks: automatic tracking of the natural constraints can be used whenever the user information about the task frame trajectory is incomplete or uncertain.

Since a compliant motion is an interaction process with the robot environment, the kinematic or natural constraints of the task geometry play an essential role. In an ideal environment, i.e. without friction or flexibility, the direction orthogonal to a surface is position or velocity constrained while the tangent direction is force constrained. On the other hand, free space is characterized by force constraints [Mason, 1981]. A compliant task is specified by a number of artificial constraints that must be satisfied during the task execution. An artificial constraint is either a desired force or a desired velocity that must be maintained in a certain direction. These artificial constraints are complementary to the natural constraints of the task geometry: a desired force is specified in a motion constraint direction, whereas a desired velocity is specified in a force constraint direction. Any compliant motion can be specified by artificial constraints given in mutually orthogonal directions.

In this view the specification of a compliant task requires two items. In the first place a reference frame must be selected. Although this frame may be chosen completely arbitrarily, it is desirable to choose its location such that the resulting task specification becomes as simple as possible. This condition is satisfied when the reference frame coincides with the directions of the natural constraints. In this case, the reference frame is called task frame or compliance frame. When doing so, the task specification becomes straightforward, since the artificial constraints are aligned with the task frame axes.

Secondly, for any of these directions the type (i.e. force or velocity) as well as the value of the artificial constraint must be given.

Besides the two items mentioned above, there is another important issue which is usually overlooked in compliant task specifications. The natural constraints have a dynamic nature, i.e. their physical location may vary with time. This implies that in order to ensure permanent validity of the task specification, the position of the task frame must be constantly updated. In other words, the task frame has to follow a trajectory in order to keep itself aligned with the natural constraints. This trajectory may or may not have a strong relation with respect to the trajectory of the end effector.

In order to satisfy the artificial constraints the compliant motion controller generates the end effector trajectory (see [De Schutter, 1986a,b]) for an example of compliant motion control). In addition the generation of the task frame trajectory also belongs to the responsibility of the compliant motion controller. However, the way in which the controller has to update the task frame during the motion has to be indicated by the user as part of the task specification. This may be rather complicated or even impossible in case of a partially known task geometry.

In [De Schutter, 1986a,b] a formalism for specifying compliant motions is presented. In addition to the specification of the artificial constraints, this formalism offers a way to specify how the task frame varies during the motion execution. In any case however, the user has to provide the explicit specification of the task frame motion.

This paper presents a technique which deduces the task frame trajectory in a more natural and automatic way. The underlying idea is to detect on-line the actual position of the natural constraints acting on the end effector, and then aligning the task frame with them. This automatic alignment of the task frame with the natural constraints, which is called 'tracking', reduces considerably the responsibility of the user with respect to the specification of the task frame trajectory.

2. Determining the artificial constraints of a task

In general, the artificial constraints may vary during the execution of a complex task, both in type and value. However, we assume that it is always possible to divide such a composed motion in a series of elementary subtasks, i.e. such that for any subtask

the artificial constraints remain constant in type and value.

In order to simplify the specification of compliant tasks, only ideal task environments are considered during the motion specification phase. In particular, an ideal task environment means absence of friction between contacting surfaces. In addition, the world, i.e. the robot and the environment, are considered infinitely stiff. Finally, the objects interacting with the robot end effector are supposed to be at rest with respect to the robot base.

The hypothesis of working in an ideal task environment implies that the controller is robust enough to cope with the approximations that are made. This aspect of the task execution is treated in detail in [De Schutter, 1986a]. Furthermore, in section 5 the influence of non-ideal circumstances on the tracking problem is described.

(1) 2-D contour tracking (figure 1)
The tip of a robot end effector has to follow an unknown and arbitrary but connected two-dimensional contour. More specifically, the end effector has to move with a constant tangential speed while applying a constant force normal to the contour.

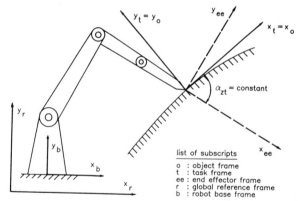

Figure 1: 2-D contour tracking

First the natural constraints are identified. In this example they are situated at the contact point between the contour and the tip of the end effector. The direction that is orthogonal to the contour is subject to a motion constraint. On the other hand the direction tangent to the contour and the rotational degree of freedom orthogonal to the plane of the contour are constrained in force.
The resulting artificial constraint types are therefore, at the tip of the end effector :

- translational direction tangent to the contour : velocity constraint;
- translational direction orthogonal to the contour : force constraint;

- rotational direction orthogonal to the plane of the contour : velocity constraint.

The numerical values for the constraints are selected by the user. In this case, the user specifies the desired tangential velocity, the desired normal force, and finally the rotational velocity. The desired rotational velocity can be used to maintain a constant orientation of the end effector either with respect to the robot base or with respect to the contour tangent and normal. In the latter case the absolute value of the desired rotational velocity (i.e. with respect to the robot base) is not known in advance

The mathematical description of the artificial constraints (i.e. direction, type and value) requires a reference frame. In order to simplify the resulting specification this reference frame is selected at the location of the natural constraints. The task frame origin therefore coincides with the contact point; the x-direction is taken tangential to the contour, and the y-axis is chosen along the normal.

In this task frame the specification of the task becomes :

x_t : velocity : v mm/sec ;
y_t : force : F N ;
α_{zt} : velocity : 0 rad/s (relative to the contour) ;

The third constraint means that the robot end effector maintains a constant orientation with respect to the contour. More precisely, the end effector maintains a constant orientation with respect to the task frame which itself has to keep itself aligned with the contour tangent and normal.

Since the constraints move along with the contact point, changing constantly in position and orientation, the task frame location has to be updated accordingly. It is the responsibility of the user to tell the controller how to update the task frame during the motion. This can be done in different ways.
If the exact task geometry is known, the user can specify explicitly the task frame trajectory, e.g. as a function of the distance travelled along the contour.
In many cases the task frame remains fixed with respect to the end effector, so that the controller can simply transfer the end effector motion to the task frame.
Finally, an approach to determine automatically the task frame trajectory during the execution, even in case of a partially known task geometry, is described in sections 3 and 6. The general idea is to detect at any moment the actual position of the natural constraints. Then the task frame is automatically aligned with the natural

constraints.

(2) Finger being drawn across the edge of a table (figure 2)
A cylindrical finger attached to the end effector slides across the edge of a table while maintaining a constant contact force, and while moving with a constant velocity parallel to the axis of the finger.

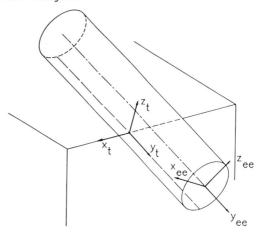

Figure 2: Finger being drawn across edge of table

The natural constraints are situated at the contact point. The direction normal to the plane which is tangent to the finger at the contact point, is naturally position constrained. All other directions are naturally constrained in force.

The task frame is chosen at the contact point, with one axis (e.g. the z-axis) parallel to the motion constraint direction. The corresponding task specification then becomes :

x_t : velocity : 0 mm/s ;
y_t : velocity : v mm/s ;
z_t : force : F N ;
α_{xt} : velocity : 0 rad/s ;
α_{yt} : velocity : 0 rad/s ;
α_{zt} : velocity : 0 rad/s .

Again, this specification is only valid if at any moment the task frame coincides with the natural constraints. In particular it is required that the task frame origin remains at the contact point (no fixed relationship between end effector and task frame), and that the y_t- and z_t-directions remain aligned with the velocity of the end effector, and the force direction respectively. The tracking method presented in this paper describes how this can be achieved without any explicit information from the user.

The same task specification remains valid when the edge of the table and the finger have an arbitrary and unknown form, or when the slide direction is not perpendicular to the table edge nor parallel to the finger axis. In such cases it is very difficult or even impossible to determine explicitly the task frame trajectory. Once again however, the task frame trajectory can be generated automatically using the method described in section 3 and 6.

3. Estimating the task frame location error with respect to the natural constraints

During the task execution automatic alignment of the task frame with the natural constraints, or 'tracking', is performed in two steps:
1) The estimation of the task frame location errors with respect to the natural constraint frame. This can be done using on-line force and velocity information as shown in this section.
2) The compensation of these errors using control loops. As explained in section 6 the outputs of the control laws are velocities which drive the task frame towards its desired position i.e. alignment with the natural constraints.

Suppose that at some instant the end effector is moving with velocity $v_t(v_{xt}, v_{yt}, v_{zt}, \omega_{xt}, \omega_{yt}, \omega_{zt})$, expressed in the task frame. This velocity is commanded by the control laws discussed in [DeSchutter 1986b]. Suppose in addition that the instantaneously measured contact forces, transformed to the task frame, are given by $F_t(F_{xt}, F_{yt}, F_{zt}, M_{xt}, M_{yt}, M_{zt})$.

Initially, we assume an ideal environment, i.e. contact between infinitely stiff objects which are at rest with respect to the robot base, and which have frictionless surfaces. Then, if the task frame is perfectly aligned with the natural constraints, the components of the velocity vector v_t which correspond to directions with natural motion constraints have to be zero, as well as the components of F_t which correspond to directions with force constraints.
This is not true however in case of an alignment error.

Suppose the alignment error between the instantaneous natural constraint frame (i.e. instantaneous desired location for the task frame) and the instantaneous actual task frame is expressed by a differential vector $\Delta(\Delta x, \Delta y, \Delta z, \Delta\alpha_x, \Delta\alpha_y, \Delta\alpha_z)$ which represents a combination of differential translations and rotations about the task frame axes. Then Δ can be found following the procedure described below.

First, the end effector velocity and contact forces, v_t and F_t, are transformed to the unknown natural constraint frame, yielding v_n and F_n. As shown in the appendix the relation between the end effector velocity and the contact forces expressed in the task frame on the one hand, and in the

natural constraint frame on the other hand is given by:

velocity relations:

$$v_{xn}= v_{xt} +\Delta\alpha_z v_{yt} -\Delta\alpha_y v_{zt} + \Delta z\omega_{yt} - \Delta y\omega_{zt}$$
$$v_{yn}=-\Delta\alpha_z v_{xt} + v_{yt} +\Delta\alpha_x v_{zt} + \Delta x\omega_{zt} -\Delta z\omega_{xt}$$
$$v_{zn}=\Delta\alpha_y v_{xt} -\Delta\alpha_x v_{yt} + v_{zt} + \Delta y\omega_{xt} - \Delta x\omega_{yt}$$
$$\omega_{xn}= \omega_{xt} + \Delta\alpha_z\omega_{yt} - \Delta\alpha_y\omega_{zt} \qquad (1)$$
$$\omega_{yn}=-\Delta\alpha_z\omega_{xt} + \omega_{yt} + \Delta\alpha_x\omega_{zt}$$
$$\omega_{zn}= \Delta\alpha_y\omega_{xt} - \Delta\alpha_x\omega_{yt} + \omega_{zt}$$

force relations:

$$F_{xn}= F_{xt} + \Delta\alpha_z F_{yt} - \Delta\alpha_y F_{zt}$$
$$F_{yn}=-\Delta\alpha_z F_{xt} + F_{yt} + \Delta\alpha_x F_{zt}$$
$$F_{zn}= \Delta\alpha_y F_{xt} - \Delta\alpha_x F_{yt} + F_{zt} \qquad (2)$$
$$M_{xn}= M_{xt} + \Delta\alpha_z M_{yt} - \Delta\alpha_y M_{zt} +\Delta z F_{yt} -\Delta y F_{zt}$$
$$M_{yn}=-\Delta\alpha_z M_{xt} + M_{yt} +\Delta\alpha_x M_{zt} +\Delta x F_{zt} - \Delta z F_{xt}$$
$$M_{zn}= \Delta\alpha_y M_{xt} - \Delta\alpha_x M_{yt} +M_{zt} + \Delta y F_{xt} -\Delta x F_{yt}$$

(1) and (2) can be rewritten as:

$$v_n - v_t = VEL_t . \Delta \qquad (3)$$
$$F_n - F_t = FOR_t . \Delta \qquad (4)$$

with

$$VEL_t=\begin{vmatrix} 0 & -\omega_{zt} & \omega_{yt} & 0 & -v_{zt} & v_{yt} \\ \omega_{zt} & 0 & -\omega_{xt} & v_{zt} & 0 & -v_{xt} \\ -\omega_{yt} & \omega_{xt} & 0 & -v_{yt} & v_{xt} & 0 \\ 0 & 0 & 0 & 0 & -\omega_{zt} & \omega_{yt} \\ 0 & 0 & 0 & \omega_{zt} & 0 & -\omega_{xt} \\ 0 & 0 & 0 & -\omega_{yt} & \omega_{xt} & 0 \end{vmatrix}$$
$$(5)$$

a matrix which contains the instantaneous end effector velocity data expressed in the task frame, and

$$FOR_t=\begin{vmatrix} 0 & 0 & 0 & 0 & -F_{zt} & F_{yt} \\ 0 & 0 & 0 & F_{zt} & 0 & -F_{xt} \\ 0 & 0 & 0 & -F_{yt} & F_{xt} & 0 \\ 0 & -F_{zt} & F_{yt} & 0 & -M_{zt} & M_{yt} \\ F_{zt} & 0 & -F_{xt} & M_{zt} & 0 & -M_{xt} \\ -F_{yt} & F_{xt} & 0 & -M_{yt} & M_{xt} & 0 \end{vmatrix}$$
$$(6)$$

a matrix which contains the instantaneous contact force information expressed in the task frame.

Define selection matrices S and S' as in (Raibert and Craig, 1981). S is a diagonal matrix containing unit or zero elements: zeros represent force constraints in the corresponding directions. Similarly $S'=I-S$ is a diagonal matrix containing unit or zero elements: zeros represent motion constraints in the corresponding directions.

Using these selection matrices the natural constraints can be expressed as:

$$S.v_n = 0 ;   (7)$$

$$S'.F_n = 0 .   (8)$$

Premultiplying (1) and (2) by S and S' respectively, and adding the result, eliminates the unknown components of v_n (in the force constraint directions) and of F_n (in the motion constraint directions). This results in:

$$(S.VEL_t+S'.FOR_t).\Delta =S(v_n-v_t)+S'(F_n-F_t).   (9)$$

Substituting the natural constraints (7) and (8) gives:

$$(S.VEL_t+S'.FOR_t).\Delta = -S.v_t - S'.F_t.   (10)$$

Finally, (10) is solved for Δ.

It is evident that this set of equations has always a solution for the tracking error, Δ, provided:
  - the user has specified a correct set of natural constraints, i.e. a set of natural constraints which is consistent with the actual task geometry;
  - the tracking error is small (because of the linearization);
  - (10) is nonsingular.
However, depending on the actual force and velocity data, the solution might not be unique.

After solving Δ, the unknown components of v_n and F_n are calculated from:

$$(S'.VEL_t+S.FOR_t).\Delta = S'(v_n-v_t)+S(F_n-F_t)   (11)$$

4. Examples of estimating the task frame location in ideal environmemts

(1) 2-D contour tracking (figure 1)
Substitution of the conditions expressing the two-dimensional nature of the problem ($\Delta z = \Delta\alpha_x = \Delta\alpha_y = 0$) into the general set of equations (1) and (2) yields :

velocity relations:

$$v_{xn} = v_{xt} + \Delta\alpha_z v_{yt} - \Delta y\omega_{zt}   (12a)$$

$$v_{yn} =-\Delta\alpha_z v_{xt} + v_{yt} + \Delta x\omega_{zt}   (12b)$$

$$\omega_{zn} = \omega_{zt}   (12c)$$

force relations:

$$F_{xn} = F_{xt} + \Delta\alpha_z F_{yt}   (13a)$$

$$F_{yn} =-\Delta\alpha_z F_{xt} + F_{yt}   (13b)$$

$$M_{zn} = M_{zt} + \Delta y F_{xt} - \Delta x F_{yt}   (13c)$$

The natural constraints of the task are expressed by:

$$v_{yn} = 0 ; F_{xn} = 0 ; M_{zn} = 0 .   (14)$$

Using the selection matrices

$$S = \begin{vmatrix} 0 & 0 & 0 \\ 0 & 1 & 0 \\ 0 & 0 & 0 \end{vmatrix} \quad \text{and} \quad S' = \begin{vmatrix} 1 & 0 & 0 \\ 0 & 0 & 0 \\ 0 & 0 & 1 \end{vmatrix} ,(15)$$

and following the procedure prescribed by equations (9) and (10), equations (12b), (13a), and (13c) are selected. They are solved for Δ, yielding ($F_{yt}\neq 0$; $\omega_{zt}\neq 0$; $F_{xt}\neq 0$):

$$\Delta\alpha_z=-F_{xt}/F_{yt}$$

$$\Delta x =-v_{yt}/\omega_{zt} - F_{xt}/F_{yt}\cdot v_{xt}/\omega_{zt}   (16)$$

$$\Delta y =-M_{zt}/F_{xt} - F_{yt}/F_{xt}\cdot v_{yt}/\omega_{zt} - v_{xt}/\omega_{zt}$$

As shown in section 5, estimation of the tracking error is subject to disturbances caused by imperfections of the environment, and, of course, by noise. Therefore it is advantageous to reduce the estimator's task by providing more user information about the task frame trajectory. In this particular case, it is clear that the task frame remains fixed with the end effector. This information can be used in two directions, namely x_t and y_t, as explained below.
In order to obtain the desired velocity in x_t-direction, a velocity controller generates the end effector motion in this direction. Similarly, a force controller generates motion commands for the end effector in y_t-direction. This is needed to maintain the desired contact force. These end effector velocities also apply to the task frame. However, in the third direction, α_z, it is the end effector which has to follow the task frame, and not vice versa (see section 2).

If the user wants the controller to update the task frame location according to the generated end effector velocities in the translational directions, tracking is no longer necessary in these directions; only $\Delta\alpha_z$ has to be estimated. If in addition the user has defined the task frame perfectly at the contact point, Δx and Δy are identically zero. The orientation error, $\Delta\alpha_z$, is then computed from either (12b) or (13a):

$$\Delta\alpha_z = v_{yt}/v_{xt}   (17a)$$

$$\Delta\alpha_z = -F_{xt}/F_{yt} .   (17b)$$

This special result has already been obtained and used in practical experiments by [De Schutter,1986a,1987].

Expressions (17a) and (17b) are equivalent when dealing with ideal environments. However, as explained in section 5, this no longer holds in non-ideal circumstances.

(2) Finger being drawn across the edge of a table
The natural constraints are expressed by:

$F_{xn} = F_{yn} = 0$;

$M_{xn} = M_{yn} = M_{zn} = 0$;   (18)

$v_{zn} = 0$.

Introducing these conditions in the general set of equations (9), and using appropriate selection matrices yields six equations in the six unknown components of Δ:

$0 = \Delta\alpha_y v_{xt} - \Delta\alpha_x v_{yt} + v_{zt} + \Delta y \omega_{xt} - \Delta x \omega_{yt}$

$0 = F_{xt} + \Delta\alpha_z F_{yt} - \Delta\alpha_y F_{zt}$

$0 = -\Delta\alpha_z F_{xt} + F_{yt} + \Delta\alpha_x F_{zt}$ (19)

$0 = M_{xt} + \Delta\alpha_z M_{yt} - \Delta\alpha_y M_{zt} + \Delta z F_{yt} - \Delta y F_{zt}$

$0 = -\Delta\alpha_z M_{xt} + M_{yt} + \Delta\alpha_x M_{zt} + \Delta x F_{zt} - \Delta z F_{xt}$

$0 = \Delta\alpha_y M_{xt} - \Delta\alpha_x M_{yt} + M_{zt} + \Delta y F_{xt} - \Delta x F_{yt}$

Again, the problem of determining the six position errors can be greatly reduced. If the user specifies that the position of the task frame has to remain fixed with respect to the robot base (which is effective in case of a cylindrical finger surface, and a velocity parallel to the finger axis), then no estimation of the tracking errors is needed. In this case the generation of the task frame trajectory becomes trivial. However, in a more general case involving an arbitrary finger surface, an arbitrary table edge, or a velocity which is not parallel to the finger axis, this simplification is not allowed, and eqs. (19) have to be solved in order to locate the instantaneous natural constraints.

5. Effects of non-ideal environments
Clearly, the estimation of tracking errors in case of non-ideal environments becomes more complex, because the ideal natural constraints expressed by (7) and (8) do not apply any more.
Two cases are considered: (1) effects of friction; (2) effects of flexibility.

(1) effects of friction

In case of friction the forces in the ideal natural force constraint directions are not identically zero, i.e.

$S'.F_n \neq 0$.   (20)

Therefore, substituting (8) into (9) causes errors in Δ.
If however a friction model is available, and reliable estimates of the friction forces can be calculated, $S'F_n$ can be replaced in (9) by $S'F_{fr}$, where F_{fr} represents the friction estimates.

Consider for example the 2-D contour tracking application, with general tracking equations:

$\omega_{zt}.\Delta x - v_{xt}.\Delta\alpha_z = -v_{yt} + v_{yn}$ (21a)

$-F_{yt}.\Delta x + F_{xt}.\Delta y = -M_{zt} + M_{zn}$ (21b)

$F_{yt}.\Delta\alpha_z = -F_{xt} + F_{xn}$ (21c)

If there is no flexibility, v_{yn} can be set to zero. Furthermore, if the surface friction coefficient, μ, is known, F_{xn} can be set to

$F_{xn} = -\,\text{sgn}(v_{xn}).\mu.\,|F_{yn}|$,   (22)

and, in case of a good point contact:

$M_{zn} = 0$ (23)

As explained in section 4, the tracking effort can be considerably reduced by providing user information about the task frame trajectory. In case $\Delta x = \Delta y = 0$ based on user specifications, eqs. reduce to:

$-v_{xt}.\Delta\alpha_z = -v_{yt}$ (24a)

$F_{yt}.\Delta\alpha_z = -F_{xt} + F_{xn}$ (24b)

In this case the effects of friction on the estimation process can be avoided by selecting the velocity relation for the calculation of $\Delta\alpha_z$.

(2) effects of flexibility

In case of contact between either a robot end effector with finite stiffness or an object in the environment with finite stiffness, the velocities in the ideal natural motion constraint directions are not identically zero, i.e.

$S.v_n \neq 0$.   (25)

Therefore, substituting (7) into (9) causes errors in Δ.
If however a flexibility model is available, and reliable estimates of these velocities can be calculated based on corresponding force derivatives, $S.v_n$ can be replaced in (9) by $S.v_{fl}$, where v_{fl} represents the velocity estimates due to flexibility.

Consider again the 2-D contour tracking application, with general tracking equations (21).

In absence of friction, F_{xn} and M_{zn} can be set to zero. Furthermore, if the surface flexibility, k_o^{-1}, is known, v_{yn} can be set to

$$v_{yn} = k_o^{-1}.(dF_{yn}/dt) . \qquad (26)$$

Again, the tracking effort can be considerably reduced by providing user information about the task frame trajectory. In case $\Delta x=\Delta y=0$, eqs. reduce to:

$$- v_{xt}. \Delta\alpha_z = -v_{yt} + v_{yn} \qquad (27a)$$

$$F_{yt}. \Delta\alpha_z = -F_{xt} \qquad (27b)$$

In this case the effects of flexibility on the estimation process can be avoided by choosing the force relation for the calculation of $\Delta\alpha_z$.

As a conclusion, non-ideal environments introduce errors in the tracking error estimation process. If a model of the 'real' environment, i.e. including friction and flexibility, is known, an attempt can be made to correct for the imperfections using the procedure described above. However, it is clear that the tracking error estimation will benefit from any information about the task frame trajectory which is provided by the user, and which restricts the tracking process to a limited number of task frame directions.

6. Tracking control
Once the task frame tracking errors have been estimated, they can be compensated using control loops (one loop per tracking direction) which are designed using well known control techniques (figure 3). In digital form the control laws are expressed as :

$$v_i(n) = k_i. \Delta_i(n) \qquad (28a)$$
and
$$\omega_i(n) = l_i. \Delta\alpha_i(n) \qquad (28b)$$

for the translational and rotational directions respectively, and with i=x,y, or z. n represents the n-th control sample interval.

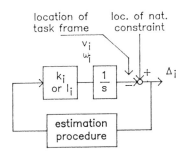

location of task frame   loc. of nat. constraint

Figure 3: Control scheme for task frame tracking (one direction)

The feedback gains k_i and l_i, which determine the bandwidths of these controllers, are selected as large as possible in order to limit tracking errors. However, their magnitude should be restricted in view of sensitivity to

estimation noise.

According to (28) the task frame is updated at every control interval. Using homogeneous transformation matrices:

$$^WA_t(n+1) = {^WA_t(n)}.{^tA_C(n)} , \qquad (29)$$

where superscript w denotes the world reference frame, and the differential update matrix, $^tA_C(n)$, is defined as:

$$^tA_C(n)=\begin{vmatrix} 1 & -\Delta\alpha_{zc}(n) & \Delta\alpha_{yc}(n) & \Delta x_c(n) \\ \Delta\alpha_{zc}(n) & 1 & -\Delta\alpha_{xc}(n) & \Delta y_c(n) \\ -\Delta\alpha_{yc}(n) & \Delta\alpha_{xc}(n) & 1 & \Delta z_c(n) \\ 0 & 0 & 0 & 1 \end{vmatrix}$$
$$(30)$$

with

$$\Delta i_c(n)=v_i(n).T ; \Delta\alpha_{ic}(n)=\omega_i(n).T \quad (31)$$

T represents the control sample interval, and i= x,y, or z. After applying (29), the rotational part of the transformation matrix has to be checked and corrected with respect to orthonormality.

As explained in previous sections the user may provide information about the task frame trajectory which reduces the tracking control effort. If he specifies that the task frame moves together with the end effector, then $v_i(n)$, and $\omega_i(n)$ in (28) are replaced by the respective end effector velocities expressed in the task frame. Similarly, if he specifies that the task frame remains fixed with respect to the robot base, then these $v_i(n)$ and $\omega_i(n)$ in (28) are set to zero.

7. Conclusion
Table 1 summarizes the artificial constraints for the end effector together with appropriate corresponding constraints for the task frame trajectory that should be at the user's disposal in an advanced compliant motion specification formalism.
This paper is concerned with the automatic generation of the task frame trajectory, in particular when the task frame has to keep itself aligned with the task, i.e. it has to track the natural constraints. This automatic alignment is performed in two steps: (1) estimation of the tracking error, and (2) tracking control. A general procedure is worked out for both steps. The influence of a non-ideal task environment on the estimation process is demonstrated in particular cases.
The constraints for the task frame trajectory can be omitted in the task specification provided the 'align with task' is selected as the default constraint. This way the effort required from the user is greatly

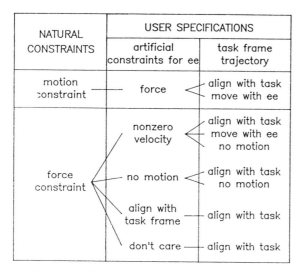

NATURAL CONSTRAINTS	USER SPECIFICATIONS	
	artificial constraints for ee	task frame trajectory
motion constraint	force	align with task move with ee
force constraint	nonzero velocity	align with task move with ee no motion
	no motion	align with task no motion
	align with task frame	align with task
	don't care	align with task

Table 1: Allowable user specifications w.r.t. artificial constraints and task frame trajectory

reduced. However, as stressed in this paper, the performance of the task frame tracking control may improve considerably by specifying one of the alternative task frame constraints (if applicable).

References

Asada H., Izumi H., 1987, Direct Teaching and Automatic Program Generation for the Hybrid Control of Robot Manipulators, Proc. IEEE Conf. on Robotics and Automation, Raleigh, 1401-1406.

De Schutter J., 1986a, Compliant Robot Motion: Task Formulation and Control, Ph. D. Thesis, Kath. Univ. Leuven (Belgium), Dept. of Mechanical Engineering.

De Schutter J., Van Brussel H., 1986b, A Methodology for Specifying and Controlling Compliant Robot Motion, Proc. 25th IEEE Conference Conf. on Decision and Control, Athens, 1871-1876.

De Schutter J., 1987a, A Study of Active Compliant Motion Control Methods for Rigid Manipulators Based on a Generic Scheme, Proc. IEEE Conf. on Robotics and Automation, Raleigh, 1060-1065.

De Schutter J. Van Brussel H., 1987b, Compliant Robot Motion. I: A Formalism for Specifying Compliant Robot Motion Tasks, Accepted for publ. Int. J. of Robotics Research.

Hirzinger G., Landzettel K., 1985, Sensory Feedback Structures for Robots with Supervised Learning, Proc. IEEE Conf. on Robotics and Automation, St.-Louis, 627-635.

Khatib O., 1987, A Unified Approach for Motion and Force Control of Robot Manipulators: The Operational Space Formulation, IEEE J. of Robotics and Automation, RA-3(1), 43-53.

Lozano-Perez T., 1983, Robot Programming, Proc. IEEE, 71(7), 821-840.

Lozano-Perez T., Mason M.T., Taylor R.H., 1984, Automatic Synthesis of Fine-Motion Strategies for Robots, Robotics Research, 3(1), 3-24.

Mason M.T., 1981, Compliance and Force Control for Computer Controlled Manipulators, IEEE Trans. on Syst. Man, and Cybernetics, SMC-11(6), 418-432.

Mason M.T., 1983, Compliant Motion, Robot Motion, M. Brady et al. eds., Cambridge, M.I.T. Press.

Paul R.P., 1981, Robot Manipulators. Mathematics, Programming and Control, M.I.T. Press.

Van Brussel H., Belien H. Thielemans H., 1985, Force Sensing for Advanced Robot Control, Proc. 5th I'nal Conf. on Robot Vision and Sensory Control, N.J. Zimmerman ed., Bedford (U.K.), IFS (Publications) Ltd.

Raibert M.H., Craig J.J., 1981, Hybrid Position/Force Control of Manipulators, ASME J. on Dyn. Syst. Meas., and Control, 103(2), 126-133.

Van Aken L. et al., 1986, LOLA (Leuven Off-Line Language): An Enhanced Manipulator Level Off-Line Robot Programming System, Proc. IFIP Working Conf. on Off-Line Programming of Industrial Robots, Stuttgart, North Holland (1987).

Whitney D.E., 1987, Historical Perspective and State of the Art in Robot Force Control, Robotics Research, 6(1), 3-14.

Appendix

With Δ (Δx, Δy, Δz, $\Delta\alpha_x$, $\Delta\alpha_y$, $\Delta\alpha_z$) the differential error vector between the natural constraint frame and the task frame, and using homogeneous transformation matrices, the relation between both frames can be expressed as:

$$^wA_n = {}^wA_t \cdot {}^tA_n , \qquad (A.1)$$

where subscript w represents the world reference frame, and

$$^tA_n = \begin{vmatrix} 1 & -\Delta\alpha_z & \Delta\alpha_y & \Delta x \\ \Delta\alpha_z & 1 & -\Delta\alpha_x & \Delta y \\ -\Delta\alpha_y & \Delta\alpha_x & 1 & \Delta z \\ 0 & 0 & 0 & 1 \end{vmatrix} \qquad (A.2)$$

represents   the   differential
transformation matrix which corresponds
to Δ.

In [Paul, 1981] it is shown that the
jacobian transformation matrix between
two frames 1 and 2, $^2J_1$, is easily
configured, based on the homogeneous
transformation matrix, $^1A_2$:

$$
^1A_2 = \begin{vmatrix} n_x & o_x & a_x & p_x \\ n_y & o_y & a_y & p_y \\ n_z & o_z & a_z & p_z \\ 0 & 0 & 0 & 1 \end{vmatrix} \qquad (A.3)
$$

corresponds to :

$$
^2J_1 = \begin{vmatrix} n_x & n_y & n_z & (pxn)_x & (pxn)_y & (pxn)_z \\ o_x & o_y & o_z & (pxo)_x & (pxo)_y & (pxo)_z \\ a_x & a_y & a_z & (pxa)_x & (pxa)_y & (pxa)_z \\ 0 & 0 & 0 & n_x & n_y & n_z \\ 0 & 0 & 0 & o_x & o_y & o_z \\ 0 & 0 & 0 & a_x & a_y & a_z \end{vmatrix}
$$

$$(A.4)$$

Applying this to the case at hand yields
the jacobian transformation matrix
between the task frame and the natural
constraint frame:

$$
^nJ_t = \begin{vmatrix} 1 & \Delta\alpha_z & -\Delta\alpha_y & 0 & \Delta z & -\Delta y \\ -\Delta\alpha_z & 1 & \Delta\alpha_x & -\Delta z & 0 & \Delta x \\ \Delta\alpha_y & -\Delta\alpha_x & 1 & \Delta y & -\Delta x & 0 \\ 0 & 0 & 0 & 1 & \Delta\alpha_z & -\Delta\alpha_y \\ 0 & 0 & 0 & -\Delta\alpha_z & 1 & \Delta\alpha_x \\ 0 & 0 & 0 & \Delta\alpha y & -\Delta\alpha_x & 1 \end{vmatrix}
$$
$$(A.5)$$

Also, in [Paul, 1981] it is shown that
transformation of velocities and forces
is performed according to:

$$v_2 = {}^2J_1 . v_1 \quad ; \quad F_2 = {}^1J_2{}^T . F_1 \qquad (A.6)$$

In this case ^tJ_n can be calculated from
^nJ_t by merely changing Δ to $-\Delta$.

Finally,   applying   (A.6)   to   the
transformation of task frame velocity,
v_t, and contact forces, F_t, from the
task task frame to the natural
constraint frame using the jacobian
transformation matrix (A.5) yields the
relations (1) and (2).

Object Manipulation in a Multi-Effector Robot System

Oussama Khatib

Robotics Laboratory
Computer Science Department
Stanford University

Abstract: This paper presents a framework for dealing with the problem of object manipulation in a system of multiple-robot manipulators. In this framework, the multi-effector/object system is treated as an augmented object representing the total masses and inertias perceived at some operational point actuated by the total effector forces acting at that point. This model is used for the dynamic decoupling, motion, and active force control of the system. The allocation of forces at the level of effectors is based on minimization of the total actuator joint force activities. The approach is extended to the case of redundant mechanisms.

1   Introduction

Object manipulation in multi-manipulator robot systems has recently received increased attention. (Alford and Belyeu, 1984) studied the coordination of two arms. Their control system is organized in a master/slave fashion, and a motion coordination procedure is used to minimize the error in the relative position between the two manipulator effectors. (Zheng and Luh, 1986) have treated the control problem of two manipulators as a "leader" and a "follower" system. The joint torques of the follower are obtained directly from the constraint relationships between the two manipulators allowing a coordinated control of the system.

The problem of motion and force control of multiple manipulators has been investigated in (Hayati, 1986). In his proposed approach, the load is partitioned among the arms. Dynamic decoupling and motion control are then achieved at the level of individual manipulator effectors. In the force control subspace, the magnitude of forces is minimized.

(Tarn, Bejczy, and Yun; 1987) developed the closed chain dynamic model of a two-manipulator system with respect to a selected set of generalized joint coordinates. Nonlinear feedback and output decoupling techniques were then used to linearize and control the system in task coordinates.

Joint space dynamic models only provide a description of the interaction between joint motions. The control of object motion and active forces requires the description of how motions along different axes are interacting, and how the apparent or equivalent inertia or mass of the object varies with configurations and directions. In this paper, the equations of motion of a multi-effector/object system are established and the

unified approach for motion and active force control (Khatib, 1987) is extended to the control of this type of robot system. This approach is also extended to the case of redunadnt mechanisms.

2   Outline of the Approach

Manipulator joints have been generally treated as motion generator devices. From this perspective, the control of the effector motion of a single manipulator is viewed as a joint motion coordination problem. In a multi-arm system, the problem of object manipulation has been formulated similarly, *i.e.* coordination of the motions of the individual arms or the individual effectors.

In the operational space framework, the control of the end-effector is based on the selection of the operational forces generated at the end-effector as a command vector. The relationships between these forces and the effector inertial and gravitional forces are used to achieve dynamic decoupling. The operational forces are produced by submitting the manipulator to the corresponding joint forces. In this approach, the involvement in the control structure of the manipulator joints is limited to the generation of joint forces. Similarly, in a multi-effector system, the manipulators are viewed as the mechanical support for the effectors to provide forces and moments at the level of the manipulated object. If the dynamics of these effectors were negligible, the equations of motion of the system would be given by the relationship between the inertial and gravitional characteristics of the manipulated object and the total effector forces acting on it. An effector, however, is not a pure generator of forces. In motion, the effector is submitted to significant inertial forces. These inertial forces are given, in the case of a single effector, by the operational space dynamic model.

A multi-effector/object system will be treated as an *augmented object* representing the total masses and inertias perceived at some operational point. This object is submitted to the vector of total force resulting from the combined action of the effectors at that point. The dynamic behavior of this system is described by the relationship between the vector of total force, *i.e.* the command vector, and the inertial and gravitional characteristics of the augmented object.

This model is then used to achieve dynamic decoupling and control of the system. The realization of the command vector is obtained by partitioning it into a set of collinear vectors allocated to the various effectors. The allocation of forces is based on the minimization of the total joint actuator activities.

3   Single Effector/Object System

In this section, the framework of operational space dynamics and control is summarized and the effect of the manipulated object on the effector dynamics is described.

3.1   Effector Operational Point

The position and orientation, with respect to a reference coordinate frame $\mathcal{R}_r(\mathcal{O}_r, \mathbf{x}_r, \mathbf{y}_r, \mathbf{z}_r)$, of the effector is described by the relationship between $\mathcal{R}_r$ and a coordinate frame $\mathcal{R}_e(\mathcal{O}_e, \mathbf{x}_e, \mathbf{y}_e, \mathbf{z}_e)$ attached to this effector. The effector position is given by the coordinate in $\mathcal{R}_r$ of the point $\mathcal{O}_e$, and its orientation is defined by the rotation transformation of $\mathcal{R}_e$ with respect to $\mathcal{R}_r$. The selection of the location on the effector of the point $\mathcal{O}_e$ (*e.g.* effector center of mass, tip) will depend on the type of operation to be performed and the way this operation is specified.
$\mathcal{O}_e$ is called the *effector operational point*. It is with respect to $\mathcal{O}_e$ that translational and rotational motions and active forces of the effector are specified.

3.2   Effector Equations of Motion

The number of independent parameters required to completely specify, in $\mathcal{R}_r$, the effector configuration is defined as the number of *effector degrees of freedom*. Various representations for the position (*e.g.* Cartesian, cylindrical, or spherical) and orientation (*e.g.* Euler angles, Euler parameters, direction cosines) can be found.

An *operational coordinate system* associated with an m-degree-of-freedom effector and a point $\mathcal{O}_e$, is a set

$\mathbf{x}$ of m *independent* parameters describing the effector position and orientation in a frame of reference $\mathcal{R}_r$. For a nonredundant n-degree-of-freedom manipulator, *i.e.* $n = m$, these parameters form a set of configuration parameters in a domain $\mathcal{D}$ of the operational space (Khatib, 1987) and constitute, therefore, a system of *generalized coordinates*. The kinetic energy of the holonomic articulated mechanism is a quadratic form of the generalized operational velocities

$$T(\mathbf{x}, \dot{\mathbf{x}}) = \frac{1}{2}\dot{\mathbf{x}}^T \Lambda(\mathbf{x})\dot{\mathbf{x}}; \qquad (1)$$

where $\Lambda(\mathbf{x})$ designates the $m \times m$ symmetric matrix of the quadratic form, *i.e.* the kinetic energy matrix. The kinetic energy can be similarly expressed with respect to other systems of generalized coordinates. Using the Jacobian matrix that relates the two systems of generalized velocities, the relationship between kinetic energy matrices associated with different generalized coordinates can be established by exploiting the identity between the two expressions of kinetic energy. With $A(\mathbf{q})$ being the kinetic energy matrix associated with the system $\mathbf{q}$ of generalized joint coordinates, and $J(\mathbf{q})$ the Jacobian matrix associated with the generalized operational velocities $\dot{\mathbf{x}}$, the matrix associated with the operational coordinates $\mathbf{x}$ is

$$\Lambda(\mathbf{x}) = J^{-T}(\mathbf{q})A(\mathbf{q})J^{-1}(\mathbf{q}). \qquad (2)$$

Let $\mathbf{F}$ be the vector of generalized operational forces associated with the generalized coordinates $\mathbf{x}$. Using the Lagrangian formalism, the end-effector equations of motion are given by

$$\frac{d}{dt}\left(\frac{\partial L}{\partial \dot{\mathbf{x}}}\right) - \frac{\partial L}{\partial \mathbf{x}} = \mathbf{F}; \qquad (3)$$

where the Lagrangian $L(\mathbf{x}, \dot{\mathbf{x}})$ is

$$L(\mathbf{x}, \dot{\mathbf{x}}) = T(\mathbf{x}, \dot{\mathbf{x}}) - U(\mathbf{x}); \qquad (4)$$

and $U(\mathbf{x})$ represents the potential energy due to gravity. Let $\mathbf{p}(\mathbf{x})$ be the vector of gravity forces

$$\mathbf{p}(\mathbf{x}) = \nabla U(\mathbf{x}). \qquad (5)$$

The effector equations of motion in operational space are given by (Khatib, 1980 and 1987)

$$\Lambda(\mathbf{x})\ddot{\mathbf{x}} + \Pi(\mathbf{x})[\dot{\mathbf{x}}\dot{\mathbf{x}}] + \mathbf{p}(\mathbf{x}) = \mathbf{F}; \qquad (6)$$

$\Pi(\mathbf{x})$ represents the $m \times m(m+1)/2$ matrix of centrifugal and Coriolis forces. The elements of the matrix $\Pi(\mathbf{x})$ can be obtained from the Christoffel symbols $\pi_{i,jk}$ given as a function of the partial derivatives of $\Lambda(\mathbf{x})$ with respect to the generalized coordinates $\mathbf{x}$,

$$\pi_{i,jk} = \frac{1}{2}\left(\frac{\partial \lambda_{ij}}{\partial x_k} + \frac{\partial \lambda_{ik}}{\partial x_j} - \frac{\partial \lambda_{jk}}{\partial x_i}\right). \qquad (7)$$

The matrix of centrifugal and Coriolis forces is given by

$$\Pi(\mathbf{x}) =$$

$$\begin{bmatrix} \pi_{1,11} & \pi_{1,12} & \cdots & \pi_{1,1m} & \pi_{1,22} & \cdots & \pi_{1,mm} \\ \pi_{2,11} & \pi_{2,12} & \cdots & \pi_{2,1m} & \pi_{2,22} & \cdots & \pi_{2,mm} \\ \cdot & \cdot & \cdot & \cdot & \cdot & \cdot & \cdot \\ \cdot & \cdot & \cdot & \cdot & \cdot & \cdot & \cdot \\ \pi_{m,11} & \pi_{m,12} & \cdots & \pi_{m,1m} & \pi_{m,22} & \cdots & \pi_{m,mm} \end{bmatrix}. \quad (8)$$

$[\dot{\mathbf{x}}\dot{\mathbf{x}}]$ represents the symbolic notation of the $m(m+1)/2 \times 1$ column matrix

$$[\dot{\mathbf{x}}\dot{\mathbf{x}}] = [\dot{x}_1^2 \ 2\dot{x}_1\dot{x}_2 \ldots 2\dot{x}_1\dot{x}_m \ \dot{x}_2^2 \ldots \dot{x}_m^2]^T \quad (9)$$

3.3 Effect of a Load

The kinetic energy matrix $\Lambda(\mathbf{x})$ associated with the operational coordinates $\mathbf{x}$ describes the inertial characteristics of the effector as perceived at the point $\mathcal{O}_e$. The addition of a load will result in an increase in the total kinetic energy.

Let m_l and I_l be the mass and inertia matrix of the load with respect to $\mathcal{R}_e$. The additional kinetic energy due to the load is

$$T_{\text{load}} = \frac{1}{2}[m_l \mathbf{v}^T \mathbf{v} + \omega^T I_l \omega]; \quad (10)$$

where $\mathbf{v}$ and ω are the vectors of linear and angular velocities.

The generalized operational velocities $\dot{\mathbf{x}}$ are related to the linear and angular velocities by a matrix $E(\mathbf{x})$ expressed as function of the operational coordinates $\mathbf{x}$,

$$\dot{\mathbf{x}} = E(\mathbf{x})\begin{bmatrix} \mathbf{v} \\ \omega \end{bmatrix}. \quad (11)$$

The matrix $E(\mathbf{x})$ is dependent on the type of coordinates selected to represent the position and orientation of the effector. By introducing the column matrices $\mathbf{x}_p$ and $\mathbf{x}_r$ defining, respectively, the selected coordinates for the position and orientation,

$$\mathbf{x}(\mathbf{q}) = \begin{bmatrix} \mathbf{x}_p \\ \mathbf{x}_r \end{bmatrix}; \quad (12)$$

$E(\mathbf{x})$ can be written as

$$E(\mathbf{x}) = \begin{bmatrix} E_p(\mathbf{x}_p) & 0 \\ 0 & E_r(\mathbf{x}_r) \end{bmatrix}. \quad (13)$$

Using equation (11), the kinetic energy due to the load can be written in the form

$$T_{\text{load}} = \frac{1}{2}\dot{\mathbf{x}}^T \Lambda_l(\mathbf{x})\dot{\mathbf{x}}; \quad (14)$$

where the matrix of kinetic energy with respect to $\mathbf{x}$ is

$$\Lambda_l(\mathbf{x}) = E^{-T}(\mathbf{x})M_l E^{-1}(\mathbf{x};) \quad (15)$$

with

$$M_l = \begin{bmatrix} m_l \mathbf{1} & 0 \\ 0 & I_l \end{bmatrix}; \quad (16)$$

where $\mathbf{1}$ and 0 are the unit and zero matrices of appropriate dimension.

For instance, for a selection of Cartesian coordinates and Euler angles, i.e. $(x, y, z, \psi, \theta, \phi)$, the matrix $E^{-1}(\mathbf{x})$ in equation (15) is

$$E^{-1}(\mathbf{x}) = \begin{bmatrix} 1 & 0 \\ 0 & E_r^{-1}(\mathbf{x}_r) \end{bmatrix};$$

where

$$E_r^{-1}(\mathbf{x}_r) = \begin{bmatrix} 0 & \cos\psi & \sin\psi\sin\theta \\ 0 & \sin\psi & -\cos\psi\sin\theta \\ 1 & 0 & \cos\theta \end{bmatrix}.$$

Lemma 1

The kinetic energy matrix of the effector and load system is the matrix

$$\Lambda_{\text{effector}+\text{load}}(\mathbf{x}) = \Lambda_{\text{effector}}(\mathbf{x}) + \Lambda_{\text{load}}(\mathbf{x}). \quad (17)$$

This is a straightforward implication of the evaluation, with respect to the operational coordinates, of the total kinetic energy of the system.

3.4 Effector/Object Equations of Motion

The equations of motion of the effector and load system become

$$\Lambda_{e+l}(\mathbf{x})\ddot{\mathbf{x}} + \Pi_{e+l}(\mathbf{x})[\dot{\mathbf{x}}\dot{\mathbf{x}}] + \mathrm{p}_{e+l}(\mathbf{x}) = \mathbf{F}; \quad (18)$$

where, using equations (7), (8), and (15), $\Pi_{e+l}(\mathbf{x})$ is given by

$$\Pi_{e+l}(\mathbf{x}) = \Pi_e(\mathbf{x}) + \Pi_l(\mathbf{x}). \quad (19)$$

$\Pi_l(\mathbf{x})$ is the $m \times m(m+1)/2$ matrix of centrifugal and Coriolis forces associated with the load and obtained from the partial derivatives of $\Lambda_l(\mathbf{x})$. Also, the resulting gravity vector can be written as

$$\mathrm{p}_{e+l}(\mathbf{x}) = \mathrm{p}_e(\mathbf{x}) + \mathrm{p}_l(\mathbf{x}); \quad (20)$$

where $\mathrm{p}_l(\mathbf{x})$ is the gravity vector obtained from the potential energy $U_l(\mathbf{x})$ associated with the load as in equation (5).

4   Multi-Effector/Object System

Let us consider the problem of manipulating an object with a system of N robot manipulators. The effectors of each of these manipulators are assumed to have the same number of degrees of freedom, m, and to be rigidly connected to the manipulated object. Let $\mathcal{O}_o$ be the selected operational point attached to this object. This point is fixed with respect to each of the effectors.
Let $\Lambda_l(\mathbf{x}_o)$ be the kinetic energy matrix associated with the load computed as in equation (15) and expressed with respect to $\mathcal{O}_o$ and the operational coordinates $\mathbf{x}_o$. Let $\Lambda_i(\mathbf{x}_o)$ be the kinetic energy matrix associated with the ith effector.

Lemma 2

The kinetic energy matrix of the N-effector/object system is

$$\Lambda_s(\mathbf{x}_o) = \Lambda_l(\mathbf{x}_o) + \sum_{i=1}^{N} \Lambda_i(\mathbf{x}_o). \qquad (21)$$

This is simply a generalization of Lemma 1. Equation (21) is obtained by evaluating the total kinetic energy of the N effectors and object system expressed with respect to the operational velocities,

$$T = \frac{1}{2}\dot{\mathbf{x}}_o^T \Lambda_l(\mathbf{x}_o)\dot{\mathbf{x}}_o + \sum_{i=1}^{N} \frac{1}{2}\dot{\mathbf{x}}_o^T \Lambda_i(\mathbf{x}_o)\dot{\mathbf{x}}_o.$$

4.1   Multi-Effector/Object Equations of Motion

The system considered here is the system resulting from rigidly connecting an object, to the effectors of N n-degree-of-freedom manipulators. This system is formed by $N(n-1)+1$ links, and one ground link connected through Nn one-degree-of-freedom joints. The number n_s of degrees of freedom of this system is given by the difference between the number of total degrees of freedom of these links obtained before the connection and the number of total degrees of freedom lost by the joint constraints after the connection. This number is given by the Grübler formula (Hartenberg and Denavit, 1964),

$$n_s = n_0(n_{\text{link}} - 1) - (n_0 - 1)n_{\text{joint}};$$

where n_{link} and n_{joint} are the numbers of total links and joints and n_0 is the number of degrees of freedom of an unconnected link (3 in the planar case and 6 in the spatial case). For the system of N n-degree-of-freedom manipulators and object considered here,

$$n_s = n_0[N(n-1)+1] - (n_0 - 1)Nn. \qquad (22)$$

With the assumption of non redundancy, the number of degrees of freedom in the planar case ($n_0 = n = m = 3$) is $n_s = 3$. This number is $n_s = 6$ in the spatial case ($n_0 = n = m = 6$).
The number of operational coordinates, m, is equal to the number of degrees of freedom, n_s, of the mechanism. These coordinates form, therefore, a set of generalized coordinates for the system.
The kinetic energy matrix of the system expressed with respect to the generalized operational coordinates $\mathbf{x_O}$ is given by equation (21). The equations of motion of the multi-effector/object system are

$$\Lambda_s(\mathbf{x}_o)\ddot{\mathbf{x}}_o + \Pi_s(\mathbf{x}_o)[\dot{\mathbf{x}}_o\dot{\mathbf{x}}_o] + \mathbf{p}_s(\mathbf{x}_o) = \mathbf{F}_o; \qquad (23)$$

where the matrix, $\Pi_s(\mathbf{x}_o)$, of centrifugal and Coriolis forces is obtained using equations (7), (8), and (15)

$$\Pi_s(\mathbf{x}_o) = \Pi_l(\mathbf{x}_o) + \sum_{i=1}^{N} \Pi_i(\mathbf{x}_o); \qquad (24)$$

where $\Pi_l(\mathbf{x}_o)$ and $\Pi_i(\mathbf{x}_o)$ are the $m \times m(m+1)/2$ matrix of centrifugal and Coriolis forces associated with $\Lambda_l(\mathbf{x}_o)$ and $\Lambda_i(\mathbf{x}_o)$ respectively. The gravity vector is

$$\mathbf{p}_s(\mathbf{x}_o) = \mathbf{p}_l(\mathbf{x}_o) + \sum_{i=1}^{N} \mathbf{p}_i(\mathbf{x}_o); \qquad (25)$$

where $\mathbf{p}_l(\mathbf{x}_o)$ and $\mathbf{p}_i(\mathbf{x}_o)$ are the gravity vectors associated with the object and the ith effector.

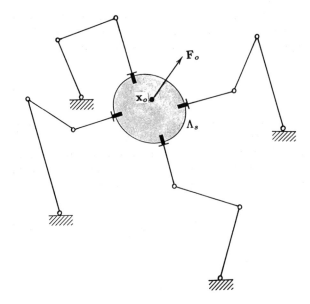

Figure 1: A Multi-Effector/Object System

4.2   Augmented Object Control

The equations of motion (23) establish the relationships between the positions, velocities, and accelerations of the multi-effector/load system and the operational forces acting on it, as illustrated in Figure 1. These equations can be viewed as describing the motion of an *augmented object* submitted to the operational forces $\mathbf{F}_o$, created by a set of effectors acting (as m-dimensional actuators) at the operational point $\mathcal{O}_o$.

The control of this object in operational space is based on the selection of $\mathbf{F}_o$ as a command vector. These generalized operational forces are the resultants of the forces produced by each of the N effectors at the operational point $\mathcal{O}_o$.

$$\mathbf{F}_o = \sum_{i=1}^{N} \mathbf{F}_{o_i}. \qquad (26)$$

The effector's operational forces $\mathbf{F}_{o_i}$ are generated by the corresponding manipulator actuators. The generalized joint force vector $\mathbf{\Gamma}_i$ corresponding to $\mathbf{F}_{o_i}$ is given by

$$\mathbf{\Gamma}_i = J_{o_i}^T(\mathbf{q}_i)\, \mathbf{F}_{o_i}; \qquad (27)$$

where $\mathbf{q}_i$ and $J_{o_i}^T(\mathbf{q}_i)$ are, respectively, the vector of joint coordinates and the Jacobian matrix computed with respect to $\mathbf{x}_o$ and associated with the ith manipulator.

The dynamic decoupling and motion control of the object in operational space is achieved by selecting the control structure

$$\mathbf{F}_o = \widehat{\Lambda}_s(\mathbf{x}_o)\mathbf{F}_o^* + \widehat{\Pi}_s(\mathbf{x}_o)[\dot{\mathbf{x}}_o\dot{\mathbf{x}}_o] + \widehat{\mathbf{p}}_s(\mathbf{x}_o); \qquad (28)$$

where, $\widehat{\Lambda}_s(\mathbf{x}_s)$, $\widehat{\Pi}_s(\mathbf{x}_o)$, and $\widehat{\mathbf{p}}_s(\mathbf{x}_o)$ represent the estimates of $\Lambda_s(\mathbf{x}_o)$, $\Pi_s(\mathbf{x}_o)$, and $\mathbf{p}_s(\mathbf{x}_o)$. $\mathbf{F}_o^*$ represents the input of the decoupled system. With perfect nonlinear dynamic decoupling, the system (23) becomes equivalent to a *single unit mass*, I_m, moving in the m-dimensional space,

$$I_m\ddot{\mathbf{x}}_o = F_o^*; \qquad (29)$$

The unified operational command vector for motion and force control can be obtained similarly to the case of a single manipulator (Khatib and Burdick, 1986; Khatib, 1987). This vector will involve in addition the generalized task specification matrices.

4.3 Allocation of Effector Forces

The control structure (28) provides the net force $\mathbf{F}_o$ to be applied to the augmented object at $\mathcal{O}_o$. The criterion for distributing this force between effectors will be based on the minimization of total actuator activities.

The force vector, $\mathbf{F}_{o_i}$, to be produced by the ith effector should be aligned with $\mathbf{F}_o$ and acting in the same direction,

$$\mathbf{F}_{o_i} = \alpha_i\mathbf{F}_o; \quad \text{with} \quad \alpha_i > 0. \qquad (30)$$

In addition, the set of N positive numbers α_i must satisfy

$$\sum_{i=1}^{N} \alpha_i = 1. \qquad (31)$$

The actuator joint forces required by the ith manipulator is

$$\mathbf{\Gamma}_i = \alpha_i J_{o_i}^T(\mathbf{q}_i)\, \mathbf{F}_o; \qquad (32)$$

The problem now is to find the set of N positive numbers, α_1, α_2,...,α_N such that the overall effort of the actuators is minimized.

Let us consider the vector of joint forces τ_i corresponding to the total operational forces $\mathbf{F}_o$

$$\tau_i = J_{o_i}^T(\mathbf{q}_i)\, \mathbf{F}_o; \qquad (33)$$

τ_i represents the actuator joint forces that would be assigned to the ith manipulator, if this manipulator alone were to produce the total operational force $\mathbf{F}_o$. Let τ_{ij} be the jth component of τ_i. Actuator joint forces are limited. Let $\overline{\gamma}_{ij}$ be the magnitude of the maximal bounds on the jth actuator force of the ith manipulator.

The number $|\tau_{ij}|/\overline{\gamma}_{ij}$ represents a measure of the effort that will be required by the jth actuator if the ith manipulator alone produced the total operational forces $\mathbf{F}_o$. The effort of the ith manipulator can be characterized by

$$r_i = \max_j\{|\tau_{ij}|/\overline{\gamma}_{ij}\}; \qquad (34)$$

which corresponds to the greatest effort. r_i is a positive number, which would be greater than one if the requested joint forces cannot be achieved by the ith manipulator alone.

In order to minimize the overall effort, the weighting numbers α_1, α_2, ..., and α_N will be selected so that the effort is equally distributed, that is

$$\alpha_1 r_1 = \alpha_2 r_2 = ... = \alpha_N r_N. \qquad (35)$$

Using equation (31), this corresponds to the solution

$$\alpha_i = \frac{\beta_i}{\beta_1 + \beta_2 + ... + \beta_N}; \qquad (36)$$

where

$$\beta_i = \frac{r_1.r_2...r_N}{r_i}. \qquad (37)$$

5 Redundant Systems

When redundant manipulators are involved, the number of degrees of freedom of the entire system might increase. Its configuration then cannot be specified by a set of parameters that only describes the object position and orientation. Therefore, the dynamic behavior of the entire system cannot be described by a dynamic model in operational coordinates. The dynamic behavior of the augmented object itself, nevertheless, can still be described, and its equations of motion in operational space can still be established. The number of degrees of freedom of the entire system, n_s, is given by (22). The number of degrees of redundancy of this system can be defined by $n_s - m_o$, where m_o is the number of degrees of freedom of the augmented object. It is important here to note that the system resulting from the connection of a set of individually redundant manipulators is not always redundant.

The freedom of the object is restricted by the freedom of the effectors. Let m_i be the number of degrees of freedom of the ith effector before connection to the object. Constrained by the effectors, the object's number of degrees of freedom is

$$m_o \leq \min_i \{m_i\}. \qquad (38)$$

The inequality in (38) reflects the fact that additional constraints can be introduced by the connection of effectors. Connected to the object, all effectors will have the same number of degrees of freedom, m_o.

In order to be able to arbitrarily specify the position and orientation of the manipulated object, m_o must be equal to three in the planar case and six in the spatial case. If n_i represents the number of degrees of freedom of the ith manipulator, the degree of redundancy of this manipulator is given by $n_i - m_o$.

5.1 Equations of Motion of a Single Manipulator

Before treating the case of a multi-effector/object system, we summarize the results in the case of a single redundant manipulator.

5.1.1 Joint Space Equations of Motion

The equations of motion of a single manipulator in joint space can be written in the form

$$A(\mathbf{q})\ddot{\mathbf{q}} + B(\mathbf{q})[\dot{\mathbf{q}}\dot{\mathbf{q}}] + \mathbf{g}(\mathbf{q}) = \boldsymbol{\Gamma}; \qquad (39)$$

where $A(\mathbf{q})$ is the $n \times n$ joint space kinetic energy matrix, $B(\mathbf{q})$ is the $n \times n(n+1)/2$ matrix of centrifugal and Coriolis forces. $\mathbf{g}(\mathbf{q})$, and $\boldsymbol{\Gamma}$ represent, re-

spectively, the gravity, and generalized forces in joint space.

5.1.2 Operational Space Equations of Motion

The dynamic behavior of the effector for a single redundant manipulator in operational space (Khatib, 1987) can be described by

$$\Lambda_r(\mathbf{q})\ddot{\mathbf{x}} + \Pi_r(\mathbf{q})[\dot{\mathbf{q}}\dot{\mathbf{q}}] + \mathbf{p}_r(\mathbf{q}) = \mathbf{F}; \qquad (40)$$

where

$$\begin{aligned}
\Lambda_r(\mathbf{q}) &= [J(\mathbf{q})A^{-1}(\mathbf{q})J^T(\mathbf{q})]^{-1}; \\
\Pi_r(\mathbf{q}) &= \bar{J}^T(\mathbf{q})B(\mathbf{q}) - \Lambda_r(\mathbf{q})H(\mathbf{q}); \qquad (41) \\
\mathbf{p}_r(\mathbf{q}) &= \bar{J}^T(\mathbf{q})\mathbf{g}(\mathbf{q});
\end{aligned}$$

and

$$\bar{J}(\mathbf{q}) = A^{-1}(\mathbf{q})J^T(\mathbf{q})\Lambda_r(\mathbf{q}). \qquad (42)$$

The matrix $H(\mathbf{q})$ is defined by

$$H(\mathbf{q})[\dot{\mathbf{q}}\dot{\mathbf{q}}] = \dot{J}(\mathbf{q})\dot{\mathbf{q}}. \qquad (43)$$

$\bar{J}(\mathbf{q})$ is actually a generalized inverse of the Jacobian matrix corresponding to the solution that minimizes the manipulator's instantaneous kinetic energy.

The $m \times m$ matrix $\Lambda_r(\mathbf{q})$ is defined as a *pseudo-kinetic energy matrix*. $\Pi_r(\mathbf{q})$ represents the matrix of Centrifugal and Coriolis forces acting on the end-effector, and $\mathbf{p}_r(\mathbf{q})$ the gravity force vector.

5.2 Augmented Object in a Redundant Mechanism

The dynamic behavior of each of the effectors is described by an equation of the form (40), the dynamic behavior of the augmented object system is

$$\Lambda_{s_r}(\mathbf{q})\ddot{\mathbf{x}}_o + \Pi_{s_r}(\mathbf{q})\mathbf{v}(\dot{\mathbf{x}}_o, \dot{\mathbf{q}}) + \mathbf{p}_{s_r}(\mathbf{q}) = \mathbf{F}_o; \qquad (44)$$

where

$$\begin{aligned}
\Lambda_{s_r}(\mathbf{q}) &= \Lambda_l(\mathbf{x}_o) + \sum_{i=1}^{N} \Lambda_{r_i}(\mathbf{q}_i); \\
\Pi_{s_r}(\mathbf{q}) &= [\Pi_l(\mathbf{x}_o)|\Pi_{1_r}(\mathbf{q}_1)|\dots|\Pi_{N_r}(\mathbf{q}_N)]; \\
\mathbf{p}_{s_r}(\mathbf{q}) &= \mathbf{p}_l(\mathbf{x}_o) + \sum_{i=1}^{N} \mathbf{p}_{i_r}(\mathbf{q}_i); \qquad (45)
\end{aligned}$$

with

$$\begin{aligned}
\mathbf{v}(\dot{\mathbf{x}}_o, \dot{\mathbf{q}}) &= [[\dot{\mathbf{x}}_o\dot{\mathbf{x}}_o]^T|[\dot{\mathbf{q}}_1\dot{\mathbf{q}}_1]^T|\dots|[\dot{\mathbf{q}}_N\dot{\mathbf{q}}_N]^T]^T; \\
\mathbf{q} &= [\mathbf{q}_1^T\mathbf{q}_2^T\dots\mathbf{q}_N^T]^T; \qquad (46)
\end{aligned}$$

and

$$\mathbf{F}_o = \sum_{i=1}^{N} \mathbf{F}_{o_i}. \qquad (47)$$

$\mathbf{F}_{o_i}$ is the operational force generated by the ith effector.

5.3 Augmented Object Control: Redundant Case

As in the case of a nonredundant system, the dynamic decoupling and control of the multi-effector/object system can be achieved by selecting an operational command vector of the form of (28), that is

$$\mathbf{F}_o = \widehat{\Lambda}_{s_r}(\mathbf{q})\mathbf{F}_o^* + \widehat{\Pi}_{s_r}(\mathbf{q})\mathbf{v}(\dot{\mathbf{x}}_o \dot{\mathbf{q}}) + \widehat{\mathbf{p}}_{s_r}(\mathbf{q}_o). \quad (48)$$

The control vector $\mathbf{F}_o$ will be distributed between the effectors as in (30), and (31)

$$\mathbf{F}_{o_i} = \alpha_i \mathbf{F}_o; \quad \text{with} \quad \sum_{i=1}^{N} \alpha_i = 1;$$

where α_i is selected to minimize the overall actuator activities as in equations (36), and (37).

5.4 Stability of the Redundant Mechanism

As in the case of a single redundant manipulator (Khatib, 1987), the stability analysis of the multi-effector/object system shows that additional stabilizing joint forces and additional gravity compensations are required to achieve asymptotic stabilization of this system.

These joint forces must be selected appropriately in order to preclude any effect of the additional forces on the multi-effector/object system and to maintain its dynamic decoupling. This can be achieved by selecting these forces from the null space of the Jacobian transpose matrix associated with each manipulator.

5.4.1 Joint Forces in a Single Manipulator

Joint forces in a single manipulator system can be decomposed into

$$\Gamma = J^T(\mathbf{q})\mathbf{F} + [\mathbf{1}_n - J^T(\mathbf{q})\bar{J}^T(\mathbf{q})]\Gamma_o; \quad (49)$$

where $\mathbf{1}_n$ is the $n \times n$ identity matrix. $\bar{J}(\mathbf{q})$, the generalized inverse that is consistent with the equations of motion of the manipulator and its effector, is given by

$$\bar{J}(\mathbf{q}) = A^{-1}(\mathbf{q})J^T(\mathbf{q})[J(\mathbf{q})A^{-1}(\mathbf{q})J^T(\mathbf{q})]^{-1}. \quad (50)$$

Γ_o is an arbitrary joint force vector. Joint forces of the form $[\mathbf{1}_n - J^T(\mathbf{q})\bar{J}^T(\mathbf{q})]\Gamma_o$ correspond to a null operational vector.

The generalized inverse given in equation (50) is consistent with the manipulator dynamic equations and is unique (Khatib, 1987). This generalized inverse is obtained as a function of the manipulator kinetic energy matrix $A(\mathbf{q})$. The determination of the generalized inverse associated with a manipulator involved

in the multi-effector/object system will require the evaluation of the inertial characteristics reflected at that manipulator.

First let us examine how the joint space kinetic energy matrix in the case of a single manipulator is affected by the addition of a load.

5.4.2 Effect of a Load on a Single Manipulator

The addition of a load to the effector of a single manipulator will result in an increase in the kinetic energy of system. Let $\Lambda_{\text{load}}(\mathbf{x}_l)$ be the kinetic energy matrix associated with the load and expressed with respect to $\mathbf{x}_o$.

Lemma 3

The joint space kinetic energy matrix of a manipulator with load is the matrix

$$A_{\text{arm+load}}(\mathbf{q}) = A_{\text{arm}}(\mathbf{q}) + [J_l^T(\mathbf{q})\Lambda_{\text{load}}(\mathbf{x}_l)J_l(\mathbf{q})]. \quad (51)$$

Replacing the operational velocities by their expressions in terms of joint velocities, the total kinetic energy is

$$T = \frac{1}{2}\dot{\mathbf{q}}^T[A(\mathbf{q}) + J_l^T(\mathbf{q})\Lambda_l(\mathbf{x}_l)J_l(\mathbf{q})]\dot{\mathbf{q}}.$$

5.4.3 Reflected Load

The pseudo kinetic energy matrix $\Lambda_{s_r}(\mathbf{q})$ describes the inertial characteristics of the N-effector/object system as reflected at the operational point $\mathcal{O}_o$. Viewed from a given manipulator, the object and the other effectors can be seen as a load attached at the point $\mathcal{O}_o$ on its effector. The additional load perceived by the ith manipulator is $\Lambda_{s_r}(\mathbf{q}) - \Lambda_{i_r}(\mathbf{q}_i)$. Following Lemma 3, the kinetic energy matrix of the manipulator resulting from this additional load is

$$A_{+_i}(\mathbf{q}) = A_i(\mathbf{q}_i) + J_i^T(\mathbf{q}_i)[\Lambda_{s_r}(\mathbf{q}) - \Lambda_{i_r}(\mathbf{q}_i)]J_i(\mathbf{q}_i). \quad (52)$$

The generalized inverse associated with the ith manipulator and consistent with the dynamic behavior of the multi-effector/object system is given by

$$\bar{J}_i(\mathbf{q}) = A_{+_i}^{-1}(\mathbf{q})J_i^T(\mathbf{q}_i)[J_i(\mathbf{q}_i)A_{+_i}^{-1}(\mathbf{q})J_i^T(\mathbf{q}_i)]^{-1}. \quad (53)$$

Finally, the ith manipulator joint forces are

$$\Gamma_i = \alpha_i J_i^T(\mathbf{q}_i)\mathbf{F}_o + [\mathbf{1}_n - J_i^T(\mathbf{q}_i)\bar{J}_i^T(\mathbf{q})]\Gamma_{i_o}; \quad (54)$$

where Γ_{i_o} is an arbitrary joint force vector. Asymptotic stabilization of the redundant system can be achieved by the addition of dissipative joint forces Γ_{i_s}. With the gravity compensation, the vector Γ_{i_o} is

$$\Gamma_{i_o} = \Gamma_{i_s} + g_i(q_i). \tag{55}$$

Joint constraints, link collision avoidance (Khatib, 1986), and control of manipulator postures can be integrated naturally in the vector Γ_{i_o}.

6   Conclusion

The augmented object model proposed in this paper constitutes a natural framework for the dynamic modelling and control of multi-effector/object systems. In this approach, the control structure only uses the necessary forces, *i.e.* net force, required to achieve the dynamic decoupling and control of the system. Compared to control structures where joint motions or effector motions are individually decoupled and controlled, the proposed control system presents a significant reduction in actuator activities. Indeed, in this approach, the inertial coupling, centrifugal, and Coriolis forces acting on one effector are used to compensate for parts of the coupling forces acting on the others. The actuator joint force activity is further minimized by the criterion used for the allocation of effector forces.

For redundant mechanism systems, the multi-effector/object equations of motion have been established, and a similar control system for dynamic decoupling and control has been developed. The expression of joint forces acting in the nullspace of the Jacobian matrix and consistent with the inertial characteristics perceived by each manipulator has been identified and used for the asymptotic stabilization and gravity compensation of the redundant mechanism.

The methodology developed in this framework constitutes a powerful tool for dealing with the problem of object manipulation in a multi-fingered hand system.

Acknowledgement

The financial support of the Systems Development Foundation and the Stanford Institute for Manufacturing and Automation (SIMA) are gratefully acknowledged. The author is grateful to Shashank Shekhar who has made valuable suggestions during the development of this work. Many thanks to Harlyn Baker for careful reading of the manuscript and to Helene Chochon for the drawing.

References

Alford, C. O. and Belyeu, S. M. 1984 (March). Coordinated Control of Two Robot Arms. Proceedings of the IEEE International Conference on Robotics and Automation, Atlanta, Georgia, pp. 468-473.

Hartenberg, R. S. and Denavit, J. 1964. Kinematic Synthesis of Linkages. McGraw-Hill, Inc.

Hayati, S., 1986 (April). Hybrid Position/Force Control of Multi-Arm Cooperating Robots. Proceedings of the IEEE International Conference on Robotics and Automation, San Francisco, California, pp. 1375-1380.

Khatib, O. 1980. Commande Dynamique dans l'Espace Opérationnel des Robots Manipulateurs en Présence d'Obstacles. Thése de Docteur-Ingénieur. École Nationale Supérieure de l'Aéronautique et de l'Espace (ENSAE). Toulouse, France.

Khatib, O. and Burdick, J. 1986 (April). Motion and Force Control of Robot Manipulators. Proceedings of the 1986 IEEE International Conference on Robotics and Automation, pp. 1381-1386, April 7-11, 1986, San Francisco.

Khatib, O. 1986 (Spring). Real-Time Obstacle Avoidance for Manipulators and Mobile Robots. International Journal of Robotic Research, vol. 5, no. 1, pp. 90-98.

Khatib, O. 1987 (February). A Unified Approach to Motion and Force Control of Robot Manipulators: The Operational Space Formulation. IEEE Journal on Robotics and Automation, vol. 3, no. 1.

Tarn, T. J., Bejczy, A. K., and Yun, X., 1987 (March). Design of Dynamic Control of Two Cooperating Robot Arms: Closed Chain Formulation. Proceedings of the IEEE International Conference on Robotics and Automation, Raleigh, North Carolina, pp. 7-13.

Zheng, Y. F. and Luh, J. Y. S., 1986 (April). Joint Torques for Control of Two Coordinated Moving Robots. Proceedings of the IEEE International Conference on Robotics and Automation, San Francisco, California, pp. 1375-1380.

MECHANICS AND MULTIPLE SENSORY BILATERAL CONTROL OF A FINGERED MANIPULATOR

T. Oomichi*, T. Miyatake*, A. Maekawa** and T. Hayashi***

*   Takasago R&D Center, Mitsubishi Heavy Industries, Ltd.
** System Engineering Department of Mitsubishi Heavy Industries, Ltd.
*** Kobe Shipyard and Engine Works of Mitsubishi Heavy Industries, Ltd.

MITI"s Agency of Industrial Science & Technology is undertaking the development of an advanced robot. Its research work on manipulation for a nuclear power plant has involved function of a four-finger manipulator model equipped with force and tactile sensors. This four-finger manipulator was further modified by Multiple Sensory Bilateral Control and its operational test indicated this control system was effective. This experiment confirmed the usefulness of the manipulator, demonstrating that it could perform various operations, including turning of a machine screw with a screwdriver, and that it required no use of its visual information to execute operations such as bolting. The Agency is planning to extend this research work to an addition of an arm with fingers, double arms and autonomous control to the manipulator.

1. Introduction

The MITI's Agency of Industry & Science is undertaking the development of an advanced robot intended to move in the working area of an actual nuclear power plant under radiation, high temperature, high humidity and other conditions hardly accessible to humans for performance of inspection, monitoring, repair and other operations with the support of a teleoperator 1).

The development of the manipulator for this robot, which performs various operations in a nuclear power plant with a high efficiency, involves the development of a multi-function manipulator provided with a high-level remote control system aided by autonomous control. This means that the Agency is aiming for the development of a sophisticated multi-function manipulator combining the dexterity for handling a general purpose tool, the delicacy required for handling of pliable objects, and the capability of performing ordinary heavy work.

This requires realization of a highly functional universal robot equipped with a double-arm fingered manipulation mechanism comparable to the human configuration, control hardware (dexterious tactile sensing fingered manipulator) and highly inteligent control software to permit its application for general work (intelligent manipulator control).

Based on the above concept, the Agency started research work in 1984 and has made favorable progress in the development of hardware required for achievement of the target with the result that it is in the process of undertaking the development of a new control technology based on this mechanism. As illustrated in Fig.1-1, which gives a description of the development of manipulation technology, this paper presents the mechanism of an experimentally fabricated master-slave control four-finger manipulator and part of the experiment conducted on its operation by control using tactile and force sensors (Multiple Sensory Bilateral Control).

2. Concept of Development and Its Features

This research and development, aimed at the robotization of the actual operation being performed in a nuclear power plant, involves research on various elements for its realization, thus having some features which distinguish it from ordinary elemental research as described below:

2.1 Coexistence of function improvement and miniturization

The investigation of a robot for its function rarely involves limitation on its configuration. This normally allows elimination of the development of hardware which consumes time and money. The fact, however, that many nuclear power plants have extremely limited working space has made it almost impossible to introduce a robot, if not reduced in size, into such plants, thus requiring great efforts to be directed toward the development of a size-reduced and highly functional robot 2). This research and development has also given high priority to this theme.

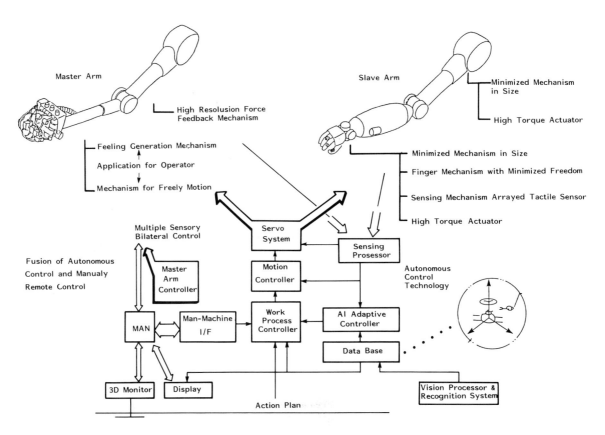

Fig.1-1 Technology for the advanced manipulation on the program

2.2 Challenge to general work and development of fingers

There are many special purpose robots already in practical use, which, however, still depend on human hand for general work. The robotization of such work may be achieved by combining special purpose jigs and tools as practiced in factory, although it is impractical where working space is limited, as mentioned above, and also requires a great variety of jigs and tools, frequently presenting a cost problem.

Therefore, this research and development has also involved the development of manipulator fingers to handle tools. Accordingly, this research aims at attaining such functions of the fingers in practical size, not simulating human fingers. Fortunately, however, experiment found it desirable that such fingers should be designed with a configuration similar to that of a human finger for handling tools used by humans 3), making the

aforementioned coexistence of miniturization and function improvement possible.

2.3 Establishment of autonomous control to secure operation speed

An experiment for providing a robot with autonomous control can be made from various standpoints. This research and development has made such an experiment to improve operation speed. Teleoperation can be made only by the adoption of a system based on master-slave operation, which, as a matter of fact, a considerable number of nuclear power plants also have adopted for areas hardly accessible to humans. This system, however, generally preforms operations at a far lower speed than when a human directly carries out the same operations. Therefore, this reserach has aimed at large-scale introduction of autonomous control into a robot for routine and stereotype work to improve the vobots operation speed so that it can operate such work at a speed as close as possible to that attained by a human.

3. Mechanism of Experimental Finger

3.1 Slave finger mechanism

(1) Number of degrees of freedom

The more the number of degrees of freedom of a manipulator's finger, the better it handles tools and other objects 4). This concept, however, is not desirable in terms of size reduction, and also involves many problems related to mechanism reliability. This research and development introduced a concept of palm axis, which provides each of the fingers with three degrees of freedom so that they can take their own positions at their tips, and added the palm axis to enables them to accommodate changes in the configuration of the ojbect and to secure their function of grasping it.

There are also opinions that manipulators for handling tools need no more than three fingers each, although many of such manipulators have a mechanism to allow ideal operation such as that provided by human fingers. This research, however, has confirmed that the proper number of fingers for a manipulator with the functions of the intended level is four with addition of redundancy. A four-finger manipulator is suitable for handling relatively large objects for its grasping stability and finger size (for example, handling a softball with the ease with which a three-finger manipulator handles a pingpong ball). This was studied in prior research, which served as a guide in designing its construction.

(2) Configuration of degrees of freedom

The configuration of degrees of freedom of the manipulator finger, if using orthogonal system, makes no

difference when only the fingers tip is considered. This research has adopted the order of swing and bending after considering the ease with which a human performs operations in this order. This was judged to allow easy comparison of the operation of a finger manipulator with that of human fingers, providing useful information for future operation analysis and algorithm study.

3.2 Master finger mechanism

The master mechanism of a finger manipulator is substantially different from that of an arm manipulator in that the latter can have its master and slave of same configuration for operation, while the former provides no practical operation if its master and slave are of the same configuration for operation. Therefore, the master finger mechanism of nearly the same configuration as the slave mechanism (Fig.3-1) cannot be recommended for operation, although it is applicable for adjustment of slave finger operation.

(a)

(b)

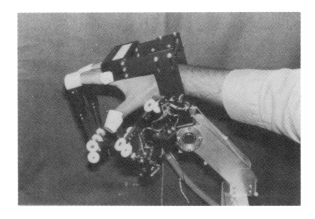

(c)

Fig.3-1 Configuration of the master finger mechanism

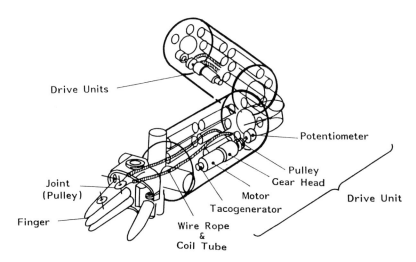

Fig.3-2 Driving mechanism of the finger

Thus, there are two types of master finger mechanism considered for study: one which is completely different in configuration from the slave finger mechanism and the other which is slightly analogous in configuration to the slave mechanism. This research experimented with the latter. In addition, the Force Feeling Generation Mechanism and Tactile Feeling Generation Mechanism to be added to the master finger must also be thoroughly studied for configuration of their installation.

3.3 Driving system

It is desirable that each joint of a manipulator finger should be driven by an actuator directly embedded in it. Such embedding, however, is impossible to make in a manipulator about the size of a human finger. This research has therefore adopted a system using a coil and wire rope. The rope, which is operated with an electric actuator built in the arm, produces friction, resulting in lowered force controllability. Thus, the concept of friction compensation control was introduced to allow microforce control. Fig.3-2 shows the concept of the finger driving system. Fig.3-3 gives a photograph of the finger manipulator.

4. Sensing Mechanism and Tactile Feeling Generation Mechanism

4.1 Sensing mechanism

The manipulator is equipped with sensors required for control of finger operation, including a joint angle sensor to measure the joint angle, a force sensor to detect the force applied to the finger and a tactile sensor.

Fig.3-3 Photograph of the version I hand

(1) Angle sensor
The present angle sensor consists of a potentiometer provided on the rope driving pulley, which produces errors due to elongation of the rope and other factors. Therefore, an angle sensor directly embedded in each joint is now under development.

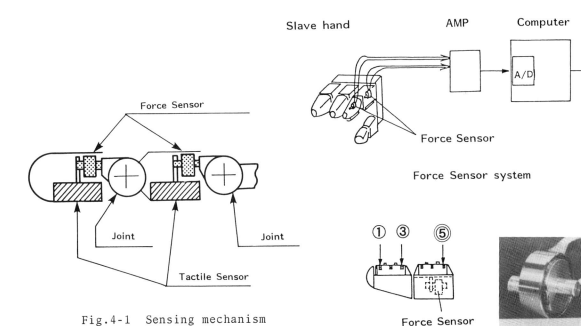

Fig.4-1 Sensing mechanism

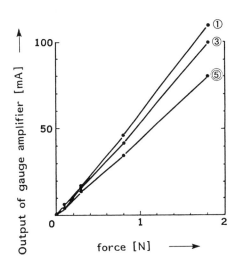

(2) Force sensor

Fig.4-1 illustrates the concept of installation of the force and tactile sensors. The force transmitted through the tactile sensor is detected with the force sensors embedded between the joints. The force sensor can detect right-angled force in two directions with a detecting ability of 0.1N and a proof stress of 100N. Fig.4-2 gives the appearance of the force sensor and an example of its characteristics.

(3) Tactile sensor

The present manipulator is equipped with an array tactile sensor of eight cells as shown in Fig.4-3 for study of its tactile sense detecting method, required quantity of cells and mounting position with concurrent research for development of an optimized tactile sensor. This sensor has a detecting ability of 0.05N, which greatly depends upon the matching of its cover attached to the inner surface of the finger. This means that such cover must be easily adaptable to the sensor and soft to provide for the fingers' stable grasping and holding operation. The functional material, however, must generally be thick, reducing the sensor's responsibility and resolution at action point. Fig.4-4 shows that the tactile sensor and its ability to detect contact force depend on the structure of its cover, indicating that the tactile sensor will not function if its cover's structure is poor. Thus, further study on the structure of the cover for a tactile sensor is very important for development of a better finger manipulator.

Fig.4-2 Output data of force sensor

Fig.4-3 Photograph of the arrayed
tactile sesor

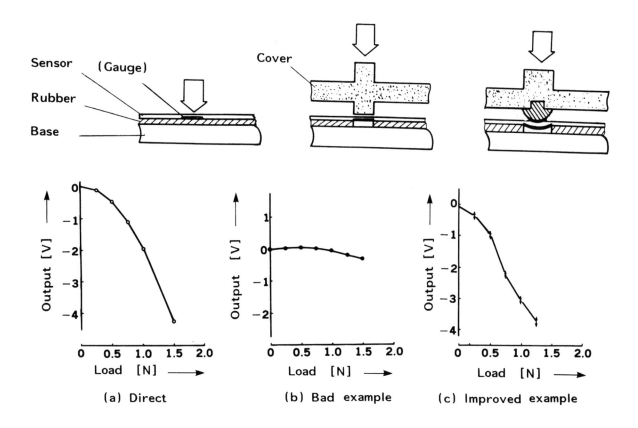

Fig.4-4 Effect of the cover

4.2 Tactile feeling generation mechanism

There is a conventional system available for application in the force generation mechanism of the manipulator presently under development, while there are few examples of Tactile Feeling Generation Mechanism applicable. In particular, the mechanism for transmission of force distribution to a human involves incorporation of all force transmitters onto the surface of the human finger, which is too complex to apply for a manipulator. Thus, the system of transmitting tactile feeling by simulating the finger surface (electric stimulation, air blow, piezoelectric vibration, etc.) was studied for its substitution for the mechanical system involving direct application of pressure to the finger surface. The study, however, showed that the former was far inferior to the latter and was not fit in terms of safety for long-term service.

The most difficult problem in the mechanical system is its size reduction and densification of the generators. Thus, further study must be conducted for densification of the mechanism from the present density, as shown in Fig.4-5, to a 3 × 3 array which has been

confirmed to be the standard required for identification of contact on the finger surface.

Fig.4-5 Photo of tactile feeling generation mechanism

5. Experiment on Operation of
   Manipulator with Multiple Sensory
   Bilateral Control

A master-slave control with a tactile sensor added to a conventional bilateral control is referred to as "Multiple Sensory Bilateral Control". Fig.5-1 gives a block diagram of the Multiple Sensory Bilateral Control applied in this experimental manipulator.

As described above, the master finger mechanism is not identical in configuration to the slave finger mechanism. Both are also completely different in the number and position of their force and tactile sense generation mechanisms. Their comparison, which requires a considerably complex calculation, is omitted here on account of space limitations.

The experiment was conducted for work categorized as about 20 items, which was considered inadequate to evaluate the performance of a manipulator which fundamentally performs work with its arm and fingers in harmony, but was good enough to evaluate the performance of the finger manipulator. As shown in Fig.5-2, the manipulator could perform bolt and nut turning and operations including pin insertion and turning of a machine screw with a screw driver. The experiment also confirmed that the manipulator could perform some operations without using a visual sensor, indicating the later was unstable in handling and grasping small objects due to its finger configuration, which suggests the need for further study to reduce the size of the finger and improve its surface adaptability.

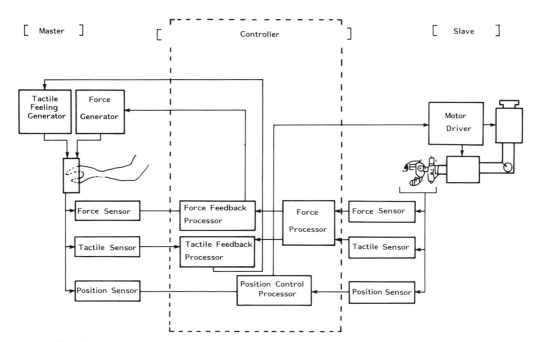

Fig.5-1 Concept of Multiple Sensory Bilateral Control

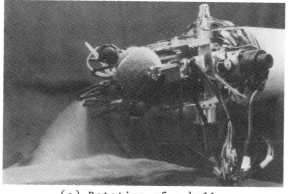

(a) Rotation of a ball

Fig.5-2 Photograph of working test (1)

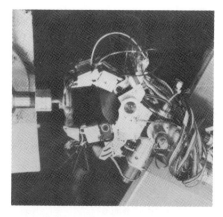

(b) Turning a valve hand

(c) Handling of a screw driver

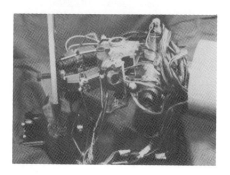

(d) Turning a bolt

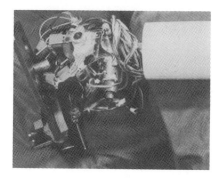

(e) Inserting a pin into a hole

(f) Holding an egg

(g) Gripping a wrench

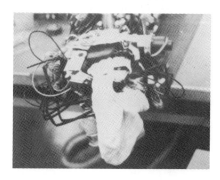

(h) Handling duster

(i) Gripping packing

Fig.5-2   Photograph of working test (2)

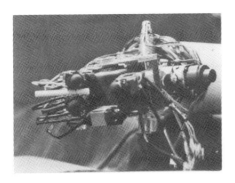

(j) Pitting a cigarette

(k) Holding an impact wrench

Fig.5-2 Photograph of working test (3)

6. Conclusion

The present research and development of nuclear power plant ultimate working robot manipulation technology provided:

- Experimental fabrication of a finger manipulator of delicacy and deterity with force and tactile sensors and Tactile Feeling Generation Mechanism, and
- Addition of Multiple Sensory Bilateral Control to this manipulator for an experiment on its operation to prove the justification for its mechanism and control concept.

7. Postscript

This paper presented the present situation of manipulation technology in the advanced robot development project, which provides prospects for realizing a manipulator equipped with a tactile sensor being concurrently developed, an actuator of capability 10 times that of the present one, an arm and double arms which allow its size reduction and function improvement. In addition, the research on intelligent control of the manipulator, which has already been undertaken, is planned to be extended to research to improve the Multiple Sensory Bilateral Mechanism, research for autonomous control to allow autonomous execution of operations using information for recognition of environment in the working area, and research for fusion of autonomous control and manual remote control to integrate them into one control system.

Reference

1 Kinichi Yamamoto; Current conditions and prospects of research and development on the most advanced robotics Technology in JAPAN, ICAR, 1985.
2 Takeo Oomichi, et al; Development of the multi-function robot for the containment vessel of the nuclear plant, ICAR, 1985.
3 Takeo Oomichi; Analysis and evaluation for fingered manipulators supported by master slave control, September, ISIR, 1985.
4 S.C. Jacobsen, et al; Design of the Utah/MIT dextrous hand, IEEE, 1986.

MEISTER: A Model Enhanced Intelligent and Skillful Teleoperational Robot System

Tomomasa SATO and Shigeoki HIRAI

Automatic Control Division
Electrotechnical Laboratory
Ministry of International Trade and Industry
1-1-4 Umezono, Sakura-mura
Niihari-gun, Ibaraki, Japan 305

Abstract: We describe a model enhanced intelligent and skillful teleoperational robot (**MEISTER**) system. The system consists of three components; a structured master-slave manipulator system, a robot model base and a motion understanding system. These components work together based on the concept of teleoperation intelligence for combining intelligence and skill in task execution. The teleoperation intelligence includes a planning intelligence, an execution intelligence, and an evaluation intelligence. The planning intelligence plans task cooperation between operator and robot. The execution intelligence realizes the skill cooperation. The evaluation intelligence keeps up with environment changes during the task executed by the operator and/or the robot. The robot model base contains the knowledge about object handling. The planning intelligence is distributed among these object models. The structured master-slave manipulator system provides a mechanism to concurrently superpose various control schemes onto the conventional master-slave control. Therefore the resulting slave manipulator motion realizes the cooperation of human skill and robot skill. The motion understanding system is the infrastructure of the evaluation intelligence. It interprets the slave manipulator motion using monitoring rules which describe typical patterns of task motions. A prototype of the MEISTER system was constructed and several scenarios were tested.

1. Introduction

A master-slave manipulator is an important tool to execute a task in hazardous environments such as space, underwater and nuclear power plants. However, the experience shows that task execution by a master-slave manipulator only is not easy and that the burden of operating the master manipulator tires the human operator easily [Johsen]. It has therefore been pointed out in the past that it is important to realize a skillful and intelligent teleoperation system.

As far as skill is concerned, we focus on fine motion. Global motions are not difficult to perform with a master-slave manipulator. On the contrary, fine motion, required after the objects are contacted, is rather difficult to perform through the operation of a master manipulator. One reason is that the operator can rely only on reduced and deformed information from the remote working site. A solution to this problem is telepresence [Akin] and tele-existence [Tachi] which try to transmit as immediate information as possible to the operator. The other reason for the difficulty is that the fine motion requires following some motion constraint. The motion constraint is imposed by either the objects to be handled or the nature of the task to be executed. Such a constraint makes the usage of a master-manipulator difficult resulting in a degradation of task execution performance. The authors have already reported on the concept of a "software jigs" [Hirai 84, Sato] to cope with this problem through the concurrent usage of a motion constraint specified by a robot language and the motion input by a master manipulator. The concept of "sharing DOF" [Vertut] has a similar effect. The present paper proposes a "structured master-slave manipulator" which is the extension of the master-slave manipulator with superposed functions of skill including software jigs.

Our system is based on the concept of "teleoperation intelligence." The teleoperation intelligence realizes cooperation between operator and robot in teleoperation task execution. The teleoperation intelligence includes a "planning intelligence" to plan the task cooperation between human operator and robot, an "execution intelligence" to realize the skill cooperation, an "evaluation intelligence" to keep up with environment changes during the task executed by either the operator or the robot. Our proposal may be discussed in the context of other system: Supervisory control [Ferrel] has been proposed to perform autonomous task execution by selecting program packages. A computer-based learning system for remote manipulator control was published [Freedy]. However, these concepts do not include the function equivalent to evaluation intelligence which maintains the consistency between a real environment and environment model even if the task is executed with a master-slave manipulator.

This paper proposes a model enhanced intelligent and skillful teleoperational robot (MEISTER) system. The overview is described in chapter 2. Chapters 3 discusses the concept of each type of teleoperation intelligence. Chapter 4 describes the MEISTER system. Chapter 5 illustrates several demonstrations of the MEISTER system. As a benchmark of MEISTER, handling an alcohol lamp is selected. Figure 1 show the set up of the working environment. The working environment includes an alcohol lamp, a match box, a stick holder and an ash tray. Chapter 6 summarizes and concludes the paper.

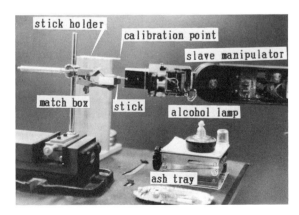

Fig. 1 Example of working environment.

2. Overview of the MEISTER System

Figure 2 shows the overview of the MEISTER system. The system consists of three components; a structured master-slave manipulator system, a robot model base and a motion understanding system.

The structured master-slave manipulator system is the interface to the human operator. It provides a mechanism to concurrently superpose various programmed control schemes onto the conventional master-slave control. The motion understanding system interprets the slave manipulator motion using monitoring rules. Both system use the robot model base storing all the knowledge of object handling in the form of numerical data and procedures.

There are two ways to start a task.

In case the operator wants to execute the task mainly by program, he or she selects the model of the object to be handled from the robot model base. The operator sends a language command to the object model. The object model arranges the task procedures retrieving the information from related object models in the robot model base. This includes explicit calculation of trajectories along with the required peripheral actions. The slave manipulator executes the arranged procedure.

It often happens that the operator wants to modify the slave motion when he or she finds that the calculated motion cannot be continued in the current environment. For example some unexpected obstacle may occur during a transportation task. Another example is stacked peg in a hole. By modification of the programmed trajectory, these troubles can be avoided and the task can be completed.

In case the operator executes the task mainly using the master manipulator, he or she can still rely on the robot skill to support the task execution. The motion understanding system tries to interpret the meaning of the slave motion. The interpreted results are used to update the model data and to look for situations where certain task may be performed autonomously. This maintenance of the models makes it possible to have the task taken over by autonomous motion.

These components of the MEISTER system mentioned above work together based on the concept of teleoperation intelligence. The detail of this concept is discussed in the next chapter.

3. Concept for Teleoperation Intelligence

Figure 3 shows the overview of the teleoperation intelligence.

3.1. Planning Intelligence

The planning intelligence is a function to utilize the robot model base effectively. In typical teleoperation situations, we cannot expect the handling objects to be fully modeled in advance. Therefore fully automatic task execution is difficult. However execution of the task in the following way is possible and effective: the robot executes a task autonomously as far as possible, while leaving to the human operator those part which the robot cannot do. Here the robot and the operator share the task execution. The planning intelligence coordinates robot plans the task procedures, asks the operator for the lacking information and initiates the procedure execution if possible. The human operator teaches the required information to the robot.

We think such a planning function is one important aspect of the teleoperation intelligence. Two main tasks of the planning intelligence are:
1) Building a queue of task procedures considering the current environment.
2) Allocation of task between man and robot.

Let us consider as an example of the teleoperation, i.e. the lighting of the alcohol lamp in the working environment shown by Fig. 1. To determine the lighting procedure, the following arrangement is needed:

Check if the cap of alcohol lamp is not already removed,
then invoke sub-task of removing the cap.
Check if the slave hand does not hold a match stick,
then invoke sub-task of picking a stick.

To specify the data, the following role allocation is required.

Retrieve the following data from the model base if it is available;
approach point, grip point, grip width, departure point, striking path, lighting point.
If any data is not determined,
then corresponding invoke teaching procedures.

With these functions of the MEISTER system, the operator can immediately begin the task of lighting an alcohol lamp. In the course of the task execution, the robot mainly executes programmed procedures, and the operator mainly teaches specific points of objects.

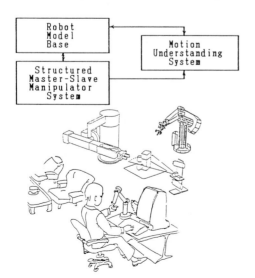

Fig. 2 Overview of MEISTER system.

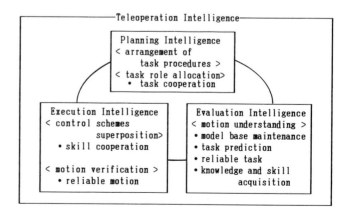

Fig. 3 Teleoperation Intelligence.

As far as the implementation is concerned, these functions of the planning intelligence are distributed in the robot model base as attached procedures and attribute values of object models. See 4-2 for detail.

3.2. Execution Intelligence

A robot is good at repeatedly moving its hand tip as specified by a program. However, programmed motions tend to lack flexibility to environmental changes. An operator is good at modifying the trajectory of the hand according to the environment conditions. However, human operator is not good at following a motion constraint resulting in a degradation of task execution performance. Thus robot skill and human skill have different features. Skill in general is a special structure of motion either in spatial and/or in time domain. A robot can realize this structure by several control schemes (refer section 3-1 for detail). By superposing these control schemes onto the conventional master-slave manipulator control, the required skill cooperation between man and robot is attainable. We think such a capability is another important aspect of the teleoperation intelligence. We call it "execution intelligence" in teleoperation. The structured master-slave manipulator is the infrastructure of the execution intelligence. Details are described in section 4.1.

The other function of the execution intelligence will be to ensure reliable motion of a programmed task by comparing the expected motion and the actual motion on-line.

3.3. Evaluation Intelligence

The system should be able to evaluate its actions even if the task is executed by master-slave manipulation and/or automatic execution. There are three reasons for this: 1) In order for the model enhanced teleoperation system to work correctly, consistency between a real environment and the environmental model should be maintained. 2) The system should predict the operator's intention and propose the autonomous execution of the predicted task in order to reduce the workload of the operator. 3) It is important to ensure a reliable task execution because arragement of the task environment is prohibited, this is usually not the case for industrial robot cells where tuning is a good method to achieve reliable results. 4) The system should acquire the knowledge and skill along with the progress of the task execution either by programmed procedures and/or by the human operation. We call such a capability "evaluation intelligence" in teleoperation.

The key function of the evaluation intelligence is realized by understanding the slave motion while the operator uses a master-slave manipulator. Motion can be interpreted and understood to a certain extent if the aim of motion is restricted to only teleoperational tasks and if the knowledge of objects in the task environment is well defined. In many cases, it is possible to predict what the final goal of the task is by knowing only the initial part of it.

Let us take the example of the handling of the alcohol lamp again. The operator grips the alcohol lamp cap. This action can be interpreted by detecting the closing of the slave fingers and knowing that the action occurs at the position of the cap. Then the operator puts the cap on a table. The action can be interpreted similarly. The new location of the cap can be calculated based on these interpretation. If the operator tries to pick the cap once again later, the system can predict that intention by knowing that the slave hand is coming closer to the cap. In this case the system can propose the autonomous execution of the predicted task. These functions enable a dynamic cooperation of the robot and the operator.

Another role of the evaluation intelligence is the task level verification of a programmed task by comparing the predicted and the achieved task state. The transfer of the human skill into robot skill should be assigned to the evaluation intelligence. But we have not achieved this part yet. These functions will be realized based on the result of slave motion evaluation.

4. Realization of MEISTER

4.1. Structured Master-slave Manipulator System

Figure 4 shows the block diagram of the structured master-slave manipulator system. As the slave-manipulator, a direct drive manipulator developed at our laboratory or a commercial industrial robot can be used. We also developed a direct drive master-manipulator, shown in Fig. 5, which allows force sensitive operation because it has no backlash or play, friction is low and inertia moment is small.

The structured master-slave manipulator system realizes the superposing of control schemes either in the spatial domain [3.1 a) to 3.1 d)] or in the time domain [3.1 e)]. Control schemes to be superposed onto conventional master-slave manipulation are as follows.

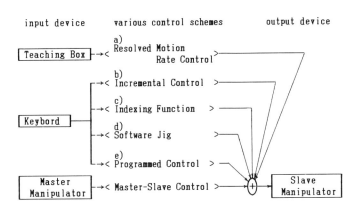

Fig. 4 Block diagram of Structured Master-Slave Manipulator System.

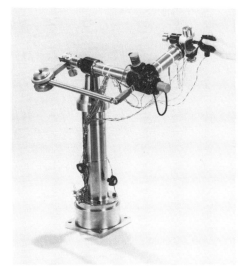

Fig. 5 Direct Drive Master Manipulator.

a) Resolved motion rate control scheme [Whitney]:

The slave manipulator is moved in the selected axis of the named coordinate system at a specified velocity while the button of the teaching box is pressed. The scheme is suited to realize precise linear motion either in joint angle space or in cartesian coordinate space.

b) Incremental control scheme:

The x, y and/or z position of the slave manipulator can be incremented in a named coordinate system at a specified amount when the operator strikes a key. Increments of rotation in each axis can be commanded in the same way. It has been reported that the scheme offers higher precision than the master-slave control scheme if signal transmission delay exists between the master and the slave [Starr].

c) Indexing scheme:

The coordinate frame of the master and the slave manipulator is automatically matched whenever the master-slave control scheme is initially activated. This implies the definition of a conversion matrix which is used to modify the coordinate value of the master manipulator into the slave manipulator coordinate value. The effects of this functions are as follows: i) Unexpected motion of the slave and/or the master manipulator caused by the miss-match of position/orientation between them can be avoided. ii) It involves placing the slave manipulator at a position/orientation suitable for a specific task and then moving the master to a position/orientation that is comfortable to the operator [Killough]. This function also virtually expands the movable range of the master manipulator. iii) If the operator selects the force as a target of the indexing function, the weight of the object gripped by the slave can be canceled out. The operator is freed from the weight of the object while moving the master manipulator. This function also solves the problem of the force reflection limitation of the master manipulator. It also enables the operator to operate within a comfortable force range.

d) Software jigs:

A software jig is a constraint of motion in the space domain superposed onto the conventional master-slave manipulator motion. It has the effect of a hardware jig, but is specified by a special software package. A master-slave manipulator language was developed to describe the software jig [Hirai 84, Sato].

Consider the task of carrying a glass filled with water. The operator must focus his attention on maintaining a vertical orientation of the glass in order not spill the water. This constrained motion increases the working load of the operator and the difficulty of the task. The software jig realizes a constrained motion by forcing the glass to be vertically oriented while the jig is active and enables the operator to concentrate on only its positional movements.

e) Programmed control scheme:

When the task is controlled by a program, the slave manipulator moves along the given trajectory. If the operator moves the master manipulator, the motion of the slave manipulator is modified correspondingly. This scheme is the cooperation of man and robot not only in the space but also in the time domain.
There are several possible realization of this scheme. The following is one example. If the master manipulator is moved such that slave leaves a space tunnel specified by absolute value of radius as threshold concentric to the calculated trajectory, the slave manipulator goes to the master position/orientation instead of following the trajectory. When the master manipulator is not moved beyond the threshold, the slave tries to return to the nearest point on the trajectory. After the slave returns to the tra-

jectory, it continues the programmed motion.

4.2. Robot Model Base

The robot model base consists of a handling model, a manipulator model, a geometric model, a vision model and a cooperative model. All these models are implemented using an object-oriented system. Each model has the data and procedures necessary in the context of its use.

The geometric model contains the geometric information of the objects. Boundary representation is used. The vision model accumulates the utilization knowledge of the vision system. The model contains the Robot Vision Language [Matsushita] instructions as its procedures. The Robot Vision Language is the instruction set which utilizes the vision system based on the light intersecting method. The cooperative model between the hand and vision functions accumulates a cooperative procedures of both. The manipulator model is constructed by collecting the knowledge needed to control the manipulator. The planning intelligence is distributed among these models.

4.2.1. Handling Model

The handling model is constructed based on the classification of the object handling knowledge [Hirai 85]. It is a set of models of objects viewed as handling or manipulation targets. It contains the information needed to manipulate objects in the form of data and procedures. It is implemented using an object oriented system and has the hierarchical structure as shown in Fig. 6. The detailed content of the handling model is shown in Fig. 7. The C-object is the model of general handling object. It contains the operational knowledge consisting of the teaching method of an object, the verifying procedures to confirm consistency of the model with the real environment and general task procedures such as grip, release, approach, depart etc. It also contains such information as base frames, approach points, grip points, and constituent points necessary for handling it. Attachment relationships between objects are included. The lower level contains more object-specific knowledge such as tool utilization procedures and related data. ALCOHOL LAMP, MATCH BOX and ASH TRAY in Fig. 6 are the models of specific objects. They contain both specific data and procedures required to handle them. The inheritance mechanism enables the system to use the general handling data and procedures of the C-object from the lower level models such as the model of ALCOHOL LAMP, MATCH BOX, and ASH TRAY.

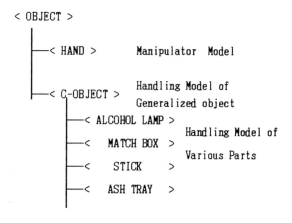

Fig. 6 Hierarchy in Handling Model.

Several object attributes are given at the construction of the model base. However, data which has to be matched with the real environment is acquired interactively during the task execution utilizing a master-slave manipulator. Details are given the next section.

4.2.2. Task execution utilizing the robot model base

Since the robot model base is implemented using an object oriented system, a task command given to the MEISTER system is actually sent to the model object which is the target of the task.

When the model object receives the task command, it tries to execute the specified procedure immediately. If the model object finds a sub-task necessary for the specified task, it sends messages to the related model objects. During the execution, the model object procedures retrieve such information as the gripping position of the object or the finger width to grasp the object from the robot model base. If any data is not available, the model object invokes the teaching procedure. In the teaching procedure, the data name is displayed on the operator's console. The operator controls the slave manipulator to teach the required data using the master manipulator and to push the teaching button at that point. The model takes in the data and saves necessary information after processing.

The task is executed with appropriate procedures because the object model selects only necessary sub-tasks considering the current state of the working environment. Maintenance of working environment data is also done by model object procedures when the locations of objects are changed by task execution. Affixment relationships between objects are equally maintained.

4.3. Motion Understanding System

The motion understanding system consists of a motion estimater and a motion symbolizer. The block diagram of the system is shown in Fig. 8.

The symbolizer is the pre-processing process of the motion understanding system. It inputs such data as position/orientation data from the slave manipulator, force data from the force sensor attached to wrist and the finger-width data from the hand, and sends the specific symbol to the motion estimater when it detects the specified event in the input analog data.

The motion estimater is based on a rule-based system similar to OPS5 [Brownston] including way of interpretation and execution of rules in event-driven way which yields high efficiency. The rule-based system consists of rules, literals (fact descriptors), working memory and a conflict set. Each component of the rule-based system is implemented as classes using the object-oriented system. The execution procedure of the rule-based system is actually stored in each class as its class methods.

The interpreting knowledge used to analyze the slave motion is described in the form of rules and stored in the handling model. The rules to interpret the basic handling motion of the general handling object is stored in the C-object. The rules to interpret the specific handling motion are stored in the specific model object of the handling model. This accumulation method gives modularity to the knowledge. It contributes not only to the easy retrieval of the knowledge but also to the suppression of redundant invocation of the interpretation as follows.

```
[class]    C-OBJECT     - name of this class
[supers]   OBJECT       - super-class of this class
[instance variables]
           frm          - base frame
           app.trn      - transformation from base
                          frame to grip position
           tlink        - information of linkage to
                          another object
           ......
[instance methods]
  :frm                  - calculates the current frame
                          of an object
  :approach             - approaches the hand to the object
  :affix                - records the junction relation
                          between objects
  :app                  - calculates the approach point
                          for an object using :frm method
  :move-to-grip         - moves the hand to grip position
  :grip                 - instructs to the hand to grip

      ( a )   Outline of C-OBJECT class

[class]   ALCOHOL LAMP - name of this class
[supers]  C-OBJECT     - super-class of this class
[instance variables]
          lighting-point - point of lighting
          ......
[instance methods]
  :light              - light the lamp

      ( b )   Outline of ALCOHOL LAMP  class
```

Fig. 7 Outline of C-OBJECT and ALCOHOL LAMP classes.

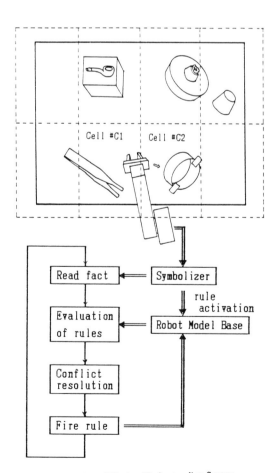

Fig. 8 Overview of Motion Understanding System.

The working space of the slave is divided into small cells. Every object in the working space is registered to cells if the object occupies any portion of them. One object can be registered to several cells. Whenever the robot hand moves from one cell to another, the symbolizer detects the change. Let C1 denote the cell which the robot hand leaves and C2 denote the cell to which the robot hand goes. The symbolizer activates rules of those objects which are registered to C2 and not registered to C1. Rules of those objects which are registered to C1 and not registered to C2 are inactivated. Rules of those objects which are registered to both C1 and C2 are left unchanged.

The detailed procedure of motion understanding is as follows:

(1) The motion estimater receives a new fact from the symbolizer and send it to the literal class.

(2) The literal class writes it into the working memory and sends it to all the rule classes which refer to the literal.

(3) If a rule class receives the new fact and is active, it evaluates the condition part using the fact.

(4) The instance of the rule whose condition part is satisfied by the fact is written into the conflict set.

(5) The conflict resolver resolves the conflict and fires a selected rule instance.

(6) The motion estimater waits for another input from the symbolizer.

The rules stored in the C-object are always active. On the other hand, the rules stored in the specific handling model are activated by the selecting mechanism described above.

5. Demonstration of MEISTER System

5.1. Demonstration using the Structured Master-slave Manipulator

a) Removing the cap from the alcohol lamp:
The master-slave control scheme is used to bring the hand tip of the slave manipulator close to the cap, because the master-slave control scheme is suited to the global motion. After this, centering the slave manipulator finger to the cap is executed by the incremental control scheme. Prior to this operation, a software jig to keep orientation of fingers horizontally is utilized to grip the cap easily. Lifting up of the gripped cap is performed with the resolved motion rate control scheme, which easily realizes linear motion at constant velocity. In this example various control schemes improve task performance effectively.

b) Obstacle avoidance during programmed motion:
An experiment of obstacle avoidance during programmed motion was executed. While the slave manipulator is executing a programmed triangle motion, an obstacle not accounted for in the program is placed on the motion path. The operator detects the obstacle and tries to avoid it with the master-slave operation superposed on the programmed motion.

5.2. Demonstration using Robot Model Base

At first, the operator types in the following command:

(send lamp1 :light box1 tray1),

where lamp1, box1 and tray1 are instances of the alcohol lamp, the match box and the ash tray class respectively. The command requires lamp1 to be lit on, i.e. to strike a match using box1, to light lamp1 and to drop used stick into tray1. Lamp1 checks conditions for the task. If any condition is not satisfied, the lamp1 send the necessary messages to the related objects. For

example, if the lamp1 finds that the manipulator hand is not holding a stick yet, it sends a 'pick' message to the stick. Scene (1) in Fig. 9 shows that the manipulator picks a stick following the message. If the lighting position of lamp1 is not determined yet, lamp1 invokes the teaching procedure. Scene (4) shows the invoked teaching procedure conducted by the operator. If all the conditions for the task are satisfied, lamp1 asks the operator to confirm the start of execution. Scene (5) to (8) shows performed autonomous execution.

In the next lighting execution using the same lamp, teaching of the lighting position will not be required because the previous data can be used.

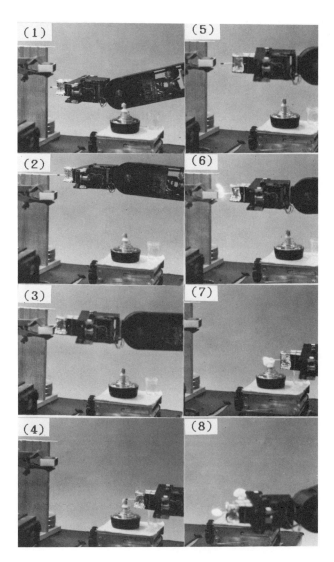

Fig. 9 Exepriment of Lighting alcohol lamp.

(1) Pciking a stick from the holder. (2) Calibrating the stick tip. (3) Teaching the match box. (4) Teaching the lighting point. (5) Starting to strike match. (6) Striking. (7) Lighting the alcohol lamp. (8) Release the stick.

5.3. Motion Understanding Experiment

5.3.1. Automatic Model Data Update

Scenario: The robot drops the "GREEN" block while it is transporting it on the table. The operator interrupts the task execution. The operator picks up the block using the master manipulator and places it on the table.

When the slave manipulator picks up the dropped object in the experiment, the system asks the operator for the name of the picked object because the object became unknown to the system at the time of dropping it. Pick and place task executions are interpreted by the system and a list describing the history of the task motion performed on the object is added to the already existing model of "GREEN." The content of the list is shown in Fig. 10. Using this history, the system can update model data.

5.3.2. Support by Autonomous Task Execution

Scenario: The operator suddenly grasps an unknown object during master-slave manipulation. The system asks the operator for the name of the object and creates a model for it. The next time the operator tries to pick it up again, the system predicts the picking task and proposes autonomous execution.

The messages from the system are shown in Fig. 11. The operator uses the master-slave manipulator to pick up a block and place it on the table. Interpretation for this action is displayed as lines (1) in Fig. 11. Following this interpretation, the system asks the operator for the name of the gripped object, because it is unknown to the system. The operator answers "GREEN," in response. Then the system generates a new model named "GREEN" as the general handling object and stores the current position of it in the model. If the operator does not give any name, the system automatically generates one. Later, the operator picks another block and places it on the table and teaches the system the name of block as "GRAY" in the similar way. The interpretation by the system for this action are given lines (2) of Fig. 11. Finally, the operator moves the master-slave manipulator toward the "GREEN" block in an attempt to pick it up again. The system predicts the attempt [line (3) of Fig. 11], and proposes an autonomous picking execution [line (4) of Fig. 11]. A "yes" is input by the operator, causing the hand to pick it up automatically [lines (5) of Fig. 11]. This experiment shows that the model of the object unknown to the system handled by the master-slave manipulator can be generated automatically and the data stored in that model can be utilized later.

6. Summary and Conclusion

In this paper, we have discussed a concept of teleoperation intelligence. It consists of a planning intelligence, an execution intelligence and an evaluation intelligence.

The planning intelligence selects the autonomous task execution procedure suitable to the working environment from the robot model base and proposes it to the operator. It also invokes the interactive data teaching procedure by checking the availability of the data in the robot model base. The execution intelligence performs superposition of robot and human skill. The evaluation intelligence enables the robot to understand the meaning of the slave manipulator motion even if it is moved by the master manipulator. The result is used to maintain consistency of the model data.

```
name   = GREEN

below        = TABLE-1    ....  There is TABLE-1 under GREEN.
above        = nil        ....  There is TABLE-1 on    GREEN.
current frame=
   (684.0 -30.0 -349.5   ....  Current base frame position
    81.2 88.6 -8.0))      ....  Current base frame orientation

alist =
  ((put on  TABLE-1       ....  GREEN is placed on the TABLE-1.
    (684.0 -30.0 -349.5   ....  position
     81.2 88.6 -8.0))     ....  orientation
    (picked up 68 159.0)  ....  GREEN is picked.
    (approached)          ....  GREEN is approached by the hand.
   ((put on  TABLE-1      ....  GREEN is placed on the TABLE-1.
    (630.6 111.3 -344.8   ....  position
     80.9 88.6 -8.2))     ....  orientation
    (picked up 66 147.0)  ....  GREEN is picked.
```

Fig. 10 Stored Data in model "GREEN" based on interpretation.

```
      ........
 *  Finger is closing.
 >  What is the new object name?              ┐
GREEN ✓                                       │
 *  Robot picks up new GREEN.                  ├─ (1)
 *  Finger is opening.                         │
 *  Robot puts GREEN on the table-1.          ┘
 *  Hand is still far from GREEN.
      ...................
 *  Hand is still far from GREEN.             ┐
 *  Finger is closing.                         │
 >  What is the new object name?              │
GRAY ✓                                         │
 *  Robot picks up new GRAY.                   ├─ (2)
 *  Hand is still far from GREEN.              │
      ...................                      │
 *  Finger is opening .                        │
 *  Robot puts GRAY on the table-1.           ┘
 *  Hand is still far from GRAY.
 *  Hand is still far from GREEN.
      ...................
 *  Hand is approaching GREEN.
 *  Hand has approached GREEN.          (3)
    point=(672.3 -46.8 -333.7 82.7 87.3 -329.9)
    point=(663.0 -36.8 -329.9 82.7 87.3 -5.1  )
 >  Shall I pick up GREEN (y/n) ?        (4)
Y ✓
 *  I have gripped GREEN.                 (5)
    Robot picks up new GREEN.
      ...................

        >  : prompt to the operator
        _  : input by the operator
        *  : report from motion
                understanding system
```

Fig. 11 Messages from Motion Understanding System during task execution.

A Model Enhanced Intelligent & Skillful Teleoperational Robot (MEISTER) system has been constructed based on the concept of teleoperation intelligence. The MEISTER system has the following sub-systems.

1) The structured master-slave manipulator: The demonstration of skill superpose is performed by concurrently considering the control signals of various control schemes and conventional master-slave control.

2) The robot model base: An object oriented system was used to construct the model and to accumulate the knowledge of object handling.

3) The motion understanding system: The system consists of the rule based motion estimater and the motion symbolizer.

Teleoperation intelligence forms the basis to upgrade the relationship between man and robot from the level of conventional "passive assistance" to that of "cooperative association." It also realizes reliable and flexible task execution utilizing the robot model base.

The MEISTER system is a prototype of an intelligent and skillful teleoperational robot system which realizes cooperative association between man and robot.

Acknowledgment

The authors would like to express their great appreciation to K. Aruga of Seiko-Epson for his assistance with the Lisp version of the motion monitors, Y.Nishida of Meiji University for his assistance with the building up the rule-based system version, and Dr. J. Takeno of Meiji University for his assistance in pursuing the research. They would also like to thank S. Hagiwara, K. Yabuuchi, Y. Maeda and M. Higuchi of Mitsubishi Electric Corp., and Y. Harada of Suzuki Motor Co., LTD. for their assistance in the production and performance measurement of the DD master manipulator. They are also indebted to K. Takase and T. Suehiro of Electrotechnical Laboratory for their providing the DD manipulator slave manipulator, Dr. T. Ogasawara and T. Matsui, who respectively implemented ETALisp and LEO, for their kind permission to use their systems. Finally, they express thanks to Dr. Y. Shirai, manager of the automatic control division of Electrotechnical Laboratory, and Dr. R. Niepold, visiting researcher at ETL from Fraunhofer Institute fuer Informations und Datenverarbeitung, Mr. K. Edsall, visiting researcher at ETL from CURTIN University of Technology, for their invaluable advice and insights.

REFERENCES

1. Akin, D.L. et al., "Space Application of Automation, Robotics and Machine Intelligence System (ARAMIS)-Phase ii," NASA Contractor Report 3734 (1983).

2. Brownston, L., Farrell, R., Kant, E. and Martin, N., "Programming Expert Systems in OPS5: An Introduction to Rule-Based Programming," Addison-Wesley, 1985.

3. Ferrell, W.R. and Sheridan, T.B., "Supervisory control of remote manipulation," IEEE Spectrum, October 1967, pp. 81-88.

4. Freedy, A., Hull, F.C., Lucaccini, L.F. and Lyman, J., "A Computer-Based Learning System for Remote Manipulator Control," IEEE Trans. SMC, Vol. SMC-1, No.4, pp. 356-363, (1971).

5. Hirai, S. and Sato, T., "A Language Based Master-Slave Manipulator System," Trans. Soc. of Instrument and Control Engineers, Vol. 20, No. 1, Janurary 1984, pp. 78-84 [in Japanese].

6. Hirai, S. and Sato, T., "Advanced Master-slave Manipulator Augmented with World Model," Proc. of 15th ISIR, pp. 137-144 (1985).

7. Johnsen, E.G. and Corliss, W.R., "Teleoperators and Human Augmentation. An AEC-NASA Technology Survey," p 65, NASA SP-5047 (1967).

8. Killough, S.M., Martin, H.L. and Hamel, W.R., " Conversion of a Servomanipulator from Analog to Digital Control," Proc. of IEEE Conf. on Robotics and Automation, pp. 734-739 (1986).

9. Matsushita, T, et al., "An Attempt to Describe Visual Functions of the Hand-eye System with an Robot Vision Language : RVL/A," Proc. of '83 Int. Conf. on Advanced Robotics, pp. 327-334 (1983).

10. Sato, T. and Hirai, S., "Language-Aided Robotic Teleoperation System (LARTS) for Advanced Teleoperation," Proc. of '85 Int. Conf. on Advanced Robotics, pp. 329-336 (1985).

11. Starr, G.P., "A Comparison of Control Modes for Time-Delayed Remote Manipulation," IEEE Trans. SMC, Vol.SMC-9, No.4, pp. 241-246, (1976).

12. Tachi, S. and Arai, H., "Study on Tele-Existence (II) -- Three-dimensional color Display with Sensation Presence --," Proc. of '83 Int. Conf. on Advanced Robotics, pp. 345-352 (1983).

13. Vertut, J., et al., "Advances in A Computer Aided Bilateral Manipulator System," Proc. of Topical Meeting: "Robotics and Remote Handling in Hostile Environments," pp. 367-376 (1984).

14. Whitney, D.E., "Resolved-motion rate control of manipulators and human prostheses," IEEE Trans., Man-Machine Syst., vol. MMS-10, no. 2, pp. 47-53, 1989.

ADVANCED TELEOPERATION WITH CONFIGURATION DIFFERING BILATERAL MASTER-SLAVE SYSTEM

Tatsuo ARAI, Satoshi HASHINO, *Eiji NAKANO and Kazuo TANI

Mechanical Engineering Laboratory, MITI
1-2 Namiki, Sakura-mura, Tsukuba Science City, Ibaraki 305, Japan

A bilateral master-slave control method for manipulators with differing master and slave arm configurations is proposed to efficiently control robots working in hazardous or remote environments such as nuclear power plants, or space and undersea. In this method any pair of master device and slave manipulator may be connected together. Therefore it has some advantages over the conventional method in which similar master and slave manipulators are used. The first advantage of this method is to improve manoeuvrability in operation, the second one is to increase versatility, and the third is that it may be applied to a teaching operation of complex tasks in industrial robots. Basic experiments using three types of manipulators have been done to check the feasibility of the proposed method. In these experiments the position trackability of the slave, the force trackability of the master and the computation time of the digital computer required for the operations of coordinate transformations, position and force servos, are examined. The results of these experiments and more practical experiments, such as a crank turning motion, show the reasonable feasibility and the broad applicability of the proposed method. Then we propose a universal master device, which is designed based on the results of the basic experiments. In this device we have introduced a position-and-orientation independent mechanism to avoid complex coordinates transformations, and a gravity compensation method using static analysis.

Introduction

In critical and hazardous environments such as nuclear power plants, space and undersea, high performance robots are required to carry out complex tasks of various kinds in place of human beings. Teleoperation techniques, where a human operator plays an important role as a supervisor, is still effective, since to date a self-sufficient intelligent robot, which is able to move around freely and to execute tasks in changing environments with some degrees of intelligence, is not yet available. The master-slave (M-S) control method is extensively used to operate remote manipulators. It has been developed for many years and applied experimentally to some projects in areas of nuclear power plants, space and undersea. The bilateral master slave control system (BMSC), which enables a human operator to sense reaction force acting at the slave end and to carry out tasks very effectively, is most commonly available. Quite a few studies on this area have been done up to now.[1] [2] [3]

In the conventional BMSC a master manipulator and a slave manipulator have the same configurations. Since analog servo controllers connect the corresponding joints of master and slave manipulators to realize the same movement in both manipulators, it is not difficult to build the system. However, we find several problems with the conventional system when we apply it to more advanced applications. In the case of controlling an anthropomorphic articulated manipulator, for example, an exoskeletal master arm is generally employed. But when we move it for teleoperation we feel it is rather bulky and heavy, since each joint must have a big actuator to feed back the reaction force acting at the corresponding joint of the slave manipulator, to a human operator. Therefore the operator feels it is very heavy and difficult to operate and cannot use it for a long time. On the other hand, when we control more than one remote slave robot in the same plant, an equal number of master arms would be required. This means that the conventional system is not economical if a large number of slave teleoperated robots are required.

To solve the above problems we have developed a new BMSC in relation to the national project of advanced robotics technology. In this paper we will introduce the configuration differing BMSC that aims at good manoeuvrability, where different types of master devices and slave manipulators are employed but not limited to the conventional style. In order to show feasibility and applicability of the new system, the design concepts, basic experiments using three types of 2 d.o.f. manipulators and a newly developed universal master device will be explained.

Concept of Configuration Differing BMSC

To meet the demand in the advanced teleoperation, the BMSC should be provided with the following features:
1) the slave manipulator should track the designated position exactly as commanded by the operator,
2) the master device should feed back the reaction force information exactly to the operator,
3) the operator should be able to operate the master device easily,
4) the master device should be used to control any types of slave manipulators,
5) the slave manipulator should be able to carry out various kinds of tasks.

In previous research, features 1) and 2) have been well discussed in terms of designing a stable control system.[4] [5] [6] On the other hand features 3)-5) have been left unsolved for many years and this is one of the main reasons why the conventional BMSC has not been used much in the fields. If any configuration of master device, even one dissimilar to the slave manipulator, can be employed, that is, a bilateral system can be made up of any type of master device and slave manipulator, the problem of manoeuvrability and universality referred to above will be greatly solved.

The main idea of our proposed BMSC is that manipulators with differing configurations are connected to each other arbitrarily. While the slave manipulator has an adequate configuration, for example, an anthropomorphous type that is suitable to various kinds of complex tasks, a light and simple master device, which has little gravitational effect and easy to operate, can be employed in this system. This method will bring the following advantages:
1) the improvement of manoeuvrability in controlling a human-like slave manipulator by avoiding the use of a bulky exoskeltal master device,
2) the increase of versatility because of easy combination of any types of master device and slave manipulator,

---

* He is currently with the University of Tohoku, Aoba, Aramaki, Sendai, Miyagi 980, Japan.

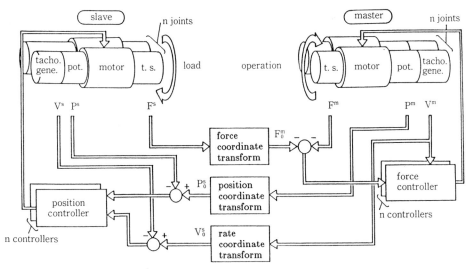

Fig.1 Block-diagram of the proposed system

3) the application to teaching of complex tasks in any industrial robots.

On the other hand it may have problems in computing such complex calculations as coordinate transformations and trigonometries in very short time compared with the conventional system in which only simple analog servos are required between the corresponding joints.

Structure of Configuration Differing BMSC

Fig.1 shows the block-diagram of the bilateral control system for manipulators with differing configurations. It is assumed here that the master and the slave manipulators have the same degrees of freedom, but that they do not necessarily have the same configurations. This restriction is not essential to the proposed system.[7] Each joint of both manipulators is equipped with a motor to provide the required torque, a potentiometer to measure angular rate and a torque sensor. The whole servo system is divided into three primary parts, that is, a position controller for the slave, a force controller for the master, and coordinate transformers. Since the configurations of the master and the slave are differing from each other, three coordinate transformers are required to compare corresponding positions, rate and force data of each manipulator.

Let the space in which the master arm is operated be an operational space and the one in which the slave manipulator works be a work space, and C^o and C^w are defined as Cartesian coordinates fixed to these spaces. The controller is required to work in such a way that the position and the orientation of the slave manipulator in C^w should be matched with those of the master manipulator in C^o, and that the force and moment of the master in C^o should be equal to those of the reaction force and moment produced in the slave manipulator in C^w.

Let p^m_i, v^m_i and f^m_i be an angular displacement, an angular rate and a torque of the master's joint i, respectively. Also let p^s_i, v^s_i and f^s_i be those of the slave's joint i. Position vectors, rate vectors and force vectors are defined as the following; $\mathbf{P}^m=(p^m_1,\ldots,p^m_n)^T$, $\mathbf{P}^s=(p^s_1,\ldots,p^s_n)^T$, $\mathbf{V}^m=(v^m_1,\ldots,v^m_n)^T$, $\mathbf{V}^s=(v^s_1,\ldots,v^s_n)^T$, $\mathbf{F}^m=(f^m_1,\ldots,f^m_n)^T$, $\mathbf{F}^s=(f^s_1,\ldots,f^s_n)^T$.

Each joint angle of the slave is controlled to track the reference value $\mathbf{P}^s_0$, which is coordinate transformed from $\mathbf{P}^m$. Let $\mathbf{x}^m$ and $\mathbf{x}^s$ be position vectors (which include both position and orientation) in C^o and C^w respectively, then they can be obtained using adequate homogeneous transformations.[8]

$$\mathbf{x}^m = \Gamma^m(\mathbf{P}^m) \tag{1}$$

$$\mathbf{x}^s = \Gamma^s(\mathbf{P}^s) \tag{2}$$

The control goal is to realize $\mathbf{x}^m=\mathbf{x}^s$, which means the slave's position in C^w should be equivalent to the master's position in C^o. The equivalence, $\mathbf{x}^m=\mathbf{x}^s$, and equations (1) and (2), yield the angular displacement of the slave, $\mathbf{P}^s_0$, corresponding to the master's present position. Therefore, the position coordinate transformation $\mathbf{P}^m$ to $\mathbf{P}^s_0$ can be described implicitly as the following.

$$p^s_{0i} = \Lambda_i(\mathbf{P}^m) \quad \text{for } 1\leq i\leq n \tag{3}$$

where Λ_i is a kinematic function that will be made clear when the actual configuration of each manipulator is given.

On the other hand, each joint torque of the master is controlled to match with the reference value $\mathbf{F}^m_0$, which is coordinate transformed from $\mathbf{F}^s$. If the dynamics of the manipulators are excluded, the force coordinate transformation $\mathbf{F}^s$ to $\mathbf{F}^m_0$ can be solved using a Jacobian matrix of the function Λ. Therefore $\mathbf{F}^m_0$ becomes

$$\mathbf{F}^m_0 = J^T\mathbf{F}^s \tag{4}$$

where J is a Jacobian matrix of the function Λ calculated as follows.

$$J_{ij} = \frac{\partial \Lambda_i}{\partial p^m_j} \quad \text{for } 1\leq i,j\leq n \tag{5}$$

The angular rate feedback can be used in each controller in order to improve the dynamic response. In the position controller, the difference between the joint angular rate $\mathbf{V}^s_0$ is used, so that $\mathbf{V}^m$ should be coordinate-transformed into $\mathbf{V}^s_0$ in the slave joint coordinates as follows,

$$\mathbf{V}^s_0 = J\,\mathbf{V}^m \tag{6}$$

which is called the rate coordinate transformation.

The position controller for the slave and the force controller for the master are constituted on the basis of PI compensation. Let u^m_i and u^s_i be the directive value for the motor driver of the master's i-th and the slave's i-th joint, respectively, then the control laws of the position and the force controllers are

$$\Delta \mathbf{P} = \mathbf{P}^s_0 - \mathbf{P}^s \tag{7}$$

$$\Delta \mathbf{V} = \mathbf{V}^s_0 - \mathbf{V}^s \tag{8}$$

$$\mathbf{U}^s = C_p \Delta \mathbf{P} + C_i \int \Delta \mathbf{P}\, dt + C_v \Delta \mathbf{V} \tag{9}$$

$$\Delta \mathbf{F} = -k_f \mathbf{F}^m_0 - \mathbf{F}^m \tag{10}$$

$$\mathbf{U}^m = d_p \Delta \mathbf{F} + d_i \int \Delta \mathbf{F}\, dt - d_v \mathbf{V}^m \tag{11}$$

where C_p, C_i, C_v, d_p, d_i and d_v are diagonal coefficient matrices, and $\mathbf{U}^s=(u^s_1,\ldots,u^s_n)^T$, $\mathbf{U}^m=(u^m_1,\ldots,u^m_n)^T$. These coefficient matrices should be selected to meet stability requirements. k_f represents a force transmission ratio. Fig.2 and Fig 3 show the block-diagram of the position and the force controllers, where G_p and k represent the actuator dynamics and the gain of the torque sensor respectively.

To check the feasibility of the proposed system, experiments using three kinds of 2 d.o.f. manipulators have been done. Fig.4 shows the schematic configurations of these manipulators. (a) is an articulated manipulator (type A), which consists of two links and two rotary joints (q_1 and q_2). (b) is a polar coordinate manipulator (type P), which consists of a rotational joint (θ) and a translational joint (r), and (c) is an orthogonal coordinate manipulator (type O), which consists of parallel pantograph link and realizes two translational movement (x and y). Each joint is driven by a geared DC servo motor, and has a potentiometer, a tachogenerator and a strain gauge based torque sensor to get joint information. Table 1 shows the specifications of these manipulators.

The position and the force controllers, the coordinate transformations and other required procedures are all executed by a TI-990 mini-computer. The position, rate and force data gathered from the sensors are fed back to the computer through an A/D converter and the motor drivers are directly controlled by the computer through D/A converters.

There are six different pairs of bilateral M-S systems, and here the combination of type A and type P manipulators is taken as an example. Let the former be the slave and the latter be the master. The coordinate transformations can be expressed as follows. Assume that the common Cartesian coordinate system C^m is fixed as in Fig.5 and that $\mathbf{P}^m=(\theta,r)^T$, $\mathbf{P}^s=(q_1,q_2)^T$. Since the slave's tip in C^w should be equivalent to the master's tip in C^o, then the following equations can be obtained.

$$l_1 \cos(q_1) + l_2 \cos(q_1+q_2) = r \cos(\theta) \tag{12}$$

$$l_2 \sin(q_1) + l_2 \sin(q_1+q_2) = r \sin(\theta) \tag{13}$$

From equations (12) and (13), the position coordinate transformation can be expressed explicitly as the following.

$$q_{10} = \theta - \phi \tag{14}$$

$$q_{20} = arccos\left(\frac{r^2-l_1^2-l_2^2}{2l_1l_2}\right) \tag{15}$$

$$\phi = atan2(l_2 sin(q_{20}),\ l_1+l_2 cos(q_{20})) \tag{16}$$

Table 1 Specifications of three manipulators

type	specification
A	$l_1 = l_2 = 300mm$ $-90° \le q_1 \le 90°$ $-160° \le q_2 \le 160°$
P	$100mm \le r \le 570mm$ $-90° \le \theta \le 90°$
O	$0mm \le x \le 600mm$ $-225mm \le y \le 225mm$

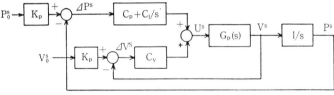

Fig.2 Block-diagram of the slave's servo

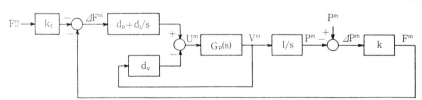

Fig.3 Block-diagram of the master's servo

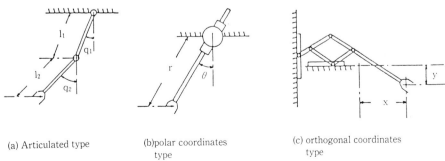

(a) Articulated type   (b)polar coordinates type   (c) orthogonal coordinates type

Fig.4 Schematic configurations of three manipulators

Differentiating equations (12) and (13) with respect to θ and r, the following Jacobian matrix can be obtained.

$$ J = \begin{pmatrix} 1 & \dfrac{cos(\alpha)}{l_1 sin(q_{20})} \\ 0 & \dfrac{-r}{l_1 l_2 sin(q_{20})} \end{pmatrix} \qquad (17) $$

where $\alpha = q_{10} + q_{20} - \theta$.

Let $\mathbf{F}^m = (\tau, f)^T$, $\mathbf{F}^s = (t_1, t_2)^T$, $\mathbf{V}^m = (\dot\theta, \dot r)^T$ and $\mathbf{V}^s = (\dot q_1, \dot q_2)^T$, where τ, f, t_1 and t_2 are the corresponding forces and torques to the coordinates θ, r, q_1 and q_2 respectively, then the force and rate coordinate transformations can be obtained from (4), (6) and (17). The coefficient matrices in (9) and (11) are selected in the following way. The dynamic characteristics of each actuator are measured using the frequency response method and its transfer function is approximated by a first order system. Each control system is modeled according to the block-diagrams of the position and force controllers in Fig.2 and Fig.3, and a zero order hold element is added to each system. The gains that ensure the stability of each system can be calculated in terms of discrete time domain. Then the system is implemented and the movement is checked and if the results are not good, the gain values are corrected by trial and error.

Photo 1 shows a general view of the experimental hardware, where the system consists of type A as the slave and type P as the master.

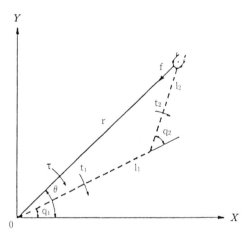

Fig.5 Relationship between two manipulators

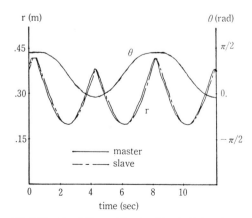

Fig.6 Results of the position tracking in P-A system

Experimental Results and Evaluations

Fundamental experiments were done from the viewpoint of checking the following characteristics:
1) the tracking capability of the slave manipulator in terms of position,
2) the tracking capability of the master manipulator in terms of force,
3) the computation time for calculating coordinate transformations and servo operations.

The tracking test of the slave is carried out in such a way that the slave is not externally loaded and the tip of the master is moved by an outer actuator, and the positional data obtained from the potentiometer is compared. Fig.6 shows the results of the position tracking with reference to the polar coordinates when type P is the master and type A the slave. The periodic movement is given to the tip of the master and the position data are compared through the master's joint coordinates (θ, r). Fig.7 shows the results when type O is the slave and type P the master, where the data are compared with respect to the slave's joint coordinates (x, y). In both cases, the position trackability of the slave is good.

The tracking test of the master is performed by fixing the end of the master and by oscillating the end of the slave regularly or at random, then comparing the force data obtained from the torque sensors of each manipulator through the same coordinates. Fig.8 shows the results of force tracking when type P is the master and type A is the slave whose tip is oscillated regularly by a vibrator. The frequency of the oscillation is 0.5 Hz. The force data are compared in the master's joint coordinates (τ, f). This shows good force trackability of the master. Fig.9 and Fig.10 show the results of the force trackability when type O is the master and type A the slave which is oscillated at random by hand. The force data are compared in the master's joint coordinates (f_x, f_y). It is clear that the slave is unstable around zero force because of the dead zone caused by joint backlash in the slave. However the trackability of the master is rather good.

The BMSC must be controlled in real time, so the question of how to execute the required calculations fast is very important. Table 2 compares each computation time executed on TI-990 minicomputer. The whole program is written in FORTRAN language and its length is about 30 lines including coordinate transformations and software servos for motors. The computation time is around 10 ms for each M-S combination.

In addition to these basic experiments, more applied experiments such as a crank turning task and a curvature tracing motion have been carried out. Throughout the experiments it has been shown that the proposed system works well and is able to carry out tasks effectively compared with the conventional method. On the other hand the following problems have been observed.
1) The difference between the working areas of master and slave manipulators may cause hardware failures, since the master can direct the position beyond the limits of the slave.
2) Each combination of master and slave requires an independent

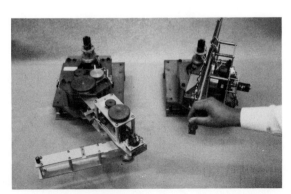

Photo 1 General view of the experimental hardware

coordinate transformation and that may prevent the system from versatility.

3) Backlash at each joint is apt to produce an unstable motion.

The following solutions can be considered for the above problems. For the first one, when the master or the slave approaches the boundary of its working area, the master device should exert a reaction force to prevent movement out of bounds.

For the second problem, a common coordinate system, Cartesian coordinates for example, should be introduced through which the required coordinate transformations can be done indirectly. In this case additional calculations are required and thus it may cause an increase in computation time. From this point of view the experiments have been again carried out and they have shown the improved system works well also. Table 3 shows computation time of each combination when the common coordinates are introduced.

For the last problem, we can suggest that the hardware must be designed carefully and it seems very efficient to adopt direct drive mechanism, as shown in the next section, to minimize backlash and joint friction.[9]

Design of Universal Master Device

In this section we are discussing the universal master device, which is specially designed to realize the proposed BMSC and will be applied to various kinds of teleoperation tasks. The master device should be designed from the following viewpoints.

1) An operator should not experience any physical fatigue or any discomfort during an operation.

2) It should provide exact information of the reaction force acting at the slave end.

3) Computation time required for the calculation of coordinate transformations should be as small as possible.

4) The mechanism should not interfere with the operator's view.

These features are essential for the master device to realize high performance teleoperation. Taking them into account, we adopt the following specifications in the hardware.

i) The configuration consists of both a 3 d.o.f. pantograph parallel link mechanism in the first three axes which can move orthogonally

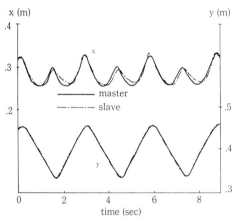

Fig.7 Results of the position tracking in P-O system

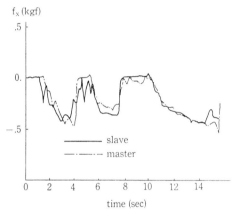

Fig.9 Results of the force tracking in O-A system (1)

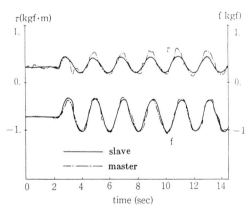

Fig.8 Results of the force tracking in P-A system

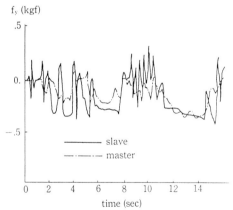

Fig.10 Results of the force tracking in O-A system (2)

Table 2 Comparison of the computation time (1)

master \ slave	A	P	O
A	7.7	9.6	10.9
P	11.2	*	10.1
O	11.0	10.1	*

(ms)

Table 3 Comparison of the computation time (2)

master \ slave	A	P	O
A	15.8	14.1	11.9
P	14.1	*	10.1
O	12.3	10.4	*

(ms)

in x, y, and z directions and contributes mainly to positioning, and a 3 d.o.f. gymbal mechanism (P_1−P_2−R_3 mechanism; P:pivot joint,R:rotation joint) in the last three axes for orientation (wrist part). This configuration is unique in that the position and the orientation of its end (or handle) are decoupled from each other, that is, the movement of the last three joints is independent of that of the first three ones. This characteristic is helpful for the reduction of computation time, since the coordinate transformations required become more easier.

ii) Each joint has a direct drive mechanism to reduce friction and to attain a high fidelity force control. The first three joints have electrical linear force motors and the last three have DC torque motors. Each joint has a force or torque sensor to realize fine force control.

iii) The first three joints have a gravity balance mechanism to allow an operator to move the device smoothly.

Fig.11 shows the structure of the developed master device. The actuators in x, y and z directions are linear induction motors which can produce constant force according to input current. The stroke of each motor is 10 cm and the maximum output force is 5 kgf. Since the linkage ratio in the pantograph mechanism is 1:4, the work space of the handle is 40×40×40 cm^3 and the maximum force produced at the handle is 1.25 kgf in each direction. The actuator of the wrist part is a DC torque motor and the maximum torque is around 5kgfcm in each joint. Each joint has a potentiometer to locate the handle end. The link mechanism protrudes upward from the platform so as not to interfere with the operator's view.

The most important factor in the design of the master device is how to eliminate its gravitational effect. There are several methods to compensate the gravity, for example, by providing a counter balance mechanism, or by controlling the exact force in actuator that cancels the actual gravitational effect.[10] We adopted a counter balance mechanism in our device. Since the device consists of several links, it is not easy to find how to realize a good balancing. In order to solve this problem, first, we analyze the statics of the whole mechanism, then, applying forces and moments in some part of the mechanism to compensate for the gravitational load, the average force that is required at the handle end over the entire work space (what we call, an operated balancing force, $\mathbf{f}_o = (f_{ox}, f_{oy}, f_{oz})^T$) is estimated. By trial and error the optimal compensating force and moment can be derived. Fig.12 shows the operated balancing force over the working area, when no compensating force is applied. In this case more than 10 kgf operated balancing force in the z direction, f_{oz} is required to hold the device. Fig.13 shows the operated balancing force and the schematic structure of the link mechanism when the compensating force Q_7 (=65.2 kgf) is applied to link 7. In this case f_{oz} is reduced, but the balancing condition is not completely attained. Fig.14 shows the structure of the link mechanism when the optimal compensation is attained. In this case the optimal compensating force and moment are given in such a way that a counter-weight is put on link 2 and the upward force Q_7 (46.5 kgf) is added to link 7. The complete balancing condition is attained where no operated balancing force is required to hold the master device.

The total weight of the master device itself is 35 kg excluding its platform and the counter balance mechanism. Photo 2 shows the overview of the developed master device. We applied this master device to the configuration differing BMSC using an R-P-P-R-P-R type slave manipulator and the computation time required for the coordinate transformations was around 60 ms.

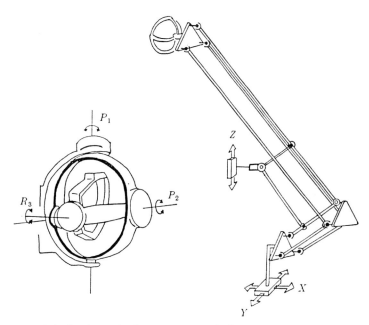

3 d.o.f. wrist mechanism   3 d.o.f. pantograph mechanism

Fig.11 Structure of the master device

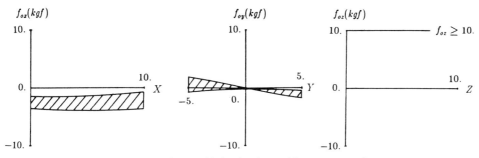

Fig.12 Operated balancing force with no compensation

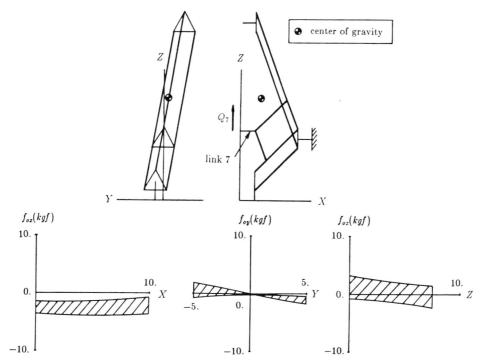

Fig.13 Operated balancing force with insufficient compensation

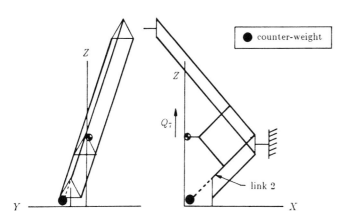

Fig.14 Schematic Structure of the link mechanism
with optimal compensation

Photo 2 Overview of the developed master device

Conclusions

In this paper a new bilateral master slave manipulator control method has been proposed and fundamental experiments using three kinds of 2 d.o.f. manipulators have been discussed. These results indicated the high feasibility and the broad applicability of the proposed method. Then we have developed a universal master device and discussed its design concept. The device is designed from the viewpoint of easy operation and simple calculations required for coordinate transformations.

Acknowledgements

The authors would like to express their appreciation to Mr. Ichiro Takeyama of Kubota Co. for his kind help in designing the master device.

REFERENCES

1. W.R. Ferrell, T.B. Sheridan, et al.: Supervisory Control of Remote Manipulation, *IEEE Spectrum*, Vol.4, No.10, pp.81-88, 1967

2. A.K. Bejzy: Sensors, Controls and Man-Machine Interface for Advanced Teleoperation, *Science*, Vol.208, pp.1327-1335, 1980

3. M. Kobayashi, S. Tachi, et al.: R&D Programs for Advanced Robot Technology "Jupiter", *Proceedings of International Conference on Advanced Robotics*, pp.39-40, 1983

4. M. Ejiri and A. Kamoi: Servo Manipulator, *Journal of the Society of Instrument and Control Engineers*, Vol.2, No.7, pp.483-490, 1963 (in Japanese)

5. N. Tominari: Analysis and Experiments of Bilateral Servomechanism through the Combination Use of Matrix and Signal-Flow Diagram, *Automatic Control*, Vol.6, No.2, pp.58-66, 1959 (in Japanese)

6. S. Fujii: Theory of Bilateral Servo Mechanism, *Journal of the Japan Society of Mechanical Engineers*, Vol.62, No.480, pp.64-69, 1959 (in Japanese)

7. T. Arai and E. Nakano: Bilateral Control System for Manipulators with Completely Different Configurations, *Proceedings of '85 International Conference on Advanced Robotics*, pp.303-310, 1985

8. R.P. Paul: Robot Maniulators, pp.217-230, *MIT Press*, 1981

9. H. Asada, T. Kanade, et al.: Design Concept of Direct-Drive Manipulators Using Rare-Earth DC Torque Motors, *Proceedings of 11th International Symposium on Industrial Robots*, pp.629-636, 1981

10. T. Arai, E. Nakano, et al.: Development of Direct Drive Human-like Manipulator, *Proceedings of 15th International Symposium on Industrial Robots*, Vol.1, pp.447-454, 1985

IV KINEMATICS AND FORCES

Most robotic devices contain mechanisms that are composed of one or more linkages. The kinematic structure of a linkage and its force and motion capabilities are its most basic characteristics.

Waldron and Hunt show that certain series and parallel mechanisms, as well as their corresponding Jacobian matrices, are related to each other through a well-known duality between velocity and force. Salisbury explores the concept of using more of a manipulator's structure than just its end-effector to perform useful tasks. This leads him to suggest a rich variety of new kinematic structures that have advantages in "whole arm" manipulation. It is often difficult to accurately determine the kinematic parameters for an actual manipulator; Hollerbach and Bennett explain how they succeeded in devising a system to automatically perform such a calibration. Their method uses a commercial motion-tracking system for acquiring the necessary experimental data.

In dealing with forces, the actual design details are often extremely important; effects that cause instabilities and noisy measurements are omnipresent. In an effort to gain basic knowledge about contacting surfaces, Cutkosky et al. have embarked on studies of material characteristics and their relationships to models of contact phenomena. Their paper describes their analytical and experimental methodologies and their early results.

Kuno et al. describe their efforts to reduce the destabilizing effects of gear-train friction and elasticity in their computer simulation of a six-axis force-controlled manipulator. They present a detailed analysis that shows the relationship of system stability to environmental stiffness. They also report on experimental verification of their simulation results.

SERIES-PARALLEL DUALITIES IN ACTIVELY COORDINATED MECHANISMS

Kenneth J. Waldron, Nordholt Professor
Department of Mechanical Engineering, Ohio State University
Columbus, Ohio 43210, U.S.A.

and

Kenneth H. Hunt, Emeritus Professor
Department of Mechanical Engineering, Monash University
Clayton, Victoria 3168, Australia

It is demonstrated that there is a deep symmetry between serial chain manipulators and fully parallel systems such as the Stewart platform. This symmetry is shown to be a result of the well known duality of motion screw axes and wrenches. The appearance of the inverse of the Jacobian matrix in force decomposition in the same role as the Jacobian in rate decomposition is also a consequence of this same duality, and of the reciprocity relationship between the motion screw system and the wrench system of a kinematic joint. A geometric meaning of the columns of the Jacobian is demonstrated. A simple example of the application of the ideas presented here to the understanding of the complex combinations of serial and parallel chains found in vehicle and multi-fingered hand problems is also presented.

Introduction

Two major modes of coordinating robotic systems have evolved: rate control [1] and force control [2]. Recently these have been brought together in hybrid force/motion coordination schemes [3,4,5]. The above studies dealt with relatively simple situations of serial chain manipulators interacting with environmental constraints. Other investigations have addressed the problems of applying these concepts to parallel, or combination series-parallel structures [6,7,8]. Yet others have addressed problems involving series-parallel structures with multiple environmental constraints such as those of grasping with multi-fingered, multi-degree of freedom hands [9-13], or of coordinating the multiple locomotion elements of legged vehicles [14,15], or actively suspended wheeled vehicles [16].

There are several symmetries between the force/torque and angular velocity/velocity vector systems. Classically it has been observed that the velocity fields of systems of interconnected rigid bodies can be described by means of systems of instantaneous screw axes [7]. At the same time, the static force systems acting on the same systems of rigid bodies can be described by means of systems of wrenches, which are vectorially homologous to the screw systems. The two types of vector system are inter-related by Ball's reciprocity relationship [18]. An instantaneous screw axis can be represented by a vector pair, or motor (ω,μ) where ω is the angular velocity of motion of a body about the screw axis, relative to a reference frame, and μ is the velocity of the point in the body which is instantaneously coincident with the origin of the reference frame. Correspondingly, a wrench can be represented by a vector pair $(\underline{F},\underline{T})$, where $\underline{F}$ is the resultant force of the force system represented by the wrench, considered to be applied at the origin of the reference frame,

and $\underline{T}$ is the corresponding resultant torque of the system. A screw axis and wrench are mutually reciprocal if:

$$\underline{\omega} \cdot \underline{T} + \underline{\mu} \cdot \underline{F} = 0 \qquad (1)$$

This is the condition for the wrench to do no work if applied to a body free to move about the screw axis.

The axes for the screw and wrench axes are actually purely geometric entities completely identical to one another. Likewise, the reciprocity condition is a geometric relationship. This is readily demonstrated by dividing the motor by the magnitude of the angular velocity, and the wrench vector pair by the magnitude of the force. Both vector pairs then assume the dimensions of normalized Plucker line coordinates [17]. They can be viewed as a generalization of Plücker line coordinates which expresses both the positions of the respective axes and their pitches. The vector pairs, in this form, are referred to as screw coordinates.

Division of equation (1) by the product of the magnitudes of angular velocity and force results in a purely geometric relationship between the screw coordinates of the screw and wrench axes. The major significance of the reciprocity relationship is that, if two rigid bodies are connected by a kinematic joint, the set of possible motions of one body relative to the other is described by a screw system consisting of all screw axes of motions permitted by the joint, and the set of force systems which can be transmitted across the joint is described by a screw system consisting of all possible wrench axes, then the two screw systems are reciprocal to one another. That is, every screw axis of one system is reciprocal to every screw axis of the other. The geometric properties of screw systems have been extensively studied [17] and are a fertile source of insights into robotic coordination problems. The terminology used here is consistent with that of reference [17].

An important example is the contact between the end effector of a manipulator and a fixed object in the environment. The contact of the two bodies constitutes a kinematic joint. The relative motion possible between the two bodies is described by a screw system of order n. The force systems which can be transmitted between them are described by a screw system of order 6-n which is reciprocal to the motion screw system. When controlling this contact using a hybrid force/rate scheme it is necessary to control n rate axes which are linearly independent members of the motion screw system, and 6-n force axes which are linearly independent members of the force screw system [5].

The Jacobian Symmetry

Another well-known symmetry between force and motion occurs when decomposing the hand velocity motor of a manipulator into commanded joint rates and, conversely, decomposing a static force system applied to the hand of the manipulator in the same position into actuator forces and torques. This can be expressed as a consequence of conservation of energy, if inertia forces are neglected. The hand velocity motor is related to the joint rates by [1]:

$$\begin{bmatrix} \omega \\ \mu \end{bmatrix} = \underline{J}\ \dot{\underline{\theta}} \qquad (2)$$

Where $(\underline{\omega},\underline{\mu})$ is the motor describing the hand velocity, $\dot{\underline{\theta}}$ is the nx1 vector of joint rates and $\underline{J}$ is a 6xn Jacobian matrix. n is the number of joints in the system.

The wrench applied at the hand is related to the joint torques and forces by:

$$\underline{T} = \underline{K}\ \begin{bmatrix} \underline{M} \\ \underline{R} \end{bmatrix} \qquad (3)$$

where $(\underline{R},\underline{M})$ is the wrench, $\underline{T}$ is the nx1 vector of joint torques and forces, and $\underline{K}$ is an nx6 matrix. Conservation of energy requires that

$$[\underline{M}^T,\underline{R}^T]\ \begin{bmatrix} \underline{\omega} \\ \underline{\mu} \end{bmatrix} = \underline{T}^T\dot{\underline{\theta}} \qquad (4)$$

Substitution from equations (2) and (3) gives:

$$[\underline{M}^T,\underline{R}^T]\ \underline{J}\ \dot{\underline{\theta}} = [\underline{M}^T,\underline{R}^T]\ \underline{K}^T\dot{\underline{\theta}}$$

which is true for arbitrary $\underline{M}$, $\underline{R}$ and $\dot{\underline{\theta}}$ if, and only if

$$\underline{K}^T = \underline{J}\ .$$

Thus, equation (3) becomes:

$$\underline{T} = \underline{J}^T\ \begin{bmatrix} \underline{M} \\ \underline{R} \end{bmatrix} \qquad (5)$$

Actually, this relationship is a direct result of the symmetry of the motion and force systems

since, as is illustrated below the columns of the Jacobian matrix $\underline{J}$ are the normalized screw coordinates of the screw axes of the manipulator joints. If n = 6 and equation (5) is inverted to,

$$\begin{bmatrix} \underline{M} \\ \underline{R} \end{bmatrix} = \underline{J}^{-1\ T}\ \underline{T}$$

the columns of $\underline{J}^{-1\ T}$ are the non-normalized screw coordinates of the wrenches produced by actuating the joints, with the direction and moment components transposed. The effect of the transposition is to make the inner product of a row of $\underline{J}^{-1}$ and a column of $\underline{J}$ equivalent to the reciprocity condition (Equation (1)). Thus, the symmetry of equations (3) and (5) is a consequence of the motor-wrench symmetry.

Series and Parallel Chains

In the serial chain configuration, shown in Figure 1, $\underline{\omega}$ and $\underline{\mu}$ are related to the joint rates by:

$$\underline{\omega} = \sum_{i=1}^{n} \dot{\theta}_i\underline{w}_i \qquad (6)$$

and

$$\underline{\mu} = \sum_{i=1}^{n} \dot{\theta}_i \underline{\rho}_i \times \underline{w}_i \qquad (7)$$

where $\underline{w}_i$ is a unit vector with the direction of axis i, θ_i is the angle of joint i (assumed to be a revolute), and ρ_i is the position relative to the fixed reference frame of any point on axis i. If joint i is a prismatic joint, $\dot{\theta}_i = 0$ eliminating the ith term from equation (6). The ith term in equation (7) is replaced by $\dot{r}_i\ \underline{w}_i$, where r_i is the prismatic joint position.

Equations (6) and (7) are readily written in the format of equation (2). Thus, if joint i is a revolute, the first three elements of column i are those of $\underline{w}_i$, the second three are those of $\underline{\rho}_i \times \underline{w}_i$. That is, column i is composed of the normalized Plücker coordinates of the axis of joint i. In this case the screw coordinates are identical to the Plücker coordinates because the pitch of the screw axis of a revolute joint is zero.

If joint i is a prismatic joint, the first three elements of column i are zero, and the second three are the elements of $\underline{w}_i$. These are the screw coordinates of a screw axis with infinite pitch with the prismatic joint sliding direction.

The force system $(\underline{R},\underline{M})$ applied to the hand of the serial chain, shown in Figure 1, is related to the joint torques by the equation

$$T_i = -\underline{w}_i \cdot \underline{\rho}_i \times \underline{R} + \underline{w}_i \cdot \underline{M}$$

or

$$T_i - \underline{w}_i \cdot \underline{M} - \underline{\rho}_i \times \underline{w}_i \cdot \underline{R} = 0 \qquad (8)$$

If joint i is a prismatic joint, the joint actuator force is given by

$$F_i = \underline{w}_i \cdot \underline{R} \qquad (9)$$

The n equations (8) or (9) corresponding to the n joints can be formatted into equation (5).

In the fully parallel Stewart platform configuration shown in Figure 2, only the prismatic joint in each limb is actuated. The force system $(\underline{R},\underline{M})$ applied to the floating member is related to the actuator forces by the equations

$$\underline{R} = \sum_{i=1}^{n} F_i \, \underline{w}_i \qquad (10)$$

$$\underline{M} = \sum_{i=1}^{n} F_i \, \underline{\rho}_i \times \underline{w}_i \qquad (11)$$

where $\underline{w}_i$ is a unit vector parallel to the sliding direction of the prismatic joint in limb i. The line joining the concurrency point of the two revolute joint axes to the center of the spherical joint is assumed to be parallel to $\underline{w}_i$. $\underline{\rho}_i$ is the position of any point on that line.

Equations (10) and (11) can be formatted into the equation

$$\begin{bmatrix} \underline{R} \\ \underline{M} \end{bmatrix} = \underline{H} \; \underline{F} \qquad (12)$$

It may be seen that $\underline{H}$ has the same form as the Jacobian matrix $\underline{J}$ of equation (2).

The joint rates of this structure can be related to the motor $(\underline{\omega},\underline{\mu})$ describing motion of the floating link by means of the equations:

$$\dot{r}_i = \underline{w}_i \cdot (\underline{\mu} + \underline{\omega} \times \underline{\rho}_i)$$

or

$$\dot{r}_i = \underline{w}_i \cdot \underline{\mu} + \underline{\rho}_i \times \underline{w}_i \cdot \underline{\omega} \qquad (13)$$

The n equations (13) can be formatted into

$$\underline{\dot{r}}_i = \underline{H}^T \begin{bmatrix} \underline{\mu} \\ \underline{\omega} \end{bmatrix} \qquad (14)$$

It can be seen that equations (12) and (14) are duals of equations (2) and (5) with $\underline{\omega}$ transposing with $\underline{R}$, $\underline{\mu}$ transposing with $\underline{M}$, $\underline{T}$ transposing with $\underline{r}$, and $\underline{\theta}$ transposing with $\underline{F}$. This duality is consistent with the motor-wrench symmetry. However, the Jacobian of the Stewart platform exists only for n = 6 and is $\underline{H}^{-1^T}$. Thus, an inverse relationship exists between the forms of the Jacobian for fully serial, and fully parallel configurations.

It is natural to wonder why the dual of the serial chain with rotary joints is a parallel chain with prismatic joints. This is best understood by viewing the limbs of the Stewart platform as force generators. The screw systems of the spherical joint, and of the crossed revolutes, are reciprocal to the pure force wrench produced by actuating the prismatic joint and, therefore, permit that wrench to be transmitted to the fixed and floating members. These joints ensure that relative movement of the fixed and floating members about any screw axis reciprocal to the wrench axis does not generate forces. Since the screw axis of a revolute joint has zero pitch, and the wrench axis of a pure force also has zero pitch, it can be seen that the limbs of the Stewart platform viewed as force generators are, in fact, duals of the revolute joints of the serial chain under the motor-wrench symmetry.

A natural question now is: "what is the dual of a prismatic joint in a serial chain?" A prismatic joint has a screw axis with infinite pitch. The wrench whose axis has infinite pitch is a couple. Figure 3 shows a limb configuration which can be inserted into a Stewart platform in place of a force generating limb, which will exert a couple on the fixed and floating members. The passive joints are selected to be reciprocal to the actuated couple at all times so that they transmit it. Correspondingly, the passive joints in the limb of the Stewart Platform are reciprocal to the actuated force at all times.

Just as use of more than three prismatic joints in a serial chain creates an internal superabundance of translatory freedom, use of more than three of the limbs of Figure 3 in a Stewart platform creates an internal redundancy. This is because no more than three couples can be linearly independent.

The duality of velocities and force systems between fully serial and fully parallel configurations can be seen to be perfect and consistent with the motor-wrench symmetry. It does not, however, extend to positions. The expressions for $\underline{w}_i$ and $\underline{\rho}_i$ in terms of the joint variables in the serial configuration are very different from the corresponding expressions of the Stewart platform. Nevertheless, the position algebras of the two system types share some important characteristics with the rate algebras. This is not surprising since the rate algebra is a generalized derivative of the position algebra in each case.

As is well known, the direct position kinematics of a serial chain are straightforward. The transformation describing the position of the hand relative to the base is obtained by simply concatenating transformations which describe the joint positions. Likewise, the direct rate kinematics are straightforward. The Jacobian matrix of equation (2) can be written in a straight-forward manner in terms of the joint positions [19], allowing $\underline{\omega}$ and $\underline{\mu}$ to be computed using that equation for specified joint rates $\underline{\dot{\theta}}$. Conversely, the inverse position kinematics of the serial chain are complex requiring solutions of systems of non-linear algebraic equations. This corresponds to the relatively complex inverse rate kinematics requiring inversion of the Jacobian matrix of equation (2).

Correspondingly, the inverse position kinematics of the Stewart platform are straightforward [6]. Given the position of the floating member relative to the base, the lengths of the limbs are readily computed:

$$(\underline{M}\underline{q}_i + \underline{m} - \underline{s}_i)^2 = r_i^2 \qquad (15)$$

where $\underline{q}_i$ is the position of the center of the ball joint on limb i relative to the floating frame, and $\underline{s}_i$ is the position of the concurrency point of the revolute axes relative to the fixed frame (Figure 2).

$$\underline{p}_o = \underline{M}\,\underline{p}_F + \underline{m} \qquad (16)$$

is the transformation relating the positions of points, $\underline{p}_F$, in the floating frame to their positions in the fixed frame, $\underline{p}_o$. This corresponds to the inverse rate kinematics expressed by equation (14) which are straightforward once the Jacobian has been constructed.

Conversely, the direct kinematics of the Stewart platform are very complex. In fact, the authors are unaware of any published solution to the general problem. Expansion of equation (15) gives

$$q_i^2 + m^2 + s_{iz}^2 + 2\underline{m}^T\underline{M}\underline{q}_i - 2\underline{s}_i^T\underline{M}\underline{q}_i - 2\underline{m}^T\underline{s}_i = r_i^2$$

where $i = 1, ..., n$.

This system of equations can be solved, in principle, when n = 6 in conjunction with 6 additional relationships obtained from

$$\underline{M}^T\underline{M} = \underline{I} \ ,$$

to give the components of $\underline{M}$ and $\underline{m}$. Once again, a system of non-linear algebraic equations is to be solved. This corresponds to the relatively complex direct rate kinematics of this system requiring inversion of matrix $\underline{H}$ in equation (14).

Contact Conditions

Multiple contacts between an actively coordinated mechanism, such as a multi-fingered hand, and a body, or a walking machine and the Earth, are a practically important example of combinations of series and parallel connections. The case of frictionless contacts has a unique solution which is discussed in reference [17]. A more important case is that of frictional point contacts with no slip, which is used as an example below.

In a serial chain, the screw system describing the motion potential of one end member relative to another is the combined linear space of the screw systems of the joints in the chain. The reciprocal screw system consists only of those screw axes which are common to the reciprocal systems of all of the joints [20]. Conversely, when two bodies are connected by joints in

parallel, they can move only about screw axes which are common to the screw systems of all of the parallel joints since all joints must simultaneously permit the motion. The reciprocal system of the parallel connection is the combined linear space of the reciprocal screw systems of the joints in parallel since wrenches may be transmitted across any combination of joints.

These properties are important in making decisions on which axes to control in force and which to control in rate. For example, consider the case of two point frictional contact without slip, shown in Figure 4. If contact moments are neglected, the screw system of each contact consists of all zero pitch axes through the point of contact (the second special three-system of reference [17]). Thus, the only screw axis common to both systems is the zero pitch axis which passes through both points of contact. Thus, the only rate axis about which movement can be commanded is this one. The reciprocal system at each contact point also consists of all zero pitch axes through the point of contact. The combination of the two reciprocal systems is a fifth order system. The zero pitch axes of this system consists of all axes which intersect the line joining the contact points, or are parallel to it. Thus, pure forces can be transmitted across the two point contact on any of these lines of action. The reciprocal system also contains all infinite pitch screws normal to the line through the contact points. Thus, couples in any direction normal to this line can be transmitted. Thus, any linearly independent combination of force and moment wrenches from this set can be commanded.

The axis which is common to the two reciprocal systems, namely the zero pitch axis through the two contact points, has particular importance. Equal and opposite forces can be exerted at the contact points along this line without affecting the resultant force across the contacts. This is the simplest example of a null system in the force decomposition. The null system is of great importance to the generation of grasping forces in multi-fingered hands.

If there are three, or more, contact points, there are, in general, no common members of the contact point screw systems. Thus, if the contacts are maintained at fixed positions, the contacted body cannot move, at least without breaking contacts. It can execute fully controlled movements if the contacting points are moved in an appropriately coordinated manner. The combined reciprocal system of the contacts is a sixth order system. Thus, any wrench can be transmitted to the contacted body, again provided that no contacts are broken.

The null space force system is a system of contact forces at each of the contact points whose resultant is zero. Since the members of the reciprocal systems at each of the contact points are all zero pitch wrenches, or pure forces, it follows that, for n contact points, the null system is a wrench system of order n-1 which has at least one zero pitch member passing through each contact point. The members at the contact points are linearly dependent, resulting in the system order being n - 1. This is required by the condition that the wrenches have a null resultant.

The reciprocal wrench system is indeterminate since three component wrenches are required to identify the contact wrench (force) at each contact point. This is a total of 3n components, or at least 9 for n = 3. Since static equilibrium of the contacted bodies produces only 6 linear, scalar equations in the screw coordinates of the component wrenches, additional conditions are necessary to resolve the indeterminacy. It has been shown [16] that a contact force distribution, which might be regarded as canonical, can be derived for any given resultant wrench in the form of a Moore-Penrose pseudo-inverse. This has also been shown to be equivalent to imposing a zero interaction force condition, where the interaction force between any two contact points is defined as the difference between the components of the contact forces at the two points directed along the line joining them [13,15]. In the light of the above discussion the interaction force may be recognized as the difference in amplitudes at the two contact points on the wrench common to the reciprocal systems at those contact points.

If the contact points are at the finger tips of a multi-fingered hand, or at the feet of a walking machine, the contact forces must be generated by the actuators in the mechanisms constituting those limbs. If they are serial chains the torques which must be commanded at the actuators to produce a given contact wrench are prescribed by equation (5). It is possible to generate any desired contact force provided there are at least three actuated joints in the limb (and no passive joints). This is because the actuator joint torques or forces combine with reactions at the base of the limb to produce a zero pitch wrench passing through the contact point. Conversely, it is not, in general, possible to produce a rotation about any desired zero pitch screw axis through the contact point unless there are at least six actuated joints in the limb. The difference is that an inverse of equation (2) giving the necessary joint rates exists only if n = 6 whereas equation (5) will give the appropriate joint torques regardless of the number of actuators. If n = 6 an appropriate set of joint rates can be obtained from equation (2) by adding n - 6 constraint equations, or by applying a generalized inverse.

Conclusions

It has been demonstrated in this paper that the duality of the rate decomposition and static force allocation problems is a direct consequence of the duality of the velocity and force-torque fields which is a basic property of screw systems. It is further demonstrated that a duality between serial and parallel manipulator structures is also a consequence of

this same fundamental duality. These properties naturally lead to an exploration of the application of screw system theory to active structures which combine serial and parallel elements. An example is the control of multiple frictional contacts between an active structure and a body. This possesses many features analogous to redundant serial structures. Notably, the force allocation among the contact points can be decomposed into a particular solution and an ensemble of null space solutions in a manner analogous to that possible in rate decomposition in redundant serial structures.

Acknowledgement

The work reported here was partially supported by a grant to Stanford University (B. Roth, Principal Investigator) by System Development Foundation. Dr. Waldron who was partially supported by that project during a sabbatical year spent as Visiting Professor in the Design Division, Department of Mechanical Engineering, Stanford University, 1986-87. Dr. Waldron would also like to acknowledge Professor Roth's contributions to this work in comments and discussions. Work reported here was also partially supported by a grant to The Ohio State University by DARPA (DAAE 07-84-K-R001).

References

1. Whitney, D.E., "The Mathematics of Coordinated Control of Prosthetic Arms and Remote Manipulators," J. Dynamic Systems, Measurement and Control, December 1972, pp. 303-309.

2. Nevins, J.L., and Whitney, D.E., "The Force Vector Assembler Concept," Proceedings of 1st IFToMM-CISM Symposium on Theory and Practice of Robots and Manipulators, Udine, Italy, 5-8 September 1983, pp. 273-288.

3. Raibert, M.H., and Craig, J.J., "Hybrid Position/Force Control of Manipulators," J. Dynamic Systems, Measurement and Control, Vol. 105, 1981, pp. 126-133.

4. Mason, M.T., "Compliance and Force Control for Computer Controlled Manipulators," IEEE Transactions on Systems, Man and Cybernetics, Vol. SMC-11, No. 6, June 1981, pp. 418-432.

5. Lipkin, H., and Duffy, J., "Hybrid Twist and Wrench Control for a Robotic Manipulator," ASME Paper no. 86-DET-74 presented at ASME Mechanisms Conference, Columbus, Ohio, October 5-8, 1986.

6. Fichter, E.F., "A Stewart Platform-Based Manipulator: General Theory and Practical Construction," International Journal of Robotics Research, Vol. 5, No. 2, Summer 1986, pp. 157-182.

7. Waldron, K.J., Roth, B. and Rhagavan, M., "Kinematics of a Hybrid Series-Parallel Manipulation System, Part I: Position Kinematics," to be presented at ASME Winter Annual Meeting, Boston, November 1987.

8. Waldron, K.J., Roth, B. and Rhagavan, M., "Kinematics of a Hybrid Series-Parallel Manipulation System, Part II: Rate and Force Decomposition," to be presented at ASME Winter Annual Meeting, Boston, November 1987.

9. Mason, M.T., and Salisbury, J.K., Robot Hands and the Mechanics of Manipulation, MIT Press, Cambridge, Mass., 1985.

10. Abel, J.M., Holzmann, W., McCarthy, J.M. "On Grasping Objects with Two Articulated Fingers," IEEE Journal of Robotics and Automation, Vol. RA-1, No. 4, December 1985, pp. 211-214.

11. Holzmann, W. and McCarthy, J.M. "Computing the Friction Forces Associated with a Three-Fingered Grasp," IEEE Journal of Robotics and Automation, Vol. RA-1, No. 4, December 1985, pp. 206-210.

12. Jameson, J.W., and Leifer, L.J., "Quasi-Static Analysis: A Method for Predicting Grasp Stability," Proceedings of IEEE International Conference on Robotics and Automation, San Francisco, April 7-10, 1986, Vol. 2, pp. 876-883.

13. Kumar, V., and Waldron, K.J. "Sub-Optimal Algorithms for Force Distribution in Multifingered Grippers," Proceedings of IEEE International Conference on Robotics and Automation, Raleigh, North Carolina, March 31-April 3, 1987, pp. 252-257.

14. McGhee, R.B., and Orin, D.E., "A Mathematical Programming Approach to Control of Joint Positions and Torques in Legged Locomotion Systems," Theory and Practice of Robots and Manipulators, A. Morecki and K. Kedzior, Eds., Elvesier, New York, 1977, pp. 225-232.

15. Waldron, K.J., "Force and Motion Management in Legged Locomotion," IEEE Journal of Robotics and Automation, Vol. RA-2, No. 4, December 1986, pp. 214-220.

16. Kumar, V., and Waldron, K.J. "Actively Coordinated Vehicle Systems," to be presented at ASME Winter Annual Meeting, Boston, November 1987.

17. Hunt, K.H., Kinematic Geometry of Mechanisms, Clarendon Press, Oxford, 1978.

18. Ball, R.S., The Theory of Screws, Cambridge, 1900.

19. Waldron, K.J., Wang, S.L., and Bolin, S.J., "A Study of the Jacobian Matrix of Serial Manipulators," J. Mechanisms, Transmissions and Automation in Design, Vol. 107, No. 2, pp. 230-238, 1985.

20. Waldron, K.J., "The Constraint Analysis of Mechanisms," J. Mechanisms, Vol. 1, 1966, pp. 101-114.

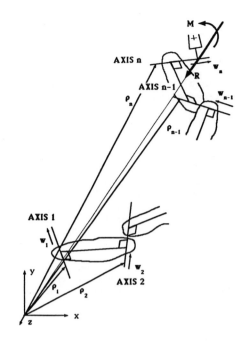

Figure 1: A serial chain. Axis 1 is fixed relative to the reference frame. $(\underline{R}, \underline{M})$ is a force system applied to the hand. The line of action of $\underline{R}$ passes through the origin of the reference frame $\underline{w}_i$ is the current direction of axis i, and $\underline{\rho}_i$ is the current position of a point on that axis.

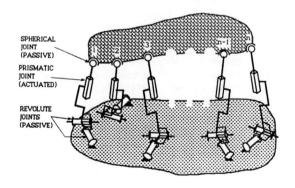

Figure 2: A fully parallel system. Each limb consists of two orthogonally intersecting revolutes, a prismatic joint normal to the second revolute, and a spherical joint. Only the prismatic joint is actuated.

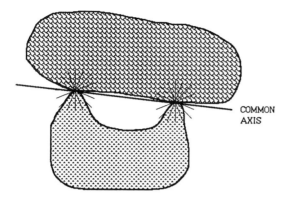

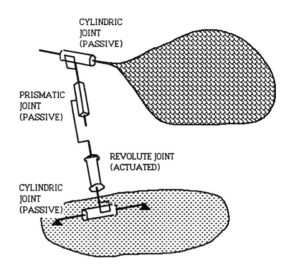

COMMON
AXIS

CYLINDRIC
JOINT
(PASSIVE)

PRISMATIC
JOINT
(PASSIVE)

REVOLUTE JOINT
(ACTUATED)

CYLINDRIC
JOINT
(PASSIVE)

Figure 3:   A limb of a parallel system which functions as a torque generator. The limb consists of a cylindric joint, a revolute whose axis intersects that of the cylindric joint orthogonally, a prismatic joint coaxial with the revolute and a cylindric joint normal to the prismatic joint. Only the revolute joint is actuated.

Figure 4:   Two-point non-sliding, frictional contact between two bodies. The screw system at each contact consists of all zero pitch screws through the point of contact. There is one common axis: that along the line through the two contact points. The screw system is self-reciprocal. That is, the reciprocal system is identical to the screw system.

WHOLE ARM MANIPULATION

Kenneth Salisbury

MIT AI Laboratory
Cambridge, MA 02139

Current manipulators use only a small percentage of their available surface area for manipulation. The use of the fingertips alone is appropriate for objects that are relatively small compared to the size of the arm. We suggest that by broadening our view of manipulation we may utilize more of the manipulator to perform useful work on objects that are relatively large compared to the manipulator itself. When properly designed, the entire arm, or a collection of arms may be used as a large hand with many of the surfaces available for constraining and manipulating objects. This approach to manipulation is particularly important in the cases of mobile terrestrial, space and undersea robots that may be called upon to work with a wide variety of object sizes in unstructured environments. In this paper we identify and classify the unique mechanisms which may be constructed from up to seven links and describe how the whole arm may be used to grasp and manipulate objects.

INTRODUCTION

Most robotic manipulation we see today involves contacting objects only with the fingertips of the robot. The current style of manipulation depends primarily on precise, predictable motion in order to succeed. While this is perhaps appropriate for highly structured environments, there is emerging a whole new class of robot applications which demand the ability to deal with unstructured, changing environments. Such applications will require that the robot be able to move about and interact with the environment in a much wider variety of ways than is now possible. Even though all the surfaces of the robot can be moved with varying degrees of freedom, it is only the fingertips that are allowed to interact physically with the environment. Thus, robots generally deal with objects that are small relative to the size and mass of the manipulator. Because our robots lack the ability to reason about tasks we attempt to build and control them so that they can assume full 6-degree-of-freedom control over their task environments. Yet many tasks require fewer degrees of actively controlled motion. The motion constraints inherent in many tasks suggest that parts of the robot less mobile than the end effector may usefully be employed to do work.

As manipulators begin to be coupled with mobile bases, the diversity of tasks they will be asked to perform will be greatly enlarged. It is easy to imagine a factory robot that will be required to retrieve a large barrel. While a large crane-like arm could be specially designed to perform the task, it may be possible to do the task using the existing structure of much smaller arms. We suggest that the intermediate links of the arm, those between the hand and base, can be used to act upon

objects by imparting forces and motions and by imposing constraints. With this view, it is easy to imagine our mobile robot using its "forearm" and "upper arm" links to push or cradle the barrel. Instead of using the fingers to pull a heavy load it would be much more advantageous to hyperflex the wrist joint and use it to hook a ring or other feature on the load. In these examples the arm is being used like a large hand relative to the mobile platform and acts more to grasp the object than to directly manipulate it. Thus, we see a continuum of functions distributed over the components of the robot. For very small objects and small motions the arm may be stationary and only the fingers would provide for movement. For medium size objects the hand may simply grasp the object securely to the the end of the arm, with the arm providing for motion control. For large objects, perhaps those on the scale of the arm itself, the links of the arm(s) may act as large fingers manipulating the object. For very large objects, the arm links may only secure the object to a mobile base which provides the necessary motion. And for even larger objects the mobile base, perhaps in concert with other mobile robots, will have to be utilized to "grasp" and "manipulate" the object much as tug boats must maneuver a large ocean vessel.

This blurring of the distinction between fingers, arms and mobile platforms suggests that we reassess the way we build robots. We may ask a number of questions: From a kinematic point of view what are the ways a set of links may be constructed to grasp and manipulate an object? From a mechanism design point of view, how can we build robot components that can assume the dual role of grasper and transporter? From a control point of view what is required to actuate these links in the variety of contexts required? From a command and planning point of view, what are the available ways of manipulating with such general mechanisms and how can we choose among them? The style of *whole arm manipulation* that we suggest brings with it the advantage of providing a given robot with much more capacity to manipulate objects for a given hardware investment (more "bang for the buck", so to speak). This is not a new theme; such efficient use of resources is familiar to us in biological systems and it is easy to cite examples of humans using all parts of their body to manipulate at one time or another.

To wisely design and control such general robot mechanisms, we need to answer the questions suggested above. In what follows mostly we will be concerned with a few of the mechanical details of building and executing simple control over robots designed for whole arm manipulation. At the moment we make no distinction between whether the robot is controlled by an autonomous control and command program or whether a human is directly included in the control process via realtime interaction with a master device. Our use of such words as grasp, manipulate, transport and push makes no assumption about which part of the robot is actually being used and, in fact, we will endeavor not to assign any functional names, such as hand, arm or mobile base to the links of the robot.

MECHANISM ENUMERATION

To explore the set mechanisms which might be available to us for performing whole arm manipulation we first systematically enumerate the devices which may be constructed from N links. We assume that the mechanism is constructed of rigid links joined together by single degree of freedom joints. The process of constructing a mechanism consists of adding a link, one at a time to an existing assembly of links. Here, we define the act of "adding a link" to an existing mechanism as simply making a choice of *which* link to add it to. Starting with a single link with no joints on it, there is only one choice of where to add the second link; it must be attached to the first. There are then 2 choices of where to add the third link, 6 choices of where to add the forth link, etc. Since we use one joint to connect each new link to the existing mechanism, there can be no closed loops in the assembly; each such mechanism is representable by an un-rooted tree structure. Since there are no joints on the first link, an N link mechanism will have $N-1$ joints.

We can enumerate all N-link mechanisms by taking all the $(N-1)$-link mechanisms and *adding* a link, one at a time, to each of the $N-1$ links. If $f(N)$ is the number of N link mechanisms constructible, then $f(N) = (N-1)f(N-1)$. With $f(1) = 1$ and $f(2) = 1$ we have

$$f(N) = (N-1)!.$$

Some of these $(N-1)!$ mechanisms will be identical to others generated and we seek a method of pruning this list of mechanisms to those which are unique. Since we do not consider the type of joint, its location, range of motion, etc., nor do we consider link dimensions, we distinguish between only those mechanisms that are topologically unique. Our analysis is concerned only with what is connected to what; the only "distance" measure considered is the relative freedom of motion between a chosen pair of links.

It is important to realize that many of the $(N-1)!$ N-link mechanisms are identical to each other; a much smaller proportion of the mechanisms is unique. When no particular link is designated as the base link, many of these mechanisms can be found to be kinematically equivalent to each other in terms of the availability of relative freedom of motion between pairs of links. The implication of this is that this set of topologically different mechanisms is relatively small and by examining the properties of each we can describe a broad class of mechanisms.

We consider two mechanisms to be equivalent when they share the following characteristics: they have the same set of link *degrees*, and the same set of *maximum relative freedoms* available between end links.

In the following discussion we define the *degree* of a link to be the number of single-degree-of-freedom joints connected to it. (This is different from the *degree of freedom* between two bodies, which is the number of independent variables required to specify the relative positions of the two bodies.) When we join a new link to an existing link, the degree, d_i, of both the link being added and the link being added to increases by 1. Thus, the sum of the degrees of all links in an N-link mechanism will be $2(N-1)$, and $\sum_{i=1}^{N} d_i = 2N$. The values of d_i must be integers between 1 and $N-1$, inclusive. We represent the set of link degrees for a particular mechanism as $\mathcal{D} = \{d_i\}$. Thus, the minimum number of distinct N-link mechanisms must be at least equal to the number of countable ways of selecting N integers which add up to $2(N-1)$, subject to the above constraints. This assumes that any such generated set of integers represents a constructible, non-disjoint mechanism with a tree structure. In fact, such a set represents one or more different constructible mechanisms. Thus, although 2 N-link mechanisms with different sets of joint degrees will be distinct from each other, the converse is not true. To determine if 2 N-links mechanisms with the same set of link degrees are different we must look further at the mechanism properties.

The second descriptor we examine for each mechanism is the set of maximum relative freedoms between end links. An end link is simply a link with degree 1. The relative freedom between two end links is the number of intervening joints along the path joining the two. This path is unique because of the tree structure of our mechanisms. If there are m end links in a mechanism, there will be $\binom{m}{2}$ parings of end links and elements in the set of relative freedoms. We designate this set of relative freedoms as $\mathcal{R}$. The number and magnitudes of these relative freedoms is important because they limit degree-of-freedom available to a mechanism for grasping and manipulating objects. For example, consider a six link mechanism with $\mathcal{D} = \{322111\}$. There are two possible ways to assemble these links, one with $\mathcal{R} = \{442\}$ and one with $\mathcal{R} = \{433\}$. In the first case there are two choices for achieving a 4-freedom pairing of end links, while in the latter there is only one way to achieve such a paring.

With these two criteria in mind, the set of link degrees, $\mathcal{D}$, and the set of relative freedoms, $\mathcal{R}$ were effectively computed for all 5914 1- through 8-link mechanisms. Table 1 lists the results found for the 25 distinct 1- through 7-link mechanisms. Figures 1-5 illustrate examples of all the 1- through 7-link mechanisms identified. In generating all candidate mechanisms it becomes readily apparent that it is not necessary to consider each of the $(N-1)!$ mechanisms when searching the N-link mechanisms for distinct combinations. It is more direct to take the already pruned list of distinct $N-1$-link mechanisms and sequentially add one link to each position to generate the next set of candidate mechanisms. In fact, the most direct way to generate a minimal set of N-link candidate mechanisms is to generate all possible sets of $\mathcal{D}$ satisfying the constraint that $\sum_{i=1}^{N} d_i = 2N$, with integers d_i satisfying $0 < d_i < N$, and then select the mechanisms with unique values of $\mathcal{R}$. With this approach we are able find the 19 unique 8-link mechanisms from among the 5040 possible 8-link combinations. It is rather remarkable that among the 5914 ways of assembling up to eight links, only 44 are distinct. This set represents the distinct topologies available for manipulator construction. While variations in dimension, shape, strength etc. will give rise to an infinite variety of real mechanisms, each will fall under one of the basic configurations given.

GRASPING AND MANIPULATING

It is important to remember that for the mechanisms identified in the previous section, we consider each link surface available for manipulating and grasping and no particular link is considered to be a base link. This alone implies that there are $2^N - 1$ ways for a given mechanism to grasp or contact an object. When we consider that each contact may impose anywhere from 1 to 6 degrees of constraint on the object, the number of potential grasps becomes extremely large. Rather than explore this vast space of possibilities, we will look at a few general properties.

The set $\mathcal{R}$ of maximum obtainable relative freedoms for each mechanism found in the previous section gives an indication of the maximum task complexity each mechanism can address and the range of choices for performing that task. The 2-link 2-1 mechanism shown in Figure 1 could perform the 1 degree of freedom task of pinching a snap together (or crushing a can, or prying open a door) in only one way, while the 6-Link 6-6 in Figure 4 mechanism has 10 different end link pairings available to perform the task. Yet, neither of these mechanisms has sufficient freedom of motion available to permit them to slide and rotate an object on a plane. Throughout the list of mechanisms we see a tradeoff between the maximum number of freedoms available for manipulating and the number of end link parings available for grasping.

We will ultimately need to consider using non-end links for contacting objects as well. For example, the top diagram in Figure 6 depicts grasping by two adjacent links. The range of object sizes which can be securely held in this grasp will depend upon the link dimensions and friction properties. In order to achieve complete restraint [Mason and Salisbury] on an object (so that the squeeze force may be increased arbitrarily) the two forces imposed on the object must lie within the friction cones at each contact. If we assume that an adjacent pair of links of length L grasp a sphere of radius r with a coefficient of friction μ, then the range of spheres which can be grasped without slipping will have $-L\mu < r < L\mu$. If instead, we grasp the same sphere between two links separated by a third link of length $2h$, as shown in the bottom diagram of Figure 6, then the range of spheres which may be successfully grasped will have $h\sqrt{1+\mu^2} - L\mu < r < h\sqrt{1+\mu^2} + L\mu$. The addition of the middle link effectively shifts the range of graspable radii so that larger objects become graspable and smaller objects become un-graspable. It is also interesting to note that as the sphere radii approach their limits, the range of locations on the link where they may be securely grasped goes to zero. Conversely, with r near the middle of its range, the range of locations on the links where the stable grasping can be achieved goes to its maximum. One useful attribute which becomes apparent as we look at grasping ranges is the need for long slender link shapes. While increasing the range of suitable grasping sites, "high aspect ratio" links loose less of the working volume to their own occupancy of it.

The modes in which such mechanisms will be able to actually manipulate objects will range from the familiar secure grasp and precise positioning approach to a wide variety of controlled slip and pushing types of motion. We have demonstrated the ability to control the slip of an object within a hand [Brock] in order to accomplish desired object motions. This involves carefully controlling the contact forces so as to achieve the desired degree of constraint or freedom in the grasped object. For the general mechanisms we have described as well, this will require the ability to control contact forces anywhere along the link. This, in turn, requires that mechanisms expected to grasp and manipulate with all available surfaces be force (or torque) controllable at the joint level. In the next section we describe our design efforts aimed at developing a basic powered link that is force controllable for use in whole arm manipulation.

PROTOTYPE LINK

Figure 7 schematically depicts a prototype link and actuation mechanism that has been designed and built in our laboratory for use in a robot capable of whole arm manipulation. The design goals were to give the links as high an aspect ratio as possible while still retaining reasonable mechanical stiffness, good force control ability and simplicity. While direct drive approaches were considered, the current state of the art in such motors requires more volume and moving mass for the motor than we considered appropriate. An analysis by [Townsend87b] showed that very high transmission efficiencies were possible using cable transmissions. In particular it was found to be more efficient to transmit the power to the joint with high speed cables rather than slow moving, high tension cables. A compact 15:1 cable reduction mechanism was placed adjacent to the joint to be powered, enabling the use of reasonable size motors. Placing the reduction near the joint rather than near the motor has two advantages: for a given maximum allowable cable stress, the effective transmission stiffness is twice as large and the compressive stresses imposed by cable pretension are reduced by a factor of 15 over most of the previous link's length. To achieve good force controllability we chose to generate accurate torques at the motor and conduct them through an efficient transmission. Rather then encumbering the system with force sensors this was achieved by concentrating on the "open loop" performance of the torque motor. This was achieved with a high quality brushless motor from the Moog corporation. Precise control of winding currents, coupled with a position dependent feed forward correction current waveform, enabled us to reduce output torque ripple to less than 1% of the average torque. The overall mechanical system has it lowest resonant frequency at around 14 Hz. The end of the 36 inch moving link can exert 5 pounds force at steady state and peak forces of 20 pounds. The back drive inertia at

the link tip is on the order of 1 lb mass. By utilizing the cable reduction we were able to achieve a relatively compact, high performance mechanism without sacrificing stiffness and back drive ability. Later versions of the device will employ slightly compliant high friction coatings to permit safe contact with and secure grasping of objects in the environment. We are currently seeking coatings with Coulomb rather than stiction friction properties so as to minimize the force control problem of sliding links across objects [Townsend87a]. A three link version of this approach is currently under development at Woods Hole Oceanographic Institute for use in under water manipulation and our project group is designing a four link version for further laboratory experimentation.

CONCLUSIONS

Our work thus far has been aimed at categorizing a large class of mechanisms in terms of their whole arm manipulation potential. Our design effort has focused on developing a high performance link module with the performance characteristics necessary for controllable and predictable interaction with the environment in a broad range of modes. We expect that preliminary experiments with the multi-degree-of-freedom version of the system will focused on achieving the stable collision, pushing and probing behaviors necessary for taking advantage of all the mechanism's potential for whole arm manipulation.

ACKNOWLEDGMENT

The author would like to gratefully acknowledge the financial support of ONR contract N00014-86-K-0685 and DARPA contract number N00015-85-K-0124.

REFERENCES

Brock, D.L., "Enhancing the Dexterity of a Multi-Fingered Hand Through Controlled Slip Manipulation," Master's Thesis, Department of Mechanical Engineering, MIT June 1987.

Chiu, S.L., "Generating Compliant Motion of Objects with an Articulated Hand," Master's Thesis, Department of Mechanical Engineering, Massachusetts Institute of Technology, May 1985.

Hunt, K.L. "Kinematic Geometry of Mechanisms", Oxford Press, 1978.

Mason, M.T. and Salisbury, J.K., "Robot Hands and the Mechanics of Manipulation," MIT Press, Cambridge, MA, 1985.

Salisbury, J.K., "Interpretation of Contact Geometries from Force Measurements," Proc. 1st International Symposium on Robotics Research, Bretton Woods, NH, MIT

Press, Sept. 1984.

Townsend, W.T. and Salisbury, J.K., "The Effect of Coulomb Friction and Stiction of Force Control," Proc. 1987 IEEE International Conference on Robotics and Automation, Raleigh, North Carolina, April 1987a.

Townsend, W.T., "The Efficiency Limit of Belt and Cable Drives", submitted for publication in the ASME Journal of Mechanisms, Transmissions, and Automation in Design, June 1987b.

Mechanism Number	Link Degrees $\mathcal{D}$	Relative Freedoms $\mathcal{R}$
1-1	[0]	[ϕ]
2-1	[1]	[1]
3-1	[211]	[2]
4-1	[2211]	[3]
4-2	[3111]	[222]
5-1	[22211]	[4]
5-2	[32111]	[332]
5-3	[41111]	[222222]
6-1	[222211]	[5]
6-2	[322111]	[442]
6-3	[322111]	[433]
6-4	[331111]	[333322]
6-5	[421111]	[333222]
6-6	[511111]	[2222222222]
7-1	[2222211]	[6]
7-2	[3222111]	[552]
7-3	[3222111]	[543]
7-4	[3222111]	[444]
7-5	[3321111]	[443332]
7-6	[3321111]	[444422]
7-7	[4221111]	[444222]
7-8	[4221111]	[433332]
7-9	[4311111]	[3333332222]
7-10	[5211111]	[3333222222]
7-11	[6111111]	[222222222222222]

Table 1. Distinct 1- through 7-link mechanisms. The first digit of each mechanism number indicates number of links. $\mathcal{D}$ is the set of link degrees for each mechanism and $\mathcal{R}$ is the set of relative freedom available between each pair of end links.

188   Salisbury

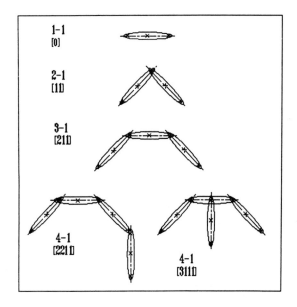

Figure 1. 1, 2, 3 and 4 link mechanisms.

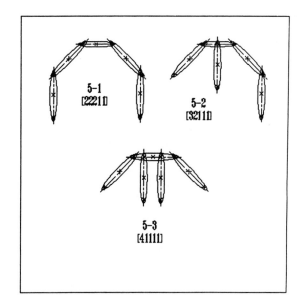

Figure 2. 5 link mechanisms.

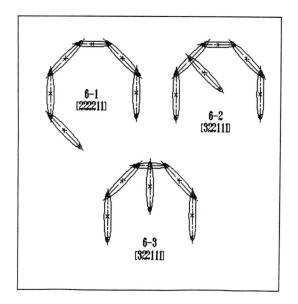

Figure 3. 6 link mechanisms, 1 through 3.

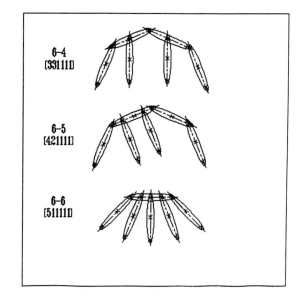

Figure 4. 6 link mechanisms, 4 through 6.

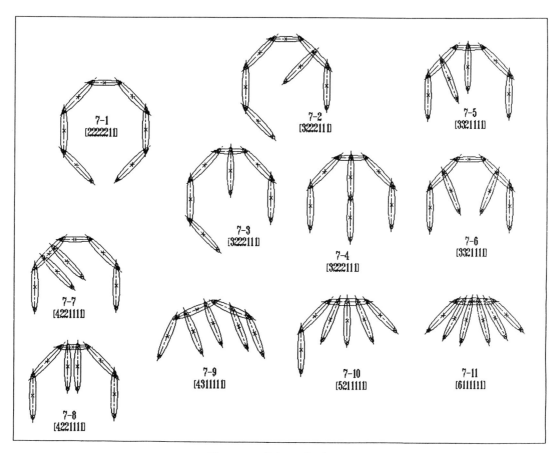

Figure 5. 7 link mechanisms.

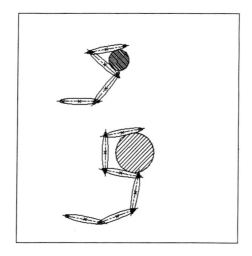

Figure 6. Two grasping configurations.

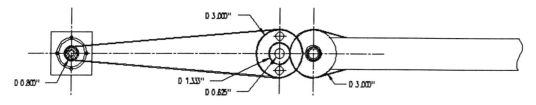

Figure 7. Single link prototype.

Automatic Kinematic Calibration Using a Motion Tracking System

John M. Hollerbach and David J. Bennett
MIT Artificial Intelligence Laboratory
545 Technology Square
Cambridge, MA 02139

The kinematic parameters of a direct drive arm have been automatically calibrated using a motion tracking system, which calculates the three-dimensional positions of active markers attached to the end link. The end link position and orientation are determined by a statistically robust procedure; in particular, it is shown that fitting a line to noisy measurements is an eigenvalue problem. An iterative least squares procedure solves for the Denavit-Hartenberg parameters. Experimental results are presented.

1 Introduction

This paper investigates the kinematic calibration of a robot manipulator using a motion tracking system. The emphasis in our research is on devising automatic calibration procedures that require minimal human involvement. We have already devised self-calibration procedures for the robot's inertial parameters (Atkeson, An, and Hollerbach, 1986), and the present effort extends self-calibration to kinematic parameters as well. Another eventual goal of our research is endpoint tracking to compensate for a manipulator on a mobile base. Hence the experimental apparatus should produce accurate estimates in real time of position and orientation. The motion tracking system was selected with these goals, and kinematic calibration falls out as a simple application of this system.

Much of the past experimental work in kinematic calibration has involved labor-intensive apparatuses and procedures. A number of investigators have employed specially machined calibration fixtures with precision points, which require that the operator manually guide an insertion tool (Foulloy and Kelley, 1984; Hayati and Roston, 1986; Veitschegger and Wu, 1987). Other investigators have employed manually operated theodolites (Chao and Yang, 1986; Chen and Chao, 1986; Judd and Knasinski, 1987; Whitney, Lozinski, and Rourke, 1986). Some computer-directed data acquisition systems have also been applied, including a stereo camera system mounted on the end effector (Puskorius and Feldkamp, 1987) and an ultrasonic range sensor (Stone, Sanderson, and Neuman, 1986; Stone and Sanderson, 1987). The stereo camera system, however, has a fairly low accuracy compared to other methods, and the cameras mounted on the end effector obviously interfere with robot operations. The ultrasonic range sensor is fairly accurate and automatic,

but the workspace area of operation is quite limited and not suitable for general endpoint tracking.

More sophisticated instrumentation for endpoint tracking has been developed but not yet applied to kinematic calibration. Laser tracking systems appear to be highly accurate (Gilby and Parker, 1982; Lau, Hocken, and Haynes, 1985), with resolutions of 1:100,000 reported. A different class of tracking systems is based on active infrared light-emitting diode markers (IREDs) and cameras with lateral-effect photodiode detectors. The Selspot I, a commercial tracking system produced by Selcom AB of Sweden, was extensively calibrated (Antonsson, 1982) and modified (Dainis and Juberts, 1985) to improve its resolution to 1:4,000. The Selspot II, an improved version, was employed as a robot teaching device, to register object features with a hand-held target and to teach a trajectory (El-Zorkany, Liscano, and Tondu, 1985). A custom-built laboratory apparatus was also used by Ishii et al. (1986) for robot teaching. Although this apparatus appears to be well done, its resolution and sampling rate are not on a par with the commercial systems.

In our experiments, we have also applied a tracking system based on IREDs and lateral-effect photodiode cameras. This Watsmart system is a commercial system produced by Northern Digital Inc. of Waterloo, Ontario, and is roughly comparable to the Selspot II. Individual markers can be sampled at 400 Hz. The resolution of this system is 1:4,000, and its accuracy is about 1 mm at a distance of 2 meters. This accuracy is not as good as that attainable with theodolites, but for our interests accuracy is sacrificed for convenience.

The contribution of this paper, in the face of a large literature in kinematic calibration, is that experimental results in arm calibration are reported for the first time with this kind of motion tracking system. We also feel that the calibration formulation is clearer and more efficient than many of the past efforts. Finally, we present a statistically robust procedure for estimating the endpoint position and orientation from noisy measurements.

2   Experimental Setup

The MIT Serial Link Direct Drive Arm (DDArm) is a three degree-of-freedom manipulator with orthogonal pairs of joint axes (Figure 1), and was designed by Haruhiko Asada (Asada and Youcef-Toumi, 1987). The robot base rotation is about the vertical axis, followed by a shoulder roll motion about a horizontal axis. This roll motion differs from the normal pitch motion of most rotary manipulators, and was designed to avoid gravity torques due to lifting the arm. The elbow rotary axis intersects and is perpendicular to this roll axis. While the geometry is a bit unusual, the three axes are able to position the forearm endpoint in a three-dimensional workspace.

Currently there are no wrist motions, so the kinematic calibration is limited to three sets of link parameters. We also consider only geometrical factors, since direct drive technology does away with gears and obviates some of the usual complexity in kinematic calibration. The non-geometric effects of backlash, gear eccentricity, and joint compliance are simply negligible. We have also not considered base deflection, which is likely to be smaller than the resolution of the measuring system due to the heavy platform construction for the DDArm.

To measure the position and orientation of the last link, a special calibration frame was attached to the third motor (Figure 1). This square frame was constructed from welded 1 in aluminum bars, with outer dimensions of 2 ft. Six infrared light-emitting diodes (IREDs) were attached at 1 ft intervals to the top half of the frame to avoid obscuration, and formed a rectangle of roughly 1 ft by 2 ft. Although three IREDs would have been sufficient to determine the position and orientation, the extra IREDs were included to improve the estimation statistics.

The three-dimensional positions of the IREDs are measured by the Watsmart System. This two-camera system triangulates the markers and calculates their three-dimensional positions after a calibration procedure. Each camera has a special lateral-effect photodiode detector, with a resolution of 1:4000. The cameras are calibrated at the factory with a four-foot plotter moving an IRED through space, to account for lens distortion and electronic effects, and the calibration tables are stored in microprocessors in the system console.

The three-dimensional coordinates of the IREDs are computed by direct linear transformations (DLTs) (Shapiro, 1978), which are set up by a 21 in calibration cube provided by the manufacturer. The 40 IREDs on this cube were presurveyed at the factory to locate their positions, and this information is stored in the system console microprocessors. The calibration procedure simply involves

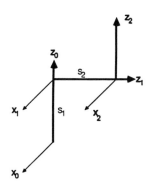

Figure 2: The Denavit-Hartenberg link parameters for the DDArm.

placing the cube at several positions in the workspace of interest, and invoking a program supplied by the manufacturer. This camera calibration procedure is convenient and fast: cameras can be placed at will and calibrated within a minute, greatly faciliting different experimental setups. The cameras in this experiment were placed at a distance of about 3 meters from the robot, and the positional accuracy of the calibration was about 1.7 mm (this information is computed by the calibration program based on the DLT fit).

For the kinematic calibration procedure, the calibration frame was placed in 125 different positions, obtained by stepping each joint through 5 increments within a 45° range. These positions and the camera placements were carefully chosen so that all IREDs remained in view. While an exact analysis has not been performed of the optimal placement of the frame for kinematic calibration, the positions were chosen based on a qualitative assessment of the identifiability of the kinematic parameters, and their adequacy was verified by the results. Bad data points were identified by calculating the perimeter of the rectangle formed by the IREDs, and were eliminated if above a certain threshold.

3   Identification Procedure

3.1   Coordinate Representation

The Denavit-Hartenberg (1955) link parameters, partially depicted in Figure 2 for the DDArm, forms the basis for the calibration procedure. The coordinate origin and axes for link i are found as follows:

- The z_i rotation axis is located at the distal end of link i, and connects links i and $i + 1$.

- The x_i axis is defined by the common normal between the rotation axes z_{i-1} and z_i.

- The coordinate origin is located at the intersection of the x_i and z_i axes, and is referred to as joint i.

The following four parameters define the location of the link i coordinate system relative to the link $i-1$ coordinate system:

- θ_i is the joint i angle about the z_{i-1} axis between the x_{i-1} and x_i axes.

- a_i is the distance between z_{i-1} and z_i measured along x_i.

- s_i is the distance between x_{i-1} and x_i measured along z_{i-1}.

- α_i is the angle between z_{i-1} and z_i measured in a righthand sense about x_i.

These link parameters also serve to identify the location of the robot base with respect to the camera coorinate system and of the calibration tool with respect to the robot's last link.

In case of near-parallel neighboring joint axes, the modification suggested in (Hayati, 1983; Hayati and Mirmirani, 1985) could be employed, where an additional skew angle β is substituted for the joint offset s. Six-parameter transformations have been proposed as another way of avoiding the parallel axis problem with the Denavit-Hartenberg parameters (Chao and Yang, 1986; Chen and Chao, 1986; Stone and Sanderson, 1987; Stone, Sanderson and Neuman, 1986; Whitney, Lozinski, and Rourke, 1986), but their added complexity and redundancy do not seem warranted given the Hayati modification. In any event, it was not necessary in our application to use this modification. Our direct drive arm has orthogonal joint axes, and the coordinate systems of the camera relative to the robot and of the calibration tool relative to the last link did not have nearly parallel z axes.

The kinematic calibration procedure must not only identify the relative transformations between the robot's links, but also the transformation between the camera coordinates and the robot base coordinates and between the calibration frame coordinates and the last link coordinates. The camera coordinates are defined by the camera calibration cube, and all IRED measurements are made with respect to these coordinates. The camera calibration cube was placed in the middle of the calibration frame movement. No model of the calibration frame was employed, and the relative location of the IREDs was presumed unknown.

In order to apply the Denavit-Hartenberg parameters to the camera origin without modifying the robot parameters, the camera origin is labeled as the -1 coordinates (Figure 3A). The calibration frame attached to the last link is defined by the x_4 and z_4 axes (Figure 3B), oriented respectively parallel to the long axis of the IRED rectangle and normal to the rectangle plane. An intermediate coordinate system defined by x_3 and z_3 is required to provide enough parameters for a six-dimensional transformation between the last link and calibration frame.

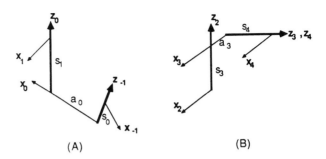

Figure 3: (A) Coordinate system of the camera relative to the robot base. (B) Coordinate system of the calibration frame relative to the last link.

3.2 Differential Relations

The direct kinematic relation between the Denavit-Hartenberg parameters and the endpoint position and orientation x is given by:

$$\mathbf{x} = \mathbf{f}(\underline{\theta}, \underline{\alpha}, \mathbf{a}, \mathbf{s}) = \mathbf{f}(\underline{\phi}) \qquad (1)$$

where $\underline{\theta}$, $\underline{\alpha}$, $\mathbf{a}$, and $\mathbf{s}$ are vectors of the Denavit-Hartenberg parameters representing all the coordinate systems, and $\underline{\phi} = (\underline{\theta}, \underline{\alpha}, \mathbf{a}, \mathbf{s})$ combines all kinematic parameters into one vector.

The calibration is based on iteration of the linearized direct kinematic equation (1), and has been employed by a number of authors (e.g., Puskorius and Feldkamp, 1987; Sugimoto and Okada, 1985; Veitschegger and Wu, 1987). The first variation $\Delta \mathbf{x}$ of the endpoint location corresponding to variations in the link parameters $\Delta \underline{\phi} = (\Delta \underline{\theta}, \Delta \underline{\alpha}, \Delta \mathbf{a}, \Delta \mathbf{s})$ is given by:

$$\Delta \mathbf{x} = \frac{\partial \mathbf{f}}{\partial \underline{\theta}} \Delta \underline{\theta} + \frac{\partial \mathbf{f}}{\partial \underline{\alpha}} \Delta \underline{\alpha} + \frac{\partial \mathbf{f}}{\partial \mathbf{a}} \Delta \mathbf{a} + \frac{\partial \mathbf{f}}{\partial \mathbf{s}} \Delta \mathbf{s} \qquad (2)$$

The differential relation may be expressed more compactly as:

$$\Delta \mathbf{x} = \begin{bmatrix} \dfrac{\partial \mathbf{f}}{\partial \underline{\theta}} & \dfrac{\partial \mathbf{f}}{\partial \underline{\alpha}} & \dfrac{\partial \mathbf{f}}{\partial \mathbf{a}} & \dfrac{\partial \mathbf{f}}{\partial \mathbf{s}} \end{bmatrix} \begin{bmatrix} \Delta \underline{\theta} \\ \Delta \underline{\alpha} \\ \Delta \mathbf{a} \\ \Delta \mathbf{s} \end{bmatrix} \qquad (3)$$

$$= \mathbf{C} \Delta \underline{\phi} \qquad (4)$$

Each of the matrices $\mathbf{J}_\theta = \partial \mathbf{f}/\partial \underline{\theta}$, $\mathbf{J}_\alpha = \partial \mathbf{f}/\partial \underline{\alpha}$, $\mathbf{J}_a = \partial \mathbf{f}/\partial \mathbf{a}$, and $\mathbf{J}_s = \partial \mathbf{f}/\partial \mathbf{s}$ represent Jacobians with respect to the particular kinematic parameters. Taking the lead from Whitney (1972), these matrices can be evaluated by simple vector relationships. This contrasts to the normal practice in the kinematic calibration literature where differential homogeneous transformations are used, yielding in our opinion a more cumbersome and less efficient development.

The first Jacobian $\mathbf{J}_\theta$ is just the normal manipulator Jacobian. If the endpoint variation $\Delta \mathbf{x} = (\Delta \mathbf{x}_p, \Delta \mathbf{x}_o)$ is taken to be composed of a positional variation $\Delta \mathbf{x}_p$

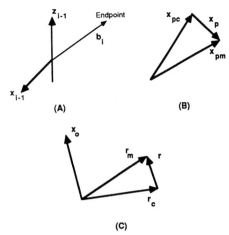

Figure 4: (A) Derivation of screw coordinates. (B) Derivation of positional error. (C) Derivation of orientational error.

followed by an orientational variation $\Delta\mathbf{x}_o$, then the Jacobian's ith column represents the screw coordinates for the ith axis of rotation $\mathbf{z}_{i-1}$ (Kumar and Waldron, 1981; Sugimoto and Okada, 1985):

$$\text{col}_i\,\mathbf{J}_\theta = \begin{bmatrix} \mathbf{b}_i \times \mathbf{z}_{i-1} \\ \mathbf{z}_{i-1} \end{bmatrix} \qquad (5)$$

where $\mathbf{b}_i$ connects joint i to a reference point on the end effector (Figure 4A). The other Jacobians can be found similarly:

$$\text{col}_i\,\mathbf{J}_\alpha = \begin{bmatrix} \mathbf{b}_i \times \mathbf{x}_i \\ \mathbf{x}_i \end{bmatrix}, \quad \text{col}_i\,\mathbf{J}_a = \begin{bmatrix} \mathbf{x}_i \\ \mathbf{0} \end{bmatrix}, \quad \text{col}_i\,\mathbf{J}_s = \begin{bmatrix} \mathbf{z}_{i-1} \\ \mathbf{0} \end{bmatrix}$$
$$(6)$$

3.3   The Endpoint Variation

For purposes of kinematic calibration, the endpoint variation $\Delta\mathbf{x}$ is the difference between the measured endpoint location $\mathbf{x}_m$ and the computed endpoint location $\mathbf{x}_c$. This variation can be expressed most conveniently by separating the positional variation from the orientational variation. The positional variation is simply (Figure 4B):

$$\Delta\mathbf{x}_p = \mathbf{x}_{pm} - \mathbf{x}_{pc} \qquad (7)$$

where $\mathbf{x}_{pm}$ is the measured position of a reference point on the end effector and $\mathbf{x}_{pc}$ is the reference point position computed from the link parameters.

The orientational variation $\Delta\mathbf{x}_o$ may be simply found by realizing that it acts like an angular velocity vector (Kumar and Waldron, 1981). Let $\mathbf{r}^*$ be any vector fixed in the end effector coordinate system, and let $\mathbf{A}_m$ and $\mathbf{A}_c$ represent the measured and computed rotation matrices from the end effector coordinate system to the global coordinate system. Then (Figure 4C)

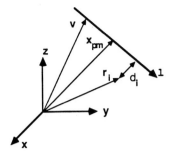

Figure 5: Least squares line fit to noisy points.

$$\Delta\mathbf{x}_o \times \mathbf{A}_c\mathbf{r}^* = \mathbf{A}_m\mathbf{r}^* - \mathbf{A}_c\mathbf{r}^* \qquad (8)$$

This equation may be solved by using the matrix form of the cross product:

$$[\Delta\mathbf{x}_o\times] = (\mathbf{A}_m - \mathbf{A}_c)\mathbf{A}_c^T \qquad (9)$$

where $\Delta\mathbf{x}_o = (\partial x, \partial y, \partial z)$ and

$$[\Delta\mathbf{x}_o\times] = \begin{bmatrix} 0 & -\partial z & \partial y \\ \partial z & 0 & -\partial x \\ -\partial y & \partial x & 0 \end{bmatrix} \qquad (10)$$

3.4   Estimating the Endpoint Location

A robust estimate of the position and orientation of the end effector can be found from a least squares fit of two straight lines to the set of IREDs. One straight line should lie parallel to the plane formed by the IREDs, while the other straight line should lie normal to this plane. Alternatively, a plane could be fit to the IREDs, but an advantage of the straight line fitting is that the IREDs do not necessarily need to lie in a plane.

Let the equation for a straight line be represented as:

$$\mathbf{v} = \mathbf{l} + \mathbf{x}_{pm} = k\hat{\mathbf{l}} + \mathbf{x}_{pm} \qquad (11)$$

where $\mathbf{v}$ is any point on the line, $\hat{\mathbf{l}}$ is a unit vector pointing in the direction of the line, k is a scalar, $\mathbf{l} = k\hat{\mathbf{l}}$ is any vector pointing along the line, and $\mathbf{x}_{pm}$ is a reference point on the straight line.

For a given IRED position $\mathbf{r}_i$, all three measured coordinates are presumed to have noise. Therefore a least squares fit should be with respect to the normal distance between an IRED position $\mathbf{r}_i$ and the straight line:

$$d_i = \frac{|(\mathbf{r}_i - \mathbf{x}_{pm}) \times \mathbf{l}|}{|\mathbf{l}|} \qquad (12)$$

The sum of squared errors λ is then:

$$\lambda = \sum_{i=1}^{6} d_i^2 = \sum_{i=1}^{6} \frac{((\mathbf{r}_i - \mathbf{x}_{pm}) \times \mathbf{l})^2}{\mathbf{l}^2} \qquad (13)$$

First we estimate the position $\mathbf{x}_{pm}$ of a reference point on the end effector from noisy measurements. Using the relation $a \cdot (b \times c) = (a \times b) \cdot c$, (13) may be rewritten as:

$$\lambda = \sum_{i=1}^{6} (\mathbf{r}_i - \mathbf{x}_{pm})^2 - \frac{1}{l^2} \sum_{i=1}^{6} ((\mathbf{r}_i - \mathbf{x}_{pm}) \cdot \mathbf{l})^2 \quad (14)$$

Taking the partial derivative with respect to $\mathbf{x}_{pm}$ and setting to zero yields

$$\frac{\partial \lambda}{\partial \mathbf{x}_{pm}} = 0 = -2 \sum_{i=1}^{6} (\mathbf{r}_i - \mathbf{x}_{pm}) + \frac{2}{l^2} \sum_{i=1}^{6} ((\mathbf{r}_i - \mathbf{x}_{pm}) \cdot \mathbf{l}) \mathbf{l} \quad (15)$$

Simplifying,

$$0 = \left(\frac{\mathbf{l}\mathbf{l}^T}{l^2} - \mathbf{I} \right) \sum_{i=1}^{6} (\mathbf{r}_i - \mathbf{x}_c) \quad (16)$$

The general solution to this equation is obtained by equating the second term on the right to zero:

$$\mathbf{x}_{pm} = 1/6 \sum_{i=1}^{6} \mathbf{r}_i \quad (17)$$

Thus the most robust estimate of a reference position $\mathbf{x}_{pm}$ is the centroid of the six IREDs forming a rectangle.

Next we estimate the direction $\mathbf{l}$ of the straight line. This estimation problem differs from ordinary least squares estimation in that it is not a linear estimation problem, because $\mathbf{l}$ appears both in the numerator and denominator. In ordinary least squares, it is presumed that only one of the coordinates has noise, and the projection of error is along that coordinate only. In our case all the coordinates must be presumed to be noisy, and the projection of error along all the coordinates must be taken, i.e., the normal distance to the plane.

Given the reference point $\mathbf{x}_{pm}$ on that line, substitute $\mathbf{x}_i = (x_i, y_i, z_i) = \mathbf{r}_i - \mathbf{x}_{pm}$ into (14):

$$\lambda = \sum_{i=1}^{6} \mathbf{x}_i^2 - \frac{1}{l^2} \sum_{i=1}^{6} (\mathbf{x}_i \cdot \mathbf{l})^2 \quad (18)$$

Taking the partial derivative of λ with respect to $\mathbf{l}$ and equating to zero,

$$\frac{\partial \lambda}{\partial \mathbf{l}} = 0 = -\frac{1}{l^4} \left(2l^2 \sum_{i=1}^{6} (\mathbf{x}_i \cdot \mathbf{l}) \mathbf{x}_i - 2\mathbf{l} \sum_{i=1}^{6} (\mathbf{x}_i \cdot \mathbf{l})^2 \right) \quad (19)$$

Sustituting (18) and rearranging,

$$\left((\sum_{i=1}^{6} \mathbf{x}_i^2) \mathbf{I} + \sum_{i=1}^{6} \mathbf{x}_i \mathbf{x}_i^T - \lambda \mathbf{I} \right) \mathbf{l} = 0 \quad (20)$$

where $\mathbf{I}$ is the identity matrix. Let $\mathbf{H} = (\sum_{i=1}^{6} \mathbf{x}_i^2) \mathbf{I} - \sum_{i=1}^{6} \mathbf{x}_i \mathbf{x}_i^T$. Then

$$(\mathbf{H} - \lambda \mathbf{I}) \mathbf{l} = 0 \quad (21)$$

$\mathbf{H}$ represents an ellipsoid of inertia with elements:

$$\mathbf{H} = \begin{bmatrix} H_{xx} & H_{xy} & H_{xz} \\ H_{xy} & H_{yy} & H_{yz} \\ H_{xz} & H_{yz} & H_{zz} \end{bmatrix} \quad (22)$$

Representative elements of this matrix are $H_{xx} = \sum_{i=1}^{6} (y_i^2 + z_i^2)$, $H_{xy} = -\sum_{i=1}^{6} x_i y_i$, and so on.

Thus the result is an eigenvalue problem (21). The cubic eigenvalue equation can be solved analytically. The eigenvectors corresponding to the eigenvalues λ_i represent the principal axes of the ellipsoid of inertia. The smallest eigenvalue λ_1 is the solution for the smallest distance, and so corresponds to an eigenvector $\mathbf{x}_4$ lying in the plane, directed along the long axis of the IRED rectangle. The largest eigenvalue λ_3 corresponds to the normal $\mathbf{z}_4$ to the plane. The vectors $\mathbf{x}_4$ and $\mathbf{z}_4$ are taken to define the coordinate system of the calibration tool, and can be used to derive the rotation matrix $\mathbf{A}_m$ straightforwardly. If the ellipsoid of inertia were symmetric, there would be ambiguity in the eigenvectors, but this is not the case for our IRED rectangular formation.

3.5   Iterative Estimation Procedure

There are 18 parameters in the vector ϕ that need to be identified for our experimental setup. A number of manipulator poses and measurements are required to determine these parameters robustly. Combine all the error vectors $\Delta \mathbf{x}_i$ and Jacobians into a single equation:

$$\begin{bmatrix} \Delta \mathbf{x}_1 \\ \Delta \mathbf{x}_2 \\ \vdots \\ \Delta \mathbf{x}_m \end{bmatrix} = \begin{bmatrix} \mathbf{C}_1 \\ \mathbf{C}_2 \\ \vdots \\ \mathbf{C}_m \end{bmatrix} \Delta \underline{\phi} \quad (23)$$

or more compactly,

$$\mathbf{b} = \mathbf{D} \Delta \underline{\phi} \quad (24)$$

The least squares solution for $\Delta \underline{\phi}$ is the pseudoinverse of $\mathbf{D}$:

$$\Delta \underline{\phi} = (\mathbf{D}^T \mathbf{D})^{-1} \mathbf{D}^T \mathbf{b} \quad (25)$$

The updated parameter values $\underline{\phi}'$ are then obtained by:

$$\underline{\phi}' = \underline{\phi} + \Delta \phi \quad (26)$$

Since this is a nonlinear estimation problem, this procedure is iterated until the variations $\Delta \underline{\phi}$ approach zero and the parameters $\underline{\phi}$ have converged to some stable values. At each iteration, the Jacobians are evaluated with the current parameters.

4   Results

Initial values for the link Denavit-Hartenberg parameters are listed in Table 1, as joint numbers 1-2, and were obtained from the nominal design parameters. To begin the iterations, initial values for the camera and calibration tool parameters also had to be chosen, and this was done with manual measurements. The camera coordinates are listed as joint 0 and the calibration tool coordinates as joint 4. Since nothing is attached after joint 4, the a_4 and α_4 parameters are not defined.

The results of the calibration are presented in Table 2. The parameters that are intrinsic to the DDArm, rather than to the placement of the camera coordinate system or the calibration frame coordinate system, are all of the index 2 parameters as well as a_1 and α_1. The calibration indicates that neighboring joint axes are not exactly perpendicular ($\alpha_1 = -1.587$ radians and $\alpha_2 = 1.613$ radians). The joint axes also do not intersect ($a_1 = -0.005$ m and $a_2 = 0.011$ m).

The index 0 camera parameters are not particularly meaningful as a point of reference. Since the camera origin defines the $\mathbf{x}_0$ axis, and hence the origin of the base coordinates through the intersection with the $\mathbf{z}_0$ axis, the parameters s_1 and $\Delta\theta_1$ are determined by the camera calibration cube placement.

The calibration frame parameters indicate that the calibration frame was mounted more orthogonally ($\alpha_3 = -1.552$ radians) and closer to intersecting ($a_3 = 0.004$ m) than the manipulator joints. Again, the index 3 and 4 parameters are defined by the placement of the calibration frame, and are not meaningful as a point of comparison.

These parameters converged after 3-6 iterations. A number of different initial conditions were tried, but the iterations always ended up with this result, indicating a global minimum. The iterative least squares method was also compared against the Levenberg-Marquardt algorithm, employed by a number of investigators (Mooring and Tang, 1984). We found that the iterative least squares method generally converged much faster than the Levenberg-Marquardt algorithm. The Levenberg-Marquardt algorithm is more conservative, partially moving along the gradient in small steps. On the other hand, if initial parameters happened to be chosen so that a singularity occurred, then the iterative least squares method could not be used. In this case, the diagonal term in the Levenberg-Marquardt algorithm was essential for convergence. In fact, the Levenberg-Marquardt algorithm is useful to determine initial parameter values for which a good estimate is not available, such as for some of the joint angle offsets. A bad initial estimate quite frequently led to a singularity in the iterative least squares method. After a good initial estimate is available, then it is much better to use the iterative least squares method to make small corrections or to track the robot.

In comparing the calibrated parameters to the initial parameters, one statistical measure is the root mean square (RMS) position and orientation error, defined as:

$$\text{RMS position error} = \sqrt{1/N \sum (\Delta\mathbf{x}_p)^2}$$

$$\text{RMS orientation error} = \sqrt{1/N \sum (\Delta\mathbf{x}_o)^2}$$

Joint	s (m)	a (m)	α (rad)	$\Delta\theta$ (rad)
0	*	*	*	*
1	*	0.0	-1.571	*
2	-.462	0.0	1.571	3.809
3	*	*	*	*
4	*	N/A	N/A	*

Table 1: Initial parameters. The * indicates unknown initial value of a parameter; N/A indicates undefined parameters.

Joint	s (m)	a (m)	α (rad)	$\Delta\theta$ (rad)
0	0.861	-0.099	3.440	0.965
1	0.228	-0.005	-1.587	5.623
2	-0.461	0.011	1.613	3.864
3	-0.542	0.004	-1.552	1.050
4	0.028	N/A	N/A	-0.485

Table 2: Calibrated parameters.

where the summation is over the N arm positions the calibration frame was placed in. The position $\Delta\mathbf{x}_p$ and orientation $\Delta\mathbf{x}_o$ error vectors were defined in (7) and (10). The RMS position error is 10 mm for the initial parameters and 7 mm for the calibrated parameters. The RMS orientation error is 0.027 rad for the inital parameters and 0.021 rad for the calibrated parameters.

Another measure is the percent variance accounted for (VAF), essentially a scaled version of the mean squared error:

$$\text{VAF in position} = 100\% \times \left(1 - \frac{\sum (\Delta\mathbf{x}_p)^2}{\sum (\mathbf{x}_{pm} - \bar{\mathbf{x}}_{pm})^2} \right)$$

$$\text{VAF in orientation} = 100\% \times \left(1 - \frac{\sum (\Delta\mathbf{x}_o)^2}{\sum (\mathbf{x}_{om} - \bar{\mathbf{x}}_{om})^2} \right)$$

For the VAF in position, the normalizing factor is the variance of the measured distance $\mathbf{x}_{pm}$ to the calibration frame centroid, relative to the mean $\bar{\mathbf{x}}_{pm}$ of all centroid positions. For the VAF in orientation, the normalizing factor is defined in terms of the variance of a vector representation of measured orientation of the calibration frame $\mathbf{x}_{om}$ relative to its mean over all orientations $\bar{\mathbf{x}}_{om}$. When this is done, the VAF is 99.88% for position and 99.92% for orientation for the initial parameters. For the calibrated parameters, the VAF is 99.99% for position and orientation.

An independent test for the two sets of parameters is an external measurement of the deviation of a reference point on the end link from a vertical straight line. A height gauge was used, as suggested in (Whitney, Lozinski, and Rourke, 1986). The reference point was placed manually at several positions along the height gauge, and the corresponding joint angles were read. The endpoint positions were then computed from the joint angles for both the initial parameters and the calibrated parameters, and a straight line was fitted to each set of end-points. The RMS error of the straight-line fit for the initial parameters was the same, namely 1.2 mm. This number has limited precision, due to problems in locating a reference point on the frame and in aligning this reference point with respect to the height gauge. With this caveat, the height gauge test indicates the two parameter sets are about equally good.

5 Discussion

In this paper we have presented an efficient procedure for kinematic calibration, based on the Denavit-Hartenberg link parameters. The procedure involves iteration of the linearized kinematic equations. One important aspect of this linearization is the use of efficient vector methods to evaluate the various Jacobians and to calculate orientation error. Another contribution is a statistically robust method for determining endpoint position and orientation. The nonlinear least squares fit for position and orientation of the calibration frame was shown to reduce to an eigenvalue problem.

Experimental results in kinematic calibration were obtained for the MIT Serial Link Direct Drive Arm using the Watsmart system, an opto-electronic motion tracking system. The height gauge test did not differentiate between the two parameter sets, since equally good results were obtained. In terms of the RMS error and VAF statistical measures, the calibrated parameters fit the Watsmart data much better than did the initial parameters.

The most probable reason for the discrepancy between the height gauge test and the other two statistical tests is errors in the Watsmart data. The current accuracy of the system is simply not good enough for kinematic calibration yet. We actually feel that the nominal values of the parameters are more correct, and provide a test for the Watsmart system rather than vice versa.

Aside from the current accuracy limitations of the Watsmart system, we feel that the approach that we have offered holds promise for the future. As mentioned earlier, the newest version of the Watsmart system has a resolution of 1:20,000 as compared to the current 1:4,000. This compares more favorably with the experimental laser ranging systems (Gilby, 1982; Lau, Hocken and Haynes, 1985), which however have not yet been experimentally applied to kinematic calibration. The advantage of our apparatus is convenience, potential accuracy, and automaticity.

We found that the iterative least squares method was sensitive to the initial parameter estimates. A bad estimate was quite likely to lead to a singularity, causing the failure of this method. Although the Levenberg-Marquardt algorithm is much slower, it nevertheless is robust with respect to singularities. Thus a good initial parameter estimate can be found using the Levenberg-Marquardt algorithm, after which the iterative least squares method can be used for updating.

Versions of the Watsmart system are available that calculate 3-dimensional positions of the markers in real time or that calculate the position and orientation of two bodies at 100 Hz. The ability to track the endpoint location in real time has other uses than just kinematic calibration. We intend to begin investigation of the control of arms on mobile platforms, for which this real-time facility is essential. Endpoint tracking is also useful for various forms of robot teaching (Ishii et al., 1987) and even teleoperator control.

Acknowledgements

This paper describes research done at the Artificial Intelligence Laboratory of the Massachusetts Institute of Technology. Support for the laboratory's artificial intelligence research is provided in part by the University Research Initiatives under Office of Naval Research contract N00014-86-K-0685 and in part by the Advanced Research Projects Agency of the Department of Defense under Office of Naval Research contract N00014-85-K-0124. Personal support for JMH was also provided by an NSF Presidential Young Investigator Award, and for DJB by a fellowship from the Natural Sciences and Engineering Research Council of Canada.

References

Antonsson, E. K. 1982. A three-dimensional kinematic acquisition and intersegmental dynamic analysis system for human motion. Ph. D. thesis, Massachusetts Institute of Technology, Mechanical Engineering.

Asada, H., and Youcef-Toumi, K. 1987. *Direct Drive Robots: Theory and Practice.* Cambridge, MA: MIT Press.

Atkeson, C.G., An, C.H., and Hollerbach, J.M. 1986. Estimation of inertial parameters of manipulator links and loads. *Int. J. Robotics Research.* 5(3): 101-119.

Chao, L.M., and Yang, J.C.S. 1986 (April 20-24). Development and implementation of a kinematic parameter identification technique to improve the positioning accuracy of robots. *Robots 10 Conference Proceedings.* Chicago: pp. 11-69 – 11-81.

Chen, J., and Chao, L.M. 1986 (April 7-10). Positioning error analysis for robot manipulators with all rotary joints. *Proc. IEEE Int. Conf. Robotics and Automation.* San Francisco: pp. 1011-1016.

Dainis, A., and Juberts, M. 1985 (March 25-28). Accurate remote measurement of robot trajectory motion. *IEEE Int. Conf. Robotics and Automation.* St. Louis: pp. 92-99.

Denavit, J., and Hartenberg, R.S. 1955. A kinematic notation for lower pair mechanisms based on matrices. *J. Applied Mechanics.* 22: 215-221.

El-Zorkany, H.I., Liscano, R., and Tondu, B. 1985 (Sept. 15-20). A sensor-based approach for robot programming. *Int. Conf. Intelligent Robots and Computer Vision, SPIE Proc. Vol. 579.* Cambridge, Mass.: pp. 289-297.

Foulloy, L.P., and Kelley, R.B. 1984 (March 13-15). Improving the precision of a robot. *Proc. IEEE Int. Conf. Robotics.* Atlanta: pp. 62-67.

Gilby, J.H., and Parker, G.A. 1982. Laser tracking system to measure robot arm performance. *Sensor Review.* 2(4): 180-184.

Hayati, S.A. 1983 (Dec. 14-16). Robot arm geometric link parameter estimation. *Proc. 22nd IEEE Conf. Decision and Control.* San Antonio: pp. 1477-1483.

Hayati, S.A., and Mirmirani, M. 1985. Improving the absolute positioning accuracy of robot manipulators. *J. Robotic Systems.* 2: 397-413.

Hayati, S.A., and Roston, G.P. 1986. Inverse kinematic solution for near-simple robots and its application to robot calibration. *Recent Trends in Robotics: Modeling, Control, and Education.*, ed. M. Jamshidi, J.Y.S. Luh, and M. Shahinpoor. Elsevier Science Publ. Co., pp. 41-50.

Ishii, M., Sakane, S., Mikami, Y., and Kakikura, M. 1987. A 3-D sensor system for teaching robot paths and environments. *Int. J. Robotics Research.* 6(2): 45-59.

Judd, R.P., and Knasinski, A.B. 1987 (March 31-April 3). A technique to calibrate industrial robots with experimental verification. *Proc. IEEE Int. Conf. Robotics and Automation.* Raleigh, NC: pp. 351-357.

Kumar, A., and Waldron, K.J. 1981. Numerical plotting of surfaces of positioning accuracy of manipulators. *Mechanism and Machine Theory.* 16: 361-368.

Lau, K., Hocken, R., and Haynes, L. 1985. Robot performance measurements using automatic laser tracking techniques. *Robotics & Computer-Integrated Manufacturing.* 2: 227-236.

Mooring, B.W., and Tang, G.R. 1984. An improved method for identifying the kinematic parameters in a six-axis robot. *ASME Proc. Int. Computers in Engineering Conf..* Las Vegas: pp. 79-84.

Puskorius, G.V., and Feldkamp, L.A. 1987 (March 31-April 3). Global calibration of a robot/vision system. *Proc. IEEE Int. Conf. Robotics and Automation.* Raleigh, NC: pp. 190-195.

Shapiro, R. 1978. Direct linear transformation method for three-dimensional cinematography. *Research Quarterly.* 49: 197-205.

Stone, H.W., and Sanderson, A.C. 1987 (March 31-April 3). A prototype arm signature identification system. *Proc. IEEE Int. Conf. Robotics and Automation.* Raleigh, NC: pp. 175-182.

Stone, H.W., Sanderson, A.C., and Neuman, C.P. 1986 (April 7-10). Arm signature identification. *Proc. IEEE Int. Conf. Robotics and Automation.* San Francisco: pp. 41-48.

Sugimoto, K., and Okada, T. 1985. Compensation of positioning errors caused by geometric deviations in robot system. *Robotics Research: The Second International Symposium.*, ed. H. Hanafusa and H. Inoue. Cambridge, Mass.: MIT Press, pp. 231-236.

Veitschegger, W.K., and Wu, C.-H. 1987 (March 31-April 3). A method for calibrating and compensating robot kinematic errors. *Proc. IEEE Int. Conf. Robotics and Automation.* Raleigh, NC: pp. 39-44.

Whitney, D.E. 1972. The mathematics of coordinated control of prosthetic arms and manipulators. *ASME J. Dynamic Systems, Meas., Control.*: 303-309.

Whitney, D.E., Lozinski, C.A., and Rourke, J.M. 1986. Industrial robot forward calibration method and results. *J. Dynamic Systems, Meas., Control.* 108: 1-8.

Figure 1: The MIT Serial Link Direct Drive Arm, with calibration frame.

Mark Cutkosky, Prasad Akella, Robert Howe, Imin Kao

Design Division
Department of Mechanical Engineering
Stanford University
Stanford, California 94305

The ability to manipulate a part in a dextrous hand depends strongly on the contact conditions between the fingers and the object. This is especially evident in fine manipulation (as in assembling components) where small motions and low velocities lead to dynamic equations that are dominated by compliance and contact conditions. In this paper, we examine the role of contact phenomena in dextrous manipulation, focusing on the relationships among contact phenomena, grasp compliance and the initiation of sliding motion. We then explore more detailed models of contact phenomena and examine the roles of tactile sensing and fingertip materials in describing and defining the contact properties.

1 Introduction

Contact phenomena are central to the study of grasping and manipulation. In dynamic and kinematic analyses they account for much of the difficulty in propagating forces and motions between the fingers and the grasped object. Ultimately, contact properties define the mobility, stability and dexterity of the grasp. For example, a grasp that is unstable for hard, pointed fingertips may be stable and controllable for soft fingertips [Cutkosky 85]. Similarly, the details of rolling and sliding at the contact points can account for the result of a manipulation exercise [Fearing 86].

In Section 2 we compute the stiffness of a grasp in terms of servo gains at the joints and structural compliances in the fingers. The analysis expands upon earlier grasp stiffness investigations by Salisbury [1985], Cutkosky [1985], and Nguyen [1987]. The contact conditions are central to this analysis, "filtering" the forces and motions transmitted through them. In addition, rolling and sliding at the contacts produce changes in the grasp geometry that affect the overall grasp stiffness and stability.

We demonstrate the stiffness computation with a simple example that approximates a human thumb and forefinger inserting a rivet into a chamfered hole. The grasp contains both redundancy due to extra finger joints in one direction, and singularity due to a lack of finger joints in other directions. However, because of structural compliance, the stiffness computation is straightforward. The resulting stiffness matrix is a useful characterization of the grasp, revealing the constrained directions, the grasp stability and whether the grasp can resist forces and moments in arbitrary directions (i.e. whether it is a force-closure grasp).

The stiffness of a grasp is also useful in determining when fingers will slip as the grasped object is acted upon by external forces and in predicting the initial direction of sliding. In Section 3 we explore the onset of sliding, and again find that it depends on the contacts. A simple example, using the Coulomb friction law, demonstrates the connection between grasp stiffness and the vulnerability of the fingers to slipping. Experiments are underway with the Stanford/JPL hand to verify the analyses of compliance and slipping, using measurements of the finger and object displacements and changes in finger forces that result from applied loads.

In Section 4 we examine contact phenomena in closer detail. While the Coulomb friction model and point-contacts are convenient for dynamic and kinematic analysis, they can lead to inaccurate results [Cutkosky and Wright 86]. Our approach is to try to characterize the behavior of real contacts through basic analyses and experiments. An improved friction model for elastic materials is reviewed. The results of static friction tests using compliant, skin-like gripping materials on smooth surfaces have been described in [Cutkosky, Jourdain and Wright 87]. Our preliminary experiments on surface texture are reported here.

In a parallel effort, we are exploring the use of tactile sensors for acquiring information about the "state" of the contact, including the nature of the coupling between the finger and the object, surface conditions, and the vulnerability of the finger to slipping. Here, too, analysis of the contact interaction will provide the fundamental basis for understanding which phenomena are important and need to be sensed.

2 Stiffness in grasping

In its most general form, the stiffness of a grasp is a linearized expression of the relationship between forces applied to the grasp and the resulting motions:

$$K = \frac{\partial f}{\partial x} \qquad (1)$$

The resulting matrix can describe force/motion relationships internal and external to the grasped object [Salisbury 85]. However, in this section we are concerned only with the stiffness of the object with respect to external forces.

As a partial derivative, the grasp stiffness permits us to look beyond instantaneous properties such as mobility[1] or force-closure[2] and to examine the *sensitivity* of the grasp to disturbances. In fact, as Salisbury [1985] points out, K is a direct measure of the grasp stability. As long as K is positive definite, the changes in the forces on the object will have a stabilizing effect.

2.1 Grasp stiffness computation

Figure 1 shows the coordinate systems for a single finger touching a grasped object. The forward force and motion relationships between the finger joints and the fingertip are:

$$^{F}J_{\theta} \; \delta\theta = \delta x_{f} \qquad (2)$$

---

[1] A grasp has full mobility if the fingers can impart arbitrary motions to the object [Salisbury 85].

[2] A grasp has force-closure if, within the limitations of friction, it can resist forces and moments from any direction [Nguyen 87].

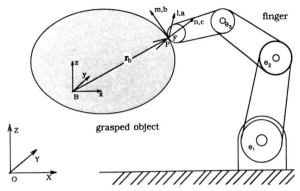

Figure 1: Coordinate systems for a single finger touching a grasped object

$$({}^{F}\mathbf{J}_{\theta})^{T}\,\mathbf{f}_{f} = \mathbf{f}_{\theta} \qquad (2b)$$

where $\mathbf{f}_{\theta}$ and $\delta\theta$ are m-element vectors of the joint torques and infinitesimal joint motions, $\mathbf{f}_{f}$ and $\delta\mathbf{x}_{f}$ are 6-element cartesian force/torque and infinitesimal motion vectors, and ${}^{F}\mathbf{J}_{\theta}$ is the $6 \times m$ Jacobian matrix relating joint motions to fingertip motions in the $F(abc)$ coordinate system.

At the contact between the fingertip and the object, the relationship between finger and object motions can be expressed as

$$\mathbf{H}\,\delta\mathbf{x}_{p} = \mathbf{H}\,\delta\mathbf{x}_{f} = \delta\mathbf{x}_{tr} \qquad (3)$$

where $\delta\mathbf{x}_{p}$ and $\delta\mathbf{x}_{f}$ are 6-element vectors of infinitesimal motions of the contact points on the body and fingertip and $\delta\mathbf{x}_{tr}$ is a vector of the components transmitted through the contact. $\mathbf{H}$ is an $n \times 6$ matrix expressing the n velocity constraints associated with the contact. For a "soft finger" as defined by Salisbury [1985],

$$\mathbf{H} = \begin{bmatrix} 1 & 0 & 0 & 0 & 0 & 0 \\ 0 & 1 & 0 & 0 & 0 & 0 \\ 0 & 0 & 1 & 0 & 0 & 0 \\ 0 & 0 & 0 & 0 & 0 & 1 \end{bmatrix}.$$

For equilibrium, the force balance at the contact point is

$$\mathbf{f}_{p} = \mathbf{f}_{f} = \mathbf{H}^{T}\,\mathbf{f}_{tr} \qquad (3b)$$

where $\mathbf{f}_{p}$ and $\mathbf{f}_{f}$ are 6-element cartesian force/torque vectors and $\mathbf{f}_{tr}$ is an n-element vector containing the non-zero force/torque components at the contact. Thus, for a point contact with friction $n = 3$, and the number of non-zero elements in $\mathbf{f}_{p}$ or $\mathbf{f}_{f}$ is three.

Finally, going from the $P(lmn)$ contact coordinate system to the $B(xyz)$ frame embedded in the object, the forward motion and force relationships are

$$ {}_{B}^{P}\mathbf{J}\,\delta\mathbf{x}_{b} = \delta\mathbf{x}_{p} \qquad (4)$$

$$ ({}_{B}^{P}\mathbf{J})^{T}\,\mathbf{f}_{p} = \mathbf{f}_{b} \qquad (4b)$$

where ${}_{B}^{P}\mathbf{J}$ is a 6×6 matrix transforming infinitesimal motions, $\delta\mathbf{x}_{b}$, in the object coordinate system to equivalent motions at the contact.

Combining equations (3b) and (4b), we can expand equation (1) by the chain rule as

$$\frac{\partial\mathbf{f}_{b}}{\partial\mathbf{x}_{b}} = \frac{\partial({}_{B}^{P}\mathbf{J}^{T}\,\mathbf{f}_{f})}{\partial\mathbf{x}_{b}} = \underbrace{({}_{B}^{P}\mathbf{J}^{T})\,\frac{\partial\mathbf{f}_{f}}{\partial\mathbf{x}_{b}}}_{\mathbf{K}_{b}} + \underbrace{\frac{\partial({}_{B}^{P}\mathbf{J}^{T})\mathbf{f}_{f}}{\partial\mathbf{x}_{b}}}_{\mathbf{K}_{J}} \qquad (5)$$

or to the first order

$$\delta\mathbf{f}_{b} \cong {}_{B}^{P}\mathbf{J}^{T}\,\delta\mathbf{f}_{f} + \Delta({}_{B}^{P}\mathbf{J}^{T})\,\mathbf{f}_{f}. \qquad (6)$$

In the first part of equation (6), $\delta\mathbf{f}_{f}$ represents the restoring forces and moments at the finger/object contact resulting from the structural and servo stiffness of the finger. In the second part, $\Delta({}_{B}^{P}\mathbf{J}^{T})\,\mathbf{f}_{f}$ represents the effects of small changes in the grasp configuration. As observed in [Cutkosky 85], these become important when the grasp forces, $\mathbf{f}_{f}$, are large compared to the restoring forces.

2.2   Computing the fingertip compliances

In this section we derive expressions for the compliances of the fingers. We begin with the individual joint and structural compliances, impose the contact constraints and transform the fingertip stiffness matrix to the body frame to obtain the servo and structural contributions to the overall grasp stiffness. For a more detailed discussion see [Kao 87].

As in previous analyses by Salisbury [1985] and Cutkosky [1985], the joint stiffnesses, due roughly to position feedback gains in a finger with m joint servos, produce an $m \times m$ joint stiffness or compliance matrix for each finger. Often, however, the fingers will be coupled [Salisbury 85]. For example, the human hand exhibits both active (servo) and passive (structural) coupling among the fingers. If we wiggle our fourth fingers, it is nearly impossible to keep the third and fifth fingers from moving in sympathy. The concatenated joint compliance matrix, including coupling among the fingers, becomes:

$$\mathcal{C}_{\theta} = \begin{bmatrix} \mathbf{C}_{\theta_{11}} & \mathbf{C}_{\theta_{12}} & \dots & \mathbf{C}_{\theta_{1,nf}} \\ \mathbf{C}_{\theta_{21}} & \mathbf{C}_{\theta_{22}} & \dots & \mathbf{C}_{\theta_{2,nf}} \\ & & \ddots & \\ & \dots & & \mathbf{C}_{\theta_{nf,nf}} \end{bmatrix}. \qquad (7)$$

In the fingertip coordinate system, the joint compliance matrix can be expressed as

$$\mathcal{C}_{j} = \mathcal{J}_{\theta}\,\mathcal{C}_{\theta}\,\mathcal{J}_{\theta}^{T} \qquad (8)$$

where $\mathcal{J}_{\theta}$ is a block-diagonal matrix composed of the Jacobians, ${}^{F}\mathbf{J}_{\theta_{i}}$, for each finger.

To the controllable joint compliances we must add the uncontrollable structural compliance. In dextrous hands the use of slender kinematic chains, cables, and soft gripping surfaces leads to significant compliance. The structural compliance is easiest to determine experimentally, applying known loads and recording deflections. For example, in recent tests on the Stanford/JPL hand, we measured the typical compliances shown in Table 1. These values were measured with the fingers extended. The combined structural compliance, at approximately $10^{-4}\,N/m$, is roughly 10% of the minimum achievable servo compliance. In anthropomorphic hands with softer links and fingertips, we expect structural compliance to be correspondingly more important. The overall fingertip compliance matrix is obtained by summing the joint and structural compliances:

$$\mathcal{C}_{f} = \mathcal{C}_{j} + \mathcal{C}_{s}. \qquad (9)$$

If $\mathcal{C}_{f}$ is invertable, which it usually will be if $\mathcal{C}_{s}$ is not negligible, we can obtain the concatenated fingertip stiffness matrix $\mathcal{K}_{f}$. However, as observed earlier, the contact matrices,

component	compliance in m/N
Cable compliance	3.1×10^{-5}
Joint and link compliance	1.0×10^{-5}
Fingertip compliance	1.1×10^{-4}

Table 1: Typical structural compliances of the Stanford/JPL hand

$\mathbf{H}_i$ "filter out" some of the motions of the fingertips. Hence not all elements of $\mathcal{K}_f$ will be experienced by the grasped object. Applying equations (3) and (3b), the concatenated stiffness matrix for the contact points on the object is

$$\mathcal{K}_p = \mathcal{H}^T \left(\mathcal{H} \, \mathcal{C}_f \, \mathcal{H}^T \right)^{-1} \mathcal{H}. \qquad (10)$$

As discussed in Section 3, $\mathcal{K}_p$ is particularly useful for sliding analyses as it contains the stiffnesses that the object "sees" at each contact point.

Finally, in terms of the $B(abc)$ coordinate system of the grasped object, we have the following:

$$\mathcal{K}_b = \mathcal{J}^T \, \mathcal{K}_p \, \mathcal{J} \qquad (11)$$

$$\mathbf{K}_b = \begin{bmatrix} I & I & ... \end{bmatrix} \mathcal{K}_b \begin{bmatrix} I \\ I \\ \vdots \\ I \end{bmatrix} \qquad (12)$$

where $\mathcal{J}$ is a block-diagonal concatenated matrix with $^P_B\mathbf{J}_i$ along the diagonals and $\mathbf{K}_b$ is the 6×6 matrix representing the stiffness of the grasped object, due to the servo and structural terms, in body coordinates.

2.3   Computing the effects of changes in geometry

When a grasped object is displaced slightly, two things happen which may affect the overall grasp stiffness and stability: the fingers shift slightly with respect to the object and, if the fingers roll or slide, the contact points move upon the object. To compute the effects of these changes in the grasp geometry we first need to find an expression for the complete motions of the fingertips with respect to the object. From the contact velocity constraints in equation (3) we can specify some, but not all, of the components of the fingertip motion when the object is displaced slightly. We need to make some assumptions about the fingertip control to determine the remaining components. One possibility is to assume that the fingertip orientation remains essentially fixed with respect to a global coordinate system [Kao 87]. For long, multijointed fingers with point contact, this is probably a reasonable assumption. A more general assumption is that the fingers will adopt a configuration that minimizes the potential energy of the grasp, subject to kinematic constraints. In this case we can solve for the motion of the fingertips using Lagrange multipliers. As in [Cutkosky 85], we combine the simultaneous equations to form a matrix, except that now the potential energy includes the combined structural and servo stiffness, expressed in fingertip coordinates:

$$\begin{bmatrix} \mathbf{K}_f & \mathbf{H}^T \\ \mathbf{H} & 0 \end{bmatrix} \begin{bmatrix} \delta \mathbf{x}_f \\ \mathbf{l} \end{bmatrix} = \begin{bmatrix} \mathbf{f}_f \\ \mathbf{H} \, \delta \mathbf{x}_p \end{bmatrix} \qquad (13)$$

where $\mathbf{l} = [\lambda_1 \ \lambda_2 \ \lambda_3 \ ...]$. For point and soft-finger contacts, a symbolic inverse can be used in solving for $\delta \mathbf{x}_f$ [Kao 87].

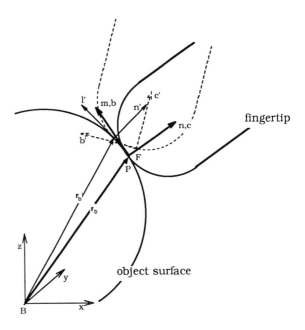

Figure 2: Coordinate systems for a finger rolling on a grasped object

If $\mathbf{C}_f$ is not invertible, one can usually solve for $\delta\theta$ in the joint space [Cutkosky 85].

While $\delta \mathbf{x}_f$ represents the absolute motion of the fingertip, $(\delta \mathbf{x}_f - \delta \mathbf{x}_p)$ represents the relative motion of the fingertip with respect to the object. Expressed in the body coordinate frame, the relative motion becomes

$$^P_B\mathbf{J}^{-1} \left(\delta \mathbf{x}_p - \delta \mathbf{x}_f \right) = \delta \mathbf{x}_b - {}^P_B\mathbf{J}^{-1} \, \delta \mathbf{x}_f. \qquad (14)$$

By comparing $\delta \mathbf{x}_f$ and $\delta \mathbf{x}_p$, it is possible for a given contact geometry and contact type (e.g. rolling contact) to determine how much the contact has moved upon the object. Figure 2 shows the contact coordinate systems before and after a fingertip has rolled slightly with respect to the object. Solutions to the complex problem of computing the contact point motion are discussed in [Kerr 85] and [Ji 87]. For our purposes, it suffices to find the change in the resultant force on the object. Put another way, from equation (3b) we know that initially $\mathbf{f}_p = \mathbf{f}_f$, but after infinitesimal motion the force acting at the contact becomes

$$\mathbf{f}'_p = \mathcal{D}^T \, \mathbf{f}_f \qquad (15)$$

where $\mathcal{D}$ is a matrix describing a small, cartesian transformation between the new position and orientation of the fingertip force, $\mathbf{f}_f$, and the initial $P(lmn)$ contact coordinate system [Kao 87]. Then, in body coordinates we have

$$\mathbf{f}'_b = {}^P_B\mathbf{J}^T \, \mathcal{D}^T \, \mathbf{f}_f = {}^P_B\mathbf{J}^T \, \mathbf{f}_f + {}^P_B\Delta\mathbf{J}^T \, \mathbf{f}_f. \qquad (16)$$

If no rolling or sliding occurs, $\mathcal{D}$ will contain only rotation terms, but in general both translations and rotations may be present. Solving for $^P_B\Delta\mathbf{J}^T$, we have

$$^P_B\Delta\mathbf{J}^T = {}^P_B\mathbf{J}^T (\mathcal{D}^T - \mathbf{I}) \qquad (16b)$$

where $^P_B\Delta\mathbf{J}^T$ represents a differential Jacobian due to the changes in the geometry. The result is similar to the differential Jacobian defined in [Cutkosky 85]. Details can be found in [Kao 87].

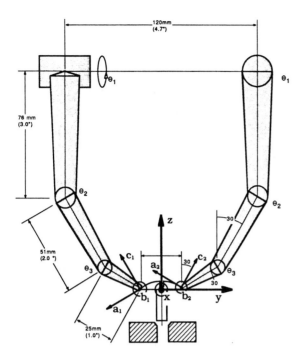

Figure 3: Assembling a rivet

Multiplying ${}^P_B \Delta \mathbf{J}^T$ by $\mathbf{f}_f$ gives us the second term in equation (5), which we will call $\mathbf{K}_J$:

$$\mathbf{K}_J = \frac{\partial({}^P_B \Delta \mathbf{J}^T \mathbf{f}_f)}{\partial \mathbf{x}_b} \qquad (17)$$

Finally, the effective stiffness is obtained by summing $\mathbf{K}_b$ from equation (12) and $\mathbf{K}_{J_i}$ for all fingers.

$$\mathbf{K}_e = \mathbf{K}_b + \sum_{i=1}^{nf} \mathbf{K}_{J_i}. \qquad (18)$$

For a force-closure grasp, $\mathbf{K}_e$ is nonsingular, so

$$\mathbf{C}_e = \mathbf{K}_e^{-1}. \qquad (19)$$

Example: Inserting a rivet into a hole
Figure 3 shows two three-joint fingers about to insert a small rivet into a chamfered hole. We assume soft fingertips and structural compliances close to those of the Stanford/JPL hand [Table 1]. The servo and structural compliances are as in Appendix I. Applying equations (8) thru (12) of the stiffness computation leads to:

$$\mathbf{K}_b = \begin{bmatrix} 76775 & -13 & -27 & 0 & 10188 & -15526 \\ -13 & 30075 & -12300 & 416 & 27 & -50 \\ -27 & -12300 & 51109 & -174 & 60 & -108 \\ 0 & 416 & -174 & 6 & 0 & -1 \\ 10188 & 27 & 60 & 0 & 1364 & -2076 \\ -15526 & -50 & -108 & -1 & -2076 & 3659 \end{bmatrix}$$

where the units are N/m and Nm for translational and rotational stiffness respectively.

Discussion: $\mathbf{K}_b$ reveals some interesting properties of the grasp. First, there is strong coupling among several directions. For example, we cannot translate in the x-direction without producing rotation in the y and z directions (so K_{x,θ_y} and K_{x,θ_z} are large). Also, since $\mathbf{K}_b$ has full rank, this grasp is a force-closure grasp. By evaluating the eigenvalues, we can find the stiffest and softest directions. More generally, the elements of $\mathbf{K}_e$ reveal stiff and soft axes. For example, rotation about the x axis is very soft compared to the others because of redundant joints for that direction.

3   Sliding analysis

Increasingly, it has been recognized that sliding is an important part of dextrous manipulation. With industrial robots and passive grippers, the goal was to avoid slipping so that the location of the part would not be lost. However, when people handle objects, they often take advantage of sliding to achieve desired motions of the part. For example, whenever we use a screw driver to turn a screw into wood, we allow the screwdriver to slip against our fingers at the end of each turn. When manipulating parts in multifingered robotic hands it has also been found that sliding must be reckoned with since it is nearly unavoidable [Fearing 86]. Consequently, we would like to be able to predict under what circumstances fingers will slide against a grasped object and in what directions they will start to slide.

A number of previous investigations have considered the vulnerability of a robotic grasp to slipping [Kerr 85, Li and Sastry 86, Jameson and Leifer 86, Nguyen 87, Ji 87]. In such analyses the fingers are treated as rigid, except for localized deformations at the fingertips so that the contact areas were finite. However, in this section we investigate two methods that make use of contact models and the grasp stiffness from Section 2 to predict when and how fingers will slip upon a grasped object. The reason for using the grasp stiffness is that it allows us to account for rates of change of the contact forces in response to external forces imposed on the object.

3.1   Changes in the contact forces

When the grasped object is acted upon by external forces and moments, $\mathbf{f}_b$, the corresponding motions at each contact point are:

$$\delta \mathbf{x}_{p_i} = {}^P_B \mathbf{J}_i\, \mathbf{K}_e^{-1} \mathbf{f}_b \qquad (20)$$

The resulting change in the forces and moments at each contact is therefore

$$\delta \mathbf{f}_i = {}^P \mathbf{K}_{p_i}\, \delta \mathbf{x}_{p_i} = {}^P \mathbf{K}_i\, {}^P_B \mathbf{J}_i\, \mathbf{K}_e^{-1} \mathbf{f}_b. \qquad (21)$$

Once the changes in the contact forces are found, we can make use of them to predict slipping according to two measures that will be discussed in this section: (1) the "worst-case finger" measure, and (2) the "progression-toward-slipping" measure.

3.2   Measures to predict Slipping
3.2.1   Worst-case finger for point contacts

Our worst-case finger measure is an extension of work by Cutkosky [1985] to a "3D worst-case finger" measure. The measure is most easily defined for point contacts and in the following discussion we assume hard, point contacts. In Section 4, however, we consider more realistic contact models and how they complicate the picture.

Initially, the grasp is in equilibrium and the contact force at each pointed fingertip is $\mathbf{f} = [f_l\; f_m\; f_n]^T$. When a new external force is applied to the object, the contact force changes according to equation (21) and the new normal and tangential force components become $f'_n = f_n + \delta f_n$ and $f'_t = \sqrt{(f_l + \delta f_l)^2 + (f_m + \delta f_m)^2}$ respectively.

According to the Coulomb law of friction, if we write the tangential force as $f_t = \alpha\,\mu\,f_n$, then slipping occurs as $\alpha \rightarrow$

1. For a grasp with several fingers, the finger closest to slipping will be the one for which α_i is closest to 1 or for which the ratio

$$\alpha_i = \frac{\sqrt{(f_{l_i} + \delta f_{l_i})^2 + (f_{m_i} + \delta f_{m_i})^2}}{\mu_i (f_{n_i} + \delta f_{n_i})} \quad (22)$$

is largest. This is the "worst-case" finger. Competing grasps can then be compared be selecting the one for which the worst-case ratio in equation (22) is smallest. This provides a conservative measure of the vulnerability of the grasp to slipping (the entire grasp is judged according to the worst-case finger) that depends both on the coefficient of friction and on $\delta \mathbf{f}_{p_i}$, which in turn depends on the grasp stiffness and geometry.

3.2.2   Progression-toward-slipping

Another way to look at the onset of slipping is to construct a potential function, V, such that

$$V = \sqrt{f_l^2 + f_m^2} - \mu f_n \quad (23)$$

which indicates how far a finger is from the edge of its friction cone. But, in general we would like to know not only how a far a finger is from the edge of the friction cone, but also whether a given force applied to the grasped object will cause it to move closer or farther from the edge, and how fast.

Therefore, we define the change in the potential function, after an external force has been applied, as

$$\begin{aligned} \delta V &= [\sqrt{(f_l + \delta f_l)^2 + (f_m + \delta f_m)^2} - \mu(f_n + \delta f_n)] \\ &\quad - [\sqrt{f_l^2 + f_m^2} - \mu f_n] \end{aligned} \quad (24)$$

Dropping small terms, this can be simplified to [Kao 87]

$$\delta V = \left(\frac{f_l \, \delta f_l + f_m \, \delta f_m}{\sqrt{f_l^2 + f_m^2}} - \mu \, \delta f_n \right) \quad (25)$$

where $\delta f_l, \delta f_m$, and δf_n are functions of $\mathbf{K}_{p_i}$ and $\delta \mathbf{x}_{p_i}$. Hence, δV depends on the initial grasping forces, the externally applied forces, the stiffnesses of the fingers, and the changes in the grasp configuration.

Example: Application of the slipping measures to a planar grasp. For the grasp configuration shown in Figure 4, we adopt servo compliances similar to those used in the Stanford/JPL hand to obtain:

$$\mathbf{C}_{\theta_1} = \mathbf{C}_{\theta_2} = \begin{bmatrix} 0.4 & 0.06 \\ 0.06 & 0.4 \end{bmatrix}$$

where the units are 1/Nm. For simplicity, we ignore the structural compliance. From equations (8)–(12), $\mathbf{K}_b$ becomes:

$$\mathbf{K}_b = \begin{bmatrix} 36803 & 0 & -954 \\ 0 & 41645 & 0 \\ -954 & 0 & 27 \end{bmatrix}$$

where the xy terms are in N/m and the θ terms are in N. Note that the y direction is decoupled from the other directions because of the symmetry of the grasp. $\mathbf{K}_J$ is neglected in this example due to the small grasp forces (1.5N). The initial forces at the contact points are:

$$\mathbf{f}_{p1} = [-0.75 \quad -1.5 \quad 0]^T \; ; \; \mathbf{f}_{p2} = [0.75 \quad -1.5 \quad 0]^T$$

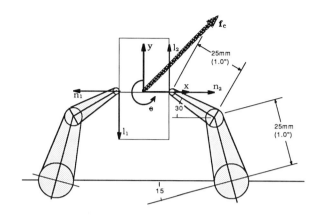

Figure 4: Slipping in a two-fingered grasp

in the (l, m, n) contact coordinates. The weight of the block is 1.5 N and $\mu = 0.6$. Suppose that now an external force $\mathbf{f}_b = [0.5 \; 0.5 \; 0]^T$ is applied, where the forces are in newtons and moments in newton-meters. From equation (21):

$$\mathbf{df}_{p_1} = \begin{bmatrix} -0.25 \\ -0.48 \\ 0 \end{bmatrix} \; ; \mathbf{df}_{p_2} = \begin{bmatrix} 0.25 \\ 0.024 \\ 0 \end{bmatrix}$$

Equation (22) gives us $\alpha_1 = 0.817$ and $\alpha_2 = 0.547$, which indicates that the first finger is the "worst-case" finger. Equation (25) leads to

$$\delta V_1 = \frac{(0.75)(-0.25)}{0.75} - (0.6)(-0.48) = 0.038$$

and, similarly, $\delta V_2 = -0.264$, which shows that the first finger is progressing toward the edge of its friction cone.

Discussion: The results of this simple example match our intuition and suggest several ways to make the grasp less likely to slip. The first, usually beyond our control, is to decrease the magnitude of the external forces. The second is to increase the initial grasp force. However, this may not be desirable since a large grasp force could damage the object and would increase $\mathbf{K}_J$, possibly destabilizing the grasp. The third possibility is to decrease the servo stiffness of the first finger. If, for example, we change the servo compliance of the first finger to

$$\mathbf{C}_{\theta_1} = \begin{bmatrix} 1.2 & 0 \\ 0 & 1.2 \end{bmatrix}$$

the two slipping measures are changed and the grasp becomes more resistant to slipping ($\alpha_1 = 0.725, \alpha_2 = 0.505, \delta V_1 = -0.04$, and $\delta V_2 = -0.34$). We note that the sign of δV_1 has changed, so that the applied force no longer tends to make the first finger slip. However, in making the first finger more compliant, we somewhat reduce the overall grasp stiffness, $\mathbf{K}_e$, resulting in larger object motions. More generally, if we reduce the stiffness of a finger that contributes greatly to the overall grasp stiffness, then the object moves more and $\mathbf{K}_J$ increases relative to $\mathbf{K}_b$, which tends to destabilize the grasp. We also note that by making *both* fingers more compliant, the object moves substantially further when external forces are applied and the slipping measures, α and δV, will be close to those of the original grasp. Stabilization schemes for both measures are summarized in Table 2.

Measure 1	α	df_l	f_b	grasp force	K_θ
finger 1	decr	decr	decr	incr	decr
finger 2	decr	decr	decr	incr	incr
Measure 2	δV	df_l	δx	grasp force	C_θ
finger 1	decr	decr	incr	incr	incr
finger 2	decr	decr	decr	incr	decr

Table 2: Changes recommended to make the grasp more resistant to slipping

4   Contact models and sensing

As in previous grasp analyses, the examples in the last section used idealized point-contact or soft fingers with Coulomb friction. However, for anthropomorphic hands with skin-like gripping surfaces, these idealized models do not accurately describe the contact characteristics. Since the contacts strongly affect the properties of the grasp, these models lead to inaccurate predictions of the grasp behavior. Consequently, there is a strong motivation to explore more accurate models of finger/object contacts. In this section we discuss ongoing analytic and experimental work to better characterize the contacts. These models rapidly become complex, and as we discuss in Section 4.4, the most practical approach is to use tactile sensing to describe the local contact conditions and to permit on-line determination of the contact type.

4.1   Friction and the Area of Contact

Unlike hard, plastically deforming materials, for which the Coulomb model of friction gives accurate results, viscoelastic materials such as rubbers usually display a coefficient of friction that varies as a function of the normal force. An improved model is described by Cutkosky and Wright [Cutkosky 86]. This model successfully predicted the variation of the frictional force with normal load for elastomers in contact with a smooth, dry surface. Because of the microscopic roughness of even apparently smooth surfaces, the actual contact between surfaces occurs only at the tops of surface asperities, where adhesion between the molecules of each surface occurs. Cutkosky and Wright's model assumes that the frictional force is proportional to the real area of contact, and an elasticity analysis shows that for many elastomers this area grows approximately as the normal force to the 2/3 power. In experiments Cutkosky, Jourdain and Wright [1987] found good correlation with this prediction, except at very light and very heavy loads.

4.2   Surface Texture

One important factor in determining the frictional forces is the geometric configuration of the surfaces of both the fingertip and the object. Not surprisingly, humans are very sensitive to variations in surface texture [Lederman 75]. In manipulation, the role of texture is determined to a great extent by the scale of the features. For example, on the smallest scale, microroughness with features as small as a fraction of a micrometer has a pronounced effect on wet friction because it breaks up the entrainment of fluid between the elastomer and the rough surface [Moore 72].

We would like to be able to predict how friction varies with texture on an object surface. Clearly one effect of texture is

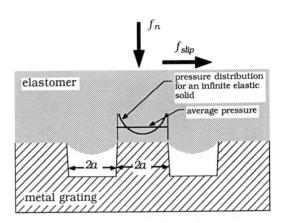

Figure 5: Profile of rubber in contact with grating, and resulting pressure distribution

to change the pressure distribution across the contact, and from the above arguments regarding elastomeric friction, this will also change the maximal frictional force.

As an idealized texture, we consider a square wave grating. The physical situation and the pressure distribution (found from classical elasticity theory [Johnson 85]) are illustrated in Figure 5. In place of a constant normal force, we must use the local pressure derived from the elasticity analysis and integrate over A_a, the apparent contact area. Since the local pressure is proportional to the total applied normal force, the result is that the limiting friction force is proportional to the applied normal force to the 2/3 power. We can express this in terms of the average pressure p as

$$f_{slip} = k\ p^{2/3}\ A_a \qquad (26)$$

where f_{slip} is the limiting force, A_a is the apparent area of the contact, and k is a constant of proportionality dependent on the pressure distribution, contact conditions, materials, etc.

To illustrate the effect of texture, we compare the friction of a flat plate to that of a ruled grating, similar to gratings used by Taylor and Lederman [1975] in experiments with human fingers. The expected pressure distributions are different due to the differences between human fingertips and rubber. Since the grating has half the surface area of the flat surface, $A_{a,f} = 2A_{a,g}$. If the same total normal force is applied to both surfaces, the average pressure on the grating ridges will be twice as large as for the flat surface, or $p_g = 2p_f$. The ratio of the friction limits is

$$\frac{f_{slip,g}}{f_{slip,f}} = \frac{k_g\ p_g{}^{2/3} A_{a,g}}{k_f\ p_f{}^{2/3} A_{a,f}} = \frac{k_g}{k_f}\ 2^{-1/3} \qquad (27)$$

where the subscripts g and f refer to the grating and flat surfaces, respectively. From this analysis we see that texture has the perhaps surprising effect of *decreasing* the effective friction at a contact. This is in contrast to the Coulomb friction model, where increased normal force results in a proportionately larger frictional force, so the change in the contact area has no effect. It is also in contrast to the effective *increase* in friction obtained when viscoelatic human fingers are pressed into a rough textured surface.

f_n	$f_{slip,g}$	$f_{slip,f}$	$f_{slip,g}/f_{slip,f}$
65	68	85	0.80
128	121	161	0.75
228	218	268	0.81
828	744	932	0.80
1428	1218	1473	0.82

Table 3: Experimental results showing the decrease in friction between flat and grooved surfaces. Forces in units of grams-weight ($9.8 \times 10^{-3} N$).

4.3   Texture and Friction Experiments

We have experimentally confirmed that texture decreases the friction of rubber on a clean, hard surface. Comparative measurements of the maximum tangential force as a function of normal force have been made for flat and grooved plates. The apparatus has been described in [Cutkosky, Jourdain, and Wright 87].

The elastomer used in this test was a soft, 3mm thick silicon rubber. The test surfaces were 45mm×25mm aluminum plates. One plate was flat, while the other was cut by parallel grooves into an approximate square wave grating [Figure 7]. The grooves and the ridges between them were 1.3mm wide. The surfaces of both plates had an identical, smooth finish, and the plates and elastomer were cleaned prior to each set of measurements.

The results of the measurements are presented in Table 3. The first column is the normal force at which the measurements were made. The second and third columns are the tangential forces at which slipping commenced for the grating and flat surface respectively. The fourth column is the ratio of the two, showing excellent agreement with the value of $2^{-1/3} \doteq 0.794$ predicted by the theory. The effects of the non-uniform pressure distribution are seen to be small in this case; the elastomer thickness is of the same order as the grating period and makes the pressure distribution "flatten out" across the grating ridges, approaching the average value shown in Figure 5.

4.4   Tactile Sensing

Because contact phenomena are influenced by such a large number of factors, an analytic approach will never produce results which reliably describe the behavior of real-world contacts. This makes tactile sensing of the state of the contact a necessity. Studies of manipulation by multi-fingered robot hands have found that without feedback from tactile sensors, the effects of the cumulative unmodeled errors eventually cause manipulation failure [Fearing 87].

In our work with robotic grasping and manipulation, we are currently exploring ways of using tactile sensing to provide information about:

- the contact location and how it is moving
- the type of kinematic coupling at the contact: point, line, soft, very soft
- forces and force distributions at the contact
- recognizable attributes of the contact surfaces (e.g. "is-oily", "is-rough") which in turn suggest which friction model is appropriate to use.

5   Conclusions and Future Work

The physical processes involved in contact phenomena can lead to useful models of the behavior of contacts. The resulting contact models figure prominently in the overall grasp stiffness and stability. We have proposed two measures that predict when and how the fingers will start to slide. The measures depend on the local finger stiffness, the contact types, the overall grasp stiffness and the grasp configuration. The first measure singles out a finger that is most prone to slipping while the second measure predicts whether a given set of external forces and moments will cause fingers to become more or less likely to slip. Using the stiffness analysis developed, we can adjust servo stiffnesses to make the grasp more resistant to slipping.

To verify these measures we are now beginning some experiments with the Stanford/JPL hand. Figure 6 shows the hand grasping a block, to which a controlled external force has been applied. The motions of the fingers and the forces at the fingertips are obtained from instrumentation in the hand. The fingertips are sheathed in rubber and dusted with a light coating of copying machine toner so that we can record the shapes and motions of the contact areas as the fingers start to slide.

More accurate models of the finger/object interaction must account for adhesion, surface contamination and texture. In this paper we discuss preliminary experimental results on texture and friction and compare them with simple theoretical models. But in the long run, since contact phenomena are extremely complex, tactile sensing will be essential for relaying the contact characteristics. To better understand the roles of surface materials, textures and contact properties in manipulation we will investigate the vibrations produced by sliding fingertips on textured surfaces.

Acknowledgements

This work was performed with the support of NSF contracts DMC8552691 and DMC8602847. The authors thank Mr. Ron Fearing for his help with experiments on the Stanford/JPL hand.

Appendix I

Example 1 For the grasp configuration and dimensions shown in Figure 3, the concatenated joint stiffness matrix is taken as:

$$
\mathcal{C}_\theta = \begin{bmatrix}
0.1 & 0 & 0 & 0.01 & 0 & 0.03 \\
0 & 0.16 & 0 & 0 & 0.05 & 0 \\
0 & 0 & 0.1 & 0 & 0 & 0.05 \\
0.01 & 0 & 0 & 0.3 & 0 & 0 \\
0 & 0.05 & 0 & 0 & 0.16 & 0 \\
0.03 & 0 & 0.05 & 0 & 0 & 0.2
\end{bmatrix}
$$

The structural compliances for the fingers are: (MKS units)

$$
\mathbf{C}_{s_1} = \begin{bmatrix}
0.0573 & 0 & -0.0088 & 0 & -0.692 & 0 \\
0 & 0.101 & 0 & 0.576 & 0 & 0.332 \\
-0.0088 & 0 & 0.0146 & 0 & 0.165 & 0 \\
0 & 0.576 & 0 & 3.76 & 0 & 2.17 \\
-0.692 & 0 & 0.165 & 0 & 13.1 & 0 \\
0 & 0.332 & 0 & 2.17 & 0 & 1.26
\end{bmatrix} \times 10^{-3}
$$

$$
\mathbf{C}_{s_2} = \begin{bmatrix}
0.128 & 0 & -0.016 & 0 & -0.931 & 0 \\
0 & 0.125 & 0 & 0.5 & 0 & 0.3 \\
-0.016 & 0 & 0.0158 & 0 & 0.102 & 0 \\
0 & 0.5 & 0 & 3.25 & 0 & 2 \\
-0.931 & 0 & 0.102 & 0 & 12 & 0 \\
0 & 0.3 & 0 & 2 & 0 & 1.25
\end{bmatrix} \times 10^{-3}
$$

Finally, the coordinate transformation matrix $\mathcal{J}$ can be found directly from the dimensions in the figure.

References

[Cutkosky 87] M.R. Cutkosky, J.M. Jourdain, and P.K. Wright. Skin materials for robotic fingers. In *Proc. 1987 IEEE Intl. Conf. on Robotics and Automation*, pages 1649–1654, March 1987.

[Cutkosky 86] M.R. Cutkosky and P.K. Wright. Modeling manufacturing grips and correlations with the design of robotic hands. In *Proc. 1986 IEEE Intl. Conf. on Robotics and Automation*, pages 1533–1539, April 1986.

[Cutkosky 85] M.R. Cutkosky. *Robotic Grasping and Fine Manipulation*. Kluwer Academic Publisher, Boston, Mass, 1985.

[Fearing 87] R. Fearing. Some experiments with tactile sensing during grasping. In *Proc. 1987 IEEE Intl. Conf. on Robotics and Automation*, pages 1637–1643, April 1987.

[Fearing 86] R. Fearing. Implementing a force strategy for object reorientation. In *Proc. 1986 IEEE Intl. Conf. on Robotics and Automation*, pages 96–102, April 1986.

[Ji 87] Z. Ji. *Dextrous Hands—Optimizing Grasp by Design and Planning*. PhD thesis, Stanford University, 1987.

[Jameson 86] J. Jameson and L. Leifer. Quasi–static analysis: a method for predicting grasp stability. In *Proc. 1986 IEEE Intl. Conf. on Robotics and Automation*, pages 876–883, April 1986.

[Johnson 85] K. L. Johnson. *Contact Mechanics*. Cambridge University Press, Cambridge, 1985.

[Kao 87] I. Kao and M.R. Cutkosky. Effective stiffness and compliance, and their application to sliding analysis. *To be published*, 1987.

[Kerr 85] J. Kerr. *Analysis of Multifingered Hands*. PhD thesis, Stanford University, 1985.

[Lederman 75] M.M. Taylor and S.J.Lederman. Tactile roughness of grooved surfaces: a model and the effect of friction. *Perception and Psychophysics*, 17(I):23–36, 1975.

[Li 86] Z. Li and S. Sastry. *Task Oriented Optimal Grasping by Multifingered Robot Hands*. Memorandum No UCB/ERL M86/43, U. C. Berkeley, May 1986.

[Moore 72] D. F. Moore. *The Friction and Lubrication of Elastomers*. Pergamon Press, New York, N. Y., 1972.

[Nguyen 87] V. Nguyen. Constructing force–closure grasps in 3-D. In *Proc. 1987 IEEE Intl. Conf. on Robotics and Automation*, pages 240–245, March 1987.

[Salisbury 85] M.T. Mason and J.K. Salisbury. *Robot Hands and the Mechanics of Manipulation*. The MIT Press, Cambridge, Mass., 1985.

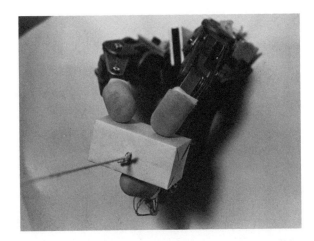

Figure 6: Sliding experiments with the Stanford/JPL hand

Figure 7: Elastomeric fingertip pressed against a ruled surface

Simulation Analysis for Force Control Six-Joint Manipulator

T. Kuno, M. Koide, N. Mimura, and H. Miyaguchi

Toyota Central Research and Development Laboratories, Inc.

Nagakute, Aichi, 480-11, Japan

Unstable vibration was observed for a hard object when Salisbury's force control method was applied to a 6-joint manipulator of speed reduction gear type. A simulation analysis was performed for the instability. A speed reduction gear has the Coulomb friction and spring characteristics, which can be eliminated by feedback of joint torque and its differential. It was found that a stable force control is possible for a variation equivalent to more than 100 times the hardness of an object, if the feedback of force from hand is suspended, while the joint torque and its differential are fed back as mentioned above. Due to the torque feedback, however, the servo damping is decreased, and the entire arm and the object spring are easily vibrated. To restrict such vibration, differential feedback of force of hands is effective. There are two problems, however. One is that the torque feedback gain cannot be increased beyond a certain level due to mutual interference of joint servos, and the other that vibration of a few hertz is generated in the control force for a hard object. Countermeasures against these problems are yet to be established. To eliminate the error force due to the arm inertia etc., which is generated in an open-loop operation, feedback of the signal of a force sensor via a low-pass filter of a band width of a few hertz is effective, but will accelerate the above vibration of a few hertz.

1. Introduction

Development of a force control manipulator requires solutions to two problems: (1) the way how to coordinate the position of a hand and the force, and (2) realization of operational stability and response characteristics. As for the problem (1) above, (a) stiffness control, (b) Impedance control, and (c) hybrid-control, are currently studied. As for the problem (2) above, active studies are being performed for these years, mainly by IBM and MIT groups[1]. A solution to the problem of stability ensures an almost identical structure for control systems, irrespective of control types of (a), (b), and (c) above. For this reason, said solution is useful for (a), (b), and (c) above universally.

We are studying the latter problem. Phenomena of instability produced when a manipulator of speed reduction gear type is controlled with force are analyzed by simulation, and measures for obtaining stability studied. This paper explains above efforts and the results.

2. Target of Study

Our target is developing of a robot capable of performing a profile operation with a high accuracy of plus or minus a few ten grams per a few centimeters per second under the condition of metal-to-metal contact for tools and works. A force control system using a position control loop as an inner loop is being studied by some other groups[2],[3]. The system is capable of performing a stable operation under the condition of the metal-to-metal contact, but the control error at a profile operation is large. J. A. Maples[3]

and others report 0.5 kg/8 mm/sec. We intend to realize a value smaller than the above by several times.

To realize the above target, we think a control system of joint torque control type is considered to be preferable, because the subject to control is not position but force. From this viewpoint, we adopted the Salisbury's method having a small amount of calculation procedures, and developing prototypes while making necessary improvements.

DD motors are normally used to study the joint torque control[1], because there are no friction and spring characteristics which deteriorate the force control characteristics, since there is no need for a DD motor to use a speed reducer. However, a DD motor inevitably has a large torque variation called cogging, and a torque feedback is required to keep it under control[4]. On the other hand, it is considered that the Coulomb friction and spring characteristics existing in a manipulator of conventional gear reduction type may be eliminated by the use of feedback control. In our development efforts, a Puma type 6-joint manipulator with speed reduction gear is used from the viewpoint of cost/performance.

3. Structure and Present Performance of Prototype

Fig. 1 shows the Salisbury's force control system adopted by us, which comprises three computer boards 8086/8087 (8 MHz) of Intel Inc. In Fig. 1, gravity torque and inertia matrix are calculated for every 100 ms, force sensor feedback 10 ms, and speed feedback 2 ms. The force sensor attached on the wrist is 6-D. O. F. sensor of Hitachi Kenki Inc.

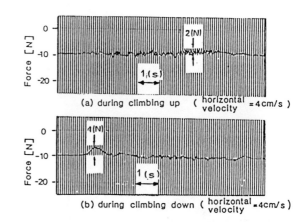

Fig. 1.   Structure of a force control system

J : Jacobian matrix
Kθ : Joint stiffness matrix
Kv : Velocity damping term
Cg : Gravity loading

Λ : Inverse coodinate transformation
KH : Virtual Compliance
CI : Instantaneous Inertia
KP, KI : Gain for torque loop

This system produces unstable vibration when a rigid tool is held against a rigid surface, and will not realize our target performance. For this reason, experiments were made by holding a light-weight and contractible jig with a built-in spring, which is mounted on the end of the sensor, against surfaces of an object. Fig. 2 shows step responses. A soft spring is stable (Fig. 2-1), but a hard one generates vibration (Fig. 2-2).

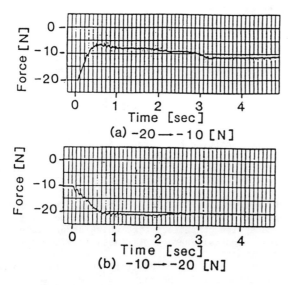

Fig. 2-1.   Experimental result of force step response (Kp = 6.3, K_I = 50, Kobj = 1.8 × 10^3 [N/m])

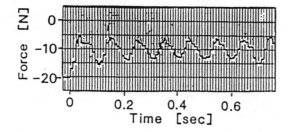

Fig. 2-2.   Experimental result of force step response (Kp = 8.9, K_I = 50, Kobj = 3.1 × 10^3 [N/m])

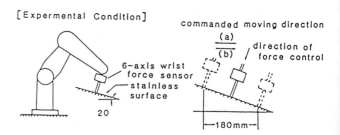

(a) during climbing up   (horizontal velocity =4cm/s)

(b) during climbing down (horizontal velocity =4cm/s)

[Experimental Condition]

6-axis wrist force sensor
stainless surface
20

commanded moving direction
(a)
(b)
direction of force control
—180mm—

Fig. 3.   Experimental results of force control during moving along the inclined plane for horizontal moving command (commanded force = 10 [N])

Fig. 3 shows response of profile operations. Force deflection is large since the force feedback gain cannot be enlarged. Meaning of the variables used in the Figures are listed in Table 1. The control system was analyzed as follows to find means of performance improvements:

4.   Analysis of Instability by Single-joint Simulation

First, instability of a single-joint was simulated. Models shown in Fig. 4 was prepared on the assumption that the springs existing in the passages for the motor torque to reach the hand as well as the friction torque characteristics are the cause of instability, where the first spring is a torsion spring of the speed reduction gear, the second one a spring of a sensor, etc., and the third one a spring of the object. As most of friction is generated at first stage and compliance at final stage of gear reducer[5], friction was exerted in front of the first spring on the motor side. Force is fed back via the sensor on the hand. A position feedback loop for the stiffness control was omitted since only stability of a force control system was to be investigated. The sample hold, delay and current limiter were installed immediately before the motor current output.

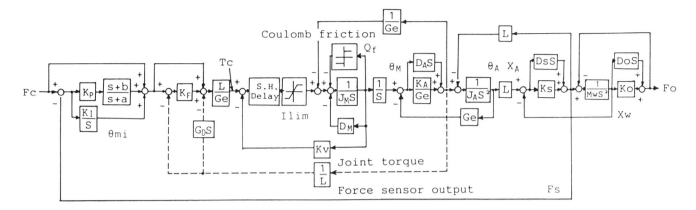

Fig. 5. Block diagram of the force control system (single-joint)

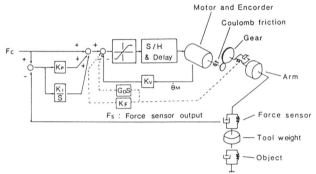

Fig. 4. Model of the force control system
(Single-joint)

Table 1. List of variables and constants

	variables / constants	value
Kp	proportional force gain of controller	$0 \sim 3$
Ki	integral force gain of controller	$0 \sim 50$
KF	joint torque feedback gain	$0 \sim 20$
a b	time constant of phase lead-lag compensator	a=0, 6.28[S] b=0 [S]
Ge	gear ratio	140.05
GD	derivative feedback gain of joint torque	0 or 0.1 [s]
L	equivalent length of 2nd link of robot arm	1.0 [m]
JM	rotor inertia of motor	3.33×10^{-4} [kg.m^2]
DM	viscous coefficient of motor	2.15×10^{-4} [Nm/$\frac{m}{s}$]
Kv	velocity feedback gain for servo system	0.1 [N/$\frac{m}{s}$]
KA	spring constant of transmission system	2.0×10^{5} [Nm/rad]
DA	viscous coefficient of transmission system	1.51×10^{-2} [Nm/$\frac{m}{s}$]
JA	arm inertia	5.157 [kg.m^2]
Ks	spring constant of wrist force sensor	4.9×10^{6} [N/m]
Ds	viscous coefficient of wrist force sensor	21.5 [N/$\frac{m}{s}$]
Mw	tool weight	1.2 [kg]
Kobj	spring constant of object	$3 \times 10^{3} \sim 3 \times 10^{6}$ [N/m]
Dobj	viscous coefficient of object	0 [N/$\frac{m}{s}$]
Qf	coulomb friction at motor bearing	0.04284 [Nm]
Ilim	limit value of motor current	20 [A]
Ts	sampling period of controller	$0.1 \sim 10$ [ms]

Block diagram is shown in Fig. 5. Variables and constants used in the analysis and the simulation are listed in Table 1.

4.1 Relationship between Hardness of Object and Instability

Transition of the characteristic root of the closed-loop system is studied. System equations of closed-loop of a linear system where Coulomb friction, etc. is omitted can be expressed as equation (1).

$$\dot{x} = Ax + Bu$$
$$y = Cx \qquad (1)$$

where

$$A = \begin{bmatrix} 0 & 1 & 0 & 0 & 0 & 0 & 0 \\ -\frac{Ks+Kobj}{Mw} & \frac{Ds+Dobj}{Mw} & \frac{KsL}{Mw} & \frac{DsL}{Mw} & 0 & 0 & 0 \\ 0 & 0 & 0 & 1 & 0 & 0 & 0 \\ \frac{KsL}{JA} & \frac{DsL}{JA} & -\frac{KA+KsL^2}{JA} & -\frac{DA+DsL^2}{JA} & \frac{KA}{JAGe} & \frac{DA}{JAGe} & 0 \\ 0 & 0 & 0 & 0 & 0 & 1 & 0 \\ \frac{KpKsL}{JMGe} & 0 & \frac{KA-KpKsL^2}{JMGe} & \frac{DA}{JMGe} & -\frac{KA}{JMGe^2} & -\frac{DA+KvGe^2}{JMGe^2} & \frac{L}{JMGe} \\ K_iKs & 0 & -K_iKsL & 0 & 0 & 0 & 0 \end{bmatrix}$$

$$B = \begin{bmatrix} 0 \\ 0 \\ 0 \\ 0 \\ 0 \\ \frac{(1+Kp)L}{JMGe} \\ K_i \end{bmatrix} \quad C = \begin{bmatrix} -Ks \\ 0 \\ KsL \\ 0 \\ 0 \\ 0 \\ 0 \end{bmatrix}^T \quad X = \begin{bmatrix} Xw \\ \dot{X}w \\ \theta_A \\ \dot{\theta}_A \\ \theta_M \\ \dot{\theta}_M \\ \theta_{mi} \end{bmatrix} \qquad (2)$$

Fig. 6 shows a root locus in a case where the
force loop gain Kp is increased. There are three
resonant roots, namely, those of a motor
inertia/arm inertia and spring of speed reducer,
 b load mass and sensor spring, and c arm
intertia and spring of object. Instability is
generated with b and c above. Increase of
spring constant of object, Kobj, will make b
above stable but will make c above unstable.
Increase in load mass and a harder spring of a
speed reducer will make b above unstable, but
countermeasures to stabilize the vibration will
not be discussed in this paper.

The responce and the vibration mode for a linear
system are shown in Fig. 7. Step input force
command of 10 N and object movement of ±10 mm/sec
are applied. In the vibration mode where an
object is hard, the spring of the speed reducer
and the spring of object are moving briskly,
suggesting that the spring of the speed reducer
has a close relationship with unstability.
However, if Kp → 0, the root enters the left side
of the S plane. In this instance, the guideline
to stabilize the system for a hard object spring
is either decrease of Kp or adoption of an open-
loop.

4.2 Characteristics of Open-Loop System

Adoption of an open-loop makes the instability
generated in Fig. 7 stable as shown in Fig. 8.

Mode of vibration for an open-loop system varies
with the relative value of object spring
constant Kobj, sensor spring constant Ks, and
speed reducer spring constant Ka. Generally,
Ka < Ks, therefore, three vibration modes, as
shown in Fig. 9, are generated as Kobj getting
larger. Vibration is observed between the entire
arm and Kobj if Kobj < Ka < Ks, and Kobj and Ka,
if Ka < Kobj < Ks. Vibration is observed around
all the springs if Ka < Ks < Kobj.

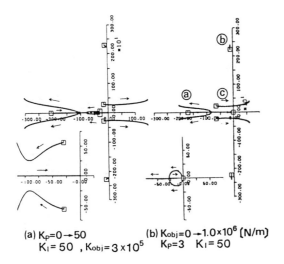

(a) $K_P = 0 \to 50$
  $K_I = 50$, $K_{obj} = 3 \times 10^5$

(b) $K_{obj} = 0 \to 1.0 \times 10^6$ (N/m)
  $K_P = 3$ $K_I = 50$

Fig. 6. Root locus for the model with wrist
         force sensor feedback when Kp or Kobj
         varies

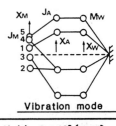

Vibration mode

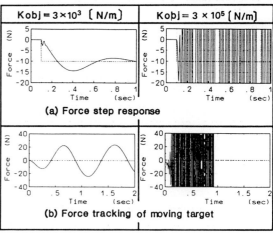

Fig. 7. Simulation for the model with force
         sensor feedback
         ($K_P = 3$, $K_I = 50$, $K_F = 0$, $Q_F = 0$)

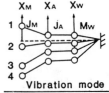

Vibration mode

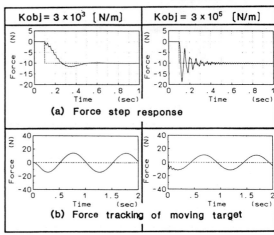

Fig. 8. Simulation for open loop model
         ($K_P = 0$, $K_I = 0$, $K_F = 0$, $Q_F = 0$)

Fig. 8 shows response of force control performance when Kobj < Ka < Ks. As Kobj is small, an appropriate damping is obtained, and a stable force control is observed. As Kobj increases, frequencies generated are gradually increased while damping is deteriorated. Since the frequency of the vibration around Ks is extremely high, a suitable damping may be achieved by a damping resistance existing in a structure. Therefore, in a practical instance, the case of Ks < Ka < Kobj need not be considered. However, vibration around Ka is required to be removed since it may deteriorate force control performance when a multiple-joint is adopted. The reaction force produced at profiling should preferably be as small as possible, but it is generated by arm inertia and velocity feedback for damping. To make it small, a feedback from the force sensor via a low-pass filter, as shown in 4.2.3 below, is effective[1].

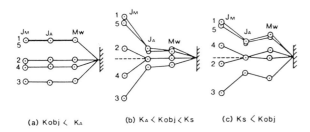

(a) Kobj < Ka   (b) Ka < Kobj < Ks   (c) Ks < Kobj

Fig. 9. Vibration mode for various Kobj

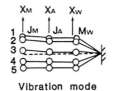

Vibration mode

Kobj = 3 × 10³ [N/m]	Kobj = 3 × 10⁵ [N/m]
(a) Force step response	
(b) Force tracking of moving target	

Fig. 10. Simulation for the model with joint torque and its differential feedback loop ($K_P = 0$, $K_I = 0$, $K_F = 10$, $G_D = 0.05$, $Q_F = 0$)

4.2.1 Effect of Joint Torque Feedback

It is aimed to make a spring of a speed reducer dynamically rigid by a feedback of joint torque. In the model of Fig. 5, if $K_s = \infty$ and $M_w = 0$ and $K_p = K_I = 0$ for simplicity purpose, the equation of motion can be expressed as follows when the torque and its differential are fed back:

$$J_M \theta_M + (D_A + G_D)(\dot\theta_M - \dot\theta_A) + (1 + K_F) K_A (\theta_M - \theta_A) = (1 + K_F) T_C$$
$$J_A \ddot\theta_A + D_A (\dot\theta_A - \dot\theta_M) + D_{obj} \dot\theta_A + K_A (\theta_A + \theta_M) - K_{obj} \theta_A = 0$$

$$(3)$$

When characteristic equation is solved as:

$$D_M + G_D \gg D_M \cdot J_M / J_A$$
$$1 + K_F \gg J_M / J_A \qquad (4)$$

then we obtain:

$$G_{(S)} = (S^2 - 2\xi\omega S + \omega n^2)\left(S^2 + \frac{D_{obj}}{J_A} S + \frac{K_{obj}}{J_A}\right) \quad (5)$$

$$\omega_n = \sqrt{K_A\left(\frac{1}{J_M} + \frac{1}{J_A}\right) + \frac{K_A K_F}{J_M}}$$

$$(6)$$

$$\xi = \frac{1}{2\omega_n}\left\{ D_M\left(\frac{1}{J_M} + \frac{1}{J_A}\right) + \frac{G_D}{J_M} \right\}$$

From the above, it is known that a speed reducer can be made rigid while ensuring a sufficient damping through feedback of torque and its differential. In other words, it is possible to limit vibration of a system to that of object spring and arm inertia only.

An example of time response and vibration mode are shown in Fig. 10, from which it is known that the speed reducer spring become more rigid than in the case of Fig. 8. A stable operation is observed over a wide range of load spring constant (3 × 10³ to 3 × 10⁵ N/M). This performance will never be realized with a force sensor feedback. The torque feedback, however, decreases damping of the arm which is generated by the velocity feedback. When Kobj becomes very large, vibration due to the above insufficient damping, and vibration of load mass and sensor spring will come out. It is necessary to find a means to increase these types of damping. As for the insufficient damping due to excessive rigidity of the entire system, it may be necessary to purposefully provide a soft spring on the wrist, for example, to avoid under damping for the entire system.

Other effective methods for achieving stability include feedback of differential of outputs of a force sensor[6]. No effect exists if Kobj < Ks. In contrast, feedback of differential of the

212   Kuno et al.

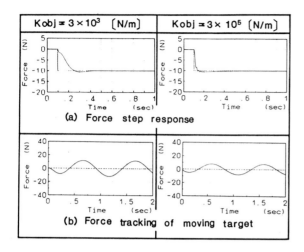

Fig. 11. Simulation for the model with differential force feedback loop (Kp = 0, K_I = 0, K_F = 10, G_F = 0.05, Q_F = 0)

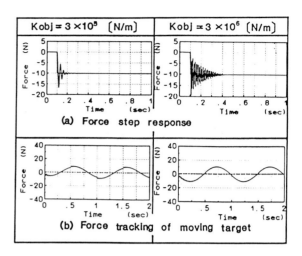

Fig. 13. The effect of joint torque feedback for Coulomb friction (Kp = 0, K_I = 0, K_F = 10, Q_F = 0.04284)

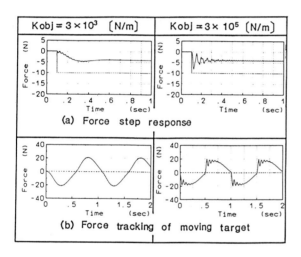

Fig. 12. The effect of Coulomb friction for the open loop model (Kp = 0, K_I = 0, K_F = 0, Q_F = 0.04284)

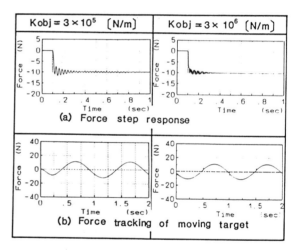

Fig. 14. The effect of joint torque and its differential feedback for Coulomb friction (Kp = 0, K_I = 0, K_F = 10, G_D = 0.1, Q_F = 0.04284)

force an object spring ensures stabilization including the above case. Fig. 11 shows an example. Excessive torque feedback gain will make the load mass and the vibration system of the sensor spring unstable.

4.2.2 Elimination of Coulomb Friction Characteristics

Actual speed reduction gears have a Coulomb friction equivalent to about 20 % of the rated motor torque. In the above analysis, it was not considered, but now it is studied here. Friction is considered to exist in the front stage of a speed reducer, or on the motor side, as shown in Fig. 4. Joint torque is to be measured at the spring existing in the final stage of the speed reducer. This assumption may not be too unrealistic, since it is considered that friction of a speed reducer is generated mostly at an area of a small torque, and flexure is considered to

be mostly generated at an area of a large torque. If the joint torque feedback is not conducted, accuracy of the force control will be considerably deteriorated as shown in Fig. 12.

Torque feedback was tried for the above condition, and it is known that damping deteriorates drastically when the Coulomb friction is large, especially under the condition of a large Kobj, as shown in Fig. 13. It is also known, however, that the torque control system is given damping and stabilizes if the torque differential is fed back as shown in Fig. 14. In this figure, the effect of Coulomb friction is eliminated. Vibrations tend to be generated easily, depending on conditions of the load side, but they are damped vibrations, and will not become unstable. Torque and differential feedback of torque will oscillate if gains are increased too much. Damping performance changes very little even if the load inertia varies.

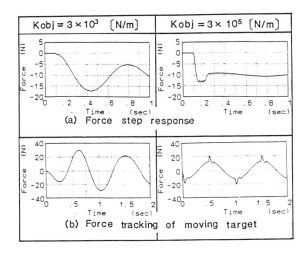

Kobj = 3×10^3 [N/m]	Kobj = 3×10^5 [N/m]

(a) Force step response

(b) Force tracking of moving target

Fig. 15. Simulation for the model with low-pass filter in force feedback loop (K_P = 3, K_I = 50, K_F = 0, Q_F = 0.04284, Cut off frequency of L.P.F. = 1 Hz)

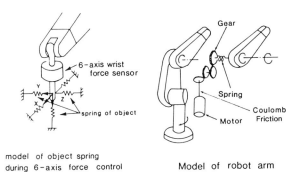

model of object spring during 6-axis force control

Model of robot arm

Fig. 16. Modeling of 6-joint manipulator

4.2.3 Improved Performance for Profile Operation

Coulomb friction has been eliminated by the feedback of joint torque. However, reaction force is generated on the hand when performing a profile operation, because of arm inertia and the viscous characteristics of a joint servo. To reduce it, it is necessary to take a force feedback from the hand. In this instance, if Kobj is large, oscillation starts for an excessive gain, as mentioned before. If feedback is exerted via a low-pass filter as in the case of An[1]), gains at high frequencies are decreased, thus ensuring a stable operation even for a hard surface. Without joint torque feedback, the above method has a very low level of control accuracy, and can not be used in practical operations. This situation is shown in Fig. 15.

4.2.4 Effect on Sampling Period

As is explained in 4.2.1 and 4.2.3 above, a satisfactory characteristic seems to be obtainable by feedback of torque and its differential. There is one problem, however, that is, the system may become unstable unless the sampling period of the torque feedback loop is in the order of 0.1 ms. An analog loop construction gives us no problem, but digitalization requires a careful study.

5. 6-joint Simulation

A simulation study was made to confirm if measures for stabilization for a single-joint are also good for a 6-joint manipulator.

5.1 Structure of Simulator

Structure of the simulation model and block diagram used are shown in Fig. 16, 17. Manipulator dynamics, spring characteristics and Coulomb friction of the speed reducer, spring characteristics of object, servo characteristics,

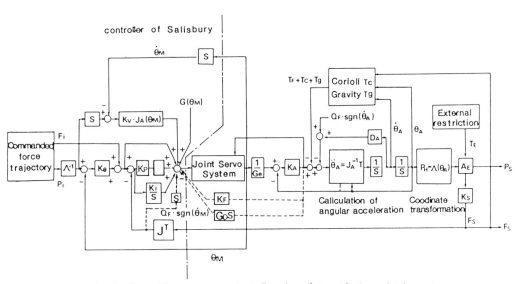

J_A : Arm inertia matrix A_E : Transformation matrix for wrist force sensor
Q_F : Coulomb friction presented in joint

Fig. 17. Block diagram of 6-joint simulation model

sample period, etc., are considered. Each motor
torque drives each link via a spring of a speed
reducer, and acceleration is generated at each
link. Use of the Newton-Euler method enables us
obtain the required torque given the acceleration
of a link, but, in our case here, it is necessary
to obtain acceleration of a link generated when
an input torque is given. For this reason, it is
impossible to use the Newton Euler method as it
is. For this reason, methods of M. W. Walker[7]
and others are used for calculation. The force
controller incorporates a Salisbury's servo. At
the present moment, characteristics of an object
include only springs. Available inputs include
target trajectory, target force, object profile
shift, etc.

5.2 Results of Simulation

5.2.1 Comparison with Characteristics of Prototype

The representative characteristic parameters of
the manipulator are listed in Table 2. Force
control is activated along the Z minus axis,
while keeping position control along X and Y axis
and around X, Y and Z axis of the hand coordinates with stiffness of 4000 N/m and 4000 Nm/deg,
respectively.

Table 2. Parameters of 6-joint manipulator

constants	axis	value					
		1	2	3	4	5	6
maximum length of arm [mm]		930					
moment of inertia around each axis [kg.m²]		4.14	3.22	0.52	2.98×10^{-3}	5.42×10^{-4}	3.06×10^{-5}
reduction gear ratio		73	140	51	51	51	42
rated output of motor [w]		300	300	300	80	80	80
motor inertia [kg.m²]		3.3×10^{4}	3.3×10^{4}	3.3×10^{4}	4.8×10^{-5}	4.8×10^{-5}	4.8×10^{-5}
spring constant [Nm/rad] of transmission system		1.16×10^{5}	1.83×10^{5}	2.89×10^{5}	1.26×10^{3}	1.27×10^{3}	8.70×10^{2}
coulomb friction [Nm]		6.76×10^{-2}	4.28×10^{-2}	1.76×10^{-2}	0.74×10^{-2}	0.38×10^{-2}	0.74×10^{-2}

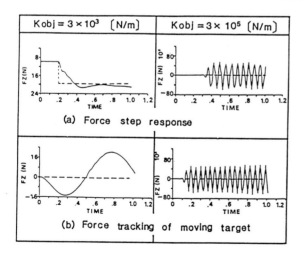

Fig. 18. Simulation for the model with the same
condition as the experiment.
Kp(Joint 2) = 7.5, K$_I$(Joint 2) = 50

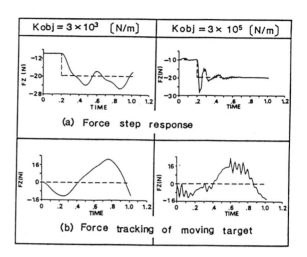

Fig. 19. Simulation for the model with low-pass
filter in wrist force feedback loop
(L.P.F. = 1.5 Hz)

Comparison of results of experiments (Fig. 2) and
simulation under the same conditions is shown in
Fig. 18. Responses to step inputs of force
instruction show a good resemblance. Constants
of the spring of the object and oscillation frequencies at which instability starts also show a
good resemblance. In both cases, also,
oscillating frequencies are constant irrespective
of the constant of the spring of the object.

Cause of oscillation is that the sampling interval is long. When the current 10 ms is reduced
to 2 ms, the constant of the spring of the object
at which instability starts is increased by five
times. The reason why the force feedback gains
Kp and KI are far larger than in the case of the
simulation of the single-joint is that the
Coulomb friction is taken into consideration.
Reduction of the sample frequency from 2 ms to 1
ms ensures further stabilization.

Like in the case of the single-joint, addition of
a low-pass filter for Kp ensures a stable step
response, even for a still harder object, as
shown in Fig. 19. On the other hand, response is
disturbed, force deflection is increased in a
profile operation, or other control performance
is deteriorated if the object is soft. Possible
causes include the spring of the speed reducer
and Coulomb friction characteristics. It is now,
therefore, tried to eliminate them with the joint
torque feedback the same as in the case of the
single-joint simulation.

5.2.2 Stabilization by Adoption of Open-Loop

Fig. 20 shows responses of force when it is
pushed against an object after adopting an open-
loop by disconnecting feedback from a force sensor. A stable push is observed although the
surface is hard. A large reaction force due to
arm inertia and viscous damping of servo is
observed. Stability is obtained even with a
system from which friction is eliminated so far
as a surface of Kobj = 3*10⁵ N/M is concerned.

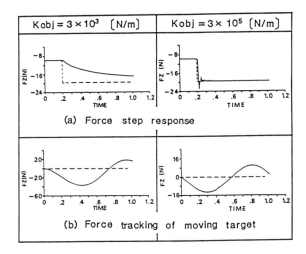

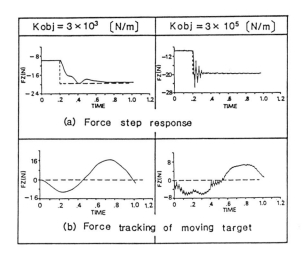

Fig. 20. Simulation for open-loop model
(Kp = K_I = 0, Q_F = 0)

Fig. 21. Simulation for the model with joint
torque and its differential feedback
(Kp = K_I = 0, Q_F = 0.04284)

If the object is further hardened, the velocity
loop becomes unstable. From the above, it is
known that a stable force control is obtainable
for 6-joint control by adopting an open-loop
control.

5.2.3 Effect of Joint Torque Feedback

The open-loop characteristics in the case when
the entire-joint torque and its differential are
fed back are studied. As shown in Fig. 21,
stable responses are available in the range of
Kobj = $3*10^3$ to $3*10^5$ N/M, and the error force
in profile operation is reduced to half comparing
to non-joint torque feedback case. But a new
vibration mode of a few hertz, which was not
observed in the case of a single-joint (Fig. 16)
and non-joint touque feedback (Fig. 20), is
observed together with a fast vibration of about
40 Hz, in the case of profiling of a hard surface. The result also shows that a stable performance is not realized unless differential
torque feedback is adopted.

The fast vibration of about 40 Hz seems to be due
to insufficient damping, which was erased when
the differential of force on object spring is fed
back (Fig. 22-(a)). Other effective methods
include addition of viscosity Dobj to object
spring, and increased velocity feedback gain.

As is clear from the above, the torque feedback
ensures rigidity of joints and decreased damping
as well. For this reason, it is necessary to
exert damping to ensure stability by using other
methods. The vibration of a few hertz is probably caused by the mutual interference of touque
feedback joint servos. And this will be the
reason of not to be able to use high touque feedback gain. Fig. 23 shows vibration of the
posture of hand. Countermeasures against this
instability are yet to be established.

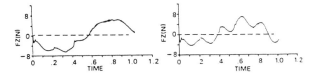

(a) with differential
force feedback
loop

(b) with low-pass fil-
tered force feedback
in addition to case
(a) (L.P.F. = 10 Hz,
Kp(Joint 2) = 0.75)

Fig. 22. Simulation for the model with differential force feedback

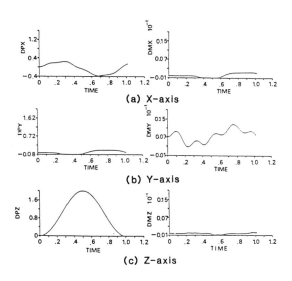

(a) X-axis

(b) Y-axis

(c) Z-axis

Fig. 23. Position and anguler error for the case
of Fig. 22(b)

5.2.4 Effect of Force Sensor Feedback

The force deflection at the time of a profile
operation is increased when a velocity feedback
is exerted to obtain stability. Fig. 22-(b)
shows response in the case when force is fed back
via a low-pass filter. The profile deflection is
smaller than in the case where there is no feedback, but the vibration of a few hertz is accelerated. Measures for compensation of this
vibration is necessary to be established, otherwise the force deflection cannot be decreased.

6. Summary

There is a possibility of designing a force
control manipulator of speed reduction gear type,
since it is known that spring characteristics and
Coulomb friction of a speed reduction gear can be
eliminated by the feedback of joint torque and
its differential. However, the effect of difference between a simulation model and an actual
machine is still to be studied. A coordinated
and precise control of multiple joint is
required, for which our current control algorism
is not sufficient. The study will be further
continued.

Acknowledgement

The authors would like to thank
Mr. Junzo Hasegawa and Mr. Riichi Takahashi of
TOYOTA R. D. Labs. Inc. for their effort to make
a chance of this research.

References

1) An, C. H. and Hollerback, J. M., "Dynamic
    Stability Issues in Force Control of
    Manipulators", Proc. IEEE Int. Conf. Robotics
    and Automation, Raleigh, March 30 - April 3,
    1987.

2) Maples, J. A. and Becker, J. J., "Experiments
    in Force Control of Robotic Manipulators",
    Proc. IEEE Int. Conf. Robotics and
    Automation, San Francisco, April 7-10, 1986.

3) Stepien, T. M. et al., "Control of
    Tool/Workpiece Contact Force with Application
    to Robotic Deburring", IEEE Journal of
    Robotics and Automation, Vol. RA-3, No. 1,
    February 1987.

4) Asada, H., "Measurement and Control of Joint
    Torques for Direct-Drive Arms", Transactions
    of the SICE, Vol. 22, No. 8, 1986.

5) Ejiri, M., "Vibrational Problems in 2 Phase
    Servomotors Used in Force Servo-mechanisms",
    Journal of the SICE, Vol. 5, No. 1, January,
    1966.

6) Khatib, O. and Burdick, J., "Motion and Force
    Control of Robot Manipulators", Proc. IEEE
    Int. Conf. Robotics and Automation,
    San Francisco, April 7-10, 1986.

7) Walker, M. W. and Orin, D. E., "Efficient
    Dynamic Computer Simulation of Robot
    Mehchanisms", Transactions of the ASME,
    Journal of Dynamic Systems, Measurment and
    Control, Vol. 104/205, September, 1982.

V RECOGNITION

In the past few years a consensus has been forming in the robotics community that the basic matching techniques required for object recognition have been developed, and that it is time to explore the other components (such as model building and vision programming techniques) required for a general-purpose recognition system. Lowe makes this point explicitly in his paper. The authors of the other papers implicitly support this opinion by the research directions they have chosen.

Pollard et al. describe components of a stereo recognition system, including a procedure for incrementally building edge models of objects viewed multiple times. Bajcsy and Tsikos describe an initial version of a system that builds object models by combining visual processing and manipulation. Their program applies an ordered sequence of operations designed to take apart an object located in range data.

The goal is to develop a functional model of the object in addition to a static shape description. Grimson describes two approaches for extending his basic matching strategy to recognize families of objects that are characterized by such parameters as scale, stretch, and rotation.

The final two papers describe techniques for predicting the appearance of object features from three-dimensional object models. The goal of this work is to provide an automatic vision programming system with descriptions of prominent features that can be used to recognize the objects. Ikeuchi and Kanade describe a framework for modeling a wide variety of sensors, and then show how it can be used to make feature predictions. Binford describes an analytic technique for predicting the observability and the type of edges associated with generalized cylinders having matte surfaces.

FOUR STEPS TOWARD GENERAL-PURPOSE ROBOT VISION

David G. Lowe

Courant Institute of Mathematical Sciences
New York University
251 Mercer Street, New York, NY 10012

General-purpose vision for robots requires the ability to identify and accurately determine the positions of all relevant three-dimensional objects within the robot workspace. These positions must be updated in real time as motion occurs, and the system must function robustly in spite of partial occlusion and unfavorable illumination. While no vision system currently can meet all of these objectives, it can be shown that they are within reach of existing technology. This paper describes four underlying capabilities that must be developed to reach these goals, including object verification and tracking, fast extraction of stable image features, automated model acquisition, and efficient indexing of the model database. Recent progress in developing each of these capabilities will be described based on our own research and that of others. We conclude that general-purpose robot vision can be implemented using these existing techniques, although much further work is necessary to produce efficient and robust implementations.

Introduction

Computer vision is a highly diverse field of research, in which it is common for different research projects to differ in their fundamental goals as well as their methods for reaching them. However, in the case of providing useful visual data for robots, there is much less disagreement regarding the appropriate goals. The robot needs to know where things are and what they are. It must be able to gather this information as quickly as needed and be able to update it as objects undergo motion at moderate rates of speed. It should function without restrictive assumptions regarding the locations or orientations in which objects may occur. While a number of recent systems [3,6,7,8,12,16] have demonstrated the ability to recognize objects from arbitrary viewpoints, these fall short of the above goals in terms of generality and speed. In this paper, we will propose four steps of research and development that would build upon previous research to satisfy the goals of general-purpose robot vision.

The following will assume that the input data for the robot consists of ordinary gray-scale images taken under normal workplace illumination. We will assume at first that the objects to be identified are known and can be modeled in advance, but we will also discuss the problem of automated model acquisition. Rather than beginning the discussion with the image input and proceeding from low-level to high-level, we will begin with what we consider to be the most fundamental capabilities and then present other components of the system that are needed to support them.

Object verification and tracking

The most basic capability required for robot vision is the ability to verify the presence of an object and accurately determine its location when given only an approximate estimate for its position. This capability is sufficient for many practical robotics applications in which the position of an object is already highly constrained. It is also the essential problem faced during motion tracking, since limits on the acceleration of an object allow its position to be predicted from frame to frame. Finally, it is also a key component for providing reliable verification during the search process that must be undertaken during more general recognition. Fortunately, this important capability is also one that is now quite well understood and for which general solutions are known. In the following paragraphs we will briefly review some of our recent work on this problem and discuss the reliability and speed of the resulting techniques.

Given an object model and an estimate for its position in an image, it is straightforward to project the model from the estimated position to predict the locations of its features in the image. However, given that the position estimate may have a significant de-

This research was supported by NSF grant DCR-8502009.

gree of error, there are likely to be many ambiguities in potential matches between image features and predicted locations of model features. The author has previously described [13] a probabilistic incremental matching technique that allows the most reliable matches in any image to be selected first. These least-ambiguous matches can be used to produce a more accurate estimate for the viewpoint, which reduces the degree of ambiguity for the more difficult cases. The ambiguity of a potential match is assessed by examining the degree of fit between the image feature and model prediction, the frequency of occurrence of the particular image feature, and the presence of any ambiguity due to competing matches in that particular image. Unless the initial viewpoint estimate is very poor, the best matches selected by these criteria are almost always correct.

A second component of the verification problem is a method for refining the viewpoint estimate given further information from the image. In previous research, the author [11,12] has described the use of Newton's method to numerically determine the best least-squares fit between a three-dimensional model and some two-dimensional image features. This method is illustrated in Figure 1 for minimizing the perpendicular errors between some image line segments and corresponding edges of a three-dimensional model. The advantages of this technique are that it is fast, robust, and capable of solving for a wide range of image and model parameters. Although the solution for position in depth from a single image is less accurate than the solution for position parallel to the camera plane, the recognition of an object in one image can be used to quickly match the object to an image taken from a different viewpoint and thereby obtain highly accurate three-dimensional position measurements.

By combining these match evaluation and viewpoint solving techniques, the model verification problem can be solved for a significant range of errors in the initial viewpoint estimate. The range over which the viewpoint estimate can be in error is determined by the potential for false matches between image and model features. In the current implementations of these methods, the features to be matched consist simply of individual straight line segments. These features have a high degree of ambiguity and therefore correct matching is achieved only when at least some parts of the model projected from the estimated viewpoint are within a roughly 30 degree orientation error and 20 pixel translation error of the correct position. However, the range for correct matching could be greatly increased by making use of more complex image features (such as curves or perceptual groupings) that do not suffer from the same degree of ambiguity as straight line segments.

Another important issue for application of these verification methods to practical robot vision is the speed with which they can be executed. Solution for viewpoint requires solving a 6×6 system of linear equations on each of several iterations (requiring roughly 150 floating point operations per iteration) and multiplying a $6 \times n$ matrix by an $n \times 6$ matrix to perform least-squares minimization for n image measurements (requiring 1400 floating point operations for a typical useful maximum of $n = 20$). It is somewhat more difficult to estimate computation times for the task of locating and evaluating the potentially matching features in an image. However, if each image feature is a line segment appropriately indexed according to position, orientation and length, then potentially matching image features can be identified with a couple of array accesses for each predicted model segment. The evaluation of each feature requires only several simple geometric calculations such as measuring the perpendicular distance of a point from a line, which can be done with integer arithmetic due to the limited precision of image data. The result is that it is quite feasible to perform the entire verification operation on a standard microprocessor within the 30ms frame time required for real-time motion tracking. This assumes, of course, that the image features are being identified simultaneously using a different piece of computational hardware. This degree of speed is also important when using verification in the inner loop of a general search for recognition.

Fast extraction of stable image features

Until recently, it was common to remark that low-level vision was the computational bottleneck in achieving fast robotic vision. However, there are now a number of examples of implemented hardware that can extract linked edge elements from images at video rates. For example, the PIPE (Pipelined Image Processing Engine) [9] can transform images at video rates into segmented straight line segments. A similar capability is reported by Moribe *et al.* [14] at Toyota Research Labs that can extract line segments from an image at a rate of 500 segments every 200ms. These capabilities will soon be widely available on relatively inexpensive hardware.

While the extraction of linked edges is sufficient for motion tracking, in which the position of an object in each frame can be quite accurately predicted, these features are at a level that is too primitive for more general object recognition. The problem is that an individual edge segment is too ambiguous and

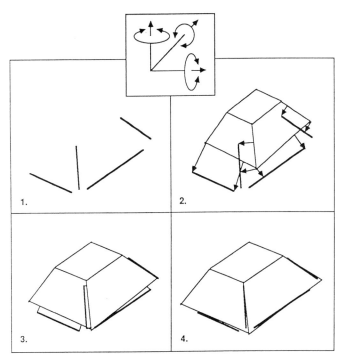

Figure 1. Viewpoint solution requires that the six parameters determining the orientation and position of an object in three dimensions (illustrated in inset at top) be adjusted to minimize the separation of the projected model lines from line segments detected in the image. Initially, we know only the two-dimensional locations of some lines in the image (1). Other components of the vision system propose some tentative matches between these image lines and some edges of a three-dimensional object. A rough initial estimate is made for the viewpoint of the object (2), and perpendicular errors are measured between the model lines projected from this viewpoint and the image lines. Newton's method is used to simultaneously solve for new values of all 6 viewpoint parameters so as to minimize these perpendicular errors. After two iterations of Newton's method, shown in (3) and (4), the optimal viewpoint has been determined to a high degree of accuracy.

could match many potentially corresponding features on each object. A very important goal for general-purpose vision is the detection of image features that are less ambiguous in their interpretation and yet are stable over changes in viewpoint. This is the goal of work in perceptual organization [10,11,17,18], in which isolated image features are grouped into structural relationships that remain stable over a wide range of viewpoints.

The author [12] has implemented perceptual grouping methods that link straight line segments on the basis of collinearity, parallelism, and proximity of endpoints. Figure 2 shows examples of these groupings detected in a bin-of-parts image. The implementation was written in Franz LISP without much attention to efficiency and takes approximately 30 seconds on a VAX 11/785 to find all significant groupings among 350 line segments. In order to perform these grouping operations at video frame rates, they must be sped up by three orders of magnitude. In addition, it would be desirable to perform many other types of grouping in order to derive the richest possi-

ble description of the image. Therefore, perceptual grouping could prove to be a significant computational bottleneck in achieving inexpensive real-time performance. In the following paragraphs, we will evaluate a number of implementation strategies to determine the intrinsic computational requirements.

If it were necessary to examine even all pairs of image features for potentially significant groupings, the combinatorial nature of the problem would render it infeasible. Fortunately, all useful groupings are based on requiring a degree of proximity between elements in addition to other relationships [11]. However, the degree of proximity is not fixed, but rather varies proportionally according to the size of the features participating in a grouping. This means that each feature must be indexed according to location at various scales of resolution, depending upon the size of the feature. Since collinearity and parallelism also depend upon the orientation of a feature, efficiency can also be gained by indexing according to orientation.

It is worth pointing out that one commonly proposed method for grouping image features is not as efficient as is often presumed. This is the method of Hough transforms [1,5], in which a feature is stored in an accumulator array under each grouping in which it could participate. Collisions in this array indicate actual groupings of multiple elements. The problem with this technique is that each image feature could participate in a large number of groupings, any one of which is quite unlikely, and that therefore the indexing process itself is very expensive. A far more economical technique is to simply index each feature under a few relevant properties such as location, orientation and size. After all features have been indexed, we can search away from each feature for other features that fall within the relevant parameter bounds to form a significant grouping with the first feature. Given that the groupings that appear in any particular image form a very sparse subset of the possible groupings in which the individual features could potentially participate, relatively little computation is wasted on the consideration of relationships that are not present in the actual data. The attraction of the Hough transform is that it can be implemented in a highly parallel and uniform manner, yet the alternative indexing methods would also seem to be highly parallelizable on existing architectures due to the locality of each grouping.

Therefore, the computational requirements for grouping sets of line segments involve indexing each segment according to a combination of position and orientation in either a hash table or multidimensional array. The quantization of the location would occur at several levels of courseness according to the size of the feature. The formation of groupings would require searching from each feature for others within the appropriate parameter bounds. This would typically require up to a dozen array accesses. Due to the courseness of the quantization in indexing, it is necessary to further check the precise relationships of each candidate grouping.

As can be seen from this discussion, the computational requirements for grouping are substantial, but represent a relatively modest and roughly constant cost for each image feature. In fact, the operations required for grouping are similar to those needed to access image features during the matching of model predictions, except that the grouping operations must be performed for every feature rather than only from locations predicted by the object model. It remains to be seen whether existing hardware is sufficiently powerful to perform a useful range of grouping operations in real time.

Object model acquisition

Much research in computer vision has been devoted to designing representations for object models. This emphasis on representation is common to many areas of artificial intelligence, since the choice of the representation for knowledge is a key step in defining the task to be implemented. However, I will argue that the key representational issues in vision are at the level of hidden intermediate structures rather than the description of a physical object model. One major requirement for representing an object is to describe its visual appearance, which is a problem that has been thoroughly explored in the field of computer graphics. However, for the purposes of recognition, it is even more important to represent the relationships between particular features and structures that can be detected in the image and corresponding components of the model. In fact, much of the research on model representation has been primarily concerned with developing this link between the image and the model. For example, models based on generalized cylinders [2] make explicit the link between symmetry axes that can be detected in the image and axes of three-dimensional model components. Similarly, a representation based upon superquadrics [15] makes explicit the relationship between various shape parameters that can be measured in the image and surfaces of model components.

However, object models must serve at least two different purposes for a wide range of object classes and feature extraction methods, which makes it unlikely that there will be any single representational primitive that will prove appropriate for the full range of requirements. One basic role for object models is to provide fast predictions for the locations of image features from particular viewpoints for use during object verification and tracking. This purpose can be met by traditional computer graphics techniques that have been developed to generate accurate descriptions of appearance from selected viewpoints. For example, for an edge-based vision system, the use of wire-frame models fulfills all of the necessary requirements and is far more efficient than most surface or volume representations. The second role for object representations is to represent associations between features that can be detected bottom-up from the image and corresponding features of particular models for use during the initial stages of recognition. Given the difficulties of recognition, it is important that the representation be able to incorporate all forms of stable image information rather than being restricted to one particular category of image descriptors.

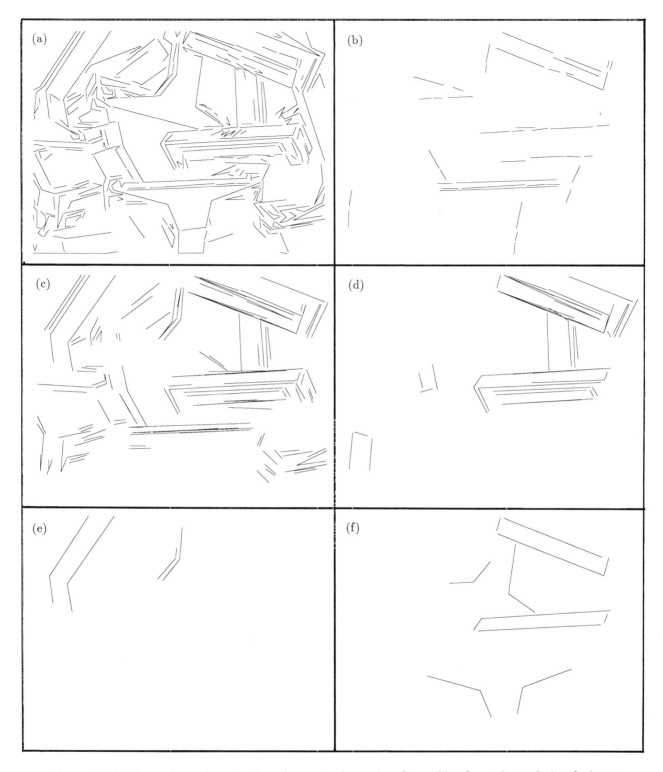

Figure 2. This figure shows the extraction of perceptual groupings from a bin-of-parts image (using the image shown in Figure 3). Frame (a) shows an initial set of 350 straight line segments detected in the original gray-scale image. The segments are first grouped on the basis of collinearity. Each segment in (b) has been found to be significantly collinear with another nearby segment, and a new segment is created joining each of these pairs. Segments are further grouped on the basis of parallelism (c) and then as sets of parallel segments with a connecting segment in close proximity to their endpoints (d). Finally, higher-level pairs of connecting parallels (e) and trapezoid or skewed-symmetry groupings (f) are formed. These viewpoint-invariant structures can be used to match specific features of object models during recognition.

This second aspect of model representation is driven more by the feature extraction capabilities of low-level vision than by properties of the models themselves. The most straightforward and reliable method for identifying these associations between image and model features is to gather data from actual images of the object. Given the inaccuracies and incompleteness of most computer graphics or CAD models, and given the difficulties in predicting the performance of most feature extraction methods, the information gathered from actual images is likely to be far more accurate than some abstract prediction. The ability to acquire object models from images of the object would also remove a significant bottleneck in the application of robot vision, since modeling can be a very time-consuming task.

There have been a number of successful examples of systems that can generate three-dimensional models from a set of images. One of the most successful is the Sheffield TINA system [16] that can build accurate edge-based models by integrating information from a number of stereo views of an object. Partial models are sufficient to recognize the object in subsequent images and to build up more complete models by integrating new information. Since model acquisition does not have the same real-time performance requirements as other aspects of robot vision, it is possible to use more time-consuming processing techniques than in other recognition applications. Since the same feature detectors and low-level processing can be used to build the model as will be used during recognition, a model built in this way is likely to be a more accurate reflection of what will actually be encountered during recognition. But the most important aspect of automated model acquisition is the representation of associations between features detected bottom-up and the database of object models, as discussed in the following section.

Efficient indexing of the model database

For general problems of visual recognition, there may be a large library of potential objects that could appear in an image and no prior information regarding their positions. Therefore, the initial stages of image processing must often proceed bottom-up without use of knowledge regarding particular objects. However, at some point it is necessary to use these features derived from the image to access particular object models for final matching and verification. This requires an indexing mechanism that can associate low-level features with the object models that are most likely to be present given those features. This indexing is a critical component of the system, since its performance determines the amount of search that must

be performed during recognition. The final step of precise viewpoint determination and verification has already been discussed above.

It is unlikely that any image feature will always result from only one possible object model. Therefore, the association between features and models must be probabilistic. At runtime, it is important to rank the hypothesized objects in decreasing order of their probability, since the amount of search required is determined by the number of objects that must be considered prior to a correct interpretation. Therefore, our goal is to find a general method for predicting the probability of each object being present given particular image features. The most straightforward and accurate method for determining these probabilities is to simply measure the probabilities from a sample of images and to continuously improve their accuracy as more instances of recognition are performed.

If we treat each image feature in isolation and ignore the effects of contextual information, then the probabilities that need to be learned are simply $P(m|f)$, the probability that model m is present at this location given that feature f has been found. However, we would also like to be able to combine the evidence from a number of different features and incorporate contextual information that may indicate the presence or absence of one object given that another object has been identified. This can be accomplished through the use of Bayes's theorem:

$$P(m|f) = \frac{P(f|m)P(m)}{P(f)} \qquad (1)$$

This incorporates the prior probability for the presence of the model, $P(m)$. Charniak [4] has suggested that this formula can be used to combine evidence from different features by remembering an updating factor, $I(m|f)$, relating each feature and model:

$$I(m|f) = \frac{P(f|m)}{P(f)}$$

From equation (1), this updating factor is multiplied by the prior probability of the model to get the updated conditional probability following detection of a feature. This process can be repeated for additional features using the updated model probability as the new prior probability, as long as the following independence assumptions are made for each pair of features, f and g:

$$P(f|g) = P(f) \qquad (2)$$
$$P(f|g, m) = P(f|m) \qquad (3)$$

Unfortunately, assumption (2) states implausibly that the features are independent of one another. This contradicts the possibility that they could both be associated with the same model, which was the original purpose for combining them in the first place. Charniak argues that this contradiction is not too important, since any error will affect all models by the same proportion and therefore leave the final probability rankings undisturbed. However, this would then require that the probability for every model be updated with the identification of each image feature, rather than just those models that are known to be related to the feature. In addition, it means that the numbers loose their interpretation as probabilities, and in fact will often have values larger than 1.

Fortunately, it is possible to eliminate independence assumption (2) and retain the use of explicit probabilities. The problem with the standard formulation of Bayes's equation, as in (1), is that the prior probability that a particular feature is present, $P(f)$, is not independent of the prior probability that a related model is present, $P(m)$. Since the model can give rise to the feature, any change in the probability that the model is present will also change the probability that the feature is present. We need to separate the probability of the feature arising from the model from the other ways in which the feature can arise. If we let $\overline{m}$ be the absence of model m, then,

$$
\begin{aligned}
P(f) &= P(f|m)P(m) + P(f|\overline{m})P(\overline{m}) \\
&= P(f|m)P(m) + P(f|\overline{m})(1 - P(m)) \quad (4)
\end{aligned}
$$

Substituting (4) into (1), we get

$$
P(m|f) = \frac{P(f|m)P(m)}{P(f|m)P(m) + P(f|\overline{m})(1 - P(m))} \quad (5)
$$

Note that this formulation requires that we keep track of two numbers for each feature-model pair, $P(f|m)$ and $P(f|\overline{m})$, and that both of these numbers can reasonably be assumed to be independent of $P(m)$. This updating formula never produces probability values greater than 1. In order to combine evidence from multiple features, the updating can simply be applied in sequence to each feature, with the updated value from one feature serving as the prior model probability for the next feature. This sequential updating is independent of the order of updating and makes the following two independence assumptions:

$$
P(f|g, m) = P(f|m)
$$
$$
P(f|g, \overline{m}) = P(f|\overline{m})
$$

These simply say that the two features are independent sources of evidence for the particular model, and are much weaker conditions than assumption (2).

How would these updating methods be applied in practice? A computer vision system would simply keep track of the number of times a particular low-level feature occurs in the image, the number of times it occurs as part of each recognized object, and the number of times that the object is recognized. As the vision system gains experience with large number of images, the resulting probabilities would increase in accuracy leading to decreased search times during recognition. Initially, the system may require a few particular features from high quality images in order to recognize the object. However, as more features are found in images of the object and their reliability is assessed, the system will be able to function with images taken under a wider range of conditions and with greater amounts of partial occlusion. If a low-level component of the system is improved, then any new features could be automatically incorporated to the extent that they are useful. There are, of course, many ways in which such a learning method can be modified to include short versus long-term memory, decay of old memories, etc., but the basic system outlined above is sufficient for most practical robotics applications. We are in the process of incorporating these learning methods in the SCERPO vision system.

Conclusions

Why has it taken so long to develop general-purpose vision systems? A major difficulty has been in developing standards for the interchange of vision system components. In the past, each research site has spent a large proportion of its effort on implementing basic tools and components that have already been developed elsewhere but cannot be reused due to a lack of standardization and documentation. This encourages a more theoretical approach to many problems in which time-consuming implementation of functioning systems is avoided. The only solution will be to define standard interfaces between vision system components and to reward the development of interchangeable modules. This provides another argument in support of a general probabilistic framework for relating image features to object models. Such a framework would allow new forms of bottom-up processing, such as image groupings, texture analysis, or shading information to be easily incorporated into an existing model-based vision system.

References

[1] Ballard, Dana H., "Generalizing the Hough transform to detect arbitrary shapes," *Pattern Recognition,* **13** (1981), 111-122.

[2] Binford, Thomas O., "Visual perception by computer," *IEEE Systems Science and Cybernetics Conference,* Miami (1971).

[3] Bolles, R.C., P. Horaud, and M.J. Hannah, "3DPO: A three-dimensional part orientation system," *Proc. of 8th International Joint Conf. on Artificial Intelligence* (Karlsruhe, West Germany, 1983), 1116-1120.

[4] Charniak, Eugene, "The Bayesian basis of common sense medical diagnosis," *Proceedings of AAAI-83* (Washington, D.C., August, 1983), 70-73.

[5] Duda, R.O. and P.E. Hart, "Use of the Hough transformation to detect lines and curves in pictures," *Communications of ACM,* **15,** 1 (1972), 11-15.

[6] Faugeras, O.D., "New steps toward a flexible 3-D vision system for robotics," *Proc. of 7th International Conference on Pattern Recognition* (Montreal, 1984), 796-805.

[7] Goad, Chris, "Special purpose automatic programming for 3D model-based vision," *Proceedings ARPA Image Understanding Workshop,* Arlington, Virginia (1983), 94-104. Also in *From Pixels to Predicates,* Alex Pentland (ed.), (Ablex Publishing Co., 1986), 371-391.

[8] Grimson, Eric, and Thomás Lozano-Pérez, "Model-based recognition and localization from sparse range or tactile data," *Int. Journal of Robotics Research,* **3** (1984), 3-35.

[9] Kent, E., M. Shneier, and R. Lumia, "PIPE (Pipelined Image Processing Engine)" *Journal of Parallel and Distributed Computing,* **2** (1985), 50-78.

[10] Lowe, David G. and Thomas O. Binford, "Perceptual organization as a basis for visual recognition," *Proceedings of AAAI-83* (Washington, D.C., August 1983), 255-260.

[11] Lowe, David G., *Perceptual Organization and Visual Recognition* (Boston, Mass: Kluwer Academic Publishers, 1985).

[12] Lowe, David G., "Three-dimensional object recognition from single two-dimensional images," *Artificial Intelligence,* **31,** 3 (March 1987), pp. 355-395.

[13] Lowe, David G., "The viewpoint consistency constraint," *International Journal of Computer Vision,* **1,** 1 (1987), 57-72.

[14] Moribe, H., *et al.,* "Image preprocessor of model-based vision system for assembly robots," *Proc. 1987 IEEE Int. Conf. on Robotics and Automation,* Raleigh, North Carolina (April 1987), 366-371.

[15] Pentland, Alex P., "Perceptual organization and the representation of natural form," *Artificial Intelligence,* **28,** 3 (1986), 293-331.

[16] Porrill, J., S.B. Pollard, T.P. Pridmore, J.B. Bowen, J.E.W. Mayhew, and J.P. Frisby, "TINA: The Sheffield AIVRU vision system," submitted to *IJCAI-87,* Milano, Italy (August 1987).

[17] Witkin, Andrew P. and Jay M. Tenenbaum, "On the role of structure in vision," in *Human and Machine Vision,* Beck, Hope & Rosenfeld, Eds. (New York: Academic Press, 1983), 481-543.

[18] Zucker, Steven W., "Computational and psychophysical experiments in grouping: Early orientation selection," in *Human and Machine Vision,* Beck, Hope & Rosenfeld, Eds. (New York: Academic Press, 1983), 545-567.

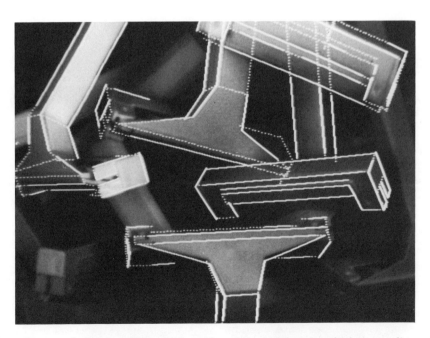

Figure 3. This photograph illustrates the final results of recognition, in which some disposable razors in a jumbled heap have been identified. The model is shown projected onto the original image from the final calculated viewpoints, with solid lines indicating a match to a corresponding image edge and dotted lines elsewhere.

Components of a Stereo Vision System

S B Pollard, J Porrill, T P Pridmore, J E W Mayhew, J P Frisby.

AI Vision Research Unit
Sheffield University
Western Bank
Sheffield S10 2TN
England
Tel (0742) 768555

We describe components of the Sheffield AIVRU 3D vision system. The system currently supports model based object recognition and location; its potential for robotics applications is demonstrated by its guidance of a UMI robot arm in a pick and place task. The system comprises:

1) The recovery of a sparse depth map using edge based passive stereo triangulation.

2) The grouping, description and segmentation of edge segments to recover a 3D representation of the scene geometry in terms of straight lines and circular arcs.

3) The statistical combination of 3D descriptions for the purpose of object model creation from multiple stereo views, and the propagation of constraints for within view refinement.

4) The matching of 3D wireframe object models to 3D scene descriptions, to recover an initial estimate of their position and orientation.

1. Introduction

Edge based binocular stereo is able to provide accurate depth data provided that the camera geometry is understood. Our current stereo algorithm, PMF (Pollard et al 1985), was designed to be largely independent of the structure of the scene. It employs the assumption that the world projects with moderate disparity gradient almost everywhere. However, in common with many other stereo algorithms, the disparity/depth data produced by PMF is largely unstructured. This paper discusses some aspects of current research at the AI Vision Research Unit concerned with the extraction and combination of geometrical information from such stereo data.

Three components of a proposed, and partially completed, vision system (Porrill et al. 1987) are discussed. These are geometrical description, scene/model matching and statistical combination. Whilst not providing complete scene descriptions (topological information being most notable by its absence) these form a substantial system in themselves which has proven to be of considerable practical potential. The system has been used, for example, to combine views of a scene to incrementally model the environment and determine position in a world coordinate frame. This has obvious application to autonomous navigation. In a similar fashion a visual model description can be compiled by simply looking at an object from a sufficient number of views. Once complete, such *models* can be matched in cluttered scenes by the same matching algorithm employed in their construction. We have coupled these visual competences with a robot arm and have been successful in picking a modelled object from a cluttered scene.

2. Low Level Processing

Early descriptions are currently recovered via edge based stereo triangulation. Edges are obtained from a single high frequency edge operator, we employ our own implementation of Canny's operator (1983) which also incorporates sub pixel acuity (obtained by quadratic interpolation of the peak). Edge data is transformed to a parallel camera geometry that is equivalent to the original camera arrangement.

The data structure resulting from the PMF stereo algorithm is essentially the edge segments of the [transformed] left image with matched segments appended with the computed disparity value. These are grouped into ordered strings corresponding to viewed curves by CONNECT (Pridmore et al 1985), a rule-based system which uses local topological and weak geometrical information to assign binary connections between data points. An initial grouping phase captures obvious, and notes potential, connectivities. The latter are either rejected or instantiated by subsequent application of the rulebase. On termination CONNECT produces a graph-like structure in which point strings join nodes marking junctions and line ends.

3. Stereo Geometry for the case of Parallel Cameras

We will use the notation (X_L, Y) for coordinates in the left image, and (X_R, Y) for coordinates of the matched point in the right image. The quantity $\Delta = X_L - X_R$ is the stereo disparity. The three dimensional space of points (X_L, X_R, Y) will be referred to as *disparity space*. (Note that this term usually refers to (X_L, Y, Δ) space). Choose the world coordinate system (x, y, z) to have its origin at the focus of the left camera and z-axis along the camera axis (this introduces an asymmetry between left and right cameras but it can be convenient to have a 'base' camera). If I is the inter-camera distance and f the common camera focal length, then points (x, y, z) in the world are related to points (X_L, X_R, Y) in disparity space by the formulae

$$X_L = \frac{fx}{z}$$

$$X_R = \frac{f(x - I)}{z}$$

$$Y = \frac{fy}{z}$$

Now suppose we have a vector $\mathbf{V} = \vec{PQ}$ joining the point P to the point Q in disparity space. We can find the associated vector $\mathbf{v}$ in the world by using the above equations to project the two points P and Q into the world to p and q and setting $\mathbf{v} = \vec{pq}$. For infinitesimal vectors (and, since the mapping projects straight lines to straight lines, for finite vectors of which only the direction and not the magnitude is of interest) this can be replaced by a linear mapping whose matrix is the Jacobian J of the stereo transformation above,

$$\begin{bmatrix} v_x \\ v_y \\ v_z \end{bmatrix} = J(X_L, X_R, Y) \begin{bmatrix} v_{X_L} \\ v_{X_R} \\ v_Y \end{bmatrix}.$$

The inverse transform (*world vector*) → (*disparity vector*) is accomplished by the inverse linear mapping J^{-1}. Hence, for example, if a line through the point $\mathbf{P}$ has direction $\mathbf{v}$ in disparity space then its direction in the world is given by the vector $\mathbf{v} = J(\mathbf{P})\mathbf{V}$. It must be remembered that projection into the world does not preserve distance, so that even though $\mathbf{V}$ may be a unit vector $\mathbf{v}$ will generally not be.

Care must be taken when transforming normal vectors (to planes and other surfaces). Though it is often customary to call them vectors they are in fact *covectors*, or *1–forms*. Such objects do not follow the above transformation law. A 1-form is defined by its scalar product with other vectors; for example the normal to a plane is defined by the fact that its scalar product with vectors in the plane is zero. The requirement that these scalar products be invariant under the mapping leads directly to the transformation law for 1-forms. In general, the transformation between a 1-form N in disparity space and **n** in the world is done according to the formulae

$$\mathbf{n} = (J^{-1})^T N \qquad N = J^T \mathbf{n}$$

(where J^T is the transpose of J). The normal vector to a plane in disparity space is therefore transformed into the world by the transpose of the inverse Jacobian, and not by the Jacobian itself as ordinary vectors are. Again it should be remembered that a unit normal will not remain unit under transformations of this kind.

4. Fitting Curves in Disparity Space

On the projection of an image point into the world errors in its disparity produce, in general, much larger errors in depth than similar errors in its image coordinates produce in its lateral position in space. If the closeness of this point to some hypothesised structure is to be measured in the world and compared with some single threshold, then, if this threshold is to allow typical errors in depth, it will allow quite unacceptable errors in lateral position; if, conversely, it is small enough to allow only reasonable errors in lateral position, it will be far too tight for the accuracy of our depth data.

We could choose to do a simple scaling of the depth dimension in the measurement of errors, but this scaling depends on scene position. In fact a correct error measure would be both anisotropic and inhomogeneous. We adopt the more rigorous, and simplifying, approach of testing closeness of fit directly in disparity space. Here the errors in horizontal position in the two images and the error in vertical position for a matched point are all generated by the similar noise processes. A simple combination of the individual errors (dX_L, dX_R, dY) into a single Euclidean distance measure dS of the form

$$dS^2 = dX_L^2 + dX_R^2 + dY^2$$

is therefore acceptable.

The drawback to fitting in disparity space is that some structures in the world, such as circles, have a less simple description there. This problem might eventually guide the choice of higher order descriptive structures; for example, cubic splines are not invariant under projectivities, but rational splines are, and so might be preferred for least squares fitting to disparity data.

4.1. Fitting Points, Planes and Lines: Orthogonal Regression

The transformation between disparity and world space is projective, and therefore preserves lines and planes. Hence if a point string is believed to be either planar or straight we can test this hypothesis directly in disparity space.

It is relatively simple to find the best fit line or plane to a given set of points (Pearson 1901). Since the technique is generally applicable, we will not make any particular reference to disparity space, and in the rest of this section points, vectors *etc.* will be denoted by lower case letters; it should however be remembered that our application of these results *is* in disparity space.

Given N points x_i in space we will find the least squares best fit plane, line, or point, where the distance of x_i from the structure to be fitted is measured by the perpendicular distance to that structure, the residual of this best fit is the standard error measure we need. This technique is sometimes called orthogonal regression, to distinguish it from the usual linear regression, where the best fitting plane is found by minimising the sum-square error in a particular coordinate direction, which would not be appropriate here.

The best fit plane, line, and point are found simultaneously, each with an associated sum square residual $\rho_{point}^2, \rho_{line}^2, \rho_{plane}^2$ which is an approximately χ^2 variable on $N-3, 2(N-2), 3(N-1)$ degrees of freedom

respectively when the errors are normally distributed. If a curve contains horizontal (which are generally difficult to stereo match reliably) or unmatched segments the best fit line is projected into the left image and the squared distance in the image plane of each such point from the line added to the sum square error, which gains one degree of freedom for each such point. The maximum likelihood test for the point string to form a structure of a given type is then

$$\frac{\rho_{structure}^2}{\text{degrees of freedom}} < \text{threshold}$$

The above residuals, related by the expression $\rho_{point}^2 < \rho_{line}^2 < \rho_{plane}^2$, are examined in decreasing order of magnitude, the first to fall below threshold being taken as representative of the true description. Should all the residuals be above threshold, a default space curve tag is assigned.

4.2. Fitting Circles

After regression curves identified as planar are passed to a three point circle fitting routine. The CONNECT string is first projected onto the best fit plane down lines of sight, assigning a depth estimate to each data point. Several point triples are then selected and the residuals (measured in disparity space) associated with arcs through them computed. The description with the lowest error is considered further. If this circle's residual is below threshold it is accepted, if it is above an upper threshold the fit is abandoned, otherwise an optimal (minimal residual) arc in the best fit plane is found. If this is also supra-threshold the best fit plane becomes the primary representation.

5. GDB: The Geometrical Descriptive Base.

The GDB is obtained by the Geometric Descriptive Filter (GDF; see Pridmore et al 1987) a program that recursively describes and segments (if descriptions prove inadequate) CONNECT strings. The result is a 3D (and 2D where 3D descriptions are not possible) description of the scene with respect to a single image (usually the left). It consists primarily of straight line and circular arc descriptors. Where such descriptions are not possible above a threshold resolution the sections of the connect string are labeled either planar or space. An example of the geometry that can be recovered is given in figure 1 for a pseudo industrial scene typical of those amenable to characterisation in such a fashion.

6. Straight Line Description and Error Estimation

Straight line segments are represented (in an overdetermined fashion) by the triple (e_1, e_2, v_0), that is, their two end points e_1 and e_2 and the direction vector between them v_0. The centroid of a line (its midpoint $(e_1 + e_2)/2$) is denoted **c**. Where the actual physical occupancy of a line is not important it is sometimes helpful to represent it by the vector pair (p_0, v_0) where p_0 is the position of a point on the line. We extend the direction vector v_0 to an orthonormal basis (v_0, v_1, v_2) and add it to our description of the line in the GDB, this then forms an intrinsic reference frame which will be carried with the line throughout its history.

Any nearby line can be described by a position vector and a direction vector

$$\mathbf{p} = p_0 + p_1 v_1 + p_2 v_2$$

$$\mathbf{v} = v_0 + v_1 v_1 + v_2 v_2$$

(note that **v** is unit to first order) and we use $\mathbf{x} = (p_1, p_2, v_1, v_2)^t$ as local coordinates on the line manifold.

Other possible measurements of the position of the line are randomly distributed close to the original measurement. To describe the error in the measurement we need only describe the error distribution of the perturbation 4-vector **x**. We make the usual assumption that the measurement process is adequately described by the measurement bias (expected error)

$$E[\mathbf{x}] = \hat{\mathbf{x}}$$

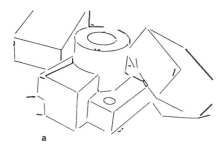

a

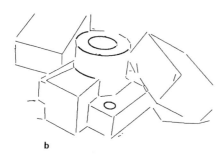

b

Figure 1

In (a) both 2 and 3 dimensional descriptions, with respect to the left hand image, are shown. Primitives of the GDB that are flagged as 2D, as a result of the fact that no depth data has been recovered for them by the stereo algorithm (perhaps as a result occlusion), are displayed bold. It is important to note that these exist only as descriptions in the image plane and not as descriptions in the world. In (b) again both 2 and 3 dimensional data are shown, but on this occasion circular sections (in three dimensions and not only in the image plane) of the GDB are the ones that have been highlighted by displaying them bold. Before segmentation each edge list is smoothed either by diffusion or by the approximately equivalent gaussian (sigma 2.5).

and the 4×4 measurement covariance matrix s

$$S = E[(\mathbf{x} - \hat{\mathbf{x}})(\mathbf{x} - \hat{\mathbf{x}})^t] = E[\mathbf{x}\, \mathbf{x}^t] - \hat{\mathbf{x}}\hat{\mathbf{x}}^t$$

This would be the case if we were sampling $\mathbf{x}$ from a normal distribution

$$p(\mathbf{x}) = \frac{1}{(2\pi)^2 \det(s)} \exp(-\frac{1}{2}(\mathbf{x}-\hat{\mathbf{x}})^t\, S^{-1}\, (\mathbf{x}-\hat{\mathbf{x}}))$$

in this case, if the mean and variance of the distribution are small, we will say that the line measurement process is approximately normal. We assume the measurement process is not biased and set $\hat{\mathbf{x}} = 0$. This leaves the task of determining s from the nature of the measurement process.

If points are assumed to be matched without error between left and right images, and the imaging process is assumed to produce equal uncorrelated errors of variance σ^2 in the three image coordinates (X_L, X_R, Y). fitting by orthogonal regression is optimal and produces a position error in the centroid of the fitted line of variance σ^2/n and an angular error of variance $12\sigma^2/nl^2$ where l is the length of the line in disparity space and these two errors are uncorrelated (these are the errors *in disparity space*). In terms of local line coordinates in disparity space the error covariance is thus

$$S_{\text{disp}} = \frac{\sigma^2}{n} \begin{bmatrix} I & 0 \\ 0 & \frac{12}{l^2}I \end{bmatrix}$$

where I is the 2×2 unit matrix. We must transform this result to world coordinates. The lateral position error coordinates transform by

$$p_i = \mathbf{v}_i{\cdot}(\mathbf{p} - \mathbf{p}_0)_{\text{world}} = \mathbf{v}_i{\cdot}J(\mathbf{p} - \mathbf{p}_0)_{\text{disparity}}$$

Since the Jacobian does not preserve the length of vectors the lateral direction error has an extra scalar factor

$$v_i = \mathbf{v}_i{\cdot}(\mathbf{v} - \mathbf{v}_0)_{\text{world}} = \frac{\mathbf{v}_i{\cdot}J(\mathbf{p} - \mathbf{p}_0)_{\text{disparity}}}{|J\mathbf{v}_0|}$$

We can thus calculate the error covariance of the description in the world to be

$$S = \begin{bmatrix} \Sigma & 0 \\ 0 & \frac{12}{l^2|J\mathbf{v}_0|^2}\Sigma \end{bmatrix}$$

where

$$\Sigma_{ij} = \frac{\sigma^2}{n}\mathbf{v}_i^t\, JJ^t\, \mathbf{v}_j \qquad i, j = 1, 2$$

where the base point $\mathbf{p}_0$ is taken as the projection of the disparity space centroid into the world. This covariance is adjoined to the description of the edge segment in the GDB.

The above idealisation is unrealistic for two main reasons. Firstly the stereo matching of *continuous* edges mixes the horizontal errors with the vertical errors; for edges with making angles θ with the horizontal which are close to zero depth values are highly inaccurate (when $\theta = 0$ matching is impossible). A crude way of compensating for this is to multiply J by a matrix producing an expansion factor of $1/\sin\theta$ in depth before using the above formulae. Secondly the points detected on continuous edges are not randomly scattered the edges, but wander slowly from one side to the other. This can be compensated for by replacing n by a smaller effective number of points on the line which counts these wanderings. Though crude, this model then captures most of the essential information about stereo errors.

7. SMM: The Scene and Model Matcher

Matches for two non-parallel line segments are sufficient to constrain all six degrees of freedom that constitute a putative transformation between a pair of scene descriptions (Faugeras *et al* 1984). Once a transformation is hypothesised, rigidity provides a powerful constraint upon other consistent matches (subject to tolerance errors). Rigidity can be exploited more cheaply (though less strongly) if expressed in terms of the consistency in a number of pairwise relationships (Grimson and Lozano-Perez 1984). Each can be stored as a range of values in look up tables, with the requirement that these ranges overlap between all pairs of consistent matches. If each pair of lines has allowable errors $|\epsilon_1|{<}\alpha_1$ and $|\epsilon_2|{<}\alpha_2$ on the location of their centroid and solid half angles ϕ_1 and ϕ_2 on their direction vector it is possible to derive suitable ranges for each of the chosen pairwise relationships (assuming that components add in a simple fashion). We adopt just three which are:

(i)   orientation differences, given by $\theta = \cos^{-1}(\mathbf{v}_{0_1}{\cdot}\mathbf{v}_{0_2})$; stored as the interval $[\max(\theta{-}\phi_1{-}\phi_2,0), \min(\theta{+}\phi_1{+}\phi_2,\pi)]$.

(ii) minimum separations between (extended) lines. That is $m = (\mathbf{c}_2{-}\mathbf{c}_1){\cdot}\mathbf{u}$; the component of the difference between the lines in the direction $\mathbf{u}$ which is normal to each. However if the lines are close to parallel it is more sensible to simply measure the perpendicular distance between the lines $m = |(\mathbf{c}_2{-}\mathbf{c}_1){-}((\mathbf{c}_2{-}\mathbf{c}_1){\cdot}\mathbf{v}_{0_1})\mathbf{v}_{0_1}|$. Stored as the interval

$$m \pm (\alpha_1 + \alpha_2 + l_1|\tan\phi_1| + l_2|\tan\phi_2|)$$

where l_i is the distance from c_i to the point of minimum separation on line i (which is defined to be zero if the lines are parallel).

(iii) distance to the beginning and end of each physical line with respect to the point of minimum separation and in the direction of the line. This relationship is only applicable for non-parallel lines. The vector between the points of closest approach is given by $\mathbf{m} = ((\mathbf{c}_2{-}\mathbf{c}_1){\cdot}\mathbf{u})\mathbf{u}$. Adding $\mathbf{m}$ to $\mathbf{c}_2$ gives $\mathbf{c}'_2$, where lines $(\mathbf{v}_{0_1},\mathbf{c}_1)$ and $(\mathbf{v}_{0_2},\mathbf{c}'_2)$ are coplanar and meet at the point of closest approach on $(\mathbf{v}_{0_1},\mathbf{c}_1)$. The signed distance to that point from $\mathbf{c}_1$ in the direction $\mathbf{v}_{0_1}$ is given by $l_1 = ((\mathbf{v}_{0_2}{\times}\mathbf{v}_{0_1}){\cdot}(\mathbf{v}_{0_2}{\times}(\mathbf{c}'_2{-}\mathbf{c}_1)))/|\mathbf{v}_{0_2}{\times}\mathbf{v}_{0_1}|^2$.

Hence the distance from p_{1_1} and p_{1_2} to that point are given by $a_1 = l_1 + (c_1 - p_{1_1}).v_{0_1}$ and $b_1 = l_1 + (c_1 - p_{1_2}).v_{0_1}$ respectively. Similarly for distances to the point of closest separation on the other line $a_2 = l_2 + (c_2 - p_{2_1}).v_{0_2}$ and $b_2 = l_2 + (c_2 - p_{2_2}).v_{0_2}$. Stored as the approximate intervals

$$a_1 \pm (\alpha_1 + \alpha_2 + |l_2||\tan\phi_2|/\sin\theta)$$

$$b_1 \pm (\alpha_1 + \alpha_2 + |l_2||\tan\phi_2|/\sin\theta)$$

$$a_2 \pm (\alpha_1 + \alpha_2 + |l_1||\tan\phi_1|/\sin\theta)$$

$$b_2 \pm (\alpha_1 + \alpha_2 + |l_1||\tan\phi_1|/\sin\theta)$$

Potential matches for each pair of descriptive elements from one scene description can be checked for geometrical consistency in the other. Rigidity implies that each of the pairwise relationships will be preserved between scene descriptions, hence any measured discrepancies must lie within a range predicted by the magnitude of allowable errors. Furthermore a pair of consistent non-parallel matches provides a powerful constraint upon the remaining matches. Hence they can be thought to represent, implicitly and weakly, a global transformation. The representation is weak because it is possible, on occasion, for matches that are not consistent with a single global transformation to satisfy the pairwise relationships. In practice such problems are not major. Furthermore if the basis of the implicit transforms is raised from a pair to a triple, quadruple or even a quintuple of matches, such inconsistencies are far less likely (additionally the margin of allowable error on each new match will be reduced).

7.1. Feature Focus

Our current approach to matching is to apply heuristics similar to those of feature focus (Bolles *et al* 1983) in order to avoid unbounded search. The strategy is to concentrate initial attention upon a number of salient features. Only matches associated with these features are subsequently entitled to *grow* hypothetical transformations. Currently processing terminates only after all focus features have been considered. The feature focus strategy adopted here differs from those considered previously as familiarity with the scene is not assumed. As a result focus features and matching strategies are not an integral component of our scene description: they must be generated at run time.

Focus features are identified in a single scene description. Currently they are chosen simply on the basis of their length, a property associated with salience. Some effort is expended to ensure that all regions of the scene are represented by chosen features, ie a feature is identified as a focus if their are not more than a certain number of longer features within a predetermined radius of it. The details of the matching algorithm are given in Pollard *et al* (1987).

An example of the performance of SMM is given in figure 2. If after matching and transformation those lines that are actually matched are replaced by their union and those that are unmatched left alone it is possible to build a more complete description of the object/scene. Furthermore descriptive primitives (such as circles) that are not currently part of the matching process itself can also be combined on the basis of their physical location. It is important to note that a circle in one scene description may be represented as a number of straight lines in the other. Once obtained this more complete scene description can be matched to yet more GDB data. This process has been repeated 8 times for the description shown in figure 3a. This description contains a large quantity of noisy data that appeared in one or other view. A cleaner model can be obtained by filtering out primitives that have never been matched (see figure 3b). In each application of the matcher statistics similar to those of the initial match were obtained. Notice that few of the occluding contours that arise from the cylinder are ever matched.

8. Statistical Combination of Multiple Stereo Views

The combination and refinement of stereo data is undertaken by the GEOMSTAT modules, which use the methods of generalised (singular covariance) Gauss-Markov estimation implemented as a recursive

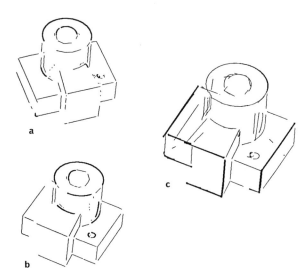

Figure 2

Figures (a) and (b) show GDB data extracted from two views of a test object (here obtained from stereograms produced by a version of the IBM WINSOM CSG body modeler). Each description consists of approximately 50 above-threshold GDB line primitives. The ten focus features chosen in view (a) obtained a total of 98 potential matches in view (b). The best consistent transformation included 9 matched lines. The best rigid rotation and translation (in that order) that takes view (a) to view (b) is computed by the least squares method discussed by Faugeras *et al* (1984) in which rotations are represented as quaternions (though for simplicity the optimal rotation is recovered before translation). In figure (c) view (a) is transformed into view (b) (the error in the computed rotation is 0.7 degrees) and matching lines are shown bold, the vast majority of the unmatched lines are not visible in both views (often as a result of noise).

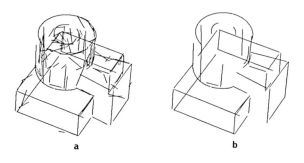

Figure 3

(a) and (b) show noisy and clean *visual* models respectively.

filter. This is similar to techniques described by Durrant-Whyte (1985) and Faugeras (1986).

The basic measurement primitives returned by the AIVRU vision system are the straight edge segments and circular arcs found in the scene. The error statistics for straight lines have already been described in §6. To describe a point measurement we choose an arbitrary basis (v_0, v_1, v_2). A general perturbation of a point r_0 can then be written as

$$r = r_0 + r_0 v_0 + r_1 v_1 + r_2 v_2$$

and the point measurement is described by the structure

$$(r_0, v_0, v_1, v_2, \mathfrak{L}, \hat{S})$$

where $\hat{x}$ and S are the mean and covariance of the perturbation vector $\mathbf{x} = (r_0, r_1, r_2)^t$.

A plane is completely described by a point $\mathbf{p}_0$ on it and its normal $\mathbf{v}_0$. Again we extend the basis and describe nearby planes $(\mathbf{p}, \mathbf{v})$ by $\mathbf{x} = (p_0, v_1, v_2)^t$ where

$$\mathbf{p} = \mathbf{p}_0 + p_0 \mathbf{v}_0$$

$$\mathbf{v} = \mathbf{v}_0 + v_1 \mathbf{v}_1 + v_2 \mathbf{v}_2$$

Finally consider the case of a small rigid motion, this might represent the small motion of an object between two views. A convenient description is by a infinitesimal rotation ω and translation τ

$$\mathbf{p}' = \mathbf{p} + \omega \times \mathbf{p} + \tau$$

These vectors can be expressed with respect to any basis $(\mathbf{v}_0, \mathbf{v}_1, \mathbf{v}_2)$

$$\omega = \omega_i \mathbf{v}_i \qquad \tau = \tau_i \mathbf{v}_i$$

(summation convention).

In general we assume that measurement primitives in three dimensions have a convenient (but probably underdetermined or constrained) description as an object ξ_0 in $\mathbf{R}^n$. We attach a frame $B = (\mathbf{v}_0, \mathbf{v}_1, \mathbf{v}_2)$ to this primitive and assume that small perturbations can be described adequately and intrinsically by a formula of the form

$$\xi = \xi_0 + F(B)\mathbf{x} + O(|\mathbf{x}|^2)$$

where $\mathbf{x} \in \mathbf{R}^m$ and $F(B)$ is an $n \times m$ matrix. A measurement of the primitive is then described by the structure

$$(\xi_0, \mathbf{v}_0, \mathbf{v}_1, \mathbf{v}_2, \hat{x}, S)$$

where

$$\hat{x} = E[\mathbf{x}] \qquad S = \text{Cov}[\mathbf{x}]$$

A composite object has a description as a list of primitives

$$\Xi = (\xi_1, \xi_2, \cdots, \xi_N)$$

with attached frames

$$B = (B_1, B_2, \cdots, B_N)$$

Any small deformation of the object can be described by a list of the perturbation vectors of each constituent relative to these frames

$$\mathbf{X} = (\mathbf{x}_1, \mathbf{x}_2, \cdots, \mathbf{x}_N)^t$$

A measurement of the composite object is completely described by the expected value $\hat{x}$ and covariance $\hat{s}$ of this 'state vector'. In the case when all the constituents of the object have been independently measured the matrix $\hat{s}$ will have block diagonal form with the covariances of the individual measurements down the diagonal. In general this will not be the case since measurements, though independent in the sensor frame, will be correlated in the world through sensor calibration error. For example the error in position of an edge in a stereo scene will not in general be affected by the presence of a second edge in the scene but any stereo rig miscalibration will affect both their positions. We will show later how the required correlations in $\hat{s}$ can be set up.

8.1. Generalised Gauss-Markov Estimation Simplified

We will deal with the case where we have sufficient measurements of Ξ to determine it completely in the absence of errors, and where we can determine a good estimate Ξ_0 from a subset of these measurements. Our aim will be to calculate the optimal estimate of the state vector $\mathbf{X}$ representing the correction required.

At any stage in the calculation we can update the linearisation point Ξ_0 by making the corrections found so far, and relinearising about the new point. The new estimated correction will be $\hat{x} = 0$ and the estimated covariance $\hat{s}$ will be unchanged by the re-linearisation.

Given a good estimate Ξ_0 of the set of primitives of interest we are interested in using our measurement devices to find the (assumed small) correction required, described by the state vector $\mathbf{X} \in \mathbf{R}^n$. Suppose previous measurements have told us that

$$E[\mathbf{X}] = \hat{x} \qquad \text{Cov}[\mathbf{X}] = \hat{S}$$

If there are no previous measurements we can take $\hat{x} = 0$ and let $\hat{S}$ be a large multiple of the unit matrix. An elegant description of the generalised (singular covariance) Gauss-Markov theory as an application of the Moore-Penrose pseudo-inverse can be found in Albert (1972). A more conventional treatment of the statistics of linear models can be found in Morrison (1976).

In order to simplify the structure of the system we have implemented our testbed programs in terms of a very simple but elegant result from Gauss-Markov theory, the optimal update rule after the imposition of a single scalar constraint. It can be shown that this is sufficient to implement any measurement or constraint equation.

Suppose we are given a single further piece of information about $\mathbf{x}$: it satisfies an exact linear constraint

$$z + \mathbf{h}^t \mathbf{X} = 0$$

where z and $\mathbf{h}$ are known. The optimal update rule is

$$\hat{S}' = \hat{S} - \frac{(\hat{S}\mathbf{h})(\hat{S}\mathbf{h})^t}{\mathbf{h}^t \hat{S} \mathbf{h}}$$

$$\mathbf{k} = \frac{\hat{S}\mathbf{h}}{\mathbf{h}^t \hat{S} \mathbf{h}}$$

$$\hat{\mathbf{X}}' = \hat{\mathbf{X}} + \mathbf{k}(z + \mathbf{h}^t \mathbf{X})$$

(note that the correction is described by an 'innovation' term proportional to the error of the old estimate, this is a simple Kalman filter). The increase in residual (weighted mean square error) is

$$\varepsilon' = \varepsilon + \frac{(z + \mathbf{h}^t \mathbf{X})^2}{\mathbf{h}^t \hat{S} \mathbf{h}}$$

If we wanted to test the plausibility of the constraint given the previous information before imposing it then maximum likelihood test treats $\varepsilon' - \varepsilon$ as χ^2 on one degree of freedom. We can impose as many of constraints as we like as long as they are independent. The method only guarantees the satisfaction of constraints to linearised order.

8.2. Applying Geometrical Constraints

The description of the scene by the GDB is an almost totally unstructured. We propose to use simple wireframe completion heuristics to give some geometrical and topological rigidity to the description. It will include such process as edge completion, hypothesising vertices and constructing missing edges. The measurement statistics for the GDB are utilised by a module GEOMSTAT which is to act as a knowledge source for the wireframe completion module. For example if two edges are hypothesised to meet at a vertex GEOMSTAT will be asked to test whether it is plausible that the lines intersect in space given the known errors of measurement. If the vertex is accepted then GEOMSTAT can correct the data optimally so that the intersection error is reduced to zero. The systematic imposition of such constraints is necessary not only to ensure geometric integrity of the wire frame but can also greatly improve accuracy since inaccurate depth measurements will be corrected by the necessity of agreeing with more accurate lateral ones.

Suppose the GDB of a scene is the list of lines $(\lambda_0, \lambda_0', \cdots)$. We amalgamate the perturbation vectors of each line into a state vector $\mathbf{X}$ describing the whole scene with error covariance s which is block diagonal

$$\mathbf{X} = \begin{bmatrix} \mathbf{x} \\ \mathbf{x}' \\ \cdot \end{bmatrix} \qquad S = \begin{bmatrix} s & 0 & \cdot \\ 0 & s' & \cdot \\ & \cdot & \cdot \end{bmatrix}$$

Suppose the first two lines in the GDB, $\lambda_0 = (\mathbf{p}_0, \mathbf{v}_0)$ and $\lambda_0' = (\mathbf{p}_0', \mathbf{v}_0')$, are hypothesised to intersect. If this were true then their true positions $\lambda = (\mathbf{p}, \mathbf{v})$ and $\lambda' = (\mathbf{p}', \mathbf{v}')$ would satisfy the constraint

$$(\mathbf{p} - \mathbf{p}') \cdot (\mathbf{v} \times \mathbf{v}') = 0$$

using the representation for lines and assuming the corrections required are small we can linearise the above expression to

$$(\mathbf{p}_0 - \mathbf{p}_0') \cdot (\mathbf{v}_0 \times \mathbf{v}_0') + p_1 \mathbf{v}_1 \cdot (\mathbf{v}_0 \times \mathbf{v}_0') + p_2 \mathbf{v}_2 \cdot (\mathbf{v}_0 \times \mathbf{v}_0')$$

$$- p_1' \mathbf{v}_1' \cdot (\mathbf{v}_0 \times \mathbf{v}_0') - p_2' \mathbf{v}_2' \cdot (\mathbf{v}_0 \times \mathbf{v}_0') + v_1 (\mathbf{p}_0 - \mathbf{p}_0') \cdot (\mathbf{v}_1 \times \mathbf{v}_0')$$

$$+ v_2 (\mathbf{p}_0 - \mathbf{p}_0') \cdot (\mathbf{v}_2 \times \mathbf{v}_0') + v_1' (\mathbf{p}_0 - \mathbf{p}_0') \cdot (\mathbf{v}_0 \times \mathbf{v}_1') + v_2' (\mathbf{p}_0 - \mathbf{p}_0') \cdot (\mathbf{v}_0 \times \mathbf{v}_2') = 0$$

This is a linear constraint on the perturbation vector $\mathbf{x}$ of the form

$$z + \mathbf{h}^t \mathbf{x} = 0$$

where

$$z = (\mathbf{p}_0 - \mathbf{p}_0') \cdot (\mathbf{v}_0 \times \mathbf{v}_0')$$

and

$$\mathbf{h} = \begin{bmatrix} \mathbf{v}_1 \cdot (\mathbf{v}_0 \times \mathbf{v}_0') \\ \mathbf{v}_2 \cdot (\mathbf{v}_0 \times \mathbf{v}_0') \\ (\mathbf{p}_0 - \mathbf{p}_0') \cdot (\mathbf{v}_1 \times \mathbf{v}_0') \\ (\mathbf{p}_0 - \mathbf{p}_0') \cdot (\mathbf{v}_2 \times \mathbf{v}_0') \\ -\mathbf{v}_1' \cdot (\mathbf{v}_0 \times \mathbf{v}_0') \\ -\mathbf{v}_2' \cdot (\mathbf{v}_0 \times \mathbf{v}_0') \\ (\mathbf{p}_0 - \mathbf{p}_0') \cdot (\mathbf{v}_0 \times \mathbf{v}_1') \\ (\mathbf{p}_0 - \mathbf{p}_0') \cdot (\mathbf{v}_0 \times \mathbf{v}_2') \\ 0 \\ 0 \end{bmatrix}$$

In the Appendix we give the formulation of other common constraints, orthogonality, parallelism, equality, as combinations of such scalar constraints.

8.3. Combining Multiple Stereo Views

Another basic application of GEOMSTAT is to the acquisition of accurate and complete wireframe models of objects or environments from multiple stereo views. Suppose we have built up a model with an associated covariance matrix from previous views, and now want to include a new view. The system uses the SMM matcher to relate the old model to the new view and calculate an approximate transformation (R_0, t_0) between the two. This is used to transform all the elements of the old model into the new frame. The transformation is non-optimal. The 'calibration error' between model and view (ω, τ) is adjoined to the state vector of the model with infinite covariance (in a mobile robot application we might use an estimate of the motion and its error given by position encoders).

For each pair of matched lines the new view of the line is adjoined to the state vector (or if a line in the model has no match in the new view an identical 'virtual' match is adjoined with infinite covariance). The constraint that they are related by the correction to the rigid motion (ω, τ) is then imposed (see Appendix). (this merges the two lines in the first case or performs the required transformation of the line and its statistics into the new frame in the second). The old version of the line is deleted from the state vector.

Figure 4a,b,c shows three details from views of the model. These have been combined optimally using the the above method program and certain obvious geometric constraints imposed using CLEANUP. The result is Figure 4d.

9. Bin Picking

It has been possible to link our visual system up to a UMI robot arm. Figure 5 shows the processing of a cluttered scene in the robots work space; it conists of three of the modeled test objects. The action of the robot, as it grasps an instance of the object, is shown in figure 6. Notice that the system is able to identify and accurately locate a modelled object in the cluttered scene. This information is used to compute a grasp plan for the known object (which is precompiled with respect to one corner of the object which acts as its coordinate frame).

10. Conclusions

We have shown the current ability of our system to recover geometrical information about a scene or object from stereo data. Furthermore we have shown how such information can be combined from multiple views and statistically improved. The possible utility of the system for model acquisition and matching has been illustrated in a cluttered scene object recognition task.

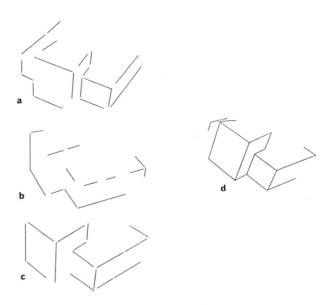

Figure 4

(a), (b) and (c) show details from real stereo views of our test object. These are matched by SMM, optimally combined, and have obvious geometrical constraints imposed (eg perpendicularity, intersection, parallelity etc) with the result given in (d).

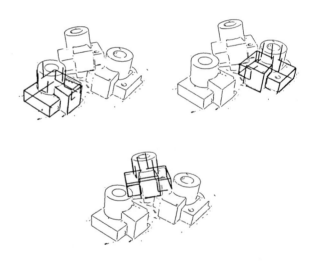

Figure 5

Model identification is depicted (in turn) for each instance of the modeled object in a cluttered scene (the model, after transformation, is shown bold).

Acknowledgements

We gratefully acknowledge Dr Chris Brown for his valuable technical assistance. This research was supported by SERC project grant no. GR/D/1679.6-IKBS/025 awarded under the Alvey programme. Stephen Pollard is an SERC IT Research Fellow.

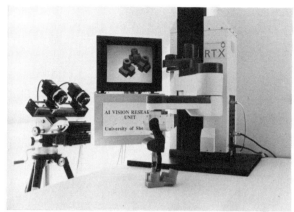

Figure 6

References

Albert, A., *Regression and the Moore-Penrose Pseudo-Inverse*, Academic Press, New York, 1972.

Ayache N, OD Faugeras, B Faverjon and G Toscani (1985) Matching depth maps obtained by passive stereo, Proc. Third Workshop on Computer Vision: Representation and Control, 197-204.

Bolles R.C, P. Horaud and M.J. Hannah (1983), 3DPO: A three dimensional part orientation system, *Proc. IJCAI 8*, Karlshrue, West Germany, 116-120.

Bowen J.B. and J.E.W. Mayhew (1986), Consistency maintenance in the REV graph environment, *Alvey Computer Vision and Image Interpretation Meeting*, University of Bristol, AIVRU Memo 20, and *Image and Vision Computing* (in press).

Burt P. and B. Julesz (1980), Modifications of the classical notion of panum's fusional area, *Perception* 9, 671-682.

Canny J.F. (1983), Finding edges and lines in images, MIT AI memo, 720, 1983.

DeKleer J. (1984), Choices without backtracking, *Proc, National Conference on Artificial Intelligence,*

Doyle J. (1979), A truth maintenance system, *Artificial Intelligence* 12, 231-272.

Durrant-Whyte H.F. (1985), Consistent integration and propagation of disparate sensor observations, *Thesis, University of Pennsylvania.*

Faugeras O.D, M. Hebert, J. Ponce and E. Pauchon (1984), Object representation, identification, and positioning from range data, *Proc. 1st Int. Symp. on Robotics Res*, J.M. Brady and R. Paul (eds), MIT Press, 425-446.

Faugeras O.D., N. Ayache and B. Faverjon (1986), Building visual maps by combining noisy stereo measurements, *IEEE Robotics conference*, San Francisco.

Grimson W.E.L. and T. Lozano-Perez (1984), Model based recognition from sparse range or tactile data, *Int. J. Robotics Res.* 3(3): 3-35.

Herman, M. (1985), Representation and incremental construction of a three-dimensional scene model, CMU-CS-85-103, Dept. of Computer Science, Carnegie-Mellon University.

Morrison, D. F. (1976) *Multivariate Statistical Methods*, McGraw-Hill.

Pearson K. (1901), On Lines and Planes of Closest Fit to Systems of Points in Space, *Phil. Mag. VI, 2*, pp 559, (1901).

Pollard S.B., J.E.W. Mayhew, and J.P. Frisby (1985), PMF: a stereo correspondence algorithm using a disparity gradient limit, *Perception*, 14, 449-470.

Pollard S.B, J. Porrill, J.E.W. Mayhew and J.P. Frisby (1985), Disparity gradient, Lipschitz continuity and computing binocular correspondences, *Proc. Third Int. Symp. on Robotics Res.*

Pollard S.B, J. Porrill, J.E.W. Mayhew and J.P. Frisby (1987), Matching geometrical descriptions in three-space, *Image and*

Porrill J., S.B. Pollard, T.P. Pridmore, J.B. Bowen, J.E.W. Mayhew, J.P. Frisby (1987) TINA: The Sheffield AIVRU vision system, submitted to IJCAI 9.

Pridmore T.P., J.E.W. Mayhew and J.P. Frisby (1985), Production rules for grouping edge-based disparity Data, *Alvey Vision Conference*, University of Sussex, and AIVRU memo 015, University of Sheffield.

Pridmore T.P., J. Porrill and J.E.W. Mayhew (1987), Segmentation and description of binocularly viewed contours, *Image and Vision Computing* Vol 5 No 2 132-138.

Appendix: Geometrical Constraints and their Linearisations

We give here some examples of condition on the state vector resulting from geometrical constraints on the pair of lines (p, v) and (p', v').

1) Orthogonality:

$$\mathbf{v} \cdot \mathbf{v}' = (v_0 + v_1 \mathbf{v}_1 + v_2 \mathbf{v}_2) \cdot (v_0' + v_1' \mathbf{v}_1' + v_2' \mathbf{v}_2') = 0$$

linearises to

$$v_0 \cdot v_0' + v_1 \mathbf{v}_1 \cdot v_0' + v_2 \mathbf{v}_2 \cdot v_0' + v_1' \mathbf{v}_0 \cdot v_1' + v_2' \mathbf{v}_0 \cdot v_2' = 0.$$

2) Intersection:

$$(\mathbf{p} - \mathbf{p}') \cdot (\mathbf{v} \times \mathbf{v}') = 0$$

linearises to

$$(\mathbf{p}_0 - \mathbf{p}_0') \cdot (\mathbf{v}_0 \times \mathbf{v}_0') + p_1 \mathbf{v}_1 \cdot (\mathbf{v}_0 \times \mathbf{v}_0') + p_2 \mathbf{v}_2 \cdot (\mathbf{v}_0 \times \mathbf{v}_0')$$
$$- p_1' \mathbf{v}_1' \cdot (\mathbf{v}_0 \times \mathbf{v}_0') - p_2' \mathbf{v}_2' \cdot (\mathbf{v}_0 \times \mathbf{v}_0') + v_1 (\mathbf{p}_0 - \mathbf{p}_0') \cdot (\mathbf{v}_1 \times \mathbf{v}_0')$$
$$+ v_2 (\mathbf{p}_0 - \mathbf{p}_0') \cdot (\mathbf{v}_2 \times \mathbf{v}_0') + v_1' (\mathbf{p}_0 - \mathbf{p}_0') \cdot (\mathbf{v}_0 \times \mathbf{v}_1') + v_2' (\mathbf{p}_0 - \mathbf{p}_0') \cdot (\mathbf{v}_0 \times \mathbf{v}_2') = 0.$$

3) Equality:

$$\mathbf{v} = \mathbf{v}'$$

$$(\mathbf{p}' - \mathbf{p}) - (\mathbf{p}' - \mathbf{p}) \cdot \hat{\mathbf{v}}' \, \hat{\mathbf{v}}' = 0 \qquad \hat{\mathbf{v}}' = \frac{\mathbf{v}}{|\mathbf{v}'|}$$

Each of these represents only two independent constraints, which can be extracted by taking the scalar product with v_1' and v_2'. The result linearises to

$$(\mathbf{p}_0' - \mathbf{p}_0) \cdot v_1' - p_1 \mathbf{v}_1 \cdot v_1' - p_2 \mathbf{v}_2 \cdot v_1' + p_1' - v_1' (\mathbf{p}_0' - \mathbf{p}_0) \cdot v_0' = 0$$
$$(\mathbf{p}_0' - \mathbf{p}_0) \cdot v_2' - p_1 \mathbf{v}_1 \cdot v_2' - p_2 \mathbf{v}_2 \cdot v_2' + p_2' - v_2' (\mathbf{p}_0' - \mathbf{p}_0) \cdot v_0' = 0$$

and

$$v_0 \cdot v_1' + v_1 \mathbf{v}_1 \cdot v_1' + v_2 \mathbf{v}_2 \cdot v_1' - v_1' = 0$$
$$v_0 \cdot v_2' + v_1 \mathbf{v}_1 \cdot v_2' + v_2 \mathbf{v}_2 \cdot v_2' - v_2' = 0$$

(the last two constraints are sufficient to impose parallelism).

4) The two lines are connected by the small motion (ω, τ) if

$$(\mathbf{p}' - \mathbf{p} - \omega \times \mathbf{p} - \mathbf{t}) - (\mathbf{p}' - \mathbf{p} - \omega \times \mathbf{p} - \mathbf{t}) \cdot \hat{\mathbf{v}}' \, \hat{\mathbf{v}}' = 0$$

$$\hat{\mathbf{v}}' - \omega \times \hat{\mathbf{v}} = 0.$$

This linearises to

$$(\mathbf{p}_0' - \mathbf{p}_0) \cdot v_1' + p_1' - p_1 \mathbf{v}_1 \cdot v_1' - p_2 \mathbf{v}_2 \cdot v_1' - v_1' (\mathbf{p}_0' - \mathbf{p}_0) \cdot v_0'$$
$$- (\mathbf{p}_0 \times v_1') \cdot \omega - v_1' \cdot \tau = 0$$

$$(\mathbf{p}_0' - \mathbf{p}_0) \cdot v_2' + p_2' - p_1 \mathbf{v}_1 \cdot v_2' - p_2 \mathbf{v}_2 \cdot v_2' - v_2' (\mathbf{p}_0' - \mathbf{p}_0) \cdot v_0'$$
$$- (\mathbf{p}_0 \times v_2') \cdot \omega - v_2' \cdot \tau = 0$$

$$-v_0 \cdot v_1' + v_1' - v_1 \mathbf{v}_1 \cdot v_1' - v_2 \mathbf{v}_2 \cdot v_1' - (v_0 \times v_1') \cdot \omega = 0$$
$$-v_0 \cdot v_2' + v_2' - v_1 \mathbf{v}_1 \cdot v_2' - v_2 \mathbf{v}_2 \cdot v_2' - (v_0 \times v_2') \cdot \omega = 0.$$

Perception via Manipulation

Ruzena Bajcsy
and
Constantinos Tsikos

Computer and Information Science Department
University of Pennsylvania
Philadelphia, PA 19104

The main argument in this paper is that one cannot discern part-whole relationships of three-dimensional objects in a passive mode without a great deal of apriori information. Perceptual activity is exploratory, probing and searching. The hypothesis is that parts are bound by a binding force that, if recognized, can be tested by an integration application of vision, force and manipulation. Concrete experiments will show the concept.

Introduction and Motivation

In the past we have argued for Active Sensing [Bajcsy, 1985] as opposed to the traditional static analysis of passively sampled data. However, it should be axiomatic that perception is not passive, but active. Perceptual activity is exploratory, probing, searching.

What is Active Sensing?

In the robotics and computer vision literature, the term *"active sensor"* generally refers to a sensor that transmits (generally electromagnetic radiation, e.g., radar, sonar, ultrasound, microwaves and collimated light) into the environment and receives and measures the reflected signals.

We believe that the use of active sensors is not a necessary condition on active sensing, and that active sensing can be performed with passive sensors (that only receive, and do not transmit, information), employed actively. Here we use the term active not to denote a time-of-flight type sensor, but to denote a passive sensor employed in an active fashion, purposefully changing the sensor's state parameters according to sensing strategies. Hence the problem of Active Sensing can be stated as a problem intelligent control strategies applied to data acquisition process which will depend on the current state of the data interpretation including recognition.

This approach has been eloquently defended by Tenenbaum [1]: "Because of the inherent limitation of a single image, the acquisition of information should be treated as an integral part of the perceptual process...Accommodation attacks the fundamental limitation of image inadequacy rather than the secondary problems caused by it". Although he uses the term *"accommodation"* rather than *"active sensing"* the message is the same.

In the spirit of active sensing we wish to further argue that stationary sensing being either non-contact (for example visual) or contact (example tactile) is necessary but not sufficient for complete determination:

a. of the part-whole relationship as opposed to two or more object arrangements

b. of flexible, i.e., moveable parts of an object.

In this paper we shall briefly review the literature related to this problem and show possible applications. Then we will present the experimental setup and the assumptions. Subsequently we shall outline the underlined theory or principles and suggest some generic experiments which will prove the hypothesis generated by the theory.

Background

During our literature search it became obvious that most of the research on object description makes the following assumptions:

a. objects are rigid, i.e., made from solid materials

b. objects have non-flexible parts

c. if two or more objects are attached to each other, the recognition whether they are one or more objects is guided by apriori information of the shape or possibly size of the object.

People have been concentrating more on the assembly process than on the disassembly process, yet if one wants to understand the structural composition of an object unless apriori given, one needs to decompose it. The closest to our thinking has come Yamada et al in building an expert system which will generate all possible procedures of disassembling the object from the 3D models. This is important for example repairs!

Another application is the Post Office where mailpieces and other packages are thrown on the conveyor belt and in order to sort them one needs to decompose the pile into singulated pieces.

Our problem however is to recognize how to take apart an object! This means to us, data driven perception which results in discerning solid and rigid separable objects and/or their parts and describing them in terms of their structural and geometric properties. Our aim is to explore complex scenes, composed of more than one object in arbitrary positions.

Our basic hypothesis is that this cannot be done only by vision, that one needs some possibilities of manipulation and the use of haptic information processing. But by the same argument this cannot be done by haptic exploration alone either!

The laboratory setup

Our laboratory setup is illustrated in Figures 1 and 2. It consists of a ranging system (WHITE SCANNER 100X), a manipulator (PUMA 560) and a simple, two fingered hand, from LORD Corporation which has force/tactile sensors on each finger.

Assumptions

We shall limit ourselves to objects and materials that are separable by mechanical but non-destructive actions, such as pushing/pulling, shaking, grasping-lifting. Later on, we may consider the action of turning.

We shall not consider mechanical forces that could damage the material that the objects are made of. This, of course, is a very delicate and sophisticated problem since one has to either have some apriori knowledge about the material or measure it in order to apply the proper amount of force without damage. In any case the general strategy must be of applying the forces gradually! Here results of Cai and Roth [Cai, 1987] on spatial motion of rigid body and the work of Rajan et al [Rajan, 1987] on dynamics of rigid body, and Peshkin, Sanderson [Sanderson, 1987] on sliding objects will be utilized.

- The manipulation selection which is driven by the goal to simplify the scene which in turn is interpreted as decomposing the scene into all rigid decomposable parts/objects. The manipulation actions to be considered are: shaking, pushing/pulling and grasping-lifting.

The most important research issue (and the most difficult one) is THE CONTROL OF EXPLORATORY MOVEMENTS OF BOTH THE CAMERA AND THE MANIPULATOR.

Our goal in this work is to discern whether objects in the scene are mechanically bound rigidly or flexibly or not at all. For that, first let us define what we mean by a binding force. The binding force is that force which holds two objects together. The binding can be rigid (like a glue) or flexible (like a hinge, or spring).

Having defined what we mean by the binding force, the main task will be to discover the existence and orientation of this force in the object ensemble. This property will in turn determine whether the sensed object is a rigid object with or without rigid parts or with flexible-linkages as parts or is composed of several separate objects.

To make all this more concrete, we shall outline a series of experiments. Each experiment will prove a certain principle. We hope to argue that these experiments are generic!

Experiment 1

Description of the scene:

Consider a series of boxes (of the same shape and size, color) or cylinders lined up on a platform next to each other as shown in Figure 3 and Figure 4. These boxes form an elongated rod like arrangement, visually indistinguishable. The binding force has only one direction!

The elements may be bound together either:

a. by glue, forming a rigid object.

b. by springs or articulations forming a flexible or an articulated object.

c. by nothing, forming an arrangement only.

The principle that we wish to prove is:

1. Vision cannot discern which of the cases (a b or c) a given object is. (this follows from our assumption).

2. The force sensing alone perhaps can distinguish a from b and c, but not b from c.

3. All three cases (a,b,c) can be distinguished by concurrent visual observation of the pushing action perpendicular to the orientation of the binding force.

This experiment is generic and it applies to any linear arrangement of uniform or similar elements with binding force that has only one direction!

Experiment 2

Description of the scene:

Consider a stack of objects, this time not horizontally but vertically arranged. Objects on top of each other. The objects can be of the same shape and size or different, as long the arrangement is stable. See Figure 5. For example, a stack of boxes (glued or connected with springs or just stacked on top of each other), a stack of plates, cups, etc. a cup and the saucer, a container with a lid, a short stack of magazines. a closet, a door, i.e., objects connected with hinges.

The binding force again has only one direction but depending on the shape/size relationship between the two neighboring objects, two different actions may be applied. These are:

a. Grasping-lifting/pulling

b. Pushing

The principle that we wish to demonstrate here is: The shape/size will first determine the manipulation action, i.e difference between grasp-lift/pull and push. Second, the economy of manipulation will determine the choices between two or more plausible actions.

The examples cited in the possible scenes should be convincing that this experiment is generic. Clearly the size and the shape determines which objects are easier to grasp and which are not. Pushing, is a more economical operation (one does not need to grasp) but the overall effect in disassembly may be less effective. We wish to study this aspect of economy of these two operations.

Experiment 3

Description of the Scene:

Two, partially contained objects. Pegg in the hole, a draw (open or closed), a box within a box, (see Figure 6 for an illustration). The binding force has more than one direction. This is the case analyzed by [Rajan et al. 1987] on Dynamics of a rigid body in frictional contact with rigid walls. They have developed formulas for computing the force torque parameters under certain motions involving one point of contact between a body and a restraining wall. This is the case for example of a draw (opening or closing). Our task is to recognize these cases and then one can compute the force torque needed to complete the task. In absence of apriori information, one will have to EXPLORE first and then iteratively get to the solution that are computed by Rajan et al.

The Model of Disassembly

Our goal is to describe a complex scene composed of one or more objects at arbitrary positions and to discern whether the objects in the scene are mechanically bound rigidly, flexibly, or not at all (touching or overlapping).

Our approach is to close the loop between vision and manipulation. A manipulator is used to simplify the scene by decomposing the scene into visually simpler scenes. In addition, the manipulator carries the contact sensors to the region of interest and performs the necessary exploratory movements that will the determine the nature of the mechanical binding between objects in the scene. Sensory data from contact sensors is collected and interpreted during manipulation. Sensory data from the visual sensors can be collected either during or after manipulation.

Our model is an Action Automaton. It is a non-deterministic finite state automaton, a quadruple: (I, O, S, T) where:

"I": Input = A set of multi-modal sensory inputs, such as:

- Range images of the scene

• Force/Torque sensory data at the gripper

• Tactile sensory data

• Gripper closure sensory data

• Data from a vacuum sensor

"O": Output = A set of manipulator actions, such as:

• Object Acquisition (grasp-lift)

• Local Displacement (push/pull)

• Global Displacement (shake-up)

"S": States = A set of states. These can be partitioned into the following:

"Se": States describing the scene:

• Scene is "Empty"

• Scene is "Dispersed" (No visible overlaps)

• Scene contains "Overlaps"

• Scene is "Ambiguous"

"Ss": States describing the actions of the sensory systems:

• Acquiring and Interpreting non-contact sensory data

• Acquiring and Interpreting contact sensory data

"Sm": States describing the actions of the manipulator:

• Object Acquisition (grasping-lifting)

• Local Displacement (pushing/pulling)

• Global Displacement (shake-up)

"T": State Transition Function, (I x S) ---> S, where:

The next state is a function of the current state and the current input. The state transition diagram is illustrated in Figure 7. Notice that the next state is not always unique. Different states and therefore different manipulation actions are possible. Clearly, the shape and size determines that some objects are easier to grasp than others. Objects too small or too big for a given gripper may be either pushed out of the scene, or be pulled out of the scene using a suction tool. The existence of highly unstable objects such as cylinders may indicate that either pushing or shaking is the appropriate action. Local and global displacements in the scene (pushing/pulling and shake-up) are obviously more economical than acquisition (grasping-lifting), but less effective in disassembly.

Another global criterion that may influence the choice of a manipulation action (besides position, orientation, size, shape, accessibility and stability of objects) is past history of the complexity of the scene. As the manipulator operates on the scene, one should expect the next scene to be visually less complex than the previous one. Reduction in visual complexity is usually a good indicator of convergence. There are exceptions. For example, a large object, totally occluding other objects, when removed from the scene will yield a scene visually more complex than the previous one.

The choice of one, out of many possible manipulator actions, is a function of current state, current data, past history, and cost of the manipulator action. In other words, the system is data and cost driven.

The self loops in the state diagram are unique. During a manipulator action, signals from the contact sensors are received, interpreted and the manipulator is essentially under the control of these sensors. For example, by monitoring the force/torque during the pushing/pulling action, it is possible to gradually apply the exploratory forces during an exploratory movement of the manipulator.

Experimental Results

Our experiments have concentrated into the domain of sorting Irregular Parcels, such as boxes, tubes/rolls, flat envelopes etc. The domain is very rich. The objects are characterized by large variations in size, shape, weight, and surface characteristics. The shape of these objects is variable because the majority of them are non-rigid objects. Finally, these objects are piled-up into random heaps. See Figure 8.

The purpose of the experiments is to sort an arbitrary heap into several streams of non-overlapping parcels. Each stream represents a generic shape. We have three generic shapes: "Flats", "Boxes", "Tubes/Rolls". Our system collects range data from the scene. This data is processed and the accessible surface segments are identified. For each surface segment, the size, shape, position, orientation, and surface normals are computed. Using geometric information, the spatial relations of the surface segments are generated. Examples of these are the "on-top-of" and "next-to" relations. Based on these relations, the scene is characterized as "empty", "dispersed", "containing overlaps", and "ambiguous".

The top-most, or most-accessible surface segments are identified for manipulation. Each manipulation action requires computation of different parameters such as, center of gravity, orientation and surface normal of the most accessible surface where the robot is going to grasp-lift, or position and orientation of the points in the scene where the robot is going to push, or the coordinates and gripper opening necessary for grasping.

Several manipulator actions are possible. We currently have implemented the pull-lift, grasp-lift, push/pull and shake actions. These actions are currently under evaluation using a large number of objects of different shapes and sizes piled-up at random. See Figure 9 and Figure 10. Work is under way to generate multiple action strategies and test these strategies on large numbers of objects and configurations.

Two, general purpose, interchangeable tools were build. The first is a suction toll and the second resembles a spatula. Depending on the manipulation action chosen, the robot can manipulate the scene by either using the gripper from LORD Corporation to grasp or push an object, or it may pick the suction tool and apply suction to the most accessible flat surface, or it may pick the "spatula" and push in an area where the LORD gripper does not fit.

The assumption we make is that the scene is decomposable. This is a rather weak assumption for the Post Office domain. In the majority of objects and heaps we have tested we have found little evidence of strong binding forces. Results of this work will be video-taped and presented at the symposium.

Conclusions and Future Work

From our experimental work in the Post Office domain we have observed that the pull-lift action is very effective for flats, boxes and large diameter tubes/rolls. The manipulator uses the LORD gripper to grasp a suction tool and to pull-lift at the center of gravity of the most accessible surface segment in the scene. In the very near future we will implement and evaluate several multiple action strategies and we will conduct the experiments we have outlined earlier.

Another area where our work may have applications is the field of Substance Testing/Exploration. Vision and manipulation may be used to explore and discern substances such as sand, dust, clay, rock and liquid. Potential applications may be autonomous vehicles exploring unknown environments in space or the ocean floor.

In substance testing, the binding forces are at a different level of resolution, the particle or the atomic level. We are working on a global level. However, we believe that it is possible to manipulate the substance, say by probing, pushing, scraping etc, and observe the global deformations of the substance.

We know, for example, that clay will look different than sand, rock or liquid after manipulation. Materials Science is using the "Rockwell Scale" to measure the hardness of metals and other solids and various other scales to measure the viscosity of liquids, or the elasticity of plastics.

Acknowledgements:

This Research was funded, in part, by the United States Postal Service, BOA Contract: 104230-87-H-0001/M-0195, DARPA/ONR grant N0014-85-K-0807, NSF grant DCR 8410771, Airforce grant AFOSR F49620-85-K-0018, Army/DAAG-29-84-K-0061, NSF-CER/DCR82-19196 A02, NIH grant NS-10939-11 as part of Crebrovascular Research Center, NIH 1-R01-NS-23636-01, NSF INT85-14199, NSF DMC85-17315, ARPA N0014-85-K-0807, by DEC Corp., IBM Corp. and LORD Corp.

References

Bajcsy, R. K.: Active Perception vs Passive Perception IEEE Computer Society Third Workshop on Computer Vision: Representation and Control, Bellaire, MI, October 13-16, 1985.

Cai, Ch. and Roth, B.: On the Spatial Motion of a Rigid Body with Point Contact, Proceedings of IEEE International Conference on Robotics and Automation, 1987, Raleigh, North Carolina, pp.686-695.

Morris, G.H., Haynes, L.S.: Robotic Assembly by Constraints, Proceedings of IEEE International Conference on Robotics and Automation, 1987, Raleigh, North Carolina, pp. 1507-1515.

Peshkin, M.A. and Sanderson, A.C.: Planning Robotic Manipulation Strategies for Sliding Objects, Proceedings of IEEE International Conference on Robotics and Automation, 1987, Raleigh, North Carolina, pp. 696-701.

Rajan, V.T., Burridge,R., and Schwartz, J.T.: Dynamics of a Rigid Body in Frictional Contact with Rigid Walls, Proceedings of IEEE International Conference on Robotics and Automation, 1987, Raleigh, North Carolina, pp. 671-677.

Rosenschein, S.J.: Formal Theories of Knowledge in AI and Robotics, Technical Note 362, SRI International, September 10, 1985.

Tsikos, C.J.: Segmentation of Complex 3-D Scenes using Multi-Modal Interaction between Machine Vision and Programmable Mechanical Scene Manipulation, Ph.D. Thesis Proposal, University of Pennsylvania, May 21, 1986.

Vijaykumar,R. and Arbib, M.A.: Problem Decomposition for Assembly Planning, Proceedings of IEEE International Conference on Robotics and Automation, 1987, Raleigh, North Carolina, pp. 1361-1366.

Yamada, S., Abe, N., and Tsuji, S.: Construction of a Consulting System From Structural Description of Mechanical Object, Proceedings of IEEE International Conference on Robotics and Automation, 1987, Raleigh, North Carolina, pp. 1413-1418.019

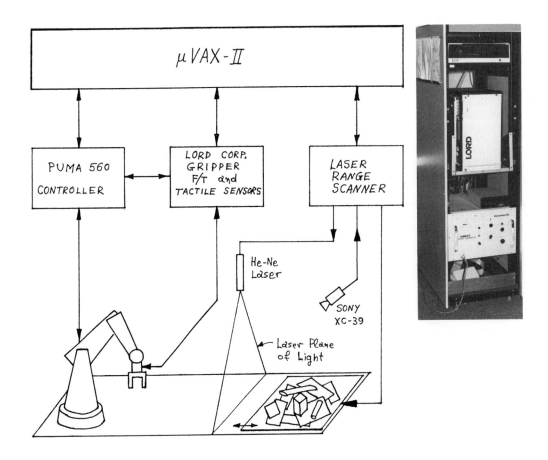

Figure 1:   System Block Diagram

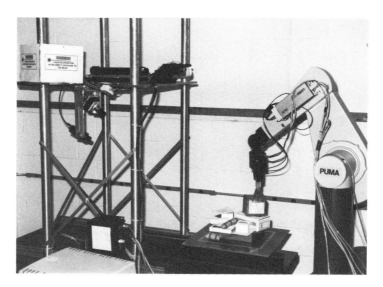

Figure 2:   Laboratory Setup

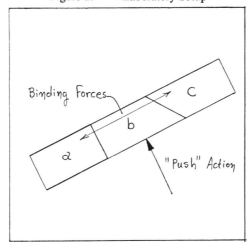

Figure 3:   Experiment - 1

Figure 4:   Experiment - 1

Figure 5:   Experiment - 2

Figure 6:   Experiment - 3

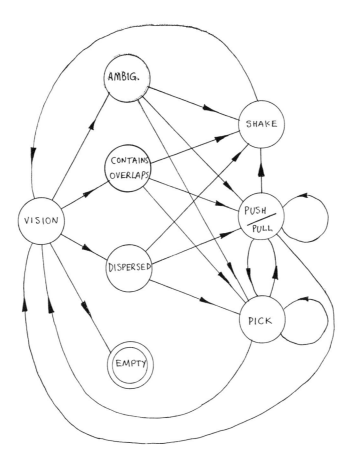

Figure 7:   State Transition Diagram

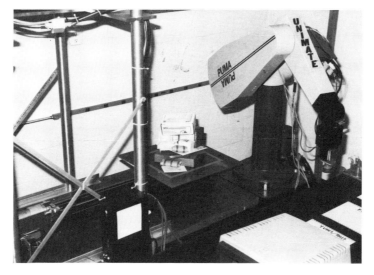

Figure 8:   A Random Heap (USPS Application)

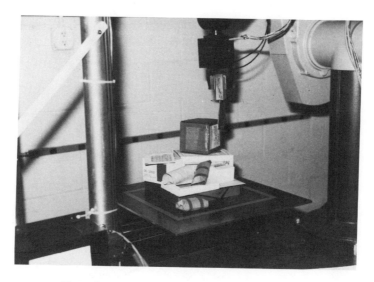

Figure 9:   An Example of the "PUSH" Action

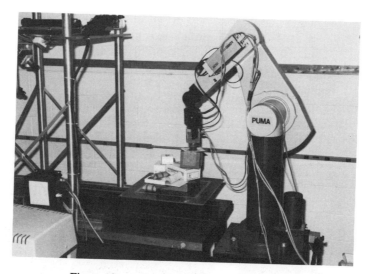

Figure 10:   An Example of the "PICK" Action

On the Recognition of Parameterized Objects[1]

W. Eric L. Grimson

MIT Artificial Intelligence Laboratory
545 Technology Square
Cambridge, Mass. 02139

Abstract. Determining the identity and pose of occluded objects from noisy data is a critical step in interacting intelligently with an unstructured environment. Previous work has shown that local measurements of position and surface orientation may be used in a constrained search process to solve this problem, for the case of rigid objects, either two-dimensional or three-dimensional. This paper considers the more general problem of recognizing and locating objects that can vary in parameterized ways. We consider objects with rotational, translational or scaling degrees of freedom, and objects that undergo stretching transformations. We show that the constrained search method can be extended to handle the recognition and localization of such generalized classes of object families.

1. Introduction

The problem considered in this paper is how to locate a known object from sensory data, especially when that object may be occluded by other unknown objects. In earlier work [Grimson and Lozano-Pérez 84, 86] we presented a constrained search method for recognizing objects from noisy, occluded data. In that work, we concentrated on rigid models of known size, so that the sensory data was metrically calibrated with the object models. It is important to be able to deal with less structured situations, however, and in this note, we consider extensions of our method to deal with families of objects that are characterized by sets of free parameters.

1.1 Input to the problem

The Sensory Data

We are interested in recognition methods that apply to a variety of sensing modalities, including visual, laser, sonar and tactile sensors. This limits the assumptions we can safely make about the sensed data. We assume only that the sensor output can be processed to provide estimates of the position and surface orientation of (possibly small and sparse) planar patches on the object. The measured positions are assumed to be accurate only to within a known error volume, and the measured surface orientations are assumed to be accurate only to within a known error cone. The data could be dense or sparse, depending on the characteristics of the sensor.

When the objects have only three degrees of positional freedom relative to the sensor (two translation and one rotational), the positions and surface normals need only be two-dimensional. When the objects have more than three degrees of positional freedom (up to three translational and three rotational), the position and orientation data must be three-dimensional.

The Object Models

In the original work, we considered only rigid objects, of fixed size. Further, we assumed that the objects could be modeled as sets of planar faces. The model faces did not have to be connected, however, nor did the model need to be complete. In this paper, we must extend the models to deal with parameterized families.

1.2 Our approach to localization

Our approach [Grimson and Lozano-Pérez 84, 86] to the localization problem has been to cast it as a search for a consistent matching between the measured surface patches and the surfaces of the known object model. The search proceeds by generating feasible interpretations, and then testing those interpretations for model consistency. Each interpretation consists of a set of pairings of sensed patches with object surfaces. Any interpretation in which the sensed data are inconsistent with local geometric constraints is discarded. All the remaining feasible interpretations are further tested for consistency with the object model, by determining if it is possible to solve for a rotation and translation that would place each sensed patch on the corresponding object surface, with an appropriate surface orientation, as specified by the interpretation pairings.

We chose to structure the search for consistent matches as one of generating and exploring of an *interpretation tree* (IT). The tree is

---

[1] An earlier version of this work appeared in the proceedings of the First International Conference on Computer Vision, London, England, June 1987

[2] This report describes research done at the Artificial Intelligence Laboratory of the Massachusetts Institute of Technology, which was funded primarily by the Advanced Research Projects Agency, under Office of Naval Research contract N00014-85-K-0214, and by the University Research Initiative under Office of Naval Research contract N00014-86-K-0685.

constructed in a depth first fashion, considering a new data patch at each level, and branching to consider the assignment of that data point to each possible object face (see Figure 1). At the first level of the tree, we consider assigning the first measured patch to all possible faces. At the next level, we assign the second measured patch to all possible faces, and so on. Each node of the tree represents a partial interpretation, as indicated in the figure.

The number of possible interpretations in the tree is astronomical, for realistically sized problems. The key to this approach is to exploit local geometric constraints to remove entire subtrees from consideration. In our earlier work, for example, we required that the distances and angles between all pairs of data elements be consistent with the distances and angles possible between their assigned model elements. If such constraints do not hold for all pairs of data/object face pairings in a partial interpretation, the subtree below that node need not be explored.

1.3 Previous work

In earlier work with rigid objects, we used local geometric constraints between pairs of data edges and their affiliated model edges to test the consistency of assigning those data edges to lie on the associated model edges. The details of such constraints, and examples of their use on simulated and real data are reported in [Grimson and Lozano-Pérez 84, 86]. A combinatorial analysis of the efficacy of such constraints is reported in [Grimson 86]. An example of the system on real two-dimensional data is shown in Figure 2. The method is described in more detail in sections below, where we discuss the extensions to parameterized objects.

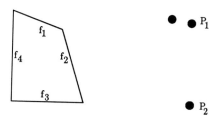

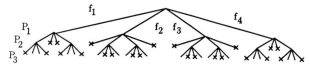

Figure 1. A simple example of constrained search. We want to find consistent matchings of the three data points to the edges of the indicated quadrilateral. If we use distance between data points as the measurement, then the table of possible ranges between the edges of the object is given by

	1	2	3	4
1	[0, 1.5]	[0, 3.25]	[2, 3.25]	[0, 2.5]
2	[0, 3.25]	[0, 2]	[0, 2.5]	[1.4, 3.25]
3	[2, 3.25]	[0, 2.5]	[0, 2]	[0, 3.25]
4	[0, 2.5]	[1.4, 3.25]	[0, 3.25]	[0, 2.5]

The tree indicates the set of possible assignments of data points to object edges, given distance as a constraint. One can see that only 16 out of 64 possible interpretations are consistent with this constraint. (Figure reproduced from Journal of the ACM, October, 1986, page 663.)

1.4 Examples of Parameterized Objects

While our previous work has illustrated the utility of our approach to the problem of rigid objects, we are interested here in extending the method to deal with parameterized objects. We consider a number of different possibilities.

Scale

Perhaps the simplest example of a parameterized family is that defined by a rigid object that can undertake a range of possible sizes, that is, the shape of the object is fixed, but the overall scale factor can vary. Many techniques for object recognition and localization can easily deal with this case, since the scale factor can simply be considered part of the coordinate frame transformation required to map the model patches into their corresponding sensed patches.

Coordinate-frame transformations

A more interesting class of parameterized objects are those that involve a limited number of moving parts. A good example is a pair of scissors, which has a single degree of freedom, namely the rotation of the two blades relative to a common joint. We would like to be able to recognize the scissors, independent of the relative orientation of the blades, and without requiring a different model to represent each orientation. This class could further be extended to include scissors of different sizes.

Stretching deformations

A third class of parameterized objects are those in which subparts can stretch along an axis. An example would be a family of hammers, for which there is a generic handle shape, but which can stretch along the axis of the handle, as indicated in Figure 3.

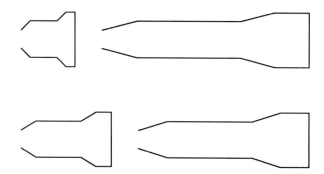

Figure 3. A set of parameterized subparts, in which the generic shape in the upper left is stretched along the axis of the shape.

Our goal is to extend our recognition method to handle such classes of parameterized families.

2. Possible approaches

A large number of methods have been explored in the literature for recognizing rigid objects, both in two dimensions and in three. When considering parameterized objects, far fewer methods have been considered. In particular, while a number of schemes have been suggested for representing parameterized objects, such as generalized cylinders and superquadrics, at this point very few actual recognition engines based on such parameterized representations have been demonstrated. The best known such system is probably ACRONYM [Brooks 1981]. Within the context of our approach to recognition, there are two distinct alternatives for extending the method to handle parameterized parts, both related in a global sense to the approach taken by Brooks.

The first approach is to extend our geometric constraints to directly incorporate the free parameters. In this case, the search process would become a constraint propagation technique, in which the current range of possible values for each of the parameters would be passed from a parent node of the IT to each of its sons. At each new node, the constraints imposed by matching the new data patch to its assigned model patch would be used to refine the range of free parameters, which would then be passed to that node's children. If any parameter is reduced to an empty range of values, the interpretation is inconsistent and the search along that subtree can be terminated.

The main difficulty with this approach is finding a clean way of representing the parameterized constraints, especially in a manner that will easily allow the computing and updating of feasible ranges for each of the parameters. Consider our example of a pair of scissors, where the parameter to be determined is the angle between the two blades. If two data fragments are being considered as belonging to two model fragments that are part of the same rigid subpart, then the constraints are the same as in our earlier approach. They either indicate consistency, in which case the range of possible values for the rotation parameter remains the same as it was before considering this pairing, or they indicate inconsistency, in which case the search must backtrack. On the other hand, suppose two data fragments are being considered as belonging to model fragments on different rigid subparts. In this case, we need a means of expressing the range of possible values for the rotation parameter as an explicit function of the relative geometry of the two model fragments and the two data fragments. This may prove difficult to obtain.

The second approach is to break the object model into rigid subparts, all of which are connected to a global model-based coordinate frame through a series of coordinate frame transformations. Each subpart can then be recognized by application of our earlier technique, including a free scale parameter. Once the subparts have been recognized and located, we must check that they are consistent by confirming that the parts satisfy a set of predetermined global coordinate-frame constraints.

Consider the earlier example of a pair of scissors, with a free overall scale factor. In this approach, we treat each blade of the scissors as a rigid subpart. Thus, we attempt to locate instances of the right and left blade in the sensory data. Once we have done this, we then confirm that the subparts are parts of a consistent whole. In the case of the scissors, this would involve checking two things: (1) the scale factor associated with each blade is roughly the same, and (2) the transformations from model coordinates to sensory coordinates associated with each blade are such that the position, in sensor coordinates, of the pin joining the two blades is roughly the same (i.e. the located instances of the blades in the data are rotated about the expected common axis). The advantage of this second method

is that the geometric constraints remain simple, yet combinatorially powerful.

Note that we can apply our search for rigid subparts in several ways. The simplest is to search the data independently for each rigid subpart, then test all possible combinations of subparts for consistent wholes. A more efficient method would be to first search the data for one subpart (e.g. the largest). For each candidate solution found in the data, we can then use limits on the ranges of the parameters to restrict the possible positions of the other subparts in the sensory data. Using this reduced data set, we can then search for instances of the other subparts, testing each instance for global consistency. If no instance of the initial seed subpart is found, (for example, it is occluded in the data) we can then consider to the next seed subpart (e.g. the next largest) and proceed as before.

In this paper, we explore both options. We first derive the set of geometric constraints on interpretations, and then illustrate the search process on some simple examples.

3. The Constraints

In this section, we develop a specific set of geometric constraints in the context of two dimensional data. Similar constraints hold for three-dimensional data. The constraints are identical to those used in [Grimson and Lozano-Pérez 84, 86]. However, a new and somewhat simpler computation of the model portion of the constraints is presented here.

In order to reduce the combinatorial complexity of exploring the large search space of possible interpretations, we need a set of constraints for determining when a partial interpretation is inconsistent. The main characteristic of the constraints is that they should be coordinate-frame independent, so that they capture information about the shape of an object, not its particular pose. The constraints we derive have two parts, a set of measurements computed from the sensory data, and a set of measurements precomputed from the object model. These are described in detail below.

In two dimensions, the basic units of processing are edge segments, since the model is assumed to consist of a set of such segments, and the sensory data is assumed to have been processed to obtain such segments. We can represent an edge (either in the data or the model) by the pair

$$\hat{\mathbf{n}}_i \qquad \text{and} \qquad \mathbf{b}_i + \alpha_i \hat{\mathbf{t}}_i, \quad \alpha_i \in [0, \ell_i]$$

where $\hat{\mathbf{n}}_i$ is a unit normal vector, $\hat{\mathbf{t}}_i$ is a unit tangent vector, oriented so that it lies $90''$ clockwise of $\hat{\mathbf{n}}_i$, $\mathbf{b}_i$ is a vector to the base point of the edge, and α_i can vary from 0 to the length of the edge ℓ_i (see Figure 4).

Angle constraint

The first constraint concerns the orientation of the edge normals. Given a pair of sensory edge fragments indexed by i, j, we can easily compute the angle between their normals, $\hat{\mathbf{n}}_i, \hat{\mathbf{n}}_j$, which we denote θ_{ij}. Given a pair of model edges indexed by p, q, we can also compute the angle between their respective normals, denoted Θ_{pq}. In the ideal case, the assignment of data edge i to lie on model edge p and data edge j to lie on model edge q would be consistent only if $\theta_{ij} = \Theta_{pq}$. In practice, of course, there is error in the data, and we must take this into account. To determine the effect of error, we assume that

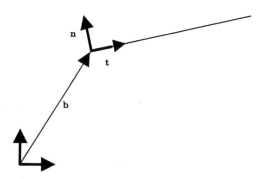

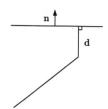

Figure 4. The representation of an edge. An edge is given by the pair

$$\hat{n}_i \qquad \text{and} \qquad \mathbf{b}_i + \alpha_i \hat{t}_i, \quad \alpha_i \in [0, \ell_i]$$

where $\hat{n}_i$ is a unit normal vector, $\hat{t}_i$ is a unit tangent vector, oriented so that it lies $90''$ clockwise of $\hat{n}_i$, $\mathbf{b}_i$ is a vector to the base point of the edge, and α_i can vary from 0 to the length of the edge ℓ_i.

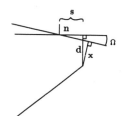 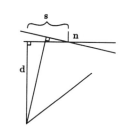

Figure 5. Errors in computing the direction constraint. (a) The component of a vector from one endpoint in the direction of the other edge's normal is given by the perpendicular distance $\mathbf{d}$ to the extended edge. (b) Since the actual normal is only accurate to within δ, one extreme case is given by rotating the extended edge about its midpoint by that amount and finding the new perpendicular distance. (c) The other extreme is obtained by considering the other endpoint.

the position of an edge point is known to within an error bound ϵ. If L is a lower bound on the length of the edges, it is straightforward to show that the maximum error in the measured angle between edge normals is given by

$$\delta = \tan^{-1} \frac{2\epsilon}{L}.$$

Thus, our angle constraint now requires that

$$\theta_{ij} \in [\Theta_{pq} - \delta, \Theta_{pq} + \delta,]$$

where all arithmetic comparisons are performed modulo 2π.

Direction constraint

The second constraint concerns the separation of the two edge fragments. In particular, we consider the range of components of a vector between the two edge fragments, in the direction of one of the edge normals. Algebraically, this is expressed by the dot product

$$\langle \mathbf{b}_i + \alpha_i \hat{t}_i - \mathbf{b}_j - \alpha_j \hat{t}_j, \hat{n}_i \rangle$$

which reduces to

$$\langle \mathbf{b}_i - \mathbf{b}_j, \hat{n}_i \rangle - \alpha_j \langle \hat{t}_j, \hat{n}_i \rangle \qquad \alpha_j \in [0, \ell_j]$$

Of course, there is an equivalent constraint for components in the direction of $\hat{n}_j$. Note that this expression actually determines a range of values, with extrema when $\alpha_j = 0, \ell_j$. These ranges can be computed both for pairs of data edges and pairs of model edges. In the ideal case, consistency will hold only if the data range is contained within the model range (since the data edges may correspond to only parts of the model edges). As in the case of the angle constraint, we also need to account for error in the measurements. We derive a simple method for doing this below.

Consider the base case, shown in Figure 5a. The perpendicular distance from the endpoint of one edge to the other edge is shown as d. In Figure 5b, the edge is rotated by $\delta(= \tan^{-1} \frac{2\epsilon}{L})$ degrees about its midpoint, and the new perpendicular distance x is shown. We need to relate x to measurable values. We already have d. We can also measure s, the distance from the midpoint of the edge to the perpendicular dropped from the endpoint of the other edge, as shown. Straightforward trigonometry then yields the new distance

$$x = (d - s \sin \delta) \cos \delta.$$

Since the position of the second edge is not known exactly, we must adjust this expression, to yield one limit on the range of possible measurements:

$$d_\ell = (d - s \sin \delta) \cos \delta - \epsilon.$$

The other extreme is shown in Figure 5c. Trigonometric manipulation yields the following upper bound

$$d_h = (s - d \sin \delta) \sin \delta + d \sec \delta + \epsilon.$$

Thus, given two model edges indexed by p, q, we can compute a range of possible measurements (modulo a known error bound), by using d_ℓ and d_h computed over all the endpoints of the edges. We denote this range by $[m_{\ell.pq}, m_{h.pq}]$. Similarly, for data edges indexed by i, j we can use the base case to compute a second range of components $[d_{\ell.ij}, d_{h.ij}]$. For the assignment of the data edges to the model edge to be consistent, we must have:

$$[d_{\ell.ij}, d_{h.ij}] \subseteq [m_{\ell.pq}, m_{h.pq}].$$

4. Search

These constraints can now be applied to the tree search process. Each node in the tree defines a set of pairings of data edges and model edges. For each node, we consider all such pairs of pairings. If each such pair passes both the angle and the direction constraints, this is a feasible partial interpretation. In this case, we can continue with the depth first search, by branching to consider the assignment of the next data edge to all possible model edges.

Such a search method will work well if all of the data edges come from a single object [Grimson and Lozano-Pérez 84, 86]. We need to modify the search in the case of extraneous data from occluding objects, however.

We model the effect of extraneous data on the search space by adding a *null face* branch below each IT node. Assigning a data patch to this node is equivalent to discarding that patch as inconsistent with the model. The null face acts as a "wild card" in the match. A straightforward application of this null-face method to data from overlapping objects will produce all consistent interpretations, including all subsets of an interpretation, but at considerable computational expense. Elsewhere [Grimson and Lozano-Pérez 86], we have investigated a number of mechanisms for improving the performance of the algorithm. Within the context of this paper, we will employ one such mechanism, namely *heuristic search ordering with cutoff*.

The method proceeds as follows. The IT is explored in a depth-first fashion, with the null face considered last when expanding a node. Now, assume an external variable, call it MAX, that keeps track of the best (longest accumulated length of matched edges) valid interpretation found so far. For a node at level i in the tree, let M denote the length of the data patches assigned to non-null faces in the partial match associated with that node. Let R be the length of the data patches below this level of the tree: $P_{i+1}, \ldots, P_n$. It is only worth assigning a null face to patch P_i if

$$M + R \geq MAX.$$

Otherwise, the length of the interpretations at all the leaves below this node will be less than that of the best interpretation already found.

This search process can be continued until all the nodes have either been examined or discarded. This can still take a long time. We have observed that the search locates the correct interpretation fairly early on, but then spends a tremendous amount of time attempting to improve on it. This phenomenon can be avoided by the use of a length threshold (as a percentage of the model's perimeter). The search is discontinued when an interpretation that exceeds that threshold passes the model test. Results of such a search cutoff are reported in [Grimson and Lozano-Pérez 86].

5. Parameterized Families

We now turn to the problem of extending our recognition method to families of parameterized objects.

5.1 Scale Factors

Perhaps the simplest family of objects to consider are those in which a single, rigid object of known shape can undergo an arbitrary global scaling, within some limits. We need to consider how to adjust the recognition process, so that it can not only recognize where an object is in the data, but also its overall size.

The angle constraint is quite straightforward in this case, since it is independent of scaling, and will remain the same. The direction constraint, however, changes.

Suppose we are considering the matching of data edges indexed by i and j to model edges indexed by p and q respectively. Further suppose that the model range associated with projecting edge p onto edge q is given by $[m_{\ell.pq}, m_{h.pq}]$. We assume that the scale factor is applied to the data, so that the transformation from a point in model coordinates, $\mathbf{v}_m$, to sensor coordinates, $\mathbf{v}_d$, is given by

$$s\mathbf{v}_d = R_\theta \mathbf{v}_m + \mathbf{t}$$

where s is a scale factor, θ is an angle, R_θ is a rotation matrix of angle θ and $\mathbf{t}$ is a translation vector. Given a range of projections of data edge i onto edge j, say $[d_{\ell.ij}, d_{h.ij}]$, we need to determine bounds on s such that

$$[sd_{\ell.ij}, sd_{h.ij}] \subseteq [m_{\ell.pq}, m_{h.pq}].$$

The following cases hold:

If $\langle \hat{\mathbf{t}}_i, \hat{\mathbf{n}}_j \rangle > 0$ then
  If $\langle \mathbf{b}_j - \mathbf{b}_i, \hat{\mathbf{n}}_j \rangle > 0$
    then $\quad s_h \leq \dfrac{m_{h.pq}}{\langle \mathbf{b}_j - \mathbf{b}_i, \hat{\mathbf{n}}_j \rangle}$

  If $\langle \mathbf{b}_j - \mathbf{b}_i, \hat{\mathbf{n}}_j \rangle < 0$
    then $\quad s_\ell \geq \dfrac{m_{\ell.pq}}{\langle \mathbf{b}_j - \mathbf{b}_i, \hat{\mathbf{n}}_j \rangle}$

  If $\langle \mathbf{b}_j - \mathbf{b}_i, \hat{\mathbf{n}}_j \rangle - \ell_i \langle \hat{\mathbf{t}}_i, \hat{\mathbf{n}}_j \rangle > 0$
    then $\quad s_\ell \geq \dfrac{m_{\ell.pq}}{\langle \mathbf{b}_j - \mathbf{b}_i, \hat{\mathbf{n}}_j \rangle - \ell_i \langle \hat{\mathbf{t}}_i, \hat{\mathbf{n}}_j \rangle}$

  If $\langle \mathbf{b}_j - \mathbf{b}_i, \hat{\mathbf{n}}_j \rangle - \ell_i \langle \hat{\mathbf{t}}_i, \hat{\mathbf{n}}_j \rangle < 0$
    then $\quad s_h \leq \dfrac{m_{h.pq}}{\langle \mathbf{b}_j - \mathbf{b}_i, \hat{\mathbf{n}}_j \rangle - \ell_i \langle \hat{\mathbf{t}}_i, \hat{\mathbf{n}}_j \rangle}$

If $\langle \hat{\mathbf{t}}_i, \hat{\mathbf{n}}_j \rangle < 0$ then
  If $\langle \mathbf{b}_j - \mathbf{b}_i, \hat{\mathbf{n}}_j \rangle > 0$
    then $\quad s_\ell \geq \dfrac{m_{\ell.pq}}{\langle \mathbf{b}_j - \mathbf{b}_i, \hat{\mathbf{n}}_j \rangle}$

  If $\langle \mathbf{b}_j - \mathbf{b}_i, \hat{\mathbf{n}}_j \rangle < 0$
    then $\quad s_h \leq \dfrac{m_{h.pq}}{\langle \mathbf{b}_j - \mathbf{b}_i, \hat{\mathbf{n}}_j \rangle}$

  If $\langle \mathbf{b}_j - \mathbf{b}_i, \hat{\mathbf{n}}_j \rangle - \ell_i \langle \hat{\mathbf{t}}_i, \hat{\mathbf{n}}_j \rangle > 0$
    then $\quad s_h \leq \dfrac{m_{h.pq}}{\langle \mathbf{b}_j - \mathbf{b}_i, \hat{\mathbf{n}}_j \rangle - \ell_i \langle \hat{\mathbf{t}}_i, \hat{\mathbf{n}}_j \rangle}$

  If $\langle \mathbf{b}_j - \mathbf{b}_i, \hat{\mathbf{n}}_j \rangle - \ell_i \langle \hat{\mathbf{t}}_i, \hat{\mathbf{n}}_j \rangle < 0$
    then $\quad s_\ell \geq \dfrac{m_{h.pq}}{\langle \mathbf{b}_j - \mathbf{b}_i, \hat{\mathbf{n}}_j \rangle - \ell_i \langle \hat{\mathbf{t}}_i, \hat{\mathbf{n}}_j \rangle}$

Thus, based on the measured and model constraint ranges, we can compute a range of scale factors $[s_\ell, s_h]$ for which the assignment of data edges to model edges is consistent. Within the context of our tree search, we can now simply require that the range of scales of a node be given by the intersection of the ranges computed for each of the pairwise constraints. If that range becomes empty, then the interpretation is inconsistent, and we proceed as in the previous case. In executing the actual search, we can propagate the current range of values downward through the tree. Thus, at the kth level of the tree, we need only consider $k - 1$ new pairs, namely the pairings of the kth data fragment and its associated model fragment, against all of the previous pairings in the interpretation. The interesection of these $k - 1$ ranges must be interesected with the current range inherited from the previous node in the tree to give the new range of possible values.

In this manner, we can naturally extend our constrained search method to recognize objects from families in which the free parameter is overall scale. An example is shown in Figure 6.

Figure 6. Examples of recognition when the free parameter is overall scale. The left part shows a set of linear edges segments, the right part shows the located object.

5.2 Rotating Subparts

More interesting classes of parameterized families include those in which parts of the object are allowed to move with respect to one another. A good example of such a family is a pair of scissors. A fixed size pair of scissors has a single degree of freedom, namely the rotation of the two blades relative to a common joint. We would like to be able to recognize the scissors, independent of the relative orientation of the blades, and without requiring a different model to represent each orientation. This class could further be extended to include scissors of different sizes.

As we suggested earlier, this could be done by generalizing the constraints to directly take the free parameters into account. However, an easier approach is to break the object up into rigid subparts, and deal with each separately. We illustrate this with our scissors example.

Suppose we treat each blade assembly as a separate part. We choose the location of the common pin as the origin of the model coordinate frame. Now suppose that we run our recognition system on each part, solving for a transformation $\theta_L, s_L, \mathbf{t}_L$ for the left blade and for a transformation $\theta_R, s_R, \mathbf{t}_R$ for the right blade. This can proceed in a manner identical to that described in section 5.1. To ensure that the two subparts are actually part of a common whole, we need to test that their interpretations are globally consistent. This can be done by means of a simple set of geometric constraints on their respective transformations. In this case, we require

$$s_L \approx s_R$$

$$\mathbf{t}_L \approx \mathbf{t}_R$$

Note that θ_L and θ_R could in principle take on any values. In practice, there is a limited range of orientations that the scissors can take on, so that a third constraint would be

$$\|\theta_L - \theta_R\| \leq C$$

where C is some threshold on the range of rotations, and the arith-

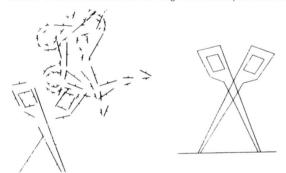

Figure 7. Examples of recognition when the free parameters are overall scale and rotation about a common axis. The left part shows a set of linear edges segments, the right part shows the located object.

metic is done modulo 2π. An example is shown in Figure 7.

Note that the search can be done independently for each part, followed by the application of the global constraints on each candidate pair of subparts. More effectively, we can first solve for the location of one of the subparts, and then use that position to restrict the possible positions of the second part, thereby directly removing some portions of the sensory data from consideration. We can also use the solution for the first subpart to restrict the values of the free parameters, for example, limiting the range of acceptable scale factors before beginning the search for the second subpart.

In this case, the data structures used to represent an object become somewhat more complex than in the case of rigid objects. Here, an object representation must include: a list of rigid subparts, each of

which is represented by a set of constraint tables as in the original recognition method; a list of the free parameters; a set of procedures for verifying the post constraints; and a procedure for generating the restricted search area for a part, as a function of the pose of solution for other parts.

5.3 Subparts that Stretch

As a third example, consider a family of tools, say a set of hammers with identical heads, but different handles. Again, we would like to extend our method to recognize both the identity and location of the hammer, and to determine which handle is attached. To model the handles, we assume that a generic shape (such as that shown in the left of figure 2) can stretch by some variable amount along an axis (in the case of the handle in figure 2 this is the axis of symmetry). The problem is to extend the search method to deal with constraints that are themselves parameterized. We do this as follows.

Without loss of generality, we assume that the model part has been oriented so that the axis of stretching is the x-axis in model coordinates. We let α denote the amount of stretching along that axis, with $\alpha = 1$ designating the base case. Note that α is likely to be restricted to some range of values, which may be specified beforehand.

Consider first the constraints on the surface normals. In the case of rigid models, our constraint was that the angle between two data normals must be the same as the angle between the corresponding model normals, to within some error. In the case of stretching parts, the normals will vary relative to one another as a function of the stretching parameter α. Suppose we let θ_{ij} denote the measured angular difference, we let ϵ denote the allowed error range in measuring the angles, and we let ϕ_i, ϕ_j denote the corresponding model angles, in model coordinates, for the base case $\alpha = 1$. By appropriate algebraic manipulation, the following cases hold.

(1) $\phi_i, \phi_j \in \{0, \pi, \frac{\pi}{2}, -\frac{\pi}{2}\}$. In this case, we need only check that $\theta_{ij} \in [\phi_i - \phi_j - \epsilon, \phi_i - \phi_j + \epsilon]$.

(2) $\phi_i \in \{0, \pi\}$. $\phi_j \notin \{0, \pi, \frac{\pi}{2}, -\frac{\pi}{2}\}$. In this case, the stretching factor is given by

$$\alpha = \frac{-\tan \theta_{ij}}{\tan \phi_j}.$$

A similar case holds when the roles of i and j are reversed.

(3) $\phi_i \in \{\frac{\pi}{2}, -\frac{\pi}{2}\}$. $\phi_j \notin \{0, \pi, \frac{\pi}{2}, -\frac{\pi}{2}\}$. In this case, the stretching factor is given by

$$\alpha = \frac{1}{\tan \theta_{ij} \tan \phi_j}.$$

A similar case holds when the roles of i and j are reversed.

(4) $\tan \phi_i \neq 0, \tan \phi_j \neq 0, \tan \theta_{ij} = 0$ In this case, $\alpha = 0$ which indicates an inconsistency.

(5) All other cases. The stretching factor is given by

$$\alpha = \frac{\tan \phi_i - \tan \phi_j}{2 \tan \phi_i \tan \phi_j \tan \theta_{ij}} \left[1 + \sqrt{1 - \frac{4 \tan^2 \theta_{ij} \tan \phi_i \tan \phi_j}{(\tan \phi_i - \tan \phi_j)^2}} \right].$$

Note that the measurement θ_{ij} is actually a range of measurements, so that the above cases will in fact produce a range of values for α.

For the edge direction constraint, we can perform a similar analysis. Suppose we are given two non-parallel data edges, each of which is designated by a base point $\mathbf{b}_i$ and an end point $\mathbf{e}_i$. These are chosen so that the tangent vector pointing from the base point to the end point is $90''$ clockwise from the normal vector $\hat{\mathbf{n}}_i$ to the edge. For these two edges, we can compute the component of the vector $\mathbf{b}_j - \mathbf{b}_i$

in the direction of the normal vector $\mathbf{n}_i$, which we call

$$d_\ell = \langle \mathbf{b}_j - \mathbf{b}_i, \hat{\mathbf{n}}_i \rangle$$

and the component

$$d_h = \langle \mathbf{e}_j - \mathbf{b}_i, \hat{\mathbf{n}}_i \rangle .$$

Then given a corresponding pair of model edges, we can compute similar components

$$m_{\ell.pq} = \langle \mathbf{b}_j - \mathbf{b}_i, \hat{\mathbf{n}}_i \rangle$$

and

$$m_{h.pq} = \langle \mathbf{e}_j - \mathbf{b}_i, \hat{\mathbf{n}}_i \rangle .$$

where in this case, the vectors to the end points of the edges are in model coordinates, rather than sensor coordinates. We also let

$$s = \text{signum} \left\{ \left\langle (\mathbf{e}_i - \mathbf{b}_i)^\perp , (\mathbf{e}_j - \mathbf{b}_j) \right\rangle \right\}$$

and we let Δx_i and Δy_i denote the x and y components respectively of the vector $\mathbf{e}_i - \mathbf{b}_i$. Then the range of values of the stretch factor α is given by the range spanned by

$$\alpha = \frac{s d_\ell \, |\Delta y_i|}{\sqrt{m_{\ell.pq}^2 - d_\ell^2 \, (\Delta x_i)^2}}$$

and

$$\alpha = \frac{s d_h \, |\Delta y_i|}{\sqrt{m_{h.pq}^2 - d_h^2 \, (\Delta x_i)^2}} .$$

In fact, one must also allow for error in the measurements, which will yield a range of values for d_ℓ and d_h, leading to a larger range of values for the stretching factor α.

To recognize the part, we must adjust the search process. In this case, we use a constraint propagation tree search. In the original search method, the constraints on a pair of measurements and a pair of model edges were used to provide a single bit of information: either the pairings had a consistent interpretation, or not. Here, we use the constraints to determine the range of values for the stretching parameter α that are consistent with that pairing of data fragments to model edges. These ranges can be propagated through the tree search, so that each node inherits the range of values consistent with its parent node. For each node, we can compute the range of values for the parameter, based on the pairing of the new data point and its associated model edge, against all other data/model pairings in the interpretation. Each such pair of pairs determines a new range, all of which are intersected to provide a new range of values. This range is intersected with the inherited range, to determine the range of values consistent with the new interpretation. If that range becomes empty, the interpretation is inconsistent, and we can backtrack in the tree and continue.

Figure 8 shows an example of a set of overlapping handles (taken from the family illustrated in Figure 3). A single instance of one of the handles is identified and located, including determining the actual value of the stretching parameter.

5.4 Combining Parameterizations

It is useful to be able to recognize objects that combine different types of parameterizations. For example, consider a pair of shears, that have both a rotational freedom between the two blades, and a stretching freedom along the axis of each blade. We can combine the methods described in Sections 5.2 and 5.3 to deal with this more general problem. An example is shown in Figure 9. Here, the system correctly solves for the position and orientation of the object, the angle of rotation between the blades and the stretching factor of the blades.

6. Relation to previous work

The literature on object recognition stretches over a period of at least twenty years. An extensive (70 page) review of much of this literature for 3D objects can be found in [Besl and Jain 1985]. A survey of model-based image analysis systems can be found in [Binford 1982].

In terms of the approach to be described here, a number of authors have taken a similar view to ours that recognition can be structured as an explicit search for a match between data elements and model elements [Ayache and Faugeras 86, Baird 85, Bolles and Cain 82, Bolles, Horaud and Hannah 83, Faugeras and Hebert 83, Goad 83, Lowe 86, Stockman and Esteva 84]. Of these, the work of Bolles and his colleagues, Faugeras and his colleagues, and that of Baird are closest to the approach presented here.

The interpretation tree approach is an instance of the consistent la-

Figure 9. Examples of recognition with different types of parameterizations. The object has a rotational free parameter and a stretching free parameter. The top part shows a set of linear edges segments, the bottom part shows the located object in isolation.

Figure 8. Examples of recognition when the free parameter is stretching along an axis. The left part shows a set of linear edges segments, the right part shows the located objects.

References

Ayache, N. J. and Faugeras, O. D. 1982. Recognition of partially visible planar shapes. *Proc. 6th Intl. Conf. Pattern Recognition,* Munich.

Ayache, N. J. and Faugeras, O. D. 1986. HYPER: A new approach for the recognition and positioning of two-dimensional objects. *IEEE Trans. Pattern Anal. Machine Intell.* PAMI-8(1):44–54.

Baird, H. 1986. *Model-Based Image Matching Using Location.* Cambridge: MIT Press.

beling problem that has been studied extensively in computer vision and artificial intelligence [Waltz 75, Montanari 74, Mackworth 77, Freuder 78, 82, Haralick and Shapiro 79, Haralick and Elliott 80, Mackworth and Freuder 85]. This paper can be viewed as suggesting a particular consistency relation (the constraints on distances and angles) and exploring its performance in a wide variety of circumstances. An alternative approach to the solution of consistent labeling problems is the use of relaxation. A number of authors have investigated this approach to object recognition [Davis 79, Bhanu and Faugeras 84, Ayache and Faugeras 82]. These techniques are more suitable for implementation on parallel machines.

The literature on recognition of parameterized objects is much smaller. The best known system is probably ACRONYM [Brooks 81], which also attacks the recognition problem by means of constraints to reduce ranges of parameterized variables.

Ballard, D. H. and Brown, C. M. 1982. *Computer Vision.* Englewood Cliffs:Prentice Hall.

Besl, P. J. and Jain, R. C. 1985. Three-Dimensional Object Recognition. *ACM Computing Surveys* 17(1): 75–145.

Bhanu, B. and Faugeras, O. D. 1984. Shape matching of two-dimensional objects. *IEEE Trans. Pattern Anal. Machine Intell.* PAMI-6(3).

Binford, T. O. 1982. Survey of model-based image analysis systems. *Int. Journ. of Robotics Research* 1(1):18–64.

Bolles, R. C., and Cain, R. A. 1982. Recognizing and locating partially visible objects: The Local-Feature-Focus method. *Int. J. Robotics Res.* 1(3):57–82.

Bolles, R. C., Horaud, P., and Hannah, M. J. 1983. 3DPO: A three-dimensional part orientation system. Paper delivered at First International Symposium of Robotics Research, Bretton Woods, N.H. (Also in Robotics Research: The First International Symposium, edited by M. Brady and R. Paul, MIT Press, 1984, pp. 413–424.)

Brooks, R., 1981. Symbolic reasoning among 3-dimensional models and 2-dimensional images. *Artificial Intel.* 17:285–349.

Davis, L. Shape matching using relaxation techniques. *IEEE Trans. Pattern Anal. Machine Intell.* PAMI-1(1):60–72.

Drumheller, M. 1987. Mobile Robot Localization Using Sonar. *IEEE Trans. Pattern Anal. Machine Intell.* PAMI-9(2): 325–332. (See also: S. B. Thesis, Dept. of Mechanical Engineering, MIT, 1984 and MIT AI Lab Memo 826, Mobile Robot Localization Using Sonar.)

Faugeras, O. D. and Hebert, M. 1983 (Aug., Karlsruhe, W. Germany). A 3-D recognition and positioning algorithm using geometrical matching between primitive surfaces. *Proc. Eighth Int. Joint Conf. Artificial Intell.* Los Altos: William Kaufmann, pp. 996–1002.

Faugeras, O. D., Hebert, M., and Pauchon, E. 1983 (June, Washington DC). Segmentation of range data into planar and quadratic patches. *Proc. CVPR'83.*

Freuder, E. C. 1978. Synthesizing constraint expressions. *Comm. of the ACM,* 21(11), pp. 958–966.

Freuder, E. C. 1982. A sufficient condition for backtrack-free search. *J. ACM,* 29(1), pp. 24–32.

Gaston, P. C., and Lozano-Pérez, T. 1984. Tactile recognition and localization using object models: The case of polyhedra on a plane. *IEEE Trans. Pattern Anal. Machine Intell.* PAMI-6(3):257–265.

Goad, C. 1983. Special purpose automatic programming for 3d model-based vision. in *Proceedings of DARPA Image Understanding Workshop.*

Grimson, W. E. L., 1986. The combinatorics of local constraints in model-based recognition and localization from sparse data. *J. ACM* 33(4):658–686.

Grimson, W. E. L., and Lozano-Pérez, T. 1984. Model-based recognition and localization from sparse range or tactile data. *Int. J. Robotics Res.* 3(3):3–35.

Grimson, W. E. L. and Lozano-Péez, T. 1986. Localizing overlapping parts by searching the iunterpretation tree. *IEEE Trans. Patt. Anal. and Mach. Intel.* to appear. (see also MIT AI Lab Memo 841, June 1985.)

Haralick, R. M. and Elliott, G. 1980. Increasing tree search efficiency for constraint satisfaction problems. *Artificial Intelligence,* Vol. 14, pp. 263–313.

Haralick, R. M. and Shapiro, L. G. 1979. *IEEE Trans. Pattern Anal. Machine Intell.* PAMI-1(4):173–184.

Lowe, D. G. 1986. Three-dimensional object recognition from single two-dimensional images. Courant Institute Robotics Report, No. 62.

Marr, D. and Hildreth, E. C. 1980. Theory of edge detection. *Proc. R. Soc. Lond.* B 207:187–217.

Mackworth, A. K. 1977. Consistency in networks of constraints. *Artificial Intelligence,* Vol. 8, pp. 99–118.

Mackworth, A. K. and Freuder, E. C. 1985. The complexity of some polynomial network consistency algorithms for constraint satisfaction problems. *Artificial Intelligence,* Vol. 25, pp. 65–74.

Montanari, U. 1974. Networks of constraints: Fundamental properties and applications to picture processing. *Inform. Sci.,* Vol. 7, pp 95–132.

Stockman, G., and Esteva, J. C. 1984. Use of geometrical constraints and clustering to determine 3D object pose. TR84-002. East Lansing, Mich.:Michigan State University Department of Computer Science.

Waltz, D. 1975. Understanding line drawings of scenes with shadows. in *The Psychology of Computer Vision,* P. Winston, Ed. New York:Mc Graw Hill, pp 19 – 91.

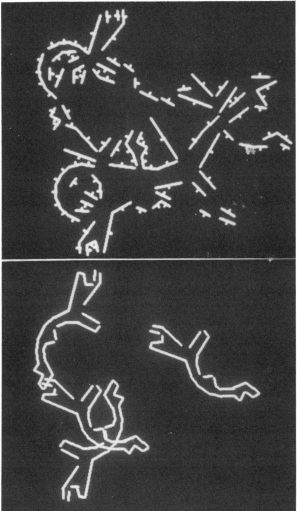

Figure 2. An example of the RAF system on two-dimensional data. A pile of
laminar parts is shown in part a. A set of linear edge fragments, extracted
by fitting linear segments to zero-crossings of a Marr-Hildreth operator are
shown in part b. The position of the identified parts in shown in part c
(the system was only interested in the smaller part).

Modeling Sensor Performance
for Model-Based Vision

Katsushi Ikeuchi
Takeo Kanade

**Department of Computer Science
and
Robotics Institute**

**Carnegie-Mellon University
Pittsburgh, PA 15213**

The model-based vision requires object appearances in the computer. How an object appears in the image is a result of interaction between the object properties and the sensor characteristics. Thus, in model-based vision, we ought to model the sensor as well as modeling the object. In the past, however, the sensor model was not used in the model-based vision or, at least, was contained in the object model implicitly.

This paper presents a framework between an object model and the object appearances. We consider two aspects of sensor characteristics: sensor detectability and sensor reliability. Sensor detectability specifies what kind of features can be detected and in what area the features are detected; sensor reliability specifies how reliable detected features are. Commonly available sensors are briefly examined in terms of their sensor characteristics. We define the configuration space to represent sensor characteristics. We propose a representation method of the sensor detectability in the configuration space. Sensor reliability distribution is also discussed in the configuration space. Under this framework, we characterize the photometric stereo and the light-stripe range finder as examples.

1. INTRODUCTION

The model-based vision requires object models in the computer. Various researchers propose many kinds of object models, ranging from generic models such as generalized cylinders [5, 28, 9, 37], extended Gaussian images [38, 19, 18], and super quadric models [35] to specific models such as aspect model [25, 11, 20], region-relation model [4, 34, 6], and smooth local symmetry [7, 8].

The object appearances, however, are determined by a *product* of an object model with a sensor model. Thus, in the model based vision, it is insufficient to consider only an object model; it is essential to exploit a sensor model as well. On the other hand, modeling sensors for model-based vision has attracted little attension; quite often, researchers who are familiar with the sensors they use tended to construct object appearances by implicitly incorporating their sensor behavior. This paper, in contrast, explores a general framework for explicitly incorporating sensor models which govern the relationship between object models and object appearances.

A sensor model must be able to specify two important characteristics: sensor detectability and sensor reliability. The sensor detectability specifies what kind of features can be detected and in what condition the features are detected. The sensor reliability specifies how reliable the detected features are. This paper, thus, present a method for modeling sensors with sensor detectability and sensor reliability. Commonly available sensors are briefly examined in terms of their sensor characteristics. Then, representation techniques for sensor characteristics are explored. We define the configuration space to represent sensor characteristics. Finally, we consider two aspects of sensor characteristics: sensor detectability and sensor reliability. We propose a representation

space on which a sensor's detectability is expressed in the uniform way. Sensor reliability analysis consists of reliability distribution and error propagation from observed data to geometric features. Under this framework, we characterize the photometric stereo and the light-stripe range finder as examples.

2. SENSORS IN THE MODEL BASED VISION

This section gives a brief survey of commonly available sensors in the model-based vision. We include both passive and active sensors. The following sensors are often used: edge detector [36, 27, 10], shape-from-shading [17, 22], binocular stereo [29, 14, 3, 33], time-of-flight range finder [24, 15], light-stripe range finder [1, 34], trinocular stereo [32], photometric stereo [40, 21], polarimetric light detector [26],and SAR (Synthetic Aperture Radar) [12, 39, 31].

Each sensor is a mapping function from object features to sensor features. Object features such as faces, edges, and verteces exist in the three-dimensional object space. These object features in the object space are mapped to sensor features such as regions, lines, and points in the sensor space. Note that the sensor features has no meaningful interpretation in the sensor space. For example, a sensor feature such as a region should be considered as a collection of points which are not grouped as one meaningful unit by a sensor. The conversion process from sensor features to geometric features will group a collection of ponits into a geometric feature such as a region.

Table 1 gives the summary of detectable features in the object space by commonly available sensors. For example, an edge detector can detect some edges in the object space as lines in the sensor space. Since it does not need special light sources, it is classified as a passive sensor.

Table 1 Detectable Object Features				
Sensor	Vertex	Edge	Face	active/passive
Edge Detector	no	yes	no	passive
Shape-from-shading	no	no	yes	passive
SAR	yes	yes	yes	active
Time-of-Flight Range Finder	no	no	yes	active
Light-stripe Range Finder	no	no	yes	active
Binocular Stereo	no	yes	no	passive
Trinocular Stereo	no	yes	no	passive
Photometric Stereo	no	no	yes	active
Polarimetric light detector	no	no	yes	active

3. REPRESENTING SENSOR CONFIGURATION

This section defines the sensor configuration space on which sensor detectablility and sensor reliability are specified. Sensor detectability and reliability depend on various factors: distance of an object, configuration of an object, reflectivity of an object, transparency of air, and background noise such as the sun's brightness. In the model-based vision, since the target object and its rough distance is a prior known, mainly angular freedom of object affects on detectability and reliability. Thus, we will define a space to spacify the relationship between the sensor coordinate and the object coordinate.

The relationship between the sensor coordinate and the object coordinate can be specified by three degrees of freedoms; two degrees of freedom in the sensor direction and one degree of freedom in the sensor rotation. Since the relationship between two coordinates is ralative, for the sake of convenience, we fix the sensor coordinate and discuss how to specify the object coordinate with respect to the sensor coordinate.

We will depict an object coordinate as a point in the following sphere. The point direction from the center denotes the z axis of the object coordinate, (θ, ϕ), where θ and ϕ specify the zenith angle and the azimuth angle of the z axis. The distance from the spherical surface to the point denotes the axis rotation around the z axis, ψ. On the spherical surface, we set points such that corresponding coordinates satisfy $\phi + \psi = 0$. The north pole of the sphere corresponds to the sensor coordinate.

Due to the bias of z axis rotation, this sphere has no discontinuity around the north pole. Actually, this sphere is a three dimensional projection of four dimensional quaternion space. Precise discussion will be found [23]. We will refer to the sphere as the configuration space.

Since the brightness change does not occur over any face, passive sensors have usually difficulty in detecting faces. An active sensor projects lights over the scene; stronger reflection can be obtained from faces; weaker or no reflection is given from edges and vertices. Thus, most active sensors are good in detecting faces, while they can detect neither edges nor vertices.

Sensor features in the sensor space are summarized in Table 2. In Table 2, a line means a line-shaped collection of detected points and a region means a region-shaped collection of detected points. For all sensors except SAR the correspondence between the object feature and the sensor feature is one-to-one. For example, an edge detector geenrates one line-shaped sensor feature corresponding to either one edge or one reflectance discontinuity line of a object feature in the object space. Photometric stereo generates a surface orientation distribution as sensor features which corresponds to one physical face in the object space. On the other hand, SAR generates either line-shaped sensor feature or point sensor feature from one edge in the object space depending on the sensor configuration. A precise discussion of SAR will be found elsewhere [12, 39, 31].

Table 2 Detected Sensor Features			
Sensor	Vertex	Edge	Face
Edge Detector	-	line	-
Shape-from-shading	-	-	region
SAR	point	point/line	line
Time-of-Flight Range Finder	-	-	region
Light-stripe Range Finder	-	-	region
Binocular Stereo	-	line	-
Trinocular Stereo	-	line	-
Photometric Stereo	-	-	region
Polarimetric light Detector	-	-	point

While this summary tells in general what object features are detectable in what forms by various sensors, it is also important to characterize in what viewing conditions those features are actually detectable and how reliable the detected features are. For that, we need to develop a representation tool for relation between object coordinates and sensor coordinates.

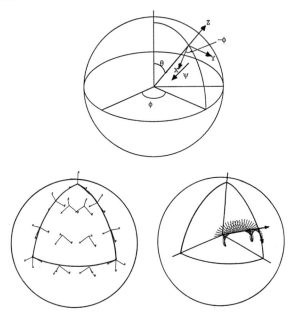

Figure 1: The configuration space

4. DETECTABILITY OF SENSORS

In the previous section, we have defined the way to represent the relationship between the sensor coordinate and the object coordinate. In this section, we will develop a constraint to determine whether an object feature can be detected at each point of the configuration space.

4.1. Constraints in Configuration Space for Feature Detection

Each sensor has two components: sources and detectors. For example, both a time-of-flight range finder and a light-stripe range finder have one source and on detector. Binocular stereo has one source and two detectors; photometric stereo has three sources and one detector. Table 3 summarizes the number of sources and detectors of each sensor.

Table 3 Source and Detector		
Sensor	Number of sources	Number of detectors
Edge Detector	1	1
Shape-from-shading	1	1
SAR	1	1
Time-of-Flight Range Finder	1	1
Light-stripe Range Finder	1	1
Binocular Stereo	1	2
Trinocular Stereo	1	3
Photometric Stereo	3	1
Polarimetric light detector	n	1

One source only illuminates one part of an object; one detector only observes one part of the object. Each sensor which consists of sources and detectors, only detect one part of the object. Thus, in order to specify the detectable area of each sensors, we need to define each source's illuminated area and each detector's visible area. We also need to define a operation method on illuminated areas and visible areas.

In the following discussion, we will consider both sources and detectors as generalized sources (G-sources). Each G-source has two properties: the illumination direction and the illuminated area. In the source case, the illumination direction and the illuminated area are the same as the nominal meanings. In the case of detectors, the illumination direction corresponds to the line of sight of the detector, and the illuminated area corresponds to the visible area from the detector.

In order to define the sensor detectability, we will use the configuration space previously defined. The illumination direction of a G-source is specified as a line in the configuration space; its illuminated area is specified as a volume in the configuration space. We will define two kinds of G-sources in terms of the distribution of illuminated areas: the uniform G-source and the directional G-source. A uniform G-source distributes its light evenly in all directions. An example of a uniform G-source is a usual light source whose illuminated area is located as a hemispherical corn of the sensor space. The center direction of the corn corresponds to the source direction.

We specify a uniform G-source as

(*NS type direction angle*)

The first argument, *type*, specifies what kind of feature the G-source illuminates, and takes one of the values; *face*, *edge*, and *vertex*. The second argument, *direction*, denotes the G-source illumination direction as a vector. The third argument, *angle* defines the illuminated area by specifying the spherical angle between the illumination direction and the surface normals associated with object features. If *type* is *face*, this angle defines the maximum allowable angle between the face surface normal and the illumination direction. If *type* is *edge*, this angle defines the maximum allowable angle of the smaller one of the two angles between the illumination direction and the two normals of incident surfaces to the edge. That is, if either or both faces are well illuminated, then the edge is considered to be illuminated. If *type* is *vertex*, we have to consider at least three faces incident to the vertex. This angle defines the maximum allowable angle of the smallest angle of those angles between the illumination diretion and the normals of incident surfaces. That is, if any of the incident faces of the vertex is illuminated, the vertex is considered to be illuminated.

Another kind of G-source is a directional G-source which projects light depending on the rotation around the light source direction. We specify a directional G-source as

(*DS type direction angle spec–direction spec–angle*)

The first argument, *type*, specifies one of the object features: *vertex*, *edge*, and *face*. The second argument, *direction*, denotes the G-source illumination direction as a vector. The third argument, *angle*, defines the spherical angle of the illuminated area, as for the uniform G-source. The fourth argument, *spec–direction* defines the constraint direction to be used in the following argument. The fifth argument, *spec–angle* defines the maximum allowable angle between the constraint direction and the principal direction such as the surface normal of a face, the edge direction of an edge, and the average surface orientation around a vertex.

An example of a directional source is a directional edge detector. As mentioned before, a detector is also considered as a source, and its illuminated area corresponds to the detectable area. Since the directional edge detector only detects edges with certain orientations, it is regarded as a directional source. The illuminated area of a directional source becomes a thin slice of the configuration space.

We can specify the sensor characteristic with AND and OR operations of these formal definitions of all component G-sources of the sensors. Figure 2 shows feature detection constraints represented by this method for all sensors listed in table 3.

4.2. Use of Feature Detection Constraints

The feature detection constraints are used together with a geometric modeler to predict how the object appears relative to the sensor. A geometric modeler generates possible attitudes of an object corresponding to each point in the configuration space. Then, detectability of each component face, edge, or vertex of the object

Sensor	Constraints in the formal definition	Constraints in the sensor space
Edge Detector	(AND (NS edge V d) (NS edge V d)) = (NS edge V d)	
Shape-from-shading	(AND (NS face V d) (NS face V d)) = (NS face V d)	
SAR	(OR (NS face V d) (NS face V d) (NS vertex V d)) (needs postprocess)	
Time-of-Flight Range Finder	(AND (NS face V d) (NS face V d)) = (NS face V d)	
Light-strip Range Finder	(AND (NS face V1 d) (NS face V2 d))	
Binocular Stereo	(AND (NS edge V1 d1) (DS edge V2 d2 VE de) (DS edge V3 d3 VE de))	
Trinocular Stereo	(AND (NS edge V1 d1) (DS edge V2 d2 VE de) (DS edge V3 d2 VE de) (DS edge V4 d2 VE de))	
Photometric Stereo	(AND (NS face V d1) (NS face V1 d2) (NS face V2 d2) (NS face V3 d2))	
Polarimetric Light Detector	(OR (AND (NS face V d) (NS face V1 d)) (AND (NS face V d) (NS face V2 d)) . . .) where V . V = cos 2d	

Figure 2: Feature detection constraints

under this attitude is determined using the constraint. The illumination direction constrains the surface shape to be detected, and the illuminated area constrains the surface orientation to be detected.

More precisely, we can imagine puting the configuration space on each point of the object in order checked whether it can be detected by the sensor. If the illumination direction from that point intersects with any of the surfaces of the object, the point cannot be detected. If the illumination direction does not intersect with any of the

surface, the point is detectable. If the surface orientation on the point is contained in the illuminated area, the point is detectable. If the surface orientation is outside of the illuminated area, the point cannot be detected. Figure 3 illustrate the outline of this operation for the illumination direction and illuminated area using this constraint.

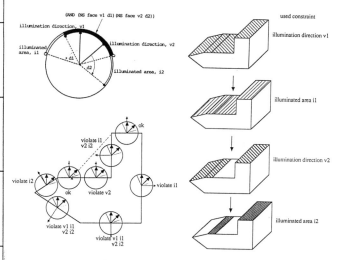

Figure 3: How to use the constraints

4.3. Detectability Distribution

The feature detection constraint gives the upper bound of the detectable areas in the configuration space. In some cases, however even though a object feature exists within the detectable area, the feature may be undetected due to noise. We define the detectability distribution such that a feature in the detectable area is actually detected. The probability is usually high in the central part and low in the peripheral part of the detectable area.

The detectability distribution can be described by multiplication of detectability distributions of the component G-sources. Namely, each G-source has a detectability distribution defined over the illuminated area. In the previous subsection, the constraint was either illuminated or non illuminated or either detectable or non-detectable. We will expand this idea to the continuous case. Namely, each G-source has its own continuous detectable distribution over its illuminated area defined in the configuration space.

Since all sensors detect features based on a brightness distribution, the detectability distribution also depends on a brightness distribution which is detected and converted to sensor features. However, there are two types of sensors in terms of the conversion method; direct sensors and indirect sensors. The direct sensor measures the brightness value and converts it to sensor features, such as surface orientation, directly from the brightness value. The indirect sensor measures the brightness value and positional information of the bright spot if the brightness value is greater than some threshold. The indirect sensor then converts the positional information to sensor features such as depth. Table 4 shows a classification of sensors based on this difference.

Since a TV camera is a most typical input device, we will examine its performance before exploring the detectability distribution. Let $P(x|d), P(d|x)$, and $P(x)$ be the conditional probability of a real value x

Table 4	Measurement method
sensor	direct/indirect
Edge Detector	direct
Shape-from-shading	direct
SAR	indirect
Time-of-Flight Range Finder	indirect
Light-stripe Range Finder	indirect
Binocular Stereo	indirect
Trinocular Stereo	indirect
Photometric Stereo	direct
Polarimetric light detector	indirect

under the observed value d, the conditional probability of the observed data d under a real value x, and the probability of x, respectively. Then, TV camera performance can be described using Bayes' theorem as

$$P(x|d) = \frac{P(d|x)P(x)}{\int P(d|x)P(x)dx}.$$

If we assume that $P(x)$ is constant, namely the brightness distribution occurs randomly,

$$P(x|d) = P(d|x).$$

The conditional probability of observed data d under the real value x is assumed as the Gaussian distribution whose mean value is x and standard deviation is σ,

$$P(x|d) = \frac{1}{\sqrt{2\pi}\sigma} e^{-\frac{(x-d)^2}{2\sigma^2}}.$$

We can obtain σ from experiments. Our SONY CCD camera has $\sigma=3$, which roughly coincides with a result elsewhere [2].

Since the detectability distribution depends on sensing methods, we will develop the distributions for the photometric stereo as a representative case of the direct sensor, and for the light-stripe range finder as a representative case of the indirect sensor.

4.3.1. Detectability distribution of photometric stereo
An direct sensor such as photometric stereo can be modeled as

$$\mathbf{y} = f(\mathbf{x})$$

where $\mathbf{x}$ is the input brightness, $\mathbf{y}$ is the output feature values, and f is the conversion function. Suppose $\mathbf{X}^*$ is the definition area of the function f; ie, the direct sensor outputs a feature value $\mathbf{y}$ from any $\mathbf{x}_i$ if $\mathbf{x}_i \in \mathbf{X}^*$. Then, the detectability distribution can be determined as the probability that the input brightness, $\mathbf{x}+\delta\mathbf{x}$, disturbed by $\delta\mathbf{x}$, is still contained in the definition area, $\mathbf{X}^*$. In order to be the problem more specific, we will examine the definition area of photometric stereo.

Photometric stereo determines the surface orientation from three images taken from the same position under different lighting directions.

$$I_1 = S_1 \bullet N$$
$$I_2 = S_2 \bullet N$$
$$I_3 = S_3 \bullet N,$$

where I_i, S_i, N are the brightness value under light source i, the i th light source direction vector, and the surface normal vector, respectively. Thus, expressing the brightness as a vector, $\mathbf{I}$, and the light source as a matrix, $\mathbf{S}$,

$$\mathbf{I} = \mathbf{SN}.$$

Applying $\mathbf{S}^{-1}$ to both sides, we obtain an explicit expression of $\mathbf{N}$,

$$\mathbf{N} = \mathbf{S}^{-1}\mathbf{I}.$$

This is the basic idea of photometric stereo [40].

Working photometric stereo has, however, two modification [21] to this theory.

1. $\mathbf{S}^{-1}$ is determined from calibration and stored in a lookup table rather than calculated from the ideal case.

2. Brightness values are normalized $\mathbf{I}/|\mathbf{I}|$ so that we can cancel the albedo effect.

We will obtain the detectability distribution of the photometric stereo. At first, we consider light source 1's detectability distribution. Assume a brightness value moves from i_1 to $i_1+\delta i_1$ due to sensor error. The normalization gives $i'_1+\delta i'_1 = (i_1+\delta e_1)/(i_1+\delta i_1+i_2+i_3)$. However, the normalized intensity $(i'_1+\delta i'_1, i'_2, i'_3)$ exists on the same plane $i'_1+\delta i'_1+i'_2+i'_3=1$. Since a continuous area on the plane is the solution area for photometric stereo, we can obtain the solution from the new triple $i'_1+\delta i'_1, i_2, i_3$. Than is, we will always succeed to obtain the feature values, ie. we will have a unit detectability distribution for the light source 1. (Though of course the resultant value may be less reliable as will be discussed in the reliability section.) The same discussion is applicable to light source 2 and light source 3. Since the total detectability distribution is given as the multiple of all three detectability distributions of sources, the detectability distribution is a constant distribution over the detectable area in the configuration space. This analysis reveals that the normalization makes the detectability to be a unit value, and thus, helps to detect features in a stable manner.

4.3.2. Detectability distribution of a light-stripe range finder
An indirect sensor projects light on the scene and determines the positional features from the observed image or signal. Thus, the detectability distribution depends on whether a sensor can detect the returned light or not. Usually, to avoid the confusion of the returned value with background noise, threshold operations are applied, such as

$$\begin{array}{ll} i \text{ is detected} & \text{if } i \geq i_0 \\ i \text{ is not detected} & \text{otherwise.} \end{array}$$

Let us consider the light-stripe range finder as an example. A light-stripe range finder projects light stripes on the scene and recovers the depth at a point from the distance between two adjacent light stripes. Thus, the detectability function depends on whether the TV camera observes the light stripes or not.

Assuming that the surface is lambertian, the brightness of the stripe is determined by the angle between the surface normal, $\mathbf{N}$, and the light source direction, $\mathbf{S}$. Then, the brightness i is given by $\mathbf{N} \bullet \mathbf{S}$, while the disturbance factor δi is given by a Gaussian distribution,

$$p(\delta i)=\frac{1}{\sqrt{2\pi}\sigma}e^{-\frac{(\delta i)^2}{2\sigma^2}}.$$

In almost all illuminated areas, $\mathbf{N}\bullet\mathbf{S}-i_0>>3\sigma$ holds, and the viewer direction does not affect the observed brightness. Thus, the detectability distribution is constant over the most part of illuminated area of the light source. In the peripheral area, however,

$$P_{detectable}(i)=P(i+\delta i\geq i_0)=\int_{i_0-i}^{+\infty}\frac{1}{\sqrt{2\pi}\sigma}e^{-\frac{(\delta i)^2}{2\sigma^2}}d(\delta i)$$

See Figure 4.

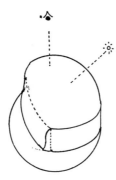

Figure 4: Detectability distribution
of a light-stripe range finder

5. RELIABILITY OF SENSORS

Once a sensor feature is detected, then the next question is how reliable the sensor feature is. This section discusses two issues of sensor reliability. The first issue is the reliability of the detected sensor feature; data detected by a sensor always contains measurement error. To determine the bound of the error is important for model based vision. For example, suppose there is a sensor feature which the geometric model takes two nominal value 100 and 90 for two distinct situations or attitudes. If a sensor has an error range of plus/minus 1 for the sensor feature, we can use the feature from that sensor as one of reliable discriminators in the recognition stage. On the other hand, if a sensor has an error range of plus/minus 20, we cannot use the feature from that sensor.

The second issue is propagation of error from sensor features to geometric features, hence the resulting reliability of those geometric features. In some cases, a detected sensor feature from a sensor is used directly as a feature; in most cases, however, geometric features are derived from sensor features and are used as features in model based vision. Thus, it is necessary to determine the error propagation mechanism.

5.1. Reliability Distribution of Sensor Feature

Table 5 shows the main sources that affect reliability of sensor features. In addition to these, various digitization such as phase digitization in a time-of-flight range finder and spatial digitization in binocular stereo must be considered but are omitted for the time being.

Table 5	Main factor of unreliability
Sensor	Factor
Edge Detector	G-source brightness (TV camera)
Shape-from-shading	G-source brightness (TV camera)
SAR	G-source direction (camera direction)
Time-of-Flight Range Finder	G-source direction (mirror direction)
Light-Strip Range Finder	G-source direction (mirror direction)
Binocular Stereo	G-source direction (camera direction)
Trinocular Stereo	G-source direction (camera direction)
Photometric Stereo	G-source brightness (TV camera, light sources)
Polarimetric light detector	G-source direction (light source direction)

As shown in Table 5, the main error comes from G-source brightness in a direct sensor and from G-source direction in a indirect sensor. Thus, we will analyze the reliability of photometric stereo and the light-stripe range finder as representatives of the direct and indirect sensors, respectively.

5.1.1. Reliability distribution of photometric stereo
For the direct sensor, $y=f(\mathbf{x})$, the disturbance of $\delta\mathbf{x}$ is propagated via f. Namely, the disturbance of the detected value, δy is

$$\delta\mathbf{y}=f'(\mathbf{x})\delta\mathbf{x}$$

Our photometric stereo can be described as two step processes. First a original brightness triple is converted to a normalized brightness triple.

$$\mathbf{I'}=\mathbf{I}/|\mathbf{I}|.$$

Then, the normalized brightness triple is converted to a surface orientation $\mathbf{N}$.

$$\mathbf{N}=\mathbf{S}^{-1}\mathbf{I'}.$$

Let us denote the brightness disturbance distribution as $N(0,\sigma^2)$. Then the normalized brightness distribution is denoted as $N(I,(\sigma f')^2)$, where f' is the first derivative of f. Figure 5a shows the distribution of f' over the detectable area. Although it is possible to approximate the distribution with polynomial, we assume it is constant (0.004) over the detectable area for simplicity. Since $\sigma=3$, $2\sigma f'=0.03$. This value corresponds to a 1.5 mesh in the lookup table.

We determine $\mathbf{S}^{-1}$ from the real data, because $\mathbf{S}^{-1}$ is represented as a lookup table. Figure 5b shows the angular distance in terms of mesh number. Namely, the figure shows angular differences between two adjacent surface normals in the lookup table. By using this result and a 1.5 mesh error from the brightness distribution, the total error becomes 5 degrees over the detectable area. This agrees with the observation from the experiment, which has plus/minus 5 degrees error in determining surface orientations over the range of detectable surface orientations. See Figure 5c.

5.1.2. Reliability distribution of a light-stripe range finder
In the case of indirect sensors, the main source of unreliability comes not from the G-source brightness but from the G-source direction. The indirect sensor can be modeled as

$$\mathbf{z}=f(\mathbf{y}(\mathbf{v}_1,\mathbf{v}_2,..\mathbf{v}_n)).$$

$\mathbf{v}_i$ denotes the ith G-source direction, and $\mathbf{y}$ denotes the conversion function from G-source directions to the positional information, while f denotes the conversion function from the positional information such as a bright spot to the observed data, and $\mathbf{z}$ specifies

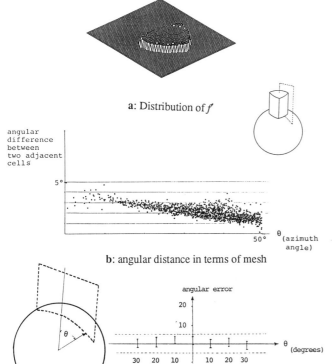

a: Distribution of f'

b: angular distance in terms of mesh

angular error

c: angular error over the detectable area

Figure 5 Reliability of photometric stereo

the deteced data such as depth or surface orientation.

$$\delta \mathbf{z} = \Sigma_i f' \frac{\partial \mathbf{y}}{\partial \mathbf{v}_i} \delta \mathbf{v}_i.$$

Thus, we will examine the disturbance based on the G-source direction.

In the light-stripe range finder, we will calculate $f'\frac{\partial \mathbf{y}}{\partial \mathbf{v}_i}$ directly from the system analysis. The angular error in the mirror is propagated to the observed error with the physical conversion process. The propagation process can be divided into three parts: mirror error to positional difference in the stripe, positional difference in the stripe to image difference, and image difference to the converted distance difference. The propagation process can be obtained analytically as follows.

Let us denote the angular error as $r\delta\theta$, where r is the distance from the light source to the physical point. At the physical place A, the laser light is intercepted. Then, due to the angular error, the physical difference, δy occurs.

$$\delta y = \frac{r}{\cos \alpha} \delta\theta,$$

where α is the angle between the light source, **S**, and the surface normal, **N**. See Figure 6a.

This physical difference is observed from the TV camera, and the image difference, δi occurs.

$$\delta i = (\cos \beta)\delta y,$$

where β is the angle between the surface normal, **N**, and the viewer

direction, **V**.

The third step is the propagation from the image plane to the distance. For the simplicity, we will assume that the camera model be orthographic projection. Then, the horizontal difference, δi, is propagated into the distance error δz as

$$\delta z = \frac{\delta i}{\tan \gamma},$$

where γ, is the angle between the viewer direction, **V**, and the light source direction, **S**. See Figure 6a.

Finally, we obtain

$$\delta z = \frac{\cos \beta}{\cos \alpha \tan \gamma} r\delta\theta$$

$$= \frac{(\mathbf{N} \cdot \mathbf{V})(\mathbf{S} \cdot \mathbf{V})}{(\mathbf{N} \cdot \mathbf{S})\sqrt{1 - \mathbf{S} \cdot \mathbf{V}}} r\delta\theta.$$

Figure 6b shows the reliability distribution over the detectable area.

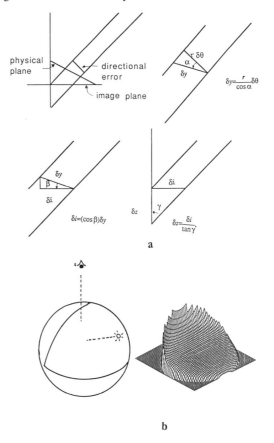

Figure 6: Reliability distribution of light-stripe range finder

5.2. Propagation of Reliability to Geometric Features

Usually raw data detected by a sensor is converted into geometric features such as distance, area, and inertia. This process propagates errors into the geometric features due to two reasons: the detectability distribution and the reliability distribution. Since this conversion process depends on the detected data, we will concentrate on faces as detected data, because most of the active sensors detect faces as the primal features.

5.2.1. Error propagation from detetability distribution

Most active sensors detect physical patches as detected pixels. Usually, these detected pixels will be grouped and converted into isolated regions. If the sensor fails to find a detectable pixel, the measured area will be reduced from the nominal area size given by a model. This process can be modeled as follows:

Suppose the detectability probability is p over a region and the nominal area size of the region is n. Under this condition, the probability to observe x pixels out of n pixels over the region is

$$P(x)=\binom{n}{x}p^x q^{n-x}$$

Namely, this probability denotes that the system executes n trials and succeeds to detect x pixels under that condition that success probability is p and fail probability is q, where $p+q=1$. This process is a binomial distribution; the mean and variance of this distribution are

$$m=np$$
$$\sigma^2=npq$$

This gives the error propagation (area reduction ratio) for the detectability distribution.

Since both photometric stereo and a light-stripe range finder give $p=1$, neither sensor causes an area reduction due to the detectability distribution.

5.2.2. Error propagation from reliability distribution

The Next factors to be considered is the reliability of detected data. We recover the geometric features such as distance, area, and inertia from skewed raw data by an affine transform, based on the observed surface orientation in either the photometric stereo or light-stripe range finder. Thus, if the raw data are erroneous, the obtained geometric features are also erroneous.

Let d be the real distance, and $d+\delta d$ be the observed one. Then, the physical system generates an observed distance $d\cos\theta$, while due to the sensor error, we will measure this surface surface orientation as $\cos(\theta+\delta\theta)$, where θ is the angle between the viewer and surface normal. Thus, for $\delta\theta$ small, we get

$$d+\delta d = d\cos\theta/\cos(\theta+\delta\theta) = d(1+\delta\theta\tan\theta).$$

In the area case,

$$a+\delta a = a(1+2\delta\theta\tan\theta).$$

In the inertia case,

$$i+\delta i = i(1+3\delta\theta\tan\theta).$$

These formulas give error propagation from angular error to features at each pixel. We will obtain geometric features from a region which consists of n pixels. Thus, the system will execute n trials of measuring $\delta\theta_i$ which is approximated as a Gaussian distribution, $N(0,\sigma^2)$, and observe the total $\Sigma_i\delta\theta$. From the theorm of the Gaussian distribution, $\delta\Theta=\Sigma_i\delta\theta$ is a Gaussian distribution, $N(0,n\sigma^2)$.

By using these formulas, we calculate error ratio of areas and inertia for photometric stereo as shown in Table 6. Predicted results are obtained based on the reliability of photometric stereo developed previously and the formulas of section. We use $n=70$, $\sigma=0.045$.

Observed results are obtained from the distribution of the real data sampled five times. Similar results are expected in the other sensors.

Table 6	Reliability of Geometric Features	
Feature	Observed	Predicted
Area	0.02	0.045
Inertia	0.05	0.067

6. CONCLUDING REMARKS

This paper discussed modeling sensors for model-based vision. Our sensor model consists of two characteristics: sensor detectability and sensor reliability. Sensor detectability specifies under what conditions a sensor can detect a feature, while sensor reliability denotes how reliable the obtained measurement is over the detectable area.

We have defined the configuration space which represents the relationship between sensor coordinates and object coordinates. The sensor detectability and the sensor reliability are expressed in this configuration space. Constraints in the configuration space involved in detecting features have been developed by using G-source illuminated area and G-source illumination direction. We have shown how to compute the sensor detectability distribution and the sensor reliability distribution for photometric stereo and a light-stripe range finder as examples.

In model based vision, expected values of various features can be computed from 3D geometric model. Those values are, however, nominal values that they should take in ideal cases or should be sensed by ideal sensors. On the other hand, actually observed sensor data contains noises and should be used accordingly. The sensor model bridges the discrepancy between these two values by modeling the distribution of the sensed value based on the characteristics of a given sensor. In model-based vision, it is possible to precompile a given 3D geometric model into a recognition strategy [20]. This precompilation cannot generate an optimal strategy without knowing each feature's reliability, because the strategy should use the most stable features at each recognition step. Thus, the sensor model is an essential component in model-based vision. We have to explore more reliable sensor models for this purpose.

We also have analyzed the error propagation mechanism from detected data to the geometric features. This is important, because quite often we are interested in geometric features derived from the detected sensor features. Once we establish the error propagation mechanism from detected sensor features to geometric features, we can also assess the reliability of the geometric features, hence we can construct a recognition system more systematically and reliably. Further study is required in this area.

To calculate detectable features of an object under the constraints of various sensors is a tedious job when we use a conventional geometric modeler. The better way is to interface a geometric modeler with the sensor model proposed. We call this a sensor modeler. The traditional geometric modeler only allows users to generate a 3D object by combining primitive objects and to display its views. In this sense, the traditional modeling system has only one sensor model which is projection. The sensor modeler we propose can generate various 2D representations under given sensor specifications. Part of this facility is being implemented in our new geometric/sensor modeler VANTAGE [16].

ACKNOWLEDGEMENT

The authors thank Richard Mickelsen, Steven Shafer, Yoshinori Kuno, Huey Chang, and the member of IUS (Image Understanding System) group of Carnegie-Mellon University for their valuable comments and discussions.

This research was sponsored by the Defense Advanced Research Projects Agency, DOD, through ARPA Order No. 4976, and monitored by the Air Force Avionics Laboratory under contract F33615-84-K-1520. The views and conclusions contained in this document are those of the authors and should not be interpreted as representing the official policies, either expressed or implied, of the Defense Advanced Research Projects Agency or of the U.S. Government.

References

[1]   Agin, G.J. and Binford, T.O.
      Computer description of curved objects.
      In *Proc. of 3rd Intern. Joint Conf. on Artificial Intelligence*, pages 629-640. Stanford, CA, August, 1973.

[2]   R. Bajcsy, E. Krotkov, M. Mintz.
      Models of errors and mistakes in machine perception.
      In *Proc. of Image Understanding Workshop*. DARPA, 1987.

[3]   Baker, H.H. and Binford, T.O.
      Depth from edges and intensity based stereo.
      In *Proc. of 7th Intern. Joint Conf. on Artificial Intelligence*. 1981.

[4]   Barrow, H.G. and Popplestone, R.J.
      Relational description in picture processing.
      Machine Intelligence 6.
      Edinburgh University Press, Edinburgh, Scotland, 1970.

[5]   Binford, T.O.
      Visual perception by computer.
      In *Proc. IEEE Systems Science and Cybernetics Conf.*. IEEE, 1971.

[6]   Bolles, R.C. and Horaud, P.
      3DPO: A three-dimensional part orientation system.
      In Kanade, T. (editor), *Three-Dimensional Machine Vision*. Kluwer, Boston MA, 1987.

[7]   Brady, J.M. and Asada, H.
      Smoothed local symmetries and their implementation.
      The International Journal of Robotics Research 3(3), 1986.

[8]   Brady, M., Ponce, J., Yuille, A., and Asada, H.
      Describing surfaces.
      In Hanafusa, H. and Inoue, H. (editors), *Proc. 2nd International Symposium on Robotics Research*. MIT Press, Cambridge, MA, 1985.

[9]   Brooks, R.A.
      Symbolic reasoning among 3-D models and 2-D images.
      Artificial Intelligence 17(1-3), 1981.

[10] Canny, J.F.
      Finding edges and lines in images.
      Technical Report AI-TR-720, Massachusetts Institute of Technology, Artificial Intelligence Laboratory, 1983.

[11] Chakravarty, I. and Freeman, H.
      Characteristic views as a basis for three-dimensional object recognition.
      In *Proc. The Society for Photo-Optical Instrumentation Engineers Conference on Robot Vision*. SPIE, Bellingham. Wash.. 1982.

[12] Cutrona, L.J.
      Synthetic Aperture Radar.
      Radar Handbook.
      McGraw Hill, New York, 1970, Chapter 23.

[13] Faugeras, O.D., Ayache, N., Faverjon, B. and Lustman, F.
      Building visual maps by combining noisy stereo measurement.
      In *Proc. of Intern. Conf. on Robotics and Automation*, pages 1433-1438. San Fransisco, April, 1986.

[14] Grimson, W.E.L.
      From Images to Surfaces: a computational study of the human early visual system.
      MIT Press, Cambridge, MA, 1981.

[15] Hebert, M. and Kanade, T.
      Outdoor scene analysis using range data.
      In *Proc. of Intern. Conf. on Robotics and Automation*, pages 1426-1432. IEEE Computer Society, San Francisco, April, 1986.

[16] Hoffman, R., Ikeuchi, K., Kanade, T., Kumar, B., and Robert, J.C.
      VANTAGE.
      Technical Report, Carnegie-Mellon University, Robotics Institute, 1987.
      in preparation.

[17] Horn, B.K.P.
      Obaining Shape from Shading.
      In Winston, P.H. (editor), *The Psychology of Computer Vision*. McGraw-Hill, New York, 1975.

[18] Horn, B.K.P.
      Extended Gaussian Images.
      Proc of the IEEE 72(12), December, 1984.

[19] Ikeuchi, K.
      Recognition of 3-D objects using the extended Gaussian image.
      In *Proc. of 7th Intern. Joint Conf. on Artificial Intelligence*. 1981.

[20] Ikeuchi, K.
      Generating an Interpretation Tree from a CAD Model for 3-D Object Recognition in Bin-Picking Tasks.
      International Journal of Computer Vision 1(2), 1987.

[21] Ikeuchi, K., Nishihara, H.K., Horn, B.K.P., Sobalvarro, P., and Nagata, S.
      Determining grasp points using photometric stereo and the PRISM binocular stereo system.
      The International Journal of Robotics Research 5(1), 1986.

[22] Ikeuchi, K. and Horn, B.K.
      Numerical shape from shading and occluding boundaries.
      Artificial Intelligence 17(1-3), 1981.

[23] Ikeuchi, K. and Kanade, T.
      Modeling sensor detectability and reliability in the sensor configuration space.
      Technical Report, Carnegie-Mellon University, Computer Science Department, .
      in preparation.

[24] Jarvis, R.A.
      A laser time-of-flight range scanner for robotic vision.
      IEEE Tran, Pattern Analysis and Machine Intelligence PAMI5(5), 1983.

[25] Koenderink, J. J. and Van Doorn, A. J.
      Geometry of binocular vision and a model for stereopsis.
      Biological Cybernetics 21(1), 1976.

[26] Koshikawa, K.
      A polarimetric approach to shape understanding of glossy objects.
      In *Proc. of 6th Intern. Joint Conf. on Artificial Intelligence*. 1979.

[27] Marr, D. and Hildreth, E.
      Theory of edge detection.
      Proc. of the Royal Society of London B 207, 1980.

[28] Marr, D. and Nishihara, H.K.
      Representation and recognition of the spatial organization of three-dimensional shapes.
      Proc. of Royal Society of London B 200, 1978.

[29] Marr, D. and Poggio. T.
      A computational theory of human stereo vision.
      Proc. of the Royal Society of London B 204, 1979.

[30] Matthies, L. and Shafer, S.A.
      Error modelling in stereo naviagtion.
      Technical Report CMU-CS-86-140, Carnegie-Mellon University, Computer Science Department, Pittsburgh, PA, 1986.

[31] Mensa, D.L.
      High Resolution Radar Imaging.
      Artech House, Dedham MA, 1981.

[32] Milenkovic, V.J. and Kanade, T.
      Trinocular vision: using photometric and edge orientation constraints.
      In *Proc. Image Understanding Workshop*. DARPA, Miami Beach, FL, December, 1985.

[33] Ohta, Y. and Kanade, T.
      Stereo by intra- and inter-scanline search using dynamic programming.
      IEEE Trans Pattern Analysis and Machine Intelligence PAMI-7(2), 1985.

[34] Oshima, M. and Shirai, Y.
      A model based vision for scenes with stacked polyhedra using 3D data .
      In *Proc. Intern. Conf. on Advanced Robot (ICAR85)*. Robotics Society of Japan, 1985.

[35] Pentland, A. P.
      Perceptual Organization and the Representation of Natural Form.
      Artificial Intelligence 28(2), 1986.

[36] Roberts, L.G.
      Machine perception of three-dimensional solids.
      In Tipplett, J.T. (editor), *Optical and Electro-Optical Information Processing*. MIT Press, Cambridge, MA, 1965.

[37] Shafer, S. A. and Kanade, T.
      The Theory of Straight Homogeneous Generalized Cylinders, and A Taxonomy of Generalized Cylinders.
      Technical Report CMU-CS-83-105, Carnegie-Mellon University, Computer Science Department, January, 1983.

[38] Smith, D.
      Using enhanced spherical images.
      Technical Report AI Memo 451, MIT Artificial Intelligence Laboratory, 1979.

[39] Tomiyasu, K.
      Tutorial review of Synthetic-Aperture Rader(SAR) with applications to imaging of the ocean surface.
      Proc. of the IEEE 66(5), May, 1978.

[40] Woodham, R.J.
      Reflectance Map Techniques for Analyzing Surface Defects in Metal Castings.
      Technical Report AI-TR-457, Massachusetts Institute of Technology, Artificial Intelligence Laboratory, Cambridge, MA, 1978.

Generic Surface Interpretation: Observability Model

Thomas O. Binford
Stanford University Robotics Laboratory

This is a generic observability model which describes properties of matte reflecting surfaces which are observable as image intensity discontinuities everywhere on the viewing sphere from which they are unoccluded except on a set of measure zero. The model is based on conjectures that humans detect only image intensity discontinuities of zeroth and first order, and curve discontinuities of zeroth, first, and second order. An example shows its utility for typical scene elements.

Introduction

This generic observability model for matte reflection describes which properties of surfaces are generically observable in images, i.e. observable except on a set of measure zero as defined below. This model provides a criterion for adequacy of internal representations of surfaces and curves in space, and for representation of the image intensity surface and curves in the image if they are to be faithful to the entities they represent.

A succession of researchers have made a beginning in labeling line drawings of complex scenes [e.g., Nalwa 87]. One goal is to understand human ability to interpret line drawings, another to exploit interpretation in machine vision. To exploit line drawing interpretation in machine vision, we make a correspondence between line drawings and real images. Line drawings are intended to relate to curves which humans or machines observe in images, but that relation is only partially defined [Binford 81].

The strong practical motivation is to use these results in a model-based vision system, SUCCESSOR, which integrates multiple sensors. Results in interpretation of line drawings have had a fundamental impact on our stereo vision programs [Arnold 80, Lim 87], and on SUCCESSOR [Binford 87]. Interpretation of line drawings was once regarded as an academic exercise when its applicability was extremely limited; despite its limitations, it is now widely relevant.

Notation

Discontinuities of order 0,1,2 are written: $\Delta_0 I$, $\Delta_1 I$ in image intensity, $\Delta_0 C$, $\Delta_1 C$, $\Delta_2 C$ in image curves, $\Delta_0 \sigma$, $\Delta_1 \sigma$, $\Delta_2 \sigma$ in a surface in space, $\Delta_1 \hat{n} \equiv \Delta_1 \sigma$ a discontinuity of order 1 in surface normal, $\Delta_0 \rho$, $\Delta_1 \rho$ in reflectivity of surface, $\Delta_0 i$, $\Delta_1 i$ in illumination on a surface. There are corresponding edges: I-edges in the image intensity surface, σ-edges in surface, ρ-edges in surface reflectivity, i-edges in illumination on a surface. Uppercase refers to the image, greek and lowercase refer to space.

Prediction

Our recognition paradigm is recognition of similarity among members of object classes, beyond recognition of identity among individuals. Figure 1 illustrates our prediction process. Prediction takes the graph of parts and produces a graph of surfaces and their intersections, edges. Intersections, holes, and affixments between surfaces are inferred to determine additional boundaries. We are modeling surface material and finish for predictions of color and specularity. A major emphasis is on prediction and hypothesis generation based on quasi-invariants. For convex polyhedra, each surface is visible over half the viewing sphere. Over most of the hemisphere, quasi-invariants for the plane are nearly constant. Predicting surfaces is $O(n)$ in the number of surfaces n.

Generic Observability Model

This model for observability for matte reflection of surfaces is typical of machine vision for passive sensors in the visible spectrum. Specular reflection from surfaces is very different. Specular reflection is typical in other parts of the electromagnetic spectrum, e.g., radar. Active sensors frequently permit simplifications, for example, enabling direct measurement of surface reflectivity. Some examples follow of sensors for which this model is not reasonable. Many materials are transparent to x-rays. Images for passive infrared sensors are dominated by temperature differences. At radar frequencies, most surfaces are smooth compared to the wavelength of the signal except at intersections of surfaces. Smooth metal surfaces scatter with strong specular reflection. Specular relections are sent off in a single direction and are usually invisible; i.e. they are visible only from a single direction.

The Model

Objects are represented as regular, connected volumes, bounded by piecewise smooth surfaces with continuity conditions satisfied at seams where there may be discontinuities of order 0, 1, .. or continuity of order 0, 1, .. It is enough to make an observability model for single smooth surfaces and for the seams between smooth surfaces.

Singularities of projections of smooth surfaces are well understood mathematically in a simple way from [Whitney 55] as presented in [Koenderink 76]. It is not clear that these singularities are observable. It will be shown that singularities of the projection are generic observables. To use Whitney's theorem, the surface patches should be C^3. The only curve singular-

ities for single smooth surfaces are occlusions, called folds in mathematics or limbs in astronomy. T's and cusps are point singularities. Figure 2 shows these singularities. Limbs are apparent boundaries of surfaces where the surface disappears, i.e., where the the line of sight is tangent to the surface. Limbs are occlusions where the surface has a zeroth order discontinuity as seen in image parameters, $\Delta_0\sigma \neq 0$. As argued below, with a qualification, discontinuities $\Delta_0\sigma \neq 0$ are generically observable, i.e. except on a set of measure one line if unoccluded. T's and cusps are observable if the corresponding limbs are observable. In order for the model to be perceptually adequate, some conditions on the representation of smooth surface patches are detailed below.

To complete the model, in addition to limbs, T's, and cusps for single smooth surface patches, there are σ-edges corresponding to tangent plane discontinuities at intersections of smooth surfaces. At intersections, the surface has tangent plane and curvature discontinuities $\Delta_1\sigma$ and $\Delta_2\sigma$ which can also be occlusions with $\Delta_0\sigma$. Surface discontinuities are shown to be generic observables.

The usual model for image intensity, I, is:

$$I = i\rho\hat{n} \cdot \hat{s} \qquad (1)$$

where i is illumination at the surface, ρ is surface reflectivity, $\hat{n}$ is the surface normal, and $\hat{s}$ is the unit vector along the source ray. The equation assumes a distant point source and matte surface reflectivity. Only those variables matter in this model.

Consider a curve on a surface in space. Normal to that curve may be discontinuities in pigment $\Delta_0\sigma$, $\Delta_1\sigma$, in illumination or shadow $\Delta_0 i$, $\Delta_1 i$, or in surface geometry $\Delta_1\sigma$, $\Delta_2\sigma$. We will speak of pigment edges or ρ-edges, shadow edges, illumination edges or i-edges, surface edges or σ-edges, or image intensity edges or I-edges for brevity, instead of discontinuity in pigmentation, illumination, surface, or image intensity. Discontinuities of order n across a curve are differences of limits from two sides of the nth derivative of the quantity along the normal.

We will argue that a discontinuity is observable at a curve if its image has a discontinuity in image intensity or its derivative, i.e., $\Delta_0 I \neq 0$

or $\Delta_1 I \neq 0$. By definition, a discontinuity is generically observable if its unoccluded image is observable except on sparse subsets of source and observer parameters, i.e., except on a set of measure zero. The discontinuity may be observable but it does not necessarily have a unique interpretation.

The sun moves during the day relative to the scene. Observers move. Object ρ-edges and σ-edges are fixed to the object and move together. It is natural to assume that motions of separate objects are unrelated, i.e., source, observer, and object. In this spirit, interpretations which are generic in source and observer parameters are made.

It is not very useful to assume that ρ-edges and σ-edges are unrelated. Surfaces of different objects vary widely in spectral reflectivity. It is moderately useful to assume that interpretations are generic with respect to reflectivity contrast between objects.

Consequences

Hypothesis 1: Humans are not sensitive to discontinuities in image intensity of second order and higher.

From this. define a curve as observable if there is an intensity discontinuity of zeroth or first order across its image. It has been observed experimentally that humans detect discontinuities in image intensity of zeroth and first order, $\Delta_0 I$ (step and delta) and $\Delta_1 I$ (slope or roof) [Cornsweet 71]. We have looked for $\Delta_2 I$ discontinuities and failed to find them in a few simple and informal experiments which are the basis for this conjecture. Better experiments are needed to quantify limits on human sensitivity to $\Delta_2 I$.

Conclusion 1: Discontinuities of surface illumination i and its derivative, i.e., $\Delta_0 i$ and $\Delta_1 i$, discontinuities in surface reflectivity ρ and its derivative, $\Delta_0 \rho$ and $\Delta_1 \rho$, and discontinuities in surface σ, its position, tangent, and curvature, $\Delta_0 \sigma$, $\Delta_1 \sigma$, and $\Delta_2 \sigma$, are observable locally on any portion of the discontinuity, generically with respect to observer and source orientation as image intensity discontinuities of order zero and one, $\Delta_0 I$, and $\Delta_1 I$. Higher order surface discontinuities are not observable as image in-

tensity discontinuities. Specifically:
a) $\Delta_1 \sigma \neq 0$, $\Delta_0 \rho \neq 0$, and $\Delta_0 i \neq 0$ all induce zeroth order discontinuities, $\Delta_0 I \neq 0$, generically with respect to observer and source orientation; b) indirectly, $\Delta_0 \sigma \neq 0$ induces $\Delta_0 I \neq 0$ generically, with the qualification described below; and c) $\Delta_2 \sigma \neq 0$, $\Delta_1 \rho \neq 0$, and $\Delta_1 i \neq 0$ all induce first order discontinuities, $\Delta_1 I \neq 0$ generically with respect to observer and source orientation.

First consider $\Delta_0 I$ nonzero, i.e., a step or delta i-edge in intensity defined normal to a curve. The image intensity discontinuity at the curve is:

$$\Delta_0 I = i_1 \rho_1 \hat{n}_1 \cdot \hat{s} - i_2 \rho_2 \hat{n}_2 \cdot \hat{s}$$

$$\Delta_0 I = i_1 \rho_1 \hat{n}_1 \cdot \hat{s} - (i_1 + \Delta_0 i)(\rho_1 + \Delta_0 \rho)(\hat{n}_1 + \Delta_1 \sigma) \cdot \hat{s} \quad (2)$$

where 1 and 2 are indices of limits from two sides normal to the curve. Of the discontinuities, only $\Delta_0 i$, $\Delta_0 \rho$, and $\Delta_1 \sigma$ have images with intensity contrast, $\Delta_0 I \neq 0$. Indirectly, $\Delta_0 \sigma$ does too, as discussed below. Consider $\Delta_1 i$, $\Delta_1 \rho$, and $\Delta_2 \sigma$ together with $\Delta_1 I$ later.

Two curves coincide locally, i.e., to first order, if they have identical position and tangent, two constraints which must be satisfied by the shadow, i.e., by the source which casts it. An i-edge $\Delta_0 i$ can coincide with a ρ-edge $\Delta_0 \rho$ or a σ-edge, $\Delta_0 \sigma$ or $\Delta_1 \sigma$ only for a special source alignment with respect to the observer, i.e., on a set of measure zero in source parameter space. There are generically two cases of interest, first, an i-edge without ρ-edge or σ-edge: $\Delta_0 i \neq 0$, $\Delta_0 \rho = 0$, $\Delta_0 \sigma = 0$, and second, a ρ-edge and/or a σ-edge with no i-edge: $\Delta_0 i = 0$, $\Delta_0 \rho \neq 0$, $\Delta_0 \sigma \neq 0$.

Shadow Edge

An i-edge is parameterized by a cone in space together with an illumination contrast, or equivalently for a single surface, by a curve on the surface, with contrast. Locally, to first order, the parameter space of source or shadow casting element is the unit sphere together with orientation of the shadow and contrast. However, generically, a shadow can coincide at a point in space with a shadow casting σ-edge, but not along a curve. This is frequent, as in figure 2. Because an i-edge does not coincide with a ρ-edge or σ-edge:

$$\Delta_0 I = i_1 \rho_1 \hat{n}_1 \cdot \hat{s} - i_2 \rho_2 \hat{n}_2 \cdot \hat{s} = (i_1 - i_2)\rho \hat{n} \cdot \hat{s}$$

$$\Delta_0 I = \Delta_0 i \rho \hat{n} \cdot \hat{s} \qquad (3)$$

If $\Delta_0 i \neq 0$ as assumed, then $\Delta_0 I = 0$ only if $\rho = 0$ or $\hat{n} \cdot \hat{s} = 0$, i.e., only if the surface is invisible.

Pigment and Surface Edges

Pigment edges, ρ-edges, are parameterized by a curve on the surface together with a tuple of color contrast components, e.g., red, green, and blue. A ρ-edge coincides with a σ-edge only on a set of measure zero in curve parameters, with two constraints, as above. However, physical mechanisms create ρ-edges which coincide with σ-edges. Include interpretations in which ρ-edges coincide withσ-edges. Manmade structures are often painted this way. Also, different parts of objects may be made of different materials; at σ-edges between parts there may be material changes which cause ρ-edges, e.g., between branches and foliage of vegetation. On the other hand, many σ-edges are not parts boundaries and many are not material edges. Also, natural and manmade camouflage have ρ-edges roughly randomly placed relative to σ-edges. There may be two distinct populations, one with ρ-edges generic relative to σ-edges. It should be worthwhile to incorporate these classes in generic prediction.

A ρ-edge cannot coincide generically with a limb. The limb on a smooth surface depends on viewpoint, while a ρ-edge is fixed on the surface. They coincide only from a constrained viewpoint, i.e., only on a set of measure zero.

Consider a combined ρ-edge and σ-edge where incident illumination is continuous across the edge. The edge is generically observable, i.e., $\Delta_0 I = 0$ occurs only for the photometric constraint:

$$\Delta_0 I = 0 = i\rho_1 \hat{n}_1 \cdot \hat{s} - i\rho_2 \hat{n}_2 \cdot \hat{s} = i(\rho_1 \hat{n}_1 \cdot \hat{s} - \rho_2 \hat{n}_2 \cdot \hat{s}) \quad (4)$$

ρ_1 and ρ_2 are reflectivities on either side, and $\hat{n}_1$ and $\hat{n}_2$ are surface normals on either side, while $\hat{s}$ is the unit vector from source to surface. Only $\hat{s}$ depends on source orientation. If $\rho_1 \neq \rho_2$, or $\hat{n}_1 \neq \hat{n}_2$ or both, then this constraint is satisfied only on a set of measure zero in source orientation on the unit sphere. There is a plane of source orientations for which this constraint is satisfied, a one constraint case with one degree of freedom. For example, if reflectivities are equal, $\rho_1 = \rho_2$, then the contrast is zero on the plane which is the angular bisector of the two tangent planes at the σ-edge. If reflectivities are unequal, then the constraint plane shifts toward the normal on the darker side. Contrast across the edge from the slope discontinuity is cancelled by a pigment discontinuity only on this plane. Since humans are sensitive to intensity discontinuities $\Delta_0 I$, they are quite sensitive to pigmentation and surface orientation discontinuities.

Occlusion

Now consider $\Delta_0 \sigma$, a zeroth order surface discontinuity, an occlusion, a limb. If a limb separates images of surfaces from two different objects, the surfaces are unrelated; their pigmentation may differ in brightness, hue, and saturation; their orientations are unrelated and not necessarily parallel. The surfaces vary in two domains. Two surfaces which are not infinitesimally close are visible across the σ-edge. If their pigments differ or if their orientations differ or both, the edge will be observable generically. If their orientations were identical generically across the boundary, then the surfaces would be parallel planes with uniform pigmentation, e.g., manmade. This follows because if one surface were curved, the apparent edge would shift over the curved surface. Parallel surface patches would be seen only from a set of measure zero in viewpoint. If the limb is not also a $\Delta_1 \sigma$ or $\Delta_2 \sigma$ edge, the surface is tangent to the line of sight there. It is an extreme alignment that the other surface is also tangent to the line of sight along that curve. For occlusion between different objects, it might be argued that surfaces of different objects are unrelated, that there is great variation in surface reflectivity, that interpretations should be generic in color (reflectivity) contrast across the occlusion. Camouflage is an exception; e.g., insects imitate leaves on which they feed to avoid being seen by birds which prey on them. If a limb separates images of two surfaces of the same object, i.e., for self-occlusion, there is often substantial reflectivity variation over a single surface of natural objects. For example, a dog's coat has substantial variation, even if it is a single color. Surfaces of manmade objects can be quite uniform.

For self-occlusion, the surfaces may have the same material and pigmentation but their orientations are not necessarily parallel. This is a shaky assumption for buildings with multiple wings which have parallel surfaces typically; manmade objects have many parallel plane surfaces. In urban areas, different buildings may have parallel surfaces, but they may typically have different surface treatments. The exception of parallel planes is a flaw; the generic interpretation appears useful however. These arguments have been local, i.e., valid on any part of an edge. Globally, a surface may occlude several surfaces; the occluding edge may be visible between some surfaces even if not between all.

First-Order Intensity Discontinuities

Now consider $\Delta_1 I \neq 0$. If $\Delta_0 I \neq 0$ then the discontinuity is observable without considering $\Delta_1 I$, thus assume that $\Delta_0 I = 0$. Using the same reasoning as above, generically there are only two cases, first, ρ-edge, σ-edge, or both coincident, and second, i-edges alone, without ρ-edge or σ-edge. First consider ρ-edge, σ-edge, or both coincident.

$$\frac{dI}{du} = i(\frac{d\rho}{du}\cos\theta - \rho\sin\theta\frac{d\theta}{du}) \qquad (5)$$

where u is the image coordinate normal to the projected edge, and $\cos\theta = \hat{n}\cdot\hat{s}$. The projection of a surface point (x, y, z) to an image point (u, v) is

$$u = \frac{w}{z}x. But\, du = \frac{w}{z}\cos\zeta\, d\tau,$$

where τ is the coordinate along the surface and normal to the edge, while $\cos\zeta$ is the cosine of the angle between the surface normal and the normal to the image plane, $\hat{n}_p$, $\cos\zeta = \hat{n}\cdot\hat{n}_p$. Here, w is the image distance.

$$\frac{dI}{du} = \frac{z}{w\cos\zeta}(\frac{d\rho}{d\tau}\cos\theta - \rho\sin\theta\frac{d\theta}{d\tau})$$

$$\frac{dI}{du} = \frac{z}{w\cos\zeta}(\frac{d\rho}{d\tau}\cos\theta - \rho\sin\theta\kappa)$$

where κ is the surface curvature. By the assumptions, $\cos\theta$ and ρ are continuous at the edge.

$$\Delta_1 I = \frac{dI}{du}\Big]^{up} - \frac{dI}{du}\Big]_{low}$$

$$\Delta_1 I = \frac{z}{w\cos\zeta}(\Delta_1\rho\cos\theta + \Delta_2\sigma\rho\sin\theta) \qquad (6)$$

But $\Delta_1\rho$ and $\Delta_2\sigma$ are independent of source angle. If either $\Delta_1\rho$ or $\Delta_2\sigma$ is nonzero, $\Delta_1 I$ vanishes only on a set of source orientations of measure zero, a plane with:

$$\tan\theta = \frac{\Delta_1\rho}{\Delta_2\sigma\rho} \qquad (7)$$

A typical assumption is that $\frac{d\rho}{du} = 0$, i.e., that pigmentation is piecewise constant.

Now consider the photometric constraint for i-edges:

$$\frac{dI}{du} = \frac{di}{du}\rho\hat{n}\cdot\hat{s} = \frac{w}{z}\frac{di}{d\tau}\rho\hat{n}\cdot\hat{s}$$

$$\Delta_1 I = 0 = (\frac{di}{d\tau}\Big]^{up} - \frac{di}{d\tau}\Big]_{low})\frac{w\rho\hat{n}\cdot\hat{s}}{z} = \Delta_1 i\frac{w\rho\hat{n}\cdot\hat{s}}{z}$$

If $\Delta_1 i \neq 0$ then $\Delta_1 I = 0$ only for $\rho = 0$ or $\hat{n}\cdot\hat{s} = 0$, i.e., if the surface is invisible.

Conclusion 1d: Perceptually adequate representations of intensity surfaces in images are piecewise smooth surfaces formed of surface patches from a second order basis which join at smooth seams where they are C^1. These pieces intersect at I-edges where they have $\Delta_0 I$ and $\Delta_1 I$ discontinuities coincident with those observable in the image.

Otherwise, intensity surfaces represented would have spurious, observable intensity discontinuities not observable in the original.

Hypothesis 2: Experiment shows that humans observe position, tangent, and curvature discontinuities in image curves with hyperresolution, $\Delta_0 C$, $\Delta_1 C$, and $\Delta_2 C$. Assume that higher order discontinuities are not observable.

The first two are obvious observations, the third has been shown in experiments concerning hyperresolution.

Conclusion 2a: Image curves should be represented as piecewise C^2 smooth curves from a third-order basis joined at knots where they are C^2. These pieces intersect at corners where there may be $\Delta_0 C$ (1-junction), $\Delta_1 C$, and $\Delta_2 C$ discontinuities which coincide with those observable discontinuities of the original.

If representations of curves were not piecewise C^2 there would be observable, spurious discontinuities in the represented curve not observable in the original.

Conclusion 2b: Object surfaces are represented as piecewise smooth C^3 surfaces formed of surface patches from a third-order basis joined at seams where they are C^2. These pieces intersect at σ-edges where they have $\Delta_0\sigma$, $\Delta_1\sigma$, and $\Delta_2\sigma$ discontinuities.

If represented surfaces were not piecewise C^2, they would have observable, spurious curvature discontinuities in projections at limbs and in intersections at σ-edges which were not observable in the original. Curvature discontinuities are observable as image intensity discontinuities of order one for which humans are significantly less sensitive than for image step discontinuities. Thus, curvature discontinuities may be barely observable.

Conclusion 2c: Representations of σ-edges of surfaces are piecewise smooth C^2 curves formed of segments from a third order basis joined at knots where they are C^2. These pieces intersect at corners where there may be $\Delta_0 C$, $\Delta_1 C$, and $\Delta_2 C$ discontinuities which correspond to those observed in their images.

If not, their projections would have $\Delta_2\sigma$ curvature discontinuities in I-edges which would introduce spurious non-observable discontinuities.

Hypothesis 3: Humans detect $\Delta_0 D$ discontinuities in dot density in random dot texture patterns but not $\Delta_1 D$ discontinuities [Vistnes 85].

Conclusion 3: Texture representations are piecewise C^0 functions formed of patches from a first-order basis joined at knots where they are C^0. They intersect at texture boundaries where they may have $\Delta_0 D$ discontinuities corresponding to those observed in images.

Physical Measurements

In this paragraph, we will comment on how generic these observables are in realizable physical situations. A generic observable is observable except on a set of measure zero in the observation hypervolume, i.e., almost everywhere. Any constraint which defines a set of measure zero defines a constraint hypersurface for one constraint or more sparse set for more constraints in the observation hypervolume. Measurement uncertainties on all variables, with probability measures, turn the constraint hypersurface into a constraint hypervolume. Constant values p_i of a joint probability measure of consistency with the constraint define a set of p_i-consistent level surfaces. If the constraint hypervolume for a chosen level of consistency is a large part of the parameter space, the generic observable is more or less useless under those conditions. If possible, measurements must be refined. Several fundamental concepts like generic and continuity have no literal perceptual translation. The concepts are so useful that we would like to extend their definitions. The aim here is to make a working definition of almost everywhere. Perceptually, we define a generic observable as one which is observable except on a sparse set, one with p_0-consistent constraint hypervolume which is a small fraction of the total observation hypervolume, for chosen value p_0.

In this case, consider the observability of an internal σ-edge for physically realistic measurements. The edge has $\Delta_1\sigma \neq 0$ with $\Delta_0\sigma = 0$ and $\Delta_2\sigma = 0$. Assume that it is an σ-edge between identical surfaces, i.e., $\Delta_0\rho = 0$, $\Delta_1\rho = 0$. The σ-edge is observable except on the plane bisecting the angle between the two surfaces. They may be curved surfaces; this is a local argument which is valid for the tangent planes. Consider the internal angle of ϕ_0. ϕ is the angle of the source with respect to the bisecting plane. The σ-edge will be potentially visible as an internal edge for $|\phi| < \frac{\phi_0}{2}$ and visible as an occluding external σ-edge for $|\phi| > \frac{\phi_0}{2}$. Based on the previous arguments, assume that the σ-edge is observable when occluding, over that part of source orientations on the unit sphere, and that the σ-edge is observable as an internal σ-edge when the contrast is large enough for existing edge operators.

At $\phi = 0$ the contrast is zero. Near $\phi = 0$, as the object rotates, $I_1 - I_2$ is the contrast difference:

$$I_1 - I_2 = i\rho(\cos\theta_1 - \cos\theta_2)$$

Under rotation of the source:

$$\theta_1 = \frac{\pi}{2} - \frac{\phi_0}{2} + \phi \qquad \theta_2 = \frac{\pi}{2} - \frac{\phi_0}{2} - \phi$$

$$dI/I = -2\tan\theta_1 d\phi$$

The intensity discontinuity will be missed if the contrast is less than threshold $k\delta$, where δ is the standard deviation of sensor noise, with k about 8 for Roberts cross, and about 1.4 for Binford-Horn. Solve for $\Delta\phi$, the angle for which contrast will be below threshold on either side of the bisector.

$$\Delta\phi = \frac{k\delta}{2\tan\theta}$$

The total range of angles over which the σ-edge is visible as an internal σ-edge is $\frac{\phi_0}{2}$. The fraction of σ-edges missed as I-edges is $\frac{\Delta\phi}{\phi_0}2 = \frac{k\delta}{\phi_0\tan\theta}$ If the signal to noise is 32 to 1, then the fraction of source angles on the unit sphere for which internal σ-edges will be missed for the right angle case is 16% for Roberts cross and 3% for Binford-Horn. For this case, the edge will be seen as an internal edge $\frac{1}{3}$ of the time and as an external edge $\frac{2}{3}$ of the time. The image dissector at MIT gave a factor of 3 better signal to noise, which would improve those results by a factor of 3. These results are for a single place along the I-edge. Binford-Horn detects an I-edge at any of many places along it and tracks the curve. Thus, global detection is better than those estimates.

As a conclusion, for high quality edge operators, few σ-edges are missed. This constrained subset is sparce and thus the generic detectability is relevant in a practical sense in detection with noise. These conditions are representative of real scenes. Experimentally, the fraction of missing internal edges was not estimated with Binford-Horn. Informally, the fraction seemed higher than this estimate. Several reasons come to mind. The operator was detuned by at least a factor of two because of noise sources which were not included in noise estimates, such as 120 cycle variation in the illumination. There were contrast reversals along edges which caused contrast to vanish. This is probably because the illumination was an extended source. The case will be significantly worse for first order image intensity discontinuities, but we have not quantified this yet.

Acknowledgements

Support for this work was provided in part by the Advanced Research Projects Agency of the Department of Defense under Image Understanding contract N00039-84-C-0211, under Knowledge Based Vision contract AIADS S1093-S-1, and by the Air Force Office of Scientific Research under contract F33615-85-C-5106.

References

[Arnold 80] Arnold, R.D., Binford, T.O.; "Geometric Constraints in Stereo Vision"; Proc SPIE Meeting, San Diego, Cal, July 1980.

[Attneave 69] F. Attneave, R. Frost; "The determination of perceived tridemensional orientation by minimum criteria"; Perception and Psychophysics, v 6, pp. 391-396, 1969.

[Binford 81] T.O.Binford; "Inferring Surfaces from Images"; Artificial Intelligence, vol. 17, pp. 205-244, Aug 1981.

[Binford 82] T.O.Binford; "Survey of Model-Based Image Analysis Systems"; Int J. of Robotics Research, v 1, p 18, 1982.

[Binford 87] T.O.Binford, T.Levitt, W.Mann "Bayesian Inference in Model-Based Machine Vision"; Proc Workshop on Uncertainty in Artificial Intelligence, 1987.

[Cornsweet 71] T. Cornsweet; "Visual Perception"; Academic Press, 1970.

[Koenderink 76] J. Koenderink, A. van Doorn; "The Singularities of the Visual Mapping"; Biological Cybernetics, vol. 24, pp. 51-59, 1976.

[Lim 87] H.S.Lim and T.O.Binford; "Stereo Correspondence; A Hierarchical Approach"; Proc ARPA Image Understanding Workshop, 1987.

[Nalwa 87] V.Nalwa; "Line Drawing interpretation: Straight Lines and Conic Sections"; IEEE Trans on Pattern Analysis and Machine Intelligence, vol. PAMI-9, no. 6, Nov. 1987.

[Whitney 55] H. Whitney; "On Singularities of Mappings of Euclidean Spaces. I. Mappings of the Plane into the Plane"; Annals of Mathematics, vol. 62, 3, pp. 374-410, 1955.

[Vistnes 85] R. Vistnes; "Detecting Structure in Random Dot Patterns"; Proc of ARPA Image Understanding Workshop, Dec 1985.

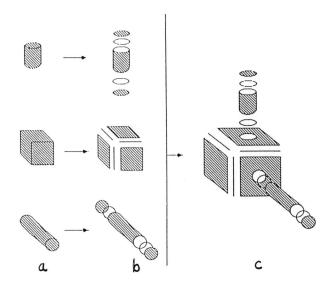

Figure 1: Prediction. a. object parts b. surfaces and edges. c. surfaces and edges with holes and hidden faces.

Figure 2: Edges and limbs. a. note shadow coincident with edge which casts it. b. limbs (folds).

VI MOTION

Sensor control of mobile robots has been one of the hottest research areas within robotics over the past three or four years. It involves three basic operations: sensor calibration, feature matching, and parameter estimation. The first two papers in part VI describe calibration techniques, the third concentrates on feature matching, and the rest of the papers present techniques for combining the information gathered by a mobile robot as it moves through an environment.

Brooks et al. describe a method for simultaneously calibrating a depth-from-motion process and a conventional stereo system. Their method consists of moving the robot in a controlled way and gathering a dense sequence of images that simplifies image-to-image matching and yet provides a long baseline for accurate parameter estimation. Tsai and Lenz describe an efficient technique for calibrating a camera with respect to an arm that is carrying it.

Thompson and Mundy combine robust model-matching with trajectory prediction to demonstrate object tracking in an increasingly complex set of tasks.

Dickmanns describes the application of Kalman filters to the task of estimating parameters from spatio-temporal data. He discusses three applications of this technique: navigating a vehicle along a road, docking a satellite, and landing an airplane. Sugihara describes a set of geometric constraints derivable from pairs of point features located by a robot moving on a planar surface, and then shows how to use these constraints to estimate the position of the robot. Matthies and Kanade describe the cyclic relationship between the world model, the robot's location, and the sensed data, and then present a strategy for iteratively updating this information as the robot gathers new data.

Ayache and Faugeras use an extended Kalman filter to incrementally build scene models in terms of lines and planes. Sandini et al. argue for a volumetric representation of a scene for integrating the information derived from stereo and motion. Brady et al. describe components of a mobile robot system for locating and picking up pallets. They include a description of the geometric reasoning required by such a robot.

Self Calibration of Motion and Stereo Vision for Mobile Robots

Rodney A. Brooks, Anita M. Flynn and Thomas Marill
MIT Artificial Intelligence Laboratory
545 Technology Square
Cambridge, MA 02139

Abstract To provide robust visual perception for navigation it is necessary to combine the outputs of more than one early vision algorithm. It is therefore necessary to have these algorithms calibrated to some common standard. In this paper we report on experiments with a mobile robot using one algorithm (forward motion vision) to calibrate another (stereo vision) without resorting to any external units of measurement. Rather, both end up being calibrated to a velocity dependent coordinate system which is natural to the task of obstacle avoidance. The foundations of these algorithms, in a world of perfect measurement, are quite elementary. The contribution of this work is to make them noise tolerant while remaining simple computationally. Both the algorithms and the calibration procedure are simple to implement and have very shallow computational depth, making them (1) run at reasonable speed on moderate uni-processors, (2) appear practical to run continuously, maintaining an up to the second calibration on a mobile robot, and (3) appear to be ideal candidates for massively parallel implementations.

1. Introduction

This paper is about vision for a mobile robot. It is about how to build a computationally cheap robust vision system which delivers data for obstacle avoidance. The vision system is continually self calibrating, making it tolerant of normal mechanical drift. But better than that, it is tolerant of severe blows to its head-like sensor platforms. After a few seconds in a trauma-induced daze it adapts to its grossly altered sensor alignments.

But wait, there's more! The algorithms require no pre-knowledge of camera focal lengths, fine orientation, or stereo baseline separation. With such quick calibration and adaption the sensors can be mounted on cheap steerable systems. We can trade cheap computation for deficiencies which arise from avoiding expensive mechanical solutions to sensor steering problems.

We begin with three observations:

- Humans are able to extract meanginful information from images without being aware of the camera geometry (e.g. baseline separation in stereo) or the focal parameters of the imaging system. They can adapt almost instantly to TV or movie images made with unknown optics and relatively quickly to disturbances in the optical pathway to their retinas. For instance a change in stereo baseline separation induced by special glasses can be adapted for in a matter of seconds. In contrast, most mobile robots today require precisely understood optics and many seconds of intense computation at the begining of an experimental run (Faugeras and Toscani (1986)) to accommodate small mechanical and electronic drifts in their systems.
- Marr (1982) points out that the *purpose of vision* depends on the task the perceiving organism is trying to achieve. His example in this section (page 32) of his philosophical treatise is the housefly. Brooks (1986) demonstrates that data from a single sensor system can be used in entirely independent channels (including independent perception systems) to control different aspects of the behavior of a mobile robot. Thus there need not be just a single purpose of vision. A useful engineering consideration in building a perception system then, is to analyze the requirements in terms of the task to be achieved using the output of the perception system.
- Much of human and animal vision is extremely fast, taking place in small fractions of a second. However, it is implemented on hardware which is extremely slow (perhaps one thousand gate delays per second) as compared with today's computer hardware (ten to one hundred million or more gate delays per second). Nonetheless biological vision is vastly superior to current computer implementations. Biological algorithms must therefore be computationally shallow in order to fit on the available hardware.

In this paper we explore some visual techniques useful for a mobile robot navigating in indoor environments. The particular task these techniques support is avoiding obstacles. Brooks (1986) shows how to separate this particular task from others that a mobile robot may concurrently be pursuing.

Man-made indoor environments give rise to images with strong vertical edges. We can make use of this fact in designing our algorithms.

Noting the earlier observations, we are interested in finding self calibrating algorithms which are tolerant of large drifts in optical properties of the imaging system, in finding algorithms which are have shallow computation depth, and in finding algorithms that are are well suited to the obstacle aviodance task, delivering outputs that are of great use in performing that task.

The experiments we describe in this paper have been performed using Allen the robot (Brooks (1987)) as a sensor platform and an offboard Lisp machine as the computational engine. The robot has two approximately forward looking CCD cameras. A standard camera mount is used to attach them to a tilt head, and so there is considerable risk of not having the cameras pointing directly forward.

This report describes research done at the Artificial Intelligence Laboratory of the Massachusetts Institute of Technology. Support for the research is provided in part by an IBM Faculty Development Award, in part by a grant from the Systems Development Foundation, in part by the University Research Initative under Office of Naval Research contract N00014-86-K-0685 and in part by the Advanced Research Projects Agency under Office of Naval Research contract N00014-85-K-0124.

1.1 Forward motion and stereo

Our primary algorithm analyzes forward motion by tracking strong vertical edges over many consecutive images. As Baker, Bolles and Marimont (1987) have pointed out, one avoids the problem of solving for corresponding points by taking closely spaced images.

Unlike Baker, Bolles and Marimont, however, we are addressing the problem of forward rather than lateral motion, and we do not assume knowledge of camera motion or of camera angle relative to motion.

Forward motion analysis relies on straight line motion of the robot at constant, but unknown, velocity, but does not require that the camera point directly ahead, nor that it point at a known angle relative to the motion. There are strong constraints on the possible motion of features if the robot motion constraints are met, so it is often possible to detect when the motion constraints are being violated.

The particular way in which forward motion analysis supports the obstacle avoidance task is to deliver distances to obstacles in units of time to collision at the current velocity. This is the perfect coordinate system for obstacle avoidance. Steering commands and velocity change commands can be given without the need to convert from an absolute coordinate system to desired velocities for the robot.

Forward motion analysis has some surprising independence properties;

- the details of the focal geometry of a perspective camera are unimportant,
- the camera need not be pointing directly in the direction of motion (there is a simple procedure which recovers the angle of the camera plane relative to the direction of motion),
- and it naturally delivers the distance to the physical artifacts giving rise to tracked features are as the time to collision with that artifact in units of the inter-frame time intervals.

These properties make forward motion analysis ideal as an input to an obstacle avoidance task on the robot. Addtionally it is easily implementable on hardware which supports only 16 bit arithmetic.

Unfortunately forward motion analysis has some drawbacks also;

- it doesn't deliver distances to obstacles which are straight ahead along the direction of motion (and clearly these are some of the most important obstacles to consider),
- and it is useless when the robot is stationary or turning in place. Thus when the robot stops to turn, it is completely blind in its new direction of motion until it has moved in that direction for a period of time.

To compensate for these shortcomings we use a second early vision algorithm whose properties exactly complement those of forward motion analysis. We use a single scanline stereo algorithm. Stereo provides depth measurements

- straight ahead,
- and when the robot is stationary.

But stereo too has a serious draw back. Even rough depth measurements rely on a knowledge of camera focal geometry and the six parameters relating the geometries of the two cameras. Alignment errors as small as $\pm 5°$ for each camera can lead to a factor of two difference in depth estimates.

The main result of this paper is a simple method of continuously calibrating the stereo system to reliably deliver depths in the same units as the forward motion analysis algorithms.

1.2 Experimental assumptions

The forward motion and stereo algorithms both assume one dimensional cameras with the optical plane parallel to the plane of motion of the robot (this was also assumed by Baker, Bolles

and Marimont (1987)). In the current experiments we use regular video CCD cameras and average a swath of 16 scanlines from the middle of the image. This highlights strong vertical edges. Grey levels are taken to 8 bits and range from 0 (white) to 255 (black).

Two cameras were mounted side by side facing forward, separated by approximately 8 inches. The cameras were only approximately aligned in the forward direction. Our analysis below assumes up to a $\pm 5°$ misalignment of each camera. It assumes the cameras are restricted to a field of view of 60°. Knowing the field of view lets us compute the focal ratio of the camera. The analysis assumes the two cameras are identical in this regard but is easily generalized to two different but known cameras.

In our experiments we used perspective lenses with approximately a 60° field of view. There is only one place, and that is in the forward motion algorithm, where knowledge of the field of view and hence focal ratio is used. It is used in correcting for errors in estimated depths due to the cameras not pointing in the direction of motion. Given our assumptions, these errors can be at most $\pm 5\%$ so only an approximate knowledge of the field of view is necessary. For a robot which can turn in place and which has appropriate encoders to measure its turn, the camera field of view could easily be calibrated each time it turns by tracking image points over a signifcant portion of the image. We did not so estimate the field of view in these experiments but assumed it *a priori*.

All computation was done offboard and offline on a Symbolics lisp machine. Total computation time for the reported experiments is on the order of a few seconds running unoptimized lisp code.

We plan on porting these algorithms to a new robot with all onboard computation. On that robot we plan on using cylindrical lenses and single scan line horizontal CCD cameras. The lenses will optically average a horizontal swath of a more conventional image highlighting strong vertical edges.

For the task of obstacle avoidance we estimate that knowledge of the distance to obstacles to within $\pm 10\%$ is quite adequate.

All our experiments described in this paper give distances in terms of the robot's current speed. We did not try to measure that quantity. Our evaluation of our experiments can not therefore be based on determinations of absolute accuracy. Rather we compare computed relative distances to pairs of tracked objects as a measure of accuracy, as in an ideal experiment all such relative distances should remain constant. On this basis we believe we have achieved $\pm 5\%$ accuracy with very computationally simple and shallow depth algorithms.

2. Forward Motion Vision

In this section we first derive the equations of forward motion vision without regard to sensitivity to noise and sampling errors. We then describe some practical algorithms to overcome those problems.

2.1 One dimensional camera geometry

Consider figure 1. It is a view from above of a perspective camera. The *image plane* is a one dimensional strip, i.e., the camera provides only a 1-D image.

The image plane has P pixels, numbered 0 through $P - 1$. The *optical center* of the camera is distance f from the image plane. We call f the *focal ratio*. The *optical center plane* is parallel to the image plane and runs through the optical center. A line, the *optical axis*, runs through the optical center and intersects the image plane at right angles. The point of intersection divides the image plane in two equal parts and is called the *center of view*.

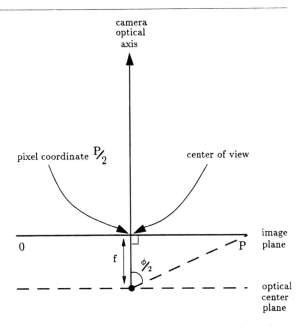

Figure 1. A one dimensional camera has an image plane f units from the optical center of the camera. The optical axis is perpendicular to the image plane, which is P pixels wide.

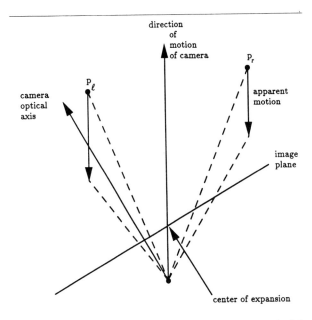

Figure 2. As a camera moves in a straight line, points to the left of the direction of motion of the camera appear to move to the left and those to the right appear to move to the right.

Points in the world are projected onto the image plane along lines that run through the optical center. The *field of view* of the camera is ϕ, the maximum angle subtended by any two visible points. The focal ratio and field of view are related by:

$$f = \frac{P}{2\tan(\phi/2)}. \qquad (1)$$

This gives f in units of pixels.

On the cameras we used in out experiments, which are 576 pixels wide with approximately a 60° field of view, f is approximately 499 pixels.

2.2 Forward motion vision geometry

Now consider figure 2. It is a view from above of a perspective camera whose optical axis is offset somewhat from the direction of motion of the camera. The camera is undergoing pure translation in a constant *direction of motion* which is offset somewhat from the optical axis. The motion direction vector, the optical axis and the image strip on the image plane are all coplanar.

This model corresponds to a 1-D camera mounted parallel to the ground plane on a mobile robot which is travelling forward without turning. Typically one would horizontally mount a cylindrical lens on such a camera to enhance the strong vertical edges found in man-made indoor environments. Without careful alignment of the camera it will not point directly in the direction of motion of the robot. Even if the camera is rigidly mounted on the body of the robot, the direction the robot travels with respect to its body will vary gradually over time due to tire wear and other mechanical processes. On our robot Allen we notice that the body and drive base of the robot can easily be misaligned by a few degrees. In this section we show how to dynamically calibrate for these effects with a few arithmetic operations over a few images taken as the robot is moving at constant velocity.

The way in which image features move in the image under the geometry of figure 2 are well known (e.g., Negahdaripour and Horn (1987)). We briefly rederive the equations here for

completeness and to lead in to some special features of the slightly more restricted case we are considering here.

The image of any point p_r which is to the right of the direction of motion will move rightwards in the image plane. The image of any point p_l which is to the left of the direction of motion will move leftwards in the image plane. Points directly ahead will not move at all in the image. The projection of such points is called the *center of expansion*. We write C_E, for its coordinate in pixels.

In an operational robot, we envision an estimator for C_E running continuously and slowly and incrementally updating the estimate as it drifts. More generally what we would like to know, for the purpose of controlling a robot, is how long it will be before the robot reaches some visible point p. The forward motion analysis described here determines the time that will elapse for the optical center of the robot's camera to travel as far as p, along the direction of motion. This assumes that the robot's velocity is constant but not that it is known.

Now consider figure 3, which illustrates the same physical setup as the last figure but with different quantities annotated. The camera has focal ratio f. Call the distance from the optical center to the center of expansion f'. The camera is misaligned by an angle α from pointing directly in the direction of motion. Suppose the camera is moving with constant velocity v and consider what happens to the image of a point p. Its physical location can be described by two non-orthogonal coordinates: x', its distance parallel to the image plane from the path taken by the optical center of the camera, and z', its distance in the direction of motion from the optical center plane. Note that the derivative of z' with respect to time, $\dot{z}'$ is the constant $-v$.

From the perspective geometry of the camera we can see that the distance, r, along the image plane, of the image of point p from the center of expansion is given by:

$$r = \frac{f'x'}{z'} \qquad (2)$$

and its derivative with respect to time is:

$$\dot{r} = -\frac{f'x'}{(z')^2}\dot{z}'.$$

We can then observe that:

$$\frac{r}{\dot{r}} = -\frac{z'}{\dot{z}'} = \frac{z'}{v}$$

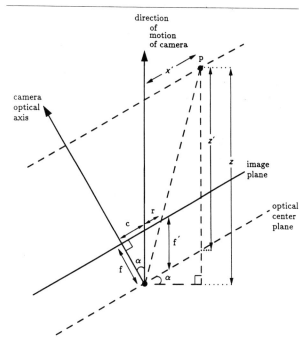

Figure 3. As a camera moves forward in some direction α offset from the optical center of the camera, we are interested in recovering the distance z to a point p.

The last term is the time it will take for the optical center plane to intersect p. Thus $r/\dot{r}$ is just the *time to collision* of the optical center plane and the physical feature whose image is being observed.

The accuracy of forward motion analysis is very sensitive to the estimate we make of the center of expansion since r is measured relative to it. The position of C_E can range over a third of the image when camera alignment of a 30° field of view camera is allowed to vary by ±5° (it is not quite so bad for larger field of view cameras). Its value clearly impacts greatly the estimates of time to collision.

With perfect measurement it turns out to be easy to recover the value of C_E by tracking a single point over a small time interval. Suppose we measure the image position of a point in a coordinate frame relative to the left end of the image. It has position R, say, in this coordinate system. Since C_E should remain constant we have that

$$r = R - C_E, \qquad \dot{r} = \dot{R}$$

so the time to collision for the optical center plane is

$$\frac{r}{\dot{r}} = \frac{R - C_E}{\dot{R}}. \qquad (3)$$

Suppose we can measure R and $\dot{R}$ at two distinct times t_0 and t_1. Then the estimate to time to collision should decrease by precisely $t_1 - t_0$. Writing our estimates as functions of time we then get that:

$$\frac{R(t_0) - C_E}{\dot{R}(t_0)} - (t_1 - t_0) = \frac{R(t_1) - C_E}{\dot{R}(t_1)}$$

whence

$$C_E = \frac{\dot{R}(t_0)R(t_1) - \dot{R}(t_1)R(t_0) + \dot{R}(t_1)\dot{R}(t_0)(t_1 - t_0)}{\dot{R}(t_0) - \dot{R}(t_1)} \qquad (4)$$

In summary then we can easily (given perfect measurement) estimate C_E and therefore compute the time to collision of the optical center plane

$$\frac{z'}{v} = \frac{R - C_E}{\dot{R}} \qquad (5)$$

However, time to collision from the optical from the optical center plane to the point p, i.e., z'/v is not exactly the information we want if the camera has been misaligned. We really want z/v where z is the component of distance from the center of the camera in the direction of motion and

$$z = z' + x'\sin\alpha \qquad (6)$$

as can be seen from figure 3.

Let $c = C_E - P/2$, the distance in pixels along the image plane from the center of view to the center of expansion, then referring to figure 3

$$\sin\alpha = \frac{c}{f'}$$

so by equation (2)

$$z = z' + \frac{cx'}{f'} = z' + \frac{crz'}{(f')^2}$$

and since

$$f' = \sqrt{c^2 + f^2}$$

we have

$$z = z' + \frac{crz'}{c^2 + f^2}. \qquad (7)$$

Notice that since we only really know z'/v (from equation (5)) this only gives us z/v, which in any case was what we wanted.

It is interesting to ask just how different z can be from z'. For a camera with a 60° field of view

$$-\tan 30° \le \frac{x'}{z'} \le \tan 30°$$

and for α restricted to ±5° we see that $z = z' + x'\sin\alpha$ is within ±5% of z'. Thus, since equation (7) is correcting such a relatively small error it is not critical to know f (which can be derived from ϕ through equation (1)) particularly accurately.

We now know z/v, or the *time to collision* with the obstacle, very accurately using only an imprecise approximation to the field of view of the camera as our *a priori* knowledge (which is easily gained by rotating the camera a roughly known amount). Since time to collision is precisely the right quantity to know for obstacle avoidance we don't need to try to compute the robot's velocity v at all. In fact we don't even need to know how our measure of passage of time t relates to external units. All we need is a steady on board clock and we can do obstacle aviodance visually.

2.3 Tracking image features

The above analysis suggests the idea of detecting image features and tracking them over many images. (An alternative is to use direct methods such as those suggested by Negahdaripour and Horn (1987)—we have not had much success with such methods due to the image and motion noise levels in our experimental situation.)

We track edges. We simply convolve the image with a derivative of a Gaussian (the actual mask is 1, 3, 5, 9, 14, 18, 20, 18, 11, 0, −11, −18, −20, −18, −14, −9, −5, −3, −1) and then look for local maximum values (Horn (1986)). We threshold the edges based on their strength of convolution with the mask. We accept only edges which have a convolution value greater than 500.

Figure 6 is a data set showing edge traces from a run with the mobile robot as the robot moves forward. It is a 2-D binary array where each row is a one dimensional image and time flows downwards. Array elements are 1 (black) where an edge was detected and 0 (white) otherwise. If the images are taken sufficiently close together (such as in this dataset) it is very simple to track edges without having to refer to the original grey level images.

It is sufficient to buffer only two rows of the array and keep track of the direction and velocity of an edge track in order to predict a small search window and direction of search in the second row. There are two cases in searching for the next edge in a trace; at the beginning of an edge trace where the direction within the image may not be known, and later when the direction is known. At all times the possibility of noise in the edge motion must be taken into account.

When the direction is not known a default symmetric window (±3 pixels) is searched in a succeeding row. If only one edge element is found, that is taken to be the next element of the trace. If more than one edge is found the current trace is abandoned.

When the direction of motion (left or right) is known we keep track of the edge velocity at each step of the trace. The trace is predicted to move the same amount at the next step plus or minus a small window of margin in order to accomodate noise in the image and edge velocity increases; −1 pixel short of prediction through +3 pixels extra. The search proceeds in the direction of motion, and the first edge encountered is taken as the correct edge. If no edge is encountered within the window then the edge trace is abandoned. No attempt is made to hypothesize a missing edge in the given one dimensional image and to try to look in the appropriate place in the next image.

There are two ways in which the direction of edge motion can be determined.

After a few elements of a trace have been tracked the direction should be clear by comparing the position of the first and most recent pixels. If the direction is not clear then the trace can be abandoned as there is no obvious depth information in it.

However, most edge traces have only one possible direction even considering only the first row in which it appears. If C_E is known then edges on the left move leftwards, and edges on the right move rightwards. Even when C_E is not known, an a priori knowledge of f and the maximum permissible range of α determines a strip within the image where it is possible that C_E might fall, and edge traces starting outside that strip have the obvious direction.

The key heuristic used by the above edge tracking algorithm to handle noise is perhaps not obvious at first glance. In fact the main idea is to abandon an edge trace when conditions get complicated. Chances are that the disturbance will last only a few images at most and the trace can be re-established as a brand new trace a few images later.

2.4 Noise and estimation

The analysis of section 2.1 assumes no noise and perfect measurement of various quantities. Real image sequences suffer from digitization effects and large sources of noise due to unstable camera platforms, unconstant velocity and curved rather than straight line motion. We must therefore fit all our measurements over many images.

To estimate the center of expansion we need to know R and $\dot{R}$ at more than one place along an edge trace. To decrease the effects of noise it is clearly best to use more than one edge trace. We use every edge trace and continually refine our estimate of C_E.

Quantity R is measured directly from the edge pixel array. We estimate $\dot{R}$, the edge velocity, by the slope of a chord between two points on a hyperbolic trace V images apart. By Rolle's theorem some point on the hyperbola between those two points has exactly that slope. We choose the midpoint in time. Thus $V\dot{R}$ is simply the distance travelled by the edge trace over V time intervals.

In the experiments reported in this paper we estimate $V\dot{R}$ at every pair of points on a trace separated by $3V$ steps in time, and use them to estimate C_E using equation (4) (by estimating $V\dot{R}$ rather than $\dot{R}$, only one division is necessary for each

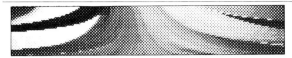

Figure 4. Image strips averaged to a single scan line and ordered in time for 100 images from the left camera.

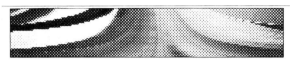

Figure 5. Image strips averaged to a single scan line and ordered in time for 100 images from the right camera.

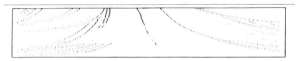

Figure 6. The edges detected in figure 4.

Figure 7. The edges detected in figure 5.

estimate of C_E). Our estimates over all time and all traces are then averaged together. We choose $3V$ so that $\dot{R}$ will have had time to change significantly and render the estimate for C_E more stable. A more sophisticated algorithm could dynamically choose the step size for the comparison based on the edge velocity.

In all our experiments reported here we have used $V = 4$.

Once C_E has been determined it is easy to compute the time to collision for a given edge point in a given edge using the same estimate for $\dot{R}$ as above. However since we are tracking edges and since edges correspond (hopefully) to a single three space feature, the time to collision should be reducing by one every image. We can therefore smooth our estimate for the time to collision by fitting a line of slope 1 over S images steps (i.e., $S + 1$ images). A least squares fit of such a line amounts to averaging the time to collision estimate along a trace over a set of $S + 1$ consecutive images.

Thus our estimates for time to collision are valid for an image $(V + S)/2$ prior to the most recently processed image.

In all our experiments reported here we have used $S = 4$.

Using this algorithm the centers of expansion are estimated at pixels 243 and 274 in figures 6 and 7 respectively. These displays of edge traces are from a stereo pair of left and right cameras mounted on our mobile robot. The cameras are 576 pixels wide so these estimates say that each camera was skewed slightly to the right, with the left one skewed more than the right. This corresponds to our visual estimate from examining the camera mounts at the beginning of the experimental run. Figures 4 and 5 show the grey level images from which these edge arrays were extracted.

2.5 Approximation errors

It is worth asking how well this scheme does for recovering depth even with synthetic data. There are a number of sources of inaccuracies; all edge locations are approximated to an integral number of pixels, divisions (such as in equation (4)) are rounded to the nearest integer, and the edge velocity estimates are only difference approximations to derivatives. With realistic camera parameters and using $V = 4$ and $S = 4$ we have experimentally found accuracy on synthetic data to be about 2%.

3. Calibrating Stereo

Recall that motion vision does not get good results close to the direction of motion since estimates for $\dot{R}$ are necessarily small and therefore susceptible to noise problems. Also it is useless when the robot is still, or not moving in straight lines. Stereo vision suffers from none of these problems but it is susceptible to camera misalignments and so must be calibrated. We calibrate it with the motion algorithm.

Our stereo algorithm matches edges in two one dimensional images. If all the camera parameters are known in advance we could then compute depth. Unfortunately it is not possible to recover all the camera parameters from a single pair of one dimensional images as it is in the case of two dimensional images (Longuet-Higgins (1981)). Rather, we use the results of the forward motion algorithms to calibrate our cameras.

3.1 The algorithm

We use the same edge operator as for forward motion and apply the operator to each of the left and right images.

Matching of edges in the two images is accomplished by means of a dynamic programming algorithm similar to that developed by Ohta and Kanade (1986) for two dimensional images and by Serey and Matthies (1987) for single scanline images, except that the cost functions here are different.

The dynamic programming algorithm searches for a minimum cost path left to right across the two images where there is a cost associated with matching two edges, and a cost with skipping an edge whether it is due to noise, occlusion, uncovering or something else.

The skipping cost is a constant (2000 in the experiments reported in this paper).

The matching cost is a larger number unless the signs of the gradients of the two edges are the same (i.e., unless the grey levels of both edges go from dark to light or vice versa). Otherwise the matching cost is the sum of squares of differences of pixel grey levels on a small window around the edge (we used 7 pixels centered on the edge, in the experiments reported here).

3.2 What needs to be calibrated

There are a large number of parameters needed to describe the optical system used for stereo vision. Each of the two cameras has a focal ratio, and each has six positional and rotational degrees of freedom relative to the robot. We are forced to calibrate for some of these parameters, we can ignore some because their effects are too small to notices, and others we take care of by our choice of stereo algorithm, camera design, and methodology.

Figure 8 illustrates the camera geometry we are assuming. The robot coordinate system has the z-axis pointing in the direction of travel of the robot. The y-axis is vertical and the x axis is perpendicular to the direction of motion.

We assume that the two cameras have the same focal ratio f or field of view.* Our forward motion algorithm assumed some *a priori* knowledge of this parameter and we suggested a simple way to determine a rough estimate for it. Rather than rely on

---

*It is possible to relax this assumption but the introduction of the necessary extra parameter in our calibration equations seems to make the calibration less stable. We do not have a theoretical basis for this remark—only empirical.

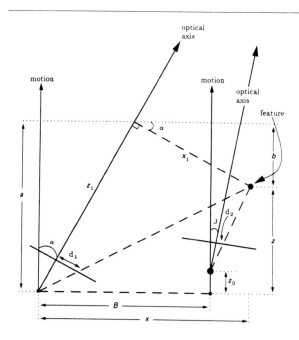

Figure 8. When there are two cameras they may both be misaligned relative to the direction of motion. They have a separation B perpendicular to the direction of motion and a misalignment z_0 in the direction of motion. Again we are interested in the forward distance z to some point.

such an estimate we calibrate the stereo system assuming no previous knowledge of f.

Now consider the geometric degrees of freedom and refer to figure 8 for definitions of geometric quantities.

x Our calibration assumes the base line separation of the cameras B in the x direction is unknown.

y In general one would assume this parameter to be small, but in any case our use of the average of 16 lines of grey level data in the current experiments, and our intention to use cylindrical lenses mean that larger values of y will not effect the stereo measurements at all.

z There may be small errors in mounting the cameras which lead to a non-zero z_0. We show below that for small z_0 the effects are minimal and can be ignored.

pitch   Again the averaging of scanlines or the use of cylindrical lenses takes care of this parameter.

roll   One would expect this parameter to be small. One could measure the fuzziness of edges (since the image is really a vertically averaged, digitally or optically, image) to estimate the amount of roll present in the cameras. We will ignore this parameter.

yaw   Each camera can swing from side to side on a standard camera mount, and in any case the orientation of the camera could easily drift mechanically from the orientation of the robot's wheels. (It certainly does on our robots.) Our calibration assumes small unknown yaw angles on each camera.

3.3 Calibration formulation

Figure 8 shows a view from above of a stereo pair of cameras mounted on a mobile robot pointing approximately in the direction of motion. We assume both cameras have focal ratio f. The optical axis of the left camera is misaligned by angle α from the direction of motion, while the right camera is misaligned by angle β. The baseline separation, B, is measured perpendicular to the direction of motion. z_0 is the misalignment offset of the optical centers in the direction of motion.

We will assume that none of these five parameters (α, β, f, B, or z_0) is known *a priori*. We will, however, assume that we know bounds on some of these quantities. We assume that α and β are no bigger than $\pm 5°$, that f, in pixels, is comparable (499 compared to 576 in our experiments) or larger than P the width of the image plane, and that z_0 is much smaller than B.

The quantities we can directly measure given some matched feature in the two images are d_1 and d_2, the distances in pixels from the centers of view of the left and right cameras respectively. Due to our assumption above about the size of f, we know that roughly

$$|d_i| < \frac{f}{2}. \tag{8}$$

The quantity we wish to compute given some matched feature in the two images is its distance z in the direction of motion. Figure 8 shows that z is measured from the optical center of the left camera. The only other parameter we could compute is x, the displacement of the feature perpindicular to the direction of motion. We use x in deriving equations for z but do not compute it explicitly in any of our experiments.

Consider the quantities labelled a and b in the figure. They both relate to the z distance of the feature from the left camera. We can write

$$z = a - b$$
$$a = z_1 \cos \alpha$$
$$b = x_1 \sin \alpha$$

where z_1 is the distance of the feature in the direction of the optical axis of the left camera and x_1 is the feature's transverse distance from that axis. Now, because we are using perspective cameras we can write

$$\frac{x_1}{z_1} = \frac{d_1}{f}$$

giving us an expression for x_1 in terms of z_1 and so we can rewrite z as

$$z = a - b = z_1 \left(\cos \alpha - \frac{d_1}{f} \sin \alpha \right) \tag{9}$$

which is a linear expression in z_1. We can get a similar linear expression for z in terms of z_2 (it also involves the constant offset z_0) and thus get a linear equation relating z_1 and z_2.

We can do the same analysis for x getting a second simulataneous linear equation relating z_1 and z_2. Solving and substituting back in equation (9) we obtain

$$z = \frac{\mu z_0 + \nu B}{\rho} \tag{10}$$

where

$$\mu = - f d_2 \cos \alpha \cos \beta + f d_1 \sin \alpha \sin \beta - f^2 \cos \alpha \sin \beta$$
$$\quad + d_1 d_2 \sin \alpha \cos \beta$$
$$\nu = f^2 \cos \alpha \cos \beta + d_1 d_2 \sin \alpha \sin \beta - f d_2 \cos \alpha \sin \beta$$
$$\quad - f d_1 \sin \alpha \cos \beta$$
$$\rho = (f^2 + d_1 d_2) \sin(\alpha - \beta) + f(d_1 - d_2) \cos(\alpha - \beta).$$

We now have an equation for z, the quantity we wish to compute, in terms of d_1 and d_2 the quantities we can measure. We now want to derive a calibration procedure to identify the unknown parameters in this equation. We begin by noting that we can safely ignore some terms.

The sines of α and β are both less than 0.1. The cosines are all greater than 0.995. Thus the dominating term in μ is roughly $f d_2$ which by equation (8) is less than half the dominating term f^2 in ν. Since we also are assuming that z_0 is much smaller then B we will simply ignore the μ term. We can also ignore all but the f^2 term in ν as the other three are each at least 20 times smaller.

Turning attention to ρ we first observe that $d_1 - d_2$ can be arbitrarily small, and that $\sin(\alpha - \beta)$ can be larger than 0.17.

Thus since either term can dominate both terms are important. The only remaining question is whether in the left hand term we can ignore $d_1 d_2$ as it is never more than $1/4$ the size of f^2. We choose to ignore it for now in our derivation of a calibration procedure, but later we compare its inclusion and exclusion experimentally and conclude that it is insignificant.

With these approximations, and dividing both the top and bottom of equation (10) through by $f \cos(\alpha - \beta)$ we get

$$z = \frac{\Lambda}{\Gamma + d_1 - d_2} \tag{11}$$

where Λ and Γ are constants to be determined by calibration.

Suppose we have a collection of stereo images of features with known distance z, i.e., we have a collection of n triples (d_{1i}, d_{2i}, z_i). For a given Λ and Γ, we could write as a measure of closeness of fit for each triple

$$\frac{\Lambda}{z_i} - \Gamma - d_{1i} + d_{2i} \tag{12}.$$

When we minimize the sum of squares of measure (12) for n calibration triples we obtain

$$\Lambda = \frac{n \sum (d_{1i} - d_{2i})/z_i - \sum (1/z_i) \sum (d_{1i} - d_{2i})}{n \sum (1/z_i{}^2) - (\sum 1/z_i)^2}$$

$$\Gamma = \frac{\sum (1/z_i) \sum (d_{1i} - d_{2i})/z_i - \sum (1/z_i{}^2)(\sum d_{1i} - d_{2i})}{n \sum (1/z_i{}^2) - (\sum 1/z_i)^2}$$

where all the sums range over the n values of i.

3.4 Calibration procedure

We collect triples to use for calibrating the stereo system by using forward motion analysis through equation (7) to get depth estimates for points visible in both the left camera and right camera. For each pair of images we know the pixel coordinates for each such point for which we have a depth estimate. We run the stereo algorithm on each pair of images and for each match it finds we check to see whether forward motion delivered a depth estimate for both the edge in the left image and the edge in the right image. If so, and if those estimates are close (within $\pm 10\%$ of their average in our experiments) we use their average as the third element of a triple which includes the left and right edge pixel coordinates.

When a few tens of triples have been collected we plug them into the least-sqaures formulation to get estimates of Λ and Γ.

3.5 Experimental results

To test the preceeding algorithms we set up our robot Allen to drive in an approximately straight line with large objects on either side of its path. Figures 9 and 10 are the left and right full frame camera views from approximately the start of its path.

The cameras were connected via cables to a Lisp machine and an image was digitized every $1/15$ of a second giving a stereo pair every $2/15$ of a second. The robot was moving at approximately 1.5 feet per second. Thus the contribution to z_0 (in figure 8) is approximately 1.2 inches which is small compared to our stereo baseline B of approximately 8 inches and justifies our disregard of μ in equation (10).

Figures 4 and 5 show the left and right grey level motion images collected from 100 stereo pairs of standard images. Each scanline in figures 4 and 5 corresponds to averaging 16 scanlines from the centers of the original images. Time flows down these pseudo images, and is approximately 13 seconds from top to bottom. Figures 6 and 7 show the edges extracted from the time images—recall that the edge detection is one dimensional along scanlines.

In these experiments we made two passes over the edge images. The first was to estimate the centers of expansions and

Figure 9. The left image of a stero pair at the beginning of a straight line motion of the robot.

Figure 10. The right image of a stero pair at the beginning of a straight line motion of the robot.

l	r	disp	org	new	l	r	disp	org	new
144	163	−19	50	52	163	189	−26	69	63
525	550	−25	60	61	521	545	−24	60	59
169	197	−28	54	68	516	541	−25	60	61
170	198	−28	62	68	512	537	−25	60	61
507	532	−25	60	61	172	202	−30	71	73
503	530	−27	60	65	174	203	−29	69	70
174	204	−30	74	73	149	137	12	28	28
175	205	−30	63	73	153	142	11	28	29
155	146	9	30	30	73	68	5	32	32
77	73	4	32	32	81	79	2	33	33
85	85	0	34	34	90	90	0	36	34
93	96	−3	36	36	102	106	−4	36	37
105	111	−6	36	38	9	48	−39	112	109
11	51	−40	115	115	435	441	−6	46	38
13	54	−41	122	123	430	439	−9	48	41
426	435	−9	49	41					

Figure 11. Display of the stereo calibration and results. Left two columns are pixel coordinates of edges in the left and right images, third column is their difference, fourth column is the average depth estimate from the motion algorithms running on the left and right image sequences and the fifth column is the depth estimate produced by the stereo system calibrated with this data.

the second to extract motion depth estimates and correlate those with the stereo matches in order to get triples for stereo calibration. On a robot running these algorithms continuously there would only be one pass, simultaneously making minor refinements to both the centers of expansion and stereo calibrations.

In the 100 image pairs the algorithms found 94 estimates for C_E in the left image, averaging to 243, and 110 estimates in the right image, averaging to 274. A total of 92 stereo matches were found, of which 31 were strongly consistent with motion depth estimates. These were used to calibrate the stereo system resulting in estimates of

$$\Lambda = 1958.8475, \quad \Gamma = 56.970116.$$

Figure 11 shows the original left and right averaged depth estimates for each of these 31 points, along with the estimate produced by the stereo algorithm with the derived calibration. The depth estimates are in units of time between collecting images. Notice that there are left to right reversals because the cameras are not particularly well aligned.

To test the stereo calibration we took four feature points corresponding to known objects in the scene. We estimated where the robot had been when the first images in the sequence were taken (to achieve the constant velocity constraint the robot had to be moving before we started collecting images) and measured

the distances to the known points in the direction of motion. We plugged the left and right image coordinates into equation (12) to get time to collision estimates, and divided each of those into the known distances (measured in feet) and averaged the result to get a calibration of the stereo system in feet. The estimate is 0.18740588 feet per image step. Figure 12 shows the unsurprising results of this procedure in the top four rows of the table.

We then took the same four features and searched for them 20 images later in the image sequences. The bottom half of figure 12 shows the stereo estimates for these four points. Ideally, all the time to collision estimates should be reduced by 20. They are reduced by 18, 14, 20, and 17. Note that the third of these points appeared roughly in the centers of the two images and no time to collision estimates were produced for it by the motion algorithms. The fourth column shows the distance in feet that would have been estimated if the stereo had come up with a decrease of exactly 20 units for each of the points. The sixth column shows the estimate that was actually obtained. The relative distances between the points known a priori from measurement given in the fourth column in the upper part of the diagram, and the estimated distances in the sixth column of the lower part of the diagram are quite good and can be summarized as:

exact	—	est
5.0	—	5.6
8.6	—	7.5
2.0	—	1.3
3.6	—	1.9
7.0	—	6.9
10.6	—	8.8

Note that these are relative distances, some of them at large distances from the robot itself.

3.6 Other calibration schemes

In experiments with synthetic data the most signifcant term omitted from equation (10) in equation (11) appeared to be $d_1 d_2$ in the denominator. We therefore repeated the above experiment using a calibration equation of the form

$$z = \frac{\Lambda}{\Gamma + \Omega d_1 d_2 + d_1 - d_2}. \tag{13}$$

The results were almost identical:

$$\Lambda = 1957.6881, \quad \Gamma = 56.864132, \quad \Omega = 2.360905 \times 10^{-6},$$

l	r	disp	**orig**	ttc	new
194	216	−22	10.5	56	10.5
314	347	−33	15.5	82	15.4
263	300	−37	19.1	98	18.4
398	414	−16	8.5	48	9.0
173	179	−6	6.7	38	7.1
336	364	−28	11.6	68	12.7
273	305	−32	14.6	78	14.6
485	479	6	5.2	31	5.8

Figure 12. The first four rows show features with known distances (fourth column) in feet, their depth (fifth column) in time to collision units as delivered by the calibrated stereo algorithm, and their depth in feet (sixth column) by calibrating the previous two columns. In the second four rows, the same points are displayed from images 20 time units later. This time the fourth column is the predicted distance based on the sixth column above.

l	r	disp	**orig**	ttc	new
194	216	−22	10.5	56	10.5
314	347	−33	15.5	82	15.3
263	300	−37	19.1	99	18.5
398	414	−16	8.5	48	9.0
173	179	−6	6.7	38	7.1
336	364	−28	11.6	68	12.7
273	305	−32	14.8	79	14.8
485	479	6	5.2	31	5.8

Figure 13. Same as for figure 12 but using a much more complex stereo calibration procedure. There is almost no difference in results.

l	r	disp	**orig**	**ttc**	**new**
194	216	−22	10.5	55	18.0
314	347	−33	15.5	37	12.1
263	300	−37	19.1	33	10.8
398	414	−16	8.5	76	24.8
173	179	−6	11.4	202	66.0
336	364	−28	5.6	43	14.0
273	305	−32	4.2	38	12.4
485	479	6	18.3	−202	−66.0

Figure 14. Same as for figure 12 but using a stereo calibration that assumes the cameras are aligned parallel to the direction of motion. The results are pure noise.

an estimate of 0.18685402 feet per image step (within 0.3% of the previous estimate), and almost identical results on the check with known distances as shown in figure 13.

These experiments convinced us that (11) is certainly sufficient. But is it necessary? To check we tried calibrating with the same data to a model of stereo that assumes the cameras are perfectly aligned, i.e., using a calibration equation of the form:

$$z = \frac{\Lambda}{d_1 - d_2}. \tag{14}$$

The results were:

$$\Lambda = -1213.2903,$$

an estimate of 0.32663247 (almost a factor of 2 off), and meaningless results on known distances as shown in 14. Clearly this naïve model is not sufficient.

4. Conclusions

In this paper we have demonstrated a number of things about forward motion analysis and stereo vision.

Forward motion analysis is fairly noisy by the unnatural standards set by most workers in computer vision and mobile robots. In this paper we first argued that those standards are not necessary, and in fact are not met by humans, most of whom operate perfectly well as autonomous mobile agents. In fact, errors of only ±10% seem more than adequate to us for mobile robot obstacle avoidance.

Forward motion analysis has some wonderful independence properties and only requires a small number of 16 bit fixed precision arithmetic operations to deliver depth in a coordinate system natural to the task of obstacle aviodance. At the same time as it is delivering depth estimates it can continually recalibrate itself for camera misalignment relative to the direction of motion. All of these computations could easily be transfered to a parallel network of simple processors.

Despite the local noise in each forward motion estimate we demonstrated that with just a few tens of such measurements we could calibrate a stereo camera system with grossly misaligned cameras.

What does this buy us?

It means we can have a vision system on board a robot that doesn't require a time consuming calibration stage at the beginning of an experimental run. Rather we can build power-up-and-go systems. If the sensor platform drifts mechanically from the drive alignment (as it does on many real robots) over time there is no calibration problem—the algorithms given in this paper continually adjust. If there is more severe and sudden misalignment, e.g., due to a hard collision, the robot will be disoriented for only a few seconds before it accommodates.

More than this however, the possibility of simple fast dynamic calibration to the world opens up the possibility of having cheap (and hence mechanically sloppy) steerable sensor platforms. If we can quickly and cheaply compute all we need to know about how such a platform is aligned we will not feel pressure to spend inordinate amounts of money building a precise platform.

Silicon is getting cheaper a lot quicker than precision machined parts are. We should search for ways, as this paper does, of trading off silicon for such precision machined parts. If the analysis and algorithms are simple we have a better chance of them being robust. Off course it is critical to back up analysis with experiment—analysis in computer vision without experiment is often a worthless intellectual pursuit.

Acknowledgements

Claudia Smith digitally drew the figures for this paper. Chris Lindblad and Dave Clemens coaxed digital images from laser printers.

References

Baker, Bolles and Marimont (1987) "Epipolar-Plane Image Analysis: An Approach to Determining Structure from Motion", Robert C. Bolles, H. Harlyn Baker and David H. Marimont, *International Journal of Computer Vision*, 1, 7–55.

Brooks (1986) "A Robust Layered Control System for a Mobile Robot", Rodney A. Brooks, *IEEE Journal of Robotics and Automation*, RA-2, April, 14–23.

Brooks (1987) "A Hardware Retargetable Distributed Layered Architecture for Mobile Robot Control", Rodney Brooks, *Proceedings IEEE Robotics and Automation, Raleigh NC*, April, 106–110.

Longuet-Higgins (1981) "A Computer Algorithm for Reconstructing a Scene from Two Projections", H. C. Longuet-Higgins, *Nature*, 293, 133–135.

Faugeras and Toscani (1986) "The Calibration Problem for Stereo", Olivier D. Faugeras and G. Toscani, *Proceedings of Computer Vision and Pattern Recognition*, Miami Beach, 15–20.

Horn (1986) "Robot Vision", Berthold K. P. Horn, *MIT Press, Cambridge*.

Marr (1982) "Vision", David Marr, *W. H. Freeman, San Francisco*.

Negahdaripour and Horn (1987) "Direct Passive Navigation", Shahriar Nagahdaripour and Berthold K. P. Horn, *IEEE Trans. on Pattern Analysis and Machine Intelligence*, PAMI-9, January, 168–176.

Ohta and Kanade (1983) "Stereo by Intra– and Inter–Scanline Search Using Dynamic Programming", Yuichi Ohta and Takeo Kanade, *CMU Tech Report*.

Serey and Matthies (1987) "Obstacle Avoidance Using 1-D Stereo Vision", Bruno Serey and Larry Matthies, *CMU Tech Report*, in preparation.

Appendix—Kludge Factors

Almost all computer vision programs have a large number of "tweakable" parameters hidden in their code. These are usually used to implement certain English phrases used in the scientific paper which describes the work. For instance there might be a phrase like "for sufficiently close edge terminations we ...". In this paper we have tried to explicity state all such *kludge factors* that we have used. For the reader's convenience we also collect them here and give the values we used for them throughout all experiments we have done.

The edge mask (derivative of a Gaussian) is:

$1\ 3\ 5\ 9\ 14\ 18\ 20\ 18\ 11\ 0\ -11\ -18\ -20\ -18\ -14\ -9\ -5\ -3\ -1$.

The threshold strength we demand of edges is 500. The same edges are used for stereo and motion algorithms.

In the dynamic programming portion of the stereo algorithm we assign a cost of 2000 to skipped matches, and the sum of squares of pixel grey level differences in a window of 7 pixels centered on the left and right edges for accepted matches.

In linking edges in the motion algorithm we start off with a search window of ± 3 pixels and later narrow that to -1 to $+3$ pixels from the most recent step.

To compute the edge velocity in the motion algorithms we use the slope of a chord joining edge locations $V = 4$ images apart. In estimating C_E we do this twice at $3V = 12$ images apart.

We smooth the time to collision estimates over $S = 4$ time intervals (i.e., 5 images).

In deciding on consistent depth estimates and stereo matches we demand that the left and right motion depth estimates lie within $\pm 10\%$ of their average.

A New Technique for Fully Autonomous and Efficient 3D Robotics Hand-Eye Calibration

Roger Y. Tsai and Reimar K. Lenz[1]

IBM T. J. Watson Research Center
Yorktown Heights, NY 10598

This paper describes a new technique for computing 3D position and orientation of a camera relative to the last joint of a robot manipulator in an eye-on-hand configuration. The calibration can be done within a fraction of a millisecond after the robot finishes the movement. To the best of our knowledge, this method is faster, simpler and more accurate than any existing technique for hand/eye calibration. A series of generic geometric properties or lemma are presented, leading to the derivation of the final algorithms, which are aimed at simplicity, efficiency and accuracy while giving ample geometric and algebraic insights. Besides describing the new technique, critical factors influencing the accuracy are analyzed, and procedures for improving accuracy are introduced. Error analysis and formulas are described and tested. Tests results of both simulation and real experiments on an IBM Cartesian robot are reported and analyzed.

Introduction

What is 3D Robotics Hand/Eye Calibration?

3D robotics hand/eye calibration is the task of computing the relative 3D position and orientation between the camera and the robot gripper in an eye-on-hand configuration, meaning that the camera is rigidly connected to the robot gripper. The camera is either grasped by the gripper, or just fastened to it. More specifically, this is the task of computing the relative rotation and translation (homogeneous transformation) between two coordinate frames, one centered at the camera lens center, and the other at the robot gripper. The gripper coordinate frame is centered on the last link of the robot manipulator, and as we shall see in this paper, the robot manipulator must possess enough degrees of freedom so as to be able to rotate the camera around two different axes while at the same time keeping the camera focused on a stationary calibration object in order to resolve uniquely the full 3D geometric relationship between the camera and the gripper.[2]

Why Isn't It Trivial?

It is obvious to see that if the robot knows the exact 3D positions of a number of points on a calibration setup in the robot world coordinate system as well as 3D location of the gripper, while at the same time, the camera can view these points in a proper way, then it is possible to determine the 3D homogeneous transformation between the camera and the calibration world coordinate frame, making it a trivial matter to compute the homogeneous transformation between the camera and the manipulator. However, it is very difficult, if possible, for the robot to acquire the accurate knowledge of the 3D positions of a number of feature points easy enough for camera to view simultaneously with the right resolution, field of view, etc., while the position information has to be known in the robot world coordinate system. Some researchers treat the difference between the calibration world coordinate system and the robot world coordinate system as a 6-degree-freedom unknown, and incorporate them into a much larger non-linear optimization process (see -- Heading id 'art' unknown --). We propose a much easier and faster approach.

Why is Hand/Eye Calibration Important?

It is important in several aspects:

Automated 3D Robotics Vision Measurement

When vision is used to measure the 3D geometric relationships between different parts of an object in a robotics work cell, it is often necessary to use the manipulator to move the vision sensor to different positions in the work space in order to see different features of the object (see Tsai and Lavin, 1984). At each position, the 3D position and orientation of the feature measured by the vision system is only relative to the vision sensor. As the manipulator moves the sensor to different positions, the measurements taken at different positions are not related to one another unless we know the 3D relative position and orientation of the sensor at different locations. If the robot system is capable of knowing where the gripper is in the robot world coordinate system to some degree of accuracy, then it should know how much 3D motion it has undertaken from one position to another. Since the camera is rigidly connected to the gripper, of course it too undergoes the same rigid body motion, BUT ONLY in the robot world coordinate system. If the hand/eye calibration is not done, one does not know the 3D homogenous transformation between the camera 3D coordinate systems at different locations simplify from the motion of the robot manipulator.

Automated Sensor Placement Planning

In order to do automated 3D measurement with robot vision, sensor planning is vital in order to automatically determine the optimum positions of the sensor in order to view all the desired features while taking care of problems of occlusion, depth of focus, resolution, field of view, etc. However, even if the robot knows where to put the sensor for optimum viewing, it does not know where the manipulator should be in order to achieve this goal, unless the 3D geometric relationships between the last link of the manipulator and the sensor is known.

Automated Part Acquisition or Assembly

When vision is used to aid the robot in grasping an object for automated assembly or part transport with eye-on-hand configuration, unless iterative visual feedback is used, the vision system may be able to determine where the part is relative to the sensor, but the robot does not know how to place the manipulator to grasp it. This problem can be resolved if the robot hand/eye calibration is done.

Stereo Vision

---

[1] Reimar K. Lenz is now with the Lehrstuhl fuer Nachrichtentechnik, Technical University of Munich, FRG.
[2] It takes at least two rotary joints and one linear joint, or three rotary joints. It is possible to use just two rotary joints, but the rotation axes for these two joints must coincide at the calibration block.

If only one camera is used to do stereo vision, one way to create a stereo base is to move the camera with the manipulator [3]. Although the robot system may know how much the manipulator has moved, it does not know the homogenous transformation between the 3D camera coordinate system, even if the camera undergoes the same rigid body motion as the gripper does (since this rigid body motion is defined only in the robot world coordinate system). Again, when the hand/eye calibration is done, this problem is solved.

Why Isn't the State of the Art Sufficient?

From our literature survey, there are two categories of approaches for doing robot hand/eye calibration:

Coupling Hand/Eye Calibration with Conventional Robot Kinematic Model Calibration

References (partial list): G. Puskorius and L. Feldkamp (1987); A. Izaquirre (1987); M. Bowman & A. Forrest (submitted for publication)

In this approach, global nonlinear optimization is done over the robot kinematic model parameters and the hand/eye parameters silmultanously, making the number of unknowns generally over 30. Such large scale nonlinear optimization is very time consuming, and needs a very good initial guess and accurate data for convergence. It also cannot easily exploit the use of redundant images and stations for reducing error since the computation would become prohibitive.

Decoupling Hand/Eye Calibration from Conventional Robot Kinematic Model Calibration

References (partial list): Y. Shiu and S. Ahmad (1987); R. Tsai and R. Lenz (1987, this paper) (partial list): G. Puskorius and L. Feldkamp (1987); A. Issaquirre (1986); M. Bowman & A. Forrest (submitted for publication)

As far as we know, Shiu and Ahmad's work and the work reported in this paper are the first attempts to decouple the hand/eye calibration from robot model calibration and not use global high dimensional nonlinear optimization. The starting point between these two works are similar (although independently developed), the solutions are very different. In Shiu and Ahmad's method, the number of unknowns to solve for is twice the number of degrees of freedom, since they treat sin and cos as independent. We found it advantageous to use redundant frames to improve accuracy, but in our algorithm, the number of unknowns stays the same no matter how many frames are used simultaneously, and for each additional frame, only 60 additional arithmetic scalar operations are needed (each operation takes less than half a microsecond on a typical minicomputer). In Shiu and Ahmond's method, the number of unknowns increases by two for each extra frame. Our procedure is simpler and faster, and the derivation procedure is also simpler. We have also done extensive error analysis, simulation or real experiments for testing the accuracy potential or problems of hand/eye calibration, and propose means for improving accuracy.

The New Approach

Basic Setup

Figure 1 is a schematic depiction of the basic setup. Figure 2 shows two photos of the actual setup. The robot carrying a camera makes a series of motions with the camera acquiring a picture of a calibration object at the pause of each motion. The calibration object is a block with an array of target points on the top surface. The position of each

calibration point is known very accurately relative to an arbitrarily selected coordinate system setup on the block (see Tsai, 1986, 1987; Lenz and Tsai, 1987; Tsai and Lenz, 1987). Detailed description of the setup can found in "Simulation and Real Experiment Results" on page 8. The following is a list of definitions for the various coordinate frames (Note: All coordinate frames mentioned here are Cartesian coordinate frames in 3D):

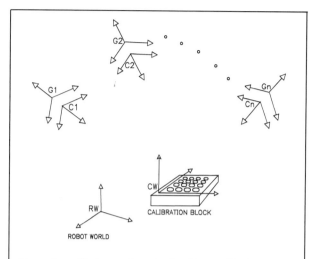

Figure 1.   Basic setup for robot hand/eye calibration. C_i and G_i are coordinate frames for the camera and gripper respectively.

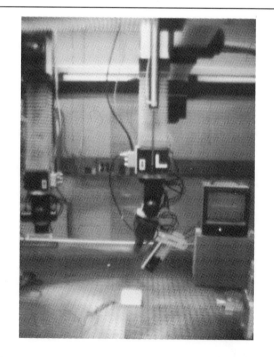

Figure 2.   The physical setup. A CCD camera is rigidly mounted on the last joint of an IBM Clean Room Robot for performing hand/eye calibration.

---

[3]   This is not highly recommendable except in low accuracy applications. It is better for the robot to carry a stereo pair of cameras or laser-camera pair, or to use one camera with model based location determination.

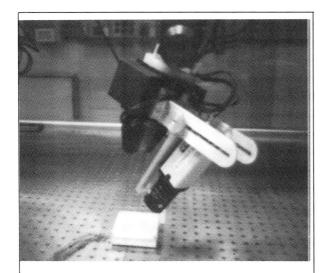

Figure 3.   The physical setup. A CCD camera is rigidly mounted on the last joint of an IBM Clean Room Robot for performing hand/eye calibration.

G_i : The gripper coordinate system. That is, the coordinate frame fixed on the robot gripper and as the robot moves, it moves with the gripper.

C_i : The camera coordinate system. That is, the coordinate frame fixed on the camera, with the z axis coinciding with the optical axis, and the x, y axes parallel to the image X, Y axes

CW : The calibration block world coordinate frame. This is an arbitrarily selected coordinate frame set on the calibration block so that the coordinate of each target point on the calibration block is known *a priori* relative to CW.

RW : The robot world coordinate frame. It is fixed in the robot work station, and as the robot arm moves around, the encoder output of all the robot joints enable the system to tell where the gripper is relative to RW.

Definition of a list of Homogeneous Transformation Matrix

H_{gi} defines coordinate transformation from G_i to RW (1)

$$H_{gi} \equiv \begin{bmatrix} R_{gi} & T_{gi} \\ 0\ 0\ 0 & 1 \end{bmatrix}$$

H_{ci} defines coordinate transformation from CW to C_i (2)

$$H_{ci} \equiv \begin{bmatrix} R_{ci} & T_{ci} \\ 0\ 0\ 0 & 1 \end{bmatrix}$$

H_{gij} defines coordinate transformation from G_i to G_j (3)

$$H_{gij} \equiv \begin{bmatrix} R_{gij} & T_{gij} \\ 0\ 0\ 0 & 1 \end{bmatrix}$$

H_{cij} defines coordinate transformation from C_i to C_j (4)

$$H_{cij} \equiv \begin{bmatrix} R_{cij} & T_{cij} \\ 0\ 0\ 0 & 1 \end{bmatrix}$$

H_{cg} defines coordinate transformation from C_i to G_i (5)

$$H_{cg} \equiv \begin{bmatrix} R_{cg} & T_{cg} \\ 0\ 0\ 0 & 1 \end{bmatrix}$$

In the above, i,j range from 1 to N, where N is the number of stations in Figure 1 on page 2 where the camera grabs pictures of the cali-

bration block. Figure 4 on page 4 illustrates the relationship between the homogeneous matrices and the various coordinate frames in Figure 1 on page 2. Note that H_{cg} does not have any station index (i or j). This is because the camera is rigidly mounted on the gripper of the robot arm and therefore, H_{cg} is the same for all stations.

What Are the Observables and What is to be computed?

The Observables or the Measurables

The Observables are H_{ci} and H_{gi} for i=1,...,N. H_{ci} is obtained from computing the extrinsic calibration parameters(see Tsai 1986, 1987; Tsai and Lenz 1987) using the image grabbed at the ith pause of robot movement. It defines the relative 3D rotation and translation from CW to C_i. For 36 calibration points, it takes about 20 msec to compute, and is accurate to one part in 4000. The other set of observables are H_{gi}s . Any robot that can supply the information of where the gripper is within the robot workstation is capable of delivering H_{gi} . This requires good robot calibration. Actually, even if H_{gi} may be bad, so long as if H_{gij} is good, there is no problem. This due to the fact the computational procedure entails only H_{gij}, but not H_{gi}.

Elements to be Computed

Intermediate: H_{gij}, H_{cij}

Since H_{gi} defines transformation from G_i to RW , and H_{gj} from G_j to RW, obviously,

$$H_{gij} = H_{gj}^{-1} H_{gi} \qquad (6)$$

Similarly,

$$H_{cij} = H_{cj} H_{ci}^{-1} \qquad (7)$$

Notice that (6) and (7) are incompatible in terms of where the inverse signs are placed. This is due to the fact that H_{gi} is from G_i to RW while H_{ci} is from CW to C_i .

Final: H_{cg}

Notice that if RW coincided with CW, it would be trivial to compute H_{cg}, which in this case would be equal to $H_{gi}^{-1}H_{ci}^{-1}$. However, it is very difficult for the coordinate system on the calibration block to be set in a fixed and precisely known 3D relationship with respect to the robot coordinate system such that the positions of all the points on the calibration block are known relative to the robot.

Some Basic Background for a General Rotation Matrix and Its Real Eigenvectors

Before describing the new technique , we introduce the representation for transformation (in particular, rotations) used below. It is well known (Rogers and Adams, 1976) that any rigid body motion or Cartesian coordinate transformation can be modelled as a rotation by an angle θ around an axis through the origin with direction cosines n_1, n_2, n_3, followed by a translation T such that

$$\begin{bmatrix} x' \\ y' \\ z' \end{bmatrix} = R \begin{bmatrix} x \\ y \\ z \end{bmatrix} + T \quad or \quad \begin{bmatrix} x' \\ y' \\ z' \\ 1 \end{bmatrix} = H \begin{bmatrix} x \\ y \\ z \\ 1 \end{bmatrix}$$

where (x, y, z) and (x', y', z') are the coordinates of any point before and after the transformation.

R is a 3 × 3 orthonormal matrix of the first kind (i.e., det(R) = 1)

$$R = \begin{bmatrix} n_1^2 + (1 - n_1^2)\cos\theta & n_1 n_2 (1 - \cos\theta) - n_3 \sin\theta & n_1 n_3 (1 - \cos\theta) + n_2 \sin\theta \\ n_1 n_2 (1 - \cos\theta) + n_3 \sin\theta & n_2^2 + (1 - n_2^2)\cos\theta & n_2 n_3 (1 - \cos\theta) - n_1 \sin\theta \\ n_1 n_3 (1 - \cos\theta) - n_2 \sin\theta & n_2 n_3 (1 - \cos\theta) + n_1 \sin\theta & n_3^2 + (1 - n_3^2)\cos\theta \end{bmatrix}$$

(8)

H is the homogeneous transformation matrix (used in (1)-(5)), and is defined as

$$H = \begin{bmatrix} R & T \\ 0\ 0\ 0 & 1 \end{bmatrix}$$

One of the eigenvector and eigenvalue of R must be the rotation axis and 1, since, by definition, R is a rotation around axis $P_R \equiv [n_1\ n_2\ n_3]^T$, and obviously,

$$R\ P_r = P_r$$

thus, P_r is an eigenvector (or principal vector) and its corresponding eigenvalue is 1. From (8) and by definition, it is obvious that specifying P_r and θ completely specifies R. Therefore, it is quite convenient to represent R by P_r scaled some function of θ. We use a modefied version of Rodrigues formula (see Junkins and Turner, 1986), and define P_r as

$$P_r = 2 \sin \frac{\theta}{2} [n_1\ \ n_2\ \ n_3]^T \qquad 0 \le \theta \le \pi \qquad (9)$$

Besides the advantages associated with Quaternions or other vector representation of rotation matrix, one advantage for us is that some error formulas hold true for even non-infinitesimal perturbation. For example, Lemma V in "Error Analysis" on page 6 is exact. Also, the error formula in (29) is simpler. Another obvious advantage is that R is a simple function of P_r without any trigonometric functions

$$R = \left(1 - \frac{|P_r|^2}{2} \right) I + \frac{1}{2} \left(P_r P_r^T + \alpha \cdot Skew(P_r) \right) \qquad (10)$$

where $\alpha = \sqrt{4 - |P_r|^2}$ and $Skew(P_r)$ is defined in (11.5). For the rest of the paper, the principal axis is defined as such, and all the computational procedure is given for P_r explicitly, and not for R.

Computational Procedures and Conditions for Uniqueness

We first give the computational procedures and conditions of uniqueness before we derive them. The derivations and proof follow from the eleven properties or lemmas in "Derivations of Computational Procedures and Conditions of Uniqueness using Eleven Lemmas" on page 5. The acutal proof for those eleven lemma will be published in a later paper that contains a fuller account of the work. The minimum number of stations is three, where station means the location where robot pauses for doing camera extrinsic calibration. Using more than three stations improves the accuracy, as to be seen in "Error Analysis" on page 6.

Some Definition of Notation:

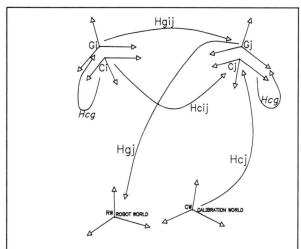

Figure 4.   Relationship between the homogeneous matrices and the coordinate frames.

θ_R : angle of rotation for R

P_{gij} : principal axis or rotation axis for R_{gij} defined in (3), which is the 3D rotation from gripper coordinate frame G_i to G_j, as defined in (9).

(11.1)

P_{cij} : rotation axis for R_{cij} in (4).

(11.2)

P_{cg} : rotation axis for R_{cg}

(11.3)

P_{cg}' : $|P_{cg}'| = \dfrac{1}{2} \cos^{-1}(\dfrac{\theta_{R_{cg}}}{2}) P_{cg} = \dfrac{1}{\sqrt{4 - |P_{cg}|^2}} P_{cg}$ (11.4)

$Skew(V)$: a skew-symmetric matrix generated by a 3D vector V such that

$$Skew(V) = \begin{bmatrix} 0 & -v_z & v_y \\ v_z & 0 & -v_x \\ -v_y & v_x & 0 \end{bmatrix}$$

(11.5)

N: number of stations described in "Basic Setup" on page 2.

Notice that the vectors defined above will also be used as a 3×1 column matrix. Also note that since P_{gij}, P_{cij} and P_{cg} are rotation axis with angle as its length, they completely specify R_{gij}, R_{cij} and R_{cg}. That is why for the procedures in the following, the formula for P_{cg} is given, not R_{cg}.

Procedure for Computing R_{cg}

Step 1: Compute P_{cg}'

For each pair of stations i,j such that the rotation angle R_{gij} or R_{cij} is as large as possible (Figure 5 illustrates a good way to select the pairing. See also section on test results), set up a system of linear equations with P_{ij}' as unknowns:

$$Skew(P_{gij} + P_{cij}) \cdot P_{cg}' = P_{cij} - P_{gij} \qquad (12)$$

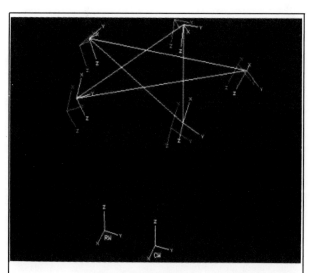

Figure 5.   Pairs of stations should be selected such that the inter-station rotation angle is as large as possible, and the angle between different inter-station rotation axes are as large as possible. The bar between stations denotes a particular selection of a pair of stations.

Since $Skew(P_{gij} + P_{cij})$ is always singular, it takes at least two pairs of stations to solve for a unique solution for P_{cg}' using linear least square technique.

Exception Handling: If $P_{gi1j1} + P_{ci1j1}$ is colinear with $P_{gi2j2} + P_{ci2j2}$ while P_{gi1j1} is not colinear with P_{gi2j2}, then the rotation angle of R_{cg} must be 180° and rotation axis the same as $P_{gi1j1} + P_{ci1j1}$.

Step 2: Compute $\theta_{R_{gc}}$

$$\theta_{R_{gc}} = 2\ \tan^{-1}|P_{cg}'| \qquad (13)$$

Note: Step 2 is not quite necessary since P_{cg} in Step 3 is sufficient to represent rotation. However, (13) may be handy.

Step 3: Compute P_{cg}

$$P_{cg} = \frac{2P_{gc}'}{\sqrt{1 + |P_{cg}|^2}} \qquad (14)$$

Procedure for Computing T_{cg}

Given at least two pairs of stations i,j, set up a linear systems of three linear equations with T_{cg} as unknowns:

$$(R_{gij} - I)T_{cg} = R_{cg}T_{cij} - T_{gij} \qquad (15)$$

For at least two pairs of stations, two sets of (15) are established and can be solved for the common unknowns T_{cg} using linear least square solutions.

Speed Performance

After the robot finishes the movement and grabbing the images, it takes only about $100 + 60N$ arithmetic operations to complete the computation. For a typical minicomputer, this only takes about $1/2$ millisecond for ten stations. This complexity figure $(100+60N)$ can be derived as follows: The majority of computation is for solving the overdetermined linear least square solutions of (12) and (15). It takes about $3 \times N \times 3^2$ to form the normal equation of either one of (11.5) and (16), and $3^3 \times 2$ to solve the 3×3 normal equation. With a minimum of three stations and two inter-station pairs, it takes about $1/10$ of a millisecond. This is negligible comparing with the robot movement and image acquisition and analysis; at the pause of each movement, it takes about 90 millisecond to grab an image, extract all the 36 feature point coordinates with high accuracy, and compute the extrinsic camera parameters defined in (4).

Derivations of Computational Procedures and Conditions of Uniqueness using Eleven Lemmas

In order to outline the derivations of the computational procedures without going into actual details, eleven lemmas will first be stated and the significance of each explained. Then, bypassing the proof for these lemma, the proof for the computational procedure for R_{cg} and T_{cg} will first be given. Then the conditions for uniqueness will be stated and proved. The proof for the eleven lemma will be published in a later paper.

Lemma I R_{gij} and R_{cij} differ by a unitary similarity transformation

$$R_{gij} = R_{cg} R_{cij} R_{cg}^T \qquad (16)$$

Significance: As a result, the eigenvector matrix of R_{gij} can be transformed from that of R_{cij} using R_{cg}.

Lemma II R_{cg} rotates the rotation axis of R_{cij} into that of R_{gij}, or

$$P_{gij} = R_{cg}P_{cij} \qquad (17)$$

Significance: Since, from "The Observables or the Measurables" on page 3, P_{cij} and P_{gij} can be readily available from the observables H_{cij} and H_{gij}, (17) establishes constraints on R_{cg} in order to solve for it. Lemma II also says that if we regard all P_{cij} and P_{gij} as two clusters of vectors or points, then R_{cg} transforms one cluster into another.

Lemma III The rotation axis of R_{cg} is perpendicular to the vector joining the ends of the rotation axes for R_{cij} and R_{gij}, or

$$P_{cg} \perp (P_{gij} - P_{cij}) \qquad (18)$$

Significance: This implies that for a given pair of distinct P_{gij} and P_{gij}, P_{cg} is confined to be in the bisecting plane of P_{cij} and P_{gij}. With two such pairs, the direction of P_{cg} can be determined. In fact, (18) implies that P_{cg} can be determined up to a scale factor s from

$$P_{cg} = s(P_{gi_1j_1} - P_{ci_1j_1}) \times (P_{gi_2j_2} - P_{ci_2j_2}) \qquad (19)$$

However, we will not use Lemma III in this manner. Instead, Lemma III is used to build up procedure for computing R_{cg} via Lemma IV,V and VI. The reason is that (19) is more error sensitive and has unnecessary degeneracies due to the fact that angle is not considered jointly.

Lemma IV $P_{gij} - P_{cij}$ is colinear with $(P_{gij} + P_{cij}) \times P_{cg}$

Significance This says that $P_{gij} - P_{cij} = s(P_{gij} + P_{cij}) \times P_{cg}$ for some scale factor s. Lemma V forces s to be 1. This lemma makes use of Lemma III, but the formula it generates is more accurate and robust than (18) (coming out of Lemma III) so far as computing P_{cg} is concerned, as to be seen.

Lemma V $P_{gij} - P_{cij}$ and $(P_{gij} + P_{cij}) \times P_{cg}'$ has the same length, where P_{cg}' was defined in (11.4).

Significance Given Lemma IV and V, Lemma VI is readily derived, which easily leads to the computational procedure for P_{cg} in (12).

Lemma VI

$$(P_{gij} + P_{cij}) \times P_{cg}' = P_{cij} - P_{gij} \qquad (20)$$

Significance Although (18) provides a constraint on the direction of P_{cg} for any pair of stations ij, (20) provides a stronger constraint since it constrians $\theta_{R_{cg}}$ as well as P_{cg}.

Lemma VII $Skew(P_{gij} + P_{cij})$ is singular and has rank 2.

Significance $Skew(P_{gij} + P_{cij})$ is the coefficient matrix for the systems of linear equation in (12) used to solve for P_{cg}'. Therefore Lemma VII implies that it is impossible to compute R_{cg} with only two stations.

Lemma VIII

$$(R_{gij} - I)T_{cg} = R_{cg}T_{cij} - T_{gij} \qquad (21)$$

Significance Lemma VIII establishes the equation in (15) used to solve for T_{cg}.

Lemma IX $R_{gij} - I$ is singular and has rank 2.

Significance $R_{gij} - I$ is the coefficient matrix for the systems of linear equation in (15) used to solve for T_{cg}. Therefore Lemma IX implies that it is impossible to compute T_{cg} with only two stations.

Lemma X If $\theta_{R_{cg}} \neq \pi/2$, or equivalently, $|P_{cg}| \neq \pm 2$, then

$$\begin{bmatrix} Skew(P_{gi_1j_1} + P_{ci_1j_1}) \\ Skew(P_{gi_2j_2} + P_{ci_2j_2}) \end{bmatrix} \qquad (22)$$

has full column rank if and only if $P_{gi_1j_1}$ and $P_{gi_2j_2}$ have different directions (or equivalently, $P_{ci_1j_1}$ and $P_{ci_2j_2}$ have different directions).

Significance (22) is just the compound matrix of two $Skew(P_{gij} + P_{cij})$ in Lemma VII, and therefore is the coefficient matrix for solving R_{cg} given two pairs of P_{gij} and P_{cij}. Thus Lemma X ensures that given a minimum of three stations, the solution for R_{cg} is unique.

Lemma XI

$$\begin{bmatrix} R_{g i_1 j_1} - I \\ R_{g i_2 j_2} - I \end{bmatrix} \tag{23}$$

has full column rank if and only if $P_{g i_1 j_1}$ and $P_{g i_2 j_2}$ have different directions (or equivalently, $P_{c i_1 j_1}$ and $P_{c i_2 j_2}$ have different directions).

Significance   (23) is just the compound matrix of two $R_{g i j} - I$ in Lemma IX, and therefore is the coefficient matrix for solving T_{cg} given two pairs of $P_{g i j}$ and $P_{c i j}$. Thus Lemma XI ensures that given a minimum of three stations, the solution for T_{cg} is unique.

Proof of the Computational Procedure for R_{cg} in (12),(13) and (14)

(12) follows from Lemma VI by considering the fact that for any two 3×1 vectors a and b,

$$a \times b = Skew(a) \cdot b \tag{24}$$

where a and b on the left denotes vectors while a and b on the right are 3×1 column matrices. (13) and (14) simply follow from the definitions of P_{cg}' in (11.4).

Proof of the Computational Procedure for T_{cg} in (15)

This follows simply from Lemma VIII.

Minimum number of Stations: Three

This follows from Lemma VII, IX, X and XI. Equivalently, the minimum number of pairs of stations needed is two.

Conditions of Uniqueness

For a minimum of three stations (or two pairs of stations), the necessary and sufficient conditions for a unique solution for R_{cg} and T_{cg} is that the inter-station rotation axes are not colinear for different pairs of stations.

Proof: This follows from Lemma VIII and X. Note that when the sum of rotation axes ($P_{g i j} + P_{c i j}$) are colinear while $P_{g i j}$ is different for different inter-station rotations, then the solution is still unique except that (12) cannot be used. In this case, $angle(R_{cg})$ is simply $180°$ and rotation axis is the same as $P_{c i j} + P_{g i j}$.

Accuracy Issues

In the following, error analysis will first be given. Then, as a result of error analysis, critical factors dominating the error, and steps for improving accuracy will be described.

Error Analysis

The purposes of error analysis are:

a.   It reveals what are the critical factors influencing the accuracy.

b.   It gives rise to various means for improving accuracies.

c.   It is essential for accuracy prediction, which is important to model-driven 3D vision planning.

d.   It helps determining whether one has properly implemented the algorithm. If the error is much larger than what the error formula predicts, something in the setup, programs or system are not in the right order.

In this section, we first give a list of definitions, followed by a list of lemma used for deriving the final error formula for R_{cg} and T_{cg}. Then the error formula for R_{cij}, T_{cij} and R_{gij}, T_{gij} due to error of R_{ci}, T_{ci} and R_{gi}, T_{gi} will be given, followed by the error formula of R_{cg} and T_{cg} will be given. Critical factors affecting the accuracy will be discussed in the next section, and test results thereafter.

Definitions

RMS: root mean square (or average of the sum of squares)

$\sigma(V)$:   RMS of the magnitude of error corrupting a 3D vector V
  $\sigma(V)$ and σ_V are equivalent.

$\sigma(R)$:   RMS of the magnitude of error of P_R (rotation axis scaled by the rotation angle, see(6.1),(11.1)-(11.3)). $\sigma(R)$ and σ_R are equivalent.

$Err(V)$:   maximum magnitude of error corrupting a 3D vector V.

$Err(R)$:   maximum magnitude of error for P_R.

List of Lemmas Leading to the Final Error Formula

Lemma I:

$$P_{\Delta R \cdot R} = P_{\Delta R} + P_R$$

where ΔR is a small perturbation rotation matrix.

Note: Lemma I says that for small error perturbation of rotation, the rotation axis are additive.

Lemma II

$$\sigma(R_1 R_2) = \sqrt{(\sigma_{R1}^2 + \sigma_{R2}^2)}$$

Lemma III

$$Err(R_1 R_2) = Err(R_1) + Err(R_2)$$

Lemma IV

$$\sigma(\Sigma V_i) = \sqrt{\sum_i \sigma_{V i}^2}$$

where V_i' are a number of 3D vectors with RMSE $\sigma_{V i}$

Lemma V

$$\sigma(R \cdot V) = \sqrt{(\frac{2}{3} \sigma_R |V|)^2 + \sigma_v^2}$$

where R is a rotation matrix with RMSE σ_R
   V is a 3D vector with RMSE σ_V

Lemma VI

$$Err(\Sigma V_i) = \sum_i Err(V_i)$$

Lemma VII

$$Err(RV) = Err(R)|V| + Err(V)$$

The proof for the above Lemma will be published in a later paper. The following formulas can be easily derived from the above lemma and the relationships between R_{cij} and R_{ci}, R_{cj} and between T_{cij} and R_{ci}, T_{ci} using (12).

Error of R_{cij} due to Error of R_{ci} and R_{cj}

$$\sigma_{Rcij} = \sqrt{\sigma_{Rci}^2 + \sigma_{Rcj}^2} \tag{25a}$$

$$Err(R_{cij}) = Err(R_{ci}) + Err(R_{cj}) \tag{25b}$$

Similar formula hold for R_g.

Error of T_{cij} due to Error of R_{ci} and T_{ci}

$$\sigma_{Tcij} = \sqrt{\frac{2}{3}(\sigma_{Rci}^2 + \sigma_{Rcj}^2)|T_{ci}|^2 + \sigma_{Tci}^2 + \sigma_{Tcj}^2} \tag{26a}$$

$$= \sqrt{\frac{4}{3} \sigma_{Rc}^2 |T_{c_1}|^2 + 2\sigma_{Tc}^2} \tag{26b}$$

(27b) is a simpler version of (27a) with σ_{Rci} and σ_{Rcj} replaced by σ_{Rc} ., etc.

$$Err(T_{cij}) = [Err(R_{ci}) + Err(R_{cj})]|T_{ci}| + Err(T_{ci}) + Err(T_{cj}) \tag{26c}$$

Error of T_{gij} due to Error of R_{gi} and T_{gi}

$$\sigma_{Tgij} = \sqrt{\frac{2}{3} \sigma_{Rgj}^2 |T_{gi} - T_{gj}|^2 + \sigma_{Tg1}^2 + \sigma_{Tg2}^2} \tag{27a}$$

$$= \sqrt{\frac{2}{3} \sigma_{Rg}^2 |T_{g1} - T_{g2}|^2 + 2\sigma_{Tg}^2} \tag{27b}$$

$$Err(T_{gij}) = Err(R_{g2}) \, | \, T_{g1} - T_{g2} | \; + Err(T_{g1}) + Err(T_{g2}) \qquad (27c)$$

Error of R_{cg}

Three-Station Case

$$\sigma_{R_{cg}} = \frac{1}{\sin[\angle(P_{g12}, P_{g23})]} \sqrt{\frac{2}{3}(\sigma_{Rg12}^2 + \sigma_{Rc12}^2)\left[\frac{1}{(\theta_{R_{g12}})^2} + \frac{1}{(\theta_{R_{g23}})^2}\right]} \qquad (28a)$$

$$Err(R_{cg}) = \frac{1}{\sin[\angle(P_{g12}, P_{g23})]}$$
$$\sqrt{(Err(R_{g12}) + Err(R_{c12})\left(\frac{1}{|\theta_{R_{g12}}|} + \frac{1}{|\theta_{R_{g23}}|}\right)} \qquad (28b)$$

where $\angle(P_{g12}, P_{g23})$ means the angle between P_{g12} and P_{g23}
$$\theta_{Rg12} = |P_{g12}| = angle(R_{g12})$$

Note that $\theta_{Rg_{ij}} = \theta_{Rc_{ij}}$ for all ij .

Since it is always easy to have θ_{Rg12} close to θ_{Rg23} (see the arrangement in "Simulation and Real Experiment Results" on page 8), (28a) reduces to

$$\sigma_{R_{cg}} = \sqrt{\frac{4}{3}(\sigma_{Rg12}^2 + \sigma_{Rc12}^2)} \; \frac{1}{\sin[\angle(P_{g12}, P_{g23})]\,|\theta_{R_{g12}}|} \qquad (28c)$$

$$Err(R_{cg}) = \frac{2}{\sin[\angle(P_{g12}, P_{g23})]} \; \frac{Err(R_{g12}) + Err(R_{c12})}{|\theta_{R_{g12}}|} \qquad (28d)$$

Redundant Stations

$$\sigma_{R_{cg}} = \sqrt{(\sigma_{Rg12}^2 + \sigma_{Rc12}^2)\left(\frac{1}{\lambda_1^2 + \lambda_2^2} + \frac{1}{\lambda_2^2 + \lambda_3^2} + \frac{1}{\lambda_3^2 + \lambda_1^2}\right)} \qquad (29)$$

where λ_is are the singular values of a matrix with the rows being the inter-station rotation eigenvectors (using definition in (9)) for the camera. A few facts worth noting (details and proofs to be published). First is that as the inter-station rotation angle increases, λ_i increases linearly, making $\sigma_{R_{cg}}$ inversely proportional to the inter-station rotation angle. The second and most important is that as the number of inter-station rotations N increases, λ_i increases by the square root of N, making $\sigma_{R_{cg}}$ inversely proportional to $\sqrt{N}$. Similarly,

$$Err(R_{cg}) = (Err(R_{g12}) + Err(R_{c12})\sqrt{\frac{1}{\lambda_1^2 + \lambda_2^2} + \frac{1}{\lambda_2^2 + \lambda_3^2} + \frac{1}{\lambda_3^2 + \lambda_1^2}} \qquad (30)$$

Error of T_{cg}

Three-Station Case

$$\sigma_{T_{cg}} \leq \frac{1}{\sqrt{2\left(\sin^2\dfrac{\theta_{R_{g12}}}{2} + \sin^2\dfrac{\theta_{R_{g23}}}{2}\right)}}$$

$$\left[\frac{16}{9} \frac{\sigma_{Rg12}^2 + \sigma_{Rc12}^2}{\sin^2[\angle(P_{g12}, P_{g23})]} \, |T_{c1}|^2 \, \frac{(\theta_{R_{c12}}^2 + \theta_{R_{c23}}^2)^2}{\theta_{R_{c12}}^2 \theta_{R_{c23}}^2}\right.$$

$$+ \; cond(A)\left(\frac{8}{3}\sigma_{Rc}^2 \, |T_{c1}|^2 \; + 4\sigma_{Tc}^2 + \frac{2}{3}\sigma_{Rg}^2(\,|T_{g1} - T_{g2}|^2\right.$$

$$+ \; |T_{g2} - T_{g3}|^2) + 4\sigma_{Tg}^2 \left.\right]^{1/2} \qquad (31)$$

where $A = \begin{bmatrix} R_{g12} & -I \\ R_{g23} & -I \end{bmatrix}$ and is the coefficient matrix for solving T_{cg} in (15)

$cond(A)$ is the condition number of A and is defined as
$$cond(A) = ||A|| \cdot ||A^{-1}||$$

To simply the formula, we can regard $\theta_{R_{cij}}$ as being close in magnitude, and $|T_{gi} - T_{gj}|$ as being close in magnitude, making (31) somewhat simpler:

$$\sigma_{T_{cg}} \leq \frac{1}{2\sin\dfrac{\theta_{R_{g12}}}{2}}\left[\frac{16}{9}\frac{\sigma_{Rg12}^2 + \sigma_{Rc12}^2}{\sin^2[\angle(P_{g12}, P_{g23})]}\,|T_{c1}|^2\right.$$

$$+ \; cond(A)\left(\frac{8}{3}\sigma_{Rc}^2\,|T_{c1}|^2 + 4\sigma_{Tc}^2 + \frac{4}{3}\sigma_{Rg}^2\,|T_{g1} - T_{g2}|^2 + 4\sigma_{Tg}^2\right) \left.\right]^{1/2} (32)$$

Similarly,

$$Err(T_{cg}) \leq \frac{1}{\sqrt{2\left(\sin^2\dfrac{\theta_{R_{g12}}}{2} + \sin^2\dfrac{\theta_{R_{g23}}}{2}\right)}}$$

$$\left\{\frac{4}{\sin[\angle(P_{g12}, P_{g23})]}\,(Err(R_{g12}) + Err(R_{c12})\,|T_{ci}|\right.$$

$$+ \; cond(A)\left[4Err(R_c) + 2Err(R_{g2})\,|T_{g1} - T_{g2}| + 4Err(T_g)\right]\left.\right\}^{1/2} \qquad (33)$$

The effect of number of stations on the error is the same as that for R_{cg} . This is verified by the test results in "Simulation and Real Experiment Results" on page 8.

Critical Factors Affecting the Accuracy and Steps in Improving Accuracy

By observing the accuracy formulas for R_{cg} and T_{cg} in "Error Analysis" on page 6, the following observations can be made:

Observation I: *The RMS error of rotation from gripper to camera $\sigma_{R_{cg}}$ is inversely proportional to the sine of the angle between the inter-station rotation axes.*

By observing (28a), it is seen that $\sigma_{R_{cg}}$ is inversely proportional to $\sin(\angle(P_{g12}, P_{g23}))$ (which is equal to $\sin(\angle(P_{c12}, P_{c23}))$). This is reasonable since, from Lemma II in "Derivations of Computational Procedures and Conditions of Uniqueness using Eleven Lemmas" on page 5, R_{cg} rotates P_{cij} into P_{gij} . With a minimum of two pairs of ij's, (17) is used to solve for R_{cg}. When $\angle(P_{g12}, P_{g23})$ becomes smaller, P_{g12} becomes closer to P_{g23} , making (17) for each ij more similar to each other, thus causing the equation to be closer to singularity. Alternatively, one can see that the coefficient matrix for solving P_{cg}' (see Lemma VII in "Derivations of Computational Procedures and Conditions of Uniqueness using Eleven Lemmas" on page 5) becomes singular as $P_{g_{i_1 j_1}}$ approaches $P_{g_{i_2 j_2}}$ and $P_{c_{i_1 j_1}}$ approaches $P_{c_{i_2 j_2}}$. In fact, it can be shown that the row vectors of the coefficient matrix in Lemma X lies in two planes, with $P_{g_{i_1 j_1}} + P_{c_{i_1 j_1}}$ and $P_{g_{i_2 j_2}} + P_{c_{i_2 j_2}}$ being the normal vectors of the two planes. Thus the greater the difference is between $P_{c_{i_1 j_1}}$ and $P_{c_{i_2 j_2}}$, the closer the two planes are to being orthogonal, making the coefficient matrix more linearly independent.

Observation 2: *The rotation and translation error are both inversely proportional to the inter-station rotation angle. That is, $\sigma_{R_{cg}} \propto^{-1} \theta_{R_{gij}}$ and $\sigma_{T_{cg}} \propto^{-1} \theta_{R_{gij}}$*

This can be seen from (28c), (28d) and (31). This is reasonable since R_{cg} is determined solely from P_{cij} and P_{gij}, and the greater $\theta_{R_{cij}}$ and $\theta_{R_{gij}}$ are, the smaller the effect of a small perturbation (with given size σ_{Rc12}, σ_{Rg12}) is on the result.

Observation 3: *The distance between the camera lens center and the calibration block has a dominant effect on the translation error.*

This comes from (31)-(33). In fact, any of the terms in (31) or (32) involving $|T_{ci}|$ or $|T_{g1} - T_{g2}|$ generates much more error than all other terms in most of the practical setup. For example, if $|T_{c1}|$ is 5 inches and the error of inter-station rotations is 3 milliradians (these are practical figures that one would encounter), then any term in (31) or (32) involving $\sigma_{Rc}|T_{c1}|$ would generate 15 mil error, which is much bigger than those other terms involving σ_{Tc}, which is the error of translation as a result of extrinsic camera calibration. The term involving σ_{T_g} however has the potential of being very big, since this depends on the positional accuracy of the robot, which can be bad.

Observation 4: *The distance between the robot gripper coordinate centers at different stations is also is a critical factor in forming the error of translation. But the distances between different camera stations are not important.*

This again comes from (31)-(33). The situation is similar to that described in Observation 3. Notice that $|T_{g1} - T_{g2}|$ is not the distance between gripper tips at different stations. It is the amount of movement of the *robot gripper coordinate center.*

Observation 5: *The error of rotation is linearly proportional to the error of orientation of each station relative to the base. The error of translation is approximately linearly proportional to this error of orientation unless the error of robot translational positioning accuracy is big.*

This comes from (28c), (28d), (31), (32) and (33).

It is convenient to define two types of critical factors. One is first degree, and the other second degree. The first degree factor is more dominant in most cases, but sometimes, some second degree factor ($\sigma_{T_{gi}}$) can be so bad such that it becomes dominant.

First Degree Critical Factors:

1. Angle between different inter-station rotation axes (e.g., $\angle(P_{g12}, P_{g23})$)

    Note: $\angle(P_{g12}, P_{g23}) = \angle(P_{c12}, P_{c23})$

2. Rotation angle of inter-station rotation $\theta_{R_{gi}}(= \theta_{R_{ci}})$

3. Distance between camera lens center and calibration block $|T_{ci}|$, and distance between robot arm coordinate centers at different stations $|T_{g1} - T_{g2}|$

4. Error of rotation of each station relative to base $\sigma_{Rgi}, \sigma_{Rci}$, or error of inter-station rotation $\sigma_{Rgij}, \sigma_{Rcij}$

Second Degree Critical Factors:

1. Error of translation of each station relative to base $\sigma_{Tci}, \sigma_{Tgi}$

Steps to Improve Accuracy

1. Adopt the setup to be described in "Simulation and Real Experiment Results" in order to achieve maximum angles between different inter-station rotation axes, no matter how many stations are used.

2. Maximize the rotation angle for inter-station rotations. This again can be done using the setup mentioned earlier.

3. Minimize the distance between camera lens center and calibration block. This requires a small calibration block and suitable optics for short range viewing.

4. Minimize the distance between robot arm coordinate centers at different stations. This requires some planning and is robot dependent.

5. Use redundant stations. The setup described in "Simulation and Real Experiment Results" is ideal for using as many stations as you wish. Since the extrinsic calibration plus feature extraction can be done within 90 msec when 36 points are used, using more frames poses no problem. The error due to non-systematic sources will be reduced by a factor of $\sqrt{N}$ where N is the number of stations. (See results in "Simulation and Real Experiment Results")

6. Use camera calibration algorithm setup that yields high accuracy to improve error on translation and rotation of each individual station.

7. Try to precalibrate the robot itself so that the position and orientation of each station is known more accurately. If this is difficult, then at least try to make inter-station translation and rotation more accurate, if possible. That is, the robot system may not be able to tell the user the absolute location and orientation of its gripper coordinate frame, it may be able to better tell the amount of relative movement from station to station.

Simulation and Real Experiment Results

Simulation Experiments

The Station Generation Process

It is important to use a process for simulating the position and orientation of gripper and camera stations that is realistic and easy for controlling the critical parameters in "Critical Factors Affecting the Accuracy and Steps in Improving Accuracy" on page 7 in order to see their effect on the final accuracy. It should allow all critical parameters to be in optimum conditions simultaneously. It also serves as a means of planning robot motion in order to generate stations in the real experiments. Figure 5 on page 4 illustrates the results of using our process for generating a five-station configuration. The bright coordinate frames are the camera coordinate frames C_i while the darker frames are for the robot gripper coordinate frames G_i. The bars in Figure 5 on page 4 indicates the selections of inter-station pairs. The station generation process is described as follows: first, set up a calibration block world coordinate frame CW and a robot world coordinate frame RW as in Figure 5 on page 4. Next, directly above CW, place a pair of coordinate frames C_0 and G_0 for camera and gripper that maintains a distance of $|T_c|$ from CW (notice that $|T_c|$ is one among the critical factors in "Critical Factors Affecting the Accuracy and Steps in Improving Accuracy" on page 7) with the z axis of C_0 pointing right at CW. C_0 and G_0 are actually not used for computing the results R_{cg} and T_{cg}, but rather for generating other stations. Next, select a number N to be the total number of stations to be generated. Then, generate N stations for camera and gripper by rotating C_0 and G_0 around N axes uniformly distributed with 360/N degrees apart, centered at CW and parallel to the xy plane of CW. The inter-station pairs are chosen using a star-drawing technique (see Figure 5 on page 4). This gives a systematic way of generating an arbitrary number of stations while at the same time allowing one to easily vary the critical parameters for testing error sensitivity.

The Control of Critical Parameters as Simulation Input Parameters

All of the critical parameters (first and second degrees) listed in "Critical Factors Affecting the Accuracy and Steps in Improving Accuracy" on page 7 can be simulated with easy control. The control of each critical parameter is listed in the following:

Inter-station rotation angle: This is controlled by varying the rotation angle used in rotating C_0 and G_0 to each individual station.

Angle between different inter-station rotation axes: This is controlled actually by varying the number of stations generated. For each case, choose only the first three traversed by doing star drawing. Obviously, the larger the number of overall stations is, the narrower the angle between successive inter-station rotation axes are.

Distance between camera and calibration block: This is controlled by varying the distance $|T_c|$ in the above generation procedure on placing C_0 and G_0

Number of Stations: This is the parameter in the process that is totally arbitrary, except that if it is even, the star drawing is not as straightforward. We always use odd number of stations.

Rotation and Translation error for each station ($\sigma_{Rci}, \sigma_{Tci}, \sigma_{Rgi}$ and σ_{Tgi}) This is extrinsic calibration error, and can be simulated by perturbing the ideal homogeneous transformation matrices for each station. From our simulation tests, they agree quite well with Lemma 5 in "Critical Factors Affecting the Accuracy and Steps in Improving Accuracy" on page 7.

Fixed Setup Parameters

In order to simulate the actual physical setup, all the setup parameters are selected to be almost the same as those used in the real experiments to be described, except that due to the x axis problem with our robot (to be described later), the station generation process used in the real experiment is modified. In the following, the setup parameters are set as follows:

$$|T_c| = 6.65\ inch \qquad |T_{cg}| = 9.5\ inch$$
$$N = 3 \qquad \sigma_{Tci} = 3\ mil$$
$$\sigma_{Tgi} = 5\ mil \qquad \sigma_{Rci} = \sigma_{Rgi} = 1.5\ milliradian$$
$$\angle(P_{g12}, P_{g23}) = \pi/3$$

In the following, we show the simulation results of four critical parameters on the error of rotation R_{cg} and translation T_{cg}. These four critical parameters are tested separately. For the testing of each parameter, all the other setup and critical parameters are set as above, while the very parameter under test will be allowed to vary over a given range. 1000 tests are done for each case, and statistics are gathered. The results are shown in figures.

Simulation Results

Effect of the Size of Inter-Station Rotation Angle on Accuracy

"Critical Factors Affecting the Accuracy and Steps in Improving Accuracy" on page 7 described the relationships between the size of inter-station rotation angle and the R_{cg} as well as T_{cg} accuracy, and gave procedures for improving the accuracy. Extensive simulation have been done and the results are consolidated into Figure 6. and Figure 7 (one for rotation error and the other translation). The curve is linear up to statistical sampling tolerance. It agrees quite well with Observation 2 in "Critical Factors Affecting the Accuracy and Steps in Improving Accuracy" on page 7, and it confirms the recommendation made in "Steps to Improve Accuracy" on page 8.

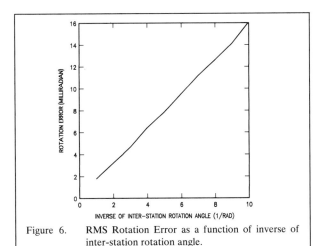

Figure 6.   RMS Rotation Error as a function of inverse of inter-station rotation angle.

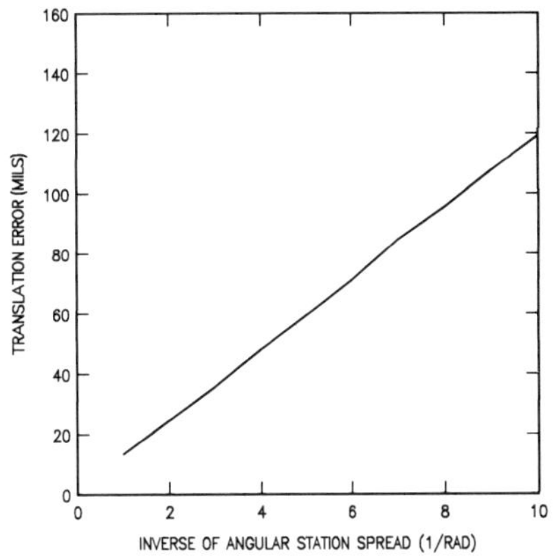

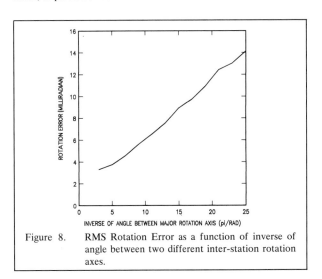

Figure 7.   RMS Translation Error as a function of inverse of inter-station rotation angle.

Effect of Angle between Inter-Station Rotation Axes on Accuracy

The situation is similar to that above except that $\angle(P_{g12}, P_{Pg23})$ is allowed to vary while θ_{Rg12} and θ_{Rg23} are fixed. The Figure 8 shows the average error of rotation as a function of $\angle(P_{g12}, P_{Pg23})$. It is again linear, as predicted in Lemma 1.

Figure 8.   RMS Rotation Error as a function of inverse of angle between two different inter-station rotation axes.

Effect of Camera-to-Calibration-Plate Distance on Accuracy

According to Lemma 3, the translation error has a dominant effect on $\sigma_{T_{cg}}$ unless σ_{Tci} or σ_{Tgi} are enormous. Figure 9 reflects this quite well. The RMS error of T_{cg} is plotted against this parameter. The curve is generally linear, but the around the origin, it bends somewhat, due to the fact that when $|T_c|$ is small, its effect is no longer dominant and the effect of σ_{Tgi} shows up.

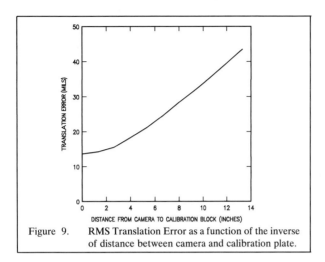

Figure 9.   RMS Translation Error as a function of the inverse of distance between camera and calibration plate.

Effect of Number of Inter-Station Pairs on Accuracy

Figure 10 and Figure 11 shows the error of translation and rotation as a function of the inverse of square root of the number of inter-station pairs. The solid line shows the RMS error, while the dashed line is the maximum error out of one thousand tests. As expected, the RMS error increases linearly as the inverse of $\sqrt{N}$. Since the proposed technique is quite efficient, and the station pose planning and robot motion are automatic, increasing the number of station is quite feasible, and pays off well.

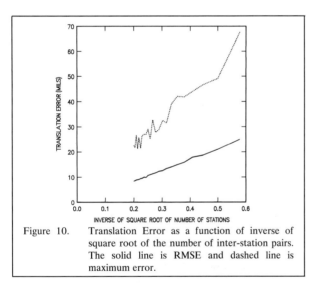

Figure 10.   Translation Error as a function of inverse of square root of the number of inter-station pairs. The solid line is RMSE and dashed line is maximum error.

Real Experiments

Setup Description

Figure 2 on page 2 shows the physical setup we used. A Javelin CCD 480 × 388 camera is fastened to the last joint of an IBM Clean Room Robot (CRR). The CRR has two manipulators, each with seven degrees of freedom (including gripper opening). We only use one of the manipulators. The CRR is an electric box frame Cartesian robot. There are three linear joints (x, y, z) and three rotary joints (roll, pitch and yaw) for each manipulator. The work volume is about 6 feet by 4 feet by 2 feet and the repeatability for linear joint is about 4 mil, and that for the rotary joints 1 milliradian. The accuracy is calibrated to a limited extent. The scale and offset for each rotary joint is calibrated to 3 milliradian accuracy. The rotation axes for the three ro-

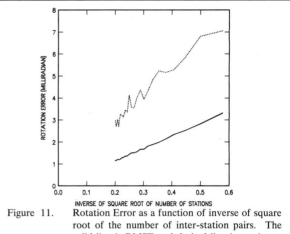

Figure 11.   Rotation Error as a function of inverse of square root of the number of inter-station pairs. The solid line is RMSE and dashed line is maximum error.

tary joints are supposed to be intersecting at the same point (origin of RW coordinate frame), but we did not calibrate that. The x axis has some problems: For our robot, the z beam sags, causing the movement in x axis to be like a pendulum. This effect is not fully calibrated yet, but we suspect that it generates about 20 mils translation and 15 millirad rotation within a work range of 15 inches. Due to this problem, we are forced to modify the station generation procedure used in the simulation in order to avoid using x axis. Either with or without moving x axis, the station placement and manipulator motion planning is automatic, and the number of stations can be arbitrary without manual intervention.

The calibration block is a clear glass plate with the center 1 inch by 1 inch area filled with 36 black disks printed on it using step-and-repeat photographic emulsion (See Figure 12 on page 11). The disks are 5000 microns apart with 2000 micron radius (accurate to 1 micron). The calibration is back lighted and sits in the middle of the work space.

Accuracy Assessment

The accuracy of our hand/eye calibration results is assessed by how accurately we can predict the placement of camera in 3D world with any arbitrary manipulator movement. As was indicated in "Why is Hand/Eye Calibration Important?" on page 1, one of the main reasons why robot hand/eye calibration is important is that robot needs to know not only where the gripper is, but also where the camera is in the work space, so that the measurement taken by vision can be related to the robot. Being able to determine where the camera is in the work space for an arbitrary manipulator movement is thus the primary goal. This is tested in the following steps:

Step 1: Move the manipulator to 2N different positions where N is greater than 2. For each station i, compute camera to calibration block homogenous transformation H_{ci} using extrinsic calibration. This takes about 90 msec per station. The robot gripper position and orientation relative to robot world, which is H_{gi}, is also recorded.

Step 2: Compute H_{cg} using procedures in "Computational Procedures and Conditions for Uniqueness" on page 4, using data from station 1 through N.

Step 3: For each station k (k from 1 to N), compute homogenous matrix H_{RC} (homogenous transformation from robot world frame RW to calibration block world frame CW) by:

$$H_{RC} = H_{gi}^{-1} H_{cg}^{-1} H_{ci}^{-1}$$

Make an average of H_{RC} computed from these N stations.

Figure 12.   Calibration block is a clear glass plate with 36 disks printed on it using photographic emulsion. The accuracy is 1 micron.

Step 4: Let stations N+1 through 2N be called verification stations. For each of the verification station, predict the position and orientation of the camera relative to robot world base coordinate RW by $H_{cg}^{-1} H_{gk}^{-1}$ where k is the station index, and H_{gk} is computed from robot joint coordinates (see "What Are the Observables and What is to be computed?" on page 3). Compare this predicted position and orientation with $H_{ck}^{-1} H_{RC}$, where H_{ck} is computed in step 1 while H_{RC} is computed in step3.

The results of a series of experiments yield the following table:

	New Camera Pose Prediction Error	
N	Rotation error	Translation error
4	4.568 mrad	23.238 mil
6	3.304 mrad	19.078mil
8	3.264 mrad	26.712 mil
10	2.888 mrad	14.642 mil
12	2.782 mrad	12.516 mil

Since there is no absolute H_{cg} ground truth to compare with, the accuracy has to be assessed as the error of new camera pose prediction, as described earlier. The effect of N is indeed very significant. We have a program that automatically plans the movement of manipulator for an arbitrary number of stations, and since the algorithm proposed in this paper is quite efficient, increasing the number of frames is quite easy. Also observe that the error of predicted camera pose includes both the error of the calibrated hand/eye relationship and the robot's positioning error. Notice from the table that for 10 stations, the translation error is about 14 mil. But the robot's positioning accuracy is worse than 10 mil. This means that the eye-to-hand relationship is calibrated to better than 10 mil. Using the error formula in (32) scaled by $\sqrt{10/3}$, the error of T_{cg} is predicted to be 10.66 mil, agreeing well with the real experiment data. The rotation error is about 2.88 millirad. Notice that the error of rotary joint is about 2.5 millirad. Therefore, the actual error of R_{cg} should also be of this order of magnitude. This agrees very well with the prediction by (28), which gives 2.557 millirad. Notice that the error in the table is not

strictly monotonic with respect to the inverse of the square root of number of stations. This is due to the fact that the simulation curves presented earlier were averaged over 1000 tests, while here, for each N, there is only one test. Also, since the robot error itself gets into it, it is more unpredictable, while the simulation curves only shows the H_{cg} error. Nevertheless, the error generally decreases nicely as the number of stations increases.

Conclusion

This paper introduced a high speed, high accuracy, versatile, simple and fully autonomous technique for 3D robotics hand/eye calibration. It is high speed since it takes only about 100+64N arithmetic operations to compute the hand/eye relationship after the robot finishes the movement, and incurs only an additional 64 arithmetic scalar operations for each additional station. This makes the current algorithm the fastest one compared with the state of the art. The speed performance is especially attractive to those applications where the hand/eye configuration needs be changed frequently. For example, the robot may pick up the camera to perform some task, and then put it right back to a holder. Since the grasping cannot be precise, hand/eye calibration must be performed frequently. It is also important to those tasks where and hand/eye relationships need be changed frequently due to different task requirements. As for the accuracy, no other reported hand/eye calibration technique does any better. The results in our real experiments could be further improved if we change the optics and the size of calibration block, as well as the mounting position, so that all of the critical factors described in the accuracy analysis section are taken into considerations.

References

1.   Bowman M. & Forrest A.,1987, Robot Model Optimization, submitted for publication.

2.   Izaguirre A., Summers J., Pu P., 1987, A New Development in Camera Calibration, Calibrating a Pair of Mobil TV Cameras, to appear in *International Journal of Robotics Research.*

3.   Jenkins J. L., and Jurner J. D., 1986, *Optimal Spacecraft Rotational Manervers,* Elsevier.

4.   Lenz, R. and Tsai, R., 1987, Techniques for Calibration of the Scale Factor and Image Center for High Accuracy 3D Machine Vision Metrology, *Proceedings of IEEE International Conference on Robotic and Automation,* Raleigh, NC.

5.   Puskorius, G. and Feldkamp, L, 1987, Calibration of Robot Vision, *Proceedings of IEEE International Conference on Robotic and Automation,* Raleigh, NC.

6.   Rogers, D. F. and Adams J. A., 1976, *Mathematical Elements for Computer Graphics,* New York, McGraw-Hill.

7.   Shiu Y. and Ahmad S, 1987, *Proceedings of IEEE International Conference on Robotic and Automation,* Raleigh, NC.

8.   Tsai, R., 1987, A Versatile Camera Calibration Technique for High Accuracy 3D Machine Vision Metrology using Off-the-Shelf TV Cameras and Lenses, to appear in IEEE Journal of Robotics and Automation, also best paper award for 1986 IEEE International Conference on Computer Visionand Pattern Recognition, Miami, Florida.

9.   Tsai, R., and Lenz, R., 1987, Review of the Two-Stage Camera Calibration Technique plus some New Implementation Tips and New Techniques for Center and Scale Calibration, *Second Topical Meeting on Machine Vision,* Optical Society of America, Lake Tahoe.

10.   Tsai, R.Y. and Lavin, M., 1984, Three-Dimensional Mechanical Part Measurement using a Vision/Robot System, *IBM Research Report RC 10506,* May 8.

Model-Based Motion Analysis—Motion From Motion*

D.W. Thompson and J.L. Mundy

Artificial Intelligence Branch
GE Corporate
Research and Development Center

The use of a geometric model in motion tracking is investigated. In particular, a simple collection of image features, called the vertex-pair is used to derive the affine transformation between a three-dimensional polyhedral object model and its projection into the image viewplane. The transformation is determined over a time sequence of images and a linear prediction model is used to determine an estimate for the transformation in subsequent frames. This predicted transform is used to constrain the search in transform space for a consistent set of model-to-scene assignments.

INTRODUCTION

There has been considerable interest in deriving the position, orientation, and shape of object surfaces from image sequences [Waxman et al., 1987]. The motion of boundaries within the image viewplane are interpreted as three-dimensional translation and rotation of object surfaces. It is possible under some circumstances to even recover primitive surface descriptions such as surface orientation and curvature. These processes have become known as determining *structure from motion*.

In structure from motion, little is assumed about the objects in the scene and the information in the time sequence is used to determine a description of the three-dimensional world. The work to be described here pursues a model-based approach instead. The view is that the interpretation of image segmentation features such as edges and regions cannot be carried out without some a priori model to guide this interpretation. The current segmentation procedures are quite error-prone in directly revealing the underlying geometry of object surfaces since the relationship between geometry and image intensity is quite complex. For example, the proper treatment of shadows requires consideration of illumination source direction and the intensity distribution of the source; these considerations are not factored into current segmentation algorithms. In this paper, motion is considered from the standpoint of model-based object recognition which is a subject of current widespread research interest [Ayache and Faugeras, 1986], [Lowe, 1985], [Grimson and Lozono-Perez, 1985], [Porrill et al. 1987], [Thompson and Mundy, 1987].

There has been prior interest in the model-directed motion analysis concept [Gennery, 1982] [Dickmanns and Wunsche, 1986]. Gennery used a Kalman filter to update the three-dimensional rotation and translation

of an object. Edge segment locations in the image are predicted by the Kalman filter and discrepancies are used to update an estimate of the transformation between the object model and the image. He assumed that an initial correct assignment of correspondences between the model edges and the scene edges is available. Dickmanns and Wunsche take a similar approach but also account for feature visibility caused by occlusion for convex bodies. They solve the initialization problem by matching the object model against all combinations of image features and select the most accurate match. The subsequent tracking is carried out by Kalman filter estimation. The three-dimensional motion is confined to three degrees of freedom (2 translation and 1 rotation).

In this paper we emphasize the object recognition aspect of motion analysis, since robust recognition in the presence of occlusion and shadowing is needed to maintain complete and continuous tracking. The motion is viewed as a trajectory in the six-dimensional space of object transformation with time as a parameter. That is, the transformation of an object with respect to the image coordinate system requires six degrees of freedom, 3 translations and 3 rotations. The transformation between an image feature and the three-dimensional model coordinate frame can be considered as a point in six-dimensional space; object motion sweeps out a curve in this transform space.

In the method to be described, a simple image feature, the vertex-pair, can be used to compute an affine approximation to the transformation between image and object coordinate frames. The transformation for all correspondences between image and object are computed, and clustering in transform space defines the group of correct correspondences [Tanaka, 1985] [Thompson and Mundy, 1987]. In the case of motion, the transformations determined from an initial image sequence are used to predict the subsequent transformation by a simple linear extrapolation in transform space. The prediction is used to initialize the search for the new transform cluster. The accuracy of the

---
* This work was supported in part by the DARPA Strategic Computing Vision Program in conjunction with the Army Engineer Topographic Laboratories under Contract No. DACA76-86-C-0007.

prediction affects the efficiency, but not the ultimate success of the recognition algorithm. The worst case recognition time would correspond to object recognition in a static scene. In most cases, the prediction is an effective search constraint and the recognition time can be reduced by orders of magnitude below that required for a complete search of transform space.

THE OBJECT RECOGNITION ALGORITHM

In this section we describe the process for generating an affine transform from a correspondence between vertex-pairs in a model and those derived from the segmentation of an intensity image. In addition, an algorithm for clustering the transform values to find an appropriate match between the model and scene is also presented.

The Model Vertex-Pair

In the work described here, we assume that a three-dimensional polyhedral model is available for the set of objects to be recognized. The use of polyhedral models does not restrict the object being viewed to be a polyhedron, but only that the significant edges and vertices that appear in an image of the object be accurately predicted from an affine projection of the model. In fact, the complete properties of a polyhedron are not required in the matching process. The two main requirements are

- Model vertices and edges are in correct geometric correspondence.

- Sufficient information is available to determine visibility of edges and vertices from all viewpoints.

For example, it is not, strictly speaking, necessary to have the faces of the polyhedron lie in planar surfaces as long as the face boundaries are in correct position and visibility calculations provide correct constraints.

We use a restricted form of perspective image formation, which is the *affine* transform [Roberts, 1965]. The affine transform preserves the parallel relation between two lines in projection. The full perspective transformation reduces to the affine approximation when the depth variations within an object are small compared with the distance of the object from the camera.

It can be shown that the six parameters of the affine transform, three translations and three rotations, can be derived from a group of model edges and vertices called the *vertex-pair*. The geometric arrangement of the vertex-pair is illustrated in Figure 1. The vertex associated with the two edges is called the base vertex. The line defined between the two vertices is called the spine. Note that the spine does not actually have to correspond to an edge in the model or in the image. The angles between each edge and the spine are defined as α and β. The rotation angles about the x,y,z axes are ϕ, ψ, ζ, respectively. These rotations define the orientation of the model vertex-pair with respect to the image plane coordinate system.

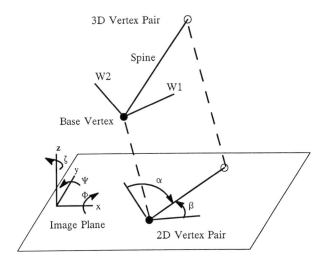

Figure 1. The geometry of the model and scene vertex-pair.

The Affine Transform — An Approximation to Perspective

Consider the coordinate system shown in Figure 2 which illustrates a general camera configuration. The camera origin and the world coordinate system are displaced by the translation vector **O**. The camera coordinate system is represented by the unit vectors, $<U,V,N>$, as shown. The object being viewed is assumed to be represented in world coordinates. In general, it is assumed that an object is represented in terms of a polyhedral surface description; a set of vertex-edge-face relations. However, the nature of the viewing transformation can be analyzed strictly in terms of the three-dimensional location of the vertices.

The general perspective viewing transformation can be represented by the matrix,

$$\mathbf{T} = \begin{bmatrix} \mathbf{U} & -\mathbf{U} \cdot \mathbf{O} \\ \mathbf{V} & -\mathbf{V} \cdot \mathbf{O} \\ -\dfrac{\mathbf{N}}{f} & (1 + \dfrac{\mathbf{N} \cdot \mathbf{O}}{f}) \end{bmatrix}$$

Note that this is a 3×4 matrix since the first column has three-dimensional coordinate vectors as elements.

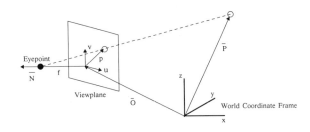

Figure 2. The perspective viewing transformation.

The last column is composed of scalar dot products. A point in space, **P** , is represented as a four element column vector corresponding to homogeneous coordinates, $<x,y,z,1>$. The image of this point in the viewplane, **p**, is a three element vector, $<u',v',w>$, where $\mathbf{p} = \mathbf{TP}$. The element w is the homogeneous scale factor, which determines the cartesian coordinates of **p**. That is,

$$u = \frac{u'}{w} \text{ and } v = \frac{v'}{w}$$

where $<u,v>$ are the cartesian viewplane coordinates.

Now suppose that the ith vertex of the object is represented as $\mathbf{P}_i = \mathbf{P}_0 + \delta\mathbf{P}_i$, where $\mathbf{P}_0$ is the centroid of the set of object vertices. $\delta\mathbf{P}_i$ is the offset from the centroid of the ith vertex. The transform of an object point is,

$$\begin{bmatrix} u' \\ v' \\ w \end{bmatrix} = \begin{bmatrix} \mathbf{U}\cdot(\mathbf{P}-\mathbf{O}) \\ \mathbf{V}\cdot(\mathbf{P}-\mathbf{O}) \\ 1 - \dfrac{\mathbf{N}\cdot(\mathbf{P}_0 - \mathbf{O})}{f} - \dfrac{\mathbf{N}\cdot\delta\mathbf{P}_i}{f} \end{bmatrix}$$

Several approximations can now be made. First assume that the object centroid is far enough from the camera so that,

$$\frac{\mathbf{N}\cdot(\mathbf{P}_0 - \mathbf{O})}{f} >> 1$$

That is, the depth (distance normal to the viewplane) of the centroid of the object is large compared to the focal length of the camera. The second, crucial, assumption is that the variation in the depth of the vertices is small compared to the depth of the centroid of the object. That is,

$$\forall_i \ \mathbf{N}\cdot\delta\mathbf{P}_i << \mathbf{N}\cdot(\mathbf{P}_0 - \mathbf{O})$$

This approximation implies that depth variations within the object do not influence image scale. The approximate transformation can thus be represented by a single scale factor for all object points,

$$w = -\frac{\mathbf{N}\cdot(\mathbf{P}_0 - \mathbf{O})}{f}.$$

Note that w is simply the depth of the object centroid, measured in units of camera focal length, f. The effect of this is to give the projection of an object that corresponds to orthographic projection except that the overall scale of the image depends on the average distance of the object from the viewplane. An orthographic projection with a scale factor is an *affine* transformation. This same approximation was observed by Roberts [Roberts, 1965], which he calls "weak" perspective.

The affine approximation is usually quite reasonable for practical viewing applications. Suppose one is im-

aging an industrial object 5 inches in diameter from 50 inches away. For an image sensor 0.5 inches square, the focal length required is about 2.5 in., assuming that the object subtends half the field of view. In this case, both approximation ratios are smaller than 10%. As another example, consider outdoor image applications such as obstacle recognition. The camera would be about 200 feet from the object which is, say, 20 feet in diameter. The focal length required in this case is still about 2.5 in.; again the approximation is valid.

The approximation is violated for cases where an object has a large extent in depth over the field of view. A typical example of this case is a scene showing a road or railroad tracks extending off to the horizon. The large depth extent requires the full perspective transformation in order to predict that parallel lines (not parallel to the viewplane) meet at a vanishing point. On the other hand, if the affine transformation approximation holds, then parallel lines in the object appear parallel in the image, independent of the orientation of the object. This latter property is the defining requirement for an affine transformation; parallelism is invariant under the transformation. The invariance of parallelism is often assumed in the selection of perceptual groups of line segments [Lowe, 1985].

The Scene Vertex-Pair

The scene vertex-pairs are derived by a standard image segmentation approach. The Canny [Canny, 1986] edge detector is used to locate object boundary points. Briefly, this edge detector applies a convolution for the first spatial derivative at each point in the image. The operator is applied in four orientations at 45-degree intervals. The direction with maximum first derivative magnitude is chosen to compute the second directional derivative. A potential edge point is defined at the zero crossing of the second derivative.

In our experiments, we do not use a threshold on first derivative magnitude to eliminate edge points, except for the unavoidable quantization of the integer calculations. That is, a threshold of 1 is used, which includes edges of any non-zero magnitude. We have adopted this policy since valid edge events in our experimental image set can occur over the full dynamic range of strength values.

The edge points are collected into connected regions and thinned into one-dimensional curves. The one-dimensional curves are approximated by a connected sequence of linear segments. The breakpoints between these segments are determined by points of maximum curvature on the curve [Asada and Brady, 1984]. We determine these locations by decomposing the curve into two functions x(t), y(t), where t is a parameter running along the curve.

These functions are smoothed at a series of spatial scales by recursively applying a 3-wide Gaussian operator to each function. The locations of extremal tangent angle change along both curves are marked at each scale. The maximum angle change is determined by the zero crossing in a second derivative operator applied to each function. A location is taken to be a segment breakpoint if the zero crossings in either x(t) or y(t) occur at many scales and the angle change is considered to be significant [Asada and Brady, 1984]. We have used a threshold of 0.2 radians to define a significant curvature maximum.

Line segments that are less than about 10 pixels in length are eliminated since they are not considered long enough to define an accurate orientation in the image view plane. For example, a variation of plus or minus one pixel at each end of an edge five pixels long corresponds to an orientation variation of more than 20 degrees. Vertices are then formed by intersecting the remaining edges. The edges are allowed to be extended by as much as one half their length at each end to discover potential intersections.

The set of scene vertex pairs consists of all possible ordered pairings of the scene vertices. For vertices occurring at the junction of three or more lines, the edges themselves are also paired to form more vertex pairs with the same pair of vertices.

Computing and Clustering the Transform

We now have two sets of vertex-pairs, model vertex pairs that are selected from a three-dimensional polyhedral model and those generated from the image as just described. The vertex-pair defines enough constraints so that all of the parameters of an affine transformation between a model vertex-pair and a scene vertex-pair can be computed. The computation is summarized in reference to Figure 1 as:

- The projected angles between the spine and each edge, α and β determine the tip and tilt angles of the model coordinate frame, ϕ and ψ with respect to the image plane.

- The orientation of the projected spine with respect to the x axis of the image plane determines the rotation about the z axis, ζ.

- The translation between the projected base vertex of the model vertex-pair and the actual image location of the scene vertex-pair gives two of the translational degrees of freedom.

- The ratio of the length of the projected model spine and the actual image spine length gives the affine scale factor.

These steps nominally produce a point in six-dimensional transform parameter space for each correspondence between a model vertex-pair and a scene vertex pair. Actually more transform values may be produced from a correspondence due to degeneracy or multiple solution in the mapping between $< \alpha, \beta >$ and $< \phi, \psi >$ [Thompson and Mundy, 1987].

The map between $< \alpha, \beta >$ and $< \phi, \psi >$ is implemented as a lookup table that is precomputed for each specific vertex-pair in the model. The visibility of each vertex-pair is considered during the formation of the table. The values of $< \phi, \psi >$ for which a vertex-pair is occluded are represented as invalid solutions in the map table.

We define a potential object match by a compact cluster in transform space [Tanaka et al., 1985, Silberberg et al., 1986]. The cluster is detected by a combination of histogramming and a form of the nearest neighbor clustering algorithm. The transformation instances are counted into a two-dimensional histogram based on values of $< \phi, \psi >$. If a bin contains at least a specified number of points, the contents of the bin are projected onto a histogram on values of ζ. Increments of five degrees are used in both histograms.

Any set of transform values that pass through the angle sieve is further tested by a nearest neighbor clustering in translation-scale space. A first point is randomly selected to serve as the center of a cluster and then other points in the set are added if they fit tolerances on translation and scale with respect to the center value. When a point is added to the cluster the center is recomputed. When a point fails the tolerance test, it becomes the center point of a new cluster.

Finally, remaining clusters, which are now coherent in transformation space, are filtered to eliminate duplicate mappings, which may occur due to overlapping sample windows, and to ensure an isomorphic mapping from model edges and vertices to scene edges and vertices.

MOTION ANALYSIS

Motion as a Trajectory in Transform Space

So far we have discussed the problem of determining the transformation of an object model with respect to the image coordinate frame for a static situation. Object motion can be viewed as a sequence of such transformations. It is reasonable to assume that the transformation does not change instantaneously with time since object motion is governed by inertia. In fact, the object motion will sweep out a continuous, one-dimensional curve, or trajectory, in transform space.

Perhaps the most important aspect of the transformation trajectory is the existence of *temporal coherence*. Coherence in this context means that the assignments between model and scene features will not change significantly from one instant to another. A few vertex-pairs will disappear and new ones will become visible as the object rotates or becomes occluded by other objects; the majority of assignments will be valid over a small time interval. The concept is illustrated in Figure 3. For cluster A, the centroid of the cluster forms a smooth trajectory and a linear prediction is appropriate. Temporal coherence, along with the assumed continuity of the transform trajectory, leads to the following matching strategy:

- From the continuity of the transform trajectory, subsequent transforms can be reasonably predicted by linear extrapolation of current trajectory data. This transform prediction can be used to focus the search for the actual transform cluster.

- The transform clusters that are due to false assignments can be discovered because these assignments will not exhibit temporal coherence.

False assignments usually arise in degenerate views of the object and these degenerate conditions will not persist over long-time intervals of general object motion. Further, the transforms computed from each vertex-pair in a false but nondegenerate cluster, will not exhibit the same individual transform trajectories and the cluster will disperse as time evolves. An example of this last case can be seen when observing a wire frame of a cube which is rotating. A human observer can easily make the incorrect assignment to the cube projection which causes the shape of cube to apparently distort as the cube rotates. This distortion would correspond to a dispersion of transform values associated with the cube vertex-pairs. This situation is shown conceptually in Figure 3 for cluster B. Thus, the presence of motion can actually contribute to the accuracy and reliability of model-based recognition, rather than be an added complication.

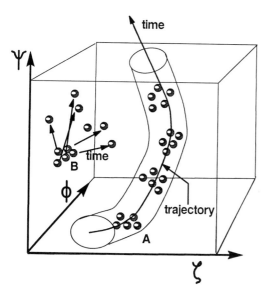

Figure 3. An interpretation of temporal coherence. The transform cluster at A evolves coherently in time. The accidental cluster at B quickly disperses as the object moves relative to the image reference frame.

Transform Prediction

In the experiments to be described here, the prediction of a new transform six-tuple, **T** is a simple linear prediction based on the time derivative of each transform parameter. That is:

$$\mathbf{T}_{i+1} = \mathbf{T}_i + \frac{d\mathbf{T}_i}{dt}\Delta t$$

The estimate for the time derivative is simply the difference between the current and previous transform,

$$\frac{d\mathbf{T}_i}{dt} = \frac{(\mathbf{T}_i - \mathbf{T}_{i-1})}{\Delta t}$$

Each translational component of the transformation is predicted exactly in this fashion. The discontinuities in the angles that describe the rotational components of the transformation are accounted for by appropriate modulo arithmetic; otherwise the prediction is the same as for translation.

This prediction mechanism can be easily extended to consider more of the trajectory history and to apply a higher order extrapolation polynomial. The Kalman filter techniques of the works mentioned in the introduction make an optimum statistical estimate of the trajectory based on the covariance matrix of observed trajectory parameters. Our main objective here is to demonstrate the temporal coherence principle in transform clustering over image sequences. The simple predictor just described serves this purpose.

One extension that is under current consideration is the use of geometric or physical models for the trajectory which have a small number of parameters that can be learned from the transform sequence. For example, in the experiments to be described below, motion along a circular arc and gravitational motion have been investigated. This extension could be considered as a type of space-time model matching where the trajectory class is recognized from constraints on the geometry of the trajectory in four dimensions.

Constraining the Search of Transform Space

The next step is to use the transform prediction, $\mathbf{T}_{i+1}$, to constrain the search transform space for an accept-

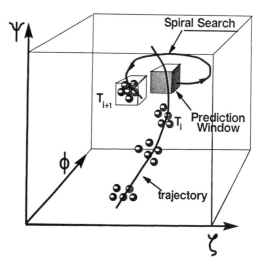

Figure 4. The use of temporal coherence to predict the next object transformation.

able assignment cluster. The search is illustrated in Figure 4 which shows the trajectory in rotation space, up to time t_i. The three-dimensional rotation space is examined within a box which is initially centered at the predicted rotation for t_{i+1}. If no transform cluster is found with at least the specified number of model-to-scene feature assignments and with the required transformational tolerance, as described previously, the box center is spiraled outward to explore areas not yet sampled. If an acceptable rotation cluster is found, the assignments are tested in translation space. Translation space is also three-dimensional, and a box is again constructed about the predicted translation.

If the transform prediction is reasonably accurate, the correct assignment cluster will be found immediately. As the accuracy of the prediction degrades, the search of rotation space expands outward from the prediction. An aspect worthy of further study is the determination of an optimum strategy for searching the neighborhood of the prediction. This investigation will involve an understanding of the errors associated with the image segmentation and their effect on the transform parameters.

The procedure outlined here is by no means foolproof, and false matches can be observed that are in the neighborhood of the prediction and with reasonably tight bounds in transform error. These false positive matches are mostly caused by degenerate transformations of the object that can still be supported by the segmentation, which might contain a considerable number of extraneous edges and vertices. Naturally, if the neighborhood can be tightened by more accurate prediction, then this problem is correspondingly reduced.

THE EXPERIMENTS

To test the ideas discussed above, we carried out a series of three experiments, with increasingly complex trajectories. The goal of the experiments was to demonstrate that model matching and transform prediction could work together to produce a continuous tracking of an object in motion. As a side product, the actual motion trajectory with the full six-degrees of freedom could be obtained. All computations were carried out on the Symbolics Lisp Machine

Pure Translation

In this experiment, a polyhedral block was moved along a purely translational trajectory at an oblique angle with respect to the camera viewing axis. Three intensity images, taken from the beginning, middle and end of the trajectory are shown in Figure 5. An instance of a segmentation for one of the images is also shown in Figure 5. Full sequence consists of twenty frames. The model matching process was carried out at approximately every fifth frame. The superposition of the block model for each of the images in Figure 5 is shown in Figure 6. In a video tape made for demonstrating the results, the model was superimposed on intermediate frames according to the linear

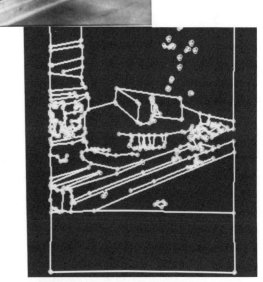

Figure 5. A set of images from the pure translation sequence.
a) Frame 1
b) Frame 10
c) Frame 20
d) The segmentation of frame 10.

prediction scheme discussed above. This process gives the impression that the model is tracking the object in the image.

Rotation

The next experiment was to use a calibrated turntable

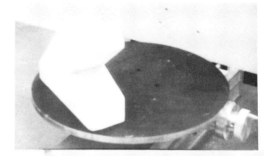

Figure 6.   The transformations found for the images in Figure 5. The matching result is indicated by projecting the model on the the image according to the transformation computed from the average over the matched assignments.
a) Frame 1
b) Frame 10
c) Frame 20

to rotate the block through a circular arc. In this case, the axis of the turntable was inclined with respect to the camera axis by about 25 degrees. The turntable was rotated by 10 degrees between each of the 36 frames in the sequence. Thus, the full sequence was a 350-degree rotation and the model matching was done every 50 degrees.

Figure 7 shows three images from the sequence with an example of the segmentation. The model matches for these images are shown in Figure 8.

Gravitational Motion

This sequence was the most difficult in that the block was tossed into the air with a twist to give it both gravitational motion and rotation. The sequence was captured by a high speed (1000 frames per second) ccd camera. This method provides a sequence of images where the moving object is not blurred by the normal integration time effects of a video camera. The total

Figure 7.   Sample frames from the rotational sequence.
a) Frame 1
b) Frame 16
c) Frame 26
d) Segmentation of Frame 16.

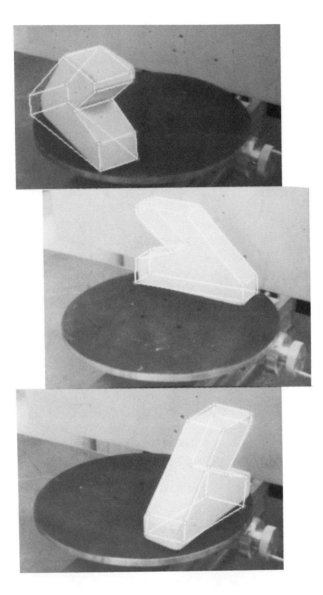

Figure 8.   Matches found for the sample images in Figure 7.
a) Frame 1
b) Frame 16
c) Frame 26

Figure 9.   Frames from the gravitational motion sequence.
a) Frame 1
b) Frame 21
c) Frame 41
d) The segmentation of frame 21.

sequence was spanned by a periodic sampling of forty-one images which, occupied approximately one second of elapsed time.

Three frames of the sequence are shown in Figure 9. Again an example segmentation is given. Two frames of the sequence are particularly interesting, since they produce a degenerate position of the cube where it is seen approximately end on. It was not possible to obtain a reliable match at these points in the trajectory and the extrapolator was used to carry on until a successful match could be obtained. A similar recovery could be expected if an object is temporarily occluded. The matches for each frame are shown in Figure 10.

ANALYSIS

Rotational Analysis

In order to quantify the accuracy of the matches found, we focused on the rotational sequence, which exhibits both rotational and translational behavior under controlled circumstances. Each consecutive match corresponds to a 50-degree clockwise rotation about the turntable axis as viewed. In order to derive this motion from the results, we first arbitrarily set the world and model coordinate systems to be equivalent. We then consider that each match provides a transfor-

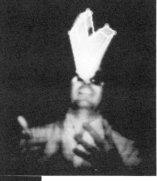

**Figure 10.   Matches found for the gravitational motion
sequence of Figure 9.**
a) Frame 1
b) Frame 21
c) Frame 41

mation of the block model within the world coordinate system, which is a right-hand system whose x-y plane is coincident with the image plane. Therefore,

$$RT_iM = T_{i+1}M$$

where **M** is the model coordinate frame, T_i is the matrix transform at time t_i, T_{i+1} is the transform at time t_{i+1}, and **R** is the transform describing the motion in the world between t and $t+1$. Thus,

$$R = T_{i+1}T_i^{-1}$$

Since the rotation sequence is constant rotation about a fixed axis, it is appropriate to interpret the matrix **R** in terms of a quaternion [Faugeras and Hebert, 1986]. Recall that a quaternion represents general rotation as rotation about a single axis, but with the axis direction determined by the required transformation. Below are the quaternions derived from each successive pair of match values in each sequence. The angle Θ is the rotation about the axis defined by the unit vector components, $<x,y,z>$. The values represent the successive model rotations needed to track the object for

each trajectory type. We expect the turntable rotation to be the most interesting.

Match Sequence Interval	Θ	x	y	z	Trajectory
1-5	0.06328774	-0.79028106	-0.5739611	-0.21471395	
5-10	0.052309066	0.9708769	0.0264449	0.23861404	Translation
10-20	0.055206552	-0.27894896	-0.9562916	-0.088843875	
1-6	0.40120396	0.3237418	0.8274006	0.45891458	
6-11	1.1686573	0.21508668	0.9468162	0.2332645	
11-21	1.7577245	0.25086188	0.9239225	0.2888524	Gravitation
21-31	1.4975253	0.18577065	0.8671058	0.46218738	
31-36	0.72890955	0.3519565	0.83358455	0.42575175	
36-41	0.83445716	0.37364966	0.68372124	0.62682676	
1-6	0.8248317	-0.08764122	-0.9044648	-0.41744846	
6-11	0.9783499	-0.09659891	-0.9945819	-0.038420383	
11-16	0.804729	0.32672945	-0.7942709	-0.5122322	Turntable
16-21	0.78189516	-0.00769019	-0.9317659	-0.36297894	Rotation
21-26	0.78858674	-0.11201641	-0.9263640	-0.35958675	
26-31	0.98708683	-0.09024005	-0.9688868	-0.23046751	
31-36	1.1550276	0.08707203	-0.9535843	-0.28826302	

In the turntable rotation sequence, the axis of rotation is generally negative in x,y and z, corresponding to an axis pointed down and into the image plane (world x-y plane). The rotational angles are positive, corresponding to a counter clockwise (right-handed) rotation about the axis when looking down the axis toward the origin, which corresponds to the actual clockwise rotation on the turntable. The average rotation is 0.9029296 radians, or 51.734 degrees (actual rotation is 50 degrees per step). The seven steps produce a total rotation of 362 degrees, more than the actual rotation of 350 degrees. The average rotational axis is (0.003, -0.925, -0.316). This axis is primarily in the y-z plane, and its angle of inclination is $\tan^{-1}(0.925/0.316)$, which is 1.241 radians, 71.139 degrees (actual angle 65 degrees).

The gravitational sequence is more difficult to analyze, as the axis of rotation, although relatively constant, is not known a priori. We may, however, consider the degree of rotation in each step and in total. Because of a relatively poor match at image 6, the rotation from image 1 to 6 is small, but the rotation from image 6 to 11 is large, with the average rotation per time slice over that sequence being 0.78 radians per match. The rest of the quaternions exhibit similar values (0.803 radians), bearing in mind that two of them are for double time slices. The block describes a total rotation of 6.388 radians, approximately 2 pi. This corresponds with a visual estimate of the block rotation. The approximate axis and sense of rotation are also in reasonable agreement with visual estimates.

The translation sequence produces quaternions of negligible rotational magnitude and incoherent axis orientation, which is to be expected with a sequence with no actual rotational motion.

Translation Analysis

The derived values for transformation translation and scale components of the transformation from the object world coordinate system to the image coordinate frame are given in the table below. Recall that scale is the ratio of the distance of the object from the camera; normalized by the camera focal length.

Image Index	X	Y	Scale	
1	155.61034	236.4964	0.4311173	
5	150.73047	236.56018	0.43545607	
10	128.03522	229.81331	0.42568496	Pure Translation
20	85.56669	219.41219	0.42400864	
1	40.70472	126.17222	0.8117685	
6	63.29604	157.3349	0.7846806	
11	143.73056	172.83398	0.697413	
16	218.30037	163.92178	0.6642433	Turntable Rotation
21	254.80548	132.60417	0.7602637	
26	223.26486	104.17795	0.8085761	
31	123.69439	92.46753	0.787468	
36	52.171467	115.97262	0.8144042	
1	76.332146	37.414	0.28231606	
6	93.513855	71.29523	0.3181397	
11	93.61582	104.93337	0.31848565	
21	112.96949	134.72246	0.29280475	Gravitational Motion
31	159.02148	114.39604	0.30877644	
36	185.7876	95.63774	0.3132562	
41	205.3817	75.22553	0.32453573	

The translational sequence is most readily interpreted in terms of image position and scale. This sequence displays a gross translation of -70 pixels in x and -17 pixels in y. The first match in the sequence is the worst of the group, and the first translational transform result is poor. The other three display constant increments in translation of -22 pixels in x and -8.5 in y. Scale (relative translation in depth) is relatively constant. The image sequence progresses slightly toward the camera, but the large relative depth of the object prevents the scale from providing much accuracy in depth estimation.

The turntable rotational sequence produces translation values corresponding approximately to an ellipse — the projection of a circular arc. The change in scale can be compared to the depth variation as the block moves on the turntable. The scale ranges from approximately 0.66 to 0.82. With a camera focal length of 12 cm, and a distance to the near edge of the turntable of 100 cm, the scale change predicts a distance of 127 cm for the block position the far side of the turntable. The actual turntable diameter is 32.5 cm (vs 27 cm from above).

The gravitational sequence exhibits parabolic translational motion in the x-y plane and negligible change in scale. The height of the block is maximum at approximately image 24, with a lateral translation of around 135 pixels. Although the number of samples is too sparse for an accurate description of the parabola, the block is translating vertically at about 35 pixels per time slice (7 pixels per image) at the beginning of the sequence. It is translating vertically at about 10 pixels per time slice near the top of the curve (2 pixels per image). Except for an anomolous result for image 11, horizontal translation is roughly constant at 20 pixels per time slice. Scale is constant, as expected, since there is essentially no translation in depth and the camera is relatively far from the block.

FUTURE DIRECTIONS

A number of important extensions to the technique are immediately obvious. If one can make a reasonably accurate prediction of the motion, then it is not necessary to segment the entire scene. It is only necessary to compute vertices and edges in the vicinity of the predicted model location in the image.

It would also be reasonable to explore the idea of incremental feature tracking where the predicted three-dimensional model motion is used to estimate feature locations in the subsequent frame. The assignments between model features and scene features could be limited to those that are reasonably consistent with the predicted locations. The model features that are predicted not to be visible in the next frame could also be eliminated from consideration.

Finally, the specification and recognition of motion models from the trajectory samples is another important avenue of investigation. For example, if it could be recognized that a trajectory represents gravitational motion, then the predictor could be made accurate over much longer time intervals than can be achieved by a linear model.

ACKNOWLEDGMENTS

We gratefully acknowledge the tireless assistance of Aaron Heller and Greg Spradlin in the generation of the results presented here.

REFERENCES

[1] Asada, H. and Brady, M., "The Curvature Primal Sketch," Proc. IEEE Workshop on Computer Vision: Representation and Control, 1984.

[2] Ayache, N. and Faugeras, O., "A New Method for the Recognition and Positioning of 2D Objects," Proc. 7th International Joint Conference on Pattern Recognition, 1986, p. 1274.

[3] Canny, J., "Finding Edges and Lines in Images, "MIT Artificial Intelligence Laboratory Report," AI-TR-720, 1986.

[4] Dickmanns, E. and Wunsche, H., "Satellite Rendezvous Maneuvers by Means of Computer Vision," Jahrbuch 1986 Bd. 1 der DGLR, Bonn, p. 251.

[5] Faugeras, O., Hebert, M., "The Representation, Recognition and Locating of 3-D Objects," International Journal of Robotics Research, Vol. 5, No. 3, 1986, p. 27.

[6] Gennery, D., "Tracking Known Three-Dimensional Objects," Proc. National Conference on Artificial Intelligence, AAAI-82, 1982, p. 13.

[7] Grimson,E. and Lozano-Perez, T., "Search and Sensing Strategies for Recognition and Localization of Two and Three Dimensional Objects," Proc. 3rd International Symposium on Robotics Research, 1985.

[8] Lowe, D., "Perceptual Organization and Visual Recognition", Kluwer Academic Publishers, Boston MA, 1985.

[9] Porrill, J., Pollard, S., Pridmore, T., Bowen, J., Mayhew, J., Frisby, J., "TINA: The Sheffield AIVRU Vision System," Proc. 10th International Joint Conference on Artificial Intelligence, 1987, p. 1138.

[10] Roberts, L., "Machine Perception of Three-Dimensional Solids, Optical and Electro-Optical Information Processing," J.T. Tippett et al., eds., MIT Press, Cambridge MA, 1965.

[11] Silberberg, T., Harwood, D., Davis, L. "Object Recognition Using Oriented Model Points," Computer Vision, Graphics and Image Processing, Vol. 35, 1986.

[12] Tanaka, H. Ballard, D., Tsuji, S. and Curtiss, M., "Parallel Polyhedral Shape Recognition," Proc. CVPR, 1985.

[13] Thompson, D. and Mundy, J., "Three Dimensional Model Matching From An Unconstrained Viewpoint," Proc. IEEE Robotics and Automation, 1987, p. 280.

[14] Waxman, A., Kamgar-Parsi, B., and Subbarao, M., "Closed-Form Solutions to Image Flow Equations, Proc. First International Conference on Computer Vision," 1987, p. 12.

4D-dynamic scene analysis with integral spatio-temporal models

E. D. Dickmanns[1]
Aerospace Technology Department
Universität der Bundeswehr München
W. Heisenberg Weg 39, 8014 Neubiberg
Federal Republic of Germany

A method for interpreting high frequency image sequences is presented that confines image data processing to the last image of the sequence and yet - by using smoothing integration-operations - allows to determine velocity components in space explicitly. This is achieved by simultaneously exploiting 3D-object and - motion models together with the laws of perspective projection. These integral models of the process observed in the world and of the (very flexible) measurement process using vision are utilized in the sense of modelbased feedback control theory (Kalman filter, observer), to estimate the state variables in space and time directly. The concept has been tested in three application areas: a planar docking maneuver between two 3D-objects, autonomous road vehicle guidance and autonomous aircraft landing.

Introduction

The usual way to process image sequences today is characterized by pictorial interpretation of single images and an ensuing comparison of the position of objects; from this the motion of objects in space is reconstructed. This procedure may be based in the historical development of digital image processing which began in the area of remote sensing taking temporally well separated single images.

It is, however, well known from biology and physiology, that pictorial vision and motion vision are two separate developments, motion vision being the phylogenetically elder one. The psychologist Yonas has shown, that also in human children motion vision is developed first <Yonas 83>.

If a slide show, say on the last vacation adventures, is copied onto a movie film and shown at normal image frequency (18-24 frames per second) the observer will turn away or close the eyes since a continuous development of action is missing. From this one can conclude that for meaningful vision, temporal continuity is an essential prerequisite. High image frequency is not detrimental since it does not alter the dynamics of the process being observed; it is, on the contrary, beneficial since it reduces the so-called correspondence problem: Within the small sampling period T, which at the usual TV-frame rate is 16 2/3 ms, features being tracked will move only by a small amount. When the process being watched is "recognized", reasonably good extrapolations to the next frame can be achieved by linear prediction with a temporal model.

If one then succeeds, by exploiting the difference between the predicted and the actually measured feature position, in determining the parameters and the state variables of the model, which served as the basis for "recognition", and in servoing these variables fast and precisely enough so that the measured values are well approximated over time, then a symbolic representation of the process in the world has been generated in the computer. This stable condition is called "recognition" of the process by computer vision or "understanding" of the dynamic scene.

It is immediately clear that because of the temporal extrapolation required, time has to be an essential component of the model. In order to achieve this, the dynamical models of modern control theory are utilized which have been developed around 1960 in the form of linearized systems of differential equations or difference equations in the discrete linear state space model for sampled control systems <Kalman 60; Kailath 80>.

This model based approach eliminates the necessity to have access to data of previous images (in order e.g. to compute differences or optical flow) and it thereby relieves computational loads considerably. This has to be paid for by having to deal with a somewhat more involved initial orientation phase when the vision process starts and when reasonable model hypotheses have to be found. However, besides confining image processing to the last image of the sequence, this approach has several additional advantages hardly to be overestimated:

+ With respect to actions required, gaps in measurement data may be bridged over a certain period in time by just using the extrapolated state variables of the model.

+ The quality of new measurement data may be judged relative to the values predicted by the model; depending on the quality of the model, the dynamics of the process and preknowledge about general environmental conditions (e.g. perturbations) a situation-specific reaction is possible: from throwing away the new data up to the initiation of a new subprocess in order to obtain a more precise analysis of the situation. In addition, the dynamical model allows the application of adapted filter algorithms for data smoothing.

+ The interpretation of the image sequence proceeds simultaneously in space and time. Meaningfull continuity conditions for features are formulated easier in 3D-space than in the 2D-image, e.g. the disappearance or appearance of features when aspect angles change or when occlusion occurs due to (spatial) object- or ego-motion.

+ Well proven spatiotemporal models allow the prediction of events or the appearance of objects, features of which can be actively looked for; in this case good hypotheses for interpretation and parameter adaptation are readily available. (It is easier to orient oneself in a "known environment" than in an unknown one. Whole objects may be recognized by detecting only a few characteristic features.)

Coming from systems dynamics this approach to image sequence interpretation is readily proposed; it does not seem to have been investigated more closely up to now, however. Except for our group at UniBw M, where dynamical models for image sequence processing have been used since 1979 <Meissner 82>, only a few hints are found in the literature to similar approaches <Gennery 81>, <Rives 86>, <Broida, Chellappa 86>. We have tested this approach at four motion control applications:

1. balance of an inverted pendulum on an electro cart <Meissner, Dickmanns 83>,<Dickmanns, Wünsche 86a>

2. autonomous road vehicle guidance <Dickmanns, Zapp 85, 86, 87>

3. planar docking maneuver between 3D-objects with a model control plant <Wünsche 86, 87>, <Dickmanns, Wünsche 86b>

4. autonomous aircraft landing (simulation) <Eberl 87>, <Dickmanns, Eberl 87>

In all four applications real-time motion control has been achieved with a real (CCD-) TV-camera and a MIMD-multi-microprocessor system for image sequence processing <Graefe 84> in the loop.

In the sequel, the approach is first described in general terms; then the applications 2 to 4 are discussed in somewhat more detail as an introduction to the references cited. Finally, an outlook is given on the growth potential up to the recognition and visual tracking of other moving objects under egomotion.

2. Integral spatio-temporal models

Figure 1 shows a juxtaposition of the usual procedure in image sequence processing (upper half) and the "cybernetic" approach based on "difference feedback" (lower half). Spatiotemporal processes in the real world (1) are imaged by a TV-camera, usually via a sequential analog video signal into an image sequence (left side). In conventional image sequence interpretation for the detection of motion two or more frames out of the sequence have to be accessed simultaneously in order to find corresponding features (corners, contours or lines) and to obtain displacement vectors in the image plane by differencing. Knowing the sampling period, the velocity components in image coordinates can theoretically be determined from this (optical flow). Due to the inevitable measurement noise, these computed velocities become the more corrupted by noise the shorter the sampling period between the two frames evaluated is (the well known roughening property of differentiation for noisy data). Based on these position and velocity data in image coordinates, one then tries to infer the imaged spatiotemporal processes (3D-motion); in this step the nonunique inversion of the perspective projection has to be performed. There are many publications to this ill-conditioned problem.

In the model-based approach, on the contrary, through a successfull recognition process over time there results a symbolic spatiotemporal model-instantiation in the computer of the dynamical scene being observed (in fig. 1 termed "world 2" (right) in accordance with <Popper 77>). The spatial symbolic representation may be done using known methods in computer vision or computer graphics; the temporal symbolic representation is realized by differential equations for the spatial position, orientation and velocity-components as state variables of the object, e.g.

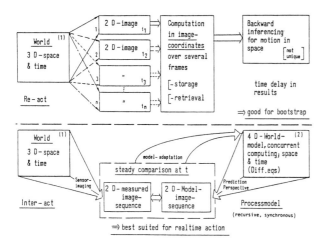

Figure 1: Two basically different ways of image sequence processing in computer vision: difference computation between images (top), model based integration (bottom).

center of gravity (c.g.) coordinates and angular orientation around the c.g..

Very often it may be sufficient to take linear approximations to the differential equations with time- or state-dependent coefficients; in a discrete formulation with respect to time and the basic sampling period, a system of difference equations results

$$x[(k+1)T] = A(k,T) \; x \; (kT) \\ + \; B(k,T) \; u(kT) + v(kT) \quad (1)$$

where x is an n-component state vector, k is the running index of the discrete time, T the sampling period, A the n*n transition matrix, B the n*m control effect matrix, u an m-component control vector and v a superimposed disturbance.

Equation (1) without the disturbance term allows to determine the state vector at time (k+1)T as extrapolation based on this model by simple matrix-vector multiplication (nominal prediction). With this 3D-state the perspective projection (3D to 2D forward) is applied to the 3D-shape features of the object model, in order to arrive at predicted positions of 2D- features to be measured in the image. This leads to an impoverished "model image", the components of which are compared to the measured actual image. The computer, therefore, needs to have access to the last image in the sequence only. In the sense of modern feedback control theory (see e.g. <Kalman 60; Kailath 80>) an additional prediction error term may now be fed back through a (yet to be determined) gain matrix in such a way that the discrepancies vanish over time. Depending on the noise statistics of the process and the measurements, either

filter- or observer-techniques may be selected.

Note, that this formulation contains the state variables in 3D-space as primary variables and that all components are reconstructed or estimated, also when a smaller number of output variables is being measured (observability assumed as given). The numerical operations required are integrations (summations in the discrete case), which tend to suppress noise effects; if the selectable error decay dynamics are chosen properly (observer-eigenvalues slightly larger than those of the plant), the resulting gain factors lead to an acceptable behaviour of this cybernetic vision process, provided the sampling period is small, compared to the characteristic time scale of the process being watched, and the model is sufficiently good.

The sequence of image comparisons (lower middle in fig. 1) thus leads to an adaptation of the model and of the state variables, converging over time towards the process running in reality. Within the computing process, thus, the dynamical scene analysed is duplicated in a symbolic form by servocontrolled instantiations of elements out of a store of components for a world model. The state variables of the dynamical model are obtained explicitly as complete time histories; they are taken instead of the state variables in the real world 1 as the basis for decisions with respect to actions, e.g. control activities. - There are interesting parallels to old philosophical ideas.[2]

A detailed treatment of special applications is not possible in the framework of this survey paper; for this, the reader is referred to the original publications cited. The following treatment of the applications investigated is intended to help clarify the general principle.

3. Automous guidance of road vehicles
Forced by gravity and the supportance of the ground, road vehicles move parallel to the local Earth surface essentially. In order to improve riding comfort, man has shaped the areas for vehicle movement with a smooth surface (roads); i.e. only radii of curvature are allowed that are large as compared to the wheel- or axle-distance. The curvatures of these "surface-strips", both in the vertical plane defined by the gravity vector and the road tangent, and in the plane tangential to the surface determine the driving behaviour of vehicles. To recognize both of those is one of the essential tasks for vehicle guidance by both man and computer using vision. This has to be achieved in a certain look ahead range concurrently while driving.

In a coordinate frame fixed to the vehicle when moving along the road, the geographically fixed road curvature appears in the car as a temporally variable state of the environment. Since the law, according to which highways are built (clotoids, i.e. linearly varying curvature over arc length), and the ranges for the parameters yielding reasonable results are known, effective filtering methods may be based on this road model for smoothing noisy image processing data <Dickmanns, Zapp 86; 87>. These methods evaluate recursively, by exploiting the dynamical model for the road being driven at speed V, the two relevant state variables in each of the two planes mentioned above: 1. the actual curvature and 2. the rate of curvature change with arc length (differential geometry road skeleton model). The image of the road in a look ahead distance, however, also depends on the position and the orientation of the camera relative to the road. If the camera position and its orientation in the vehicle are fixed, then the state variables of the vehicle relative to the road (lateral position y and heading angle ψ) determine its perspective image. This holds true spatially. Temporal continuity conditions result from the vehicle having only limited mobility: Its wheels revolve in a plane normal to their axis; the sliding angle ß due to soft tires and slipping are small, but not negligeable. From this, side constraints in the form of differential equations for vehicle motion result: If the vehicle does have an angle relative to the road not equal to zero, there will be resulting a lateral offset y in the future; this, in addition, depends on the centrifugal force ($\sim V^2$) and the steering control. Introducing the knowledge of these interactions into the process of image sequence interpretation, again a very effective recursive approach for estimating the entire state vector of the vehicle results. Though only some feature positions are being measured, all position and speed components are determined exploiting always the last image of the sequence only <Dickmanns, Zapp 85, 86, 87>. Fig. 2 shows the cooperation of the two dynamical models for curvature determination (upper part) and for vehicle state estimation (lower part) in the feedback loop.

Road curvature c determined in the look ahead range is not only used for driving the anticipatory part of the lateral control $u_{a\ lat}$, but also for automatically adapting longitudinal speed V. This is adjusted in such a way that the lateral acceleration $a_y = cV^2$ stays below a preset limit value (e.g. 0.1 of Earth gravity g). Both in simulations with real sensors in the loop and in

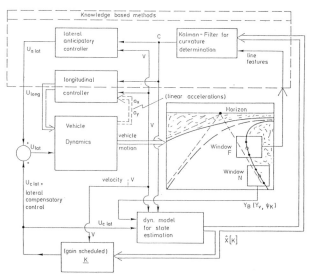

Figure 2: Block diagram for high speed road vehicle guidance by computer vision: model based estimation of curvature (upper right) and vehicle state relative to the road (lower right).

real experiments with our 5-ton test vehicle for autonomous mobility and computer vision, VaMoRs (fig. 3), this method has proven to be very efficient.

Figure 3: The UniBw M test vehicle for autonomous mobility and computer vision VaMoRs.

In fully automatic test runs speeds up to 60 km/h have been achieved, where the vehicle adapted speed to the curvature of the track automatically. One of these test tasks is shown in figure 4. Image sequence evaluation- and control cycle time has been 0.08 to 0.1 seconds.

Other vehicles as partners in road traffic may be observed and tracked using very similar methods and the same camera (see below).

4. Planar relative positioning
A frequent task in robotics is to position a controllable three-dimensional vehicle relative to another 3D-object. Using the dynamic approach to computer

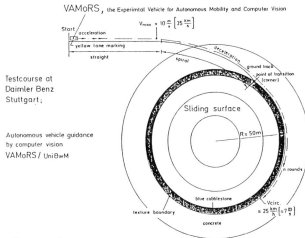

Figure 4:
One of the test runs for VaMors.

vision described above, H.J. Wünsche developed several important implementational details and demonstrated its performance and efficiency in fully autonomous docking maneuvers with a model control plant in the laboratory <Wünsche 87>. Fig. 5 shows the aircushion vehicle with a computer controlled reaction jet propulsion system on a planar table together with several docking partners. The convex prismatic shapes of the bodies are assumed to be known. They are represented in the computer by wire frame models. The

controlled vehicle carrying a CCD-TV-camera has the task to recognize its docking partner, drive towards it, recognize the precise position of the docking port, position itself axially relative to it and finally to maneuver towards the partner until mechanical lock-in is achieved. During this maneuver relative position and velocity have to be evaluated steadily in order to guarantee safe process control. Partial occlusions of the target body over a finite period of time may occur but are not allowed to disrupt the docking procedure.

In <Wünsche 86; 87; Dickmanns, Wünsche 86b)> application specific details are given. Corners in the perspective projection are chosen as features to be tracked; the complete state vector of the vehicle relative to the docking partner is estimated recursively by tracking a varying number of these features in the monocular image sequence over time. The state vector consists of two translatory positions and speed components and one angular orientation and rate; together with the camera pitch angle and a rotatory disturbance acceleration, eight state components are steadily estimated.

Kalman filter techniques in a sequential stabilized formulation are used based on tracking up to four feature positions. By continuously checking a performance index, _those_ features are automatically selected which yield the best estimation results. Occlusions due to changes in aspect angle are predicted and feature tracking is redirected autonomously. If a sudden occlusion of a feature by an unexpected object occurs, after a short period of repeated trials at the old feature position a new combination of features is selected yielding the next best performance index. Due to the strong perspective distortion of imaged features at small distances, the algorithms have to be tolerant against changes in feature shape. Fig. 6 shows a block diagram form of fig. 1 (lower part) for this application. In figure 7 results of a test run over 90 seconds are given, in which the vehicle first turns towards the docking partner (- reduction for t<9s, first row then moves towards it (R-reduction for 13<t<20s,5-th row), circumnavigates it at constant R (for 20<t<60s, last two rows, being the polar angle and VT the tangential velocity component) and finally closes in for docking (t>60s, see R and VR).

The approach developed in this application for 3D-object recognition and-tracking is generally applicable and is presently being transferred to the task of recognizing other vehicles, distance keeping and collision avoidance in road

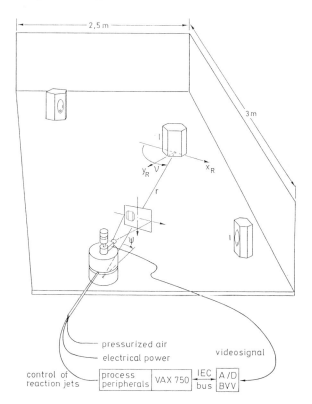

Figure 5: Satellite model plant for visually controlled docking.

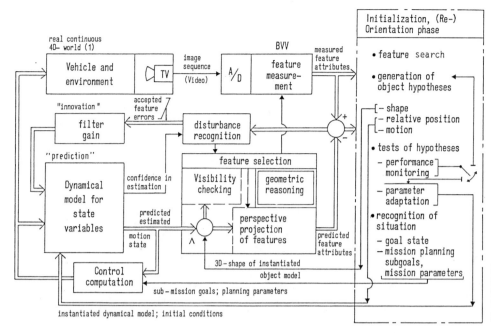

Figure 6:
Block diagram for the "dynamic-" or "4D-" vision concept

scenes. Here, the object shape and its relative motion state have to be determined simultaneously. Background knowledge on road-vehicle shapes and their mobility parameters is exploited to alleviate the task of generating simultaneously both spatial and temporal interpretation hypotheses.

In this case, both shape- and dynamical model-instantiations from a long term model-base have to be tested against feature aggregations from the image sequence; simultaneous reasoning in space and time is required. Shape models will be based on the normalized-curvature-function (NCF) representation proposed in <Dickmanns 85>.

In order to alleviate the solution of this task, the next generation of our image sequence processing system BVV provides the capability of active (fast) control of the viewing direction (see <Mysliwetz, Dickmanns 86>) and of analyzing video data of two TV cameras in parallel (e.g. for tele- and wide angle lenses yielding images of different resolution).

5. Landing approach by computer vision

This is the most complex real-time motion control task solved by computer vision up to now. Aircraft motion occurs simultaneously in six degrees of freedom: three translatory and three rotary ones. In each degree of freedom, according to Newton's law, one differential equation of second order is required to model the dynamical behaviour, so twelve state variables are necessary to describe the rigid body motion.

An aircraft is controlled by selecting four control variable time histories: Elevator for pitch and altitude, aileron for roll, rudder for yaw and sideslip and throttle for thrustlevel control; in addition diverse flaps may be set for certain flight regimes (start and landing). To direct such a vehicle in a well controlled maneuver requires skill and concentration even for a trained human pilot; he has to acquire this capability in an extended learning process. In case that he would like to switch to a different type of aircraft, he has to submit to a type rating procedure. Here, he not only has to become acquainted with the positions of knobs and dials but he has to develop a feeling for the normal dynamic behaviour of the vehicle following certain control inputs. Typical motion sequences in time are essential knowledge elements with respect to his task of reacting correctly in given situations.

Exactly this knowledge, coded in differential equations as side constraints to the development of trajectories, should be available to an automatic system for recognizing and controlling landing approaches by computer vision. Though it is possible to obtain the actual position and relative orientation of a camera (up to a scaling factor) from a single image containing the rectangular landing strip and the horizon, it is hard to extract velocity components from a sequence of noise corrupted images by differencing in the conventional manner, especially when control activation is based on these noisy data.

Simultaneously exploiting spatial and temporal models as shown in section 2

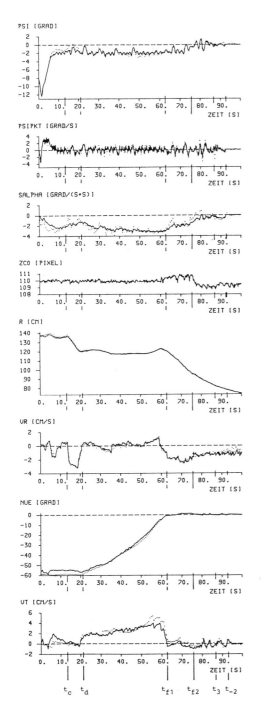

Figure 7: Time histories of state variables for a docking maneuver by computer
vision in real time (from <Wünsche 87>).

and figure 6, G. Eberl has shown that
the problem of controlling landing
approaches by visual feedback to the
computer may be tackled successfully
relying on present day microprocessors
<Eberl 87>. In a six-degree-of freedom
simulation with real-time image sequence
processing hardware in the loop, complete landings starting from 2 km
distance have been performed fully
autonomously with aerodynamic speed V

being the only quantity not determined
from vision. Twelve state variables and
four control time histories have to be
determined depending on the perspective
distortions and its rates in the image
of a rectangular planar landing strip.
The problem has been solved using three
cooperating Kalman filters (of sixth,
fifth and second order) on a Perkin
Elmer computer PE 3252 which was able to
compute both the motion simulation and
the state- and control-evaluation in 100
ms cycle time (fig. 8). It seems unlikely that such a complex task can be
handled by computer vision without using
integrated spatio-temporal process models.

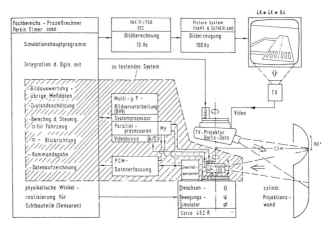

Figure 8: Hardware in the loop simulation for automatic visual landing approach of an aircraft

6. Conclusions
By unifying dynamical models, 3D-shape
representation and (forward) perspective
projection and by using this integrated
model in the sense of observer-/filter-
methods of modern control theory, a
formulation of the recognition process
simultaneously in space and time has
been achieved. Though only data of the
last image of a sequence are being
processed, by exploiting spatio-temporal
models of the process in the scene being
watched, also speed components in 3D-
space can be determined using smoothing
integration (summation) operations over
time. The inversion of the perspective
projection is bypassed by extrapolating
the motion-state with the dynamical
model over time in order to obtain the
model-state variables at the next measurement point in time. For this state
the features to be evaluated in the real
image are computed in the "impoverished
model image" by forward projection. The
measured differences between these
feature positions and the actually
measured ones are used to improve the
model state in space and time (velocity
components) directly; only the partial
derivative matrix of the perspective
projection equations with respect to the

state variables of the dynamical model is needed here; the error decay rate may be selected fixing the corresponding feedback gain matrix as known from modern control theory.

This approach offers a sufficiently rich imbedding for the interpretation process in space and time and is computationally efficient. The models may be time-varying (e.g. vehicle dynamics as function of speed); the method even then works reasonably well provided the model rate of change is slow as compared to the image frequency. The results achieved up to now in four application areas are encouraging; they have been obtained with sampling rates from 8 to 25 Hz. Development steps are being done presently towards the capability of handling more complex situations where (several) objects of unknown shape may occur having unknown dynamical models.

[1]Dr.-Ing., Prof. for Control Engineering This research has been partially supported by BMFT and DFG.

Literature:

<Broida, Chellappa 86> T.J. Broida, R. Chellappa: Estimation of Object Motion Parameters from Noisy Images. IEEE Trans. PAMI Vol.8 No.1, Jan.1986, pp 90-99.
<Dickmanns 85> E.D. Dickmanns: 2D-Object recognition and representation using normalized curvature functions. In M.H. Hamza (ed.): Proc. IASTED Int. Symp. on Robotics and Automation '85, Acta Press, 1985, pp 9-13.
<Dickmanns, Zapp 85> E.D. Dickmanns, A. Zapp: Guiding Landvehicles Along Roadways by Computer Vision. Proc. Congres Automatique 1985, AFCET, Toulouse.
<Dickmanns, Zapp 86> E.D. Dickmanns, A. Zapp: A Curvature-based Scheme for Improving Road Vehicle Guidance by Computer Vision. In: "Mobile Robots", SPIE-Proc. Vol. 727, Cambridge, Mass., Oct. 1986, pp 161-168.
<Dickmanns, Wünsche 86a> E.D. Dickmanns, H.-J. Wünsche: Regelung mittels Rechnersehen. Automatisierungstechnik (at) 34, 1/1986, pp 16-22.
<Dickmanns, Wünsche 86b>: Satellite Rendezvous Maneuvers by Means of Computer Vision. Jahrestagung DGLR München, Okt. 86. Jahrbuch 1986 Bd 1, DGLR, Bonn, pp 251-259.
<Dickmanns, Zapp 87> E.D. Dickmanns, A. Zapp: Autonomous High Speed Road Vehicle Guidance by Computer Vision. Preprint 10th IFAC-Congress, München, July 1987.
<Dickmanns, Eberl 87> E.D. Dickmanns, G. Eberl: Automatischer Landeanflug durch maschinelles Sehen. (To appear in DGLR-Jahrbuch 1987) Jahrestagung der DGLR, Berlin, Oct. 1987.

<Eberl 87> G. Eberl: Automatischer Landeanflug durch Rechnersehen. Dissertation UniBw München, LRT, 1987.
<Gennery 82> D.B. Gennery: Tracking Known Three-Dimensional Objects. American Assoc. for AI, AAAI, Pittsburgh, Aug. 1982, Proc., pp 13-17.
<Graefe 84> V. Graefe: Two Multi-Processor Systems for Low-Level Real-Time Vision. In: J.M. Brady e.a. (eds.): Robotics and Artificial Intelligence, Springer-Verlag, 1984, pp 301-308.
<Kalman 60> R.E. Kalman: A new Approach to Linear Filtering and Prediction Problems. Trans. ASME, Series D, J. Basic Eng., 1960, pp 35-45.
<Kailath 80> Th. Kailath: Linear Systems. Englewood Cliffs, N.J., Prentice Hall, 1980.
<Meissner 82> H.G. Meissner: Steuerung dynamischer Systeme aufgrund bildhafter Informationen.. Dissertation HSBw München, LRT, 1982.
<Meissner, Dickmanns 83> H.G. Meissner, E.D. Dickmanns: Control of an Unstable Plant by Computer Vision. In: T.S. Huang (ed.): Image Sequence Processing and Dynamic Scene Analysis. Springer-Verlag, 1983.
<Mysliwetz, Dickmanns 86> B. Mysliwetz, E.D. Dickmanns: A Vision System with Active Gaze Control for Real-Time Interpretation of Well Structured Dynamic Scenes. Conf. On Intelligent Autonomous Systems, Amsterdam, Dec. 1986, Proc., pp
<Popper 77> K.R. Popper, J.C. Eccles: The Self and Its Brain - An Argument for Interactionism. Springer Internat., Berlin, 1977.
<Rives e.a. 86> P. Rives, E. Breuil, B. Espian: Recursive Estimation of 3D Features Using Optical Flow and Camera Motion. Conf. on Intelligent Autonomous Systems, Amsterdam, Dec. 1986, pp 522-532.
<Wünsche 86> H.-J. Wünsche: Detection and Control of Mobile Robot Motion by Real-Time Computer Vision. In: "Mobile Robots", SPIE-Proc. Vol. 727, Cambridge, Mass., Oct. 1986, pp 100-109.
<Wünsche 87> H.J. Wünsche: Erfassung und Steuerung von Bewegungen durch Rechnersehen. Dissertation UniBw München, LRT, 1987.
<Yonas 83> A. Yonas: Development Stages of Depth Perception in Human Infants. In: D. Ingle etal. (eds.): Brain Mechanisms and Spatial Vision, NATO-ASI, Lyon 1983, Springer Verlag.

LOCATION OF A ROBOT USING SPARSE VISUAL INFORMATION

Kokichi Sugihara

Department of Mathematical Engineering and Information Physics
Faculty of Engineering, University of Tokyo
Hongo, Bunkyo-ku, Tokyo 113, Japan

The paper considers an approach to a problem of locating a robot using visual information. It is assumed that a robot carries a camera and moves on a flat floor in a room. The problem is to find the location of the robot by establishing a correspondence between a model of the room and an image taken by the camera. The present approach is such that vertical edges are extracted from the image and they are matched with vertical lines in the model of the room. A relatively efficient method is constructed and its sensitivity to noises is analyzed. The problem of designing marks is also touched upon.

Introduction

Every mobile robot should possess some mechanism to know, while moving, its own location and posture with respect to the outside world. Many sensing techniques have been developed and used for this purpose. One method is the use of electric marks such as guide cables buried under the floor, but it is not flexible because the cables should be re-buried when the tasks of the robot are changed. Another method is to continually integrate its own motion by detecting inertial force or by counting the number of rotation of the wheels. This method is advantageous in the sense that it does not require any preparation in the outside world, but it is sensitive to noises because errors are accumulated in the the course of integration.

Another approach to this problem is the use of remote sensors, such as a range finder and a camera. These remote sensors are divided into two classes: active and passive. Active sensors transmit prove signals and receive reflected signals; they include an ultrasound radar [Tachi and Komoriya, 1985; Drumheller, 1987], a laser radar [Duda et al., 1978; Hebert and Kanade, 1987], a slit-light range finder [Shirai and Suwa, 1971; Ishii and Nagata, 1974; Sato and Inokuchi, 1984], and projected pattern detectors [Will and Pennington, 1972; Sugihara et al., 1985]. They can obtain relatively reliable information for locating objects with respect to the sensor position. However, these sensors cannot be used when two or more robots work simultaneously, because it is difficult for a robot to judge whether the detected signal is of its own or the one that another robot transmits.

The passive sensors, on the other hand, receive information from the outside world without disturbing the environment; a typical example is an image sensor. If two such sensors are used, range information is also obtained by the principle of binocular vision [Moravec, 1979; Grimson, 1981; Ohta and Kanade, 1983], but the correspondence problem (i.e., the problem of establishing a correspondence between features in two images) requires tremendous time in processing.

An image taken by a single camera, in general, does not convey enough information for a robot to find its location with respect to the unknown outside world, because an image is two-dimensional while the outside world is three-dimensional. However, in many practical situations, especially in industrial situations, geometrical structures of the outside world are *a priori* known. In such situations it is often possible to determine the location of the robot from only one image. There have been proposed many methods for locating a robot in a fixed outside world (or, equivalently, for locating a known object with respect to a fixed camera) [Shimasaki, 1979; Hannah, 1980; Fischler and Bolles, 1981; Nakamura, 1981; Nakamura and Ueda, 1982; Haralick et al., 1984].

It seems that most of these methods assume that features can be extracted correctly from the images. Unfortunately, however, image processing is not always perfect. For example, when an edge detecting operator is applied to an image, all edges are not always detected correctly; some edges may be missing, and some spurious edges may be detected. It is of course important to search for better image processing techniques, but it is likewise important to search for methods that work even if the image processing stage is not perfect.

This paper considers a situation in which only a simple and poor result of the image processing stage is available. Our assumptions are as follows. A robot has a map of a room, and carries a camera whose optical axis is kept parallel to the floor. From an image taken by the camera, only vertical edges are extracted, and in the map is given the points where vertical edges can arise. All vertical edges are identical, that is, we cannot tell locally which vertical edge corresponds to which point in the map. The problem is to search for the point where the image is taken by establishing the correspondence between the vertical edges in the images and those in the map.

We first review a theoretical method that can solve this location problem [Sugihara, 1987], and next modify it so that it works for vertical edge data containing position errors. The method is applied to computer-generated data, and the experimental results are considered from a viewpoint of the design of marks for visual navigation.

2. Point Location Problem

We consider a robot that moves on a flat floor, takes an image by a camera whose optical axis is parallel to the floor, and extracts vertical edges from this image. We do not expect perfectness in the image processing stage, and hence we assume that some edges may be missing. The robot has a map of the room, in which the points of vertical poles are marked. Then, the problem is to establish the matching between the vertical edges in the image and the vertical poles in the map, and thus to find the position at which the image is taken. This problem can be formulated in the following way.

Let e be a point on a two-dimensional plane, and let $r_1, r_2, ..., r_k$

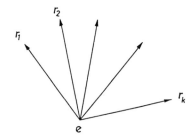

Fig. 1. Bunch of rays.

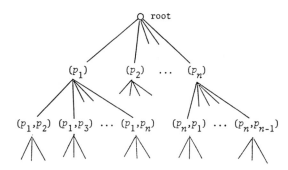

Fig. 2. Interpretation Tree.

be half lines emanating from e. Then, $B=(e;r_1,...,r_k)$ is called a *bunch of rays*, and e and r_i $(i=1,...,k)$ are called the *center* and the *i-th ray*, respectively, of the bunch of rays B (see Fig. 1). A bunch of rays B represents information given by vertical edges in the image; the center corresponds to the point at which the image is taken, and the rays correspond to the directions in which vertical edges are observed. Thus, the set of vertical edges extracted form the image can be represented as the corresponding bunch of rays with respect to a certain coordinate system fixed to the moving robot.

When the robot moves on the floor, the coordinate system fixed to the robot admits two-dimensional translations and rotations. A transformation M is called a *motion* if it is a composition of a rotation and a translation. For any motion M, let $M(B)$ represent the bunch of rays that is obtained when the transformation M is applied to the coordinate system on which B is defined. Furthermore, let $M(e)$ and $M(r_i)$ denote the center and the ith ray, respectively, of $M(B)$. Here we consider only 'two-dimensional' motions; consequently the motion never generates a mirror image of B. Now, our problem can be stated in the following way.

Problem 1. Let $p_1,...,p_n$ be n points on a plane, and $B=(e;r_1,...,r_k)$ be a bunch of rays. Find all the motions M such that every ray in $M(B)$ passes through at least one point.

Problem 1 intuitively means the following. The points $p_1,...,p_n$ represent positions at which vertical poles stand. The poles are slender so that they correspond to simple vertical edges in the image. There is no obstacles that occlude poles form the camera, and hence every pole is visible unless another pole is in front of it. The points $p_1,...,p_n$ in Problem 1 are called *mark points*.

If M^* is a motion required in Problem 1, $M^*(B)$ represents a possible location and posture of the camera with respect to the outside world. Note that we do not expect perfectness in the edge detection. Even if the edge extraction stage fails in finding some edges (and consequently they are not included in the bunch of rays B), Problem 1 still corresponds to the robot location problem; indeed, the points that are not on any ray can be considered as poles that cannot be detected from the image.

3. Interpretation Tree

Suppose that we are given n mark points $p_1,...,p_n$ and a bunch of rays $B=(e;r_1,...,r_k)$. Let $I=(p_{j_1},...,p_{j_m})$ be a sequence of m mark points chosen from $\{p_1,...,p_n\}$ arbitrarily, where $m\leq k$. We consider that I represents an interpretation of the ray data such that the ray r_i is caused by the mark point p_{j_i}. I is called an *interpretation* of B and m is called the *depth* of the interpretation I. In particular, I is called a *partial* interpretation if $m<k$, and a *total* interpretation if $m=k$. Interpretation I of depth i is said to include interpretation J of depth j if $i<j$ and I coincides with the partial sequence composed of the first i elements of J. Re-

garding that interpretation J is a *son* of interpretation I if I includes J and the depth of J is one greater than the depth of I, we get a tree whose root is the interpretation of depth 0, and whose leaves are total interpretations, as shown in Fig. 2. This tree is called an *interpretation tree* [Gaston and Lozano-Perez, 1984].

To solve Problem 1 is nothing but to find the set of total interpretations that are consistent in the sense that each ray passes through the corresponding mark point specified by the interpretations. However, the number of total interpretations (i.e., the number of leaves of the interpretation tree) is equal to $n(n-1)\cdots(n-r+1)$, which is very large; for example, even if $n=20$ and $r=5$, the number of total interpretations is greater than one million. Therefore, to check the consistency of each total interpretation one by one is a time consuming task. Fortunately, this combinatorial explosion can be avoided. In this section we will see that almost all inconsistent interpretations can be pruned out only by checking inconsistency of partial interpretations with small depths.

An interpretation of depth k can be regarded as the representation of one correspondence of k rays to k of mark points, implying that each ray comes from the corresponding mark point. Therefore, to check the inconsistency of this interpretation is a small subproblem of Problem 1, and can be restated formally in the following way.

Problem 2. Let $p_1,...,p_k$ be points on a plane, and $B=(e;r_1,...,r_k)$ be a bunch of rays. Find the motion M such that the ith ray in $M(B)$ passes through p_i for all $i=1,...,k$.

The solution of this problem is well known in elementary geometry.

If $k=1$, a solution of Problem 2 can be obtained by first choosing any translation T and next finding a rotation R around $T(e)$, the translated center of B, such that the ray transformed by $M=RT$ passes through p_1, where RT represents the transformation obtained by applying T and R in this order.

If $k=2$, the possible camera position is restricted to part of a circle. Let C be a circle passing through p_1 and p_2 such that the angle α between p_1 and p_2 at the circumference is equal to the angle between the two rays r_1 and r_2, as shown in Fig. 3. Here, we measure the angle with a fixed order; that is, the angle between r_i and r_j being equal to α means that r_i coincides with r_j if r_i is rotated by the angle α in the clockwise manner around the center e. Hence, if the angle between r_i and r_j is equal to α, the angle between r_j and r_i is equal to $2\pi-\alpha$. In this way we can avoid the ambiguity between the two circles C and C' shown in Fig. 3, one of which is the mirror image of the other with respect to a mirror placed along the line connecting p_1 and p_2 perpendicular to the plane.

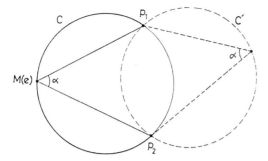

Fig. 3. Circular arc formed by possible camera positions.

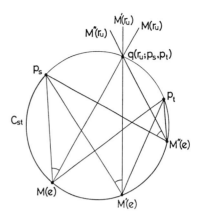

Fig. 5. Fixed point through which a ray should pass.

The circle C is divided at points p_1 and p_2 into two portions. Let C^+ be the portion such that the angle between p_1 and p_2 at the circumference is equal to the angle between r_1 and r_2; C^+ is represented by the bold line in Fig. 3. Obviously, the arc C^+ exhausts the possible positions of the camera. Thus, in the case of $k=2$, there is exactly one degree of freedom in the choice of a solution of Problem 2.

If $k=3$, the camera position, if exists, is determined uniquely except for some special cases. Let C_{ij} be the circle passing through p_i and p_j such that the angle of the arc p_ip_j at the circumference is equal to the angle between r_i and r_j, and let C_{ij}^+ be the portion of C_{ij} such that the angle between p_i and p_j at the circumference is equal to the angle between r_i and r_j. As shown in Fig. 4, the camera should be on both arcs C_{12}^+ and C_{23}^+; the two arcs have at most two points of intersection but one of them is point p_2, and therefore the other point of intersection is the only possible position for the camera. If p_3 is on circle C_{12}, then C_{23} is identical with C_{12} and consequently the camera position cannot be determined uniquely.

In the case where $k \geq 4$, on the other hand, Problem 2 does not necessarily admit a solution. Using the first three rays, r_1, r_2, and r_3, we can in general determine the unique candidate for the possible camera position; the candidate for the possible motion, say M^*, is determined. Then, using the other rays, we can check whether M^* is a true solution. M^* is a solution if the ray $M^*(r_i)$ passes through p_i for all $i = 4, ..., k$; otherwise the problem has no solution.

Problem 2 corresponds to the situation where the mark points are distinguishable from each other. This situation can arise when a boat floating on a dark sea wants to determine its location using the directions of the light from lighthouses; where the lighthouses correspond to the mark points. If the light sources have different colors or different cycles of rotary scan, the correspondence between the rays and the lighthouses can be established easily; thus the problem of finding the location of the boat is reduced to Problem 2.

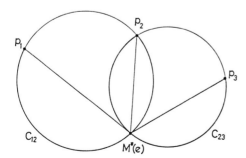

Fig. 4. Unique camera position determined by three rays and the corresponding mark points.

4. Point Location Using Identical Marks

Here we return to Problem 1. As shown in section 3, if three pairs of rays and the associated mark points are given, a unique candidate for the camera position is determined, and if the fourth pair of a ray and the associated mark point is also given, the consistency of the candidate can be checked. Therefore, all the solutions of Problem 1 can be obtained if we first choose and fix any four rays, say $r_1, ..., r_4$, and next, for any interpretation (p_i, p_j, p_l, p_m) of depth 4, solve Problem 2 on the assumption that r_1, r_2, r_3, and r_4 respectively correspond to p_i, p_j, p_l, and p_m. There are $n(n-1)(n-2)(n-3)$ different interpretations of depth 4, and hence the above naive procedure can solve Problem 1 in $O(n^4)$ time.

In what follows we shall show that the time complexity can be decreased to $O(n^3)$. For this purpose the next observation is useful. Let $B = (e; r_1, ..., r_k)$ be a bunch of rays, and suppose that the first two rays pass through p_s and p_t respectively. Then, the center $M(e)$ should be on a certain circular arc, as we have seen in Fig. 3. Let C_{st} be the circle on which $M(e)$ moves. When $M(e)$ moves along the circular arc, the rays of B also move. However, each ray $M(r_u)$ intersects the circle C_{st} at a certain fixed point. This is a direct consequence of the elementary theorem on the angle at a circumference; see Fig. 5. For $u = 3, ..., k$, let the fixed point of intersection between C_{st} and $M(r_u)$ be denoted by $q(r_u; p_s, p_t)$. If the uth ray corresponds to the ith mark point p_i, the ray $M(r_u)$ should be on the line connecting p_i and $q(r_u; p_s, p_t)$.

Next, let $R(r_u; p_s, p_t)$ denote the region swept by the ray $M(r_u)$ when the motion M is taken so that the first and the second rays pass through p_s and p_t respectively. $R(r_u; p_s, p_t)$ represents the region to which the mark point corresponding to the uth ray should belong on the assumption that the first and the second rays correspond to p_s and p_t. The region is shown by the shaded area in Fig. 6, where (a) shows the case in which r_u is on the arc connecting r_1 and r_2, whereas (b) shows the case in which r_u is outside the arc.

Consider a 'rotatable' line that passes through the fixed point $q(r_u; p_s, p_t)$ and that turns around at the fixed point as the center of rotation. Suppose that the rotatable line first passes through the point p_s, and next turns continuously until it reaches the other point p_t. As it turns, it hits all the mark points in the region $R(r_u; p_s, p_t)$ one by one. Let $L(r_u; p_s, p_t)$ be the list of the mark points in $R(r_u; p_s, p_t)$ representing the order in which they are hit by the rotatable line. The list can be constructed at most in $O(n \log n)$ time [Aho, Hopcroft and Ullmann, 1974], because it can be obtained by merging two sorted lists of mark points, one consisting of the points in $R(r_u; p_s, p_t)$ that are inside the circle

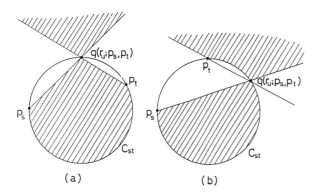

Fig. 6. Region swept by a ray when the camera moves on the circular arc.

C_{st} and the other consisting of the points in the opposite side with respect to the fixed point, where the points are sorted in the arguments with respect to a certain coordinate axis with the origin at $q(r_u; p_s, p_t)$.

Note that the point of intersection of the rotatable line and the circle C_{st} represents the point at which the center $M(e)$ should be if the uth ray is on the rotatable line. Let $w(r_u, p_i; p_s, p_t)$ be the point of intersection between circle C_{st} and the rotatable line that passes through p_i; see Fig. 7. Since $w(r_u, p_i; p_s, p_t)$ represents the point at which the center $M(e)$ should be, we get

$$(1) \quad w(r_3, p_i; p_s, p_t) = w(r_4, p_j; p_s, p_t)$$

if the four rays $r_1, ..., r_4$ correspond to the four mark points p_s, p_t, p_i, p_j, respectively. If eq. (1) does not hold, we can reject the correspondence.

Now, we can construct the following algorithm to solve Problem 1.

Algorithm 1 (Location using identical marks).
Input: n mark points $p_1, ..., p_n$, and a bunch of rays $B = (e; r_1, ..., r_k)$ ($k \geq 4$).
Output: Solution of Problem 1.
Procedure:
1. Make stack F empty.
2. For every ordered pairs (p_s, p_t) ($1 \leq s, t \leq n$, $s \neq t$), do Steps 3, 4, and 5.

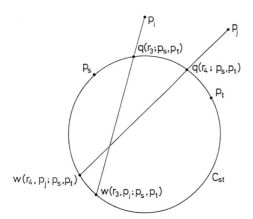

Fig. 7. Rotatable lines associated with the third and the fourth rays.

3. Find the circle C_{st} on which the center $M(e)$ should lie when $M(r_1)$ and $M(r_2)$ pass through p_s and p_t, respectively. Also find the fixed points $q(r_3; p_s, p_t)$ and $q(r_4; p_s, p_t)$ through which $M(r_3)$ and $M(r_4)$ respectively should pass.
4. Construct the ordered lists of hits $L(r_3; p_s, p_t)$ and $L(r_4; p_s, p_t)$.
5. Let p_i be the first point in $L(r_3; p_s, p_t)$ and p_j be the first point in $L(r_4; p_s, p_t)$. Until p_i and p_j respectively visit all the points in $L(r_3; p_s, p_t)$ and $L(r_4; p_s, p_t)$, do 5.1 and 5.2.
   5.1. If $w(r_3, p_i; p_s, p_t) = w(r_4, p_j; p_s, p_t)$, check whether all the other rays $r_5, ..., r_k$ pass through some mark points; if they do, add to the stack F the motion M such that $M(e) = w(r_3, p_i; p_s, p_t)$ and $M(r_1)$ goes through p_s.
   5.2. If the arc length between p_s and $w(r_3, p_i; p_s, p_t)$ is smaller than the arc length between p_s and $w(r_4, p_j; p_s, p_t)$, then let p_i be the next point in $L(r_3; p_s, p_t)$. Otherwise let p_j be the next point in $L(r_4; p_s, p_t)$.
Return F.

We see that the algorithm examines all the correspondences between the rays and the mark points; Step 2 exhausts the correspondences between the first two rays with all the mark points, and Step 5 exhausts the possibility of the correspondence between the third and the fourth rays with all the other points.

Steps 1, 3, and 6 require only $O(1)$ time, and Step 4 can be done in $O(n \log n)$ time by means of any sorting algorithm. Step 5.1 requires $O(n)$ time in the worst case, that is, in the case when $w(r_3, p_i; p_s, p_t) = w(r_4, p_j; p_s, p_t)$ is satisfied. This condition, however, is satisfied only rarely; indeed it is satisfied only when the associated correspondence gives a solution or accidental alignment occurs. Hence, we can assume that the worst cases occur less than some constant times that does not depend on n. Step 5.2 requires $O(1)$ time, and consequently, Step 5 itself is carried out in $O(n)$ time. Since Steps 3, 4, and 5 are repeated $O(n^2)$ times in Step 2, the algorithm can be done in $O(n^3 \log n)$ time. It is easy to see that the space complexity is of $O(n)$.

In the case where preprocessing is allowed, the time complexity can be decreased to $O(n^3)$. Indeed, the dual-representation method [Chazelle, Guibas and Lee, 1985; Edelsbrunner, O'Rourke and Seidel, 1986; Asano, Asano, Guibas, Hershberger, Imai, 1986] enables us to sort the marking points in the arguments with respect to any origin in $O(n)$ time with the cost of $O(n^2)$ space and $O(n^2)$ preprocessing time. Hence, Step 4 can be done in $O(n)$ time, and consequently the algorithm can be done in $O(n^3)$ time with $O(n^2)$ space.

Thus, Algorithm 1 runs in $O(n^3 \log n)$ time with $O(n)$ space, or in $O(n^3)$ time with $O(n^2)$ space.

5. Point Location Using Noisy Rays

5.1. Preliminary Observation

We have considered the location problem on the assumption that angles between rays contain no errors. However, since a bunch of rays is obtained by digital image processing, it is difficult to expect that the relative directions of rays are completely accurate. In this section, we consider how to find the robot position using these noisy ray data.

Suppose that the observed angle, say α, between two rays r_i and r_j passing p_i and p_j, respectively, contains error at most by δ. Then, as shown by shaded area in Fig. 8, the possible positions of the camera center e form a crescent-shape area bounded by two circular arcs at which angles at circumferences between p_i and p_j are $\alpha - \delta$ and $\alpha + \delta$, respectively. Let us denote this crescent-shape area by $Q(p_i, p_j; \alpha, \delta)$. Next, suppose that we observe k rays $r_1, ..., r_k$ that pass through mark points $p_1, ..., p_j$

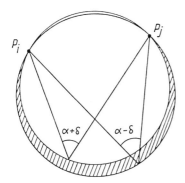

Fig. 8. Possible positions of the camera center determined by a noisy angle between two rays.

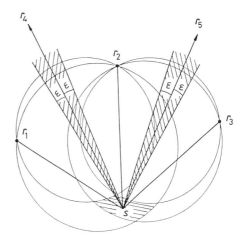

Fig. 10. Range search due to noisy rays.

respectively, and know that observed angle α_i between two rays r_i and r_{i+1} contains an error whose value is at most δ for $i = 1$, ..., $k-1$. Then the set of possible locations of the camera center is obtained as the region

(2) $R_k = \bigcap_{1 \le i \le k-1} Q(p_i, p_{i+1}; \alpha_i, \delta)$.

In Fig. 9, the region is illustrated for $k = 4$.

Thus the theoretical solution of the location problem with noisy rays is given by eq. (2). However, this answer is not practical from a computational complexity point of view. Recall that, when rays contain no noise, the camera center is determined uniquely by establishing (or assuming) a correspondence between three rays and three mark points. For the case of noisy ray data, on the other hand, the possible locations form a region as represented by eq. (2). In other words, the possible points, if exist, cannot be determined uniquely even if we utilize all k rays. This implies that we have to check nonemptyness of R_k defined in eq. (2) for all cases of the correspondences between k rays and n mark points. Since there are $n(n-1) \cdots (n-k)$ such cases, it takes much time to find possible locations; for example, even if $k = 5$ (that is, if the image contain only five vertical edges), we have to check $O(n^5)$ different cases.

In order to circumvent the combinatorial explosion, we can make use of the following expedient. First, using a subset, say

$\{r_1, ..., r_m\}$ ($3 \le m \le k$) of the rays, we determine the region R_m. We choose a point, say s, in R_m as the camera center and treat it as if it is a correct position. Next, we have to check the existence of mark points through which the other rays pass. Here, inaccuracy of the observed directions of the rays are taken into account in such a way that, instead of checking the existence of mark points 'on' the rays, we check the existence of mark point 'near to' the rays. For this purpose, we choose small angle ε and, for each ray, see if any mark point exists in the fan-shaped area that is obtained when the ray is swept around the center s both clockwise and counterclockwise by angle ε. See Fig. 10.

Note that the tolerance angle ε must be larger than the original error range δ, because the camera center s in Fig. 10 is an approximation of the true position. Now the question is what value of ε is enough to cover the original error range δ.

5.2. Error Analysis

In order to answer this question, we next see how much the camera position is disturbed when the observed rays are not accurate. Suppose that two mark points p_i and p_j are observed at the camera center in visual angle α. Let a be the distance between p_i and p_j, and h be the greatest distance from the midpoint of p_i and p_j to a point on the circler arc C_{ij}^+, as shown in Fig. 11. Then, we get

(3) $h = \dfrac{a}{2} \tan \dfrac{\alpha}{2}$.

Let us assume that the angle α is changed to $\alpha+\delta$, where δ is small, and as a result of it, h is changed to $h+\Delta h$, that is

(4) $h+\Delta h = \dfrac{a}{2} \cot \dfrac{\alpha+\delta}{2}$.

Since

$\sin(\dfrac{\alpha}{2}+\dfrac{\delta}{2}) = \sin\dfrac{\alpha}{2}+\dfrac{\delta}{2}\cos\dfrac{\alpha}{2}+O(\delta^2)$,

$\cos(\dfrac{\alpha}{2}+\dfrac{\delta}{2}) = \cos\dfrac{\alpha}{2}-\dfrac{\delta}{2}\sin\dfrac{\alpha}{2}+O(\delta^2)$,

we get

$h+\Delta h = \dfrac{a}{2}(\cos\dfrac{\alpha}{2}-\dfrac{\alpha}{2}\sin\dfrac{\alpha}{2}+O(\delta^2))(\sin\dfrac{\alpha}{2}+\dfrac{\delta}{2}\cos\dfrac{\alpha}{2}+O(\delta^2))^{-1}$

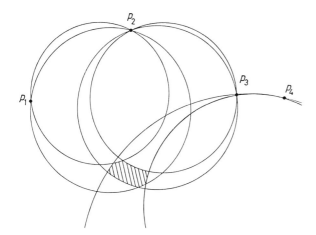

Fig. 9. Region formed by the possible locations of the camera center determined by four noisy rays.

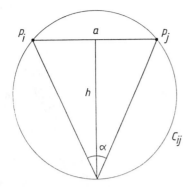

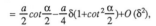

Fig. 11. Point on the circumference that is furthest from the two mark points.

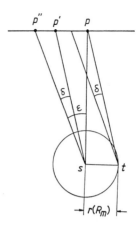

Fig. 12. Tolerance angle.

$$= \frac{a}{2}cot\frac{\alpha}{2} - \frac{a}{4}\delta(1+cot^2\frac{\alpha}{2}) + O(\delta^2),$$

and hence the magnitude of Δh can be approximated by

(5) $|\Delta h| = \frac{a}{4}\delta(1+cot^2\frac{\alpha}{2})$.

Since $cot^2\frac{\alpha}{2}$ is monotonically decreasing in α for $0\le\alpha\le\pi$, eq. (5) implies that the deviation of the camera center caused by the error δ in the observed ray angle decrease as α increases. For example, in the circumstance where $a = 500$cm and $\delta=1^o$, $|\Delta h| = 14.8$cm if $\alpha=45^o$ whereas $|\Delta h| = 72.3$cm if $\alpha=20^o$. Thus, the crescent-shape region becomes slant as the ray angle α becomes larger. Therefore, we can expect that the region R_m becomes smaller if we use m rays whose mutual angles are larger.

Next let us consider how large the tolerance angle ε should be to compensate inaccuracy of the camera center s in Fig. 10.

Let δ is the maximum error angle of the observed rays. Suppose that, using m rays $r_1, ..., r_m$, we get the region R_m in which the camera center should be, as we saw in eq. (2). Let $C(R_m)$ be the smallest circle that contain R_m, and $r(R_m)$ be the radius of $C(R_m)$. We choose the center of the circle $C(R_m)$ as the approximated position of the camera center. Then, the radius $r(R_m)$ represents the maximum difference between the true camera center and the approximated center.

Let us suppose that mark point p stands in distance from the approximated camera center s, and that the true position of the camera center t is in distance $r(R_m)$ from s in the direction perpendicular to the line connecting s and p, as shown in Fig. 12. The true ray passing though p is tp, but in the worst case it is observed as tp' in Fig. 12. Since the approximated position of the camera center is at s, the ray tp' is displaced to sp''. Let ε be the angle between two lines tp and tp'', From Fig. 12 we get

$$\frac{r(R_m)}{l} = \tan(\varepsilon-\delta).$$

Since both ε and δ are small, $\tan(\varepsilon-\delta) \approx \varepsilon-\delta$, and consequently we get

(6) $\varepsilon = \delta + \frac{r(R_m)}{l}$.

Eq. (6) tells us that the tolerance angle ε decreases as the error range δ or the radius $r(R_m)$ decreases, and increases as the distance l decreases.

Note that if the camera center is very close to the mark point, l decreases and hence ε becomes larger; in that case the use of the tolerance angle will become useless. However, if a mobile robot is equipped with tactile or ultrasonic sensors, it can keep itself off from walls and thus prevents the distance l from becoming too small. If the lower bound of l is set appropriately, the tolerance angle ε in eq. (6) can be small enough for the practical purpose. For example, if $l = 200$cm, $r(R_m) = 10$cm, and $\delta=1^o$, we get $\varepsilon=3.9^o$.

5.3. Location Algorithm

Keeping the above error analysis in mind, we construct an algorithm for locating the robot using noisy ray data.

Recall that for accurate ray data, we need to traverse the interpretation tree from the root node down to only level 4 nodes, because most of interpretations can be judges as inconsistent if we check the first four rays and the corresponding mark points.

If the rays contain noises, on the other hand, it is not always sufficient to traverse down to level 4 nodes because the possible camera positions form a region, but not a point. For interpretation $I=(p_{i_1}, ..., p_{i_m})$, let us define

(7) $R(I) = \bigcap Q(p_{i_j}, p_{i_{j+1}}; \alpha_i, \delta)$,

where the intersection is taken over all $j = 1, ..., m-1$. $R(I)$ represents the region to which the camera center is restricted if we adopt the interpretation I.

In terms of the interpretation tree, we can construct an algorithm to find the camera locations from noisy ray data in the following way.

Algorithm 2 (Location using noisy rays).
Input: n mark points $p_1, ..., p_n$ on the plane, a bunch of rays $B = (e; r_1, ..., r_k)$ (where $k\ge4$, and mutual angle α_i between r_i and r_{i+1} may be different from the true value by δ at largest), limit ρ of the diameter, and the tolerance angle ε.
Output: Solution of Problem 1.
Procedure:
1. Make stack F empty.
2. Traverse the interpretation tree from the root node toward leaves in the depth first order, and do Step 3 for every node I that is visited.
3. Construct $R(I)$.
    Case 3.1) If $R(I)$ is empty, prune all subtrees of I and go to the next node.

Case 3.2) If $r(R(I))>\rho$, then
  (i) if I is a leaf, add I to F, and
  (ii) if I is not a leaf, go down to the next node.
Case 3.3) Otherwise (i.e., if $R(I)$ is nonempty and $r(R(I))\leq\rho$), choose the center of the smallest circle containing $R(I)$ as the approximated camera center, and for every node in the subtree whose root is I, do the range search (shown in Fig. 10) with the tolerance angle ε. If there is a total interpretation (contained in I) in which every ray contains a mark point in its fan-shaped area defined by the tolerance angle ε, add it to F.
Return F.

This algorithm checks consistency of interpretations in two modes. In the first mode, the region $R(I)$ formed by possible camera positions is updated until it becomes small enough. In the second mode, a tentative camera position is chosen inside $R(I)$ and existence of mark points that correspond to the remaining rays is checked. The time complexity depends on how many branches are pruned in the course of the processing.

6. Computer Simulation

Preliminary experiments are carried out using computer-generated data.

An example is shown in Fig. 13; (a) illustrates the shape of a room having 33 mark points on walls (mark points are represented by small black squares, and walls by double lines), and (b), ..., (e) represent the possible camera positions for various ray data that are shown at the bottom of the figures. In (b), the given bunch of rays consists of only three rays, and the number of possible positions is 694. In (c), one more ray is added, and the number of possible locations decreases to 40. Here, the candidates of possible camera positions are calculated using the first three rays on the assumption that they do not contain errors, and the range search for the fourth ray is carried out with the tolerance angle $0.5°$. In a similar manner, five rays are used in (d), resulting only two possible camera positions as shown there. However, as the tolerance angle becomes a little larger, the number of possible camera positions increases rapidly. Fig. 13(e) shows the possible positions for the same ray data as in (d) determined with the tolerance angle $2°$; the number of possible camera positions increases to 25.

7. Concluding Remarks

We have considered the problem of locating a mobile robot using a map of mark points and visual angles of the mark points. First, efficient method, which works in $O(n^3)$ time where n is the number of mark points, is constructed for the case in which

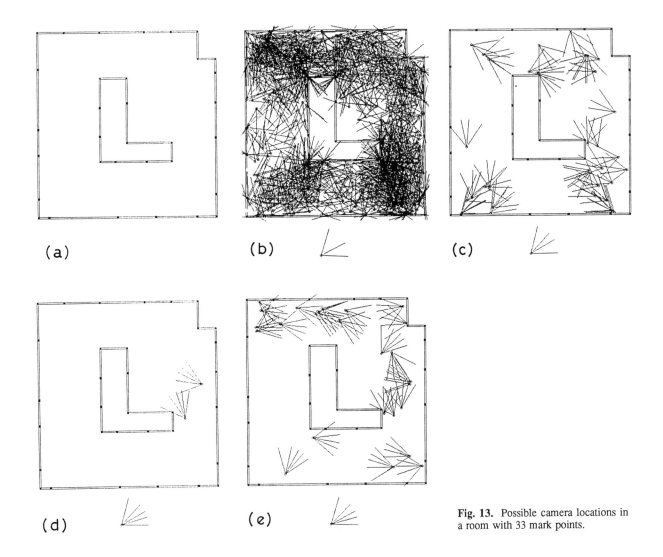

Fig. 13. Possible camera locations in a room with 33 mark points.

the directions of the rays contain no errors, and next, it is modified for noisy ray data.

One of our main motivations of this study is to see how much load is imposed in later stages of the analysis if we extract only simple (and hence sparse) information in an image processing stage. In this paper we have observed that the load imposed in later stages is very large; even in the case where ray directions contain no noises, it takes $O(n^3)$ time to find all possible positions of the robot. In the case of noisy ray data, our result is worse; we cannot bound the time complexity in $O(n^3)$ because the pruning mechanism does not work until we go down along the interpretation tree to nodes with four or greater depth. Moreover, if the error range becomes larger, the number of possible positions increases rapidly, resulting the formulation of the problem itself being nonsense.

It seems that one of the most effective way to overcome the difficulties is to place distinguishable marks in the room. For example, if vertical lines are drawn on the walls with different color and an image is taken by a color camera, we can easily find the correspondence between vertical edges in the image and the vertical lines on the walls. Another example of distinguishable marks is sources of light going on and off in different cycles; observing the cycles of twinkling, we can distinguish one mark point from another. If one of the rays is distinguishable, the number of interpretations decreases by factor of n, and if two are distinguishable, it decreases by factor of n^2. Thus, we can expect that the load of finding robot location will much decrease if there are several mark points that can be distinguished from each other. To search for easily distinguishable marks and for an effective way of their layout seems the most important and the most promising direction of extending the present study.

Acknowledgments

The author would like to express his thanks to Prof. Masao Iri of the University of Tokyo, Prof. Takao Asano of Sophia University, Prof. Tetsuo Asano of Osaka Electro-Communication University, Prof Hiroshi Imai of Kyushu University, and Prof. Ken-ichi Kanatani of Gumma University for valuable comments. The work is partly supported by the Grant in Aid for Scientific Research of the Ministry of Education, Science and Culture of Japan (Grant No. 62580017), and by the Secom Science and Technology Foundation.

References

Aho, A. V., Hopcroft, J. E., and Ullman, J. D., 1974. *The Design and Analysis of Computer Algorithms,* Addison-Wesley, Reading.

Asano, T., Asano, T., Guibas, L., Hershberger, J., and Imai, H., 1986. Visibility of disjoint polygons, *Algorithmica,* **1**, pp. 49-63.

Chazelle, B., Guibas, L. J., and Lee, D. T., 1985. The power of geometric duality, *BIT,* **25**, pp. 76-90.

Drumheller, M., 1987. Mobile robot localization using sonar, *IEEE Trans. Pattern Anal. Machine Intell.,* **PAMI-9**, pp. 325-332.

Duda, R. O., et al., 1978. Use of range and reflectance data to find planar surface regions, *IEEE Trans. Pattern Anal. Machine Intell.,* **PAMI-1**, pp. 259-271.

Edelsbrunner, H., O'Rourke, J., and Seidel, R., 1986. Constructing arrangements of lines and hyperplanes with applications, *SIAM J. Comput.,* **15**, pp. 341-363.

Fischler, M. A., and Bolles, R. C., 1981. Random sample consensus --- A paradigm for model fitting with applications to image analysis and automated cartography, *Comm. ACM,* **24**, pp. 381-395.

Gaston, P. C. and Lozano-Perez, T., 1984. Tactile recognition and localization using object models --- The case of polyhedra on a plane, *IEEE Trans. Pattern Anal. Machine Intell.,* **PAMI-6**, pp. 257-266.

Grimson, W. E. L., 1981. *From Images to Surfaces*, MIT Press, Cambridge.

Hannah, M. J., 1980. Bootstrap stereo, *Proc. DARPA Image Understanding Workshop*, Maryland, Science Appl. Inc., pp. 201-208.

Haralick, R. M. et al., 1984. Matching wire frame objects from their two dimensional perspective projections, *Pattern Recogn.,* **17**, pp. 607-619.

Hebert, M. and Kanade, T., 1987. 3-d vision for an autonomous vehicle, *Proc. IEEE Int. Workshop Industrial Appl. Machine Vision Machine Intell.,* Tokyo, pp. 375-380.

Ishii, M., and Nagata, T., 1974. Feature extraction of 3-dimensional objects with a laser tracker (in Japanese), *Trans. Soc. Instrument Control Eng. Japan,* **10**, pp. 599-605.

Moravec, H. P., 1979. Visual mapping by a robot rover, *6th Int. Joint Conf. Artif. Intell.,* Tokyo, pp. 589-600.

Nakamura, T., 1981. A method of slit code detection for the position measurement of a robot vehicle (in Japanese), *Trans. Soc. Instrument Control Eng. Japan,* **17**, pp. 492-498.

Nakamura, T., and Ueda, M., 1982. Matching method of vertical edge patterns for locating a mobile robot (in Japanese), *Trans. Soc. Instrument Control Eng. Japan,* **18**, pp. 576-582.

Ohta, T., and Kanade, T., 1983. Stereo by intra- and inter-scanline search using dynamic programming, CMU-CS-83-162, Carnegie-Mellon Univ., Computer Science Dept., Pittsburgh.

Sato, S., and Inokuchi, S., 1984. Range imaging by Gray coded projection (in Japanese), Nation. Convent. 1984 Instit. Electron. Comm. Eng. Japan, Part 6, pp. 283-284.

Shimasaki, M., 1979. Some discussions on inverse of projection (in Japanese), Tech. Rep. of Working Group on Image Engineering, IE79-15, Instit. Electron. Comm. Eng. Japan.

Shirai Y., and Suwa, M., 1971. Recognition of polyhedrons with a range finder, *2nd Int. Joint Conf. Artif. Intell.,* pp. 80-87.

Sugihara, K., 1987. Some location problem for single-eye robot navigation, *Proc. IEEE Int. Workshop Industrial Appl. Machine Vision Machine Intell.,* Tokyo, pp. 250-255.

Sugihara, K., Okazaki, K., Feng, K., and Sugie, N., 1985. Regular pattern projection for surface measurement, in Hanafusa, H. and Inoue, H. (eds.), *Robotics Research --- The Second International Symposium*, MIT Press, Cambridge, pp. 17-24.

Tachi, S. and Komoriya, K., 1985. Guide dog robot, in Hanafusa, H. and Inoue, H. (eds.), *Robotics Research --- The Second International Symposium*, MIT Press, Cambridge, pp. 334-340.

Will, P. M., and Pennington, K. S., 1972. Grid coding --- A novel technique for image processing, *Proc. IEEE,* **60**, pp. 669-680.

The Cycle of Uncertainty and Constraint in Robot Perception

Larry Matthies and Takeo Kanade

Computer Science Department
Carnegie-Mellon University
Pittsburgh, PA 15213

Abstract

Uncertainty and constraint are central themes in robot perception. To interpret sensor data, robots apply constraints that allow them to build an initial model of the world. In principle, the model makes it easier to interpret new data, which in turn improves the model and further simplifies the interpretation process. Explicit representations of uncertainty quantify this cycle by characterizing the amount of information in the model, the amount of constraint the model supplies to interpretation, and the amount of information gained from new data.

We illustrate this cycle with two implemented systems. The first system estimates the motion of a mobile robot by using stereo to track landmarks in the environment. It models the uncertainty in the landmark locations, uses Kalman filtering to reduce this uncertainty, and uses the landmark model to constrain stereo correspondence. The second system employs Kalman filtering to extract depth from known camera motion. The camera is translated in very fine steps horizontally and vertically, parallel to the image plane, in a pattern resembling trinocular stereo. Depth is computed incrementally at edges tracked as the camera moves. Note that the two systems can be combined by using fine camera motion to get coarse depth information to guide stereo. This combination gives a simple but powerful illustration of the use of constraint when there are large uncertainties in the world model. We conclude by reviewing the cyclical structure of these systems and discussing how uncertainty and constraint are manifested at each point in the cycle.

1. Introduction

Uncertainty and constraint are important, complementary aspects of 3D robot perception. In a statistical sense, uncertainty implies measurement noise in sensor data, which leads to uncertainty in 3D models created from the data. In a broader sense, uncertainty also implies a lack of knowledge, which is reflected in the absence of a 3D model before sensing begins.

Constraint is related to both types of uncertainty. In the latter sense, it is difficult to interpret sensor data when the structure of the world is unknown. Classical examples are stereo matching and object recognition, which entail large amounts of search when applied to unknown scenes. In this case, constraint is imposed by invoking world model assumptions or by employing sensing strategies that limit the search. Once a 3D model of the scene is constructed, in principle it can guide the interpretation of subsequent data. However, the former sense of uncertainty now comes to bear. Noise makes the existing model and the sensor data uncertain, so to properly employ constraint we must quantify the levels of uncertainty in both.

In this paper, we examine the effects of uncertainty and constraint in two implemented systems. The first is a stereo vision system that estimates the incremental motion of a mobile robot travelling through an unknown environment [17]. The system extracts landmark points from the images and tracks the landmarks to estimate motion. Two important aspects of the system are its use of 3D normal distributions to model the uncertainty in landmark locations and its use of Kalman filters to reduce this uncertainty over time. Experimental results show convincingly both the quality of the motion estimates and the importance of the uncertainty model in achieving those estimates.

Whereas the first system applies models of uncertainty to motion estimation, the second applies them to incrementally acquiring depth from known, fine motion of a single camera. The camera translates horizontally and vertically, parallel to the image plane, in a pattern that resembles trinocular stereo [21]. The system tracks edgels through the image sequence and uses Kalman filtering to incrementally refine the depth of each edgel. The system performs well with difficult scenes; it also illustrates the value of orthogonal camera motions in acquiring more complete depth maps than possible from motion in one direction alone. In this system, the sensing strategy limits search and the uncertainty model leads to better depth information over time.

These systems illustrate the importance of uncertainty in motion and depth estimation and show how constraint can be imposed through both the sensing strategy and the world model. They also lead us to two interesting observations. First, the systems can be combined. Known, fine motion can be used to acquire coarse depth information to guide stereo fusion [11]. This reflects our philosophy of using sensing strategies to supply constraint when the 3D model is largely unknown. Second, both of our systems are essentially point-based, because we track and model the uncertainty of edgels and landmark points. Although similar methods have also been applied to lines and planes [10], we are very clearly limited in our ability to represent uncertainty in 3D shape. Cellular representations, such as *occupancy grids* [8, 9, 23], may be a solution to this problem. We will expand on these issues in the final section of this paper.

2. Stereo navigation

Our first illustration is a stereo vision system built for robot navigation [17, 24, 28]. This system uses stereo cameras onboard a robot to track landmark points, then uses the apparent motion of the landmarks to estimate the frame to frame motion of the robot. The system models the uncertainty in the landmark positions, employs Kalman filters to reduce this uncertainty over time, and uses knowledge of the landmark positions together with predictions of the robot's motion to locate the landmarks in new stereo images. In this section we will review the main features of the system and discuss extensions currently in progress.

2.1. System overview

The structure of the system is shown in Fig. 1. The main data structures are a set of 3-D points $\{P_i\}$, called the local model and described in robot-centered coordinates, and the robot's position in a fixed, global reference frame. The points in the local model are

This research was supported in part by the Office of Naval Research under contract N00014-81-K-0503 and in part by a postgraduate fellowship from the FMC Corporation. The views and conclusions contained in this document are those of the authors and should not be interpreted as representing the official policies, either expressed or implied, of the funding agencies.

obtained by stereo matching and are used as landmarks. When a new stereo pair is digitized, points from the local model are matched in the images to determine their current locations $\{Q_i\}$ relative to the robot. A motion estimation algorithm computes the rotation and translation (R and T) relating the new and old robot coordinates. A landmark updating system transforms the old local model into the current coordinate frame and combines it with the new stereo measurements to create a new local model. Finally, the motion estimate is used to update the robot's global position. The cycle then repeats with the acquisition of a new pair of images. We will examine four operations of the system: representing 3D uncertainty, estimating the robot motion, updating the landmark positions, and using the landmark model to constrain stereo matching in new images.

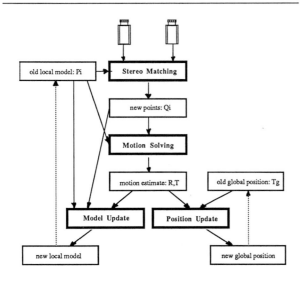

Figure 1: Structure of the stereo navigation system

2.2. Representing uncertainty in stereo triangulation

The geometry of stereo triangulation is shown schematically in Fig. 2 for the case of 2-D points projecting onto 1-D images. The tick marks on the image planes denote pixel boundaries and the radiating lines extend these boundaries into space. Suppose point P projects onto the left image at x_l and the right image at x_r. Because of errors in measurement, the stereo system will determine x_l and x_r with some error, which in turn causes error in the estimated location of P. Fig. 2 illustrates this for errors caused by image quantization; because of resolution limits, the estimated location of P can lie anywhere in the shaded region surrounding the true location [4, 27]. Random contributions to measurement error will blur the boundaries of this region, but the qualitative shape will be similar.

We construct a model of the landmark's position by treating it as a 3D, normally distributed random vector. The mean value of the distribution (the landmark's position) is taken to be the coordinate vector computed by standard stereo triangulation methods. The covariance matrix of the distribution is computed in the following manner. Let the image coordinates be given by $l=[x_l, y_l]$ and $r=[x_r, y_r]$ in the left and right image, respectively. Consider these as normally distributed random vectors with means μ_l and μ_r and covariance matrices V_l and V_r. From l and r we need to estimate the coordinates $[X, Y, Z]^T$ of the 3-D point P. We use the ideal, noise-free triangulation equations $P=[X,Y,Z]^T=f(l,r)$, or

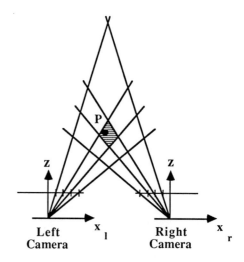

Figure 2: Stereo geometry showing triangulation uncertainty

$$X = b(x_l+x_r)/(x_l-x_r)$$

$$Y = b(y_l+y_r)/(x_l-x_r) \qquad (1)$$

$$Z = 2b/(x_l-x_r)$$

(assuming a unit focal length and a baseline of $2b$) to infer the distributions of X, Y, and Z as functions of the random vectors l and r. If equation (1) was linear, P would be normal [7] with mean $\mu_p=f(\mu_l,\mu_r)$ and covariance

$$V_p = J\begin{bmatrix} V_l & 0 \\ 0 & V_r \end{bmatrix} J^T \qquad (2)$$

where J is the matrix of first partial derivatives of f or the Jacobian. Since f is nonlinear these expressions do not hold exactly, but we use them as satisfactory approximations.

The true values of the means and covariances of the image coordinates needed to plug into (1) and (2) are unknown. We approximate the means with the coordinates returned by the stereo matcher and the covariances with identity matrices. This is equivalent to treating the image coordinates as uncorrelated with variances of one pixel. Better covariance approximations can be obtained by several methods [1, 12].

Geometrically, the normal distribution represents the uncertainty in landmark positions as ellipsoidal contours of constant probability centered on the nominal position of the landmark. This is illustrated in Fig. 3, where the ellipse represents a contour of the distribution and the diamond represents the quantization error of Fig. 2. For nearby points, the contours will be close to spherical; the farther away the points, the more eccentric the contours become. The *true* error distribution will have longer tails than the normal distribution; however, the normal approximation yields good results in practice.

2.3. Estimating robot motion

After processing two stereo pairs, the robot has two sets of 3-D points that have been obtained by stereo matching: a local model of points $\{P_i\}$ defined relative to its previous position and the coordinates $\{Q_i\}$ of these points relative to its current position. The correspondences between P_i and Q_i are known, but the motion

Figure 3: Quantization error with normal approximation

between them is not. Thus, we have a set of equations

$$\{ Q_i = R P_i + T \}$$

in which P_i and Q_i are known point vectors, R is the matrix of the unknown rotation, and T is the unknown translation. We will describe how we use the landmark uncertainty in computing R, T, and the uncertainty in R and T.

For simplicity, we will begin with purely translational motion, for which the motion equation is

$$Q_i = P_i + T$$

We rewrite this as

$$Q_i - P_i = M_i = T$$

to emphasize the role of $M_i = Q_i - P_i$ as measurements of T. From our earlier discussion, P_i and Q_i are modelled as normally distributed, uncorrelated random vectors with covariances U_i and V_i, respectively. Therefore, M_i will also be normally distributed with covariance $U_i + V_i$. If we consider M_i to be a sequence of noisy measurements of T, each corrupted by noise with zero mean and covariance $U_i + V_i$, application of the maximum likelihood method leads to minimizing the following expression over possible values of T [7]:

$$\sum_{i=1}^{n} \varepsilon_i^{\mathrm{T}} W_i \varepsilon_i \qquad (3)$$

where $\varepsilon_i = M_i - T$ and $W_i = (U_i + V_i)^{-1}$. The solution to this is

$$T = (\sum_{i=1}^{n} W_i)^{-1} \sum_{i=1}^{n} W_i M_i$$

and the covariance matrix of the estimation errors is

$$V_T = (\sum_{i=1}^{n} W_i)^{-1}$$

The covariance matrix can be analyzed to assess the quality of the motion estimate.

Generalizing this method to handle motion with translation *and* rotation is complicated by the fact that the equations become nonlinear. The expression to be minimized is

$$\sum_{i=1}^{n} \varepsilon_i^{\mathrm{T}} W_i \varepsilon_i \qquad (4)$$

$$\textit{with } \varepsilon_i = Q_i - R P_i - T$$
$$\textit{and } W_i = (R U_i R^{\mathrm{T}} + V_i)^{-1}$$

We have not been able to find direct solutions to this problem. Our approach is to use a direct solution involving a simpler error model [25] to get an initial estimate of the transformation, then to iteratively refine the estimate with the Gauss-Newton method [13]. Convergence is fast unless all points are very distant; for example, in the experiments with real data described later, the final estimates were obtained after four to eight iterations. We obtain a covariance estimate for the motion parameters in this case by linearizing the solution about the final estimate and performing an approximate error propagation [20] from the covariances of the landmarks to the covariance of the motion parameters.

2.4. Updating landmark positions

The landmark update involves transforming the old local model to the current coordinate frame, inflating its uncertainty to account for the uncertainty of the transformation, and filtering the old model with the new measurements to create the updated model. Let P_{t-1}^+ be the coordinate vector of a single point in the old local model at time $(t-1)$ and let V_{t-1}^+ be its covariance. For purely translational motion, P_{t-1}^+ is transformed to the current frame by

$$P_t^- = P_{t-1}^+ + T \qquad (5)$$

where T is the translation from time $(t-1)$ to time t. The translation has covariance matrix V_T, so the transformed point has covariance

$$V_t^- = V_{t-1}^+ + V_T \qquad (6)$$

Equation (5) introduces some correlation between points that is not accounted for in (6), but we assume this is small enough to ignore. To extend this to rotation, we rewrite (5) as

$$P_t^- = R P_{t-1}^+ + T \qquad (7)$$

This is nonlinear, so to compute V_t^- we proceed by analogy to equation (2); that is, we pre-multiply the covariance of R, T, and P_{t-1}^+ by the Jacobian of the transformation and post-multiply by the Jacobian transposed. Since we treat P_{t-1}^+ as uncorrelated with R and T, this leads to

$$V_t^- = J_m V_m J_m^{\mathrm{T}} + R V_{t-1}^+ R^{\mathrm{T}}$$

where J_m contains the derivatives of (7) with respect to the motion parameters and V_m is the covariance of the motion parameters.

Now let Q_t be the measurement of the same point at time t and let U_t be the covariance of this measurement. Some manipulation of the basic Kalman filter equations leads to the following estimates of the updated point location and covariance:

$$V_t^+ = \{ (V_t^-)^{-1} + U_t^{-1} \}^{-1} \qquad (8)$$

$$P_t^+ = P_t^- + V_t^+ U_t^{-1} (Q_t - P_t^-) \qquad (9)$$

This procedure assumes that the error in the motion estimate is uncorrelated with the error in the landmark points. When the motion estimate is obtained by the stereo system this will not be true, but if other sensors also contribute to the motion estimate it will be approximately true.

2.5. Constraining correspondence in the next image

Knowledge of the landmark positions, together with predictions of the robot's motion between frames, allows the robot to constrain its search for the landmarks in new images. We currently implement this by limiting the search to fixed-sized image windows around the projected location of each landmark. This can be extended to use the probabilistic information in the landmark model by computing a covariance matrix for the projected image coordinates.

The first step of this process is to predict the landmark positions relative to the robot at time $t+1$. This step is identical to the prediction stage of the Kalman filter above. Since the robot's motion will be uncertain, this increases the uncertainty in the landmark positions. Following this, the landmarks are projected on the new images and the covariance of the *image* coordinates is estimated from the covariance of the 3D coordinates. This is the inverse of the error propagation we performed in section 2.2 to compute the original 3D error model. Briefly, we denote the perspective projection as

$$(x_l, y_l, x_r, y_r) = f(X, Y, Z),$$

take the Jacobian J of this transformation, and approximate the uncertainty of the image coordinates with the covariance propagation

$$\Sigma_{image} \approx J \Sigma_{X,Y,Z} J^T$$

Confidence intervals derived from the resulting covariance matrix can be used to define search windows or to weight the acceptability of alternate matching candidates. These procedures are being explored.

2.6. Experimental results

These algorithms were tested in the FIDO stereo obstacle avoidance system built in CMU's Mobile Robot Lab [16, 24, 28]. FIDO uses the Moravec interest operator and correlation procedure [22] to track point features through stereo pairs. The points serve as landmarks for motion estimation and as obstacles for path planning [29]. We will show the performance of the motion estimation subsystem on two stereo image sequences obtained by driving a vehicle through the Mobile Robot Lab. For comparison, we will also show results obtained on the same data with a previous version of the system that modelled the uncertainty in landmark positions with scalars instead of full 3D normal distributions (see [17, 22] for details of the scalar model).

Fig. 4 shows the layout of the room used for these experiments. The dimensions of the room are approximately 17x30 feet. Fig. 5 shows the floorplan of the room and the actual path of the vehicle for the first experiment; the dots in the path mark where each stereo pair was digitized. For this experiment, the paths estimated by the vision system are shown in Figs. 6 and 7 for the scalar and

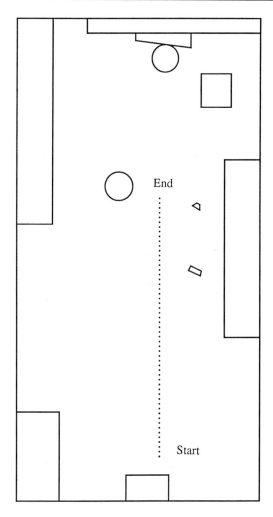

Figure 5: Floorplan of the room. The dotted line shows the actual path of of robot in the first experiment. Each dot marks the robot's position when one stereo pair was taken.

the 3D normal uncertainty models, respectively. Performance with the scalar model is very poor; on the other hand, performance with the 3D normal model is extremely good.

Figs. 8 and 9 show the results of the second experiment. The results are comparable to the first experiment, except for two larger errors that occurred with the 3D normal model. We attribute these to undetected errors in stereo correspondence that have corrupted the motion estimates. We expect that multivariate outlier detection methods [3] based on covariance matrices of the landmark model will give better rejection of correspondence errors. This is under development.

2.7. Discussion

Two strong conclusions can be drawn from these results. The first is the specific observation that accurate visual motion estimation *is* feasible, contrary to much previous experience in computer vision. Exactly how accurate it can be remains to be seen. A mathematical answer to this question can be obtained by perturbation or covariance analysis techniques and Monte Carlo simulations. However, a practical answer also involves the question of how to obtain more reliable correspondence. We are

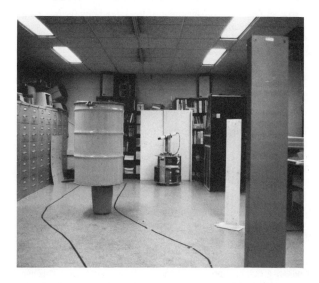

Figure 4: Room used for the motion experiments

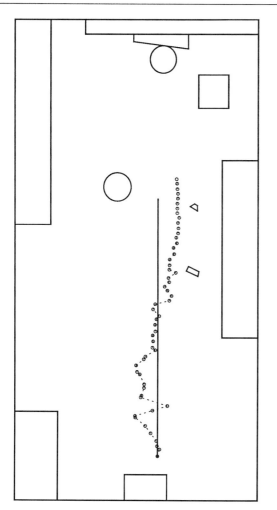

Figure 6: First experiment: path estimated with landmark position uncertainty modelled by scalars.

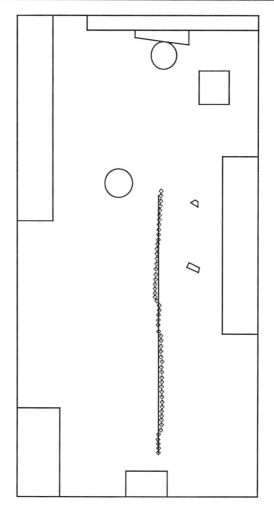

Figure 7: First experiment: path estimated with the landmark position uncertainty modelled by 3D normal distributions.

currently addressing this by enhancing the constraints in the stereo matcher and by developing statistical outlier detection methods that use the 3D landmark covariances to reject incorrectly tracked landmarks. Beyond this, more effective landmark tracking will require more extensive stereo matching and 3D modeling.

The second conclusion is that models of uncertainty have an important role to play in computer vision in general. This section has demonstrated their value in estimating motion and updating the 3D positions of sparse sets of points. Related methods have been applied to updating 3D line and plane descriptions [10], representing uncertain transformations in mapping [20, 26], and recognizing objects [2]. By explicitly representing the level of uncertainty in shape or motion descriptions, such work allows different pieces of data, with different levels of uncertainty, to be combined in a near-optimal fashion. The natural question to ask is how can these techniques contribute to more extensive shape and motion estimation? Applications of Kalman filtering to motion estimation are dealt with at length in the optimal estimation [19] and aerospace navigation [30] literatures. However, the shape estimation problem is less well developed. In the following section, we will discuss one approach to using Kalman filters to obtain image-based depth maps. We will touch briefly on modeling uncertainty in 3D representations in the final section of the paper.

3. Incremental depth from known motion

Our second system illustrates the use of uncertainty models and constraint in the incremental acquisition of depth from known camera motion. The central problem in getting depth from images is finding correspondences in two views. In stereo, this is typically overcome by assuming restrictions on the shape of the world, minimum and maximum disparity limits, and by using powerful but slow search and optimization algorithms. Known, fine camera motion [5] and trinocular stereo [21] both alleviate these problems by adding constraint. In fact, they can be complementary techniques. In this section we combine the small, lateral motion insights of the *epipolar plane image* method [5] with Kalman filtering to represent uncertainty and to achieve incremental depth acquisition. We also use orthogonal motions of the camera to obtain more complete depth information than available from motion in a single direction.

3.1. Equations for recursive depth estimation

We assume that the scene is stationary while the camera undergoes small changes in position. This implies that image features will undergo small shifts, which allows us to use simple algorithms to track the features without making strong assumptions about the structure of the scene. Camera translations parallel to the image plane, which cause image features to flow along the rows or

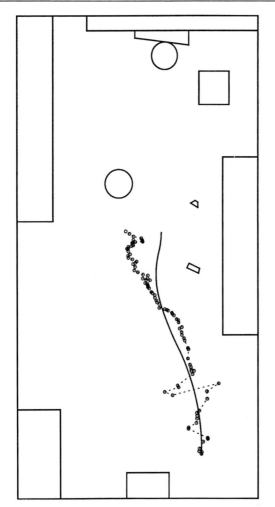

Figure 8: Second experiment: path estimated with uncertainty modelled by scalars.

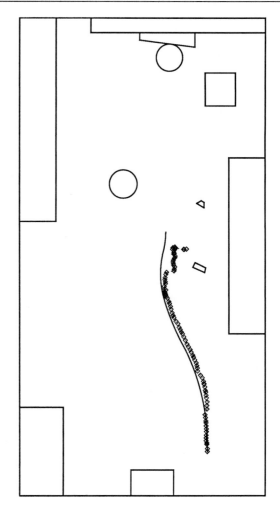

Figure 9: Second experiment: path estimated with uncertainty modelled by 3D normal distributions.

columns of the image, lead to the simplest depth from motion equations, the simplest image processing algorithms, and provide more depth information than other modes of motion; therefore, these are the motions we use. Since small motion results in low depth resolution, the question we address is how to refine depth estimates over the course of several frames. We answer this question with Kalman filtering.

Suppose the camera translates laterally, parallel to the image plane, in constant steps between frames. Then image features flow at a constant rate along image rows, with the rate depending on the distance to the corresponding 3D surfaces. The image position x_t of a feature in the tth frame depends on the depth Z of the surface and the camera translation T in the following way:

$$x_t = \frac{sTt}{Z} + x_0$$

where x_0 is the position of the feature in the first frame and s is a scale factor that encapsulates the resolution of the camera and the focal length of the lens. Since s, T, and Z are constant, the coordinates x_t trace out a straight line in the x–t plane (Fig. 10). This observation was the basis of the epipolar plane image approach [5], which explicitly formed such x–t images from the original image sequence and extracted lines in the x–t plane. In

this paper, we process the images incrementally by extracting edge points (*edgels*) on each scanline in the first frame, tracking them through the image sequence, and recursively updating the line parameters by Kalman filtering.

The parameters we fit are the intercept of the x–t line with the *current* image and the frame-to-frame displacement of the feature (the inverse slope of the line). Our Kalman filter formulation propagates this information from frame to frame, so that we always compute the intercept in the current image. Let the slope and intercept parameters be $P = [\, d \, c \,]^T$ (*depth* and *current x*). The Kalman filter will model these parameters as a 2D, normally distributed random vector and will estimate the covariance matrix Σ of their distribution. The filter models the extracted edge positions x_t as a sequence of noisy measurements in which the noise has zero mean and known variance σ^2. For simplicity, we assume here that the noise variance is constant over time.

If x_0 and x_1 are the positions of an edgel in the first two frames, the parameters for this edgel are initialized from the linear fit of $P = [\, d \, c \,]^T$ to x_0 and x_1:

$$\begin{bmatrix} x_0 \\ x_1 \end{bmatrix} = \begin{bmatrix} -1 & 1 \\ 0 & 1 \end{bmatrix} \begin{bmatrix} d \\ c \end{bmatrix}$$

with the result that

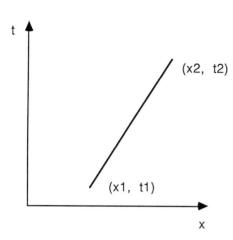

Figure 10: Image flow under lateral camera translation is constant, so the column coordinate (*x*) of a feature traces out a straight line in the *x-t* plane.

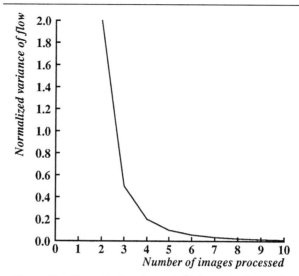

Figure 11: Normalized variance (σ_d^2/σ^2) in the image flow estimate *d* as a function of the number of frames processed.

$$c = x_1$$

$$d = x_1 - x_0$$

$$\Sigma = \sigma^2 \begin{bmatrix} 2 & 1 \\ 1 & 1 \end{bmatrix}$$

The covariance matrix comes from inverting the normal equations in the standard approach to linear statistical problems [19].

The motion equations that transform the parameters and covariance matrix between frames are

$$P_t^- = \begin{bmatrix} c_t \\ d_t \end{bmatrix} = \begin{bmatrix} 1 & 1 \\ 0 & 1 \end{bmatrix} \begin{bmatrix} c_{t-1} \\ d_{t-1} \end{bmatrix} = M P_{t-1}$$

$$\Sigma_t^- = M \Sigma_{t-1} M^T$$

The superscript minuses indicate that these estimates do not incorporate the measured edge position at time *t*. The newly measured edge position x_t is incorporated by computing the updated covariance matrix Σ_t^+, a gain matrix *K*, and the updated parameter vector P_t^+:

$$\Sigma_t^+ = \{ (\Sigma_t^-)^{-1} + S \}^{-1} \quad where \ S = \frac{1}{\sigma^2} \begin{bmatrix} 0 & 0 \\ 0 & 1 \end{bmatrix}$$

$$K = \frac{1}{\sigma^2} \Sigma_t^+ \begin{bmatrix} 0 \\ 1 \end{bmatrix}$$

$$P_t^+ = P_t^- + K [x_t - c]$$

In order to see how the uncertainty decreases as the number of measurements increases, we can compute the series of covariance matrices Σ_t^+. For example, the variance of the frame-to-frame displacement (slope) parameter *d* is plotted in Fig. 11 as a function of the number of images processed. This curve indicates the number of frames needed to achieve a given level of precision in the depth estimates. From the figure, it is clear that the estimates converge rapidly and that little information will be added after the tenth frame.

3.2. Experimental results

We have applied this procedure to images taken with horizontal and vertical camera translations parallel to the image plane (Fig. 12). Edges were extracted by applying the Canny operator [6] to each image and fitting quadratic curves around gradient maxima to localize edges to sub-pixel resolution. The maximum edge displacement between frames was known to be less than two pixels, so edges were matched by scanning a two-pixel window for match candidates and comparing the edge gradient magnitudes and directions. The flow parameters *P* were also used to predict where an edge from the previous frame would appear in the current image; the difference between the predicted position of the edge and that of potential matches was used as a final acceptance test. Depth estimates from the combined horizontal and vertical camera motions were interpolated to produce dense depth maps. These were shaded with the original image intensity and rendered in 3D from different viewpoints to produce the results in Fig. 13.

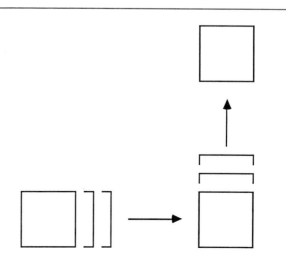

Figure 12: Camera motions used to acquire depth.

Figure 13: Depth from motion results: one of the raw images, the edges that were extracted, and two perspective views of the final depth map.

The main structure of the scene is recovered quite well. Errors tend to occur near the ends of line segments, such as at corners of walls and buildings. This is not surprising, since edge extraction will not work well at such locations without considerable tailoring. This is a weakness of edge-based approaches to image matching. It suggests that techniques based on more complete image descriptions, such as correlation or local expansions in terms of derivatives [15] or frequency components [14], will lead to better matching. Nevertheless, the results will edges are quite good. They underscore the power of incremental depth estimation methods and the value of orthogonal camera motions in obtaining more complete depth maps.

3.3. Discussion

This system reflects our approach to uncertainty and constraint in several ways. By using such small motion, it applies a great deal of constraint to initialize its depth model. With the Kalman filter, it gradually reduces the uncertainty in the model as more images are processed. The depth model applies constraint to the next image through the matching test based on predicted edge positions. A more general application of constraint, not implemented in the current system, is to allow the camera to move further between frames as the precision of the depth model improves.

The most important extension of this work may be the use of fine motion to constrain or corroborate stereo [11]. One or both cameras of the stereo system can be moved in small steps before attempting to match between cameras. In this case, creating a dense depth map by interpolation with the monocular depth estimates may allow us to identify occluding boundaries *before* stereo matching begins.

Our work in this system only begins to scratch the surface of incremental approaches to depth from motion. By fitting a line to the edge points in all images of the sequence, our Kalman filter approach retains *all* depth information available for the edges it tracks. However, it must be possible to obtain denser depth

measurements, either by improving the edge tracking (perhaps with a multi-scale approach) or by exploring an alternate type of feature or flow estimation process [1, 14]. There is also the intriguing possibility of formulating a Kalman filter that estimates depth at *pixels* in the image rather than at edges [18]. These possibilities are the subject of current research.

4. Conclusions

In summary, we have demonstrated the importance of uncertainty and constraint in two implemented systems. Bringing the systems together, we see that they reflect the three-stage processing cycle of Fig. 14. For example, in stereo navigation, the system repeatedly constructs a 3D model, matches the model to new images, and computes the position of the robot. In this cycle, the output of two consecutive stages is used by the third. In one revolution,

- the robot's estimated position and the existing 3D model are used to interpret new images,
- the 3D model and the images are used to refine the estimate of the robot's position, and
- the images and the position estimate are used to update the 3D model.

In principle, each trip around the cycle will improve the 3D model, leading to more constraint on subsequent image matching and motion estimation. Explicit representations of uncertainty quantify this cycle in terms of normal distributions. This allows us to specify the amount of information in the model, the amount of constraint that can be applied to matching, and the amount of improvement new data can made to the model. Eventually, this may also allow us to describe the effects of combinations of sensors, externally supplied information, and perturbations of the system by appropriately representing the uncertainty in each piece of information and each disturbance [19].

In terms of Fig. 14, our second system draws on external information by using precisely controlled motion to build the 3D model. This defines a sensing strategy that balances uncertainty in the 3D model with precision of the camera motion. An important potential application of this strategy is to initialize stereo fusion [11]. Plots such as Fig. 11, which indicate depth uncertainty as a function of camera motion, can define disparity limits each image

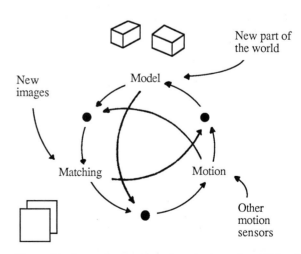

Figure 14: Processing cycle used to obtain motion and depth from image sequences.

feature for a given stereo baseline. Conceivably, the amount of camera motion and the size of the baseline can be tuned to keep the range of possible disparities for each feature very small. We are currently exploring this avenue.

Finally, in this paper we have dealt with 3D models consisting only of points. Although Kalman filtering has been applied to lines and planes [10], there is clearly a need for more general methods of describing 3D shape and shape uncertainty. The cellular representation known as the *occupancy grid* or *certainty grid* [8, 23] may be a solution to this problem. We have begun to apply this technique to building an integrated depth representation from sonar and single-scanline stereo [9].

Acknowledgements

Discussions with Jim Crowley helped to formulate the use of the error model in constraining stereo correspondence. Steve Shafer provided guidance and valuable comments throughout this work. The stereo motion estimation results would not have been possible without the support and the work of Hans Moravec and Chuck Thorpe.

References

1. P. Anandan and R. Weiss. Introducing a smoothness constraint in a matching approach for the computation of displacement fields. Proc. of ARPA IUS Workshop, December, 1985, pp. 186-197.
2. N. Ayache and O.D. Faugeras. "HYPER: A new approach for the recognition and positioning of two-dimensional objects". *IEEE Trans. on Pattern Analysis and Machine Intelligence PAMI-8*, 1 (January 1986), 44-54.
3. V. Barnett and T. Lewis. *Outliers in Statistical Data.* John Wiley & Sons, New York, NY, 1984.
4. S.D. Blostein and T.S. Huang. Quantization errors in stereo triangulation. Proc. 1st Int'l Conf. on Computer Vision, June, 1987, pp. 325-334.
5. R.C. Bolles, H.H. Baker, D.H. Marimont. "Epipolar-plane image analysis: an approach to determining structure from motion". *Int'l J. Computer Vision 1* (1987), 7-55.
6. J. Canny. "A computational approach to edge detection". *Trans. Patt. Anal. & Mach. Intell. PAMI-8*, 6 (Nov. 1986), 679-698.
7. T.F. Elbert. *Estimation and Control of Systems.* Van Nostrand Reinhold Co., New York, NY, 1984.
8. A. Elfes. "Sonar-based real-world mapping and navigation". *IEEE J. Robotics and Automation RA-3*, 3 (June 1987), 249-265.
9. A. Elfes and L. Matthies. Sensor integration for robot navigation: combining sonar and stereo range data in a grid-based representation. Proc. 26th IEEE Conf. on Decision and Control, Los Angeles, CA, December 9 - 11, 1987. In press.
10. O.D. Faugeras, N. Ayache, B. Faverjon, F. Lustman. Building visual maps by combining noisy stereo measurements. IEEE Int'l Conf. on Robotics and Automation, April, 1986, pp. 1433-1438.
11. D. Geiger and A. Yuille. Stereopsis and Eye-Movement.
12. D.B. Gennery. *Modelling the environment of an exploring vehicle by means of stereo vision.* Ph.D. Th., Stanford University, June 1980.
13. P.E. Gill, W. Murray, and M.H. Wright. *Practical Optimization.* Academic Press, 1981.
14. D.J. Heeger. Depth and flow from motion energy. Proc. AAAI, August, 1986, pp. 657-663.
15. M. Kass. A computational framework for the visual correspondence problem. Proc. 8th Int'l Joint Conf. on Artifical Intelligence, Karlsruhe, W. Germany, August, 1983, pp. 1043-1045.
16. L.H. Matthies, C.E. Thorpe. Experience with visual robot navigation. Proc. IEEE OCEANS'84 Conf., September, 1984, pp. 594-7.
17. L.H. Matthies and S.A. Shafer. "Error modeling in stereo navigation". *IEEE J. Robotics and Automation RA-3*, 3 (June 1987), 239-248.
18. L. Matthies, R. Szeliski, and T. Kanade. A Kalman filter approach to estimating depth from motion. *In preparation.*
19. P.S. Maybeck. *Stochastic Models, Estimation, and Control.* Academic Press, New York, NY, 1979.
20. E.M. Mikhail. *Observations and Least Squares.* University Press of America, Lanham, MD, 1976.
21. V.J. Milenkovic, T. Kanade. Trinocular vision using photometric and edge orientation constraints. Proc. DARPA Image Understanding Workshop, Dec., 1985.
22. H.P. Moravec. *Obstacle avoidance and navigation in the real world by a seeing robot rover.* Ph.D. Th., Stanford University, September 1980.
23. H.P. Moravec. Certainty grids for mobile robots. JPL/NASA Space Telerobotics Workshop, Pasadena, CA, January, 1987.
24. H.P. Moravec. The Stanford Cart and the CMU Rover. Proceedings of the IEEE, July, 1983, pp. 872-884.
25. P.H. Schonemann and R.M. Carroll. "Fitting one matrix to another under choice of a central dilation and a rigid motion". *Psychometrika 35*, 2 (June 1970), 245-255.
26. R. Smith, M. Self, P. Cheeseman. Estimating Uncertain Spatial Relationships in Robotics. In *Uncertainty in Artificial Intelligence*, North Holland, to appear.
27. F. Solina. Errors in stereo due to quantization. MS-CIS-85-34, U. Pennsylvania, September, 1985.
28. C.E. Thorpe. *Vision and navigation for a robot rover.* Ph.D. Th., Carnegie-Mellon University, December 1984.
29. C.E. Thorpe. Path relaxation: path planning for a mobile robot. Proc. AAAI, August, 1984.
30. J.R. Wertz (ed). *Spacecraft Attitude Determination and Control.* D. Reidel Publishing Company, 1978.

Maintaining Representations of the Environment of a Mobile Robot[1]

Nicholas Ayache and Olivier D. Faugeras

INRIA
Domaine de Voluceau-Rocquencourt
BP 105 - 78153 Le Chesnay Cédex - France

Abstract In this paper we describe our current ideas related to the problem of building and updating 3D representations of the environment of a mobile robot that uses passive Vision as its main sensory modality. Our basic tenet is that we want in these representations both geometry and uncertainty. We first motivate our approach by defining the problems we are trying to solve and giving some simple didactic examples. We then present the tool that we think is extremely well adapted to solving most of these problems: the Extended Kalman Filter (EKF). We discuss the notions of minimal geometric representations for 3D lines, planes, and rigid motions. We show how the EKF and the representations can be combined to provide solutions for some of the problems listed at the beginning of the article, and give a number of experimental results on real data.

Keywords: Mobile Robots, 3D Visual Maps, Fusion of Sensory Data, Geometric Representations, Uncertainty, Extended Kalman Filtering, Motion Estimation.

1 Introduction

In the last few years, Computer Vision has gone wildly into the area of 3D analysis from a variety of sensing modalities such as Stereo, Motion, Range Finders and sonars. A book that brings together some of this recent work is [Kan87].

Most of these sensing modalities start from pixels which are then converted into three-dimensional structures. A characteristic of this work as compared to previous work where images were the starting and the ending point (like in image restoration for example)is that noise in the measurements is of course still present but, contrary to what has happened in the past, it has to be taken into account all the way from pixels to 3D geometry.

Another aspect of the work on 3D follows from the observation that if noise is present, it has to evaluated, i.e. we need models of sensor noise (sensor being taken here in the broad sense of sensory modality), and reduced. This reduction can be obtained in many ways. The most important ones are:

- First, the case of one sensor in a fixed position: it can repeat its measurements and thus, maybe, obtain better estimations.

- Second, the case of a sensor that can be moved around: given its measurements in a given position, what is the best way to move in order to reduce the uncertainty and increase the knowledge of the environment in a way that is compatible with the task at hand.

- Third, is the case of several different sensors that have to combine their measurements in a meaningful fashion.

Interesting work related to these issues has already emerged which is not reported in [Kan87]. In the area of robust estimation procedures and models of sensors noise, Hager and Mintz [HM87] and Mc Kendall and Mintz [MM87] have started to pave the ground. Bolle and Cooper [BC86] have developed maximum likelyhood techniques to combine range data to estimate object positions. Durrant-Whyte [Dur86], in his Ph.D. Thesis has conducted a thorough investigation of the problems posed by Multi-Sensory systems. Applications to the navigation of a mobile robot have been discussed by Smith and Cheeseman [SC87] and by Matthies and Shafer [MS86]. The problem of combining stereo views has been attacked by Ayache and Faugeras [FAF86], [AF87b], Porril et al. [P*87], and Kriegman [KTT87].

Several problems related to these preliminary studies need more attention. Modelling sensor noise in general and more specifically visual sensor noise appears to us an area where considerable progress can be achieved ; relating sensor noise to geometric uncertainty and the corresponding problem of representing geometric information with an eye toward describing not only the geometry but also the uncertainty on this geometry are key problems to be investigated further as is the problem of combining uncertain geometric information produced by different sensors.

2 What are the problems that we are trying to solve

We have been focusing on a number of problems arising in connection with a robot moving in an indoor environment and using passive vision and proprioceptive sensory modalities such as odometry. Our mid-term goals are to incrementally build on the robot an increasing set of sensing and reasoning capabilities such as:

- build local 3D descriptions of the environment.

- use the descriptions to update or compute motion descriptions where the motion is either the robot's motion or others.

- fuse the local descriptions of neighboring places into more global, coherent, and accurate ones.

---

[1]This work was partially supported by esprit project P940.

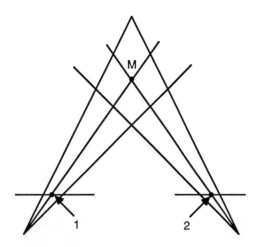

Figure 1: Effect of pixel noise on 3D reconstruction

- "discover" interesting geometric relations in these descriptions.

- "discover" semantic entities and exhibit "intelligent" behavior.

We describe how we understand each of these capabilities and what are the underlying difficulties.

2.1 Build local 3D descriptions of the environment

Up until now, our main source of 3D information has been Stereo [AF87c,AL87] even though we have made considerable progress toward the use of structure from motion also [FLT87]. In any case the problems are very similar for both sensing modalities and we concentrate on Stereo. As announced in the introduction, our main concern is to track uncertainty all the way from pixel noise to geometric descriptions. Figure 1 shows for example that in a Stereo system, if pixels positions are imperfectly known, then the corresponding 3D point varies in an area with a quite anisotropic diamond shape. This is a clear example of a relation between pixel uncertainty and geometric (the position of point M) uncertainty. Another source of uncertainty in Stereo is the calibration uncertainty. In a stereo rig, intrinsic parameters of the cameras such as focal length, and extrinsic parameters such as relative position and orientation of the cameras have to be calculated. Figure 2 shows the effect on the reconstruction of a point M of an uncertainty on the focal lengths of the two cameras. Again, M varies in a diamond like shape. Of course this source of uncertainty adds itself to the previous pixel uncertainty.

Another example of the propagation of uncertainty is given in Figure 3 where pixels in left and right images are grouped into line segments: pixel uncertainty is converted into 2D line uncertainty. Line segments are then matched and used to reconstruct 3D line segments : 2D line uncertainty and calibration uncertainty are converted into 3D uncertainty. Yet another set of examples of this kind of propagation is shown in Figure 4 where coplanar and cocylindrical line segments are grouped together ; again, the question is, what is the uncertainty on the plane or on the cylinder ?

From these examples, we see that the main problem that needs to be solved in order to build local 3D descriptions of the environment is how geometric uncertainty propagates when we

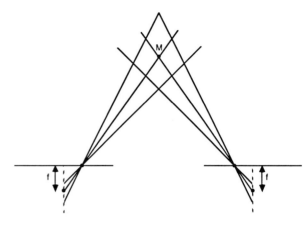

Figure 2: Effect of calibration errors on 3D reconstruction

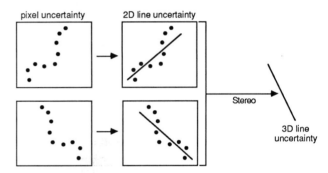

Figure 3: From pixel uncertainty to 3D line uncertainty

build up more complex primitives from simpler ones. This in turn generates two questions:

1. How do we represent geometric primitives.

2. How do we represent uncertainty on these primitives.

2.2 Update position and motion information

Figure 5 shows a measurement of a physical point made in two positions 1 and 2 of a mobile vehicle. In position 1, it "sees" M with some uncertainty represented by the ellipse around it. In position 2, it "sees" P with another uncertainty. Assuming that the displacement between 1 and 2 is exactly known, it is possible to express P and M in the same coordinate system. If the displacement estimate is wrong, as it is in Figure 5, the two zones of uncertainty do not intersect and it is very unlikely that the observer will realise that the points M and P are instances of the same physical point. If we now take into account the uncertainty on the displacement (assuming that we can estimate it) we have Figure 6 where the combination of displacement uncertainty and measurement uncertainty produces a larger ellipse around P which intersects the one around M : the observer can now infer that the probability of M and P being the same physical point is quite high and use the two measurements to obtain a better estimate of the displacement and reduce its uncertainty. The measurements can also be used to produce better estimates of the positions (Figure 7). This is related to what we call geometric fusion.

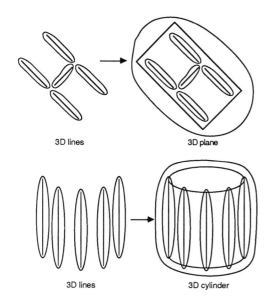

3D lines   3D plane

3D lines   3D cylinder

Figure 4: From 3D line uncertainty to 3D surface uncertainty

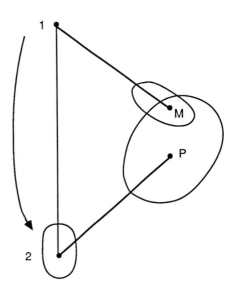

Figure 6: Measuring a point in two positions (displacement and uncertainty estimation)

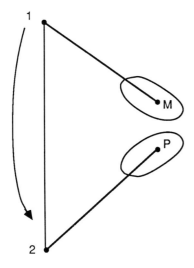

Figure 5: Measuring a point in two positions (wrong displacement estimation)

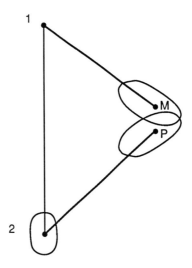

Figure 7: Improving the estimation of the points position

340 Ayache and Faugeras

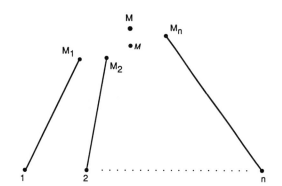

Figure 8: Fusing n points measured from different positions

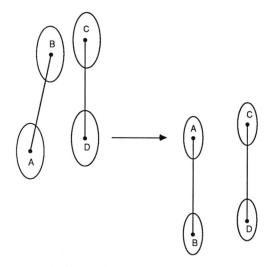

Figure 9: Discovering that AB and CD are parallel

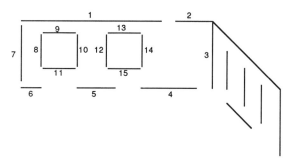

Figure 10: Hypothesizing walls, windows, and doors

2.3 Fusing geometric entities

Figure 8 shows a slightly more general case than what is depicted in Figure 7. The mobile vehicle has measured the physical point M in n positions numbered from 1 to n. Each measurement yields a point $M_i, i = 1, ..., n$ and some uncertainty in the coordinate system attached to the robot. Displacement uncertainty is also available. Using the ideas described in Section 5, we can improve the estimates of the displacements and reduce their uncertainty by discovering that points $M_1, ..., M_n$ are all instanciations of the same point. We can also use this observation to reduce the uncertainty on, let us say M_1, by combining the n measurements and produce a point M, fusion of $M_1, ..., M_n$, as well as its related uncertainty. The points $M_1, ..., M_n$ can then be erased from the representation of the environment, they can be forgotten. What remains is the point M expressed in the coordinate system attached to position 1 for example, and the displacements from 1 to 2, 2 to 3, etc ..., which allow to express M in the other coordinate systems.

Fusing geometric entities is therefore the key to "intelligent" forgetting which in turn prevents the representation of the environment of growing too large.

2.4 Discovering "interesting" geometric relations

Using this approach also allows us to characterize the likelyhood that a given geometric relation exists between a number of geometric entities and to use this information to obtain better estimates of these entities and reduce their uncertainty. For example, as shown in Figure 9, segments AB and CD which have uncertainty attached to their endpoints have a high likelyhood to be parallel. Assuming that they are, we can update their position (they become more parallel) and reduce the uncertainty of their endpoints. The same reasoning can be used for the relation "to be perpendicular".

2.5 Discovering semantic entities

Figure 10 shows the kind of "semantic" grouping that is of interest to us in the context of a mobile robot moving indoors, to combine geometry and some a priori description of the environment. The line segments numbered from 1 to 15 are found, using the ideas described in Section 2.4, to be coplanar with a high probability ; the corresponding plane is found to be vertical with a very high probability which can be deduced from the geometric uncertainty of the line segments. This observation can then be used to infer that the plane has a high probability to be a wall. If we also observe that segments 8 to 11 and 12

to 15 form approximately two rectangles this can be used to infer that they have a high probability to be parts of a window or a door.

3 What is the tool that we are using

In this third section, we introduce the Extended Kalman Filter (EKF) formalism which is applied in sections 4 and 5 to solve the problems we have just listed in section 2.

3.1 Unifying the problems

In all these previously listed problems, we are confronted with the estimation of an unknown parameter $a \in \mathbb{R}^n$ given a set of k non necessary linear equations of the form

$$f_i(x_i, a) = 0 \qquad (1)$$

where $x_i \in \mathbb{R}^m$ and f_i is a function from $\mathbb{R}^m \times \mathbb{R}^n$ into $\mathbb{R}^p$. The vector x_i represents some random parameters of the function f_i in the sense that we only measure an estimate $\hat{x}_i$ of them, such that

$$\hat{x}_i = x_i + v_i \qquad (2)$$

where v_i is a random error. The only assumption we make on v_i is that its mean is zero, its covariance is known, and that it is a white noise :

$$E[v_i] = 0$$

$$E[v_i v_i^t] = \Lambda_i \geq 0$$

$$E[v_i v_j^t] = 0 \quad \forall i \neq j$$

These assumptions are reasonable. If the estimator is biased, it is possible to substract its mean to get an unbiased one. If we do not know the covariance of the error (or some other confidence measure on it), the estimator is meaningless. If two measurements $\hat{x}_i$ and $\hat{x}_j$ are correlated, we take the concatenation of them $\hat{x}_k = (\hat{x}_i, \hat{x}_j)$ and the concatenated vector function $f_k = [f_i^t, f_j^t]^t$. The problem is to find the optimal estimate $\hat{a}$ of a given the functions f_i and the measurements $\hat{x}_i$.

3.2 Linearizing the equations

The most powerful tools developed in parameter estimation are for linear systems. Before using complicated nonlinear optimization techniques, it is worthwhile to try applying the linear tools to a linearized version of our equations. This is the EKF approach that we now develop.

For each nonlinear equation $f_i(x_i, a) = 0$ we need to know an estimate $\hat{a}_{i-1}$ of the solution a, and again a measure S_i of the confidence we have in this estimate[2]. We assume that $\hat{a}_{i-1}$ is given by

$$\hat{a}_{i-1} = a + w_i \tag{3}$$

where w_i is a random error. The only assumptions we make on w_i are the same as for v_i, i.e.

$$E[w_i] = 0$$

$$E[w_i w_i^t] = S_i \geq 0$$

where S_i is a given positive matrix. Here again, no assumption of gaussianness is required.

Having an estimate $\hat{a}_{i-1}$ of the solution, the equations are linearized by a first order Taylor expansion around $(\hat{x}_i, \hat{a}_{i-1})$:

$$f_i(x_i, a) = 0 \approx f_i(\hat{x}_i, \hat{a}_{i-1}) + \frac{\widehat{\partial f_i}}{\partial x}(x_i - \hat{x}_i) + \frac{\widehat{\partial f_i}}{\partial a}(a - \hat{a}_{i-1}) \tag{4}$$

where the derivatives $\widehat{\partial f_i}/\partial x$ and $\widehat{\partial f_i}/\partial a$ are estimated at $(\hat{x}_i, \hat{a}_{i-1})$:

Equation 4 can be rewritten as :

$$y_i = M_i a + u_i \tag{5}$$

where

$$y_i = -f_i(\hat{x}_i, \hat{a}_{i-1}) + \frac{\widehat{\partial f_i}}{\partial a} \hat{a}_{i-1}$$

$$M_i = \frac{\widehat{\partial f_i}}{\partial a}$$

$$u_i = \frac{\widehat{\partial f_i}}{\partial x}(x_i - \hat{x}_i)$$

Equation 5 is now a linear measurement equation, where y_i is the new measurement, M_i is the linear transformation, u_i is the random measurement error. Both y_i and M_i are readily computed from the actual measurement $\hat{x}_i$, the estimate $\hat{a}_{i-1}$ of a, the function f_i and its first derivative. The second-order statistics of u_i are derived easily from those of v_i :

$$E[u_i] = 0$$

$$W_i \stackrel{\Delta}{=} E[u_i u_i^t] = \frac{\widehat{\partial f_i}}{\partial x} \Lambda_i \frac{\widehat{\partial f_i}^t}{\partial x}$$

---

[2]In practice, we shall see that only an initial estimate $(\hat{a}_0, S_0)$ of a is required prior to the first measurement $\hat{x}_1$, while the next ones $(\hat{a}_i, S_i)$ are provided automatically by the Kalman filter itself.

3.3 Recursive Kalman Filter

When no gaussianness is assumed on the previous random errors u_i, v_i and w_i, the Kalman Filter equations provide the best (minimum variance) linear unbiased estimate of a. This means that among the estimators which seek $\hat{a}_k$ as a linear combination of the measurements $\{y_i\}$, it is the one which minimizes the expected error norm,

$$E[(\hat{a}_k - a)^t(\hat{a}_k - a)]$$

while verifying

$$E[\hat{a}_k] = a$$

The recursive equations of the Kalman Filter which provide a new estimate $(\hat{a}_i, S_i)$ of a from $(\hat{a}_{i-1}, S_{i-1})$ are the following ones [Jaz70]:

$$\hat{a}_i = \hat{a}_{i-1} + K_i(y_i - M_i \hat{a}_{i-1}) \tag{6}$$

$$K_i = S_{i-1} M_i^t (W_i + M_i S_{i-1} M_i^t)^{-1} \tag{7}$$

$$S_i = (I - K_i M_i) S_{i-1} \tag{8}$$

or equivalently

$$S_i^{-1} = S_{i-1}^{-1} + M_i^t W_i^{-1} M_i \tag{9}$$

One can see that the previously estimated parameter $\hat{a}_{i-1}$ is corrected by an amount proportional to the current error $y_i - M_i \hat{a}_{i-1}$ called the inovation. The proportionality factor, K_i, is called the Kalman gain. At the end of the process, $\hat{a}_k$ is the final estimate and S_k represents the covariance of the estimation error :

$$S_k = E[(\hat{a}_k - a)(\hat{a}_k - a)^t]$$

The recursive process is initialized by $\hat{a}_0$, an initial estimate of a, and S_0, its error covariance matrix. Actually, the criterion minimized by the final estimate $\hat{a}_k$ is :

$$C = (a - \hat{a}_0)^t S_0^{-1}(a - \hat{a}_0) + \sum_{i=1}^{k}(y_i - M_i a)^t W_i^{-1}(y_i - M_i a) \tag{10}$$

It is interesting to note that the first term of equation 10 measures the squared distance of a from an initial estimate, weighted by its covariance matrix, while the second term is nothing else than the classical least-square criterion, i.e. the sum of the squared measurement errors weighted by their covariance matrices. Indeed, intializing the process with an arbitrary $\hat{a}_0$ and $S_0^{-1} = 0$, criterion 10 provides the classical least-square estimate $\hat{a}_k$ obtained from the measurements only, while the initial estimate does not play any role.

The enormous advantage of such a recursive solution, is that if we decide, after a set of k measurements $\{x_i\}$, to stop the measures, we only have to keep $\hat{a}_k$ and S_k as the whole memory of the measurement process. If we decide later to take into account additional measurements, we simply have to initialize $\hat{a}_0 \equiv \hat{a}_k$ and $S_0 \equiv S_k$ and to process the new measurements to obtain exactly the same solution as if we had processed all the measurements together.

3.4 Gaussian assumption

Up to now, we did not introduce any gaussian assumption on the random measurement errors $v_i = x_i - \hat{x}_i$ of equation 2 and on the prior estimate error $w_0 = a - \hat{a}_0$ of equation 3. However, in practice, these errors usually come from a sum of independent random processes, which tend toward a gaussian process (Central Limit theorem). If we actually identify v_i and w_0 with gaussian processes, i.e.

$$v_i \equiv N(0, \Lambda_i)$$

$$w_0 \equiv N(0, S_0)$$

then, it follows that the noise u_i in equation 5 is also gaussian, i.e.

$$u_i \equiv N(0, W_i)$$

and that all the successive estimates provided by the recursive Kalman filter are also gaussian

$$\hat{a}_k = N(a, S_k)$$

Moreover, in this case, the Kalman filter provides the best (minimum variance) unbiased estimate $\hat{a}_k$ among all, even non-linear, filters. This estimate $\hat{a}_k$ is also the maximum likelihood estimator of a. This comes from the fact that in the gaussian case, the solution is the conditional mean $\hat{a}_k = E[a/y_1, ..., y_k]$ which both minimizes the variance and maximizes the likelihood while being expressed as a linear combination of the measurements y_i. Therefore in this case, the minimum variance and minimum variance linear estimates are the same, namely the estimate $\hat{a}_k$ provided by the Kalman filter [Jaz70].

In conclusion, in the gaussian case, the Kalman filter provides the best estimate with the advantage of preserving gaussianness of all the implied random variables, which means that no information on the probability density functions of the parameters is lost while keeping only their mean and covariance matrix.

3.5 Rejecting Outlier Measurements

At iteration i, we have an estimate $\hat{a}_{i-1}$ and an attached covariance matrix S_{i-1} for parameter a. We also have a noisy measurement $(\hat{x}_i, \Lambda_i)$ of x_i and we want to test the plausibility of this measurement with respect to the equation $f_i(x_i, a) = 0$.

If we consider again a first order expansion of $f_i(x_i, a)$ around $(\hat{x}_i, \hat{a}_{i-1})$ (equation 4), considering that $(\hat{x}_i - x_i)$ and $(\hat{a}_{i-1} - a)$ are independent centered gaussian processes, we see that $f_i(\hat{x}_i, \hat{a}_{i-1})$ is also (up to linear approximation) a centered gaussian process whose mean and covariance are given by:

$$E[f_i(\hat{x}_i, \hat{a}_{i-1})] = 0$$

$$Q_i = E[f_i(\hat{x}_i, \hat{a}_{i-1}) f_i(\hat{x}_i, \hat{a}_{i-1})^t] = \frac{\widehat{\partial f_i}}{\partial x} \Lambda_i \frac{\widehat{\partial f_i}^t}{\partial x} + \frac{\widehat{\partial f_i}}{\partial a} S_{i-1} \frac{\widehat{\partial f_i}^t}{\partial a}$$

Therefore, if the rank of Q_i is q, the generalized Mahalanobis distance :

$$d(\hat{x}_i, \hat{a}_{i-1}) = [f_i(\hat{x}_i, \hat{a}_{i-1})]^t Q_i^{-1} [f_i(\hat{x}_i, \hat{a}_{i-1})] \qquad (11)$$

has a χ^2 distribution with q degrees of freedom [3].

Looking at a χ^2 distribution table, it is therefore possible to reject an outlier measurement $\hat{x}_i$ at a 95 % confidence rate by setting an appropriate threshold ϵ on the Mahalanobis distance, and by keeping only those measurements $\hat{x}_i$ which verify:

$$d(\hat{x}_i, \hat{a}_{i-1}) < \epsilon \qquad (12)$$

---

[3] If $q < p$ = the size of the measurement vector f_i, Q_i^{-1} is the pseudo-inverse of Q_i.

3.6 Enforcing a perfect measurement

The recursive equations of the Kalman filter allow for the exact verification of a linear equation ([P*87]). This is done simply by setting the covariance of the linear measurement equation 5 to zero:

$$W_i = 0;$$

By doing this, it is easy to see that the Kalman gain becomes

$$K_i = S_{i-1} M_i^t (M_i S_{i-1} M_i^t)^{-1}$$

and that :

$$M_i K_i = I.$$

Therefore after processing the measurement, we have:

$$y_i - M_i \hat{a}_i = y_i - M_i \hat{a}_{i-1} - M_i K_i (y_i - M_i \hat{a}_{i-1}) = 0$$

which shows that the measurement equation 5 exactly holds. This fact yields a singularity of the covariance matrix, as can be seen by computing

$$S_i M_i^t = S_{i-1} M_i^t - S_{i-1} M_i^t (M_i S_{i-1} M_i^t)^{-1} M_i S_{i-1} M_i^t = 0$$

As was pointed out by Porrill [P*87], one can impose exact measurements only as long as they are independent. Before imposing a new exact measurement, one must verify that

$$S_{i-1} M_i^t \neq 0 \qquad (13)$$

otherwise $M_i S_{i-1} M_i^t$ cannot be inverted. If $S_{i-1} M_i^t = 0$, it means that the new exact measurement is not independant of the previous ones. Either it verifies

$$y_i = M_i a_{i-1} \qquad (14)$$

which means that it is already verified, or it is inconsistent with the previously enforced exact measurements and must be either rejected or considered as a noisy neasurement, i.e. with a covariance matrix $W_i > 0$. Of course in practice the tests of equations 13 and 14 are corrupted by numerical errors, and we did not test their sensitivity to such errors.

3.7 Iterated Extended Kalman Filter

Up to now we have found a powerful tool to deal with linear noisy systems of equations. But these linear equations come from the first order expansion of nonlinear equations. If the estimate $\hat{a}_i$ around which the expansion is performed is too far from the correct parameter a, the approximation of equation 4 is not very good, and the optimal solution of the linear system may differ significantly from the true one.

A method to reduce the effect of nonlinearities is to apply the iterated Kalman filter (cf. [Jaz70], pp. 279 and 353–355). This consists in applying equation 6 as long as $\hat{a}_i - \hat{a}_{i-1}$ is large enough, computing at each iteration a new value of K_i, y_i and M_i obtained from a re-linearization of f_i about the new estimate $\hat{a}_i$. In general, after a few iterations (especially at the begining of the process), $\hat{a}_i$ is so close to a that the linearization error is almost zero, yielding an almost optimal filter.

3.8 Extension to non-stationary process

We assumed in the previous sections that the parameter vector a of the measurement equations 1 was constant at each iteration i, i.e.

$$a_i = a_{i-1} \qquad \forall i$$

In fact, the Kalman filter naturally extends to non stationary processes for which the parameter vector a is the solution of a gauss-markov state equation at each iteration, i.e.

$$a_i = F_i a_{i-1} + r_i$$

where r_i is a gaussian centered white noise :

$$r_i \equiv N(0, R_i)$$

and

$$E[r_i r_j^t] = 0 \quad \forall\, i \neq j$$

In this case the Kalman equations are only slightly modified [Jaz70] but the general formalism remains the same.

This powerful extension of the Kalman filter has not been used up to now in our experiments. Nevertheless, it could provide elegant solutions in cases where the parameter a is non stationary, for instance to consider elastic deformations which are modeled by a slightly varying locally rigid transformation.

4 Geometric Representations

In this Section, we give the details of the geometric representations that we have found useful at various stages of our work. It is first important to note that we have been dealing so far only with points, lines, and planes, i.e. with affine geometric entities. This may appear to be quite a restriction on the type of environments that we can cope with. This is indeed the case but there are a number of reasons why we think that our approach is quite reasonable:

1. The obvious one is that for the kind of environment that our mobile robot moves into, these primitives are very likely to cover most of the geometric features of importance.

2. A second reason is that more complicated curved features can be first approximated with affine primitives which are then grouped into more complicated non affine primitives.

3. A third reason is that we believe that the techniques we have developed for representing and combining uncertainty of affine primitives are generic and directly applicable to non affine primitives.

Let us now discuss specifically lines, planes, and rigid displacements.

4.1 Line representations

The 3D segments that we deal with are usually constructed from stereo [AF87c,AL87]. Their endpoints may be quite unreliable, even though they can be of some usefulness from time to time, and we largely depend on the infinite lines supporting those line segments.

We concentrate here on how to represent 3D lines. The obvious representation we mention here only for pedagogical reasons, is by two points; this representation is 6-dimensional and, as we will see next, not minimal. Another way to represent a line is to choose a point on it (3 parameters), and a unit vector defining its direction (2 parameters). The corresponding representation is 5-dimensional and, again, not minimal. In fact, the set of affine 3D lines is a manifold of dimension 4 for which we will exhibit later an atlas of class C^∞. This implies

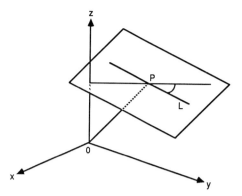

Figure 11: 3D line representation

that a minimal representation of a straight line has four parameters. One such representation can be obtained by considering the normal to the line from the origin (if the line goes through the origin it is the same as a vector line and can be defined by two parameters only). The point of intersection between the normal and the line is represented by three parameters. If we now consider (see Figure 11) the plane normal at P to OP, the line is in that plane and can be defined by one more parameter, its angle with an arbitrary direction, for example the line defined by P and one of the axis of coordinates (in Figure 11, the z-axis). Of course, when the line is parallel to the xy-plane this direction is not defined and we must use either the x- or y-axis. This brings up an interesting point, namely that there does not exist a global minimal representation for affine lines, i.e. one which can be used for all such lines. We must choose the representation as a function of the line orientation. Mathematically, this means that the manifold of the affine straight lines cannot be defined with only one map. This is quite common and is also true for affine planes and rotations of $\mathbb{R}^3$, as will be shown next.

The previous representation for a line is not in fact the one we have been using. The one we use considers a line (not perpendicular to the z-axis) as the intersection of a plane parallel to the y-axis, and a plane parallel to the x-axis:

$$\begin{cases} x = az + p \\ y = bz + q \end{cases} \tag{15}$$

The intersection is represented by the four-dimensional vector $L = [a, b, p, q]^T$ which has the following geometric interpretation. The direction of the line is that of the vector $[a, b, 1]^T$, and the point of intersection of the line with the xy-plane has coordinates p and q. Since the last coordinate of the direction vector is equal to 1, the line cannot be perpendicular to the z-axis or parallel to the xy-plane. If we want, and we do in pratice, represent such lines, we must choose another representation, for example:

$$\begin{cases} y = ax + p \\ z = bx + q \end{cases} \tag{16}$$

which cannot represent lines parallel to the yz-plane, or perpendicular to the x-axis, or:

$$\begin{cases} z = ay + p \\ x = by + q \end{cases} \tag{17}$$

which excludes lines parallel to the zx-plane.

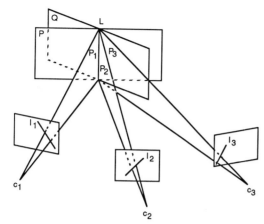

Figure 12: Reconstruction of 3D lines

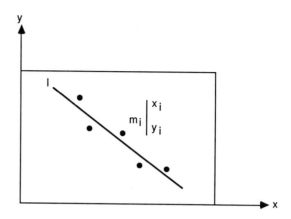

Figure 13: 2D line approximation

Each representation defines a one to one mapping between $\mathbb{R}^4$ and a subset (in fact an open subset) of the set of affine 3D lines and it can be shown that these three mapping define on this set a structure of C^∞-manifold for which they form an atlas.

In practice, this means the representation is not exactly four-dimensional, but is made of the four numbers a, b, p, and q and an integer i taking the values 1, 2, and 3 to indicate which map 15, 16, or 17 we are currently using.

The fact that the set of affine 3D lines has been given a structure of C^∞-manifold implies that the a', b', p', q' of a given representation are C^∞-functions of the a, b, p, q of another representation for all lines for which the two representations are well defined (for example all lines not parallel to the xy- and yz-planes).

The representation of a line also includes a 4×4 covariance matrix Λ_L on the vector L. It is interesting at this stage to trace the computation of this covariance matrix all the way from pixel to 3D. In order to do this, we must briefly explain how 3D lines are computed in our current Stereo system [AL87]. We use three cameras as indicated in Figure 12. In theory, the three planes defined by the 2D lines l_1, l_2, and l_3 and the optical centers C_1, C_2, and C_3 belong to the same pencil and intersect along the 3D line L. In practice they do not because of noise and we have to find the "best" line satisfying the measurements, i.e. l_1, l_2 and l_3. This can be done by using the idea of pencil of planes, described more fully in [FLT87]. We assume that in the coordinate system attached to camera 1, for example, the equation of the ith plane P_i, $i = 1, 2, 3$, is given by

$$u_i x + v_i y + w_i z + r_i = 0$$

where the 4 vectors $P_i = [u_i, v_i, w_i, r_i]^T$ are known, as well as their covariance matrix Λ_{P_i} (we show later how to compute them). If we use representation 15 for the 3D line, it is represented as the intersection of the two planes P of equation $x = az + p$ and Q of equation $y = bz + q$. Writing that the five planes P, Q, and P_i, $i = 1, 2, 3$, from a pencil allows us to write 6 equations :

$$\begin{cases} w_i + au_i + bv_i = 0 \\ r_i + pu_i + qv_i = 0 \end{cases} \quad i = 1, 2, 3.$$

in the four unknowns a, b, p, and q.

We can apply directly the Kalman formalism to these measurement equations and choose $a = [a, b, p, q]^T$, and x_i as the 4-vector P_i. We can therefore simply compute an estimate $\hat{a}$ of a and its covariance matrix $\Lambda_{\hat{a}}$ from the P_i's and Λ_{P_i}'s.

Let us now show how we can compute the P_i's and Λ_{P_i}'s. Each line $l_i, i = 1, 2, 3$, is obtained by fitting a straight line to a set of edge pixels which have been detected using a modified version of the Canny edge detector [Can86,Der87]. Looking at Figure 13, let $x\cos\theta + y\sin\theta - p = 0$ be the equation of the line l which is fit to the edge pixels m_i of coordinates x_i, y_i ($0 \leq \theta < 2\pi, \rho \geq 0$). We assume that the measured edge pixels are independent and corrupted by a gaussian isotropic noise and take the parameter a equal to $[\theta, \rho]^T$ and the measurement x as the vector $[x, y]^T$. The measurement equation is therefore

$$f(x, a) = x\cos\theta + y\sin\theta - \rho$$

Applying the EKF formalism to the n edge pixels forming the line provides the best estimate $\hat{a}$ of the line parameters and its covariance matrix. Having done this for all three cameras, it is easy to deduce the equations of the three planes P_i and the covariance matrixes on their coefficients.

4.2   Plane representations

Planes can receive pretty much the same treatment as lines. A plane is defined by three parameters, and this is minimal. A possible representation is the representation by the normal n (a unit norm vector), and the distance d to the origin. The problem with this representation is that it is not unique since $(-n, -d)$ represents the same plane. It is possible to fix that problem by assuming that one component of n, let us say n_z, is positive, i.e. we consider planes not parallel to the z-axis. For these planes we must choose another convention, for example that n_x positive. Again, this works well for planes not parallel to the x-axis. The third possible representation is to assume n_y positive which excludes planes parallel to the y-axis.

So, we have three one to one mappings of open subsets of the product $S_2 \times R$, where S_2 is the usual gaussian sphere, into open subsets of the set of planes :

$$\begin{array}{lll} (n, d), \ n_z > 0 & \longrightarrow & \text{planes non parallel to } Oz \\ (n, d), \ n_x > 0 & \longrightarrow & \text{planes non parallel to } Ox \\ (n, d), \ n_y > 0 & \longrightarrow & \text{planes non parallel to } Oy \end{array}$$

It is easy to show that these three mappings define on the set of 3D planes a structure of C^∞-manifold of dimension 3.

One practical disadvantage of the previous representations is that the normal n is constrained to lie on the unit sphere S_2

i.e. must satisfy the constraint $\|n\| = 1$. A possibly simpler representation is obtained by considering the mapping from R^3 to the set of 3D planes defined by :

$$p_1 : (a, b, c) \longrightarrow ax + by + z + c = 0 \qquad (18)$$

this can represent all planes except those parallel to Oz and it is a one to one continuous mapping from $\mathbb{R}^3$ to the open subset of the set of 3D planes constituted of the planes not parallel to the z-axis. In order to obtain all possible plane, we must also consider the mappings :

$$p_2 : (a, b, c) \longrightarrow x + ay + bz + c = 0 \qquad (19)$$

$$p_3 : (a, b, c) \longrightarrow bx + y + az + c = 0 \qquad (20)$$

p_2 (resp. p_3) excludes planes parallel to the x-axis (resp. the y-axis). It is easy to show that p_1, p_2, p_3 also define on the set of 3D planes a structure of C^∞-manifold of dimension 3.

4.3   Rigid displacements

In a previous paper [AF87b] we have proposed to use the exponential representation of rotation matrixes. This is the same as saying that a rotation is defined by its axis u (a unit vector) and its angle θ. The vector $r = \theta u$ can be used to represent the rotation and we have :

$$R = e^H$$

where H is an antisymmetric matrix representing the cross-product with the vector r (i.e. $Hx = r \wedge x$, for all x).

Let us see how we can define a structure of manifold on the set of rotations using this representation. If we allow θ to vary over the semi-open interval $[0, 2\pi[$, the vector r can vary in the open ball $B(0, 2\pi)$ of $\mathbb{R}^3$ of radius 2π. But the mapping $f : B(0, 2\pi)$ into the set of rotations is not one to one because (u, π) and $(-u, \pi)$ represent the same rotation. To enforce uniqueness we can assume that one of the coordinates, for example u_z, of the rotation axis u is positive. We can then represent uniquely the open subset of the set of rotations for which the axis is not perpendicular to the z-axis, and has a positive component along that axis, and the mapping is continuous. If we consider the open set of rotations defined by (u, θ), $u_z < 0$, we have another one to one continuous mapping. With these two mappings, we cannot represent rotations with an axis perpendicular to the z-axis. In order to obtain all possible rotations, we have to introduce the other four mappings defined by (u, θ) and $u_x > 0$ (resp. $u_x < 0$, $u_y > 0$, $u_y < 0$) which represent rotations with an axis not perpendicular to the x-axis (resp. the y-axis). We are still missing the null vector, i.e we have no representation for the null rotation, the identity matrix. In order to include it, we have to add a seventh map by considering for example the rotations defined by the "small" open ball $B(0, \epsilon)$ where ϵ must be smaller than π. These seven mappings define on the set of rotations a structure of C^∞-manifold of dimension 3.

It is interesting that in all three cases (3D lines, planes, and rotations), there does not exist a unique global representation and that we must live with at least three local mappings.

It is now instructive to study how the group of rigid displacements operates on the representations for lines and planes.

4.3.1   Line transformation

The easiest way to derive how representation 15 changes under rotation and translation is by considering that the line is defined by two points. The details can be found in the INRIA

report corresponding to this paper. We give here the results. a, and b are only sensitive to rotation:

$$\begin{bmatrix} a \\ b \end{bmatrix} \rightarrow \begin{bmatrix} a' \\ b' \end{bmatrix}$$

and:

$$a' = \frac{r_1.\alpha}{r_3.\alpha} \qquad b' = \frac{r_2.\alpha}{r_3.\alpha}$$

where $\alpha = [a, b, 1]^T$, and the r_i's are the row vectors of matrix R. This is true only if $r_3.\alpha \neq 0$; if $r_3.\alpha = 0$, the transformed line is perpendicular to the z-axis and representation 16 or 17 must be used.

The case of p and q is similar and we find:

$$\begin{bmatrix} p' \\ q' \end{bmatrix} = \frac{1}{r_3.\alpha} H(R\beta + t \wedge R\alpha)$$

where we have taken $\beta = [q, -p, bp - aq]^T$.

4.3.2   Plane transformation

Given a plane represented by its normal n and its distance to the origin d, if we apply to it a rotation along an axis going through the origin represented by a matrix R followed by a translation represented by a vector t, the new plane is represented by Rn and $d - t.Rn$ [FH86].

This allows us to compute how the representation 18, for example, is transformed by the rigid displacement. From the previous observation :

$$\begin{pmatrix} a \\ b \\ 1 \end{pmatrix} \rightarrow R \begin{pmatrix} a \\ b \\ 1 \end{pmatrix} \text{ and } c \rightarrow c - t.R \begin{pmatrix} a \\ b \\ 1 \end{pmatrix}$$

Introducing the three row vectors r_1, r_2, r_3 of matrix R, we have, assuming that $r_3.\alpha \neq 0$:

$$a' = \frac{r_1.\alpha}{r_3.\alpha} \quad b' = \frac{r_2.\alpha}{r_3.\alpha} \quad c' = \frac{c - t.R\alpha}{r_3.\alpha}$$

if $r_3.\alpha = 0$, this means that we cannot use the same representation for the transformed plane since it is parallel to the z-axis, therefore we must choose the representation 19 or 20.

5   Registration, Motion and Fusion of Visual Maps

In this section we show how to solve the problems listed in section 2 within the formalism and the representations explicited in sections 3 and 4.

5.1   Initial assumptions

We are given two visual maps $\mathcal{V}$ and $\mathcal{V}'$, each of them attached to a coordinate reference frame $\mathcal{F}$ and $\mathcal{F}'$ (see Figure 14).

Each visual map $\mathcal{V}$ is composed of primitives $\mathcal{P}$, described by a parameter vector P. We dispose of an estimate $\widehat{P_0}$ of P and of an error covariance matrix W_{P_0}.

The coordinate frames $\mathcal{F}$ and $\mathcal{F}'$ are related by a rigid displacement $\mathcal{D}$ such that each point M' of $\mathcal{F}'$ is related to a point M of $\mathcal{F}$ by the relation

$$O'M' = R\,OM + t$$

where R is the rotation matrix and t the translation vector of the displacement $\mathcal{D}$. We also have an estimate $\widehat{D_0}$ of D, with an error covariance matrix W_{D_0}.

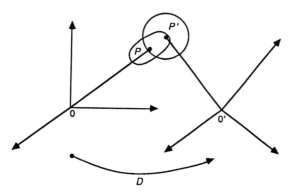

Figure 14: The general registration motion fusion problem

relations	points	lines	planes
points	$\equiv$	$\subset$	$\subset$
lines		$\equiv // \perp$	$\subset // \perp$
planes			$\equiv // \perp$

Table 1: Relations between the primitives; $\equiv$: identical to; $\subset$: included in; $\parallel$: parallel to; $\perp$: orthogonal to.

5.2   Defining geometric relations

We define a set of geometric relations between the primitives P and P' of two visual maps $\mathcal{V}$ and $\mathcal{V}'$. These relations are given in table 1.

This list of relations/primitives is not exhaustive but only demonstrative. The relation "identical" expresses the fact that the primitives P and P' represented in $\mathcal{V}$ and $\mathcal{V}'$ actually describe the same physical primitive. The relation "included" expresses that P describes a physical primitive which is part of the physical primitive described by P'. The relations "parallel" and "orthogonal" are interpreted in a similar fashion.

Each geometric relation can be expressed by a vector equation of the form :

$$f_i(P, P', D) = 0 \qquad (21)$$

5.3   Expliciting geometric relations

We now explicit equation 21 for the geometric relations of table 1. We denote by $\overline{P}$ the parameters of the primitive $\overline{P} = D(P)$, the image of P by the rigid displacement D. The computation of $\overline{P}$ from P is, in the case of points, $\overline{OM} = ROM + t$. The case of lines and planes was explicited in the previous Section. The measurement equations are the following ones :

Point-Point:

$$\text{relation} \equiv : O'M' - \overline{OM} = 0$$

Point-Line: assuming the line is not orthogonal to the z-axis :

$$\text{relation} \subset : \begin{cases} \bar{x} - a'\bar{z} - p' = 0 \\ \bar{y} - b'\bar{z} - q' = 0 \end{cases}$$

Point-Plane: assuming the plane is not parallel to the z-axis :

$$\text{relation} \subset : a'\bar{x} + b'\bar{y} + \bar{z} + c' = 0$$

Line-Line: assuming the two lines are not orthogonal to the z-axis :

$$\begin{aligned}\text{relation} &\equiv : (a', b', c', d')^t - (\bar{a}, \bar{b}, \bar{c}, \bar{d})^t = 0 \\ \text{relation} &\parallel : (a', b')^t - (\bar{a}, \bar{b})^t = 0 \\ \text{relation} &\perp : a'\bar{a} + b'\bar{b} + 1 = 0\end{aligned}$$

Line-Plane: assuming the line is not orthogonal and the plane not parallel to the z-axis :

$$\begin{aligned}\text{relation} &\subset : \begin{cases} a'\bar{a} + b'\bar{b} + 1 = 0 \\ a'\bar{p} + b'\bar{q} + c' = 0 \end{cases} \\ \text{relation} &\parallel : a'\bar{a} + b'\bar{b} + 1 = 0 \\ \text{relation} &\perp : (a', b')^t - (\bar{a}, \bar{b})^t = 0\end{aligned}$$

Plane-Plane: assuming the plane not parallel to the z-axis :

$$\begin{aligned}\text{relation} &\equiv : (a', b', c')^t - (\bar{a}, \bar{b}, \bar{c})^t = 0 \\ \text{relation} &\parallel : (a', b')^t - (\bar{a}, \bar{b})^t = 0 \\ \text{relation} &\perp : a'\bar{a} + b'\bar{b} + 1 = 0\end{aligned}$$

This approach should be compared to that of [Mun86].

5.4   Registration

The registration (or matching) of two primitives P and P' consists in detecting that their parameters P and P' verify equation 21 for one of the above listed geometric relations, with respect to the current noisy estimates $(\hat{P}_0, W_{P_0})$, $(\hat{P}'_0, W_{P'_0})$, and $(\hat{D}_0, W_{D_0})$ of P, P' and D.

This "detection" is done by computing between each pair of primitive the generalized Mahalanobis distance explicited by equation 11, and by matching a pair of primitive each time the χ^2 acceptation test given by inequality 12 is verified, i.e. when

$$d(\hat{P}_0, W_{P_0}, \hat{P}'_0, W_{P'_0}, \hat{D}_0, W_{D_0}) < \epsilon$$

In order to avoid a $0(n^2)$ complexity algorithm, it is of course possible to use additional control structures to select a subset of candidate primitives for each test. For instance, to test the relation "$\equiv$" between points or lines, bucketing techniques can be used with efficiency (see for instance [AFFT85]).

5.5   Motion

Having registered two primitives P and P', the motion problem consists in reducing the uncertainty on the *motion parameters* D while taking into account the uncertainty on the parameters P, P' and D.

This is done by setting $a = D$ and $x = (P, P')^t$, and by using the relation equation 21 as a measurement equation 1:

$$f_i(x, a) \equiv f_i((P, P'), D) = 0$$

Starting from the initial estimate $\hat{a}_0 = \hat{D}_0$, $S_0 = W_{D_0}$, and using the measurement $\hat{x}_1 = (\hat{P}_0, \hat{P}'_0)^t)$ with

$$W_1 = \begin{pmatrix} W_{P_0} & 0 \\ 0 & W_{P'_0} \end{pmatrix}$$

one applies the EKF formalism to obtain a new estimate $\hat{a}_1$ of the motion with a reduced covariance matrix $S_1 < S_0$. (In the sense $S_0 - S_1$ non-negative.)

This process is recursively repeated: at iteration i, if a new pair of primitives can be registered with the new motion estimate $(\hat{a}_{i-1}, S_{i-1})$, the additional measurement equations they bring lead to a new better estimate $\hat{a}_i$ of the motion with a still reduced covariance matrix S_i. This process ends after the matching of k primitives with a final estimate $(\hat{a}_k, S_k)$ of the motion parameter D.

5.6   Fusion

5.6.1   General Fusion

The fusion problem is exactly the dual of the motion problem, as it consists, after the registration of 2 primitives, in reducing the uncertainty on the *primitive parameters* P and P' while taking into account the uncertainty on the parameters P, P' and D.

This is done by "switching the attention", i.e. by choosing $a = (P, P')^t$ and $x = D$ while using again the relation equation 21 as a measurement equation 1:

$$f_i(x, a) \equiv f_i(D, (P, P')) = 0$$

The initial estimate is taken as $\hat{a}_0 = (\hat{P}_0, \hat{P'}_0)^t$ and

$$S_0 = \begin{pmatrix} W_{P_0} & 0 \\ 0 & W_{P'_0} \end{pmatrix}$$

and one uses the measurement $\hat{x}_1 = \hat{D}_0$ with $W_1 = W_{D_0}$ to apply the EKF formalism and obtain a new estimate $\hat{a}_1$ of the primitive parameters with a reduced covariance matrix $S_1 < S_0$.

If additional relations hold between these primitives and other ones, the same treatment allows for a further reduction in their parameters uncertainty, and therefore a more accurate estimation of the primitive parameters.

5.6.2   Forgetting primitives

After the treatment of a constraint, the parameters P_1 and P'_1 of the primitives are usually correlated, which means that the covariance matrix

$$\mathrm{cov}(\hat{P}_1, \hat{P'}_1) = \begin{pmatrix} W_{P_1} & W_{P_1 P'_1} \\ W_{P'_1 P_1} & W_{P_1} \end{pmatrix}$$

contains $W_{P'_1 P_1} = W_{P_1 P'_1}^t \neq 0$.

Therefore, it is no longer possible to treat independently P and P' in successive measurement equations. One as to consider them as a new primitive, either by keeping only one of them, or the union of them.

For instance, if one updates the parameters of P' with those of an "identical" primitive P observed in a previous visual map, one keeps only the updated parameters of P' in the new map, with their covariance matrix $W_{p'}$, forgetting the previous paramaters P after having used them.

On the other hand, if one updates the parameters of two lines by detecting that they are orthogonal, one keeps the new primitive formed by the union of the updated two lines, with the corresponding covariance matrix. One must use this kind of relation carefully, in order to control the size of the state parameter a.

5.6.3   Autofusion

In the special case where $\mathcal{V} \equiv \mathcal{V}'$, all primitives come from the same visual map, and the motion parameters vanishes as they correspond to the identity transform and are perfectly known.

Nevertheless, one can still detect the previous geometric relations between pairs of primitives P and P', and use them to reduce the uncertainty on the primitives parameters.

6   Experimental Results

The basic principles presented in this paper were tested on a variety of synthetic and real data. The interested reader can find registration and motion results with real points and lines in [AF87b], registration and fusion results with synthetic and real points and lines in [AF87a] and results on the building of global 3D maps from passive strereovision in [AL87]. In this paper we only present results of the motion estimation from two 3D maps, of the fusion of several inaccurate 3D maps, and of the detection of colinearity within a single 3D map (what we called "autofusion"). In each of these examples, the 3D map is made of 3D lines.

6.1   Registration and Motion

Figure 15 shows the edges of a triplet of images taken by the mobile robot in a first position. From these edges, the trinocular stereovision system computes a set of 3D segments. Each 3D segment is represented by the parameters (a, b, p, q) of the 3D line supporting it and by the error covariance computed — as it is explained in section 4.2 — from the uncertainty on the edge points in the three images (we took an isotropic gaussian density function of covariance 1 pixel around each edge point). Each 3D line is bounded by 2 endpoints obtained from the endpoints measured in the 3 images which are projected on the reconstructed 3D line.

We show in figures 16 and 17 respectively the horizontal and vertical projections of the reconstructed 3D segments. We also show the uncertainty attached to the reconstructed 3D lines by showing the uncertainty it produces on the coordinates of their endpoints. The 95% confidence regions of the endpoints positions are ellipsoids whose projections are the ellipses shown in figures 16 and 17. One can see the anisotropic distribution of the uncertainty on the three coordinates of the points and its variation as a function of their position relative to the cameras (which are located grossly in the middle of the front view and at the bottom of the top view).

The robot now moves a little, a new triplet of images is taken (figure 18) and another set of 3D lines is computed. Initially, the robot is given a very crude estimate of its motion between the two views. Applying this crude estimate to the 3D lines obtained in position 1, and projecting them in one of the images obtained in position 2 (the image of camera 3), one obtains the crude superimposition observed in figure 19. Solid lines are the transformed 3D segments computed in position 1, while the dotted lines are the 2D segments observed in position 2.

We now ask the system to discover the relation "$\equiv$" between the 3D lines (see section 5.3) reconstructed in positions 1 and 2, given the initial crude motion estimate and its uncertainty. The program takes each 3D line in position 1, applies the noisy current motion estimate to place it in the 3D map obtained in position 2 with a new covariance matrix (combining the initial uncertainty with the motion uncertainty), and computes its Mahalanobis distance (equation 11) to all the other lines of position 2.

The program detects a match each time a pair of lines passes the χ^2 test of equation 12. If a line in position 1 can be matched to several lines in position 2, this is an *ambiguous* match, and nothing is done. On the other hand, each time an *unambiguous* match is found, the parameters of the motion are updated as it is explained in section 5.5. As the uncertainty on motion decreases after each new match, some previously am-

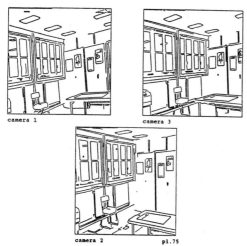

Figure 15: Triplet of images taken in position 1

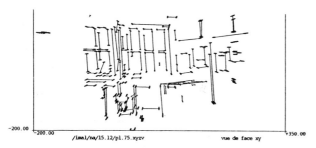

Figure 16: Front view of reconstructed 3D lines

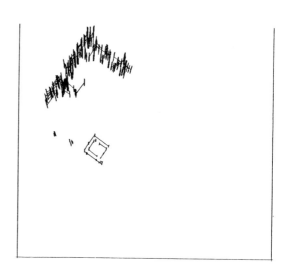

Figure 17: Top view of reconstructed 3D lines

Figure 18: Triplet of images taken in position 2

Figure 19: Superimposition of 3D segments of position 1 with 2D edges of position 2 (crude initial motion estimate)

biguous matches can now become unambiguous. Therefore the entire matching process is repeated until no more line can be matched (3 iterations in this example). The final estimate of the motion is very accurate, as can be seen in figure 20 where the obtained superimposition is now almost perfect.

Applying exactly the same technique to a set of 6 triplets of views taken during the motion of the robot, the sytem was able to build a global 3D map of the room (figure 21) where rotating segments at the bottom right are the computed successive robot positions.

6.2   Registration, Motion and Fusion

In this experiment, the robot is looking from 4 different positions at a regular pattern (figures 22 and 23) formed by vertical lines floating in front of horizontal lines, and builds in each position a local 3D map. Exactly the same technique as in the previous example was used to register each successive local 3D map, and put all of them in a single absolute reference frame. Figure 24 shows the resulting 3D map before fusion. Fusion is achieved by discovering the relation "≡" computed between lines in the global 3D map, and taking into account the uncertainty on the 3D lines due to their reconstruction and to the successive motion estimations. Fusion yields a reduction from 1808 to 650 segments and improved accuracy, as can be seen by looking at the front and top view of the reconstructed 3D pattern after fusion (Figure 25).

6.3   Detecting colinearity in space

In this experiment, the robot is looking at the regular pattern only once. We show in figure 26 the vertical and horizontal

/imal/der/imal5.12/pl.c3.70.a   /imal/na/15.12/pl.75.xyzv

Figure 20: Superimposition of 3D segments of position 1 with 2D edges of position 2 (final motion estimate)

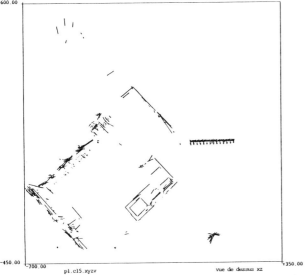

Figure 21: Top view of a global 3D map of the room computed from 6 local 3D maps

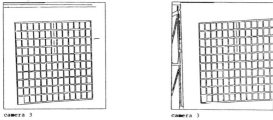

camera 3   camera 3

Figure 22: A regular grid observed from positions 1 and 2

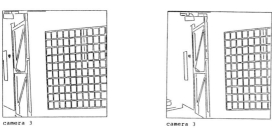

camera 3   camera 3

Figure 23: A regular grid observed from positions 3 and 4

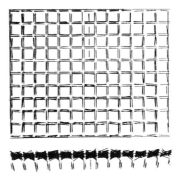

Figure 24: Front and top view of reconstructed 3D lines before identical lines are detected

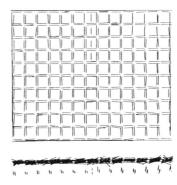

Figure 25: Front and top view of 3D lines after the fusion of identical lines

projections of the initially reconstructed 3D segments. We also show the uncertainty attached to reconstructed 3D lines by showing the uncertainty it produces on the coordinates of their endpoints. (in the same way as in the first experiment).

We now ask the system to discover the relation "≡" between the 3D lines (see section 5.3). The program takes a first 3D line, computes its Mahalanobis distance (equation 11) to all the other lines of the scene, and accepts the first line which passes the χ^2 test of equation 12. The two lines are fused using the technique of section 5.6 and one keeps only the parameters of the optimal line representing both of them with an updated covariance matrix. The remaining lines are now compared to this new virtual line still with the Mahalanobis distance of

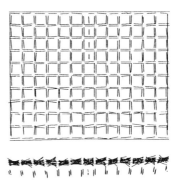

Figure 26: Front and top view of reconstructed 3D lines, before colinearity is detected

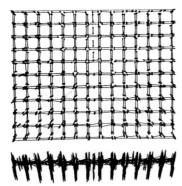

Figure 27: Initial uncertainty attached to 3D lines endpoints

equation 11 but with the new updated covariance matrix, while the χ^2 test of equation 12 remains unchanged. This process is repeated until no more line can be matched with the first one, and then repeated with all the remaining unmatched lines.

The result is a reduced set of virtual lines on which the endpoints of the original segments have been projected, as shown in figure 28. The uncertainty on the line parameters has been greatly reduced: figure 29 shows the resulting uncertainty on the lines endpoints, which agrees very well with the reality.

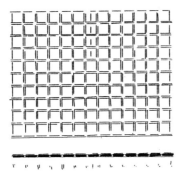

Figure 28: Front and top view of 3D lines when colinearity is discovered and enforced

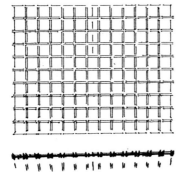

Figure 29: Uncertainty attached to 3D lines endpoints after the fusion of colinear segments

References

[AF87a]   N. Ayache and O.D. Faugeras. Building a consistent 3d representation of a mobile robot environment by combining multiple stereo views. In *Proc. International Joint Conference on Artificial Intelligence*, August 1987. Milano, Italy.

[AF87b]   N. Ayache and O.D. Faugeras. Building, registering and fusing noisy visual maps. In *Proc. First International Conference on Computer Vision*, pages 73–82, IEEE, June 1987. London, U.K., also an INRIA Internal Report 596, 1986.

[AF87c]   N. Ayache and B. Faverjon. Efficient registration of stereo images by matching graph descriptions of edge segments. *The International Journal of Computer Vision*, 1(2), April 1987.

[AFFT85]   N. Ayache, O.D. Faugeras, B. Faverjon, and G. Toscani. Matching depth maps obtained by passive stereovision. In *Proceedings of Third Workshop on Computer Vision: Representation and Control*, pages 197–204, IEEE, October 1985.

[AL87]   N. Ayache and F. Lustman. Fast and reliable passive trinocular stereovision. In *Proc. First International Conference on Computer Vision*, pages 422–427, IEEE, June 1987. London, U.K.

[BC86]   Bolle and Cooper. On optimally combining pieces of information, with application to estimating 3d complex-object position from range data. In *IEEE Transactions on PAMI*, pages 619–638, 1986.

[Can86]   J. Canny. A computational approach to edge detection. *IEEE Transactions on Pattern Analysis and Machine Intelligence*, 8 No6:679–698, 1986.

[Der87]   R. Deriche. Using canny's criteria to derive an optimal edge detector recuresively implemented. *The International Journal of Computer Vision*, 2, April 1987.

[Dur86]   H.F. Durrant-Whyte. Consistent integration and propagation of disparate sensor observations. In *Proc. International Conference on Robotics and Automation*, pages 1464–1469, April 1986. San Francisco, CA, USA.

[FAF86]   O.D. Faugeras, N. Ayache, and B. Faverjon. Building visual maps by combining noisy stereo measurements. In *Proc. International Conference on Robotics and Automation*, pages 1433–1438, April 1986. San Francisco, CA, USA.

[FH86]   O.D. Faugeras and M. Hebert. The representation, recognition, and locating of 3d shapes from range data. *The International Journal of Robotics Research*, 5, No 3:27–52, 1986.

[FLT87]   O.D. Faugeras, F. Lustman, and G. Toscani. Motion and structure from motion from point and line matches. In *Proc. First International Conference on Computer Vision*, pages 25–34, IEEE, June 1987. London, U.K.

[HM87]   Hager and M. Mintz. *Estimation Procedures for Robust Sensor Control, in the integration of sensing with actuation to form a robust intelligent control system*. GRASPLAB Report 97, Department of Computer and Information Science, Moore School, University of Pennsylvania, March 1987.

[Jaz70]   A.M. Jazwinsky. *Stochastic Processes and Filtering Theory*. Academic Press, 1970.

[Kan87]   T. Kanade. *Three-Dimensional Machine Vision*. Kluwer Academic Publishers, 1987.

[KTT87]   D.J. Kriegman, E. Triendl, and Binford T.O. A mobile robot: sensing, planning and locomotion. In *Proc. International Conference on Robotics and Automation*, pages 402–408, IEEE, 1987. Raleigh,North Carolina.

[MM87]   McKendall and M. Mintz. *Models of Sensor Noise and Optimal Algorithms for Estimation and Quantization in Vision Systems*. GRASPLAB Report 97, Department of Computer and Information Science, Moore School, University of Pennsylvania, March 1987.

[MS86]   Matthies and Shafer. *Error modelling in Stereo Navigation*. Technical Report, University of Carnegie-Mellon, Department of Computer Science, 1986. pp. 86–140.

[Mun86]   J.L. Mundy. Reasoning about 3-d space with alebraic deduction. In O. D. Faugeras and Georges Giralt, editors, *Robotics Research, The Third International Symposium*, pages 117–124, MIT Press, 1986.

[P*87]   J. Porrill et al. Optimal combination and constraints for geometrical sensor data. March 1987. to appear.

[SC87]   R.C. Smith and P. Cheeseman. On the representation and estimation of spatial uncertainty. *International Journal of Robotics Research*, 5(4):56–68, 1987.

MOTOR AND SPATIAL ASPECTS IN ARTIFICIAL VISION

G. Sandini, P. Morasso, M. Tistarelli

University of Genoa
Department of Communication, Computer and Systems Science
Via Opera Pia 11A — I16145 Genoa

The integration of vision and movement is investigated within the framework of stereo and motion analysis. In particular the extraction of depth information from multiple images is discussed and the results of algorithms applied to stereo images and image sequences are presented. Such processes end up with a common stereometric format: a visual bas−relief (VB) representing both an iconic component (a depth map) and a motor/proprioceptive component (the spatial location and orientation of the viewer). Moreover in order to integrate the spatio−temporal flow of information coming from a moving observer we need some sort of *accumulator*. We hypothesize that this accumulator is a volumetric representation of a portion of space dynamically updated by the flow of information. An example of such mechanism based on an oct−tree representation, and applied to multiple stereo images is presented.

1. Stereometric Strategies Related to Movement

Visually−guided behavior is intrinsically a *data flow problem*: hundreds of megabits per second that need some kind of data−reduction. This can be performed immediately at the sensor level in high−speed servo−mechanisms that destroy the greatest part of the available information, extracting a few peculiar features. They are able to *react* but are unable to *understand*. A reaction−type behavior is ego−centric, it cannot discriminate among situations that, although similar from the purely sensory point of view, are significantly different from the environmental point of view and require, accordingly, different behaviors.

However, in advanced applications in unstructured environments that imply the kind of flexibility displayed by humans, we need to contrast ego−centric with eco−centric behavior, i.e. a behavior based on the environment (the layout and the nature of objects and free space). Eco−centric behavior cannot afford to destroy information during data reduction. On the contrary, it requires to *accumulate* it, in order to build up knowledge about the environment. Knowledge acquisition and knowledge interrogation should be uncoupled and should proceed asynchronously, in such a way to free action from "ego−centric slavery".

In order to perform data reduction in an eco−centric way, we need some sort of *accumulator*, i.e. an internal representation where we can *accumulate* spatial information derived from the input flow. We hypothesize that this accumulator is a volumetric representation of a portion of space that allows incremental generation and metric operations such as computation of volumes, areas, distances, size parameters, volumetric set operations, etc.

In our view, vision *is* essentially such a constructive process and this requires that all the cooperating visual processes end up with a common stereometric format: a visual bas−relief (VB). VB's are mixed representations that have both an iconic component (a depth map) and a motor/proprioceptive component (the spatial location and orientation of the viewer). In such a framework, that emphasizes the ecological nature of vision [Gibson 1979], active motor exploration has obviously a strategic significance: a passive observer could never really *see* because he could not look at objects from many viewpoints. However, active control of ego−motion is not only important at the *strategic* level, it is also important at the *tactical* level in determining specific stereometric methods.

A basic form of stereometric method is *triangulation*. The same object point is observed from two different vantage points and its position in space is evaluated by intersecting the two rays which are generated by the corresponding picture elements. Stereometric triangulation, applied systematically to a carefully selected set of picture elements, induces a depth map, i.e. a bundle of line segments emanating from either picture plane and passing through the corresponding center of projection.

From the *computational point of view*, stereometric triangulation requires the knowledge of the relative positioning of the two cameras (6 parameters), the optical parameters (4 or 5), and of the patterns of iconic correspondence (i.e. the identification of pairs of picture elements that correspond to the same object point).

From the *operational point of view*, stereometric triangulation can be implemented in two ways:

♦ *Binocular*. In this case, the couple of corresponding icons is provided by two cameras with a base line of (approximately) constant length and the relative movement of the two cameras may be constrained in such a way that the two optical axes and the base line are coplanar. In binocular stereometry the relative positioning parameters are reduced to two rota-

This research was partially supported by Esprit Project 419 and by the Italian Ministry of Education (projects on robotics and artificial intelligence).

tions only — rotations around two parallel axes perpendicular to the base line. Moreover, the correspondence pattern between the two images, expressed by the family of epipolar lines, has a prevalent "horizontal" structure.

◆ *Kinetic.* In this case, the couple of corresponding icons is provided by one camera that moves in space — the egomotion. The base line is generated by movement. In qualitative terms, there is a complete analogy with the binocular case. The difference is that the movement may generate an arbitrary relative positioning of the two frames of the triangulation. Therefore arbitrary patterns of correspondence may occur that require complex computations. Special patterns of movement, however, may generate special correspondence patterns that reduce the complexity[1]. Egomotion generates an apparent motion of iconic features on the picture plane that is characterized by a focus of compression (FOC) or a focus of expansion (FOE): This focus is the epipole.

The shape—formation role of triangulation is based on an explicit computation of depth, the depth of visible points of the face of an object, up to the occluding contours. When approaching these contours, however, the straight triangulation may become inaccurate unless the contours correspond to sharp edges of the object surface. For smooth occluding surfaces, it is better to use a weaker method than triangulation, a method that uses rays without computing distance explicitly. For this purpose, a good candidate is a method that uses a volumetric representation of occluding contours and performs explicit *solid intersections* among them without passing through a depth map[2].

Let us now compare the pros and cons of different stereometric strategies:

● Binocular stereo is good for detecting the depth of edges which are close to vertical, e.g. the legs of a chair. This is due to the fact that the epipolar lines are about horizontal and edges can be detected best if they are orthogonal to the direction of search.

● Kinetic stereo on the horizontal plane gives information of the same nature as binocular stereo because the epipolar lines follow a similar pattern. Therefore this method is a surrogate of binocular stereo for a monocular observer.

● Kinetic stereo on the vertical plane gives a performance which is complementary of that given by binocular stereo, i.e. it detects best horizontal edges like the seat of a chair because the pattern of epipolar lines is about vertical.

● As regards kinematic stereo in the axial direction, the same complementarity that characterizes kinematic stereo on the vertical plane holds only in the central part of the visual field and not in the two lateral parts, according to the radial structure of the epipolar lines.

● The occluding contour method has two roles. One is to improve the estimate of the object shape in the neighborhood of the occluding contour and the other is to provide the 3D support for the integration of sequences of bas—relief evaluation by means of the other methods.

The knowledge of the weak and strong points of every method may suggest a way of integrating them, for example by means of a fuzzy formulation of the volumetric representations and of the composition operators. The solution to this problem must be based on the estimate of the accuracy achieved by the different methods in the recovery of 3D data. In fact the depth information derived from stereo or optic flow have different intrinsic accuracy and must be made homogeneous as a first step toward integration.

Another point concerns the limits of the analogy between binocular stereo and kinetic stereo. In the former case, couples of corresponding images are the source data, whereas in the latter case the source data is a time varying image. The movement of the observer in a 3D world generates an optical flow field on his retina [Pradzny 1980] and it is this optical flow the starting point of any computational formulation of kinetic stereo. In kinetic stereo, the problem consists of processing the optical flow *while controlling the egomotion*, in such a way that patterns of correspondence can be established for images at different instants of time. A further difference between the two computational problems arises from the fact that the motion of the camera can be actively controlled in case of egomotion whereas in stereo vision it is fixed by the stereo geometry (it is only a virtual motion). Moreover, binocular stereo is intrinsically discontinuous in space (the distance between the two sensors is fixed) whereas the egomotion that induces kinetic stereo is continuous is space and time. For this reasons, kinetic stereo requires a *tracking* strategy while binocular stereo must be based on *matching* procedures.

We should point out that this kind of problem is different from the problem usually faced by people working with optical flow, i.e. the problem of deducing egomotion from time—varying imagery. Of course this problem, that concerns passive (unknown) movements, is much harder than the problem formulated in this paper, that concerns active movements, because knowledge of egomotion is an extremely powerful source of perceptual structure.

2. Binocular Stereo

In our approach, the binocular stereo process is based on two computational steps — regional stereo and edge stereo — where the latter refines the initial rough estimate provided by the former, down to the accuracy of one pixel. From the precise measurement of disparity along the edges, a depth—map is then computed by means of interpolation.

Two major classes of factors affect the accuracy of the stereo algorithm: one is related to the local energy of the stereo image pairs and the other to the stereo set—up and the optical factors. At the present level of implementation we only considered the first factor, by actually measuring the local energy of the stereo images and by ranking the results of the stereo matching according to it. The algorithm follows a *coarse to fine* approach: Each image of the stereo pair is band—limited with filters of increasing center frequency (Laplacian of Gaussian) and the disparity, which is first measured at low spatial frequency, is refined at medium and high spatial frequency. The resulting measure is used as a first approximation of edge disparity. Edge disparity is measured by explicitly matching edges extracted from the high spatial frequency images. The rationale for this choice is the fact that a direct matching of isolated edge points would produce many false matches because unable to enforce a *smoothness constraint*. Let us now consider in more detail the computational modules[3].

▶ *Filtering and extraction of zero−crossings.* Each image of the stereo pair is filtered by a convolution with a Laplacian of Gaussian operator. The band−pass procedure sets an upper limit to the maximum achievable accuracy or, in other words, limits the range of measurements to be performed. Moreover, after having removed the low−spatial frequencies, the regions of high energy *are* the regions of luminance discontinuities where measurements are performed. This is a necessary condition to assure that the gross and the fine measurements are actually congruent (i.e. they measure the same thing). The choice of the Laplacian of Gaussian is related to the fact that the edges that are used for the final step of the computation of disparity are obtained by extracting the zero crossings of the filtered images [Marr and Hildreth 1980].

▶ *Measurement of local energy.* The stereo pair filtered at low frequency is used to isolate the patches of the images where the disparity will be measured. This is obtained by measuring the energy over patches of one image. The size of the patches is proportional to the spatial frequency band of the filtered image (4 times the size of the central lobe of the Laplacian of Gaussian) and centered over the zero crossings of the filtered image.

The rationale for this procedure is that the disparity cannot be reliably measured over the all the image[4] but only over those patches where the probability of finding an edge is high. It should be noted that the edges extracted at this spatial frequency are different from those that will be used in the final step of the procedure. At that stage, the accuracy could be much higher and the resolution will also be higher.

▶ *Correlation* The disparity among patches of the stereo pair is computed using a correlation procedure similar to that proposed by Nishihara in the PRISM system [Nishihara 1984], but the procedure is changed in two major ways in order to overcome a significant defect of the algorithm: if an error occurs early in the coarse−to−fine approximation, it is very unlikely that this error can be corrected later on.

The first modification is that at each level of accuracy also orientational infomation is considered. In fact in the original implementation proposed by Nishihara the cross−correlation function was measured from the sign of the images filtered with a Laplacian of Gaussian without taking into consideration any structural information. In our experimental situation this caused a high number of wrong matches. In order to overcome this problem, without loosing the "regional" approach of the method, the average direction of the intensity gradient is also measured in the left and right image patch and for each value of the correlation. The difference between the two values (left and right) is used to weight the correlation function and produces a reliability factor linked to disparity. In this way disparity (identified by the peaks of the correlation function) is dependent of local orientation.

The second fundamental modification is that each level of the process does not only produce one disparity value, but multiple disparity measures are propagated from one level to the next one, each measurement being characterized by a reliability factor.

By using this procedure, the reliability measure of a disparity value may change as a consequence of the new information introduced by the different spatial frequency bands of the second and third iteration. And in fact in all those instances where the details are actually relevant to the matching procedure the reliability measure increases with the iterations. The overall result is that early wrong matches may be corrected later on in the procedure.

The degree of refinement achieved by the three successive approximation is proportional to the spatial frequency band selected both through the size of the patches and through the unitary shift of the correlation procedure. For the values we have used in the example of figure 1 (with standard deviations of 8, 4 and 2) the disparity is computed with a resolution of 8, 4, and 2 pixels. This means that at the last stage disparity is known with a resolution of $+-2$ pixels.

▶ *Edge Matching.* If the resolution achieved during the previous steps of the algorithm is in the range of $+-2$ pixels, as in the example of fig. 1, edge matching simply reduces to a search for the closest edge.

▶ *Interpolation* The results of edge matching, which are localized on edge points, are propagated to all the pixels of the image by a linear interpolation procedure.

3. Kinetic Stereo

Tracking contour points on successive images of a sequence has much in common with the correspondence problem in stereo matching. On the other hand the tracking strategy necessary for an arbitrary and unknown egomotion is a very complex computational problem which can be simplified substantially by actively controlling the navigation parameters. In this case the two dimensional direction of motion (i.e. the projection of the direction of motion on the image plane) is known and it is possible to compute the two dimensional velocity vector completely. In order to facilitate the computation of the egomotion parameter, a constrained egomotion strategy was adopted in which the position of the fixation point is stabilized during the navigation. This egomotion strategy, which can also be seen as if the observer was tracking an environmental point, has been already analyzed in the past [Bandopadhay et.al. 1986, Sandini and Tistarelli 1986], and is one of the basic assumption of the approach presented here.

Besides the constraints imposed on navigation we also based our algorithm on the assumption that the images of the sequence vary slowly with respect to the sampling frequency. This need is partly related to the *discrete* visual world typical of todays computer vision. In humans, in fact, spatio−temporal interpolation actually produces a perception of moving objects which is either continuous or blurred. In our experimental set−up, where we are forced to emulate real−time processing by sampling image sequences at a much slower sampling rate, the *stroboscopic effect* due to a sub−sampling in time must be considered as an *artificial* source of noise, which, on the other hand may greatly change the overall performance of the algorithm. In a real−time environment (i.e. in a situation where the computational power is sufficient to perform a real−time computation) the spatio−temporal interpolation produced by the sensor or by appropriate filtering mechanisms [Bliss 1986] will actually perform like a time band−pass filtering actually improving the overall performance of the system. In other words, the continuous nature of motion information can be used to derive, strictly on a local basis, the component of velocity perpendicular to the contour, while the egomotion parameters can be used to derive the direction of motion.

The position in space of the image points is computed with a triangulation procedure applied on points that have been matched across a given number of images. This last step, again, requires the knowledge of navigation parameters.

The kinetic stereometric process is divided into the following computational modules (the first is common with binocular stereo):

▶ *Filtering and extraction of the zero−crossings*

▶ The *time derivative* is computed using a classical 5−point interpolation formula in order to increase the accuracy of the following processing step.

▶ The *velocity component perpendicular to the local orientation of the contour* is computed as the ratio between the time derivative and the intensity gradient [Hildreth 1983].

▶ The computation of the *true direction of iconic motion* requires to estimate egomotion, first. This is a complex process indeed that in humans has many components: motor, vestibular, proprioceptive, visual, etc. Let us only consider here the visual strategy of egomotion estimate, in relation with the well known human technique of visual stabilization by means of fixation/smooth pursuit [Carpenter 1977]. This quasi−automatic behavior has the interesting consequence that during egomotion the visual axis is rotated in such a way to be invariantly aimed at a fixation point in the environment, therefore creating an "egomotion triangle": The base of the triangle is the (unknown) ego−displacement, the lengths of the sides are distances from the fixation point that can be computed by binocular stereo, and the base angles measure "ocular rotations". Solving the triangle gives a description of egomotion, from which it is possible to derive the iconic position of FOC or FOE and then the true direction of iconic motion. This approach has two advantages: firstly, camera motion is simpler to control with respect to other active control strategies (like manteining the parallelism of the optical axis) and can take advantage of visual feedback and secondly, the measurement of the parameters of the camera motion is easier than with other motion strategies. It is also worth noting the analogy between this kind of egomotion triangulation and the triangulation applied to the optic flow pattern that generates the depth map.

▶ The *instantaneous optic flow* is computed by searching from a contour point on the image at time T, the corresponding point in the image at time T+1. This search (which is similar to a tracking procedure) is performed along the "true direction of motion" and within the range derived from the perpendicular component.

▶ The *integrated optic flow*, necessary to achieve a sufficient base for triangulation, is obtained by joining the instantaneous optical flow of a given number of successive images of the sequence. The implications related to the choice of this number are currently investigated (in the experiment presented here a fixed number of 5 successive instantaneous optical flows were integrated to obtain the integrated optical flow".

▶ The computation of the *depth map* is done straightforwardly from the knowledge of the optic flow by a stereometric triangulation between corresponding edge points identified by the previous step. The depth map itself is "filled" by interpolating the depth measurements performed on contour points. Figure 2 gives an example of the computational process.

4. Volumetric Integration with Oct−trees

Oct−trees are data structures that imply a recursive decomposition of a region of space − the *Universe*− into subregions − *Octants* − the decomposition being terminated when an octant may be considered uniform as regards some measurable feature that is spatially distributed, such as density of matter [Jackins and Tanimoto 1980].

In its simplest form, an oct−tree is used to discriminate between objects and free space and in this case it is sufficient to store only a bit in each voxel. Augmented oct−trees have been proposed to make explicit some additional information [Jackins and Tanimoto 1983, Chien and Aggarwal, 1986].

In general, although oct−trees have been proposed originally as a tool for efficient memory storage of volumetric structures, such as 3D binary array descriptions of objects, we feel that they have more fundamental properties that make them attractive from the point of view of vision and knowledge representation:

● Oct−tree represent objects and free space at the same time and in the same way, i.e. they capture the essential complementarity between figure and ground.

● Oct−trees provide a variable resolution representation, self−adapting to the structural complexity of an universe.

● An oct−tree stores multiple representations of the same universe at the same time: from a given oct−tree it is easy to extract a lower resolution representation simply by reducing the number of levels of the tree.

● It is easy to perform volumetric set operations (union, intersection, etc.) that are the basis of many problems of visual integration, planning and navigation.

On the other hand, oct−trees have two main problems: locality and rotation. Locality is lost in the tree−structure and rotation affects an oct−tree in a complex and highly unstructured way. We are not facing these problems here.

Let us now focus on the central problem of incremental volumetric representation: integration of the sequences of views obtained during active navigation/exploration of the environment [Massone and Morasso 1986, Morasso and Sandini 1985, Sandini et al. 1986].

We assume that each view provides a basic visual representation: a *depth image*. A depth image is an *ego−centric* representation, i.e. it is implicitly referred to the observer's coordinate system. In order to use it in active navigation/exploration, we need to convert it to an *eco−centric* representation, i.e. a representation referred to an environmental coordinate system. The reason is that only eco−centric representations can allow us to *integrate* multiple views by means of *volume intersection techniques*. This requires *proprioception*, i.e. a measurement of the position/orientation of the self with respect to the environment, and the construction of the corresponding representation.

In other words, depth images plus proprioception are the basic ingredients to build an eco−centric 3D visual representation, what we define as a *visual bas−relief* (VB). Visual integration can then be expressed as the process of intersecting sequences of visual bas−reliefs. We propose oct−trees as a convenient representational basis to carry out the task.

Volume intersection techniques applied to oct−trees have been used by Chien and Aggarwal [1986]. They assume that three orthogonal views are available and that the viewer is at infinity. We relax both constraints.

A visual bas−relief (VB) is an infinite portion of 3D space that stays beyond a depth image. A VB can be identified by two vectors (a translation and a rotation) plus an image (a depth image). Figure 3 shows an example of the VB of an object.

For building the oct−tree representation of a VB, we need a basic primitive, which compares a generic voxel with VB. In the approach that we followed, the voxel is assimilated to the surrounding sphere because it is easier to project a sphere than a cube on the depth image. The projection requires only to estimate the spherical coordinates of the ray passing through the center of the voxel and the visual angle subtended by it. These parameters are mapped onto the depth image plane, generating a discretized circle, whose pixels identify a couple of z−values that are then compared with the depth image and classified as either 'white', 'black', or 'gray'.

In the process of environment exploration, a sequence of VBs can be constructed, one for each viewpoint. The cumulative oct−tree of the object can be obtained recursively by means of a volume intersection strategy, according to which the current object oct−tree is intersected with the current VB. Volumetric intersection can be performed efficiently exploiting the tree−structure of oct−trees.

In such a constructive process, the object−oct−tree may be initially set to full−universe. Subsequent views *chisel out* solid chunks − in analogy with the action of a sculptor − improving more and more the volumetric fidelity of the representation. Figure 4 shows the construction of a clown face from several views.

It is important to point out that the complexity of the volumetric integration process is independent of the number of views: the current oct−tree summarizes the result of an arbitrarily long exploration. This must be contrasted with other solid modeling approaches, such as CSG, in which the complexity grows exponentially with the number of constructive operations.

The variable resolution capability of oct−trees can play a major role in shaping *smart exploration strategies*. Since the time to build an oct−tree is an exponential function of the number of levels, it is important to limit this number according to the pragmatic requirements of the exploration and to the accuracy granted by the perceptual data. As regards this point, in particular, if depth images are characterized by a fixed iconic resolution (number of pixels), the size of the smallest detectable voxel for a given depth map is linearly related to the smallest depth value. Therefore, the intrinsic available accuracy of the VB construction process increases when the observer

approaches the object. However, the exploration strategy may decide to exploit this limit fully only when necessary, for example when some gross feature has been identified which requires some closer inspection. Moreover, since a portion of an oct−tree is still an oct−tree, when attention is focused on a portion of the universe, the visual integration process can be restricted to it.

A foundamental issue related to volume intersection techniques is that of *uncertainty*. The sources of uncertainty in the computation and intergration of depth maps are, mainly, three:

- i) The nature of the matching process with respect to local image features (like orientation of edges with respect to direction of camera displacement);
- ii) The nature of stereometric triangulation with respect to geometric and optical factors;
- iii) The intrinsinc uncertainty of proprioception due to either a limited accuracy of the sensors or to environmental disturbances

If all these factors are made explicit the volumetric information extracted from different information sources can be made homogeneous and, subsequently, integrated. How this goal can be achieved is still subject to discussion but a stochastic model of both the process of building VBs and the process of integrating them will certainly be necessary. For example a *depth−uncertainty image* registered with the depth−map, and representing the probability of correct measure can be associated to each depth−map, and a volumetric representation whose elements (e.g the leaves of a oct−tree, or each voxel) stores a probablity of free space can be used to . explicitly represent uncertainty during volumetric integration.

---

[1] Let us consider a few examples: If the camera movement is in the horizontal plane, the effect is similar to that of the binocular case; If the movement is in the direction of the optical axis, then the epipoles are in the center of each image and the patterns of correspondence have a polar structure; If the camera movement is in the vertical plane, the epipoles stay on the vertical axes and the patterns of correspondence are vertical−like, and so on.

[2] In a sense, however, an occluding contour defines a degenerate depth map, a map for which we can assume a zero distance value inside the contour and an infinite value outside it.

[3] These modules do not require a sequential execution, that is forced on our present implementation by the nature of the available hardware. On the contrary, the appropriate hardware should allow parallel distributed processing.

[4] For example, in the PRISM system, proposed by Nishihara, the energy of the image is artificially made constant over the all image by projecting random dot patterns.

REFERENCES

Bandopadhay, A., B. Chandra, and D. H. Ballard, "Active Naviga tion: Tracking an Environmental Point Considered Beneficial," *Proc. of "Workshop on Motion: Representation and Analysis"*, pp. 23−29, IEEE Computer Society, May 7−9, 1986.

Bliss, J. G., "Velocity−tuned Filters for Spatio−temporal Interpolation," *Proc. of "Workshop on Motion: Representation and Analysis"*, pp. 61−66, IEEE Computer Society, May 7−9 1986.

Carpenter, R. H. S., *Movements of the Eyes,* Pion, London, 1977.

Chien, C. H. and J. K. Aggarwal, "Identification of 3D objects from Multiple Silhouettes Using Quadtree/Octree," *Computer Vision Graphics and Image Processing*, vol. 36, pp. 256−273, 1986.

Gibson, J. J., in *The Ecological Approach to Visual Perception*, Houghton Mifflin, Boston, 1979.

Hildreth, E. C., *The Measurement of Visual Motion,* MIT Press, Cambridge, USA, 1983.

Jackins, C. L. and S. L. Tanimoto, "Quad−trees, Oct−trees and k−trees − A Generalized Approach to Recursive Decomposition of Euclidean Space," *IEEE Trans. PAMI,* vol. 5 No.5, pp. 533−539, 1983.

Jackins, C. L. and S. L. Tanimoto, "Oct−trees and their Use in Representing Three−Dimensional Objects," *Computer Vision, Graphics and Image Processing,* vol. 14, pp. 249−270, 1980.

Marr, D. and E. Hildreth, "Theory of Edge Detection," *Proc. R. Soc. Lond.,* vol. B 207, pp. 187−217, 1980.

Massone, L. and P. Morasso, "Analogical and Propositional Knowledge in Intelligent Path Planning," *Proc. ECAI '86,* pp. 507−517, Brighton, July 1986.

Morasso, P. and G. Sandini, "3D Reconstruction from Multiple Stereo Views," *Proc. III Intl. Conf. on "Image Analysis and Processing",* Rapallo October 1−2, 1985.

Nishihara, H.K., "PRISM: a practical real−time imaging stereo matcher," A.I. Memo 780, MIT A.I. Laboratory, Boston, Mass., May, 1984.

Prazdny, K., "Egomotion and Relative Depth Map from Optical Flow," *Biol. Cybernetics,* vol. 36, pp. 87−102, 1980.

Sandini, G. and M. Tistarelli, "Recovery of depth Information: Camera Motion as an Integration to Stereo," *Proc. of the Workshop: on Motion: Representation and Analysis,* IEEE−CS, Charleston, South Carolina, May 7−9, 1986.

Sandini, G., V. Tagliasco, and M. Tistarelli, "Analysis of Object Motion and Camera Motion in Real Scenes," *Proc. IEEE Intl. Conference on "Robotics & Automation",* IEEE−CS, San Francisco, April 7−10, 1986.

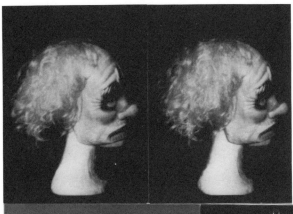

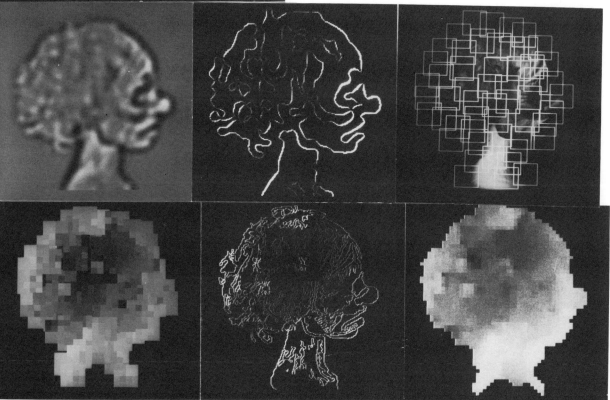

Figure 1. Computation of depth map from stereo images. Top row: Stereo pair; Middle row: the left image represent the result of the filtering procedure; the middle image represent the zero crossings extracted (gray level codes intensity gradient); the squares of the right image represent the regions of the image where the disparity will be computed. lower row: disparities measured at the end of the regional computation (left image), at the end of the edge matching procedure (middle image), and after the interpolation of the edge disparity. Gray level codes distance (darker meaning closer). disparity

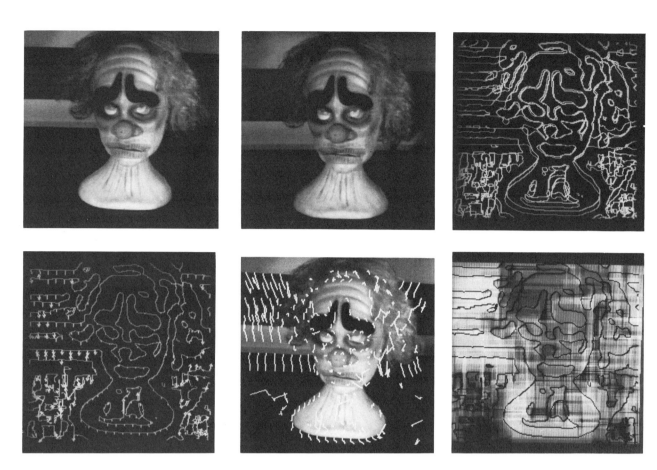

Figure 2. Computation of depth map from egomotion. Camera motion was constrained on a vertical plane and the fixation point is stabilized over the nose of the clown. Top row: First (left) and last (middle) image of a the sequence of 5 images used in this experiment; the right image represents the contours of the first and last image of the sequence superimposed. Bottom row: the left image represent the instantaneous optical flow (i.e. the optical flow computed from a pair of successive images); middle image represent the integrated optical flow measured over the five images; the right image shows the depth map obtained by interpolation of the depth values computed along the contours (darker means closer);

Figure 4 (*NEXT PAGE*). Construction of an object (a clown face) from several views. First row Samples of the three stereo pairs used in the experiment. Second row Depth images obtained with the stereo algorithms described in the text. Distance is coded with density (lighter means closer). Third row: Oct−tree bas−relief obtained from the depth maps of the upper row (note that the left image was measured at a lower resolution level). Fourth row: left image represent the volumetric intersection of the left and middle bas− reliefs of the upper row while the right one represent the volumetric intersection of all the three bas−reliefs.

Figure 3. Visual bas−relief of a synthetic object (the viewer location is outside of the oct−tree universe). This image shows the simulation of a bas−relief obtained by a virtual camera positioned over the object (a mug with a cylindrical shape). The conical shape obtained is caused by the position of the camera.

Progress toward a system that can acquire pallets and clean warehouses

Michael Brady, Stephen Cameron,
Hugh Durrant-Whyte, Margaret Fleck,
David Forsyth, Alison Noble,
and Ian Page
Robotics Research Group,
Department of Engineering Science,
University of Oxford,
Oxford OX1 3PJ,
U.K.

Abstract

Mobile robots are a paradigm of the challenge of systems integration in Robotics. We discuss work at Oxford on the development of an Autonomous Guided Vehicle that can acquire free-standing pallets and can clean warehouses. The work is based on a commercially-available, free-ranging AGV that can plan paths and sense its position using an infrared laser triangulation system. We describe work aimed at providing the AGV with: vision, sonar, and a direct ranging sensor; the ability to integrate these sensors; and 3D geometric reasoning capabilities.

Introduction

The challenge of systems integration is ubiquitous in Robotics, in topics that seem, at first sight, to be completely different: sensor-based assembly; compliant process control; legged locomotion; and, perhaps most comprehensively, path-planning and guidance of mobile robots. Integration is necessary because actuators need to be integrated with sensors and with systems that can reason about geometry and forces. Integration is also necessary because a system that combines the processing of several sensors, or sensor modalities such as stereo and motion, can overcome the inadequacies of each individual sensor. It is partly for this reason that there has recently been a spate of mobile robot research projects, also partly because another round of system building is considered timely by some Robotics researchers and by some funding agents. Outside research laboratories, the use of Automated Guided Vehicles in industry tripled in 1985 alone (Hollier 86), and they constitute one of the fastest growing sectors of the Robotics business. This paper reports work on an Autonomous Guided Vehicle (AGV) at Oxford University. The work springs from a need and an opportunity.

- The *opportunity* arises because the FAST Division of the GEC Company has recently marketed a free-ranging AGV (constructed by Caterpillar) that is designed for the movement of material in factories (Figure 1). The AGV is free-ranging in that it does not require specially prepared roadways or wire guides, it can plan alternative routes to a goal (say, to a pallet or to a machine tool) and it can re-plan when it is confronted with an unexpected obstacle as detected by the touch bar on the front of the AGV. The GEC AGV plans movements in a 2D representation of the factory floor. It is equipped with a rotating infrared laser scanner that reads bar codes attached to the factory wall. By reading three or more bar codes it can find its position by triangulation. The AGV is accurate to better than half a centimetre over thirty metres. Though odometry is available to the AGV controller, it is rarely used in practice because of wheel slippage on factory floors. The AGV communicates over a radio link to a controlling computer, which maintains a "map" of the factory layout that includes details of processing centres and the "roadways" between such centres. The system software can plan a path between processing centres that avoids obstacles (including other AGVs). The GEC-Caterpillar system is an impressive advance on the technology and controlling software of industrial AGVs. GEC have generously donated an AGV to the Oxford Robotics Research Group.

- The *need* arises because the GEC AGV, like every other mobile robot, is limited in scope. The primary application of the GEC-Caterpillar AGV is in the development of flex-

Figure 1: The GEC Autonomous Guided Vehicle. See text for details.

ible manufacturing systems in which parts and partially manufactured objects are individually routed through a series of processing centres. For many such applications, the sensing and planning capabilities of the GEC-Caterpillar AGV may well be sufficient (though operating machinery has already posed problems for the infrared sensors). For some applications, however, the sensory capabilities, and as a result the planning capabilities, clearly need to be augmented. The GEC AGV can accurately locate itself within its *known* environment as specified by the set of bar charts, whose locations are accurately determined at set-up time. The AGV is cannot sense objects that are not in pre-determined positions other than by colliding with them, and even in that case it simply assumes that the obstacle fills an entire lane of a roadway through the factory. Similarly, the AGV's representation is restricted to a two-dimensional "bird's eye view" of the factory layout. It is incapable of 3D reasoning of the sort required for stacking and palletising.

For these reasons, our work is aimed at extending the GEC AGV's repertoire to the following applications:

1. The GEC-Caterpillar AGV is regularly commanded to move to a place where it can pick up a pallet for delivery to a processing centre. Typically, pallets are placed by fork-lift trucks. Inevitably, they are positioned inaccurately and sometimes the wrong way round. Often, several pallets accumulate at the reception centre, and this complicates the pick-up procedure. We intend to use a mixture of range sensing and vision to determine the position and configuration of a pallet. The information produced by our programs should support spatial reasoning to determine which of several pallets should be picked up, and how.

2. It is intended that the GEC-Caterpillar AGV will be used for applications such as cleaning a large, unattended area. Related applications include warehousing and crop harvesting. So long as the "avenues" to be cleaned are clear, the AGV can perform its job predictably and well. Obstacles, however, pose a problem. Consider, as a typical domain, clearing a baggage handling area at a major airport: if the obstacle is determined to be an item of luggage, it should be pushed gently out of the avenue; but if the obstacle is a trolley, a slight deviation should be planned to take the AGV around it. Note that only a few different types of obstacles may be expected and this information can be utilised in the interpretation programs.

In our current design, the AGV will be equipped with vision, a thirty-two element sonar system (Steer 85), and a novel ranging device (Reid, Rixon, and Messer 84). The vision processes, we are developing include mixed active/passive stereo, motion, and shape from contour. Progress in vision is described in the next section. The responses of the various sensor processes are being integrated using the methods of Durrant--Whyte, and progress is sketched in Section 5. The geometric capabilities of the enhanced GEC AGV are being provided by the S-bounds technique of (Cameron 84) and recent progress, including a computer model of the AGV environment at Oxford and path planning algorithms for the computer model, are described in Section 4. Work on sonar and ranging will be reported elsewhere. Clearly, an AGV of the type we are constructing demands computational power in excess of that provided by serial processors of reasonable cost (M68020 Workstations for example). We are implementing several algorithms on a SIMD/MIMD processor, called the Disputer, designed by (Page 87) and which consists of an array of Transputers coupled to a SIMD engine that implements RasterOp (alias BitBlt) as a primitive. The Disputer is described in Section 3.6

Rich representation of image structure

This section describes some of our recent progress in vision. We begin by noting that representations that capture some the tight constraint available at colour and texture edges and at loci of two-dimensional image change potentially support fast

algorithms for the computation of motion, shape from contour, and stereo (see (Brady 87) for more details). We then show that the information we seek can in fact be computed reliably. First, we describe Fleck's *Phantom Edge Finder* (Fleck 87), and we sketch some recent work on the differential geometry of image surfaces by (Noble 87). Then we introduce the work of (Forsyth 87) on a system that can detect and describe colour edges. Finally, we describe a powerful SIMD-MIMD processor which has been constructed at Oxford on which the algorithms described in this Section are being implemented.

Seeds of perception

Not all information is created equal. Different locations in an image (or range image) offer different levels of constraint to visual processes. Generally, a region of an image that is the projection of a portion of a smooth surface imposes less constraint on visual interpretation than do one-dimensional loci of change, which often correspond to visual edges. Informally, we shall refer to loci of one-dimensional intensity change as "edges" despite the fact that the step edges ubiquitously studied in computer vision are only one of a number of important kinds of change (Canny 83) (Ponce and Brady 87) (Asada and Brady 86). Edges offer even more constraint if they can be elaborated by descriptions that relate to important visible surface characteristics such as texture or colour (see below). We call regions that correspond to smooth surface patches *loci of zero-dimensional change*, and they are roughly characterized by two large eigenvalues in the image autocorrelation function as the image "looks" the same in all directions. Similarly, we call edges *loci of one-dimensional change*. By analogy, the autocorrelation function has a large eigenvalue whose eigenvector lies along the edge and a small eigenvalue whose eigenvector lies in the direction of the normal to the edge. Similarly, we refer to corners, points of occlusion (eg T-junctions and X-junctions), various curvature maxima, and configurations of edges that have nearby terminations as *loci of two-dimensional change*.

This observation suggests that the computation of the parameters of a visual process might be computed most effectively by basing that computation first on loci that offer most powerful and then decreasingly powerful constraint. Often this corresponds to working from loci of two-dimensional change, then on loci of one-dimensional change, and finally on loci of smooth change. Indeed, it seems possible that models can be invoked very early in this computation, possibly even on the basis of the determination of the most constraining information available in the image. This suggests in turn that the refinement of model invokation and the determination of rich image descriptions can proceed hand in hand. According to this broad scheme, points of tightest constraint are *seeds of perception* from which are grown more extensive descriptions of change and, eventually, image descriptions. (Brady 87) has explored this theme in a number of visual problems: shape from contour; optic flow and structure from motion; stereo; shape from shading; and model-based recognition of objects. We summarise the main results here.

The computation of *shape from contour* is one of the most powerful passive ranging techniques in human vision. Analysis has concentrated mostly on smooth, planar contours. However, the determination of shape from contour is most effective when there are curvature discontinuities along a curve. Consider a planar curve $\gamma(s)$ that is imaged after undergoing a general affine transform $\mathbf{T}$, that is, a translation, rotation, and scaling. Under affine transforms, as well as under orthographic or perspective image projection **P**, the zero-crossings and curvature peaks of γ appear as zero-crossings and curvature peaks of the image of $\mathbf{P}(\mathbf{T}(\gamma))$ (see also (Marr 77) (Huttenlocher and Ullman 87)). In general, metric quantities such as angles, lengths, and ratios of lengths associated with the shape γ are not preserved in $\mathbf{P}(\mathbf{T}(\gamma))$, and so they are of limited usefulness for determining shape from contour. There are, however, at least two constraints that *can* be used to effect the determination of γ from its oriented projection $\mathbf{P}(\mathbf{T}(\gamma))$:

1. *the order constraint*: the order of curvature changes around the projected planar shape is unaffected by affine transformation. Other shapes may occlude the shape of interest, as for example when an aeroplane is partly occluded by cloud. In such cases, curvature changes not associated with the shape of interest may obtrude into the curvature change sequence; nevertheless, subsequences of curvature changes associated with the shape to be recognised are generally visible.

2. *the type constraint*: there are many different types of curvature change; for example, Asada and Brady consider *corner, crank, end, smooth join, bump* and *dent*, whereas (Hoffman and Richards 82) propose a number of different *codon types* for representing curvature changes. Under a broad range of values for the scaling factor of the affine transformation (determined by the object shape and by the viewing conditions), the type of a curvature change of γ is the same as that of the corresponding curvature change in $\mathbf{P}(\mathbf{T}(\gamma))$. For example, in Asada and Brady's notation, the projection of a transformed crank change is typically a crank.

Asada and Brady implemented an unpublished program that recognised a variety of shapes (aeroplanes) that had undergone affine transformation and partial occlusion. The model was represented as a sequence of curvature changes, each with an associated type. Recognition consisted of a Waltz-like labelling of curvature changes to match subsequences of the curvature changes found in an image to subsequences of the model. Significantly, though not surprisingly, composite types such as cranks and ends were most effective for constraining the subsequence match.

Shape matching and recognition based on local salient features by Asada and Brady and by Turney, Mudge, and Volz may be contrasted with the approach of (Grimson and Lozano-Pérez 86). They argue that matching based on salient features is unreasonable when data is noisy (precluding the accurate computation of salient features) or when objects are overlapped (salient features are more likely to be occluded than gross features). There is a law of excluded middle operating here: salient features cannot be *relied upon* for recognition, for the reasons advanced by Grimson and Lozano-Pérez. However, recognition can be more effective, reliable, and efficient if such salient features are available. Recently, working in our Laboratory, (Stein 87) implemented a recognition program that was a blend of (Turney, Mudge, and Volz 85) and (Grimson and Lozano-Pérez 86). Figure 1 shows a typical recognition result obtained by Stein's program.

Most work on *optic flow* is based on the *motion constraint equation*:

$$\mathbf{N}\cdot\mu = \frac{I_t}{\|\nabla I\|} \qquad (1)$$

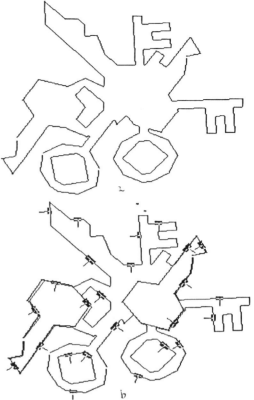

Figure 2: **a.** Outline of a set of overlapped shapes. **b.** Key shapes found in the pile shown in a.

which is a first-order Taylor series expansion of $I(\mathbf{x}+\delta\mathbf{x}, t+\delta t)$ (Nagel 87). In this equation, $\mu(\mathbf{x})$ is the optic flow field and **N** is the image unit normal $\nabla I/\|\nabla I\|$. Since the image gradient $\|\nabla I\|$ occurs in the denominator of the motion constraint equation, the computation of $\mathbf{N}\cdot\mu(\mathbf{x})$ is poorly conditioned unless $\|\nabla I\|(\mathbf{x})$ is large. Often, points $\mathbf{x}$ at which the gradient is large correspond to edges. This is the basis of Hildreth's (Hildreth 84) scheme for the computation of visual motion. Her algorithm identifies points $\mathbf{x}$ at which the image gradient is large with zero-crossings of a Laplacian of a Gaussian filter (Marr and Hildreth 80). The main novelty of her approach is based on a theorem that states that if $\gamma(s)$ is a closed contour (as zero-crossing contours must be unless they are thresholded or cross the image boundary) then there is a unique optic flow field $\mu(\mathbf{x})$ that minimises the smoothness expression:

$$\oint_\gamma \left(\frac{d\mu}{ds}\right)^2 ds$$

so long as the optic flow is different at at least two different points along the closed curve. Hildreth combines the edge smoothing term with the motion constraint equation using a Lagrange multiplier, and solves the resulting minimisation problem using a conjugate gradient descent algorithm. This minimisation algorithm is inherently sequential (Gong 87), rendering it difficult to implement Hildreth's algorithm in parallel. One way to proceed is to replace the conjugate gradient algorithm by a scheme such as Terzopoulous' multigrid relaxation algorithm (Terzopoulos 83) or graduated non-convexity (Blake and Zisserman 87). We are exploring an alternative approach.

Nagel (Nagel 87) (Dreschler and Nagel 82) has shown that, in practice as well as principle, the *full* optic flow field is computable at what he calls "grey-level corners". Noble (Noble 87) critically analyses Nagel's grey-level corner model. Recently, Nagel (Nagel 86) (Nagel and Enkelmann 86) has shown that the smoothness assumptions underlying the algorithms of Horn and Schunck, of Hildreth, and others amount to special cases of an "oriented smoothness" assumption that is implicit in the use of higher order derivatives. We have proved a generalisation of Nagel's result (see (Brady 87) for the proof.)

Theorem 1. If $\mathbf{H}(\mathbf{x})$ is the image Hessian, and κ is the (planar) curvature of a level contour of the intensity function whose tangent is $\mathbf{T}$ and whose normal is $\mathbf{N}$, then

$$(\mathbf{N}^\top \mathbf{H}\mathbf{T})\mathbf{N} \cdot \mu = \|\nabla I\|\kappa \mathbf{T} \cdot \mu.$$

Since $\mathbf{T}\cdot\mu$ is required to compute the full flow field, it follows that

1. the full optic flow can be computed at any location along a level contour (including zero crossings) at which the curvature is non-zero.

2. the reliability, or numerical conditioning, of the computation of the full flow increases as the curvature increases. Hence it is most reliable at corners.

Nagel (Nagel 87) suggests using the full flow field at corners to determine the optic flow elsewhere. This makes sense since the computation is most well conditioned at those points. Dreschler and Nagel write down the second *spatial* derivative and first *temporal* derivative of the flow field *everywhere* in the image. They note the crucial role played by the image Hessian. This is to be expected from elementary fluid mechanics (Landau and Lifschitz 59). Similarly, in a series of theoretical papers, Koenderinck and van Doorn [1975, 1976, 1981, 1985, 1986] have noted invariant properties of the motion parallax field due to the movement of rigid bodies relative to an observer. Barnard and Thompson (Barnard and Thompson 82) have pursued a similar approach. Similarly, (Davis, Wu, and Sun 83) have studied the motion of image corners in the relatively easy case of images of moving polyhedra.

Returning to Hildreth's computation, we noted above that zero-crossing contours are closed as is required for the application of her main theorem. In general, however, zero-crossing contours of a Laplacian-of-a-Gaussian filter do not necessarily belong to a single object, so that motion smoothing can produce poor results. The Laplacian-of-a-Gaussian does not provide as good an edge map as is produced by a directional operator such as Canny's. In turn, Canny's edge map is not as good, particularly at loci of two-dimensional change, as that produced by Fleck's phantom edge finder (Fleck 87). Although Hildreth's theorem relies upon closed contours, it is straightforward to show that:

Theorem 2: If the full optic flow is specified as $\mu(s_1) = \mu_1$ and $\mu(s_2) = \mu_2$ at two points s_1, s_2 along a level contour, then there is a unique flow field $\mu(s)$ which minimises Hildreth's edge smoothness integral and satisfies the given boundary conditions. $\square$

Theorem 2 can be used to speed the convergence of Hildreth's conjugate gradient scheme by restricting it to portions of contours between loci of two-dimensional change at which the full optic flow field can be computed. Between such loci, one might either:

1. Use the Hessian-based formula developed in Theorem 1 directly. This would be a bad idea because the computation of $\mathbf{T}\cdot\mu$ is poorly conditioned when the curvature is small.

2. or, develop a relaxation formula to interpolate the optic flow between known values μ_1, μ_2 as in Theorem 2.

We are pursuing the latter approach. Note that the situation is trivial for straight edges for which the optic flow linearly interpolates the values at the corners (Murray, Castelow, and Buxton 87). More generally, it is easy to show that:

$$(\mathbf{T}\cdot\mu)(s+\delta s) = (\mathbf{T}\cdot\mu)(s) + \delta s\, \kappa(\mathbf{N}\cdot\mu) \qquad (2)$$

Note that $\delta s\,\kappa = \delta\alpha$, the incremental change in the tangent angle along the curve.

In its usual formulation (Buxton 87), the geometry of *stereo* is a simple case of the geometry of 3-d rigid body motion. This assumes that the stereo cameras have previously been rectified, perhaps mechanically. The term "stereo" vision is also coined for stereo-mapping and aerial reconnaisance in which the aeroplane motion between successive images is well approximated by a translation, rotation, and magnification in the image plane. In such applications, rectification may or may not be a separate pre-process prior to stereo matching (Hannah 80) (Gennery 79). Rectification processes typically determine the global image rotation, magnification, and translation by applying a least squares process to a suitable set of sampled points $\mathbf{x}_j^i$, where $i = 1, 2$ denotes the image from which the sample point is taken. The sample set needs to be sparse (for efficiency) and sufficiently constraining to determine the rectification parameters. Points with low autocorrelation are often chosen as the sample set.

Evidently, rectification can be viewed as a partial stereo match. Indeed, some authors have based stereo algorithms on the sparse point sets that are also suitable for rectification. In perhaps the earliest example of this (Moravec 77) developed an "interest operator" that isolated small image areas with large intensity variation in the four principal directions. His algorithm worked from a coarse to a fine scale choosing the fifty most "interesting" points to match in order to compute a rough range map for his roving vehicle. A variation of Moravec's operator was developed and used by (Hannah 80) in her work on aerial passive navigation and by (Barnard and Thompson 82) in their work on optic flow.

Moravec's stereo matcher restricted attention to a few points for reasons of efficiency. This may not be the only reason to base a stereo matching algorithm upon seeds that are loci of two-dimensional intensity change. Recently, Rogers has noted that the (relative) disparity between two matched scene points varies inversely with the square of their depth difference (see (Brady and Hopkins 87) for a precise statement of this). Similarly, the disparity gradient between those points varies inversely with the difference in depth. Rogers has pointed out that the second derivative of disparity (which, by analogy, is called disparity curvature) of those points does not vary with depth, which makes it a particularly attractive parameter on which to base object recognition. In general, the computation of disparity curvature is ill-conditioned. However, as disparity curvature is related to surface curvature, it is best conditioned at loci of two dimensional image change. The computation of such points is also well suited to computation on SIMD processors. We are currently exploring the use of such points as seeds for stereo.

3.3   The phantom edge finder

Figures 3 and 4 illustrate results with a new edge finding algorithm, named the *Phantom Edge Finder* because of its resemblance to the (Watt and Morgan 87) *MIRAGE* algorithm for one-dimensional boundaries. It also owes a considerable debt to (Pearson and Robinson 85) for the "cartoon" representation of intensity changes. The *Phantom Edge Finder* removes camera noise while preserving fine texture and sharp corners. Its output boundaries are thin, without "feathering" or multiple responses. Results from different scales are combined into a single edge map, and extraneous edges in staircase patterns are removed during scale combination.

The *Phantom Edge Finder* is, in many ways, similar to existing edge finders. Its performance derives from a new view

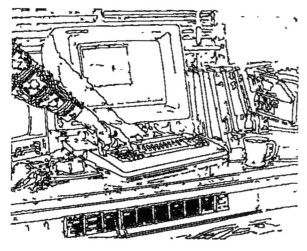

Figure 3: Output of the Phantom Edge Finder on an image of a computer console. Top left: original image. Top right: cartoon, in which black cells are on the dark side of an edge, white cells on the light side, and grey cells both or neither. Bottom left: edge map. Bottom right: reconstructed intensities.

of the relationship between regions and boundaries that is discussed more fully in (Fleck 87). According to this view, *regions* represent subsets of space while *boundaries* represent the topology of space. In vision, regions are represented by sets of cells, such as the receptors in a CCD camera. Boundaries are placed between adjacent cells, that is, between cells sharing an edge or a vertex. In the *Phantom Edge Finder*, most processing takes

place at cells. Function values (e.g. intensity) and labels used in computation are stored at cell locations. Boundaries are only represented implicitly, by putting contrasting labels on pairs of adjacent *edge* cells that are separated by boundaries. In fact, the *Phantom Edge Finder* does not compute boundaries directly, but identifies edge cells and deduces the boundary locations from them. Many edge finder computations are done over all cells with significant second difference responses, which form wide bands of cells near boundaries. These algorithms do not fit neatly into the traditional distinction between region-based and boundary-based algorithms.

The *Phantom Edge Finder* detects boundaries using second differences, for three reasons:

1. The sign of a first difference depends on the direction of motion along the corresponding one-dimensional path; that of the second difference does not.

2. A first difference responds at the boundary itself. The second difference, however, gives a high response *near* boundaries. Since processing is done at cell locations and boundaries are located between cells, this is the most useful type of response.

3. Roof edges are signalled by peaks and valleys in the second differences; they are not signalled explicitly in first difference responses.

The *Phantom Edge Finder* detects boundaries using directional second differences. For the rectangular arrays assumed by the current program, second differences are taken in four directions: horizontal, vertical, and two diagonal directions. The operator used is $[1, 0, -2, 0, 1]$. To equalize the responses of step edges and thin bars, the second difference response $a - 2b + c$ is normalized by $\|max(a - b, c - b)\| / \|(a - b) + (c - b)\|$. Because noise is suppressed later in the program, prior smoothing with a Gaussian or related filter is not needed, and a small operator can be used to preserve fine detail. The noise suppression relies on the fact that camera noise is added *after* optical blurring. Noise is identified by the following criterion:

- A cell response due to a real edge has a star-convex neighborhood of responses of the same sign, where the sum of the responses over that neighborhood is high.

The *Phantom Edge Finder* avoids the problem of "feathering" by combining responses from different directions *before* extracting zero crossings. Specifically, it tries to classify each cell with a significant second difference response as either on the light side ("light") or on the dark side ("dark") of a boundary. Cells with no significant response are unlabelled. It is, however, possible for a cell to be on the light side of one boundary and to be on the dark side of another. This happens when the intensity surface has a saddle. Intensity saddles can be images of a saddle on the imaged three-dimensional surface, or they may be caused by smoothing a junction of three or more regions. Such cells are labelled as both light and dark.

The classification of cells as dark or light is based on computing the maximum-amplitude positive and negative responses over all directional differences. For an isolated step edge, the maximum amplitude response is in the direction closest to perpendicular to the boundary. If more than one boundary is involved, the maximum-amplitude response(s) reflect differences perpendicular to the boundaries with the largest intensity changes Since a cell can be on both the light and dark sides of different boundaries, separate positive and negative responses are computed for each cell.

This method of combining directional responses has been designed to give good performance on sharp corners and places where several regions meet at a point. For example, Figure 5 illustrates the performance of the *Phantom Edge Finder* on the tines of a fork. Most edge finders combine responses in ways that are not good indicators of the boundary strengths involved in such cases; examples include: the sum of the directional responses, other non-directional center-surround operators (Marr and Hildreth 80), and the sum of the responses of the correct sign. Such techniques tend to give overly high values to the insides of sharp corners and overly low values to the outsides. In theory (Berzins 84), the zero-crossing of the Laplacian of a Gaussian is closed around a sharp corner but balloons out. In practice, the weak outside response of this type of operator causes the zero-crossing to randomly merge into the background noise. The combination method used in the *Phantom Edge Finder* does not require that the directional responses conform to any particular pattern, e.g. have a unique maximal response, peak responses in some directions, or responses that can be modelled as a linear transformation. Previous work has tended to depend on such assumptions (Canny 83) and (Haralick, Watson, and Laffey 83), although they break down at sharp corners and boundary intersections. Canny's edge finder, for example, tends to leave small gaps at such points.

The maximum-amplitude positive and negative responses

Figure 4: Output of the Phantom Edge Finder on an image of four textured patterns.

are then used to classify each cell as dark or light. Presence of a non-noise response of one type is not sufficient grounds for assigning that label to the cell, since cells near the zero-crossing in a step edge may have both negative and positive responses. In such cases, one response is significantly larger than the other, unless the cell is actually straddling the boundary. Only in cases where the two responses are of similar strength does the program assign both labels. When one response is more than 1.5 times the other response, *Phantom Edge Finder* gives the cell only a label reflecting the larger response.

From the dark/light classification of cells, the algorithm then extracts boundaries. A boundary is considered to exist between a pair of cells when they have opposite dark/light labels. These boundaries correspond to step edges. Thin bars, even as thin as one cell wide, are found as a pair of step edges. Because cells may not be labelled, or may be assigned both labels, boundaries can end abruptly. Roof edges are determined as regions of dark or light response that are not near dark/light transitions. Currently, the algorithm does not detect roof edges which are close to step edges robustly. Further detail, particularly on the combination of information from different scales and the elimination of staircase phenomena, are described in (Fleck 87).

The local geometry of images

The inadequacy of edge finders that are based on detecting large differentials stems from the implicit assumption that edges are loci of one-dimensional change. The simplest example of two-dimensional image structure is provided by the 'L'- junction or gray-level corner, which corresponds to a corner of a polyhedral surface in the real-world. Another important intensity structure is the 'T'-junction, typically arising where three polyhedra surfaces meet. Whereas it is possible to write down a mathematical definition for an 'L'-junction (Dreschler and Nagel 82), a multitude of parameters are required for a 'T'-junction. 'T'-junctions are relatively simple two-dimensional structures.

With the ultimate goal of defining a two-dimensional image representation, we have investigated some of the differential geometric properties of the intensity image structure. We have shown how the geometry of a simple facet model can characterise idealised instances of features such as intensity junctions and corners. The analysis given here and in (Noble 87) provides the *Phantom Edge Finder* with a theoretical underpinning in differential geometry.

(Haralick, Watson, and Laffey 83) proposed a eigenstructure representation for the Topographic Primal Sketch. Gradients, first and second derivatives, and the Hessian were used to derive ten pixel labels based on surface and edge properties. The calculations of principal curvatures (a crucial part of the scheme) proved complex. Further, there is an inherent ambiguity problem with the labelling scheme. An equivalent surface description is provided by using the Gaussian (K) and Mean (H) curvatures. Whereas the principal curvatures are the eigenvalues of the Weingarten Map (defined as the matrix $\mathbf{G}^{-1}\mathbf{D}$ where $\mathbf{D}$ is the Second Fundamental Form and $\mathbf{G}$ is the First Fundamental Form), H and K correspond to the natural algebraic invariants. However, H and K are scalar quantities. Thus a representation based on their characteristics removes the need to consider directional quantities. Motivated by this, and by the performance of Haralick's *Topographic Primal Sketch*, we propose to use the characteristics of the Second Fundamental Form.

The foundations of the scheme are derived from the image surface description provided by the facet model (Haralick 80), (Haralick 84). We approximate the image surface locally as a linear combination of (the first eight) Chebychev polynomials, to distribute noise evenly through the window. In practice, we work with a (5×5) window; here we derive the simpler

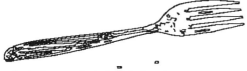

Figure 5: An image of a fork with sharply pointed tines, cartoon output, and edge map.

case of a (3×3) window centered on the origin, and covering $(x,y) : x = -1, 0, 1; y = -1, 0, 1$.

The intensity function $I(x, y)$ is approximated as:

$$I(x,y) = \sum_{n=0}^{8} a_n P_n(x,y)$$

where P_i refers to the *ith* Chebychev polynomial:

$$
\begin{aligned}
P_0(x,y) &= 1 & P_1(x,y) &= x \\
P_2(x,y) &= y & P_3(x,y) &= x^2 - 2/3 \\
P_4(x,y) &= xy & P_5(x,y) &= y^2 - 2/3 \\
P_6(x,y) &= xP_5(x,y) & P_7(x,y) &= yP_3(x,y) \\
P_8(x,y) &= P_3(x,y)P_5(x,y)
\end{aligned}
$$

The coefficients $a_0, a_1, \ldots, a_8$ may be found using the orthogonality of the Chebychev polynomials:

$$a_n = \frac{\sum_x \sum_y P_n(x,y)I(x,y)}{\sum_i \sum_j P_n^2(i,j)}$$

This implies that the fitting coefficients can be computed as a linear combination of the data values in $I(x, y)$ with coefficients

$$\frac{\sum_x \sum_y P_n(x,y)}{\sum_i \sum_j P_n^2(i,j)}$$

Solving for each of the parameters produces the following nine convolution masks.

$$
\begin{array}{ccc}
\frac{1}{9}\begin{bmatrix} 1 & 1 & 1 \\ 1 & 1 & 1 \\ 1 & 1 & 1 \end{bmatrix} &
\frac{1}{6}\begin{bmatrix} -1 & 0 & 1 \\ -1 & 0 & 1 \\ -1 & 0 & 1 \end{bmatrix} &
\frac{1}{6}\begin{bmatrix} -1 & -1 & -1 \\ 0 & 0 & 0 \\ 1 & 1 & 1 \end{bmatrix} \\
a & b & c \\[2mm]
\frac{1}{6}\begin{bmatrix} 1 & -2 & 1 \\ 1 & -2 & 1 \\ 1 & -2 & 1 \end{bmatrix} &
\frac{1}{4}\begin{bmatrix} 1 & 0 & -1 \\ 0 & 0 & 0 \\ -1 & 0 & 1 \end{bmatrix} &
\frac{1}{6}\begin{bmatrix} 1 & 1 & 1 \\ -2 & -2 & -2 \\ 1 & 1 & 1 \end{bmatrix} \\
d & e & f \\[2mm]
\frac{1}{4}\begin{bmatrix} -1 & 0 & 1 \\ 2 & 0 & -2 \\ -1 & 0 & 1 \end{bmatrix} &
\frac{1}{4}\begin{bmatrix} -1 & 2 & -1 \\ 0 & 0 & 0 \\ 1 & -2 & 1 \end{bmatrix} &
\frac{1}{4}\begin{bmatrix} 1 & -2 & 1 \\ -2 & 4 & -2 \\ 1 & -2 & 1 \end{bmatrix} \\
g & h & j
\end{array}
$$

Each mask may be applied independently to the image data to determine parameter estimates for all image pixels. In principle, this implies that it is possible to express $I(x, y)$ up to the fourth degree. Now consider the differential geometry of the image surface:

$$\mathbf{S}(x,y) = x\mathbf{i} + y\mathbf{j} + I(x,y)\mathbf{k}$$

The First Fundamental Form is defined by the equation,

$$\Phi_1 = d\mathbf{S}.d\mathbf{S} = E dx^2 + 2F dx dy + G dy^2$$

Assuming a fourth order Chebychev model,

$$
\begin{aligned}
I(x,y) &= a + bx + cy + d(x^2 - 2/3) + exy + f(y^2 - 2/3) \\
&\quad + gx(y^2 - 2/3) + hy(x^2 - 2/3) + j(x^2 - 2/3)(y^2 - 2/3)
\end{aligned}
$$

the First Fundamental Form coefficients can be derived in terms of the parameter estimates:

$$
\begin{aligned}
E &= 1 + I_x.I_x &&= 1 + (b - 2/3g)^2 \\
G &= 1 + I_y.I_y &&= 1 + (c - 2/3h)^2 \\
F &= I_x.I_y &&= (b - 2/3g)(c - 2/3h)
\end{aligned}
$$

$$EG - F^2 = 1 + I_x^2 + I_y^2 = 1 + (b - 2/3g)^2 + (c - 2/3h)^2$$

Similarly, the Second Fundamental Form is given by,

$$\Phi_2 = -d\mathbf{S}.d\hat{\mathbf{N}} = Ldx^2 + 2Mdxdy + Ndy^2$$

where $\mathbf{N}$ is the local surface normal. In terms of estimated parameters:

$$
\begin{aligned}
L &= I_{xx}\Big/\sqrt{1 + I_x^2 + I_y^2} &= 2(d - 2/3j)\Big/\sqrt{EG - F^2} \\
N &= I_{yy}\Big/\sqrt{1 + I_x^2 + I_y^2} &= 2(f - 2/3j)\Big/\sqrt{EG - F^2} \\
M &= I_{xy}\Big/\sqrt{1 + I_x^2 + I_y^2} &= e\Big/\sqrt{EG - F^2}
\end{aligned}
$$

$$LN - M^2 = 4(d - 2/3j)(f - 2/3j) - e^2 \Big/ (EG - F^2)$$

The matrix of coefficients of the Second Fundamental Form is denoted by $\mathbf{D}$. The determinant of $\mathbf{D}$ can be used to provide a pixel label describing the local surface geometry. As is well-known, a planar point is defined by $L = M = N = 0$, a

Figure 6: Characterisation of idealised 2D image structures; 2D structures identified by the algorithm are highlighted on the original. (a) 'Y'-junction, (b) 'T'-junction, (c) 'X'-junction,(d) Corner.(e) shows the distribution of elliptics(black),hyperbolics(dark grey) and parabolics(light grey) around the corner in (d).

parabolic point $LN - M^2 = 0$, a hyperbolic point $LN - M^2 < 0$, and an elliptic point $LN - M^2 > 0$.

For noise-free images, this geometric classification is complete. 'Interesting' points are associated with neighbourhoods containing strong evidence of two-dimensional intensity variation (elliptic and hyperbolic points). Results are presented for running the algorithm on synthetic and real data. Figure 6 shows the characterisation of common idealised two-dimensional image structures. Groups of localised two-dimensional (elliptic and hyperbolic) labels correctly identify corners and intersections. The two-dimensional structure identified by the algorithm for an asymmetric chess board is shown in Figure 7a. A Canny operator assumes that a discontinuity has the local structure of a step. Figure 7b illustrates the result of applying

the Canny algorithm to the chess board image.

For real images a purely geometric model is inadequate. Figure 8a, show the pixel classification for one image of a cup from a motion sequence. Clusters of hyperbolic and elliptic points appear around object corners and at 'T'- junctions; an observation consistent with Nagel's gray-value corner definition, namely that a gray-value corner lies between the local maxima of positive Gaussian curvature (elliptic point) and local maxima of negative Gaussian curvature (hyperbolic). Preliminary empirical investigations suggest that a suitable measure (C) on which to base statistical noise analysis is

$$C = \sqrt{EG - F^2}.\frac{|\kappa_1| + |\kappa_2|}{2}$$

This measure is closely related to that proposed for the Kitchen-Rosenfeld and Zuniga-Haralick corner detectors. Figure 8b shows the result of thresholding the Cup Image hyperbolic points at a 95 % confidence level on this measure.

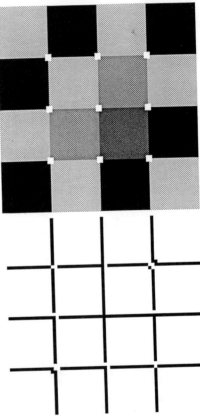

Figure 7: Chess board: (a) 2D structure identified by the algorithm (highlighted white), (b) a Canny operator fails to correctly mark the intersections.

A system that finds changes in colour

Colour provides additional constraint for intermediate vision processes by enriching the descriptions attached to edges with information that concerns properties of the imaged surface. Colour information can be of considerable use in vision applications:

- *Colour makes segmentation more reliable.* The reader might care to look for four impala ram and one lamb in Figure 9. If you cannot, try looking at the colour version of the picture. (Horn 86) has described how the grey level

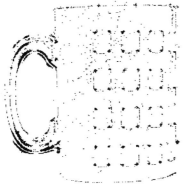

Figure 8: Cup image: (a) Clusters of hyperbolic (black) and elliptic (white) points appear around object corners and along curved edges. Pixel classification of entire image after smoothing with a Gaussian of $\sigma = 5$, (b) Thresholding hyperbolics on a measure of cornerness suppresses false labelling due to noise.

information at pixels depends both on the reflectance and the orientation of a surface. However, the colour of a pixel also depends as well on the shape of the surface reflectance function, which, by making assumptions about the spatial variation of the spectral composition of the illuminant, we are able to recover.

- *Colour constrains matching.* Consider matching edges from a pair of edges, as is usually done in stereo, motion, and in computing shape representations such as *Smoothed Local Symmetries*. Complex images often pose considerable picket-fence problems. Matches may be disambiguated by recording the colour present on each side of an edge in each image.

- *Colour can aid visual monitoring of processes.* For example, the problem of visually monitoring the cooking of meat is most reliably determined from its hue.

The most useful information is concentrated at changes, and so we need to be able to find changes in colour.

To digitize scenes, we use a CCD camera and a number of different gelatine filters. The following differences between our camera setup and the human eye may be noticed:

- The chromatic aberration of a camera lens is so small (at the frequencies of interest) that it can be neglected. As a result, each colour channel has the same spatial resolution.

- There are as many kinds of receptors at each point as we

care to put there, within the limitations of the physics of available filters.

These differences are considerable, but the kernel of the problem still remains: *given a set of receptor responses, and knowing the receptor sensitivities, recover the surface reflectance function, up to a constant* (we refer to this rather loosely as the *shape* of the surface reflectance function.) It is clear that this is not possible without additional constraints. Fundamental to all computational work on computing the shape of surface reflectances is the assumption that illumination changes slowly over space. This is equivalent to the assumption that a sharp change in the colour signal is due to a sharp change in the world of reflecting objects, rather than to a sharp change in illumination.

For this reason, the following seems to be a reasonable account of early colour vision:

1. Compute the best approximation to the colour signal, and find the colour changes.

2. From those changes, construct an estimate of the spatial structure of the illuminant.

3. From this, construct a map of the surface reflectance functions that are presumed to have caused the original colour signal.

In our current work on finding colour changes, we avoid the problem of colour constancy by assuming that the spectral content of the illuminant varies slowly over space. Thus, all perceivable spatial changes in colour in images of a given scene are due to changes in the shape of the surface reflectance function. This assumption underlies all colour constancy work, but it is not the same as assuming isochromatic illuminants from scene to scene.

In related work, Nevatia constructed a colour edge detector by applying the Hückel operator to the red, green and blue filtered images with the intention of using the additional information to improve the original edge map, but concluded that most edge information was in the intensity image (Nevatia 77). It turns out that this is essentially correct; but it is an unfortunate conclusion: rather than being a source of *new* edges; the available colour information is a *source of rich descriptors* to attach to existing edges. (Machuca and Philips 83) proposed a colour edge detector operating on the phase of the IQ vector (effectively a representation of hue), but presented few results. (Gershon 85) proposed a colour edge detector based on the presence in the cortex of double opponent cells, but few experimental results.

If we wish to use the spatial bandwidth of our system, the option of inspecting the colour at either side of a brightness change must be rejected. Cameras plus filters are able to spatially localise isoluminant changes in colour, a task on which humans perform poorly. We can exploit this ability. Since we are attempting to find a property of surfaces from images we need to detect changes in the *shape* of the colour signal, and these are assumed to correspond to changes in the shape of the spectral reflectances of the world. An opponent coding of a colour signal determines the shape of the colour signal, if we normalise it by the intensity of the two components involved. For example, $\frac{(B-Y)}{(B+Y)}$, where B is the blue component of the colour signal and Y is yellow, determines the relative size of the "humps" at the long wavelength and short wavelength ends of the spectral energy density. Similarly, $\frac{(R-G)}{(R+G)}$ deter-

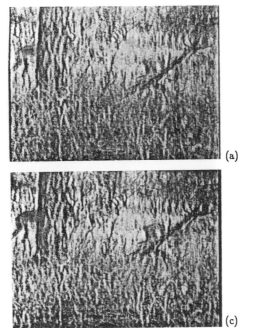

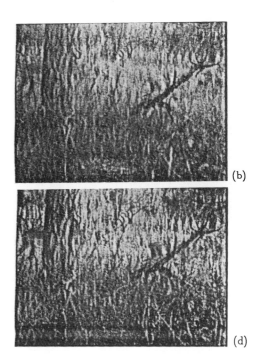

Figure 9: **Impala Rams:** there are four impala rams and
one lamb in this image. (a) shows the intensity image of the
impala. (b) shows the red component of the colour version
of this picture. (c) shows the green component of the colour
version. (d) shows the blue component of this picture.

mines the finer scale shape at the long wavelength end of the
spectrum. It follows that the opponent cell responses represent
a sensible decomposition of the colour signal that the sensors
can reconstruct.

Recall that the only signal available to the system is the
projection of the colour signal onto three functions. We can
represent the colour signal as an infinite sum relative to any
given set of basis functions. For the first three basis functions,
we may choose any set of functions that span the space spanned
by the receptor sensitivity functions. Then, to reconstruct the
signal, we simply compute the coefficients of the receptor sensitivity functions in the expansion: in essence, we are blind to
the rest of the signal, by construction. This is contrary to the
proposal of (Barlow 82), who analysed the response of the receptors to a Fourier decomposition of the spectrum presented.
There is a natural basis, namely an orthogonalisation of the
three receptor sensitivity functions.

Double opponent cells (see for example (Daw 72), (Gershon 85) or (Livingstone and Hubel 84)) assume a particular
significance in this analysis. Consider the receptor sensitivity
functions in Figure 10. Notice that there is a clear separation
between the hump at the blue end of the spectrum, whereas the
receptors at the longwave end of the spectrum are rather close
together. Thus, a signal reconstructed as a linear combination
of these functions can qualitatively be described by considering
two questions:

1. (i) is the hump at the shortwave end of the signal larger or
   smaller than the composite hump at the longwave end?

2. (ii) considering the finer scale structure of the longwave
   end of the signal, which hump is larger?

The responses of opponent cells can be viewed as answering these questions. This suggests that colour edges may be
detected by applying a conventional edge detector to an oppo-

nent encoding of the image. In our implementation, the colour
edge finder works as follows:

The opponent signals are computed, and a pyramid of scaled
and resampled versions is constructed for the opponent signals,
the intensity signal, and the opponent intensity signals. For
those regions in the image where the opponent intensity signal
is below some threshold, the opponent signals are adjusted to
be in balance, as reliable information about the nature of the
colour signal and its changes is not available at such points.

The response regions for each opponent at each scale are
calculated. Notice that at this stage we do not use the normalised opponent intensity signals since we wish to force the
edges in the opponent signals to line up with those in the intensity signal. We have found that using the opponent signals
leads to an average error of less than a pixel (or rather, an occasional error of a pixel, and no greater errors), whereas using the
normalised opponents leads to a larger error which is difficult
to deal with in a principled way. The response regions label
the image with areas where the opponents have swung one way
or the other. In this way, we can isolate the isoluminant colour
changes.

We construct zero crossing maps of the image, where the
zero crossings are labelled with (i) the colour in the original
image; and (ii) with the nature of the change in colour across

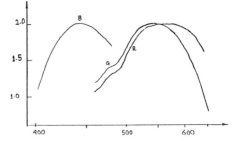

Figure 10: **Receptor sensitivity functions:** The graph
shows human cone sensitivity functions plotted as log relative
sensitivity against wavelength. The graphs were simplified from
Bowmaker and Dartnall, 1980.

the zero crossing. Keeping the images in register is relatively straightforward: the fact that the *Phantom Edge Finder* is so accurate at localising changes, means that the response regions coincide to within at most a single aberrant pixel. Locally, we then require edges in the opponents either to be in register with edges in the brightness image, or to be far from them.

This can easily be enforced. For each pixel marked by the *Phantom Edge Finder* as being on the 'light' side of a zero crossing, we inspect its neighbours that are marked similarly. The neighbours of these pixels which are not marked as being on either side of a zero crossing, are sorted by opponent response, and the majority vote is accepted as a labelling for all pixels visited. The same must be done for all pixels marked as being on the 'dark' side of a zero crossing, *mutatis mutandis*. This technique deals with registration errors in the response images that are one pixel wide and this is the worst case in practice.

As noted in the previous subsection, phantom edges are zero crossings generated from an image by inflexions in the image surface. These occur when, for example, a red region is separated from a green region by a white region: the white region is then redder than the green region and greener than the red region. (Clark 86) has suggested that these may be rejected when one marks zero crossings by considering the actual change over the puported zero crossing: our colour change program is based on an idea due to (Fleck 87), which works by considering the way these zero crossings tend to arise when one combines a map of responses obtained at a coarse scale with a set obtained at a finer scale. A version of Clark's technique is also used, as these spurious edges, although not terribly common in intensity images, are for some reason a real problem in opponent encoded images. Opponent zero-crossings are subjected to this technique as well.

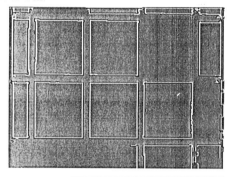

Figure 11: **ColorChecker Edges:** (a) shows the zero crossings of the R-G opponent. (b) shows the zero crossings of the B-Y opponent. The red (blue, resp.) sides of edges are marked white, the green (yellow, resp.) black.

We show results in Figures 11 and 12; the images are presented as a set of three component images, and the response regions and zero crossing maps are shown for a number of examples.

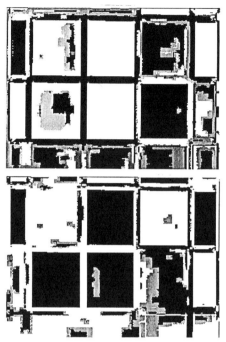

Figure 12: **ColorChecker Edges:** (a) shows the response regions of the R-G opponent. (b) shows the response regions of the B-Y opponent. The red (blue, resp.) responses are marked white, the green (yellow, resp.) black.

The *Disputer*: a dual-paradigm parallel processor for graphics and vision

The *Disputer* is a parallel processor which is a closely coupled arrangement of a 256-processor SIMD machine and a 42-processor MIMD machine. Algorithms at the "back-end" of the graphics pipeline and at the "front-end" of machine vision applications, are often characterised by local-support operations on large arrays of pixels. The data-parallelism of early vision and late graphics computations are well suited to SIMD processing. Later vision, earlier graphics, and many robot control tasks typically exhibit task parallelism that is better matched to the MIMD model of computation. The *Disputer* is the combination of: a SIMD array processor called *DisArray*; a MIMD network of Inmos Transputers; and controller hardware which has been designed to link them together. The two parallel machines are closely coupled and the SIMD machine has a real-time video output channel. The entire system is programmed in Occam 2. This machine is now allowing us to investigate dual-paradigm algorithms very effectively.

Earlier work on a SIMD machine for graphics applications (Page 83) resulted in a system called *DisArray* (Display Array) that significantly reduced one of the major bottlenecks of real-time graphics: rendering the image into a frame buffer. The initial motivation for building *DisArray* was to execute RasterOp (BitBlt), an important operation in bitmap-based graphics, in parallel at very high speed. Though it was primarily intended for exploring parallel algorithms for graphics applications, *DisArray* is a general purpose SIMD machine that is similar to the AMT (previously ICL) *Distributed Array Processor* (S.F.

73). Because it is a general purpose SIMD processor, *DisArray* has proved an effective base for developing a broader class of algorithms than originally envisaged. Parallel algorithms have been developed for many vision and graphics problems, such as polygon rendering.

DisArray is an array of 256 single processing elements (PEs) in a 16×16 arrangement with four nearest-neighbour communications. Row-based and column-based broadcast lines transmit data, addressing, and control information to the PEs. In addition, a video shift register is threaded through the PEs, which supports real-time display of a 512×512, 16-colour bitmap from some part of the array memory. A proposed re-design of the video board will upgrade the screen resolution and allow real-time video input as well. Each PE has 256k by 1-bit memory, implemented by a single dynamic RAM. All processors in the array execute the same, globally broadcast, instruction at the same time. The array has a low-level scheduler which arbitrates between requests for such computational cycles and video refresh cycles.

A sequential controller (a Transputer) generates the instructions for the SIMD array. Having given a single instruction to the array, the controller and array operations then proceed in parallel. The array instructions are generally of the form :

$$\text{Mem [addr] := F (Mem [addr], Register, RowData AND ColumnData)}$$

where F is an arbitrary Boolean function and the operation takes place between two 256-bit square words. The instruction register for the array, together with various address and data registers for communication are mapped into the address space of the controller. The controller itself is a 20MHz, 32-bit, 1Mbyte RISC machine, based on the T414 transputer.

The MIMD array is a six-by-seven array of Transputers, each of which is a 20MHz T414 with no external support chips. The memory for each Transputer is limited to the 2kbytes of on-chip, 50nS static RAM. The nearest-neighbour connections in the array are hard-wired and the 26 edge connections are brought out to a patch panel. The edge connections are also used to communicate with the *DisArray* controller and with the Transputer development system. We have recently augmented the MIMD processor network with a further 40 Transputers each with 256kb of external RAM.

There is a 16-bit DMA link between the *DisArray* controller and a Unix host processor. A running application on the *Disputer* can arbitrarily access the Unix memory. This link is often used to locate and continuously refresh the screen picture from a display file, or other applications-oriented data structure, in the address space of some Unix process. We also use the DMA link to get image data into the *Disputer* from a Datacube frame grabber/processor which is acessible from the Unix host over an Ethernet.

At present, all of the software for the *Disputer* is in Occam 2 and the software development is carried out on a 2Mbyte T414 transputer with an IBM PC/AT acting as terminal and filestore. The complete SIMD/MIMD application can be expressed as a single Occam program, even though it might consist of many hundreds of processes. The development system (transputer and/or IBM PC) can also act as a host to the *Disputer* system, in which case communication is by up to 4 transputer links rather than the DMA link.

Currently, we have a simple low level vision system working on the SIMD hardware and we will soon extend this to incorpo-

rate Fleck's *Phantom Edge Finder* described earlier. We then intend to develop some simple intermediate-level vision algorithms running on the MIMD engine performing, for instance, parallel matching against a database of models. It has become increasingly clear that there is a great deal of computational commonality between graphics algorithms and those being developed by the machine vision community, most obviously in the data-parallel algorithms. This is perhaps not too surprising, as graphics and vision are two sides of the same coin, whose currency is computational geometry. Indeed we now feel that the degree of commonality is such that it warrants the development of a *virtual machine* for graphics and vision and we are actively working on its definition. This will provide an interface between applications programs and the highly parallel hardware which implements the kernel algorithms of the application. It is the intention that the virtual machine is not heavily orientated towards any particular hardware model, but should be implementable in a number of different ways.

Geometric reasoning

Geometric reasoning will play a key role within the AGV project. The main geometric reasoning system will perform three major functions:

- Planning collision-free paths for the vehicle, including adjusting the plan to avoid unexpected obstacles (detouring);

- Planning pallet acquisition, using a fork-lift attachment to the vehicle;

- Providing geometric modelling support for the sensor systems, including visibility information.

The last of these functions affects mainly the organisation of the geometric data bases, and will not be discussed in detail here. Providing the first two functions involves the use of a number of techniques/algorithms from different branches of A.I. and robotics, notably different forms of path-planning, path-checking, and search techniques. Although our short-term goal is to provide the three major functions listed above, we are also interested in building a computational framework that will support other geometric reasoning tasks and queries, for example the cleaning application; thus we are putting some effort into the organisation of the geometric reasoning system.

The World Model

The world model is a central database that defines what the AGV believes its surroundings to be. The central role of the world model is illustrated by the system architecture, shown in figure 13. (This diagram is, of course, only a first approximation to the truth!) In this architecture the primary flow of information is from top to bottom, as information from the different sensors is combined, sifted, pruned, and "interesting" features lodged in the world model. In fact, to avoid the AGV sitting and thinking about its surroundings for long periods of time it is necessary for *predictive* information to flow from the world model to the sensors, and so there is a secondary flow of information to be catered for. One important feature of this architecture is that the planning system believes the world model to be accurate; in particular, there is no direct link between the planner and the sensors. Such an approach is not normally recommended in most robotic systems as uncertainty abounds. However we believe that such an approach

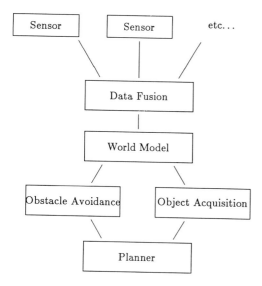

Figure 13: Overall System Architecture

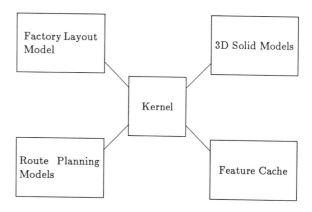

Figure 14: World Model Components

can be tolerated, at least for the work described herein, for three reasons. Firstly, the environment of the vehicle is reasonably friendly; it is not liable to be attacked, and reaction time is not critical. Secondly, the vehicle itself is a relatively inaccurate machine (by normal robotic standards) operating in a fairly coarse environment: there should be little need for the precise, guarded motions of the type required, say, in robotic assembly work. Thirdly, the reliability of the system is not critical; if the vehicle does occasionally fail to find a way of performing its task it can sit and bleep to itself, awaiting human interaction. We see the world model itself as consisting of four components, accessed through a kernel (figure 14). Two of the components are essentially static, namely the Factory Layout Model and the 3D Solid Models. The factory model "looks" like a two-dimensional plan of the factory, on which are marked static items (e.g., machining centres, pillars, doorways), quasi-static items (e.g., waste bins, doors), and nominal roadways. The 3D models are three-dimensional representations of objects that the vehicle senses or (literally) comes into contact with, for which a simplified two-dimensional projection will not suffice. (If there are many instances in the factory of, say, parts bins, only a single instance is stored in this component.) The other components of the world model will change, both due to the discovery of unexpected objects and due to the movement of the vehicle itself. One component is the feature cache—it will store features that are useful for sensing. For example, once a convenient landmark has been identified in a view and its position computed the prominent features can be stored in the cache, as being potentially useful and probably (but not necessarily) invariant. (Of course, such a cache needs a regime for disposing of information that has outlived its usefulness.) The route-planning component has a similar function to the feature cache, namely to save information that was expensive to produce and that could be useful. In this case, the information will consist of local detours around obstacles that can be reused (providing the obstacle does not move). Local C-space maps, which are generated during the obstacle avoidance phases, may also be cached.

Obstacle Avoidance

The fact that the environment of the AGV is reasonably well-

structured means that we can take advantage of very simple path planning algorithms; in particular, much of the time the AGV can use generate-and-test, whereby a path is proposed and then checked for validity. In turn, proposing paths for the AGV is normally quite simple, as unless there are reasons to do otherwise the vehicle can just uses the factory roadways. The only real problem occurs when an unexpected obstacle is encountered, when we expect one of three strategies to be used:

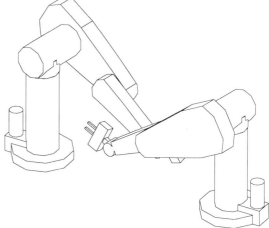

Figure 15: Two robots almost interfering

- If the obstacle is small we will use a potential-field approach to attempt to define a detour motion around it (Khatib 85); this motion is verified by the path-checker before being accepted.

- If the obstacle is larger the system will use a C-space approach, using a number of two-dimensional C-space maps covering a small number of vehicle orientations (Lozano-Pérez 83; Lozano-Pérez 85).

- If the route is blocked the vehicle will try to backtrack to find another route.

To perform collision detection we will use the routines already built into the ROBMOD system (Cameron 85; Cameron 84). These routines have been optimised to perform intersection tests using S-bounds, which is a simple method to reason about the bounding volumes. (Cameron 87). As an example, figure 15 shows two robots that almost interfere. The S-bounds system generates an initial set of spatial bounds for the various parts of the model, and then refines this set to reduce the volume that needs to be searched for interferences (figure 16).

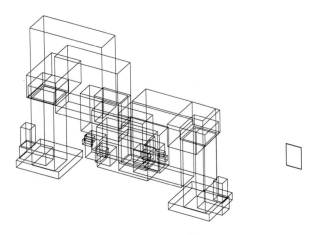

Figure 16: S-bounds in action. The initial spatial bounds for the two robots (left) are reduced to a single, small bound (right).

Object Acquisition

The purpose of the object acquisition experiment is to introduce the AGV into a space into which a number of loaded pallets have been positioned in an irregular manner. The AGV will have a fork-lift attachment, and has to identify the pallets, compute their orientations, and plan how the acquire the pallets using the fork-lift. In doing so it must take into account the positions of other objects and pallets in the area in order to avoid collisions. The path planning required in this case is thus of a different calibre from that required for obstacle avoidance, as it is necessary for the forks of the vehicle to come into close proximity with other objects. However, the class of objects that has to be tackled is restricted—namely, in the first instance, to pallets. Thus our approach is to use simple skeletonised plans to propose paths for the vehicle, which are then tested for validity. This will clearly work in simple cases; the challenge will come in getting the system to work well in relatively cluttered cases.

Three Dimensional Modelling

To test the system we will require realistic, three-dimensional models of the AGV and its environment. Such support will be provided by the ROBMOD modelling system (Cameron and Aylett 87). Developed at Edinburgh University ROBMOD is a Constructive Solid Geometry based system (Requicha and Voelcker 82), which can also produce boundary information and visibility maps for vision work. Figure 17 shows a ROBMOD model of our laboratory. Figure 18 shows another view of the laboratory, but this time from within the room. ROBMOD also provides support for many of the basic geometric functions required by the geometric reasoning system, such as collision detection, and distance computations.

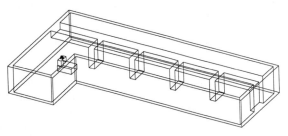

Figure 17: Our AGV Laboratory

Sensor integration

The AGV described will operate in an unknown, but relatively structured environment. A number of different sensors will be used to provide the robot with navigation and part acquisition information. To make effective use of the observations provided by these sensors, it is important that we develop techniques to integrate the available information.

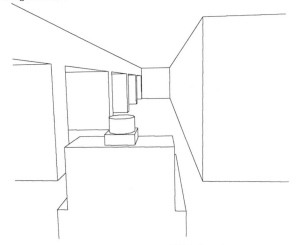

Figure 18: Interior View of the AGV Laboratory

We recall that the AGV will be equipped with stereo-vision, a sonar array, a laser scanner, and proximity switches. These sensors will be used to locate and navigate the robot, provide environment information for path planning, and obtain object information for the acquisition stage. In each of these tasks, different sensors will provide different information, which must be combined to provide a full and complete description of the task domain. The observations made by the different sensors will always be uncertain, usually partial, occasionally spurious or incorrect and often geographically or geometrically incomparable with other sensor views. It is the goal of the integration processes to combine inbformation from all these different sources into a robust and consistent description of the environment

We will consider the environment in terms of geometry and describe all locations and features in terms of parameterized functions. To operate efficiently, the robot system must be able to represent, account for, and reason with the effects of uncertainty in these geometries in a consistent manner. We will describe uncertainty in the environment in terms of a probability distribution defined on the parameter vectors of feature description functions. A description of the environment will be developed in terms of a network of uncertain geometric features. Techniques for manipulating, transforming and combining these stochastic geometric descriptions have been developed (Durrant-Whyte 87c), and will be used as a basis for integrating sensor information.

A general model of sensor characteristics will be used to describe the dependence of sensor observations on the state of the environment, the state of the sensor itself, and other sensor observations or decisions. This sensor model describes a sensor in terms of it's ability to extract uncertain geometric descriptions of the environment (Durrant-Whyte 87b). A constrained Bayesian decision procedure will be used to cluster and integrate sparse, partial, uncertain observations from these diverse sensor systems (Durrant-Whyte 87a).

Acknowledgements

The project described in this paper is a collaborative effort between Oxford University and a number of industrial companies, and is supported by the ACME (Applications of Computers in Manufacturing Engineering) Directorate of the UK Science and Engineering Research Council. We particularly thank our collaborators, Alan Davies, Mike Robbins, and Malcolm Roberts of GEC's FAST Division who designed and developed the GEC AGV. We thank our other industrial collaborators for their continuing contributions to our work: Tony Williams (Thorn--EMI), Roger Hake (IBM), David May (Inmos), Peter Bateman and John Waddington (RARDE), and Jack Betteridge (BP). The Oxford AGV project has benefited substantially from the active involvement of members of the ACME Directorate: Peter Smith, Guy Richards, and Bill Hillier.

References

H. Asada and M. Brady, 1986. The Curvature Primal Sketch. *IEEE Trans. Pattern Anal. Machine Intell.*, PAMI-8(1):2–14.

H.B. Barlow, 1982. What causes trichromacy?: a theoretical analysis using comb filtered spectra. *Vision Research*, 22:635–643.

S. T. Barnard and W. B. Thompson, 1982. Disparity analysis of images. *IEEE Trans. Pattern Anal. Machine Intell.*, PAMI-2:333–340.

V. Berzins, 1984. Accuracy of Laplacian Edge Detectors. *Comput. Graphics Image Processing*, 27:195–210.

A. Blake and A. Zisserman, 1987. *Visual Reconstruction.* MIT Press, Cambridge, Mass.

J.M. Brady, 1987. Seeds of Perception. In *Proc. Alvey Vis. Conf.*, page , Cambridge, UK.

Michael Brady and P. J. Hopkins, 1987. *Disparity curvature.* Technical Report, Oxford University (in preparation).

B. F. Buxton, 1987. *Notes on computer vision.* Technical Report, GEC Hirst Research Laboratory.

S. A. Cameron, 1984. *Modelling Solids in Motion.* PhD thesis, University of Edinburgh. Available from the Department of Artificial Intelligence.

S. A. Cameron, 1985 (March 25–28). A study of the clash detection problem in robotics. In *Int. Conf. Robotics and Automation*, pages 488–493, St. Louis.

S. A. Cameron, 1987. Efficient intersection tests for objects defined constructively. Submitted to Int. J. Robotics Research.

S. A. Cameron and J. Aylett, 1987. ROBMOD *Users Guide.* Software Report, Department of Artificial Intelligence, University of Edinburgh (U.K.).

J.F. Canny, 1983. *Finding Edges and Lines.* Technical Report Tech.Rep. 720, Massachusetts Inst. Technol.

J.J. Clark, 1986. Authenticating Edges produced by Zero Crossing Algorithms. submitted to PAMI.

L. S. Davis, Z. Wu, and H. Sun, 1983. Contour based motion estimation. *Comput. Graphics Image Processing*, 23:313–326.

N. Daw, 1972. Color-coded cells in goldfish, cat and rhesus monkey. *Investigative Opthalmology*, 11:411–417.

L. Dreschler and H. -H. Nagel, 1982. Volumetric model and 3-d trajectory of a moving car derived from monocular tv frame sequences of a street scene. *Comput. Graphics Image Processing*, 20:199–228.

H. F. Durrant-Whyte, 1987a. Consistent Integration and Propagation of Disparate Sensor Observations. *Int. J. Robotics Research*, 6.

H.F. Durrant-Whyte, 1987b. *Integration, Coordination and Control of Multi-Sensor Robot Systems.* Kluwer, Boston.

H.F. Durrant-Whyte, 1987c. Uncertain Geometry in Robotics. In *Proc. IEEE Int. Conf. Robotics and Automation*, page 851, Raleigh, NC.

Margaret M. Fleck, 1987 (). The phantom edge finder. In *Proceedings of the Alvey Vision Conference*, Cambridge, England.

David Forsyth, 1987. The use of colour in vision. In *Proc. Alvey Vis. Conf.*, Cambridge, UK.

D. B. Gennery, 1979. Stereo camera calibration. In *Proc. Image Understanding Workshop*, page , Science Applications Inc., Silver Springs, Md.

R. Gershon, 1985. Empirical results with a model of color vision. In *Proc. CVPR*, San Francisco.

Shaogang Gong, 1987. *Parallel computation of visual motion.* Technical Report , Oxford University MSc report.

W. Eric L. Grimson and Tomás Lozano-Pérez, 1986 (). Search and sensing strategies for recognition and localization of two- and three- dimensional objects. In *Third Symp. Robotics Research*, pages 73–82, Gouvieux, France.

Marsha Jo Hannah, 1980. Bootstrap stereo. In *Proc. Image Understanding Workshop*, page , Science Applications Inc., Silver Springs, Md.

R.M. Haralick, 1980. Edge and Region Analysis for Digital Image Data. *Comput. Graphics Image Processing*, 12:60–73.

R.M. Haralick, 1984. Digital Step Edges from Zero-crossings of Second Directional Derivatives. *IEEE Trans. Pattern Anal. Machine Intell.*, PAMI-6(1):58–68.

R.M. Haralick, L.T. Watson, and T.J. Laffey, 1983. The Topographic Primal Sketch. *International Journal of Robotics Research*, 2(1):50–72.

E. C. Hildreth, 1984. *The Measurement of Visual Motion.* MIT Press, Cambridge, Ma.

D. D. Hoffman and W. A. Richards, 1982. Representing smooth plane curves for recognition: implications for figure-ground reversal. In *Proc. Nat. Conf. Artif. Intell.*, pages 5–8, Pittsburgh, Pa.

R. H. Hollier, 1986. *Automated Guided Vehicle Systems.* IFS, London.

B. K. P. Horn, 1986. *Robot Vision.* MIT Press, Cambridge, Ma.

D. P. Huttenlocher and S. Ullman, 1987 (June). Object recognition using alignment. In *Proceedings of the First International Conf. Comp. Vision.*, pages 102–111, London, England.

L. D. Landau and E. M. Lifschitz, 1959. *Fluid Mechanics*. Pergamon Press, Oxford.

M.S. Livingstone and D.H. Hubel, 1984. Anatomy and Physiology of a color system in the primate visual cortex. *J. Neuroscience*, 4:309–356.

T. Lozano-Pérez, 1983 (February). Spatial planning—a configuration space approach. *IEEE Transactions on Computers*, 108–120.

T. Lozano-Pérez, 1985. Motion planning for simple robot manipulators. In *3rd Int. Sym. Rob. Res.*, Gouvieux.

R. Machuca and K. Philips, 1983. Applications of vector fields to image processing. *IEEE Trans. Pattern Anal. Machine Intell.*, PAMI-5.

D. Marr, 1977. Analysis of occluding contour. *Proc. R. Soc. London*, B 197:441–475.

D. Marr and E. C. Hildreth, 1980. Theory of edge detection. *Proc. Roy. Soc. London*, B207:187–217.

H. P. Moravec, 1977. Towards automatic visual obstacle avoidance. In *Proc. Int. Jt. Conf. Artif. Intell.*, page 584, Cambridge, Ma.

D. W. Murray, D. A. Castelow, and B. F. Buxton, 1987. From an image sequence to a recognised polyhedral object. In *Proc. Alvey Vis. Conf.*, Cambridge, UK.

H. -H. Nagel, 1986. Image sequences– ten (octal) years from phenomenology towards a theoretical foundation. In *Proc. 8th Int. Conf. Patt. Recog.*, page , Paris.

H. -H. Nagel, 1987. On the estimation of optical flow. *Artificial Intelligence*, (to appear):.

H. -H. Nagel and W. Enkelmann, 1986. An investigation of smoothness constraints for the estimation of displacement vector fields from image segments. *IEEE Trans. Pattern Anal. Machine Intell.*, PAMI-8:565–593.

R. Nevatia, 1977. A Color edge detector and its use in scene segmentation. *IEEE Trans. Sys. Man and Cyb.*, SMC-7:820–826.

J.A. Noble, 1987. The Geometric Structure of Images. M.Sc. report.

I. Page, 1983. DisArray : A Graphics-Oriented Fifth Generation Workstation. In *Nicograph '83*, Tokyo.

Ian Page, 1987. The DisPuter. In *Parallel Architectures for Computer Vision (Page, Ian ed.)*, page , Oxford University Press.

Don E. Pearson and John A. Robinson, 1985. Visual Communication at Very Low Data Rates. *Proc. IEEE*, 73:795–812.

J. Ponce and M. Brady, 1987. Towards a surface primal sketch. In *Three-dimensional vision (Kanade ed.)*.

G. T. Reid, R. C. Rixon, and H. I. Messer, 1984. Absolute and comparative measurements of three-dimensional shape by phase measuring Moire topography. *Optics and Laser technology*.

A. A. G. Requicha and H. B. Voelcker, 1982 (March). Solid modeling: a historical summary and contemporary assessment. *IEEE Computer Graphics and Applications*, 2.

Reddaway S.F., 1973. DAP - A Distributed Array Processor. In *First Annual Symposium on Computer Architecture*, Gainsville, Fla.

B. Steer, 1985. *Navigation for the guidance of a mobile robot*. PhD thesis, Warwick University.

Fridtjof Stein, 1987. *Recognition of overlapped objects*. Technical Report OU-RRG-87-11, Oxford University Robotics Research Group.

D. Terzopoulos, 1983. The role of constraints and discontinuities in visible-surface reconstruction. In *Proc. 7th Int. J. Conf. Artif. Intell.*, pages 1073–1077, Karlsrühe.

J. L. Turney, T. N. Mudge, and R. A. Volz, 1985. Recognizing partially occluded parts. *IEEE Trans. Pattern Anal. Machine Intell.*, PAMI-7:410–421.

R.J. Watt and M.J. Morgan, 1987. A theory of the primitive spatial code in human vision. *Vision Research*.

VII ROBOT PROGRAMMING

The large number of papers in part VII is a reflection of the strong interest in high-level programming techniques for robotic systems. Although progress has been made in the areas of semiautomatic and automatic programming, much remains to be done. The need is now more apparent then ever: it is now possible to perform complex manipulation and perception tasks, but in many practical cases it is not yet economical to apply such techniques, because the programming is too tedious and time consuming. These nine papers address different aspects of the problem.

Craig presents a discussion of the central issues that need to be considered in developing any off-line manipulation programming system. He also outlines the basic design of one such system. Fehrenbach and Smithers describe the progress to date on a very ambitious demonstration project named the "Design-to-Product" project. The goal is to use computer-aided design information to automatically generate off-line programming for sensor-based robotic assembly of a product. In a similar vein, Asano describes the concept of a model-based software system to supervise remote maintenance tasks done by a master-slave manipulator system. This system is intended to be used in conjunction with a human operator who can issue high-level supervisory commands without relying on knowledge of computer programming. Bartenstein and Inoue introduce a learning algorithm that automatically converts easy-to-write user-oriented programs into more complex programs for use in connection with robotic systems. They illustrate the use of their algorithm in connection with applications to two-dimensional robot vision, manipulation, and navigation.

Taylor et al. introduce the idea of automatically creating a motion program for a sensor-based manipulator by using a game tree created for a game-theoretic model of manipulation. In this model there are two players: the manipulator and nature. The manipulator makes "moves" in the game by choosing a control signal to its actuators, and nature moves by choosing a signal to the sensors. Ghallab et al. take account of the fact that time is an important variable in planning and execution monitoring. They propose a programming structure based on a hierarchical representation of temporal goals and events, and explain how this can be used to program and monitor a flexible assembly cell.

In many robotic applications, errors are important factors that must be dealt with explicitly. The next three papers are concerned with overcoming problems due to different types of errors. If a robot is expected to complete a complex set of actions but errors occasionally occur in the middle of the sequence, what can be done? Trevelyan et al. address this problem and show how a recursive approach to motion-control programming can provide for robust error recovery. Pertin-Troccaz and Puget consider the errors caused by uncertainty. They propose adapting program-proving techniques for use in the automatic generation of robot programs. They use a backward propagation technique for patching programs found to generate actions whose uncertainties could lead to errors. Their paper assumes that valid estimates of uncertainty exist. In the next paper, Smith et al. present a general method for estimating uncertainties in relative spatial relationships between a series of objects that are themselves located by spatial relationships having uncertainties associated with them.

Issues in the Design of Off-Line Programming Systems

John J. Craig
SILMA Inc.
2111 Grant Rd.
Los Altos, Ca. 94022

Off-line programming systems are important both as aids in programming present day industrial automation as well as platforms for robotics research. Numerous issues must be considered in the design of such systems. A discussion of these issues is presented, followed by the basic design of one such system. Among the topics discussed are the spatial representation of solids, graphical rendering of these objects, automatic collision detection, incorporation of kinematics, path planning, and dynamic simulation, simulation of sensors, concurrent programming, translation by post processors to various target languages, and workcell calibration.

Introduction

In the last decade the growth of the industrial robot market has not been nearly as rapid as predicted. One primary reason for this is that robots are still too difficult to use. A great deal of time and expertise is required to install a robot in a particular application and bring the system to production readiness. For various reasons, in some applications this problem is more severe than others, and hence, we see certain application areas (e.g. spot welding, spray painting) being automated with robots much sooner than other application domains. It seems that lack of sufficiently trained robot system implementors is limiting growth in some if not all areas of application. At some manufacturing companies, management encourages the use of robots to an extent greater than that which can be realized by available applications engineers. It is also the case that a large percentage of the robots delivered are being used in ways which do not fully make use of their capabilities. These symptoms indicate that current industrial robots are not easy enough to use to allow successful installation and programming in a timely manner.

There are many factors that make robot programming a difficult task. First of all, it is intrinsically related to general computer programming, and so shares many of the same problems encountered in that field. But programming robots, or any programmable machine, has particular problems which make the development of production ready software even more difficult. Most of these special problems arise from the fact that a robot manipulator interacts with its physical environment [Goldman, 1985]. Even simple programming systems maintain a "world model" of this physical environment in the form of locations of objects and have "knowledge" about presence and absence of various ob-

jects encoded in the program strategies. During development of a robot program (and especially later during production use) it is necessary to keep the internal model maintained by the programming system in correspondence with the actual state of the robot's environment. Interactive debugging of programs with a manipulator requires frequent manual resetting of the state of the robot's environment - parts, tools, etc., must be moved back to their initial locations. Such state resetting is especially difficult (and sometimes costly) when the robot is performing a non-reversible operation on one or more parts (e.g. drilling, routing, etc.). The most spectacular effect of the presence of the physical environment is when a program bug manifests itself in some unintended non-reversible operation on parts, tools, or on the manipulator itself.

Although there are difficulties in maintaining an accurate internal model of the state of the manipulator's environment, there seems no question that there are great benefits to be obtained by doing so. Whole areas of sensor research, perhaps most notably computer vision, are aimed at developing techniques by which world models may be verified, corrected, or discovered. Clearly, in order that any computational algorithm be applied to the robot command generation problem, the algorithm needs access to a model of the robot and its surroundings.

In the development of programming systems for robots, advances in the power of programming techniques seem directly tied to the sophistication of the internal model referenced by the programming language. Early joint space "teach by showing" robot systems employed a limited world model, and there were very limited ways in which the system could aid the programmer in accomplishing a task. Slightly more sophisticated robot controllers were developed with kinematic models so that the system could at least aid the user in moving the joints so as to accomplish Cartesian motions. Robot programming languages (RPLs) evolved which support many different data types and operations which the programmer may use as needed to model attributes of the environment and compute actions for the robot. Some RPLs support world modelling primitives such as affixments, data types for forces and moments, and other features [Mujtaba and Goldman, 1981].

The robot programming languages of today might be called "explicit programming languages" in that every action that the system takes must be programmed by the application engineer. At the other end of the spectrum, are the so-called "task level programming" (TLP) systems in which the programmer may state high level goals such as "insert the bolt", or perhaps even "build the toaster oven". Such systems are built using techniques from artificial intelligence research to automatically generate motion and strategy plans. However, these task level languages do not exist yet, although various pieces of such systems are under development by researchers [Lozano-Perez, 1983]. Task level programming systems will require a very complete model of the robot and its environment in order that these automated planning operations can be performed.

We will define an off-line programming (OLP) system to be a robot programming language which has been sufficiently extended, generally by means of computer graphics, that the development of robot programs can take place without access to the robot itself. Although this paper is focused to some extent on the particular problem of robot programming, the notion of an OLP system extends to any programmable device on the factory floor. A common argument raised in their favor is that an OLP system will not tie up production equipment when it needs to be reprogrammed, and hence, automated factories can stay in production mode a greater percentage of the time. They also serve as a natural vehicle to tie computer aided design (CAD) data bases used in the design phase of a product to the actual manufacturing of the product. In some applications, this direct use of CAD design data can dramatically reduce the programming time required for the manufacturing machinery.

Off-line programming of robots offers other potential benefits which are just beginning to be appreciated by industrial robot users. We have discussed some of the problems associated with robot programming, and most have to do with the fact that an external, physical workcell is being manipulated by the robot program. This makes backing up to try different strategies tedious. Programming of robots in simulation offers a way of keeping the bulk of the programming work strictly internal to a computer - until the application is nearly complete. Thus, many of the problems peculiar to robot programming tend to diminish.

Off-line programming systems should serve as the natural growth path from explicit programming systems to task level programming systems. The simplest OLP system is merely a graphical extension to a robot programming language, but from there can slowly be extended towards a task level programming system. This gradual extension is accomplished by providing automated solutions to various sub-tasks as these solutions become available, and letting the programmer use them to explore options in the simulated environment. Until we discover how to build task level systems, the user must be in the loop to evaluate automatically planned sub-tasks and guide the development of the application program. If we take this view, an OLP system serves as an important basis for research and development of task level planning systems, and indeed, in support of their work many researchers have developed various components of an OLP system (e.g. 3-D models and graphic display, language post processors, etc.). Hence, OLP systems should be a useful tool in research as well as an aid in current industrial practice.

Central Issues in OLP systems

In this section we raise many of the issues that must be considered in the design of an OLP system. The collection of topics discussed will help to scope the definition of an OLP system.

User Interface

Since a major motivation in developing an OLP system is to create an environment in which manipulators are easier to program, the user interface is of crucial importance. However, the other major motivation is to remove reliance on use of the physical equipment during programming. Upon initial consideration, these two goals seem to be in conflict – robots are hard enough to program when you can see them, how can it be easier when the physical device is not present? This question is the essence of the OLP design problem.

Manufacturers of industrial robots have learned that the RPLs they provide with their robots cannot be successfully utilized by a large percentage of manufacturing personnel. For this, and other historical reasons, many industrial robots are provided with a 2-level interface [Shimano et al, 1984], one for programmers and one for non-programmers. Non-programmers utilize a teach pendant and interact with the robot to develop robot programs. Programmers write code in the RPL and interact with the robot in order to teach robot workpoints and to debug program flow. In general, these two approaches to program development trade off ease of use versus flexibility.

Viewed as an extension of a RPL, it is natural for an OLP system to contain an RPL as a subset of its user interface. This RPL should share features which have already been discovered valuable in present robot programming systems. For example, for use as an RPL, interactive languages are much more productive than compiled languages which force the user to go through the "edit - compile - run" cycle for each program modification.

While the language portion of the user interface inherits much from "traditional" RPLs, it is the lower level (i.e. easier to use) interface which must be carefully considered in an OLP system. A central component to this interface is a computer graphic view of the robot being programmed and its environment. Using a pointing device such as a light pen or a mouse, the user can indicate various locations or objects on the graphics screen. The design of the user interface addresses exactly how the user interacts with the screen to specify a robot program. The same pointing device can be used to point at items in a "menu" in order to specify modes or invoke various functions.

A central primitive is that of teaching a robot work point or "frame" which has six degrees of freedom by means of interaction with the graphics screen. Due to the availability of 3-D models of fixtures and workpieces in the OLP system, this task is often quite easy. The interface provides the user with the means to indicate locations on surfaces, allowing the orientation of the frame to take on a local surface normal, and then provides methods for offsetting, re-orienting, etc. Depending on the specifics of the application, such tasks are quite easily specified via the graphics window into the simulated world.

With a well designed user interface it should be possible for non-programmers to accomplish certain applications from start to finish. In addition, frames and motion sequences 'taught' by non-programmers can be translated by the OLP system into textual RPL statements. These simple programs can be maintained and embellished in a RPL form by more experienced programmers. For programmers, the RPL availability allows arbitrary code development for more complex applications.

3-D Modelling

A central element in OLP systems is the use of graphic depictions of the simulated robot and its workcell. This requires the robot and all fixtures, parts, and tools in the workcell to be modelled as three dimensional objects. To speed up program development, it is desirable to use any CAD models of parts or tooling that are directly available from the CAD system on which the original design was done. As CAD systems become more and more prevalent in industry, it becomes more and more likely that this kind of geometric data will be readily available. Because of the strong desire for this kind of CAD integration from design to production, it makes sense for an OLP system to contain a CAD modelling subsystem, or to be itself a subsystem of a CAD design system. If an OLP system is to be a stand alone system, it must have appropriate interfaces to transfer models

to and from external CAD systems. However, even a stand alone OLP system should have at least a simple local CAD facility for quickly creating models of non-critical workcell items, or for adding robot specific data to imported CAD models.

Multiple representations of spatial shape are generally required. For many operations, an exact analytic description of the surface or volume is generally present, while in order to benefit from display technology another representation is often needed. Present technology is well suited to systems in which the underlying display primitive is a planar polygon. Hence, while an object shape may be well represented by a smooth surface, practical display (especially for animation) requires a faceted representation. User interface graphical actions such as pointing to a point on a surface should internally act so as to specify a point on the true surface, even if graphically the user sees a depiction of the faceted model.

An important use of the three dimensional geometry of the object models is in automatic collision detection. That is, when any collisions occur between objects in the simulated environment, the OLP system should automatically warn the user, and indicate exactly where the collision is taking place. Since applications such as assembly involve many desired "collisions", it is necessary to be able to inform the system that collisions between certain objects are acceptable. It is also valuable to be able to generate a collision warning when objects are within a specified tolerance of a true collision. The exact collision detection problem for general 3-D solids is quite difficult, whereas collision detection for the same faceted models used for display is somewhat more tractable.

Kinematic Emulation

A central component in maintaining the validity of the simulated world is the faithful emulation of the geometrical aspects of each manipulator that is simulated. Concerning inverse kinematics, there are two possiblities for how the OLP system interfaces to the robot controller. First, it is possible for the OLP system to replace the inverse kinematics of the robot controller, and always communicate robot positions in mechanism joint space. The second choice is to communicate Cartesian locations to the robot controller and let the controller use the inverse kinematics supplied by the manufacturer to solve for robot configurations. The second choice is almost always preferable especially as manufacturers begin to build in *arm signature* style calibration to their robots. These calibration techniques effectively customize the inverse kinematics for each individual robot. If this is the case, then it is desirable to communicate information at the Cartesian level to robot controllers.

These considerations generally mean that the forward and inverse kinematic functions used by the simulator must reflect the nominal functions used in the robot controller supplied by the manufacturer of the robot. There are several details of the inverse kinematic function as specified by the manufacturer which must be emulated by the simulator software. Any inverse kinematic algorithm must make arbitrary choices in order to resolve singularities. For example, when joint 5 of a Puma 560 robot is at its zero location, axes 4 and 6 line up, and a singular condition exists. The inverse kinematic function in the robot controller can only solve for the sum of joint angles 4 and 6, and then uses an arbitrary rule to choose individual values for joints 4 and 6. Whatever algorithm is used, it must be emulated in the OLP system. Another example is that of choosing the nearest solution when many alternate solutions are possible. The simulator must use the same algorithm in making the selection as the controller will use in order to avoid potentially catastrophic errors in simulating the actual manipulator. A helpful feature occasionally found in robot controllers is the ability to command a Cartesian goal, but specify which of the possible solutions is to be used. If this feature is available, the simulator need not emulate the choice of solution algorithm as the OLP system can force its choice on the controller.

Path Planning Emulation

In addition to kinematic emulation for static positioning of the manipulator, it is desirable for an OLP system to accurately emulate the path taken by the manipulator in moving through space. Again, the central problem is that the OLP system needs to simulate the algorithms in the robot controllers, and these path planning and execution algorithms vary considerably from one robot manufacturer to another. Simulation of the spatial shape of the path taken is important for detection of collisions between the robot and its environment. Simulation of the temporal aspects of the trajectory are important in predicting the cycle times of applications. When a robot is operating in a moving environment (for example, near another robot) accurate simulation of the temporal attributes of motion is necessary to accurately predict collisions, and in some cases to predict communication or synchronization problems such as deadlock.

Dynamic Emulation

The motion of manipulators can be simulated without dynamic attributes if the OLP system does a good job of emulating the trajectory planning algorithm of the controller and if the actual robot follows desired trajectories with negligable errors. However, at high speed or under heavy loading conditions, trajectory tracking errors can become important. Simulation of these tracking errors necessitates modelling the dynamics of the manipulator and objects which it moves, as well as the control algorithm used in the manipulator controller. Presently there are practical problems in obtaining sufficient in-formation from the robot vendors to make this kind of dynamic simulation of practical value, but in some cases dynamic simulation can be fruitfully pursued.

Multi-Process Simulation

Some industrial applications involve two or more robots cooperating in the same environment. Even in single robot workcells there may often be a conveyor belt, transfer line, vision system, or some other active device with which the robot must interact. For this reason, it is important that an OLP system be able to simulate multiple moving devices and other activities that involve parallelism. As a basis for this capability, the underlying language in which the system is implemented should be a multi-processing language. In such an environment it is possible to write independent robot control programs for each of two or more robots in a single cell, and then simulate the action of the cell with the programs running concurrently. If signal and wait primitives are added to the language, the robots can interact with each other just as they might in the application being simulated.

Simulation of Sensors

Studies have shown that a large portion of robot programs are not motion statements but rather initialization, error checking, I/O and other kinds of statements [Taylor et al, 1982]. Hence it is important that the OLP system provide an environment in which complete applications can be simulated, including interaction with sensors, various I/O, and communication with other devices. Within an OLP system which supports simulation of sensors and multi-processing, not only are robot motions checked for feasibility, but also debugging of the communication and sychronization portion of the robot program can be accomplished.

Language Translation to Target System

An annoyance for present users of industrial robots (and other programmable automation) is that almost every supplier of such systems has invented a unique language for programming their product. If an OLP system aspires to be universal in the equipment it can handle, it is forced to deal with the problem of translating to and from several different languages. One choice for dealing with this problem is to choose one single language to be used by the OLP system, and then post process the language in order to convert it into the format required by the target machine. It is also desirable to be able to upload programs which already exist on the target machines and bring them into the OLP system.

Two potential benefits of OLP systems are directly related to this language translation topic. The one offered most frequently by proponents of OLP systems is that one universal interface which can be used to program a variety of robots solves the problems that users face of learning and dealing with several automation languages.

The second benefit stems from economic considerations in future scenarios in which hundreds or perhaps thousands of robots fill factories. The cost associated with a powerful programming environment (such as a language and graphical interface) may prohibit placing this at the site of each robot installation. Rather, it seems to make economic sense to place a very simple, "dumb", but cheap controller with each robot, and have it downloaded from a powerful, "intelligent" OLP system which is located in an office environment. Hence, the general problem of translating an application program from a powerful universal language to a simple language designed to execute in a cheap processor, is an important issue in OLP systems.

Workcell Calibration

An inevitable reality of a computer model of any real world situation is that of inaccuracy in the model. In order to make programs developed on an OLP system usable, methods for workcell calibration must be an integral part of the system. The magnitude of this problem varies greatly depending upon the application, and makes off-line programming of some tasks much more realistic than others. In applications in which the majority of the robot work points must be retaught with the actual robot to solve inaccuracy problems, OLP systems loose their effectiveness.

A large class of applications involve many actions performed relative to a rigid object. Consider, for example, the task of drilling several hundred holes in a bulkhead. The actual location of the bulkhead relative to the robot can be taught using the actual robot by taking three measurements. From that data, the locations of all the holes can be automatically updated if they are available in part coordinates from a CAD system. In this situation, only these three points need be taught with the robot rather than hundreds. Most tasks involve this sort of "many operations relative to a rigid object" paradigm, for example, PC board component insertion, routing, spot welding, arc welding, palletizing, painting, deburring, etc..

CimStation

In this section we consider the core design of CimStation, an OLP system under development by SILMA Inc [Kehmeier, 1987]. By "core design" we mean the fundamental portion of the system that maintains a world model which describes arbitrarily many objects each having attributes such as spatial shape, position, velocity, and others. The way in which this world model is programmed and the way in which resulting programs are converted to operate the corresponding real world devices will be discussed.

Models and Graphics

CimStation contains a facility to build CAD models

from scratch, or to import them from external CAD systems via the IGES (Initial Graphical Exchange Specification) interface. In either case, models are represented by a boundary representation of the surface or solid. Internally these boundaries or surfaces are represented with collections of planar polygons, or facets. The *model* data structure stores edges that are shared between facets only once, and likewise, points that are shared between edges are stored only once. This data structure also includes information which allows groups of facets to be regarded as a single *surface*, for example, the facets making up the curved surface of a cylinder. In addition to this faceted representation, an analytic repesentation of the surface may be stored with the model as well. For compatibility with existing CAD systems, wireframe models, which are collections of line segments, can be handled also.

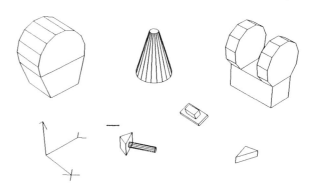

Figure 1 *Examples of a Faceted Models.*

On computer systems without hardware assist for graphics, models are displayed as in figure 1, using backface elimination. On platforms with graphics hardware, facets are sorted, projected, and filled so as to render shaded hidden surface scenes.† Collision detection is implemented for collisions between any two surfaced models, and uses the faceted repesentation for the computation. To speed up collision detection, all objects in the world model have *bounding boxes* precomputed. On platforms without graphics hardware, a software collision detection algorithm similar to [Bobrow, 1987] is used.

When available, graphics hardware can be exploited for the collision detection computation. In CimStation this is done with an algorithm related to, but more general than, the method presented in [Smith, 1985]. In our algorithm, the hardware used for clipping polygons to a 3-D volume (normally used in display) is used to quickly determine if any object intrudes into a specified volume.

---

† All figures is this paper were generated on a black and white Apollo DN3000 computer, on which CimSation does not perform polygon filling.

The hardware restricts the nature of this 3-D volume to have straight edges and to be topologically equivalent to a cube. The collision detection algorithm to detect a collision with object 'A' proceeds roughly as follows:

1) Check whether any polygons intrude into the bounding box of 'A'.

2) For each intruding polygon found in step 1, construct its bounding box, and check for intrusion by any polygon of object 'A'.

3) If any intrusions are found in step 2, use software routine for determining if and where the planar polygons intersect.

As an elaboration of the above algorithm, in CimStation near misses within a specified tolerance can also be detected by "expanding" all objects by the desired tolerance.

Objects and the World Model

Every simulated entity such as a workpiece, fixture, or link of a robot is repesented by an *object*. The object data structure contains the model of the entity, several other attributes, plus room to add future data. A simple example of another attribute stored with an object is a *label* by which the object is referenced. Objects can be built from their models and stored in database libraries for later use.

It is natural to group objects into *structured objects* in a tree structure. For example, an n-jointed robot is a structured object having a null model at its root, and having $n + 1$ sub-objects ('link0' through 'linkn'). Sub-objects are referred to by pathnames, for example, 'puma1/link3'. The entire simulated world is a single structured object with a null model at the root named 'world'. Anytime an object is moved, all of its descendants move with it, but the motion of a child-object does not affect its parent-object.

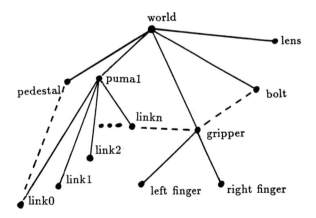

Figure 2 *Example of the World Model Tree.*

Figure 2 shows an example of a simple world model containing a robot, an end-effector, a part ('bolt'), and an object upon which the robot is mounted ('pedestal'). Dashed lines in figure 2 indicate *affixments* which are used to temporarily create a rigid connection between two objects. Affixments are used to connect an end-effector to the final link of the robot. It is also by means of these affixments that a simulated manipulator picks up a simulated bolt. In the situation shown in figure 2, a command to move 'puma1/linkn', 'gripper', or 'bolt' would result in motion of the manipulator.

Anytime an object is moved, other objects in the world may move with it either due to their position in the world tree or because of affixments. The set of objects to be moved are computed as the transitive closure of two binary relations: the parent-child relation of the world model tree, and the affixment relation.

The world model always contains an object called 'lens' whose position specifies the location from which the world is to be viewed. The focal length is stored as an attribute of this object. The 'lens' can be moved anywhere to obtain various views and might, for example, be affixed to the gripper in order to generate an animation of what would be seen if one rode along on the gripper.

Attachment of Kinematics to Structured Objects

In order to simulate the motion of connected linkages such as manipulators, kinematic routines may be associated with any structured object in the world model. In CimStation these kinematics are associated with the outermost link of the robot, always called 'linkn'. The fact that kinematics are associated with an object earns that object the distinction of being *magic*. Anytime a move command is issued to any object which belongs to an affixment class containing a magic object, the motion becomes dictated by the kinematics associated with the magic object. Hence, a command to move 'bolt' (of the figure 2 example) causes the inverse kinematics of 'puma1' to be executed, and all moving linkages and affixed objects moved as a consequence.

In CimStation the kinematic routines are generally *closed form* [Craig, 1986], but may be iterative if need be. Kinematic routines supplied by the robot vendor may be used directly if available.

Structured objects are by no means restricted to the class of open serial chains, but may have a completely general topology. For example, figure 3 shows a Cincinnati Milacron T3-776 industrial robot, which is slightly more complex than an open kinematic chain due to some additional linkages.

Attachment of Paths to Objects

To add the dimension of time to the world model, a *path* becomes associated with an object anytime that object is asked to move. A path is essentially a frame-valued

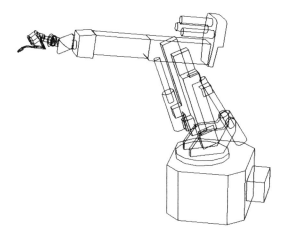

Figure 3 *The Cincinnati Milacron T3-776 robot is an example of a structured object.*

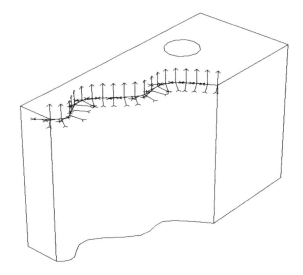

Figure 4 *A path derived from CAD data.*

function of time, hence specifying the evolution of the position and orientation of an object as a function of time. At any instant several paths can be associated with different objects in the world, forming the basis of simulation of simultaneous motion.

The geometric properties of a path can be specified in several ways using CimStation. Often they are specified as in typical RPLs, by a sequence of *via points.* Each of these via points can be specified graphically or numerically. Another way a path can be specified is computationally – a user-written SIL routine might compute a list of frames based on some algorithm. Finally, and perhaps most importantly, paths can often be specified more or less directly from CAD data. Figure 4 shows a path (indicated by an equally spaced sequence of frames) which was generated very rapidly from a CAD model that had been imported via the IGES format from another CAD system.

Dynamics and Evaluation of World State

Paths associated with objects play the role of desired paths, which are equivalent to actual paths if CimStation is not simulating dynamics. If dynamic simulation is enabled, then the desired path, present state, and control law associated with a given object are used to determine the actual position of the object at any future time. In either mode, when a graphic depiction of the world state is desired, the system updates the positions of all objects and calls the display function to render a scene. This rendering is a function of the location of the 'lens' and its current focal length, either of which could themselves be changing over time.

The SIL Language

Users develop application programs through interaction with the mouse-menu interface, or directly in a powerful programming language called SIL [Pearce, 1987]. In program generation mode, actions described from the mouse-menu interface generate corresponding SIL statements, so whether used by programmers or non-programmers, CimStation creates SIL programs. CimStation makes use of the local facilities of the host platform for text editing, file system, hardcopy output, etc..

SIL has PASCAL syntax, and a great many predefined types, procedures, and functions. Examples of predefined types are a variety of geometric types such as **types zyz** (an Euler angle set), **ypr** (yaw, pitch, and roll about fixed axes), **point** which is a vector, **frame** which is a homogeneous transform, and dozens of others. An example of a predefined procedure is the **moveto** procedure, which is used to accomplish most motion specification in SIL.

SIL procedures may be *polymorphic* in that the same procedure name can be used for different routines as long as the two can be distinguished by the types and number of arguments. This feature is taken advantage of in building a robot programming language which has a minimum number of keywords for the user to remember. For example, the statement **moveto('tool',foo)** will move the 'tool' to **foo**, where **foo** may be a joint vector, a frame, a position vector (implying translate only), or a rotation type (implying rotate only). Hence, SIL does not need a proliferation of command names as found in most motion control languages (e.g. move, jmove, jog, rotate, translate).

Another major feature of SIL is *automatic coercion* of types. This allows the system to be informed of **data** types that are semantically equivalent, and for the specification of mapping functions between these types. For example, types which represent three-space rotations can automatically coerce to one another in SIL. Hence if a subroutine is developed which accepts an argument of the type **zyz** Euler angles, it can immediately be called with argument of type **ypr**, or any other rotation type. This also leads to a "clean" syntax and non-proliferation of function names.

A major extension beyond standard PASCAL is that SIL is an interactive language. A single statement can be typed at the system at any time, and the results can be observed. The SIL environment is a LISP-like environment in which global variables, functions, and procedures are all immediately available. When a user defines a new function, it becomes part of the global state. Unlike LISP, SIL is a typed language and has the relatively easy syntax of PASCAL. The great majority of CimStation is itself written in SIL, so when users add new functions to the system, they are expanding the system just as its developers have. Fully debugged SIL code can be compiled for efficiency.

The single largest extension to PASCAL that SIL offers is that it is a concurrent or multi-processing language. Users may define a *process* with syntax exactly like that of a procedure declaration (very simple examples are shown in figure 5 and 6). Later several processes may be run concurrently. Processes communicate through global variables or by means of message passing. The message passing primitives are called **signal** and **wait**. The type of data signaled (and waited for) can be any legal SIL type, so messages can range from simple booleans to complex structured types. In most automation simulations, booleans are used as signals, as this mimics the simple binary I/O ports found on many controllers.

In summary, SIL can be thought of as an interpreted, concurrent PASCAL with many predefined types and functions apropos to the robot programming problem.

Simulation of Sensors

CimStation allows the simulation of several kinds of sensors. In general, using the multi-processing environment and other features of the system, the user is free to write elaborate simulations of sensors if desired. In this section some simple capabilities to simulate sensors are discussed.

Simulation of force sensing for *guarded moves* is possible using the multi-processing environment and the collision detection capability. In a guarded move, the collisions between the end-effector (including anything affixed to it) and the rest of the environment are checked at the force sample rate, and if a collision occurs, motion of the robot is stopped. This force monitor is implemented as a separate process that "wakes up" at the force sample rate and checks for a new collision.

Similarly, the simulation of limit switches and light-beam interrupt sensors are simulated using the collision detection apparatus.

Vision systems can be simulated using a process to emulate the vision system. This process can be signalled to determine the position and orientation of any workcell object. The simulation consists of delaying for some specified processing time and then returning the frame of the workcell object to the calling process. Failure to detect the object can be signalled if the object is not in the simulated camera's field of view.

Translation to Target System Languages

The SIL environment provides a universal language with several advanced features as well as access to the world model. This environment is designed to be powerful and easy to use, to maximally aid in the difficult task of developing robot programs. The resulting program, in order to be useful, must be translated into the native language of the simulated robot (or other programmable automation). The native languages found in present day robot controllers vary widely as regards the types, operations, and program structures which they support. A portion of CimStation is a subsystem which accomplishes this translation from a universal language (SIL) to a restricted language. A large part of this computational machinery is common regardless of the target language, and another portion is target language dependent.

The language translation problem in an OLP system is more complex than that of a cross compiler between two universal languages. The problems are due to the fact that the target language is restricted, and also in that the source program makes references to a world model which will generally not be present on the target system. Consider a SIL program which makes use of affixments while manipulating the world model, and also refers to robot goal positions given relative to the location of various objects in the world. In a target system which does not support a world model and affixments, such a program may not be implementable. Likewise, if a SIL program makes use of certain types or operations which are not supported on the target platform, the translation may not be possible. Hence, a large portion of the translation algorithm in CimStation has to do with analyzing the SIL program in light of a description of the target language to determine if the program is *translatable*. This analysis is not as simple as merely checking to see if non-supported types or operations appear in the SIL code.

Consider the two simple example SIL programs in figures 5 and 6. They are intended for download to a controller which supports the type frame, but does not support the operation **rel** (frame multiplication). Although both programs contain the use of the **rel** operator on frames, one is downloadable (fig. 6), and one is not (fig. 5). In the version shown in figure 6, the **rel** operator only appears in expressions whose operands are program-flow invariant, and hence can be precomputed.

Program analysis procedes roughly as follows. The source SIL program is converted into a graph in which each node is a block of code which begins with a label, contains only sequential instructions, and which ends in a "go to" or a conditional "go to". The arcs of the graph are program jumps which may or may not be taken at

```
process puma1(is_ok: boolean);
var x,bin1,bin2,drop: frame;
begin
  bin1:= [40,40,0,0,90,-90] as crt_zyz;
  bin2:= [20,80,0,0,90,-90] as crt_zyz;
  drop:= [0,0,15,0,180,0] as crt_ypr;
  signal(sensor,ready,true);
  wait(is_ok);
  if is_ok then
    x:=bin1
  else
    x:=bin2;
  moveto('bolt', drop rel x);
end;
```

Figure 5 *A non-downloadable SIL program.*

```
process puma2(is_ok: boolean);
var x,bin1,bin2,drop: frame;
begin
  bin1:= [40,40,0,0,90,-90] as crt_zyz;
  bin2:= [20,80,0,0,90,-90] as crt_zyz;
  drop:= [0,0,15,0,180,0] as crt_ypr;
  signal(sensor,ready,true);
  wait(is_ok);
  if is_ok then
    x:=drop rel bin1
  else
    x:=drop rel bin2;
  moveto('bolt', x);
end;
```

Figure 6 *A downloadable SIL program.*

run time depending on the value of external inputs, etc. The entire SIL program is analyzed to determine its use of variables, and these variables are collected in a *state vector*. By querying a tabular description of correspondences between SIL types and opertions and those supported in the target system, certain elements of this state vector are marked as non-represented. At each node of the program's graph, we ask if there is any way to enter that node such that a non-represented variable can have different values. If this is possible, and if the non-represented variable is used in the node in question, the program is not downloadable. If analysis shows that non-represented operations are only performed on operands that are program-flow invariant, then these expressions can be precomputed, with only the result appearing in the target code. More details of the translation process can be found in [Pearce et al, 1988].

If the program is downloadable, the translator will produce a native language program complete with program structures and I/O. For many target languages, most all SIL programs are downloadable. Users who have some familiarity with the target systems limitations can generally avoid creating SIL programs which are non-downloadable. Figure 7 shows the KAREL language [GMF, 1986] source which results from translation of the SIL program in figure 6. Note that because KAREL supports the **rel** operator, both SIL programs shown above are downloadable to this controller. Note that the translator has taken care of the details of changing the representation of orientation used (from **zyz** to a KAREL type which is equivalent to **ypr**), and the units used (from cm to mm).

```
PROGRAM PUMA2

CONST
IS_OK = 2
SENSORREADY = 3

VAR
X,DROP,BIN1,BIN2: POSITION

BEGIN
$MOTYPE = JOINT
$TERMTYPE = COARSE
$UFRAME = POS(0.0,0.0,-950.0,0.0,0.0,0.0,'')
$UTOOL = POS(-0.0,-0.0,334.962,-0.0,0.0,0.0,'')
$SPEED = 346.41
G336::
BIN1 = POS(400.0,400.0,0.0,-89.9994,0.000508,-89.9999,'')
BIN2 = POS(200.0,800.0,0.0,-89.9994,0.000508,-89.9999,'')
DROP = POS(0.0,0.0,150.0,0.0,180.0,0.0,'')
DOUT[SENSORREADY] = TRUE
IF DIN[IS_OK] THEN
GO TO G329
ENDIF
GO TO G332
G329::
X =  (BIN1:DROP)
GO TO G326
G332::
X =  (BIN2:DROP)
G326::
MOVE TO X NOWAIT
END PUMA2
```

Figure 7 *The KAREL version of the program in fig. 5.*

Calibration Facilities

CimStation can temporarily be connected to a robot controller in *online* mode. In this mode, the simulated and actual robots move together as the user interacts with CimStation. The main purpose of online mode is to allow the robot to be used to re-teach object locations, and to upload such data to CimStation to correct the world model. If the robot is remote from CimStation, this reteaching can occur independently and a data file uploaded.

The major calibration procedure makes use of feature point correspondence between modelled features and the locations of those features obtained by teaching with the robot. The algorithm uses n feature points (where n must be at least three) to update the location of a rigid body. The system computes the RMS position error for the taught points in order to allow the user to assess the accuracy of the robot, and thus his chances for success.

Another calibration procedure called *warp* may be used to deform the shape of a continuous path derived from a CAD model by reteaching n points along the path. This routine uses a cubic error spline to smoothly warp the original (CAD-derived) space curve so that it interpolates the taught points while as much as possible maintaining its original shape.

Automating Sub-Tasks in OLP Systems

In this section we briefly mention some advanced features which might be integrated into the "baseline" OLP system concept already presented. Most of these features accomplish automated planning of some small portion of an industrial application.

Automatic Robot Placement

One of the most basic tasks that can be accomplished by means of an OLP system is the determination of the workcell layout so that the manipulator(s) can reach all of the required workpoints. Determing correct robot or workpiece placement by trial and error is more quickly completed in a simulated world than in the physical cell. An advanced feature which automates the search for feasible robot or workpiece location(s) goes one step further in reducing burden on the user.

Automatic placement can be computed by direct search, or perhaps by heuristic guided search techniques. Since most robots are mounted flat on the floor (or ceiling), and have their first rotary joint perpendicular to the floor, it is generally only necessary to search by tesselation of the three dimensional space of robot base placement. The search might optimize some criterion or might halt upon location of the first feasible robot or part placement. Feasibility can be defined as collision-free ability to reach all workpoints, or perhaps given an even stronger definition. A reasonable criterion to maximize might be some form of a *measure of manipulability* as in [Khatib, 1985]. An implementation using a similar measure of manipulability has been discussed in [Nelson et al, 1987]. The result of such an automatic placement is a cell in which the robot can reach all of its workpoints in *well-conditioned* configurations.

Collision Avoidance and Path Optimiztion

Research on the planning of collision free paths [Brooks, 1983] and the planning of time optimal paths [Sahar and Hollerbach, 1985] are natural candidates for inclusion

in an OLP system. Some related problems which have a smaller scope, and smaller search space are also of interest. For example, consider the problem of using a six degree of freedom robot for an arc welding task whose geometry specifies only five degrees of freedom. Automatic planning of the redundant degree of freedom can be used to avoid collisions and avoid singularities of the robot [Craig, 1987].

Automatic Planning of Coordinated Motion

In many arc welding situations, details of the process require a certain relationship between the workpiece and the gravity vector to be maintained during the weld. The result is a two or three degree of freedom orienting system on which the part is mounted operating simultaneously with the robot in a coordinated fashion. In such a system their may be nine or more degrees of freedom to coordinate. Such systems are generally programmed today using teach pendant techniques. A planning system that could automatically synthesize the coordinated motions for such a system might be quite valuable [Craig, 1987].

Force Control Simulation

In a simulated world in which objects are represented by their surfaces, it is possible to investigate the simulation of manipulator force control strategies. This task involves the difficult task of modelling some surface properties and expanding the dynamic simulator to deal with the constraints imposed by various contacting situations. In such an environment it might be possible to assess various force controlled assembly operations for feasibility [Peshkin and Sanderson, 1987].

Automatic Scheduling

Along with the geometric problems found in robot programming, there are often difficult scheduling and communication problems. This is particularly the case if we expand the simulation beyond a single workcell to a group of workcells. While some discrete time simulation systems offer abstract simulation of such systems [Russell, 1983], few offer planning algorithms. Planning schedules for interacting processes is a difficult problem and an area of research [Kusiak and Villa, 1987; Akella and Krogh, 1987]. An OLP system would serve as an ideal test bed for such research, and would be immediately enhanced by any useful algorithms in this area.

Automatic Assesment of Errors and Tolerances

An OLP system might be given some of the capabilities discussed in recent work in modeling positioning errors sources and the effect of data from imperfect sensors [Smith et al, 1987; Durrant-Whyte 1987]. The world model could be made to include various error bounds and tolerancing information, and the system could assess the likelihood of success of various positioning or assembly tasks. The system might be able to suggest the use and placement of sensors so as to correct potenial problems.

Conclusion

Off-line programming systems are useful in present day industrial applications and can serve as a basis for continuing robotics research. A large motivation in developing OLP systems is to fill the gap between the explicitly programmed systems available today, and the task level systems of tomorrow.

References

Akella, R., and Krogh, B., "Hierarchical Control Structures for Multi-Cell Flexible Assembly System Coordination", IEEE Conference on Robotics and Automation, Raleigh, N.C., April, 1987.

Bobrow, J., "The Efficient Computation of the Minimum Distance Between Convex Polyhedra", UC Irvine, to appear.

Brooks, R., "Planning Collision-Free Motions for Pick and Place Operations", International Journal of Robotics Research, Vol. 2, No. 4, 1983.

Craig, J.J., "Introduction to Robotics: Mechanics and Control", Addison Wesley, Reading Mass., 1986.

Craig, J.J., "Coordinated Motion of Industrial Robots and 2-DOF Orienting Tables", Proceedings of the 17th International Symposium on Industrial Robots, Chicago, Illinois, April, 1987.

Durrant-Whyte, H., "Uncertain Geometry in Robotics", IEEE Conference on Robotics and Automation, Raleigh, N.C., April, 1987.

GMF Inc., "KAREL Language Reference", Version 1.20p, Troy, Michigan, 1986.

Goldman, R., "Design of an Interactive Manipulator Programming Environment", UMI Research Press, Ann Arbor, Mi., 1985.

Kehmeier, D., "The CimStation User's Manual", Version 3.0, Available from Silma, Inc., 2111 Grant Rd., Los Altos, Ca. 94022. 1987.

Khatib, O., "The Operational Space Formulation in the Analysis, Design, and Control of Manipulators", Third International Symposium of Robotics Research, MIT Press, Gouviex, France, October, 1985.

Kusiak, A., and Villa, A., "Architectures of Expert Systems for Scheduling Flexible Manufacturing Systems", IEEE Conference on Robotics and Automation, Raleigh, N.C., April, 1987.

Lozano-Perez, T., "Spatial Planning: A Configuration Space Approach", IEEE Transactions on Systems, Man, and Cybernetics, Vol. SMC-11, 1983.

Mujtaba, S., and Goldman, R., "AL User's Manual", Third Edition, Stanford Dept. of Computer Science, Report No. STAN-CS-81-889, December, 1981.

Nelson, B., Pedersen, K., and Donath, M., "Locating Assembly Tasks in a Manipulator's Workspace", IEEE Conference on Robotics and Automation, Raleigh, N.C., April, 1987.

Pearce, J., "Concurrent Programming in SIL", Available from Silma, Inc., 2111 Grant Rd., Los Altos, Ca. 94022. 1987.

Pearce, J., Speight, D., and Craig, J., "Translation from a Universal Language into Restricted Languages", to appear, 1988.

Peshkin, M., and Sanderson, A., "Planning Robotic Manipulation Strategies for Sliding Objects", IEEE Conference on Robotics and Automation, Raleigh, N.C., April, 1987.

Russel, E., "Building Simulation Models with Simcript II.5", C.A.C.I., Los Angeles, Ca., 1983.

Sahar, G., and Hollerbach, J., "Planning of Minimum-Time Trajectories for Robot Arms", IEEE Conference on Robotics and Automation, St. Louis, Mo., March, 1985.

Shimano, B., Geschke, C., and Spalding, C., "VAL - II: A Robot Programming Language and Control System", SME Robots VIII Conference, Detroit, June, 1984.

Smith, R., "Fast Robot Collision Detection Using Graphics Hardware", Symposium on Robot Control, Barcelona, Spain, November, 1985.

Smith, R., Self, M., and Cheeseman, P., "Estimating Uncertain Spatial Relationships in Robotics", IEEE Conference on Robotics and Automation, Raleigh, N.C., April, 1987.

Taylor, R., Summers, P., and Meyer, J., "AML: A Manufacturing Language", International Journal of Robotics Research", Vol.1, No.3, Fall, 1982.

Design and Sensor - Based Robotic Assembly in the "Design to Product" Project

Paul Fehrenbach
GEC Research Limited
Marconi Research Centre
Great Baddow, Chelmsford
England.

Tim Smithers
Department of Artificial Intelligence
University of Edinburgh
Edinburgh
Scotland.

The "Design to Product" project is part of the UK Government's programme of collaborative research into advanced information technology, known as the Alvey Programme. The project's objective is to demonstrate the application of Artificial Intelligence techniques in the integrated computer-based support of the lifecycle of light electro-mechanical products from design, through manufacture to service. This paper describes the progress made to date in the areas of design and sensor-based robotic assembly. The operation of a demonstration system that links these two aspects is described and some of the problems encountered are discussed. There is a brief outline of intended future development within the project in these areas.

1. Introduction

The "Design to Product" (DtoP) project is one of four large scale demonstrator projects set up under the UK's programme of collaborative research into advanced information technology. It is known as the Alvey Programme after the chairman of the committee that recommended that such a national research effort be started [Alvey 82].

The consortium of universities and companies collaborating on the DtoP project comprises the Universities of Edinburgh, Leeds and Loughborough, the HUSAT Research Centre, GEC Electrical Projects Ltd., GEC Research Ltd., GEC Avionics Ltd. and Lucas CAV Ltd. and is managed by GEC Electrical Projects. A more detailed description of the project and the respective areas of interest and expertise of the different collaborators can be found in [Smithers 85].

The aim of the DtoP project is to show that in a selected area of mechanical engineering the tools and techniques developed by Artificial Intelligence (AI) research can be applied to the integration of the product lifecycle: from design, through manufacture, to field servicing and maintenance. The project, which started in March 1985, is split into two phases of two and half years each. The first, or "pilot", phase is intended to prove the viability of the Design to Product concept. The second, "demonstrator" phase will aim to establish an integrated demonstration of the principles developed during the pilot phase.

2. Background

There is a widely recognised need for improved efficiency and flexibility in the manufacture of engineering products, particularly for small batch production. This need has played a large part in stimulating the development of today's Computer Aided Design (CAD), Computer Aided Manufacture (CAM) and Computer Integrated Manufacturing (CIM) techniques and systems. By applying existing AI techniques and by researching new ones, the DtoP project aims to develop the technology required for the next generation of computer integrated manufacturing systems and to demonstrate these techniques in a realistic factory environment.

One aspect of manufacture being investigated by the DtoP project is that of flexible, sensor-based robotic assembly. In this paper we discuss the approach to the integration of an AI-based design support system and a sensor-based robotic assembly facility being investigated by Edinburgh University and GEC Research's Marconi Research Centre. Section 3 presents the objectives of the pilot phase robotic assembly work at GEC Research. A description of the research into AI-based engineering design support systems being carried out at Edinburgh is presented in Section 4. Sections on the generation of assembly data, robotic assembly and a description of the assembly cell being developed follow in Sections 5, 6 and 7. Section 8 presents a discussion of the results gained so far and Section 9 contains some conclusions which can be drawn from these results.

3. Pilot Phase Sensor-Based Robotic Assembly Objectives

Two robotic assembly demonstrations are planned for the end of the DtoP pilot phase in September 1987. One will allow the design and assembly of a range of simple products using off-line programming of a novel robot, at GEC Research, and the other will show the partial assembly of a more complex product using conventional teach-mode programming techniques

for industrial robots, at Lucas Systems and
Engineering Ltd. This paper is concerned with
the first of these demonstrations only.

The GEC Research demonstration aims to show
that the information generated during the
design of a new variant for an existing product
range can be used to produce the instructions
necessary to assemble the product from a set of
standard components using a flexible, robotic
assembly cell. The most important part of the
demonstration is the generation of the assembly
data used to program the cell. The assembly
cell is the testbed for the assembly data. The
whole demonstration, except for operation of
the assembly hardware, is controlled by the
user.

In the course of a day, it is hoped to describe
some of the background to the project and to
show the design and assembly of two new
variants to add to the existing product range.
This should provide proof of the flexibility of
the assembly system. Some of the design
decisions for one of the variants will be made
by the audience. The different functions of
design, assembly data generation and robotic
assembly will be taken in sequence. Since time
will not permit iterations for refinement, the
operators must have a high level of confidence
in their data. This will be ensured, so far as
is possible, by keeping the design tasks simple
and by checking the output of each stage before
proceeding to the next. Integration of the
different functions will not be advanced, so
the users will be relied upon to transfer and
access appropriate data files and to plug any
gaps between software modules. All the
software, except that controlling the cell
hardware, will be running on the same Sun 3
workstation.

The product chosen for the demonstration is a
single cylinder diesel fuel injection pump,
created specially for the project, Figure 1.
The pump has over 20 components which can be
assembled in more than 400 different ways to
produce a range of different variants on the
same basic theme. The basic pump design, and
that of each component, has been considered for
ease of assembly and adapted to produce a
product which presents a tractable but
realistic assembly problem, involving the
precise mating of components, use of
sub-assemblies and the use of screw fasteners.

4.   AI-Based Engineering Design Support System

Good design is a prerequisite of good assembly
because in an integrated system poor design
information will lead to unreliable assembly
instructions, with possibly disastrous
consequences. The DtoP project's effort in
design is concentrated on research into the
application of new and existing AI techniques
to support engineering design. The work is
centred at the Department of Artificial
Intelligence, Edinburgh University. Part of

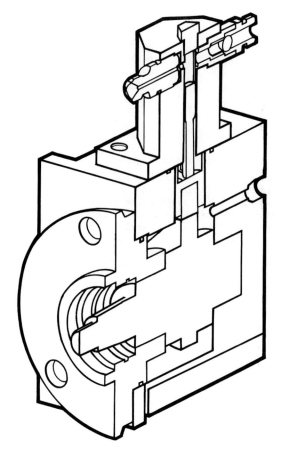

Fig.1 : The Simple Fuel Pump

the overall engineering design support system
being built by the project is called the
Edinburgh Designer System (EDS).

4.1   The Edinburgh Designer System Architecture

The EDS is intended to provide an integrated
knowledge base, knowledge management system and
coherent set of intelligent sub-systems to
support engineers engaged in the design of a
product. Here design is taken to mean the
functional and geometric design of a product,
together with the design of its cost,
manufacture, test, installation, maintenance
and repair. The EDS knowledge base is thus
intended to include knowledge relevant to all
aspects of the design of a product. Similarly,
the set of intelligent sub-systems is being
developed to support the wide range of
activities carried out during the design
process and the knowledge management system is
being designed to structure and maintain the
large amounts of knowledge generated in a
flexible, coherent and consistent way.

The primary representation scheme used in the EDS distinguishes if from today's Computer Aided Draughting (CAD) systems. In the EDS the representation scheme, or formalism, for building a description of a particular design primarily expresses functionality. In current CAD systems the representation schemes used are geometric. The reason for this different approach is that, for the EDS to support the full range of activities which constitutes the design process, it has to be able to represent and reason about the functionality required of a product with respect to many other aspects affecting its cost, manufacture, testing and maintenance and this cannot be done by representing and manipulating geometry alone [Smithers 85, Popplestone, Smithers et al 86].

The architecture of the EDS contains a number of tightly coupled core sub-systems. It is, however, designed to be an open architecture so that other sub-systems can be linked to it in a consistent way. The main components of the present EDS architecture are:

(1) A Declarative Knowledge Base (DKB). This is a hierarchically structured multi-levelled knowledge base containing the engineering knowledge to be used to support the exploration of the design space and the building of a design description. A set of software tools is also provided for building and maintaining the DKB.

(2) A Design Description Document (DDD). This has a dynamic knowledge base which conceptually serves to maintain a record of the design process and a full description of the final design, or designs.

(3) An Assumption based Truth Maintenance Systems (ATMS) [deKleer 84]. This sub-system manages the contents of the DDD, recording how new knowledge is derived, on what it depends, and to what other sub-systems it can sensibly be given for further reasoning. It is also responsible for preventing inferences being made from inconsistent knowledge by any of the reasoning sub-systems.

(4) A Designer System Manager (DSM). The control of the EDS is based upon a blackboard model [Nii 86]. The DSM is designed to control the invocation of the various sub-systems within the EDS and the interaction with users.

(5) A set of forward inferencing sub-systems which provide knowledge sources, or "engines", able to reason about: algebraic expressions and equations; spatial relationships; geometric shapes and tabulated data. The algebraic engine draws on the work of Bundy et al [Bundy et al 82], the spatial reasoning engine

implements some of the robot programming ideas of Popplestone et al [Popplestone et al 80] and the geometric modelling engine uses two constructuve solid geometry (csg) [Requicha and Tilove 78] type modellers: the "Noname" modeller from Leeds University [Armstrong 82] and the "Robmod" modeller from Edinburgh [Cameron 84]. The table engine is based on the Codd relational algebra [Codd 70].

(6) A set of backward chaining and model-based reasoning systems which provide support for higher level design activities. These are intended to support the design of a product's manufacture, reliability, maintenance, testing and cost, for example.

(7) A System Development Interface (SDI) which provides the current interface to the system. It is distinguished from an engineering designer's interface since it is primarily intended to meed the needs of those engaged in building, testing and debugging the system.

A more extensive and detailed description of the Edinburgh Designer System may be found in [Smithers 87].

4.2   Support of Design for Robotic Assembly

When designing a product for which manufacture will include assembly by robot, consideration must be given to how it is to be assembled from an early stage. Failure to do so can, and often does, result in a product design that is either difficult, or impossible, to assemble using a robot.

Answers to the questions "What can and cannot be assembled?" or "Which design is easier to assemble?" depend on a large number of different pieces and types of knowledge: about the manipulative capabilities of the robot and gripper, for example. If during the design of a product such questions are going to be answered with the aid of the design support system, this knowledge needs to be available to the system. It must be made available in such a way that the right piece of knowledge can be accessed at the right time and be presented in the most appropriate form. For example, at an early stage in the design of a particular product decisions often have to be taken as to how to decompose a required functionality into component sub-systems. In deciding upon an appropriate decomposition it may be appropriate to consider the maximum gripping dimension of the assembly robot that is available, and also its maximum payload. Later in the design process more detailed information about the geometry of the gripper may be required to decide if a proposed part acquisition strategy will work for a particular component shape.

To represent such knowledge in a way that is both consistent and flexible with respect to the level of detail required is a difficult knowledge representation problem, and one that is being investigated as part of the development of the EDS. By including knowledge about the assembly process it is intended that the functional, geometric and robotic assembly aspects of a product's design can be supported in a more tightly coupled way than is possible with present day CAD systems.

4.3   Robotic Assembly Knowledge Generated at Design Time

As a result of considering, at the appropriate level of detail, the robotic assembly of a product during its functional and geometric design, knowledge about how it is to be assembled will be built up and recorded in the Design Description Document of the EDS. This knowledge will include descriptions of the goemetric shape of the parts that constitute the assembly, the way these parts are spatially related and some information about the order in which they are to be assembled. The ordering information will not typically represent a full ordering since there will often by a number of different orders in which at least some of the parts can be put together. This information is important, since such partial ordering can be used during the assembly process to allow dynamic scheduling.

As an example, if, during the design of a particular geometric feature, a detailed investigation of how the robot would grasp the part by this feature had to be carried out to establish a suitable geometric shape for the feature, then significant amounts of knowledge about this part of the robot program will have been generated. This knowledge should not have to be re-generated when the full assembly program comes to be built.

5.   Robotic Assembly Data Generation

The design and assembly knowledge generated using the EDS will be used to derive assembly programs for the sensor-based robotic assembly cell in two stages:

(1) Assembly planning
(2) Cell programming

5.1   Assembly Planning

A simple assembly planning package has been written for the demonstration in September. It is simple in the sense that it is intended to plan for the simple fuel pump in the context of a demonstration and the range and complexity of the problems that it is required to tackle are therefore restricted.

The planner takes as its input the knowledge in the Design Description Document of the EDS and considers the spatial constraints on all pairs of assembled components to generate possible sequences of disassembly. Using concepts of gravity, stability and support and applying a set of disassembly rules, the planner generates a disassembly graph that shows the possible ways of disassembling the pump. Each arc of the graph has a cost attached, generally as a function of the time required for the operation, and generation of the graph is directed by a concurrent AO* search to minimise the cost, so not all possibilities are generated. When the graph is complete it is traversed in the reverse direction to produce an assembly graph where all possible paths are optimal, i.e. lowest cost. This plan is reviewed by the user and stored.

The planner is generative, producing a totally new plan for each pump variant. This takes several hours and for the demonstration some pre-computed plans will be available to save time. The planner is ignorant of the number of products to be assembled and plans for only one, the plan requiring to be repeated if there are more than one to be assembled. It also has no knowledge of resource availability and assumes that all necessary resources are available. Resource scheduling is dealt with at a later stage.

5.2   Cell Programming

When all the fuel pump variants that are to be assembled in the same batch have been designed and been through assembly planning, then the assembly cell can be programmed. A high level cell scheduler takes as input the number of each type of variant that is to be assembled and the assembly plans for each variant and produces a program for the assembly cell in a special assembly cell control language. The high level scheduler has knowledge of the equipment in the assembly cell and its capabilities, but relies on the user for decision making and for all knowledge of resource availability and constraints external to the cell. For the demonstration all the necessary resouces will be available when first required, the components being supplied as kits of parts on pallets.

The assembly cell control language has three basic constructs: SEQ, PAR and TRY. SEQ is used to produce strict sequences of machine operations that must all execute correctly in sequential order for the SEQ command to return a successful outcome. PAR allows operations to be executed in parallel fashion by the distributed control system in the cell and imposes no sequence at all. All the operations must execute correctly for the PAR command to return a successful outcome. TRY is a means of allowing different alternative operations to be tried until one is successful. A list of alternative operations that achieve the same end result is specified and the TRY command will execute the first of these. If it fails then the second will be executed and likewise the third and subsequent operations until one is successful or the end of the list is reached. If any one of the alternative is successful then the TRY command ends and returns a successful outcome. This facility is useful for delicate assembly processes that have a high risk of failure but which can be attempted in different ways, for example putting a nut on the end of a screw and engaging the thread.

6.   Sensor-Based Robotic Assembly

The program in the assembly cell control language is interpreted by the assembly cell control system and converted into a petri net of cell operations which is displayed graphically to the user. The start node of the petri net is marked and markers move round the network as the program is executed, once it has been given the command to run by the user. The net, combined with the position of the markers in the net, represents the state of the cell.

The major pieces of equipment in the assembly cell have controllers running communications processes which communicate with each other mainly via RS232C serial lines to form a distributed control system. An identical communications process runs on the Sun and together they operate as a message passing system, interfaced to the petri net representation of the cell program via the UNIX file system on the Sun. Messages are transmitted as ascii text.

The controllers also run the MICCON (Methodology for Integrated Command and Control) software environment, developed by GEC Research, which controls the operation of individual pieces of equipment. MICCON provides an extensive library of low level robot, gripper and other functions which can be called with parameters and which return a status or success/failure response on termination. It is these MICCON functions and macros built from them that make up the majority of the commands in the assembly cell program.

When the command to run the assembly program is given, and assuming that the necessary resources are available, the petri net control program puts a message into a file which is accessed by the communications process on the Sun. The communications process sends a suitably packaged message to the appropriate machine controller, where it is read by that communications process, stripped and passed to MICCON for execution. The response is awaited and sent back via the reverse route to a different file on the Sun where it is picked up by the petri net program. The markers on the petri net advance to the next node and the next message is sent. If a PAR construct is found in the petri net then two or more messages will be transmitted simultaneously and be routed to different machines in the cell.

At the level of individual MICCON commands the response of the assembly cell hardware to the cell program cannot be precisely determined in advance. The use of sensors to control some motions, such as the later stages of part mating, means that the exact path by which the desired end is achieved is not always specified.

The process of passing messages back and forth continues until the end of the program is reached, when the completed fuel pumps should be on pallets in the pallet rack awaiting manual unloading.

7.   Sensor-Based Robotic Assembly Cell

The equipment in the assembly cell comprises a pallet handling system and an assembly station. The pallet handling system is centred on a GEC PRW10 process robot and delivers pallets between an input/output rack and the assembly station. The assembly station uses the GEC Tetrabot robot developed at GEC Research and performs all the assembly operations on a pallet of components to build a pump. The Sun workstation is located close by, so that the user can see the cell in operation, but is separated from it by a light beam safety interlock. The layout of the cell is shown in Figure 2.

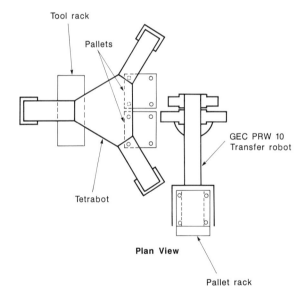

Fig.2 : Assembly Cell Layout

7.1   Tetrabot

The Tetrabot is an experimental six degree of freedom robot designed and built by GEC Research for this project. It is partly parallel and partly serial in configuration, using three rods extending from a triangular top plate and meeting at a point to provide three translational degrees of freedom and a three axis serial wrist to provide three rotational degrees of freedom. Figure 3 shows a photograph of the Tetrabot. The design owes much to the earlier Gadfly robot [Potton 83] which is wholly parallel in configuration.

The Tetrabot is capable of accelerating payloads of 6 kg at up to 10 ms^{-2} and with a top speed of 1 ms^{-1} over a cylindrical volume with a diameter of 1 m and height of 0.7 m. It has been designed with assembly applications in mind and is expected to be highly accurate when fully calibrated. The Tetrabot is controlled by a single M68020 with M68881 maths coprocessor for the kinematics.

7.2   Marconi Gripper

The Marconi gripper on the Tetrabot is a simple, parallel action two fingered gripper. The fingers move in and out together over a range of 200 mm and the servo system can resolve their positions to 0.1 mm. The finger ends are detachable and can be manually replaced by sensors or other special purpose fingers. The Marconi gripper is controlled by an M68000 microprocessor.

7.3   Force Sensors

The plain fingers on the Marconi gripper have been replaced by a pair of six degree of freedom force and torque sensors built into finger shells. Each sensor transduces three orthogonal components for force and three torques, with maximum loads of 100N and 4Nm respectively. The twelve streams of data are fed into a Weitek WTE 5330 array processor supervised by an M68020. This combination provides a nominal 16 Mflops of processing which is used for real-time force feedback control of the Tetrabot and Marconi gripper. The force control allows active compliance of the robot and gripper structure to be used during assembly to increase the reliability of part mating operations.

7.4   Pallet Handling Equipment and Tools

The pallet handling robot is a standard industrial robot with five degrees of freedom and a maximum payload of 10 kg. It has a simple, passive gripper. The pallets are 400mm square with a matrix of holes for locating components, jigs and fixtures and four larger holes for location of the pallet.

Before and after use pallets are stored in a rack accessible by the pallet handling robot. The robot transfers them, when required, to a table underneath the Tetrabot and locks them in place using a mechanical toggle arrangement. The robot also unlocks the pallets and replaces them in the rack once assembly is complete.

During assembly the Tetrabot can use a powered screwdriver that is available in the assembly station. This can be grasped by the Tetrabot and used to tighten a range of screws, a task which the robot would find difficult unaided. Other tools such as a glue applicator could be added if required.

7.5   Calibration

The equipment in the assembly cell was precisely located before being secured to the floor, so that, for instance, the position of the assembly table is known accurately in the Tetrabot's coordinate frame. The coordinate frames of the different items could therefore be related easily and the different parts of the cell calibrated with respect to each other.

To improve the off-line accuracy of the Tetrabot beyond that achievable using its internal position transducers and the nominal kinematic model, it was calibrated before use. The actual position of the end point of the robot in six-dimensional space was measured relative to a world coordinate frame using an optical technique. This was compared with the position that the robot's internal sensors and kinematic model thought it had attained. Measurements were made for a large number of positions and with a range of loads and as a result an error map for correction of the kinematic model was produced. This was incorporated into the Tetrabot's controller and increased the off-line programming accuracy achievable. Measurements were also made of the robot in motion to study dynamic effects such as overshoot. These were used to tune the dynamic behaviour of the robot. The static and the dynamic measurements were made for GEC Research by the UK's National Engineering Laboratory. The static calibration of the Tetrabot is described in [Woodward 87].

8.   Discussion

8.1   Some Problems Encountered

The main problems encountered in building the system described in this paper were in two areas: assembly knowledge representation and provision of a suitable assembly robot.

The most fundamental of the knowledge representation problems was representing assembly knowledge in the EDS. Some assembly knowledge has been incorporated with the functional component descriptions in the Declarative Knowledge Base, as text for the user to read. Assembly knowledge is also being included in one of the high level toolkits for support of design of manufacture. This knowledge is encoded as rules for application by the user. The representations used are adequate for present purposes but more powerful representations will be needed before any kind of automated reasoning about assembly can be incorporated into the EDS.

The attachment of assembly knowledge to functional descriptions of individual components and sub-assemblies in the Declarative Knowledge Base of the EDS presents an opportunity to reason about the effects of this knowledge on the combined function of two components when they are assembled. Reasoning is currently done by the user but ways of assisting the user are being investigated. Making use of the assembly knowledge available at all stages of design should lead to better products that are easier to assemble using sensor-based robotic systems.

The last of the knowledge representation problems concerns the need to work in an uncertain world with systems that find uncertainty difficult to handle. The approach being adopted is to try and quantify the uncertainty in real world parameters and design assembly cell behaviours that cater for a specified range of uncertainty with a high degree of confidence [Smithers and Malcolm 87]. Assembly cell programs can then be written with a high level of overall confidence that they will succeed if uncertainty is contained within the expected bounds.

The robot related problems derived from the need to provide an accurate assembly robot that can be off-line programmed easily and which can respond to sensor input in real-time to implement sensor-based control. Although many suitable robot mechanisms are available commercially, none provide access to the control software at the detailed level necessary to implement, say, active compliance in response to force sensor input. Therefore GEC Research decided to design the Tetrabot as an assembly robot with mechanics that provide the desired accuracy, speed, range of movement and load carrying capability and a controller that is totally accessible for experimental and developmental purposes.

Once the Tetrabot had been built it needed to be calibrated in order to achieve the required accuracy for reliable off-line programming. Calibration is a time consuming process and one that can be continued indefinitely unless a firm acceptance criterion is fixed. Sufficient measurements were made to improve the accuracy of the Tetrabot significantly by producing an error map for the kinematic model. Initial calibration must be maintained throughout the service life of the robot and a jig has been designed and built to check the calibration of the Tetrabot at intervals in the future. The device measures the error from the expected calibration position in six coordinates and allows the error map for the kinematic model to be adjusted.

8.2   Future Developments

The demonstration described in this paper is one of the halfway milestones for the DtoP project and will be followed by further work to improve its capabilities until the end of the project in 1990.

The main objective of the coming years' work will be closer integration of the design, assembly data generation and robotic assembly functions to make better use of the knowledge and data in the system and reduce the dependence on the human user. These functions will also become parts of a larger computer integrated manufacturing system incorporating machining and product service functions.

Refinement of the assembly planning and cell programming techniques are envisaged that should allow planning for a wider range of products, including fully engineered production fuel pumps, at least in part, and generic planning for whole ranges of simple products, so that each variant does not have to be planned separately. Intermediate stages of plan refinement will be introduced and it should be made easier to iterate between design and assembly planning and cell programming to achieve more nearly optimal results overall. Computationally tractable approaches to handling uncertainty will continue to be investigated outside the DtoP project and it is hoped to incorporate the results of this work at an appropriate stage.

The assembly cell will be expanded to include a second assembly station using a different type of assembly robot and the pallet handling system will be changed to a conveyor based system to cater for this. The design of the present assembly cell could easily be expanded to include more assembly stations, but the load carrying capacity of the pallet handling robot is not sufficient for the wider range of products to be assembled. The cell control system already has the capability to handle more than one assembly station.

The Marconi gripper is intended to be replaced by a more complex, reconfigurable gripper capable of grasping and manipulating a wide range of objects. A prototype reconfigurable gripper has already been built by GEC Research and used to study gripping strategies for objects, based on their geometric design data. The new gripper will be fitted with force and torque sensors but the design of these will depend on the structure and modes of operation of the gripper and may not require the complexity of the present six degree of freedom sensors.

Overall, the design to assembly part of the DtoP project will be made more robust over the next two years and have its capabilities enhanced to produce a more advanced demonstration in March 1990.

9.   Conclusions

The achievements of the DtoP project to date in the areas of design and robotic assembly show that an intelligent knowledge-based approach to integration of these activities is effective, for the purpose of mounting a demonstration. The demonstration system is not fully automated and relies on the user for some important decision making and control functions. The potential of using product design knowledge to derive instructions for a flexible, robotic assembly cell can be demonstrated and some indications of how this potential should be developed have been discussed. There is still a long way to go, but systems of the type described should lead to more economical and more effective product design and manufacture with reduced lead times and a more flexible response to customer demands.

Acknowledgements

The work described in this paper has been conducted as part of the Alvey "Design to Product" large scale demonstrator project and the authors are grateful for the support received from other project collaborators in carrying out the work presented here. Funding for the parts of the project described has been provided by the Science and Engineering Research Council, the Department of Trade and Industry, GEC Research Ltd. and GEC Electrical Projects Ltd.

References

[Alvey 82] - Alvey, J., "A Programme for Advanced Information Technology", the Report of the Alvey Committe, pub Department of Trade and Industry, UK HM Stationery Office, 1982.

[Armstrong 82] - Armstrong et al, "Noname Description and Users Manual", Department of Mechanical Engineering, Leeds University, 1982.

[Bundy et al 82] - Bundy, A., Stirling, L., Byrd, L., O'Keefe, R., and Silver, B., "Solving Symbolic Equations with PRESS", DAI Research Report, No. 171, Department of Artificial Intelligence, Edinburgh University, 1982.

[Cameron 84] - Cameron, S., "Modelling Solids in Motion", Ph.D Thesis, Department of Artificial Intelligence, Edinburgh University, 1984.

[Codd 70] - Codd, E.F., "A Relational Model of Data for Large Shared Data Banks", CACM V.13, No. 6, 1970.

[deKleer 84] - deKleer, J., "Choices Without Backtracking", Proc. Conf. AAAI, 1984.

[Nii 86] - Nii, P., "Blackboard Systems", Parts one and two, the AI Magazine, Vol. 7, Nos. 2 and 3, 1986.

[Popplestone et al 80] - Popplestone, R.J., Ambler, A.P., and Belos, I., "An Interpreter for a Language for Describing Assemblies", AI Vol. 14, No. 1, 1980.

[Popplestone, Smithers et al 86] - Popplestone, R.J., Smithers, T., Corney, J., Koutsou, A., Millington, K., and Sahar, G., "Engineering Design Support Systems", DAI Research Paper, No. 286, Department of Artificial Intelligence, Edinburgh University, 1986.

[Potton 83] - Potton, S.L., "GEC Advanced Device for Assembly", proc. 15th CIRP International Seminar on Manufacturing Systems, University of Massachusetts, Amherst, 20-22 June 1985.

[Requicha and Tilove 78] - Requicha, A.A.G., and Tilove, R.B., "Mathematical Foundations of Constructive Solid Geometry: General Topology of Closed Regular Sets", TM277a, Production Automation Project, University of Rochester, USA, 1978.

[Smithers 85] - Smithers, T., "The Alvey Large Scale Demonstrator Project 'Design to Product'", proc. conf. Artifical Intelligence in Manufacturing Key to Integration?, Gottlieb Duttweller Institute, Zurich, 7-8 November 1985.

[Smithers 87] - Smithers, T., "The Edinburgh Designer System: An Intelligent Knowledge Based Systems Approach to Supporting Engineering Design", in preparation, 1987.

[Smithers and Malcolm 87] - Smithers, T., and Malcolm, C.A., "A Behavioural Approach to Robot Task Planning", presented at the Advanced Robotics Programme Workshop on Manipulators, Sensors and Steps Towards Mobility, Karlsruhe, May 1987. Also available as DAI Research Paper No. 306.

[Woodward 87] - Woodward, C.A.W., "Practical Experiences with the Wild-Leitz RMS 2000 System", proc. Second Industrial and Engineering Survey Conference, University College, London, September 1987.

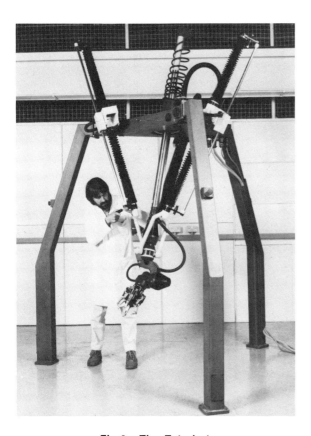

Fig.3 : The Tetrabot

Kuniji Asano

A model databased remote maintenance system, named TAROS, is being developed in order to make up for inherent shortcomings in a conventional master slave manipulator system.
In this system, knowledge about manipulator and other objects moving together with the manipulator is described with respect to manipulator coordinate frame. On the other hand, knowledge about handling objects and handling procedures is described in terms of object coordinate frame. By measuring the relation between manipulator and object coordinate frame, using a range finder at the spot, TAROS can execute remote work autonoumusly. Task instructions are limited to as few as possible, so as to make TAROS operation easy.

1. INTRODUCTION

One robot application, which is expected to be in large demand in the near future, is maintenance work in hostile environments. Although a fairly long time has passed since this kind of robot was talked about, it has not yet reached the stage of practical use. There are many reasons which make the problem so difficult. People say that one great reason is that remote maintenance mostly involves unstructured task, whose details are not defined beforehand. In order to perform an unstructured task, a robot must be, more or less, able to carry out a part of human actions involving intelligence.
However, people in general understand that present robot technology has not yet become sufficiently mature that a robot can successfully play such a role. Therefore, remote manipulation systems, being planned for nuclear fuel reprocessing plant, for fusion reactor plant or an actually used system in space, adapts a master slave manipulator.

The master slave manipulator was developed originally without considering unstructured tasks. It was made for only protecting a worker from radioactive rays [1]. However, a remote manipulation system using a master slave manipulator seems apparently suitable for unstructured tasks, because the operator is included in the closed loop, as shown in Fig. 1. Also, operator and manipulator share intelligent and hostile parts of works with each other.

Many master slave manipulators for remote maintenance technology development, have been developed in TOSHIBA, for example, for nuclear fuel reprocessing plant, fusion reactor plant, decommissioning of nuclear power reactor and hot electric power distribution line. The lessons obtained through these experiences are
1. Operation of master slave manipulator is very hard, because it is difficult to always secure an optimum view point for a monitor camera.
2. A master slave manipulator does not have good dexterity and operability.
3. For the above reasons, operation is time consuming and brings physical and mental fatigue to an operator.

Shortcomings described above seem basically inherent in a master slave manipulator. To cope with these problems, some research efforts have been carried out [2]-[6]. TOSHIBA Advanced Robot System (TAROS) development is also for increasing remote maintenance work efficiency by making up the above shortcomings. The TAROS project was started in April, 1987 on a four-year plan. This paper describes the TAROS concept.

2. TAROS DEVELOPMENT PURPOSE

In remote maintenance, it is nonsense to teach robot motions or to input a lot of control instructions and to debug them on the spot, after the maintenance work became clear. Such work is very troublesome, time consuming and liable to error. Therefore, automatic control program generation, that is, robot planning, is

essential. Many interesting reports on
robot planning have been published [7]-
[22]. However, almost of them are end
effector level planning. There seems to
be a tendency to search **excessively** for
generality.

Now, let us reexamine the property of an
unstructured task which must be done in
remote maintenance.
Nuclear fuel reprocessing plant is mainly
composed of tower, tank and pipe line,
which are used for dissolution, separation, purification and transport of nuclear material [23]. When trouble occurs
in tower or tank, generally, no maintenance work is done on the spot. The
tower or tank is brought to a decontamination room by gantry crane, and problems
are corrected by direct maintenance after
decontamination work has been accomplished.
So, remote work necessary in this case
involves pipe connector connection and
disconnection. The pipe connector, specially made to easily accomplish connection and disconnection and to remain leak
free, is generally standardized [24].
Therefore, a geometrical connector model
and its connection and disconnection task
procedure, described in terms of connector coordinate frame, can be strictly
defined beforehand [25]. That is, connection and disconnection tasks for pipe
connector are regarded as structured
tasks on these points.
If a pipe leaks, cutting and welding work
on the pipe become necessary. In this
case, no one expects that the robot can
do these tasks directly using a saw or
welding torch. All the tasks the robot
has to carry out, are to set and to remove specially made pipe cutter or welder
on and from the pipe. Setting and removing task procedure for such tools are
also easily described beforehand in terms
of pipe coordinate frame.
The robot, being developed in Japan National Project "Jupitor", has a wrench in
its image picture. Now, considering disassembly of a pipe flange in a nuclear
power plant, this task also can be regarded as a structured task, since a
geometrical flange model and fastening
and loosening procedure for the bolt are
easily described beforehand in terms of
flange coordinate frame.
Then, what is not obvious beforehand?
It is the positional relation between
robot and object. Now, the task, wherein
a **geometrical** model of handling object
and its handling procedure can be defined
beforehand, in terms of the object coordinate frame, though the object position with respect to the robot is not
obvious previously, is named a semistructured task.
If it were feasible to measure the positional relation of the handling object
with respect to the robot coordinate
frame, all semistructured tasks, described above, become structured tasks

by applying homogeneous transform [26].

The TAROS development purpose is to realize a remote maintenance system, which
can be applicable to semistructured tasks
immediately, on the spot, without having
a well trained operator fully conversant
with computer programming, using knowledge database and robot planner.
A situation when a geometrical model or
task procedures for the handling object
can not be described beforehand in terms
of object coordinate frame, that is, when
it is a completely unstructured task, appears when object is damaged. For this
case, a conventional master slave manipulator operation will be applied by switching control from the robot to a slave arm.

3. REFERENCE TASK FOR TAROS

Since no robot can handle all tasks, some
reference task must be determined for developing and evaluating TAROS. Assembly
and disassembly task for the gear box,
shown in Fig. 2, were chosen as the
reference task. The reference task includes mostly basic tasks, which a remote
maintenance system must be able to handle,
for example, screwing a bolt into and out
of a threaded hole, setting a wrench on a
bolt head, fastening and loosening a bolt
with the wrench and setting and removing
a gear to and from a shaft.
Here, fastening and loosening a bolt with
a robot using a wrench may be a little
unrealistic, without using a motor driven
impact wrench, because the required
torque reaches several hundred kilogram·
cm in actual practice. Also, the gear
box is not made so as to play the role of
gear box itself, but as an example of a
simple mechanical assembly.

4. STRUCTURE OF TAROS

TAROS structure is shown in Fig. 3. TAROS
planner is composed of problem solver,
knowledge database, called a world model
database and state monitor.
Downstream side is composed of manipulator controller and seven degrees-of-freedom manipulator.
First, TAROS planner generates a primitive task instruction process from a task
instruction, while referring to the world
model database. Then, TAROS planner
translates the primitive task instruction
into a robot control program. This is
called a minimum unit in a task, formed
by a set of motion control instructions
a primitive task. Table 1 shows task instructions in TAROS. Table 2 shows primitive task instructions. A special
feature of TAROS, worth mentioning, is
that the number of task and primitive
task instructions are limited to as few
as possible, so as to make TAROS operation easy. Prefix "P-" in the primitive

task instructions separates a primitive task instruction from a task instruction. Needless to say, TAROS operation is possible with any level of instructions.

4.1 World model database

All knowledge about handling an object, its handling procedure and the manipulator concerned is fed into the world model database. Since the manipulator moves to the handling object in remote maintenance, geometrical models of the manipulator and other objects moving together with the manipulator are described in terms of manipulator coordinate frame. Also, a geometricla model of the handling object and its handling procedure are described in terms of object coordinate frame. Database has a hierarchical structure. Knowledge about the gear box, that is, origin of gear box coordinate frame, gear box size and its component list, is stored in the parent frame. Knowledge about each component is described in the child frame. Table 3 shows BOLT frame example. Here, knowledge is divided into three categories, knowledge used as argument in motion control program, knowledge used for planning and knowledge regarding bolt handling procedures.

4.2 State monitor

State monitor watches state of the world and updates the world model database every time the state of the world changes. Although a human becomes cognizant of the state of the world through using various sansations, such as visual, auditory, touch, pressure and deep sensation, the monitor function in TAROS is very poor, because manipulator has only force, position, speed and proximity sensors. Therefore, it is being considered to allow an operator to share the state monitoring role. In this case, it is definite that the man machine interface problem will be serious, provided that the operator is relatively untrained in regard to computer programming.

4.3 Problem solver

Since TAROS planner adopts means ends analysis [27]-[30], precondition expressions, which must be satisfied before executing task instruction in table 1, are described here. Assembly and disassembly order for components and connection relation between components are expressed in the preconditions.
First, problem solver generates a primitive task instruction process from task instruction, while referring to the world model database. The planning method is based on means ends analysis. Table 4 shows the primitive task instruction generating process, when planner receives the instruction, "remove (GEAR 2)" from the operator. Prefix "rt-" means "ready

to" and "rt-remove (GEAR 2)" expresses preconditions for executing "remove (GEAR 2)". Table 4 data were compiled for the case that all right hand side terms for all precondition expressions are not satisfied. Instruction (11) $\sim$ (23) are primitive task instructions generated. Adoption of means ends analysis markedly reduces the state space for search.
Then, problem solver converts the primitive task instruction into a motion control program, while referring to the world model database. Though many "p-remove (OBJECT)" instructions appear in Table 4, task procedure for "p-remove (GEAR 3)" is quite different from that for "p-remove (BOLT(i))". In TAROS, a motion control program is set up by referring to the database for the designated object in the primitive task instruction.
For example, the motion control program for "p-remove (BOLT(i))" is made by referring to the BOLT data frame shown in Table 3. Table 5 shows an example of "p-remove (BOLT(i))" procedure. Since coordinate values, bolt(i), apbolt(i), dpbolt(i) in Table 3 are described with respect to gear box coordinate frame, they are transformed into those values in the manipulator coordinate frame by instructions (3) $\sim$ (5). The point to which special attention should be paid is that coordinate values for apbolt(i) and dpbolt(i) are end effector coordinate values. In this case, they show hand coordinate values at approach and departure points.
Then, the hand moves to the bolt head via the approach point by following instructions (6) $\sim$ (8). Next, the hand grasps the bolt head and repeats the motion for turrning the bolt anticlockwise by 120 degrees, while pulling the bolt head according to instructions (11) $\sim$ (14) and (21) $\sim$ (26).
If the bolt comes out of the threaded hole, the hand transports it to departure point, according to instructions (15) $\sim$ (18). "p-remove (BOLT(i))" procedure ends by reporting that BOLT(i) is in the hand, according to instructions (19)(20).
The state monitor updates both BOLT frame and MANIPULATOR frame in the world model database, upon receiving this report. Then, the next primitive task instruction, "store (BOLT(i))", is executed.

Compliant control of end effector is essential in assembly and disassembly tasks for the gear box. However, it is not complete now. Therefore, the "p-remove (BOLT(i)) procedure is written, provided that compliant control problems, required here, are solved.

5. DECISION STRATEGY FOR HAND POSTURE AND TRAJECTORY

The previous section does not mention how to give the hand posture at grasp and approach points. These problems are very important, to achieve successful robot planning. If these problems are solved, including obstacle avoidance, it is not too much to say that robot planning has half succeeded. This is the reason why many papers on the robot planning have treated these problems. However, it seems that no general and simple solution exists, because of their difficulties. So, it is necessary to prepare a suitable strategy for these problems, whatever the case may be.

In TAROS, in order to avoid collision between manipulator and environment, grasping, removing and setting tasks are accomplished via approach and departure points as a rule. The grasp and approach or departure point positions are always designated beforehand. Plural approach or departure points are given, if necessary. Then one hand posture is, at least, designated beforehand for the approach and grasp points, and used in common. If both hand postures are designated, the hand posture at the approach point has priority. In the relation between grasp and departure points, posture data handling is the same as in the case of approach and grasp points. However, if both hand postures are designated, the grasp point posture has priority.

In a remote maintenance system, the manipulator moves to a work object, as previously mentioned. If the strategy described here is not sufficiently complete for the work, manipulator moves so that the work space comes to a point in front of the manipulator.

6. MANIPULATOR AND ITS CONTROLLER

Figure 4 shows the appearance of the manipulator used in phase 1 of the TAROS project. Finally, in phase 2, a dual arm system, as shown in Fig. 5, is assumed to be used. They are 7 degrees of freedom manipulators. Although many interesting reports have been published, regarding dealing with redundant manipulator [31]-[34], in TAROS, they are used as 6 degrees of freedom manipulator, fixing at some joint, until an efficient method is found in the future.
This manipulator has a torque sensor in each joint. Therefore, compliant control experiments are possible in both cases of using distributed force signals or concentrated force signals measured by 6 axes force sensor. In order to minimize mechanical friction, a low reduction gear (10:1) is adopted. Also, application of a new torque sensor to the manipulator is being studied [35]. The gauge factor for the new sensor is about $100 \sim 1000$ times that for conventional resistive foil strain gauge. Therefore, realization of stiffer manipulator is expected in the dual manipulator system in Fig. 5. Figures 6 and 7 show the computer structure for the manipulator controller and its appearance.

7. OBJECT COORDINATE FRAME MEASUREMENT

In order to control the manipulator using coordinate values and task procedures, described in terms of object coordinate frame, the relation between object coordinate frame and manipulator coordinate frame must be measured.
In a practical manipulator system, a range finder, shown in Fig. 8, will be installed on the manipulator system in order to measure the object coordinate values in the manipulator coordinate frame. The light spot position, made by hitting certain standard point of the object with a light beam, is measured by dual TV camera image signals, posture and position of the range finder and triangulation principle. Therefore, coordinate values for the object, described in the manipulator coordinate frame, can be obtained by repeating the above measurement on three specific standard points on the object, decided upon beforehand. Range finder operation is carried out by the operator. When assembly and disassembly tasks for the gear box are carried out, even if the position and posture of the gear box changes with respect to the manipulator system, the TAROS project becomes successful.

8. CONCLUSION

The TAROS concept is described here. By TAROS development, realizing the following items is expected.
1. Remote maintenance system, which can respond to a semistructured task immediately.
2. Remote maintenance system, which an operator can operate easily, without the need for having any computer programming knowledge.
3. Remote maintenance system, which can reduce the working time and operator fatigue.

The first target for TAROS application is a remote maintenance system for a fusion experimental reactor.

REFERENCES

[1] D. Tesar et al.: "Summary Report of The Nuclear Reactor Maintenance Technology Assessment" DOE-OR-6102-T-1, 1980.

[2] D. E. Whitney: "State Space Models of Remote Manipulation Tasks", proc. 1st IJCAI, 1969.

[3] W. R. Ferrell et al.: "Supervisory Control of Remote Manipulation", IEEE Spectrum October, 1967.

[4] S. Hirai et al.: "Language Directed Master-Slave Manipulation Method Using LARTS/T", J. of the Robotics Society of Japan Vol. 2, No. 6 December 1984, (in Japanese).

[5] T. Sato et al.: "Design of Tele-operator System Utilizing the World Model", J. of the Robotics Society of Japan, Vol. 4, No. 4, August 1986, (in Japanese).

[6] A. K. Bejczy: "Remote Applications of Robot", Proc. of '83 ICAR, 1983.

[7] J. H. Munson: "Robot Planning, Execution, and Monitoring in an Uncertain Environment", Proc. 2nd IJCAI, 1971.

[8] T. Lozano-perez: "Automatic Planning of Manipulator Transfer Movements", IEEE Trans. on S. M. C., Vol. SMC-11, No. 10, 1981.

[9] C. Laugier: "A Program for Automatic Grasping of Objects with a Robot Arm", Proc. of the 11th ISIR, Tokyo 1981.

[10] R. A. Brooks: "Solving the Find-Path Problem by Good Representation of Free Space", 2nd AAAI Confer., Aug. 1982.

[11] R. A. Brooks: "Planning Collision Free Motions for Pick and Place Operations", Proc. of the 1st International Symposium on Robotics Research, The MIT Press (1983).

[12] T. Lozano-perez et al.: "Automatic Synthesis of Fine-Motion Strategies for Robots", ibid.

[13] B. Dufay et al.: "An Approach to Automatic Robot Programming Based on Inductive Learning", ibid.

[14] R. A. Brooks et al.: "A Subdivision Algorithm in Configuration Space for Findpath with Rotation", IJCAI, Karlsruhe 1983.

[15] M. T. Mason: "Atuomatic Planning of Fine Motions: Correctness and Completeness", Proc. of International Confer. on Robotics, Atranta (1984) IEEE Computer Soci.

[16] B. Faverjon: "Obstacle Avoidance using an Octree in the Configuration Space of a Manipulator", Proc. of International Confer. on Robotics, Atranta (1984) IEEE Computer Soci.

[17] H. Farreny et al.: "Tackling Uncertainty and Imprecision in Robotics", Proc. of 3rd International Symposium on Robotics Research, The MIT Press (1986).

[18] R. P. Paul et al.: "A Robust, Distributed Sensor and Actuation Robot Control System", ibid.

[19] M. Ghallab: "Coping the Complexity in Inference and Planning System", ibid.

[20] B. R. Fox: "A Representation for Opportunistic Scheduling", ibid.

[21] C. Laugier et al.: "SHARP: A System for Automatic Programming of Manipulation Robots", ibid.

[22] T. Lozano-perez: "Motion Planning for Simple Robot Manipulators", ibid.

[23] J. T. Long: "Engineering for Nuclear Fuel Reprocessing", ANS (1978).

[24] J. M. Mckibben et al.: "The SAVANNA RIVER Plant Purex Plant - 25 Years of Successful Remote Operation", Proc. of the 27th Confer. on Remote System Technology, 1979.

[25] K. Takase et al.: "A Structured Approach to Robot Programming and Teaching", IEEE Trans. on S. M. C., Vol. SMC-11, No. 4, April, 1981.

[26] R. P. Paul: "Robot Manipulators: Mathematics, Programming, and Control", The MIT Press (1981).

[27] R. E. Fikes et al.: "STRIPS: A New Approach to the Application of theorem Proving to Problem Solving", Artificial Intelligence 2 (1971), 189-208.

[28] R. E. Fikes et al.: "Learning and Executing Generalized Robot Plans", Artificial Intelligence 3 (1972), 251-288.

[29] R. E. Fikes et al.: "Some New Directions in Robot Problem Solving", Machine Intelligence, Vol. 7 (1972), 405-430.

[30] P. R. Cohen et al. (Ed.): The Handbook of Artifical Intelligence, Vol. 3, PITMAN (1982).

[31] H. Hanafusa et al.: "Analysis and Control of Articulated Robot Arms with Redundancy", Prep. 8th IFAC World Congress, vol. XIV, 1981.

[32] A Liegeoise: "Automatic Supervisory Control of the Configuration and Behavior of Multibody Mechanisms", IEEE Trans. on S. M. C., Vol. SMC-7, No. 12, 1977.

[33] T. Yoshikawa: "Analysis and Control of Robot Manipulators with Redundancy", Proc., of the 1st International Symposium on Robotics Research, The MIT Press (1983).

[34] C. A. Klein et al.: "Review of Pseudoinverse Control for Use with Kinematically Redundant Manipulators", IEEE Trans. on S. M. C., Vol. SMC-13, No. 3, 1983.

[35] M. Sahashi et al.: "A New Torque Sensor of Circumferential Excitation Type Using Magnetostrictive Amorphous Ribbons" Proc. of the 6th Sensor Symposium, 1986.

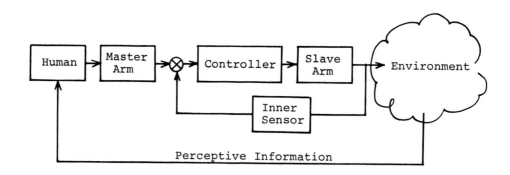

Fig. 1   Master-Slave Manipulator Work.

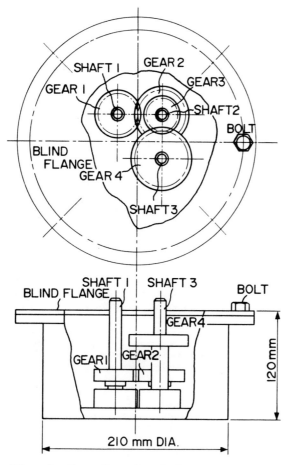

Fig. 2   Gear Box for Reference Task.

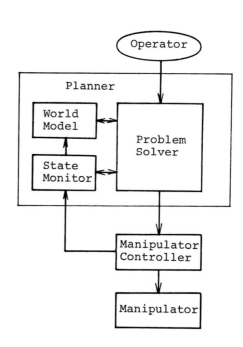

Fig. 3   TAROS Blockdiagram

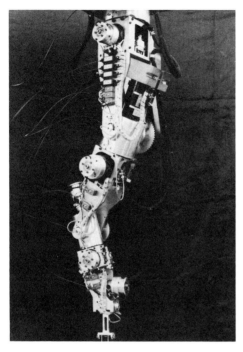

Fig. 4   Manipulator Appearance.

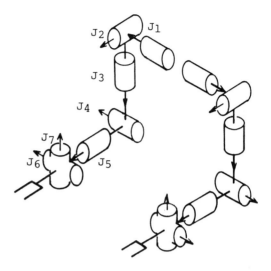

Fig. 5   Dual Arm System Configuration.

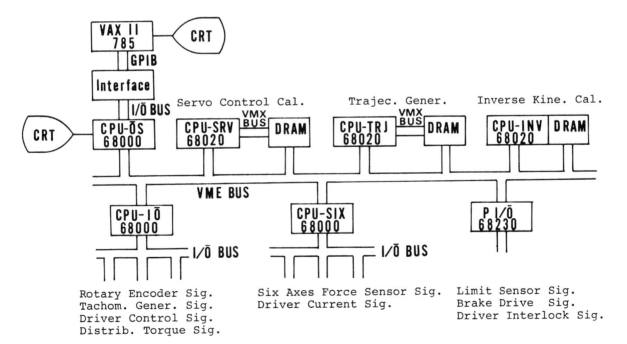

Fig. 6   Manipulator Controller Computer Structure.

Fig. 7   Controller Appearance.

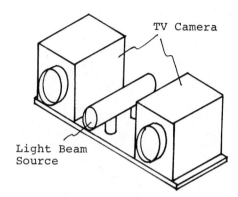

Fig. 8   Range Finder.

assemble(OBJECT)	This instruction includes all primitive tasks necessary to make the OBJECT complete state from current disassemble state.
remove(OBJECT)	This instruction includes all primitive tasks necessary to remove the OBJECT from current state of the OBJECT.
fasten(OBJECT) loosen(OBJECT)	These instructions include all primitive tasks necessary to fasten or loosen the OBJECT.

Table 1   Task Instruction List.

grasp(OBJECT)

set(OBJECT, POSITION)

put(OBJECT, POSITION)

p-remove(OBJECT)

p-fasten(OBJECT)

p-loosen(OBJECT)

hold(OBJECT, POSITION)

store(OBJECT)

Table 2   Primitive Task Instruction List.

```
BOLT :
Kind                                  Hexagon
Size                                  D= 10 mm
Head Width                            HW= 17 mm
Head Height                           HH= 7 mm
Length                                L= 20 mm
Number                                N= 8
Tool                                  WRENCH
Set Position of BOLT(i)               bolt(i)=
  i=1,···,N
Approach Point of Set BOLT(i)         apbolt(i)=
  i=1,···,N
Departure Point of Set BOLT(i)        dpbolt(i)=
  i=1,···,N
Store Position of BOLT(i)             sbolt(i)=
  i=1,···,N
Approach Point of sbolt(i)            apsbolt(i)=
  i=1,···,N
Departure Point of sbolt(i)           dpsbolt(i)=
  i=1,···,N
Fastening Torque of Bolt              FT=      kg.cm
Loosening Torque of Bolt              LT=      kg.cm
Current State of BOLT(i)              fastened(BOLT(i)) or loosened(BOLT(i))
  i=1,···,N
Current Position of BOLT(i)           at(BOLT(i), bolt(i)) or ·····
  i=1,···,N
p-fasten(BOLT) Procedure
p-loosen(BOLT) Procedure
set(BOLT) Procedure
p-remove(BOLT) Procedure
store(BOLT) Procedure
grasp(BOLT) Procedure
```

Table 3   An Example of BOLT Frame.

```
(1)  remove(GEAR2)
(2)  rt-remove(GEAR2)= at(GEAR3, stocker(G3))& at(GEAR4, stocker(G4))
                        & handempty.
(3)  remove(GEAR3).
(4)  rt-remove(GEAR3)= at(BLIND FLANGE, stocker(BF))& handempty.
(5)  remove(BLIND FLANGE).
(6)  rt-remove(BLIND FLANGE)= at(BOLT(i), sbolt(i))& handempty
                        i=1,···,N.
(7)  remove(BOLT(i)) i=1,···,N.
(8)  rt-remove(BOLT(i))= loosened(BOLT(i))& handempty
                        i=1,···,N.
(9)  loosen(BOLT(i)) i=1,···,N.
(10) rt-loosen(BOLT(i))= have(WRENCH)& at(WRENCH, bolt(i))
                        i=1,···,N.
(11) grasp(WRENCH).
(12) set(WRENCH, bolt(i)).         repeat i=1,···,N
(13) p-loosen(BOLT(i)).
(14) store(WRENCH).
(15) p-remove(BOLT(i)).            repeat i=1,···,N
(16) store(BOLT(i)).
(17) p-remove(BLIND FLANGE).
(18) store(BLIND FLANGE).
(19) p-remove(GEAR3).
(20) store(GEAR3).
(21) p-remove(GEAR4).
(22) store(GEAR4).
(23) p-remove(GEAR2).
```

Table 4   Primitive Task Generating Process for
          remove(GEAR2).

```
(1)   begin  "p-remove bolt"

(2)      frame bolt(i), apbolt(i), dpbolt(i)
         scalar HW, RN1, RN2

(3)      trans(bolt(i));
(4)      trans(apbolt(i));
(5)      trans(dpbolt(i));
(6)      move ARM to (apbolt(i));
(7)      open HAND to (1.5*HW);
(8)      move ARM to (bolt(i));
              on force(z·axis of bolt(i))≧ 50 gr. do stop;
(9)      RN1= 1;
(10)     RN2= 1;

(11)     while(RN1 > 0) do
(12)       begin "repeat"
(13)       close HAND with force= 500 gr. ;
(14)       turn ARM 120 deg. around(z·axis of bolt(i))
               with force= 200 gr. along(z·axis of bolt(i))
               on torque(z·axis of bolt(i))= 0 do RN2= 0;
(15)       if (RN2= 0) then
(16)         begin "finish"
(17)         stop ARM;
(18)         move ARM to (dpbolt(i));
(19)         report(have(BOLT(i)));
(20)         end "finish"
(21)       else
             begin "continue"
(22)         open HAND to (1.5*HW);
(23)         turn ARM 120 deg. around(-z·axis of bolt(i));
(24)         end "continue";
(25)       if (RN2= 0) then RN1= 0 else RN1=1;
(26)       end "repeat";
(27)   end "p-remove bolt";
```

Table 5 An Example of p-remove(BOLT(i)) Procedure.

LEARNING-ASSISTED ROBOT PROGRAMMING

Oskar Bartenstein and Hirochika Inoue
Department of Mechanical Engineering
The University of Tokyo

This paper introduces a learning algorithm and case studies of possible applications. The learning algorithm improves robot programs given in the form of "SITUATION implies ACTION" inference rules by specialization and generalization, and by correctness preserving transformations. The system takes easy to specify user oriented programs as approximations of desired target programs and converts them incrementally into final programs. Programs are represented as sets of inference rules, and the inference rules are changed by the learning system whenever it detects program insufficiencies during application runs. The paper explains the learning algorithm, outlines an implementation in a logic programming language and describes results of its application to 2D robot vision, motion and navigation.

1. INTRODUCTION

Economy of robotic systems is determined by both programmer productivity, i.e. how much time and effort the user has to spend to program a given task, and by device productivity, i.e. how expensive equipment has to be used and which cycle times can be achieved within the limits of the devices. System designers have to balance programmer productivity and device productivity, because programming systems today incur inefficient execution for human oriented programs with high programmer productivity, or they incur high programming cost for efficient programs that take domain characteristics into account. Furthermore, high level programming systems have a hard time to deal with low level effects always present in physical systems, such as sensor tolerances or unmodelled dynamics.

This paper presents how to obtain efficient robot oriented programs from easy to program human oriented programs using a learning algorithm. The system takes a user provided imperfect program as an approximation of the desired target program and improves it into a finally efficient, device and domain dependant program, incrementally introducing domain knowledge into the target program body. This approach has two merits: first, the learning system incorporates knowledge obtained during program application into the target program, thus automatically taking care of low level effects, and second the system shifts the major part of the programming burden from the user to the robot's computer, so that non expert users also can effectively use robotic equipment.

The following sections introduce the learning algorithm that manipulates target programs represented by sets of inference rules, give a logic programming implementation of the learning system, and explain its application to three subproblems in robotics: vision, motion and navigation, before discussing some experiences with the system.

2. LEARNING ALGORITHM

To explain the learning algorithm we describe its input and output data, i.e. the target programs, and how target programs are executed. Then we introduce types of possible errors of target programs and how they are corrected. Finally we explain the learning loop and how it is invoked by the evaluation of results obtained running the target programs.

2.1 Target Program Representation

Programs to be manipulated by other programs must have a simple, uniform syntax and modular structure, so that the manipulating programs can treat them easily and changes have only local scope. Moreover, they must have clearly defined semantics so that they can be understood by the learning system. For these reasons programs are represented as sets of inference rules of the form

$$SITUATION\ implies\ ACTION$$

where the right hand side specifies the next action and the left hand side tells under which conditions or sensor input data the ACTION is to be performed. Each single rule reads "in this and this SITUATION do that and that ACTION"; together the rules form a program that tells the robot what to do in every conceivable situation. This discussion is restricted to a finite number of different actions. A rule taken from section 6 about an application of the learning system to mobile robot navigation is given in figure 1,

```
observe((large_box,(-340,-340),(305,305)) AND
        (large_box,(-335,-335),(225,225)) AND
            :          :
        (small_box,(160,160),(90,90))     AND
        (triangle,(-290,-290),(10,10))))
                                implies forward
```

Figure 1: Example: SITUATION implies ACTION rule

where each part of the conjunction refers to an object identified and observed by the robot at a certain lateral and longitudinal distance. It is obvious that a set of rules of that kind can form a robot program.

2.2 Target Program Execution

The set of inference rules of a given task forms an executable target program if interpreted as a whole: it can be viewed as a big IF...THEN...ELSE decision tree where the left hand sides have to be evaluated to get an applicable right hand side, or as a simple production system, or as a logic program that infers the truth of the right hand side statement from the conditions stated left hand and information provided by the sensors. If all conditions in *SITUATION* are satisfied, then *ACTION* is executed. After execution of the action the system is confronted with the next input situation and the execution cycle repeats. Here, the logic programming view is preferred for reasons explained below: an *ACTION* is inferred by the *SITUATION implies ACTION* rules which in turn call the sensors. The sensors give the ground facts, i.e. the axioms for the inference process.

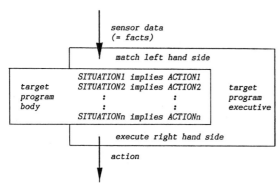

Figure 2: Target program execution

2.3 Classification of Target Program Faults

A learning system by definition has to improve imperfect target programs. For error detection and error correction, problems with target programs are divided into two classes. Consider to learn how to recognize objects with a visual sensor. If an object X is presented to the camera, the learner should respond with "the identity of the object is X"; any other response is incorrect and is caused by one or both of the following primitive mistakes:

    a) the learner recognized an object that is
       different from the correct one
    b) the learner did not recognize the correct
       object

Since target programs are represented as

    SITUATION1 implies ACTION1
    SITUATION2 implies ACTION2
           :
    SITUATIONn implies ACTIONn

the two above errors are either an error of the first kind:

    The target program inferred an *ACTION* that
    it should not have inferred

or an error of the second kind:

    The target program failed to infer an *ACTION*
    that it should have inferred

and there are no other types of errors. Thus the representation of target programs as inference

rules helps to confine errors to specified rules, limits the scope of corrections and reduces the space of possible corrections.

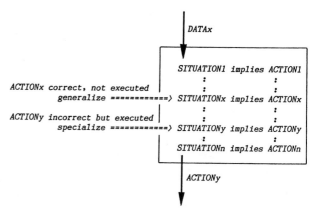

Figure 3: Target program faults

2.4 Specialization and Generalization

To obtain correct target programs it is sufficient to correct the two kinds of errors introduced above, compare figure 3. An error of the first kind, i.e. inference of an undesired *ACTIONy*, is caused by a corresponding *SITUATIONy* whose conditions have all been satisfied in spite of the fact that the input data did not justify to apply *ACTIONy*. Therefore *SITUATIONy* is too permissive, too general and has to be further constrained, or specialized. An error of the second kind, i.e. the failure to infer the desired *ACTIONx* is caused by a corresponding *SITUATION* whose conditions could not be satisfied in spite of the fact that the input data did justify to apply *ACTIONx*. *SITUATIONx* is too special and has to be relaxed, or generalized. Specialization and generalization

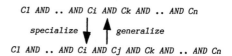

Figure 4: primitive generalization and specialization step

are dual operations. In cooperation they are able to derive any program expressible in the language used for *SITUATION*s, including the two borderline cases of the universal situation that matches always and the absurd situation that matches never, compare figure 5.

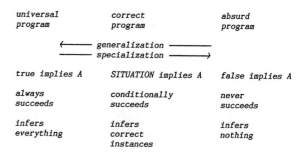

Figure 5: Effect of specialization and generalization

For specialization the learning system introduces a constraint measured by the sensors but until then not used in the *SITUATION implies ACTION* rule, for example it introduces color. For generalization the system either drops a condition from the conjunction, or, to cover a numerical value x it extends the range of the interval [a,b] to [min(a,x), max(b,x)]. This amounts to a special form of a disjunction that is well known from expert systems research. For physical systems as encountered in robotics this is very practical and important, because pattern matching with an exact numerical value will never succeed. Intervals (or probabilistic values) have to take care of tolerances.

It must be decided how to select constraints for specialization of situations and how to select

```
SITUATION  implies  ACTION

    true  implies   A_1
    true  implies   A_2
     :       :       :
    true  implies   A_N
```

Figure 6: initial target program: the universal program

constraints to be dropped. In robotics, time is scarce and learning systems must construct compact and fast programs. Because of this requirement the system here first drops all conditions, i.e. starts with the universal programs (compare figure 6) and then introduces one constraint at a time upon need as detected during application, to be discussed in section 2.6.

2.5 The Learning Loop
The learning system consists of two levels: the level of the target program and the level of the learning program which manipulates the target program. Figure 7 shows the execution cycle of the target program as before and in addition the "meta" loop of the learning program. The learning program takes as input the target program I/O, the target program body, and from the domain or the user information on the quality of the reponse, and if necessary replaces rules of the body with new ones. The meta loop monitors the execution of the lower level one. If the action performed by the learner and the required action are identic, then the learning system does nothing, since this

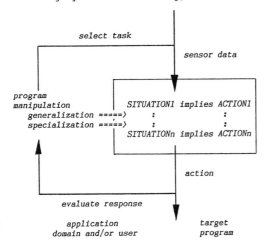

Figure 7: Target program manipulation

part of the program is correct. Programs have been simplified before this stage, so there is no need at this point to simplify programs any more. However, if the action performed is not correct, then the system first locates the at most two faulty rules concerned and specializes and generalizes them, respectively. It is not required that one single correction step suffice.

The learning algorithm does not impose a particular way of scheduling the learning loop and the application loop with respect to each other. It is as well possible to invoke learning incrementally after each application of a rule as to apply the learning process in a one shot fashion to a whole set of experiments once in a while. What method is best seems to depend on the application and on the user interface: to invoke learning early may alleviate the teaching phase, but is only possible if learning does not prolong the teaching process, otherwise the user will not like it. To collect complete records of training examples for later processing may quickly exhaust system resources, so it is necessary to start learning early if the example data are overwhelming. We applied the system both ways and found a combination useful: incremental learning to reduce the bulk of the experiment data, and time and again learning without user interaction.

2.6 Failure Driven Learning
The learning system introduces constraints from examples into initially empty conjunctions of *SITUATION implies ACTION* rules in order to get simple target programs. When and which constraints are introduced has influence on the efficiency of the learning process and on the target programs. If the learner can select the sequence of problems to learn, then several methods are available: breadth first introduction of only as few as possible new constraints into a given *SITUATION* and exhaustive check with respect to different *ACTION*s, depth first introduction of constraints in order to achieve working but suboptimal programs fast, or "lazy" methods that do not change an application program until absolutely necessary. Experimentally we found that breadth first introduction of new constraints is much faster than depth first methods, in spite of the larger search space for breadth first program generation. This result was obtained from sensors with a rich set of data and quite high resolution, so that in most cases the conjunctions of learned programs had only one or two components.
The eager algorithms make sure that all programs are correct for all known examples, while the lazy algorithm invokes program correction only when actually an error occurred. Therefore the lazy algorithm is not sensitive to the number of examples, and is much faster. The eager algorithms are summarized in figure 8, where the difference between depth first and breadth first lies in the implementation of "introduce constraints".

The eager algorithm requires exhaustive verification of all *SITUATION*s with respect to their examples, and exhaustive falsification with respect to their counterexamples, so it is at least quadratic. To invoke learning only after problems with the target program have been detected in a lazy way gives a lazy algorithm, compare figure 9.

To learn about a problem, learn about all ACTIONS

To learn about an ACTION, assume a rule

     "SITUATION infers ACTION"

as a solution, and improve as follows

If any example which lead to a different ACTION satisfies SITUATION, then SITUATION is too general, specialize SITUATION by introduction of constraints from examples.

If any example which lead to ACTION does not satisfy SITUATION, then SITUATION is too special, generalize SITUATION by relaxing constraints.

Figure 8: Eager learning algorithm

To learn about a problem, learn about every subproblem

To learn about a subproblem, do it and evaluate the solution

If a solution A is correct, there is nothing to learn

if a solution B is wrong,

    then specialize the rule for B so that
      it does not give the wrong answer B for
      the current subproblem

    and generalize the rule for A so that
      it does give the right answer A for
      the current subproblem

    and learn once more about subproblems A and B

Figure 9: Lazy learning algorithm

The lazy algorithm permits any sequence of the problems to be learned, so it is particularly suitable for incremental learning. Figure 10 compares learning times for a vision application, figure 11 summarizes some characteristics.

execution time (seconds) of the learning algorithm

objects learned	depth first	breadth first	lazy
1	6	5	14
2	19	12	17
3	689	35	24
4	843	49	28
5	10267	114	29
:	:	:	:
26	--	4023	236

Figure 10: execution time of one shot learning of a set of 26 objects from 2D numerical information, comparison of eager depth first, breadth first and lazy learning

goal:	assert generality	assert speciality	initial program	final program
method: breadth f.	search	test	universal	minimal
depth f.	search	test	universal	not min
lazy	remove constraint upon need	add constraint upon need	universal	not minimal

Figure 11: Comparison of eager and lazy learning

3.   IMPLEMENTATION

The learning algorithm is implemented in Prolog. There are several reasons to select Prolog: First, the target program representation as *SITUATION implies ACTION* blend without further effort to programs executable in the host language. For example a recognition program can be written as

    recognize(IDENTITY) <-
      SITUATION implies IDENTITY,
      meta_call(SITUATION).

where the second line looks up a candidate inference rule and the last line executes it. The last line in the program does the hard work of verifying the conditions required by *SITUATION* with the sensor data. That last line is implemented using the Prolog meta call by

    meta_call(S) <- S.

which takes a chunk of data and executes it as a program. Second, the host language allows to both generate and test examples and situations, also using the meta call facility: An inference rule *SITUATION implies ACTION* executed with respect to given sensor data can not only test an instantiated *SITUATION* for truth, but also create an instance of a *SITUATION*. This is important for learning systems that create their own test data, and is used extensively. For example a call to the sensor system

    sensor(distance,X)

can be used to test for a distance, if X is instantiated at call time, or it can be used to retrieve a value for X. Third, the notions "too_general" and "too_special" introduced in this paper map directly into the logic programming execution model of programs that either succeed or fail: Programs that succeed on counterexamples are too general, programs that fail on examples are too special. The resulting learning programs are very compact because they make direct use of the underlying language model. Finally, it is possible to rewrite the inference rules

    SITUATION implies ACTION

so that they become Prolog programs themselves

    ACTION <- SITUATION

which can even be compiled by a good host system into machine language. This last step completes the cycle from user provided input examples to final machine language programs all within one programming environment. Figure 12 lists the main algorithm of the learning system, figure 13 the failure driven lazy version.

```
learn :- action(ACTION),learn(ACTION),fail ; true.

learn(ACTION) :-
        experience(ExpdSituation,ACTION),
        generalization(ExpdSituation,SITUATION),
        special_enough(SITUATION,ACTION),
        remember(SITUATION implies ACTION).

generalization(Sit,GenSit) :- drop_conditions(Sit,GenSit).
special_enough(SIT,ACT) :- not too_general(SIT,ACT).

too_general(S,A)  :-
        otheraction(A,OA), experience(OS,OA),
        create_situation(S),
        meta_call(S),              % make instance of S
        create_situation(OS),
        meta_call(S).              % verify S with OS
```

Figure 12: the pure learning algorithm

```
learn :- action(A),learn(A),fail ; true.

learn(A) :- invoke_sensor(A), recognize(B), learn(B,A), !.

learn(A,A) :- !.
learn(RecObj,CorrObj) :- !,
        generalize_program_for(CorrObj),
        specialize_program_for(RecObj),
        learn(CorrObj),
        learn(RecObj).

specialize_program_for('UNKNOWN') :- !.
specialize_program_for(A) :- implies(Conditions,A),
        ( new_constraint(A,Conditions,NewC),
        retract(implies(Conditions,A)),
        assertz(implies((NewC,Conditions),A))
        ; panic_sensor_insufficient ), !.

generalize_program_for(A) :- exists_program(A),
        ( sufficiently_general(A) ; relax_program(A)),!.
generalize_program_for(A) :- introduce_program(A), !.

exists_program(A) :- implies(Conditions,A).

sufficiently_general(A) :- recognize(A).

relax_program(A) :-
        retract(implies(Conditions,A)),
        relax_conditions(A,Conditions,NewConditions),
        assertz(implies(NewConditions,A)).
```

Figure 13: failure driven learning algorithm

The following sections on application case studies show how the system is actually used, and how the user and the system share the programming task.

4. APPLICATION TO VISION

We use an industrial vision machine based on 2D SRI vision features and want to enable the robot to recognize parts as depicted in figure 14 after the parts have been introduced to the robot. It is not required to deal with unknown parts. The robot is allowed to use any primitive provided by the vision machine, but the robot is not given a vision program or hints on the parts or useful

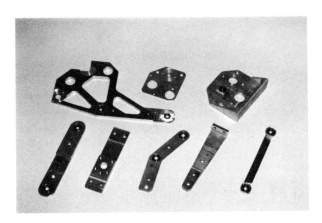

Figure 14: parts of a robot finger

primitives. On the other hand the robot shall recognize objects fast, so the fewer features it has to use the better. Hence the learner has to make best use of the vision machine and of the redundancies in the application domain to obtain

as fast programs as possible. Learning time itself is not an issue, and the robot can even request the user to show a desired object.

The trace of the learning algorithm and the target programs depend on the difficulty the sensor has to distinguish objects. In figure 15 a trace for 7 objects shows that e.g. parts e and c are more difficult than part g.

```
learning a
  generalize program for a
  specialize program for UNKNOWN
learning b
  generalize program for b
  specialize program for a
    generalize program for a
    specialize program for b
learning c
  generalize program for c
  specialize program for UNKNOWN
learning d
  generalize program for d
  specialize program for a
    generalize program for d
    specialize program for c
      generalize program for c
      specialize program for d
learning e
  generalize program for e
  specialize program for c
    generalize program for c
    specialize program for e
      generalize program for e
      specialize program for c
        generalize program for c
        specialize program for e
          generalize program for e
          specialize program for c
            generalize program for c
            specialize program for e
              generalize program for e
              specialize program for c
                generalize program for c
                specialize program for e
                  generalize program for e
                  specialize program for c
                    generalize program for c
                    specialize program for e
learning f
  generalize program for f
  specialize program for e
    generalize program for e
    specialize program for f
      generalize program for f
      specialize program for e
        generalize program for e
        specialize program for f
          generalize program for f
          specialize program for e
learning g
  generalize program for g
  specialize program for UNKNOWN
```

Figure 15: learning sequence of 7 objects

In this paper we discuss only the case where the whole object is visible, without overlap or touching objects. How to deal with these cases is discussed in [Bartenstein and Inoue,86]. Learning determines what features to use and what features to ignore, depending on the objects at hand. For the learning algorithm it is easy to recognize the eight engineering parts above. In order to study the time and cost of the learning algorithm itself we applied the system to a much harder case: recognition of 26 alphabetic characters, which is sort of a worst case for an SRI machine, because the objects are similar on purpose, especially if seen with a sensor that does not concentrate on structure and contours, but on numerical features like area, hight, width etc., which are all designed to be about the same for an even printed image. Results obtained from application of the learning system to the set of 26 very similar objects are summarized in figures 10 above and 16. The experiments show that both breadth first learning for compact programs and incremental learning for quick results are good methods, while depth first learning is too inefficient for a rich problem space.

file length in bytes of the learned programs:

objects learned	orig data	depth first	breadth first	incre-mental
A-C	4323	182	110	
A-D	5767	319	146	
A-E	7205	675	196	
A-F	8646	766	249	
A-G	10087	1087	291	
:	:	:	:	
A-Z	37466	--	1211	5284

Figure 16: length of recognition programs generated by learning of a set of 26 objects from 2D numerical information, comparison of results obtained using depth first, breadth first and incremental learning

5. APPLICATION TO MOTION

5.1 The Task
We use the learning system for the two main joints of a simulated SCARA robot. This type of robot is typically used for high speed, repetitive precision work. The size of the robot has to be selected to closely match the application to achieve both precision and speed. Programs for pick and place operations are given as a series of points in world coordinates. The points specify a collision free trajectory from start to goal position. Intermediate points are not so important as long as there is no collision. The path is easy to program; however, since it is programmed in the subjective space of the human user and not in the objective joint space of the robot, it contains parts that are not optimal with respect to the robots kinematics. The effect is worsened because the robot is adapted in size to its task, so that the influence of its kinematics becomes both important and harder to imagine except for experienced programmers. This results in uneven acceleration profiles for the actuators, putting unreasonable strain on the robot sometimes and wasting time at other places.
The learning process enables the robot to change its path according to its own needs, while observing task imposed constraints: fixed start and end points and collision avoidance. As a result, programming can be done in the programmer's device independant world and the final program is still adapted to robot and task.

5.2 The Robot and its Sensors
The simulated two joints of the SCARA robot move in a plane above the work surface, the robots tip has to avoid collision with obstacles standing out of the work surface. The learning system knows the geometry of the robot, the path, and it must be able to detect collision. The simulation just checks whether the position of the tip falls

within an obstacle, the tip is assumed round with known diameter. In the simulation the diameter is added to the obstacles and the tip has zero size. Sensors provide to the learning system data about angular displacement, speed and acceleration of each joint. The simulator obtains the values from two numerical derivations of the path with respect to the path run length in joint space; in reality the values will come from torque sensors at the actuators and thus include dynamics, which the simulation now does not. Figure 17 shows a top view of an application with two obstacles: a path defined by start, end, and intermediate points.

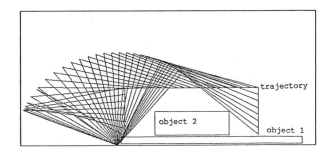

Figure 17: path programmed in cartesian coordinates

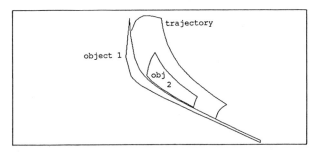

Figure 18: same path plotted in joint coordinates

5.3 The Learning Process
The learning system transforms the raw path incrementally. There is always a complete and executable program available, which serves both as an approximation of the path to be learned and as a lower bound on the quality of the new path. The learner works in the robots joint space, changing joint positions locally and then verifying the obtained result: it checks whether the path is still collision free and whether the maximal acceleration in the new path is not higher than in the previous path. The learning algorithm terminates when the maximal acceleration of the new path increases.
Since the method to remove old and propose new constraints to the system for evaluation will be applied very often, it must be simple and should converge fast to locally straight lines in joint space. We use the following heuristic: for a path segment defined by joint space points $P[i-1]$, $P[i]$, $P[i+1]$, replace the position of point $P[i]$ with the position of the center of gravity of the triangle $P[i-1], P[i], P[i+1]$. This lends itself to extension beyond two dimensions. Experiments show that it converges fast if the distance between

points on the trajectory is not too small with respect to the overall path length. The influence of the tesselation step size on the time required for the learning process is a shortcoming of our implementation now and we are thinking about methods to include selection of adequate tesselation into the learning algorithm. Another shortcoming of the system as it is now is the global evaluation function; learning may terminate due to a local acceleration peak, but it could be useful to continue learning at other places. Recursive learning on path segments seems to be a solution, which is not integrated now.

5.4 Examples

Application of the learning system to the task above gives the new path shown in figure 19. The new path requires less joint displacement and less acceleration. Raw and learned motions of a more involved example show figures 20 and 21.

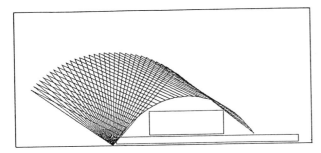

Figure 19: Learned trajectory

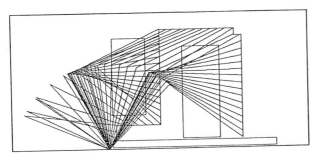

Figure 20: Raw trajectory

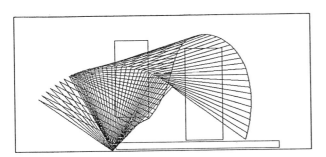

Figure 21: Learned trajectory

6. APPLICATION TO NAVIGATION

6.1 The Task

Consider a mobile robot for use in known static

environment, for example an unmanned materials transportation unit on a factory floor, with range finder and visual sensor. The robot unit must find its way through the shop (compare figure 22) from work area to work area after being guided once by its user. Hence the learner has to extract from the large amount of information from the sensors about the environment (figure 23) only as much as is really needed for the particular path and workshop (see figure 24): the learner will realize what objects or object groups are unique landmarks in the shop area and can be used for reliable guidance, and the learner will also be able to disregard and skip information about objects that are too frequent to be useful as unambiguous markers, or just not necessary because simpler landmarks are readily available.

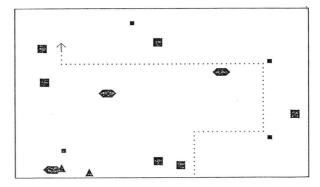

Figure 22: Mobile robot environment and path

```
observe((large_box,(-340,-340),(305,305)) AND
        (large_box,(-335,-335),(225,225)) AND
        (large_box,(-90,-90),(320,320))   AND
        (small_box,(-140,-140),(360,360)) AND
        (small_box,(160,160),(270,270))   AND
        (large_box,(-40,-40),(30,30))     AND
        (large_box,(210,210),(150,150))   AND
        (small_box,(-290,-290),(60,60))   AND
        (diamond,(-190,-190),(190,190))   AND
        (diamond,(60,60),(240,240))       AND
        (diamond,(-310,-310),(10,10))     AND
        (large_box,(-90,-90),(40,40))     AND
        (small_box,(160,160),(90,90))     AND
        (triangle,(-290,-290),(10,10)))
                                   implies forward
```

Figure 23: part of an initial navigation program
(one of 91 rules)

```
observe((large_box,(-50,-50),(15,35)))    implies forward
observe((large_box,(45,45),(60,480)))     implies forward
observe((large_box,(-490,-490),(55,195))) implies forward
observe((small_box,(-170,-170),(20,150))) implies forward
observe((large_box,(-340,-340),(215,305))) implies forward
observe((small_box,(-170,-170),(10,10)))  implies left
observe((large_box,(-490,-490),(45,45)))  implies left
observe((large_box,(-340,-340),(205,205))) implies right
observe((large_box,(45,45),(50,50)))      implies right
observe((large_box,(-50,-50),(5,5)))      implies stop
```

Figure 24: final navigation program (complete)

For "programming", the user leads the robot once through the path and gives the robot time to look at the environment. After the learning phase, which can either be one-shot after the training run or incremental during later application runs, the program will be heavily domain dependant: useful only for one particular factory floor.

6.2 The robot and its sensors

The robot is mobile in two dimensions on a plane surface. In order to limit the complexity of the training and learning task later, the robot is restricted in its movements, it can either go straight ahead by multiples of a length unit or turn plus or minus 90 or 180 degrees around its vertical axis. So the robot cannot go curved lines and it cannot perform combined step sequences except straight ones, but it can move freely on a square grid, which is sufficient for our purposes. The sensors give the a set of triples

$$observe(Identity, Long\_Dist, Latl\_Dist),$$

where each triple stands for an observed object and the set of triples represents the factory environment as far as it is observable by the robot. Longitudinal and lateral distances are in fact intervals, accounting for the precision (or lack of precision) of the range finder. Thus the robot can recount the environment in phrases like "Now there is an object X at a place between 3 and 5 length units in front and between 10 and 15 length units to the right of me; and there is an object Y at... ; and... ".

6.3 The Learning Process

When the user leads the robot through its path at training time, information about the environment will be overwhelming, and most of it will be redundant, if the environment is not really sparsely populated. Learning finds out what objects are informative enough for orientation, or, if single objects are insufficient, what groups of objects can be used as landmarks.

Data Acquisition and Program Execution

During training the robot remembers what it experienced in the form of *SITUATION implies ACTION* rules, one rule for every grid point on the path. *ACTION* is what the user made the robot do at that time (e.g. "turn left") and *SITUATION* is the conjunction of the observe triples. During training, *SITUATION* is just a record of the sensor data. During application, *SITUATION* will be interpreted as requests to the sensors to verify expected objects. The next time the robot is at the same position, *SITUATION* will be evaluated to 'true' and the rule does in fact infer *ACTION*. If the *SITUATION* cannot be reduced to 'true', then *ACTION* is not eligible for execution. There is one inference rule acquired at each grid point on the robots path during the training phase, and *SITUATION* holds information on every visible object. Hence the memory requirement grows about linearly with the number of objects in the environment and with the length of the route.

Program Manipulation and Verification

The learning process reduces the complexity of the raw program as acquired during training in two ways: First, the complexity of the original *SITUATION*s is reduced until only as many objects are verified as necessary to justify *ACTION*, so the single inference rules become shorter. Learned programs execute faster than the raw programs, and require much less memory. Second, the learning process combines inference rules that use the same landmarks on contiguous stretches of the path, enabling the robot to go straight on if new orientation is not needed. Thus the number of

inference rules decreases, further reducing memory and time requirements, and eliminating stops for unnecessary reevaluation of the environment. The implementation uses breadth first search to find landmark objects or groups of objects. Breadth first search yields short conjunctions to define the *SITUATION*s, which in turn yield fast navigation programs. Data obtained during training serves as database to verify the validity of derived programs. Verification is exhaustive.

6.4 Examples

Consider the robot working on a factory floor, as in figure 22. 15 objects of 4 different kinds populate the work area. The user leads the robot through a path with 91 points on the grid accessible to the robot. At every point the robot observes its environment and records the action told. The robot has 180 degree field of view, so it records a total of 91 rules with up to 15 constituents in each condition part, using 29495 bytes of memory. Execution of the raw program takes 207 seconds. After the learning process, the robot has a knowledge base of now only 11 rules with an average of 1 constituent in the conjunctions, requiring 601 bytes of memory. Execution time of the learned program is 3.18 seconds, about 60 times faster than the raw program. The robot stops for orientation at 11 places, including 5 places where it has to stop anyway to make a left or right turn. Figure 25 shows the result: marked are points on the path where the robot stopped for orientation and objects that it actually used as landmarks.

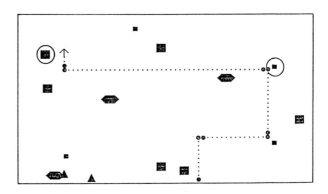

Figure 25. Learned environment and path

7.   DISCUSSION

7.1 Monotonic Program Manipulation

The learning system manipulates programs by two primitive operations, "generalize" and "specialize". Generalization expands the scope of a condition, increases the applicability of an inference rule. Generalization repairs errors of the first kind. Specialization reduces the scope of an inference rule, and therefore corrects errors of the second kind. To generalize a program, one can either add a relaxant or remove a constraint, and to specialize a program one can either add a constraint or remove a relaxant.

Since specialization and generalization are dual operations one has to take care not to cause infinite loops. We limit the learning algorithm to either monotonic specialization or monotonic generalization. This choice drastically reduces the search space for program generation, and includes two special cases: either to generate a target program by specialization from the universal program, or to generate a target program by generalization from the absurd program. Our goal are fast target programs, so we construct programs by specialization from universal programs. Even the use of breadth first search for the most compact target program is not prohibitively expensive for example in the vision case: the off-the-shelf vision hardware provides by far more data than really needed for our experiments, so breadth first search is in fact an efficient method to use.

7.2 Heuristics

Dealing with physical systems, we have to cope not only with qualitative, structural data, but also quantitative, numerical data. With respect to numerical data we use the assumption that intervals are closed. If a numerical descriptor has the value X during one experiment and a value Y during another experiment, we assume that the descriptor in question can assume any value of the interval between X and Y. This may not hold in some cases and cause to reject correct programs, but the rule is very powerful. The rule is also safe because it does not generate wrong rules, even if correct rules can be rejected. In other words the assumption is a heuristic but it does not compromise the target program correctness.

7.3 Memory Hierarchy

The algorithm as given in section 5 has severe limitations because if run as it is without further refinement it will require to verify every inference rule with all positive and all negative examples, which necessarily leads to combinatorical explosion of the verification process. This is tolerable for applications with few objects and few examples, where the complexity lies within the pattern matching of examples and not in the numbers of experiments.

In application fields with many expected experiments we use three levels of memory: momentaneous memory that records everything, short term memory that groups examples, and long term memory, which is equivalent to the finally learned program. Momentaneous memory is only used during data acquisition, since it would grow linearly with the number of experiments the data is discarded immediately after integration into short term memory. Short term memory holds data of groups of experiments and grows linearly with the number of inference rules. The learning algorithm relies on short term memory if it has to introduce new constraints into inference rules. Long term memory holds only the information known to be necessary by that time. Long term memory is identic with learned programs after termination of the learning process, and only the information held in long term memory will be used during application of the target programs.

8.   CONCLUSION

We introduced a learning algorithm by

generalization, specialization and program transformation. We found that all three types are valuable, depending on the initial knowledge of the learner. In the vision case we produced programs by specialization from the universal program, in navigation we sped up programs by speciality preserving generalization, and in the motion example we replaced constraints guided by heuristics and verification. We selected the approach to be taken by the learner manually. However, a more powerful learner might be able to select its strategy by itself without running into termination problems.

Research on learning has accompanied intelligent robotics for twenty years now, and has yet to find its way into industrial use. This paper focussed on an down-to-earth approach to introduce learning into the user machine interaction in order to improve the programmability of robotic equipment. We do not claim to have a universal learning system, nor that it is useful to use learning for every aspect of robotics. However we demonstrated cases where learning helps to achieve better robot programs with less effort.

REFERENCES

[1] L.V. Aken, H.V. Brussel
On-line robot trajectory control in joint coordinates by means of imposed acceleration profiles
in: Proc. 15th ISIR, Tokyo, 1985, pp 1003

[2] O. Bartenstein, H. Inoue
Automatic Synthesis of Vision Programs using a Logic Programming Approach
Proc. Japan-U.S.A. Symp. on Flexible Automation, Osaka, 1986

[3] Hirochika Inoue
Building a Bridge between AI and Robotics
in: Proc. 9th IJCAI, Los Angeles, 1985, pp 1231

[4] Michael Lebowitz
Concept Learning in A Rich Input Domain: Generalization Based Memory
in: Machine Learning II, Kaufmann, Palo Alto 1986

[5] Tomas Lozano-Perez, W. Eric Grimson
Recognition and Localization of Overlapping Parts from Sparse Data
2nd ISRR, 1984, Kyoto, Japan

[6] Ehud Shapiro
Algorithmic Debugging
MIT Press, Cambridge, MA, 1983

[7] J.A. Robinson
Logic: Form and Function
Edinburgh University Press, 1979

[8] Paul E. Utgoff
Shift of Bias for Inductive Concept Learning
in: Machine Learning II, Kaufmann, Palo Alto, 1986

Sensor-based manipulation planning
as a game with nature

Russell H. Taylor
IBM T. J. Watson Research Center
Yorktown Heights, NY, 10598

Matthew T. Mason
Carnegie-Mellon University
Pittsburgh, PA 15213

Kenneth Y. Goldberg
Carnegie-Mellon University
Pittsburgh, PA 15213

This paper explores a game-theoretic approach to automatic planning of sensor-based robotic manipulation programs. To win the game, the robot must provably attain a specified task state. The robot moves by choosing a control signal, and nature moves by choosing a sensor signal. Planning is accomplished by searching the game tree. In some task domains, the approach provides a straightforward method of reasoning about uncertainty, non-deterministic actions, and imperfect sensors. We demonstrate the approach in two different task domains: orienting an object using an instrumented tilting tray; and orienting and and grasping an object with an instrumented parallel-jaw gripper.

1   Introduction

This paper approaches robotic manipulation as a game being played between the robot and nature. To win the game, the robot must attain a task state that provably satisfies a specified goal, such as uniquely orienting a polygonal object or achieving a stable grasp. The robot chooses the motor signals, and nature chooses the sensor data. To plan for the worst case, the robot must search the game tree for a winning strategy.

Our approach treats manipulation planning as a tree search. Uncertainty in the robot's world model, error in the robot's actions, and noisy sensors, are all explicitly modeled and accounted for in the construction of the tree. We are implementing planners for two different task domains. First, to extend Erdmann and Mason's (1986) work on orienting objects with tilting trays, we have incorporated the use of sensory feedback. Second, based on Brost's (1986) earlier work on planning parallel-jaw grasping motions, we have implemented a system that plans a sequence of squeezes to orient and ultimately grasp an object, using measurements of finger separation when appropriate.

The rules of the manipulation game are determined by the actions and sensory events that are possible from any given state of the task. To avoid combinatorial explosion, it is imperative that we consider only those actions and sensory events that have different effects. In some cases, it is possible to reduce the number of alternatives from infinity to a small finite number without compromising the planner's scope.

1.1   Previous work

Our approach originates in the desire to construct plans that model uncertainty in the robot's model of the world. Taylor (1976) describes a system that predicts possibile uncertainties, using them to choose among alternative strategies, and to adjust the parameters of the chosen strategy. Brooks' (1982) system verifies and re-works robot plans, based on bounds on uncertainty. Brooks' work can be viewed as complementary to the present paper, since Brooks' plans use sensory information in a continuous fashion, rather than for conditional branching. Our plans use sensory data exclusively for conditional branching.

A formal framework for planning in the presence of uncertainty is developed in Lozano-Pérez, Mason, and Taylor (1984), Mason (1984), Erdmann (1986), Buckley (1987), and Donald (1986). Buckley provides the link to the present paper by his use of AND/OR graphs. Buckley applied the approach to planning of generalized damper and generalized spring motions. The present paper adopts Buckley's notation for AND/OR graphs, explores the general application of the idea, and illustrates the concept with implementations in two task domains.

The present paper describes planners for two different task domains: *tray-tilting* and *squeeze-grasping*. Tray-tilting is the process of orienting a planar object in a tray by moving the tray through a sequence of tilt angles, and squeeze-grasping is the orienting and grasping of a planar object by a sequence of squeezes with a parallel-jaw gripper. The first work on tray-tilting was Grossman and Blasgen (1975), followed by Erdmann and Mason (1986). For earlier work on the mechanics of pushing, and squeeze-grasping in particular, see Mason (1986), Mani and Wilson (1984), Brost (1986), and Peshkin (1985).

Our work is also related to the problem of choosing tactile probe motions to determine the position and orientation of an object (Grossman and Blasgen 1975, Grimson and Lozano-Pérez 1984, Grimson 1986, Ellis 1987). The problem is easily cast as an AND/OR graph search. Ellis' *ambiguity tree* is similar, but describes the interpretation of probe data, with the probe sequence fixed, yielding a pure AND tree.

2   Example

We will begin with a simple example, contrived to illustrate the basic concepts and avoid the many complications. Consider a rectangular object in the plane, constrained to have one of its edges aligned with a fixed reference line. Due to the symmetry of the block, we will distinguish two states, SHORT and TALL. The robot can rotate the block through 90 degrees, which turns a SHORT into a TALL, and vice versa. An optical interrupt type sensor is mounted so as to detect the block's state (see Figure 1).

We can summarize the options of the robot as follows: at any given time it can decide to rotate the block to its other state, an action we

422   Taylor et al.

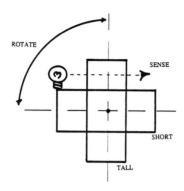

Figure 1: An illustrative example.

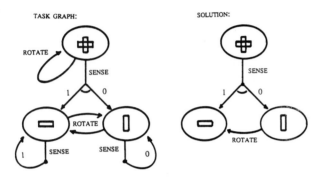

Figure 2: Task graph and solution sub-graph for the example.

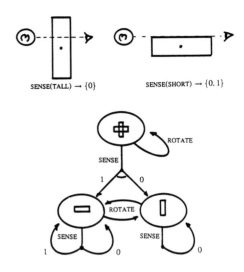

Figure 3: The example with ambiguous sensing.

will call ROTATE, or it can consult the sensor, obtaining either a 0 or a 1 depending on whether the light beam is broken, or not, respectively. We will assume that the block's state is initially unknown, and the goal is to force the block into the SHORT state. Starting with the rectangle in either of two orientations, we construct a graph (Figure 2) that captures every possible sequence of events in the task. An initial ROTATE changes nothing, the object state is still unknown. An initial SENSE determines the object state, after which it can be meaningfully ROTATEed. Additional SENSEs are redundant. A strategy to accomplish the given task can be expressed as a sub-graph of the task graph, as shown in the figure.

The key features of the task graph are:

- Each node is a set of possible world states.

- Each action, and each sensory event, is a transition from a set of possible initial world states to a set of possible resultant world states.

- The graph has an AND/OR structure. The robot can choose its actions, and can guarantee a win if *any* of its actions lead to a win. But nature chooses the sensory outcomes, so the planner must ensure that *all* sensory outcomes lead to a win.

To represent model uncertainty, each node corresponds to a set of possible world states, not a specific world state. Hence a search node does not represent a state of the world, but rather the state of the robot's model of the world during plan execution (Brooks 1982; Lozano-Pérez, Mason, and Taylor 1984). The distinction is subtle, but important. It is useless to achieve a desired state of the world in ignorance; the robot must know that the goal is achieved. Hence we search not for a specified world state, but for a specified model state. In principle, we can encode the state of the robot's world model, i.e. summarize all information available to the robot, as the set of states consistent with this information. Hence our search nodes are defined by a set of possible states of the world.

For many problems, it may be impossible, or inadvisable, to boil the robot's world model down to a set of all possible world states. For example, we might have a system that calibrates the location of a pallet, using touch probe information obtained through a sequence of guarded moves. The sensible thing is to collect the information, then apply a single routine that predicts the pallet location, rather than computing a set of all possible pallet locations after each probe. To express such strategies in a graph, we could augment the state encoded at a node to fully represent the computational state of the robot's world model (Brooks 1982).

Besides representing uncertain knowledge of the state of the world, we have to represent and reason about under-determined actions and noisy sensors. For instance, we can modify our earlier example by introducing noise in our sensory data. Suppose that the optical sensor's location is not precisely known, with the consequence that a broken beam is inconclusive, although an unbroken beam still implies a state of SHORT. The resulting graph is shown in Figure 3. In this case, there is no winning strategy, because the sensor might never give the robot any information. This example shows a shortcoming of our worst-case approach to planning. We might want to consider a strategy that tries to get lucky, i.e. hopes that nature cooperates. In principle, the graphs can be extended using probabilistic models of actions and sensors to construct probabilistic plans.

When we turn our attention from contrived examples to more realistic task domains, planning becomes more complicated. The example above is contrived to have a finite number of world states, a finite number of actions, and a finite number of sensory events. In more realistic problems, we often must deal with continuous spaces of task state, action, and sensory data. Modeling uncertainty, actions, and sensing, are accordingly more complicated. The most striking difference is the combinatorial nature of the search, especially when branching factors of the order of the continuum are contemplated. This paper deals with continuous spaces of choices in two ways. First, we partition a continuous space of actions into classes that have identical effect. Continuous spaces of action were handled thus by Brost (1986) and by Erdmann and Mason (1986). Second, we deal with continuous spaces of sensory events by sampling. There are many variations; we simply sample the space at a fixed, fairly coarse, resolution. Other possibilities are discussed later in the paper.

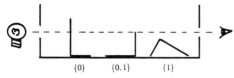

Figure 4: The sensor model.

3 Graphs and searching

A planning problem is defined by the task state space, the sensory and action functions, a set of possible initial states, and a set of goals, with each goal expressed as a set of states. We adopt the following notation:

X	the task state space, i.e. the set of possible states of the physical world.
D	the sensor space, i.e. the set of possible sensor data.
U	the action space, i.e. the set of possible actions.
$I \subset X$	the set of possible initial states.
$G_i \subset X$	the ith goal.
$a : U \times X \to \mathcal{P}(X)$	the task state-transition function, expressing the effect of actions.
$s : X \to \mathcal{P}(D)$	the sensor function, expressing the meaning of sensory data.

where $\mathcal{P}(\cdot)$ is the power set, to express the multi-valued character of actions and measurements.

Each planning problem is transformed into a graph search problem. A node in the graph is a set of possible task states, i.e. a subset of X. A node encodes the robot's knowledge of the task state during execution of the plan. Hence the initial node is the set of possible initial states I, and success is achieved by reaching any subset of any goal G_i. Actions and sensory events cause transitions among the nodes of the graph:

$V = \mathcal{P}(X)$	the nodes of the task graph
$\xrightarrow{u}$	a relation on the nodes V, defining the action arcs for action u. $X_1 \xrightarrow{u} X_2$ iff $a : (u, X_1) = X_2$.
$\xrightarrow{d}$	a relation on the nodes V, defining the sensing arcs for sensor datum d. $X_1 \xrightarrow{d} X_2$ iff $s^{-1}(d) \cap X_1 = X_2$.

Here, and throughout the paper, we are treating action and sensing as mutually exclusive concepts. Some problems, though, treat action and sensing as indivisible. For example, the guarded moves described by Lozano-Pérez, Mason, and Taylor (1984) involve choices by the robot and by nature. Buckley's formulation of the AND/OR graph uses sensor data interpreted during the motion to define alternative result nodes for the motion. Another example combining choices by the robot with choices by nature is when the robot has two different sensors to choose between. Our formulation of the graph is easily generalized to deal with such situations, but this paper focuses on the extreme cases: pure sensing and pure action.

A solution to a planning problem can be described by a subgraph of the task graph. The subgraph should lead to a goal in finite time, so cycles and infinite subgraphs are not allowed. Each node (except leaf nodes) should include exactly one outgoing action arc, or *all* of the outgoing sensing arcs, reflecting the AND/OR structure of the problem. We will seek solutions that minimize the worst-case number of arcs, i.e. we seek the solution sub-graph that minimizes the maximum path-length. We presently employ a breadth-first search, hashing the nodes for efficiency. Simple searches converge in a few seconds on a Symbolics 3600.

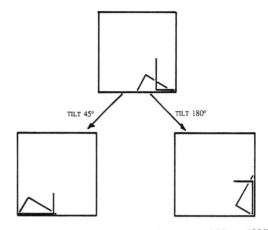

Figure 5: A typical set of tilt actions (Erdmann and Mason 1986).

4 Automatic planning of sensor-based tray-tiltin programs

Our first application is the problem of orienting an object with an instrumented tilting tray. A polygonal object slides freely in a rectangular tray, which is instrumented with simple optical-interrupt sensors. The robot can tilt the tray at any angle desired and query the sensors. The object slides and rolls along the sides and into and out of the corners. Starting from an initially unknown orientation, the problem is to obtain any completely determined orientation and position. In the modeling of the mechanics of tray-tilting we follow Erdmann and Mason (1986), which should be consulted for more details. Briefly:

- A rigid polygonal object, with known shape and center of mass, slides about in a rectangular planar tray.

- The forces acting on the object are gravity, forces of constraint, and friction. Coulomb friction occurs between the object and the tray walls. Friction with the tray bottom is negligible.

- The system is quasi-static: inertial and impact forces are negligible.

- The object is initially in one of a finite number of stable orientations, in the middle of one of the tray walls.

- The attitude of the tray is directly controllable.

To complete the problem definition, we must define the allowed sensory modalities:

- A light beam passes parallel to each wall. The sensor reports whether the beam is broken or not.

- The distance from the beam to the wall lies in some known interval.

For any given orientation of the object against some wall, there are three possibilities, illustrated in Figure 4. If the object's profile is definitely less than the sensor's distance from the wall, a 1 is obtained. If the object's profile is definitely greater than the sensor's distance from the wall, a 0 is obtained. If the object's profile falls inside the interval of possible sensor distances, we cannot predict which sensor datum will occur.

The first problem is to characterize the possible states of the task. For the tray-tilting task domain, we can get by with a finite number of possible configurations. By definition, the initial set of configurations is finite. If

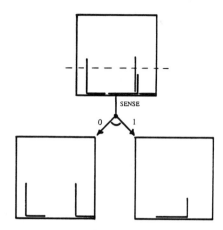

Figure 6: A typical set of sensor events.

we avoid motions that move the object into the center of the tray, and if we wait long enough for the object to complete its motion, then the number of possible configurations remains finite.

A typical tilting action is shown in Figure 5. Initially there are two possible configurations of the block in the tray. Two different choices of tilt angle are shown, with the corresponding result nodes. Searching the graph requires that the effect of a tilt action be predicted automatically, using the methods (in fact, using the actual code) described in Erdmann and Mason (1986) and Erdmann (1984). An interesting type of indeterminacy enters when Coulomb friction and rigid bodies are allowed in Newtonian mechanics. Multiple solutions are possible, and there may even be situations that admit no solutions.[1] Erdmann's system finds multiple solutions. Since the nodes of the task graph are represented by a set of world states, multiple solutions are easily accommodated in the task graph. We have not observed any cases without solutions, and do not know whether they can occur. The result node would be the empty set, i.e. there are no world states consistent with such an action. The meaning of such a situation is that our assumptions of the mechanics of the world are inconsistent, and hence our planner is invalid. This is one case of what we have come to call "confusing nodes": a node which is in some way beyond the scope of the planner, and must perforce be avoided.

Figure 6 shows a typical sensory operation. If the beam is broken, we construct the result node by eliminating every configuration in the initial node that is too short to break the beam. If the beam is not broken, the result node is obtained by eliminating every configuration that is too tall to not break the beam. Some configurations, on the fuzzy edge between short and tall, will appear in both resultant nodes. The most straightforward implementation of sensor interpretation is to begin by computing off-line, for every possible sensor datum, the set of world states consistent with that datum. Now, during the search, we can interpret any hypothetical sensor datum by intersecting the set of possible states with those consistent with the sensor datum, as previously computed. This is only feasible with very simple sensors, such as our optical interrupt sensor. At the opposite extreme, computer vision, for instance, it is not practical to enumerate and interpret every possible image, even if we do it off-line!

It should be apparent that the demonstration system is not limited to the optical interrupt sensors, which were introduced for concreteness. In fact, the available sensors are actually described to the system by their interpretations, i.e. by a mapping from some sensor data space to sets of consistent world states.

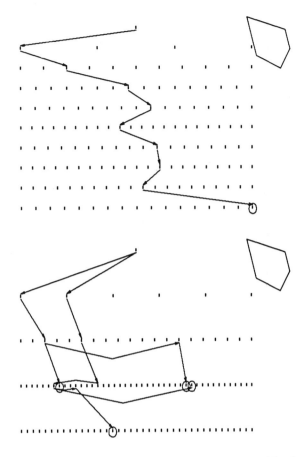

Figure 7: Typical solutions, with sensing (below) and without (above).

At this writing, the planner seems to be running reliably, but we have not tested it systematically, nor have we tested the plans generated by the planner. A typical case is shown in Figure 7, which shows two plans, one with sensing and one without. The goal nodes are circled. All arcs other than those in the solution have been suppressed for readability. For each node, one outgoing arc indicates an action; two outgoing arcs indicates a sensory operation. The planner seems to work very well on randomly-generated polygons, although there are some polygons that are not orientable.

5 Automatic planning of sensor-based squeeze-grasping programs

Our second example application is the problem of planning a sequence of squeezes to completely orient and grasp an object, with sensory data arising from measurement of the finger separation at the completion of a squeeze. The mechanics closely follows the work of Brost (1986), which addresses the problem of planning a single squeeze without sensory feedback. Our assumptions are:

- The object is a rigid planar polygon, in planar motion.
- The two fingers are infinitely broad, rigid, parallel half-planes, approaching from arbitrarily far away.
- The finger motions are symmetric: the tangential components of velocity are equal, and the normal components are opposite, but equal in magnitude. The motions continue until further motion would imply distortion of the object.

---

[1]The existence of problems admitting no solution consistent with Newton's laws, rigid bodies, and Coulomb friction, has been widely accepted for some time. Lötstedt (1981) for example, describes such a problem, but see Mason and Wang (1987) for a solution to Lötstedt's problem.

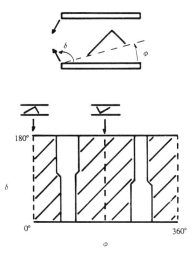

Figure 8: A squeeze-grasp diagram (Brost 1986).

- The forces acting on the object are gravity, normal to the support plane, contact with the support plane, and contacts with the fingers. All contact forces observe Coulomb's law. We assume the static and dynamic coefficients of friction are equal.

- The system is quasi-static: inertial and impact forces are negligible.

Brost assumes that the initial object orientation falls within some known interval of angles, that the coefficient of friction is known to fall in some known interval, and that the angle of finger motion is controlled to within known tolerances. These assumptions result in a two-parameter family of actions—only the finger orientation, relative to the object, and the direction of finger motions, measured as an angle relative to one of the finger's faces, are necessary to predict the object's motion. Brost's analysis leads to simple diagrams, partitioning the two-parameter family of possible actions into equivalence classes that will rotate the object to a completely determined orientation (see Figure 8).

We will extend Brost's results in two ways. First, we have to extend the planning from a single action to sequences of actions. Second, we have to model the sensory operations and incorporate them in the planning. To simplify the constructions we will assume that the coefficient of friction is known exactly, and that the finger motions can be controlled perfectly. To incorporate Brost's methods dealing with these errors would distract us from our main goal, which is to incorporate sensor-based strategies.

To plan sequences of squeezes, we have to represent sets of orientations more general than Brost's intervals. For example, let the initial orientation of a rectangle be completely unconstrained, and consider the orientations possible after one squeeze, represented as a set of points on the unit circle. Typically, there will be four isolated points, corresponding to the four aligned orientations of the rectangle, and four intervals, corresponding to four possible cocked configurations. We will model the set of possible orientations by a finite set of intervals on the unit circle, including singular intervals.

In considering sequences, rather than isolated squeezes, we introduce another complication. Brost's diagrams, such as the diagram of Figure 8, identified regions that would rotate the object to a single determined orientation. However, we have to analyze and identify regions of weaker operations, which do not orient the object by themselves, but which might be useful in a sequence. Figure 9 shows a diagram that is similar to Brost's diagram and is for the most part derived from Brost's analysis, but which identifies all distinct operations, not just those that orient the object completely and immediately.

In order to reduce the number of choices of actions from a continuum to a finite number, we need to identify entire classes that can be represented

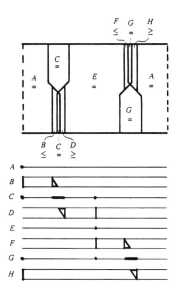

Figure 9: The partitioned space of squeezes.

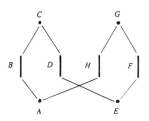

Figure 10: The partial order holding among the squeezes of Figure 9.

as a single choice. Both Brost (1986) and Erdmann and Mason (1986) partitioned their action spaces into a finite number of equivalence classes. In Figure 9 regions A, C, G and E are equivalence classes, i.e. every action gives the same result and can be represented by a single node apiece. Regions B, D, F and H illustrate a refinement on the use of equivalence classes. Under certain conditions discussed later, we can prune nodes that are proper supersets of other nodes. For example, the continuum of nodes arising from actions in region B are all supersets of the nodes arising from regions A and E, and can be pruned.

The regions of Figure 9 are labeled to indicate whether they are equivalence classes, or whether a subset relation holds. Each region labeled "=" is an equivalence class, and each region labeled "$\leq_i$" or "$\geq_i$" is totally ordered. Both of these types of region can be represented by a single node in the graph. Although we have not encountered one yet, there can also be unordered classes of actions, which in principle should not be pruned. There are several approaches to unordered continua of actions; at present we are simply pruning them. Depending on our results, we may sample them. The ordering among the actions of Figure 9 is shown in Figure 10. It is a partial order, with two minimal elements. If we encountered this situation in a search, we would consider the two minimal actions only.

This leaves us with the problem of modelling sensory operations. We assume that the finger separation sensor measures the distance between the fingers with a tolerance of ± 1 mm.[2] To interpret such data, consider the typical construction of Figure 11, showing finger separation as a function of object orientation. For a measured finger separation of d, the true finger separation lies in an interval $[d - 1, d + 1]$ mm, and the feasible

---

[2]The sensor is implemented by a Sony Magnascale position transducer that is part of the Lord hand. The real sensor has micron resolution, and will no doubt have accuracy much better than ± 1 mm.

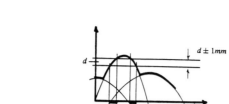

Figure 11: For the triangle, finger separation as a function of object orientation.

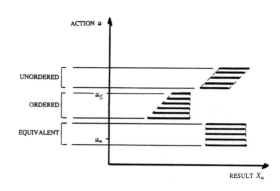

Figure 12: Equivalent, ordered, and unordered continua of actions.

object orientations are obtained by inverting the function shown in the diagram.

During the planning stage, this sensory model leads to an infinite branching factor, and needs to be amended. We will divide the sensor range into m equal intervals, and will ignore any information beyond this coarse sampling of the sensory data. Other possible approaches are discussed later in the paper.

At the time of this writing, we have implemented the computation that predicts the outcome of a tilting operation, but not the sensory modeling component.

6   Continua of actions and sensor operations

A key property of task graphs is to have a finite branching factor, and, in practice, this branching factor should be as small as possible. Obviously, a finite branching factor occurs when the sensor data space D and the action space U are finite. A finite branching factor is also obtained when the task state space X is finite, since there are only a finite number of possible search nodes. Even when the sensor space, action space, and state space are all continuous, it may be possible to obtain small finite branching factors. The key method is to define a *dominance* relation among alternative actions. The dominance relation is defined as follows: for a given search node X_i, we say that an action u dominates an action v, $u \leq_i v$, iff $a(u, X_i) \subseteq a(v, X_i)$. If there is a finite set of actions that dominate the entire class of actions U, then we have a finite branching factor at node X_i.

Figure 12 illustrates different types of dominance relations among a continuum of actions, for a given search node X_i. For each action u, we have plotted the corresponding result X_u. In this case, the action space U falls into three continua, one comprised of equivalent actions, one with the actions ordered, and one with the actions unordered. We can choose any action from the class of equivalent actions, and we can choose the minimal action from the ordered actions, but each action in the unordered continuum is different, and potentially useful.

Although we have had no occasion to use it, a similar construction exists for alternative sensory events, with the sense of the relation reversed. From a node X_i, we will say that sensory datum d dominates sensory datum e iff $s^{-1}(d) \cap X_i \supseteq s^{-1}(e) \cap X_i$, written $d \geq_i e$. The reason for the reversed sense is that we are dealing with the opponent's move. In the case of action, we can choose the best, i.e. most specific outcome. In the case of sensing, we must anticipate the worst, i.e. most ambiguous outcome. For action, we seek a finite set of minimal nodes. For sensing, we seek a finite set of maximal nodes.

It is evident that pruning away dominated nodes does not affect the existence of a solution sub-graph. Suppose we are contemplating two different actions u and v from a given node, with results X_u and X_v, and suppose that $u \leq_i v$, i.e. $X_u \subseteq X_v$. The relation between the two nodes is that X_u is *more specific* than X_v, i.e. the robot has *more information* at node X_u. If there is a plan starting from X_v, then there is also a plan, indeed, the

same plan, starting from the more specific node X_u. Hence, pruning X_v will not affect the existence of a plan.

A more difficult question is whether pruning a dominated node affects the search for, rather than the existence of, a solution sub-graph. We require our search procedure to have the following property:

> If a search from node X_v succeeds, and if $X_u \subset X_v$, then a search from node X_u will also succeed.

I.e., we require that our planner cannot be foiled by giving it more specific pre-conditions. We refer to this property as "pre-condition monotonicity"—the scope of the planner is monotonic non-decreasing as the pre-conditions become more specific.

Pre-condition monotonicity may seem to be a property that any respectable planner would have, but it is not as trivial a property as it may seem. Exhaustive breadth-first search, pruning dominated nodes, would seem to have this property, but not if an unordered continuum of nodes occurs. Suppose state A leads to a continuum of result states, and suppose state B leads to the union taken over this continuum, no matter which action is applied. Suppose that a solution is easily found from the union. Starting from node $\{A, B\}$, the search would obtain a single node, the union of the continuum, and would proceed easily to a solution. Starting from node $\{A\}$, however, the search would obtain the continuum, and would never converge on the solution.

The searches implemented for the tray-tilting and squeezing domains depart from the ideal exhaustive search, by neglecting certain nodes, which we have been referring to as "confusing nodes". There are four different situations that give rise to confusing nodes:

- Due to the possibility of inconsistencies in Newtonian mechanics with Coulomb friction and rigid bodies, we may someday generate a null node. By definition, the empty set is a subset of all sets, hence the null sequence satisfies any goal, and pre-condition monotonicity holds. There is a paradox, though, because this reasoning suggests that a planner should steer the task state toward inconsistencies in Newton+Coulomb+rigid body mechanics. The philosophical difficulties apply not only to nodes that have links to the null node, but to supersets of nodes (other than the null node) that have links to the null node. Presumably our theory doesn't tell us all possible outcomes, in certain degenerate situations. (Either that, or there are states of the physical world that truly have no possible outcomes, which should surely be avoided at all costs.) We ought to avoid situations where our theory *might* be deficient, not just situations where our theory is *certain* to be deficient.

- Our representation of the tray-tilting task state requires that all possible configurations at a node have contact with a common wall. If an action would lead to a *multi-wall node* that violates this restriction, the node is labeled "confusing," and pruned. A multi-wall node is more ambiguous than its single-wall subset nodes. If an initial node leads to a multi-wall result, a more ambiguous initial node leads to a more ambiguous multi-wall result, so pre-condition monotonicity seems to hold.

- The tray-tilting planner avoids sliding an object into the center of the tray, losing all contacts. If a sequence of actions leads from an initial node to a no-contact node, the same will occur starting from a more ambiguous initial node. Pre-condition monotonicity seems to hold.

- In the squeezing domain, we prune all the nodes in an unordered continuum of actions. The same example we constructed above, to illustrate the limitations of exhaustive breadth-first search, can also be applied to show that a search that prunes the nodes of an unordered continuum does not satisfy pre-condition monotonicity.

This leaves us in an interesting position. We are justified in pruning dominated nodes, as long as the pruning in every instance produces a finite branching factor. If an un-pruneable continuum arises at any point during a search, our earlier prunings might have prevented us from finding a solution. At this point, variant search strategies might be considered, but we have not pursued them yet.

Action and sensing continua are important in many problems. As an extreme example, consider the *shooting gallery problem*: a point bear, either alive or dead, is at some location on the real line. A sensor tells the exact location of the bear, and an action (shooting), given the exact location of the bear, changes the state from alive to dead. The possible initial states are any live state, and the goal state is any dead state. The solution is obvious: look and shoot, aiming the gun at the location returned by the sensor. Unfortunately, following the initial sensory operation we obtain a completely unordered continuum of nodes. Further, we know that this continuum is not full of superfluous nodes—pruning of any nodes in the continuum would lead to an incorrect plans. A number of approaches suggest themselves.

One approach is to allow nodes in the search that do not correspond to a definite set of states, but rather correspond to some undetermined set of states, presumably using symbolic descriptions depending on one or more parameters. We would have a two-step plan: locate the bear, then shoot at the bear's location. The node between the two steps would represent the state of the execution-time model, but with a parameter, representing the bear's location, that would be resolved at execution time, rather than at planning time. Similarly, the shooting action would be expressed in terms of the parameter.

The introduction of such symbolic descriptions into plan graphs corresponds to the introduction of variables into robot programs, and has been studied by Taylor (1976) and Brooks (1982). In our example, the sensing operation would set a runtime variable modelling the bear's position, which would then be passed as a parameter to the gunlaying function. More generally, we must augment our planning states to encode both the *locus* of the bear, (i.e., the set of places it may be at plan execution time) and the *determination* of the bear (i.e., how accurately the runtime variables will model its true location). Within this paradigm, sensing actions modify the determination attributes of planning states and manipulation actions modify both locus and determination attributes. This interrelationship becomes clearer if we consider the *extended shooting gallery problem* in which "looking" returns a short interval of positions in which the bear might be, and the bear will be killed if and only if the gun's aiming point is accurate within some (other) specified interval. The initial locus of the bear is some (long) interval on the real line. In the absence of other information, the determination is the same interval. Looking leaves the bear locus unchanged but reduces the determination interval to that of the sensor. If this interval is short enough, then a single point-and-shoot strategy will suffice, if we can verify that all points in the bear locus are within range of the gun. Otherwise, it will be necessary to fire several shots to cover the determination interval or to use some other actions ("beating the bush") to drive the bear into range. Further complexities

arise if the bear is not sedentary, so that shooting and missing may cause him to run away from the shot, thus restricting the locus but possibly lengthening the determination interval.

A more realistic example is the squeeze-grasping problem. Measurements of finger separation lead to unordered continua, which might be more appropriately addressed with program variables. The straightforward approach is to measure the finger separation and use an inverse trigonometric function to determine the possible orientations. If an unambiguous answer is obtained, the hand can simply be rotated to the correct orientation. An ambiguous answer might still require search to further reduce the possible orientations.

A second approach to the shooting-gallery problem is to redefine our actions. We could wrap up the look and shoot sequence by defining a single action, called "point the gun at the bear." In fact, we have done precisely the same thing in our definitions of the tray-tilting and squeeze-grasping domains. In reality, our actions are implemented using sensory data from joint encoders. The servos hide their sensory data from our planner. In effect, this is equivalent to the idea of using a symbolic description of the entire continuum of nodes, but with the hard part done off-line in the definition of the problem.

A third approach is to pursue a more interactive, less contemplative approach to manipulation. If the robot were to just take a look, and then make a plan, the problem is trivial. Sensing is good during execution, and for the same reasons is good during planning: it eliminates lots of states. What isn't clear is why the robot decides to take a look—unless there is a plan at a more abstract level.

The fourth and simplest approach to continua, besides the option of just pruning them, is to sample. This describes a wide variety of search strategies, corresponding to the large variety of different ways of mapping an infinite set into a finite set. Some examples are:

- Ignore the information, and construct a node that is the union over all nodes in the continuum. For a continuum of actions, this means applying any action, and forgetting which one was applied! For a continuum of sensing, the original node is obtained, and is equivalent to doing nothing.

- Fixed resolution sampling. The sensor range or action space is divided into a finite number of regions. For a sensing continuum, the result nodes must be constructed by taking the union over each region. For an action continuum, any action from the region could be selected.

- Variable resolution sampling. The sensor range or action space is first divided into a finite number of regions, but at a later point of the search may be divided into smaller regions.

A useful view of the variable resolution approach is that we begin by using the first bit of the sensor datum (or action), and, if not successful, we try again with the second bit, and so forth. This still allows many different sampling approaches, corresponding to the infinity of possible binary encodings of the sensor range or action space.

7 Stochastic models

There is one extension of our work which might be very instructive. So far, we represent uncertainty in task state by a set of possible tasks. If we introduce probability distributions, we may be able to plan strategies more effectively. More importantly, we may be able to quantify and compare the effectiveness of different manipulation and sensing techniques in solving a task. We will briefly sketch the extension.

To begin, we require an a priori probability distribution, rather than just an initial set of possible states. The origin of the a priori distribution is context dependent, but in many cases we would probably assume a uniform distribution over our present initial set.

The difficult part is extending the mechanics so that probability distributions are obtained, rather than the set of possible result states. When the mechanics are deterministic, this is straightforward in principle. When the mechanics are non-deterministic, e.g. when a given tilt angle and a completely determined orientation can lead to two different orientations, it will be necessary to assign probabilities to the alternative events. This might be done empirically, it might be founded on analysis of a more detailed model (such as an elastic model of the object in the tray), or it might be hypothesized with no rationale.

The goal criteria could be unchanged, requiring that a goal be achieved with complete uncertainty. Or, if desired, goal satisfaction might be modified to allow specified confidence levels, e.g. a strategy represents a solution if it will orient the object with probability 0.99. Different objective criteria are possible for choosing among alternative solution strategies. Instead of our present minimum worst-case number of operations, we might consider minimizing the expected number of operations.

The chief attraction of this approach is that it allows us to quantify the uncertainty at a node, and to quantify the effect of an action or sensory operation. For each node we would compute an entropy to measure the uncertainty, and for each link we would compute the change in entropy, measuring in bits the reduction (if any) of uncertainty. (See Sanderson (1984) for the use of entropy in robotic assembly.) We would then be in a position to answer such questions as, "how much information does a tilt operation give me?" and "how many bits am I *really* getting from my sensor?"

8   Extensions to identification and shape uncertainty

Our approach of planning is readily extended to problems in object identification and shape uncertainty. We simply extend the task state space X to incorporate the additional variables. A successful search of the graph would result in a sequence of actions and sensor operations terminating at some some singleton node, implying a completely determined object in a completely determined location. For instance, Erdmann and Mason (1986) considered the problem of an Allen wrench in the tilting tray, with its reflection unknown. The two reflections correspond to two different shapes in the plane: a J wrench and an L wrench. If we augment the task state variable a binary state variable, taking on either of the values J or L to indicate the wrench's reflection state, our planner can immediately be applied to determine which type of wrench is present, as well as its location in the tray. The construction is equivalent to Donald's (1986) definition of "generalized configuration-space" to include variables describing possible shape variations.

We can also deal with problems in "configurable" sensors, which are in principle no different from the problems we have already considered. For example, suppose that our tilting-tray's light beam can be moved closer to or further from the wall on command. The task state space X would be augmented with a variable describing the light beam position, which could then be selected to provide the most information.

There are some interesting variations on this. If we hypothesize that sensor re-configurations are applicable only as the first motion, we have a sensor design problem. For any given object, the graph search will choose a sensor location and the orientation program. Similarly, we can pose sensor calibration problems, asking the robot to resolve uncertainty in the sensor model. Suppose the light beam's position is fixed, but unknown. We augment the task state with a variable that reflects the sensor's position, and proceed as before. During the course of execution of the plan, the robot would simultaneously deduce the sensor location and the object orientation.

9   Conclusion

The paradigm of treating robot planning as a game with nature generalizes readily and provides a very powerful framework for reasoning about robot task planning. Our experience with the example problems shows that this approach can be applied fruitfully to real task domains, not just toy problems. For more complex domains the introduction of symbolic relationships and explicit representation of uncertainty may be necessary. We are also interested in exploring extensions to stochastic models, identification, and calibration problems.

Acknowledgements

We would like to thank Randy Brost and Mike Erdmann, who allowed us to use the code from their earlier work, and contributed to the present work through numerous discussions. The ongoing experimental work depends heavily on contributions from Tom Wood and Dan Christian. We would also like to thank the Lord Corporation, who donated the instrumented gripper system, and the System Development Foundation and National Science Foundation, who provided support for Goldberg and Mason.

References

R. A. Brooks. 1982. Symbolic error analysis and robot planning. *Int J Robotics Research*, v5 n1, pp 29–68.

R. C. Brost. 1986. Automatic grasp planning in the presence of uncertainty. *Proceedings, 1986 IEEE Int Conf on Robotics and Automation*, San Francisco.

S. J. Buckley. 1987. Planning and teaching compliant motion strategies. Ph.D. thesis, MIT Department of Electrical Engineering and Computer Science.

B. R. Donald. 1986. Robot motion planning with uncertainty in the geometric models of the robot environment: a formal framework for error detection and recovery. *Proceedings, 1986 IEEE Int Conf on Robotics and Automation*, San Francisco.

R. E. Ellis. 1987. Acquiring tactile data for the recognition of planar objects. *Proceedings, 1987 IEEE Int Conf Robotics and Automation*. Raleigh, NC.

M. A. Erdmann. 1984. On motion planning with uncertainty. MIT Artificial Intelligence Laboratory, AI-TR-810.

M. A. Erdmann. 1986. Using backprojections for fine motion planning with uncertainty. *Int J Robotics Research*, v5 n1, pp. 19–45.

M. A. Erdmann and M. T. Mason. 1986. An exploration of sensorless manipulation. *Proceedings, 1986 IEEE Int Conf on Robotics and Automation*, San Francisco.

W. E. L. Grimson and T. Lozano-Pérez. 1984. Model-based recognition and localization from sparse range or tactile data. *Int J Robotics Research*, v3 n3, pp. 3–35.

W. E. L. Grimson. 1986. Sensing strategies for disambiguating among multiple objects in known poses. *IEEE J Robotics and Automation*, v2 n4, pp. 197–213.

D. D. Grossman and M. W. Blasgen. 1975. Orienting mechanical parts by computer-controlled manipulator. *IEEE Transactions on Systems, Man, and Cybernetics*, vSMC-5 n5.

P. Lötstedt. 1981. Coulomb friction in two-dimensional rigid body systems. *Zeitschrift fur Angewandte Mathematik un Mechanik*, v61 n12 pp. 605–615.

T. Lozano-Pérez, M. T. Mason, and R. H. Taylor. 1984. Automatic synthesis of fine-motion strategies for robots. *Int J Robotics Research*, v3 n1, pp 3–24.

M. Mani and W. R. D. Wilson. A programmable orienting system for flat parts. *Proceedings, NAMRI XIII.* Berkeley, CA.

M. T. Mason. 1984. Automatic planning of fine-motions: correctness and completeness. *Proceedings, IEEE Int Conf Robotics,* Atlanta.

M. T. Mason. 1986. Mechanics and planning of manipulator pushing operations. *Int J Robotics Research,* v5 n3, pp. 53–71.

M. T. Mason and Y. Wang. 1987. On the inconsistency of rigid-body frictional planar mechanics. CMU-CS-87-130. Computer Science Department, Carnegie-Mellon University.

M. A. Peshkin. 1985. The motion of a pushed, sliding object (part 1: sliding friction and part 2: contact friction). CMU-RI-TR-85-18, Robotics Institute, Carnegie-Mellon University.

A. C. Sanderson. 1984. Parts entropy methods for robotic assembly system design. *Proceedings, Int Conf Robotics.* IEEE Computer Society, Atlanta, GA.

R. H. Taylor. 1976. A synthesis of manipulator control programs from task-level specifications. Stanford Artificial Intelligence Laboratory AIM-282.

Dealing with Time in Planning and Execution Monitoring

Malik Ghallab, Rachid Alami, Raja Chatila

LAAS-CNRS, 31077 Toulouse cedex, France

Two generic classes of robotics applications, the structured environment class, and the unstructured environment class, are considered with respect to planning and execution monitoring. The paper analyzes the common and distinct requirements in these 2 classes for representing time and dealing with time and real-time in planning and execution monitoring tasks. An original approach is proposed. It is base on a hierarchical representation of temporal relations between goals, events, actions and their effects, together with an efficient management of the time lattice. This approach is developed in the context of an experimental project: a flexible assembly cell.

1 Introduction

Robotics researches focus usually on one of the two generic classes of robotics applications:

- the structured environment class, and

- the unstructured environment class.

A good paradigm of the first class is that of flexible assembly cells, whereas autonomous mobile robots, for example in public safety applications, are prototype elements of the second class. Although there are some applications that fall in between (e.g. a flexible maintenance and repair cell), these two classes present a significant spectrum of research problems that have to be solved in third generation robots.

There are several common points and differences between the two classes, for example in space representation and geometric reasoning, in control problems, or in perception systems. We will be concerned here solely by planning and execution monitoring aspects involved in these two classes.

The Robotics Group at LAAS has been developing for several years two experimental projects, one in each class: HILARE, a mobile robot [16] [8], and NNS an environment for managing a flexible assembly cell [1] [11]. Two distinct approaches to planning and execution monitoring have been implemented in these two projects. Common points were mainly rule based formalisms and tools, such as production rules compilers. None of our previous approaches was able to represent explicitly and deal with time and real-time at the planning level, and at the action and reaction level.

The first goal of this work was thus to analyze the common and distinct requirements in these 2 generic classes for representing time and dealing with time and real-time in planning and execution monitoring tasks. A subsequent goal was to come up with a satisfactory approach for meeting these requirements, and to apply it to our experimental projects.

This paper reports on our findings and the actual state of the work. The next section analyzes the temporal structures required, surveys known methods, and develops the proposed approach that relies on an original data structure, called an *Indexed Time Table* (**IxTeT**). An *IxTeT* is a hierarchical representation of temporal relations in a plan (relations between goals, events, actions and their effects), together with an efficient management of the time lattice. Section 3 develops and illustrates through an example of realistic complexity

the embodiment of the proposed approach for one of the 2 generic classes considered: the flexible assembly cell environment.

2 Temporal structures for planning and acting

Different types of actions may involve different kind of resources (space, tools, sensors, particular abilities of the robot, programs and computer resources...). But every action involves time. Information describing an action exhibit a rich temporal structure: the time at which the action has been (or will be) considered and decided, when it could be carried out, when it did (or may) start, its duration, when each of its effects held (or will hold), and the various relations (before, during, at the same moment...) between these time points or intervals. Events that take place in a dynamic environment have similarly a temporal structure (except that they are not under the robot control).

Such knowledge is difficult to represent and manage, it lacks precision and certainty, and leads to huge combinatorics. It is however absolutely required if a robot has to act in a dynamic environment coherently and efficiently towards some goal, and to react sensibly and in real-time to external events. Let us analyze the requirements for representing explicitly and reasoning on temporal knowledge in planning and execution monitoring tasks: what we would like to express and do concerning time.

2.1 Temporal knowledge required in planning

Planning for a goal, i.e. deciding in a given situation what to do and when to do it, is a projection over a desirable future. Such projection relies on the knowledge of past and current states of the world, and results from the analysis of several possible futures where goals and expected events have been tentatively set and tried to be met or dealt with through actions. It is thus mainly a reasoning on time: a processing of the temporal structures of goals, actions and events.

Goals: in general they may be given with both relative and absolute time links. The "conjunctive goals" planning problem [7] is just a particular case of the situation where goals are partially ordered. For example: "pack up bolts A and assemble sub-system B then bring back both".

Goals may also be linked by synchronization, overlapping and duration constraints, e.g. "feed parts A and B simultaneously" ; "keep spring A loaded while inserting shock absorber". Similar relations may be used to set goals relatively to expected events, e.g. "heat until but no more than the red point" ; "unload wagon A during its next stop".

Achievement of goals may also be specified with regards to absolute time bounds: "reach location A before sunset" ; "fix the leak or leave area B before end of count-down timer" .

Thus in general a goal corresponds to an interval of time (or a time point) during which a property should hold, and one may need to constrain the length or position of this interval relatively to other goals, events or absolute references.

Actions: they take place during a time span that has a constrained length (duration). Their effects and conditions should be located with respect to this interval. Some effects hold from the beginning of an action, others during it or when the actions ends; indirect effects may lag well behind the action.

A decomposition operator (or a skeleton of plan) may describe a structure of elementary actions together with their relative position in time and their compound effects.

Actions that share resources or are done by the same agent may have additional time constraints that do not result from their elementary description (such as overlapping, disjoining or synchronization relations).

Events and world description: the current state of the world is just a part of what needs to be described in a dynamic environment where changes may result from other causes then the robot own actions.

Past events and states could be important for future decisions. This is the case for events without effects on the present but that may have future results; for example an intermittent failure, or a fixed failure that could have a delayed effect.

Information about the expected future are evidently essential in planning: what will or may happen in the environment if the robot does not act. This concerns:

- **scheduled events:** bound to happen at known time (relative or absolute); e.g. "workshop garbage is collected at 07:00" ; "feeding cart comes every 20 minutes".

- **conditional events:** will happen when some conditions are met (immediately or after a delay); e.g. "overflow of a bin or storage place at some threshold", "failure in computers room cooling equipment, if not fixed, will results approximately 1 hour later in an automatic shut down of all computers".

A robot may plan to act in order to prevent some expected events (the above shut down). It may also plan to take profit from their known effects to reach its goals, thus synchronizing its actions with world changes. Processes that take place in the environment may be considered just like events, except that they have durations that could be constrained.

In summary the various knowledges required as input by a planner, i.e. goals, actions, events and world properties, have time intervals that can be constrained in duration, are related to each others and to absolute references.

The output of a planner should be a conditional plan: several sets of actions, temporally structured, and whose projected effects achieve the given goals and their temporal constraints, taking into account current and past states of the environment together with the expected events. This conditional plan should be generated together with an execution model that specifies:

- the conditions and rules that will be evaluated at execution time to resolve non deterministic choices,

- the properties to be monitored for checking direct or indirect effects of actions,

- the sensorial informations to focus attention on in order to detect expected events.

The corresponding temporal knowledge would be: when and for how long checking, monitoring and focusing should be done. The plan execution model should also detail synchronization steps and other critical phases, taking into account the real duration of actions, delays of their effects, length of processes...

As it will be argued and illustrated later, the differences between a structured environment planner and an unstructured one cannot be grasped into a unified approach unless planning is considered as a hierarchical process that is pursued deeper opportunistically as conditions (knowledge, time for planning...) permit or require.

2.2 Time in Execution Monitoring

Execution monitoring is used here in a broader sense than the restricted literal interpretation. In fact we are interested in most decision making aspects related to acting and reacting.

Acting requires necessarily a plan. There is however a large overlapping between planning and acting. Plans need refinement at execution time: an action considered elementary at planning level may require at execution level a further decomposition chosen such that it fits the current situation. Conditional plans involve choices between alternatives, eventually only one of which (the most likely one) has been fully pursued at planning time but another one may need to be developed and resubmitted to the planner at execution time. Unexpected events may require partial modification or rejection of current plan. Even current goals may have to be discarded or postponed for more urgent ones.

Tasks devoted to a robot execution monitor are thus: monitoring, keeping track of the state of achievement of current plan, refining adequately actions and implementing them, chosing among alternatives, focusing the attention of sensory systems, deciding about short terms reactions to unexpected events. Those tasks involve mainly 2 temporal aspects: how one keeps track and defines permanently the present time, and how one deals with real-time.

The present is defined relatively to the projected future. It evolves normally as planned, or may "jump" backward in the plan, or forward, or even out of the plan. The advance of time is discontinuous and driven by asynchronous events (although a robot may have a clock that gives the absolute time). Each expected event when observed instantiate a particular future: if P and Q are expected next, Q happening before P reduces uncertainty for what should come later. Observing the occurrence of an event expected much later may change locally or significantly the rest of the plan, e.g. if it was to result from a forthcoming action, the purpose of this action has to be reconsidered. A "positive" event (forward jump in the plan) may achieve directly part of the goals, e.g. a motor that resumes operations while the robot is in its way to reach it for repair. On the opposite a "negative" event (backward jump) may cancel the effects of a previous actions and make them necessary again or show them ineffective and require another plan.

The real-time requirement is mainly due to the dynamic feature of the environment, i.e. to unexpected changes and events that happen asynchronously, at a speed not under the robot control, but that require from it adequate reactions. Such events should be perceived, identified, and at least partially understood before a decision about how to react can be taken. We are talking here about unexpected events that the robot knows about, and can deal with.

To perceive and identify an unexpected event a robot should be looking for its eventual happening. This awareness or focus of attention relies on execution monitoring: critical actions or phases of a plan should trigger particular monitorings. The real-time reaction to an event should correspond to a set of actions hierarchically ordered by response time, e.g. with the following 3 levels:

- an immediate reflex action: most of the time a direct mapping from the event identification;

- a short term adaptation to the new situation: to permit full assessment, goals evaluation and replanning;

- a long term reaction according to the new plan

For example: a fast autonomous vehicle faces a closed path

- reflex: it brakes to avoid collision

- short term adaptation: it parks safely and replan

- long term reaction: it takes another itinerary (this can overlap with the previous level).

2.3   Time in structured and in unstructured environment applications

A scenario for a structured environment application is that of a multisensory, multi-arm, flexible cell for robotics assembly that has to carry out the same task for a short time (few days) with the maximum degree of robustness, error recovery and efficiency (see detail in section 3.1)

A scenario for an unstructured environment application is that of mobile robot working in a hazardous area that is required to go to some place, to find and fix a leak, or to leave that place before an automatic shut down.

The following table sketches the main differences of interest to us between this two classes:

	structured	unstructured
- variability of the environment	low	high
- variability of goals	low	high
- degree of knowledge modelization and programming	high	low
- degree of autonomy	low	high
- degree of parallelism	high	low

How time is involved in this two classes of applications ?

Structured environment:

- off-line tasks : time is involved only at the reasoning level

- on-line tasks :

  -each agent in this distributed multi-agent system has the same share of time (other resources are shared differently);

  - at a macroscopic level time is seen as periodic (repetition of the task);

  - time has to be optimized

Unstructured environment:

- there are almost no off-line tasks (except high level learning), most planning has to be done in real-time;

- there are more constraints on a unique agent, less parallelism and almost no repetitive tasks

- a clock giving the absolute time is required

These differences have several consequences for planning and execution monitoring. In the structured case most of the planning can be done off-line. Giving the a priori knowledge about the environment and its low variability, one may aim for a conditional plan, or a scheme of plans, that foresees a large number of possible futures, and organize this set of plans into a detailed execution model.

In the unstructured case a detailed plan, even if it can be generated, would be useless (not achievable). The task at hand could be decomposed into a plan skeleton that specifies the main subgoals, constraints and choices involved in this task. Further refinements will be carried out at execution time.

Planning being done on-line in the unstructured case, it is just like any other action: it has a duration (unknown, but constrained) and overlaps with other actions. As time permit, planning can be pursued into deeper levels of detail, or stopped at just a sketchy skeleton together with the first action required to start the plan. Thus planning should be a hierarchical process. Planning and execution controlling are both involved at action time. Unexpected events that make the plan non achievable are easily checked, those not involved in the plan but that make it obsolete require a limited replanning.

In the structured case the on-line system relies on the execution model to instantiate a particular plan, among the schema of plans, that fit the current situation. No simultaneous use of the off-line planner and the on-line system is required.

2.4   Temporal Knowledge in known Planners and Execution Monitors

Now that we have freely prospected what knowledge we would like to express and what should be done with it, let us briefly survey what

can be done with known planning and execution monitoring technics.

Situation calculus and state-space representations: The paradigm here is STRIPS [13]. There is no explicit representation of time in such systems, just a linear sequence of states. Actions are modeled by a triple <pre-conditions, delete-list, add-list>. They do not have a duration, and their effects take place in a single instantaneous transition from state to state. The goal is a single state. No coming event can be taken into account. The world is assumed to be static but of the only actions planned for (thus there is no real time).

Some discrepancy with planned states can however be taken into account at execution time. Execution monitoring relies on the Triangle Table method [12]. A Triangle Table is a data structure that summarizes all conditions and effects of a sequences of STRIPS-like actions and their relationships. The "kernel" of the table defines what has been consistently achieved so far. If permanently computed at execution time it will enable to locate the present state of the world in the plan and to inform the execution monitor about what to do next [19] and [20]. Replanning will be required if the kernel is empty.

Procedural or task networks: They have been developed in NOAH [21] and NONLIN [23]. Planning is a hierarchical process based on task decomposition. For efficiency reasons and in order to avoid unnecessary constraints and backtrackings ("early commitment") concurrent sub-tasks are considered. A decomposition is a partial order of actions and sub-tasks to be achieved by further decomposition. Ordering constraints are later on added by a critical assessment of the network (if not possible a backtracking is performed). The planner's output is thus a partial order of instantaneous actions, opportunistically ordered at execution time.

Windows and durations: They are temporal concepts used in DEVISER [25] to extend the task network approach. A window is one or 2 numerical bounds on a forthcoming time point. Goals are constrained relatively to absolute references, e.g. (goals ((window between 10 50) (duration 1000)) (P) (Q)) requests that properties

P and Q should be achieved simultaneously sometime between t=10 and t'=50, and should hold for at least 1000 time units. Actions are represented by the usual triples <pre-conditions, del, add> in addition to a fixed duration. All effects take place at the end of an action. Unconditional events scheduled at times bounded by known windows can be expressed. Planning is performed as in NONLIN by node decomposition, this is done in addition to a propagation of numerical inequalities along the task network, that constrain further allowed windows and may lead to backtracking. The planner's output is similar to a PERT chart.

Thus DEVISER represents time as points, bounds and values on the real axis, that are processed only when given numerical values. No relative relationships (between goals, events, actions and their effects) are allowed, neither are conditional events.

Temporal logic of intervals: It has been developed in [2] and [4], and proposed for planning in [3]. It is a general world model where each assertion is temporally qualified by a symbolic interval over which it holds. An interval is related to another one by a temporal relation or a disjunction of (mutually exclusive) relations, such as: during, start, overlap. Each interval is represented as a node in a complete graph whose consistency is maintained by transitive closure propagation, e.g. adding "A overlaps or meets B" propagates to all other intervals related to A and B, thus adding new constraints that propagate at their turn... eventually leading to a contradiction. Past and current properties of the world are directly expressed in this temporal graph. Even non temporal properties are represented as quantified expressions on intervals.

Future events are temporally related to the conditions that trigger them. Goals and their relationships appear like expected events except that they should result from actions to be added in the graph.

An action is also an interval temporally linked to the intervals of its conditions and effects intervals, e.g.

```
"if action STACK(x,y) occurs over interval I-stack then
   I-stack finishes the interval I-clear-y over which
CLEAR(y) holds, and
   I-stack meets the interval I-on-xy over which
ON(x, y) holds, and
   I-stack is during the interval I-clear-x over which
CLEAR(x) holds".
```

The planner's output is a consistent temporal graph that includes the one given as input, and where every goal results from (has been causally explained by) the effects of planned actions.

This approach has some nice features: time is explicitly dealt with at the symbolic level, general qualitative relations can be expressed, intervals are very flexible (they are implicitly stretched or moved to allow insertion of other actions as planning progresses), synchronized, overlapping and parallel actions can be generated.

But the temporal logic of interval has also several drawbacks and restrictions:

- at the knowledge representation level: it is a strictly relative model that does not allows scheduled dates, deadlines, durations, or absolute delays (thus a solution given by this approach may not be feasible);

- at the programmer's level: a large number of intervals have to be explicited and described;

- at the planning level: the plan output is non conditional, i.e. it is a single projected future of what will happen if every thing goes well;

- at the problem solving level: the homogeneous representation of all knowledge as relations on temporal intervals leads to a very large graph, the management of which is an exponential process (that also requires a vast amount of memory); this does

not reduce the usual complexity of planning (backtracking is still required), thus making the practicality of the approach questionable.

A recent paper [22] unifies that approach with that of [18] into a more rigorous theory (based on time points instead of intervals). It formalizes clearly the syntax and semantics of formulas in this temporal logic. However it does not address the above mentioned problems.

2.5   The Indexed Time Table approach to Planning and Execution Monitoring

This section introduces a knowledge representation formalism and structure, called an *Indexed Time Table* (**IxTeT**) that will enable us to express absolute and relative temporal relations between properties, events, goals and actions. It will be argued through simple examples and informal algorithms that the proposed representation is a promising approach towards filling the requirements previously set for planning and execution monitoring.

2.5.1   A formalism for actions, goals and events

We need to express intervals and time points, together with their relationships:

- qualitative relations between 2 intervals: before, meet, overlap, start, during, end, equal, and their inverses (after, is-met-by... see [2]):

- qualitative relations between an interval and a time point: before, during, start-at, end-at, after. Other relations can be expressed by combining those above, e.g.

  (disjoin A B) is equivalent to
  (or (before A B) (meet A B) (after A B))

  (start-before A T) is equivalent to
  (or (during A T) (end-at A T) (before A T))

- quantitative relations between 2 time points or extremities of intervals, e.g.
  (> (span (beginning Interv1) (termination Interv2))
  (span Interv3))
  Some absolute time references can be used, e.g.
  (clock Value-A), (end Timer-B).

Planning being a hierarchical process, we will rely on decomposition operators to specify the steps required to achieve a task. Such operators will be described as in the following example that defines a 3 actions and 2 pre-conditions operator:

```
(to (achieve (on ?x ?y))
    (when    (on ?x ?z))
    (do    steps  s1 (achieve (clear ?x))
                  s2 (achieve (clear ?y))
                  s3 (pickup ?x ?z)
                  s4 (holdmove ?x (position ?y))
                  s5 (putdown ?x ?y)
           such-that (meet s1 s3)
                     (meet s2 s5)
                     (meet s3 s4)
                     (meet s4 s5)))
```

The "when" field specifies the context of decomposition; the "do" field can be a single action or task, e.g.

```
(to (achieve (clear ?x))
    (when (and (on ?y ?x) (clear ?z)))
    (do   (achieve (on ?y ?z))))
```

Actions and their affects are described independently of decomposition operators. For example:

```
(describe (pickup ?x ?y)
          (effects  met-by (clear ?x)
                    meet   (clear ?y)
                    end    (on ?x ?y))
          (duration 20))

(describe (putdown ?x ?y)
          (effects  met-by (clear ?y)
                    start  (on ?x ?y)
                    meet   (clear ?x))
          (duration 20))
```

A "when" field can be added to specify different effects and durations in various situations. The duration field can be any evaluable expression on the action variables. Quantitative delays can be added to temporal relations between an action and its effects. Note that the preconditions of an action that are not affected by it do not appear in its description: they are subtasks in a decomposition operator. This clean separation between decomposition operators and the description of actions (as in [23]) leads to a modular and powerful formalism (there are different ways to combine a "to" operator with its actions).

Expected events, scheduled or conditional, are expressed by the following operator:

```
(expect event
        (when context)
        (effects temporal-relation1 property1
                 temporal-relationN propertyN))
```

The context in the "when" field can be:

- a scheduled time, e.g. (starts-at (clock 0700)); or

- a conjunction of conditions that trigger the event together with temporal links to it.

A duration field can also be associated to an event.

Finally the required goals are defined by an achieve operator:

```
(achieve goals goal1 absolute-constraint1
               goalN absolute-constraintN
         such-that (temporal-relations between goals)* )
```

Absolute constraints are temporal relations between the required goals and known intervals or time points.

2.5.2   The Indexed Time Table

Temporal relations in the above formalism link implicit intervals; this make the knowledge easier to specify and read. But this knowledge cannot be used unless an internal representation make the corresponding intervals explicit: the same property may have several instances, each one can be true and false at different intervals (e.g. there are 6 instances of (clear ?u) in the above example). Thus an analysis of each decomposition operator and its actions is needed in order to explicit and match consistently the right intervals.

The output of this preprocessing analysis is represented as a time table, called an OTT, that summarizes action positions and truth values for all properties involved in the operator (effects and subgoals) along a sequence of symbolic time points. The time table corresponding to the previous example is given in *Figure 1*. Three contiguous actions, thus 4 time points are needed for this operator. Few simple temporal relations have been propagated to check possible matching of intervals, e.g. effect (clear ?x) of putdown cannot be the same interval as that of (clear ?x) of step s1 otherwise we would have a loop. All logical relations (non temporal) between properties involved in the operator are taken into account, e.g.
$\forall$ x,y (clear ?x) $\longleftrightarrow$ (not (on ?y ?x)). The usual hypothesis for negation by failure for closed world is assumed.

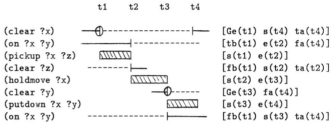

Figure 1

In this table a solid line denotes a true property, a broken line a false property, a rectangle is the interval of an action. End points of intervals are marked whenever known. Those corresponding to subgoals are indicated by circles. A complete symbolic representation of an OTT (given on the right of the figure) needs specification of truth values together with temporal relations. We use the symbols **tb, ta, fb, fa** for respectively true before, true after, false before and false after; **s** stands for start-at (was false, became true), **e** stands for end-at (from true to false), **G** denotes a subgoal. Notice for example how step s1 and the relation (meet s1 s3) is translated in the first row as **Ge(t1)**, whereas the 3rd effect of action **putdown** corresponds for the same row to **[s(t4) ta(t4)]**.

An important property of this structure: it is not allowed to introduce an interval in a row between 2 time points one of which being an **s** or an **e** not prefixed by a **G**, e.g. an new interval for (clear ?x) is not allowed between t1 and t4. The corresponding interval is said to be **non breakable** for that property.

An Indexed Time Table ($IxTeT$) is a structured organization of several OTTs, that is generated by a planner and corresponds to a complete plan together with its time structure. It starts initially from a time table describing current and past properties of the world, expected events and required goals together with their temporal relations. A goal is expanded using an appropriate decomposition operator, its OTT is inserted in the current $IxTeT$. This satisfies one or several pending goals (at least the expanded one), and introduces new subgoals to be expanded later.

The most important and difficult step here is the insertion of an OTT into an $IxTeT$. Time points have to be located with respect to those of the $IxTeT$: subgoals and effects in the OTT should be matched to properties in the $IxTeT$ taking into account and checking several temporal and logical relations.

Let us illustrate some aspects of this process through a simple example (borrowed from [3]) using the above OTT. A 2 arms robot has to permute the first 2 parts of a stack of 3 parts, e.g. starting from

(and (on b a) (on a c)),

we require the un-ordered conjunction of 2 goals:

(and (on a b) (on b c)).

The initial $IxTeT$ is thus (Ist and Last are first and last time points):

```
(on b a) : [tb(Ist) fa(Last)]
(on a c) : [tb(Ist) fa(Last)]
(on a b) : [fb(Ist) Gta(Last)]
(on b c) : [fb(Ist) Gta(Last)]
```

Goal (on b c) is expanded: an instance of the above OTT is simply inserted between time points Ist and Last, giving the sequence (Ist t1 t2 t3 t4 Last). Two interesting rows in the current $IxTeT$ are:

```
(clear b) : [tb(Ist) Ge(t1) s(t4) ta(t4) fa(Last)]
(on b c)  : [fb(Ist) fb(t1) s(t3) ta(Last)]
```

Replacing the goal (on b c) at Gta(Last) in the initial $IxTeT$ by ta(Last), and removing ta(4), makes the interval [t3 Last] non breakable: no other interval for this property can be inserted in it unless a backtracking in this goal decomposition is performed. Similarly subgoal (clear b), when later on expanded, will be immediately satisfied if no other interval for that row is inserted between Ist and t1 (note however that the interval [Ist t1] remains breakable since the goal is still pending).

In the next step goal (on a b) requires insertion of another instance of the same OTT (with time points t'1 through t'4):

- t'1 is characterized by the subgoal (clear a), this property is true in the current $IxTeT$ starting at t2, thus we should have: t'1 after t2 ;

- t'3 requires the subgoal (clear b) that is true either between Ist and t1 (but this will make the previously pending subgoal harder to meet), or after t4, thus : t'3 after t4 ;

- t'2 is not constrained by a subgoal, but it provides the effect (clear c) that is a pending subgoal at t3, thus: t'2 before t3 ;

- t'4 is just constrained to be between t'3 and Last.

Luckily in this example all insertion constraints can be met and lead to a completely ordered sequence of time points. The corresponding $IxTeT$ is given graphically in *Figure 2* (matched intervals have been drawn separately).

Remaining subgoals are immediately satisfied without further expansion. Notice how interactions between overlapping actions have been explicitly and quite simply taken into account (as a mater of comparison, the same example requires the explicit definition of 23 input intervals and propagation of 945 temporal constraints in the approach of [3]).

2.5.3 Planning with an $IxTeT$

The basic principles have been explained above along with the definition of the $IxTeT$. Several essential topics remain however to be developed. Let us go through some of them here.

How one should manage the agenda of pending goals ? The idea is to follow the hierarchy of decomposition: first all goals in the initial $IxTeT$, then those pending from the first level of decomposition, and so on. However if a goal can be immediately satisfied, without decomposition, by making an interval non breakable, we will leave it pending and put it back at the end of the agenda (unless all goals are in the same situation). This avoids constraining unnecessarily the $IxTeT$: a relation such as [tb(t) Ge(t')] is easily checked in the table, and the planner will chose if possible insertions that do not break it, otherwise nothing has been invested yet in decomposing this goal (and no backtracking will be required if it has to be decomposed).

Such strategy solves the classical problem where starting from:

(and (on c a) (clear b)), we require

(and (on c a) (on a b)).

Goal (on c a) will simply stay unexpanded until expansion of (on a b) needs (clear a), that in turn makes expansion of (on c a) necessary.

This strategy also enhances the planner robustness with regards to goals ordering in the agenda.

Another important issue is where in the $IxTeT$ to insert an OTT when there are several alternatives. In addition to the time position of the goal being expanded and to the subgoals and effects of the decomposition operator used, one has also to consider the decomposition context (the "when" field) that may restrict possible insertion points.

A first heuristic here is to leave whenever possible variables of the context non instanciated. This can be done for variables that are required for achieving the OTT subgoals. For example the "to" operator for (clear ?x) can be used with variable ?z non instanciated (but it requires variable ?y). This again avoids unnecessary constraints in the $IxTeT$: remaining variables are opportunistically matched when needed to satisfy a pending subgoal.

A second heuristic in this issue is to introduce only the constraints that may solve pending subgoals. Most of the time this should lead to an $IxTeT$ whose time points are partially but not completely ordered.

The efficient management of this partial order relies on one of the two indexing schemes proposed for the $IxTeT$ approach. Let us introduce an example using the above OTT. Starting from
(and (on a b) (on a d) (clear c)) we require
(and (on b c) (on a b)) . Expansion of the first goal is done as before. The 2nd instance of the OTT for goal (on a b) is however inserted in the current $IxTeT$ with less constraints:

- t'1 requires (clear a) : t'1 is before t2

- t'3 requires (clear b) : t'3 is after t4

- t'2 does not provide any needed effect, its is not constrained by this insertion; neither is t'4. We have thus the following partial order (*Figure 3*):

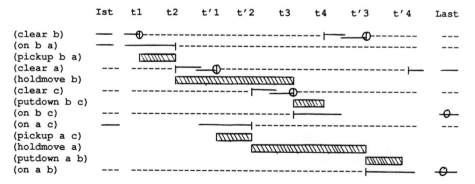

```
          Ist   t1    t2    t'1   t'2   t3    t4    t'3   t'4   Last
(clear b)  ——————⊘— - - - - - - - - - - - -|— —⊘— - - - - -     - - -
(on b a)   ———————————|- - - - - - - - - - - - - - - - - - - -   - - -
(pickup b a)  ——▨▨▨——|
(clear a)  - - -   - - - - - |— —⊘— - - - - - - - - - - - - - -|—  ———
(holdmove b)        ▨▨▨▨▨▨▨▨▨▨▨▨▨▨▨▨▨▨|
(clear c)  - - -   - - - - - - - - - - - -|— —⊘——▨▨▨▨▨▨▨—          - - -
(putdown b c)                            ▨▨▨▨—|
(on b c)   - - -   - - - - - - - - - - - - - - - - - - - - - - -   —⊘
(on a c)   ——————————————————|— - - - - - - - - - - - - - - - -   - - -
(pickup a c)              ——▨▨▨▨—|
(holdmove a)                  ▨▨▨▨▨▨▨▨▨▨▨▨▨▨▨▨▨▨▨—|
(putdown a b)                                     ——▨▨▨▨——|
(on a b)   - - -   - - - - - - - - - - - - - - - - - - - - |—————   —⊘
```

Figure 2

```
Ist ──→ t1 ──→ t2 ──→ t3 ──→ t4 ──→ t'3 ──→ t'4 ──→ Lst
              └──→ t'1 ──→ t'2 ──┘
```

Figure 3

Two interesting rows in the corresponding *IxTeT* (that cannot be drawn graphically) are given bellow:

```
(clear b) : [tb(Ist) Ge(t1) s(t4) Ge(t'3) fa(Lst)]
(clear a) : [fb(Ist) fb(t1) s(t2) Ge(t'1) s(t'4) fa(Lst)]
```

The important property here is, although the *IxTeT* time points are partially ordered, those used in any given row correspond to a complete order. From the point of view of a single property, time is non ambiguously seen as a simple sequence. We know when the property is required to be true or false, when a new interval can be inserted for it, and whether it corresponds to a pending goal that can be readily satisfied or that request expansion.

The algebraic structure of a set of time points in an *IxTeT* is thus a lattice. It can be represented as a directed acyclic graph with a root (Ist) and a sink (Last). Two basic operations have to be performed on this time lattice:

- finding if two points are ordered and their relative position;

- inserting time points and links consistently (i.e. without loops).

The obvious method for both operations relies on path finding, but it is too costly for such a heavy use. The proposed approach relies on a hierarchical indexing scheme.

Let R be any convenient range of numbers (integers or reals) with a conventional Min and Max; i, j, $i_1, \ldots, i_k$ are elements of R. Each time point t in the lattice is given an index: a sequence noted $t(i_1.i_2 \ldots i_k)$, of one or several elements of R. Ist and Last are indexed Ist(Min) and Last(Max). The rest of the lattice is indexed such that if t is immediately before t' (no other point is between t and t') then:

- either $t(i_1. .i_k.j)$ and $t'(i_1. i_k.j')$ are such that $j < j'$ and there is no other index $(i_1. i_k.j'')$ in the lattice with: $j < j'' < j'$ (i.e. t' is the next sibling of t in the index hierarchy) ;

- or $t(i_1. .i_k)$ and $t'(i_1. i_k.j)$ are such that there is no index $i_1..i_k.j'$ with: $Min < j' < j$ (i.e. t' is the first son of t in the hierarchy).

For example we would have (*Figure 4*):

```
Ist ──→ t(1) ──────→ t(2) ──→ t(3) ──→ t(4) ──→ t(5) ...
       └──→ t(1.1) ┬──→ t(1.2) ──────┘↑
                   └──→ t(2.1) ──→ t(2.2) ──┘
```

Figure 4

Indexes as stored as a tree with a pointer from each index to the corresponding time point. A node in the lattice has pointers to its immediate successors.

The relative position of $t(i_1. .i_n)$ and $t'(j_1. .j_m)$ is found as follow:

- if $(n < m)$ and $(i_1. .i_{n-1}) = (j_1. .j_{n-1})$ and $(i_n < j_n)$ then t is before t' (e.g. $t(3.4.5)$ is before $t(3.4.7.2)$; $t(6)$ is before $t(9.1.3)$), in this case t and t' are said to be directly comparable, and we note $t < t'$

- otherwise successor nodes of t are followed along the same level of the indexing hierarchy until a node t'' at a higher level is found:

- if $t'' < t'$ then t is before t'

- if $t' < t''$ then nothing can be said: we restart from t' and try to compare its higher successors to t

- otherwise the path from t'' is pursued higher up until a direct comparison can be made.

If no direct comparison can be made at the highest indexing level up from t, then we try up from t'. If it does not succeed then t and t' are not ordered.

A direct comparison involve few operations (of constant complexity). A path up in the indexing hierarchy is of logarithmic length. Thus it should be a very fast algorithm. The same procedure provides a loop checking test: there is a cycle between t and t' iff t is before t' and t' is before t.

More work is needed to insert time points and links in the lattice while keeping the indexing structure as defined. The main idea is to have nodes in the lattice as high as possible in the indexing hierarchy (to "flatten" up the lattice). For example we may want to insert in the previous lattice (*Figure 4*) a time point t after t(2.2) and before t(1.2). Previously to this insertion we had the path $t(2.2) \longrightarrow t(5)$, after the insertion we would have $t(2.2) \longrightarrow t \longrightarrow t(1.2) \longrightarrow t(4)$. But $t(4) < t(5)$: the insertion adds a constraint into the lattice that has to be taken into account by changing pointers and indexes. Pointer t(2.2) is removed (less constrained), t is indexed t(2.3), t(1.2) is re-indexed t(2.4), thus giving (*Figure 5*):

```
t(1) ──→ t(2) ──────────→ t(3) ──────────→ t(4) ──→ t(5)
 │      └──→ t(2.1) ──→ t(2.2) ──→ t(2.3) ──→ t(2.4) ┘↑
 └──────────→ t(1.1) ──────────────────────────┘↑
```

Figure 5

The general procedure for inserting a link (or a sequence of nodes) between t and t' would be:

- if t' is before t then the link cannot be inserted (it would make a loop);

- if the path up from t goes through a node t'' such that t' is before t'' then the link adds a constraint in the lattice, nodes in the 2 involved pathes and their offsprings have to be re-indexed;

- otherwise we just add the new link or sequence of nodes as offsprings of t up to t' (if $t(i_1. .i_k)$ has already a son node $t''(i_1. .i_k.i_{k+1})$, we just add a dummy node indexed $(i_1. .i_k.i_{Min})$ between them and make it father of the newly inserted nodes).

The complexity of this procedure has not yet been analyzed.

With the time lattice being defined we are now ready to take into account absolute constraints on the duration of actions and position of time points for goals and events. The lattice is an additive graph with durations as positive or null labels on arcs. The maximum cumulative sum of arc labels between t and t', over all existing paths from t to t', corresponds to the minimum required time to go from t to t'. This minimum will eventually be compared to absolute constraints attached to the 2 time points t and t'. A non satisfied constraint will lead to rejecting the faulty path. PERT-like technics such as those implemented in DEVISER [25] will be used to check the consistency of each insertion of an *OTT* into the *IxTeT*. A good processing of the uncertainty and imprecision necessarily attached to such information has however to be added to such technics.

A final point about the structure of an *IxTeT*: its temporal dimension is indexed through the time lattice, it would improve the planner efficiency to also index its second dimension. We would like to find easily the rows to look into and those to be added to an *IxTeT*, while inserting an instance of an *OTT*. We would also need to have all logical relations concerned by those rows, and the rows that will be checked through those relations. The indexing scheme proposed here relies on a unification tree, a structure that results from the compiling of a set of patterns [14].

2.5.4 Execution Monitoring with an *IxTeT*

This topic will be discussed in more detail in the next section, in the context of a flexible assembly cell application. Let us survey briefly here what could be the main benefits for monitoring a plan expressed as an *IxTeT*.

As time advances, the lattice is reduced to an ordered sequence. This is achieved either:

- through an opportunistic choice made by the Execution Monitor, or

- through the occurrence of an event.

For example we just passed time t. In the *IxTeT* t is followed in any order by:

- t', defined as the end of action A synchronized with the beginning of action B; and

- t", defined as the occurrence of a scheduled event.

If t' happens before t", the corresponding relation is propagated through the 2 pathes. Eventually this will add constraints in the lattice, and resolve future choices.

Another issue is when to expect a conditional event: the indexing of the *IxTeT* enables to find easily when a conditional event may occur (its effects have been taken into account at planning level). The observed (or chosen) ordering of time points non previously ordered will enable to tell (or decide) if the conditions triggering the event do or do not hold simultaneously.

How an *IxTeT* can be of any help to reacting to an unexpected event? We assume that such event is relevant to the task at hand but does not require postponing or canceling current goals. The event and its logical consequences are put into the *IxTeT* at the current time. Any contradiction with what was expected is compared to the past and to the previously projected future:

- properties required later for a forthcoming action or goal but that are not true any more (were true initially or resulted from some previous action) should be considered as new subgoals inserted in the rest of the *IxTeT* and decomposed by the planner;

- properties that were planned to hold only later on, as a result of some forthcoming actions, will lead to reconsider the need of such actions and those before them.

Detailed examples will be given in the following section.

3   A Structured Environment Application: The NNS project

In this section, we discuss how the proposed approach could be used to tackle problems of *Task Planning* and *Execution Control* for a project developed at LAAS that represents a structured environment application: the NNS project [5] [6] [10].

The NNS project aims at developing methods and tools for the programming and the robust execution control of complex manipulation tasks to be performed by a multi-robot flexible assembly cell.

Clearly, such a system involves decision-making capabilities available off-line and on-line. The originality of our system lies mainly in the

fact that the *Off-Line System*, instead of producing a "rigid" program, generates a more "flexible" structure called *Task Execution Model* that will be used on-line in order to take into account sensor information, to interpret what happens in the workcell and to react to various asynchronous events *(Figure 6)*.

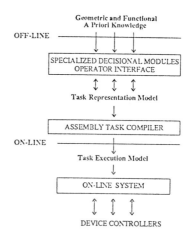

Figure 6: NNS organization and Knowledge Representation

The *Off-Line System* includes various planners based on geometric reasoning in order to structure the space of the workcell, to synthesize the various actions that can be executed [17] [24] and to provide rules for action selection and scheduling [1].

The *On-Line System* is a *Knowledge-Based System* [11]; it uses the *Task Execution Model* in order to completely instanciate and schedule the actions to be performed given the current state of the workcell, as well as to control their execution in a multi-agent environment.

We will restrict ourselves, in the following, to the problem of Action Scheduling and Execution Control.

3.1   Task Modeling

The highest level of abstraction used by our system for an assembly task is modeled as follows: the workcell is supplied with several primary elements and delivers products according to a predefined process.

Example: The assembly task concerns three types of parts:*A*, *B* and *C*. Parts *A* are introduced by the conveyor 1. Parts *B* and *C* are introduced in random order on conveyor 2. The workcell produces sub-assemblies *BA* (*B* on *A*) and *BC* (*B* on *C*). The sub-assembly *BC* must be inspected before unloaded. Defective parts are put in a specific storage.

We introduce three concepts that allow to specify an assembly task at this level of abstraction: the *identity of part*, the *site* and the *posture* of a *part* in a *site*.

The identity of a part corresponds to a specific step in an assembly process (primary part, sub-assembly...)

Example:

- the identity "part A" corresponds to a part of type *A*.

- the identity "?(partA1 partA2 ... partAn)" corresponds to a part of type *A1* or *A2* or .. or *An*. This is an arbitrary notation to represent parts that belong to a class of parts but that are not yet identified. This case may arise after a feeding operation if parts arrive in random order, after an identification operation that does not discriminate completely the identity of a part or after the analysis of a failure that makes the identity of a part doubtful.

A *site* corresponds to a place in a workcell which is intended to hold parts (such as a robot gripper, a storage place on a table or on a conveyor belt...). A symbolic name is attached to each site (*rob1, sto1, conv1*). The parts present in a cell are always in one of its sites. A site contains only one part at a time. Sites may be fixed or may move in a cell. In the case of sites representing conveyors, these sites may be AWAY.

A *part posture* provides a qualitative description of the geometric and dynamic constraints that achieve stable position of a part. On *Figure 7* different postures of part *B* are represented.

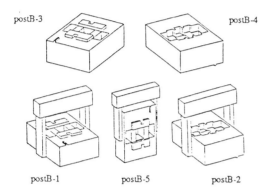

Figure 7 : Different Postures of part B

Each part has a discrete number of possible (and useful) postures. It is limited by the devices and the tools available in a cell and by the set of part postures imposed to perform operations. A number is associated to each part posture: *PostB-1, PostB-2...*

The three basic concepts of *site*, *identity* and *posture* constitute the major ingredients that allow us to specify and to represent an assembly task. The *Task State* is represented by the state of all the sites in the workcell:

$$< TaskState > ::= (< Site >< SiteState >)^*$$

$$< SiteState > ::= < part >:< posture > |\ EMPTY\ |\ AWAY$$

Example: *Figure 8* shows the different sites in a cell and their role in the assembly task introduced earlier.

♠ *cnv1*: conveyor belt for loading parts *B* and *C*; this site is equipped with a camera for part identification and localization;

♠ *cnv2*: conveyor for loading parts *A*;

♠ *cnv3*: conveyor for unloading sub-assemblies *BA* and *BC*;

♠ *garb*: storage where defective parts *BC* (noted *BC-*) are rejected;

♠ *rob1* and *rob2*: robot grippers;

♠ *asm1*: site for the part-mating of *A* and *B*;

♠ *asm2*: site , equipped with a camera, for the part-mating of *B* and *C* and the inspection of the result;

♠ *sto1, sto2, tab1*: storage sites.

Actions are defined as operators that change the *Task State*. An action either modifies the identity of a part present in a site, or transfers

it from one site to another site, changing its posture. There are several action classes that can be represented as follows:

Feeding
$$(site\ AWAY) \mapsto (site\ partX : postX)$$

Inspection
$$(site\ partX : postX) \mapsto \begin{array}{l} (site\ partX^+ : postX^+) \\ or \\ (site\ partX^- : postX^-) \end{array}$$

Part-Mating
$$\begin{array}{l}(site1\ partX : postX_1) \\ (site2\ partY : postY_2)\end{array} \mapsto \begin{array}{l}(site1\ partXY : postXY_3) \\ (site2\ EMPTY)\end{array}$$

Pick or Place
$$\begin{array}{l}(site1\ partX : postX_1) \\ (site2\ EMPTY)\end{array} \mapsto \begin{array}{l}(site1\ EMPTY) \\ (site2\ partX : postX_2)\end{array}$$

3.1.1 Action Planning

As it has been emphasized earlier, a robotics workcell that performs repeatedly over time the same assembly task is an a priori known environment (though very difficult to model and to structure) where most problems - or at least those that need heavy decisional processes - can be addressed off-line. Yet, there remain decisions that must be taken on-line in order to provide a robust behavior and a better efficiency to the system.

For instance, action planning cannot be done completely off-line because of:

- the presence of non-deterministic actions (use of sensor information);

- the occurrence of asynchronous events (failures, random arrival of parts, interactions with the shop level..);

- the difficulty to evaluate precisely the duration of actions particularly in the case of a multi-agent system.

However, it is not useful to have a "complete" and "permanent" planning system on-line, that will, again and again, rediscover interrelations between actions, goals... Such a situation is useless and very time-consuming particularly in the case of a multi-agent system.

For all these reasons, the *Task Execution Model*, produced by the *Off-Line System*, contains what we call a *Task Plan*; it is a scheme of plans that will reduce the planning activity of the *On-Line System*. Note that the planning activity is reduced not suppressed. This is a key issue as it emphasizes an interesting link between *Planning* and *Execution Control*. The *Planner* prepares the decisions using a global knowledge of the task. The *Execution Controller* has a planning activity based on this knowledge; it generates "small plans" in a close interaction with the actual environment.

There exists a first version of the software that implements these ideas. It has been used, with reasonable performance, to program and control a complex assembly task involving 4 types of parts on a two-robot assembly cell equipped with various sensors. The reader may refer to [1] [11] [9] [10].

Our intent here below is to analyze how the temporal structures and the formalisms, presented in section 2, could be used in such a system to overcome some of its limitations by introducing an explicit representation of time in the planning process off-line and on-line.

3.1.2 The Task Plan

The *Task Plan* is a part of the *Task Execution Model*; it is used on-line to determine the set of "admissible" actions that can be performed

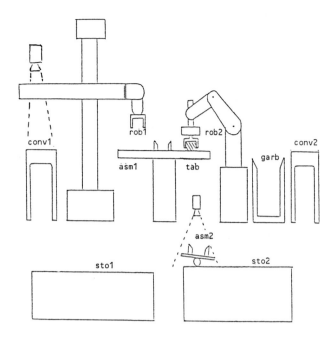

Figure 8: Spatial Organization of a Cell

from any *Task State*. An action is "admissible" if it is feasible from the current *Task State*, relevant (the action is necessary and other actions that are "better" are not feasible) and if the action does not lead to a "deadlock" situation or a situation where the task has to "backtrack".

The *Task Plan* representation is not explicit: the number of possible task states is finite but very important, if we consider that asynchronous events may occur during the execution. The *Task Plan* consists of a set of rules. Each rule represents a condition on the Task State that makes an action admissible. All rules are terminal and made of simple propositional forms without quantified variables. They can be compiled into a decision tree according to the techniques described in [15].

Using temporal relations, it will be possible to analyze the *Task State* at various moments; this will lead to more subtle conditions like: *Action* i *is admissible if the situation* sj *is verified in a "close" future*. We give here an example of a rule corresponding to the *Task Plan* of the assembly task described above.

Example: If a part *A* is stored in *sto1* and there is no expected arrival of another part *A* on *cnv2* for a given duration (*DELTA2 time units*), and if the site *asm1* will be empty in a close future (less than *DELTA1 time units*), then the action 26 of picking part *A* from *sto1* is "admissible" (**at** represents the time at which the action will be executed)

```
(if ((sto1 A:3)
     (rob2 EMPTY)
     (< (span *at* (begin (asm1 EMPTY))) DELTA1)
     (> (span *at* (end (cnv2 AWAY))) DELTA2))
 then
     ((ADMISSIBLE action-26)))
```

Other conditions can be taken into account. For instance, two actions

that make use of the same tool cannot overlap.

The effects of the actions are provided as follows:

```
(describe (pick ?site1 ?site2 ?part ?post1 ?post2)
    (effects
            met-by (?site1 ?part : ?post1)
            met-by (?site2 EMPTY)
            meet   (?site1 EMPTY)
            meet   (?site2 ?part : ?post2)))
```

Note that value of the properties is changed somewhere between the beginning of an action and its end. However, at the level of action planning, the states of the sites are "protected" during all the duration of an action. Lower levels manipulate a more precise description of actions. For example, a Pick action is composed of several steps: gross motion and preparation of the tools, approach motion, grasping operation, disengage motion. The change of state is situated in a small interval - called "uncertainty interval" - where we cannot define what is exactly the state. This description is used by the *Execution Controller* in order to monitor the task state.

Starting from this general description, the *Off-Line System* will instanciate specific description for each action taking into account information such as the effectors to be used, the position of the sites... in order to determine the duration of the action (for some actions, it is possible to do it off-line) or a minimum and a maximum bound of it.

We will show later how all this knowledge is used on-line to produce *Execution Plans* that describes the sequences of actions to be performed with respect to the actual workcell state.

3.1.3   The Task Plan construction or "compilation phase"

The *Assembly Task Compiler* is the last step in the *Off-Line System*. It generates the *Task Execution Model* which contains the *Task Plan*. It performs various processings, like verifying that no information is missing, that there is a way for each part entering the cell to be processed..

For this purpose, a graph representation is built for the assembly task. It describes all the actions that can be performed on parts. This graph represents the possible evolutions of each part independently *(Figure 9)*. Nodes are site states; arcs are oriented and represent actions.

This graph illustrates various difficulties encountered in action planning:

- Problems of parallel execution: several parts, even parts of the same type, may "traverse" the graph at the same time. Various actions can be executed in parallel as we assume a multi-agent system. Some actions cannot be performed simultaneously as they use the same resource (tool, sensor, space region ...)

- Special care must be taken in order to manage appropriately "critical resources" like sites linked to manipulators;

- Temporal relations and estimation of action duration (depending on the context) are clearly very useful in such application; it should be interesting to take into account the fact that a conveyor cannot stay idle more than a specified time...

- It could be also useful to preselect paths for parts, that could be chosen under certain preconditions (normal functioning, periodical arrival of parts...)

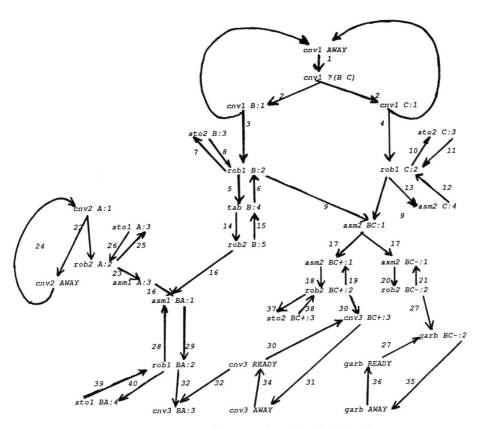

Figure 9: Assembly Task Graph

3.1.4 Execution Control

An *Execution Plan* is a particular set of action sequences - among possible sequences implicitly contained in the *Task Plan* - together with synchronization constraints between these sequences. This plan selection and instanciation will take place at the completion of non deterministic actions, after feeding and unloading actions and when a failure arises that causes a mismatch between the actual state and the state expected in the current *Execution Plan*.

In the current implementation, a new *Execution Plan* is generated as if the cell was not working; its initial state is the state that will be obtained if the the current *Execution Plan* is completely achieved. We would like to proceed more smoothly by taking into account current plan i.e. "merging" a new *Execution Plan* plan with the current one.

An example: In the first situation, the cell activity is stopped (no action is currently performed) and we have the current *Task State*:

$ES0 = (... (cnv B:1) (sto1 A:3) (asm2 C:4) (rob1 EMPTY) (rob2 EMPTY) ...)$

(the two robots are empty, a part *B* is available on the conveyor belt *cnv1*, a part *A* and a part *C* are respectively stored in *sto1* and in *asm2*)

The *Execution Controller* constructs an *IxTeT* (partially) illustrated in *Figure 10a* and *Figure 10b*.

Time points for the beginning and the end of action *i* will be noted $si/j/k$ and $ei/j/k$ where *j* is the number of the *Execution Plan* et *k* is a complementary index (used only in the case when an action appears more than one time in a plan). The time point representing the beginning of the *Execution Plan* number *j* is noted *1st/j*.

The Execution Plan that has been produced contains the sequences: [3-5-14-16-29...], [26-23] and [1-2]. The temporal structure of this plan is given in *Figure 10b*.

Note that:

- In constructing the table after action 3, the *Execution Controller* has chosen action 5 while action 9 was also admissible; this is because of a task-dependent heuristic;

- the set of actions 26-23 could be placed before or after 14; as the action 23 has to be placed before action 16 (rendez-vous for part-mating), the reasonable choice has been made;

- the manipulator linked to *rob1* does nothing between $e(5/0)$ and $s(29/0)$;

- a new planning step is expected after the execution of action 2 (identification of parts provided in random order by conveyor 1); this is represented in *Figure 10a* by an arrow.

The execution begins. Actions 3/0 and 26/0 can be started in parallel. Let us suppose that action 2/0 finishes with the identification of a new part of type B while actions 5/0 and 23/0 are still executing.

If we assume that the planning process is sufficiently fast and that we can estimate a time bound for its duration, then it is possible to consider a "scenario" where a complementary plan is "merged" with the plan under execution. This assumption is reasonable because of the fact that the planning activity of the *Execution Controller* is based on decisions prepared off-line.

The *Execution Controller* would then generate the *IxTeT* presented in *Figure 11a* and *Figure 11b*.

Note that:

- actions 3/1 and 9/1 have been inserted between 5/0 and 29/0;

- two actions will cause a new plan to be constructed; action 2/1 and action 17/1.

A lot of work remains to be done in order to validate the ideas and the mechanisms sketched here. However, let us summarize here below some key issues under investigation. The availability of a temporal structure for plans and of a flexible projection in the future will allow a better control of the cell.

An important issue is to be able to permanently verify the relevance of plans (or sub-plans) under execution. The *Execution Controller* has to decide when to "merge" a new plan with a plan already in execution, when to replan completely... Task dependent heuristics should be prepared off-line in order to allow the *Execution Controller* to evaluate a situation and to react to it efficiently.

References

[1] R. Alami and H. Chochon. Programming of flexible assembly cells: task modeling and system integration. In *IEEE, International Conference on Robotics and Automation, St Louis (USA)*, March 1985.

[2] J. F. Allen. An interval-based representation of temporal knowledge. In *7th IJCAI, Vancouver (Canada)*, August 1981.

[3] J. F. Allen. Planning using a temporal world model. In *8th IJCAI, Karlsruhe (FRG)*, August 1983.

[4] J. F. Allen. Towards a general theory of action and time. *Artificial Intelligence*, 23:123–154, 1984.

[5] ARA. *Journées Annuelles du Programme ARA, Toulouse (France)*. September 1984.

[6] ARA. *Journées Bilan du Programme ARA, Paris (France)*. June 1986.

[7] D. Chapman. Planning for conjunctive goals. *Artificial Intelligence*, 32:333–377, 1987.

[8] R. Chatila. Mobile robot navigation: space modeling and decisional processes. In *Robotics Research 3, Faugeras and Giralt (Eds), MIT Press*, 1986.

[9] H. Chochon. *Programmation de tâches d'assemblage robotisées: modélisation et processus décisionnels.* Thèse de l'Université Paul Sabatier, Toulouse (France), Laboratoire d'Automatique de d'Analyse des Systèmes (C.N.R.S.), November 1986.

[10] H. Chochon and R. Alami. A knowledge-based system for programming and execution control of multi-robot assembly cells. In *'87 International Conference on Advanced Robotics (ICAR), Versailles (France)*, October 1987.

[21] E. D. Sacerdoti. *A Structure for Plans and Behaviour.* Elsevier North-Holland, 1977.

[22] Y. Shoham. Logics in AI: semantical and ontological considerations. *Artificial Intelligence*, 33:89–104, 1987.

[23] A. Tate. Generating project network. In *5th IJCAI*, August 1977.

[24] J. M. Valade. Geometric reasonning and synthesis of assembly trajectory. In *'85 International Conference on Advanced Robotics (ICAR), Tokyo (Japan)*, September 1985.

[25] S. A. Vere. Planning in time: windows and durations for activities and goals. *IEEE Transactions PAMI*, 5(3), May 1983.

[11] H. Chochon and R. Alami. NNS, a knowledge-based on-line system for an assembly workcell. In *IEEE, International Conference on Robotics and Automation, San Fransisco (USA)*, April 1986.

[12] R. E. Fikes, P. Hart, and N. J. Nilsson. Learning and executing generalized robot plans. *Artificial Intelligence*, 3(4), 1972.

[13] R. E. Fikes and N. J. Nilsson. STRIPS: a new approach to the application of theorem proving to problem solving. *Artificial Intelligence*, 2, 1971.

[14] M. Ghallab. Coping with complexity in inference and planning systems. In *Robotics Research 3, Faugeras and Giralt (Eds), MIT Press*, 1986.

[15] M. Ghallab. *Optimisation de processus décisionnels pour la Robotique.* Thèse d'état, Université Paul Sabatier, Laboratoire d'Automatique et d'Analyse des Systèmes (C.N.R.S.), Toulouse (France), October 1982.

[16] G. Giralt, R. P. Sobek, and R. Chatila. A multi-level planning and navigation system for a mobile robot: a first approach to HILARE. In *6th IJCAI, Tokyo (Japan)*, August 1979.

[17] L. Gouzènes. Strategies for solving collision-free trajectories problems for mobile or manipulator robot. *International Journal of Robotics Research*, 3(4), Winter 1984.

[18] D. V. McDermott. A temporal logic for reasoning about processes and plans. *Cognitive Science*, 6, 1982.

[19] N. J. Nilsson. *Triangle Tables: a proposal for a robot programming language.* Technical Note 347, AI Center, SRI, 1985.

[20] J. F. Picardat. *Contrôle d'exécution, compréhension et apprentissage de plans d'action: Développement de la méthode de la table triangulaire.* Thèse de l'Université Paul Sabatier, Toulouse (France), Université Paul Sabatier, 1987.

Figure 11.a

rob1 EMPTY	-ta(e5/0)	tb(s3/1)-fa(e3/1)	fb(s9/1)-ta(e9/1)	tb(s29/0)-fa(e29/0)
rob1 B:2	-fa(e5/0)	fb(s3/1)-ta(e3/1)	......	
rob1 BA:2	fa(1st/1)	fb(s29/0)-ta(e29/0)		
rob2 EMPTY	-ta(e23/0)	tb(s14/0)-fa(e14/0)	fb(s16/0)-ta(e16/0)	
rob2 A:2	-fa(e23/0)	fb(s14/0)-ta(e14/0)	tb(s16/0)-fa(e16/0)	
rob2 B:5	fa(1st/1)	fb(s14/0)-ta(e14/0)		
tab EMPTY	-fa(e5/0)	fb(s14/0)-ta(e14/0)		
tab B:4	-ta(e5/0)	tb(s14/0)-fa(e14/0)		
sto1 EMPTY	fa(1st/1)	fb(s26/0)-ta(e26/0)		
sto1 A:3	ta(1st/1)	tb(s26/0)-fa(e26/0)		
asm EMPTY	-fa(e23/0)	fb(s29/0)-ta(e29/0)		
asm A:4	-ta(e23/0)			
asm BA:1	fa(1st/1)	fb(s16/0)-ta(e16/0)	tb(s29/0)-fa(e29/0)	
asm2 EMPTY	fa(1st/1)			
asm2 C:4	ta(1st/1)	tb(s9/1)-fa(e9/1)		
asm2 BC:1	fa(1st/1)	fb(s9/1)-ta(e9/1)	tb(s17/1)-fa(s17/1)	
asm2 BC+:1	fa(1st/1)	fb(s17/1) ⟹		
asm2 BC-:1	fa(1st/1)	fb(s17/1) ⟹		
cnv1 AWAY	fa(1st/1)	fb(s3/1)-ta(e3/1)	tb(s1/1)-fa(e1/1)	
cnv1 ?(B C)	fa(1st/1)	fb(s1/1)-ta(e1/1)	tb(s2/1)-fa(e2/1)	
cnv1 B:1	ta(1st/1)	tb(s3/1)-fa(e3/1)	fb(s2/1) ⟹	
cnv1 C:1	fa(1st/1)	fb(s2/1) ⟹		
cnv3 AWAY	fa(1st/1)			
cnv3 READY	ta(1st/1)			
cnv3 BA:3	fa(1st/1)			

Figure 11.a

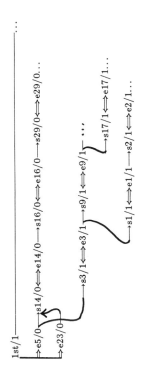

Figure 11.b

Figure 11: Indexed Time Table for Execution Plan 1

Figure 10.a

rob1 EMPTY	ta(1st/0)	tb(s3/0)-fa(e3/0)	fb(s5/0)-ta(e5/0)	tb(s29/0)-fa(e29/0)
rob1 B:2	fa(1st/0)	fb(s3/0)-ta(e3/0)	tb(s5/0)-fa(e5/0)	
rob1 BA:2	fa(1st/0)	fb(s29/0)-ta(e29/0)	......	
rob2 EMPTY	ta(1st/0)	tb(s26/0)-fa(e26/0)	fb(s23/0)-ta(e23/0)	tb(s14/0)-fa(e14/0)
rob2 A:2	fa(1st/0)	fb(s26/0)-ta(e26/0)	tb(s23/0)-fa(e23/0)	
rob2 B:5	fa(1st/0)	fb(s14/0)-ta(e14/0)	tb(s16/0)-fa(e16/0)	
tab EMPTY	ta(1st/0)	tb(s5/0)-fa(e5/0)	fb(s14/0)-ta(e14/0)	
tab B:4	fa(1st/0)	fb(s5/0)-ta(e5/0)	tb(s14/0)-fa(e14/0)	
sto1 EMPTY	fa(1st/0)	fb(s26/0)-ta(e26/0)		
sto1 A:3	ta(1st/0)	tb(s26/0)-fa(e26/0)		
asm EMPTY	ta(1st/0)	tb(s23/0)-fa(e23/0)	fb(s29/0)-ta(e29/0)	
asm A:4	fa(1st/0)	fb(s23/0)-ta(e23/0)		
asm BA:1	fa(1st/0)	fb(s16/0)-ta(e16/0)	tb(s29/0)-fa(e29/0)	
asm2 EMPTY	fa(1st/0)			
asm2 C:4	ta(1st/0)			
cnv1 AWAY	fa(1st/0)	fb(s3/0)-ta(e3/0)	tb(s1/0)-fa(e1/0)	
cnv1 ?(B C)	fa(1st/0)	fb(s1/0)-ta(e1/0)	tb(s2/0)-fa(e2/0)	
cnv1 B:1	ta(1st/0)	tb(s3/0)-fa(e3/0)	fb(s2/0) ⟹	
cnv1 C:1	fa(1st/0)	fb(s2/0) ⟹		
cnv3 AWAY	fa(1st/0)			
cnv3 READY	ta(1st/0)			
cnv3 BA:3	fa(1st/0)	......		

Figure 10.a

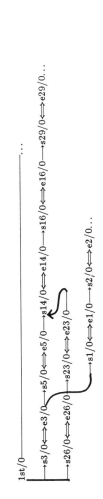

Figure 10.b

Figure 10: Indexed Time Table for Execution Plan 0

ADAPTIVE MOTION SEQUENCING FOR PROCESS ROBOTS

James P. Trevelyan, Technical Director, Automated Sheep Shearing Project
Mark Nelson, Graduate Student, Department of Computer Science
Peter Kovesi, Research Engineer

University of Western Australia, Nedlands, Western Australia 6009

A process robot uses a special purpose end effector to perform a process during some of its motions. If an error occurs during the process, some recovery movements may be needed before the original process motion can be resumed. In this paper we show how a recursive approach to motion control can provide a convenient arrangement for adaptive motion sequencing as an integral part of an automatic error recovery system. This leads in turn to more convenient adaptive programming, greater robot productivity and greater safety in operation. While these developments arise particularly from the requirement of sheep shearing robots they are applicable to other industrial process robots.

INTRODUCTION AND BACKGROUND

Research on sheep shearing with robots has been conducted at the University of Western Australia since 1977 and two experimental shearing robots have been constructed together with an automatic restraint and manipulation platform to hold the sheep. Over 500 sheep have been shorn under experimental conditions in seven years of experiments with live animals. Reliability of both hardware and software has been of paramount importance in maintaining an excellent safety record for both sheep and operators. Automatic error recovery was incorporated as a basic part of the robot control system in 1984 and has been improved and developed since then.

Representation of Manual Skills

Like many other industrial processes sheep shearing is considered to be a manual skill and automated sheep shearing was implemented by transferring the manual skills to a manipulator robot equipped with a shearing handpiece. The manual skill is described in terms of a basic procedure. Figure 1 shows part of the standard instructions on issue to all shearers in Australia and illustrates what can be termed 'basic procedure' for shearing. The movements shown will take place assuming that no corrective actions are required. The need for corrective action arises when the shearer makes an error or when conditions on the sheep are different to what the shearer expects. Typically, the shearer stops, moves the handpiece back a short distance and resumes shearing at a different angle or position to correct for the perceived difference.

In doing this the operator has:-

(a)   detected an operating error

(b)   diagnosed the condition

(c)   selected an appropriate corrective action

(d)   implemented the corrective action

(e)   has resumed the originally planned sequence of movements

The ability to implement corrective actions, to diagnose and decide which corrective action should be used is part of the skills which have to be acquired through learning from shearer trainers and practise. Considerable experience is required before a shearer can correctly diagnose most problems and can implement recovery movements which have minimal impact on productivity.

Many manual skills are described in this form. First the basic procedure is described which is executed if nothing goes wrong. Secondly, there is a series of statements which take the form 'if..... then do....'

In processes where the movement itself is part of the process (such as shearing, welding, gluing) corrective actions are often required in the middle of process movements. Therefore as part of our research on sheep shearing robots we have looked for a method of programming movements which enables us to specify recovery motions. The biggest step in this direction occurred when we were forced, by a major software failure, to take a serious look at automatic error recovery.

Importance of Automatic Error Recovery

Automatic recovery from errors is important for two reasons; first to improve the safety of the robot, and second to improve the productivity of the robot.

The safety implication is particularly important in the case of adaptive robots. An adaptive robot tends to exhibit a much wider range of behaviour than a fixed program robot, and it will therefore be more difficult for a human supervisor to detect a malfunction. We have also discovered that the adaptability of the robot which is intrinsic to the software can often mask significant faults.

Automatic error recovery permits increased productivity because the robot requires less supervision, and because it is capable of recovering from unusual operating conditions which could otherwise require manual intervention or adjustment. In the case of sheep shearing, certain types of sheep require different shearing strategies to normal sheep. Often, the need for a different strategy is not apparent until shearing has commenced, and may only be required for part of the sheep. There is, therefore, a major potential productivity gain arising from the ability of a robot to recover from a range of faults or unusual operating conditions.

Automatic error recovery was first implemented in our research robot ORACLE for safety reasons. However, it was soon apparent that unusual operating or shearing conditions could be treated in the same manner as faults and, therefore, an automatic error recovery feature in the control system could provide a convenient way of extending the adaptability of the robot to motion sequencing.

A survey of the literature has shown that research in the field of automatic error recovery is comparatively scarce (Nelson 1986). Parallel developments to the ideas presented in this paper have been reported by Lee et al (1985) and Smith and Gini (1986). The work by Lee has developed into an automatic system for producing robot operating systems for industrial robots. The work by Smith and Gini is based on an augmented programming language which has built in mechanisms for intelligent forward recovery from operating errors.

In our research, we have decided that a practical system for automatic error recovery is an immediate requirement. The technique which we describe does not have the ultimate flexibility of the 'expert systems' type of approach described in the literature. However, it has been shown to be convenient to implement, and can be programmed with relatively simple extensions to our existing techniques.

An important feature of our work has been the emphasis on software failures. Experimentation with robots for sheep shearing involves frequent tests with development software in an environment in which it is usually impossible to repeat an experiment. Not only are software failures probable, but there are typically only rare opportunities to observe such errors and collect information which is essential for correction of errors.

After two years of routine use this feature is now seen as perhaps the most important in the entire robot control system. It has not only provided a means of implementing intelligent adaptive motion sequencing and protected sheep and operators from potentially hazardous robot operations but has also been used as an invaluable debugging tool.

HOW THE ROBOT WORKS

The SM robot (figure 2) consists of a mechanical arm with hydraulic actuators, and in this respect is similar to robots which are used in factories for welding car bodies, painting and lifting. The essential feature required for shearing is an ability to react quickly to unpredictable bumps in the skin and sheep movements such as breathing. To do this, the robot has sensors in the cutter mechanism which measure the distance between the cutter and the skin. The positions of the follower actuator at the cutter and of the arm actuators are changed to keep the cutter at the correct height and orientation over the sheep skin.

The robot needs to be programmed with knowledge about sheep and shearing. Part of this is a three dimensional geometric model of sheep surface shapes called a 'software sheep'. The robot uses the map to move the cutter close enough to the skin for the sensors to start working, and then for finding the right way across the surface. The map also helps the sensing by calculating the likely cutter movements required to follow the surface immediately ahead of the cutter. Each sheep is different, but by measuring the approximate size and shape of each one as it is loaded for shearing, the computer can calculate an approximate map

which has been adapted for each sheep. As shearing progresses, the robot discovers the actual shape of the sheep through sensing and this can be used to improve the accuracy of map prediction. (Trevelyan 1986)

CONTROL SYSTEM SOFTWARE STRUCTURE

The main conclusion of this paper is that a recursive structure in the robot motion control software provides a convenient method for implementing automatic recovery movements and for adaptive motion sequencing. To introduce the later discussion of this we will first present the structure of the software which we have used for adaptive control without automatic error recovery. This arrangement is similar in principle to RCCL as presented by Paul and Hayward (1986) with the addition of a further real time level to perform joint space interpolation. A recursive motion control structure can be built by re-arranging these software elements and by the addition of some important new elements. Figure 3. illustrates the major process modules of the software and Figure 4. shows the functional arrangement of blocks to achieve adaptive motion control. The following sub sections describe the function of each block:

The interpreter executes shearing sequences consisting of predominantly procedural definitions of shearing operations on different parts of the sheep.

Each sequence consists of a text file containing parameter definitions, explicit motion commands such as moving the robot to a defined position over the sheep, or executing a single shearing movement on the sheep (a blow) or implicit motion commands which require a number of individual movements.

The motion planner interprets commands which perform explicit or implicit motions. The module performs geometric calculations which define the location of the movement relative to the sheep and, in the case of implicit commands, repeats this step for each of the movements required. The motion planner constructs data objects defining each motion and the way in which the robot is to execute each motion.

Both the interpreter and motion planner operate in the background, that is, they execute only when there is a need to plan robot movements and the rest of the time waiting for those movements to be completed.

The motion control and computation module receives requests for motions specified by the motion planner described above. The module determines which action will be programmed and in what order depending on priority and results to be achieved. It uses a series of movement modules to perform robot movements.

There are specific motion modules for each type of robot movement such as shearing and repositioning for the next shearing movement. Each movement module interprets the data object defining the movement and calculates the movement of the robot arm and orientation of the wrist in cartesian space over the next motion step (typically 70 msecs).

The inverse arm solution module calculates the movements required in the six main actuators of the robot arm to produce the demanded arm position and wrist orientation changes. (See Trevelyan et al, 1984, Trevelyan 1985, Kovesi 1985 and Trevelyan et al 1986 for further details of the geometric calculations and arm solution techniques.)

The interpolator module linearly interpolates movements of

the six main arm actuators in joint space to calculate actuator set point voltages at a sufficiently fast rate to provide smooth actuator operation between successive motion steps. The arm trajectory is modified in joint space to partially compensate for movements of the follower actuator.

The sensing module interprets inputs from sensors mounted on the cutter and generates movements for the fast response follower actuator which moves the cutter up and down relative to the surface of the sheep. Data is provided by the motion modules to help make best use of the information from sensors.

EXAMPLES OF OPERATING ERRORS

Adaptive motion sequencing typically occurs in response to operating errors. Other types of errors which can occur within a robot and its control system are hardware errors and software errors and these have been described elsewhere by Trevelyan and Nelson (1986).

The term 'operating errors' is introduced to describe situations in which the adaptation of robot motion by path modification, wrist re-orientation, movement speed or cutter drive speed is inadequate, or exceeds pre-set limits. Some examples follow:

Model error

A typical operating error is a situation in which the position of the skin under the cutter measured by sensors deviates from the predicted surface model by more than a certain distance, say 60 millimetres.

Response: The sensor calibration should first be checked to ensure that the sensors have correctly detected the skin of the sheep. This can be done by moving the cutter away from the sheep. Next, the shearing is recommenced further back. If the error fails to recur, then it is possible that wool characteristics may have caused the sensors to measure the distance to the skin incorrectly, and the sensor characteristics may require modification. If the error does recur, the shearing is still possible, but at a slower speed, and with tighter limits placed on allowable wrist orientation changes.

Excessive drag force

A simpler kind of operating error can be detected by measuring the drag force required to push the cutter through the wool. If the drag force exceeds a certain value then it can be assumed that exceptional wool conditions are being encountered and an alternative shearing action is required.

Response: Use periodic interruptions of shearing to reduce the drag force. If the problem recurs in the same location, move the cutter forwards and up relative to the skin at each interruption, with the effect of 'hacking' off difficult shearing wool. This is slow, and reduces the value of the fleece, but may be the only way to remove the wool.

Skin cut

A third example of an operating error is that of a skin cut. The characteristics of sensor signals can be monitored to detect when one or more teeth of the shearing comb has penetrated the skin of the sheep. The normal adaptive response of the robot to such signals is to lift the cutter away from the skin; however if forward motion of the robot continues this action will make the cut worse.

Response: The robot must be temporarily moved backwards to withdraw the comb teeth from the skin and then shearing can be resumed from a recovery point memorised before the skin cut was encountered.

NOTE: Sheep are often cut many times in the course of manual shearing, because they have a soft, wrinkled skin. However they heal very quickly. Cuts occur far less often in automated shearing.

TECHNIQUES FOR AUTOMATIC ERROR RECOVERY

Two types of error recovery have been described by Smith and Gini (1986) citing Randell et al (1978). *Backward recovery* consists of going back to a previous system state that is known to be correct. In this context the recovery from a skin cut described from above is seen to be a type of backward recovery. *Forward recovery* consists of performing alternate actions with the robot that lead it to a state which it would have reached had it been able to continue with the planned actions. The planned actions can then be resumed from that state.

It is not appropriate to attempt to implement the equivalent software techniques in the context of an adaptive robot. Backward error recovery typically involves the notion of rolling back the system to a known correct previous state. However, it may be neither possible nor desirable to move the robot exactly in reverse through previous states. Instead, it is necessary to implement a sequence of actions (including movements) by which the robot can reach some known correct previous state. Before re-starting the robot in this previous state it may be necessary to alter some of the parameters which govern the robot's behaviour, based on a diagnosis of the likely cause of the problem.

Smith and Gini (1986) define forward recovery as a determination of the difference between the actual state and the desired state of the robot and then developing a sequence of operations to achieve the desired state (p285). It is implied from their paper that the notion of 'desired state' is the successful completion of a sequence of movements, each of which is explictly defined in the robot programming language. In sheep shearing, most of the movements are process steps; it is necessary to perform shearing along the path of movement to remove wool, and it is not sufficient simply to reach the end of a shearing movement by some alternate route.

Let us define the term *interruption point* as the point (or state) at which motion of the robot was interrupted in response to an error, and *recovery point* as the point at which normal motion can be resumed.

An alternative notion to describe forward error recovery which we have found useful is:

Execution of an alternate sequence of task movements, after which the original sequence can be resumed at a recovery point forward of the point of interruption, the recovery point being either later in the interrupted motion, or later in the current group of implied motions, or at the commencement of a later sequence command.

This alternate notion permits resumption of the originally interrupted movement, or pattern of movements, within a single sequence motion command.

This can be applied to the operating error example above in which the 'hacking' style of shearing can be adopted for just part of one shearing blow; the original blow may be resumed in the original manner at some point ahead of the area of difficulty.

If the recovery point is considered to be located before the interruption point, then the same notion embraces backward recovery too, with the necessary addition of the movements needed to reach the recovery point. Thus, for the context of our application, we can unify the notions of forward and backward recovery, and proceed to define the implementation requirements. These are summarised below.

Implementation requirements for automatic error recovery

Error recovery requires the following steps to be implemented:

a) Detection of errors. The techniques for this are discussed in Trevelyan and Nelson (1986).

b) Diagnosis of errors. We have chosen to calculate signatures which are rules that provide diagnosis of error conditions.

c) Selection of appropriate response. Signatures define the appropriate response actions. The principal difficulties arise when more than one set of responses are requested.

d) Planning and execution of response. From the discussions above, a recursive motion control structure seems to be the most appropriate.

Diagnosis

The concept of signatures (Lee et al, 1985) defines an error in terms of a variable being outside a range of values in one of a group of machine states, for which the range limits apply. We have extended this concept to introduce frequency counting since a single instance of an error may only indicate a transient 'deviation' which can be tolerated.

We have chosen to calculate three kinds of signature; an alarm signature, an event signature, and a fault signature. Alarm signatures are defined as:

Alarm number, description
Variable selection
Lower limit
Upper limit
Pattern of machine states in which range limits are valid

Faults (typically for software errors such as illegal states, and incorrect array addressing) are detected by code inserted into the appropriate sections of software.

Selection of an appropriate recovery action requires some form of diagnosis and this is implemented with a series of rules called 'event signatures'. They are somewhat more complex than the simpler kinds of signatures defined above for alarms and introduce time and space dependency and a boolean combination of inputs comprising alarm signatures and other event signatures. By this means we can set up a decision tree which implements a crude method of diagnosis. Events at the ends of the decision tree have actions associated with them which will perform the necessary sequence modification and recovery movements.

Event signatures are defined as:

Event number, description
Boolean combination of alarms and/or events
Incidence rate
Forget rate
Accumulator
Rate selection (time, distance)

Selection of state transitions for resetting accumulator
Pattern of machine states (as for alarm signature)
Response actions and attributes

The 'incidence rate' and 'forget rate' parameters form a frequency counting facility. The accumulator value (initially zero) is incremented at the 'incidence rate' at every motion step at which the boolean combination is 'true', and decremented at the 'forget rate' at every step when it is 'false'. The response actions are requested only if the accumulator value exceeds 1.0. Different types of operating errors can be detected using this facility by selecting different incidence and forget rate values:

Example of simple frequency count

> incidence rate 2 per sec
> forget rate 0

Response requested when fault has been detected on 0.5 seconds of total motion step time (if motion step is 0.07 sec, this requires 8 steps)

Example of frequency count, with forget rate as well

> incidence rate 2 per sec
> forget rate 0.2 per sec

Response requested if fault detected for 0.5 seconds continuously, or occurs more than 10% of motion steps, on average.

We have found that it is possible to represent quite complex operating error conditions using these relatively simple signatures.

Specification and selection of response

Each response associated with a signature consists of a set of action requests such as:

shut down robot power
stop sensing
stop motion
re-load real time software
record prior events
move off sheep

Each of these is a simple action which can be implemented by the action scheduler module of the real time software. Each response is given a priority level so that a priority ordered queue can be constructed in the event of multiple faults.

When automatic recovery requires more complex actions than the simple ones listed above a change to the motion sequence can be requested through the interpreter. One of the options for response actions is 'programmed response' for which the action scheduler sets a flag which causes the sequence interpreter to search the current sequence for a procedure specifying a programmed response. Within such a procedure, changes to parameters, additional shearing actions, or alternative shearing actions can be specified. Once all these have been executed, and if it is appropriate, the action scheduler will calculate a suitable recovery point and resume the interrupted motion.

The principal difficulty which has to be resolved is that a single fault in shearing can give rise to a shower of consequent faults. An instance of high drag force can be caused by attempting to penetrate a skin fold with the comb teeth; at the same instant as the drag force limit is exceeded, a skin cut can occur, and the cutter drive motor can stop due to temporary overload. Some mechanism is required within the action scheduler to avoid an accumulation of successive response requests, especially when the responses are similar as in the case just given.

We have chosen to include a set of motion attributes with the response request. A set of dynamic motion attributes is updated at each step to describe the current motion of the robot. Examples of possible attributes are:

moving up (relative to cutter)
moving down
moving forward
moving back
stopped
etc.

Response requests from successive faults are added to a queue. Each request in the queue is scanned and if the motion attributes match the current dynamic attributes, then the set of 'non motion' responses is added by union with the set of non motion actions being executed, and the request is removed from the queue.

This has the effect of removing from the queue those requests which are for motions similar to what the robot is in the process of doing as a result of earlier errors.

SOFTWARE STRUCTURE FOR IMPLEMENTATION

Figure 5 shows the elements of software required to implement the system described. The diagram is similar to Figure 4, but shows more detail of TOM. Only the additional interactions required for error recovery have been shown.

Each movement module (such as shearing, repositioning) implements an adaptive movement of the robot in real time and has associated with it information specifying the path that the robot is intended to take, the path that the robot actually has executed (which will normally be different) and local information used to control time and distance dependent aspects of the motion. If we are to provide the ability to interrupt a programmed motion of the robot and resume it later we must arrange for all this information to be saved in such a way that firstly a recovery position can be calculated and secondly the original motion can be resumed. Furthermore we must provide the facility to perform similar movements as part of the recovery sequence, for example, it may be necessary to perform a short corrective shearing blow to recover from an operating error in the originally programmed blow.

One of the most convenient ways of handling this situation would be to use recursive movement modules in which data pertaining to a particular motion is stored on a stack and corrective motions are implemented at deeper levels of recursion using new data. Recovery to the originally programmed motion can be implemented by dropping the level of recursion.

Typical real time processes are implemented by programs which are re-executed at regular time intervals. This makes it difficult to implement a fully recursive approach. Instead of executing an entire process at each real time step we have chosen an arrangement where the process is suspended and then re-started from the point of suspension at each real time step.

The block 'motion control and computation' of Figure 4 has been expanded in Figure 5 to show the inter-relationship between the action scheduler and the motion modules to permit recursive formation of movements. Initially, the action scheduler calls a motion module to initiate a movement. The motion module computes the movement for the current motion step, then calls the action scheduler recursively via (B) to suspend Tom (the suspension point is located in the action scheduler). On restarting, the action scheduler checks the results of signature calculations and response requests and other system status information before returning control via (B) to the motion module to calculate movement for the next motion step. If a recovery movement is required, the action scheduler will call the appropriate motion module(s) via (A) again to initiate the recovery movement at a deeper level of recursion. When the motion module calculates that a motion has been completed, it returns control to the action scheduler via (A). Figures 6 and 7 show more detail of the internal structure of the action scheduler and motion modules.

The motion interface module is non recursive; this module converts movements calculated by motion modules into a simple combination of position and orientation change for the cutter which can then be passed to the kinematics module.

The recursive structure of real time computation needs to be complemented by a recursive interpreter so that recovery sequences can be programmed through procedures in the main sequence of commands. When a recovery sequence is completed control passees back to the original point of interruption in the main sequence. In terms of the original requirements of programming manual skills the main sequence implements the basic procedure. Rules in the form of event signatures implement the 'if.......then....' parts of the corrective actions and the procedures implement the 'do......' part of the corrective actions which form the other part of the manual skills.

EVENT LOGGING

One of the most important parts of the software required to implement automatic error recovery is automatic event logging to record sufficient information to enable skilled engineers to understand the actions of the robot and to develop new and improved responses for operating errors. This is particularly important in practical situations where operating errors seldom occur in isolation; typically several operating errors are diagnosed at the same time and combined recovery action is required. It is vital to be able to check that the robot did take appropriate recovery action and to understand the sequence of decision making in the diagnosis.

It would be impractical to record all of the results of all of the significant calculations performed by the robot's control systems. Instead we have implemented an arrangement for recording the sequence of calculations and signatures leading up to selected events and can record, optionally the details of the recovery action itself. This is implemented by using a series of ring buffers in memory into which are placed all the results of significant calculations and signatures. The data in the ring buffers is organised in frames each of which embraces all the data pertaining to a single motion step. When one of the selected events occurs, the ring buffers are copied to an event log in disc storage, thereby preserving a record of what preceded the event.

The event log is later processed by a special program which rearranges data recorded in ring buffers into a consecutive time history of significant decisions and calculations made by the robot. The program allows interactive access to more detailed data so that more detailed aspects of all operating software can be examined. We have found this facility for automatic recording, and later, examination of minute details of operation of software in an otherwise unrepeatable experiment to be of immense value in debugging software. The difficulties of debugging complex, real time software systems have been described in other literature (Harmon, 1986) but we have found testing to be relatively straightforward given automatic event logging and software error detection as described in Trevelyan and Nelson (1986).

OPERATING EXPERIENCE

The first implementation of error recovery software provided detection capabilities for all the types of errors described, but only a limited diagnosis and response capability; no recursion was possible in the motion control modules so a separate motion module was used for all recovery actions. Signatures were calculated by explicit coding, and frequency counting applied to only a few. Options available in programmed response procedures were limited.

The results were strikingly successful. A suprising number of errors in the original software were detected; the adaptability of the software had previously masked the effects of the errors. In several experiments with live sheep, software failures were detected, and the potentially hazardous consequences pre-empted. Experience with this implementation in nearly 200 live sheep trials has led to the specification of the arrangement described in this paper which is currently being implemented. We hope to describe some of the results by the time this paper is presented.

ACKNOWLEDGEMENTS

The authors would like to acknowledge the contributions of their colleagues of the automated sheep shearing team to this aspect of the research project. The project is commissioned by the Australian Wool Corporation and funded by the Wool Research and Development Fund.

REFERENCES

Harmon, S.Y. (1986): Practical implementation of autonomous systems: problems and solutions. Proc. Int. Conf. on Intelligent Autonomous Systems, Amsterdam, December 8th-11th, Elsevier, ISBN 0 444 70168 0.

Hayward, V., and Paul, R.P. (1986): Robot manipulator control under Unix RCCL: a robot control "C" library. Inc.J. of Robotics Research.

Kovesi, P. D., (1985): Obstacle avoidance. Proceedings of 2nd International Conference on Advanced Robotics (ICAR), Tokyo, pp 51-58.

Lee, M. H., Barnes, D. P. and Hardy, N. W., (1985) Research into error recovery for sensory robots. Sensor Review, October, p. 194.

Nelson, M. J. (1986): Automatic error recovery for adaptive robots. Technical report 86/3, Department of Computer Science, University of Western Australia.

Randell, P., Lee, P.A., and Treleaven, P. C., (1978): Reliability issues in computing system design. Computing Surveys, Vol 10, No. 2, p. 123.

Smith, R. E. and Gini, M., (1986): Reliable real-time robot operation employing intelligent forward recovery. Journal of Robotic Systems, Vol 3, No. 3, p. 281.

Trevelyan, J. P., Elford, D., Kovesi, P. and Ong, M., (1986): ET: a wrist mechanism without singular positions. Int. J. Robotics Research, Vol 4, No. 4, Winter, p. 71.

Trevelyan, J. P., Kovesi, P. and Ong, M., (1984): Motion control for a sheep shearing robot. Proceedings of 1st International Symposium on Robotics Research, MIT Press, p. 175.

Trevelyan, J. P., (1985): Skills for a shearing robot: dexterity and sensing. Proceedings of 2nd International Symposium on Robotics Research, MIT Press, p. 273.

Trevelyan, J. P. (1986): Automated sheep shearing - Introduction. Technical report, Automated sheep shearing group, University of Western Australia.

Trevelyan, J. P. and Nelson, M.J (1986): Adaptive robot control incorporating error recovery, ICAR 1987, Versailles, France (to appear).

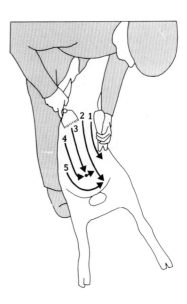

Figure 1 Part of instructions issued to shearers.

Corrective actions are taught at shearing schools or learned from other shearers.

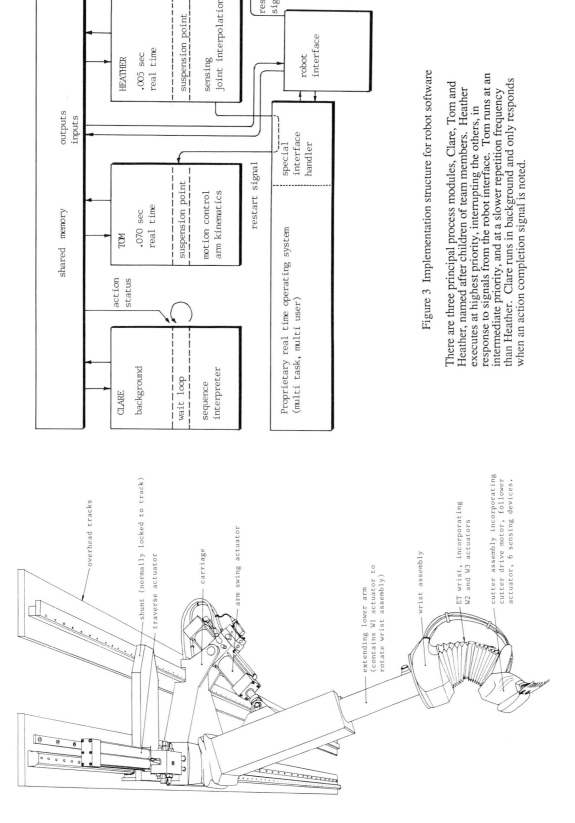

Figure 3 Implementation structure for robot software

There are three principal process modules, Clare, Tom and Heather, named after children of team members. Heather executes at highest priority, interrupting the others, in response to signals from the robot interface. Tom runs at an intermediate priority, and at a slower repetition frequency than Heather. Clare runs in background and only responds when an action completion signal is noted.

Figure 2 SM robot

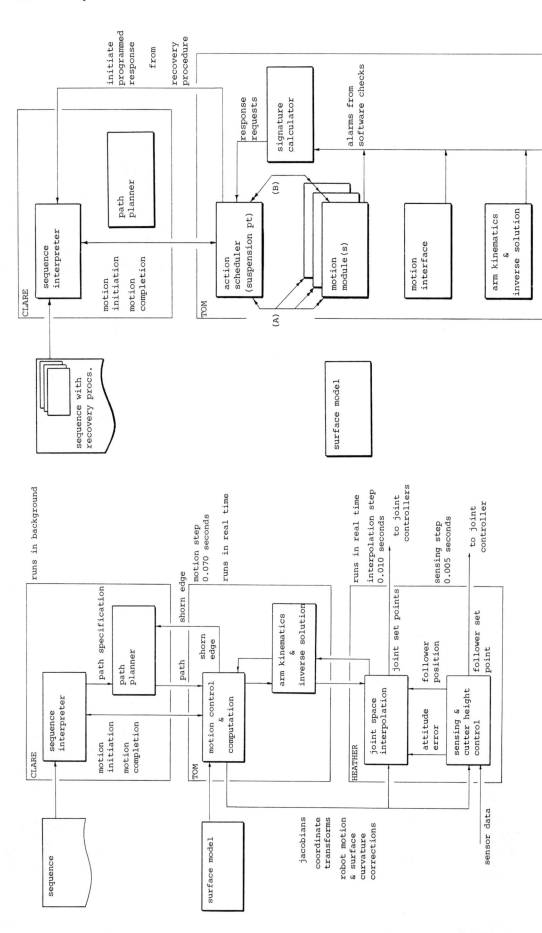

Figure 5 Elements of software structure for error recovery

Action scheduler - motion module relationship. (A) - the action scheduler calls a motion module to initiate a movement, the motion module returns when the movement is completed. (B) - motion modules call the action scheduler to suspend execution until the next motion step.

Figure 4 Software function for motion control

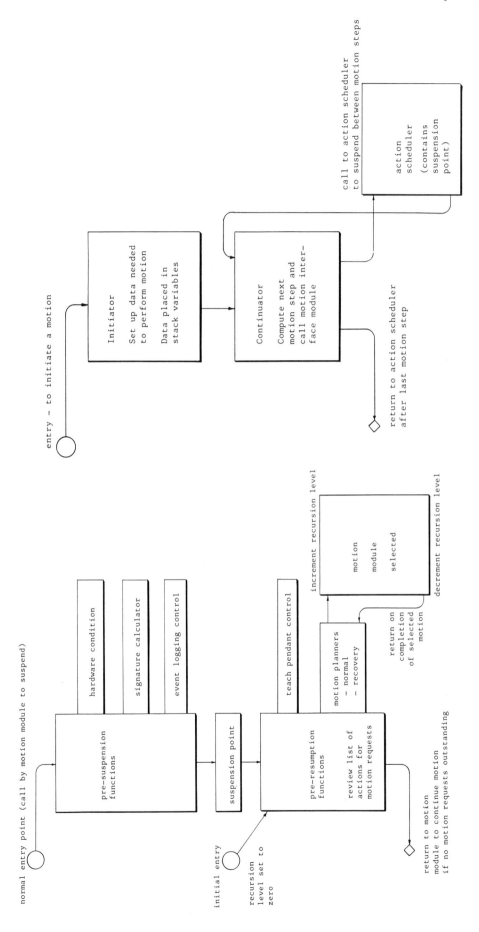

Figure 7 Structure of motion module

There are several different motion modules, for different types of movements such as shearing, repositioning, repositioning close to the sheep surface, etc. Each has a different method for calculating the robot movements.

Figure 6 Structure of action scheduler

At the zero level of recursion, before any motion is requested, the action scheduler is called from a dummy module.

Dealing with uncertainty in robot planning using program proving techniques

Jocelyne Pertin-Troccaz and Pierre Puget

LIFIA laboratory
Institut National Polytechnique de Grenoble
46, Avenue Félix Viallet
38031 Grenoble Cedex - France

Abstract: A global approach for dealing with uncertainties using program proving techniques in Robotics is presented. We consider a manipulation program automatically generated by a planner according to spatial and geometric criteria and ignoring uncertainties. Such a program is correct only if, at each step, uncertainties are smaller than the tolerances imposed by the assembly task. We propose an approach which consists in verifying the correctness of the program with respect to uncertainties in position and possibly modifying it by adding operations in order to reduce uncertainties. These two steps based on a forward and a backward propagation borrowed from formal program proving techniques are described in a general framework suitable for robotics environments. Forward propagation consists in computing successive states of the robot world from the initial state and in checking for the satisfaction of constraints. If a constraint is not satisfied, backward propagation infers new constraints on previous states. These new constraints are used for patching the program. The approach is described in technical details in the case of a simple manipulation language and of a relational model of the world including a representation of uncertainties.

1 Introduction

One of the major issues addressed by automatic robot programming is to deal with uncertainties. Uncertainties may be due to the initial environment, the robot control or the sensing operations. The difficulty of reasoning about them largely depends on the fact that they are mainly side-effects of motion commands that propagate dependencies across operations such as grasping, transfer motions, and assembly motions. Therefore, they must be considered both from a global viewpoint (analyzing the robot control program) and from a local viewpoint (generating fine-motion strategies for example).

In this paper we will focus on the global treatment of uncertainties in a planning system. Our approach consists in using a *planner* that reasons exclusively in geometrical terms in order to generate a nominal plan using path finding methods. This first plan is a program written in a particular robot programming language. Constraints are then added to the plan which is analyzed by a *prover*. If some constraints are not satisfied, a regression[1] technique is used for amending the plan.
The purpose of this paper is to describe the prover through its main components: the forward and the backward constraint processes.

A few works were done in the past with close motivations. The most famous is [Brooks 82]. The work presented in this paper uses a completely different formalism borrowed from formal program proving used in computer science theory.

The aim of the next section is to define formally both the programs and their data. Data specify states of the world. In the following section, this framework is applied to the particular context of robotics. A model is given, a language is defined and our approach is illustrated with this language. Then, an analysis of related works is presented and finally a discussion of this approach is given. The appendix presents an example by this approach.

2 General framework

A conventional computer program describes *operations* on *data*. To reason about it, it is necessary to introduce a formal framework for which it is possible to describe these two notions. Our framework partly comes from the one used in classical program proving. In the context of robot programming, the meaning of "operations" and "data" is different from what they mean in classical programming languages. "Data" are states of the real world, and these states are partially known and unperfectly modeled. "Operations" are actions on this real world, whose effects are sometimes complex, not necessarily deterministic, and unperfectly modeled.

2.1 Representing the physical world with uncertainty

In order to describe a physical system, it is necessary to choose k physical quantities which characterize any state of the system.
These physical quantities define k *state variables* $(x_1, x_2, \ldots, x_k)$. The choice of these variables requires a compromise between the quality of the description and the complexity of its use. By quality we mean that it allows the description of the relevant phenomena (mechanical, electrical, ...) with a sufficient realism. For us, this physical system is both the robot and its environment, also called *world*.
Knowing an actual state of the world requires determining the value a_i of each state variable x_i by measuring the corresponding physical quantity. Since the measurement can never be

---

[1]In terms of AI plan generation systems (see [Nilsson 82])

exact, there exists a difference between the state described by $(a_1, a_2, \ldots, a_n)$ and the actual state of the world. This difference is called *error*. Generally we have an information on this error and we can represent it as a set of possible errors. This representation can be said "set-oriented", by opposition to the "probabilistic" representation which consists in assigning a probability to every state of the world [Smith 87a].

An error may be very large while the set it belongs to is very small, i.e., that is to say that the actual state of the world can be well approximated from its measurement when sensors are calibrated. Assuming this is the case, representing the difference between the actual state and its calibrated measurement corresponds to representing an *uncertainty*[2].

Example:

Let us consider a world consisting of a 3 degrees of freedom cartesian manipulator. The relevant physical parameters for a position-control of the manipulator are $(X_{rob}, Y_{rob}, Z_{rob})$. Other parameters such as temperature or hygrometry can be neglected. Since the accuracy of the robot is known to be 2 mm in each direction, the real position of the robot corresponding to a theoretical one $(X_{rob}^0, Y_{rob}^0, Z_{rob}^0)$ will be within a sphere of radius 2 mm, centered on the point $(X_{rob}^0, Y_{rob}^0, Z_{rob}^0)$. This sphere represents the uncertainty.

Let us consider a n-tuple $(w_1, w_2, \ldots, w_n)$ that consists of k state variables and k variables describing the uncertainty on their values. The state defined by the value of the k state variables is named *nominal state* of the world.

A *model* of the world is a function W which associates to each $(w_1, w_2, \ldots, w_n)$ a set of possible actual states of the world "around" the nominal state. This set will be noted $W(w_1, w_2, \ldots, w_n)$.

2.2 Program proving

A program is written for implementing a particular function f; it transforms a set of initial data I into a set of final results O. Intuitively, the correctness of a program is twofold:

1. the program has to terminate and to meet its requirement, i.e., implementing the function f ($O = f(I)$)

2. the program has to be feasible, i.e., each instruction is executable from I (no division by zero, no array index out of bounds, ...).

In computer science, these two features are respectively known as *program proving* and *data flow control*. Although we are mainly interested in the second feature - the first one is implicitly treated by the planner that has to generate the suitable program - our approach will use some concepts introduced in the context of formal proof [Hoare 69].

Our purpose is to verify the feasibility of a program and to modify it locally in case of no feasibility.

Let us consider a *program* as an ordered set of instructions $\{I_1, I_2, \ldots, I_m\}$; we make no assumption on the type of these instructions.

A *constrained program* is a program in which a feasibility constraint is associated to each instruction I_i. We note: $CP = \{(C_1, I_1), (C_2, I_2), \ldots, (C_m, I_m)\}$ with each constraint

of the form $C_i(w_i^1, w_i^2, \ldots, w_i^{p(i)})$ where $w_i^j \in \{w_1, w_2, \ldots, w_n\}$ and $p(i) \leq n$. Note that $p(i) < n$ means that the constraint is indifferent to the value of some parameters defining the state of the world.

Let E and F be two conditions and P a program. We note $E\{P\}F$ the statement which means "if E holds before executing P then F will hold after the execution of P. E is called *precondition* and F is called *postcondition*[3] of P. Program proving consists in proving such statements using specific inference rules.

To any logical condition C one can associate the set: $W(w_1, w_2, \ldots, w_n)/C(w_C^1, w_C^2, \ldots, w_C^{p(C)})$ of all the possible states of the world verifying C. The shorter notation W/C will also be used. When $C = (true)$, then W/C is the set of all the possible states of the world.

We can give two equivalent formulations of the proof (a state formulation and a condition formulation), thanks to the following property.

Property 1 *If W/E (resp. W/F) is the set of worlds verifying E (resp. F) and if P implements the function f_P then $E\{P\}S \Longleftrightarrow f_P(W/E) \subseteq W/F$.*

Property 2 *if $F \Longrightarrow F'$ and $E\{P\}F$ then $E\{P\}F'$; F is a stronger postcondition than F'.*

Proof:

$$(F \Longrightarrow F') \iff (W/F \subseteq W/F')$$
$$E\{P\}F \iff f_P(W/E) \subseteq W/F$$

It follows that $f_P(W/E) \subseteq W/F'$; therefore $E\{P\}F'$

2.2.1 Verifying the correctness of a program by forward propagation

Let W_{act_0} be the actual state of the world before running the program. Let W_{act_i} be the intermediate actual state of the world resulting from the execution of the first i instructions.

Definition 1 *Let $CP = \{(C_1, I_1), (C_2, I_2), \ldots, (C_m, I_m)\}$ be a constrained program, CP will be correct iff for each $i \in \{1, 2, \ldots, m\}$, the actual state of the world $W_{act_{i-1}}$ before the execution of instruction I_i belongs to W/C_i, i.e., verifies the constraint C_i.*

As mentioned in the previous section, every actual state W_{act_i} is unknown. We suppose that the set of possible W_{act_i} can be characterized by a condition S_i. Hence, another definition of the correctness of a program can be given:

Definition 2 *If $CP = \{(C_1, I_1), (C_2, I_2), \ldots, (C_m, I_m)\}$ is a constrained program and if S_0 is the condition characterizing the set of possible states of the world before running CP, CP is said correct for S_0 iff $\forall i \in \{0, 1, \ldots, m-1\}$ $S_i \Longrightarrow C_{i+1}$.*

A state W_{act_i} results from $W_{act_{i-1}}$ after the execution of I_i. In other words, if I_i implements the function f_{I_i} then $W_{act_i} = f_{I_i}(W_{act_{i-1}})$. Therefore, S_i is the condition such that $W/S_i = f_{I_i}(W/S_{i-1})$. From property 1 we can deduce that S_i is a special postcondition of S_{i-1} for I_i such that W/S_i is "minimal". Property 2 and its proof show that S_i is in fact the strongest postcondition (defined bellow) of I_i for S_{i-1}.

---

[2]In the following, the words *error* and *uncertainty* will be also used for the physical quantities.

[3]Definitions and properties come from [Berlioux 83]

Definition 3 *Let E and F be two conditions and P a program such that F is a postcondition of P for E. E is the* strongest postcondition *of P for E, iff for each postcondition F' of P for E, $F \Longrightarrow F'$. We will note it $F = SPost(P,E)$.*

Property 3 *If W/E (resp. W/F) represents the set of worlds verifying E (resp. F), and P implements the function f_P, then $W/F = f_P(W/E) \Longleftrightarrow F = SPost(P,E)$.*

The statement $(x \geq 0)\{x := x * 2\}(x \geq -5)$ is true but $(x \geq -5)$ is not the strongest postcondition of $\{x := x+2\}$ for $(x \geq 0)$. $SPost(\{x := x * 2\},(x \geq 0)) = (\frac{x}{2} \geq 0)$

Example:
Let us consider the following constrained program:
$CP = \{((true), \{x := x+1\}), ((1 \leq x \leq 10), \{y := tab[x]\})\}$
The initial world is characterized by: $S_0 = (-15 \leq x \leq 15)$
S_0 implies C_0; S_1 is computed as the strongest postcondition of S_0.
$SPost(\{x := x+1\}, S_0) = (-14 \leq x \leq +16) = S_1$
Since S_1 does not imply C_1, then CP is not correct for S_0.

Supposing that any postcondition is used instead of the strongest postcondition, if one constraint is not satisfied then we cannot conclude on the uncorrectness of the program (see property 1). For example: $(x \geq 0)\{x := x+2\}(x \geq -4)$ is true. If the constraint to be verified afterwards is $(x \geq 1)$ then it is wrong to conclude that the program is not correct. On the other hand, since $SPost(\{x := x+2\},(x \geq 0)) = (x \geq 2)$, we can conclude that the program is correct.

In practice, we will define the semantics of a language i.e. the effects of the execution of each instruction I by giving $SPost(I,C)$ for a general condition C. The method used for verifying the correctness of a program consists in: (1) iteratively computing each S_i using the recurrent definition $S_i = SPost(I_i, S_{i-1})$, (2) verifying at each step that S_i implies C_{i+1}. We call this *forward propagation*.

2.2.2 Amendment of a program by backward propagation

Let us assume that for some S_0, the constrained program is not correct, i.e., there exists $j \in \{1, 2, \ldots, m\}$ such that S_{j-1} does not imply C_j. The purpose of this second phase is to modify the program in order to make it correct. One may want to modify S_0 in S_0' such that for each $i \in \{1, 2, \ldots, m\}$, S_{i-1}' implies C_i. This is not always possible when the initial environment is fixed by some external devices (part feeders for example) or when the planner fix it according to its own criteria (collision avoidance for example).

A more general way of making the program correct consists in propagating C_j backward in order to determine new constraints $C_j^{j-1}, C_j^{j-2}, \ldots, C_j^1$ on previous states $S_{j-2}, S_{j-1}, \ldots, S_0$ such that when one of them is satisfied then C_j is also satisfied. In other words, $C_j^i\{I_i; I_{i+1}; \ldots; I_{j-1}\}C_j$ must be true for each $i \in \{1, 2, \ldots, j-1\}$[4]. Each C_j^i is a precondition of $\{I_i; I_{i+1}; \ldots; I_{j-1}\}$ for C_j. We determine C_j^i as the *weakest precondition* because, intuitively, it will be the easiest one to sat-

---

[4] We use a "composition rule": $E\{P\}G \land G\{Q\}F \Longrightarrow E\{P;Q\}F$

isfy among the whole set of preconditions of $\{I_i; I_{i+1}; \ldots; I_{j-1}\}$ for C_j.

Definition 4 *Let E and F be two conditions and P a program, E is the* weakest precondition *of P for F iff E is a precondition of P for F and for any other precondition E' of P for F, $E' \Longrightarrow E$; we will note it $WPre(P,F) = E$.*

Property 4 *If W/E (resp. W/F) represents the set of worlds verifying E (resp. F) and if P implements f_P then $WPre(P,S) = E \Longleftrightarrow W/E = f_P^{-1}(W/F)$*

For example:
$WPre(\{x := 2\},(x = 2)) = (true)$
$WPre(\{x := x+1\},(x \leq 3)) = (x+1 \leq 3)$

Computing these new constraints at each step of the program necessitates a composition rule:

Property 5

$$WPre([P;Q],F) = WPre(P,WPre(Q,F))$$

We determine for $i \in \{0, 1, \ldots, j-1\}$ new conditions C_j^i as

$$
\begin{aligned}
C_j^i &= WPre([I_i; I_{i+1}; \ldots; I_{j-1}], C_j) \\
&= WPre(I_i, WPre(I_{i+1}, WPre(\ldots, WPre(I_{j-1}, C_j)\ldots)))
\end{aligned}
$$

Since $SPost(WPre(P,F))$ implies F we are sure that if any of the C_j^i is verified before the execution of I_i then C_j will hold before the execution of I_j.

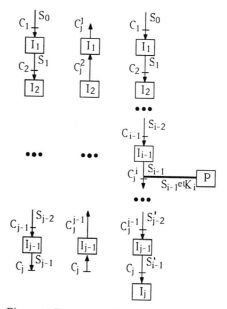

Figure 1: Forward and backward propagation

Satisfying one of these new constraints can be done by locally modifying the program, *adding* some new instructions called *patch*. The patch has to modify some S_i while at the same time maintaining the global behavior of the program.

For each C_j^i (resp. for C_j), we have to determine a condition K_i (resp. K_j) such that $S_{i-1} \wedge K_i \Longrightarrow C_j^i$ and $K_i \neq (false)$ (resp. $S_{j-1} \wedge K_j \Longrightarrow C_j$ and $K_j \neq (false)$).

If it is possible to choose a patch that transforms W/S_{i-1} in $W/(S_{i-1} \wedge K_i)$ for some $i \in \{1, 2, \ldots, j-1\}$ then the constraint C_j will be satisfied (see figure 1). Because we compute weakest preconditions, if no patch is available for satisfying at least one of them, then the program cannot be corrected.

The choice of both the location of the patch and the patch itself may rely on different criteria; for the location of the patch it could be: weakest K_i among all in terms of the number of parameters, weakest K_i among all in terms of the discrepancy between the real values of the parameters and the desired ones, etc...

3   Instantiating the framework

In order to generate a program, the planner reasons in terms of both theoretical positions and links between objects. The prover has to verify the feasibility of the program according to uncertainties. Therefore, a patch will have to reduce uncertainties, globally conserving theoretical positions and links. Such a patch may be: a sensing operation, a grasp/ungrasp strategy, a fine-motion strategy, or a sensorless motion strategy [Mason 86]. Using some of these patches necessitates a call to the planner.

3.1   A possible representation of the world under uncertainty

As mentioned earlier, the physical system to represent is the robot and its environment. This environment consists of solid objects which are manipulated by the robot. In this paper, we focus on proving the correctness of a program only concerned with uncertainties on the location of the objects and the robot; we will call them position uncertainties. We do not consider shape and dimension uncertainties. We do not either consider any physical phenomenon like elasticity or friction. These points are discussed in a following section.

Since we are not interested in geometric reasoning, every object will be known by means of its position; it will be modeled by a coordinate frame whose position is given by a geometric transform relatively to a reference frame. A position *error* is the geometric transform between a nominal position and a real position. So, according to our convention, a position uncertainty is a set of geometric transforms.

Using only position information both about the robot and the objects is not sufficient for reasoning about the real world since the behavior of any object depends on its interactions with the other objects. In the context of assembly, the relevant interactions are physical contacts of objects occuring when grasping an object, putting an object onto another, or affixing two objects together.

In this section, a model to represent objects positions, position uncertainty, and frame bindings is proposed.

3.1.1   Modeling W/S

As the robot is an articulated object it is represented by two cartesian frames; the first, named robot, represents the position of the robot while the second, named gripper, corresponds to the position of its end-effector. Any other object is represented by a single cartesian frame, object. A particular object, named workspace (or wsp), is the absolute reference of the manipulation: it can lie on a table, on the floor of a workshop, etc...

At any time of the manipulation, every object of the environment, except workspace, is located relatively to either workspace or another object it is in contact with. Therefore, a state of the world can be represented as a tree whose root is workspace, for which each node is a frame that represents an object and each link corresponds to a binding of two frames (i.e., to a contact of the objects). To each link $ARC(obj_i, obj_j)$ are associated both the relative position of the two nodes $ARC(obj_i, obj_j) : P$ and the uncertainty on this position $ARC(obj_i, obj_j) : U$. The first information is represented by a geometric transform. The description of the representation of the second information is the topic of the following subsection.

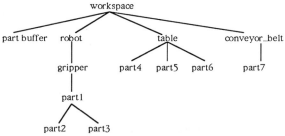

Figure 2: Representing W/S

Figure 2 represents a world where an assembly is held by the gripper and the other objects lie either on a table or on a conveyor belt. Finished assemblies are kept in a part buffer.

Later on, the robot puts the assembly in the part buffer and grasps the object part7; the tree is shown in figure 3.

Representing W/S as described, S is a conjunction of predicates of the following form:
$ARC(object_i, object_j) : P = P_0 \wedge ARC(object_i, object_j) : U = U_0$ where the two items respectively specify the position of $object_j$ relatively to $object_i$ and the uncertainty on this position.

3.1.2   Modeling position uncertainties

Since an uncertainty is a set of geometric transforms, the representation of position uncertainty is based on an underlying

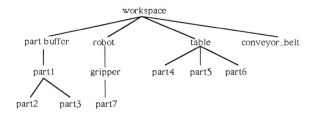

Figure 3: Another W/S

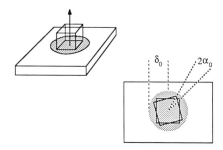

Figure 4: Object on a plane

representation of geometric transforms. A geometric transform can be decomposed into a translation and a rotation. The corresponding representation is a 3-tuple: translation vector, rotation axis (as a unit vector), and rotation angle. We have chosen this representation because of its geometrical meaning. Indeed, an algebraic representation with homogeneous coordinate matrices is not well-adapted for expressing the relative degrees of freedom between objects.

In the most general case, a position uncertainty should be represented by a subset of $\mathbf{R}^3 \times \mathbf{S}(1) \times [-\pi, +\pi]$ (where $\mathbf{R}$ is the set of real numbers, $\mathbf{S}(1)$ is the unitary sphere). In fact, a subset of this cartesian product will be approximated by the smallest recovering subset of the form:

$$Tr \times U \times A$$

where

- Tr is a sphere, a disk, or a line segment

- U is the whole sphere or a single unitary vector

- A is an interval $[-\alpha, +\alpha]$ where α is a "small" angle

The consequence of this approximation is a loss of information, resulting in overconstraining uncertainties for program proving. This representation was not only chosen for the sake of simplicity but it also corresponds to a large number of geometrical situations with different types of contact.

Example: Object lying on a plane $z = K$:
The object can slide on the plane and can rotate around the plane's normal vector. Its uncertainty relatively to the plane is such that (see figure 4):

- Tr is a disk whose radius is δ_0 and axis is $\vec{k}$

- U is the single vector $\vec{k}$

- A is an interval $[-\alpha_0, +\alpha_0]$

3.1.3 Using the model for constraint evaluation

Constraints C_i bear on the value of the relative uncertainty of any object with respect to any other one. Since the model of the world is not complete, these constraints cannot be directly evaluated from the tree structure. Therefore making this evaluation possible requires the development of some tools operating on the model. The purpose of this paragraph is to list the necessary tools. Their technical description can be found in [Puget 85], and [Pertin 86].

Let $WAY(obj_i, obj_j)$ be the path from obj_i to obj_j in the tree; if obj_j is a son of obj_i, then $WAY(obj_i, obj_j)$ will be noted $ARC(obj_i, obj_j)$.

$WAY(obj_i, obj_j) : P$ denotes the position of obj_i relatively to obj_j when $WAY(obj_i, obj_j) : U$ is the uncertainty on this relative position. Computing these items from the tree necessitates two operators: compose and reverse.

$$\text{compose}[WAY(obj_i, obj_j), WAY(obj_j, obj_k)]$$
$$= WAY(obj_i, obj_k)]$$

$$\text{reverse}[WAY(obj_i, obj_j)] = WAY(obj_j, obj_i)$$

While these operators are well-known for positions, they have to be defined for uncertainties (see [Puget 85] for more details).

In the following, these operators will be noted respectively $*$ and $^{-1}$.

As explained in the next section, two more operators are necessary when computing the effects of some actions.

The first operator is used for determining the relative uncertainty when a contact occurs between two objects. This is a projection operator with the following syntax:

$$\text{project}[WAY(obj_i, obj_j) : U,$$
$$\{WAY(workspace, obj_k) : P, type, parameters\}]$$

The first term is the uncertainty to be projected; the second term contains: (1) the frame in which the projection is determined, (2) the type of the contact (plane or line), and (3) its parameters in this frame.

The second operator is used for updating the model when a sensor operation is made. It is noted:
$$\text{merge}[ARC(obj_k, obj_l), sense(obj_i, obj_j)].$$

$sense(obj_i, obj_j)$ is a fictive arc, consisting of:
$sense(obj_i, obj_j) : P$, the nominal transform given by the sensor
$sense(obj_i, obj_j) : U$, the uncertainty on the relative position between obj_i and obj_j estimated from the accuracy of the sensor.

This operator propagates the information onto $ARC(obj_k, obj_l)$. The principle is shown on figure 5. It is performed in two steps:

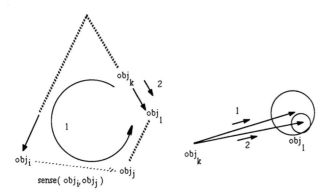

$$sense(\,obj_i, obj_j\,)$$

Figure 5: The merging operator

1. $WAY(obj_k, obj_l)$ is computed as the composition:
   $WAY(obj_k, obj_i) * sense(obj_i, obj_j) * WAY(obj_l, obj_j)^{-1}$
   (path 1 on the figure).

2. the intersection of the resulting uncertainty volume with the previous uncertainty volume given by $ARC(obj_k, obj_l)$ (path 2 on the figure) gives a new nominal position and a new uncertainty volume for $ARC(obj_k, obj_l)$

Hence, a constraint C_i will be defined as follows:

< constraint > ::= < relative uncertainty > $\subseteq U_i$
< relative uncertainty > ::= $WAY(obj_i, obj_j) : U$ |
< relative uncertainty $>^{-1}$ |
< relative uncertainty > * < relative uncertainty >|
project[< relative uncertainty >,
        { frame, type, parameters }] |
merge[< relative uncertainty >, < sensor result >]

Evaluating one of these constraints poses a problem when some parameters of the model are not instantiated. It occurs when a sensing operation is made. In this case, some parameters are represented by a non-instantiated variable whose value depends on the result given by the sensor. As we do not have any method for symbolically computing the operators compose, reverse, project, and merge, we use estimations on the result given by the sensor. If uncertainties are small compared to nominal transforms, it is possible to compute approximate uncertainty volumes by taking the previous nominal values instead of the values measured by the sensor. This will be described in detail in [Puget 87]. A particular case can be seen in the example.

3.2   Representing the effects of actions

A robot programming language consists of three types of instructions: moving commands, end-effector operations and sensing operations. We will illustrate the processes of forward and backward propagation on the following language:

MOVE < obj > TO < position >
where:
< position >   ::= < object > | < object > * < transform >
< transform >   ::= < elem-transf > |
                    < elem-transf > * < transform >
< elem-transf >::= translat(vector,distance) | rot(vector,angle)

< object > is any object except robot and workspace

This instruction specifies a pure position-controlled movement of the manipulator. At the destination, object is located at position.

GRASP < object >
where object is any object except workspace, robot and gripper.
This instruction specifies the grasping of an object by the robot. The gripper is already at the right position. We consider a two parallel jaw gripper.

DROP < object > ONTO (< object > , < contact >)
where:
< contact > ::= < type > < parameters >
< type > ::= plane | line
< parameters > ::= < point > < vector >
< point > ::= < coordinates >
< vector > ::= < coordinates >

A planar contact is specified by a point on the plane and the outcoming normal; a linear contact is given by a point on the line and the vector supporting the line. The first object is any object except workspace, robot and gripper; the second one is any object except robot and gripper.
It specifies the action of releasing an object onto another object with the establishment of a single contact. Gripper is already at the right position.

LOCATE obj_i RELATIVELY TO obj_j
This instruction specifies a sensing operation (mainly a vision operation) which gives the nominal position and the relative uncertainty between obj_i and obj_j. The uncertainty is estimated from the accuracy of the sensor.

Although this language will be discussed later on, let us notice right now that it has been chosen to be semantically homogeneous for the purpose of the proof. We do not consider complex algorithmic constructions (loops, conditional statements, ...). Proving these constructions has already received significant attention in computer science.

3.2.1   Forward propagation

Formally, executing any of the specified instructions MOVE, GRASP, DROP, and LOCATE is equivalent to making assignments to some parameters of the model. For example "MOVE gripper TO position" is equivalent to assign to the link between robot and gripper both a new value for the relative position of gripper and a new uncertainty.

It is not easy to give a general formulation of the strongest postcondition $SPost(\{x := expr\}, C)$ of an assignment. Indeed, this necessitates the introduction of an extra fictive variable representing the value of x before the assignment (see [Berlioux 83] for more details). The resulting condition cannot reasonably be used for further forward propagation since it contains existential quantifiers. Our particular problem is to compute strongest postconditions of conditions describing the state of the world. These conditions are conjunctions of predicates as $(w_k = expr)$ where w_k is a parameter of the model, and *expr* is an expression (see §3.1.1). Thanks to this particular type of constraints extra variables are not necessary for computing strongest postconditions. It can be done using two more properties:

Property 6
$$SPost(\{w_k := expr_1\}, (w_l = expr_2)) = (w_l = expr_2) \; \textit{if} \; k \neq l$$
$$= (w_l = expr_1) \; \textit{if} \; k = l$$

Property 7

$$\bigwedge_{i=1}^{p} (E_i\{P\}S_i) \Longrightarrow (\bigwedge_{i=1}^{p} E_i)\{P\}(\bigwedge_{i=1}^{p} S_i)$$

Therefore, in order to compute $SPost(I_i, S_{i-1})$, it is only necessary to know how the parameters of the model are modified by the execution of the instruction. This can be seen as a *symbolic interpretation* of the program (see [Cousot 75], [King 74]).

Coming back to the given language, we will only express the part of the model modified by the execution of the instruction. It will be specified by a delete-list and an add-list.

    MOVE obj_1 TO $obj_2 * T$
T may be the identity transform. We consider that the uncertainty on the position of the gripper is determined by the resolution of the robot U_{move}.

delete-list:
    $ARC(robot, gripper) : P = T_0 \wedge$
    $ARC(robot, gripper) : U = U_0$
add-list:
    $ARC(robot, gripper) : P =$
        $WAY(robot, obj_2) : P * T * WAY(obj_1, gripper) : P$
    $\wedge ARC(robot, gripper) : U = U_{move}$

    GRASP obj
Grasping makes the uncertainty of obj relatively to the gripper be projected on the plane of the jaws (see figure 6). Positions are not modified.

delete-list:
    $ARC(father(obj), obj) : P = T_0 \wedge$
    $ARC(father(obj), obj) : U = U_0$
add-list:
    $ARC(gripper, obj) : P = WAY(gripper, obj) : P \wedge$
    $ARC(gripper, obj) : U =$
        $project[WAY(gripper, obj) : U,$
            $\{WAY(workspace, gripper), plane, (000), (010)\}]$

DROP obj_1 ONTO $(obj_2, contact)$
Dropping makes the relative uncertainty of obj_1 and obj_2 be projected according to the contact. obj_1 is already at the right position. Positions are not modified.

delete-list:
    $ARC(gripper, obj_1) : P = T_0 \wedge$
    $ARC(gripper, obj_1) : U = U_0$
add-list:
    $ARC(obj_2, obj_1) : P = WAY(obj_2, obj_1) : P \wedge$
    $ARC(obj_2, obj_1) : U =$
        $project[WAY(obj_2, obj_1) : U,$
            $\{WAY(workspace, obj_2) : P, contact\}]$

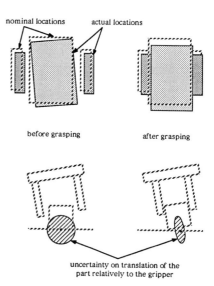

before grasping   after grasping

uncertainty on translation of the
part relatively to the gripper

Figure 6: The effect of grasping

LOCATE obj_1 RELATIVELY TO obj_2
The information provided by measuring the relative position between obj_1 and obj_2 allows to update every arc of $WAY(obj_1, obj_2)$.
For all $ARC(obj_k, obj_l)$ of $WAY(obj_1, obj_2)$:

delete-list:
    $ARC(obj_k, obj_l) : P = T_0 \wedge$
    $ARC(obj_k, obj_l) : U = U_0$
add-list:
    $ARC(obj_k, obj_l) : P =$
        $merge \; [sense(obj_1, obj_2), ARC(obj_k, obj_l)] : P$
    $\wedge ARC(obj_k, obj_l) : U =$
        $merge \; [sense(obj_1, obj_2), ARC(obj_k, obj_l)] : U$

3.2.2 Backward propagation

In formal program proving, the weakest precondition of an assignment is given by:

$$WPre(\{x := exp\}, F) = F(x \mid exp)$$

For example:
$$WPre(\{x := x * 2\}, (x \leq 4)) = (x * 2 \leq 4) = (x \leq 2)$$

Using this axiom, backward propagation is mostly a rewriting process. As the tree structure is a data given to the prover, it can be used in the backward propagation in order to simplify the expression of the constraints. When backchaining, we will never have expressions like: $(ARC(obj_1, obj_2) \wedge C) \vee (\neg ARC(obj_1, obj_2) \wedge C')$ as the presence of $ARC(obj_1, obj_2)$ may be evaluated from the tree.

    MOVE obj_1 TO $obj_2 * T$
This instruction has an effect on the $ARC(robot, gripper)$. So the weakest precondition of this instruction for a constraint C will be obtained by substituting each item $WAY(obj_i, obj_j)$ in C:

- if $ARC(robot, gripper)$ belongs to $WAY(obj_i, obj_j)$[5] in the direct way by:

---
[5]$WAY(...)$ is computed on the tree resulting of the action

$WAY(obj_i, robot) * A_{move} * WAY(gripper, obj_i)$ where
$A_{move} : P =$
$WAY(robot, obj_2) : P * T * WAY(obj_1, gripper) : P$
and $A_{move} : U = U_{move}$

- if $ARC(robot, gripper)$ belongs to $WAY(obj_i, obj_j)$ in the indirect way by:
$WAY(obj_i, gripper) * A_{move}^{-1} * WAY(gripper, obj_j)$

- otherwise $WAY(obj_i, obj_j)$ remains the same

GRASP obj

This instruction modifies the uncertainty between $gripper$ and obj. The weakest precondition of grasping for a constraint C is obtained by substituting each item $WAY(obj_i, obj_j)$ in C:

- if $ARC(gripper, obj)$ belongs to $WAY(obj_i, obj_j)$ in the direct way by
$WAY(obj_i, gripper) * A_{grasp} * WAY(obj, obj_j)$ where
$A_{grasp} : P = WAY(gripper, obj) : P$
and $A_{grasp} : U = project[...]$ (see §3.2.1)

- if $ARC(gripper, obj)$ belongs to $WAY(obj_i, obj_j)$ in the indirect way by:
$WAY(obj_i, obj) * A_{grasp}^{-1} * WAY(gripper, obj_j)$

- otherwise $WAY(obj_i, obj_j)$ remains the same

DROP obj_1 ONTO (obj_2, contact)

This instruction modifies the uncertainty between obj_1 and obj_2. Its weakest precondition for a constraint C is obtained by substituting each item $WAY(obj_i, obj_j)$ in C:

- if $ARC(obj_1, obj_2)$ belongs to $WAY(obj_i, obj_j)$ in the direct way by:
$WAY(obj_i, obj_1) * A_{drop} * WAY(obj_2, obj_j)$ where
$A_{drop} : P = WAY(obj_1, obj_2) : P$ and
$A_{drop} : U = project[...]$ (see §3.2.1)

- if $ARC(obj_1, obj_2)$ belongs to $WAY(obj_i, obj_j)$ in the indirect way by: $WAY(obj_i, obj_2) * A_{drop}^{-1} * WAY(obj_1, obj_j)$

- $WAY(obj_i, obj_j)$ remains the same

LOCATE obj_1 RELATIVELY TO obj_2

This intruction has an effect on each arc of $WAY(obj_1, obj_2)$. Its weakest precondition for a constraint C is obtained by substituting each item $WAY(obj_i, obj_j)$ in C:

- if $WAY(obj_1, obj_2)$ intersects $WAY(obj_i, obj_j)$ in the direct way and
$WAY(obj_1, obj_2) \cap WAY(obj_i, obj_j) = WAY(obj_k, obj_l)$ by:
$WAY(obj_i, obj_k) * A_{locate} * WAY(obj_l, obj_j)$

$A_{locate} = merge[ARC(obj_k, ...), sense(obj_1, obj_2)] *$
$\quad\quad ... *$
$\quad\quad merge[(ARC(..., obj_l), sense(obj_1, obj_2)]$

- if $WAY(obj_1, obj_2)$ intersects $WAY(obj_i, obj_j)$ in the indirect way and
$WAY(obj_1, obj_2) \cap WAY(obj_i, obj_j) = WAY(obj_k, obj_l)$ by:
$WAY(obj_i, obj_l) * A_{locate}^{-1} * WAY(obj_k, obj_j)$

- otherwise $WAY(obj_i, obj_j)$ remains the same.

4   Related works

A large amount of work has focused on the problem of uncertainty in robotics. Among them, much attention has been paid to uncertainty modeling. Recent works on this topic are based on probabilistic models of uncertainty. The purpose of [Smith 87a, Smith 87b] is very close to the manipulation of the tree structure presented above. This paper presents a general theory for estimating uncertain relative spatial relationships between reference frames in a network of uncertain spatial relationships. [Durrant 87] presents a probabilistic viewpoint of uncertain geometry. A major problem addressed in his paper is how to maintain the topological consistency of relations between geometric features when updating the model. The resulting analysis has been applied to the problem of developing maximal information sensing.

Some general methods for incorporating error information in planning have been developed in [Taylor 76], [Brooks 82]. Both works take place in the framework of a hierarchical planning system using skeleton refinement. Taylor propagates errors and tolerances forward through algebraic relations describing a physical situation for deciding the correctness of the manipulation program. Except that we manipulate uncertainty hypervolumes instead of real numbers, the basic idea of this approach is rather close to our forward propagation. Brooks generalizes Taylor's work in order to allow a backward reasoning by using symbolic constraints manipulation. The system manipulates inequations on uninstantiated variables either forward for verifying a plan or backward in order to restrict choice on plan variables or to amend the plan. Unlike in our approach, in his method, there is no difference between the backward and the forward propagation except that the unknown variables of the inequations manipulated by the system change. Brooks gives no particular attention to the problem of modeling both a structured environment and the effects of actions.

Another way of tackling the uncertainty problem consists in taking it into account when planning motion strategies. The preimage approach of [Lozano 84] focuses on fine motions strategies. Such a method can be said local compared with the previous one. Much attention is paid to uncertainty on control; it is modeled by means of a velocity cone and a position error ball. The approach is a backward propagation of geometric regions in a configuration space. Being given a goal, the problem is to find the region from which the goal is reachable from a single motion (a compliant motion). It is a geometric representation of weakest preconditions. The entire process may be seen as the proof/amendment of <starting region>{compliant MOVE}<goal region> in a generalized-damper model. Such a configuration space model cannot be used for describing structured environments and so cannot be used, alone, in a global approach to deal with uncertainties.

Another very different approach presented in [Mason 86] consists in generating sensorless motion strategies for reducing uncertainties combining frictional forces and geometric constraints. It is based on a mechanical reasoning allowing a taxonomy of physical situations represented in what is called an operation space. Each region of this space associates a single final situation to a set of parameters for a particular operation (grasping for example). This work could be very useful for making global methods more realistic regarding mechanics.

[Donald 86] develops a method in the context of execution monitoring. The problem initially introduced in [Lozano 84] is to generate plans that allow to reach a goal recognizably. The problem comes from the fact that two situations might not be distinguishable because of uncertainty when one is in the goal and the other is not. Donald proposes an approach that generates motion strategies which achieve the goal when it is recognizably reachable and signals error when it is not. Sensing errors, control errors and uncertainty on geometry are represented as a position uncertainty in a generalized configuration space.

5 Discussion

A framework allowing the verification of the correctness of a manipulator program, taking explicit account of uncertainty has been presented in this paper. This approach lies on several basic assumptions which are discussed here.

Static representation of operations

We consider the execution of a program as an alternate sequence of states and operations. This allows to reason about static states of the world, and to avoid temporal aspects of manipulation. A major drawback of this simplification is that it is very difficult to represent uncertainties occuring during operations. One could imagine to represent states of the world and operations as functions of time. A constraint would be a predicate which has to hold between two dates. This has never been done. Uncertainties occuring during operations are represented in [Buckley 87] or [Lozano 84] by cones containing the planned trajectory of the effector.

Representation of the world

The problem of world modeling has been studied extensively but it still remains open. We can distinguish several different aspects of modeling that are important for planning robot operations in presence of uncertainty:

- to compute motions and trajectories, we must have a model of the geometry of objects. We have not mentionned much about of the representation of uncertainty on shape and size of objects. We do not have any real efficient tool to deal with this aspect. In [Donald 86], the author proposes to represent the uncertainty on a parameter defining the geometry of an object by incrementing the dimension of a generalized configuration space. For real scenes, the great number of parameters should lead to an unmanageable complexity.

- we must have also a representation of spatial relationships between objects. As knowledge about existence and nature of contacts between objects is very interesting to determine their relative position uncertainty, it is very important to have a good representation of contacts between objects. In Smith's work [Smith 87a], the "relational" aspect of the world is well represented. Except that he has chosen a probabilistic representation of uncertainty, his representation is close to ours.

- it can be also important to model physical aspect of the world such as forces, friction, or elasticity to estimate the exact effect of actions. The model presented in this paper is limited regarding this feature. Especially, our method could be very well improved if we were able to represent compliant motions with our model. A representation similar to the one in [Donald 86], or in [Lozano 84] is better suited from this particular point of view.

Choice of a programming language

The whole method of program proving relies on the assumption that the language is defined by giving strongest postconditions and/or weakest preconditions of each instruction. This raises the problem of defining the semantics of a robot programming language. As we know, this problem has never been specifically studied. To allow program verification/amendment, a language has to meet several requirements:

- its semantics has to be "homogeneous". This means that the effect of all the instructions can be represented at a single level of abstraction. This is not the case with actual industrial robot programming languages because they mix quite high level instructions (for moving the effector, for example) and very low level instructions (generally I/O operations and sensors readings)

- the effect of the operations has to be predictable, i.e., operations have to be deterministic. Even if there is uncertainty on the effect of actions, this uncertainty has to be predictable. This is not always obvious. For example, force controled motions do not always stop in an entire predictable state.

These two requirements are not met by existing robot programming languages. We are convinced that these needs necessitate new formulations of robot control as [Khatib 85]. Although, we are conscious of the difficulty of implementing well-adapted manipulation primitives, specific developments seem a necessary stage of automatic robot programming.

References

[Berlioux 83] P.Berlioux, Ph. Bizard: "Construction, preuve et évaluation de programmes", Dunod Publisher, October 1983, (In French)

[Brooks 82] R.A.Brooks: "Symbolic error analysis and robot planning", International Journal of Robotics Research, Vol.1, No.4, Winter 1982

[Buckley 87] S.J.Buckley: "Planning and teaching compliant motions stategies", Ph.D dissertation, MIT AI lab., AI-TR-936

[Cousot 75] P.Cousot, R.Cousot: "Static verification of dynamic type properties of variables", Research Report IMAG no 25, Grenoble, November 1975

[Donald 86] B.R.Donald: "A theory of error detection and recovery: robot motion planning with uncertainty in the geometric models of the robot and environment", International Workshop on Geometric Reasoning, Oxford University, July 1986

[Durrant 87]   H.F.Durrant-Whyte: *"Uncertain geometry in robotics"*, IEEE International Conference on Robotics and Automation, Raleigh, March/April 1987

[Hoare 69]   C.A.R.Hoare: *"An axiomatic basis for computer programming"*, Communications of the ACM, no 12, pp576/580, 1969

[Khatib 85]   O.Khatib: *"The operational space formulation in the analysis, design, and control of robot manipulators"*, 3rd International Symposium on Robotics Research, Gouvieux, October 1985

[King 74]   J.C.King: *"Symbolic execution and program testing"*, IBM Thomas J. Watson Research Report RC 5082, Yorktown Heights, October 1974

[Lozano 84]   T.Lozano-Pérez, M.T.Mason, R.H.Taylor: *"Automatic Synthesis of fine-motion strategies for robots"*, International Journal of Robotics Research Vol.3, No.1, Spring 1984

[Mason 86]   M.T.Mason, R.C.Brost: *"Automatic grasp planning: an operation space approach"*, 6th Symposium on Theory and Practice of Robots and Manipulators, Cracow, Poland, September 1986

[Nilsson 82]   N.J.Nilsson: *"Principles of Artificial Intelligence"*, Springer Verlag, 1982

[Pertin 86]   J.Pertin-Troccaz, P.Puget: *"Contrôle dans le système de programmation automatique SHARP"*, Research Report LIFIA no.50, Grenoble, June 1986, (In French)

[Puget 85]   P.Puget: *"Problèmes de prise en compte des incertitudes en robotique d'assemblage"*, DEA Report, LIFIA, Grenoble, June 1985, (In French)

[Puget 87]   P.Puget: *"Utilisation de techniques de preuve de programme pour la programmation automatique des robots"*, Ph.D Thesis (forthcoming), LIFIA, Grenoble, 1987, (In French)

[Smith 87a]   R.Smith, M.Self, P.Cheeseman: *"A stochastic map for uncertain spatial relationships"*, IEEE International Conference on Robotics and Automation, Raleigh, March/April 87

[Smith 87b]   R.Smith, M.Self, P.Cheeseman: *"Estimating uncertain spatial relationships in robotics"*, to appear in the International Journal of Robotics Research, Winter 1987

[Taylor 76]   R.H.Taylor: *"Synthesis of manipulator control programs from task-level specifications"*, AIM 228, AI Laboratory, Stanford, July 1976

Example

The purpose of this example is to show the method rather than to illustrate the computations. This is the reason why we have chosen a simplified representation of uncertainty. We only consider translation movements and do not consider rotation errors. Thus uncertainty volumes can be represented as cartesian products of intervals $[-\Delta x, +\Delta x] \times [-\Delta y, +\Delta y] \times [-\Delta z, +\Delta z]$. This set will be noted $|\Delta x|\Delta y|\Delta z|$

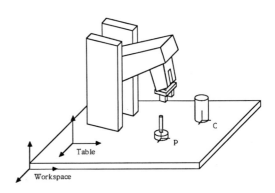

Figure 7: A manipulation

Composition and inversion operators are very simple because position and uncertainty are decoupled:
$$(Tr_1, |\Delta x_1|\Delta y_1|\Delta z_1|) * [(Tr_2, |\Delta x_2|\Delta y_2|\Delta z_2|)$$
$$= (Tr_1 * Tr_2, |\Delta x_1 + \Delta x_2|\Delta y_1 + \Delta y_2|\Delta z_1 + \Delta z_2|)$$
$$(Tr, |\Delta x|\Delta y|\Delta z|)^{-1} = (Tr^{-1}, |\Delta x|\Delta y|\Delta z|)$$

Let us consider a manipulation consisting in grasping a piston P and placing it into a cylindrical part C (figure 7). Assuming that the initial position of the different parts is known, this task is theoritically achievable by the following program:

```
MOVE gripper TO P*Transl(z,200);
GRASP P;
MOVE P TO C*Transl(z,250);
DROP P;
MOVE gripper TO Workspace;
```

We suppose that we have a manipulator whose accuracy is 0.1mm in the x and y directions, and 0.2mm in the z direction. We suppose also that we have a vision sensor which gives the position of an object with an accuracy of 0.3mm in each direction. Because of the design of the gripper, the relative position error between the gripper and a part to be grasped has to be smaller than 3mm in each direction. The clearance between the piston and the cylinder is 1mm in the x and y directions and 3mm in the z direction. Thus, we have to prove the following constrained program for a particular S_0:

$$CP = \{ ((true),\{\text{MOVE gripper TO P*Transl(z,200)}\}),$$
$$(C_1,\{\text{GRASP P}\}),$$
$$((true),\{\text{MOVE P TO C*Transl(z,250)}\}),$$
$$(C_3,\{\text{DROP P}\}),$$
$$((true),\{\text{MOVE gripper TO workspace}\})\}$$

where:
$$C_1 = [WAY(P, gripper) : U \subseteq |3.0|3.0|3.0|]$$
$$C_3 = [WAY(P, C) : U \subseteq |1.0|1.0|3.0|]$$

Forward propagation

Let us suppose that the initial state can be represented by the tree structure of figure 8[6].

W/S_1 resulting from the first move differs only from W/S_0 by the transform between robot and gripper. With our conventions, the position uncertainty of gripper is not changed. We can check for the satisfaction of C_1:

---

[6]In order to keep the figures readable, we will only specify uncertainties in them

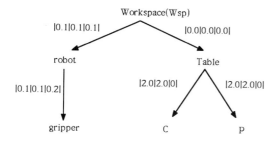

Figure 8: W/S_0

$$WAY(P, gripper) : U$$
$$= [ARC(P, Table) * ARC(Table, Wsp)$$
$$\quad * ARC(Wsp, robot) * ARC(robot, gripper)] : U$$
$$= |2 + 0 + 0.1 + 0.1|2 + 0 + 0.1 + 0.1|0 + 0 + 0.1 + 0.2|$$
$$= |2.2|2.2|0.3|$$

C_1 is satisfied and we can compute the next state.

W/S_2 is computed using the rules given in §3.2. The tree structure is given by figure 9. W/S_3 resulting from the second move differs from W/S_2 only by the transform between robot and gripper. The position uncertainty of gripper is not changed. We can check for the satisfaction of C_3:

$$WAY(P, C) : U$$
$$= [ARC(P, gripper) * ARC(gripper, robot) * ARC(robot, Wsp)$$
$$\quad * ARC(Wsp, table) * ARC(table, C)] : U$$
$$= |2.2 + 0.1 + 0.1 + 0 + 2|0 + 0.1 + 0.1 + 0 + 2$$
$$\quad |0.3 + 0.2 + 0.1 + 0 + 0|$$
$$= |4.4|2.2|0.6|$$

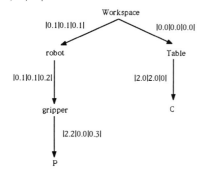

Figure 9: W/S_2

C_3 is not satisfied. We have to compute its weakest preconditions.

Backward propagation

From the rules given in §3.2.2 for computing weakest preconditions, we get:

$$C_3^2 = WPre(\{\text{MOVE P TO C*Transl(z,250)}\}, C_3)$$
$$= (WAY(P, gripper) * A_{move}^{-1} * WAY(robot, C)) : U \subseteq |1.0|1.0|3.0|$$

where

$$A_{move}^{-1} : P$$
$$= (WAY(robot, C) : P * Transl(z, 250) * WAY(P, gripper) : P)^{-1}$$
$$= ARC(gripper, P) * Transl(z, -250) * WAY(C, robot)$$
$$A_{move}^{-1} : U$$
$$= |0.1|0.1|0.2|$$

$$C_3^1 = WPre(\{\text{GRASP P}\}, C_3^2)$$
$$= (A_{grasp}^{-1} * A_{move}^{-1} * WAY(robot, C)) : U \subseteq |1.0|1.0|3.0|$$

where A_{move}^{-1} is same as above and

$$A_{grasp}^{-1} : U$$
$$= project[WAY(gripper, P) : U,$$
$$A_{grasp}^{-1} : P$$
$$= WAY(P, gripper) : P$$

C_3^0, which is $WPre(\{\text{MOVE gripper TO P*Transl(z,200)}\}, C_3^1)$ is computed in the same way.

Searching for a patch

If we decompose C_3^1 and C_3^2 in elementary arcs, we get:

$$C_3^2 = [ARC(gripper, P)^{-1} * A_{move}^{-1} * ARC(Wsp, robot)^{-1} *$$
$$\quad ARC(Wsp, table) * ARC(table, C)] : U \subseteq U_3$$
$$C_3^1 = [A_{grasp}^{-1} * A_{move}^{-1} * ARC(Wsp, robot)^{-1} *$$
$$\quad ARC(Wsp, table) * ARC(table, C)] : U \subseteq U_3$$

In C_3^2, $A_{move}^{-1} : U$, $ARC(Wsp, robot)^{-1} : U$, $ARC(Wsp, table)$ are irreducible and "relatively small" terms (0.1 or 0.2mm). On the other hand, $ARC(gripper, P) : U$ and $ARC(table, C) : U$ have a larger contribution (relatively $|2.2|0.0|0.3|$ and $|2.2|2.2|0.0|$) and can be reduced by a sensing operation.

In C_3^1, there are also some irreducible terms: $A_{move} : U$, $ARC(Wsp, robot) : U$, and $ARC(Wsp, table) : U$. $ARC(table, C) : U$ can be reduced by a sensing operation. A_{grasp} depends on WAY(gripper,P):U, i.e. $ARC(robot, gripper) : U$, $ARC(Wsp, robot) : U$, $ARC(Wsp, table) : U$, and $ARC(table, P) : U$. All these terms are irreducible except $ARC(table, P) : U$ which can be reduced by a sensing operation.

A modified program could be:

```
LOCATE C RELATIVELY TO Table;
LOCATE P RELATIVELY TO Table;
MOVE gripper TO P*Transl(z,200);
GRASP P;
MOVE P TO C*Transl(z,250);
DROP P;
MOVE gripper TO Workspace;
```

The execution of the first instruction makes $ARC(C, Table)$ become $merge(sense(C, Table), ARC(C, Table))$, which is easy to compute. The resulting uncertainty is the intersection of $|0.3|0.3|0.3|$, volume given by the vision sensor and $|2.0|2.0|0|$, initial uncertainty volume. This intersection is $|0.3|0.3|0|$. The resulting nominal value is unknown. As nominal values and uncertainties are decoupled, this will make no trouble to evaluate constraints.

The state resulting from the execution of the two first instructions is given by figure 10.

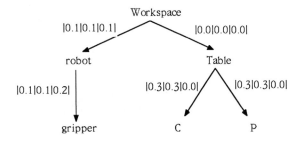

Figure 10: The effect of the patch

Then we have to propagate this state forward to verify C_1 and C_3. Propagating and then checking for the satisfaction of the constraints is left to the reader.

Acknowledgments

This research is supported by Agence De l'Informatique and a contract with Industrie et Technologie de la Machine Intelligence. This paper greatly benefited from discussions with Professor Jean-Claude Latombe.

A Stochastic Map
For Uncertain Spatial Relationships

Randall Smith[†] Matthew Self[‡] Peter Cheeseman[§]

SRI International
333 Ravenswood Avenue
Menlo Park, California 94025

[‡]Currently at UC Berkeley.

[†]Currently at General Motors Research Laboratories,
Warren, Michigan.

[§]Currently at NASA Ames Research Center,
Moffett Field, California.

In this paper we will describe a representation for spatial relationships which makes explicit their inherent uncertainty. We will show ways to manipulate them to obtain estimates of relationships and associated uncertainties not explicitly given, and show how decisions to sense or act can be made *a priori* based on those estimates. We will show how new constraint information, usually obtained by measurement, can be used to update the world model of relationships consistently, and in some situations, optimally. The framework we describe relies only on well-known state estimation methods.

1 Introduction

Spatial structure is commonly represented at a low level, in both robotics and computer graphics, as local coordinate frames embedded in objects and the transformations among them — primarily, translations and rotations in two or three dimensions. These representations manifest themselves, for example, in transformation diagrams [Paul 1981]. The structural information is *relative* in nature; relations must be chained together to compute those not directly given, as illustrated in Figure 1. In the figure the nominal, initial locations of a beacon and a robot are indicated with coordinate frames, and are defined with respect to a fixed reference frame in the room. The *actual* relationships are x_{01} and x_{02}, (with the zero subscript dropped for relations defined with respect to the reference frame). After the robot moves, its relation to the beacon is no longer explicitly described.

Generally, nominal information is *all* that is given about the relations. Thus, errors due to measurement, motion (control), or manufacture cause a disparity between the actual spatial structure and the nominal structure we expect. Strategies (for navigation, or automated assembly of industrial parts) that depend on such complex spatial structures, will fail if they cannot accommodate the errors. By utilizing knowledge about tolerances and device accuracies, more robust strategies can be devised, as will be subsequently shown.

1.1 Compounding and Merging

The spatial structure shown in Figure 1 represents the *actual* underlying relationships about which we have explicit information. Given a method for combining serial "chains" of given relationships, we can derive the implicit ones. If the explicit relationships are not *known* perfectly, errors will *compound* in a chain of calculations, and be larger than those in any constituent of the chain.

With perfect information, relationship x_{21} need not be measured — it can be computed through the chain (using x_2 and x_1). However, because of imperfect knowledge, the computed value and the measurement will be different. The difference is resolved by *merging* the pieces of information into a description *at least* as "accurate" as the most accurate piece, no matter how the errors are described. If the merging operation does not do this, there is no point in using it.

The real relationships x_1, x_2, and x_{21} are mutually constrained,

and when information about x_{21} is introduced, the merging operation should improve the estimates of them all, by amounts proportional to the magnitudes of their initial relative uncertainties. If the merging operation is *consistent*, one updated relation (vector) can be removed from the loop, as the relation can always be recomputed (by compounding the others).

Obviously, a situation may be represented by an arbitrarily complex graph, making the estimation of some relationship, given all the available information, a difficult task.

1.2 Previous Work

Some general methods for incorporating error information in robotics applications([Taylor 1976], [Brooks 1982]) rely on using worst-case bounds on the parameters of individual relationships. However, as worst-case estimates are combined (for example, in the chaining above) the results can become *very conservative*, limiting their use in decision making.

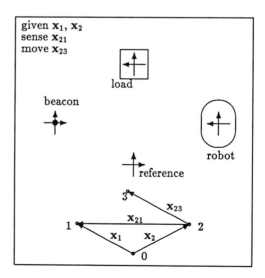

given x_1, x_2
sense x_{21}
move x_{23}

load

beacon

robot

reference

Figure 1: Robot Navigation: Spatial Structure

A probabilistic interpretation of the errors can be employed, given some constraints on their size, and the availability of error models. Smith and Cheeseman[Smith, 1984] described six-degree-of-freedom relationships by their mean vectors and covariance matrices, and produced first-order formulae for compounding them. These formulae were subsequently augmented ([Smith, 1985]) with a merging operation — computation of the conditional mean and covariance — to combine two estimates of the same relation. A similar scalar operation is performed by the HILARE mobile robot [Chatila, 1985].

Durrant-Whyte [Durrant-Whyte 1986] takes an approach to the problem similar to Smith and Cheeseman, but propagates errors differentially rather than using the partial derivative matrices of the transformations. Both are concerned with integrating information consistently across an explicitly represented spatial graph. Others [Faugeras 1986],[Bolle and Cooper, 1986] are exploiting similar ideas for the optimal integration of noisy geometric data in order to estimate global parameters (object localization).

This paper (amplified in [Smith 1986]) extends our previous work by defining a few simple procedures for representing, manipulating, and making decisions with uncertain spatial information, in the setting of recursive estimation theory.

1.3   The Example

In Figure 1, the initial locations of a beacon and a mobile robot are given with respect to a fixed landmark. Our knowledge of these relations, $\mathbf{x}_1$ and $\mathbf{x}_2$, is imprecise, however. In addition, the location of a loading area (the box) is given very accurately with respect to the landmark. Thus, the vector labeled $\mathbf{x}_3$, has been omitted.

The robot's task is to move to the loading area, so that it's center is within the box. It can then be loaded.

The robot reasons:

"I know where the loading area is, and approximately where I am (in the room). Thus, I know approximately what motion I need to make. Of course, I can't move perfectly, but I have an idea what my accuracy is. *If I move*, will I likely reach the loader (with the required accuracy)? If so, then I will move."

"If not, suppose that I try to sense the beacon. My map shows its approximate location *in the room*; but of course, I don't know exactly where *I am*. Where is it in relation to me? Can I get the beacon in the field of view of my sensor without searching around?"

"*Suppose* I make the measurement. My sensor is not perfect either, but I know its accuracy. Will the measurement give me enough information so that I can then move to the loader?"

Before trying to answer these questions, we first need to create a map, and place in it the initial relations described.

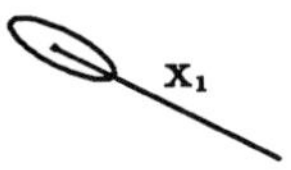

2   The Stochastic Map

In this paper, uncertain spatial relationships will be tied together in a representation called the *stochastic map*. It contains estimates of the spatial relationships, their uncertainties, and the inter-dependencies of the estimates.

2.1   Representation

A *spatial relationship* will be represented by the vector of its *spatial variables*, $\mathbf{x}$. For example, the position and orientation of a mobile robot can be described by its coordinates, x and y, in a two dimensional cartesian reference frame and by its orientation, ϕ, given as a rotation about the z axis. An *uncertain* spatial relationship, moreover, can be represented by a *probability distribution* over its spatial variables.

The complete probability distribution is generally not available. For example, most measuring devices provide only a nominal value of the measured relationship, and we can estimate the average error from the sensor specifications. However, the full distribution may be unneccesary for making decisions, such as whether the robot will be able to complete a given task (e.g. passing through a doorway). For these reasons, we choose to model an uncertain spatial relationship by estimating the first two moments of its probability distribution—the *mean*, $\hat{\mathbf{x}}$ and the *covariance* (see Figure 2). Figure 2 shows our map with only one object located in it — the beacon. The diagonal elements of the covariance matrix are just the variances of the spatial variables, while the off-diagonal elements are the covariances between the spatial variables. The interpretation of the ellipse in the figure follows in the next section.

Similarly, to model a system of n uncertain spatial relationships, we construct the vector of *all* the spatial variables, called the *system state vector*. As before, we will estimate the mean of the state vector, $\hat{\mathbf{x}}$, and the *system covariance matrix*, $\mathbf{C}(\mathbf{x})$. In Figure 3 the map structure is defined recursively (described below), providing the method for building it by adding one new relation at at time.

The current system state vector is appended with $\mathbf{x}_n$, the vector of spatial variables for a new uncertain relationship being added. Likewise, the current system covariance matrix is augmented with the covariance matrix of the new vector, $\mathbf{C}(\mathbf{x}_n)$, and its cross-covariance with the new vector $\mathbf{C}(\mathbf{x}, \mathbf{x}_n)$, as shown. The cross-covariance matrix is composed of a column of sub-matrices — the cross-covariances of each of the original relations in the state vector with the new one, $\mathbf{C}(\mathbf{x}_i, \mathbf{x}_n)$. These off-diagonal sub-matrices encode the dependencies between the estimates of the different spatial relationships and provide the mechanism for updating all relational estimates that depend on any that are changed.

Thus our "map" consists of the current estimate of the mean of the system state vector, which gives the nominal locations of objects in the map with respect to the world reference frame, and the associated system covariance matrix, which gives the uncertainty of each point in the map and the inter-dependencies of these uncertainties.

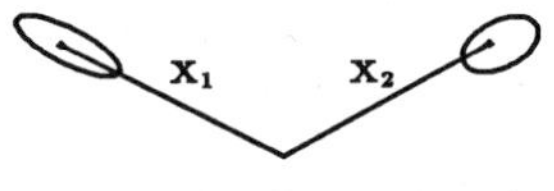

$$\hat{\mathbf{x}} = \hat{\mathbf{x}}_1 = \begin{bmatrix} \hat{x} \\ \hat{y} \\ \hat{\phi} \end{bmatrix}, \quad \mathbf{C}(\mathbf{x}) = \begin{bmatrix} \sigma_x^2 & \sigma_{xy} & \sigma_{x\phi} \\ \sigma_{xy} & \sigma_y^2 & \sigma_{y\phi} \\ \sigma_{x\phi} & \sigma_{y\phi} & \sigma_\phi^2 \end{bmatrix}$$

Figure 2: The Map with One Relation

$$\hat{\mathbf{x}}' = \left[\begin{array}{c} \hat{\mathbf{x}} \\ \hline \hat{\mathbf{x}}_n \end{array} \right], \quad \mathbf{C}(\mathbf{x}') = \left[\begin{array}{c|c} \mathbf{C}(\mathbf{x}) & \mathbf{C}(\mathbf{x}, \mathbf{x}_n) \\ \hline \mathbf{C}(\mathbf{x}_n, \mathbf{x}) & \mathbf{C}(\mathbf{x}_n) \end{array} \right]$$

Figure 3: Adding A New Object

The map can now be constructed with the initial estimates of the means and covariances of the relations $\mathbf{x}_1$ and $\mathbf{x}_2$, as shown in Figure 3. If the given estimates are independent of each other, the cross-covariance matrix will be 0.

2.2 Interpretation

For some decisions based on uncertain spatial relationships, we must assume a particular distribution that fits the estimated moments. For example, a robot might need to be able to calculate the probability that a certain object will be in its field of view, or the probability that it will succeed in passing through a doorway.

Given only the mean, $\hat{\mathbf{x}}$, and covariance matrix, $\mathbf{C}(\mathbf{x})$, of a multivariate probability distribution, the principle of maximum entropy indicates that the distribution resulting from assuming the least addtional information is the normal distribution. Furthermore if the relationship is calculated by combining many different pieces of information, the central limit theorem indicates that the resulting distribution will tend to a normal distribution.

We will graph uncertain spatial relationships by plotting contours of constant probability from a normal distribution with the given mean and covariance information. These contours are concentric ellipsoids (ellipses for two dimensions) whose parameters can be calculated from the covariance matrix, $\mathbf{C}(\mathbf{x})$ [Nahi, 1976]. It is important to emphasize that we do not assume that the individual uncertain spatial relationships are described by normal distributions. We estimate the first two central moments of their distributions, and use the normal distribution only when we need to calculate specific probability contours.

In the figures in this paper, a line represents the *actual* relation between two objects (located at the endpoints). The actual object locations are known only by the simulator and displayed for our benefit. The robot's information is shown by the ellipses which are drawn centered on the estimated mean of the relationship and such that they enclose a 99.9% confidence region (about four standard deviations) for the relationships. The mean point itself is not shown.

We have defined our map, and loaded it with the given information. In the next two sections we must learn how to read it, and then change it, before discussing the example.

3 Reading the Map

Having seen how we represent uncertain spatial relationships by estimates of the mean and covariance of the system state vector, we now discuss methods for estimating the first two moments of unknown multivariate probability distributions. See [Papoulis, 1965] for detailed justifications of the following topics.

3.1 Uncertain Relationships

The first two moments computed by the formulae below for nonlinear relationships on random variables will be first-order estimates of the true values. To compute the actual values requires knowledge of the *complete* probability density function of the spatial variables, which will not generally be available in our applications. The usual approach is to approximate the non-linear function

$$\mathbf{y} = \mathbf{f}(\mathbf{x})$$

by a Taylor series expansion about the estimated mean, $\hat{\mathbf{x}}$, yielding:

$$\mathbf{y} = \mathbf{f}(\hat{\mathbf{x}}) + \mathbf{F}_{\mathbf{X}}(\mathbf{x} - \hat{\mathbf{x}}) + \cdots,$$

where $\mathbf{F}_{\mathbf{X}}$ is the matrix of partials, or Jacobian, of $\mathbf{f}$ evaluated at $\hat{\mathbf{x}}$:

$$\mathbf{F}_{\mathbf{X}} \triangleq \frac{\partial \mathbf{f}(\mathbf{x})}{\partial \mathbf{x}}(\hat{\mathbf{x}}) \triangleq \begin{bmatrix} \frac{\partial f_1}{\partial x_1} & \frac{\partial f_1}{\partial x_2} & \cdots & \frac{\partial f_1}{\partial x_n} \\ \frac{\partial f_2}{\partial x_1} & \frac{\partial f_2}{\partial x_2} & \cdots & \frac{\partial f_2}{\partial x_n} \\ \vdots & \vdots & \ddots & \vdots \\ \frac{\partial f_r}{\partial x_1} & \frac{\partial f_r}{\partial x_2} & \cdots & \frac{\partial f_r}{\partial x_n} \end{bmatrix}_{\mathbf{x}=\hat{\mathbf{x}}}.$$

This terminology is the extension of the f_x terminology from scalar calculus to vectors. The Jacobians are always understood to be evaluated at the estimated mean of the input variables.

Truncating the expansion for $\mathbf{y}$ after the linear term, and taking the expectation produces the linear estimate of the mean of $\mathbf{y}$:

$$\hat{\mathbf{y}} \approx \mathbf{f}(\hat{\mathbf{x}}). \qquad (1)$$

Similarly, the first-order estimate of the covariances are:

$$\begin{aligned} \mathbf{C}(\mathbf{y}) &\approx \mathbf{F}_{\mathbf{X}}\mathbf{C}(\mathbf{x})\mathbf{F}_{\mathbf{X}}^T, \\ \mathbf{C}(\mathbf{y}, \mathbf{z}) &\approx \mathbf{F}_{\mathbf{X}}\mathbf{C}(\mathbf{x}, \mathbf{z}), \qquad (2) \\ \mathbf{C}(\mathbf{z}, \mathbf{y}) &\approx \mathbf{C}(\mathbf{z}, \mathbf{x})\mathbf{F}_{\mathbf{X}}^T. \end{aligned}$$

Of course, if the function $\mathbf{f}$ is *linear*, then $\mathbf{F}_{\mathbf{X}}$ is a constant matrix, and the first two moments of the multivariate distribution of $\mathbf{y}$ are computed exactly, given correct moments for $\mathbf{x}$. Further, if $\mathbf{x}$ follows a normal distribution, then so does $\mathbf{y}$.

In the remainder of this paper we consider only first order estimates, and the symbol "$\approx$" should read as "linear estimate of."

3.2 Coordinate Frame Relationships

We now consider the spatial operations which are necessary to reduce serial chains of coordinate frame relationships between objects to some resultant (implicit) relationship of interest: compounding, and reversal. A useful composition of these operations is also described.

Given two spatial relationships, $\mathbf{x}_2$ and $\mathbf{x}_{23}$, as in Figure 1, *with the second described relative to the first*, we wish to compute the resultant relationship. We denote this binary operation by $\oplus$, and call it compounding.

In another situation, we wish to compute $\mathbf{x}_{21}$. It can be seen that $\mathbf{x}_2$ and $\mathbf{x}_1$ are not in the right form for compounding. We must first invert the sense of the vector $\mathbf{x}_2$ (producing $\mathbf{x}_{20}$). We denote this unary inverse operation $\ominus$, and call it reversal.

The composition of reversal and compounding operations used in computing $\mathbf{x}_{21}$ is very common, as it gives the location of one object coordinate frame *relative* to another, when both are described with a common reference.

These three formulae are:

$$\begin{aligned} \mathbf{x}_{ik} &\triangleq \mathbf{f}(\mathbf{x}_{ij}, \mathbf{x}_{jk}) \triangleq \mathbf{x}_{ij} \oplus \mathbf{x}_{jk} \\ \mathbf{x}_{ji} &\triangleq \mathbf{g}(\mathbf{x}_{ij}) \triangleq \ominus \mathbf{x}_{ij} \\ \mathbf{x}_{jk} &\triangleq \mathbf{h}(\mathbf{x}_{ij}, \mathbf{x}_{ik}) \triangleq \mathbf{f}(\mathbf{g}(\mathbf{x}_{ij}), \mathbf{x}_{ik}) \triangleq \ominus \mathbf{x}_{ij} \oplus \mathbf{x}_{ik} \end{aligned}$$

Utilizing (1), the first-order estimate of the mean of the compounding operation is:

$$\hat{\mathbf{x}}_{ik} \approx \hat{\mathbf{x}}_{ij} \oplus \hat{\mathbf{x}}_{jk}.$$

Also, from (2), the first-order estimate of the covariance is:

$$\mathbf{C}(\mathbf{x}_{ik}) \approx \mathbf{J}_{\oplus} \begin{bmatrix} \mathbf{C}(\mathbf{x}_{ij}) & \mathbf{C}(\mathbf{x}_{ij}, \mathbf{x}_{jk}) \\ \mathbf{C}(\mathbf{x}_{jk}, \mathbf{x}_{ij}) & \mathbf{C}(\mathbf{x}_{jk}) \end{bmatrix} \mathbf{J}_{\oplus}^T$$

where the Jacobian of the compounding operation, $\mathbf{J}_\oplus$ is given by:

$$\mathbf{J}_\oplus \triangleq \frac{\partial(\mathbf{x}_{ij} \oplus \mathbf{x}_{jk})}{\partial(\mathbf{x}_{ij}, \mathbf{x}_{jk})} = \frac{\partial \mathbf{x}_{ik}}{\partial(\mathbf{x}_{ij}, \mathbf{x}_{jk})} = \begin{bmatrix} \mathbf{J}_{1\oplus} & \mathbf{J}_{2\oplus} \end{bmatrix}.$$

The square sub–matrices, $\mathbf{J}_{1\oplus}$ and $\mathbf{J}_{2\oplus}$, are the left and right halves of the compounding Jacobian.

The first two moments of the reversal function can be estimated similarly, utilizing its Jacobian, $\mathbf{J}_\ominus$. The formulae for compounding and reversal, and their Jacobians, are given for three degrees–of–freedom in Appendix A. The six degree–of–freedom formulae are given in [Smith 1986].

The mean of the composite relationship, computed by $\mathbf{h}()$, can be estimated by application of the other operations:

$$\hat{\mathbf{x}}_{jk} = \hat{\mathbf{x}}_{ji} \oplus \hat{\mathbf{x}}_{ik} = \ominus\hat{\mathbf{x}}_{ij} \oplus \hat{\mathbf{x}}_{ik}$$

The Jacobian can be computed by chain rule as:

$$\begin{aligned}
{}_\ominus\mathbf{J}_\oplus &\triangleq \frac{\partial \mathbf{x}_{jk}}{\partial(\mathbf{x}_{ij}, \mathbf{x}_{ik})} = \frac{\partial \mathbf{x}_{jk}}{\partial(\mathbf{x}_{ji}, \mathbf{x}_{ik})} \frac{\partial(\mathbf{x}_{ji}, \mathbf{x}_{ik})}{\partial(\mathbf{x}_{ij}, \mathbf{x}_{ik})} \\
&= \mathbf{J}_\oplus \begin{bmatrix} \mathbf{J}_\ominus & \mathbf{0} \\ \mathbf{0} & \mathbf{I} \end{bmatrix} = \begin{bmatrix} \mathbf{J}_{1\oplus}\mathbf{J}_\ominus & \mathbf{J}_{2\oplus} \end{bmatrix}.
\end{aligned}$$

The chain rule calculation of Jacobians applies to any number of compositions of the basic relations, so that long chains of relationships may be reduced recursively. It may appear that we are calculating first-order estimates of first-order estimates of ..., but actually this recursive procedure produces *precisely* the same result as calculating the first-order estimate of the composite relationship. This is in contrast to min-max methods which make conservative estimates at each step and thus produce *very* conservative estimates of a composite relationship.

3.3   Extracting Relationships

We have now developed enough machinery to describe the procedure for estimating the relationships between objects which are in our map. The map contains, by definition, estimates of the locations of objects with respect to the world frame; these relations can be read of out the estimated system mean vector and covariance matrix directly. Other relationships are implicit, and must be extracted, using methods developed in the previous sections.

For any relationship on the variables in the map we can write:

$$\mathbf{y} = \mathbf{g}(\mathbf{x}).$$

where the function $\mathbf{g}()$ is general (not the function described in the previous section). *Conditioned on all the evidence in the map*, estimates of the mean and covariance of the relationship are given by:

$$\begin{aligned}
\hat{\mathbf{y}} &\approx \mathbf{g}(\hat{\mathbf{x}}), \\
\mathbf{C}(\mathbf{y}) &\approx \mathbf{G}_\mathbf{x} \mathbf{C}(\mathbf{x}) \mathbf{G}_\mathbf{x}^T.
\end{aligned}$$

4   Changing the Map

Our map represents uncertain spatial relationships among objects referenced to a common world frame. It should change if the underlying world itself changes. It should also change if our knowledge changes (even though the world is static). An example of the former case occurs when the location of an object changes; e.g., a mobile robot moves. An example of the latter case occurs when a constraint is imposed on the locations of objects in the map, for example, by measuring some of them with a sensor.

To change the map, we must change the two components that define it — the (mean) estimate of the system state vector, $\hat{\mathbf{x}}$, and the estimate of the system variance matrix, $\mathbf{C}(\mathbf{x})$.

Figure 4 shows the changes in the system due to moving objects, and the addition of constraints. A similar description appears in Gelb [Gelb 1984] and we adopt the same notation.

We will assume that new constraints are applied at discrete moments, marked by states k. The update of the estimates at state k, based on new information, is considered to be instantaneous. The estimates, at state k, *prior* to the integration of the new information are denoted by $\hat{\mathbf{x}}_k^{(-)}$ and $\mathbf{C}(\mathbf{x}_k^{(-)})$, and *after* the integration by $\hat{\mathbf{x}}_k^{(+)}$ and $\mathbf{C}(\mathbf{x}_k^{(+)})$. At these discrete moments our knowledge is increased, and uncertainty is reduced.

In the interval between states the system may be changing dynamically — for instance, the robot may be moving. When an object moves, we must define a process to extrapolate the estimate of the state vector and uncertainty at state $k-1$, to state k to reflect the changing relationships.

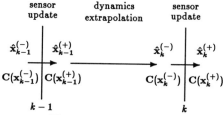

Figure 4: The Changing Map

4.1   Moving Objects

In our example, only the robot moves, so the process model need only describe its motion. A continuous dynamics model can be developed given *a particular robot*, formulated as a function of time (see [Gelb, 1984]). However, if the robot only makes sensor observations at discrete times, then a discrete motion approximation is quite adequate.

Assume the robot is represented by the Rth relationship in the map. When the robot moves, it changes its relationship, $\mathbf{x}_R$, with the world. The robot makes an uncertain relative motion, $\mathbf{y}_R$, to reach a final world location $\mathbf{x}_R'$. Thus,

$$\mathbf{x}_R' = \mathbf{x}_R \oplus \mathbf{y}_R.$$

Only a portion of the map needs to be changed due to the change in the robot's location from state to state — specifically, the Rth element of the estimated mean of the state vector, and the Rth row and column of the estimated variance matrix.

In Figure 5,

$$\hat{x}'_R \approx \hat{x}_R \oplus \hat{y}_R,$$

$$C(x'_R) \approx J_{1\oplus}C(x_R)J_{1\oplus}^T + J_{2\oplus}C(y_R)J_{2\oplus}^T,$$

$$C(x'_R, x_i) \approx J_{1\oplus}C(x_R, x_i).$$

For simplicity, the formulae presented assume independence of the errors in the relative motion, y_R, and the current estimated robot location x_R. As in the desciption of Figure 3, $C(x, x'_R)$ is a column of the individual cross-covariance matrices $C(x_i, x'_R)$.

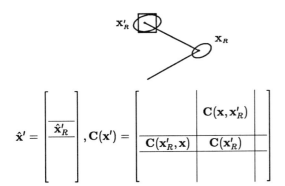

$$\hat{x}' = \begin{bmatrix} \hat{x}'_R \\ \end{bmatrix}, C(x') = \begin{bmatrix} & C(x, x'_R) \\ \hline C(x'_R, x) & C(x'_R) \end{bmatrix}$$

Figure 5: The Moving Robot

4.2   Adding Constraints

When new information is obtained relating objects *already in the map*, the system state vector and variance matrix do not increase in size; i.e., no new elements are introduced. However, the old elements are *constrained* by the new relation, and their values will be changed.

Constraints can arise in a number of ways:

- A robot measures the relationship of a *known* landmark to itself (i.e., estimates of the world locations of robot and landmark already exist).

- A geometric relationship, such as colinearity, coplanarity, etc., is given for some set of the object location variables.

In the first example the constraint is noisy (because of an imperfect measurement). In the second example, the constraint could be absolute, but could also be given with a tolerance.

There is no mathematical distinction between the two cases; we will describe all constraints as if they came from measurements by *sensors* — real sensors or pseudo-sensors (for geometric constraints), perfect measurement devices or imperfect.

When a constraint is introduced, there are two estimates of the geometric relationship in question — our current best estimate of the relation, which can be extracted from the map, and the new sensor information. The two estimates can be compared (in the same reference frame), and together should allow some improved estimate to be formed (as by averaging, for instance).

For each sensor, we have a *sensor model* that describes how the sensor maps the spatial variables in the state vector into sensor variables. Generally, the measurement, z, is described as a function, h, of the state vector, corrupted by mean-zero, additive noise v. The covariance of the noise, $C(v)$, is given as part of the model.

$$z = h(x) + v. \tag{3}$$

The expected value of the sensor and its covariance are easily estimated as:

$$\hat{z} \approx h(\hat{x}).$$

$$C(z) \approx H_X C(x)H_X^T + C(v),$$

where:

$$H_X \triangleq \frac{\partial h_k(x)}{\partial x}\left(\hat{x}_k^{(-)}\right).$$

The formulae describe our best estimate of the sensor's values under the circumstances, and the likely variation. The actual sensor values returned are usually assumed to be conditionally independent of the state, meaning that the noise is assumed to be independent in each measurement, even when measuring the same relation with the same sensor. The actual sensor values, corrupted by the noise, are the second estimate of the relationship.

In Figure 6, an over-constrained system is shown. We have two estimates of the same node, labeled x_1 and z. In our example, x_1 represents the location of a beacon about which we have prior information, and z represents a second estimate of the beacon location derived from a sensor located on a mobile robot at x_2. We wish to obtain a better estimate of the location of the robot, and perhaps the beacon as well; i.e., more accurate values for the vector $\hat{x}$. One method is to compute the conditional mean and covariance of x given z by the standard statistical formulae:

$$\widehat{x \mid z} = \hat{x} + C(x, z)C(z)^{-1}(z - \hat{z})$$

$$C(x \mid z) = C(x) - C(x, z)C(z)^{-1}C(z, x).$$

Using the formulae in (2), we can substitute expressions in terms of the sensor function and its Jacobian for $\hat{z}$, $C(z)$ and $C(x, z)$ to obtain the Kalman Filter equations [Gelb, 1984] given below:

$$\hat{x}_k^{(+)} = \hat{x}_k^{(-)} + K_k\left[z_k - h_k(\hat{x}_k^{(-)})\right],$$

$$C(x_k^{(+)}) = C(x_k^{(-)}) - K_k H_X C(x_k^{(-)}),$$

$$K_k = C(x_k^{(-)})H_X^T\left[H_X C(x_k^{(-)})H_X^T + C(v)_k\right]^{-1}.$$

For linear transformations of Gaussian variables, the matrix H is constant, and the Kalman Filter produces the *optimal minimum-variance Bayesian estimate*, which is equal to the mean of the *a posteriori conditional density function* of x, given the prior statistics of x, and the statistics of the measurement z. Since the transformations are linear, the mean and covariances of z are exactly determined by (1) and (2). Since the orignal random variables were Gaussian, so is the result. Finally, since a Gaussian distribution is completely defined by its first two moments, the conditional mean and covariance computed define the conditional density.

No non-linear estimator can produce estimates with smaller mean-square errors. For example, if there are *no angular errors* in our coordinate frame relationships, then compounding is linear in the (translational) errors. If only linear constraints are imposed, the map will contain optimal and consistent estimates of the frame relationships.

For linear transformations of non-Gaussian variables, the Kalman Filter is not optimal, but produces the optimal *linear* estimate. The map will again be consistent. A non-linear estimator might be found with better performance, however.

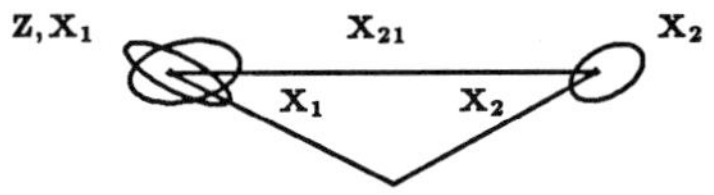

$$\hat{\mathbf{x}}' = \begin{bmatrix} \hat{\mathbf{x}} \\ \hline \hat{\mathbf{z}} \end{bmatrix}, \quad \mathbf{C}(\mathbf{x}') = \left[\begin{array}{c|c} \mathbf{C}(\mathbf{x}) & \mathbf{C}(\mathbf{x}, \mathbf{z}) \\ \hline \mathbf{C}(\mathbf{z}, \mathbf{x}) & \mathbf{C}(\mathbf{z}) \end{array} \right]$$

Figure 6: Overconstrained Relationships

For non-linear transformations, Jacobians such as **H** will have to be evaluated (they are not constant matrices). The given formulae then represent the Extended Kalman Filter, a sub-optimal non-linear estimator. It is one of the most widely used non-linear estimators because of its similarity to the optimal linear filter, its simplicity of implementation, and its ability to provide accurate estimates in practice.

The error in the estimation due to the non-linearities in **h** can be greatly reduced by iteration, using the Iterated Extended Kalman Filter equations [Gelb, 1984]. Such iteration is necessary to maintain consistency in the map when non-linearities become significant. Convergence to the true value of **x** cannot be guaranteed, in general, for the Extended Kalman Filter, although as noted, the filter has worked well in practice on a large number of problems, including navigation.

5   The Example

Our example is designed to illustrate a number of uses of the information kept in the Stochastic Map for decision making. An initial implementation of the techniques described in this paper has been performed. The uncertainties represented by ellipses in the illustrations, were originally computed by the system on a set of sample problems with varying error magnitudes. This description, however, will have to remain qualitative until a more extensive investigation can be performed.

5.1   What if I Move?

We combine discrete robot motions by compounding them, as shown in Figure 5. It is assumed that any systematic biases in the robot motion have been removed by calibration. The robot's best estimate of its location is $\hat{\mathbf{x}}_2$, with error covariance $\mathbf{C}(\mathbf{x}_2)$ (given in the map). Since the location of the loading area is known very accurately in room coordinates, the robot can compute the nominal relative motion that it would like to make, $\hat{\mathbf{y}}_{2,load}$. From an internal model of its own accuracy, the robot estimates the covariance of its motion error as $\mathbf{C}(\mathbf{y}_{2,load})$. If there were no errors in the initial estimate of the robot location, and no motion errors incurred in moving, the robot would arrive with its center coincident with the center of the loading area. When the two uncertain relations are compounded, the first-order estimate of the mean of the robot's final location is also the center of the loading area, but the covariance of the error has increased.

In order to compare the likely locations of the robot with the loading zone, we must *now* assume something about the probability distribution of the robot's location. For reasons already discussed, a multi-variate Gaussian distribution which fits the estimated moments is assumed. Given that, we can determine the elliptical region of 2-D space in which the robot should be found, with probability approximately determined by our choice of confidence levels—more than likely corresponding to 4 or 5 standard deviations of the estimated errors, for relative certainty.

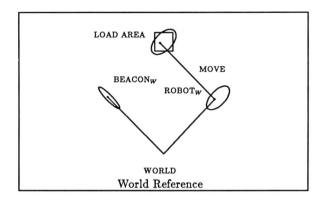

Figure 7: A Direct Move *Might* Fail

All that remains is to determine if the ellipse is completely contained in the desired region; for purposes of illustration, Figure 7 shows that it is not. The robot decides it cannot achieve its goal reliably by moving directly to the load area.

5.2   Where is the Beacon?

Before moving, the robot can attempt to reduce the uncertainty in its initial location by trying to spot the beacon. The relative location of the beacon to the robot is computed by $\ominus \mathbf{x}_2 \oplus \mathbf{x}_1$. The two estimated moments of each relation are pulled from the map, and the moments of the result are estimated, as described in section 3.2.

Given the estimate, an elliptical region in which the beacon should be found with high confidence can be computed as before; but this time the relational estimate, and hence the ellipse are described in robot coordinates. The robot can compare this region with the region swept out by the field of view of its sensor to determine if sensing is feasible (without repositioning the sensor, or worse, turning the robot). The result is illustrated in Figure 8.

The robot determines that the beacon is highly likely to be in its field of view.

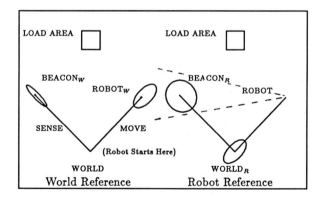

Figure 8: Is the Beacon Viewable?

5.3   Should I Use the Sensor?

Even if the robot sights the beacon, will the additional information help it estimate its location accurately enough so that it can then move to the loader successfully? If not, the robot should pursue a different strategy to reduce its uncertainty.

For simplicity, we assume that the robot's sensor measures the relative location of the beacon in Cartesian coordinates. Thus the sensor function is the functional composition of reversal and compounding, already described. The sensor produces a measurement with additive, mean-zero noise $\mathbf{v}$, whose covariance is given in the sensor model as $\mathbf{C}(\mathbf{v})$. Given the information in the map, the conditional mean and covariance of the expected sensor value can be estimated:

$$\mathbf{z} = \mathbf{x}_{21} = \ominus\mathbf{x}_2 \oplus \mathbf{x}_1 + \mathbf{v}.$$

$$\hat{\mathbf{z}} = \hat{\mathbf{x}}_{21} = \ominus\hat{\mathbf{x}}_2 \oplus \hat{\mathbf{x}}_1.$$

$$\mathbf{C}(\mathbf{z}) = {}_\ominus\mathbf{J}_\oplus \left[\begin{array}{cc} \mathbf{C}(\mathbf{x}_2) & \mathbf{C}(\mathbf{x}_2,\mathbf{x}_1) \\ \mathbf{C}(\mathbf{x}_1,\mathbf{x}_2) & \mathbf{C}(\mathbf{x}_1) \end{array} \right] {}_\ominus\mathbf{J}_\oplus^T + \mathbf{C}(\mathbf{v}).$$

In the Kalman Filter Update equations described in section 4.2, the system covariance matrix can be updated *without an actual sensor measurement having been made*; it depends only on $\mathbf{C}(\mathbf{x})$, $\mathbf{C}(\mathbf{v})$, and the matrix $\mathbf{H}_\mathbf{X}$. In the example, $\ominus\mathbf{J}\oplus$ takes the place of $\mathbf{H}_\mathbf{X}$, and is evaluated with the current values of $\hat{\mathbf{x}}_2$ and $\hat{\mathbf{x}}_1$, the robot and beacon locations. The updated system covariance matrix can be computed *as if* the sensor were used. The reduction in the robot's locational uncertainty due to applying the sensor can be judged by comparing the old value of $\mathbf{C}(\mathbf{x}_2)$ with the updated value. The magnitudes of this "updated" robot covariance estimate, and $\mathbf{C}(\mathbf{y}_{2,load})$ (from 5.1), can be used to decide if the robot will be able to reach its goal with the desired tolerance.

In our example, it is determined that the sensor should be useful. Figures 9 shows the result of a simulated measurement, with the location and measurement uncertainties transformed into either map or robot coordinates, respectively. Figure 10 illustrates the improvement in the estimations of the robot and beacon locations following application of the Kalman Filter Update formulae with the given measurement. Finally, Figure 11 shows the result of compounding the uncertain relative motion of the robot with its newly estimated initial location. The robot achieves its goal.

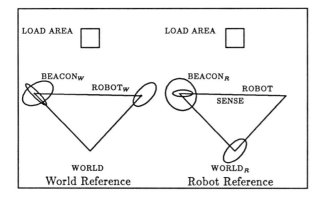

Figure 9: The Robot Senses the Beacon Again

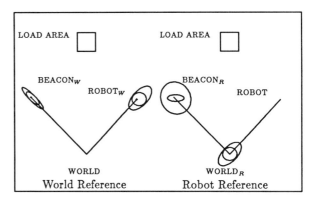

Figure 10: Updated and Original Estimates

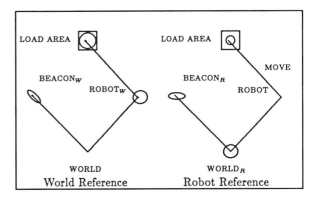

Figure 11: The Robot Moves Successfully

6   Discussion and Conclusions

This paper presents a general method for estimating uncertain relative spatial relationships between reference frames in a network of uncertain spatial relationships. Such networks arise, for example, in industrial robotics and navigation for mobile robots, because the system is given spatial information in the form of sensed relationships, prior constraints, relative motions, and so on. The methods presented in this paper allow the efficient estimation of these uncertain spatial relations and can be used, for example, to compute *in advance* whether a proposed sequence of actions (each with known uncertainty) is likely to fail due to too much accumulated uncertainty; whether a proposed sensor observation will reduce the uncertainty to a tolerable level; whether a sensor result is so unlikely given its expected value and its prior probability of failure that it should be ignored, and so on. This paper applies state estimation theory to the problem of estimating parameters of an entire spatial configuration of objects, with the ability to transform estimates into any frame of interest.

The estimation procedure makes a number of assumptions that are normally met in practice, and can be summarized as follows:

- Functions of the random variables are relatively smooth about the estimated means of the variables within an interval on the order of one standard deviation. In the current context, this generally means that angular errors are "small". In Monte Carlo simulations[Smith, 1985], the compounding formulae used on relations with angular errors having standard deviations as large as 5°, gave estimates of the means and variances to within 1% of the correct values. Wang [Wang] analytically verified the utility of the first-order compounding formulae as an estimator, and described the limits of applicability.

- Estimating only two moments of the probability density functions of the uncertain spatial relationships is adequate for decision making. We believe that this is the case since we will most often model a sensor observation by a mean and variance, and the relationships which result from combining many pieces of information become rapidly Gaussian, and thus are accurately modelled by only two moments.

Although the examples presented in this paper have been solely concerned with *spatial* information, there is nothing in the theory that imposes this restriction. Provided that functions are given which describe the relationships among the components to be estimated, those components could be forces, velocities, time intervals, or other quantities in robotic and non-robotic applications.

Appendix A: Three DOF Relations

Formulae for the full 6DOF case are given in [Smith 1986].

The formulae for the compounding operation are:

$$\mathbf{x}_{ik} \triangleq \mathbf{x}_{ij} \oplus \mathbf{x}_{jk}$$
$$= \begin{bmatrix} x_{jk} \cos \phi_{ij} - y_{jk} \sin \phi_{ij} + x_{ij} \\ x_{jk} \sin \phi_{ij} + y_{jk} \cos \phi_{ij} + y_{ij} \\ \phi_{ij} + \phi_{jk} \end{bmatrix}.$$

where the Jacobian for the compounding operation, $\mathbf{J}_\oplus$ is:

$$\mathbf{J}_\oplus \triangleq \frac{\partial(\mathbf{x}_{ij} \oplus \mathbf{x}_{jk})}{\partial(\mathbf{x}_{ij}, \mathbf{x}_{jk})} = \frac{\partial \mathbf{x}_{ik}}{\partial(\mathbf{x}_{ij}, \mathbf{x}_{jk})} =$$

$$\begin{bmatrix} 1 & 0 & -(y_{ik} - y_{ij}) & \cos \phi_{ij} & -\sin \phi_{ij} & 0 \\ 0 & 1 & (x_{ik} - x_{ij}) & \sin \phi_{ij} & \cos \phi_{ij} & 0 \\ 0 & 0 & 1 & 0 & 0 & 1 \end{bmatrix}.$$

The formulae for the reverse operation are:

$$\mathbf{x}_{ji} \triangleq \ominus \mathbf{x}_{ij} \triangleq \begin{bmatrix} -x_{ij} \cos \phi_{ij} - y_{ij} \sin \phi_{ij} \\ x_{ij} \sin \phi_{ij} - y_{ij} \cos \phi_{ij} \\ -\phi_{ij} \end{bmatrix}.$$

and the Jacobian for the reversal operation, $\mathbf{J}_\ominus$ is:

$$\mathbf{J}_\ominus \triangleq \frac{\partial \mathbf{x}_{ji}}{\partial \mathbf{x}_{ij}} = \begin{bmatrix} -\cos \phi_{ij} & -\sin \phi_{ij} & y_{ji} \\ \sin \phi_{ij} & -\cos \phi_{ij} & -x_{ji} \\ 0 & 0 & -1 \end{bmatrix}.$$

Acknowledgments

The research reported in this paper was performed at SRI International, and was supported by the National Science Foundation under Grant ECS-8200615, the Air Force Office of Scientific Research under Contract F49620-84-K-0007, and by General Motors Research Laboratories.

References

Bolle R.M., and Cooper, D.B. 1986. On Optimally Combining Pieces of Information, with Application to Estimating 3-D Complex-Object Position from Range Data. *IEEE Trans. Pattern Anal. Machine Intell.*, vol. PAMI-8, pp. 619-638, Sept. 1986.

Brooks, R. A. 1982. Symbolic Error Analysis and Robot Planning. *Int. J. Robotics Res.* 1(4):29-68.

Chatila, R. and Laumond, J-P. 1985. Position Referencing and Consistent World Modeling for Mobile Robots. *Proc. IEEE Int. Conf. Robotics and Automation.* St. Louis: IEEE, pp. 138-145.

Durrant-Whyte, H. F. 1986. Consistent Integration and Propagation of Disparate Sensor Observations. *Proc. IEEE Int. Conf. Robotics and Automation.* San Francisco: IEEE, pp. 1464-1469.

Faugeras, O. D., and Hebert, M. 1986. The Representation, Recognition, and Locating of 3-D Objects. *Int. J. Robotics Res.* 5(3):27-52.

Gelb, A. 1984. *Applied Optimal Estimation.* M.I.T. Press

Nahi, N. E. 1976. *Estimation Theory and Applications.* New York: R.E. Krieger.

Papoulis, A. 1965. *Probability, Random Variables, and Stochastic Processes.* McGraw-Hill.

Paul, R. P. 1981. *Robot Manipulators: Mathematics, Programming and Control.* Cambridge: MIT Press.

Smith, R. C., *et al.* 1984. Test-Bed for Programmable Automation Research. Final Report-Phase 1, SRI International, April 1984.

Smith, R. C., and Cheeseman, P. 1985. On the Representation and Estimation of Spatial Uncertainty. SRI Robotics Lab. Tech. Paper, and *Int. J. Robotics Res.* 5(4): Winter 1987.

Smith, R. C., Self, M., and Cheeseman, P. 1986. Estimating Uncertain Spatial Relationships in Robotics. *Proc. Second Workshop on Uncertainty in Artificial Intell.*, Philadelphia, AAAI, August 1986. To appear revised in Vol. 2, *Uncertainty in Artificial Intelligence.* Amsterdam: North-Holland, Summer 1987.

Taylor, R. H. 1976. A Synthesis of Manipulator Control Programs from Task-Level Specifications. AIM-282. Stanford, Calif.: Stanford University Artificial Intelligence Laboratory.

Wang, C. M. 1986. Error Analysis of Spatial Representation and Estimation of Mobile Robots. General Motors Research Laboratories Publication GMR 5573. Warren, Mich.

VIII PATH PLANNING

Interest in automatic path planning has increased in recent years for two reasons. First, it parallels the increased interest in mobile robots. And second, it is derived from the fact that computers are getting inexpensive enough that it will soon be possible to have economical real-time collision-prediction and path-planning computers for every robot. The papers in this section present new techniques in this area.

For efficiency reasons Arimoto et al. argue for multiple representation systems and multiple levels of analysis. They use solid models of objects and boundary models of manipulators; they use a graph-based global planner and a forced-based local planner. Kawabe et al. present analytic techniques for detecting collisions between moving polyhedra. Jarvis and Byrne describe their exploration of methods for making three-dimensional measurements of an environment and then estimating a mobile robot's position. They conclude their discussion with a brief description of how to extend a distance transform technique into a method for computing several types of paths, including ones that explore unknown regions and others that exhaustively cover an area for tasks such as mowing and sweeping. Canny describes exact solutions to two path-planning problems: the shortest-path problem and the velocity-limited motion planning problem. These solutions are based on a new method for solving systems of polynomial equations.

A Feasible Approach to Automatic Planning of Collision-Free Robot Motions

S. Arimoto[*], H. Noborio[*], S. Fukuda[*], and A. Noda[**]

*Faculty of Engineering Science, Osaka University,
Toyonaka, Osaka, 560 Japan

**Mitsubishi Electric Corporation, Amagasaki, Hyogo,
661 Japan

Abstract: A feasible approach to the problem of automatic path planning for collision-free robot motions is proposed. Key ideas of this approach is 1) to use two different schemes of solid modeling, one being boundary representations for representing a robot and the other being octree representations for doing a set of obstacles in the robot's workspace, 2) to apply an efficient algorithm based on such modeling schemes for checking any existence of interference between the robot and the obstacles, and 3) to propose and use a feasible algorithm that can fast determine nearly the shortest distance between the robot and the set of obstacles and find such a point on a surface of the robot that is nearly the closest to the obstacles. The resolution of calculation of the shortest distance depends on the octree decomposition level r and can be determined less than $(\sqrt{3}L)/2^r$ where L denotes the length of one side of the whole space.

A collision-free path can be determined locally by introduction of a reactive force vector for each robot link, which is calculated based upon the knowledge on the closest pair of points that give nearly the shortest line between the link and the obstacles, and an attractive force vector, which is defined as the difference vector from the present position and posture of the endeffector of the robot to its target position and posture. Together with this local path planning, an automatic path planning in a global sense is proposed, which is constructed by introducing a cost function defined on possible triangular mobility planes and searching for an optimal path with the minimum cost in a finite graph generated by those mobility triangles.

1. INTRODUCTION

It has long been recognized that the problem of automatic planning of collision-free paths for a computer controlled manipulator among obstacles is central to off-line programming of robot assembly operations. This incentive gives rise to a good many of research works on collision-free path planning problems[1]-[7]. Most of these previous papers can be classified roughly into the following two categories. The one represents obstacles and moving objects in a space of configuration parameters, then constructs a free (mobility) space in terms of the cartesian or joint coordinates, and finally finds a good collision-free path in some sense. The other tries to construct or realize a collision-avoiding trajectory or movement respectively on the basis of geometric shapes of the manipulator and the obstacles represented directly in the three dimensional real space.

An original work in the former category was given by Lozano-Perez[1], who proposed a novel concept of configuration space and an interesting idea of representing manipulator trajectories as movements of a reference point by expanding conceptually the workspace obstacles. Then, Brooks[2] proposed a method that can construct the free space as union of generalized cones and find good collision-free paths among obstacles represented as unions of convex polygons. Faverjon[3] and Hasegawa[4] represented the free volume in the manipulator-joint space and proposed a method of searching for a path in that volume. However, such proposed methods in line with this direction present several difficulties, among which the burden of required computation for finding the volume swept by the moving manipulator and the overlap between the swept volume and the obstacles is of enormous importance. In fact, most of these proposed key algorithms need a huge amount of computation depending combinatrically on the complexity of shapes of the manipulator and the obstacles and exponentially on the degree of freedom of the manipulator.

In the latter category, much attention has been paid to the potential method[5]-[7]. One of serious drawbacks of this method is that, when shapes of the obstacles are complicated, it becomes hard to represent an adequate reactive potential. In addition, any efficient way for choosing adequate points on manipulator links at which reactive force vectors can be evaluated is not found so far.

In view of such difficulties arised in previous approaches, one is led to consideration of what a burning issue is, whose solution approach may gain access to a practical system for actualizing the automatic design of collision-free robot motions. This paper claims that the crucial issue is to find a closest pair of points between a given robot link and the obstacles. As a matter of course, it has implicitly been known that such a three-dimensional closest-pair problem is one of the most difficult problems in computational geometry. Nevertheless, once a closest pair of points between the link and the obstacles is obtained, it is possible to employ one of systematic methods proposed previously or to use even good heuristics to find a good collision-

-free path. By reason of this, this paper
attempts to find a feasible approach to the
intersection and closest-pair problems in the
three dimensional cartesian space. This is
eventually accomplished by an idea occurred. It
is to use two different ways of solid modelling,
one of which is the octree[8)-10)] that represents
the set of obstacles in the robot's workspace
and the other is the boundary representations[10)]
that represents the set of links constituting
the robot manipulator. The proposed algorithm
consists of 1) finding a minimal bounding box
which contains a given link on the basis of
tree-searching in the octree and 2) recursive
decomposition of the bounding box until reaching
a cubic volume with the specified finest
resolution scale that is the closest to the
obstacles. As a result a pair of points that
are nearly the closest each other between the
link and the obstacles can be found and its
resolution is bounded below $\sqrt{3}L/2^r$, where L
denotes the length of one side of the whole
environment space and r does the highest
decomposition level. The first half of the
algorithm is almost the same as an interference
check algorithm proposed recently by the
authors[11)-13)]. A specialized case of the
second half of the algorithm is treated in
details in the authors' recent paper[14)].

Once such a nearly closest pair of points
between each of manipulator links and the
obstacles is found, it is easy to assign a
reactive force vector to each link though it is
hard to construct a reactive potential in
general. This overcomes some drawbacks of the
potential method mentioned above and thereby may
yield a feasible technique to realize collision-
-avoiding robot motions in a local sense. In a
final section a new approach to finding a
collision-free path is proposed in a global
sense, where the manipulator is represented
grossly by a straight line segment. The
approach is based on 1) construction of a finite
graph that represents a mobility space
consisting of triangles swept by such a line
segment, 2) assignment of a cost function to
those swept triangles, and 3) finding an optimal
collision-free path by applying a dynamic
programming method for realization of an
efficient tree-search in the graph.

2. CHOICE OF SOLID MODELING SCHEMES

For attaining feasible solutions to the
real-time path planning for collision-free robot
motions, it is the most crucial to choose
adequate schemes for representing solid objects:
the robot and its workspace. The key idea of
this paper is to choose two different modelling
schemes, that is, to use octree representations
for representing the workspace and boundary
representations for doing the robot.

2.1 Octree Representations

An octree to be used for modelling the
workspace is a solid model with a hierarchical
data structure obtained by decomposing
recursively the space, as shown in Fig.1. In

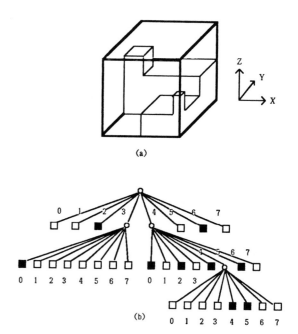

Fig.1 Working space (a) and its octree (b).

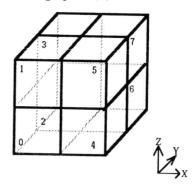

Fig.2 The order of octants.

the octree, each node is labeled according to
its position with respect to the set of all
solids (called "Obstacles" in this paper)
constituting the workspace to represent:
exterior (called a "white" node), interior (a
"black" node), and recursively decomposed (a
"mixed" node). A cubic region (called a "cube")
corresponding to a mixed node is divided into
eight subregions ("subcubes") which are called
"child" nodes of the mixed node. The
enumeration of eight octants that defines the
order of child cubes is given in Fig.2.

The decomposition is recursively processed by
the depth-first search until the finest
resolution level (r) of the octree. At the
finest level r, all mixed nodes are converted to
black nodes. If a set of all eight octants at
this level becomes black by this conversion,
then the set of these child nodes is merged into
their parent node, which must be labeled as a
black node. As a result, every external node
(or called a "terminal" or "leaf" node) becomes
white or black. In other words, all internal
nodes consist of only mixed nodes.

Roughly speaking, the octree decomposition proceeds further in the vicinity of the boundary surface between the free space and obstacles.

2.2 Boundary Representation

Boundary representations that are used to represent solid links of the robot are a solid model with a set of patches as shown in Fig.3. A patch of the B-reps. is represented by a sequence of verteces which are counterclockwise ordered for the normal vector of the plane that includes the patch as shown in Fig.3. Since the B-reps. retains the topological information of the solid, translational and rotational movements of robot links are easily represented by renovating a set of cartesian coordinates that correspond to moving vertices.

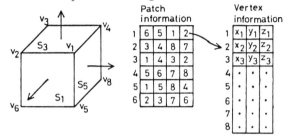

Fig.3 Boundary representation.

3. DETERMINATION OF A SET OF CUBES (A BOUNDING BOX) THAT CONTAINS A ROBOT LINK

For the effective realization of obstacle avoidance for the robot in the cartesian coordinates space, it is necessary to begin with examining whether any interference arises or not between the robot and the set of obstacles constituting the robot's workspace. This can be done by an interference check algorithm proposed in our previous papers [11]-[13]. In fact it can check efficiently the existence or non-existence of interference between the B-reps. for representing the robot and the octree for representing the workspace. Since it plays also a principal role in determination of an approximate for the minimum distance between a robot link and the obstacles, it is important to summarize its concept and basic process in what follows.

The basic process of the algorithm is to divide a cubic region C that includes some patches or a portion of patches of robot links (B-reps.) into eight child cubes and simultaneously to let each child cube inherit patches within his cubic region from his father's cube. By this rule of succession, eight child cubes can be classified into three states: "inside" (inside the robot), "outside" (outside the robot), and "intersection" (intersection with the robot), as shown in Fig.4. On the other hand, the attribute for such a child cube (node) is retained in the octree, that is, eight child cubes are classified into a "black" node (interior of the obstacles), a "white" node (free space), and a "mixed" node (obstacles and free space).

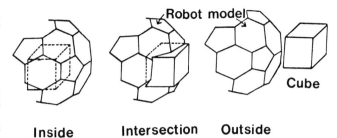

Fig.4 Relation between robot and cube.

Attribute	State		
	inside	intersetion	outside
black	interfere	interfere	non-interfere
mix	interfere	undecidedness	non-interfere
white	non-interfere	non-interfere	non-interfere

Table 1 Relation between attribute of the cube in the octree and state of the cube for the robot.

Putting in order these results on the state and attribute of a concerned child cube yields Table 1, which can determine the status of each child cube as "interference", "non-interference", or "undecidedness" (see Fig.4 and Table 1).

After starting from the undecidedness cube that represents the whole space, succeeding undecidedness cubes are treated recursively by applying the basic process mentioned above. In the sequel, the complete checking for any interference or non-interference of the robot with all obstacles in the workspace is accomplished. In the algorithm it is seen that, as long as a concerned intersection cube is "mixed", any portion of patches in the cube are inherited by its succession (one of child cubes). Hence, every patch of robot links is alloted eventually to a subset of terminal nodes which are only white or black in the octree representation of the workspace.

It is now possible to consider a basic problem for finding a minimal set of cubic regions that encloses an arbitrarily given patch in the space. In fact, by virtue of the interference check algorithm mentioned above it is easy to see that, given a patch of robot links, a minimal set of cubes that encloses the patch can be selected immediately by making a list of terminal nodes that intersect with this patch. Therefore, this set of cubes can be regarded as a bounding box that contains the whole patch. After dealing with every patch of a given robot link and finding its minimal bounding box, it is then possible to obtain the minimal bounding box that contains the link as a set of union of all resultant bounding boxes. For example, given a link as illustrated in Fig.5, such a minimal set of cubes consists of U=(A,B,C,D,E), each of which is "white" if there is no interference between the link and the set of all obstacles in the workspace.

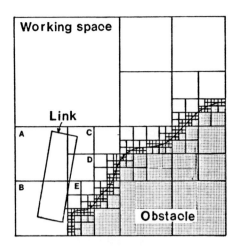

Fig.5 Determination of a set of cubes
      that contains a link.

* To explain the algorithm with clarity
  a two-dimensional case (a quad-tree)
  is illustrated where a link and its patches
  are represented by a parallelepiped and
  its edges, respectively.

4. FINDING THE CLOSEST PAIR OF POINTS

For the design of automatic path planning for
robot motions it is quite helpful to know the
shortest Euclidean distance between a robot link
and the set of obstacles in the robot's
workspace. To do this, it is necessary to find
a pair of points such that one point lies on a
link patch and the other lies on a surface of
the obstacles and the straight line between
these two points is the shortest among such
pairs of points. This can be established in an
approximation sense by using an algorithm for
finding a pair of cubic regions such that one is
a cube with the finest resolution level r that
is succession to a "white" cube of the bounding
box for the link and the other is a "black" cube
of the octree for representing the workspace and
this pair gives the shortest distance among such
pairs. The algorithm consists of the following
two successive steps.

4.1 Finding a "Black" Cube That Is the
         Nearest to a Given "White" Cube

Given a "white" cube w, it is possible to
find a "black" node in the octree that its
corresponding cubic region is the nearest to the
white one by a modified scheme of "Depth-First
Search"[15].
[Pre-Processing] Set the present input node N
as the root node of the octree and set Dm=∞.
[Basic Processing] Search for a child node Ni
being not yet processed of the input node N
according to the priority of shorter distance to
the "white" cube. The algorithm that can
determine the order of this priority in the
sense of "shorter" distance is given later. If

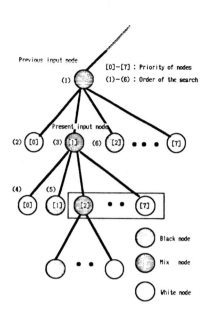

Fig.6 Pruning of nodes in the algorithm.

all child nodes have been already processed, go
back to the node N's father node (set the
present input node to the node N's father
node).
1) When Ni is "black": Retain this black node
if and only if the distance Dp between the node
Ni's corresponding cubic region and the white
cube w is less than the shortest distance Dm at
the present stage and update Dm by Dp. Then, or
if it is not so, go back to its grandfather node
(set the present input node to the node Ni's
grandfather node), since other brother nodes
need not be further searched for because of
their posteriority of the sense of "shorter"
distance as shown in Fig.6.
2) When Ni is "mixed": Set the present input
node to the node Ni and return to [Basic
Processing] if and only if the distance Dp
between the node Ni's corresponding cube and the
"white" cube w is less than the shortest
distance Dm at the present stage. Otherwise,
return to [Basic Processing].
3) When Ni is "white": Return to [Basic
Processing].

It should be remarked that it is easy to
calculate the distance Dp between any two
cubes.

<Determination of the Order of Priority>

Denote a concerned node of the octree by N
and call it the present input node. The
distance from the white cube w to each of the
node N's eight child cubes can be determined by
the vector (x,y,z) from the center of mass of N
to that of w, the length of one side of N, and
the length of one side of w. However, in some
cases it is possible to determine the order of
priority of child cubes Ni in the sense of
"shorter" distance by comparing the magnitudes
of vector components x, y, and z. In other
cases, comparison of the magnitudes of x, y, and
z determines at least the order of priority of

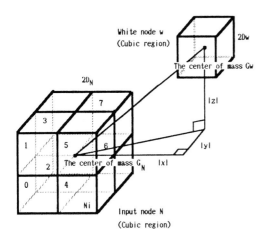

Fig.7 Decision of the priority
of eight child nodes.

"shorter" distance among six child nodes. In other words, it is at most necessary to calculate the actual distance to w for only two child cubes. The details of the proof is given in Appendix 1. The algorithm itself can be described in the following two steps:

(a) When $D(w) \leq D(N)$ (where $D(*)$ denotes the level of node $*$):

[Step 1] Denote the vector from the center of mass of the input cube N to that of the "white" cube w by (x,y,z), the length of one side of the input cube N by $2Dn$, that of the "white" cube w by $2Dw$, and the length D by $Dn+Dw$.
[Step 2] First let $S \leftarrow 0$, and then let $S \leftarrow S + 4$ if $x \geq 0$. Next if $y \geq 0$, let $S \leftarrow S + 2$. Finally, if $z \geq 0$, let $S \leftarrow S + 1$. As a result, it is concluded that $Order[0] = S$.
[Step 3] Define a function $Max[i]$ $(i=1,2,3)$ as the ith maximum value among $\{|x|,|y|,|z|\}$. And define a function $Number[i]$ $(i=1,2,3)$ as follows: When $Max[i] = |x|$, define $Number[i] = 4$ if $x \geq 0$ and $Number[i] = -4$ if $x < 0$. When $Max[i] = |y|$, define $Number[i] = 2$ if $y \geq 0$ and $Number[i] = -2$ if $y < 0$. When $Max[i] = |z|$, define $Number[i] = 1$ if $z \geq 0$ and $Number[i] = -1$ if $z < 0$. Then, let
$$Order[1] = Order[0] - Number[3],$$
$$Order[2] = Order[0] - Number[2].$$
Next, define $h = 2(Max[1] - Max[2] - Max[3]) + D + Dw$ if $Max[3] \geq D$ and $h = Max[1]^2 - Max[2]^2 - Max[3]^2 - 2Dw(Max[1] - Max[2] - Max[3]) - Dw^2$ if $D \geq Max[1]$. Then, if $h \geq 0$, let
$$Order[3] = 7 - Order[0] + Number[1]$$
and if $h < 0$, let
$$Order[3] = Order[0] - Number[1].$$
If $Max[3] < D < Max[1]$, let
$$Order[3] = 7 - Order[0] + Number[1].$$
Finally, let
$$Order[i] = 7 - Order[7-i] \quad (i = 4,...,7).$$
Since h can be calculated straightforwardly, it is quite easy to determine $Order[i]$, $(i = 0,...,7)$, (the order of priority).

(b) When $D(w) > D(N)$: Define $Order[i]$ as the order of priority of the input node N's father.

4.2 Determination of the Closest Pair of Points Between a Robot Link and the Obstacles

In Chapter 2 it is shown that, given a robot link, a minimal bounding box that encloses the link can be obtained straightforwardly via the interference check algorithm.

It is now possible to propose an algorithm for selecting a black node in the octree that is nearly the closest to the link. The algorithm consists of the following four steps, among which the step 3) plays a principal role:
1) Let U be a bounding box that contains the robot link. For each white node $w_i \in U$, find a black node b_i in the octree that is the closest to w_i by using the algorithm proposed in Section 4.1. Denote the shortest distance between w_i and b_i by d_i. Then, all of triplets (w_i, b_i, d_i) for $w_i \in U$ are registered in a list.
2) Arrange all triplets in order of larger distance of di in the list.
3) Take out the last triplet with the smallest distance from the list and examine the decomposition level of the white node in this triplet. If the level is equivalent to the finest resolution level r, go to step 4). Otherwise, decompose this white cube into eight subcubes and register in the list only such subcubes that intersect with some patch of the link. Then, go back to step 2).
4) The triplet presently taken out from the list gives the closest pair that consists of a white cube w_0 with level r and a black cube b_0. Hence, denote the distance in this triplet by d and end.

Since the resultant white cube w_0 is the smallest cube with the finest resolution level r, the real shortest distance dmin between the robot link and the set of obstacles in the workspace can be approximated by d in the following way:
$$d \leq dmin \leq d + (\sqrt{3}L)/2^r.$$
where L denotes the length of one side of the whole space. The details of the proof is given in Appendix 2.

It should be remarked that the proposed algorithms in sections 4.1 and 4.2 are also valid for the case that cubic regions used in the octree representation are not a real cube but a parallelepiped region, provided that the determination algorithm of the order of priority is modified correctly.

5. LOCAL PATH PLANNING

It is now possible to suppose that, by applying the algorithm described in the previous section for a given manipulator link, a pair of white and black cubes is found. Here the white cube is of the smallest with the finest resolution level r, and has some intersection with the link and is the closest to the obstacles. The black one corresponds to a terminal node registered in the octree that represents the obstacles. At that time a pair of vertices of the white cube and the black cube that are the closest each other among such pairs can be found, too. This shortest distance between them is denoted by d and such a vertex of the black cube is denoted by P_1.

Now draw a straight line from P_1 to the closest vertex of the white cube and find a point P_0 as an intersection point of the link with this line. If such a straight line does not happen to intersect with the link inside the white cube, choose an appropriate point P_0 on a patch of the link within the white cube. Anyway, it is possible to define a reactive force vector in the following manner:

$$\vec{v} = f(d) \overrightarrow{P_1 P_0}$$

where the symbol $\overrightarrow{PQ}$ means a unit vector with direction from point P to point Q. A scalar function f(d) can be chosen appropriately to adjust the magnitude of the reaction force. Note that at each joint its corresponding reactive force to be artificially exerted on it is calculated by a corresponding vector component of the following:

$$\vec{u} = \Sigma \ J^T(P_0) \vec{v}$$

where the summation is taken over the finite set of manipulator links. It should be remarked that each reactive force vector can be defined without knowing any closed-form description of the reactive potential function.

A collision-avoiding motion is then realized locally by introducing an attractive force in addition to those reactive force vectors as shown in Fig.8. The attractive force can be derived by defining an artificial potential function of the difference between a pair of present location and direction vectors of the endeffector and a pair of its target location and direction vectors, as proposed previously by the authors[16],[17] and Khatib[6].

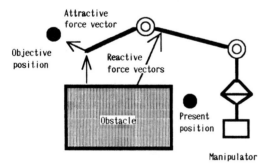

Fig.8 An artificial potential field.

6. GLOBAL PATH PLANNING

Now suppose that the manipulator can be locally controlled to move without colliding with the obstacles in the workspace by such an artificial potential method as explained in the previous section. Then it is necessary to design a collision-free path in a global sense. In this paper the "global" sense implies the assumption that the manipulator can be simply represented as a straight line segment in the

space. One end of the segment which is called the origin and denoted by a point B corresponds to a location of the basement link and thereby is assumed to be fixed. The other end point corresponds to a location of the endeffecter. It is further assumed that the direction of the endeffector is planned in the local sense and hence is not taken into consideration in this global path planning. The validness of this simplification must be examined at once by applying the local path planning strategy, after a global path is planned automatically by the proposed method mentioned below.

Given a starting point S and a goal point G in the three dimensional real space, then select appropriately several intermediate points P_i. If the free end point of the line segment moves along a straight line from such a point P_i to its succeeding point P_{i+1}, a triangular plane is formed by the sweep of the segment movement. This plane surrounded by the triangle $\triangle P_i B P_{i+1}$ is called a mobility triangle. If a mobility triangle does not intersect any obstacle in the workspace, it is said to be free. It is now possible to propose a feasible approach to finding a good path in the global sense. The approach consists of the following three important concepts.

6.1 Definition of a Cost Function

To each triangular plane Ti a cost is assigned, which is defined as an area Q of an intersection R of Ti with the set of black cubes in the octree that represents the obstacles. The determination of the intersected region R is carried out efficiently by the interference check algorithm mentioned in Section 3.

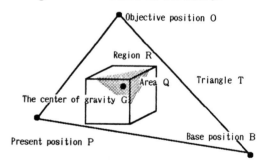

Fig.9 Calculation of cost for a triangle T.

6.2 Branching Out

If the cost of a concerned mobility triangle T is not zero, the manipulator can not move in a neighborhood of an intersection region R with the obstacles inside T. Then, denote this triangle by $\triangle$ PBO, define a plane A that is perpendicular to the vector PO and contains the center of mass of the intersection region R, and select new intermediate points, each of which is a center of the intersection of a white cube registered in the octree with the plane A. For such a new intermediate point F, define two different triangles $T_1(\triangle PBF)$ and $T_2(\triangle FBO)$ as shown in Fig.10 and replace the triangle T with

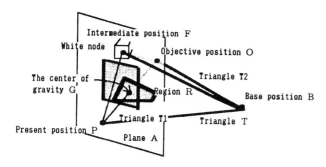

Fig.10 Selection of intermediate position and expansion of triangle T.

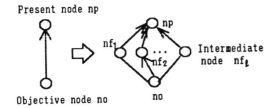

Fig.11 Expansion of an edge in graph.

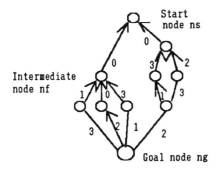

Fig.12 General graph.

1) Find a path with the minimal cost among all paths from n_s to n_g. To accomplish this straightforwardly, from every node except n_s the pointer and the minimal cost should be assigned to each node along the minimal cost path backward from that node to n_s so that it is possible to trace backward the optimal path from n_g to n_s. This assignment of pointer and minimal cost is carried out whenever branching out arises as described below.

2) If the chosen path with the minimal cost is of zero cost, end the algorithm. Otherwise, select a branch with maximal cost on the path and let it branch out.

Whenever branching out occurs, first attach the pointer from every node n_f to the node n_p and register every minimal cost at its corresponding node n_f. At the same time, find an optimal path from n_o to n_p via one of nodes n_f, and attach the pointer on such branch from n_o and present the minimal cost to node n_o. Then, if this resultant optimal cost at n_o becomes less than or equal to the previous cost at n_o before branching out, return to step 1). Otherwise, consider a set V of the node n_o and nodes of its all descendants to n_g as shown in Fig.13, and change the assignment of pointers and minimal costs at all branches and nodes inside V in the following ways:

(a) For each node in V, erase the pointer to its parent node and discard its minimal cost to n_s retained before. Denote the present node to be processed by v, let $v \leftarrow n_g$, and execute (b) recursively.

(b) At each of the node v's parent nodes, execute the following processing:

1) If this parent node retains the value of its minimal cost, do not anything at all.

2) If this parent node does not retain the cost value, replace the present node with this parent node and go to (b).

these two triangles T_1 and T_2. If a set of such triangles is represented by a graph, from the starting point to the goal point, the replacement of T with T_1 and T_2 is represented by branching out as shown in Fig.11, where nodes of triangles corresponding to intermediate target points P, O, and F are denoted by n_p, n_o, and n_f, respectively. A cost assigned to a triangular plane is given to its corresponding branch.

6.3 Algorithm for Finding a Path

A collision-free path can be found by searching for a free (cost-free) path from the starting node n_s to the goal node n_g in the graph as shown in Fig.12. Here the cost for a path from n_s to n_g is defined as the sum of all costs of branches that constitute the path. A path whose cost is zero is said to be free, which consists only of free triangles that do not collide with any obstacle in the workspace. Hence, the problem is to search for such a free path in the graph. The algorithm that can solve this efficiently is constructed on the basis of dynamic programming in the following way:

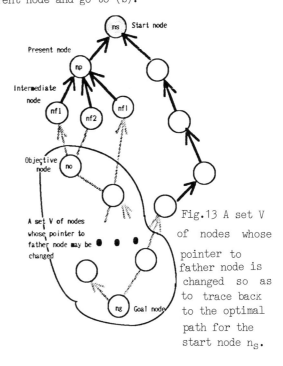

Fig.13 A set V of nodes whose pointer to father node is changed so as to trace back to the optimal path for the start node n_s.

9) C.L Jackins and S.L. Tanimoto, "Oct-trees and Their Use in Representing Three-Dimensional Objects," Computer Graphics and Image Processing 14, Nov. 1980.

10) A.A.G. Requicha and H.B.Voelcker, "Solid Modeling: Current States and research directions," IEEE Computer graphics and Application, Vol.3, No.7, pp.25-27, 1983.

11) H. Noborio, S. Fukuda, S. Arimoto, "A New Interference Check Algorithm Using Octree," presented at the 1987 IEEE International Conference on Robotics and Automation, Raleigh, North Calorina, 1987.

12) H. Noborio, "Input and Usage of Spatial Information Based on the Octree Representation," Ph.D Dissertation, Dept. of Mechanical Engineering, Faculty of Engineering Science, Osaka University, March 1987.

13) H. Noborio, S. Fukuda, S. Arimoto, "A New Interference Check Algorithm Using Octree Representation," J. of Robotics Society of Japan, Vol.5, No.3, pp.190-199, 1987, (in Japanese).

14) H. Noborio, H. Hata, S. Arimoto, "An Octree-Based Algorithm for Selecting the Closest Pair of Two Points on a Robot and Its Obstacles," submitted to J. of Robotics Society of Japan (in Japanese).

15) D.A. Nilsson, "Principles of Artificial Intelligence," Tioga, Palo, Alto, Calif., 1980.

16) M. Takegaki and S. Arimoto, "A New Feedback Method for Dynamic Control of Manipulators," Trans. of ASME, J. of Dynamic Systems, Measurement and Control, 103, pp.119-125, 1982.

17) F. Miyazaki and S. Arimoto, "Sensory Feedback for Robot Manipulators," Journal of Robotic Systems, Vol.2, No.1, pp. 53-72, Spring 1985.

18) S.K. Kambhampati and L.S. Davis, "Multiresolution Path Planning for Mobile Robots," IEEE Journal of Robotics and Automation, Vol.RA-2, No.3, pp.135-145, Sept., 1986.

APPENDIX I

A proof for the validity of the determination algorithm of the order of priority for eight child nodes is given.

Let (x,y,z) be a vector from the center of mass of N to that of w. When there is a relation $x \geq y \geq z \geq 0$, the order of priority of child nodes Ni within the node N in the sense of "shorter" distance is considered. By symmetry of elements x, y, and z, the proof of the other relations can be similarly devised from the proof for the case $x \geq y \geq z \geq 0$. The enumeration of eight octants that defines the order of child nodes is given in Fig.2. Then, the distances between the white node w and such child nodes Ni are denoted by $d(i)$, respectively.

(a) $|z| \geq D$:

$$d(0)^2 = (|x|-Dw)^2 + (|y|-Dw)^2 + (|z|-Dw)^2,$$
$$d(1)^2 = (|x|-Dw)^2 + (|y|-Dw)^2 + (|z|-D)^2,$$
$$d(2)^2 = (|x|-Dw)^2 + (|y|-D)^2 + (|z|-Dw)^2,$$
$$d(3)^2 = (|x|-Dw)^2 + (|y|-D)^2 + (|z|-D)^2,$$
$$d(4)^2 = (|x|-D)^2 + (|y|-Dw)^2 + (|z|-Dw)^2,$$
$$d(5)^2 = (|x|-D)^2 + (|y|-Dw)^2 + (|z|-D)^2,$$
$$d(6)^2 = (|x|-D)^2 + (|y|-D)^2 + (|z|-Dw)^2,$$
$$d(7)^2 = (|x|-D)^2 + (|y|-D)^2 + (|z|-D)^2.$$

Obviously, the inequalities $d(0) \geq d(1) \geq d(2) \geq d(3)$, $d(4) \geq d(5) \geq d(6) \geq d(7)$, $d(2) \geq d(4)$, $d(3) \geq d(5)$ are obtained. This implies that Order[0]=7, Order[1]=6, Order[2]=5, Order[5]=2, Order[6]=1, and Order[7]=0.

Further, let $d(3)^2 - d(4)^2 = (D-Dw)\{2(|x|-|y|-|z|)+D+Dw\}$.
If $h = 2(|x|-|y|-|z|)+D+Dw \geq 0$, let Order[3]=4 and Order[4]=3. Otherwise, let Order[3]=3 and Order[4]=4.

(b) $|y| \geq D \geq |z|$:

$$d(0)^2, d(1)^2 = (|x|-Dw)^2 + (|y|-Dw)^2,$$
$$d(2)^2, d(3)^2 = (|x|-Dw)^2 + (|y|-D)^2,$$
$$d(4)^2, d(5)^2 = (|x|-D)^2 + (|y|-Dw)^2,$$
$$d(6)^2, d(7)^2 = (|x|-D)^2 + (|y|-D)^2.$$

Obviously, the equalities and inequalities $d(0) = d(1) \geq d(2) = d(3) \geq d(4) = d(5) \geq d(6) = d(7)$ are obtained. This implies that Order[0]=7, Order[1]=6, Order[2]=5, Order[3]=4, Order[4]=3, Order[5]=2, Order[6]=1, and Order[7]=0.

(c) $|x| \geq D \geq |y|$:

$$d(0)^2, d(1)^2, d(2)^2, d(3)^2 = (|x|-Dw)^2,$$
$$d(4)^2, d(5)^2, d(6)^2, d(7)^2 = (|x|-D)^2.$$

Obviously, the equalities and inequalities $d(0) = d(1) = d(2) = d(3) \geq d(4) = d(5) = d(6) = d(7)$ are obtained, which mean that Order[0]=7, Order[1]=6, Order[2]=5, Order[3]=4, Order[4]=3, Order[5]=2, Order[6]=1, and Order[7]=0.

(d) $D \geq |x|$:

$$d(0)^2 = (|x|-Dw)^2 + (|y|-Dw)^2 + (|z|-Dw)^2,$$
$$d(1)^2 = (|x|-Dw)^2 + (|y|-Dw)^2,$$
$$d(2)^2 = (|x|-Dw)^2 + (|z|-Dw)^2,$$
$$d(3)^2 = (|x|-Dw)^2,$$
$$d(4)^2 = (|y|-Dw)^2 + (|z|-Dw)^2,$$
$$d(5)^2 = (|y|-Dw)^2,$$
$$d(6)^2 = (|z|-Dw)^2,$$
$$d(7)^2 = 0.$$

Obviously, the inequalities $d(0) \geq d(1) \geq d(2) \geq d(3)$, $d(4) \geq d(5) \geq d(6) \geq d(7)$, $d(2) \geq d(4)$, $d(3) \geq d(5)$ are obtained. This shows that Order[0]=7, Order[1]=6, Order[2]=5, Order[5]=2, Order[6]=1, and Order[7]=0.

Further, if $d(3)^2 - d(4)^2 = h = |x|^2 - |y|^2 - |z|^2 - 2lw(|x|-|y|-|z|) - Dw^2 \geq 0$, let Order[3]=4 and Order[4]=3. Otherwise, let Order[3]=3 and Order[4]=4.

Finally, three values $|x|$, $|y|$, and $|z|$ are replaced by Max[1], Max[2], and Max[3], respectively. The order of priority of child nodes Ni can now be determined.

If all of the node v's parent nodes have retained their own minimal costs, choose such one that gives the smallest sum of the cost for the branch from v to it and its own cost. In other words, choose one of paths starting from v to ns such that its cost is minimal among such paths. Then, return to the previous node just before the node v is called (let v be one of v's descendants), and go to (b).

Note that this recursive tree-search processing is based on the "principle of optimality" in dynamic programming. Thus, it is possible to find the optimal path immediately by tracing the sequence of pointers from the node n_g to the node n_s.

7. EXPERIMENTAL RESULTS

The proposed algorithm is tested by using two different solid models. A PUMA manipulator is composed of a set of base, arm, and hand, which is represented by ten boundary representations. A working space includes a box composed of four paralellepipeds as only one obstacle, and is represented by the octree whose resolution level is eight. Figure 14 illustrates the location of the manipulator and the obstacle.

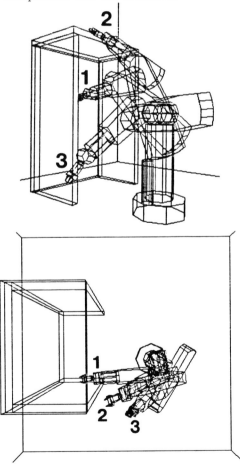

Fig.14 A path (denoted by 1->2->3) is planned by the proposed global path planning algorithm for the PUMA manipulator.

The algorithm is implemented by C language on a Unix operating system. To produce a collision-free path (1 → 2 → 3) in Fig.14, a computational time of about one minute was eventually required on a MELCOM 360-50 computer (3.7MIPS, 8MB), though less than one second was required for each execution of the closest-pair algorithm.

8. CONCLUSIONS

A feasible approach to the automatic planning of collision-free robot motions is proposed. The approach is based on an efficient algorithm for checking the existence or nonexistence of interferences between a manipulator link and the obstacles and for finding the closest pair of points between them. A local path planning is realized by a modified artificial potential method. A reactive force vector for each link can be defined by using the obtained data on the closest pair, even if any reactive potential is not available. In addition, a new approach for planning a collision-free path in a global sense is proposed. This approach is constructed by introducing a concept of mobility triangles which are considered to be planes swept by straight line movements of the manipulator, a cost function defined on such mobility triangles, a graph representation of the set of such triangles and an efficient way for searching for a path with the minimal cost in the graph, which yield a collision-free path in a global sense.

REFERENCES

1) T. Lozano-Pérez, "Automatic Planning of Manipulator Transfer Movements," IEEE Trans. System, Man, and Cybernetics Vol.SMC11, No.10, pp.681-689, 1981.
2) R.A. Brooks, "Planning Collision-Free Motions for Pick-and Place Operations," International Journal of Robotics Research, Vol.2, No.4, pp.19-44, 1983.
3) B. Faverjon, "Obstacle Avoidance Using an Octree in the Configuration Space of a Manipulator," IEEE Conf. Robotics, Atranta, pp.504-512, 1984.
4) T. Hasegawa, "Collision Avoidance Using Characterized Description of Free Space," International Conf. Advanced Robotics, Tokyo, Japan, pp.69-76, Sept. 1985.
5) O. Khatib and J.F.Le Maitre, "Dynamic Control of Manipulators Operating in a Complex Environment," 3rd CISM-IFToMM Sympo., pp.267-282, 1978.
6) O. Khatib, "Real-time Obstacle Avoidance for Manipulators and Mobile Robots," International Journal of Robotics Research, Vol.5, No.1, Spring 1986.
7) M. Okutomi and M. Mori,"Decision of Robot Movement by Means of a Potential Field," Advanced Robotics, Vol.1, No.2, pp.131-141, 1986.
8) D. Meagher, "Geometric Modeling Using Octree Encoding," Computer Graphics and Image Processing 19, pp.129-147, 1982.

APPENDIX II

Let d be the distance calculated by the algorithm shown in Section 4, and dmin be the minimum distance between the whole link and the obstacles. Here, the difference between the two distances d and dmin is evaluated.

Suppose that the algorithm selected a white node A and finished. Then, the distance between the white node (cubic region) A and the obstacles is the smallest than any other distances between white nodes within the list and the obstacles. The level of the white node A is the finest resolution level (r) of the octree. Denote by B a white cube containing a point P on a link surface which is really the closest to the obstacles with the same resolution r.

In Fig.15, the minimum distances between nodes A and B and the nearest obstacle are defined by da' and db', respectively. Further, the minimum distances between the link in nodes A and B and the nearest obstacle are defined by da and db, respectively.

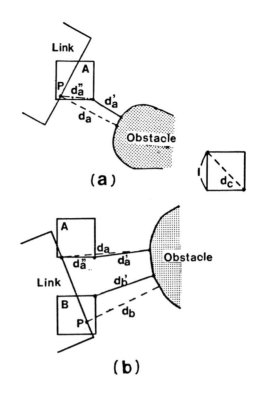

Fig.15 Relation of the closest cube A and the closest point P for the obstacle.

(a) In the case that the point P exists in the node A (See Fig.15(a))

$$da' \leq da = dmin \leq da' + da'' \leq da' + dc.$$

(b) In the case that the point P exists in the node B (See Fig.15(b))

$$da' \leq da, \quad db' \leq db, \quad da' \leq db'.$$

$$da' \leq db' \leq db = dmin \leq da \leq da' + da'' \leq da' + dc.$$

The inequalities give that the magnitude of difference between d and dmin is bounded below by dc ($=\sqrt{3}*L/2^r$, L is the length of one side of the whole space).

Collision Detection among Moving Objects in Simulation

Shinji Kawabe, Akira Okano, and Kenji Shimada

IBM Japan, Tokyo Research Laboratory
5-19 Sanbancho, Chiyoda-ku, Tokyo 102
Japan

Abstract: This paper describes an algorithm of collision detection between moving objects in simulation. Graphical simulation of robot motion has been recognized to be useful for industrial applications, since the programmer's intention can be easily confirmed by the visual check-up of the programmed 3-dimensional motion. But it is still difficult to visually detect a collision between moving objects. Therefore, in this paper, the requirements necessary for detecting collisions among moving objects in simulation are described first, and an algorithm meeting them is proposed. In this method, we assume that the motion of each moving object is described by a cubic function of time. A collision occurs in one of the two cases; a vertex touches a plane, or an edge touches another edge. By solving the equations that satisfy the conditions of intersection between the geometric elements, we obtain the time and position of the collision between moving objects. The equations are shown and the computation cost is evaluated. Finally, some issues in implementation are addressed and experimental results are shown to prove the effectiveness of the algorithm proposed in this paper.

Introduction

As more and more robotic systems have been utilized in various industrial applications, off-line programming methods have been developed to reduce the time and labor of teaching motions at the site and to avoid suspending the production lines. In off-line programming, the control data of robotic systems is generated by using languages, graphics, or the combination of them. In addition to the capabilities of off-line programming, the functions of graphically simulating the programmed motion are very useful. In fact, there are many graphical programming and simulation systems commercially available.

The purposes of using those simulation capabilities are to confirm the motion, trajectories, synchronization with other machines, cycle time, etc. By using the graphical simulation, we can easily understand the status of the robots. But it is still difficult to visually detect collisions while objects are moving on the graphics screen. Therefore, it is desirable for the simulation system to have the capabilities of automatic collision detection.

Subsequent sections of this paper describe the requirements for collision detection in simulation, an algorithm that meets the requirements, issues in implementation, and some experimental results.

Requirements for Collision Detection

Since collision or interference detection among 3-D objects is a fundamental issue in the simulation of their behavior, several methods have been proposed so far [*Ozawa*, 1986] , [*Boyse*, 1979] , [*Canny*, 1986] , [*Cameron*, 1985] , [*Esterling*, 1984]. In [*Ozawa*, 1986], [*Boyse*, 1979] , a collision or interference between a moving object and a stationary object is detected, while in [*Canny*, 1986] , [*Cameron*, 1985] , the problem of detecting a collision or interference among moving objects is dealt with. The word "collision" refers to the state where an object begins to touch another object, while the word "interference" refers to the state where more than two objects occupy the same area of the space at a specific time. The methods of detecting a collision or interference are divided into three categories;

- Multiple interference detection
  The position and orientation of the object is calculated at a reasonably sampled time and interference check is performed at each of the positions. Since methods of detecting interferences among stationary objects by using solid models are well known, they are easy to implement. But if the time interval is too large, a collision might be missed. On the other hand if the time interval is too small, the computation time might be too long for practical purposes.

- Swept volume
  Methods of generating the swept volume of a moving object have been developed in solid modelling. By using these methods, the collision detection problem may be solved as an interference problem between the swept volumes. But at present, it is difficult to obtain a swept volume unless the motion of the object is described by linear or quadratic equations. Besides, even if a collision is detected, it may be very difficult to obtain the exact time and position of the collision.

- Intersection calculation
  When the trajectories of the faces, edges, and vertices of an object are described by the functions of time, we derive the equations that satisfy the conditions of intersection among the geometric elements. By solving the equations, we obtain the exact time and position of the collision. This idea was proposed in [2,3]. But in [3], the motion of the object is limited to linear translation or rotation around an axis. Simultaneous translation and rotation is dealt with in [4], but the method is difficult to implement, if the trajectory is not simple. In fact, in the example, the object is uniformly translated and rotated.

Considering these characteristics, in this paper, we take the third method, intersection calculation, for the following reasons;

- No detection miss
  Multiple interference detection is not satisfactory in this respect.

- Exact time and point of the earliest collision
  In many applications such as robotics, we need to know the exact time and position at which the object begins to touch another object for the first time, because the object wants to move avoiding the collision at the next step. This method, intersection calculation, is suitable for this purpose.

- Desired accuracy

    Since it is generally difficult to accurately describe the motion of a moving object by a function of time, approximation of the motion is necessary. As the accuracy required for each application is different, the accuracy should be specified when the motion is approximated. This may be achieved by this method.

In the following sections, we describe a collision detection algorithm that meets these requirements and that can be applied to the collision problem among moving objects as well as between a moving object and a stationary obstacle.

An Algorithm of Collision Detection

Outline of the algorithm

We assume that an object is represented as a polyhedron whose faces are planes surrounded by straight lines. Two moving objects thus represented collide with each other, if either of the following two cases occurs;

Type 1 Contact:
a vertex of an object touches a face of the other object (Fig.1)
Type 2 Contact:
an edge of an object touches an edge of the other object (Fig.2)

where an edge contains its two end vertices, and a face contains its boundary edges.

The algorithm of detecting a collision works as follows. We assume that the two objects do not interfere with each other at the initial position. The motion of every vertex, edge, and face is described by a function of time. An equation that satisfies the Type 1 condition where a vertex is on a face of the other object is obtained for every pair of vertices and faces. The other type of equation that satisfies the Type 2 condition where two edges intersect is obtained for every pair of edges of two objects. By solving these equations for the time, we obtain the candidate times when a collision may occur. The answer we want to obtain is the minimum of the answers that exist between the initial and final times.

The equations for the two types of intersection are derived as follows.

Type 1 Contact

Let's assume that the motion of vertices and faces is described by the function of time,

$$X(t)$$
$$P(t)u + Q(t)v + R(t)$$

respectively, where t is the parameter of time, $P(t)$ and $Q(t)$ are vectors on the face, $R(t)$ is a point on the face, and u and v are parameters.

When the vertex touches the face, a geometric relation

$$X(t) = P(t)u + Q(t)v + R(t)$$

is required. Thus, we obtain

$$[P(t) \quad Q(t) \quad R(t) - X(t)] \begin{bmatrix} u \\ v \\ 1 \end{bmatrix} = 0$$

If this matrix equation has answers, the determinant equation

$$|P(t) \quad Q(t) \quad R(t) - X(t)| = 0 \qquad (1)$$

must be satisfied. By solving this equation, we obtain the answers that may be the time when a Type 1 collision occurs. The collision time must be between the initial and final times of the motion. In addition, unless the position of the collision at that time is located inside the boundary of the face, the collision never occurs. This type of equation is solved for all the pairs between the vertices and faces of two objects.

Type 2 Contact

Assuming that the motion of the vertices of an edge is described by a function of time, the edge can be described by

$$A(t)u + B(t) \qquad (0 \leq u \leq lu, |A(t)| = 1)$$

where $A(t)$ is the direction vector of the edge and $B(t)$ is one of the two end vertices, u is a parameter, and lu is the length of the edge. Similarly, another edge is described by

$$C(t)v + D(t) \qquad (0 \leq v \leq lv, |C(t)| = 1)$$

where v is a parameter and lv is the length of the edge.

When two edges touch each other, a geometric relation

$$A(t)u + B(t) = C(t)v + D(t)$$

is required. Thus, we obtain

$$[A(t) \quad -C(t) \quad B(t) - D(t)] \begin{bmatrix} u \\ v \\ 1 \end{bmatrix} = 0$$

If this matrix equation has answers, the determinant equation

$$|A(t) \quad -C(t) \quad B(t) - D(t)| = 0 \qquad (2)$$

must be satisfied. By solving this equation, we obtain the answers that may be the time when a Type 2 collision occurs. The collision time must be between the initial and final times of the motion. In addition, unless the position of the collision at that time is between the end vertices of the both edges, the collision never occurs. This type of equation is solved for all the pairs between the edges of two objects.

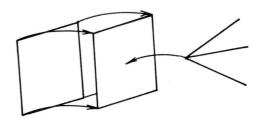

Fig.1. Collision between a plane and a vertex.

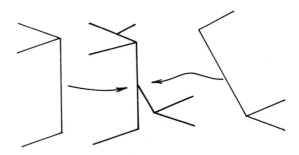

Fig.2. Collision between an edge and another edge.

So far we have the candidate times of possible collisions, but an actual collision occurs at the minimum of them obtained by solving the two types of equations.

Detailed algorithm

In our study, we make use of cubic functions of time to describe the motion of 3-D objects. Instead of using cubic functions, the degree of the function may be one, two, or more than three, but linear or quadratic functions are generally not enough for describing the motion of robot links, and on the other hand the functions of higher degrees are difficult to handle.

Each element of the homogeneous transformation matrix that represents the motion of a 3-D object is described by a cubic function of time. One way of defining such a homogeneous transformation is to obtain a cubic function of time for each element from given four homogeneous transformations that represent the positions and orientations of the object at the initial, final, and two intermediate times.

Then, we have a homogeneous transformation matrix $T_i(t)$ whose elements are described by cubic functions of time t, where i specifies the object.

The shape of a 3-D object is represented by the boundary representations (B-rep) and the solid is surrounded by planes. The coordinate of each vertex of the solid with respect to the object coordinate system is described by a homogeneous coordinate

$$X_{ij} = (x, y, z, 1).$$

An edge is described by

$$p = A_{ij}u + B_{ij} \quad (0 \le u \le lu, |A_{ij}| = 1)$$

where A_{ij} is the direction vector of the edge, B_{ij} is one of the two vertices of the edge in the object coordinate system, and lu is the length of the edge. The subscript i specifies the object and j specifies the edge. A face is described by

$$q = P_{ij}u + Q_{ij}v + R_{ij}$$

where P_{ij} and Q_{ij} are vectors on the face and R_{ij} is a point on the face in the object coordinate system.

When a homogeneous transformation $T_i(t)$ of an object is given, the coordinate of a vertex X_{ij} of the object is described by

$$T_i(t)X_{ij}$$

in the world coordinate system. An edge is similarly described by

$$p = T_i(t) (A_{ij}u + B_{ij}) \quad (0 \le u \le lu, |A_{ij}| = 1)$$

and a face is described by

$$q = T_i(t) (P_{ij}u + Q_{ij}v + R_{ij})$$

in the world coordinate system.

Type 1 Contact

When we deal with two objects i and k, and homogeneous transformations $T_i(t)$ and $T_k(t)$ are given to the each object, the determinant equation (1) becomes

$$|T_i(t)P_{ij} \quad T_i(t)Q_{ij} \quad T_i(t)R_{ij} - T_k(t)X_{kl}| = 0 \quad (3)$$

where the subscript j and l specify the element. We solve this type of equation for every pair of j and l. Since every element of the homogeneous matrices $T_i(t)$ and $T_k(t)$ is described by a cubic function of time t, the degree of the equation (3) is 9. By using the general method of solving the equation of N degrees [IBM, 1974] , we have 9 answers that is the time when a Type 1 collision may occur. Finally, we get one answer that meets the following conditions, if there is one.

1. Real answer between the initial and final times.
2. A collision point $T_k(t)X_{kl}$ is obtained at that time.
3. The collision point exists inside the boundary of the face.
4. Minimum of the answers that meet the above three conditions.

Type 2 Contact

In this type of contact, the determinant equation (2) is described by

$$|T_i(t)A_{ij} \quad - T_k(t)C_{ij} \quad T_i(t)B_{ij} - T_k(t)D_{kl}| = 0 \quad (4)$$

where the subscripts j and l specify the elements. We solve this type of equation for every pair of j and l. The degree of the equation (4) is 9. By solving the equation, we obtain 9 answers that is the time when a Type 2 collision may occur. We finally get one answer that meets the following conditions, if there is one.

1. Real answer between the initial and final times.
2. A collision point is obtained at that time.
3. The collision point exists between the end vertices of the both edges.
4. Minimum of the answers that meet the above three conditions.

By solving these two types of equations for every pair, we have obtained the candidate times of possible collisions so far, but an actual collision occurs at the earliest time t_m of them. The position of the earliest collision is also obtained, and the positions and orientations of the objects i and k, when they collide, are expressed by $T_i(t_m)$ and $T_k(t_m)$ respectively.

Relative Motion between Moving Objects

A general way of solving the collision problem between moving objects is described in the previous section. But the the degree of the equations is 9 and we get 9 answers, though at most 6 answers exist in the real situation. The degree can be reduced by introducing the relative motion of the objects. By calculating the motion of a moving object relative to another moving object, the collision problem of the two moving objects becomes that of a moving object and a stationary object.

A moving object and a stationary object may collide with each other in one of the following three cases;

Type 1 Contact:
a vertex of a moving object touches a face of a stationary object
Type 2 Contact:
a face of a moving object touches a vertex of a stationary object
Type 3 Contact:
an edge of a moving object touches an edge of a stationary object.

As explained in the previous section, the motion of each moving object is described by a cubic function of time. Namely, every element of the homogeneous transformation matrix that represents the position and orientation of the object is a cubic function of time. One way of obtaining the homogeneous transformation matrix that represents the relative motion of an object i with respect to another object j is as follows. When four transformation matrices are given to each object to describe its positions and orientations at the initial, final, and two intermediate times,

$$T_{i1}, T_{i2}, T_{i3}, T_{i4}$$
$$T_{j1}, T_{j2}, T_{j3}, T_{j4},$$

the relative position and orientation of the object i with respect to the object j at each of the four times is described by

$$
\begin{aligned}
T_{k1} &= T_{j1}^{-1} \ T_{i1} \\
T_{k2} &= T_{j2}^{-1} \ T_{i2} \\
T_{k3} &= T_{j3}^{-1} \ T_{i3} \\
T_{k4} &= T_{j4}^{-1} \ T_{i4}
\end{aligned}
$$

where $T_{j1}^{-1}, T_{j2}^{-1}, T_{j3}^{-1}$, and T_{j4}^{-1} are the inverse matrices of T_{j1}, T_{j2}, T_{j3}, and T_{j4} respectively. From these four transformation matrices T_{k1}, T_{k2}, T_{k3}, and T_{k4}, we obtain a homogeneous transformation matrix $T_k(t)$, each of whose elements is described by a cubic function of time. This matrix $T_k(t)$ represents the motion of the object i relative to the object j.

Now, collisions between two moving objects can be detected by checking collisions between the moving object i whose motion is represented by the transformation matrix $T_k(t)$, and the stationary object j. Two objects A and B are moving in Fig.3 and the same motion can be described by the relative motion shown in Fig.4. We derive the equations for each of the three types of intersection as follows.

Type 1 Contact (Moving vertex vs. stationary face)

A stationary face and a vertex P of the moving object i whose motion is represented by the homogeneous transformation matrix $T_k(t)$, are described by

$$
\begin{aligned}
ax &+ by + cz + d = 0 \\
T_k(t)P &= (X_k(t), Y_k(t), Z_k(t))
\end{aligned}
$$

respectively, where a, b, c, and d are constants, and X_k, Y_k, and Z_k are cubic functions of time. When the vertex touches the face, a geometric relation

$$
aX_k(t) + bY_k(t) + cZ_k(t) + d = 0 \qquad (5)
$$

is required. The degree of this equation is three, and we obtain three answers. We finally get the time of possible collisions of Type 1 as the minimum of the answers that exist between the initial and the final times, and at which the intersection is inside the boundary of the stationary face.

Type 2 Contact (Moving face vs. stationary vertex)

A stationary vertex and a face of the moving object whose motion is represented by the homogeneous transformation matrix $T_k(t)$, are described by

$$
\begin{aligned}
&(X, Y, Z) \\
&a(t)x + b(t)y + c(t)z + d(t) = 0
\end{aligned}
$$

respectively, where $a(t), b(t), c(t)$, and $d(t)$ are cubic functions of time. When the face touches the vertex, a geometric relation

$$
a(t)X + b(t)Y + c(t)Z + d(t) = 0 \qquad (6)
$$

is required. The degree of this equation is three, and we obtain three answers. We finally get the time of possible collisions of Type 2 as the minimum of the answers that exist between the initial and the final times, and at which the intersection is inside the boundary of the moving face.

Type 3 Contact (Moving edge vs. stationary edge)

A stationary edge and a moving edge whose motion is represented by the homogeneous transformation matrix $T_k(t)$, are described by

$$
\begin{aligned}
x &= cv + d \\
x &= a(t)u + b(t)
\end{aligned}
$$

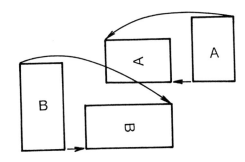

Fig.3. Motion of objects A and B.

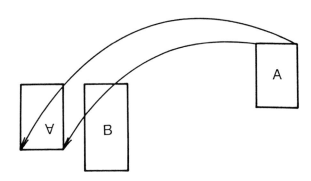

Fig.4. Motion of the object A relative to the object B.

respectively, where c and d are constant vectors, and $a(t)$ and $b(t)$ are the vectors each of whose element is a cubic function of time. When an edge touches the other edge, a geometric relation

$$
a(t)u + b(t) = cv + d
$$

is required. We obtain

$$
[a(t) \quad -c \quad b(t) - d]\begin{bmatrix} u \\ v \\ 1 \end{bmatrix} = 0
$$

Then,

$$
|a(t) \quad -c \quad b(t) - d| = 0 \qquad (7)
$$

The degree of this equation is six, and we obtain six answers. We finally get the time of possible collisions of Type 3 as the minimum of the answers that exist between the initial and the final times, and at which the intersection is on the both edges.

The minimum value t_{col} of all the answers obtained in the three cases is the time when a collision occurs for the first time during the motion. The positions and orientations of the two objects at the collision time is represented by the transformation matrices $T_i(t_{col})$ and $T_j(t_{col})$.

Computational Cost

The computation time of the method of detecting a collision between moving objects is proportional to the number of the pairs between vertices of an object and faces of the other, and between edges of the two objects. When the numbers of the vertices, edges, and faces that belong to the objects i and j are V_i, V_j, E_i, E_j, F_i, and F_j respectively, the order of the number of the pairs is

$$O(V_iF_j + F_iV_j + E_iE_j).$$

For each computation, an equation of 9 degrees must be solved.

In the same way, the computation time of the method of detecting a collision between a moving object and a stationary object is also proportional to the number of the pairs between vertices of an object and faces of the other, and between edges of the two objects. Therefore, the order of the number of the pairs is

$$O(V_iF_j + F_iV_j + E_iE_j).$$

This is the same order the first method has, but an equation of 3 or 6 degrees is solved for each pair, while the degree of the equation is 9 in the first method. This evaluation means that collisions between moving objects can be detected by the simpler method whose computation time for each pair is much shorter, and which requires the same order of the number of computations.

Approximation of Motion

Since it is generally impossible to accurately describe the motion of a moving object, we need to approximate it. When the motion is described by a cubic function of time, namely every element of the homogeneous transformation matrix is a cubic function of time, there are several ways of obtaining the function. As described before, one way of obtaining the matrix is to calculate the coefficients of the function from four given homogeneous transformation matrices at the initial, final, and two intermediate times. As a result of this approximation, the obtained homogeneous matrix $T_i(t)$ is not necessarily normalized at an arbitrary time except four given times. Namely,

$$|rot(T_i(t))| \neq 1.$$

Therefore, the object does not necessarily take the exact position and orientation and the shape of the object may be distorted.

In our method, we can control the level of approximation. When m homogeneous transformation matrices are given along the trajectory of a moving object, we should be able to determine the number of segments each of which is described by a cubic function. We first obtain a cubic function for every element of the homogeneous transformation matrix from the given m homogeneous transformation matrices. By using the transformation matrix thus obtained, we calculate the positions of a specific point of the object at the given m times. Each position is compared with the position calculated by the given transformation matrix, and the maximum difference is obtained. If the maximum difference is larger than a certain threshold, the trajectory represented by the m homogeneous transformation matrices is divided into two. And the same procedures taken for the whole trajectory are performed for each of the divided trajectories. This process continues until the maximum difference becomes smaller than the threshold.

Issues in Implementation

We implemented the algorithm of detecting collisions among moving objects for our graphical robot simulation system. The relative motion of a moving object with respect to another object is utilized. Since we need to solve the equations of 3 and 6 degrees, the computation cost is not very low. Therefore, several measures are taken to reduce the computation time in the implementation. They are categorized into two classes;

1. Reduce the number of pairs
2. Stop the process to avoid unnecessary calculations.

Since the computation time is proportional to the number of the pairs, i.e. edge vs. edge, vertex vs. face, and face vs. vertex, we should try to reduce the number. If we can localize the part of an object that may touch another object, namely, if we can extract the faces, edges, and vertices that may touch another object, the number of the pairs can be reduced and, as a result, the computation time becomes shorter. But it is difficult to automatically localize such a part of an object at present, we basically deal with the whole parts of an object, although most of them may not contribute to collision.

Utilizing the local characteristics of a polyhedron, we can eliminate the edges and vertices that never touch another polyhedron before other parts of the polyhedron touch it. This applies to concave edges, and vertices that connect to only concave edges. Since these characteristics depend on the shape of the polyhedron, it is useful to mark these edges and vertices before the collision detection process begins, so that the process can skip these elements.

In addition to the pre-processing for reducing the number of the computations, the computation time may be reduced by stopping the further processes, when certain conditions are found.

Assuming that we have a moving object A whose motion is represented by a homogeneous transformation matrix $T(t)$, and a stationary object B, the algorithms of detecting a collision may be expressed in pseudocode as follows. The pre-processing described above may or may not be performed. The initial time of the motion is 0 and the final time is 1.

Type 1 Contact (Moving vertex vs. stationary face)

```
t <-- BigNumber             {collision time}
p <-- Unknown               {collision point}
for each face F of solid A do
 for each vertex V of solid B do
  ((t1,p1),(t2,p2),(t3,p3)) <-- MoveVintF (F,V,T)
                {T is transformation matrix}
                { 0 ≤ t1 ≤ t2 ≤ t3 ≤ 1}
  if t1<t then
   if ClassPoint(p1,F) = insideF or onF then
    t <-- t1; p <-- p1
   else if t2<t then
    if ClassPoint(p2,F) = insideF or onF then
     t <-- t2 ; p <-- p2
     else if t3<t then
      if ClassPoint(p3,F) = insideF or onF then
       t <-- t3 ; p <-- p3
       end { t3 classification }
      end { t3 test }
     end { t2 classification }
    end { t2 test }
   end { t1 classification }
  end { t1 test }
 end { Vertex loop }
end { Face loop }
```

This flow is straightforward. The function MoveVintF returns three pairs of the collision time and point in the ascending order of the time, by solving the equation (5), if three real answers exist, otherwise existing real answers are returned in the ascending order. The cubic equation can be analytically solved. Since the initial time is 0 and the final time is 1, if an answer does not exist within this range, it is not the answer we want.

Even if a collision point is on the surface, it may not be located inside the boundary of the face. The function ClassPoint checks whether the point is inside the boundary or not. This algorithm is well known, but expensive. Therefore, we refine the function MoveVintF to reduce the candidates for classification.

A face has another form of description using three vectors a, b, and c as shown in Fig.5, so that the parallelogram defined by

$$p = au + bv + c \quad (0 \le u \le lu, 0 \le v \le lv)$$

contains the original face, where lu and lv are the length of the parallelogram, and $|a| = 1$ and $|b| = 1$. If the collision point does not exist in the area where $0 \le u \le lu$ and $0 \le v \le lv$, it never exist inside the boundary of the face. This simple refinement greatly reduces the execution of the function ClassPoint.

Type 2 Contact (Moving face vs. stationary vertex)

```
{ t : collision time }
{ p : collision point}
for each vertex V of solid A do
 for each face F of solid B do
  ((t1,p1),(t2,p2),(t3,p3)) <-- MoveFintV (V,F,T)
                  {T is transformation matrix}
                   { 0 ≤ t1 ≤ t2 ≤ t3 ≤ 1}
    if t1<t then
     T1 <-- T(t1)     {Transformation at t1}
     F1 <-- T1 * F    {Transform every vertex of F}
     if ClassPoint(p1,F1) = insideF or onF then
      t <-- t1 ; p <-- p1
     else if t2<t then
      T2 <-- T(t2)    {Transformation at t2}
      F2 <-- T2 * F   {Transform every vertex of F}
      if ClassPoint(p2,F2) = insideF or onF then
       t <-- t2 ; p <-- p2
      else if t3<t then
       T3 <-- T(t3) {Transformation at t3}
       F3 <-- T3 * F{Transform every vertex of F}
       if ClassPoint(p3,F3) = insideF or onF then
        t <-- t3 ; p <-- p3
       end { t3 classification }
      end { t3 test }
     end { t2 classification }
    end { t2 test }
   end { t1 classification }
  end { t1 test }
 end { Face loop }
end { Vertex loop }
```

The function MoveFintV returns three pairs of the collision time and point in the ascending order of the time, by solving the equation (6), if three real answers exist, otherwise existing answers are returned in the ascending order. The cubic equation can be analytically solved. Since the initial time is 0 and the final time is 1, if an answer does not exist within this range, it is not the answer we want.

In the same way taken in Type 1, the function ClassPoint checks whether the collision point is inside the face or not. But the situation is different from Type 1, because the face moves in Type 2, while the face is fixed in Type 1. Therefore, every vertex that surrounds the face must be transformed by the matrix $T(t)$ at each time, before the classification of the collision point is carried out. This process is obviously expensive. But by describing the moving face by three vectors as explained in Type 1, the classification process becomes easy and the execution of the function ClassPoint is reduced.

We refine the function MoveFintV. As shown in Fig.6, a face at the initial position has another form of description

$$p = au + bv + c \quad (0 \le u \le lu, 0 \le v \le lv)$$

where a, b, and c are constant vectors, lu and lv are the length of the parallelogram, and $|a| = 1$ and $|b| = 1$. When a collision point

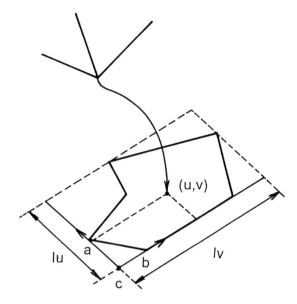

Fig.5. A moving vertex touching a stationary face.

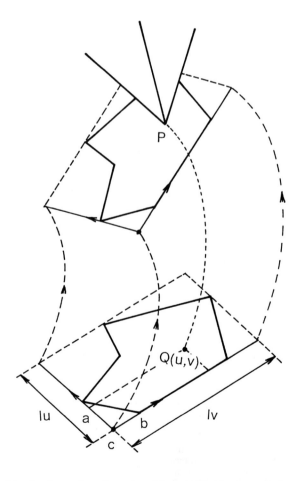

Fig.6. A moving face touching a stationary vertex.

P is given, in fact this is the coordinate of a stationary vertex, the original point Q that moves to the collision point P at the time is obtained by

$$Q = T^{-1} P$$

where T^{-1} is the inverse matrix of T at that time. Then, the face parameters u and v for the point Q are obtained. If the point Q does not exist in the area where $0 \leq u \leq lu$ and $0 \leq v \leq lv$, the collision point P is not inside the boundary of the face.

The point Q is returned by the function MoveFintV as well as the collision time t and point P. This method enables the classification of the collision point P without transforming the vertices of the moving face, because it is obvious that the collision point P is inside the boundary of the face, if the original point Q is inside the boundary at the initial position. This refinement greatly reduces the execution time in this case.

Type 3 Contact (Moving edge vs. stationary edge)

```
{ t : collision time }
{ p : collision point}
for each edge Ea of solid A do
 for each edge Eb of solid B do
  (t1,p1) <-- MoveEintE (Ea,Eb,T)
                  {T is transformation matrix}
                  { 0 ≤ t ≤ 1}
  if t1<t then
    t <-- t1 ; p <-- p1
  end { t1 test }
 end { Edge B loop }
end { Edge A loop }
```

A moving edge and a stationary edge are described by

$$R = a(t)u + b(t) \qquad (0 \leq u \leq lu)$$
$$S = cv + d \qquad (0 \leq v \leq lv)$$

respectively, where $a(t)$, $b(t)$, c, d are vectors, $|a| = 1$, $|c| = 1$, and lu and lv are the length of the edges. The collision point should exist on the both edges, namely in the range of $0 \leq u \leq lu$ and $0 \leq v \leq lv$. The function MoveEintE returns the minimum time $t1$ of collision points obtained by solving the equation (7). If the time $t1$ is larger than the collision time t obtained so far, a collision occurs before the time $t1$, and the answer is not necessary.

After these three procedures, if the collision time t is still the BigNumber that is given before the collision detection process begins, a collision does not occur in this motion, otherwise, a collision occurs at the time t, at the position p. The positions and orientations of the objects are obtained by the transformation matrices at the time t.

Experimental Results

The solids used for experiments are shown in Fig.7 and the numbers of faces, edges, and vertices of each solid are listed in Table 1. The relative computation time for collision detection among these solids resulted in Table 2. The real computation time for detecting a collision between two cuboids is less than 1 sec., which is acceptable for practical applications.

Another example in Fig.8 shows the simulation of two moving robots. It is obviously difficult to detect collisions by looking at the motion on the graphical terminal, but by using the method developed in this research, we can obtain the exact time and position of the collision in the moderate computation time as shown in Fig.9.

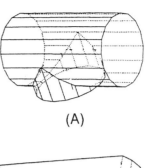

(A)

(B)

(C)

Fig. 7. Objects used for experiments of collision detection.

Table 1. The number of vertices, edges, and faces of the objects in Fig.7.

	vertex	edge	face
Object A	102	150	55
Object B	16	24	10
Object C	8	12	6

Table 2. The ratio of computation time for collision detection among the objects in Fig.7.

	Object A	Object B	Object C
Object A	160	27.5	12.5
Object B		4.6	2.0
Object C			1.0

496   Kawabe et al.

Conclusions

In this paper, we have described two basic types of intersection between two moving polyhedra and derived equations for each type of intersection. The types are face vs. edge, and edge vs. edge. The motion of each polyhedron is described by a cubic function of time. This algorithm can detect collisions without missing, and the exact time and position of the collision can be obtained. We then showed that the problem of collisions between moving objects can be solved by the problem of detecting collisions between a moving object and a stationary object. We derived equations for each of three types of intersection between an object and an obstacle and showed an example of its implementation. The experimental examples have proved that the algorithm developed in this research works sufficiently for practical applications, in terms of reliability and computation time.

Acknowledgements

We are grateful to Hideo Matsuka for many valuable suggestions on the technical issues and for his management support to this research project. We would like to thank C. K. Chow for his management help in working on this project and in the preparation of this paper.

References

1. Boyse, J., "Interference Detection Among Solids and Surfaces," Comm. of ACM, Vol.22, No.1, 1979, pp.3-9.

2. Canny, J., "Collision Detection for Moving Polyhedra," IEEE Transaction on Pattern Analysis and Machine Intelligence, Vol.8, No.2, 1986, pp.200-209.

3. Cameron, S., "A Study of the Clash Detection Problem in Robotics," Proc. of International Conference on Robotics and Automation, IEEE, 1985, pp.488-493.

4. Esterling, D.M. and Rosendale, J.V., "An Intersection Algorithm for Moving Parts," NASA Symposium on Computer Aided Geometric Modelling, 1984, pp.119-123.

5. IBM System/360 and System/370, IBM 1130 and 1800, Subroutine Library-Mathematics, User's Guide, SH12-5300-1, 1974.

6. Ozawa, K., Kumamoto, K., Akashi, K., and Nakata, H., "A Fast Interference Check Method in Off-line Robot Teaching," Journal of Robotics Society of Japan, Vol.4, No.2, 1986, pp.3-14, (in Japanese).

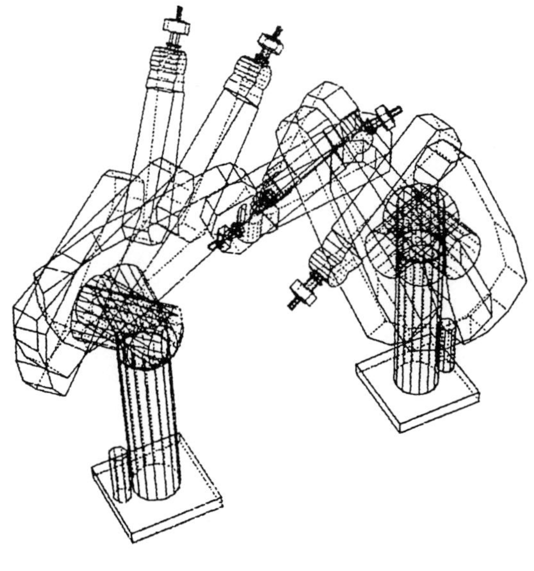

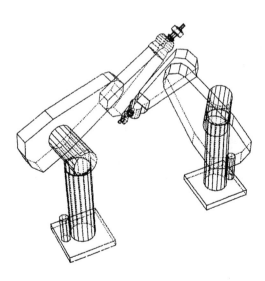

Fig.8. Two robots moving simultaneously.

Fig.9. A collision detected by the system.

An Automated Guided Vehicle with Map Building and Path Finding Capabilities

R.A. Jarvis and J.C. Byrne
Department of Electrical Engineering
Monash University
CLAYTON VIC. 3168
Australia

This paper presents preliminary work aimed at applying a previously reported optimal collision-free path finding algorithm, which was shown capable of operating in known and initially unknown environments, to a Denning DRV-1 mobile robot. This means having to accommodate the physical realities of sensory based environmental mapping, position/orientation determination and collision-free path following, within the energy and pay load constraints of the robot and meeting the requirement of reasonable speed of operation.

1. Introduction

There are three essential components to a robot navigation task. Firstly, it is necessary to be provided with or have the capability of sensory-based learning a model of the environment with sufficient detail and accuracy to permit safe route planning. In some cases, a balance of local and global detail might suffice provided that some refinement can be achieved in the process of carrying out the navigation task. In the situation where the model of the environment must be built from data acquired by sensory transduction devices aboard the robot, considerable complexities of implementation arise from the need to both derive the appropriate mapping data and to register these findings in a globally consistent way despite robot movement. If the main processing resources are not aboard, there is also the problem of communicating with the host, possibly at high bandwidth.

Secondly, given an environmental model, possibly incomplete, it is necessary to devise a collision-free plan of movement of the robot which combines exploratory and goal seeking behaviour. The robustness, speed and optimality properties of this algorithm are critical to the quality of the resulting navigation action. In the case of operation in a partially unknown environment, the path planning strategy must include some type of incremental adjustment to take advantage of further details of the environmental model which can be acquired by the roving robot.

Thirdly, unless it is possible to know or determine the location and orientation of the robot at fairly short intervals of movement, it will not be possible to complete the navigation task confidently, since modelling distortions might accumulate and global registration be lost. Thus, the problem of position/orientation tracking must be solved in an efficient and sufficiently accurate manner.

If all the above three requirements can be met, it is clear that such a navigation system could support automated guided vehicles in a wide range of applications in industrial, office, hospital, domestic, outdoor, mining and space environments. The main goals might be to improve efficiency, reduce human tedium and improve human safety in hazardous environments.

In this paper we address ourselves to the problems of using on-board sensory data acquisition for environmental modelling (ultrasonic and image based ranging), beacons for obviating dead reckoning based robot position/orientation determination and applying robust and versatile distance transform based path planning algorithms when a physical robot (Denning DRV-1) is involved.

In the next section the Denning DRV-1 will be described along with the overall navigation system components which are collectively the subject of this paper.

The next three sections will deal with environmental modelling, position/orientation tracking and collision-free path finding, respectively. Finally, the current status and future plans of the project will be clarified.

2. The Denning DRV-1 Robot and the Proposed Navigation System.

The Denning DRV-1 robot (See Figure 1) moves on three wheels which are steered and rotated in unison, enabling it to move in any direction without turning its body. A rotating platform which follows the steering rotation is provided for on-board sensory devices. A number of on-board microcomputers direct movement and collection of range data from a set of 24 ultrasonic range sensors distributed around the 'waist' of the drum like robot at intervals of 15°. The ultrasonic sensors are fired in three groups of eight (every third) to avoid overlap of their coverage volumes. Using a terminal or host computer attached via an RS 232 serial link, simple movement, status and ultrasonic sensor firing commands can be issued and appropriate data returned to the operator. Whilst there are several ways of controlling the robot, simple terminal emulation interchanges were chosen for the purposes of this investigation. Initially, the processing power for environmental mapping, position/orientation determination and collision-free path planning are to be handled by a dedicated VAX 11/750, but plans are well advanced towards using an IBM AT plus 68020/68881 board combination enhanced by considerable image processing capability (Matrox MVP-AT) to provide this service, possibly on-board; this should provide at least VAX 11/780 power for compute bound work.

The overall schematic of the proposed navigation scheme is shown in Figure 2. Dead-reckoning position/orientation data based on accumulated steering and driving commands can be collected at will, but this will not be necessary with the use of the beacon detection system. Both ultrasonic and stripe light ranging data is made available to support environmental mapping. Video images can be transmitted to a video processing system [1] attached to the VAX. The environmental mapping data (possibly incomplete) and position/orientation tracking data are used by the collision-free path finding algorithm which directs the robot to a prespecified absolute position goal.

3.   Environmental Modelling

Since, for navigational purposes, a volumetric model of the environment is of more immediate importance than one which describes the properties of surfaces and the identity of objects, range sensing would seem the appropriate means by which such a model should be constructed. Whilst, for simplicity, a 2D floor map (indicating filled and free areas) is sufficient, in the main, for navigation on a flat surface, it should be clear that some conservative floor projections of obstacle protrusions at any height which could effect the selected path for the robot are required in the model. Thus, ideally, 3D ranging should be used; however, cost, payload and time restrictions favour a more modest approach.

A number of alternatives to range based environmental mapping were considered. Initially, it was hoped that a coded stereo [2] system developed in the department could be applied directly to this problem, although the experimental apparatus so far built was aimed at high resolution small volume 3D modelling. It was found that limited contrast and intensity made mapping of volumes up to 10m x 10m x 3m unfeasible for the current equipment; however, some further development could make this approach viable. Its chief attraction is that, with views at approximately 60⁰ intervals around the robot, a fairly complete 3D model could be constructed using well tested hardware and software.

Since the DRV-1 is provided with 24 ultrasonic range sensors, it was hard to resist the temptation of trying to develop an acceptable floor map using them despite serious misgivings about the use of ultrasonic ranging [3] for this purpose. The polaroid ultrasonic range sensors have a 30⁰ solid angle main lobe energy spread characteristic which severely limits the accuracy of location of targets. More seriously, at the ultrasonic frequencies used (50 to 60 Khz), many common surfaces exhibit specular reflection effects which can cause non-return of signal, or, which is worse, false return from secondary reflection surfaces. In all, the data available is not only statistically coarse, but highly unreliable in a way which makes statistical averaging unhelpful, since the multiple reflection errors are systematic. Figure 3 illustrates some of the problems encountered through the use of ultrasonic ranging techniques and also shows some actual ultrasonic ranging based maps.

Another, seemingly straightforward and elegant approach to 360⁰ ranging, is to use cone mirror optics (See Figure 4) to transmit sheets of light and gather triangulation based range data for the whole line of sight surrounding space in a single image. A mirror cone was fabricated but proved not to be of sufficient quality or size to be useful; however, the idea is valid enough and will be pursued further. Figure 5 shows a cone image and its geometrically corrected version.

In the wake of these earlier disappointments of implementation rather than concept, it was decided to revert to single stripe ranging using a vertical slit projector and a horizontally displaced video camera, both mounted on a rotating platform on the DRV-1. Without the advantage of the logarithmic complexity coding mechanism essential to the method of Alexander and Ng [2], a 5⁰ interval scan would involve the analysis of 72 image frames, each containing a single light stripe. Since the processing time for this analysis could prove unacceptable, a simpler alternative scheme has been devised but not yet implemented. It consists of aligning the camera so that the image of the light stripe on the floor is along a known scan line and detecting the first 'kink' of that line which corresponds to where the floor meets with an obstacle supported by it (see Figure 6).

The line length to that first kink is directly related to the radial range to the first obstacle. To improve the light stripe contrast without imposing an unacceptable energy supply problem (since only on-board batteries must be used) both the special projector design of Figure 7 and the use of flash strobes are being investigated.

4.   Position/Orientation Robot Tracking

Measuring steering and wheel driving motor turns is an unreliable way of determining the position and orientation of the robot relative to an initial home position since incremental errors associated with wheel slippage and alignment creep in. The availability of a high resolution laser gyroscope or satellite based navigation system would, of course, be an ideal solution, but these are not economically or technically feasible at this time. The first solution planned was the use of on board ultrasonic transmitters and spatially distributed ultrasonic microphones at known locations; however, the company which was to supply the appropriate equipment disappeared and could not be contacted after the order was placed. Another option was the use of lateral effect diode position detection cameras and fish-eye lens or cone mirror optics to enable the angular positions of light emitting diodes fixed around the room to be determined. Ambient light interference and other problems made this approach less attractive after some early tests. The use of ultrasonic range data and a given map to hypothesise position/orientation data has been reported in the literature [4]; both the unreliability of ultrasonic range data and the dependence of the method on the availability of the environmental map makes this approach unacceptable for this project.

A beacon based system was eventually chosen. When an inexpensive infra-red transmitter/receiver system used for intrusion detection (when the beam to and from a cat's eye reflector is broken) showed excellent reliability over 10 metres, confidence in this approach rose considerably. It was envisaged that mounting such a device on a rotating platform on the robot (the same one used for light stripe ranging) and fixing cat's eye reflectors at suitable positions in the room would provide a simple, reliable and inexpensive solution; the angles at which return beams were detected would be sufficient to determine robot position/orientation if at least 3 readings were available from any location. It was later discovered that some glossy paint surfaces could cause false alarms. The cat's eye reflectors were replaced by active light emitting diode sources driven at the frequency detected by the receiver and the transmitter window blocked. The geometry of position determination for this system is illustrated in Figure 8.

Orientation can be easily recovered by either attaching a target source to the body of the robot in such a way that the receiver on the rotating table can 'see' it and distinguish it from the others (say by the time length of sighting since it is so close) or by using a micro switch which determines when the rotating table is at a known robot body reference position. Rather conveniently, the beacon detection signal is transmitted to the VAX on the sound channel of the same transmitter user by the video camero to send its images to the frame grabber attached to the VAX. The transmitted beacon trigger pulses are time stamped by the VAX parallel I/O device service routine and this information used for position/orientation detection assuming short term constant angular velocity of the rotating platform.

5. Optimal Collision-Free Path Finding

Optimal collision-free path finding is an important issue for both robotic manipulators and automated guided vehicles. In the general case, in high dimensional configuration space (one dimension for each degree of freedom), path finding algorithms can be computationally expensive and may well be prohibitively so where real-time robotic applications are concerned. When the environment is known beforehand, the problem can already be difficult (e.g. dense mapping the free space of a six degree of freedom anthropomorphic robotic manipulator into configuration space and then finding an appropriate trajectory); if operation in an initially unknown environment is required, the complexity could expand rapidly.

Most earlier work reported in the literature [5,6,7,8,9] concerns the known environment situation. One approach is to test a hypothesised trajectory for the overlap of the swept volume with obstacle volumes and to suggest adjustments which reduce the insection volumes to nil. A more elegant approach due to Lozano-Perez and Wesley [10] is to grow the obstacles to accommodate the physical extent of the robot and to reduce the problem to finding the optimal point path trajectory in the resulting configuration space into which the grown obstacles are mapped. For convex polygonal obstacles and robotic vehicles in the plane, a translation only solution can be easily found using A* free search [11]. An example of this approach is shown in Figure 9. If non-convex polygons are involved, segmentation into convex components must precede application of the algorithm. When vehicle rotation is included, finding the solution is more complex. In even higher dimensional configuration spaces, the computational complexity becomes extremely high and the problem of mapping obstacles into that configuration space can also be difficult and computationally expensive.

More recently, Brooks [12,13] developed the idea of free space pathways (freeways) modelled using generalised cylinders; in cluttered situations with complex shaped free space volumes, such an approach is likely to be unwieldy. An entirely different approach [14] is to base planning on semantically driven components which relate examined situations with appropriate action (e.g. approaching an object on a table from above).

When the obstacle field is initially partially or totally unknown, optimal collision-free path planning becomes a problem in which environmental modelling and path finding activity must be combined, hopefully in an efficient way. Some work along these lines has been reported by Iyengar et al [15].

For the path-finding component of this project, the distance transform based method previously reported by Jarvis [16] and Byrne [17] is used. A more detailed and extended version of this paper is in preparation [18]. The method is based on the propagation of distance outwards from the goal to all free space, flowing around the obstacles, thus creating a distance potential landscape where downhill from any part of free space leads optimally to the goal. Efficient sequential processing algorithms can generate this result very simply. Where complex and convoluted obstacles are involved, multiple passes of the raster and reverse raster order sequential algorithm are required; usually 2 to 5 passes are sufficient. Not only does this approach allow inclusion of non-convex obstacles but also accommodates multiple goals, multiple start points, variations in free space distance weighting, partial updates, sensory based incrementally developed environmental maps and systematic coverage of all free space. Exploring all unknown areas with or without a secondary goal is also easily achieved. Furthermore, in the simple case of a circularly symmetric vehicle (such as the Denning DRV-1) in the plane, the method allows the growing of the obstacle field to account for the vehicle diameter in a trivial manner. Figure 10 shows some collision-free path solutions for complex but known environments. In Figure 10(d) multiple goals are defined.

In initially unknown environment, sensory device acquired data can be used to incrementally develop an environmental map. The learning modes so far experimented with are by touch and by ranging (called 'seeing' in the earlier work). For the touch mode, the vehicle is able to discover only whether cells in its immediate neighbourhood are filled or empty. In the ranging mode, a radial line of sight range scan is considered to provide information of empty and filled space along a ray emanating from the robot and systematically rotated around it. In general, this latter mode is able to acquire information about the environment at a much greater rate than for the touch alternative. If the unknown space is assumed to be empty (optimistic assumption), the path can proceed in a manner which is optimal subject to that assumption and the current knowledge of the environment. It is possible to weigh distances in favour of avoiding or seeking out unknown space or to grade the positions of obstacle boundaries to account for uncertainty and to accommodate some probabilistic estimates of the obstacle content of as yet unknown space.

Exploration of all unknown space is elegantly achieved by initially defining all unknown space to be a collective goal and subsequently allocating filled and empty space labels to cells as they are 'discovered' through goal seeking behaviour of the robotic vehicle. This results in a non-optimal but reasonably efficient exploration strategy. Both learning by touch and by ranging can be used for mapping the environment during exploration. Figure 11(a) shows an exploration experiment in progress with shades of grey indicating filled (light grey) and unfilled (dark grey) cells which have not yet been sensed by the robotic vehicle and black and white indicating discovered empty and filled cells, respectively. A further extension permits the robotic vehicle to visit every empty cell and finish up at a specified goal point; it is also possible to mark each cell in such a way that no cell is marked twice. The implication here is that, if the robotic vehicle were washing or painting the free floor area, one cell at a time, it could be made to do so without ever crossing over wet areas; it never paints itself into a corner. Figure 11(b) shows such a space filling trajectory which, although not optimal, is acceptable enough. The method is entirely robust no matter how complex the obstacle map.

Another example of distance transform based collision-free trajectory planning was reported by Jarvis [19]. The waist, shoulder and elbow joints of a Unimate 250 robotic manipulator computer model were driven along an optimal collision-free trajectory derived by 3D distance transforms in the corresponding configuration space into which the obstacles were previously mapped. Figure 12 shows such a trajectory. Although the obstacle mapping is a tedious process, the trajectory calculation is not. Such an approach could be extended up to the whole 6 degrees of freedom of the robot manipulator if desired.

6.   Progress to Date and Anticipated Development

The well proven distance transform based collision-free path planning algorithms previously reported have been modified to operate on sensory based mapping data and to give movement directions to the DRV-1 robot. Robot navigation in known environments using the dead reckoning position/orientation data drived from accumulating steering angle and drive increments have been successfully carried out but accumulated errors severely limit the lengths of the paths which can be navigated safely. In the immediate future it is anticipated that beacon tracking data will be available to correct this deficiency. Whilst a number of range finding techniques for environmental mapping have been experimented with, the final equipment design is not yet complete although implementation is not expected to extend beyond several months, since considerable experience in ranging techniques already exists within the group. As yet to be decided is whether to put all computational resources on-board or to rely on radio communication for data transfer to and from a stationary host computer. It is expected that a complete demonstration of tracking, mapping and path finding will be possible by the end of the year.

7.   Conclusions

This paper has presented preliminary work on implementing well proven path-planning algorithms developed by the authors for use in controlling a physical automated guided vehicle which will map its environment and navigate through it using beacon tracking techniques. This vehicle will soon be capable of path finding, exploring and free space covering for target applications in industrial, office, hospital and domestic environments. The current experiments are expected to lead to a complete prototype system which could be the basis of a commercially viable product, perhaps developed cojointly with a suitable industrial partner. Many other projects using the DRV-1 as a research platform for sensory-based robot guidance are anticipated. Attaching a robot arm to the DRV-1 is also being contemplated; this would permit both 'eye-in-hand' vision analysis studies and the extension of the domains of applicability to include object manipulation.

1.   Jarvis, R.A. and Ewin, R.E., "A Vax-Based Robotic Vision Laboratory", Proc. 8th Australian Computer Science Conference, Melbourne, 6-8 Feb., 1985, pp.4-1 to 4-10.

2.   Alexander, B.F. and Ng K.C., "3D shape measurement by active triangulation using a projected array of coded dots or stripes of light", Proc. Conf. on Robots in Australia's Future", Perth, 13-16 May, 1986, pp.243-250.

3.   Jarvis, R.A., "A Perspective on Range Finding Techniques for Computer Vision", Vol. PAMI-5, No.2., March 1983, pp.122-139.

4.   Drumheller, M., "Mobile Robot Localization Using Sonar", Trans. IEEE PAMI, Vol. PAMI-9, No.2, March 1987, pp.325-332.

5.   Ahuja, N., Chien, R.T., Yen, R. and Bridwell, N., "Interference Detection and Collision Avoidance Among Three Dimensional Objects", the 1st Annual National Conference on Artificial Intelligence, Stanford University, Aug. 18-21, 1980, pp.44-48.

6.   Chattergy, R., : "Some Heuristics for the Navigation of a Robot", The International Journal of Robotics Research, Vol. 4, No. 1, 1985, pp.59-66.

7.   Crowley, J.L., "Navigation for an Intelligent Mobile Robot", IEEE Journal of Robotics and Automation, Vol. RA-1, March 1985, pp.31-41.

8.   Gilbert, E.G. and Johnson, W.J., "Distance Functions and Their Application to Robot Path Planning in the Presence of Obstacles", IEEE Journal of Robotics and Automation, Vol. RA-1, No. 1, March 1985, pp.21-30.

9.   Udupa, S.M., "Collision Detection and Avoidance in Computer Controlled Manipulators" , 5th International Joint Conference on Artificial Intelligence , M.I.T., Aug. 22-25, 1977, pp.737-748.

10.   Lozano Perez, T., and Wesley, M.A., "An Algorithm for Planning Collision-Free Paths Among Polyhedral Obstacles", ACM, Vol. 22, No. 10, Oct. 1979, pp.560–570.

11.   Nilsson, N.J., "Problem Solving Methods in Artificial Intelligence", McGraw-Hill, 1972.

12.   Brooks, R.A., "Planning Collision-Free Motions for Pick-and-Place Operations", The International Journal of Robotics Research, Vol. 2, No.4, winter 1983, pp.19-44.

13.   Brooks, R.A., "Solving the Find-Path Problem by Good Representation of Free Space", IEEE Transactions on Systems, Man, and Cybernetics, Vol. SMC-13, No.3, March/April 1983, pp.190-196.

14.   Kang, K.H. and Jarvis, R.A., "A New Approach to Robot Collision-Free Path Planning", Proc. Conf. on Robots in Australia's Future, Perth, 13-16 May 1988, pp.72-79.

15.   Iyenger, S.S., Jorgenson, C.C., Rao, S.V.N. and Weisbin, C.R., "Robot Navigation Algorithms Using Learned Spatial Graphs", Robotica (1986), Vol. 4, pp.93-100.

16.   Jarvis, R.A., "Collision-Free Trajectory Planning Using Distance Transforms", Mechanical Engineering Trans. of The Institution of Engineers, Australia, Vol. ME 10, No. 3, Sept. 1985, pp.187-191.

17.   Jarvis, R.A. and Byrne, J.C., "Robot Navigation : Touching, Seeing and Knowing", Proc. 1st Australian Artificial Intelligence Congress, Melbourne, 18-20 Nov.,1986, Section e.(12 pages).

18.   Jarvis, R.A. and Byrne, J.C., "Robot Navigation in Known and Unknown Environments", in preparation.

19.   Jarvis, R.A., "Configuration Space Collision-Free Path Planning for Robotic Manipulators", Proc. 10th Australian Computer Science Conference, Deakin University, Victoria, 4-6 Feb., 1987, pp.193-204.

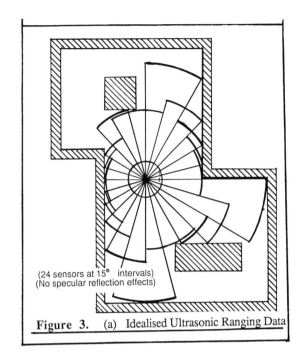

(24 sensors at 15° intervals)
(No specular reflection effects)

Figure 3.   (a)   Idealised Ultrasonic Ranging Data

Figure 1.   Denning DRV-1 Mobile Robot

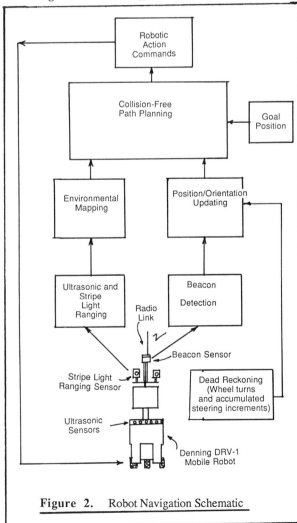

Figure 2.   Robot Navigation Schematic

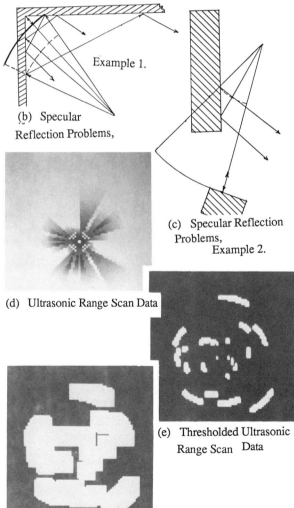

Example 1.

(b) Specular
Reflection Problems,

(c) Specular Reflection
Problems,
       Example 2.

(d) Ultrasonic Range Scan Data

(e) Thresholded Ultrasonic
Range Scan Data

(f) Grown Obstacle Field Using Map from 3(e)

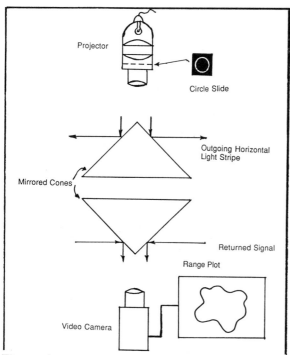

Figure 4.   Cone Optics for Simultaneous 360° Ranging

(a) Cone Image

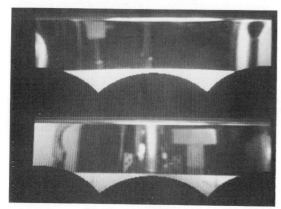

(b) Geometrically Corrected Cone Image

Figure 5.

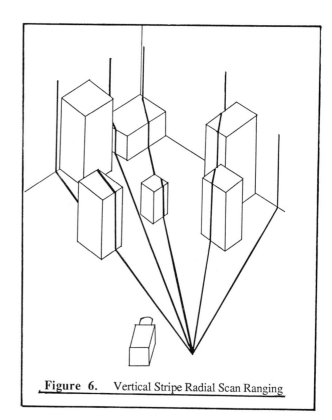

Figure 6.   Vertical Stripe Radial Scan Ranging

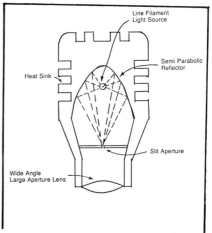

Figure 7.   High Intensity Light Stripe Projector

(a)   The Circular Arc Loci of Vehicle
        Location.

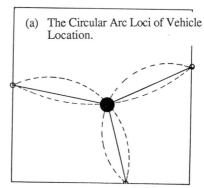

Figure 8.   Determining Robotic Vehicle
                Position/Orientation Using Three Beacons.

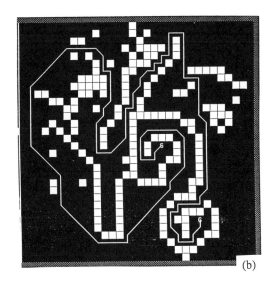

(b)

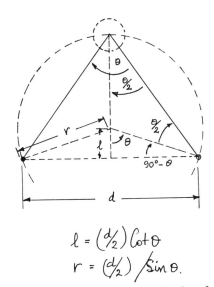

$$\ell = \left(\frac{d}{2}\right) \cot \theta$$
$$r = \left(\frac{d}{2}\right) / \sin \theta.$$

8. (b) Determining the Centre and Radius of
the Circles Depicted in (a).

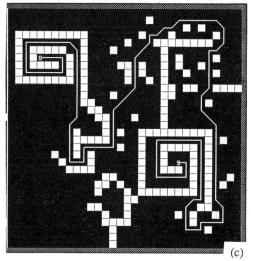

(c)

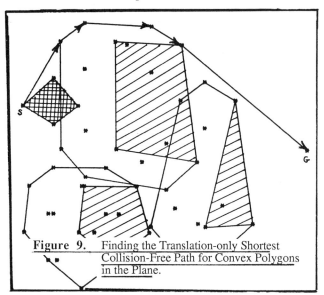

Figure 9.   Finding the Translation-only Shortest
Collision-Free Path for Convex Polygons
in the Plane.

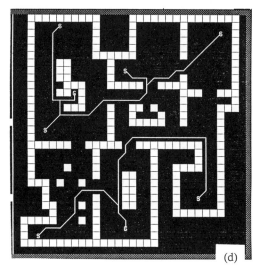

(d)

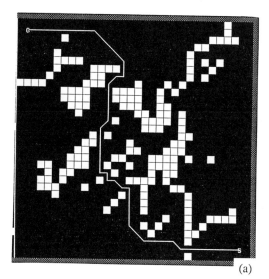

(a)

Figure 10. Optimal Collision-Free Paths found Using
Distance Transforms.

504   Jarvis and Byrne

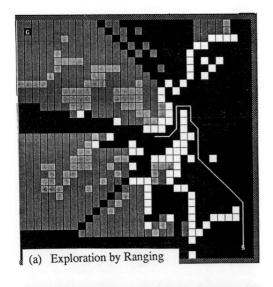

(a) Exploration by Ranging

Figure 11. (b) Covering all Free Space

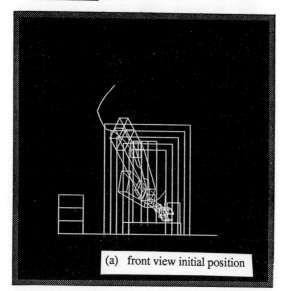

(a) front view initial position

Figure 12. Collision-Free Trajectory for Robotic Manipulation.

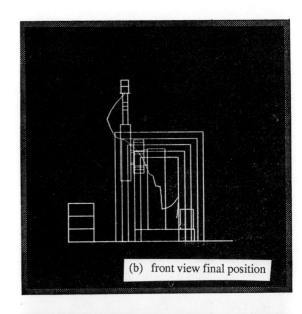

(b) front view final position

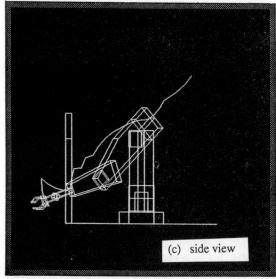

(c) side view

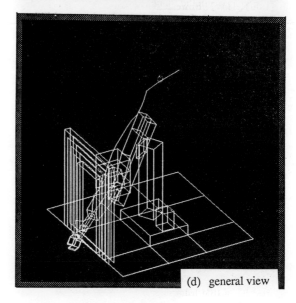

(d) general view

Exact Solution of some Robot Motion Planning Problems

John Canny

Artificial Intelligence Laboratory
Massachusetts Institute of Technology

and

Computer Science Division
University of California, Berkeley

Abstract

We give exact solutions for two natural extensions of the basic robot motion planning or piano-movers' problem in three dimensions. These are the euclidean shortest path problem and dynamic motion planning with velocity limits. While both planning problems are NP-hard, we give algorithms that efficiently find a simple solution (one with few via points) if one exists. The algorithms are based on a new method for solving systems of polynomial equations, and on a gap theorem which allows exact computation on algebraic numbers using binary approximations of sufficient accuracy.

1 Introduction

We are interested here in algorithms for various robot motion planning problems which are exact, that is which will always find a solution if one exists, and will never output an incorrect solution. Planning the motion of a robot with arbitrarily many links was shown to be PSPACE-hard (i.e. at least as hard as the well known NP-hard problems) by Reif [Rei]. This result applied to the basic motion planning or "piano-movers'" problem, which is the problem of finding an obstacle-avoiding path, without consideration of the dynamic constraints of the robot. However, if the number of degrees of freedom is fixed, as it usually is, Schwartz and Sharir [SSh] showed that the basic motion planning problem is solvable in polynomial time. Their result was based on the configuration space transformation [Udu], [LW]. However, the polynomial exponents for the Schwartz-Sharir method were very large for typical problems, and it involved large constants. Thus while their method gave a theoretical solution to the problem, it was impractical for most problems. Recently, Canny [Can] described a new general method which solves the movers' problem in polynomial time, with exponent equal to the number of degrees of freedom of the robot, which is worst-case optimal. Its algebraic complexity is also much lower than previous methods, leading to smaller constants in running time. Using some of the techniques in that paper, we present solutions for two extensions of the basic movers' problem.

Acknowledgements. This report describes research done at the Artificial Intelligence Laboratory of the Massachusetts Institute of Technology. Support for the Laboratory's Artificial Intelligence research is provided in part by the Office of Naval Research under Office of Naval Research contract N00014-81-K-0494 and in part by the Advanced Research Projects Agency under Office of Naval Research contracts N00014-80-C-0505 and N00014-82-K-0334. John Canny is supported by an IBM fellowship.

If dynamic constraints are added to the movers' problem, or if a minimal time or minimal distance path is sought, there is strong evidence that motion planning cannot be done in polynomial time [RSh], [CR], even if the number of degrees of freedom is fixed at two or three. In this paper, we give improved solutions for planning shortest paths, and for planning motions with moving obstacles in three dimensions. These algorithms take exponential time in the worst case, but will run in polynomial time if the problem has an "easy" solution. Both algorithms make use of an efficient method for solving systems of equations which is described in section 5.

In section 2, we review the shortest path problem in three dimensions, giving the known lower and upper bounds on the problem. We then describe a simple algorithm based on enumeration of edge sequences and equation solving for locally shortest paths. In section 3, we review work on dynamic motion planning, and give an algorithm for dynamic motion planning for obstacles moving uniformly in straight lines. This algorithm is more complex than the shortest path method, but has roughly the same complexity. It uses a simplified version of the roadmap algorithm of [Can]. Section 4 gives the mathematical basis for the algebraic methods described in the paper. Section 5 contains a gap theorem which allows exact computation via binary approximation, and then gives an algorithm for solving systems of polynomial equations.

2 The Shortest Path Problem

The shortest path problem is of interest in robotics because it is the simplest instance of a minimum cost path planning problem. The shortest path may be defined using a variety of metrics, but we consider here only the usual euclidean distance. The environment is assumed to be polyhedral, with vertex coordinates etc. described as rational binary numbers. The objective is to find a continuous path between two given points which avoids the obstacles in the environment, and which has minimum length, (see figure 1).

Efficient algorithms for two dimensional euclidean shortest path have been known for some time. This problem was first studied by Lozano-Pérez and Wesley [LW]. They showed that a shortest path can be found by searching the visibility graph of the vertices of the polygonal environment. No upper bounds were given in their paper, but their algorithm should run in $O(n^3)$ time. Improvements were given by Sharir and Schorr [SSc], and by Reif and Storer [RSt] to $O(n(k + \log n))$ time, where k is the number of convex parts of the obstacles.

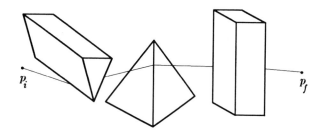

Figure 1: The shortest obstacle avoiding path from p_i to p_f

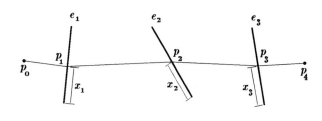

Figure 2: The positions of via points p_i along edges e_i

While the euclidean shortest path has efficient solutions in two dimensions, the three-dimensional problem is more difficult. In [CR] it is shown that this problem is NP-hard for any L^p metric, which is strong evidence that exponential time may be required in the worst case. There have been a number of papers on restricted versions of the problem. Mount [Mou], and Sharir and Baltsam [SB] gave polynomial time algorithms for environments consisting of a small fixed number of convex polyhedra. Papadimitriou [Pap] gave a polynomial time approximate algorithm which finds a path at most a small multiplicative constant longer than the shortest path. The general problem has been dealt with by Sharir and Schorr [SSc] who gave an $2^{2^{O(n)}}$ algorithm by reducing the problem to an algebraic decision problem in the theory of real closed fields. The best previous bound is due to Reif and Storer [RSt] who gave both $2^{n^{O(1)}}$-time, and $(n^{O(\log n)})$-space algorithms by using the same theory but with a more efficient reduction.

2.1   An algebraic Method

We describe a new method for the shortest path problem under the euclidean (L^2) metric whose running time is $O(n^{k+1}6^{5k})$ for finding the shortest path which touches k edges. We use the fact that a shortest path consists of a sequence of straight line segments with endpoints that lie on the edges of the environment. The globally shortest path can touch at most n edges, so this algorithm will find the shortest path in time $n^{O(n)}$, improving slightly the exponential-polynomial bound of Reif and Storer.

The algorithm is simple. First, all sequences of k edges are enumerated. For each sequence of edges $e_1, \ldots, e_k$, we solve a system of k polynomials in k variables $x_1, \ldots, x_k$ to find all the *locally* shortest paths through these edges, ignoring the obstacles. The variable x_i represents the position of the contact point along the length of the edge e_i. See figure 2. The system of polynomials specifies that a locally shortest path makes equal opposite angles when entering and leaving the edge, (see the figure). Then for each locally shortest path, we test every straight line segment of the path against all the faces of the obstacles. If any line segment of the path pierces any face of an obstacle, then the entire path is discarded. For those locally shortest paths that remain, we compare their lengths using binary arithmetic to sufficient accuracy to decide which is the globally shortest path.

Specifically, let p_0 denote the source point, and p_{k+1} denote the destination point. Then, we wish to find the k intermediate points $p_1, \ldots, p_k$ where each p_i lies on the edge e_i. If H_{e_i} denotes the head (vertex) of e_i and T_{e_i} denotes the tail of e_i, then

$$p_i = (1 - x_i)T_{e_i} + x_i H_{e_i} \tag{1}$$

that is, p_i is the convex combination of T_{e_i} and H_{e_i} specified by x_i. The condition that the locally shortest path make equal angles on entering and leaving the edge e_i can be formulated as

$$\frac{(p_i - p_{i-1}) \cdot D_{e_i}}{|(p_i - p_{i-1})|} = -\frac{(p_{i+1} - p_i) \cdot D_{e_i}}{|(p_{i+1} - p_i)|} \tag{2}$$

where $D_{e_i} = H_{e_i} - T_{e_i}$ is a vector in the direction of the edge e_i. Squaring and cross multiplying, the above condition can be written as a algebraic function of the p_i,

$$\begin{aligned} &((p_i - p_{i-1}) \cdot D_{e_i})^2((p_{i+1} - p_i) \cdot (p_{i+1} - p_i)) \\ &= ((p_{i+1} - p_i) \cdot D_{e_i})^2((p_i - p_{i-1}) \cdot (p_i - p_{i-1})) \end{aligned} \tag{3}$$

and substituting for p_i etc. from equation (1) we see that the previous identity can be written as a polynomial in the x_i of degree 4. There is one such equation for each intermediate edge e_i, and for a path which touches k edges, we obtain a system of k polynomials in k variables, all of degree 4. This system can be solved using the algorithm described in section 5 in time single exponential in k. Once the via points (x_i) are found, we can determine whether the straight line path segment between two consecutive via points is collision free by intersecting this path segment with every face in the environment. This test is the same as for a face and edge segment with rational endpoints, but here the edge has algebraic endpoints. However, the algebraic case reduces to the rational case using the gap theorem of section 5. The intersection test can be done in $O(n)$ time for each path segment.

For each sequence of k edges, finding all sets of via points takes time $O(k^3 4^{5k} \log^2 w)$ binary operations, where w is the coefficient size of the edge endpoints in the description of the environment. Since there are $O(n^k)$ sequences, and each takes $O(n)$ time to verify, the algorithm overall takes time $(n^{k+1} 2^{O(k)} \log^2 w)$.

3   Dynamic Motion Planning with Velocity Bounds

We consider motion planning for a robot with a fixed number of degrees of freedom in an environment in which the obstacles are moving, and in which the robot has constraints on its velocity. If there are no motion constraints, and the trajectories of obstacles can be described algebraically, then the problem is solvable in polynomial time [RSh]. However, if velocity limits are added, the problem is more difficult. In [RSh] it was shown that motion planning in 3-d with rotating dynamic obstacles is PSPACE-hard in the presence of velocity bounds, and NP-hard in the absence of bounds. However, the rotating obstacles have non-algebraic trajectories. In [CR] it is shown that dynamic motion planning with velocity bounds is NP-hard even if the obstacles are convex polygons moving in the plane with constant velocity and without rotation.

We define the *asteroid avoidance problem* in two or three dimensions as the problem of determining a collision-free path for a point with bounded velocity, and polygonal or polyhedral obstacles moving with constant velocity and without rotation. Reif and Sharir [RSh] gave algorithms for both the two and three dimensional problems. Their two-dimensional algorithm ran in time $O(n^{2(k+2)}k)$ for an environment with k convex polygons with a total of n edges. They also gave a $(2^{n^{O(1)}})$-time algorithm for the three dimensional problem. In this paper we give improved bounds for the three dimensional problem, using the equation solving technique described in section 5.

3.1 An Algorithm for Three Dimensional Asteroid Avoidance

Our algorithm is closely based on that of Reif and Sharir [RSh], and we will use their notation. In their paper, they show that if an obstacle-avoiding path (satisfying the velocity bound) exists, then there exists a "normal movement". A normal movement is an obstacle-avoiding motion that satisfies the velocity bound, and has a canonical form. It consists of an alternating sequence of direct movements and maximal contact movements. A direct movement is a motion of constant velocity in a straight line between edges or vertices of obstacles. A contact motion is a sequence of straight line (constant velocity) motions between the edges or vertices of a particular obstacle. There is an additional condition that contact movements cannot visit the same obstacle more than once. The fact that contact motions need not visit the same edge more than once on each obstacle imply that the number of straight line path segments is at most equal to the number of edges in the environment.

Reif and Sharir then construct an explicit formula in the existential theory of real closed fields with $O(n)$ variables which is satisfiable if and only if there exists a successful normal motion. The $O(n)$ variables define the coordinates of the via points in between consecutive straight line path segments. Using exactly the same technique, it is possible to construct a formula F_k in $O(k)$ variables which is satisfiable if and only if there exists a successful normal motion *consisting of k straight line motions*. While k may be almost equal to n in the worst case, it seems worthwhile to consider paths consisting of only a few segments, since these can be computed much more efficiently.

Given such a formula, we then make use of the roadmap algorithm described in Canny [Can]. This algorithm constructs a skeleton of the set of points which satisfy a semi-algebraic formula. The formula F_k above which defines the set of successful normal motions is semi-algebraic. The roadmap algorithm will return a skeleton of this set in time $(n^{O(k)}2^{O(k^2)})$, and in particular, it returns sample points for which the formula is true. That is, it returns assignments to the $O(k)$ variables, and each such assignment will define a successful motion sequence. In fact, the roadmap algorithm computes more information (connected components) than is required here. For our application the point linking phase ([Can]) of the roadmap algorithm can

be eliminated, and the time complexity then drops to $n^{O(k)}$.

4   Resultants and Equation Solving

At the heart of the motion planning algorithms which we describe in this paper is an algorithm for computation of a generalized resultant for a system of polynomials. The resultant of a system of polynomials $f_1, \ldots, f_n$ in variables $x_1, \ldots, x_n$ is a single polynomial *in the coefficients of the f_i*, whose vanishing is a necessary and sufficient condition for the system to have a solution. The resultant can be used to find the solutions of a system of polynomials via the u-resultant [Wae]. There was a considerable amount of work on resultants late last century and early this century, and a general method was given by Cayley (described in Salmon's book [Sal]) for n polynomials, which was simplified by Macaulay [Mac]. Both methods are based on division of determinants and subdeterminants of certain matrices in the coefficients of the f_i, Cayley's method requiring n divisions and Macaulay's method requiring only two.

For large problems, Cayley's and Macaulay's methods require division of determinants which are much larger than the resultant itself. Furthermore, some of these determinants may vanish, and this must be recognised and different determinants computed. In this section we describe a new method for resultant computation which avoids these problems. Like the older methods, it involves division of determinants of matrices in the coefficients of the f_i. In the new method, we introduce an indeterminate offset to certain coefficients of the f_i. Instead of dividing determinants, we divide characteristic polynomials of the same matrices. This has a number of advantages. Firstly, the resultant depends on only some of the coefficients of the characteristic polynomials, in fact only on those coefficients smaller (roughly speaking) than the resultant. The others need never be computed. Secondly, no branching or division over the coefficient field of the polynomials is necessary, since characteristic polynomials always have leading coefficient one. This allows a fast parallel algorithm for resultant computation. Finally, we are able to obtain better bounds on the size of the resultant itself, and this leads to a tighter "gap" theorem for the minimum size of roots of polynomial systems. Gap theorems can be used to find the accuracy required for computations with algebraic numbers via binary approximations.

4.1   Mathematical Formulation

For n homogeneous polynomials $f_1, \ldots, f_n$ of degrees $d_1, \ldots, d_n$ in the n variables $x_1, \ldots, x_n$, there exists a single resultant R, which is a homogeneous polynomial in the coefficients of the f_i, [Wae]. The vanishing of this resultant is necessary and sufficient for the polynomials to have a non-trivial simultaneous zero (a zero distinct from 0) in the algebraic closure of the base field. This resultant has degree $d_1, d_2, \ldots, d_{i-1}d_{i+1}, \ldots, d_n$ in the coefficients of f_i. While R is not readily expressible as the determinant of a single matrix, it can be defined as the greatest common divisor of the determinants of n matrices $A^1, \ldots, A^n$. As we shall see below, it is also possible to define the resultant as a rational function of certain subdeterminants of the A^k thereby avoiding the GCD computation. In the special case $n = 2$, the determinants of A_1 and A_2 are identical, and both are equal to the Sylvester resultant of f_1 and f_2.

The matrices A^k are constructed as follows. This construction follows that given in [Wae]. First we define the degree d

of monomials that index the columns of A^k:

$$d = 1 + \sum_{i=1,\ldots,n} (d_i - 1) \tag{4}$$

Let $\alpha \in Z^n$ represent the exponents of a monomial in $x_1, \ldots, x_n$, i.e. if $\alpha = (\alpha_1, \alpha_2, \ldots, \alpha_n)$ we use the notation x^α for the monomial

$$x^\alpha = x_1^{\alpha_1} x_2^{\alpha_2} \cdot \ldots \cdot x_n^{\alpha_n}$$

Then the set of monomials of degree d, denoted X^d is

$$X^d = \{x^\alpha \mid \alpha_1 + \alpha_2 + \cdots + \alpha_n = d\} \tag{5}$$

and we observe that the cardinality of X^d is

$$N = |X^d| = \binom{d+n-1}{d} \tag{6}$$

We now partition X^d into n subsets as follows:

$$X_1^d = \{x^\alpha \in X^d \mid \alpha_1 \geq d_1\}$$

$$X_2^d = \{x^\alpha \in X^d \mid \alpha_2 \geq d_2 \text{ and } \alpha_1 < d_1\}$$

$$\vdots \qquad \vdots$$

$$X_n^d = \{x^\alpha \in X^d \mid \alpha_n \geq d_n, \ \alpha_i < d_i, \text{ for } i = 1, \ldots, n-1\} \tag{7}$$

and it is readily shown that every element of X^d is contained in exactly one of these subsets. Now for each X_i^d we define a set of polynomials F_i as

$$F_i = \frac{X_i^d}{x_i^{d_i}} f_i \tag{8}$$

that is, $F_i = \{x^\beta f_i \mid x^\beta x_i^{d_i} \in X_i^d\}$. Then the polynomials in F_i, for $i = 1, \ldots, n$, have degree d. The union F of the F_i is a collection of N polynomials of degree d. Since there are N monomials of degree d, we can construct a square matrix whose columns correspond to the N monomials in X^d, and each row of which contains the coefficients of those monomials in some polynomial in F. Specifically, we choose any ordering of the N elements of X^d, and then construct an $N \times N$ matrix A^n where A_{ij}^n is the coefficient of the ith monomial of X^d in the jth polynomial of F. The determinant of A^n has degree $d_1 d_2 \ldots, d_{n-1}$ in the coefficients of f_n, because the number of power products in X_n^d is $d_1 d_2 \ldots, d_{n-1}$.

The A^k for $k = 1, \ldots, n-1$ are defined similarly, but the power products X_i^d are different. In the definition (7) each X_i^d is the set of elements of X^d which are multiples of $x_i^{d_i}$, which are not contained in previous X_i^d's. For A^k, we reorder the X_i^d so that X_k^d appears last in the definition, so that it is the set of all multiples of $x_k^{d_k}$ which are not multiples of $x_i^{d_i}$ for any $i \neq k$. Thus X_k^d has $d_1, \ldots, d_{k-1} d_{k+1}, \ldots, d_n$ elements, and this number is also the degree of $\det A^k$ in the coefficients of f_k.

From now on, we will let a^k denote the determinant of A^k. These a^k are known as inertia forms [Hur]. They are characterized by the following property:

$$x_j^p a^k = 0(f_1, \ldots, f_n) \tag{9}$$

holds for some p and some (in fact every) j.

Now the resultant of $f_1, \ldots, f_n$ is the greatest common divisor of the a^k *as polynomials in the indeterminate coefficients of* $f_1, \ldots, f_n$ (see [Wae], section 82). This is a crucial point. We are interested in the value of the resultant for a certain specialization of the coefficients. By a specialization of the coefficients, we mean the introduction of polynomial relations on the indeterminate coefficients, e.g. $u_1 = 5$ or $u_1 = 2u_2$. This only succeeds up to a point. Specialization commutes with addition and multiplication and therefore with determinant computation. Thus we get the same result for each a^k by evaluating a^k formally and substituting for the coefficients as we do by substituting first and evaluating the determinant numerically.

However, specialization does not commute with the greatest common divisor step. For example, consider the greatest common divisor of ax and bx, where a and b are indeterminates. Suppose that a and b are both specialized to zero. If we compute the GCD before specialization, we get x, but both terms vanish if we specialize before the GCD step. For the Sylvester resultant, the GCD step is unnecessary, because the two a^k are identical. Similarly, if all the polynomials are linear, then all the a^k are identical, and equal to the determinant of the system. For the general case, the a^k are different, and the GCD step is non-trivial. One can require that the specialization of the coefficients be sufficiently "generic", since the GCD step succeeds for almost all specializations of the coefficients. However, this is an unnecessary restriction. At the other extreme, it is possible to compute the determinants symbolically, and then compute the GCD of the a^k as polynomials in *all* the symbolic coefficients of the f_i. However, this is a massive task, and generates terms of size double exponential in d.

4.2   Partial Coefficient Specialization

In the method described here, we instead specialize all but n of the coefficients (Strictly speaking, rather than leaving some coefficients indeterminate, we add an indeterminate offset to those coefficients). This ensures that the GCD of the a^k is the resultant. Furthermore, it allows the resultant to be recovered without a true GCD step, in fact without division over the base field. The resultant is computed from the a^k by a sequence of $2n$ polynomials divisions involving only *monic* polynomials. Division of monic polynomials does not involve division of their coefficients.

We define a new system of polynomials $\hat{f}_i$ from the f_i as follows:

$$\hat{f}_i(x_1, \ldots, x_n) = f_i(x_1, \ldots, x_n) + u_i x_i^{d_i} \tag{10}$$

where the u_i are indeterminates. Notice that the u_i appear on the leading diagonal of every matrix A^k. In fact u_i occupies the leading diagonal position in the columns indexed by monomials in X_i^d. The product of the diagonal u_i's appears as the leading term of a^k, treating a^k as a polynomial in $u_1, \ldots, u_n$, and its coefficient is 1. It follows that a^k has degree $d_1, \ldots, d_{k-1} d_{k+1}, \ldots, d_n$ in u_k. But the resultant R also has degree $d_1, \ldots, d_{i-1} d_{i+1} \ldots, d_n$ in u_i for all i. In fact the resultant (before specialization) has a single term of maximal degree in all the u_i, and this term has coefficient 1 (see [Wae]). Since the resultant divides all the a^k, we can write

$$a^k(u_1, \ldots, u_n) = b^k(u_1, \ldots, u_{k-1}, u_{k+1}, \ldots, u_n) R(u_1, \ldots, u_n) \tag{11}$$

where b^k is a polynomial independent of u_k because R and a^k have the same degree in u_k. Knowing the a^k, and knowing that the leading coefficients of both the a^k and R are 1, we can actually solve for all the coefficients of R (and b^k if desired). First we need:

Definition A multivariate polynomial $p(x_1,\ldots,x_2)$ of degree d_i in x_i is said to be *rectangular* if its leading term is of maximal degree in all the x_i, i.e. the leading term is of the form $cx_1^{d_1}x_2^{d_2}\ldots,x_n^{d_n}$. The product or quotient of two rectangular polynomials is also rectangular.

In particular $R(u_1,\ldots,u_n)$ is rectangular and monic, i.e. its leading coefficient is one. All the $a^k(u_1,\ldots,u_n)$ are rectangular and monic, so the $b^k(u_1,\ldots,u_{k-1},u_{k+1},\ldots,u_n)$ are rectangular and monic. To compute the resultant we can use:

The Basic Recurrence

Let $R_j(u_1,\ldots,u_j)$ be the leading coefficient of R considered as a polynomial in $u_{j+1},\ldots,u_n$. Since R is rectangular, it follows that the leading coefficient of R_j equals the leading coefficient of R, so that R_j is monic. Let $b_j^k(u_1,\ldots,u_j)$ be the leading coefficient of b^k, considered as a polynomial in $u_{j+1},\ldots,u_n$. Then b_j^k is also monic. Finally, let $a_j^k(u_1,\ldots,u_j)$ be the leading coefficient of a^k considered as a polynomial in $u_{j+1},\ldots,u_n$. Now the polynomial identity (11) implies a corresponding identity on the leading coefficients of the polynomials, so the following relationships hold:

$$R_{k-1}b_{k-1}^k = a_{k-1}^k \qquad \text{for } k = 1,\ldots,n$$

$$R_k b_{k-1}^k = a_k^k \qquad \text{for } k = 1,\ldots,n \qquad (12)$$

Where the second expression exploits the fact that $b_k^k = b_{k-1}^k$ since b^k is independent of u_k. So if we know R_{k-1}, we can compute R_k by first dividing a_{k-1}^k by R_{k-1} to get b_{k-1}^k, and then dividing b_{k-1}^k into a_k^k. Since we know $R_0 = 1$, after $2n$ divisions we obtain $R_n = R$. Notice that all of the polynomials in the division process are monic, and division by a monic polynomial involves only multiplication and subtraction steps on the coefficients. Thus, the computation of the GCD using the recurrence in (12) commutes with specialization. The identities (12) are valid irrespective of whether the coefficients of the polynomials in (12) are indeterminates or elements of the base field. Having finally obtained R as a polynomial in $u_1,\ldots,u_n$, we specialize $u_1,\ldots,u_n$ to zero, yielding the desired resultant.

4.3   Method 1

The recurrence relations just described allow the resultant to be computed for any specialization of the coefficients of the f_i, but involve computation of determinants which are high degree polynomials in $u_1,\ldots,u_n$, rather than elements of the base field. In fact we are only interested in the constant term of $R(u_1,\ldots,u_n)$, since the original system corresponds to the specialization $u_i = 0$ for all i. The polynomial identities in (12) imply corresponding identities on the *constant terms* of these polynomials.

So if $R_{k,0}$ denotes the constant term of R_k etc., we have

$$R_{k,0} = \frac{a_{k,0}^k R_{k-1,0}}{a_{k-1,0}^k} \qquad (13)$$

where once again $R_{0,0} = 1$. Each $a_{j,0}^k$ is a subdeterminant of a^k with u_i specialized to zero, so that no manipulation of polynomials in u_i is necessary. This method involves only slightly more

computation than evaluation of the determinant of A^n for the *original polynomial system.*

The disadvantage of this method is that it is not guaranteed to succeed, since some of the $a_{j,0}^k$ may vanish, even if the resultant does not. One possible fix is to evaluate (12) by evaluating *only a term of lowest degree* in each R_k and b_{k-1}^k, since computing the term of lowest degree in a polynomial quotient only requires knowledge of the term of lowest degree in the divisor. However, in the worst case, this may involve evaluation of all the terms in the a^k. Furthermore, for large n, the intermediate $a_{j,0}^k$ will be much larger than the resultant itself, so that their computation seems wasteful. Instead we describe a second method for which the a_j^k cannot vanish, so that branching is unnecessary. In the latter method, division over the base field is never necessary, and intermediate terms larger than the resultant are never generated.

4.4   Method 2

The recurrence relation in (12) is valid for any specialization of the $u_1,\ldots,u_n$. The problem with the recurrence as it stands is that it involves polynomials of quite high degree in n variables. If we add the specialization $u_1 = u_2 = \cdots = u_n$, then all polynomials become univariate in the single variable u_1. The effect of this specialization is to collapse all the terms of a given degree (by summation) into the coefficient of u_1 of that degree. From the definition of rectangularity, it should be clear that the polynomials remain monic after this specialization. Thus the method now involves only division of monic polynomials in the single variable u_1. We denote the polynomials after this specialization by $\bar{R}$, $\bar{a}_j^k$, $\bar{b}_j^k$, so that $\bar{R}(u_1) = R(u_1, u_1,\ldots,u_1)$ and $\bar{a}_j^k(u_1) = a_j^k(u_1, u_1,\ldots,u_1)$, etc. Then we have the recursion

$$\bar{b}_{k-1}^k(u_1) = \frac{\bar{a}_{k-1}^k(u_1)}{\bar{R}_{k-1}(u_1)} \qquad \text{for } k = 1,\ldots,n$$

$$\bar{R}_k(u_1) = \frac{\bar{a}_k^k(u_1)}{\bar{b}_{k-1}^k(u_1)} \qquad \text{for } k = 1,\ldots,n \qquad (14)$$

Recall from the properties of the A^k, that the indeterminates u_i lie along the leading diagonal. Since a_j^k is the leading coefficient (term of highest degree) with respect to the variables $u_{j+1},\ldots,u_n$, a_j^k is the determinant of the submatrix of A^k obtained by deleting all those rows and columns that contain any of the variables $u_{j+1},\ldots,u_n$.

For notational expendiency, we define A_j^k as the submatrix of A^k whose determinant is a_j^k. In fact we can define A_j^k without making use of any of the introduced indeterminates u_i. Let A_j^k be the submatrix of A^k obtained by deleting all rows and columns that contain the coefficient of $x_i^{d_i}$ in f_i for $i > j$. This definition simply follows from the fact that these are the rows and columns that *would have* contained the introduced variables $u_{j+1},\ldots,u_n$.

Then the constant coefficient $a_{j,0}^k$ is simply the determinant of A_j^k with no indeterminates introduced. For $\bar{a}_j^k(u_1)$, we notice that the indeterminate $u_1 = \cdots = u_j$ appears on the leading diagonal of A_j^k, so that $\bar{a}_j^k(u_1)$ is the characteristic polynomial of A_j^k. For computation in parallel, the known fast methods for computing the determinant [Csa] in fact compute the coefficients of the characteristic polynomial as a side effect, so method 2 is as fast as method 1 using current parallel alorithms.

Notice also that division by monic polynomials does not require division in the base field. To see this, let $a(s)$ and $b(s)$ be two polynomials of degree m, n respectively, $m > n$, and where b is monic. Then to find the quotient of a and b we form the following matrix:

$$Q = \begin{pmatrix} a_m & a_{m-1} & a_{m-2} & \cdots & a_{n+1} & \cdots & a_1 & a_0 \\ -1 & -b_{n-1} & -b_{n-2} & \cdots & -b_{2n-m+1} & \cdots & 0 & 0 \\ 0 & -1 & -b_{n-1} & \cdots & -b_{2n-m+2} & \cdots & 0 & 0 \\ \vdots & \vdots & \vdots & & \vdots & & \vdots & \vdots \\ 0 & 0 & 0 & \cdots & -1 & \cdots & -b_0 & 0 \end{pmatrix}$$
(15)

then this matrix has $m - n + 1$ rows. The left-most $m - n + 1$ columns form a square matrix, and it is readily seen that the principal subdeterminants are the coefficients of the quotient a/b. That is, the coefficient of s^i in a/b is the determinant of the submatrix containing the first $m - n - i + 1$ rows and columns of Q. This relationship shows also that the quotient depends only on the leading $m - n + 1$ coefficients of both polynomials, so that it is not necessary to compute the lower order terms. The leading r terms of a product of polynomials also depends only on the leading r terms of each of the polynomials. So in the recurrence (14), we need only evaluate a number of terms in each of the polynomials equal to the degree of the result polynomial $\bar{R}_n(u_1)$.

It turns out that for characteristic polynomials, the coefficient size of the higher order terms is lower (see section 3.3 on polynomial height for a precise characterization of this). Thus the higher order terms are the least expensive to compute. Using the method described in [Csa], the higher order characteristic polynomial coefficients can be computed independently of the lower order terms. For a system of n polynomials of degree d, the characteristic polynomial of an A^k has degree approximately $(d\epsilon)^n$ in u_1 where ϵ is the base of natural logarithms, while the resultant has degree $nd^{(n-1)}$. For certain problems, such as equation solving, the saving caused by evaluating only leading coefficients of the a_j^k dominates the extra effort involved in doing division of polynomials in u_1 rather than elements of the base field (which may themselves be multivariate polynomials). The computation of leading characteristic polynomial coefficients only can be done in parallel, with similar saving.

Since method 2 involves only computation of matrix determinants of matrices of single exponential size, and since monic polynomial division can also be performed using determinant computations, Csanky's $\log^2$ parallel time algorithm [Csa] implies that the resultant can be computed in polynomial parallel time.

An Example   We compute the resultant of a system of 2 quadrics and a linear polynomial in three variables x, y, z. The polynomials are:

$$f_1 = a_{xx}x^2 + a_{xy}xy + a_{xz}xz + a_{yy}y^2 + a_{yz}yz + a_{zz}z^2$$

$$f_2 = b_{xx}x^2 + b_{xy}xy + b_{xz}xz + b_{yy}y^2 + b_{yz}yz + b_{zz}z^2 \quad (16)$$

$$f_3 = c_x x + c_y y + c_z z$$

Then to construct the matrix A^1, we first notice that $d = \sum(d_i - 1) + 1 = 3$. For the purposes of the construction, we order the polynomials as f_2, f_3, f_1 so that f_1 is last in the list. Then we split the monomials of degree 3 into three groups, each of which contains all the remaining monomials which are divisible

by $x_i^{d_i}$. In this case, the monomials in each group are divisible by y^2, z and x^2 respectively:

$$X_2^3 = \{y^3, y^2z, y^2x\}$$

$$X_3^3 = \{yz^2, yzx, z^3, z^2x, zx^2\} \quad (17)$$

$$X_1^3 = \{yx^2, x^3\}$$

We use these monomials to index the rows and columns of A^1. Each row of A^1 is filled with the coefficients of $\frac{x^\alpha}{x_i^{d_i}} f_i$ where the monomial x^α is the row index, and is contained in X_i^3.

$$A^1 = \begin{pmatrix} b_{yy} & b_{yz} & b_{xy} & b_{zz} & b_{xz} & 0 & 0 & 0 & b_{xx} & 0 \\ 0 & b_{yy} & 0 & b_{yz} & b_{xy} & b_{zz} & b_{xz} & b_{xx} & 0 & 0 \\ 0 & 0 & b_{yy} & 0 & b_{yz} & 0 & b_{zz} & b_{xz} & b_{xy} & b_{xx} \\ 0 & c_y & 0 & c_z & c_x & 0 & 0 & 0 & 0 & 0 \\ 0 & 0 & c_y & 0 & c_z & 0 & 0 & 0 & c_x & 0 \\ 0 & 0 & 0 & c_y & 0 & c_z & c_x & 0 & 0 & 0 \\ 0 & 0 & 0 & 0 & c_y & 0 & c_z & c_x & 0 & 0 \\ 0 & 0 & 0 & 0 & 0 & 0 & 0 & c_z & c_y & c_x \\ a_{yy} & a_{yz} & a_{xy} & a_{zz} & a_{xz} & 0 & 0 & 0 & a_{xx} & 0 \\ 0 & 0 & a_{yy} & 0 & a_{yz} & 0 & a_{zz} & a_{xz} & a_{xy} & a_{xx} \end{pmatrix}$$
(18)

Notice that the coefficients of $x_i^{d_i}$ in f_i, namely b_{yy}, c_z and a_{xx} appear along the leading diagonal. A^2 is similar to A^1 and can be formed by simply interchanging x and y.

$$A^2 = \begin{pmatrix} a_{xx} & a_{xz} & a_{xy} & a_{zz} & a_{yz} & 0 & 0 & 0 & a_{yy} & 0 \\ 0 & a_{xx} & 0 & a_{xz} & a_{xy} & a_{zz} & a_{yz} & a_{yy} & 0 & 0 \\ 0 & 0 & a_{xx} & 0 & a_{xz} & 0 & a_{zz} & a_{yz} & a_{xy} & a_{yy} \\ 0 & c_x & 0 & c_z & c_y & 0 & 0 & 0 & 0 & 0 \\ 0 & 0 & c_x & 0 & c_z & 0 & 0 & 0 & c_y & 0 \\ 0 & 0 & 0 & c_x & 0 & c_z & c_y & 0 & 0 & 0 \\ 0 & 0 & 0 & 0 & c_x & 0 & c_z & c_y & 0 & 0 \\ 0 & 0 & 0 & 0 & 0 & 0 & 0 & c_z & c_x & c_y \\ b_{xx} & b_{xz} & b_{xy} & b_{zz} & b_{yz} & 0 & 0 & 0 & b_{yy} & 0 \\ 0 & 0 & b_{xx} & 0 & b_{xz} & 0 & b_{zz} & b_{yz} & b_{xy} & b_{yy} \end{pmatrix}$$
(19)

Finally, for A^3, we use the order f_1, f_2, f_3, and the monomials:

$$X_1^3 = \{x^3, x^2y, x^2z\}$$

$$X_2^3 = \{xy^2, y^3, y^2z\} \quad (20)$$

$$X_3^3 = \{xyz, xz^2, yz^2, z^3\}$$

and the matrix itself is

$$A^3 = \begin{pmatrix} a_{xx} & a_{xy} & a_{xz} & a_{yy} & 0 & 0 & a_{yz} & a_{zz} & 0 & 0 \\ 0 & a_{xx} & 0 & a_{xy} & a_{yy} & a_{yz} & a_{xz} & 0 & a_{zz} & 0 \\ 0 & 0 & a_{xx} & 0 & 0 & a_{yy} & a_{xy} & a_{xz} & a_{yz} & a_{zz} \\ b_{xx} & b_{xy} & b_{xz} & b_{yy} & 0 & 0 & b_{yz} & b_{zz} & 0 & 0 \\ 0 & b_{xx} & 0 & b_{xy} & b_{yy} & b_{yz} & b_{xz} & 0 & b_{zz} & 0 \\ 0 & 0 & b_{xx} & 0 & 0 & b_{yy} & b_{xy} & b_{xz} & b_{yz} & b_{zz} \\ 0 & c_x & 0 & c_y & 0 & 0 & c_z & 0 & 0 & 0 \\ 0 & 0 & c_x & 0 & 0 & c_y & c_z & 0 & 0 & 0 \\ 0 & 0 & 0 & 0 & 0 & c_y & c_x & 0 & c_z & 0 \\ 0 & 0 & 0 & 0 & 0 & 0 & 0 & c_x & c_y & c_z \end{pmatrix}$$
(21)

Since the matrices all have symbolic coefficients, none of the intermediate terms will vanish, so we can use method 1. Now to start the recurrence we have $a_{0,0}^1 = 1$. and $R_{0,0} = 1$. $a_{1,0}^1$ is the determinant of the matrix A_1^1 which is obtained by deleting all the rows and columns of A^1 which contain the coefficient of $x_i^{d_i}$, for $i > 1$, that is, all the rows and columns containing b_{yy} or c_z. Hence

$$A_1^1 = \begin{pmatrix} a_{xx} & 0 \\ a_{xy} & a_{xx} \end{pmatrix} \qquad (22)$$

so that $a_{1,0}^1 = a_{xx}^2$. Dividing by $b_{0,0}^1 = 1$ we obtain $R_{1,0} = a_{xx}^2$. Next we need $a_{1,0}^2$ and $a_{2,0}^2$ which are the determinants of the matrices:

$$A_1^2 = \begin{pmatrix} a_{xx} & a_{xz} & a_{xy} \\ 0 & a_{xx} & 0 \\ 0 & 0 & a_{xx} \end{pmatrix} \qquad (23)$$

$$A_2^2 = \begin{pmatrix} a_{xx} & a_{xz} & a_{xy} & a_{yy} & 0 \\ 0 & a_{xx} & 0 & 0 & 0 \\ 0 & 0 & a_{xx} & a_{xy} & a_{yy} \\ b_{xx} & b_{xz} & b_{xy} & b_{yy} & 0 \\ 0 & 0 & b_{xx} & b_{xy} & b_{yy} \end{pmatrix} \qquad (24)$$

So that $a_{1,0}^2 = a_{xx}^3$, $b_{1,0}^2 = a_{1,0}^1/R_{1,0} = a_{xx}$, and

$$
\begin{aligned}
a_{2,0}^2 &= a_{xx}(a_{xx}^2 b_{yy}^2 - a_{xx}a_{xy}b_{xy}b_{yy} - 2a_{xx}a_{yy}b_{xx}b_{yy} \\
&\quad + a_{xx}a_{yy}b_{xy}^2 + a_{xy}^2 b_{xx}b_{yy} - a_{xy}a_{yy}b_{xx}b_{xy} + a_{yy}^2 b_{xx}^2)
\end{aligned} \qquad (25)
$$

and since $R_{2,0} = a_{2,0}^2/b_{1,0}^2$, we have

$$
\begin{aligned}
R_{2,0} &= a_{xx}^2 b_{yy}^2 - a_{xx}a_{xy}b_{xy}b_{yy} - 2a_{xx}a_{yy}b_{xx}b_{yy} \\
&\quad + a_{xx}a_{yy}b_{xy}^2 + a_{xy}^2 b_{xx}b_{yy} - a_{xy}a_{yy}b_{xx}b_{xy} + a_{yy}^2 b_{xx}^2
\end{aligned} \qquad (26)
$$

The next step is the computation of $a_{2,0}^3$ which is the determinant of

$$A_2^3 = \begin{pmatrix} a_{xx} & a_{xy} & a_{xz} & a_{yy} & 0 & 0 \\ 0 & a_{xx} & 0 & a_{xy} & a_{yy} & a_{yz} \\ 0 & 0 & a_{xx} & 0 & 0 & a_{yy} \\ b_{xx} & b_{xy} & b_{xz} & b_{yy} & 0 & 0 \\ 0 & b_{xx} & 0 & b_{xy} & b_{yy} & b_{yz} \\ 0 & 0 & b_{xx} & 0 & 0 & b_{yy} \end{pmatrix} \qquad (27)$$

which can be factored as

$$
\begin{aligned}
a_{2,0}^3 &= (a_{xx}b_{yy} - a_{yy}b_{xx})(a_{xx}^2 b_{yy}^2 - a_{xx}a_{xy}b_{xy}b_{yy} - 2a_{xx}a_{yy}b_{xx}b_{yy} \\
&\quad + a_{xx}a_{yy}b_{xy}^2 + a_{xy}^2 b_{xx}b_{yy} - a_{xy}a_{yy}b_{xx}b_{xy} + a_{yy}^2 b_{xx}^2)
\end{aligned} \qquad (28)
$$

so that $b_{2,0}^3 = a_{2,0}^3/R_{2,0} = a_{xx}b_{yy} - a_{yy}b_{xx}$. To complete the computation, we compute the determinant of $A_3^3 = A^3$ and divide it by $b_{2,0}^3$ to yield the resultant. Unfortunately, both the determinant and the quotient are too large to be given in this text. However, they have both been computed using Macsyma and the computation time for this problem was about a minute on a Symbolics 3600 Lisp Machine.

4.5   The u-Resultant

We can use the multivariate resultant defined above to find the solutions of a system of polynomials when the number of solutions is finite. Let $f_1, \ldots, f_{n-1}$ be $n - 1$ homogeneous polynomials in the unknowns $x_1, \ldots, x_n$. We introduce the linear polynomial with indeterminate coefficients:

$$l = v_1 x_1 + v_2 x_2 + \cdots + v_n x_n \qquad (29)$$

If we now compute the resultant of $f_1, \ldots, f_{n-1}, l$ in the variables $x_1, \ldots, x_n$, we obtain a resultant $R(v_1, \ldots, v_n)$ which is a homogeneous polynomial whose degree is the product of the degrees of the f_i. This polynomial is called the u-resultant of $f_1, \ldots, f_{n-1}$ [Wae]. If the solution set of $f_1, \ldots, f_{n-1}$ is finite, then the system $f_1, \ldots, f_{n-1}, l$ has no solution for almost all linear forms l. Thus the resultant must be non-vanishing. It is easily shown that the u-resultant factors completely over the complex numbers into linear factors of the form:

$$s_1 v_1 + s_2 v_2 + \cdots s_n v_n \qquad (30)$$

and that each vector $(s_1, s_2, \ldots, s_n)$ is a solution of the original system.

4.6   Degree bounds and Gap Theorems

For the remaining algebraic algorithms, we will be making use of finite precision binary numbers to approximate algebraic numbers. Although this only allows us to evaluate expressions approximately, if we are careful, we can still determine the values of certain expressions exactly using "Gap" theorems. Specifically, these theorems state that for any collection of integral polynomials of a certain size (bounded number of bits in each coefficient and bounded degree) there is a non-zero minimum spacing between any two distinct roots of the polynomials in the collection. We may speak about the size of an algebraic number, this size being the size of the minimal polynomial which has this number as a root.

Thus if the binary approximations to two algebraic numbers of a certain size are sufficiently close (their difference is smaller than the gap), then the two algebraic numbers must be identical. In particular, if the binary approximation to an algebraic number of a certain size is sufficiently small, then the algebraic number must be zero.

It turns out that manipulation of these binary approximations is much more efficient than the manipulation of "exact" algebraic numbers as described by Schwartz and Sharir. Roughly speaking, the approximate computations can be done in exponential time, while the exact arithmetic representation grows doubly exponentially with the number of arithmetic operations.

Theorem 4.1 *(Gap Theorem) Let $\wp(d, c)$ be the class of polynomials of degree d and coefficient magnitude c. Let $f_1(x_1, \ldots, x_n), \ldots, f_n(x_1, \ldots, x_n) \in \wp(d, c)$ be a collection of n polynomials in n variables which has only finitely-many solutions when projectivized. Then if $(\alpha_1, \ldots, \alpha_n)$ is a solution of the system, then for any j either*

$$\alpha_j = 0 \quad or \quad |\alpha_j| > (3dc)^{-nd^n} \qquad (31)$$

The proof of this result is given in [Can]. It gives a nearly tight bound on the number of bits $O(nd^n \log dc)$ required to represent an algebraic number. To see that it implies a gap between distinct algebraic numbers, consider two algebraic numbers α and β, which are defined by polynomials f and g of a certain size (degree and coefficient length). That is we have $f(\alpha) = 0$ and $g(\beta) = 0$, with f, g integral polynomials. Now let h be the polynomial $\delta - \alpha - \beta = 0$. The gap theorem applied to the system of polynomials f, g, h implies a lower bound on the magnitude of δ, that is, on the difference between α and β. To get this lower bound using the theorem, we do not need to know what f and g are, only bounds on their degree and coefficient size.

5   Solution of Polynomial Systems

Algorithm 5.1 Input: *non-homogeneous polynomials* $f_1, \ldots f_r$ *in variables* $x_1, \ldots x_{r-1}$, *or homogeneous* $f_1, \ldots f_r$ *in variables* $x_1, \ldots x_r$.
Output: *a necessary and sufficient condition (in the form of an integral polynomial in the coefficients of the f_i) that the homogeneous (or homogenized) system have a solution over the complex numbers.*

Description   Let d_i be the degree of f_i. We use the method 2 above to compute the resultant of the system. This requires the computation of the characteristic polynomials of r matrices of size at most

$$N = \binom{r + d - 1}{r - 1} \qquad (32)$$

where $d = 1 + \sum(d_i - 1)$ as before. Each characteristic polynomial can be computed using $O(N^4)$ operations on elements of the coefficient ring, and the maximum degree of any intermediate result in the polynomial coefficients is N. The $2r$ polynomial divisions require at most $O(N^2)$ operations each on the coefficient ring, and so the overall number of operations on the coefficient ring is $O(rN^4)$ (naively). Once again the maximum degree of intermediate values in the coefficient ring is N. Notice that we cannot compute the time complexity of the method without knowing the cost of multiplication and addition on elements of the coefficient ring as a function of their degree, e.g. this function is pseudo-linear for integers, at least quadratic for polynomials in two variables etc.

On the other hand we can use method 1, which involves the computation of determinants of submatrices of the A^k, and therefore has time complexity $O(rN^3)$.

For the simple case where all the d_i are equal, the above expressions may be simplified, since $N = \binom{rd_1}{r-1} = O((rd_1)^{(r-1)})$. Thus the number of coefficient operations is $O(r(rd_1)^{4(r-1)})$ for method 2, and $O(r(rd_1)^{3(r-1)})$ for method 1.

Algorithm 5.2 Input: *Homogeneous polynomials* $f_1, \ldots f_{r-1}$ *of degree d in r variables* $x_1, \ldots x_r$ *which have a finite number of distinct solutions. The solutions are assumed to have distinct x_1 coordinates (this occurs with probability one after a change of coordinates).*
Output: *A list of the real root vectors* $(s_1, \ldots s_r)$, $s_r \neq 0$, *which are solutions of the system.*

Description   We use the u-resultant defined in the last section. However, rather than computing the complete u-resultant as a polynomial in $v_1, \ldots v_r$, we compute several resultants in three indeterminates, and then match solutions by v_1-coordinate. Each resultant includes the original polynomials and one of the linear forms:

$$l_i = v_1 x_1 + v_r x_r + v_i x_i \qquad \text{for } i = 2, \ldots r - 1 \qquad (33)$$

and let the corresponding resultants be denoted R_i. The R_i are homogeneous in v_1, v_r, v_i . Now by setting $v_r = 1, v_i = 0$ in R_i, R_i becomes a univariate polynomial in v_1. We can isolate

the real roots of this polynomial to any precision using Sturm sequences. Let $v_1 = \alpha_j$ be one such approximate root. Now let $v_r = 1$, $v_1 = 0$, we can isolate a root of R_i in the same way and we get an approximation to a solution $v_i = \beta_{k_i}$. Now for each α_j, there is a corresponding β_{k_i} such that $v_1 = \alpha_j$, $v_i = \beta_{k_i}$, $v_r = 1$ is a solution of $R_i = 0$. We check this by substitution, making use of the gap theorem to bound the numerical precision we require. Doing this for all i, we obtain all the solution vectors $(\alpha_j, \beta_{k_2}, \ldots, \beta_{k_{r-1}}, 1)$ by identify α_j values. (Note that this works because what we are really doing is examining the terms of highest power in v_1, v_r, v_i in the *full* u-resultant)

Using the defining polynomials for α_j, β_k and R_i, the gap for values of R_i is $O(rd^{3r} \log dw)$ bits, where w is the maximum absolute value of any coefficient of any f_i. By simple error analysis, using the upper bounds for α_j and β_k, and the fact that R_i has degree d^r, we need $O(rd^{3r} \log dw)$ bits of accuracy in the value of each root to ensure that the error in the value of R_i is within the gap. Once we have a sufficiently good approximation to a root, Newton's method can be used to isolate the root to this accuracy in time $O(r^3 d^{3r} \log^3 dw)$. Evaluation of R_i for each solution β_k takes time $O(r^2 d^{3r} \log^2 dw)$. (Both of the previous two bounds make use of a simple divide-and-conquer scheme for polynomial evaluation, and rounding to $O(rd^{3r} \log dw)$ bits). To find all three-element solution rays (solution rays for some R_i) takes time $O(r^2 d^{5r} \log^2 dw)$. Once we have these for each R_i, we can immediately obtain all n-element real root vectors by comparing their v_1-coordinates. Since the cost for evaluation dominates the time for computation of the resultants themselves, the overall cost for this algorithm is $O(r^3 d^{5r} \log^2 dw)$ binary operations.

6   Conclusions

We described two methods for extensions of the basic robot motion planning or piano movers' problem. In both cases, the paths to be found consisted of a small number of straight line path segments (in space or space-time). The problems considered were the euclidean shortest path problem in three dimensions, and the asteroid avoidance problem in three dimensions. We showed that the via points for these paths can be efficiently computed using algebraic methods based on the multivariate resultant and on gap theorems. This lead to algorithms which were single exponential in the number of via points, and in polynomial time if the number of via points is fixed.

References

[Can]   Canny J. F. "A New Algebraic Method for Robot Motion Planning and Real Geometry", to appear in Proc. 28th IEEE Conf. FOCS, (Oct. 1987).

[CR]   Canny J. F. and Reif J. "New Lower Bound Techniques for Robot Motion Planning", to appear in Proc. 28th IEEE Conf. FOCS, (Oct. 1987).

[Csa]   Csanky L., "Fast Parallel Matrix Inversion Algorithms" SIAM J. Comp., Vol. 5, No. 4, (Dec. 1976).

[LW]   Lozano-Pérez T., and Wesley M., "An algorithm for Planning Collision-Free Paths Among Polyhedral Obstacles", Comm. ACM, vol 22, no 10, (Oct 1979), pp. 560-570.

[Mac]   Macaulay F. S., "Some Formulae in Elimination" Proc. London Math. Soc. (1) 35, (1902) pp 3-27.

[Mou]   Mount D. M., "On finding shortest paths on convex polyhedra", Tech. Rept., Computer Science Department, University of Maryland, (1984).

[Rei]   Reif J., "Complexity of the Mover's Problem and Generalizations," Proc. 20th IEEE Symp. FOCS, (1979). Also in "Planning, Geometry and Complexity of Robot Motion", ed. by J. Schwartz, J. Hopcroft and M. Sharir, , Ablex publishing corp. New Jersey, (1987), Ch. 11, pp. 267-281.

[RSh]   Reif J., and Sharir M., "Motion Planning in the Presence of Moving Obstacles", Proc. 25th IEEE symp. FOCS, (1985), pp. 144-154.

[RSt]   Reif J., and Storer J., "Shortest Paths in Euclidean Space with Polyhedral Obstacles", Tech. Rep. CS-85-121, Comp. Sci. Dept., Brandeis University, (April 1985).

[Sal]   Salmon G., "Modern Higher Algebra", G. E. Stechert and Co. New York, reprinted 1924, (1885).

[SSh]   Schwartz J. and Sharir M., "On the 'Piano Movers' Problem, II. General Techniques for Computing Topological Properties of Real Algebraic Manifolds," Comp. Sci. Dept., New York University report 41, (1982). Also in "Planning, Geometry and Complexity of Robot Motion", ed. by J. Schwartz, J. Hopcroft and M. Sharir, Ablex publishing corp. New Jersey, (1987), Ch. 5, pp. 154-186.

[SB]   Sharir M., and Baltsam A., "On Shortest Paths amid Convex Polyhedra", Proc. ACM Computational Geometry Conf., Yorketown Heights, 1986.

[SSc]   Sharir M., and Schorr A., "On Shortest Paths in Polyhedral Spaces", Proc. 16th ACM STOC, (1984), pp. 144-153.

[Udu]   Udupa S., "Collision Detection and Avoidance in Computer Controlled Manipulators", Proc. 5th Int. Joint. Conf. on Art. Intell., Mass. Inst. Tech. (1977) pp 737-748.

[Wae]   van der Waerden B. L., "Modern Algebra", (third edition) F. Ungar Publishing Co., New York (1950).

Participants

Russell L. Andersson
Room 4B607
AT&T Bell Laboratories
Crawfords Corner Road
Holmdel, NJ 07733
(201) 949-2440

Tatsuo Arai
Mechanical Engineering Laboratory
MITI
1-2 Namiki, Sakura-mura
Tsukuba Science City
Ibaraki 305
Japan

Suguru Arimoto
Department of Mechanical Engineering
Faculty of Engineering Science
Osaka University
Toyonaka, Osaka, 560
Japan
06-844-1151, ext. 4505

Haruhiko Asada
Department of Applied Systems Science
Faculty of Engineering
Kyoto University
Kyoto, 606
Japan

Kuniji Asano
Energy Science and Technical Laboratory
R&D Center, Toshiba Company
4-1, Ukishimacho, Kawasaki-ku
Kawasaki, 210
Japan
044-277-3111

Christopher G. Atkeson
MIT AI Laboratory, NE43-759
545 Technology Square
Cambridge, MA 02139
(617) 253-0788
cga%oz@mc.lcs.mit.edu

Nicholas Ayache
INRIA
Domaine de Voluceau-Rocquencourt
BP105-78153 Le Chesnay Cedex
France
33 1 39 63 53 20
seismo!mcvax!Inria!Ayache

Ruzena Bajcsy
Department of Computer and Information
Science
Moore School
University of Pennsylvania
Philadelphia, PA 19104
(215) 898-6222
Bajcsy@CIS.UPENN.EDU

Antal K. Bejczy
MS 198-330
Jet Propulsion Laboratory
California Institute of Technology
Pasadena, CA 91109
(818) 354-4568

Thomas O. Binford
Artificial Intelligence Laboratory
Computer Science Department
Stanford University
Stanford, CA 94305
(415) 723-2797
TOB@sail.stanford.edu

Robert C. Bolles
SRI International, EK290
333 Ravenswood Avenue
Menlo Park, CA 94025
(415) 859-4620
Bolles@iu.ai.sri.com

J. Michael Brady
Department of Engineering Science
Oxford University
19 Parks Road
Oxford OX1 3PJ
England
011-44-865-273154
jmb%robots.oxford.as.uk.@CS.UCL.AC.UK

Rodney A. Brooks
MIT AI Laboratory, Room 836
545 Technology Square
Cambridge, MA 02139
(617) 253-5223
brooks%oz@mc.lcs.mit.edu

John Canny
543 Evans Hall
University of California
Berkeley, CA 94720
(415) 642-9955
jfc@ernie.berkeley.edu

Brian Carlisle
Adept Technology, Inc.
150 Rose Orchard Drive
San Jose, CA 95134
(408) 434-5011

Y. T. Chien
National Science Foundation
1800 G Street NW
Washington, DC 20550
(202) 357-9572

John J. Craig
SILMA Inc.
2111 Grant Road
Los Altos, CA 94022
(415) 967-5878
JJC@sail.stanford.edu

Mark R. Cutkosky
Mechanical Engineering Department
Stanford University
Stanford, CA 94305
(415) 723-1588
Cutkosky@Whitney.Stanford.Edu

Ronald W. Daniel
Department of Engineering Science
Oxford University
19 Parks Road
Oxford OX1 3PJ
England
(0865) 73153

Paolo Dario
Department of Engineering Science
University of Pisa
2-56100 Pisa
Italy
50-44478 or 500827
LFCMAST@icnucevm.BITNET

J. De Schutter
Department of Mechanical Engineering
Katholieke Universiteit Leuven
Celestijnenlaan 300B
B-3030 Leuven
Belgium
32-16-28 62 11, x 2480

E. D. Dickmanns
Fakultät für Luft- und Raumfahrttechnik
Universität der Bundeswehr München
Werner-Heisenberg-Weg 39
D-8014 Neubiberg
West Germany
089 6004 2077/3583

S. Dubowsky
Room 3-469A
Massachusetts Institute of Technology
77 Massachusetts Avenue
Cambridge, MA 02139
(617) 253-2144

Olivier Faugeras
INRIA
Domaine de Voluceau Rocquencourt
78153 Le Chesnay Cedex
France
(331) 39635438
mcvax!inria!robotics-hawaii!faugeras

Paul Fehrenbach
GEC Research Ltd.
Marconi Research Centre
West Hanningfield Road
Great Baddow, Chelmsford CM2 8HN
England
(0245) 73331, ext. 3232

Eckhard Freund
Institut für Roboterforschung
Universität Dortmund
Postfach 500 500, D-4600
Dortmund 50
West Germany
02371/51773

Malik Ghallab
LAAS-CNRS
7 Av Colonel Roche
31077 Toulouse Cedex
France
61-33-68-59
Mcvax!inria!laas!malik

George Giralt
Laboratoire d'Automatique et d'Analyse des
Systemes
Centre National de la Recherche Scientifique
7 Avenue de Colonel Roche
31400 Toulouse
France
mcvax!lasso!giralt@seismo.css.gov

W. Eric L. Grimson
MIT AI Laboratory, Room 725
545 Technology Square
Cambridge, MA 02139
(617) 253-5346
welg%oz@mc.lcs.mit.edu

G. Hirzinger
DFVLR
D-8031 Wessling
West Germany
08153/28401

John M. Hollerbach
MIT AI Laboratory
545 Technology Square
Cambridge, MA 02139
(617) 253-5798
jmh%oz@mc.lcs.mit.edu

Ralph Hollis
T. J. Watson Research Labs
P.O. Box 218
Yorktown Heights, NY 10598
(914) 945-2894

Masanori Idesawa
Institute of Physical and Chemical Research
2-1, Hirosawa, Wako-Shi
Saitama, 351-01
Japan
Telephone: 0484-62-1111
idesawa%riken.junet@relay.cs.net

Katsu Ikeuchi
Computer Science Department
Carnegie-Mellon University
Pittsburgh, PA 15213
(412) 268-6349
ikeuchi@n.sp.cs.cmu.edu

Hirochika Inoue
Department of Mechanical Engineering
University of Tokyo
7-3-1 Hongo, Bunkyo-ku
Tokyo, 113
Japan
(03) 812-2111, ext. 6285

Kanji Inoue
Bridgestone Corporation
3-1-1 Ogawahigashi-Cho, Kodaira-Shi
Tokyo, 187
Japan

Roberta Ishihara
System Development Foundation
One Maritime Plaza, Suite 1770
San Francisco, CA 94111
(415) 362-0480

Steve Jacobsen
Center for Engineering Design
3176 Merrill Engineering Building
University of Utah
Salt Lake City, UT 84112
(801) 581-6499
Cetron@ced.utah.edu

Ray A. Jarvis
Department of Electrical Engineering
Monash University
Wellington Road
Clayton, Vic. 3168
Australia

Takeo Kanade
Department of Computer Science and Robotics
Institute
Carnegie-Mellon University
Pittsburgh, PA 15213
(412) 268-3016
Kanade@N.SP.CS.CMU.EDU

Shinji Kawabe
Tokyo Research Laboratory
IBM Japan, Ltd.
5-9 Sanbancho, Chiyoda-ku
Tokyo, 102
Japan
03-265-9242
BITNET:Kawabe@JPNTSCVM

Oussama Khatib
AI Laboratory, Cedar Hall
Stanford University
Stanford, CA 94305
(415) 723-9753
ok@sail.stanford.edu

Toshitaka Kuno
Toyota Central R&D Laboratory, Ltd.
41-1, Aza Yokomichi, Oaza Nagakute
Nagakude-cho, Aichi-gun
Aichi-ken, 480-11
Japan
(05616) 2-6111

Jean-Claude Latombe
Computer Science Department
Stanford University
Stanford, CA 94305

David Lowe
Computer Science Division
Courant Institute of Mathematical Science
New York University
251 Mercer Street
New York, NY 10012
(212) 460-7260
Lowe@NYU.ARPA

Tomás Lozano-Pérez
MIT AI Laboratory
545 Technology Square
Cambridge, MA 02139
(617) 253-7889
tlp%oz@mc.lcs.mit.edu

Matthew T. Mason
Computer Science Department
Carnegie-Mellon University
Pittsburgh, PA 15213
(412) 268-8804
Matt.Mason@C.CS.CMU.EDU

John E. Mayhew
AI Vision Research Unit
Sheffield University
Sheffield S10 2TN
England
0742-768555, ext. 6551

Hirofumi Miura
Department of Mechanical Engineering
University of Tokyo
7-3-1 Hongo, Bunkyo-ku
Tokyo, 113
Japan
03-812-2111, ext. 6316

J. L. Mundy
Rm. 4129, Bldg. K-1, Box 8
General Electric R&D Center
Schenectady, NY 12301
(518) 387-6418
Mundy@GE-crd.arpa

Yoshihiko Nakamura
Center for Robotic Systems in Microelectronics
University of California
Santa Barbara, CA 93105
(805) 961-4976
Ucbvax!ucsbcsl!asgard!Nakamura

David Nitzan
SRI International, EL221
333 Ravenswood Avenue
Menlo Park, CA 94025
(415) 859-2575
nitzan@sri-robotx.arpa

Takeo Oomichi
Machinery Laboratory
Takasago R&D Center
Mitsubishi Heavy Industries, Ltd.
2-1-1 Shinhama Arai-cho, Takasago
Hyogo, 676
Japan
0794-42-2121

Richard Paul
Department of Computer and Information Science
Moore School
University of Pennsylvania
Philadelphia, PA 19104
(215) 898-1592
Lou@CIS.UPENN.EDU

Jocelyne Pertin-Troccaz
LIFIA/IMAG Laboratory, BP 68
Insitut National Polytechnique de Grenoble
46, Avenue Félix Viallet
38031 Grenoble Cedex
France
76-51-46-90
VVCP:Jocelyne@Lifia@MCVAX

Marc H. Raibert
NE43-765, Massachusetts Institute of
Technology
545 Technology Square
Cambridge, MA 02139
(617) 253-2478
raibert%oz@mc.lcs.mit.edu

Stanley Rosenschein
SRI International, EJ247
333 Ravenswood Avenue
Menlo Park, CA 94025
(415) 859-4167
Stan@stripe.sri.com

Bernard Roth
Department of Mechanical Engineering
Stanford University
Stanford, CA 94305
(415) 723-3657
BXR@SAIL.Stanford.EDU

Kenneth Salisbury
MIT AI Laboratory, NE43-820A
545 Technology Square
Cambridge, MA 02139
(617) 253-5834
jks%oz@mc.lcs.mit.edu

Guillio Sandini
Department of Communication, Computer, and
Systems Science
INFORMATICS
University of Genoa
via Opera Pia 11-AI16145
Genoa
Italy
39 10-31-02-23

Tomomasa Sato
Electrotechnical Laboratory
1-1-4, Umezono
Sakura-mura, Niihari-gun
Ibaraki, 305
Japan
0298-54-5445

Victor Scheinman
Automatix, Inc.
499 Seaport Court
Redwood City, CA 94063
(415) 369-7400

Yoshiaki Shirai
Electrotechnical Laboratory
1-1-4 Umezono
Sakuramura, Niihari-gun
Ibaraki, 305
Japan
0298-54-5412

Randall C. Smith
Computer Science Department
General Motors Research Labs
Warren, MI 48090
(313) 986-1461
Smith@GMR.COM(Csnet)

Kokichi Sugihara
Department of Mathematical Engineering and
Information Physics
Faculty of Engineering
University of Tokyo
Hongo, Bunkyo-ku
Tokyo, 113
Japan
03-812-2111, ext. 6906

Russell H. Taylor
T. J. Watson Research Center
P.O. Box 218
Yorktown Heights, NY 10598
(914) 945-1796
RHT@IBM.COM

James P. Trevelyan
Department of Mechanical Engineering
University of Western Australia
Nedlands, Western Australia 6009
380.3058 or 380.3148

Roger Tsai
T. J. Watson Research Center
P.O. Box 218
Yorktown Heights, NY 10598
(914) 945-1437
RTSAI@ibm.com

Ken Waldron
Department of Mechanical Engineering
Ohio State University
206 West 18th Avenue
Columbus, OH 43210
(614) 292-0500

Daniel E. Whitney
Charles Stark Draper Laboratory
555 Technology Square
Cambridge, MA 02139
(617) 258-2917

Carl York
System Development Foundation
One Maritime Plaza, Suite 1770
San Francisco, CA 94111
(415) 362-0480

The MIT Press, with Peter Denning, general consulting editor, and Brian Randell, European consulting editor, publishes computer science books in the following series:

ACM Doctoral Dissertation Award and Distinguished Dissertation Series

Artificial Intelligence, Patrick Winston and Michael Brady, editors

Charles Babbage Institute Reprint Series for the History of Computing, Martin Campbell-Kelly, editor

Computer Systems, Herb Schwetman, editor

Exploring with Logo, E. Paul Goldenberg, editor

Foundations of Computing, Michael Garey and Albert Meyer, editors

History of Computing, I. Bernard Cohen and William Aspray, editors

Information Systems, Michael Lesk, editor

Logic Programming, Ehud Shapiro, editor; Fernando Pereira, Koichi Furukawa, and D. H. D. Warren, associate editors

The MIT Electrical Engineering and Computer Science Series

Scientific Computation, Dennis Gannon, editor